Human Resource Management

Functions, Applications, Skill Development

Robert N. Lussier, *Springfield College*

John R. Hendon, *University of Arkansas at Little Rock*

Active learning to engage today's students

This textbook is designed to provide an opportunity to "learn by doing" in a way that will appeal to today's students. The text can be used in traditional lecture-based teaching, and it also offers a wide range of engaging activities that accommodate a variety of contemporary learning styles. Many of the specific learning preferences of today's students are addressed in the book's overall approach, organization, and distinctive features.

- Students' preferences for **active learning** are addressed with a large variety of activities and skill-building tools.

- **Applications and skills** that students can put into practice right away are provided in a variety of Work Applications, Concept Applications, Self-Assessments, and Skill Building Exercises.

- Students' **visual learning** styles are catered to with colorful exhibits, models, and figures throughout the text.

Explains functions, provides applications, and builds students' skills!

This comprehensive textbook is intended to develop the full range of human resource management (HRM) competencies through a balanced, three-pronged approach to the curriculum.

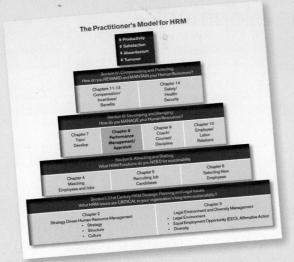

Key features of this text:

1. Provides a clear understanding of the traditional HRM **concepts and functions**, as well as the current trends and challenges facing HR managers.

2. Includes **applications** of HRM concepts and functions through developing critical thinking.

3. Assists in the development of critical HRM **skills**.

1. Outlines the Key Concepts and Functions

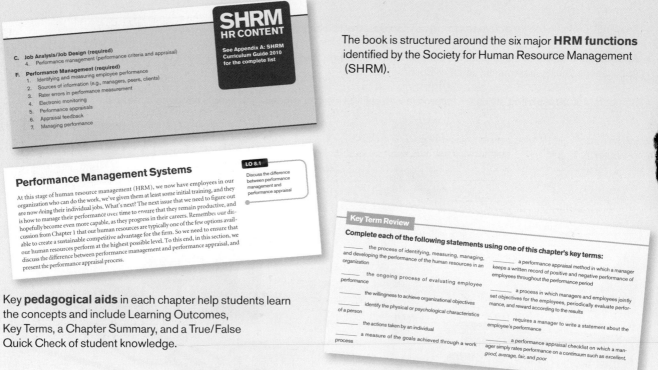

SHRM HR CONTENT

See Appendix A: SHRM Curriculum Guide 2010 for the complete list

C. Job Analysis/Job Design (required)
   4. Performance management (performance criteria and appraisal)
F. Performance Management (required)
   1. Identifying and measuring employee performance
   2. Sources of information (e.g., managers, peers, clients)
   3. Rater errors in performance measurement
   4. Electronic monitoring
   5. Performance appraisals
   6. Appraisal feedback
   7. Managing performance

The book is structured around the six major **HRM functions** identified by the Society for Human Resource Management (SHRM).

Performance Management Systems

LO 8.1
Discuss the difference between performance management and performance appraisal

At this stage of human resource management (HRM), we now have employees in our organization who can do the work, we've given them at least some initial training, and they are now doing their individual jobs. What's next? The next issue that we need to figure out is how to manage their performance over time to ensure that they remain productive, and hopefully become even more capable, as they progress in their careers. Remember our discussion from Chapter 1 that our human resources are typically one of the few options available to create a sustainable competitive advantage for the firm. So we need to ensure that our human resources perform at the highest possible level. To this end, in this section, we discuss the difference between performance management and performance appraisal, and present the performance appraisal process.

Key **pedagogical aids** in each chapter help students learn the concepts and include Learning Outcomes, Key Terms, a Chapter Summary, and a True/False Quick Check of student knowledge.

Key Term Review

Complete each of the following statements using one of this chapter's key terms:

_____ the process of identifying, measuring, managing, and developing the performance of the human resources in an organization

_____ the ongoing process of evaluating employee performance

_____ the willingness to achieve organizational objectives

_____ identify the physical or psychological characteristics of a person

_____ the actions taken by an individual

_____ a measure of the goals achieved through a work process

_____ a performance appraisal method in which a manager keeps a written record of positive and negative performance of employees throughout the performance period

_____ a process in which managers and employees jointly set objectives for the employees, periodically evaluate performance, and reward according to the results

_____ requires a manager to write a statement about the employee's performance

_____ a performance appraisal checklist on which a manager simply rates performance on a continuum such as excellent, good, average, fair, and poor

Key areas from the *SHRM Human Resource Curriculum: An Integrated Approach to HR Education: Guidebook and Templates for Undergraduate and Graduate Programs* (SHRM, 2010) are annotated for easy reference where they appear in each chapter of the text, and an appendix covers the entire undergraduate SHRM curriculum guide.

SHRM
Guide – F:3
Rater Errors in Performance Measurement

2. Richly Illustrated With Applications

Performance Management Miscue

Most managers don't look forward to performance appraisals. As soon as Heather stuck her head in my office and asked me to sit in on her performance appraisal, I knew I had two employees who needed some coaching— Heather and her supervisor, Christine. Our company bases many employment decisions on performance appraisals, so the results are important.

When I entered the room, it became apparent that although Heather believed she had been doing a great job, Christine did not agree. Christine recorded Heather's performance as needing improvement over- all, but did not offer any reason beyond a vague charge that Heather had a poor attitude and wasn't a team player.

I quickly suggested a small interruption to the meeting, and asked Heather to step out of the room. It soon became clear that the overall problem was Heather's failure to report to work on time. When Heather was late, it impacted her entire work group as the other employees then had to answer Heather's phone calls.

What's going on here? Why don't Heather and Christine agree on Heather's performance? Where did Christine go wrong? How can Christine get Heather to agree with her performance review now? How can this problem be avoided during the next formal performance appraisal ses- sion? The answers to these questions are based on having a good performance management system. By reading this chapter, you will learn how you can avoid these problems.

Opening vignettes illustrate how a real-life HR manager—currently employed by Saxon Drilling Services in Arkansas—works within the various HRM functions in her daily activities. Other **organizational examples** of HRM concepts and functions appear throughout the book.

WORK
APPLICATION 8-3

Assess the effectiveness of an evaluative performance appraisal you had. Did the manager present both positive and negative performance areas? Did you "really" listen? Where there any surprises? Explain any problems and how the evaluation could be improved.

Work Applications incorporate open-ended questions that ask students to explain how the HRM concepts apply to their own work experience. Student experience can be present, past, summer, full-time, or part-time employment.

8-2 APPLYING THE CONCEPT

Assessment Options

Which of the following assessment options for measuring performance is being described in each of the given situations?

a. traits
b. behavior
c. results

_____1. This is the second time you got upset and yelled at customers. This has to stop.

_____2. You have produced 15 products again this week. You know the standard is 20, so I'm giving you a formal warning that if you don't get up to standard in two weeks, you will be fired.

_____3. When you promote one of the women from waitress to hostess, be sure she is attractive so customers have a good impression of our restaurant and want to come back.

_____4. I'm really surprised. Since you started working from home, you have actually increased your data entry numbers by 5 percent.

_____5. On item number 5, willingness to take responsibility, I'm giving you an aver- age rating.

Applying the Concept features ask students to determine the most appropriate concept to be used in a specific short example.

Case 2. Performance Evaluation at DHR: Building a Foundation or Crumbling Ruins?

DHR Construction was managed by Richard Davis, operat- ing manager and senior partner. Homes were built on-demand to customer specifications. Richard Davis was in charge of the financial management of the firm including working with suppli- ers, creditors, and subcontractors (obtaining bids and construc- tion loans). Davis and Richard Hodgetts, the general partner, met on a weekly basis and communicated through phone calls and

e-mail. The role of project foreman was delegated to either one of their subcontractors or a hired employee and, in the worst-case scenario, filled by a reluctant Hodgetts (who had a full-time job outside of the business and had minimal free time).
DHR earned a reputation for honesty, promptness in paying bills, and professionalism—rare commodities for a small home builder in the area. However, DHR was also very demanding of suppliers—if

Cases at the end of each chapter illustrate how specific organizations use the HRM functions.

Video Link 8.1:
Video on human resource management

Videos on the Student Study Site are accompanied by questions for discussion in the book.

3. Focuses on Skill Development

6-1 SELF-ASSESSMENT

INTERVIEW READINESS

Select a professional job you would like to apply for. Indicate how confident you are that you can give an answer that would make a positive impression on an interviewer by placing a number from 1 to 7 on the line before each question.

I have a confident answer   I don't have a confident answer

7   6   5   4   3   2   1

_____ 1. Why did you choose the job for which you are applying?
_____ 2. What are your long-range career goals over the next five to 10 years?
_____ 3. What are your short-range goals and objectives for the next one to two years?
_____ 4. How do you plan to achieve your career goals?
_____ 5. What are your strengths and weaknesses? Describe a situation in which you did so.
_____ 6. What motivates you to put forth your greatest effort? Describe a situation in which you did so.
_____ 7. What two or three accomplishments have given you the most satisfaction? Why?
_____ 8. Why do you want the job?
_____ 9. In what kind of an organizational culture do you want to work?
_____ 10. Why did you decide to apply for a position with our organization?
_____ 11. What do you know about our organization?
_____ 12. In what ways do you think you can make a contribution to our organization?

Self-Assessments help students to gain personal knowledge of how they will complete the HRM functions in the real world. All information for completing and scoring is contained within the text.

Skill Builders help students to develop skills that can be used immediately in their life and on the job.

SKILL BUILDER 6-1

Questions for a Professor to Teach This Course

Objective
To develop your ability to develop interview questions.

Skills
The primary skills developed through this exercise are:
1. *HR Management skill* – Technical, business, and conceptual and design skills
2. *SHRM 2010 Curriculum Guidebook* – G: Staffing: Recruitment and Selection

Preparation
Assume you are the dean of your college and you need to hire a professor to teach this course next semester. Develop a list of at least 10 questions you would ask the candidates during a job interview for the position.

Apply It
What did I learn from this experience? How will I use this knowledge in the future?

_____

Your instructor may ask you to do this Skill Builder in class in a group by sharing your interview questions. If so, the instructor will provide you with any necessary information or additional instructions.

Communication Skills

The following critical-thinking questions can be used for class discussion and/or for written assignments to develop communication skills. Be sure to give complete explanations for all answers.

1. Other than an annual evaluation, what would you do to "manage" the performance of your employees? Explain why you chose the items that you did.

2. What would you do as the manager in order to make sure that your employees knew the standards that they would be evaluated against? Explain your answer.

3. Do you really think that it is possible for a performance appraisal to be motivational? Why or why not?

4. Can you think of a situation where a trait-based evaluation would be necessary? Explain your answer.

5. You are in charge, and you want to evaluate a group of assembly workers. Who would you choose as the evaluator(s)? What about an evaluation of the director of operation? Explain your answer.

6. How would you minimize the chance that stereotyping could affect the evaluation process in your company?

Communication Skills sections at the end of each chapter include questions for class discussion, presentations, and/or written assignments to help students develop critical thinking communication skills.

Behavior Models that show step-by-step actions to follow when implementing an HRM function, such as conducting a job interview, conducting a performance appraisal, or coaching and disciplining, are presented throughout the text.

Model 8-2 The Evaluative Performance Appraisal Interview

Preparation for the Appraisal Interview
1. Make an Appointment → 2. Have the employee perform a self-assessment → 3. Assess the employees performance → 4. Identify strengths and areas for improvement → 5. Predict the employee's reactions and plan how to handle them

Conducting the Appraisal Interview
1. Open the interview → 2. Go over the assessment form → 3. Agree on strengths and areas for improvement → 4. Conclude the interview

Accompanied by High-Quality Ancillaries!

Comprehensive online resources at www.sagepub.com/lussier support and enhance instructors and students' experiences.

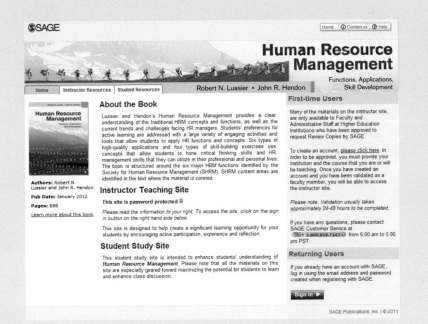

For the Instructor: Password-protected resources include:

- A test bank
- PowerPoint slides
- Answers to in-text exercises and case questions
- Course syllabi
- Video links
- Web resources
- Skill Builder assessment tools in downloadable format
- SHRM Resource Guides to cases and videos, which are available to instructors who are members of the organization
- Tables, figures, and artwork from the book in PDF form

For Students: Open-access study materials include:

- Web quizzes
- E-flash cards
- Full-text articles from SAGE's celebrated journal collection with critical thinking questions
- Video links
- Web resources

Los Angeles | London | New Delhi
Singapore | Washington DC

FOR INFORMATION:

SAGE Publications, Inc.
2455 Teller Road
Thousand Oaks, California 91320
E-mail: order@sagepub.com

SAGE Publications Ltd.
1 Oliver's Yard
55 City Road
London EC1Y 1SP
United Kingdom

SAGE Publications India Pvt. Ltd.
B 1/I 1 Mohan Cooperative Industrial Area
Mathura Road, New Delhi 110 044
India

SAGE Publications Asia-Pacific Pte. Ltd.
33 Pekin Street #02-01
Far East Square
Singapore 048763

Executive Editor: Patricia Quinlin
Associate Editor: Maggie Stanley
Editorial Assistant: Mayan White
Production Editor: Brittany Bauhaus
Typesetter: C&M Digitals (P) Ltd.
Copy Editor: Melinda Masson
Proofreader: Theresa Kay
Cover and Interior Designer: Gail Buschman
Marketing Manager: Nicole Elliott
Permissions Editor: Karen Ehrmann

Copyright © 2013 by SAGE Publications, Inc.

Printed in Canada

A catalog record of this book is available from the Library of Congress.

9781412992428

11 12 13 14 15 10 9 8 7 6 5 4 3 2 1

Human Resource Management

To my wife Marie and our six children—Jesse, Justin, Danielle, Nicole, Brian, and Renee

—Bob

To my mother and to Krista, my great love, and her two greatest loves—Jordan and Brooke

—John

Human Resource Management

Functions, Applications, Skill Development

Robert N. Lussier
Springfield College

John R. Hendon
University of Arkansas at Little Rock

Los Angeles | London | New Delhi
Singapore | Washington DC

Brief Contents

Detailed Contents

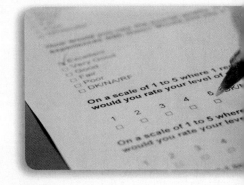

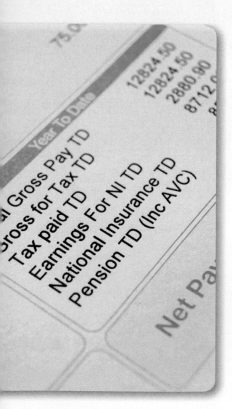

About the Authors

Robert N. Lussier is a Professor of Management at Springfield College. Having taught management for more than 25 years, he has developed innovative and widely copied methods for applying concepts and developing skills that can be used both personally and professionally. He served as founding director of Israel Programs and taught courses in Israel. His international experience also stretches to Namibia and South Africa.

A prolific writer, Dr. Lussier has more than 350 publications to his credit, including the best-selling textbooks *Human Relations in Organizations* (8th ed., McGraw-Hill), *Leadership: Theory, Application, and Skill Development* (4th ed., South Western/Cengage), and *Management Fundamentals* (4th ed., Cengage). He has published articles in *Academy of Entrepreneurship Journal, Business Horizons, Business Journal, Entrepreneurial Executive, Entrepreneurship Theory and Practice, Journal of Business and Entrepreneurship, Journal of Business Strategies, Journal of Management Education, Journal of Small Business Management, Journal of Small Business Strategy, SAM Advanced Management Journal,* and others. He holds a bachelor of science in business administration from Salem State University, two master's degrees in business and education from Suffolk University, and a doctorate in management from the University of New Haven.

A seven-time entrepreneur and former director of operations for a $60 million company, **John R. Hendon** brought his experience and interests to the classroom full-time in 1994 and has been a Management Instructor at the University of Arkansas at Little Rock for more than 14 years. Mr. Hendon is an active member of the Society for Human Resource Management (SHRM) and he teaches in the areas of strategy, human resources management, and organizational management and researches in a number of areas in the management field, specializing in entrepreneurial research.

Mr. Hendon is also currently the president of The VMP Group, a 20-member, Arkansas-based business consulting firm. The company consults with a variety of businesses on human resources, family business, strategic and business planning, organizational design, and leadership.

Over the past 20 years, Mr. Hendon has provided professional assistance in the start-up and operation of dozens of Arkansas- and California-based businesses and nonprofits, along with government agencies and utilities. In addition, he has more than 20 years' experience as an operations and logistics manager, business owner, and U.S. Navy Supply Corps Officer. Mr. Hendon holds an MBA from San Diego State University and a bachelor of science in education from the University of Central Arkansas.

Preface

In his book *Power Tools* (1997), John Nirenberg asks, "Why are so many well-intended students learning so much and yet able to apply so little in their personal and professional lives?" The world of business and human resource management (HRM) has changed, and so should how it is taught. Increasing numbers of students want more than lectures to gain an understanding of the concepts of HRM. They want their courses to be relevant, they want to apply what they learn, and they want to develop skills they can use in their everyday life and at work. It's not enough to learn about HRM; they want to learn how to *be* HR managers. This is why we wrote this book. After reviewing and using a variety of HRM books for more than a decade, we didn't find any that (1) could be easily read and understood by students and (2) effectively taught students how to *be* HR managers. Our text is designed to better prepare students to be successful HR managers. As the subtitle states, this book not only presents the important HRM concepts and functions, but it also takes students to the next levels by actually teaching them to apply the concepts through critical thinking and to develop HRM skills they can use in their personal and professional lives.

Market and Course

This book is for undergraduate- and graduate-level courses in HRM including personnel management. It is appropriate for a first course in an HRM major, as well as for required and elective courses found in business schools. This textbook is also appropriate for HRM courses taught in other disciplines such as education and psychology, particularly industrial and organizational psychology. The level of the text assumes no prior background in business or HRM. This book is an excellent choice for online and hybrid courses in HRM.

Learning by Doing: A Practical Approach

I (Lussier) started writing management textbooks in 1988—prior to the calls by the Association to Advance Collegiate Schools of Business (AACSB) for skill development—to help professors teach their students how to apply concepts and develop management skills. Pfeffer and Sutton (*The Knowing-Doing Gap*, 2000) concluded that the most important insight from their research is that knowledge that is actually implemented is much more likely to be acquired from learning by doing than from learning by reading, listening, or thinking. We designed this book to give students the opportunity to "learn by doing" with the following approaches:

- A practical **"how to manage"** approach that is strategy driven
- Specific identification of each primary content area listed in the Society for Human Resource Management (SHRM) **2010 curriculum guidebook** for undergraduate students in the text where the material is covered
- Six types of high-quality **application materials** using the concepts to help students develop critical thinking skills

- Four types of high-quality **skill builder exercises** that actually help students develop HR management skills that they can utilize in their professional and personal lives
- A comprehensive **video** package that reinforces HRM-related abilities and skills
- An approach that meets the preferred learning styles of **NetGens**

A New Generation of Learners: "Netgens"

Today's students are called "Digital Millennials" or "NetGens." They need to be fully engaged in learning on multiple levels, and traditional methods of teaching do not Always meet their needs. Our text is flexible enough to accompany lecture-based teaching and also offers a wide range of engaging activities that accommodate a variety of contemporary learning styles. Many of the specific learning preferences of NetGens (Matulich, Papp, & Haytko, 2008) have been addressed in the book's overall approach, organization, and distinctive features:

- **Active Learning**

  A desire for active learning is addressed with a large variety of activities and skill-building tools.

- **Practical Approaches**

  A desire for **application and skills** in personal and professional realms is addressed by the variety of features throughout the text. **Immediate feedback and ongoing self-assessment** are found in the True/False Quick Checks, Work Application prompts, and Self-Assessment tools. Organization tools such as **checklists, summaries, and "how to"** instructions—for example, the marginal references to SHRM guidelines—are integrated throughout.

- **Accessible Content**

  Chunking of content into easily digested segments helps students to organize study time. **Visual learning** preferences are accommodated in colorful exhibits, models, and figures throughout the text, along with an ancillary package that includes visual learning options. **Internet learning** preferences are recognized in a robust web-based package, which includes video and interactive features for students.

A Three-Pronged Approach

We have created a comprehensive textbook intended to develop the full range of HRM competencies. As the title of this book implies, we provide a balanced, three-pronged approach to the curriculum.

Concepts/Functions

The following features are provided to support the first step in the three-pronged approach.

HRM functions. Chapter 1 presents the six major HRM functions identified by SHRM with questions that need to be answered. The book is structured around the six functions in four parts; see the Table of Contents for details. These six functions are emphasized in order to show students the depth of knowledge that is required of a 21st-century HR manager.

Pedagogical aids. Each chapter includes Learning Outcomes, a Chapter Summary and Key Terms, and a True/False Quick Check of student knowledge. Marginal icons indicate the points at which international human resources is discussed in the text, and where online videos are appropriate to use.

SHRM's required and integrated content, as well as many secondary HR content areas from the *SHRM Human Resource Curriculum: An Integrated Approach to HR Education: Guidebook and Templates for Undergraduate and Graduate Programs* (SHRM, 2010), are annotated for easy reference where they appear in each chapter of the text. A margin note identifies the *SHRM Human Resource Curriculum* topic being covered, and, in a feature unique to this book, a reference number links to an appendix covering the entire undergraduate guide. *Every* primary content area and subtopic identified in the *SHRM Human Resource Curriculum* is at least introduced within the text, and virtually all are covered in significant depth.

Applications

The following features are provided to support the second step in the three-pronged approach.

Opening vignettes illustrate how a real-life HR manager, Cindy Wright, currently employed by Saxon Drilling Services in Arkansas, works within the various HRM functions in her daily activities.

Organizational examples of HRM concepts and functions appear throughout the book.

Work Applications incorporate open-ended questions that require students to explain how the HRM concepts apply to their own work experience. Student experience can be present, past, summer, full-time, or part-time employment.

Applying the Concept features ask students to determine the most appropriate HRM concept to be used in a specific short example.

Cases at the end of each chapter illustrate how specific organizations use the HRM functions. **Critical thinking questions** challenge the students to identify and apply the chapter concepts that are illustrated in each case. Also, longer, more comprehensive **SHRM** cases, which are available to members, are summarized in a **Case Matrix.** There are two longer cases in the book itself.

Video resources to demonstrate specific skills and HR functions are offered online, with marginal icons pointing to the corresponding chapter content. Additional video resources available to **SHRM** members are summarized in a **Video Matrix,** which designates appropriate chapters for SHRM video programs.

Skill Development

The following features are provided to support the third step in the three-pronged approach.

Self-Assessments help students to gain personal knowledge of how they will complete the HRM functions in the real world. All information for completing and scoring is contained within the text.

Communication Skills at the end of each chapter include questions for class discussion, presentations, and/or written assignments to help students develop critical thinking communication skills; they are based on HR content areas.

Behavior Models that show step-by-step actions to follow when implementing an HRM function, such as conducting a job interview, conducting a performance appraisal, or coaching and disciplining, are presented throughout the text.

Skill Builders help students develop skills that they can use in their personal and professional lives. Many of the competitor exercises tend to be discussion-oriented exercises that don't actually help students develop a skill that can be used immediately on the job.

Ancillaries

For the Instructor

A password-protected **Instructor Teaching Site** at www.sagepub.com/lussier gives instructors access to a full complement of resources to support and enhance their HRM course, from large lecture courses to smaller, interactive classes. The following assets are available to instructors using this book:

- A **test bank** with a variety of test questions for each chapter of the book, including multiple-choice, true/false, short-answer, and essay questions. Tests are available in Microsoft Word and in Diploma computerized testing software
- **PowerPoint slides** for each chapter summarizing key material suitable for lecture and review
- **Answers** to in-text exercises and case questions
- **Course syllabi** for semester, quarter, and online courses
- **Video links** that feature relevant interviews, lectures, personal stories, inquiries, and other content for use in independent or classroom-based explorations
- **Web resources** offering opportunities for extended inquiry and investigation
- **Skill Builder** assessment tools in downloadable form
- **SHRM Resource Guides** to cases and videos, which are available to instructors who are members of the organization
- **Tables, figures, and artwork** from the book in PDF form

Instructor materials for this book are available in the **Blackboard** course management system.

For Students

An open-access Student Study Site at www.sagepub.com/lussier provides materials and tools to be used in conjunction with the textbook to enhance understanding of key concepts, facilitate class discussion, and provide ideas for course projects and research. Resources include web quizzes, e-flash cards, and full-text articles from SAGE's celebrated journal collection with critical thinking questions, video links, and web resources.

Acknowledgments

We would like to thank our team at SAGE Publications, which helped bring this book to fruition. Our editor Lisa Cuevas Shaw brought us to SAGE and shepherded the development of *Human Resource Management* from its inception. Eve Oettinger, MaryAnn Vail, Mayan White, and Maggie Stanley provided additional assistance and support. We are grateful to Gail Bushman for a distinctive interior design that sets this book apart. During the production process, Melanie Birdsall, Brittany Bauhaus, and Melinda Masson provided their professionalism and valuable support. Helen Salmon lent her marketing experience and skills to promoting the book.

We would like to acknowledge our colleagues at SHRM who provided organizational resources to ensure that *Human Resource Management*—in particular the 2010 *SHRM Human Resource Curriculum*—is *the* textbook of choice for future HR practitioners. We would also like to recognize Cindy Wright of Saxon Drilling Services in Arkansas for her vital contribution of chapter opening vignettes, which feature her personal insight and experience as an HR professional. Excellent case material has been provided by Herbert

Sherman and Theodore Vallas of the Department of Management Sciences, School of Business Brooklyn Campus, Long Island University, by Gundars Kaupins of Boise State University, and by Robert Wayland, University of Arkansas at Little Rock.

Thanks to the following reviewers who participated throughout all stages of the book's development:

Vicki Baker, *Albion College*

Carrie Belsito, *Utah State University at Logan*

Ralph R. Braithwaite, *University of Hartford*

Larry K. Bright, *The University of South Dakota*

Eugene P. Buccini, *Western Connecticut State University*

Anthony DiPrimio, *Holy Family University*

W. Randy Evans, *University of Tennessee at Chattanooga*

Gerald P. Ferguson, *Community College of Allegheny County*

John T. Fielding, *Mount Wachusett Community College*

Melissa L. Gruys, *Wright State University*

Kim Hester, *Arkansas State University*

Sujin K. Horwitz, *University of St. Thomas*

Gary Hunt, *University of Maryland*

Gundars Kaupins, *Boise State University*

Rebecca Kelly, *University of Georgia at Athens*

George G. Klemic, *Lewis University*

Jack N. Kondrasuk, *University of Portland*

William C. Kostner, *Doane College, Lincoln Campus*

Debbie Mackey, *University of Tennessee*

Debbie L. Mackey, *University of Tennessee*

Rick Maclin, *Missouri Baptist University*

Kathleen W. Mays, *East Texas Baptist University*

Kelly A. Mollica, *University of Memphis*

Gary R. Murray, *Rose State College*

Arlene J. Nicholas, *Salve Regina University*

Thomas J. Norman, *California State University–Dominguez Hills*

Fidelis Ossom, *Northwestern Oklahoma State University*

Kern Peng, *Santa Clara University*

Allison Pratt, *Brandman University* and *Saddleback College*

Bill Price, *University of Texas of the Permian Basin*

Carlton R. Raines, *Lehigh Carbon Community College*

Roxanne Roske, *University of California at Los Angeles*

Romila Singh, *University of Wisconsin–Milwaukee*

Brenda Smith, *Southwest Tennessee Community College, Macon Cove Campus*

Lisa Stafford, *Fairfield University*

Howard R. Stanger, *Canisius College*

Frederick Tesch, *Western Connecticut State University*

Thomas R. Tudor, *University of Arkansas at Little Rock*

Lisa Turner, *Missouri State University*

Antoni Vianna, *University of Phoenix, San Diego Campus*

Amy Wojciechowski, *West Shore Community College*

References

Matulich, E., Papp, R., & Haytko, D. (2008). Continuous improvement with teaching innovations: A requirement for today's learners. *Marketing Education Review, 18,* 1–7.

Nirenberg, J. (1997). *Power tools.* New York: Prentice Hall.

Pfeffer, J., & Sutton, R. I. (2000). *The knowing-doing gap.* Boston: Harvard Business School Press.

Society for Human Resource Management. (2010). *SHRM human resource curriculum: An integrated approach to HR education: Guidebook and templates for undergraduate and graduate programs.* Alexandria, VA: Author. Retrieved August 15, 2011, from http://www.shrm.org/Education/hreducation/Documents/2010%20Curriculum%20Guidebook%20Final%203.31.10.pdf

21st-Century Human Resource Management Strategic Planning and Legal Issues

1

The New Human Resource Management Process

Learning Outcomes

After studying this chapter you should be able to:

 1.1 Identify the difference between the traditional view of Human Resource Management and the 21st-century view

1.2 Describe the major HRM skill sets

1.3 Discuss the line manager's HRM responsibilities

1.4 Identify and briefly describe the major HRM discipline areas

1.5 Explain the Practitioner's Model for HRM and how it applies to this book

1.6 Define the following terms:

Human resources
Employee engagement
Cost center
Revenue center
Productivity center
Productivity
Effectiveness
Efficiency
Job satisfaction
Turnover
Absenteeism
Sustainable competitive advantage

Information Age
Knowledge worker
Technical skills
Human relations skills
Conceptual and design skills
Business skills
Line manager
Staff manager
Society for Human Resource Management (SHRM)

Chapter 1 Outline

Why Study Human Resource Management?

HRM Past and Present
    Past View of HRM
    Present View of HRM

21st-Century HRM
    HRM Challenges
    The HRM Strategic View
    Technology and Knowledge
    Labor Demographics
    Productivity and Competitiveness Through HRM

HRM Skills
    Technical Skills
    Human Relations Skills
    Conceptual and Design Skills
    Business Skills

Line Managers' HRM Responsibilities
    Line Versus Staff Management
    Major HR Responsibilities of Line Management

HR Managers' Responsibilities: Disciplines Within HRM
    The Legal Environment: EEO and Diversity Management

Staffing
Training and Development
Employee Relations
Labor and Industrial Relations
Compensation and Benefits
Safety and Security
Ethics and Sustainability

HRM Careers
    The Society for Human Resource Management
    Other HR Organizations
    Professional Liability

The Practitioner's Model for HRM
    The Model
    Sections of the Model

Trends and Issues in HRM
    Technology and High-Performance Work Systems
    Increasing Globalization
    Ethical Issues—Reverse Discrimination

A. Employee and Labor Relations (required)
    4. Employee engagement
    5. Employee involvement
    6. Employee retention
    20. Attendance

B. Employment Law (required)
    22. Professional liability

D. Organization Development (required)
    5. Improving organizational effectiveness
    6. Knowledge management
    9. Ongoing performance and productivity initiatives
    10. Organizational effectiveness

H. Strategic HR (required)
    6. Internal consulting (secondary)
    9. Ethics (integrated)
    11. Organizational effectiveness

Case 1-1. Welcome to the World of 21st-Century HRM

SHRM
HR CONTENT

See Appendix A: *SHRM 2010 Curriculum Guidebook* for the complete list

HRM *Is* a Profession!

In my personal opinion, the increase in employer requirements for professional certification exemplifies the transition in Human Resource Management from record keeper to strategic partner status. I'm glad I was encouraged to certify as soon as possible. The investment in certification paid off in tangible proof of expertise in the body of knowledge deemed essential for work in Human Resources, and helped me advance my employment opportunities.

Actually, my professional progress was set in motion with membership in professional HR organizations. First I became a Society for Human Resource Management (SHRM) student member, which provided access to SHRM's website— valuable for research while I was a college student, and still an often used resource in my work.

Next, my involvement spread to the local HR association. The chapter meetings provide excellent opportunities to network, swap "best practice" policies, and learn from colleagues. It was here that I discovered the HR Certification Institute training classes. I am still good friends with many of the people I met during those classes. In fact, the people who invest in certification are the ones who tend to become more involved in their profession and, by extension, to become more successful as well.

I, Cindy Wright, invite you to join me throughout this textbook as we explore real-life HR situations highlighting important information from each chapter. Continue reading Chapter 1 to discover more about Human Resource Management as a profession.

❖   ❖   ❖

Cindy came late to the Human Resources profession, and perhaps that explains some of her passion for the field. As she explains: "It's not often that one is lucky

enough to be able to decide as an adult exactly what it is you really want to do and then go out and do it." Bringing her background experience as an involved parent, community volunteer, and family business manager to bear on her education, Wright graduated summa cum laude with a Business Administration degree, HR emphasis. Cindy tested for her Human Resource Certification Institute (HRCI) Certification as a Professional in Human Resources (PHR) at her initial date of eligibility because she believes certification is a crucial element of professionalism.

Cindy's first position as a benefits specialist for a Caterpillar dealer with 500 employees allowed her to conduct the company's first ever employee benefit satisfaction survey and revamp a paid time off arrangement for the hourly workers as a result. After further employment as a benefits administrator for seven thousand telecommunication's retirees, she has shifted to an HR Generalist position with Saxon Drilling, a gas well drilling company employing just under 500 workers.

Besides membership in the profession's national organization—the Society for Human Resource Management (SHRM), Wright has been active in the local affiliated chapter—the Central Arkansas Human Resources Association (CAHRA). Wright serves as Vice President of Administration for the chapter's Board as well as Chair of the College Relation's Committee. She was recognized by her peers with the "Rising Star" award for her work in creating a student chapter membership. Currently involved in organizing a CAHRA satellite chapter in Conway, AR, Wright's mission is to provide assistance to others interested in entering into and advancing within the Human Resources profession.

WHY STUDY HUMAN RESOURCE MANAGEMENT?

It's natural at this point to be thinking, "What can I get from this book?" or "What's in it for me?" These questions are seldom asked or answered directly. But they should be answered.[1] Success in our professional and personal lives is about creating relationships,[2] and students understand the importance of relationships.[3] So the short answer is that the better you can work with people— and this is what most of this book is about—the more successful you will be in your personal and professional lives as an employee, a manager, or a Human Resource Manager.

Today's students want courses to have practical relevance.[4] So that is the focus of this book; we designed it to be the most relevant "how to" book you ever used. As indicated by its subtitle, "Functions, Applications, and Skill Development," this book uses a three-pronged approach, with these objectives:

- To teach you the important functions and concepts of Human Resource Management (HRM)
- To develop your ability to apply the HRM functions and concepts through critical thinking
- To develop your HRM skills in your personal and professional lives

The book offers some unique features to further each of these three objectives, as summarized in Exhibit 1-1.

Let's go on to the longer answer to why we study HRM. Human Resource issues are emerging as some of the most prominent concerns for owners and managers.[5] You've probably heard buzzwords floating around about managers—and particularly Human Resource Managers—needing to be more strategic, business focused, customer focused, and generally in tune with the overall operational success of the organization.[6] Think about it for a minute. What is happening in today's business environment that might be causing Human Resource Managers to rethink their way of doing business? One of the primary items that is causing this process of rethinking management is that there is much greater competition within most industries today compared to 20 or 30 years ago.[7] As a result, Human Resource Managers as well as Operational Managers have been forced to think in more strategic terms about how their organization can win against their competitors by utilizing their human resources.[8]

One simple fact is that, in the 21st-century organization, **human resources**—*the people within an organization*—are one of the primary means of creating a competitive advantage for the organization, because management of human resources affects performance.[9] Why is this? It's simply because most organizations of comparable size and scope within the same industry generally have access to *the same* material and facilities-based resources. This being the case, it's very difficult to create a competitive advantage based on material, facility, or other tangible or economic resources. What this leaves is people. If the organization can manage its people (human resources) more successfully than its competitors can, if it can get employees involved in the day-to-day success of the organization, it has a much greater chance of being successful—with the term *successful* defined as being more productive and more profitable than the competition. Managers are responsible for getting the job done through employees,[10] so the organization's human resources are its most valuable resource.[11] (As you can see, there is a SHRM Guide box next to this section. We will explain them in the sixth section of this chapter.)

Companies who fall "in the top 10% on employee engagement beat their competition by 72% in earnings per share during 2007–08."[12] Also in a 2009 study it was shown that "during a span of 12 months, companies with high levels of engagement outperformed

SHRM

Guide – A:5
Employee involvement

SHRM

Guide – A:4
Employee engagement

Exhibit 1-1	Features of This Book's Three-Pronged Approach
Features That Present HRM Functions and Concepts	• Learning Outcome statements • Key terms • Step-by-step behavior models • Chapter summaries with glossaries • Review questions
Features to Apply the HRM Functions and Concepts That You Learn	• Opening thoughts • Organizational examples • Work Applications • Applying the Concepts • Cases • Videos
Features That Foster Skill Development	• Self-Assessments • Communication Skills questions • Skill Builder exercises

those with less engaged employees in operating income, net income growth rate and earnings per share growth rate."[13] In this context, we define engaged employees as those who understand what they need to do to add value to the organization and are satisfied enough with the organization and their roles within it to be willing to do whatever is necessary to see to it that the organization succeeds. While employee satisfaction (which we will talk about at length later) can be a part of engagement, the concept of **employee engagement** is much larger. It is *a combination of both job satisfaction and a willingness to perform for the organization at a high level and over an extended period of time.*

This book will teach you how to operate successfully within your organization and compete productively in a 21st-century organization—as an employee, a Human Resource (HR) Manager, or any other type of manager—to get your employees involved or engaged, and to get the results necessary to succeed in the new century against tough competitors.[14] We will focus on Human Resource Management, but the principles within this text apply to any form of management. The bottom line for you here is that if you learn these skills and apply them successfully in your role as a manager, you *will* get your employees engaged and improve productivity, and *that* is what will get you noticed by senior management and allow you to move up the organizational ladder. So let's get started.

HRM Past and Present

First, let's look at how Human Resource Management has changed over the past 40 years, taking us from the past traditional view of HRM to the present 21st-century view of HRM.

Past View of HRM

Back in the dark ages around the mid-1970s (there weren't even any computers available to most managers!), Human Resource Manager (we usually called them Personnel Managers then) were sometimes selected for the job because they had limited skills as an Operational Manager—they might have had less experience or been considered "a people person" rather than a "tough boss." In other words, they weren't considered to be as capable of managing what were considered to be *real* operations, so we put them in HR. Why? In general, Human Resource Management was considered to be a bit easier than other management jobs. Human Resource Managers were only expected to be "paper pushers" who could keep all of the Personnel files straight. They maintained organizational records on the people who worked for the company but had very little to do with the management of the organization's business processes. Since all they had to do was manage paper, we frequently put those with more limited skills in Personnel.

In this environment, most Human Resource Departments provided limited services to the organization—keeping track of job applicants, maintaining employee paperwork, and filing annual performance evaluations. The line managers were the ones responsible for directly managing the people within the organization.

Cost centers. In these types of organization, the Human Resource Department was considered to be a cost center for the organization. What's a cost center? In simple terms, a **cost center** is *a division or department within the organization that brings in no revenue or profit—it only costs money for the organization to run this function.* As you can easily see, we don't want many (or any) cost centers in an organization if we can help it. We need revenue centers instead.

Revenue centers. **Revenue centers** are a *division or department that generates monetary returns for the organization.* Where cost centers eat up available funds, revenue centers provide funds for the organization to operate in the future. So, what's a good HR Manager to do?

Present View of HRM

The old workplace, in which managers simply told employees what to do, is gone. You will most likely work in a team and share in decision making and other management tasks. Today, people want to be involved in management,[15] and organizations expect employees to work in teams and participate in managing the firm.[16]

Productivity centers. Welcome to the 21st century and the productivity center. A **productivity center** is *a revenue center that enhances profitability of the organization through enhancing the productivity of the people within the organization.* So, why does a modern organization worry so much about HRM? Today's Human Resource Manager is no longer running an organizational cost center. Their function, along with all other managers within the organization, is to improve organizational revenues and profits—to be a profit center. How does HR create revenue and profits for the organization? They do it through enhancing the productivity of the people within the organization. **Productivity** is *the amount of output that an organization gets per unit of input, with human input usually expressed in terms of units of time.*

SHRM

Guide – D:9
Ongoing performance and productivity initiatives

We must be more competitive in today's business environment in order to survive for the long term. As a manager of any type, we do things that will improve the productivity of the people who work for us and our organization—we create productivity centers.

But, how can we become more productive? Productivity is the end result of two components that managers work to create and improve within the organization:

– **Effectiveness**—*a function of getting the job done whenever and however it must be done; it answers the question "Did we do the right things?"*

– **Efficiency**—*a function of how many organizational resources were used in getting the job done; it answers the question "Did we do things right?"*

Both of these are important, but most of the time we are focused on efficiency. Human resources (our people) allow us to be more efficient as an organization *if* they are used in the correct manner. This course is about how to make *our people* more efficient.

Recall that efficiency is a function of how many organizational resources we use up in order to get the job done. It doesn't matter what kind of resource we are talking about. We burn up material resources doing our jobs, we burn up monetary resources doing our work, and we burn up facility resources doing our jobs. Do we burn up *human* resources? Well, not literally, but we burn up people's time. This is the value that we have in our people—their time. We physically use up monetary resources, facility resources, and material resources, but we use up the time available from our people.

Today's technology improves the effectiveness and efficiency of HR Managers leading to higher levels of productivity throughout the organization.

Managing HR deals primarily with improving the efficiency of the people within your organization. If your people are inefficient, it can kill you—literally kill your organization. Your organization will fail if your people are inefficient over long periods of time. If we don't use our people efficiently, we're ultimately going to be forced out of business by somebody who is better at using those resources than we are. So the primary reason we're worried about HR Management within an organization is to improve efficiency of our human beings.

So how do we make our people more efficient? Well, the problem is that we can't really *directly* affect the performance of individuals within the organization. We can't force an

SHRM

Guide – D:5, D:10, H:11
Improving organizational effectiveness;
Organizational effectiveness

employee to act in a certain way all of the time within the organization. We have the ability to sanction (punish) them when they don't do what we need them to do, but we *don't* have the ability to directly control all of their actions. As managers for the organization, we have to do things that will have an indirect effect on our people's productivity—their efficiency and effectiveness. We have certain things within our control as managers that can cause our people to do things that we need them to do.

21st-Century HRM

In this section, we discuss some of the issues facing today's HR Managers, including challenges, the strategic view, technology and knowledge, changing labor demographics, and productivity and competitiveness through HRM.

HRM Challenges

Before we go further, let's look at some of the things that managers tell us make their jobs more difficult and that they can't *directly* control.[17] Every time that we survey managers in any industry, in any department, about managing others, they bring up the following issues as among the most important and most difficult things that they deal with:

1. Productivity—defined above

2. Job satisfaction—a feeling of well-being and acceptance of one's place in the organization

3. Turnover—permanent loss of workers from the organization (People who quit would be considered *voluntary* turnover, while people who were fired would be *involuntary* turnover.)

4. Absenteeism—temporary absence of employees from the workplace

Note that all of these issues deal with people—not computers, not buildings, not finances—people! Also, the manager has no *direct* control over these things. The manager only affects these items through indirect actions. In other words, we can't *force* employees to come to work in order to avoid absenteeism or to be happy with their work. We have to create conditions where employees are willing to, or even want to, come to work and where they enjoy their job. We can (and should) do this through employment practices that the employee perceives as fair and reasonable, such as providing acceptable pay for the tasks performed by the employee.

We have already introduced you to productivity. What about the other three items? Why do we care about job satisfaction, turnover, and absenteeism? Let's take a moment to have a more detailed look at each of them.

Job satisfaction, as noted above, *is the feeling of well-being that we experience in our jobs—basically whether or not we like what we do and the immediate environment surrounding us and our jobs,* or "the extent to which people like (satisfaction) or dislike (dissatisfaction) their jobs."[18] Why do we as managers worry about our employees' job satisfaction? Well, there is a wealth of research that shows that if our employees are highly dissatisfied with their jobs, they will be far more likely to have lower than average productivity. Is the opposite true? If we have highly satisfied employees, will they necessarily have higher productivity? Not necessarily, although they could have.[19] But let's leave that discussion for later. For right now, just understand that low job satisfaction typically leads to lower productivity, so we want to maintain high job satisfaction.

What about turnover? **Turnover** is *the permanent loss of workers from the organization.* Does turnover cost the organization? Absolutely![20] What costs are associated with turnover

WORK
APPLICATION 1-2

Recall your most recent job. Did you work in a traditional cost or revenue center or a present productivity center? Briefly describe the firm and department and what made it a cost, revenue, or productivity center.

Video Link 1.1
HRM Challenges

SHRM

Guide – A:6
Employee retention

within the organization? Well, first we have the cost of the paperwork associated with the departing employee and—if they left involuntarily—we may have increases in our unemployment insurance payments. Next, we must find someone else to do the job—we have job analysis costs, recruiting costs, and selection costs (we will talk about all of these later). Once we hire someone new, we have orientation and other training costs, costs associated with getting the new worker "up to speed" on their job—something we call a learning curve—and costs associated with them just not knowing our way of doing business (every company has a unique culture, and not knowing how to act within that culture can cause problems). So, again, we have many costs associated with the process of turnover in the organization, and as a result, we want to minimize turnover.

How about absenteeism? **Absenteeism** is *the failure of an employee to report to the workplace as scheduled.* What's the big deal here? If employees don't come to work, we don't have to pay them, right? Well, that's true for some of them, but not when we give sick pay. So why do managers worry about absenteeism? Well, for one thing, it *does* cost the organization money[21]—not necessarily directly, but indirectly. Even if we don't have to pay employees when they are absent from work, we still have to maintain all of their benefits like health insurance; that costs the organization, doesn't it? We also likely lose productivity in other employees because they are there to do our work and others depend on them; that costs us money. In addition, if some of our workers are frequently absent, it causes lower job satisfaction in others who have to "take up the slack" for their absent coworkers. And there are other issues as well. So, we can quickly see that even though we don't have to pay some of our workers if they don't come to work, absenteeism still costs the organization money. So managers are concerned with absenteeism.

Note that the four HR challenges are interrelated. Absenteeism is costly; it is often due to the result of low job satisfaction, and usually leads to lower productivity.[22] People tend to leave their jobs (turnover) when they don't have job satisfaction, and while they are being replaced, and sometimes after, productivity in the organization goes down.[23] Because it can affect absenteeism, turnover, and productivity, we will discuss job satisfaction in Chapter 10.

So now that we have reviewed these four big issues that managers can't directly control, we can see how important they are. The bottom line for this section is that, as managers, we always need to be looking for things to do that will improve productivity and job satisfaction and reduce absenteeism and turnover. These four items are *critical*. Everything in HRM revolves around these four things.

The HRM Strategic View

Strategy and strategic planning deal with a process of looking at our organization and environment—both today and in the expected future—and determining what we as an organization want to do to meet the requirements of that expected future. We work to predict what this future state will look like and then plan for that eventuality. Line managers in organizations have participated in strategic planning for around 70 years, but their HR cousins did not really get involved until about the mid-1980s at the earliest.

Only in the last 30 or so years has HR Management really gone from reactive to proactive in nature. Instead of waiting for someone to quit and then going out and finding a replacement, HR Managers are now actively seeking talent for their organizations.[24] Good HR Managers are constantly looking at processes within the organization and, if there is something going wrong, figuring out how to assist the line management team in fixing the problem, whether it is a training problem, a motivation problem, or any other people-oriented problem. The function of HR has been redesigned to enhance the other (line) functions of the business.

SHRM

Guide – A:20
Attendance

WORK
APPLICATION 1-3

How would you rate your level of productivity, job satisfaction, turnover, and absenteeism in your current or a past job?

Sustainable competitive advantage. Why has HR been redesigned? To make our organizations more competitive and create sustainable competitive advantages. This is the basis for strategic HRM.[25] Strategy and strategic planning deal with the concept of creating "sustainable competitive advantages." **Sustainable competitive advantage** is *a capability that creates value for customers that rivals can't copy quickly or easily, and allows the organization to differentiate its products or services from competitor products or services.* An organization creates a sustainable competitive advantage over its industry rivals by doing something that creates value for its customers that rivals can't copy quickly or easily,[26] and that allows it to differentiate its products or services from competitor products or services.

So the question then is: Can we get an advantage from our buildings or physical facilities? Can we gain an advantage from our equipment? Can we create machinery that our competitors can't create or imitate? Do we have access to computers that they don't have access to? Of course not—not in most cases anyway. It is very rare that we can create any *real* technological advantage over any significant period of time, even if our technology is proprietary. If we create a technological advantage in today's business environment, it's usually overcome, or at least closely matched, fairly quickly. So where within the organization can we create sustainable competitive advantage? The only place we can consistently create advantage that our rivals can't quickly match is through the successful use of our human resources—getting them to be more productive than our rivals. If we can create an organization where people want to come to work, and as a result of wanting to come to work they are more productive, less likely to leave, less likely to be absent, and more creative and innovative—if we create that kind of organization, guess who wins? We win; you lose; you die. It's that simple.

The main goals of strategic HRM. So then, what are the main goals of strategic HRM? In the 21st-century organization, the primary HRM function is no longer just ensuring that the company has (1) the correct number of employees with the levels and type of skills the organization requires and (2) control systems to make sure employees are working toward the achievement of the goals in the strategic plan. This is a control model for organizational management that doesn't work in today's organization.

While we must successfully do these things sometimes, we also have to encourage our human resources to the maximum extent possible through motivation, leadership, environmental analysis, and organizational changes that work to improve job satisfaction. The model for a successful HR Manager has evolved to encompass the processes required to get that necessary employee engagement and the associated increases in productivity and job satisfaction while lowering absenteeism and turnover. That's a full plate for any manager. As a result, HR Managers *have to be* part of the strategic planning team today.

Analyze strategic direction for HR fit. One of the most interesting and exciting jobs within the HRM field is as part of the strategic planning efforts for the organization. Why is it so interesting and exciting? It is because, if you play a role in creating the strategy for the organization, you have a hand in creating the organization's future. As we have already noted, HRM efforts are critical in order to be able to carry out organizational plans and reach goals that have been defined by the strategic plan. While this is not usually an option for those who are early in their HR careers, it is certainly an option as they get experience in four skill sets—human relations skills, technical skills, conceptual and design skills, and especially business skills (see "HRM Skills" later in this chapter).

Technology and Knowledge

Why has the job of the HR Manager changed so drastically? It has changed primarily because of the type of work that we do today in organizations compared to the type of work that was common in the last century. The 20th century saw the growth and decline of the

WORK
APPLICATION 1-4

Recall your most recent job. What is the firm's competitive advantage, and how would you rate its sustainability?

Industrial Age in the United States and most other developed countries around the world. However, as we neared the end of the 20th century we started to enter the **Information Age**—*an era that began around 1980 in which information became one of the main products used in organizations and that is characterized by exponential increases in available information in all industries.* This is when assembly line work began to be taken over more and more by computers and robots, and the humans in our organizations were beginning to provide more than just labor. They started to provide intelligence—or knowledge. In this Information Age, we began to see a new kind of worker.

Guide – D:6
Knowledge management

Knowledge workers and the knowledge-based firm. **Knowledge workers** are *workers who "use their head more than their hands"—knowledge workers gather and interpret information in order to improve a product or process for their organization.* There has been a lot written in the past 20 years on knowledge workers, but we can boil it down to the fact that most workers in your generation are not going to be working primarily with their hands; they will be working with their minds. Knowledge workers "manage knowledge" for the firm.

The pace of technological change. One of the most critical issues that we face in the 21st century is that technology is currently outstripping our ability to use it. In other words, we are creating computers and other technological systems that we can't figure out how to use as quickly as they are created. Computers get faster and faster, but the human beings who have to use them don't. What does this mean to a business? It means that if we (the *people* in the organization) can figure out ways to take advantage of the technology better and quicker than our competitors, then we can create a sustainable competitive advantage. Notice that we didn't say that we create *better technology*—that wouldn't give us a sustainable advantage. Our competitors could just copy the technology in one form or another once we designed it. We create the ability to continually figure out ways to *use the technology* more successfully. So, as the technology changes, our people continually figure out ways to take advantage of it before our competitors' people do. This ability within our people is the thing that creates a continuing advantage over competitors who either don't have people with as much knowledge and as many varied skill sets, or don't have people who want to assist the organization because they are not engaged and not satisfied.

Knowledge is precious in an organization. We never have enough knowledge. There is a continuous shortage of knowledge workers for our organizations—those people with specialized sets of knowledge that they can apply to the problems within our companies. They don't work with their hands; they work with their heads. In fact, "the majority of jobs being created in the United States require skills possessed by only twenty percent of the current workforce."[27] And the United States is not alone. In most countries of the world, the news is the same—too few knowledge workers with too many knowledge jobs open and waiting for them. This means that for the foreseeable future, we will have a shortage of knowledge workers in our organizations across the globe.

What does this mean to the organization's HR Manager? It means that they are going to be competing for talent (20% of adults) with every other HR Manager in the world. If the organization has a reputation as a difficult place to work, will the organization succeed in getting people to come to work for them when they have so many other opportunities? I think not! Only if the organization manages their human resources successfully and maintains a reasonable working environment will they have any chance of filling most of the jobs that they have available.

Labor Demographics

In addition to the issue of knowledge workers and knowledge-based organizations, we face significant demographic changes over the next 20 years in the labor force that will be available to our companies.

Part of the diversity in today's workforce is people retiring later in life and working part-time.

Companies are already seeing a reduction in the number and quality of potential employees, as well as greater gender, ethnic, and age diversity than at any time in the past. The lack of skilled workers for increasingly complex jobs is considered to be a major, ongoing problem.[28] Partly as a result of this shortage of skilled labor, we are seeing more older employees with high-level skill sets remain in the workforce. Some agencies estimate that over 90% of the growth in the U.S. labor force between 2006 and 2016 will be from workers ages 55 and older.[29] So as a manager in a 21st-century organization, your workforce will look much older than has historically been the case.

Your organization will also look more culturally diverse—even compared to today. The growth in immigrant workers will be substantial. Hispanic workers (of all nationalities) alone are predicted to be approximately 24% of the workforce in 2050, but today they compose only about 14% of the workforce. Asian workers are expected to move up from about 4% of the workforce to about 8%. But the gender mix will stay fairly close to what it is today. The percentage of women in the workforce has stabilized at about 47%–48%.[30]

What does all of this mean? It means that managers of a 21st-century organization will need to be more culturally aware and able to deal with individuals with significantly different work ethics, cultural norms, and even languages.

Productivity and Competitiveness Through HRM

Remember that managing productivity is the main job of any manager in an organization. However, the only way that we can get top-notch productivity is to manage job satisfaction, absenteeism, and turnover indirectly through the things that are within our control as managers. If we succeed in increasing productivity, we directly affect our company's competitiveness. Why? Because increased productivity leads to increased profitability, and if we are more profitable, we have many options for increasing our competitiveness over the long term, creating that sustainable competitive advantage that we talked about earlier.

HRM SKILLS

LO 1.2

Describe the major HRM skill sets.

What skills will an HR Manager need in order to succeed in their job? All managers require a mix of technical, human relations, conceptual and design, and business skills in order to successfully carry out their jobs (consider Exhibit 1-2). HR Managers are no different—all leaders need management skills to improve organizational performance.[31] The set of necessary skills for HR Managers is similar to the one for other managers, but of course it emphasizes people skills more than some other management positions would.

Technical Skills

The first set of skills necessary for successful HR Managers is technical skills, the easiest of the four sets to develop.[32] **Technical skills** are defined as *the ability to use methods and techniques*

Exhibit 1-2	HRM Skills

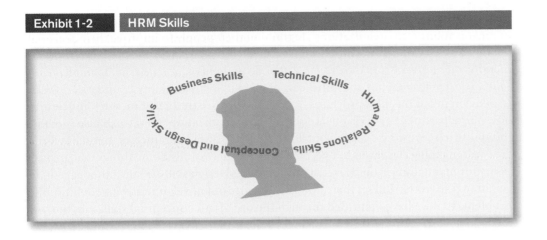

to perform a task. Being successful as an HR Manager requires comprehensive knowledge of laws, rules, and regulations relating to HR; computer skills, because everything in HR is now computerized, including some Equal Employment Opportunity (EEO) reporting requirements; skills in interviewing; training knowledge and skills; understanding of performance appraisal processes; and cultural knowledge (so we don't make a culture-related mistake), among many others. We will cover many of these skills in the remaining chapters of this book.

Human Relations Skills

The second major skill set is human relations (people) skills. **Human relations skills** are *the ability to understand, communicate, and work well with individuals and groups through developing effective relationships.* The resources you need to get the job done are made available through relationships, both inside (employees, coworkers, supervisors) and outside (customers, suppliers, others) the firm.[33] Organizations are seeking employees with good human relations skills,[34] and business schools are placing more emphasis on people skills.[35] We will focus on interpersonal skills throughout the book, and you will have the opportunity to develop your human relations skills through this course.

HR Managers must have strong people skills. This does not mean that HR Managers have to always be gullible or sympathetic to every sob story, but it does mean that they have to be *empathetic*. What is empathy? Empathy is simply being able to put yourself in another person's place—to understand not only what they are saying but why they are communicating that information to you. Empathy involves the ability to consider what the individual is feeling, while remaining emotionally detached from the situation.

Human relations skills also involve the ability to work well with others in teams, to persuade others, to mediate and resolve conflicts, to gather information from others, and to jointly analyze, negotiate, and come to a collective decision.

Finally, human relations skills involve the ability to relate to, as well as influence, both employees and the executive staff of the organization. The HR Manager must be able to work both sides of this issue. There are many times where they have to speak with the executive suite about issues that are uncomfortable or that, at least in the short term, affect organizational productivity. These conversations are delicate and require significant ability to sway the thoughts and opinions of others.

Conceptual and Design Skills

Conceptual and design skills are another skill set required in a successful HR Manager, and it is based on decision making. Clearly, the decisions you have made over your

WORK
APPLICATION 1-5

Give examples of how your present or a past boss used each of the four HRM skills.

lifetime have affected you today. Leadership decisions determine the success or failure of organizations,[36] so organizations are training their people to improve their decision-making skills.[37] **Conceptual and design skills** include *the ability to evaluate a situation, identify alternatives, select a reasonable alternative, and make a decision to implement a solution to a problem.* The conceptual part of this skill set is an ability to understand what is going on in our business processes—the ability to "see the bigger picture" concerning how our department or division and the overall organization operates. It also includes the ability to see if we are getting outside expected process parameters. In other words, are we doing things we shouldn't be, or are we not successfully doing things that are necessary for maintaining a high level of productivity? Design skills are the other part of the equation. This is the skill set that allows us to figure out novel or innovative solutions to problems that we have identified through the use of our conceptual skills. So, the first part of this skill set is identification of any problems that exist, and the second part is decision making to solve problems.

Business Skills

Lastly, HR Managers must have strong general business skills. Like technical skills, business skills are easier to develop than human relations and conceptual and design skills.[38] **Business skills** are *the analytical and quantitative skills, including in-depth knowledge of how the business works and its budgeting and strategic planning processes, that are necessary for a manager to understand and contribute to the profitability of their organization.* HR professionals must have knowledge of the organization and its strategies if they are to contribute strategically. This also means that they must have understanding of the financial, technological, and other facets of the industry and the organization.

1-1 APPLYING THE CONCEPT

HRM Skills

Identify each activity as one of the following types of HRM skills:

a. technical
b. human relations

c. conceptual and design
d. business

_____ 1. The HR Manager is giving a few department members a sincere thanks for finishing a job analysis ahead of schedule.

_____ 2. The HR Manager is scheduling employee work hours for next week.

_____ 3. The HR Manager is writing an e-mail.

_____ 4. The HR Manager is working on the budget for next year.

_____ 5. The HR Manager is trying to figure out why company attendance has dropped recently.

_____ 6. The HR Manager is making copies of a report for the meeting.

_____ 7. The HR Manager is being introduced to a new employee and talking socially with her for a few minutes before she goes to her new job.

LINE MANAGERS' HRM RESPONSIBILITIES

So, what if you are not planning on becoming an HR Manager? Why do you need to understand the topics that we are discussing throughout this book? Well, line managers are the first point of contact with most employees when they have questions about Human Resource policies or procedures. As a result, you have to have a basic understanding of the management of your organization's human resources. You need to be able to answer employee HR questions, and if you don't follow the HR policies you can get disciplined and fired, not to mention causing legal problems for your firm and potentially spending time in jail. In this section we explain the difference between line and staff management, and line managers' major HRM responsibilities.

LO 1.3

Discuss the line manager's HRM responsibilities.

Line Versus Staff Management

Line managers are *individuals who create and maintain the organizational processes and the people who create whatever it is that the business sells*, whether it is a pair of shoes or a technical service. They are simply the people who control the actual operations of the organization—what the organization *does*. A line manager may have direct control over staff employees, but a staff manager would not generally have any direct control over line employees.

HR Managers, on the other hand, would generally be staff managers. **Staff managers** are *individuals who advise line management of the firm in their area of expertise*. These managers act basically as internal consultants for the company within their fields of specialized knowledge. For example, a company accountant and lawyer would usually have staff authority within a manufacturing firm— they would be there to *advise* the operational managers concerning what is legal or illegal. However, in a law firm, a lawyer would usually be a line manager, because the organization's end product is knowledge and application of the law. In this case, the lawyer would have the ability to control the organization's processes to produce their output—a legal briefing, a lawsuit, or a contract agreement, for instance.

Line and staff employees can work more effectively together with today's technology.

SHRM

Guide – H:6
Internal consulting
(secondary)

Major HR Responsibilities of Line Management

So, what would a line manager need to know about HR Management? A lot! Remember that every manager's primary job is to manage the resources of the organization, including the *human* resources. The following list shows some of the major items that a line manager would need to understand in order to successfully do their job:

Legal considerations. Line managers can inadvertently violate the law if they don't know what the various employment laws say and what actions are prohibited in dealing with company employees. Laws that a line manager needs to understand include employment laws, workplace safety and health laws, labor laws, and laws dealing with compensation and benefits.

WORK
APPLICATION 1-6

Give examples of line and staff positions for an organization you work or have worked for.

Labor cost controls. What can and can't line managers do to minimize labor costs? All managers need to know how they can manage labor costs, both from an efficiency standpoint and from the standpoint of understanding the state and federal laws that limit our ability to manage our labor resources.

Leadership and motivation. Obviously, one of the major reasons we have managers is to provide motivation and leadership to employees in our organizations. Managers are worth "less than nothing" if they don't improve their workers' performance and productivity through use of motivation and leadership of those followers.

Training and development. Line managers are generally the first to see when there is a problem with organizational processes. This is frequently an indication that some type of tr loyees on their annual performance appraisals. This is another situation in which a manager might recognize the need for further training of the workforce. Finally, line managers are the people responsible for making changes to organizational processes. As a result of these changes, we frequently need to train our people on the new methods of doing our work.

Finally in this area, line managers are the people responsible for identifying the talented workers in the organization that we need to develop so that they can move into higher-level positions when they are needed. The organization needs to have these people "in the pipeline" so that as people leave the company or retire we have qualified individuals to take their place.

Appraisal and promotion. Line managers should almost always be responsible for the appraisal (also called evaluation) of the people who work for them as well as the process of debriefing these individuals on their annual (or more frequent) work evaluations. The line manager would also have a strong voice in who should be eligible for promotions in the organization, since their job is to know their people and each of their capabilities and limitations.

Safety and security of employees. Line management has primary responsibility for seeing to the safety and security of our workforce. They must know federal and state laws concerning occupational safety and health as well as procedures for security of the organization's workspaces and people from both outsiders and employees who would want to harm them. They need to monitor the areas under their physical control to minimize the hazards that can occur inside our companies.

So line managers have a lot to do with the human resources in the organization, don't they? Every line manager needs to know all of these things and more in order to be successful in their jobs. We will discuss the HRM process further as we go through this text.

WORK
APPLICATION 1-7

Give examples of HR responsibilities performed by your present or a past boss.

HR MANAGERS' RESONSIBILITIES: DISCIPLINES WITHIN HRM

LO 1.4

Identify and briefly describe the major HRM discipline areas.

But what if you *are* planning to become an HR Manager? HR Managers take the lead in the management and maintenance of the organization's people. It is an exciting field with many different paths that you can take over the course of your career. You can do such things as recruiting and selecting people into the company, training and developing talent, and managing compensation and benefits, among many others. The field is so broad that you could do something different each year for a 40-year career and never duplicate an earlier job exactly.

So if you have decided that you would like to explore the field of HRM as a career, what kind of jobs could you expect to fill inside your organization? What are your options for a career, and what kinds of specialized training and certification are available for you in the field? Although there are many different jobs in the field, most of them fall into a few functions. Let's take a look at each of these disciplines or specialties briefly. We will provide details in later chapters.

What areas are covered by the HR department in an average organization? Quite a few, actually. Most HR jobs are either *generalist* jobs, where the HR employee works in many different areas, or *specialist* jobs, where the employee focuses on a specific discipline of HR. What specialties are available? Here is a partial list of some of the major specialist careers that you can get into if you so desire. But first, complete Self-Assessment 1-1 to help you better understand your overall interest in HR and which specialties interest you most.

The Legal Environment: EEO and Diversity Management

Equal Employment Opportunity (EEO) and Diversity Management specialists are involved with the management of the organization's employee-related actions to ensure compliance with Equal Opportunity laws and regulations as well as organizational Affirmative Action plans when they are required or desired. These managers also have responsibilities related to the management of the diverse employee groups within the company. There are many issues in the diversity effort that require managing, including intergroup conflict, creating cohesiveness, combating prejudice, and others. We will discuss some of these issues later in the text.

The Human Resource legal and regulatory environment is critical to every organization today. This is also quite likely the area that changes more than any other in HRM. Every court case that deals with the Human Resource environment inside any organization has the potential to affect every organization with its results. Even if the court ruling doesn't change the way a company has to do business, if Congress sees that a ruling was unfair, they may change the law at either the federal or the state level, and that affects each organization under their jurisdiction. This, briefly, is how the Lilly Ledbetter Fair Pay Act (among other laws) was created. The Supreme Court ruled in a case of unequal pay based on existing laws, and because the U.S. Congress felt that the ruling was unfair, a law was enacted to change certain rules on how and when an equal pay complaint can be filed. We will talk a little more about this law in Chapter 2.

So, if every court case that deals with Equal Opportunity, or compensation and benefits, or harassment, or discrimination in any form has the opportunity to change the way every company does business, then you can quickly see that this is an area of critical importance to your company and that people with strong expertise in HR law are equally critical to the organization. So if you want a job where you *really* never do the same thing twice, look at the HR legal and regulatory environment.

Video Link 1.2

HR Managers' Responsibilities

Staffing

This is all of the things that we need to do in order to get people interested in working for our company—going through the recruiting process, selecting the best candidates who apply, and getting them settled into their new jobs. This is likely one of the most rewarding areas in HRM. We get to hire people into the organization who want to work for us. However, it is also a highly complex job where we have to understand the jobs for which we are hiring and the people who apply to fill those jobs, as well as the legalities involved with the hiring process. This is the first line of defense for the company. This area can literally make or break the organization in its ability to be productive. If we attract and hire the right types of people with the right attitudes and skills, the organization has a good start at being successful. If we hire the wrong types—people who don't want to work or don't have the correct skill sets—the organization will have a very difficult time being successful in the long term.

1-1 SELF-ASSESSMENT

HR DISCIPLINES

Following are 24 HR activities that you could be involved in. Rate your interest in each specialty with a number (1–7) that represents your interest in the activity.

I'm not really interested in doing this   I'm really interested in doing this

| | 1 | 2 | 3 | 4 | 5 | 6 | 7 |

1. _____ Working to make sure everyone in the firm is treated fairly.
2. _____ Working against discrimination and helping minorities to get hired and promoted.
3. _____ Knowing the HR laws, helping the firm implement them, and reporting how the firm complies with them.
4. _____ Working to get people to apply for jobs, such as writing advertisements and attending job fairs.
5. _____ Interviewing job candidates.
6. _____ Orienting new employees to the firm and their jobs.
7. _____ Teaching employees how to do their current jobs.
8. _____ Developing employees' general skills so they can progress in the firm.
9. _____ Designing curricula and lesson plans for others to teach employees.
10. _____ Coaching, counseling, and disciplining employees not working to standards.
11. _____ Working with teams and helping resolve conflicts.
12. _____ Working to understand and improve the level of job satisfaction throughout the firm.
13. _____ Working with union employees.
14. _____ Collective bargaining with unions.
15. _____ Solving employee complaints.
16. _____ Working to determine fair pay for different jobs, such as finding out competitor pay scales.
17. _____ Creating incentives to motivate and reward productive employees.
18. _____ Finding good benefit providers, such as lower-cost and higher-quality health care coverage.
19. _____ Making sure that employees don't get hurt on the job.
20. _____Working to keep employees healthy, such as developing diet and exercise programs.
21. _____ Ensuring the security of the facilities and employees, issuing IDs, and keeping employee records confidential.
22. _____ Ensuring that employees are ethical, such as working on and enforcing codes of ethics.
23. _____Enforcing ethical standards, such as maintaining methods for employees to confidentially report ethics violations.
24. _____ Working to help the organization develop methods to improve efficiency while protecting our environment.

Scoring and Interpreting Individual Discipline Results

Place your rating numbers (1–7) below and total the three scores for each discipline:

Legal Environment: EEO and Diversity Management

1 _____

2 _____

3 _____

_____ Total (rank total _____ [1–8])

Staffing

4 _____

5 _____

6 _____

_____ Total (rank total _____ [1–8])

Training and Development

7 _____

8 _____

9 _____

_____ Total (rank total _____ [1–8])

Employee Relations

10 _____

11 _____

12 _____

_____ Total (rank total _____ [1–8])

Labor and Industrial Relations

13 _____

14 _____

15 _____

_____ Total (rank total _____ [1–8])

Compensation and Benefits

16 _____

17 _____

18 _____

_____ Total (rank total _____ [1–8])

Safety and Security

19 _____

20 _____

21 _____

_____ Total (rank total _____ [1–8])

Ethics and Sustainability

22 _____

23 _____

24 _____

_____ Total (rank total _____ [1–8])

Based on the totals in each discipline, rank each of them from 1 to 8. The higher the score, the greater your interest in this area of HR, at this point in time in this book. It can change as you learn more about each discipline. You will also be doing self-assessments in other chapters that relate to these eight disciplines.

Scoring and Interpreting Total Discipline Results

Place the total of all eight disciplines (24 activities) here _____ and on the continuum below.

Low interest in HR 24   50   75   100   125   150   168   High interest in HR

The higher your score, the greater your overall interest in HR, again at this time only.

You should realize that this self-assessment is designed to show your interest. If you rated yourself low in an HR discipline, but you actually got a real job in that area, you could find it very interesting, and vice versa. The self-assessments throughout this book are designed to give you a better understanding of your interest and aptitudes that are open to your interpretations. For example, some people tend to rate themselves much lower and higher than others even though they have the same level of interest—so don't be too concerned about your score. There are *no* correct answers or scores. Some people with lower scores may actually enjoy the course more than those with higher scores. The objective is to gain personal knowledge and get you thinking about how the topic relates to "you."

So at this point, you should have a better idea of what the eight HR disciplines are and which areas are of more and less interest to you. But as you read the rest of this chapter and the others and learn more about each discipline, you may change your mind.

Training and Development

Next, we have the developing Human Resource discipline. This is where the training for the organization's human resources occurs. A modern organization won't get very far without constantly training their employees. Research supports that employees participating in more training and development are less likely to leave the company (turnover) and less likely to engage in neglectful behavior.[39] We train people for a variety of reasons, from teaching them their basic job to teaching them the things that they will need in order to move up in the organization as people above them resign or retire. If you enjoy teaching and learning, this might be an area to consider as a career field in HRM. Many HR Managers stay in training and development for their entire careers because they like it. They get to interact with many different people within the organization and get to learn about many different parts of the company as they go through the training processes.

As a Training and Development specialist, you would have responsibility for the training processes within the organization as well as curricula, lesson plans, and delivery of training courses. You would also be involved with the development of talent within the company in order to provide employees who are trained and able to move into more senior positions as they become vacant.

Employee Relations

What happens in the Employee Relations area of HR Management? This specialty covers a very wide array of items associated with management and employee relations. It involves such things as coaching, conflict resolution, counseling, and disciplining of the workforce as needed. It also involves leadership and team building efforts within the organization. Virtually every 21st-century organization operates with at least some teams as part of its structure, and teams create unique problems within the company. HR Managers also measure and evaluate job satisfaction as part of employee relations. We constantly evaluate the level of satisfaction in our organizations because we know that job satisfaction has a strong relationship with productivity. For right now, just understand that HR Managers in this function have to keep up with the many and varied laws relating to labor relations.

The Employee Relations specialty also involves the management of employee communication and work-related stress. These managers would typically be responsible for the management of job satisfaction and employee engagement within the company.

Labor and Industrial Relations

The Labor and Industrial Relations specialist works with the laws and regulations that control the organization's relationships with their workforce. This is also the area where any relationships that the organization has with unions are dealt with. HR Managers who work in this area might be involved in union votes, negotiations for union agreements, contract collective bargaining, handling grievances, and other items that affect the union-management relationship within the organization. This area also includes all relations activities, even in nonunion businesses. These managers have to maintain a working knowledge of all of the federal labor relations laws such as the National Labor Relations Act and the Taft-Hartley Act. Again, we will cover this in more detail later.

Compensation and Benefits

In the area of Compensation and Benefits, a manager might find jobs in compensation planning, salary surveys, benefits management, incentive programs, and much more. This area deals with how we reward the people who work for us. Rewards come in many styles and types, and this is where the organization decides on the total compensation package that they will use in order to attract and retain the best mix of people for their particular type of company. Here again, a manager will have to understand the federal and state laws that deal with compensation management within businesses, including the Fair Labor Standards Act and other major discrimination laws. Compensation management also includes issues such as pay secrecy, comparable worth, and wage compression—topics that we will cover in some detail in later chapters.

In this specialty, you will have a hand in setting pay scales, managing pay of various types, and administering benefits packages. All of the processes within this discipline are designed to help the organization attract and keep the right mix of employees. You would also deal directly with all of the federal and state compensation laws to ensure compliance in organizational pay and benefits procedures.

Safety and Security

We also need to protect our human resources. In this discipline, a manager might work in the area of occupational safety and/or health to make sure we don't injure our people or cause them to become sick because of exposure to some substance they work with. It also includes fields such as stress management and employee assistance programs that help employees cope with the demands of their jobs on a daily basis. And finally, this function works to ensure that employees are secure from physical harm by other workers, outsiders, or even acts of nature. We have to protect our people if we are going to expect them to do their jobs.

As a Safety and Security specialist, the HR Manager works to ensure that the work environment is safe for all workers so that on-the-job injuries and illnesses are minimized to the extent possible. They also have responsibility for managing the organization's plans for securing the workforce, both from being harmed by other people and from natural disasters such as earthquakes or tornados. These managers also have to maintain employees' confidential HR files.

Ethics and Sustainability

In this specialty, HR Managers bear responsibility for seeing to it that the organization acts in an ethical and socially responsible manner. They work on codes of ethics and making sure employees live by the codes, such as by maintaining ways in which employees can report violations of ethics (whistle-blowing).

ESR

SHRM

Guide – H:9
Ethics (integrated)

Environmental issues are now a major social concern,[40] and sustainable development has become one of the foremost issues facing the world.[41] *Sustainability* is meeting the needs of today without sacrificing future generations' ability to meet their needs.[42] All developed societies and a growing number of developing countries expect sustainability, or for managers to use resources wisely and responsibly; protect the environment; minimize the amount of air, water, energy, minerals, and other materials used in the final goods we consume; recycle and reuse these goods to the extent possible rather than drawing on nature to replenish them; respect nature's calm, tranquility, and beauty; and eliminate toxins that harm people in the workplace and communities.[43] Some companies operating in less developed countries have historically done a relatively poor job of maintaining the environment. In fact, in many cases, these companies decided to operate out of a particular country to minimize the costs associated with conservation and sustainability.

Recycling contributes to our present and future sustainability.

If you take a look at the table of contents as well as the Practitioner's Model below, you will realize that this book is organized to discuss these eight areas of HRM. We went through the disciplines pretty quickly, but each will be dealt with in much more detail as we continue through this text. For right now, just understand the basic idea that there are many different functions and areas in which an HR Manager can work as part of their organization. It is pretty much a guarantee that you won't get bored in your role as a 21st-century HR Manager if you don't want to. Next, let's take a look at some of the professional organizations that are out there that can help you get where you want to go in HRM.

WORK
APPLICATION 1-8

Give brief examples of the HR disciplines performed by the HR department (or individual responsible for HR) where you work or have worked.

1-2 APPLYING THE CONCEPT

HRM Disciplines

Match each activity to its HRM discipline:

a. Legal Environment: EEO and Diversity Management
b. Staffing
c. Training and Development
d. Employee Relations

e. Labor and Industrial Relations
f. Compensation and Benefits
g. Safety and Security
h. Ethics and Sustainability

_____ 8. The HR Manager is meeting with a union steward to resolve an employee grievance.

_____ 9. The HR Manager is working on an ad for the newspaper giving a brief description of a job opening.

_____ 10. The HR Manager is checking the cleanliness of the food processing equipment.

_____ 11. The HR Manager is working on the bonus system for production workers to motivate them to produce more.

_____ 12. The HR Manager is following the company policy of giving preference to African Americans so they can advance.

_____ 13. The HR Manager is teaching the new employee how to run the cash register.

_____ 14. The HR Manager is referring an employee to a drug counselor.

_____ 15. The HR Manager is interviewing a job candidate.

_____ 16. The HR Manager is investigating an employee sexual harassment case.

_____ 17. The HR Manager is working on a master's degree in HRM.

_____ 18. The HR Manager is working with an insurance company to offer employees a new dental plan.

_____ 19. The HR Manager is replacing the window air conditioners with a more energy-efficient model that emits less pollution.

_____ 20. The HR Manager is having the computer department install a new software program to make sure that no one can hack into the employee records.

HRM CAREERS

If you are interested in HRM as a career, there are several professional associations and certification programs in areas associated with HR Management that will help you get into these jobs and advance more quickly in the future. Here are some of them, and there are others within HR disciplines that are not discussed here.

The Society for Human Resource Management

Video Link 1.3
HRM Careers
SHRM

The first organization to deal with HR Managers was SHRM. **SHRM** is *the Society for Human Resource Management, the largest and most recognized HRM advocacy organization in the United States.* According to their website, SHRM is "the world's largest association devoted to human resource management . . . representing more than 250,000 members in over 140 countries."[44]

What does SHRM do? Probably the biggest part of their work is dedicated to two areas—first, advocacy for national HR laws and policies for organizations, and second, training and certification of HR professionals in a number of specialty areas. They also provide members with a place to network and learn from their peers as well as a vast library of articles and other information on HR Management. SHRM is such an outstanding organization that anyone thinking about a career in Human Resources should consider joining. Student memberships have always been, and continue to be, very inexpensive, especially considering all that is available to members of the organization. Does your school have a student SHRM chapter? If it does, and you are serious about a career in HR, join. If your school doesn't have a chapter, consider starting one.

SHRM operates the Human Resource Certification Institute (HRCI), which provides some of the top certifications for HR personnel anywhere in the world. The two biggest certification programs are the PHR and SPHR certifications. PHR stands for Professional in Human Resources, and SPHR is Senior Professional in Human Resources. Both of these certifications are recognized as verification of a high level of training by virtually any senior manager in organizations worldwide.

In addition to the HRCI, SHRM provides a curriculum guide for colleges and universities that offer HRM degree programs. The guide identifies specific areas in which SHRM feels students should gain competence as HRM majors. The curriculum areas are broken down into required, secondary, and integrated sections. Because SHRM is such a significant force in each of the HRM fields, we have decided to indicate where each of the required curriculum areas is covered within this text in order to show you the depth of knowledge that is required of a 21st-century HR Manager. In each chapter, you will see notes on the side of the page when an *SHRM required* topic is discussed. These notes are alphanumerically keyed to the information in Appendix A: SHRM 2010 Curriculum Guidebook. You might want to pay special attention to these side notes if you plan to become an HR Manager after school.

If you do decide to work toward a goal of becoming an HR Manager, you will need to think about the SHRM Assurance of Learning exam. This exam is sort of a student version of the PHR certification noted above. According to the SHRM website, "First and foremost, passing the assessment will help students show potential employers they have acquired the minimum knowledge required to enter the HR profession at the entry level."[45] To get more information about the Assurance of Learning exam, go to the SHRM website at www.shrm.org/assessment.

WORK
APPLICATION 1-9

Will you join a professional association and seek certification? Explain why or why not.

SHRM

Guide – B:22
Professional liability

Other HR Organizations

In addition to SHRM, two other significant organizations have recognized HR certification programs in the United States. They are the American Society for Training and Development (ASTD) and WorldatWork. As its name implies, ASTD primarily focuses on the training and development functions of HR Managers.[46] WorldatWork mainly deals with compensation, benefits, and performance management programs.[47] Both are quite high in quality within their area of focus. Each of the above organizations has an extensive website. If you are interested in them, take a look as you have time.

Professional Liability

One of the more important things that you need to understand if you are thinking about becoming a Human Resources Manager of any sort is the issue of professional (personal) liability for the actions that you take on behalf of the organization. You most likely don't know that HR Managers can be held personally liable for some of the actions that they take as part of their job. For instance, two federal laws, the Fair Labor Standards Act and the Family and Medical Leave Act (we will discuss these in detail in later chapters), "have both been construed by courts to provide for individual liability."[48] Both the organization and managers who have authority to make decisions for the organization can be sued by an employee who feels that their rights under these laws have been violated. This is one of the many reasons that if you plan to manage people, you really want to understand all of the HRM concepts as well as possible. These are only two examples of potential professional liability that an HR Manager can incur if they fail to take federal and state laws into account. There are many others. So you need to be aware of the potential for personal liability, and in some cases you may even need to consider professional liability insurance—for instance, if you are an HRM consultant to outside organizations.

LO 1.5

Explain the Practitioner's Model for HRM and how it applies to this book.

THE PRACTITIONER'S MODEL FOR HRM

We have given you a (really) brief history of the HRM world and what HR Management does for the organization. Now we need to get into the meat of the matter and start talking about some of the detailed information that you will need to know in order to be a successful HR (or other) manager for your organization once you earn your degree. How will we do that? We are going to work through what you need to know using a Practitioner's Model for HRM (Exhibit 1-3).

The Model

The Practitioner's Model is designed to show you how each of the sections of HRM interact and which items must be dealt with before you can go on to successfully working on the next section, kind of like building a foundation before you build a house. The model first provides you with knowledge of which organizational functions are *critical* in order to ensure that the organization can be viable over the long term. Second, you will learn what the organization needs to do in order *to sustain itself* over the long term. Third, the model discusses the critical issues in *managing* the organization's human resources successfully. Fourth and finally, the model discusses how to *maintain your human resources* through managing the compensation and benefits provided to your people and through making sure that they remain safe and secure while at work.

Exhibit 1-3	The Practitioner's Model for HRM

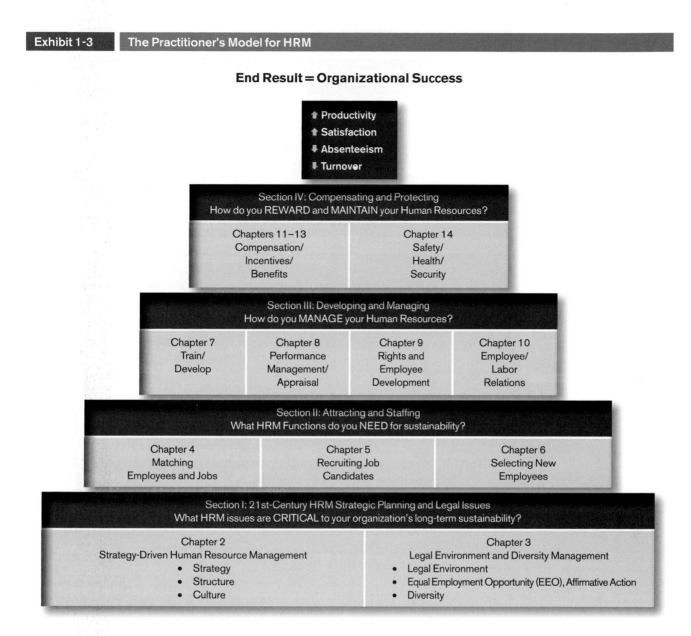

Sections of the Model

Let's discuss the details of each section of the model separately.

Section I: 21st-century HRM, strategic planning, and HR laws. Let's take it section by section. You have already begun Section I (Exhibit 1-4), where we talk about HRM in the 21st century along with the necessity for strategy-driven HRM and a strong understanding of the basic HR legal environment. This is the basis for everything else that a 21st-century HR Manager will do, so it is the foundation of our diagram. These things are *most critical* to the organization's basic stability and success because if we don't get them right, we will probably not be around long enough as an organization to be successful in the sections resting on this one.

Section II: Attracting and staffing. Once we have a stable organization with some form of direction, we will start to look at getting the right people into the right jobs in Section II (Exhibit 1-5). This section includes the items that will allow the organization to get its work done successfully over long periods of time. We first look at identifying the jobs that will

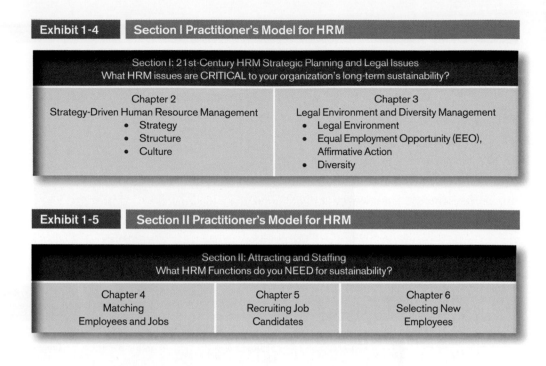

Exhibit 1-4	Section I Practitioner's Model for HRM

Section I: 21st-Century HRM Strategic Planning and Legal Issues
What HRM issues are CRITICAL to your organization's long-term sustainability?

Chapter 2 Strategy-Driven Human Resource Management	Chapter 3 Legal Environment and Diversity Management
• Strategy • Structure • Culture	• Legal Environment • Equal Employment Opportunity (EEO), Affirmative Action • Diversity

Exhibit 1-5	Section II Practitioner's Model for HRM

Section II: Attracting and Staffing
What HRM Functions do you NEED for sustainability?

Chapter 4 Matching Employees and Jobs	Chapter 5 Recruiting Job Candidates	Chapter 6 Selecting New Employees

need to be filled and then work through how to recruit the right numbers and types of people to fill those jobs. Finally, we find out what our options are concerning methods to select the best of those job candidates that we have recruited. The items in Section II are absolutely *necessary* for long-term organizational sustainability and success.

Section III: Developing and managing. In the third section (Exhibit 1-6), we learn how to manage our people once they have been selected into the organization. We have to train (and retrain) our people to do jobs that are ever-changing in today's organization; we have to evaluate them in some formal manner so that they know how well they are doing in the eyes of their management; and we have to develop them so that they can fill higher-level positions as we need people to step up into those positions. We unfortunately sometimes have to counsel and/or discipline our employees as well, so we need to learn how to do that so we can improve motivation when possible and so, if we can't improve motivation and can't overcome poor work behaviors, we know how to correctly and humanely separate the individuals from the organization (terminate them). Finally, Section III addresses the role of employee and labor relations, with emphasis on the function of unions within organizations. So Section III shows us how to *manage* our human resources on a routine basis.

Section IV: Compensating and protecting. The last section of the model (Exhibit 1-7) will cover the compensation and benefits packages that we work with in order to keep

Exhibit 1-6	Section III Practitioner's Model for HRM

Section III: Developing and Managing
How do you MANAGE your Human Resources?

Chapter 7 Train/ Develop	Chapter 8 Performance Management/ Appraisal	Chapter 9 Rights and Employee Development	Chapter 10 Employee/ Labor Relations

Exhibit 1-7	Section IV Practitioner's Model for HRM

Section IV: Compensating and Protecting How do you REWARD and MAINTAIN your Human Resources?	
Chapters 11–13 Compensation/ Incentives/ Benefits	Chapter 14 Safety/ Health/ Security

our people satisfied (or at least not dissatisfied). In this section, we also cover the area of worker safety and health and how organizations have changed in their attitudes concerning the well-being of their human resources. Again, the employees of a 21st-century organization are almost always the basis for at least some of our competitive advantage over our rivals in any industry, so we need to keep them healthy and happy. Section IV shows us how to *reward and maintain* our workforce, since they are so critical to our ongoing success.

TRENDS AND ISSUES IN HRM

In each chapter of this text, we will discuss some of the most important issues and trends in HRM today. These issues and trends will cover areas such as technology in HRM, globalization of businesses, ethical issues in HR, and diversity and equal opportunity. For this chapter, we chose the following three issues: technology and high-performance work systems, the ever-increasing globalization in virtually all types of industries, and the hotly debated issue of reverse discrimination.

Technology and High-Performance Work Systems

The 21st-century organization obviously uses computers and technology as an integral part of managing its business. We already discussed knowledge workers, who can only succeed if we give them the tools necessary to use their knowledge. One of the ways in which we use technology to manage knowledge and increase performance is through the use of so-called High-Performance Work Systems (HPWSs). An HPWS is "a set of HR practices, including comprehensive employee recruitment and selection procedures, compensation and performance management systems, information sharing, and extensive employee involvement and training, [that] can improve the acquisition, development and retention of the talented and motivated workforce."[49] "Leading organizational behavior specialists believe that [the] HPWS has the greatest potential to provide sustained competitive advantage to companies adopting it."[50] Organizations must get better at managing their technology in order to take advantage of the opportunities provided by HPWSs.

As you can see, creation of this "set of practices" would be impossible without the use of technology. We utilize technologies in the form of a Human Resource Information System (HRIS) to help us analyze individual applicants for employment; to maintain information on compensation packages, performance management, training, and retention; and to systematically capture knowledge from the people resources within our companies. You will be part of the generation of leaders that has to incorporate these technologies so that your organization can improve effectiveness and efficiency. The 21st-century organization cannot be successful in managing these items without significant use of technological

WORK
APPLICATION 1-10

Explain how technology is used where you work or have worked.

systems. Those organizations that are successful in adapting to the capabilities of technology will be the ones that create the sustainable competitive advantage that is required for long-term viability in today's world.

Increasing Globalization

There is little argument that globalization continues to increase in most industries worldwide. Why is this the case, and what does it mean to a 21st-century manager? Globalization occurs in a variety of ways, from sales and customer relations efforts in new country markets to where and how we source new workers. Outsourcing is one way that globalization is expanding. Outsourcing to companies that happen to be in another country (sometimes called offshoring) is increasing at a significant rate, due to the fact that many processes can be performed in other countries at a significant discount to their cost in the United States.

Video Link 1.4

Increasing Globalization

Whether you feel that this is right or wrong is of little importance. Let's say that you (and your company) decide that it is wrong to offshore jobs, and you don't do it even though you could save substantial amounts of money. In the meantime, your primary competitors *do* offshore those jobs and their processes, saving 20% of the cost of the goods produced. As a result, they can sell their products for 20% less than you can. Who is going to win in the marketplace? Will the average consumer pay 20% more for your goods because you were "saving your workers' jobs"? You know the answer to this—the average consumer will buy the cheaper goods.

So, globalization is going to continue as long as there are savings to be had. As a result, HR Managers will have to deal with a more global workforce as we move through the 21st century. They will have to be able to recruit and select workers in many different country markets; they will have to be able to train them and evaluate those workers' abilities; they will have to understand and adapt to cultural differences in work ethics; and they will have to be well versed in the HR laws of many countries. Globalization is a significant challenge to any manager, but it is a much more significant issue to HR Managers than to those in most other management fields.

WORK
APPLICATION 1-11

How has globalization affected where you work or have worked?

Ethical Issues–Reverse Discrimination

ESR

In 2009, a case claiming "reverse discrimination" came to the Supreme Court. What is reverse discrimination? It is discrimination against a majority group rather than a minority group—in general in the United States this would be White employees or applicants. Is reverse discrimination wrong? We protect many different minority groups within the United States, but how do we, and how should we, protect the majority group? At what point does the protection of minority groups cross over to discrimination against the majority?

The case that brought back discussions about reverse discrimination was *Ricci v. DeStefano*, 129 S. Ct. 2658 (2009),[51] and it renewed the discussion of race-based decision making in employment. While there are many nuances to the case and ultimately to the Supreme Court decision, the end result was that reverse discrimination was deemed to have occurred in this case. The basic issue is that a written promotion exam for firefighters was considered by the city of New Haven, Connecticut, to be discriminatory when no Black and only one Hispanic test taker passed the exam. As a result, the city threw the entire exam out due to *disparate impact* (we will discuss this term in Chapter 3) and didn't promote anyone. The firefighters who scored highest on the exam sued based on reverse discrimination. According to the local newspaper, the justices concluded that some of the city's arguments justifying its actions to the high court "are blatantly contradicted by the record" and found that the city "turned a blind eye to evidence supporting the exam's validity."

WORK
APPLICATION 1-12

What is your opinion regarding reverse discrimination? Have you experienced or seen discrimination at work?

Was the decision right or wrong? We can't make that determination here, but the area of employment discrimination (of all types) continues to be one that HR Managers have to be very aware of and guard against to the best of their ability. The HR department is, and will continue to be, the organization's watchdog on the topic of workforce discrimination.

Video Link 1.5
Reverse Discrimination

Wrap-Up

As we bring this chapter to a close, let's take a look at what we have accomplished. We started out by showing you how HRM has changed in the past several decades and how it has become much more important to the organization due to continuing demands to increase productivity. We showed you how productivity, job satisfaction, turnover, and absenteeism are issues that we have to deal with but have no direct control over, and we showed you how they affect work in organizations. We then identified several skills that you will need in order to be successful as a 21st-century HR Manager and identified the functional areas and the specialties that you can choose from if you decide to pursue a career in HRM. Finally, we gave you a model for success as a practitioner of HR Management and showed you just a few of the issues that HR Managers will face in the coming years. That's enough text for one chapter, so let's close this one out and move to giving the answers to the Learning Outcomes and Applying the Concepts and developing skills.

Chapter Summary

Visit www.sagepub.com/lussier for helpful study resources.

1.1 Identify the difference between the traditional view of Human Resource Management and the 21st-century view.

The traditional view of Human Resource Management is that of a cost center. A cost center is a department or division within an organization that uses up organizational resources but doesn't create revenues for the company. In the 21st-century organization, we view human resources as a productivity center for the company. As a productivity center, HR has a revenue-generating function by providing the organization with the right people with the right skills in the right place so that organizational productivity can be improved.

1.2 Describe the major HRM skill sets.

The HRM skill sets include technical skills, human relations skills, conceptual and design skills, and business skills. Technical skills include the ability to use methods and techniques to perform a task. Human relations skills provide the ability to understand, communicate, and work well with individuals and groups through developing effective relationships. Conceptual and design skills provide the ability to evaluate a situation, identify alternatives, select an alternative, and implement a solution to the problem. Finally, business skills provide the analytical and quantitative skills, including in-depth knowledge of how the business works and its budgeting and strategic planning processes that are necessary for a manager to understand and contribute to the profitability of the organization.

1.3 Discuss the line manager's HRM responsibilities.

Line managers require knowledge of each of the following topics:

- Major employment laws—line managers must know all of the major employment laws so that they don't accidentally violate them in their daily interactions with their employees.
- Labor cost controls—line managers have to understand what they are legally and ethically allowed to do to control labor costs.
- Leadership and motivation—probably the most significant function of a line manager is that of being a leader and motivator for the people who work for them. Managers are worth "less than nothing" if they don't improve employee performance.
- Training and development—line managers are typically the first point of contact to determine that training or development is required in order for their workforce to perform at eye level. They are also the people responsible for making changes to organizational processes. Training in new processes is typically required in order to create maximum productivity in our workforce.

- Employee safety and security—line managers have primary responsibility for safety and security of the workers in an organization. They have to know the laws that deal with occupational safety and health as well as security procedures to protect their people from individuals who might want to do them harm.

1.4 Identify and briefly describe the major HRM discipline areas.

- EEO and Diversity Management—specialists in this area deal with Equal Opportunity laws and regulations as well as management of a diverse workforce.
- Staffing—these specialists manage the processes involved in job analysis, recruiting, and selection into the organization.
- Training and Development—these managers take responsibility for the training processes within the organization as well as curricula, lesson plans, and delivery of training courses. They are also involved with development of talent within the company in order to provide a group of employees able to move into more senior positions as they become vacant.
- Employee Relations—this area involves coaching, counseling, and discipline processes along with employee communication and stress management. Employee Relations Managers are also typically responsible for the management of job satisfaction and employee engagement.
- Labor and Industrial Relations—these managers work with the laws and regulations that control organizations' relationships with their workforce. They also work with any union-management contracts, including but not limited to union votes, grievances, contract negotiations, and bargaining with union representatives.
- Compensation and Benefits—in this discipline, the individual will work with pay of various types and benefits packages, all of which are designed to attract and keep the right mix of employees in the organization. Compensation and Benefits Managers also deal directly with federal and state compensation laws to ensure compliance.
- Safety and Security—in the Safety and Security field, HR Managers work to ensure that the environment on the job is safe for all workers so that on-the-job injuries and illnesses are minimized to the extent possible. They also manage the organization's planning for securing the workforce, both from being harmed by other people and from natural disasters such as earthquakes and tornadoes.
- Ethics and Sustainability—in this field, HR Managers bear responsibility for seeing to it that the organization acts in an ethical and socially responsible manner, to minimize harm

to the environment and its various stakeholders. They manage the sustainability efforts in the organization in order to minimize its "footprint" on the environment—in other words to minimize the depletion of worldwide resources caused by the organization carrying out its processes.

1.5 Explain the Practitioner's Model for HRM and how it applies to this book.

The Practitioner's Model is designed to show the relationships between each of the functions and disciplines within HRM. On the first level are the items that are absolutely critical to the organization if it is going to continue to operate (and stay within federal and state laws while doing so) and be stable and successful for a significant period of time. The second level encompasses those things that are required in order to identify the kinds of jobs that must be filled, and then recruit and select the right types of people into those jobs in order for the company to maximize productivity over the long term. These are the items that will allow the organization to get its work done successfully over long periods of time. As we get into the third tier, we concern ourselves with management of the human resources that we selected in the second level. We have to get them training to do their jobs, and allow them to perform those jobs for a period of time. We then have to appraise their performance and if necessary correct behaviors that are not allowing them to reach their maximum potential through the coaching, counseling, and disciplinary processes. As this is occurring, we need to ensure that we maintain positive relationships with our employees so that they remain engaged with the organization and remain productive. We manage these positive relationships in many ways, from measuring and assessing job satisfaction periodically to managing relationships with union employees where we work for unionized employers. Finally, in the top tier, we want to make sure that we reward and maintain our workforce to minimize unnecessary turnover and dissatisfaction. We do this both through fair and reasonable compensation planning and through the maintenance of a safe and secure workplace.

Key Terms

Absenteeism	Employee engagement	Line manager	Staff manager
Business skills	Human relations skills	Productivity	Sustainable
Conceptual and design skills	Human resources	Productivity center	competitive advantage
Cost center	Information Age	Revenue center	Technical skills
Effectiveness	Job satisfaction	Society for Human Resource	Turnover
Efficiency	Knowledge worker	Management (SHRM)	

Key Term Review

Complete each of the following statements using one of this chapter's key terms:

_____ are the people within an organization.

_____ is a combination of both job satisfaction and a "willingness to perform" for the organization at a high level, and over an extended period of time.

_____ is a division or department within an organization that brings in no revenue or profit—in other words it costs money for the organization to run this function.

_____ is a division or department that generates monetary returns for the organization.

_____ is a revenue center that enhances profitability of the organization through enhancing the productivity of the people within the organization.

_____ is the amount of output that an organization gets per unit of input, with human input usually expressed in terms of units of time.

_____ answers the question "Did we do the right things?" It is a function of getting the job done whenever and however it must be done.

_____ is a function of how many organizational resources were used in getting the job done. It answers the question "Did we do things right?"

_____ is the feeling of well-being that we experience in our work—basically whether or not we like what we do and the immediate environment surrounding us and our work.

_____ is the permanent loss of workers from the organization.

_____ is the failure of an employee to report to the workplace as scheduled.

_____ is a capability that creates value for customers that rivals can't copy quickly or easily, and allows the organization to differentiate its products or services from competitor products or services.

_____ is an era that began around 1980 in which information became one of the main products used in organizations; it is characterized by exponential increases in available information in all industries.

_____ are workers who "use their head more than their hands" to gather and interpret information in order to improve a product or process for their organizations.

_____ include the ability to use methods and techniques to perform a task.

_____ are the ability to understand, communicate, and work well with individuals and groups through developing effective relationships.

_____ are made up of the ability to evaluate a situation, identify alternatives, select an alternative, and make a decision to implement a solution to a problem.

_____ are the analytical and quantitative skills, including in-depth knowledge of how the business works and its budgeting and strategic planning processes, that are necessary for a manager to understand and contribute to the profitability of their organization.

_____ create and manage the organizational processes and the people that create whatever it is that a business sells.

_____ are the individuals who *advise* line management of the firm in their area of expertise.

_____ is the largest and most recognized of the HRM advocacy organizations in the United States.

Quick Check (True-False)

Answer the following true-false questions. The answers are provided following the questions.

1. Revenue centers in a company eat up available funds, while cost centers provide funds for the organization to operate in the future. T F

2. Turnover, whether voluntary or involuntary, costs the organization money, and therefore the organization should generally attempt to minimize turnover. T F

3. The main goal of strategic HRM isn't just ensuring the correct number of employees have the levels and types of skills the organization requires; we also have to encourage our people through motivation, leadership, environmental analysis, and organizational changes that work to improve job satisfaction. T F

4. Cultural diversity within organizations has just about peaked, and will change very little over the next 20 years or so. T F

5. Technical skills for HR Managers include the ability to understand, communicate, and work well with individuals and groups through developing effective relationships. T F

6. Required skills for line managers include Legal Considerations, Labor Cost Control, Leadership and Motivation, Training and Development, Appraisal and Development, and the Safety and Security of Employees. T F

7. HR Training and Development Specialists are responsible for the training processes within the organization, including curricula, lesson plans, and delivery of training courses, as well as development of talented individuals within the company. T F

8. According to the Practitioner's Model, each section of the model stands alone—there is very little if any interaction required between the sections in order to create organizational success. T F

Communication Skills

The following critical-thinking questions can be used for class discussion and/or for written assignments to develop communication skills. Be sure to give complete explanations for all answers.

1. Why is it important for all business majors to take this course in HRM?

2. Are you interested in becoming an HR Manager? Why or why not?

3. Do you agree with the statement that "the people resources within the organization are one of the few ways to create a competitive advantage in a modern business"? Why or why not?

4. Is "employee engagement" possible in an age when people tend to have very little loyalty to their employers and vice versa? How would you work to increase employee engagement as a manager?

5. Can HRM *really* create revenue for the organization? If so, how?

6. Identify some things that could be done by a manager to increase productivity and job satisfaction and decrease absenteeism and turnover. Make a list for each item.

7. If you were an HR Manager for your organization, what would you do to increase the number of applicants who apply for "knowledge worker" positions in your organization? Assume you can't pay them more. What would you do then?

8. Is there anything that the individual within an organization can do to help improve relations among diverse workers? If so, what?

9. Some say that the hard skills (technical and business skills) are more important than the soft skills (human relations and conceptual and design skills) for a manager. What do you think, and why?

10. Are external certification programs (in all jobs) becoming more important? Why?

Video

Please visit the student study site at **www.sagepub.com/lussier** to view the video links in this chapter.

Answers

REVIEW QUESTIONS (TRUE-FALSE) Answers

1. F 2. T 3. T 4. F 5. F 6. T 7. T 8. F

Case

Case 1-1. Welcome to the World of 21st-Century HRM

Angie was standing at her (former) desk picking up her personal items and wondering how she had gotten into this mess. At one shoulder was the head of HR and at the other was one of the security officers. They were there to escort her out of the building as soon as she retrieved her personal items. Thinking back, the last hour or so had been a whirlwind. She had come to work like she had for the past several months, maybe a little late and a little hungover, but she was there.

Shortly after she had sat down at her desk to start making phone calls, her supervisor had called her into his office. He asked her to accompany him to the HR Manager's office. Once there, she saw a printout of her Facebook page and the blog that she kept on pretty much a daily basis. She was a little embarrassed by the photos on the printouts from her Facebook page, but at least they weren't as racy as some she had considered putting up. She was really glad that when she graduated from college she had purged her account of all of those pictures of the Florida vacations on the beach (and other places).

Angie knew, like all of the other employees, that company management had recently been going through some of the social networking sites to review potential recruits before they decided to hire them, but she didn't know anything about management reviewing current employees' personal webpages. *Well*, she thought, *my pages are pretty clean since I was warned about this by career services in college.*

However, what she saw next really bothered her. There was the highlighted section of her blog from last Thursday. She had forgotten about that! In the post, she had noted that she had a whopping hangover because of the girls' night out on Wednesday, and "I think I'll call in sick because I just can't face working for that idiot with this headache." Well, they knew that she wasn't sick. How could she have been that stupid?

As she sat there, she suddenly realized that this was no normal conversation—it looked more like an inquisition. And when the HR Manager informed her that the company was going to terminate her employment, she couldn't believe it. What had happened to freedom of speech? What had happened to a person's right to have a life outside of work? Could they monitor her personal communications that had nothing to do with work and then use them against her? She wasn't sure, but she thought that was wrong. Nonetheless, here she was cleaning out her desk.

According to a recent study by the company Harris Interactive for CareerBuilder.com, almost half of employers are using social networks to screen job candidates.[52] Over a third of employers had decided not to offer jobs to potential candidates based on content from their social networking sites including Facebook, LinkedIn, Myspace, Twitter, and others. CareerBuilder notes in another article how a person can get fired because of social media. They give the following five reasons as among the most prevalent: posting a scandalous photo; viewing or updating your profile on company time; posting information that conflicts with your employer's values; revealing why you're a lousy employee; and venting about your employer, boss, or job.[53]

Social media sites are no longer just a location where you can connect with your friends. Companies are routinely using these sites to research both recruits for employment *and* the actions of current employees. The Internet is full of references to people fired for things that they said on their personal webpages. And it doesn't necessarily matter if you set your pages to private. Your friends may still capture comments that you've made on their pages without you even knowing about it. In addition, recruiters may use your "friend" list to find people to call for references, and if your friend is unaware of the purpose for the call, they might say something that you'd rather they didn't. Employers can look at who has recommended you on sites such as LinkedIn and may approach those references as well.[54]

Social media is here to stay and companies are using it, but is Angie right? Can the company use her personal pages on social media sites against her as an employee? Should the employer be able to discipline an employee because of a personal social media page? Even if they can, is it ethical? Can an employee have any expectation that their personal rants, whether against their employer or the local store or their former boyfriend or girlfriend, are private? Isn't free speech protected by the Constitution? Organizations (and many employees and former employees) are now struggling with these questions. We will discuss these questions as we explore the world of 21st-century HRM over the next 14 chapters, but right now, what do you think?

1. Does Angie have a right to say what she wants on her Facebook page or in her blog? Why or why not?

2. What if she harmed the company or its reputation in some way with what she posted? Would that change your answer?

3. What if she gave out confidential information about new products or services?

4. Is it legal for the company to terminate an employee because of something they did away from work?

5. If it is legal for the company to terminate an employee for something they did on their own time, in what circumstances would this be legal? For example:

   - Would it be legal for the company to terminate an employee because the employee campaigned for a politician who was writing legislation that would harm the interests of the company?

   - Would it be legal for the company to terminate someone who wrote in their blog that they had physically assaulted another person because they were angry?

   - Would it be legal to terminate someone who wrote that they carried a gun to work, even though they really didn't?

6. Does Angie have any legal recourse because of the company firing her over her social media posts?

SKILL BUILDER 1-1

Getting to Know You

Objectives

1. To get acquainted with some of your classmates.

2. To gain a better understanding of what the course covers.

3. To get to know more about your instructor.

Skills

The primary skills developed through this exercise are:

1. *HR Management skill*—Human relations

2. *SHRM 2010 Curriculum Guidebook*—A: Employee relations

Procedure 1 (5–8 minutes)

Break employees into groups of five or six, preferably with people they do not know. Have each member tell his or her name and two or three significant things about himself or herself. Then have them ask each other questions to get to know each other better.

Procedure 2 (4–8 minutes)

Can everyone in the group address every other person by name? If not, have each member repeat his or her name. Then each person in the group should repeat the names of all the group members, until each person knows everyone's first name.

Application

What can you do to improve your ability to remember people's names?

_____

_____

_____

Procedure 3 (5–10 minutes)

Have each group elect a spokesperson. Then have the group members look over the following categories and decide on some specific questions they would like their spokesperson to ask the instructor from one or more of the categories. The spokesperson will not identify who asked the questions. Groups do not have to have questions for each area.

- *Course expectations.* What do you expect to cover or hope to learn from this course?
- *Doubts or concerns.* Is there anything about the course that you don't understand?
- *Questions about the instructor.* List questions to ask the instructor in order to get to know him or her better.

Procedure 4 (10–20 minutes)

Each spokesperson asks the instructor one question at a time until all questions have been answered. Spokespeople should skip questions already asked by other groups.

Apply It

What did I learn from this experience? How will I use this knowledge in the future?

_____

_____

SKILL BUILDER 1-2

Comparing HR Management Skills and HR Responsibilities

Objective

To better understand the importance of good HR Management skills and implementing HR responsibilities effectively.

Skills

The primary skills developed through this exercise are:

1. *HR Management skill*—Conceptual and design

2. *SHRM 2010 Curriculum Guidebook*—A: Employee relations

Compare Your Supervisors' HR Management Skills and HR Responsibilities Effectiveness

Recall the best supervisor or boss (preferably line managers, not HR) you ever worked for and the worst one you ever worked for. Compare these two people by writing brief notes in the following chart about each person's HR Management skills and HR responsibilities.

HR Management Skills and HR Responsibilities

Best Supervisor or Boss		Worst Supervisor or Boss
	Technical	
	Human Relations	
	Conceptual and Design	
	Business Skills	
	Legal Considerations	
	Labor Cost Control	
	Leadership and Motivation	
	Training and Development	
	Appraisal and Promotion	
	Safety and Security	

Apply It

Based on your own experiences with a good boss and a poor one, what do you believe are the key differences between good and poor managers?

_____

_____

_____

2

Strategy-Driven Human Resource Management

Learning Outcomes

After studying this chapter, you should be able to:

2.1 Identify and explain the major components of the business environment

2.2 Describe the three major organizational factors that affect our strategy options

2.3 Discuss how the vision and mission help organizations focus their resources

2.4 Identify and describe the major components of organizational structure and why it is important to understand them

2.5 Describe organizational culture and tell how it affects the members of the organization

2.6 Identify the common measurement tools for strategic HRM

2.7 Describe an HRIS and identify how it can help HR make decisions

2.8 Define the following terms:

Strategy
Vision
Mission statement
Objectives
Organizational structure
Complexity
Formalization
Centralization
Organizational culture
Economic Value Added
 (EVA)

Return on Investment (ROI)
Balanced Scorecard (BSC)
HR scorecard
Human Resource
 Information System (HRIS)
Outsourcing
Sustainability

Chapter 2 Outline

Strategy and Strategic Planning in the 21st Century

The External Environment

Strategy

    What Is Strategy?

    Visions and Missions

    Types of Strategies

    How Strategy Affects HRM

    Strategic Analysis

    Designing a Strategy

    How HR Promotes Strategy

Structure

    Basics of Organizational Structure

    How Structure Affects Employee Behavior

    How Structure Affects HRM

Organizational Culture

    What Is Organizational Culture?

How Culture Controls Employee Behavior
in Organizations

Measurement Tools for Strategic HRM

    Economic Value Added

    Return on Investment

    Balanced Scorecard

    HR Scorecard

Human Resource Information Systems

    What Is an HRIS?

    How HRISs Assist in Making HR Decisions

Trends and Issues in HRM

    Globalization Increases the Need for Strategic Planning

    Ethics—Outsourcing and Employee Leasing

    Does a Small, Entrepreneurial Organization Need a
    Strategic Plan?

    Can Sustainability Create a Competitive Advantage?

SHRM HR CONTENT

See Appendix A:
SHRM 2010 Curriculum Guidebook **for the complete list**

A. **Employee and Labor Relations (required)**

    3.   Managing/creating a positive organizational culture

C. **Job Analysis/Job Design (required)**

    9.   Organization design (missions, functions, and other aspects of work units for horizontal and vertical differentiation)

E. **Outcomes: Metrics and Measurement of HR (required)**

    1.   Economic value added

    2.   Balanced scorecard (HR and organization level)

    7.   Return on Investment (ROI)

    8.   HR scorecard

    9.   Organizational scorecard

H. **Strategic HR (required)**

    1.   Strategic management

    2.   Enhancing firm competitiveness

    3.   Strategy formulation

    4.   Strategy implementation

    5.   Sustainability/corporate social responsibility

    7.   Competitive advantage

    8.   Competitive strategy

    10. Linking HR strategy to organizational strategy

    13. Mission and vision

    14. Quality management

I. **Total Rewards (required)**

B. **Employee Benefits**

    14. Outsourcing

Case 2-1. Building Up Our Assets: DHR Construction

A Positive Culture Is a Critical Component

One thing many family get-togethers have in common is storytelling—reminiscing about common experiences and outstanding family members. The same is true for your work "family." Shared experiences and leadership tales help mold the company culture. The most often recited anecdote at my company is about the man who founded the U.S. operations—Mr. Dave. As the story goes, one employee brought a box of donuts into work one day, and someone took just half of a donut.

Mr. Dave called everyone in and chided his employees for the action. "From now on, never leave half a donut!" The story became a metaphor for his whole-hearted, jump-in-with-both-feet method of doing business. Whenever we need to get in and get the job done, someone is sure to mention the donut story. What else defines company culture? Chapter 2 examines strategies, mission statements, visions, and values—all important pieces of a company's identity.

The Practitioner's Model for HRM

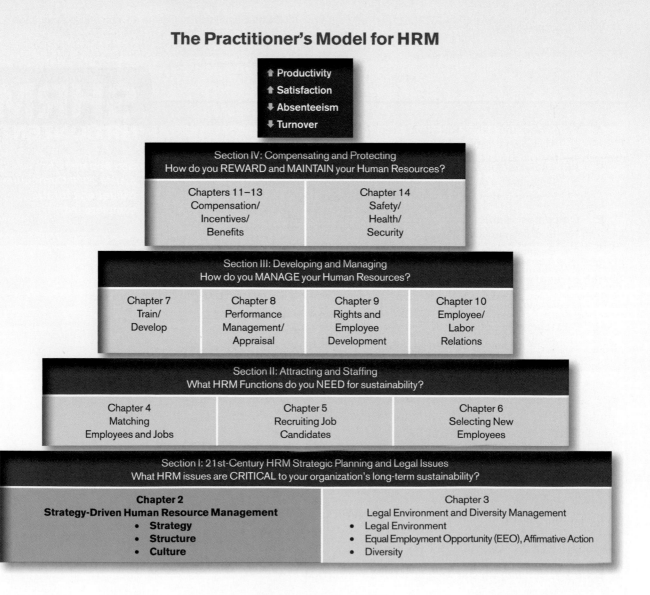

⬆ Productivity
⬆ Satisfaction
⬇ Absenteeism
⬇ Turnover

Section IV: Compensating and Protecting
How do you REWARD and MAINTAIN your Human Resources?

| Chapters 11–13 Compensation/ Incentives/ Benefits | Chapter 14 Safety/ Health/ Security |

Section III: Developing and Managing
How do you MANAGE your Human Resources?

| Chapter 7 Train/ Develop | Chapter 8 Performance Management/ Appraisal | Chapter 9 Rights and Employee Development | Chapter 10 Employee/ Labor Relations |

Section II: Attracting and Staffing
What HRM Functions do you NEED for sustainability?

| Chapter 4 Matching Employees and Jobs | Chapter 5 Recruiting Job Candidates | Chapter 6 Selecting New Employees |

Section I: 21st-Century HRM Strategic Planning and Legal Issues
What HRM issues are CRITICAL to your organization's long-term sustainability?

Chapter 2
Strategy-Driven Human Resource Management
- **Strategy**
- **Structure**
- **Culture**

Chapter 3
Legal Environment and Diversity Management
- Legal Environment
- Equal Employment Opportunity (EEO), Affirmative Action
- Diversity

Strategy and Strategic Planning in the 21st Century

We briefly introduced you to the concept of strategy and strategic planning in Chapter 1. As indicated there, strategy and strategic planning deal with a process of looking at our organization and its environment—both today and in the expected future—and determining what we as an organization want to do to meet the requirements of that expected future. This process of strategic analysis is more critical   and more important—today than it has ever been. This is because in most industries today we have far more competition than ever before, making it more difficult to create that sustainable competitive advantage that we need in order to survive over the long term.

Strategic planning is about planning, and to be successful, you need to plan with goals and measurable standards.[1] There is an old saying: "When you fail to plan, you plan to fail." Research supports this saying and confirms the importance of planning.[2] Some managers complain that they don't have time to plan, yet research shows that managers who plan are more effective and efficient than nonplanners. Before we get into the details of strategic planning, complete Self-Assessment 2-1 to determine your level of planning.

Strategic planning is about determining our Strategy Choice (see Exhibit 2-1). Our external environments have a series of factors that determine to a great extent how we as managers must act in order to provide the right combination of people in the organization to do the necessary

Strategic planning is a key foundation of organizational success.

work so that we can reach our strategic goals. In addition, internal capabilities and operations dictate some of our options. Analysis of the environment and internal operations should lead to a choice of a particular strategy type.

HRM is a critical component of meeting organizational goals, because without the right people with the right types of education and the right mind-set, we cannot ever expect to be able to accomplish the objectives that we set for ourselves. Again, people are one of the most difficult resources to imitate, and because this is true, they give us the potential for a powerful competitive advantage over our rival firms.

In this chapter, we focus primarily on the environment. The environment has two parts: internal and external. In the first section, we discuss the external environment. Then we take three separate sections to describe the internal environment: strategy, structure, and culture.

The External Environment

The external environment consists of a series of influences from outside the organization that you cannot control. Each of these forces acts on your firm and cause it to have to adapt to that particular outside force. Strategic responses are needed to adjust to environmental changes.[3] The nine major external business forces are shown in Exhibit 2-2 followed by an explanation of each.

LO 2.1

Identify and explain the major components of the external environment.

2-1 SELF-ASSESSMENT

LEVEL OF PLANNING

Indicate how well each statement describes your behavior by placing a number from 1 to 5 on the line before the statement.

Describes me				Does not describe me
5	4	3	2	1

_____ 1. I have a specific end result to accomplish whenever I start a project of any kind.

_____ 2. When setting objectives, I state only the end result to be accomplished; I don't specify how the result will be accomplished.

_____ 3. I have specific and measurable objectives; for example, I know the specific grade I want to earn in this course.

_____ 4. I set objectives that are difficult but achievable.

_____ 5. I set deadlines when I have something I need to accomplish, and I meet the deadlines.

_____ 6. I have a long-term goal (what I will be doing in 3–5 years) and short-term objectives to get me there.

_____ 7. I have written objectives stating what I want to accomplish.

_____ 8. I know my strengths and weaknesses, am aware of threats, and seek opportunities.

_____ 9. I analyze a problem and alternative actions, rather than immediately jumping right in with a solution.

_____ 10. I spend most of my day doing what I plan to do, rather than dealing with emergencies and trying to get organized.

_____ 11. I use a calendar, an appointment book, or some form of "to do" list.

_____ 12. I ask others for advice.

_____ 13. I follow appropriate policies, procedures, and rules.

_____ 14. I develop contingency plans in case my plans do not work out as I expect them to.

_____ 15. I implement my plans and determine if I have met my objectives.

Add up the numbers you assigned to the statements to see where you fall on the continuum below.

Planner						Nonplanner
75 ___	65 ___	55 ___	45 ___	35 ___	25 ___	15 ___

Don't be too disappointed if your score isn't as high as you would like. All of these items are characteristics of effective planning. Review the items that did not describe you and consider making an effort to implement the characteristic of planning.

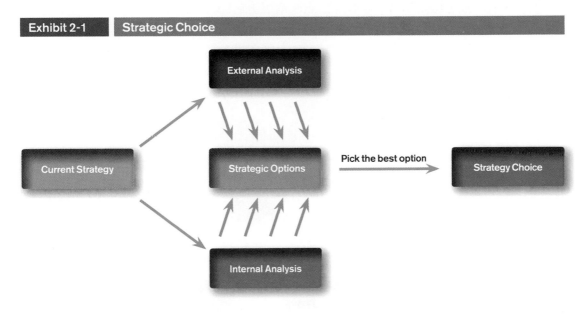

Exhibit 2-1   Strategic Choice

- **Customers.** Customers have more power today than ever before, as they have a major effect on the organization's performance through their purchase of products. Without customers, there's no need for an organization. Therefore, companies must continually improve products to create value for their customers.[4] This process of product improvement requires skilled employees who are willing to use their creativity to further the organization's knowledge, and as a result create new products and services for their customers. McDonald's listened to its customers wanting more choice and variety, so it offers salads and now sells just about as much chicken as beef.[5]

- **Competition.** Businesses must compete for customers, and firm performance is not simply a function of its own actions but must be understood relative to the actions of its rival *competitors*.[6] Wal-Mart continues to drop its prices to take customers away from competitors.[7] If Southwest lowers its price, rivals generally have to match the lower price, and they can counterattack.[8] Organizations also frequently compete for the same employees and sometimes suppliers. Competitors' changing strategic moves affect the performance of the organization.[9] Almost everyone has heard of one organization stealing employees from another similar organization, especially in high technology fields.

- **Suppliers.** Organizations buy resources from suppliers. Therefore, partnerships with *suppliers* also affect firm performance.[10] Dell, Lenovo (IBM), Toshiba, and Fujitsu all had to recall laptop computer batteries made by Sony.[11] Therefore, it is important to develop close working relationships with your suppliers, and close relationships require employees who have the ability to communicate, empathize, negotiate, and come to mutually advantageous conclusions.

- **Labor Force.** The available recruits and the employees of an organization have a direct effect on its performance. Management recruits human resources from the available labor force outside its boundaries. Employees perform or monitor all processes within the organization. Unions also provide employees for the organization, and they are considered an external factor because they become a third party when dealing with the organization. Google is a fast-growing company, recruiting thousands of new workers.[12]

- **Shareholders.** The owners of a corporation, known as shareholders, influence management. Most shareholders of large corporations are generally not involved in the day-to-day operation of the firm, but they do vote for the directors of the corporation. The board

WORK
APPLICATION 2-1

Give examples of how customers, competitors, and suppliers affected an organization where you work or have worked.

Exhibit 2-2	The External Environment

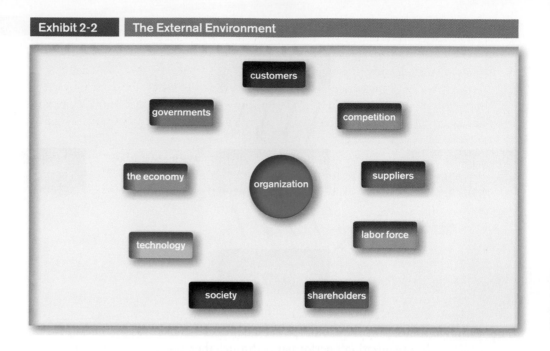

of directors is also generally not involved in the day-to-day operation of the firm. However, it hires and fires top management. The top manager reports to the board of directors. If the organization does not perform well, managers can be fired.[13]

- **Society.** Our *society*, to a great extent, determines what acceptable business practices are.[14] Individuals and groups have formed to pressure business for changes. People who live in the same area with the business do not want it to pollute the air or water or otherwise abuse natural resources. Monsanto was pressured because of its bioengineered agricultural products. Mothers Against Drunk Driving (MADD) pressures Anheuser-Busch and other alcohol companies to promote responsible alcohol consumption.

- **Technology.** Few organizations operate today as they did even a decade ago. Products not envisioned a few years ago are now being mass produced. Computers and the Internet have changed the speed and the manner in which organizations conduct and transact business, and they're often a major part of the firm's systems process, including, for example, Frito-Lay using handheld computers to track real-time inventories. Changing technologies require technologically savvy employees who have the ability to adapt to new processes. Without employees who are comfortable with changing technologies, organizations today will soon find themselves unable to compete.

- **The Economy.** No organization has control over economic growth, inflation, interest rates, foreign exchange rates, and so on. In general, as measured by Gross Domestic Product (GDP), businesses do better when the economy is growing than during times of decreased economic activity, or recession.

  During periods of inflation, businesses experience increased costs. When interest rates are high, it costs more to borrow money. Foreign exchange rates affect businesses both at home and abroad. Thus, the economy has a direct impact on the firm's performance-profits. We always have to take the economy into account when performing strategic planning activities.

- **Governments.** National, state, and local governments all set laws and regulations that businesses must obey. For firms employing 20 or more employees, the annual cost of

WORK
APPLICATION 2-2

Give examples of how society and technology affected an organization where you work or have worked.

WORK
APPLICATION 2-3

Give examples of how the economy and government affected an organization where you work or have worked.

complying with government regulations is almost $7,000 per employee.[15] The Occupational Safety and Health Administration (OSHA) sets safety standards, and the Environmental Protection Agency (EPA) sets pollution standards that must be met. Merck cannot market drugs without Food and Drug Administration (FDA) approval. In other words, to a large extent, business may not do whatever it wants to do; the government tells business what it can and cannot do.[16] So government matters, as it affects how business is conducted.[17] Due to the financial crises, Congress worked to create new financial regulations to help prevent another crisis and recession.

Governments create both opportunities and threats for businesses. Allstate insurance left the state of Massachusetts because of the unfavorable government environment there. To learn more about the U.S. federal government, visit its official web portal, www.usa.gov.

2-1 APPLYING THE CONCEPT

The External Environment

Identify which external environmental factor is referred to in each statement.

a. customers
b. competition
c. suppliers
d. labor force
e. shareholders

f. society
g. technology
h. the economy
i. governments

_____ 1. Procter & Gamble has developed a new biodegradable material to replace the plastic liner on its diapers so that they don't take up landfill space for so long.

_____ 2. At one time, AT&T was the only long-distance company, but then MCI, Sprint, and others came along and took away some of its customers.

_____ 3. I applied for a loan to start my own business, but I might not get it because money is tight these days due to the financial crisis.

_____ 4. The owners of the company have threatened to fire the CEO if the business does not improve this year.

_____ 5. Management was going to sell our company to PepsiCo, but that would be in violation of antitrust laws. What will happen to our company now?

Strategy

In addition to our analysis of the major external business environmental factors above, we have to review some internal organizational factors to decide what we want to do as an organization as we move into the future. The major factors in our analysis of our organizational environment are shown in Exhibit 2-3 and discussed in this and the next two sections.

LO 2.2

Describe the three major organizational factors that affect our strategy options.

Exhibit 2-3	The Internal Environment

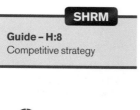

SHRM

Guide – H:8
Competitive strategy

Video Link 2.1

What is Strategy?

Strategy and the strategic planning process have a long history. "Many military historians, and contemporary business students, view the Chinese military strategist, Sun Tzu (ca. 500 B.C.) as the developer of 'the Bible' of strategy . . . Sun Tzu's principles are divided into basically two components: 1) knowing oneself and 2) knowing the enemy."[18] In other words, know your environment and know your organization. So, competitive strategies and strategic planning principles have been around a very long time. Businesses have adapted these principles to their own use. But how does a modern business go about creating and implementing a strategic plan? Strategic planning follows a process.[19] Let's discuss the process.

What Is Strategy?

At its basic level, **strategy** is *a plan of action to achieve a particular set of objectives.* Several studies have shown that HRM is an important strategic business function that influences the performance of both large and small firms.[20] What does strategy take into account? It looks at the external environment and the internal (organizational) environment in order to create strategic advantage. Strategic advantage occurs when you analyze the environment better and react quicker than your competitors, and thus create the sustainable competitive advantage that we introduced in Chapter 1.

SHRM

Guide – H:1
Strategic management

We look at three big strategic questions in order to analyze what kind of plan we need to write. These questions are:[21]

1. What is our present situation (where are we now)?

2. Where do we want to go?

3. How do we plan to get there?

These questions are both very simple and very complex. On the surface, you would think it's easy to identify what our present situation is (Question 1). But many factors go into identifying "where we are now." These factors include such things as "Are we making a profit?" "Do our products satisfy our customers' current needs?" "Do we have the right kind of workforce in place at this time?" "Is our technology working like it should?" "Do we have sufficient physical resources, such as plants, machinery and equipment, and retail

SHRM

Guide – H:7
Competitive advantage

locations?" and "Are our advertising and marketing programs successful?" as well as many more. This is a snapshot of your organization at a particular point in time, and it has to be comprehensive so that we know what is happening, good and bad, within the organization in significant detail. If you think about each of these factors for just a second, you will see how complex the answer to Question 1 really becomes.

Questions 2 and 3 are just as complex. Question 2 is basically asking us what we plan to look like as an organization at a particular point in the future. In other words, what is our *vision and mission* for the organization? Question 3 deals with the creation of the plan that will allow us to reach the goals that we identify in our answer to Question 2, in order to become the organization that we envision and, at the same time, create a sustainable competitive advantage.

Visions and Missions

The vision. A **vision** is *what we expect to become as an organization at a particular future point in time.* The vision by necessity is a fuzzy thing; it is not specific in that we don't say *how* we're going to do a particular thing, but we identify a future state of being. It is "who we are, what we stand for, what we believe in, and what we want to become." Visions, however, are very powerful when used correctly. The vision provides a *focus point* for the future; it tells the company where it is headed.[22] The company will look into the future and see what they want to look like as a company at that time—what do they want to be when they "grow up"? If everyone is focused on the same future end state, they will work toward that same end state. So, basically the question that we answer with the vision is "What do we want to become as an organization?" But the firm is only successful when the followers share the leader's vision.[23]

The mission. In contrast, the mission is where we start to become specific. The **mission statement** is *our expectations of what we're going to do in order to become the organization that we envisioned.* The mission statement is a statement of what the various organizational units do and what they hope to accomplish, in alignment with the organizational vision. The mission is generally narrower and more specific than a vision, which means that it generally must be a bit longer-winded. Who do we serve (in terms of customer groups, types of products and services, technologies we use, etc.), and how do we serve them? So, the mission statement answers the question "What do we need to do in order to become what we have envisioned?"

Putting the vision and mission together. Let's put this in simpler terms. We will use as an example the vision and mission for the College of Business at the University of Arkansas at Little Rock. Their vision is as follows: "The College of Business serves as a catalyst to advance education and economic development in the State of Arkansas."[24] Notice that this vision does not tell you how they will be a catalyst. It doesn't say what the college is going to *do*. All it tells you is that they expect to be a catalyst. What is a catalyst? A catalyst is "a substance that modifies and increases the rate of a reaction without being consumed in the process."[25] So,

SHRM

Guide – H:13
Mission and vision

LO 2.3

Discuss how the vision and mission help organizations focus their resources.

Video Link 2.2

Vision and Mission

All employees need to understand the vision and mission in order to focus on achieving it.

what is the college going to *be*? It is going to be an organization that increases the rate of change in education and economic development in its home state. However, this does not tell us anything about how the college is going to do this. If we look at the mission of the organization, we will find out *how the organization expects to do what the vision puts forth.* Let's look at the mission of this College of Business. "The mission of the College of Business is to prepare students to succeed as business professionals in a global economy and to contribute to the growth and viability of the region we serve."[26] So, what is the College of Business going to do? It is going to provide education to the students in order to give them the tools to succeed in business and create change in the state. This, in turn, will act to improve the state's economic fortunes.

Video Link 2.3

Differences Between
Vision and Mission

When you put the vision and mission together, the people in the organization get a more complete picture of what direction they are expected to go. This allows the people in the organization to focus on that particular direction. Once everyone is focused on the same direction, it makes it much easier to achieve our goals. *This focus is the thing that makes a vision and mission so powerful.* If everyone in the organization is focused on the same end result, it is much more likely that the organization will achieve that end result.

This also gives everyone a clearer picture of what is expected of them individually. Think of it as follows: If you're bricklayer and you're laying bricks, you may not pay close attention to each of the bricks you lay if you have no mental picture of the finished project. However, if you're building a beautiful art museum and you have been shown a picture of what the museum will look like when finished, you're more likely to pay close attention to each brick because you want to be able to say that you helped create something beautiful.

A strong vision and a good mission statement are critical parts of the strategic planning process. *Everything* else in strategic planning comes from the vision and mission.

Vision + Mission = FOCUS!

WORK
APPLICATION 2-4

Identify the vision and mission of an organization where you work or have worked.

Finally, organizations go through a series of analyses of both external and internal factors in order to come up with the plan of action that answers Question 3. Strategic planners look at each of the environmental factors that we noted above as well as analyzing the company's capabilities and limitations in order to come up with a workable plan. We will discuss some of these factors in the following sections.

Types of Strategies

There are several generic (general) strategy types that we are able to categorize. Some researchers break these down into just two or three options while others have several more. We will try to keep this as simple as possible right now, since for our purposes we only need to know the major divisions in strategy types. So we will break the types down into three options—Cost Leadership, Broad Differentiation, and Focus or Niche Strategies.[27] Take a look at each one below.

Cost Leadership. Cost Leaders do everything that they can in order to lower organizational costs required to produce their products or services. Cost Leaders do not necessarily provide their product or service to the customer for a lower price. They can choose to keep their prices down and maintain the same margin as their higher-cost competitors, or they can alternately choose to charge the same price as their competitors, which will increase their margins above their competitors' on each of the goods or services sold. Wal-Mart has had great success with this strategy, and during the recession and coming out of it, Wal-Mart reduced prices even more aggressively.[28] In Europe, McDonald's opened McCafé coffee shops to compete head on with Starbucks with lower cost to become the continent's number-one coffee shop chain.[29]

Broad Differentiation. This strategy attempts to create an impression of difference for the company's product or service in the mind of the customer. The differentiator company stresses its advantage over its competitors.[30] If they are successful in creating this impression, they can charge a higher price for their product or service than their competitors. Differentiation, it should be noted, is based not necessarily on real difference but on the perception of difference by the customer, which is often created through advertising.[31] Nike, Ralph Lauren, Calvin Klein, and others place their names on the outside of their products to differentiate them from those of the competition. According to Coca-Cola, the three keys to selling consumer products are differentiation, differentiation, differentiation, which it achieves with its scripted name logo and contour bottle.

Focus or Niche Strategy. With this strategy the company focuses on a specific portion of a larger market. For instance, the company may focus on a regional market, a particular product line, or a buyer group. Within a particular target segment, or market niche, the firm may use differentiation or cost leadership strategy. Businesses can win big by thinking small.[32] It is hard to compete head-on with the big companies like Coca-Cola and PepsiCo, but the much smaller Dr Pepper Snapple Group's two noncolas have a differentiation taste for a much smaller target market, but it is very profitable.[33]

WORK APPLICATION 2-5

Identify the strategy of an organization where you work or have worked and explain how it uses the strategy against its competitors to gain customers.

2-2 APPLYING THE CONCEPT

Strategies

Identify which strategy is used by each brand or company listed.

a. Cost Leadership
b. Broad Differentiation
c. Focus or Niche Strategy

_____ 6. Polo clothes/shirts

_____ 7. Target stores

_____ 8. Mercedes-Benz cars

_____ 9. *Golf Digest* magazine

_____ 10. Secret deodorant

How Strategy Affects HRM

There are several areas where the generic corporate strategy affects how we do our jobs within HR. Let's take a look at a few of the significant differences between generic strategies. We will also review how HRM affects the ability to commit to a particular corporate strategy a little later in this chapter. We will continue to discuss these areas in greater detail as we progress through the book.

HRM and Cost Leadership. If our organization is following a generic Cost Leader strategy, we are going to be most interested in minimizing all internal costs, including employee costs. So we are concerned with maximum efficiency and effectiveness. Because we are concerned with maximum efficiency, we will probably create highly specialized jobs within the organization so that we have people doing the same thing repeatedly. This will generally cause the employee to get much better and faster at their job. We will also have specific job descriptions for each position and job-specific training—very little, if any, cross-training. We will hire new workers based on technical skills and abilities, and will most likely emphasize job-based pay where the employee gets paid more if they perform their job faster and better. We would also provide incentives that emphasize cost controls and efficiency. Finally, it's quite likely in this situation that managers will use performance appraisals as a control mechanism to allow them to weed out less efficient and effective employees.

HRM and Differentiation. If, on the other hand, our organization is following a differentiator strategy, we're going to be more concerned with employees who are flexible and adaptable, who have the ability to innovate and create new processes, and who can work in uncertain environments within cross-functional teams. In a differentiator organization we would most likely have much broader job classifications, as well as broader work planning processes. Individuals would be hired and paid based on individual knowledge and skill sets, not specifically based on the job that they fill at the point in time that they enter the organization. Here, our incentive programs would reward innovation and creativity. Finally, in the differentiator organization, performance appraisals will generally be used as a tool to develop the skill sets of the valuable knowledge workers within the organization, not as a tool to punish and weed out poor performers. So you can see very quickly that HRM will need to do its job in a significantly different way based on the type of generic strategy that the company decides to follow.

Strategic Analysis

There are two primary components of strategic analysis used by most organizations. The first is called Five-Forces Analysis, and it is the primary tool that most organizations use to analyze the external environment. The second is called SWOT Analysis (SWOT stands for Strengths, Weaknesses, Opportunities, and Threats). There are many other strategic analysis tools, but let's save those for another course.

Five-Forces Analysis. Five-Forces Analysis is again brought to us by Michael Porter. Porter identified competition within an industry as being a composite of five competitive forces that should be considered in analyzing competitive situations.[34] See Exhibit 2-4 for a list of the Five Forces.

Exhibit 2-4	Five-Forces Competitive Analysis

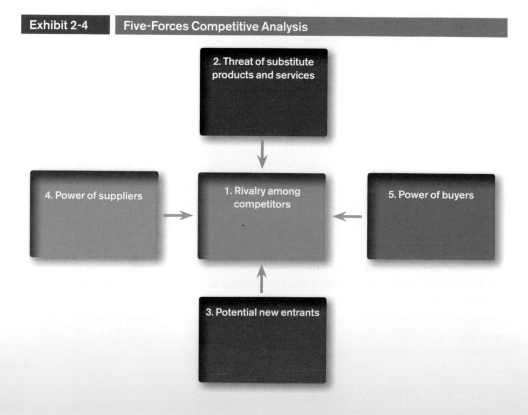

1. *Rivalry among competitors.* Porter calls this rivalry scrambling and jockeying for position. Examples of this jockeying for position include questions such as "How do businesses compete for customers (e.g., on the basis of price, quality, or speed)?" "How competitive is the industry?" "Which competitors are targeting the same customer groups?" and others. The company needs to anticipate the moves of its competitors. Coke and Pepsi are longtime rivals.

2. *Threat of substitute products and services.* Companies in other industries may try to take your customers away. Newer methods of storing and playing music and videos—for example, Apple iPods and other MP3 players—are displacing CDs and DVDs at a fairly rapid rate today. Companies to provide CD- and DVD-based music and videos have a threat of substitution from companies using these newer methods.

Video Link 2.4
Review of Five-Forces
Competitive Analysis

3. *Potential new entrants.* How difficult and costly is it for new businesses to enter the industry as competitors? Does the company need to plan for new competition? In many industries today, all it takes to enter is the ability to create and host a website. If it is easy to enter an industry and profitability is significant, then the threat of new entrants is much higher. If it's more difficult to enter an industry, for instance, because of high capital equipment costs, and profitability is lower, possibly because the product is a commodity (think about the steel manufacturing industry), then the threat of new entrants is significantly lower.

4. *Power of suppliers.* How much does our business depend on its suppliers? If the business has only one major supplier of a critical component, without alternatives available, the supplier has greater bargaining power over the business. However, if our business can get its major supplies from any one of many different suppliers, then the suppliers will have very little power over the business.

WORK
APPLICATION 2-6

Conduct a Five-Forces
Competitive Analysis for an
organization where you work
or have worked.

5. *Power of buyers.* How much does our business depend on its buyers? If one, or a few, large buyers purchase most of what we provide, then the buyer has significant bargaining power over our company. As an example, almost every business student has heard of the power Wal-Mart holds over its suppliers because of the volume of goods that it buys. However, if we provide products or services to many different buyers, none of which provides us with a major portion of our business, then the buyers generally have very little bargaining power.

Companies use industry and competitive situation analysis primarily at the corporate level to make decisions regarding which lines of business to enter and exit and how to allocate resources among existing lines of business.

SWOT Analysis. An organization's strengths and weaknesses, as well as opportunities and threats, are determined through the use of SWOT Analysis. Basically, in the process of SWOT Analysis, the organization creates a list of its strengths, weaknesses, opportunities, and threats. See Exhibit 2-5 for a setup in which to list SWOTs. Once this list is created, the organization evaluates each of the sections of the list in order to decide where it can use its resources most effectively.

If, for example, we have an organizational strength that is critical to maintain in order to serve our most important customer groups, then we will allocate resources toward maintenance of that strength. If, however, we have strengths in our list that no longer provide us with the potential for advantage over our competitors, then we may choose not to use organizational resources to maintain that strength. So as you can see, the process of SWOT Analysis is a process of balancing our available resources in order to make the most of our strengths and opportunities, and to minimize any danger to the organization from its weaknesses and threats.

WORK
APPLICATION 2-7

Conduct a SWOT Analysis
for an organization where you
work or have worked.

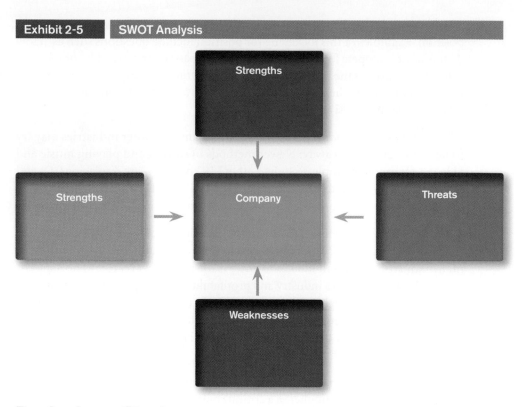

| Exhibit 2-5 | SWOT Analysis |

Designing a Strategy

Once we have identified an organizational vision and mission, decided on which generic strategic type we're going to pursue, and done some analysis of the external environment and our organizational capabilities, we're ready to start designing our organization's strategy. The next steps in our design process include setting objectives, creating a strategic plan, implementing that plan, and then once the plan has been put into place monitoring and evaluating its success. Let's take a brief look at each of these.

Setting objectives. Successful strategic management requires a commitment on the part of managers to a defined set of objectives. Successful managers have a goal orientation,[35] which means they set and achieve objectives, and goal orientation can be learned.[36] After developing our vision and mission and completing a situation analysis, the next step is to set objectives that flow from the mission to address strategic issues and problems identified through the situation analysis. **Objectives** *state what is to be accomplished in singular, specific, and measurable terms with a target date.* The organization has to write at least one objective for every major goal that is set forth in its strategy. You begin with the end in mind, and objectives do not state how they will be accomplished (plan)—just the end result you want to accomplish.[37]

Here is a model adapted from Max E. Webber to help you write effective objectives, followed by a few company examples.

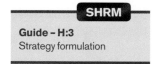

WORK
APPLICATION 2-8

Write an objective for an organization where you work or have worked that is specific, is measurable, and has a target date.

To + action verb + singular, specific, measurable result + target date

Marvel Entertainment:[38] To produce 10 movies by 2117.

Nike:[39] To increase annual revenues 41% by 2015.

Dell:[40] To cut cost by $4 billion in 2011.

Create a strategy. Once we've identified our set of objectives, the next step is to weave them into a cohesive organizational plan. This is the point at which we determine what we're going

2-3 APPLYING THE CONCEPT

Writing Objectives

For each objective, state which "must" criteria is not met.

a. single result b. specific
c. measurable d. target date

_____ 11. To sell 5 million Nissan Leaf electric cars.

_____ 12. To sell 5% more Ford and 8% more Lincoln cars in 2013.

_____ 13. To decrease sales by year-end 2013.

_____ 14. To be perceived as the best restaurant in the Chicago area by 2015.

_____ 15. To write objectives within two weeks.

to do in order to achieve the objectives that we have set. Taking into account the vision and mission that we have decided on as well as our environment and each of the strengths, weaknesses, opportunities, and threats, we begin to plan activities within the organization that will allow us to reach those objectives. Looking at this process, you should be able to quickly see that no organization should ever just copy another organization's strategy—even if that strategy has been successful for the company that is being copied. Why would this be the case? Well, the simple answer is that no two organizations have *the same* vision and mission, organizational environment, or strengths, weaknesses, opportunities, and threats, and as a result no two organizations should have the same objectives. Therefore, no two organizations could *ever* expect to be successful by following the same straegy.

Implementing, monitoring, and evaluating strategies. Dr Pepper's executive Tony English said, "Strategy is fantastic, but execution is what brings the results."[41] The last items in the strategic planning process are implementing and then monitoring and evaluating the plan's success. The goal here is to ensure that the mission and objectives of the organization are achieved. Successful implementation of strategies requires effective and efficient support systems throughout the organization. It also requires a dedication to the plan at all levels in the organization. Although strategic planning usually goes well, implementation is often a problem.[42] One reason is that strategic plans often end up buried in bottom drawers; no action is taken to implement a strategy.

As strategies are implemented, they must also be monitored and evaluated. This process is called controlling. *Controlling* is the process of establishing and implementing mechanisms to ensure that objectives are achieved. An important part of controlling is measuring progress toward the achievement of the objective and taking corrective action when needed. Another important part of controlling is staying within budgets when appropriate, or changing them when necessary to meet changes in the environment.

Quality management is one example of where the controlling process allows the company to adjust their internal processes in order to reach a predetermined level of quality control. Quality must consistently be monitored because quality costs, but lack of quality costs much more. So, as part of strategy, we always need to watch quality through the controlling process.

SHRM

Guide – H:4
Strategy implementation

SHRM

Guide – H:14
Quality management

SHRM

Guide – H:10
Linking HR strategy to
organizational strategy

How HR Promotes Strategy

So, what does HRM have to do with a particular strategy? Do HR Managers need to recruit, select, train, evaluate, and interact with organizational employees differently based on different organizational strategies? Of course they do. We showed you earlier how we might manage people differently based on different generic strategies. The same holds true when looking at different sets of objectives, different competitors, and different organizational strengths and weaknesses, as well as many other industry and company characteristics. HR Managers have to evaluate all of these characteristics in order to determine what kinds of people to bring into the organization and then how to maintain those people once they have become a part of the company. This is the reason that it's so critical for HR Managers to understand organizational strategy. In fact, as you go through the remainder of this book, you will see continuing references to how HRM will affect the company's ability to do its work over the long term. Everything that HR does must mesh with the chosen strategy in order to provide the right kinds of employees, who will learn and do the right types of jobs so that the company can achieve its goals.

SHRM

Guide – H:2
Enhancing firm
competitiveness

Structure

Organizational structure refers to *the way in which an organization groups its resources to accomplish its mission.* Strategies require an organizational structure to be implemented.[43] Why do firms that seem equal execute at different levels of efficiency? The answer must be in how their resources are structures and managed.[44] Thus, the proper selection of the organizational structure is critical to business success.[45]

HR Managers also need to have an understanding of organizational structure in order to do their jobs correctly. An organization is a system, typically structured into departments such as finance, marketing, production, human resources, and so on. Each of these departments affects the organization as a whole, and each department is affected by the other departments. Organizations structure their resources to transform inputs and outputs. All of an organization's resources must be structured effectively to achieve its mission.[46] As a manager in any department, you will be responsible for part of the organization's structure.

LO 2.4

Identify and describe the major components of organizational structure and why it is important to understand them.

Basics of Organizational Structure

One way to look at organizational structure is to identify a series of fundamental components. Each of these components identifies part of how we divide the organization up and group its resources in order to make them more efficient and effective. Let's discuss complexity, formalization, and centralization structure.

SHRM

Guide – C:9
Organizational design

Complexity. The first component that we will talk about is called complexity. Complexity is *the degree of three types of differentiation within the organization.* Complexity is divided into these three subparts: vertical differentiation, horizontal differentiation, and spatial differentiation.

Vertical differentiation deals with how we break the organization up vertically or, in other words, how many layers there are in the organization from the top to the bottom. How many bosses are there, and to whom does each one report? To whom does the HR Manager report? The organization chart is used to show the chain of command. You need a

clear boss who is accountable for results.[47] At Yahoo! there was a problem because it wasn't clear who the bosses were and who should be making decisions.[48]

Horizontal differentiation identifies how we break the organization up horizontally. The normal way that we break organizations up horizontally is into departments. HR is commonly a department within the organizational structure advising and assisting all the other departments in the firm. But there are other ways in which we can segment the organization horizontally including by customer type, product or process type, and geographic division, as well as many other options.

Spatial differentiation deals with the physical separation of different parts of the organization. For instance, we may have headquarters in Los Angeles while we have a production plant in Indonesia. Spatial differentiation can make it much more difficult to manage the organization due to the fact that it's spread out among many locations. American Express does business in over 130 countries.[49] Now that is complex.

So, complexity involves the way that we divide the organization into different segments, both physically and within artificial boundaries such as departments. Why does this matter to the organization's managers? The more the organization is broken into segments, the more difficult it becomes to manage within it. If we have many vertical layers in the organization (vertical differentiation) and many horizontal divisions of the organization (horizontal differentiation), and the organization has many different physical locations (spatial differentiation), it is much more difficult to conduct business than if there are fewer divisions. Higher complexity makes it more difficult to communicate between the different parts of the organization, to make decisions within the organization, and to find information that we need when it's in another part of the organization. As a result of this difficulty in making decisions in communicating, the cost of managing this type of organization goes up. So, it's harder to manage a highly complex organization and it costs more, so we want to minimize complexity as much as possible. However, we can't always minimize complexity completely.

Formalization. Formalization is *the degree to which jobs are standardized within an organization.* In other words, have we created policies, procedures, and rules that "program" the jobs of the employees? If we make things routine by creating standard operating procedures and other standard processes in the organization, we can usually increase the efficiency and effectiveness of the people within the organization, in turn making the entire organization more productive on a per-unit basis. So, the more that we can formalize the jobs within the organization, the easier it is to manage the people in those jobs. We also tend to have lower costs in organizations that are highly formalized because jobs are done in a routine, repetitive manner.

As a result, we generally want to formalize all of the processes that we can within the organization, but we can't always formalize everything that we do. How much we're able to formalize jobs within the organization depends on what the organization is designed to do. If the organization is designed to do the same thing over and over, then we can usually formalize many of its procedures. If the organization is, on the other hand, designed to do unique and nonroutine things (never does the same thing twice), then we will probably not be able to formalize very much in this type of organization.[50]

Centralization. The third major component of structure is called centralization. **Centralization** is *the degree to which decision making is concentrated within the organization.* The degree of centralization in an organization has to do with dispersion of authority for decision making and delegation of authority. If we can concentrate authority in decision making within one or a few individuals, we can concentrate on hiring people who are very good at making business decisions in those few positions and not worry about the decision-making skills of the rest of our employees.

Centralization of decision making tends to create greater control within the organization, because those few decision makers will soon find that they make similar decisions over and over, and they become very good at determining the best course of action in a particular situation. In other words, there is a learning curve in decision making. The more decisions you make, the better you get at making high-quality decisions.

However, there's a trade-off to centralized decision making. As the organization gets larger, we may have to go through many layers of the organization in order to get a decision made. This can slow down the processes within the firm—in some cases to such an extent that by the time a decision is made, it becomes irrelevant. BP was criticized for having a complex, balky, unmanageable decision-making structure that led to the oil disaster in the Gulf Coast. Managers knew there were problems, but nobody made the decision to shut down the well.[51] So we have to balance centralization and decentralization within our firms, and the trend is toward decentralization.[52] However, we know that centralized decision making gives us greater control and as a result generally tends to lower our costs for decision making. So if everything else were held constant, we would rather have highly centralized decision making.

So what is the best structure? Is there one "best" structure? No. The best structure is one that fits the firm's current competitive situation as well as its internal capabilities that enable it to implement its strategies successfully. Warren Buffett advises to keep things simple.[53] Peter Drucker may have said it as well as anyone when he noted: "The simplest organization structure that will do the job is the best one. What makes an organization structure 'good' is the problems it does not create. . . . To obtain both the greatest possible simplicity and the greatest 'fit' organization design has to start out with a clear focus on KEY ACTIVITIES needed to produce KEY RESULTS."[54]

How Structure Affects Employee Behavior

We now know that structure is made up of complexity, formalization, and centralization. Does the way that we combine these components cause employees within the organization to act in different ways? In fact, it does. Think for a second of a company that in your mind is a bureaucracy. It might be a government agency, it might be a corporation that you've worked for, or it might be the college or university at which you study. Chances are that this organization is highly complex, has many standard procedures or ways of doing things (formalization), and is probably at least partially centralized (only certain individuals can make major decisions). If you are part of this organization and someone asks you to do something that is outside the scope of your job, then you most likely would say, "That's not my job," and tell them to go to a different person to accomplish that task. You don't have the authority or the knowledge to be able to help them.

Now let's look at a different kind of organization. You have taken a job with a brand-new, entrepreneurial firm. There are no departments, there are no standard procedures,

WORK
APPLICATION 2-9

Briefly describe the complexity, formalization, and centralization of the organizational structure where you work or have worked.

and you were hired at least in part because of your ability to "think on your feet" and make decisions. Someone again asks you to do something that is outside the scope of your normal job. In this environment, you're much more likely to take upon yourself the task of figuring out a way to assist the other person instead of passing the task to someone else. The structure of the organization has changed the way that you react to a request to do something that is outside the scope of your job, or it becomes your job.

How Structure Affects HRM

As the HR Manager, would your job change because of the different structures in the two companies above? In a small entrepreneurial firm, there usually is no HRM Department, but someone has to perform the HR functions. Would you need to recruit and hire different types of people in a bureaucratic organization than you would in an entrepreneurial organization? Indeed you would. In the more bureaucratic organization, you would most likely look for and hire people who had significant depth of expertise in a narrow area within their field of knowledge so that they could apply that expertise in a highly efficient manner, because that would make the organization more productive over the long term.

Your training programs would probably be more specific, and geared toward particular jobs. In addition, your performance appraisal processes would be aimed at evaluating more specific tasks and functions than would be the case in the entrepreneurial organization. In fact, the organizational structure will affect virtually every function of the HR Manager. So in order to be a successful HR Manager you have to understand and adapt to the particular organizational structure of your firm.

Organizational Culture

Organizational culture is another characteristic that affects how the HR Manager operates within the firm. Fostering the right organizational culture is one of the most important responsibilities of the chief executive.[55] Management needs to be involved in establishing the shared values, beliefs, and assumptions so that employees know how to behave.[56] Every group of humans that gather together anywhere, and at any point in time, create a unique group culture. They have their own group standards, called norms, and they create pressure to conform to the group's standards. Social groups have societal cultures, nations have country cultures, and organizations have their own distinct cultures.

> **SHRM**
>
> **Guide – A:3**
> Managing/creating a positive organizational culture

What Is Organizational Culture?

Organizational culture consists of *the values, beliefs, and assumptions about appropriate behavior that members of an organization share.* Culture describes how employees do what they do (behavior, values) and why they do what they do (profits, customers, employees, society). Every organization has a culture, and success depends on the health and strength of its culture.[57] Therefore, leaders should be spending a lot of time building the organization's culture.[58] Executive John Tolva says that success comes from the values that IBM has instilled in us; it's a professional code that isn't written down, but it's there.[59] Organizational culture is primarily learned through observing people and events in the organization.

> **LO 2.5**
>
> Describe organizational culture and tell how it affects the members of the organization.

Artifacts. There are five artifacts of organizational culture, which are important ways that employees learn the organizations culture:

1. *Heroes*, such as founders Tom Watson of IBM, Sam Walton of Wal-Mart, Herb Kelleher of Southwest Airlines, Frederick Smith of FedEx, and others who have made outstanding contributions to their organizations.

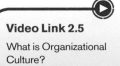

Video Link 2.5

What is Organizational Culture?

WORK
APPLICATION 2-10

Briefly describe some of the organizational culture artifacts where you work or have worked.

Video Link 2.6

How to Strategize

2. *Stories*, often about founders and others who have made extraordinary efforts, such as Sam Walton visiting every Wal-Mart store yearly or someone driving through a blizzard to deliver a product or service. Public statements and speeches can also be considered stories.

3. *Slogans*, such as the McDonald's Q, S, C, V slogan (or Quality, Service, Cleanliness, and Value).

4. *Symbols*, such as plaques, pens, jackets, or a Mary Kay cosmetics pink Cadillac.

5. *Ceremonies*, such as awards dinners for top achievers at Mary Kay cosmetics.

Three levels of culture. The three levels of culture include behavior, values and beliefs, and assumptions. Exhibit 2-6 illustrates the three levels of culture.

Level 1: Behavior. Behavior includes the observable things that people do and say or the actions employees take. *Artifacts* result from behavior and include written and spoken language, dress, material objects, and the organization's physical layout. Heroes, stories, slogans, symbols, and ceremonies are all part of behavior-level culture. The behavior level is also called the *visible level*. Values, beliefs, and assumptions are considered the *invisible level*, as you cannot actually observe them.

Level 2: Values and Beliefs. Values represent the way people believe they ought to behave, and beliefs represent "if-then" statements: "If I do X, then Y will happen." Values and beliefs provide the operating principles that guide decision making and shape the behaviors that result in Level 1 culture. Values and beliefs cannot be observed directly; we can only infer from people's behavior what they value and believe.[60] There is a benefit to making values a part of the daily or weekly conversation within the organization.[61]

Although organizations use heroes, stories, symbols, and ceremonies to convey the important values and beliefs, the slogan is critical to Level 2 culture. A slogan expresses key values. Slogans are part of organizational mission statements, while a philosophy (FedEx People-Service-Profit) is a formal statement of values and beliefs.

Level 3: Assumptions. Assumptions are values and beliefs that are so deeply ingrained that they are considered unquestionably true. Because assumptions are shared, they're rarely discussed. They serve as an "automatic pilot" to guide behavior. In fact, people often feel threatened when assumptions are challenged. If you question employees on why they do something or suggest a change, they often respond with statements like "That's the way it's always been done." Assumptions are often the most stable and enduring part of culture and are difficult to change.

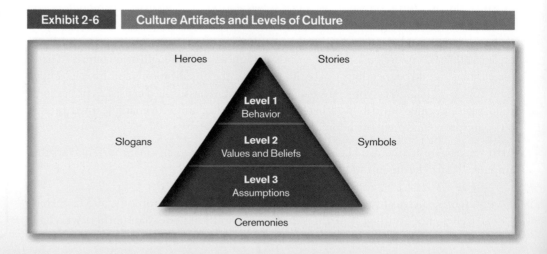

| Exhibit 2-6 | Culture Artifacts and Levels of Culture |

Notice that behavior is at the top of the diagram in Exhibit 2-6. Assumptions and values and beliefs affect behavior, not the other way around; in other words, cause and effect work from the bottom up.

How Culture Controls Employee Behavior in Organizations

Because organizational culture is based at least partly on assumptions, values, and beliefs, the culture can control how people act within its boundaries. For instance, if the culture says that we *value* hard work and productivity, but an individual on one of the teams fails to do his or her part, work hard, and be productive, the other members of the team are quite likely to pressure the individual to conform to the culture. Since assumptions, values, and beliefs are so strong, the individual will most likely change their actions to conform to those that the culture values.

You may not believe that culture has the ability to cause you to change the way you act, but it does. Have you ever done something to fit in, or something you really didn't want to do because of *peer pressure*? Doesn't peer pressure control most people? Think about the way that you act as part of your family and then compare that to the way you act as a student at school, or with a group of your friends, or as an employee at work. Chances are quite high that you act differently within these different "cultures." We all act to conform, for the most part, to the culture that we happen to be in at that point in time, because the cultural values push us to act that way.

In a strong organizational culture, employees tend to dress and behave in similar ways.

WORK
APPLICATION 2-11

Give examples of how culture controls employee behavior where you work or have worked.

2-4 APPLYING THE CONCEPT

The Internal Environment

Identify which internal environmental factor is referred to in each statement.

a. strategy   c. culture
b. structure

_____ 16. Walking around the Bank of America department during my job interview, I realized that I would have to wear a jacket and tie every day.

_____ 17. I work in the Production Department of Procter & Gamble, and my boss's title is Production Department Supervisor.

_____ 18. At Gillette, we sell personal products to men, including shaving, cleaning, and deodorizing products.

_____ 19. I process monthly payments at GMAC Mortgage all day long.

_____ 20. At Ford, quality is Job 1.

Reviewing the environment. Recall that there is an internal and an external environment. See Exhibit 2-7 for a review of the components making up the environment.

Measurement Tools for Strategic HRM

LO 2.6

Identify the common measurement tools for strategic HRM.

Just as we have to quantify and measure any other part of the organization, we also have measurement tools in HRM. Some of the most common tools are Economic Value Added; balanced scorecards, including organizational scorecards and HR scorecards; and Return on Investment. Let's take a brief look at each of these tools.

Economic Value Added

SHRM

Guide – E:1
Economic value added

Economic Value Added is designed as a method for calculating the creation of value for the organization's shareholders. Basically, **Economic Value Added (EVA)** is *a measure of profits that remain after the cost of capital has been deducted from operating profits*. It provides shareholders and managers with a better understanding of how the business is performing overall. As an equation, EVA would look like this: [62]

EVA = **net operating profit after tax – (capital used x cost of capital)**

So, EVA is a measure of how much money we made through our operations minus the amount of money that we had to spend (at a particular interest rate) in order to perform those operations. For a company to grow, it must generate average returns higher than its capital costs.

Exhibit 2-7	The Internal and External Environment

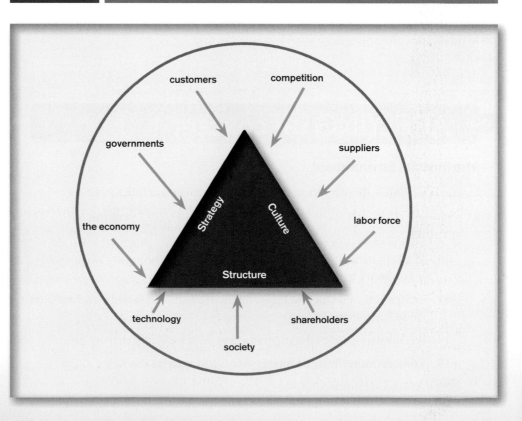

Return on Investment

The concept of Return on Investment is, at its core, very simple. **Return on Investment (ROI)** is a *measure of the financial return we receive because of something that we do to invest in our organization or its people*. ROI is most commonly used in financial analyses, but there are many areas of HR that lend themselves to ROI calculations such as training, outsourcing, benefits, diversity, and many others. In each of these areas, we can calculate the cost of providing the process—whether that process is training or diversity management or anything else—and compare that to the returns we get from the process. To calculate ROI, you need two figures. The first figure that you need is the cost of the investment. The second figure that you need is the gain that you receive from making the investment. From here, the calculation is pretty simple:

SHRM

Guide – E:7
Return on Investment (ROI)

$$ROI = \frac{\text{Gain From Investment} - \text{Cost of Investment}}{\text{Cost of Investment}}$$

Let's use a quick example to illustrate. Assume that we create a training course to improve the skills of our assembly workers and send those workers through the program. To send all of the workers through the training costs us $1 million. We know that historically, during a normal year of production, the assembly workers have been able to assemble $5 million worth of our product. However, after the training is complete, we measure our assembly process over the ensuing year and find that our average amount of product created has increased to $8 million. This gives us a gain from the investment of $3 million. We can plug these numbers into our calculation and find out that:

$$ROI = \frac{\$3\text{ million} - \$1\text{ million}}{\$1\text{ million}} = \frac{\$2\text{ million}}{\$1\text{ million}} = 2 \text{ or } 200\%$$

So in this case our Return on Investment over the course of one year is two times the cost of the investment.

It is always important to calculate at least a rough ROI for any investment in organizational resources. There's a definite need to understand how much we get in return for an investment in our people. Don't just make an assumption that the Return on Investment is always positive—because it's not.

Balanced Scorecard

Is your organization achieving its mission? If you don't have a quick and accurate answer, then, besides financial measures, you need a Balanced Scorecard.[63] The Balanced Scorecard is one of the most highly touted management tools today.[64] The Balanced Scorecard concept is credited to Robert Kaplan and David Norton.[65] Basically, the scorecard says that measurement of an organization's success using purely financial measures is not sufficient.

SHRM

Guide – E:2, E:9
Balanced scorecard /
organizational scorecard

The organization also has to take into account nonfinancial measures designed to help the organization compete strategically within its industry, including learning and growth of its human resources.[66] **The Balanced Scorecard (BSC)** *measures financial, customer service, internal process, and learning and growth (or sustainability) measures*. All four dimensions of the scorecard are equally important, because the results in each area affect results in the other areas of performance. We're not going to get into the details of each of these measurement forms in this text. Suffice it to say that the organization needs to analyze its performance on multiple levels.

SHRM

Guide – E:8
HR scorecard

HR Scorecard

In addition to the organizational Balanced Scorecard, an HR scorecard has also been designed and is being used by many businesses in operation today. The four dimensions of the HR scorecard are as follows:[67] *The* **HR scorecard** *identifies HR deliverables, identifies HR system alignment, compares HR alignment with strategy, and measures organization gains created by HR practices.* Let's explain each part.

1. Identifying HR deliverables—what functions does HR perform, and what services does HR deliver that provide value to the organization?

2. Identifying HR system alignment through the use of the High-Performance Work System (HPWS)—recall from Chapter 1 that an HPWS is a set of HR practices, including comprehensive employee recruitment and selection procedures, compensation and performance management systems, information sharing, and extensive employee involvement and training that can improve the acquisition, development, and retention of the talented and motivated workforce.[68]

3. Alignment of the system with company strategy—this is the process of comparing the HPWS with the organization's strategic plan and making sure that the HR procedures being followed match well with a strategic direction of the company.

4. Identifying HR efficiency measures—this is the process of measuring the returns that the organization gets from its HR Management policies through the use of items such as EVA and ROI.

WORK
APPLICATION 2-12

Which measurement tools do they use where you work or have worked? If you don't know, ask a financial manager if EVA, ROI, BSC, and/or the HR scorecard are used.

Human Resource Information Systems

LO 2.7

Describe an HRIS and identify how it can help HR make decisions.

Strategic planning requires the management and manipulation of large amounts of data. HR serves as a broad-based system using data to influence organizational performance.[69] As a result, most organizations today use computer systems to manage and manipulate that data. Human Resource Information Systems are simply one type of system used to manage data in organizations.

What Is an HRIS?

A **Human Resource Information System (HRIS)** is an *interacting database system that "aim[s] at generating and delivering HR information and allow[s] us to automate some human resource management functions."*[70] HRISs are primarily database management systems, designed for use in HR functions. Some of the most common HRIS features include modules for attendance and leave tracking, job and pay history, appraisal scores and review date tracking, benefits enrollment and tracking, succession management, training management, and time logging. There are also other modules available depending on the size and type of the organization.

How HRISs Assist in Making HR Decisions

HRISs allow us to maintain control of our HR information and make it available for our use during the strategic planning process. Organizations can access things such as training records, job descriptions, work histories, and much more. Having this information immediately available makes the strategic planning process both quicker and smoother. We can also use the information stored in the database to make daily decisions within the

HR Department. For example, since training records are available in the HRIS, if we need to determine who has been trained in a particular process, it is fairly easy to identify those individuals who have had the correct training. We can also use the same databases when considering promotions, transfers, team assignments, and many other daily activities that are required inside the organization.

Trends and Issues in HRM

WORK
APPLICATION 2-13

How does the HR Department where you work or have worked use an HRIS? If you don't know, ask an HR Manager

We continue our discussion of some of the most important issues and trends in HRM today. For this chapter, we chose the following issues: globalization increasing the need for strategic planning; ethics—outsourcing and employee leasing; whether a small entrepreneurial organization needs a strategic plan; and whether sustainability and corporate social responsibility create a competitive advantage. Let's discuss each of these topics separately.

Globalization Increases the Need for Strategic Planning

As business in most industries becomes more and more global, competition almost inevitably increases.[71] Why has this happened? It is primarily due to the fact that as industries globalize, competitors who used to be limited to one country or a few countries gain access to many more markets. As more and more competitors gain access to more and more markets, it is obvious that competition is likely to increase. This increasing competition puts pressure on businesses to create a plan to overcome their competitors' advantages.

As we noted earlier in this chapter, the process of strategic planning is designed to analyze the competitive landscape that our organization faces and create a workable plan that will allow us to compete within that landscape. So as competition increases, a good solid "global" strategy and continuous reviews of our strategic plans become more and more significant.

Ethics–Outsourcing and Employee Leasing

Outsourcing and employee leasing are two ways in which organizations are changing the employee-employer relationship. Outsourcing is the process of *hiring another organization to do work that was previously done within the host organization.* Two common areas in which companies outsource today are payroll and benefits management. In some cases, the organization to which we outsource a particular process may be located in another country. In this case the outsourcing is often referred to as *offshoring.* Either one of these situations can have the effect of lowering the number of employees in the host organization and as a result lowering the cost of managing the human resources within that company.

Employee leasing is a little bit different than outsourcing. In an employee leasing arrangement, an organization called a *Professional Employment Organization (PEO)* is the company responsible for hiring

SHRM

Guide – I:B14
Outsourcing

Going global takes effective strategic planning.

ESR

WORK
APPLICATION 2-14

How has outsourcing, employee leasing, temporary workers, and/or replacing full-time employees with part-time employees been used where you work or have worked? Do you believe the use of these techniques to save money is ethical?

the employee and maintaining all of the records related to that employee. In this case, the employee who is hired by the PEO is called a "leased employee." In addition, the PEO will be responsible for HR-related services such as payroll, benefits, and training. The PEO is the employer of record for all of the employee services, releasing the host organization from having to provide the day-to-day HR services required for the leased employees.[72]

So, why is this an ethical issue? The ethical question in each of these cases first involves the potential for job loss within the host organization and possibly shipping jobs overseas. In the case of outsourcing or offshoring, the organization may cut entire divisions' worth of employees and send that work to the outsourcing organization. In the case of leased employees, the employee is also put in a position of working "in reality" for both the host employer and the PEO. This can create significant conflict for the employee. Finally, there are also potential tax-related implications in dealing with PEOs. According to *HR Magazine*, "The complicated hiring arrangements between PEOs and client corporations can make it difficult to determine which company is ultimately responsible for withholding and reporting an employee's income and payroll taxes. . . . Some business owners allegedly have taken advantage of complicated employee leasing arrangements to evade paying payroll taxes and to skim substantial sums of money from employee withholding funds."[73]

Does a Small, Entrepreneurial Organization Need a Strategic Plan?

OK, IBM and General Motors need strategic plans in order to determine how they're going to compete against strong entrenched competitors within their industries. However, does a small business need to have a strategy, even if they don't have significant large-scale competition? The answer here is an emphatic yes. A recent study compared successful to failed small businesses. The successful companies did significantly more planning than those that failed.[74]

There *are* organizations that survive for many years without a formal strategy, whether through luck or because of the managerial skill of the leader of the firm, but they are the exception rather than the rule. However, in virtually every successful situation there will come a point where competition begins to increase, and new competitors begin to encroach on the once safe customers and territories of the business. When this happens, if the organization is not prepared to compete and win, it is almost always too late to create a strategy at that point. The company is quite likely going to fail if faced with these circumstances.

So, even small organizations in minimally competitive industries should take the time to create and follow a reasonably detailed strategic plan. Remember, strategic planning is all about forecasting *future* conditions and how to compete and succeed within a particular industry. Don't assume that because the organization doesn't currently feel competitive pressure, they don't need a strategic plan. If you start a business and make money, the question isn't "Will competition come and take business away?" It's "When they come, how can I keep my customers?" And this takes strategic planning.

Can Sustainability Create a Competitive Advantage?

SHRM

Guide – H:5
Sustainability/corporate
social responsibility

Environmental issues are now a major social concern,[75] and sustainable development has become one of the foremost issues facing the world.[76] You've all heard about the greening of corporate America. Organizations from Wal-Mart to the corner drugstore—both for profit and nonprofit—are paying more attention than ever to their impact on the environment and are making attempts to minimize that impact through sustainability efforts.[77]

What is sustainability? **Sustainability** is *meeting the needs of today without sacrificing future generations' ability to meet their needs.*[78] Society expects sustainability, or for managers to use resources wisely and responsibly; protect the environment; minimize the amount of air, water, energy, minerals, and other materials found in the final goods we consume; recycle and reuse these goods to the extent possible rather than drawing on nature to replenish them; respect nature's calm, tranquility, and beauty; and eliminate toxins that harm people in the workplace and communities.[79]

In order for the earth to retain its ability to sustain us and allow us to continue to thrive over the long term, we collectively have to attempt to lower our impact on the environment by lowering the number and amount of resources that we use up in our daily activities. All of us must also do things to allow that environment to regenerate and increase its ability to maintain the population of the earth over time. At the corporate level this is part of the concept of corporate social responsibility. Corporations have a responsibility to the societies that surround them to maintain and support those societies and not do unnecessary harm.

Can this commitment to sustainability and corporate social responsibility create a competitive advantage for the organization? Many corporations have determined that it can.[80] Today, most businesses view the green of the environment and the green money of economics and financial returns go hand-in-hand, so they are embracing green management.[81] Thus, the trend is toward green management.[82] Every day another corporation is in the news with a new sustainability campaign. What is the purpose of these campaigns? In most cases, the primary purpose appears to be an attempt to show the organization's customers that they are a careful and caring steward of the environment. Most customer groups are increasingly aware of the dangers of environmental pollution and destruction, and as such are becoming more concerned individually with preventing such pollution and destruction. Organizations have noticed this and determined that customers will make buying decisions at least in part based on their perception of the corporation's "greenness." If it is true that customers make buying decisions at least partly based on corporate social responsibility and sustainability efforts, then those efforts can be part of creating a competitive advantage.

Wrap-Up

So, you have learned in this chapter that strategy, structure, and culture affect Human Resources and that our Human Resource Management processes affect our ability to carry out a strategy while remaining within a certain structure and culture. You've also learned that we have to measure and analyze HR's contributions to the organization and its profitability. We can't just shovel money into a particular function such as training and assume that it provides us with a positive return. We showed you some of the common tools that you can use in order to do those measurements and analyses. We also identified how an HRIS allows us to keep track of employee information that is critical both to the day-to-day operation of the organization and to the strategic planning process. That's probably enough for this chapter, so we will close it out for now and go to the answers to the learning outcomes and then to Applying the Concepts and developing skills.

ESR

Video Link 2.7

Long Term Strategy Planning

WORK
APPLICATION 2-15

Identify some of the green management initiatives being conducted for sustainability where you work or have worked.

Chapter Summary

 Visit www.sagepub.com/lussier for helpful study resources.

2.1 **Identify and explain the major components of the business environment.**

There are nine major external forces: customers, competition, suppliers, labor force/unions, shareholders, society, technology, the economy, and governments. Each factor is briefly discussed below.

- *Customers*. Customers have great power over most organizations today. Therefore, companies must continually improve products to create value for their customers.
- *Competition*. Organizations must compete against each other for customers. Organizations also frequently compete for the same employees, and sometimes for suppliers. Competitors' changing strategic moves affect the performance of the organization.
- *Suppliers*. The firm's performance is affected by its suppliers. Therefore, it is important to develop close working relationships with your suppliers, and close relationships require employees who have the ability to communicate, empathize, negotiate, and come to mutually advantageous conclusions.
- *Labor force unions*. The available recruits and the employees of an organization have a direct effect on its performance. Management recruits human resources from the available labor force outside its boundaries. Employees perform or monitor all processes within the organization.
- *Shareholders*. The owners of a corporation, known as shareholders, influence management. Most shareholders of large corporations are generally not involved in the day-to-day operation of the firm, but they do vote for the board of directors of the corporation, and the directors have the ability to hire and fire top management. The top manager reports to the board of directors.
- *Society*. Individuals and groups within society have formed to pressure business for changes. People who live in the same area with the business do not want it to pollute the air or water or otherwise abuse natural resources.
- *Technology*. Computers and the Internet have changed the speed and the manner in which organizations conduct and transact business, and they're often a major part of the firm's systems processes. Changing technologies require technologically savvy employees who have the ability to adapt to new processes. Without employees who are comfortable with changing technologies, organizations today will soon find themselves unable to compete.
- *The economy*. No organization has control over economic growth, inflation, interest rates, foreign exchange rates,

and so on. In general, as measured by Gross Domestic Product, businesses do better when the economy is growing than during times of decreased economic activity, or recession.
- *Governments*. National, state, and local governments all set laws and regulations that businesses must obey. Governments create both opportunities and threats for businesses. To a large extent, business may not do whatever it wants to do; the government tells business what it can and cannot do.

2.2 **Describe the three major organizational factors that affect our strategy options.**

Our strategic options are governed to a great extent by our current strategy, our organizational structure, and our culture. Strategy deals with how the organization competes within its industry. Strategy is just a plan of action to achieve a particular set of objectives. It looks at the external environment and the organizational environment in order to create strategic advantage. Strategic advantage occurs when you analyze the environment better and react quicker than your competitors, and thus create a sustainable competitive advantage.

Organizational structure refers to the way in which an organization groups its resources to accomplish its mission. An organization is a system, typically structured into departments such as Finance, Marketing, Production, Human Resources, and so on. Each of these departments affects the organization as a whole, and each department is affected by the other departments. Organizations structure their resources to transform inputs and outputs. All of an organization's resources must be structured effectively to achieve its mission. As a manager in any department, you will be responsible for part of the organization's structure.

Organizational culture consists of the values, beliefs, and assumptions about appropriate behavior that members of an organization share. Organizational culture is primarily learned through observing people and events in the organization.

2.3 **Discuss how the vision and mission help organizations focus their resources.**

A vision is *what we expect to become as an organization at a particular future point in time*. The vision is fuzzy; it is not specific in that we don't say *how* we're going to do a particular thing, but we identify a future state for the organization. So, the question that we answer with the vision is "What do we want to become as an organization?"

In contrast, the mission is more specific. The mission statement is *our expectations of what we're going to do in order to become the organization that we envisioned*. The mission is a statement of what the various organizational units will do and what they hope to accomplish, in alignment with the organizational vision. So, the mission statement answers the question "What do we need to do in order to become what we have envisioned?"

When you put the vision and mission together, the people in the organization get a more complete picture of what direction they are expected to go. This allows the people in the organization to focus on that particular direction. Once everyone is focused on the same direction, it makes it much easier to achieve our goals. *This focus is the thing that makes the vision and mission so powerful*. If everyone in the organization is focused on the same end result, it is much more likely that the organization will achieve that end result.

2.4 Identify and describe the major components of organizational structure and why it is important to understand them.

All of an organization's resources must be structured effectively to achieve its mission. Structure is made up of three major components:

- Complexity—the degree of three types of differentiation within the organization: vertical differentiation, horizontal differentiation, and spatial differentiation. The more the organization is divided, whether it is vertically, horizontally, or spatially, the more difficult it is to manage.
- Formalization—the degree to which jobs are standardized within an organization. The more we can standardize the organization and its processes, the easier it is to control those processes.
- Centralization—the degree to which decision making is concentrated within the organization at a single point, usually at the top of the organization. A highly centralized organization would have all authority concentrated at the top of the organization while a decentralized organization would have authority spread throughout. If authority can be centralized, we can take advantage of learning curve effects that help to improve our decision making over time.

2.5 Describe organizational culture and tell how it affects the members of the organization.

Organizational culture consists of the values, beliefs, and assumptions about appropriate behavior that members of an organization share. Organizational culture is primarily learned through observing people and events in the organization.

Because organizational culture is based at least partly on assumptions, values, and beliefs, the culture can control how people act within its boundaries. Since assumptions, values, and beliefs are so strong, individuals will generally act to conform to the culture. We all act to conform, for the most part, to the culture that we happen to be in at that point in time, because the cultural values push us to act that way.

2.6 Identify the common measurement tools for strategic HRM.

There were four common tools that we discussed in the chapter: Economic Value Added (EVA), Return on Investment (ROI), the Balanced Scorecard (BSC), and the HR scorecard.

EVA is a measure of profits that remain after the cost of capital has been deducted from operating profits. ROI is a measure of the financial return we receive because of something that we do to invest in our organization or its people.

The BSC says that measurement of an organization's success using purely financial measures is not sufficient. The organization also has to take into account nonfinancial measures designed to help the organization compete strategically within its industry. While financial measurement is one of the four perspectives in the organizational Balanced Scorecard, it also includes customer measures, internal process measures, and learning and growth (or sustainability) measures.

The HR scorecard is also being used by many businesses today. The four dimensions of the HR scorecard are (1) identifying HR deliverables, (2) identifying HR system alignment through the use of the High-Performance Work System, (3) alignment of the system with company strategy, and (4) identifying HR efficiency measures.

2.7 Describe an HRIS and identify how it can help HR make decisions.

Human Resource Information Systems (HRISs) are interacting database systems that "aim at generating and delivering HR information and allow us to automate some human resource management functions." They are primarily database management systems, designed for use in HR functions.

HRISs allow us to maintain control of our HR information and make it available for use during the strategic planning process. Having this information immediately available makes the strategic planning process both quicker and smoother. We can also use the information stored in the database to make daily decisions within the HR Department, such as a decision on whom to send to a particular training class. We can also use these databases when considering promotions, transfers, team assignments, and many other daily activities that are required inside the organization.

Key Terms

Balanced Scorecard (BSC)

Centralization

Complexity

Economic Value
  Added (EVA)

Formalization

HR scorecard

Human Resource Information
  System (HRIS)

Mission statement

Objectives

Organizational
  culture

Organizational structure

Outsourcing

Return on Investment (ROI)

Strategy

Sustainability

Vision

Key Term Review

Complete each of the following statements using one of this chapter's key terms:

_____ is a plan of action to achieve a particular set of objectives.

_____ is what we expect to become as an organization at a particular future point in time.

_____ is our expectations of what we're going to do in order to become the organization that we envisioned.

_____ state what is to be accomplished in singular, specific, and measurable terms with a target date.

_____ refers to the way in which an organization groups its resources to accomplish its mission.

_____ is the degree of three types of differentiation within the organization.

_____ is the degree to which jobs are standardized within an organization.

_____ is the degree to which decision making is concentrated within the organization at a single point, usually at the top of the organization.

_____ consists of the values, beliefs, and assumptions about appropriate behavior that members of an organization share.

_____ is a measure of profits that remain after the cost of capital has been deducted from operating profits.

_____ is a measure of the financial return we receive because of something that we do to invest in our organization or its people.

_____ measures financial, customer service, internal process, and learning and growth (sustainability).

_____ identifies HR deliverables, identifies HR system alignment, compares HR alignment with strategy, and measures organization gains created by HR practices.

_____ are interacting database systems that aim at generating and delivering HR information and allow us to automate some human resource management functions.

_____ is the process of hiring another organization to do work that was previously done within the host organization.

_____ is meeting the needs of today without sacrificing future generations' ability to meet their needs.

Quick Check (True-False)

1. Strategy and strategic planning are more important today than ever, due to increased competition. T F

2. The three major organizational factors that affect our strategy options are structure, culture, and government. T F

3. A vision statement is plenty. Most organizations don't need a mission statement because it is redundant. T F

4. A Broad Differentiation strategy attempts to create an impression of difference for a company's products or services in the mind of their customer. T F

5. If an organization follows a Cost Leader strategy, they will likely have broad job classifications and use incentive programs to reward innovation and creativity. T F

6. SWOT Analysis is a process of balancing our available resources in order to make the most of our strengths and opportunities, and to minimize any danger to the organization from its weaknesses and threats. T F

7. It is frequently possible, and in fact usually desirable, to copy the industry leader's strategy in order to achieve success in a specific industry. T F

8. Controlling is the process of establishing and implementing mechanisms to ensure that objectives are achieved. T F

9. The three main components of organizational structure are complexity, differentiation, and formalization. T F

10. Differing organizational structures will have very little if any effect on HR Managers and their jobs. T F

11. Organizational culture describes how employees do what they do, and why they do what they do. T F

12. Values and beliefs cannot be observed directly; we can only infer from people's behavior what they value and believe. T F

13. The HR scorecard is based on the assumption that "purely financial measures" of the organization's success are not sufficient, but the organizational scorecard only measures financial returns. T F

Communication Skills

The following critical-thinking questions can be used for class discussion and/or for written assignments to develop communication skills. Be sure to give complete explanations for all answers.

1. Can you name a business that you know of in which competition has increased significantly in the past few years? Why do you think their competition has occurred in this case?

2. What are some of the ways that the environmental factors that we discussed in the chapter directly affect the organization?

3. Do you agree that every organization needs a strategic plan? Why or why not?

4. Think about the technological changes that have occurred since you were born. Do you think those changes have affected the strategic planning process? How?

5. What should a mission statement focus on—customers, competitors, products/services, employee environment, or something else? Identify why you chose a particular answer.

6. We discussed the three major generic strategies in this chapter. Can you think of examples of each of the three strategies in businesses that you know of? In your opinion, how successful have these companies been with their strategy?

7. If you were going to design the structure for a new, innovate startup company, what kind of structure would you try to create (high or low complexity, formalization and centralization)? Why would you set up this type of structure?

8. Which of the five artifacts, or important ways that employees learn about culture, do you think is most important? Why?

9. Name some situations in HRM when you would want to use either Economic Value Added (EVA) or Return on Investment (ROI) as an analytical tool.

10. Do you agree that Balanced Scorecards are a good way to evaluate the organization's performance overall? Why or why not? What measures would you add to the scorecard to improve it?

11. Is outsourcing good or bad for the organization overall? Why?

Video

Please visit the student study site at **www.sagepub.com/lussier** to view the video links in this chapter.

Answers

REVIEW QUESTIONS (TRUE-FALSE) Answers

1. T 2. F 3. F 4. T 5. F 6. T 7. F 8. T 9. F 10. F 11. T 12. T 13. F

Case

Case 2-1. Building Up Our Assets: DHR Construction

In August 2011, when the Dow Jones Industrial Average dipped under 8,000 from a high of almost 11,500, Richard Davis and Stephen Hodgetts, academics, friends, and coauthors, were lamenting their ever-shrinking retirement funds. As Hodgetts was fond of saying,

"America believes in education: The average professor earns more money in a year than a professional athlete earns in a whole week."

After a long discussion, they decided that they needed to take direct control of their investments and not be prisoners to the rise and fall of the stock market. Davis had done enough preliminary research on the real estate market in their area and convinced Hodgetts that there was money to be made in property ownership and renting starter homes (three bedrooms, two baths) to individuals with poor credit who could not afford a home but who had excellent rental track records. Davis and Hodgetts formed D&H Management and found six families in three months who were happy to rent and eventually purchase homes in the $175K price range. The deal was so attractive that D&H even had a waiting list of new tenants. The six homes, though, gobbled up their initial investment and required additional capital.

The New Firm: DHR Construction, LLC

Their construction company started off as just a small capital-raising venture. Hodgetts and Davis would finish off the basements of their rental homes, get the homes reappraised, and then remortgage the properties, pulling out an additional $10K–$20K per home. These funds could then be used as down payments for future rental homes.

In chatting about this matter with some of their renters, Davis and Hodgetts were approached by one of them to perform all of the nonlicensed work (excluding electrical, plumbing, HVAC, etc.). Davis explained to the renters (Alan and Wilma Bronson) that they would have to form their own company and act as any other subcontractor. After completing a few basements, Alan and Wilma enjoyed working on these basements so much that they approached Davis and Hodgetts about figuring out a way that Davis and Hodgetts could keep them occupied all year-round. In essence, Alan would quit his job and work as a subcontractor for Davis and Hodgetts. This was not possible, though, since there was not enough work to keep Alan and Wilma busy. Yet a few days later the situation dramatically changed.

One of Davis's students, David Russ, who was designing their basements, said that he thought that Davis and Hodgetts could cut out the middleman in terms of the rental business if they built their own homes. Davis thought that Russ was crazy at the time, but they talked after class and Russ said that he would be happy to act as the general contractor and that he knew all of the subcontractors who were needed in order to construct new homes. Alan and Wilma would do all of the interior work, and Alan could hire some part-time workers to help himself out. Davis and Hodgetts could then build the rest of their homes under a different company name, sell it to themselves for a small profit, and then make a profit renting the homes.

In around nine months, the preliminary profits derived from their construction operation led Davis and Hodgetts to build homes not only to be purchased by D&H Management but also for public consumption. In May DHR Construction broke ground on their first home to be sold to the public.

In November, Davis and Hodgetts bought out David Russ's interests in DHR Construction due to differences in management and business philosophies. Davis was left to act as contractor while Hodgetts handled D&H Management. By January 2004, they had completed three homes at St. Andrews subdivision. Alan quickly took over the role of foreman/contractor when DHR shifted their building site to another location, the Florence Development, which had a much more upscale look. DHR was no longer building starter homes; they shifted into the mid-size market (four bedrooms, $300K) where they could make a higher profit margin. By April, DHR had built three homes in Florence, had plans to build five more in that area, and were looking at other developments for future growth and expansion.

Branching Out: Patio Homes

In June, Davis located a brand-new development about 10 miles east of where they currently were building, in an area called Snowy Mountains. Snowy Mountains was a unique project for the area since the developers had built lakes, a golf course, and a clubhouse (including a three-star restaurant) and had very specific designs for community development. The housing currently in the development (Phase 1) ran the gamut of homes, from four-bedroom patio homes (that started around $450K) to multimillion-dollar estates on the lake.

DHR Patio Homes was formed by Davis and Hodgetts (run under the corporate label of DHR Construction), who decided to build the lower-end patio homes; these homes would yield them their highest profit margins to date. Using the same management and work crew as DHR, Davis acted as the architect and head of operations for construction while Alan acted as foreman and continued his own subcontracting work. Hodgetts remained in charge of the rental operation but served as an advisor to Davis on an "as needed" basis.

Questions

1. Describe Davis and Hodgetts's strategic planning process. What seems to be the driving force for their planning?

2. What was Davis and Hodgetts's original strategy for managing their retirement funds? How did that strategy change?

3. What type of strategy did Davis and Hodgetts first use in their business? How did that strategy change with the change in their business?

4. What HRM issues might Davis and Hodgetts have to address given their changing business strategy?

5. Describe the structure of DHR Construction.

6. In your opinion, how does this structure affect HRM?

Case created by Herbert Sherman, PhD, and Mr. Theodore Vallas, Department of Management Sciences, Long Island University School of Business, Brooklyn Campus

SKILL BUILDER 2-1

Writing Objectives

For this exercise, you will first work at improving ineffective objectives. Then you will write nine objectives for yourself.

Objective

To develop your skill at writing objectives.

Skills

The primary skills developed through this exercise are:

1. *HR Management skill*—Conceptual and design

2. *SHRM 2010 Curriculum Guidebook* – H: Strategic HR

Part 1

Indicate which of the criteria each of the following objectives fails to meet in the model and rewrite the objective so that it meets all those criteria. When writing objectives, use the following model:

To + action verb + single, specific, and measurable result + target date

1. To improve our company image by the end of 2014

    Criteria not met: _____

    Improved objective: _____

    _____

2. To increase the number of customers by 10%

    Criteria not met: _____

    Improved objective: _____

    _____

3. To increase profits during 2014

    Criteria not met: _____

    Improved objective: _____

    _____

4. To sell 5% more hot dogs and 13% more soda at the baseball game on Sunday, June 14, 2013

    Criteria not met: _____

    Improved objective: _____

    _____

Part 2

Write three educational, three personal, and three career objectives you want to accomplish. Your objectives can be short-term (something you want to accomplish today) or long-term (something you want to have accomplished 20 years from now) or in between those extremes. Be sure your objectives use the model and meet the criteria for effective objectives.

Educational Objectives

1 _____
_____
_____

2 _____
_____
_____

3 _____
_____
_____

Personal Objectives

1 _____
_____
_____

2 _____
_____
_____

3 _____
_____
_____

Career Objectives

1 _____
_____
_____

2 _____
_____
_____

3 _____
_____
_____

Apply It

What did I learn from this experience? How will I use this knowledge in the future?

_____
_____

Your instructor may ask you to do this Skill Builder in class in a group. If so, the instructor will provide you with any necessary information or additional instructions.

SKILL BUILDER 2-2

The Strategic Planning at Your College

This exercise enables you to apply the strategic planning process to your college or university as an individual and/or a group. Complete each step by typing/writing out your answers.

This exercise can also be conducted for another organization.

Objective

To develop your strategic planning skills by analyzing the internal environment of strategy, structure, and culture.

Skills

The primary skills developed through this exercise are:

1. *HR Management skill*—Conceptual and design
2. *SHRM 2010 Curriculum Guidebook* – H: Strategic HR

PART A. STRATEGY

Step 1. Developing a Mission

1. What is the vision and mission statement of your university/college or school/department?
2. Is the mission statement easy to understand and remember?
3. How would you improve the mission statement?

Step 2. Identify Strategy

Which of the three generic strategies is used?

Step 3. Strategic Analysis

1. Conduct a Five-Forces Competitive Analysis, like that in Exhibit 2-4 (page 50).
2. Complete a SWOT analysis, like that in Exhibit 2-5 (page 52).
3. Determine the competitive advantage (if any) of your university/college or school/department.

Step 4. Setting Objectives

What are some objectives of your university/college or school department?

Step 5. Implementing, Monitoring, and Evaluating Strategies

How would you rate your university/college's or school/department's strategic planning? How could it be improved?

PART B. STRUCTURE

Describe the organizational structure in terms of its complexity, formalization, and centralization.

PART C. CULTURE

1. Identify artifacts in each of the categories of heroes, stories, slogans, symbols, and ceremonies.
2. Identify the cultural levels of the organization's behaviors, values and beliefs, and assumptions.

Apply It

What did I learn from this experience? How will I use this knowledge in the future?

_____

_____

Your instructor may ask you to do this Skill Builder in class in a group. If so, the instructor will provide you with any necessary information or additional instructions.

3

The Legal Environment and Diversity Management

Learning Outcomes

After studying this chapter, you should be able to:

3.1 Describe the OUCH test and its four components and identify when it is useful in an organizational setting

3.2 Identify the major Equal Employment Opportunity laws and the groups of people that each law protects

3.3 Describe the three main types of discrimination in the workplace

3.4 Discuss the organizational defenses to accusations of discrimination

3.5 Briefly discuss the two major federal immigration laws and how they affect the workplace

3.6 Briefly discuss and identify the major functions of the Equal Employment Opportunity Commission

3.7 Discuss the difference between Equal Employment Opportunity, Affirmative Action, and diversity

3.8 Identify the two primary types of sexual harassment

3.9 Define the following terms:

Discrimination
Illegal discrimination
→ OUCH test
Four-fifths rule
Disparate treatment
Disparate impact
Pattern or practice discrimination
Bona Fide Occupational Qualification (BFOQ)
Business necessity
Job relatedness
Disability
Reasonable accommodation
Essential functions
Undue hardship
Compensatory damages
Punitive damages
Race-norming

Right-to-sue
Retaliation
Adverse employment action
Constructive discharge
Affirmative Action (AA)
Reverse discrimination
Diversity
Creativity
Innovation
Divergent thinking
Conflict
Functional conflict
Dysfunctional conflict
Cohesiveness
Sexual harassment
Quid pro quo
Hostile work environment
Reasonable person

Chapter 3 Outline

SHRM
HR CONTENT

See Appendix A: *SHRM 2010 Curriculum Guidebook* **for the complete list**

B.   Employment Law (required)
   1.   The Age Discrimination in Employment Act of 1967
   2.   The Americans With Disabilities Act of 1990 and as Amended in 2008
   3.   The Equal Pay Act of 1963
   4.   The Pregnancy Discrimination Act of 1978
   5.   Title VII of the Civil Rights Act of 1964 and 1991
   6.   Executive Order 11246 (1965)
   10. The Rehabilitation
        Act of 1973
   16. The Uniformed Services Employment and Reemployment Rights
        Act of 1994
   18. Enforcement agencies (EEOC, OFCCP)
   25. Disparate impact
   26. Disparate treatment
   27. Unlawful harassment

        Sexual
        Religious
        Disability
        Race
        Color
        Nation of origin
   28. Retaliation
   29. Reasonable accommodation

        ADA
        Religious
   31. The Lilly Ledbetter Fair Pay Act of 2009
   32. The Genetic Information Nondiscrimination Act of 2008
   35. The Immigration Reform and Control Act of 1986
   38. The Immigration and Nationality Act of 1952

C.   Job Analysis/Job Design (required)
   6.   Compliance with legal requirements

        Equal employment (job relatedness, Bona Fide Occupational Qualifications, and the reasonable accommodation process)

G.   Staffing: Recruitment and Selection (required)
   15. Bona Fide Occupational Qualification (BFOQ)

Case 3-1. English-Only: One Hotel's Dilemma

Case 3-2. When Religion Is on the Agenda

The Legal Compliance Minefield

A major component of HR Management is compliance—ensuring that the organization complies both with government rules and regulations and with its own policies and procedures. Different treatment of individuals who are in similar circumstances opens the door to legal liability. Just such a situation had an impact on one of our supervisors. Zac was a great employee—enthusiastic, pleasant, and efficient—and his supervisor, Jim, was sympathetic when Zac explained he was facing difficulties at home with child care arrangements due to a change in his wife's working hours. Jim became lenient in permitting Zac to leave a little early on days he had additional child care duties. Meanwhile, Destiny, a single mom, often had to leave work early to manage child care issues of her own. She was disorganized, unenthusiastic, and often in a sour mood at work. After a particularly rough week, Jim called Destiny into his office for an official reprimand for leaving work early too many times in a two-week period. Destiny promptly threatened to file a discrimination suit against Jim. Did she have a valid claim? What should Jim have done differently? Chapter 3 provides armor for the minefield of legal compliance.

The Practitioner's Model for HRM

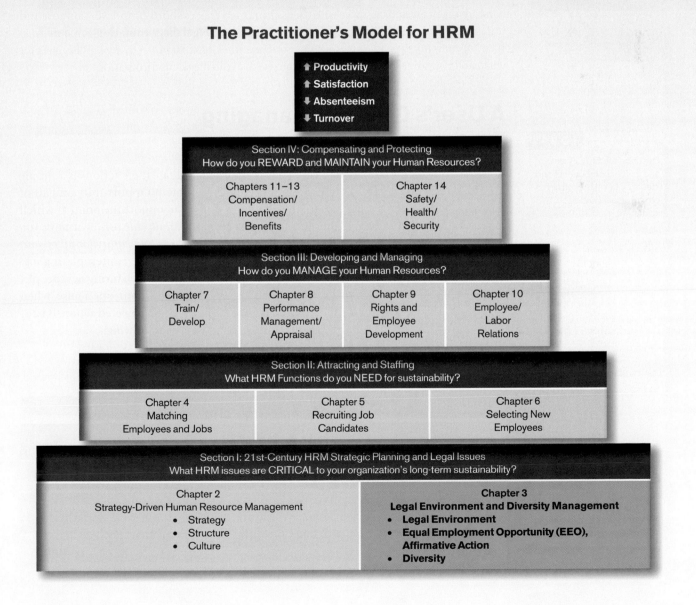

The Legal Environment for HRM–Protecting Your Organization

The HRM environment has become much more complex in the past 30 years. Why? Well, there have been a significant number of laws enacted during and immediately prior to that period that affect how organizations do business. In addition, we have grown to believe in the value of a diverse workforce much more so than in the 1960s and '70s. In this chapter, we will explore some of the laws that HR Managers have to work with on a daily basis as well as looking in some more depth at diversity and why it is valuable in an organization.

One of the primary jobs of an HR Manager in any type of organization is to assist in avoiding any discriminatory situations that can create legal, ethical, or social problems with employees, former employees, the community, or other stakeholders.

As a result, one of the first things we need to do in this chapter is to identify what is meant by the term *discrimination*. **Discrimination** is *the act of making distinctions, or choosing one thing over another—in HR, it is distinctions among people.* So you can see very quickly that we *all* discriminate every day. If a manager does not discriminate, then they're not doing their job. However, we want to avoid *illegal* discrimination based on a person's membership in a protected class (we will discuss protected classes shortly), and we want to avoid unfair treatment of any of our employees at all times. **Illegal discrimination** is *making distinctions that harm people by using a person's membership in a protected class.* This chapter will teach you some of the tools that we can use to avoid illegal discrimination.

WORK APPLICATION 3-1

Give examples of how you and other employees legally discriminate at work.

A User's Guide to Managing People–The OUCH Test

LO 3.1

Describe the OUCH test and its four components and identify when it is useful in an organizational setting.

The first and simplest tool that any manager can use to evaluate their actions is a simple thumb rule. Before we start talking about Equal Employment Opportunity and all of the forms of illegal discrimination in the workplace, this is an opportune point at which to introduce you to the OUCH test.[1] The **OUCH test** is *a thumb rule used whenever you are contemplating any employment action, to maintain fairness and equity for all of your employees or applicants.* You should use this test whenever you are contemplating *any action that involves your employees.* For example, you should use it when hiring new people, when promoting employees, when deciding whether or not to give someone a raise, when analyzing disciplinary action against an employee, or in any other job-related action. It is, of course, an acronym (see Exhibit 3-1). The acronym stands for the following:

Exhibit 3-1	The OUCH Test
Objective	Fact-based and quantifiable, not subjective or emotional
Uniform in Application	Apply the same "tests" in the same ways
Consistent in Effect	Ensure the result is not significantly different for different groups
Has Job Relatedness	Action *must* relate to the essential job functions

Objective

Is the action *objective*, or is it subjective? What's the difference? Something that is objective is based on fact, cognitive knowledge, or quantifiable evidence. Something that is subjective is based on your emotional state, an opinion, or how you feel in a certain circumstance, not on cognitive knowledge. We should make our employment actions as objective as we possibly can in all cases. Now, this does not mean that we can always make our employment actions objective—we simply need to make them as objective as we possibly can.

Uniform in Application

Is the action being uniformly applied? In other words, if you apply an action in an employment situation, are you applying that same action in all cases of the same type? For example, if you have one applicant for a position take a written test, you need to have all the applicants for that same position take the same written test, under the same conditions, to the best of your ability. *Uniform in application* is more difficult than most people think it is.

If you ask someone to perform a test (whether written, verbal, or physical), you need to provide the exact same circumstances, as much as you can control them. If performing a physical test, you would need to use the same physical items if possible, and if you asked people to take a written exam, you would need to provide the exact same type of setting for the test. If one person took the exam in a quiet room and the other in a noisy hallway, you would not be uniform in application.

Consistent in Effect

Does the action taken have a significantly different effect on a protected group than it has on the majority group members? *Consistent in effect* is a little bit more difficult than the other three OUCH test characteristics. There are many protected groups in U.S. law. We have to try and make sure that we don't affect one of these protected groups disproportionately with an employment action. How do we know? The Department of Labor and the Equal Employment Opportunity Commission (EEOC) have given us a test called the four-fifths rule.[2] The **four-fifths rule** is *a test used by various federal courts, the Department of Labor, and the EEOC to determine whether disparate impact exists in an employment test*.

The best way to quickly explain the four-fifths rule is to give you a simple example. Take a look at Exhibit 3-2. Let's suppose that we live in an area that is basically evenly split between African American and White populations. You are planning on hiring about 40 new employees for a general position in your company. You decide to give each of the potential employees a written test. If the results of the test disproportionately rule out the African American portion of the population, then your written test is not consistent in effect. Let's use the four-fifths rule to find out whether or not you were being consistent. To make this example simple, we will assume that you had 100 White male applicants and 100 African American male applicants. What would show that you were consistent in effect? Look at the following numbers.

If we are outside the four-fifths rule, have we automatically broken the law? No. We have to investigate why we are outside the four-fifths parameter, though. If there is a *legitimate reason* (we will discuss these shortly) for the discrepancy that would be able to be proven in a court case, we are probably OK with a selection rate that is outside the parameters. By the way, we *can* also look at six fifths to determine the possibility of reverse discrimination, so we would want to be between 16 and 24 African American males selected in the first example, since six fifths of 20 is 24.

Exhibit 3-2	The Four-Fifths Rule

You are planning to hire about 40 new employees. The statistical information on applicants is below:

Example 1:

	White Males	African American Males
Applicants	100	100
Selected	20	17
Selection rate	20% (20/100)	17% (17/100)

Four-fifths = 80%, so 80% of 20% (.80 x .20) = 16%.

The selection rate of 17% is greater than 16%, so the four-fifths rule is met.

Example 2:

	White Males	African American Males
Applicants	100	40
Selected	29	9
Selection rate	29%	22.5% (9/40)

Four-fifths = 80%, so 80% of 29% (.80 x .29) = 23.2%

The selection rate of 22.5% is less than the 23.2% required, so the four-fifths rule is *not* met.

You would have to hire 9.28 or more people (23.2% of 40 = 9.28) in this case to be within the four-fifths rule. You can't have .28 of a person, so you need to round up to 10 to be within the requirement, and you need one more African American male to get up to 10.

Since the selection rate of African American males (the protected group in this case) in the first example is 17%, it is above the four-fifths rule threshold of 16%. Therefore we are "consistent in effect" based on the four-fifths rule.

However, in the second example, the selection rate of the African American males is 22.5%, and the minimum value by the four-fifths rule is 23.2%. As a result, we are outside the boundaries of being "consistent in effect" in this case.

Consistent in effect is by far the most complex of the four OUCH test factors. However, it is also a very important factor to show consistency in our actions as managers in an organization. Are we treating all groups *fairly*? Do the results show that we are? *Consistent in effect* will show us the answer visually.

Has Job Relatedness

Is the action directly related to the *primary* aspects of the job in question? The word *primary* will become very important later when we discuss the Americans With Disabilities Act, which calls these factors "essential factors." For right now, just understand that our actions have to be directly job related (i.e., *have job relatedness*). In other words, if your

WORK
APPLICATION 3-2

Select an employment policy where you work or have worked. Give it the OUCH test, stating if it does or does not meet each of the four criteria.

job has nothing to do with making coffee for the office in the morning, I cannot base any employment action such as a hiring or firing on whether or not you can make coffee.

Remember, however, that the OUCH test is a thumb rule and does not work perfectly. It is not a legal test by itself. You have to understand the limits of any rule of thumb. It is a good guide to nondiscriminatory practices, but it is only a guide.

Major Employment Laws

In any management position within any organization today, you need a basic understanding of the major employment laws that are currently in effect. If you don't understand what is legal and what isn't, you can inadvertently make mistakes that may cost your employer significant amounts of money and time, and if that happens they may not be your employer anymore. You don't want that to happen, so let's take a chronological look at some of the laws listed in Exhibit 3-3. These are some of the major laws that you'll need to know about as you start to manage people for your organization.

LO 3.2

Identify the major Equal Employment Opportunity laws and the groups of people that each law protects.

Exhibit 3-3	Major EEO Laws in Chronological Order
Law	**Description**
Equal Pay Act of 1963	Requires that women be paid equal to men if they are doing the same work
Title VII of the Civil Rights Act of 1964	Prohibits discrimination on the basis of race, color, religion, sex, or national origin in all areas of the employment relationship
Age Discrimination in Employment Act of 1967	Prohibits age discrimination against people 40 years of age or older and restricts mandatory retirement
Vietnam Era Veterans' Readjustment Assistance Act of 1974	Prohibits discrimination against Vietnam veterans by all employers with federal contracts or subcontracts of $100,000 or more. Also requires that Affirmative Action be taken.
Pregnancy Discrimination Act of 1978	Prohibits discrimination against women affected by pregnancy, childbirth, or related medical conditions as unlawful sex discrimination
Americans With Disabilities Act of 1990	Strengthened the Rehabilitation Act of 1973 to require employers to provide "reasonable accommodations" to allow disabled employees to work
Civil Rights Act of 1991	Strengthened civil rights by providing for possible compensatory and punitive damages for discrimination
Uniformed Services Employment and Reemployment Rights Act of 1994	Ensures the civilian reemployment rights of military members who were called away from their regular (nonmilitary) jobs by U.S. government orders
Veterans' Benefits Improvement Act of 2004	Amends USERRA to extend health care coverage while away on duty, and requires employers to post a notice of benefits, duties, and rights of reemployment
Genetic Information Nondiscrimination Act of 2008	Prohibits the use of genetic information in employment, prohibits intentional acquisition of same, and imposes confidentiality requirements
Lilly Ledbetter Fair Pay Act of 2009	Amends the 1964 CRA to extend the period of time that an employee is allowed to file a lawsuit over pay discrimination

The Equal Pay Act of 1963

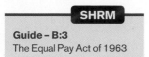

SHRM

Guide – B:3
The Equal Pay Act of 1963

The first modern Equal Employment Opportunity law that we will review is the Equal Pay Act. The act requires that women who do the same job as men, in the same organization, receive the same pay. It defines *equal* in terms of "equal skill, effort, and responsibility, and [job tasks] which are performed under similar working conditions."[3] However, if pay differences are the result of differences in seniority, merit, quantity, or quality of production, or *any factor other than sex* (e.g., shift differentials, training programs), then differences are legally allowable.[4] This wording makes the act a somewhat weaker law than was probably originally intended. Even though the Equal Pay Act was weaker than expected, it was followed the next year by a law that was much tougher concerning equality and nondiscrimination.

Title VII of the Civil Rights Act of 1964

SHRM

Guide – B:5
Title VII of the Civil Rights
Act of 1964 and 1991

Title VII of the Civil Rights Act of 1964 was probably the most significant single piece of legislation regulating Equal Employment Opportunity in the history of the United States. It changed the way that virtually every organization in the country did business, and even helped change employers' attitudes about discrimination. Even in cases where the law does not directly apply to an organization, it has been used to evaluate internal policies to attempt to ensure fairness and equality for all of our workers.

The 1964 Civil Rights Act (CRA) states that it is illegal for an employer "(1) to fail or refuse to hire or to discharge any individual, or otherwise to discriminate against any individual with respect to his compensation, terms, conditions, or privileges of employment, because of such individual's race, color, religion, sex, or national origin; or (2) to limit, segregate, or classify his employees or applicants for employment in any way which would deprive or tend to deprive any individual of employment opportunities or otherwise adversely affect his status as an employee, because of such individual's race, color, religion, sex, or national origin."[5]

The act applies to organizations with 15 or more employees working 20 or more weeks a year that are involved in interstate commerce. Why does the organization have to be involved in interstate commerce? Mainly because of the Tenth Amendment to the U.S. Constitution, which deals with states' rights. The federal government can't make any laws that apply wholly within the borders of a single state. The law also generally applies to state and local governments; educational institutions, public or private; all employment agencies; and all labor associations of any type.

Important concepts introduced by the CRA of 1964 include:

– Disparate treatment

– Disparate (also called adverse) impact

– Pattern or practice

– Bona Fide Occupational Qualification

– Business necessity

– Job relatedness

LO 3.3

Describe the three main
types of discrimination in the
workplace.

Types of Discrimination

The 1964 CRA identified, really for the first time, three types of discrimination. While it didn't specifically name these types, it did describe the process of each of the three in at least some detail. Once this was done, court rulings helped to further define the three types, which we have come to call *disparate treatment, disparate impact,* and *pattern or practice.* Disparate treatment and impact are also sometimes called "adverse" treatment or impact.

In addition to the three types of discrimination that were more or less directly identified in the 1964 CRA, a fourth and fifth type have been determined to exist by federal courts based on the wording of the CRA. These other two types of discrimination are *religious discrimination* and *sexual harassment.* For now, let's discuss the three forms of discrimination that were directly identified in the CRA. We will save the fourth and fifth items for later in the chapter.

Disparate (adverse) treatment. **Disparate treatment** exists when individuals in similar situations are intentionally treated differently and the different treatment is based on an individual's membership in a protected class. In a court case, the plaintiff must prove that there was a discriminatory motive—that is, that the employer intended to discriminate in order to prove disparate treatment.[6] Disparate treatment is generally illegal unless the employer can show that there was a Bona Fide Occupational Qualification (BFOQ—we will talk about these shortly) that caused the need to intentionally disallow members of a protected group from applying for or getting the job.

SHRM

Guide – B:26
Disparate treatment

Disparate (adverse) impact. **Disparate impact** occurs when an officially neutral employment practice disproportionately excludes the members of a protected group; it is generally considered to be unintentional, but intent is irrelevant. For there to be discrimination under disparate treatment, there has to be intentional discrimination. Under disparate impact, intent does not matter.[7]

SHRM

Guide – B:25
Disparate impact

Some characteristics (height and strength are two examples) are not distributed equally across race and gender groups, and in some jobs these characteristics may be related to successful performance in the job. Therefore, disparate impact is not *necessarily* illegal. The important question is whether the characteristic is related to successful performance on the job (has job relatedness). Disparate impact is generally judged by use of the four-fifths rule. Both the Department of Labor, through their Uniform Guidelines on Employee Selection Procedures (UGESP)— we will talk about these more in Chapter 6—and the EEOC have expressed a preference for using the four-fifths rule to determine disparate impact.[8] If the four-fifths requirement is not satisfied,

Effective HRM practices can help to prevent lawsuits.

discrimination is considered to have occurred; however, *illegal* discrimination has not necessarily been proven.

The four-fifths rule requires that, if we fall outside of its boundaries, we must investigate to ensure that we haven't used an *illegal protected class characteristic* to bias an employment outcome. If our investigation shows that an employment test or measure was biased toward or against a certain group, then we would have to correct the test or measure, unless there was a legitimate reason to measure that particular characteristic (discussed below). However, if our investigation shows that the test was valid and reliable, and that there was some other legitimate reason why we did not meet the four-fifths standard, then illegal discrimination *may* not exist. The bottom line here is that we always need to investigate thoroughly if we fall outside the four-fifths standard.

Pattern or practice. Pattern or practice discrimination occurs when a person or group engages in a sequence of actions over a significant period of time that is intended to deny the rights provided by Title VII (the 1964 CRA) to a member of a protected class. If there is reasonable cause to believe that a state or local government, or a nongovernmental organization, is engaging in a "pattern or practice" that denies the rights provided by Title VII, the U.S. Attorney General may bring a federal lawsuit against them.[9] In general, no individual can directly bring a pattern or practice lawsuit against an organization. As with the disparate treatment concept, it must be proven that the employer intended to discriminate against a particular class of individuals, and did so over a protracted period of time. See Exhibit 3-4 for types of discrimination and organizational defenses to illegal discrimination charges.

Exhibit 3-4	Types of Discrimination and Organizational Defenses to Illegal Discrimination Charges	
Discrimination Type	**Intent**	**Organizational Defense**
Disparate Treatment	Intentional	BFOQ
Disparate Impact	Unintentional	BFOQ or Business Necessity and Job Relatedness
Pattern or Practice	Intentional	BFOQ (Unlikely Defense)

Organizational Defenses to Discrimination Charges

LO 3.4

Discuss the organizational defenses to accusations of discrimination.

The organization *does* have some defenses to charges of illegal discrimination. We can defend ourselves by showing that there was a need for a particular characteristic or qualification for a specific job or that there was a *requirement* that the business do certain things in order to remain viable and profitable so that we didn't harm *all* of our employees by failing and shutting down. Let's go through each of the defenses and show you what we're talking about.

SHRM

Guide – G:15
Bona Fide Occupational Qualification (BFOQ)

Bona Fide Occupational Qualification. The first defense is called a Bona Fide Occupational Qualification. A **Bona Fide Occupational Qualification (BFOQ)** is *a qualification that is absolutely required in order for an individual to be able to successfully do a particular job.* The qualification cannot just be a *desirable* quality within the job applicant, but must be *mandatory*. A BFOQ would be a legitimate defense against a charge of disparate treatment. As an example, an employer who is staffing the members of a theater troupe for a production of *Romeo and Juliet* might legitimately require that only women be allowed to apply for the role of Juliet. A male actor would not have to be considered for this role due to the fact that he is not a woman and cannot legitimately fill the role of a woman on stage. Another example of a BFOQ would be a requirement in some cases that only persons of particular religious faith be allowed to apply for a job as a worker within a mosque, a church, or a synagogue. In this case there's a reasonable expectation that people who do not share the same faith would not have the knowledge (qualifications) to be able to fill the job, and would in fact almost certainly violate some of the rules of the faith if they were to be employed in such a position.

On the other hand, there was a very famous case of an employer attempting to use the BFOQ defense in response to a lawsuit against them. In this case, their BFOQ defense was considered to be invalid. In 1971, a man named Celio Diaz sued Pan Am World Airways in the United States for discrimination based on the fact that he was denied the opportunity to apply for a flight attendant position with the airline. The airline required at the time that flight attendants be female only. In court, the airline defended the requirement that flight attendants be female based on the fact that passengers *expected* the role of a flight attendant to be filled by a woman. In their arguments, they maintained that the passenger expectation was tantamount to a requirement. However, as most of you know, the courts ruled against the airline and allowed men to apply for, and be accepted into, positions as flight attendants. The reasoning of the courts was that expectation or "customer preference" does not create a requirement in the eyes of the law.[10] A BFOQ defense can be used against both disparate impact and disparate treatment allegations.

Business necessity. **Business necessity** exists when a particular practice is necessary for the safe and efficient operation of the business, and there is a specific business purpose for applying a particular standard that may, in fact, be discriminatory. A business necessity defense is applied by an employer in order to show that a particular practice was necessary for the safe and efficient operation of the business, and that there is a specific business purpose for applying a particular standard that may, in fact, be discriminatory.

Business necessity defenses must be combined with a test for job relatedness (discussed next). If an organization can show a legitimate business necessity for the test that they apply in an employment action, then they have a legitimate defense to disparate impact. Business necessity is specifically prohibited as a defense to disparate treatment.[11]

Job relatedness. **Job relatedness** *exists when a test for employment is a legitimate measure of an individual's ability to do the essential functions of a job.* For job relatedness to act as a defense to a discriminatory action, first it has to be a business necessity, and then the employer must be able to show that the test for the employment action was a legitimate measure of an individual's ability to do the job.[12] (It doesn't have to be a paper-and-pencil test. The federal government defines a "test for employment action" as the full range of assessment techniques, including written exams, performance tests, training programs, probationary periods, interviews, reviews of experience or education, work samples, and physical requirements.)[13]

If the employer is unsuccessful in showing that the employment test measures a legitimate requirement of the job, the job relatedness test will fail. If, however, the employer can show that the test was a legitimate measure of the job requirements, then this can be a legitimate defense to discrimination.

There is one thing that all good managers, especially HR Managers, should keep in mind, though. The best way to defend against illegal discrimination charges is to avoid actions that could bring such charges about. If the company follows the laws and regulations, the potential for charges of discrimination become significantly less likely, so HR needs to ensure that we do everything possible to avoid those charges.

The Age Discrimination in Employment Act of 1967

The Age Discrimination in Employment Act of 1967 (ADEA) prohibits discrimination against employees age 40 or older. In this case, it applies if the organization has 20 or more workers instead of 15. This act almost exactly mirrors Title VII with the exception of the 20-worker minimum. This mirroring of the 1964 CRA is true with almost all of the protected class discrimination laws that came about after 1964.

**WORK
APPLICATION 3-3**

Give examples of BFOQ for jobs at an organization where you work or have worked.

SHRM

Guide – B:1
The Age Discrimination in Employment Act of 1967

3-1 APPLYING THE CONCEPT

BFOQ

State if each of the following would or wouldn't meet the test of a BFOQ.

a.   It is a legal BFOQ.

b.   It is not a legal BFOQ.

_____ 1.   For a job of loading packages onto trucks to be delivered: Applicants must be able to lift 50 pounds.

_____ 2.   For the job of teaching history at a Catholic college: Applicants must be practicing Catholics.

_____ 3.   For the job as an attendant in a women's locker facility at a gym or resort: Applicants must be female.

_____ 4.   For the job of a prison guard with male inmates: Applicants must be men.

_____ 5.   For the job of modeling men's clothing: Applicants must be men.

Video Link 3.1

Age Discrimination in
Employment Act

The act again notes that "it shall be unlawful for an employer: (1) to fail or refuse to hire or to discharge any individual or otherwise discriminate against any individual with respect to his compensation, terms, conditions, or privileges of employment, because of such individual's age; (2) to limit, segregate, or classify his employees in any way which would deprive or tend to deprive any individual of employment opportunities or otherwise adversely affect his status as an employee, because of such individual's age," and it adds a third condition: "(3) to reduce the wage rate of any employee in order to comply with this chapter."[14] The law also applies to employers, all employment agencies, and all labor associations of any type, as well as generally applying to state and local governments and educational institutions.

Why did Congress pass the ADEA? It was passed in response to a business practice that started to become a significant issue in the 1960s. Companies began to lay off older workers who tended to have higher salaries and then hire younger workers who would usually work for significantly less money. Congress became aware of these actions and decided that this was an unfair form of discrimination against people who had spent many years of their lives working for these same companies. The law that resulted was the ADEA.

Age discrimination complaints make up a large percentage of those filed with the EEOC, and these cases can be very costly. Most of the cases settle out of court, but the settlements run between $50,000 and $400,000 or more per employee. ADEA cases were nearly 20% of the total EEOC complaints filed in 2009,[15] and the median award in an ADEA verdict was $255,100.[16]

The Vietnam Era Veterans' Readjustment Assistance Act of 1974

This act provides basically the same protection as the CRA, but for Vietnam veterans. However, it only applies to federal contractors. Why was this law enacted? It was primarily due to the fact that after the war in Vietnam, soldiers came home to a public that was largely opposed to our participation in the war. As a result, some employers would discriminate against Vietnam veterans for taking part in a war that they personally had been opposed to. Congress decided that it was not legitimate for employers to single out veterans who had only done what the country had required of them, so they passed the Vietnam Era Veterans' Readjustment Assistance Act (VEVRAA) to prohibit such behaviors. The law requires that "employers with Federal contracts or subcontracts of $100,000 or more provide equal opportunity *and* affirmative action for Vietnam era veterans, special disabled veterans, and veterans who served on active duty during a war or in a campaign or expedition for which a campaign badge has been authorized."[17]

The Pregnancy Discrimination Act of 1978

The Pregnancy Discrimination Act of 1978 (PDA) required that employers treat any woman who was pregnant in the same manner as they would any other employee with a medical condition. It prohibits discrimination against women affected by pregnancy, childbirth, or related medical conditions as unlawful sex discrimination under Title VII and requires that they be treated as all other employees for employment-related purposes, including benefits.[18]

Here, too, one wonders why this law was necessary. As insurance costs started to rise in the 1970s, companies started to look for ways to lower their insurance costs. One way they found was to exclude pregnancy from their health insurance policies. By the mid-1970s, only a minority of employers covered pregnancy and related illnesses in their health policies, even though women made up about 45% of the workforce.[19] Finally, in 1976, a Supreme Court decision ruled that to deny benefits for pregnancy-related disability was *not* discrimination based on sex.[20] This ruling outraged many women's advocacy organizations that in turn put pressure on Congress, which passed the PDA in 1978. Again, this law is mandatory for companies with 15 or more employees, including employment agencies, labor organizations, and state and local government.

SHRM

Guide – B:4
The Pregnancy Discrimination Act of 1978

The Americans With Disabilities Act of 1990 as Amended in 2008

The first major federal law dealing with discrimination against disabled individuals was the 1973 Rehabilitation Act. This act stated that agencies of the federal government, federal contractors, and subcontractors with contracts exceeding $10,000 had to take Affirmative Action and could not discriminate on the basis of disabilities in any employment actions.[21] However, this act only applied to a relatively small number of companies in the United States. Conversely, the Americans With Disabilities Act (ADA) is one of the most significant employment laws ever passed in the United States. It also prohibits discrimination based on disability in all employment practices such as job application procedures, hiring, firing, promotions, compensation, and training. However, it applies to virtually *all* employers with 15 or more employees in the same basic ways as the CRA of 1964.

There are many things about the ADA that make it difficult for employers to act in concert with the law. The first of these is the definition of the word *disability*. The ADA defines a **disability** as *a physical or mental impairment that substantially limits one or more major life activities, a record of having such an impairment, or being regarded as having such an impairment.*[22] According to rulings on the law, conditions such as obesity, substance abuse, and left-handedness are not covered disabilities (you may laugh, but it's true!), but something like obesity—if caused by a medical condition that would qualify as a disability—could be covered in some cases.

The definition of a disability is interesting because of the fact that anyone who has a record of having an impairment covered by the ADA is considered in the same manner as someone who has a current disability. It is the same with someone who is regarded as having an impairment. How can someone be regarded as being impaired or disabled when they aren't? Well, as an example, if you have ever seen someone who has been severely burned on their face and hands, you may have had some questions as to whether the individual was disabled or not. Under the ADA, you must treat that person as if they were

SHRM

Guide – B:10
The Rehabilitation Act of 1973

SHRM

Guide – B:2
The Americans With Disabilities Act of 1990 and as Amended in 2008

LO 3.5

Define the terms *disability, reasonable accommodation, undue hardship,* and *essential function* in accordance with the Americans With Disabilities Act of 1990.

HRM should be focusing on abilities to do the job, not eliminating applicants based on job-related disabilities.

SHRM

Guide – B:29
Reasonable
accommodation (ADA)

▶

Video Link 3.2

The Americans With
Disabilities Act Overview

disabled because of your concerns that they may have a disability. You would have to consider the individual for a job for which they applied if they can perform the essential functions of the job, regardless of their appearance or your expectation of a disability.

What Does the ADA Require of Employers?

What are some of the things an employer has to do in order to comply with the ADA? An organization must make "reasonable accommodations" to the physical or mental limitations of an individual with a disability *who was otherwise qualified* to perform the "essential functions" of the job, unless it would impose an "undue hardship" on the organization's operation.[23]

So, what is a reasonable accommodation? **Reasonable accommodation** is *an accommodation made by an employer to allow someone who is disabled but otherwise qualified to do the essential functions of a job to be able to perform that job*. Reasonable accommodations are usually inexpensive and easy to implement. Here again, an example works best. If a job in a particular company requires that the employee use a computer keyboard in their work and a blind individual applies for that particular job, the organization can make a reasonable accommodation to the individual by purchasing a Braille keyboard. In this case, Braille keyboards are inexpensive and provide the blind individual with the ability to do the job based on the "reasonable accommodation" provided.

In defining reasonable accommodations, it is also necessary to distinguish between "essential" and "marginal" job functions. Although essential functions are noted in the ADA, they are not defined there. Our understanding of essential functions comes mainly from court decisions concerning ADA cases. Based on these court cases, **essential functions** *are the fundamental duties of the position*. A function can generally be considered essential if it meets one of the following criteria:

1. The function is something that is done routinely and frequently in the job.

2. The function is done only on occasion, but it is an important part of the job.

3. The function may never be performed by the employee, but if it was necessary it would be critical that it be done right.

Marginal job functions, on the other hand, are those that may be performed in the job but need not be performed by all holders of the job. Individuals with disabilities cannot be denied employment if they cannot perform marginal job functions.[24]

What would be an example of a marginal job function? Let's say that in a clerical job, one of the job holder's duties is to file paperwork. However, the filing cabinet is a vertical five-drawer cabinet, and if someone was in a wheelchair, they would not be able to file papers in the upper drawers. The person in the job only spends about five minutes per day filing, and only a portion of that is taken up for filing in the upper two drawers of the filing cabinet. Would filing be an essential function in this job? No, it wouldn't—for a couple of reasons. First, it takes up a very small part of the day, so it is not something that they would do a lot. Second, in most cases the company could buy horizontal filing cabinets that the disabled individual could reach, thus providing a reasonable accommodation to the disability. Finally, if for some reason the company could not put horizontal filing cabinets into the area (there were severe space limitations and no way to expand at a reasonable cost), then someone else could do the filing in the upper drawers for a couple of minutes per day. So in this case, filing would be a marginal job function.

Generally, although not always, we find a list of the essential functions of the job in the organization's job descriptions and specifications. If the function is not listed as essential in the job description and specification, we may have difficulty using it as a defense in a disability case. Therefore, we generally want to ensure that we list all of the essential functions of the job in the job description and specification documents. We cover job descriptions and specifications in Chapter 4.

OK, we have to make reasonable accommodations, but do employers have to take the initiative to make every job disability-friendly? No. Under the ADA, employers are:[25]

- Not required to make reasonable accommodations if the applicant or employee does not request it.
- Not required to make reasonable accommodations if applicants don't meet required qualifications for a job.
- Not required to lower quality standards or provide personal use items such as glasses or hearing aids to make reasonable accommodations.
- Not required to make reasonable accommodations if to do so would be an undue hardship.

What is an undue hardship? An **undue hardship** is *when the level of difficulty for an organization to provide accommodations, determined by looking at the nature and cost of the accommodation and the overall financial resources of the facility, becomes a significant burden on the organization.* In general, the Department of Labor notes that most accommodations are relatively easy and inexpensive (usually less than $500—think of the Braille keyboard above, which costs about $25).[26] However, we must note that an undue hardship may be different for different companies. For instance, a small company with only a few million dollars in revenue per year may have an undue burden based on a relatively low-cost accommodation to a disabled individual, while a larger company could not claim undue hardship for the same accommodation.

An example helps here, too. If we were the owners of a small company housed on the second floor in a downtown historic district building and had an applicant for a job who was wheelchair bound, would we be required to consider that applicant for a job and accommodate the individual by rebuilding the historic building? The answer is most likely no, because of the fact that the accommodation required in one of the historic houses in such a district would require a major rebuilding effort, since stairways and doors in such houses were typically very narrow. This effort would likely cost a significant amount of money—an amount that would be unreasonable for the organization to pay. However, if we're faced with the same disabled individual and we are a large company headquartered in the modern building, we would certainly be required to make the reasonable accommodation necessary to allow an individual in a wheelchair to work within the confines of our building.

The biggest problem that employers have with the ADA is the fact that it contains a number of words and phrases that can be interpreted in a wide variety of ways. Many of these were further defined in the 2008 amendment to the ADA, but there still remains significant room for interpretation of many of these terms. For example, the term *reasonable accommodation* is open to broad interpretation, and the term is not defined very specifically in the ADA. *Essential function* is another term where *essential* can be defined in a wide variety of ways, although continuing court cases have narrowed it down some over the past 20 years. Because of these poorly defined terms, companies have had a very difficult time in applying the ADA in a consistent manner, and as a result have been involved in quite likely more lawsuits per disabled employee than with any other protected group.[27] Companies have worked for nearly 20 years to get clarification of the meaning of some of these words in the ADA without success to this point. The 2008 amendment does clarify some of the points in the ADA, but leaves others without satisfactory answers. However, there is an ongoing effort on the part of businesses to redefine some of the terms in the law so that they can more easily comply.

The Civil Rights Act of 1991

SHRM

Guide – B:5
Title VII of the Civil Rights
Act of 1991

The Civil Rights Act of 1991 was enacted as an amendment in order to correct a few major omissions of the 1964 CRA as well as to overturn several U.S. court decisions.[28] One of the major changes in the amendment was the addition of compensatory and punitive damages in cases of intentional discrimination under Title VII and the ADA. The 1991 act allows compensatory and punitive damages when intentional or reckless discrimination is proven. **Compensatory damages** are *monetary damages awarded by the court that compensate the person who was injured for their losses.* They can include such things as future pecuniary loss (potential future monetary losses such as loss of earnings capacity), emotional pain, suffering, and loss of enjoyment of life. **Punitive damages** are *monetary damages awarded by the court that are designed to punish the injuring party when they intentionally inflicted harm on others.* They are meant to discourage employers from discriminating by providing payments to the plaintiff beyond the actual damages suffered.

Recognizing that one or a few discrimination cases could put an organization out of business, thus adversely affecting many innocent employees, the CRA of 1991 provides for a sliding scale of upper limits or "caps" on the combined amount of compensatory and punitive damages based on the number of employees employed by the employer. The limitations are shown in Exhibit 3-5.[29]

Another major area in which the 1991 act changed the original CRA is in the application of quotas for protected group members. Many companies, after the 1964 CRA, created and used quotas for hiring and promotion. The quotas were made explicitly illegal by the 1991 act. In addition, the act prohibits "discriminatory use," also called race-norming, of test scores. **Race-norming** exists *when different groups of people have different scores designated as "passing" grades on a test for employment.* One group may have higher requirements for passing grades while another is allowed to pass at a lower level. The 1991 act basically equated this with quotas and as such made it illegal.[30]

Exhibit 3-5	Caps on Compensatory and Punitive Damages by Employer Size
• 15 to 100 employees:	$ 50,000
• 101 to 200 employees:	$100,000
• 201 to 500 employees:	$200,000
• 501 employees or more:	$300,000

The Uniformed Services Employment and Reemployment Rights Act of 1994

The Uniformed Services Employment and Reemployment Rights Act of 1994 (USERRA) was passed to ensure the civilian reemployment rights of military members who were called away from their regular (nonmilitary) jobs by U.S. government orders. According to the U.S. Department of Labor website, "USERRA is intended to minimize the disadvantages to an individual that occur when that person needs to be absent from his or her civilian employment to serve in this country's uniformed services. USERRA makes major improvements in protecting service member rights and benefits by clarifying the law and improving enforcement mechanisms. It also provides employees with Department of Labor assistance in processing claims."[31]

USERRA covers virtually every individual in the country who serves, or has served, in the uniformed services and applies to all employers in the public and private sectors, including federal employers. The law seeks to ensure that those who serve their country in military service can retain their civilian employment and benefits, and can seek employment free from discrimination because of their service. USERRA also provides protection for disabled veterans, requiring employers to make reasonable efforts to accommodate the disability.

SHRM

Guide – B:16
The Uniformed Services Employment and Reemployment Rights Act of 1994

The Veterans' Benefits Improvement Act of 2004

The Veterans' Benefits Improvement Act of 2004 (VBIA) was enacted as an amendment to USERRA. It made two significant changes to USERRA—it extended the requirement for employers to maintain health care coverage over employees who were serving on active duty in the military. Originally, this period was 18 months. VBIA changed it to 2 years. It also required employers to post a notice of benefits, duties, and rights under USERRA/VBIA where it is visible to all employees who might be affected.[32]

Title II of the Genetic Information Nondiscrimination Act of 2008

The Genetic Information Nondiscrimination Act of 2008 (GINA) includes two sections. The one that is applicable to us here is Title II of the act, which "prohibits the use of genetic information in employment, prohibits the intentional acquisition of genetic information about applicants and employees, and imposes strict confidentiality requirements."[33]

Here is another law where some of you are wondering why it was enacted. GINA was created basically because of recent advances in genetic testing. We are now able to identify some genetic information that relates to a predisposition to contract certain diseases or disorders, such as Alzheimer's and Huntington's disease. In order to prevent increases in medical premiums, some companies were starting to use these tests as a decision tool in hiring of employees, and some insurance companies were using such tests to determine health care coverage. There was some question about "preexisting conditions"—if you have the genetic marker for a disease, does that mean it is a preexisting condition and therefore not covered by some insurance policies?

Because these tests were starting to be used to make employment and health care decisions, Congress decided to address their use. The result was GINA. The law prohibits discrimination based on genetic information and restricts acquisition and disclosure of such information so that the general public will not fear adverse employment—or health coverage–related consequences for having a genetic test or participating in research studies that examine genetic information.[34]

SHRM

Guide – B:32
The Genetic Information Nondiscrimination Act of 2008

Research has shown benefits of having a diverse workforce.

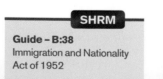

SHRM

Guide – B:31
Lilly Ledbetter Fair Pay Act
of 2009

The Lilly Ledbetter Fair Pay Act of 2009

The Lilly Ledbetter Fair Pay Act of 2009 (LLFPA) adds a provision to amend Title VII of the 1964 CRA, which says:

> "(3)(A) For purposes of this section, an unlawful employment practice occurs, with respect to discrimination in compensation in violation of this title, when a discriminatory compensation decision or other practice is adopted, when an individual becomes subject to a discriminatory compensation decision or other practice, or when an individual is affected by application of a discriminatory compensation decision or other practice, including each time wages, benefits, or other compensation is paid, resulting in whole or in part from such a decision or other practice."[35]

So, what does this mean? In practical terms, the LLFPA extends the period of time in which an employee is allowed to file a lawsuit for compensation (pay) discrimination. The 1964 CRA only allowed 180 days from the time of the last discriminatory act for an individual employee to file a lawsuit. The LLFPA allows an individual to file a lawsuit within 180 days after "any application" of that discriminatory compensation decision, including every time the individual gets paid, as long as the discrimination is continuing, which would usually be for the entire period of their employment.

One of the most significant aspects of the LLFPA is that the amendments to the time allowed to file a discrimination complaint *could* also apply to other antidiscrimination laws like the Age Discrimination in Employment Act and the Americans With Disabilities Act, which borrow Title VII's limitations period.

Immigration Laws Relating to Employment and Equal Opportunity

LO 3.6

Briefly discuss the two major federal immigration laws and how they affect the workplace.

Immigration and employment of immigrant workers is controlled by a series of federal laws. In general, these laws are designed for two purposes—to require verification of the legal right to work within the United States and to avoid potential discrimination against immigrant workers who are legally allowed to work in the country. The two major laws in this area are the Immigration and Nationality Act of 1952 (as amended) and the Immigration Reform and Control Act of 1986. While immigration law is extremely complex, for our purposes in an introductory HR text we will only discuss the basic employment provisions of these two laws.

The Immigration and Nationality Act of 1952

SHRM

Guide – B:38
Immigration and Nationality
Act of 1952

The Immigration and Nationality Act of 1952 (INA) was designed to take a variety of different immigration laws and combine them into a single act. Before the INA, a number of federal laws governed immigration but they were not consistent and were not organized in one location under one authority.[36] The INA allows companies in the United States to employ immigrant workers in certain specialty occupations. For example, foreign workers such as engineers, teachers, computer programmers, medical doctors, and physical therapists may be employed under the INA.[37] However, there are specific requirements to apply for such employment, and there are annual limits to the number of workers who can apply for work visas in these specialty occupations.

Because Congress could foresee the potential to discriminate against *all* alien workers to avoid any accusation of hiring undocumented workers, the INA also has a nondiscrimination requirement when dealing with alien workers who have the right to work in the United States. Such workers become another protected class for the purposes of Equal Employment Opportunity.

The Immigration Reform and Control Act of 1986

Under the Immigration Reform and Control Act of 1986 (IRCA), employers may only hire individuals who are authorized to legally work in the United States. The IRCA has a provision that prohibits employers from knowingly hiring undocumented workers and requires employers to verify each employee's eligibility for employment. The employer has a requirement to verify the identity and employment eligibility of anyone hired through the use of a form called the Employment Eligibility Verification Form (I-9). However, the act also provides employers complying "in good faith" with the requirements of IRCA with what is called an affirmative defense to inadvertently hiring an unauthorized alien. An affirmative defense means basically that if we made a *legitimate and complete effort* to verify a person's legal status and it turns out that they provided false documents, or that we were tricked or lied to in some other way, we won't be held liable for any potential fines that would have otherwise been assessed for hiring undocumented workers.[38]

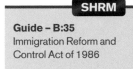

SHRM
Guide – B:35
Immigration Reform and Control Act of 1986

Reminder–State and Local Laws May Be Different

As with any introductory textbook, we can't tell you all of the laws that would apply in the various locations across the United States, and certainly in other countries around the world. We can only cover the major laws that affect virtually everyone in each of the United States. Each state as well as many cities has their own equal opportunity laws that employers within that state must follow. It's up to the HR Manager to brief themselves on the local and state laws and regulations concerning equal opportunity.

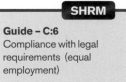

WORK
APPLICATION 3-4

Give examples of how major employment laws have affected an organization where you work or have worked, preferably as the law relates directly to you. Be sure to specify the law and what the firm does or doesn't do because of the law.

The Equal Employment Opportunity Commission

The various federal Equal Employment Opportunity laws are enforced by the Equal Employment Opportunity Commission (EEOC). The EEOC was created by the 1964 CRA as an enforcement arm for the act. It is a federal agency that has significant power over employers in the process of investigating complaints of illegal discrimination based on "race, color, religion, sex (including pregnancy), national origin, age (40 or older), disability or genetic information."[39]

SHRM
Guide – B:18
Enforcement agencies (EEOC)

What Does the EEOC Do?

The EEOC is the federal agency primarily charged with enforcement of the federal Equal Employment Opportunity laws. The EEOC basically has three significant responsibilities: (1) investigating and resolving discrimination complaints through either conciliation or litigation, (2) gathering and compiling statistical information on such complaints, and (3) education and outreach programs on what constitutes illegal discrimination.[40]

General EEO timelines:

- Individuals must typically file a complaint within 180 days of the incident (or the last occurrence of the incident if it is ongoing).

SHRM
Guide – C:6
Compliance with legal requirements (equal employment)

3-2 APPLYING THE CONCEPT

Employment Laws

State which law would apply in each of the following statements.

a. Equal Pay
b. Title VII CRA 1964
c. ADEA
d. VEVRAA
e. PDA
f. ADA

g. CRA 1991
h. USERRA
i. VBIA
j. GINA
k. LLFPA
l. Immigration laws

_____ 6.   I serve in the National Guard and will be deployed overseas for a year. As a result, my boss is laying me off, and I will have to find a new job when I get back.

_____ 7.   I worked here for 20 years, and what do I get for my dedication? The firm is laying me off to hire some new younger person for less compensation to save money.

_____ 8.   I got the job because the employer never asked me any questions about my being legally eligible to work in the United States. Now the company is in trouble with the INS.

_____ 9.   They are paying me less than the men who do the same jobs just because I'm a woman. I complained to the HR Department, but nothing has been done about it.

_____ 10.   The firm hired this new guy and bought a special low desk because he is so short.

_____ 11.   The company intentionally discriminated against me and then fired me when I complained. So I'm suing the firm for lost wages.

_____ 12.   The firm made me take this medical test and found out that I am at high risk to get cancer, so it decided not to hire me to save money on medical insurance.

_____ 13.   My manager intentionally passed me over for promotion because I am Hispanic.

_____ 14.   I didn't want to go and fight overseas, but I was drafted into the Army in 1969 and had no choice; I didn't want to go to jail for draft evasion. I can't understand why this firm doesn't want to hire me for service to my country.

– The complainant must give the EEOC up to 60 days to investigate the complaint.

– Generally, if the complainant is dissatisfied with the outcome, legal charges must be filed before 300 days have passed from the last date of discrimination. If not, the case cannot go forward in court. However, recall from our discussion of the LLFPA above that this law will change the length of time that complainants have to file a lawsuit in at least those cases relating to pay or other compensation.

– The complainant has sole responsibility for ensuring that deadlines are met. If the individual does not file required items by their due dates, then the case is generally not able to be taken forward.

If the EEOC determines that discrimination has taken place, it will attempt to provide reconciliation between the parties without burdening the courts. If the EEOC cannot come to an agreement with the organization, there are two options:

1. The agency may aid the alleged victim in bringing suit in federal court.

2. It can issue a "right to sue" letter to the alleged victim. A **right-to-sue** is *a notice from the EEOC, if they elect not to prosecute an individual discrimination complaint within the agency, which gives the recipient the right to go directly to the courts with their complaint.*

If the EEOC does not believe the complaint to be valid or fails to complete the investigation, the complainant still may sue in federal court on their own. However, without a right-to-sue letter, it will generally be difficult for a complainant to succeed in getting a judgment against the employer.

Employee Rights Under the EEOC

The employee has a right to bring discrimination complaints against their employer by filing a complaint with the EEOC. Employees also have a right to participate in an EEOC investigation, hearing, or other proceeding without threat of retaliation. The employee also has rights related to the arbitration and settlement of the complaint. Employees also have the right to sue the employer directly in court over claims of illegal discrimination even if the EEOC does not support their claim.

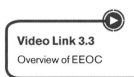

Video Link 3.3
Overview of EEOC

Employer Prohibitions

The employer has some rights as well. The employer has a right to defend their organization using the defenses noted earlier—BFOQ, business necessity, and job relatedness. However, the employer does not have a right to retaliate against individuals who participate in an EEOC action either through filing charges or through participating in the above investigations, hearings, or proceedings. The employer also is prohibited from creating a work environment that would lead to charges of constructive discharge. Both of these items are prohibited in each employment law that deals with harassment, including harassment based on race, religion, sex, disability, color, or national origin.

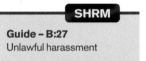

SHRM

Guide – B:27
Unlawful harassment

Retaliation

In addition to providing defenses against discrimination claims, the 1964 Civil Rights Act also identifies a situation in which organizations can be held liable for harming the employee because of retaliation.[41] **Retaliation** is *a situation where the organization takes an "adverse employment action" against an employee because the employee brought discrimination charges against the organization or supported someone who brought discrimination charges against the company.* An **adverse employment action** is *any action such as a firing, demotion, schedule reduction, or change that would harm the individual employee.*

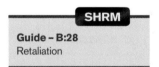

SHRM

Guide – B:28
Retaliation

Retaliation is a form of harassment based on the individual filing a discrimination claim. Each of the EEO laws identifies retaliation as illegal harassment based on the protected class identified within that law. The EEOC is responsible for compliance with the 1964 CRA concerning retaliation. As stated on its website: "All of the laws we enforce make it illegal to fire, demote, harass, or otherwise 'retaliate' against people (applicants or employees) because they filed a charge of discrimination, because they complained to their employer or other covered entity about discrimination on the job, or because they participated in an employment discrimination proceeding (such as an investigation or lawsuit)."[42]

There are severe penalties for engaging in retaliation against an employee or applicant for participating in such activity. Every manager needs to be aware of this concept in order to avoid actions that might be construed as retaliatory.

Constructive Discharge

In addition to retaliation, the organization can be guilty of "constructive discharge" due to discriminatory actions on the job. Again, the EEOC would generally be the agency responsible for initially investigating claims of constructive discharge.[43]

Basically, **constructive discharge** *exists when an employee is put under such extreme pressure by management that their continued employment becomes intolerable and as a result of the intolerable conditions the employee quits, or resigns from the organization.* This result would be constructive discharge. In a Supreme Court decision in 2004,[44] the Court noted, "The constructive discharge concept originated in the labor-law field in the 1930's; the National Labor Relations Board (NLRB) developed the doctrine to address situations in which employers coerced employees to resign, often by creating intolerable working conditions, in retaliation for employees' engagement in collective activities." The Supreme Court noted in this same case that the U.S. Court of Appeals had identified constructive discharge as the following: "(1) he or she suffered harassment or discrimination so intolerable that a reasonable person in the same position would have felt compelled to resign . . . ; and (2) the employee's reaction to the workplace situation—that is, his or her decision to resign—was reasonable given the totality of circumstances."[45]

So based on the above information, if an individual can show constructive discharge caused them to resign from the organization, then the individual would be eligible for all employee rights associated with being involuntarily terminated from the company. If, in fact, the individual suffered sexual harassment or discrimination that resulted in their constructive discharge, the organization would suffer liability for those employment actions. The EEOC would be the agency charged with investigating and arbitrating the results of this conduct by the employer. The 2004 Supreme Court case set new standards for demonstrating constructive discharge from a company, and in so doing created a more difficult employment environment for the organization. Every employer or manager needs to understand this concept.

EEO, Affirmative Action, and Diversity–What's the Difference?

LO 3.7

Discuss the difference between Equal Employment Opportunity, Affirmative Action, and diversity.

As a manager, you need to understand the terms *Equal Employment Opportunity, Affirmative Action,* and *diversity.* These are significantly different concepts, but many employees, employers, and even some educators tend to use them interchangeably. *Equal Employment Opportunity* is the term that deals with a series of laws and regulations put in place at the federal and state government level in the last 45 years. As such, *Equal Employment Opportunity* is very specific and narrowly defined within U.S. and various state laws.

On the other hand, Affirmative Action as a concept was created in the 1960s through a series of policies at the presidential and legislative levels in the United States. Affirmative Action, except in a few circumstances, does not have the effect of law.[46] We will discuss those circumstances in the next section. Therefore, Affirmative Action is a much broader concept based on policy; EEO is more narrowly based on law.

Finally, diversity is not law, nor is it *necessarily* even policy within organizations. Diversity is a very broad set of concepts that deal with the differences among people within organizations. Today's organizations view diversity as a valuable part of their Human Resource makeup. However, there are no specific laws that deal with requirements for diversity within organizations beyond the EEO laws that specifically identify protected class members and require that organizations deal with those protected class members in an *equal* way when compared to all other members of the organization.

While this certainly creates *some* greater diversity in organizations, the concept of diversity goes much further than just Equal Employment Opportunity. We have already discussed many

WORK
APPLICATION 3-5

Has an organization where you work or have worked had any potential or actual cases brought to the EEOC against it? If so, explain the complaint. The HR staff may not be too eager to talk about this, but you can do some research on larger corporations.

of the major equal employment opportunity laws. Now, let's take a look at Affirmative Action and the concept of diversity. Exhibit 3-6 provides a summary of these three concepts.

Affirmative Action

So, what is Affirmative Action? **Affirmative Action (AA)** is *a series of policies, programs, and initiatives that have been instituted by various entities within both government and the private sector, which are designed to prefer hiring of individuals from protected groups in certain circumstances, in an attempt to mitigate past discrimination.* However, Affirmative Action policies and programs do not generally have the same effect as EEO laws.

There are actually only two specific cases in which Affirmative Action can be mandated, or *required*, within an organization. In all other cases today, creation of an Affirmative Action program is strictly voluntary. The two situations where Affirmative Action is mandatory are:

Executive Order 11246

If the company is a contractor to the federal government and receives more than $10,000 per year, they are required by presidential order (Executive Order 11246) to maintain an Affirmative Action program. Exemptions from this order include the following:

> **SHRM**
>
> **Guide – B:6**
> Executive Order 11246
> (1965)

- The order "shall not apply to a Government contractor or subcontractor that is a religious corporation, association, educational institution, or society, with respect to the employment of individuals of a particular religion to perform work connected with the carrying on by such corporation, association, educational institution, or society of its activities. Such contractors and subcontractors are not exempted or excused from complying with the other requirements contained in this Order."[47]
- "The Secretary of Labor may also provide, by rule, regulation, or order, for the exemption of facilities of a contractor that are in all respects separate and distinct from activities of the contractor related to the performance of the contract: provided, that such an exemption will not interfere with or impede the effectuation of the purposes of this Order: and provided further, that in the absence of such an exemption all facilities shall be covered by the provisions of this Order."[48]

Federal Court Orders for AA Programs

If an organization is presented with a federal court order to create an Affirmative Action program to correct past discriminatory practices, they must comply. This is usually only done when there is an egregious history in the organization of past discriminatory practices.

Exhibit 3-6	Equal Employment Opportunity, Affirmative Action, and Diversity

Topic	Governance	Concept
EEO	Federal (and state) law	Narrow, specific requirements and prohibitions
Affirmative Action	Executive orders, federal court orders, or voluntary	Policies that broadly define situations in which actions should be taken to balance a workforce with its surroundings
Diversity	Organizational policies	Generally no legal requirement; designed to better serve a more diverse customer base

The following web links do an excellent job of telling you about the current body of information on the concept of Affirmative Action and its history to date:

http://www.infoplease.com/spot/affirmative1.html

http://plato.stanford.edu/entries/affirmative-action/

The Bakke decision noted in the above Stanford University link is the basis for the concept of **reverse discrimination**, which is *discrimination against members of the majority group in an organization, generally resulting from affirmative action policies within an organization.*

The Office of Federal Contract Compliance Programs

The Office of Federal Contract Compliance Programs (OFCCP) is in charge of monitoring and enforcing Executive Order (EO) 11246, Section 503 of the 1973 Rehabilitation Act and the 1974 VEVRAA.[49] We have already discussed VEVRAA above, so let's take a look at EO 11246 and the Rehabilitation Act as they relate to the OFCCP.

The OFCCP is in charge of federal contract compliance, and both EO 11246 and the Rehabilitation Act require that federal contractors who receive more than a certain dollar value in contracts from the federal government per year provide equal opportunity and take Affirmative Action toward protected class individuals. In the case of EO 11246, those groups are race, color, religion, sex, and national origin, and in the case of the Rehabilitation Act it is disabled individuals.

Diversity in the Workforce

What is diversity? **Diversity** is simply *the existence of differences—in HRM, it deals with different types of people in an organization.* This brings up a number of questions. Why do we want to have diversity in organizations? What are the advantages that we create by having a more diverse workforce? Are there any disadvantages to having a more diverse work group? What can we do about any disadvantages? Let's discuss diversity as it provides both opportunities and challenges.[50]

Demographic Diversity

Is diversity really all that important? The answer is yes.[51] For one thing, there is currently a shortage of skilled workers, so to exclude a qualified person because he or she is different in some way is counterproductive to business success. Also, as we have already discussed, discrimination is against the law.

In 2011, the world population hit 7 billion people.[52] However, the world Caucasian population is actually shrinking as more Whites die each year than are born. It takes 2.1 children per family to replace the current generation. However, Western European women are only having 1.59 babies and U.S. women are having 2.09 babies, while women worldwide, mostly non-Caucasian, are having 2.56 babies.[53]

In 2011, White babies are a minority in the United States, or less than half of the births. White women are having fewer children than non-Whites, while the growth of mixed marriages has led to more multiracial births. Among Hispanics, there are roughly nine births for every one death, compared with about a one-to-one ratio for Whites.[54] In 2010, Caucasians under 18 were only 54% of this age group.[55] In 10 states, more than 50% of the under-15 population are minorities.[56]

Whites will constitute less than half of the total U.S. population by 2042, with the current number-two Hispanics driving minority growth.[57] The state of California is already less than 50% Caucasian. Whites currently make up only 40% of the populations in large cities.[58]

With these statistics, it should be clear that increasing cultural diversity in the workforce poses one of the most challenging human resource and organizational issues of our time.[59]

Why Do We Need Diversity?

Diversity is also important and needed because as the White population continues to shrink and minorities grow, selling your goods and services to a variety of groups increases sales, revenues, and profits—or embracing diversity creates business opportunities.[60] Organizations today have begun to value the diversity of their workforces simply due to the fact that they have found that as companies have become more diverse, they have been able to serve a larger and more diverse customer base.[61] Diverse employees allow us to see the diversity around us in our customers and other stakeholders much better than if our work groups were more homogeneous.[62] As a result, we are better able to provide products and services that will appeal to the larger and more diverse groups that we come into contact with during the course of doing business.[63]

Advantages of Diversity

The primary advantages of a diverse workforce come from the ability to stimulate more creative and innovative solutions to organizational problems. How does a more diverse workforce add to the creativity and innovation in an organization? **Creativity** is *a basic ability to think in unique and different ways and apply those thought processes to existing problems,* and **innovation** is *the act of creating useful processes or products based on creative thought processes.*

Basically, if we look at a problem from different perspectives, we find out that there are more facets to the problem than we originally realized. Have you ever been in a situation where you just couldn't find something and you asked someone else to help you search for it and they found it almost immediately? A diversified group looking at a problem will look at the problem from different directions and in different ways, and therefore discover more of the aspects of the problem than would a single person or a more homogeneous work group.[64]

But why is creativity necessary in a business today? Creativity is necessary in organizations in order for the organization to innovate. OK, but why do we need to innovate? Organizations in today's fast-moving industries have to be able to innovate and change to adapt to their external environment—their competitors, their customers, and changes in technology. If an organization is unable to innovate, they will almost certainly die in today's business world.

Also, creativity is a rare commodity in organizations. Why is it so hard to be creative? Most of us have learned not to be creative due to the fact that we have been told over and over as we grow up that we should do things the way everyone else does them. Over time this has the effect of causing most of us to give up on being very creative and just go along with the way that the majority of people do something. We lose the ability to think differently. This ability is called divergent thinking and is necessary in order to come up with creative solutions to a problem.[65] **Divergent thinking** is *the ability to find many possible solutions to a particular problem, including unique, untested solutions.*

By introducing diversity into our workforce, we assist the process of divergent thinking. Different people think differently because they have different backgrounds and have solved problems differently in the past. We all bring this unique set of problem-solving skills to our work. Luckily, we don't all have the same background, so this has the effect of increasing the creativity and innovation in the organization without the individual having to relearn the ability to be highly creative.

Challenges of Diversity

Of course diversity has its challenges. There are several things that can cause diversity to break down the organization instead of allowing it to become better and more creative.[66] The first issue is conflict. **Conflict** is simply *the act of being opposed to another.* Conflict occurs in all interactions between individuals. There are many reasons for conflict. However, conflict is typically greater when people are significantly different from each other, which means that if we create a more diverse workforce there's a greater likelihood for more significant conflict.

Is conflict bad? Not necessarily. Conflict can basically be broken down into functional conflict and dysfunctional conflict. **Functional conflict** is *how organizations go through the process of creating new things—the opposition itself drives the organization to change.* If we don't have conflicts, the organization never changes. However, **dysfunctional conflict** is *when conflict gets to the point where creativity is stifled and in fact almost all work becomes difficult or impossible because of the conflict's intensity.* Dysfunctional conflict breaks down the organization while functional conflict allows it to grow.

The second big issue is group cohesiveness. **Cohesiveness** is *an intent and desire for group members to stick together in their actions.* In organizations, we have learned that in order for a work group to become as good as it possibly can the group has to become cohesive. The members have to learn to *want* to be part of the group and want to interact with other members of the group in order for the group to perform at a high level. So we need cohesiveness to be high. However, the more diversity there is within the group, the more difficult it is to create the cohesiveness necessary for high performance. So, more diverse groups tend to be less cohesive—not always, but as a general rule.

A third significant issue in diversity is *resistance to change.* If organizations are used to being less diverse, then diversity can be something that is scary to the people in the organization. If they are uncomfortable with the change, they *will* resist. This resistance can be taken care of through a number of methods including the creation of a more participative decision-making environment, creating cognitive dissonance, or coercion, plus a number of other methods. However, this is not the class to discuss change management. We would get into a topic that would significantly sidetrack us. Suffice it to say here that resistance to change *can* be managed in the organization.

There are several other things that make diversity a challenge. The above items are some of the most significant, but if you are interested you can always read more in a variety of organizational management, psychology, or sociology literature.

Managing Diversity

Diversity affects bottom-line profits. In other words, if all the diverse employees don't work well together, the organization does not work well.[67] Creating a cohesive, operational, and highly successful diverse workforce doesn't just happen. Management has to work to create success with diversity. Managing diversity so that we gain the benefits available is one of the most critical jobs of a 21st-century manager. Diversity can be managed successfully only in an organizational culture that values diversity.[68] While the details of a diversity management program are the topic for discussion in another course (due to time constraints in an introductory course), we can briefly review what managers need to be concerned with.

Exhibit 3-7 illustrates the process of managing diversity. Successfully managing diversity requires top management support and commitment.[69] Senior managers have to "walk the talk" of the diversity program if it is going to succeed. Employees throughout an organization look to top management to set an example. If the management is committed to maintaining a diverse workplace characterized by dignity, others at all levels of the organization will be as well.

Managing diversity further requires leadership.[70] Diversity leadership refers to having top-level managers responsible for managing diversity. The diversity leaders must also set policies and practices relating to maintaining diversity.

Finally and most important, employees must be provided with training so that they can work together as teams despite differences in race, gender, age, ability, and other factors.[71] Therefore, corporations are providing diversity training for their managers and

WORK
APPLICATION 3-7

Discuss how demographic diversity and the need for diversity are affecting an organization you work or have worked for. What are some of the advantages and challenges faced by the firm? Also, describe how diversity is managed at the organization.

employees.[72] In fact, training is one of the most common activities included in diversity initiatives.[73] The primary goal of diversity training is to remove obstacles faced by members of the organization that might prevent their professional and personal growth.[74]

Through managing diversity, affirmative action and diversity programs have been used to help women and minorities advance in organizations. Complete Self-Assessment 3-1 to determine your attitude toward women and minorities advancing at work.

Exhibit 3-7	Managing Diversity

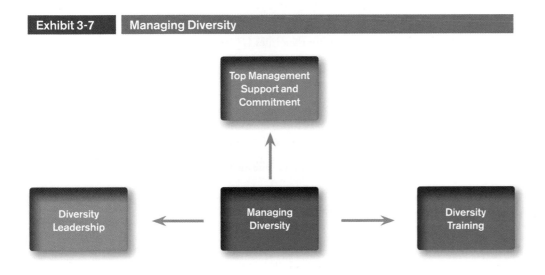

Sexual Harassment– A Special Type of Discrimination

Sexual harassment is a special type of discrimination identified as part of the 1964 CRA (the prohibition of discrimination based on sex), but it is one of the two items we mentioned earlier in the chapter that was not specifically recognized as a separate type of discrimination until the federal courts started hearing cases on the act. In the case of sexual harassment, it was a Supreme Court decision in the 1980s that finally identified such harassment as specifically violating the CRA. The case was *Meritor Savings Bank v. Vinson*, and it confirmed the intent of the 1964 CRA that sexual harassment was specifically prohibited by the act. Sexual harassment is a pervasive issue in organizations, and we as managers need to understand what it is and how to avoid creating a situation where it can occur at work. So, in this section, let's discuss the types of sexual harassment, what constitutes it, and how to reduce it.

Video Link 3.4

Hostile Work Environment

Types of Sexual Harassment

Sexual harassment is defined by the EEOC as follows: "*Unwelcome sexual advances, requests for sexual favors, and other verbal or physical conduct of a sexual nature constitutes sexual harassment when submission to or rejection of this conduct explicitly or implicitly affects an individual's employment, unreasonably interferes with an individual's work performance or creates an intimidating, hostile or offensive work environment.*"[75] There are two types of sexual harassment specifically delineated in the *Vinson* case:[76] "quid pro quo harassment" and "hostile work environment." Both are discussed below.

LO 3.8

Identify the two primary types of sexual harassment.

3-1 SELF-ASSESSMENT

ATTITUDE TOWARD WOMEN AND MINORITIES ADVANCING

Be honest in this self-assessment, as your assessment will not be accurate if you don't. Also, you should not be asked to share your score with others.

Answer the 10 questions below twice—once related to women and the other related to minorities. Place the number 1, 2, 3, 4, or 5 on the line before each statement for women and at the end of the statement for minorities.

| Agree | 5 | 4 | 3 | 2 | 1 | Disagree |

Women   **Minorities**

_____ 1. Women/Minorities lack motivation to get ahead.   1. ____

_____ 2. Women/Minorities lack the education necessary to get ahead.   2. ____

_____ 3. Women/Minorities working has caused rising unemployment among White men.   3. ____

_____ 4. Women/Minorities are not strong enough or emotionally stable enough to succeed in high-pressure jobs.   4. ____

_____ 5. Women/Minorities have a lower commitment to work than White men.   5. ____

_____ 6. Women/Minorities are too emotional to be effective managers.   6. ____

_____ 7. Women/Minorities who are managers have difficulty in situations calling for quick and precise decisions.   7. ____

_____ 8. Women/Minorities have a higher turnover rate than White men.   8. ____

_____ 9. Women/Minorities are out of work more often than White men.   9. ____

_____ 10. Women/Minorities have less interest in advancing than White men.   10. ____

_____ Total   _____ Total

Women—To determine your attitude score toward women, add up the total of your 10 answers on the lines before each statement and place it on the total line and on the following continuum.

10 _____   20 _____   30 _____   40 _____   50

Positive attitude   Negative attitude

Minorities—To determine your attitude score toward minorities, add up the total of your 10 answers on the lines after each statement and place it on the total line and on the following continuum.

10 _____   20 _____   30 _____   40 _____   50

Positive attitude   Negative attitude

Each statement is a negative attitude about women and minorities at work. However, research has shown all of these statements to be false; they are considered myths. Such statements stereotype women and minorities unfairly and prevent them from advancing in organizations through gaining salary increases and promotions. Thus, part of managing diversity and diversity training is to help overcome these negative attitudes to provide equal opportunities for *all*.

Quid Pro Quo

Literally, *quid pro quo* means "this for that." **Quid pro quo** is *harassment that occurs when some type of benefit or punishment is made contingent upon the employee submitting to sexual advances.* "If you do something for me, I will do something for you, or conversely if you refuse to do something for me, I will harm you." Quid pro quo is a direct form of harassment aimed at an individual and is most commonly seen in supervisor-subordinate relationships, although this is not always the case. It is, however, based on the power of one individual over another. If the harasser has no power to reward or punish the individual who is the object of the harassment, then it is difficult for quid pro quo harassment to exist. In the case of coworkers where one is pressuring the other concerning a relationship, the situation would more likely be considered to be a hostile work environment.

All employees should feel comfortable with coworkers on the job.

Hostile Work Environment

Hostile work environment means *harassment that occurs when someone's behavior at work creates an environment that is sexual in nature and makes it difficult for someone of a particular sex to work in that environment.* Hostile environment sexual harassment happens when a "reasonable person" would determine that the environment went beyond normal human interactions and the jokes and kidding that went with those interactions rose to the level that such a reasonable person would consider the act or acts to be both harassing and sexual in nature.[77] A **reasonable person** would be *the "average" person who would look at the situation and its intensity to determine whether the accused person was wrong in their actions.*

What Constitutes Sexual Harassment?

Can sexual harassment in any form occur between a female supervisor and a male subordinate? Can sexual harassment occur between two male employees or two female employees? The answer is *absolutely!* Sexual harassment does not have to occur between a male supervisor and female subordinates. Again, there is a famous Supreme Court case of male-on-male harassment on an offshore oil platform. It is *Oncale v. Sundowner Offshore Services.*[78] In the case, Joseph Oncale quit his job on an oil rig and filed a harassment suit against his employer. The Court ruled that he was harassed to the point that it met the standard where a reasonable person would have considered it sexual harassment.

As in other forms of illegal discrimination, the plaintiff only has to show a prima facie (literally "on the face of it," meaning it "looks" like harassment to our reasonable person) case that harassment has occurred. This includes:[79]

1. The plaintiff is a member of a protected class,

2. The harassment was based on sex,

3. The person was subject to unwelcome sexual advances, *or*

4. The harassment was sufficiently severe enough to alter the terms, conditions, or privileges of employment.

In order for the organization to be considered for liability, two critical conditions must exist:[80]

1. The plaintiff cannot solicit or incite the advances.

2. The harassment must be undesirable, and severe enough to alter the terms, conditions, and privileges of employment.

Some cases are clearly sexual harassment on the first offense, such as requesting sex as part of the job and any touching in the private bathing suit areas. However, some offenses are not so obvious, such as touching in nonprivate areas and asking a person to go on a date. In these gray areas, you should tell people that you find the behavior offensive and if they repeat the behavior you will report them for sexual harassment. For example, "I am uncomfortable with you hugging me, so don't do it again or I will report you for sexual harassment."

Reducing Organizational Risk From Sexual Harassment Lawsuits

Once the plaintiff has shown a prima facie case for the accusation, and it is determined that the harassment was potentially severe enough to alter the terms, conditions, and privileges

---

WORK
APPLICATION 3-8

A high percentage of people, especially women, have been sexually harassed. Have you or anyone you know been sexually harassed at work? Briefly describe the situation, stating if it was quid pro quo or a hostile work environment.

3-3 APPLYING THE CONCEPT

Sexual Harassment

Indicate which kind of behavior is described in each statement.

a. sexual harassment—after the harassment letter, write in if it is (1) quid pro quo or (2) hostile work environment (a1 or a2)
b. not sexual harassment

_____15.   Karl, the supervisor, tells Mary-Joe, the department's administrative assistant, that he'd like to take her out for the first time today.

_____16.   Helen tells her assistant Jose that he will have to go to a motel with her if he wants to be recommended for a promotion.

_____17.   Carlos and Sue have each hung up pictures of nude men and women on the walls near their desks, in view of other employees who walk by.

_____18. As coworker Sandy talks to John, he is surprised and uncomfortable because she gently rubs his buttock.

_____19. Gordon tells his coworker Tina an explicitly sexual joke, even though twice before Tina told him not to tell her any dirty jokes.

_____ 20. Roberto typically puts his hand on his secretary's shoulder as he talks to her, and she is comfortable with the way he treats her.

of work (and assuming that the organization can't show the plaintiff invited or incited the advances, in the case of quid pro quo harassment), the courts will then determine whether the organization is liable for the actions of its employee based on the answers to two primary questions:

1. Did the employer know about, or should they have known about, the harassment?

2. Did the employer act to stop the behavior?

In general, if the employer knew or should have known and did nothing to stop the behavior, they can be held liable.

So how do you protect your organization from liability in the case of a charge of sexual harassment, either quid pro quo or hostile work environment? Exhibit 3-8 shows five important steps to follow.[81]

In general, management in the organization should probably determine that sexual harassment is a "one strike and you're out" offense. In other words, it is a major disciplinary infraction for which a person should be terminated. Why should we have such low tolerance for this type of action? Well, consider if you had an employee who was guilty in the past of harassing another employee. You did the investigation, found that the harassment did occur, and disciplined the harasser but did not terminate them. What if, months or even years later, the same employee harasser acted in the same manner toward another individual in your organization? You might be put in the position where you would have to go to court and defend your earlier actions.

In a case such as this, it would be very difficult to claim that you and the organization did not know or could not have known that the harassment might occur. The result would quite likely be that your organization would lose this case in court and might have to pay a significant settlement to the aggrieved individual. This is not a position that we should be willing to put ourselves in as managers of our organizations and their resources. Sexual harassment should be treated very seriously, because the consequences can be grave for the organization if they don't do what they should to prevent it.

WORK
APPLICATION 3-9

Describe the sexual harassment policy where you work or have worked. If you are not sure, check the company HR handbook or talk to an HR Department staff member to get the answer.

Exhibit 3-8	Limiting Organizational Liability for Sexual Harassment

1. Develop a policy statement making it clear that sexual harassment will not be tolerated. You have to delineate what is acceptable and what is not. The policy should also state that anyone participating in a sexual harassment complaint or investigation should not be retaliated against.

2. Communicate the policy by training all employees to identify inappropriate workplace behavior. Make sure that everyone is aware of the policy.

3. Develop a mechanism for reporting sexual harassment that encourages people to speak out. It is critical in this case to create a mechanism outside of the normal chain of command. The typical case of harassment is between an individual's immediate supervisor and that individual. Because of this, if the organization does not have a way to report the behavior that is outside the normal supervisory chain of command, the courts will consider that the company does not have a mechanism for reporting.

4. Ensure that Just Cause procedures (we will talk about these in Chapter 9) are followed when investigating the complaint.

5. Prepare to take, and then carry out, prompt disciplinary action with those who commit sexual harassment.

SHRM

Guide – B:29
Reasonable
accommodation (religious)

Religious Discrimintion

As we noted earlier in the chapter, the federal courts have also determined that religious discrimination is a violation of the 1964 CRA through its identification of religion as a protected class of individuals. Because religion was specifically identified in the CRA, we can't use it as a factor in making "any employment decision" with our employees. Religion is a less obvious characteristic than gender or race, so it is usually not a characteristic on which we base decisions. However, if a person's religion requires a certain type of dress or observation of religious holidays or days of worship that are not in keeping with the normal workday practices of the organization, and if the individual requests accommodation for their religious beliefs, then we generally would need to make every reasonable effort to accommodate such requests.

So, the bottom line is that employers must provide a "reasonable accommodation" for requests that are based on "employees' sincerely held religious beliefs or practices unless doing so would impose an 'undue hardship' on their business operations."[82] We have already defined reasonable accommodations and undue hardship in the section on the ADA in this chapter. The general result of a series of federal court rulings on religion and religious practices has been that if such practices can be accommodated by the organization without creating an excessive burden on the organization, then they must be accommodated, under penalty of law.

However, if the job description and specifications require employees to work specific days and hours of the day, and applicants accepts the job, the employer does not need to accommodate them. For example, many health care workers are religious Christians and don't want to work on Christmas, Good Friday, Easter, and other holy days; but they do because it is part of the job. On the other hand, if a Muslim wants to take a break at a certain time of the workday to pray, that is reasonable to accommodate. Some companies have even built quiet rooms for prayer, for meditation, or just to relax.

Trends and Issues in HRM

As always, we end this chapter with some significant trends and issues that are affecting HRM. In this chapter, we will cover four items that have been recent issues with employers—both large and small. These issues include religious discrimination, managing EEO as a path to organizational stability, global corporations and their susceptibility to U.S. EEO laws, and small organizations' compliance issues under EEO.

Religious Discrimination

As we noted in the last section, religion has generally not been a large-scale issue in organizations in the past, because a person's religion is not generally "visible" to others and as a result we generally don't make decisions with religion in mind. However, an issue of standards of dress in a number of religions, most notable Islam's standards for women's attire in public, has become a point of discussion in some workplaces. Is there the potential for discrimination with a front-desk employee or with a secretary who deals with the public if that employee is wearing a niqab or hijab (Muslim head coverings)? Are there dangers involved with allowing people (of any faith) to come into a bank or a government building with their faces obscured?

Are the hijab and the niqab symbols of the second-class citizenship of women in the Islamic faith? If they are symbols of discrimination against women, do governments have the right to ban them, at least in certain situations? French President Nicolas Sarkozy says, "The problem of the burqa [women's robes] is not a religious problem. . . . It is a problem of liberty and the dignity of women. It is a sign of servitude and degradation."[83] Do you agree?

How about employers? If an employer sees the niqab as a symbol of repression, can the employer deny the right to wear such head coverings and use the antidiscrimination statutes concerning gender as justification? These are some of the questions that we are dealing with in companies today, and there are certainly no easy answers.

What should you do, as the HR Manager, if one of the other managers or the president of the company came to you wanting to ban such head coverings for employees? Well, Title VII (the 1964 CRA) requires "reasonable accommodation of employees' sincerely held religious beliefs, observances, and practices when requested, unless accommodation would impose an undue hardship on business operations."[84] So, in order to comply, the rules that we talked about under the 1964 CRA would apply here as well.

You have to make accommodations *if* the individual requests them and they are based on sincerely held beliefs, *unless* there is a business necessity requiring you to do something that conflicts with the religious belief or if doing so would create an undue hardship on the organization. For instance, according to the EEOC, "If a security requirement [for example, wearing a scarf covering the head] has been unilaterally imposed by the employer and is not required by law or regulation, the employer will need to decide whether it would be an undue hardship to modify or eliminate the requirement to accommodate an employee who has a religious conflict."[85]

Is Managing Diversity the Path to Corporate Sustainability?

Does equal opportunity for all employees lead to success for the organization that manages to create such a workplace? Is diversity a trait that helps create sustainable organizations? A lot of evidence says the answer to both questions is yes. Although evidence shows that in some cases diversity creates barriers to team performance, the overwhelming majority of research identifies significant potential for organizational growth and long-term sustainability.

ESR

One recent study reviewed the performance of a set of businesses that concentrate on sustainability and corporate social responsibility, including diversity initiatives, with similar businesses that do not.[86] While the results were not conclusive, they do show that organizations that focus on sustainable operations generally did better than their counterparts. The group of sustainable organizations provided an average 18.2% growth in share value versus only 8.7% for the counterpart companies, and gave an average 6.5% return on assets versus 5.4% in the comparison companies. The same study, however, emphasizes that just being "sustainable" doesn't guarantee better-than-average results. Additional characteristics of the top companies include (1) inspirational, visionary leadership; (2) a link between corporate strategy and sustainability; (3) setting goals and monitoring progress; and (4) a link between sustainability and performance.

The above is just one study on sustainable corporations. There are many others out there that support the link between sustainability, diversity, and corporate success. And the fact is that, even if the company doesn't increase revenues from its sustainability efforts, such efforts are almost certainly not responsible for losing the corporation money. So, based on the positive social returns that the organization gets from having a reputation for sustainable operations, it just makes sense to operate in a sustainable manner.

Are Global Employees Subject to U.S. EEO Laws?

After reading this chapter, you now know that most organizations in the United States are subject to a variety of EEO laws. But are employees in foreign companies subject to the same laws, and are employees of U.S. companies in other countries subject to these laws? Again, the EEOC gives us guidance on these situations. Let's take a look at the rules for coverage.

According to the EEOC, "All employees who work in the U.S. or its territories . . . are protected by EEO laws, regardless of their citizenship or work authorization status. Employees who work in the U.S. or its territories are protected whether they work for a U.S. or foreign employer."[87] So if you are in the United States or a U.S. territory, you are covered by U.S. EEO laws.

But what about Americans working outside the United States? According to the EEOC, "U.S. citizens who are employed outside the U.S. by a U.S. employer—or a foreign company controlled by an U.S. employer—are protected by Title VII, the ADEA, and the ADA." However, "U.S. employers are not required to comply with the requirements of Title VII, the ADEA, or the ADA if adherence to that requirement would violate a law of the country where the workplace is located."[88] Finally, if you are employed by a foreign company in a country other than the United States, the laws of that country would apply, so you would not have the protection of U.S. EEO laws in such a case.

Different countries have different employment laws that must be obeyed. So think about the complexity of the HR executive working for a multinational company doing business in more than 100 countries! Thus, multinationals need HR legal specialists in each country.

Help! My Small Organization Can't Comply With This Law!

Many owners of small, entrepreneurial businesses work extremely long hours, and certainly don't need extra work (and more paperwork!) added to what they have to do already. They worry about whether or not they are violating the various federal EEO laws and corresponding state statutes, but don't have a lot of time to review all of the rules and regulations concerning EEO.

What should such employers do? The easy answer is that they generally don't have to worry about any potential violation of the EEO laws until their organization reaches the employee threshold noted in each of the laws. If you recall, the threshold for most of the EEO laws is 15 or more employees working 20 or more weeks per year. So if the organization doesn't have 15 employees they would not be covered by the federal EEO statute that has such a limitation. However, a warning here: Some states (California being one) have lower personnel thresholds for their versions of the various EEO laws, so an employer, small or large, needs to check to see if their state has a different limit for a given law or regulation.

If a small company is in doubt about their state's laws, one of the best places to go is to the state's Small Business Development Center (SBDC). Every state has these centers, although they are not exactly the same from state to state, and one of their assigned tasks is assisting small companies within their state in the start-up and operation of such businesses.[89] They know the rules, and know how to help small companies comply with the rules and laws of their state.

Wrap-Up

Well, that's about enough for this chapter. We presented a definition for the word *discrimination* as well as the term *illegal discrimination*—remember, they are not the same! You have learned an easy-to-use thumb rule for managing people (the OUCH test) and a rather large number of Equal Employment Opportunity laws, including when and how each of them applies to an organization. We also discussed the main organizations that monitor these laws and regulations—the EEOC and the OFCCP. We reviewed some special cases of discrimination that have been getting a lot of attention lately, sexual harassment and religious discrimination, and discussed how to manage the organization's liability in these situations. And, finally, we looked at the similarities and differences between equal opportunity laws, Affirmative Action policies, and the concept of diversity in organizations. Let's close this one out.

Chapter Summary

Visit www.sagepub.com/lussier for helpful study resources.

3.1 Describe the OUCH test and its four components and identify when it is useful in an organizational setting.

The OUCH test is a thumb rule used whenever you are contemplating any employment action, to maintain fairness and equity for all of your employees or applicants. OUCH is an acronym that stands for [O]bjective, [U]niform in application, [C]onsistent in effect, and [H]as job relatedness. An employment action should generally be objective, instead of subjective; we should apply it the same every time with everyone to the best of our ability; it should not have an inconsistent effect on any protected groups; and anything we do must be directly related to the job to which we are applying it. You should use this test whenever you are contemplating any action that involves your employees.

3.2 Identify the major Equal Employment Opportunity laws and the groups of people that each law protects.

The Equal Pay Act of 1963 requires that women be paid equal to men if they are doing the same work.

Title VII of the Civil Rights Act of 1964 prohibits discrimination on the basis of race, color, religion, sex, or national origin in all areas of the employment relationship.

The Age Discrimination in Employment Act of 1967 prohibits age discrimination against people 40 years of age or older and restricts mandatory retirement.

The Vietnam Era Veterans' Readjustment Assistance Act of 1974 prohibits discrimination against Vietnam veterans by all employers with federal contracts or subcontracts of $100,000 or more. VEVRAA also requires that Affirmative Action be taken.

The Pregnancy Discrimination Act of 1978 prohibits discrimination against women affected by pregnancy, childbirth, or related medical conditions as unlawful sex discrimination.

The Americans With Disabilities Act of 1990 strengthened the Rehabilitation Act of 1973 to require employers to provide "reasonable accommodations" to allow disabled employees to work.

The Civil Rights Act of 1991 strengthened civil rights by providing for possible compensatory and punitive damages for discrimination.

The Uniformed Services Employment and Reemployment Rights Act of 1994 ensures the civilian reemployment rights of military members who were called away from their regular (nonmilitary) jobs by U.S. government orders.

The Veterans' Benefits Improvement Act of 2004 amends USERRA to extend health care coverage while away on duty, and requires employers to post a notice of benefits, duties, and rights of reemployment.

The Genetic Information Nondiscrimination Act of 2008 prohibits the use of genetic information in employment, prohibits intentional acquisition of same, and imposes confidentiality requirements.

The Lilly Ledbetter Fair Pay Act of 2009 amends the 1964 CRA to extend the period of time in which an employee is allowed to file a lawsuit over pay discrimination.

3.3 Describe the three main types of discrimination in the workplace.

Disparate treatment is discrimination that exists when individuals in similar situations are intentionally treated differently and the different treatment is based on an individual's membership in a protected class.

Disparate impact occurs when an officially neutral employment practice disproportionately excludes the members of a protected group. It is generally considered to be unintentional, but intent is irrelevant. For there to be discrimination under disparate *treatment*, there has to be intentional discrimination. Under disparate *impact*, intent does not matter.

Finally, pattern or practice discrimination occurs when a person or group engages in a sequence of actions over a significant period of time that is intended to deny the rights provided by the 1964 CRA to a member of a protected class. If there is reasonable cause to believe that a state or local government, or a nongovernmental organization, is engaging in a "pattern or practice" that denies the rights provided by Title VII, the U.S. Attorney General may bring a federal lawsuit against them.

3.4 Discuss the organizational defenses to accusations of discrimination.

The first defense is called a Bona Fide Occupational Qualification (BFOQ)—a qualification that is absolutely required in order for an individual to be able to successfully do a particular job. The qualification cannot just be a desirable quality within the job applicant, but must be mandatory. A BFOQ would be a legitimate defense against a charge of disparate treatment.

A "business necessity" defense exists when a particular practice is necessary for the safe and efficient operation of the business, and there is a specific business purpose for applying a particular standard that may, in fact, be discriminatory.

A business necessity defense *may* be a defense to disparate impact charges. Business necessity defenses must be combined with a test for "job relatedness." For job relatedness to act as a defense to a discriminatory action, first it has to be a business necessity, and then the employer must be able to show that the test for the employment action was a legitimate measure of an individual's ability to do the job.

3.5 Briefly discuss the two major federal immigration laws and how they affect the workplace.

In general, the federal immigration laws are designed for two purposes—to require verification of the legal right to work within the United States and to avoid potential discrimination against immigrant workers who are legally allowed to work in the country. The two major laws in this area are the Immigration and Nationality Act of 1952 (INA) (as amended) and the Immigration Reform and Control Act of 1986 (IRCA).

The INA allows the employment of immigrant workers in certain specialty occupations. However, there are specific requirements to apply for such employment, and there are annual limits to the number of workers who can apply for work visas in these specialty occupations. Because Congress could foresee the potential to discriminate against all alien workers to avoid any accusation of hiring undocumented workers, the INA also has a nondiscrimination requirement when dealing with alien workers who have the right to work in the United States.

The IRCA prohibits employers from knowingly hiring undocumented workers and requires employers to verify each employee's eligibility for employment through the use of a form called the Employment Eligibility Verification Form (I-9). The act also provides employers complying "in good faith" with the requirements of the IRCA with an affirmative defense to inadvertently hiring an unauthorized alien.

3.6 Briefly discuss and identify the major functions of the Equal Employment Opportunity Commission.

The EEOC is a federal agency that has significant power over employers in the process of investigating complaints of illegal discrimination based on race, color, religion, sex (including pregnancy), national origin, age (40 or older), disability, or genetic information.

The EEOC has three significant functions: investigating and resolving discrimination complaints through either conciliation or litigation, gathering and compiling statistical information on such complaints, and education and outreach programs on what constitutes illegal discrimination.

3.7 Discuss the difference between Equal Employment Opportunity, Affirmative Action, and diversity.

Equal Employment Opportunity is the term that deals with a series of laws and regulations put in place at the federal and state government levels in the last 45 years. As such, Equal Employment Opportunity is very specific and narrowly defined within U.S. and various state laws.

Affirmative Action was initiated in the 1960s through a series of policies at the presidential and legislative levels in the United States. Affirmative Action, except in a few circumstances, does not have the effect of law. Therefore, Affirmative Action is a much broader concept based on policy than is EEO, which is more narrowly based on law.

Finally, diversity is not law, nor is it *necessarily* even policy within organizations. Diversity is a very broad set of concepts that deal with the differences among people within organizations. Today's organizations view diversity as a valuable part of their Human Resource makeup; however, there are no specific laws that deal with requirements for diversity within organizations beyond the EEO laws that specifically identify protected class members and require that organizations deal with those protected class members in an *equal* way when compared to all other members of the organization.

3.8 Identify the two primary types of sexual harassment.

Quid pro quo harassment occurs when some type of benefit or punishment is made contingent upon the employee submitting to sexual advances. In other words, "If you do something for me, I will do something for you, or conversely if you refuse to do something for me, I will harm you."

Hostile work environment harassment occurs when someone's behavior at work creates an environment that is sexual in nature and makes it difficult for someone of a particular sex to work in that environment. Hostile environment sexual harassment happens when a "reasonable person" would determine that the environment went beyond normal human interactions and the jokes and kidding that went with those interactions rose to the level that such a reasonable person would consider the act or acts to be both harassing and sexual in nature.

Key Terms

Adverse employment action	Disability	Hostile work environment	Race-norming
Affirmative Action (AA)	Discrimination	Illegal discrimination	Reasonable accommodation
Bona Fide Occupational Qualification (BFOQ)	Disparate impact	Innovation	Reasonable person
Business necessity	Disparate treatment	Job relatedness	Retaliation
Cohesiveness	Divergent thinking	OUCH test	Reverse discrimination
Compensatory damages	Diversity	Pattern or practice discrimination	Right-to-sue
Conflict	Dysfunctional conflict	Punitive damages	Sexual harassment
Constructive discharge	Essential functions	Quid pro quo	Undue hardship
Creativity	Four-fifths rule		
	Functional conflict		

Key Term Review

Complete each of the following statements using one of this chapter's key terms:

_____ is the act of making distinctions, or choosing one thing over another—in HR, it is distinctions among people.

_____ is making distinctions that harm people by using a person's membership in a protected class.

_____ is a thumb rule used whenever you are contemplating any employment action, to maintain fairness and equity for all of your employees or applicants.

_____ is a test used by various federal courts, the Department of Labor, and the EEOC to determine whether disparate impact exists in an employment test.

_____ exists when individuals in similar situations are intentionally treated differently and the different treatment is based on an individual's membership in a protected class.

_____ occurs when an officially neutral employment practice disproportionately excludes the members of a protected group; it is generally considered to be unintentional, but intent is irrelevant.

_____ occurs when a person or group engages in a sequence of actions over a significant period of time that is intended to deny the rights provided by Title VII (the 1964 CRA) to a member of a protected class.

_____ is a qualification that is absolutely required in order for an individual to be able to successfully do a particular job.

_____ exists when a particular practice is necessary for the safe and efficient operation of the business, and there is a specific business purpose for applying a particular standard that may, in fact, be discriminatory.

_____ exists when a test for employment is a legitimate measure of an individual's ability to do the essential functions of a job.

_____ is a physical or mental impairment that substantially limits one or more major life activities, a record of having such an impairment, or being regarded as having such an impairment.

_____ is an accommodation, made by an employer, to allow someone who is disabled but otherwise qualified to do the essential functions of a job to be able to perform that job.

_____ are the fundamental duties of the position.

_____ occurs when the level of difficulty for an organization to provide accommodations, determined by looking at the nature and cost of the accommodation and the overall financial resources of the facility, becomes a significant burden on the organization.

_____ are monetary damages awarded by the court that compensate the person who was injured for their losses.

_____ are monetary damages awarded by the court that are designed to punish the injuring party when they intentionally inflicted harm on others.

_____ occurs when different groups of people have different scores designated as "passing" grades on a test for employment.

_____ is a notice from the EEOC, if they elect not to prosecute an individual discrimination complaint within the agency, which gives the recipient the right to go directly to the courts with their complaint.

_____ is a situation where the organization takes an "adverse employment action" against an employee because the employee brought discrimination charges against the organization or supported someone who brought discrimination charges against the company.

_____ is any action such as a firing, demotion, schedule reduction, or change that would harm the individual employee.

_____ exists when an employee is put under such extreme pressure by management that their continued employment becomes intolerable and as a result of the intolerable conditions the employee quits, or resigns from the organization.

_____ is a series of policies, programs, and initiatives that have been instituted by various entities, within both government and the private sector, that are designed to prefer hiring of individuals from protected groups in certain circumstances, in an attempt to mitigate past discrimination.

_____ is discrimination against members of the majority group in an organization, generally resulting from Affirmative Action policies within an organization.

_____ is the existence of differences—in HRM, it deals with different types of people in an organization.

_____ is a basic ability to think in unique and different ways and apply those thought processes to existing problems.

_____ is the act of creating useful processes or products based on creative thought processes.

_____ is the ability to find many possible solutions to a particular problem, including unique, untested solutions.

_____ is the act of being opposed to another.

_____ is how organizations go through the process of creating new things—the opposition itself drives the organization to change.

_____ occurs when conflict gets to the point where creativity is stifled and in fact almost all work becomes difficult or impossible because of the conflict's intensity.

_____ is an intent and desire for group members to stick together in their actions.

_____ is unwelcome sexual advances, requests for sexual favors, and other verbal or physical conduct of a sexual nature when submission to or rejection of this conduct explicitly or implicitly affects an individual's employment, unreasonably interferes with an individual's work performance, or creates an intimidating, hostile, or offensive work environment.

_____ is harassment that occurs when some type of benefit or punishment is made contingent upon the employee submitting to sexual advances.

_____ is harassment that occurs when someone's behavior at work creates an environment that is sexual in nature and makes it difficult for someone of a particular sex to work in that environment.

_____ would look at the situation and its intensity to determine whether the accused person was wrong in their actions.

Quick Check (True-False)

Answer the following true-false questions. The answers are provided following the questions.

1. If a manager does not discriminate, then they're not doing their job. T F

2. The four-fifths rule tells you that you need to hire four-fifths of your employees from the local community. T F

3. The OUCH test is a legal measure used to determine whether or not discrimination has occurred. T F

4. The Civil Rights Act of 1964 says it is illegal to use "race, color, religion, sex, or national origin" as a determining factor in any employment actions. T F

5. Disparate impact is an intentional form of discrimination. T F

6. Bona Fide Occupational Qualifications are qualities that are either mandatory or highly desirable in someone chosen for a particular job. T F

7. The Americans With Disabilities Act says that an organization must make "reasonable accommodations" to the physical or mental limitations of an individual with a disability *who was otherwise qualified* to perform the "essential functions" of the job, unless it would impose an "undue hardship" on the organization. T F

8. The Civil Rights Act of 1991 strictly limits the combined amount of compensatory and punitive damages that can be awarded in a court verdict based on the number of employees in an organization. T F

9. The Lilly Ledbetter Fair Pay Act of 2009 requires an individual to file a lawsuit within 180 days after the initial application of a discriminatory compensation decision, or the individual will never be able to file such an action. T F

10. U.S. immigration law requires employers to verify the identity and employment eligibility of anyone hired through the use of a form called the Employment Eligibility Verification Form (I-9). T F

11. One of the primary responsibilities of the Equal Employment Opportunity Commission is federal contract compliance for Executive Order 11246 and the 1973 Rehabilitation Act. T F

12. Affirmative Action policies are required of every organization with more than 50 employees by federal law. T F

13. Quid pro quo sexual harassment occurs when someone's behavior at work creates an environment that is sexual in nature and makes it difficult for someone of a particular sex to work in that environment. T F

14. All employees who work in the United States or its territories are protected by Equal Employment Opportunity laws, regardless of their citizenship or work authorization status. T F

Communication Skills

The following critical-thinking questions can be used for class discussion and/or for written assignments to develop communication skills. Be sure to give complete explanations for all answers.

1. Do you agree that applying the OUCH test to an employment situation will minimize illegal discrimination? Why or why not?

2. Are there any groups of people in the United States that you think should be covered by federal laws as a protected group, but are not currently covered? Why or why not?

3. Is most discrimination unintentional in the United States (disparate impact), or is most discrimination intentional (disparate treatment)? Why do you think so?

4. What is your opinion on organizations using Bona Fide Occupational Qualifications to limit who they will consider for a job?

5. Do we *really* need all of the laws that protect the Equal Employment Opportunities of different groups (age, military service, pregnant women, etc.)? Why or why not?

6. Do you agree that most employers probably *want* to obey the Americans With Disabilities Act, but don't know exactly what they are required to do? Do you think that most employers would rather not hire disabled people? Justify your answer.

7. How would *you* define the terms *reasonable accommodation* and *undue hardship* if you were asked by one of your company managers?

8. Has Affirmative Action gone too far in creating a *preference* for historically underrepresented groups over other employees and applicants instead of treating everyone equally?

9. Is illegal immigration really hurting this country, when most illegal immigrants take jobs that Americans don't want to do anyway?

10. Do you think that sexual harassment in the workplace is overreported or underreported? Justify your answer.

Video

Please visit the student study site at **www.sagepub.com/lussier** to view the video links in this chapter.

Answers

REVIEW QUESTIONS (TRUE-FALSE) Answers

1. T   2. F   3. F   4. T   5. F   6. F   7. T   8. T   9. F   10. T   11. F   12. F   13. F   14. T

Cases

Case 3-1. English-Only: One Hotel's Dilemma

Erica, the Human Resource Manager, was frustrated by many of her hotel staff speaking Spanish in the hallways and rooms as they were cleaning them.

The Sawmill Hotel where Erica works is situated in downtown Minneapolis, Minnesota. Its target market includes sports enthusiasts attending nearby professional (Twins, Vikings, Timberwolves, Wild) games but also business professionals and families. This four-star hotel features an indoor and outdoor swimming pool, a message center, three stores, two restaurants, and a beauty shop. Total staff includes about 10 managers, 30 cleaning assistants to take care of rooms, 10 front desk specialists, and 25 who are involved with the stores, restaurants, and beauty shops. All are required to focus on customer service as their number-one value.

Erica hires everyone in the hotel except for the Chief Executive Officer, Vice President of Finance, and Vice President of Marketing. For the rest of the managers, the 30 cleaning assistants, and the store, restaurant, and beauty shop workers, she advertises for openings with the local job service and the Minneapolis *Star Tribune* (with the associated website). A typical *Tribune* ad for a cleaning assistant reads as follows: Cleaning Assistants Wanted, Sawmill Hotel, $9–$11/hour. Prepare rooms for customers and prepare laundry. Contact: Erica Hollie, Human Resource Manager, 555-805-1234.

As a result of the advertising, Erica has been able to obtain good help through the local target market. Twenty-seven of the 30 cleaning assistants are women. Twenty of the 30 have a Hispanic background. Of the Hispanics, all can speak English at varying levels.

Rachel, the lead cleaning assistant, believes that maximizing communication among employees helps the assistants become more productive and stable within the hotel system. She uses both English and Spanish to talk to assistants under her. Spanish is useful with many assistants because they know Spanish much better than English. Spanish also is the "good friends" language that allows the Spanish speakers to freely catch up on each other's affairs and that motivates them to stay working at the hotel. The use of the Spanish language among cleaning assistants has been common practice among them for the two years since the hotel opened.

In the last few months, top management decided to have an even greater focus on customer service by ensuring customer comment cards are available in each room and at the front desk. Customers also can comment online about their stay at the hotel.

There have been several customer complaints that cleaning assistants have been laughing about them behind their back in Spanish. One customer, Kathy, thought that staffers negatively commented about her tight pink stretch pants covering her overweight legs. Other customers have complained they didn't think asking staff for help was easy given the amount of Spanish spoken. In all, about 15 out of 42 complaints in a typical month were associated with the use of the Spanish language.

Though bellhops and front desk clerks are typically the workers who handle complaints first, Erica, the Human Resource Manager, has the main responsibility to notify workers about customer complaint patterns and to set policy in dealing with the complaints. The prevalence of complaints concerning workers speaking Spanish each month led Erica to make a significant change in policy concerning the use of Spanish. In consultation with top management, Erica instituted the following employee handbook policy effective immediately:

"English is the main language spoken at the hotel. Any communication among employees shall be in English. Use of Spanish or other languages is prohibited unless specifically requested by management or the customer."

In an e-mail explanation for the new policy, Erica stated the number of complaints that had come from the use of Spanish and the need for customer courtesy and communication.

Rachel immediately responded to Erica's e-mail by stating that the new policy was too harsh on the native Spanish-speaking assistants at the hotel. She thought that a better policy is to allow her assistants to communicate with each other through Spanish but by quietly doing so away from customer earshot. If there is a general discussion in front of a customer, it is recommended to speak English. There should never be discussions in any language about customer appearances.

Though Rachel grumbled, the policy stuck because Erica and top management wanted to stop customer complaints. As a result of the policy, 10 of the 20 Spanish-speaking assistants quit within two months. These were high-quality assistants who had been with the hotel since the start. Their replacements came from a job service and have not worked out as well in their performance.

Questions

1. What law(s) do you think might apply in this case?

2. Should a complete ban of Spanish be instituted among staff of the hotel unless customers use Spanish themselves, or should the use of Spanish be completely allowed by staff among themselves as long as it is quiet (why or why not)?

3. What rules, if any, would you put into effect in this situation, knowing about the customer complaints? Explain your answer.

Case created by Gundars Kaupins of Boise State University

Case 3-2. When Religion Is on the Agenda

The Loxedose Company near Chicago transfers computer models into hard physical copies. Computer programmers design the representation, and machines sculpt the product line by line from the bottom to the top by adding levels of materials that adhere and are durable.

Two managers who founded the company celebrate individual and company successes. For example, Founders Day, August 25, features all 30 members of the company (or whoever is available) helping blow out the company birthday cake. Labor Day features a camping trip for those interested, at a manager's cabin at the largest lake in the area. Halloween features most employees wearing a costume, unless they are out on a sales or delivery run. Thanksgiving features a turkey lunch, whether vegetarians like it or not.

The managers believe that everyone should be working together and celebrating together. Accordingly, Christmas is not only a great year-end celebration but also a super holiday party. Traditionally, gifts are exchanged, Christmas carols are sung, and computer-designed trophies are given to the employees with bonus checks attached. Employees have to be present to receive the prizes made from Loxedose computer designs and materials.

This year, Loxedose hired a married couple, Omar and Judy, to be a part of the sales staff. Omar was from Saudi Arabia and also was studying in a university in Chicago. His wife was an American who was going to the same university.

Judy joined the Islamic faith when she married Omar. She was a Christian early in her life and then was unchurched through many years before she met Omar.

The upcoming Christmas party was a mandatory meeting and celebration. Employees had to be there to pick up their trophy along with the $200 bonus check. Judy was OK with going to the celebration, but Omar was not because it was a Christian celebration. Judy decided to go to the Christmas party without Omar to pick up Omar's statue along with hers.

The party started just fine with an exchange of presents, a birthday cake for Jesus, and a bunch of thank-yous from top management. When it came to giving out the celebratory statues and money, the managers stated you had to be there. Omar and Judy were mentioned together so Judy started picking up both statues when the company managers said Omar had to be there. Judy protested saying this was part of a Christmas celebration that was not part of his religion. Omar's statue and money were forced to remain.

Judy and Omar protested to management that they were discriminating based on religion because the bonus based on performance was distributed through the Christmas party and not offered if the employee didn't attend. All employees should have an equal right to get the bonus. Furthermore, not everyone will always be able to attend the parties because of illnesses, family matters, and other issues.

The managers proposed creating a new employee handbook policy associated with celebrations, awards, and religion. The following choices were suggested in a company meeting:

1. Celebrations within the company are important because they bring the employees together beyond the basic job. Employees will be required to attend Christian celebrations during work hours because that is the dominant religion.

2. Celebrations within the company are important because they bring the employees together beyond the basic job. Employees will be required to attend celebrations unless there are religious reasons or other reasons approved by management.

3. Celebrations within the company are important because they bring the employees together beyond the basic job. However, no celebrations shall be related to any, or for any, religious holiday, in order to respect the beliefs of those who do not celebrate as such. Anyone missing any party needs prior approval from management.

4. Celebrations within the company are optional. However, rewards will be provided for performance at a December party. If no reward is received at the party, it will be delivered to the employee the next day.

5. No statues or awards will be given at company celebrations. They will be mailed to employees or added to payroll automatically.

Top management strongly opposes the last two proposals because they would actually destroy the effect of providing awards in front of everyone. They prefer the second proposal because everyone would need to contact management and management would have control of who would be at the celebration. Omar and Judy do not like the fact that they would be forced (in Proposal 2) to reject the Christmas party because it is Christian. They much prefer Proposal 3 that eliminates religion-related celebrations. Top management does not like the proposal because it thinks religion-based celebrations are an important part of life.

Questions

1. Which employment law or laws does this case involve? How would the law(s) that you identified apply in this case?

2. Which employee handbook proposal should the company incorporate (if any) and why?

3. How effective in the company's culture is giving out awards in front of everyone else?

4. Should religious parties be optional? Mandatory? Offered? Not offered?

Case created by Gundars Kaupins of Boise State University

SKILL BUILDER 3-1

The Four-Fifths Rule

For this exercise, you will do some math.

Objective

To develop your skill at understanding and calculating the four-fifths rule.

Skills

The primary skills developed through this exercise are:

1. *HR Management skill* — Analytical and quantitative business skills

2. *SHRM 2010 Curriculum Guidebook* — E: Outcomes: Metrics and Measurement in HR

Complete the following Four-Fifths Problems

1.

	Males	Females
Applicants	100	100
Selected	50	40
Selection rate	50% (50/100)	40% (40/100)

Four-fifths = _____ %.
The selection rate of _____% is equal to, less than, or greater than _____% or four-fifths.
Therefore, the four-fifths rule is or is not met. How many total females and how many more females should be hire

2.

	White	Non-White
Applicants	120	75
Selected	80	25
Selection rate	_____	_____

Four-fifths = _____ %.
The selection rate of _____% is equal to, less than, or greater than _____% or four-fifths.
Therefore, the four-fifths rule is or is not met. How many total and how many more non-Whites should be hired? _____ _____

3.

	White	Non-White Females
Applicants	63	109
Selected	17	22
Selection rate	_____	_____

Four-fifths = _____ %.
The selection rate of _____% is equal to, less than, or greater than _____% or four-fifths.
Therefore, the four-fifths rule is or is not met. How many total and how many more non-White females should be hired? _____ _____

SKILL BUILDER 3-2

Diversity Training

Objective

To become more aware of and sensitive to diversity.

Skills

The primary skills developed through this exercise are:

1. *HR Management skill*—Human relations skills
2. *SHRM 2010 Curriculum Guidebook*— J: Training and Development

Answer the following questions.

Race and Ethnicity

1. My race (ethnicity) is ____.

2. My name, ____, is significant because it means ____. [or]

   My name, ____, is significant because I was named after ____.

3. One positive thing about my racial/ethnic background is ____.

4. One difficult thing about my racial/ethnic background is ____.

Religion

5. My religion is ____.

6. One positive thing about my religious background is ____.

7. One difficult thing about my religious background is ____.

Gender

8. I am ____ (male/female).

9. One positive thing about being (male/female) is ____.

10. One difficult thing about being (male/female) is ____.

Age

11. I am ____ years old.

12. One positive thing about being this age is ____.

13. One difficult thing about being this age is ____.

Other

14. One way in which I am different from other people is ____.

15. One positive thing about being different in this way is ____.

16. One negative thing about being different in this way is ____.

Prejudice, Stereotypes, Discrimination

17. Describe what happened if you have ever been prejudged, stereotyped, or discriminated against. It could be minor, such as having a comment made to you about your wearing the wrong type of clothes/sneakers or being the last one picked when selecting teams.

Apply It

What did I learn from this experience? How will I use this knowledge in the future?

_____

_____

Your instructor may ask you to do this Skill Builder in class in a group. If so, the instructor will provide you with any necessary information or additional instructions.

Staffing

4

Matching Employees With Jobs

Learning Outcomes

After studying this chapter you should be able to:

4.1 Describe the process of work flow analysis and identify why it is important to HRM

4.2 Identify the four major options available for the job analysis process

4.3 Discuss the four major approaches to job design

4.4 Identify and briefly describe the components of the Job Characteristics Model

4.5 Describe the three major tools for motivational job design

4.6 Discuss the three most common quantitative HR forecasting methods

4.7 Identify the seven major options for decreasing organizational numbers when faced with a labor surplus

4.8 Discuss the problems that need to be considered in offering an early retirement program

4.9 Identify the seven major options for overcoming a labor shortage

4.10 Define the following terms:

Work flow analysis
Job analysis
Job description
Job specification
Job design
Mechanistic job design
Biological job design
Perceptual-motor job design
Motivational job design
Job Characteristics
  Model (JCM)

Job simplification
Job expansion
HR forecasting
Quantitative forecast
Trend analysis
Ratio analysis
Regression analysis
Qualitative forecasting
Layoff
Hoteling

Chapter 4 Outline

Employee and Job Matching

Work Flow Analysis
- Organizational Output
- Tasks and Inputs

Job Analysis
- Why Do We Need to Analyze Jobs?
- Databases
- Job Analysis Methods
  - Questionnaires
  - Interviews
  - Diaries
  - Observation
- Do We Really Have "Jobs" Anymore?
- Task or Competency Based?
- Outcomes: Job Description and Job Specification

Job Design/Redesign
- Organizational Structure and Job Design
- Approaches to Job Design and Redesign
- The Job Characteristics Model

Designing Motivational Jobs
- Job Simplification
- Job Expansion
  - Job Rotation
  - Job Enlargement
  - Job Enrichment
- Work Teams
  - Integrated Work Teams
  - Self-Managed Work Teams

Applying the Job Characteristics Model
- Job Design for Flexibility
- Job Design Is Country Specific

HR Forecasting
- Forecasting Methods
  - Quantitative Forecasting
  - Qualitative Forecasting
- Measuring Absenteeism and Turnover

Reconciling Internal Labor Supply and Demand
- Options for a Labor Surplus
  - Downsizing and Layoffs
  - Pay Reduction, Work Sharing, Natural Attrition, Hiring Freeze, Retraining, and Transfer Options
  - Early Retirement
- Options for a Labor Shortage
  - Overtime
  - Temporary or Contract Workers
  - Retrain Workers, Outsourcing, or Turnover Reduction
  - New Hires and Technological Innovation

Succession Planning

Trends and Issues in HRM
- Work Flows and Job Design for Sustainability
- Diversity and Job Design
- High-Velocity and Entrepreneurial Organizations Need Flexibility in Job Design

SHRM
HR CONTENT

See Appendix A: *SHRM 2010 Curriculum Guidebook* for the complete list

C. Job Analysis/Job Design (required)
1.   Job/role design (roles, duties, and responsibilities)
7.   HR planning (skill inventories and supply/demand forecasting)
8.   Work management (work processes and outsourcing)

D. Organization Development (required)
12. Organizational structure and job design
15. Succession planning

E. Outcomes: Metrics and Measurement of HR (required)
3.   Measuring absenteeism
4.   Measuring turnover
5.   Trend and ratio analysis projections
10. Quantitative analysis
12. Analyzing and interpreting metrics
13. Forecasting

G. Staffing: Recruitment and Selection (required)
1.   Employment relationship (employees, contractors, and temporary workers)

H. Strategic HR (required)
12. Trends and forecasting in HR

K. Workforce Planning and Talent Management (required)
1.   Downsizing/rightsizing
2.   Planning (forecasting requirements and availabilities, gap analysis, action planning, core/flexible workforce)
5.   Retention (measurement)
6.   Labor supply and demand
7.   Succession planning

Case 4-1. The Explosion at DHR Construction

Is There a Painless Way to Reduce the Workforce?

Besides employing people with the skills and knowledge necessary to work today, the HR Manager must also plan for the employees, skills, and knowledge that will be needed in the future. Our President had a grim look on his face as he joined us around the conference table. The economic recession had taken its toll on our company, and now we had to face some tough choices to make some immediate and significant cuts in the budget. Richard suggested a layoff. Pat suggested a percentage cut in salaries. John suggested rotating mandatory unpaid vacation time The discussion went on and on because each solution would impact our employees in a negative way. Which suggestion do you think is the best way to reduce labor costs? How might this dilemma have been avoided? Chapter 4 will show you not only how to manage a labor surplus, but also how to forecast your future labor needs to help avoid an imbalance.

The Practitioner's Model for HRM

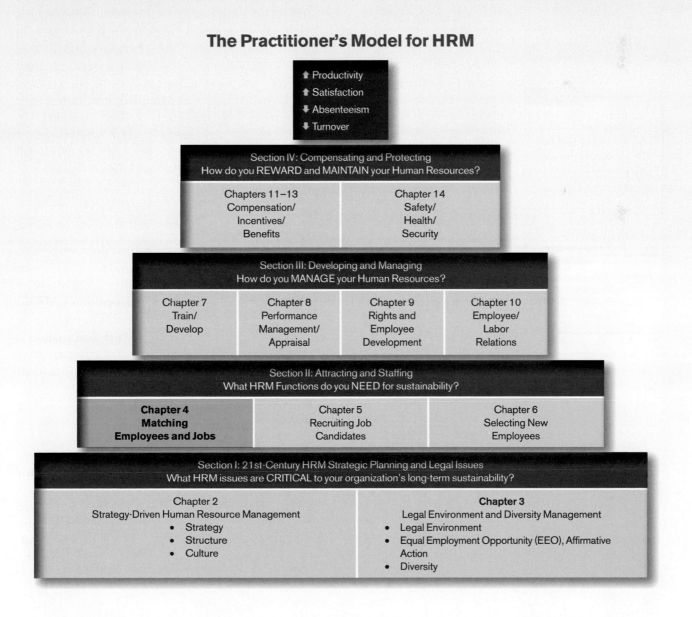

Video Link 4.1

Job Description
and Specifications

Employee and Job Matching

Now that we have learned some of the basics concerning how to treat our human resources fairly and equitably in Chapters 1–3, we need to start putting them to work in the organization. Let's start with the realization that in order for our organization to maximize productivity, it is imperative that we match the right people with the right jobs.[1] Why? Because mismatched workers tend to have low job satisfaction leading to absenteeism, turnover, and lower levels of productivity than those who are matched effectively. The first step is to determine what jobs we need to have performed and the qualifications needed to do the job (job description and specifications), and then we can match employees to those jobs.

This chapter deals with how we design the flow of work and subsequently the jobs in our organizations. Work flows create the need for certain types of tasks to be performed within each part of the organization. Once we have identified the tasks that will have to be performed, we then determine how to lump those tasks into jobs, and then design the resulting jobs in certain specific ways depending on what our priorities are as an organization. For instance, motivational job design allows us to provide jobs with more extrinsic motivating potential to our employees. We can use motivational job tools to assist us in improving job satisfaction and lowering absenteeism and turnover in at least some situations. We will also take a look at another part of matching people and jobs in the section on HR forecasting, which tries to match number and types of people that we will need with number and types of jobs that will require filling within a specified period of time. This process can tell us whether or not we might need to shed some types of employees from our rosters, retrain them to do other jobs, potentially hire more people with skill sets that we expect will be in short supply, or do some other things that can make employee supply match employee demand within the company. It may not sound too clear right now, but this chapter will go through each of these processes, and hopefully it will become clearer to you as we go. Let's start by taking a brief look at *work flow analysis.*

LO 4.1

Describe the process of work flow analysis and identify why it is important to HRM.

Work Flow Analysis

SHRM

Guide – C:8
Work management
(work processes
and outsourcing)

Let's imagine that we are starting up a brand-new company. The first thing we have to know is what we expect the organization to do. Do we plan to make products (things to be manufactured such as Apple iPhones), or do we plan to provide services (as AT&T offers service for cell phones including the iPhone)? Who is going to depend on whom, and what processes are going to be accomplished in what ways, and how quickly?[2] The way that we put the organization together will depend on what we expect it to do. **Work flow analysis** is *the tool that we use to identify what has to be done within the organization to produce a product or service.* For each product or service that we provide in the organization, we have to identify the work flows that create that product or service.

Organizational Output

Work flow analysis is a bit different from some of the other things that we do, though, because we have to do it backward. The first thing we analyze is the end result of our processes—our organizational outputs. In other words, we need to know what the customer wants from us.[3] Why do we do it this way? Well, if you think about this backward method, it starts to make sense fairly quickly. As we noted in the strategic planning chapter (Chapter 2), "How can we design the steps to do something if we don't know what it is supposed to look like when we are finished?"

If our product organization decides we are going to make desks, but we don't identify what kind of desks we're going to make, do we need skilled craftsmen who can work with hardwoods and design a beautiful handmade wooden desk, or do we need metal workers who can bend tubing and attach Formica surfaces to a metal frame to make a standard office desk? The answer is, of course, it depends on what kind of desk we plan to make. So identifying the end result is a critical first step in identifying the work flows to create that result.

Tasks and Inputs

So we start our work flow analysis by looking at the end result. Once we identify the result we expect, we can then determine the steps, or activities required in order to create the end result that we've identified. This is basically an analysis of the tasks that are going to have to be performed in order to create the output that we expect. Finally, based on the steps that we identify and the tasks that will have to be performed, we can then identify the inputs that are going to be necessary to carry out the steps and perform the same tasks.

There is a simple mnemonic (a memory tool) available to remember what resource inputs we have available. It is called the 3 Ms:

1. Material—any physical resource such as tools, equipment, or real estate that we use in production

2. Manpower—the people who are needed in a particular production process (both quantity and types)

3. Money—the capital that must be spent to perform our processes

These are the three large categories of resources that we use up in the organization in doing what we are designed to do.[4] Whenever we look at work flow analysis, we have to identify which of the 3 Ms and how much of each we are using up in a particular process. So the final result of our work flow analysis is shown in Exhibit 4-1.

Exhibit 4-1	Work Flow Analysis

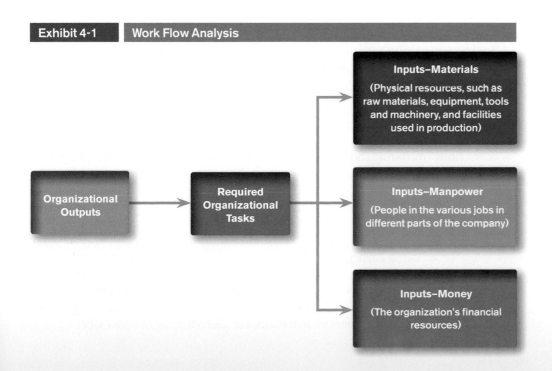

Work flow analysis almost always shows us that some steps or jobs within the organization can be combined, simplified, or even eliminated (we will talk more about work simplification shortly). In some cases, the work flow analysis will show that groups or teams rather than individual workers should be the basic building blocks of our processes.

Does HR do all of this work flow analysis? No, the organization's line management is typically responsible for mapping out work flows. However, HR Managers need to understand the process so that they can assist line managers in identifying the tasks and the human inputs required to do those tasks, and so that they can design appropriate organizational systems for the human resources who will be performing the tasks so that those people are both motivated and efficient.

Job Analysis

Once we understand the work flows in the organization, the next thing that we need to do is figure out which parts of the work flows are done where. This is the basic concept of job analysis. **Job analysis** is *the process used to identify the work performed and the working conditions for each of the jobs within our organizations.* Job analysis results will include duties, responsibilities, skills, knowledge required, outcomes, conditions under which the worker must operate, and possibly other factors.[5]

The two primary outcomes for most job analysis projects are the *job description* and the *job specification*. The **job description** *identifies the major tasks, duties, and responsibilities that are components of a job*, while the **job specification** *identifies the qualifications of a person who should be capable of doing the job tasks noted in the job description.*

Why Do We Need to Analyze Jobs?

Job analysis is at the core of HRM. It is the basis of just about everything that HR does. If you think about it for just a minute, you will realize that we have to have the jobs in the organization identified and correctly analyzed in order to perform *any* of the following functions:

1. Human resource planning—Job analysis helps us design jobs better to get the results that we need (we will talk about job design shortly).

2. Job evaluation for compensation—If we don't know what the job consists of, how can we determine how much the job is worth to the organization so we know how much to pay the person?

3. Staffing (recruiting and selection)—If we don't know what the person is going to do and how much we will pay, then how do we know whom to recruit and hire?

4. Training—If we don't know what the job consists of, how can we teach people to do the job?

5. Performance management—How can we evaluate the performance of someone if we don't know what their job consists of?

6. Maintain a safe work environment—Job analysis will help us identify hazards that the job incumbent will need to understand, as well as any required personal protective equipment and training requirements for safely carrying out their job.

Other things that can be affected by job analysis include individual career planning and development, organizational strategy and structure, employee relations and legal compliance, and many other HRM tasks.

OK, so job analysis is important to the HR Department. How does it affect other managers? Think about the following issues that any organizational manager may face on a routine basis:

1. Managers must have detailed information about all the jobs in their work groups to understand the work flow processes.

2. Managers need to understand the job requirements to make intelligent hiring, training, and promotion decisions.

3. Every manager is responsible for ensuring that all employees are performing their jobs satisfactorily through performance evaluation.

So, we can see that job analysis is very important to both HR Managers and line managers in the organization. But, how do you analyze a job? Read on.

Databases

Job analysis can be assisted through the use of various databases. The Department of Labor's Dictionary of Occupational Titles, and now O*NET,[6] provide data on over 900 different job titles, and the list is continually updated. The information is free for use (unless you are going to use it to develop other products, software, or applications) by anyone who has a need. O*NET data give you general information on these job titles that then have to be adjusted for your company's specific circumstances. Other databases are also available commercially. This database information can be used to help with analysis of a large number of jobs that are common across many different companies, and can be modified as necessary for the specific organization and job.

Therefore, a good starting point of job analysis can be a database. However, as stated, if you find a job analysis, it will most likely need to be customized. A database job analysis can be customized by conducting your own job analysis, and if you can't find one, you need to conduct your own job analysis. How to do so is our next topic.

Job Analysis Methods

Four commonly used methods to analyze jobs include questionnaires, interviews, diaries, and observation.[7] No matter how the process is completed, the result that we are looking for is a description of what goes on in that particular job and what qualifications are needed in order for a person to be successful in the position. Let's take a closer look at the four options.

LO 4.2

Identify the four major options available for the job analysis process.

Questionnaires

There are a number of highly valid and reliable questionnaires available for the job analysis process. The questionnaire can be given to many different people in order to analyze the job in question. It may be given to the current job holder (incumbent), the supervisor, or others who are affected by the way the job is completed in the organization. Most of the questionnaires follow similar processes. Each asks questions that help to identify the functions that are a part of a particular job and then, in most cases, assigns a point value to that function.[8] For example, one function might be preparing and distributing budget reports using a spreadsheet, and this function may be worth 25 points in a particular questionnaire, while the function of analyzing complex financial data for trends might be worth 65 points in such a questionnaire.

Questionnaire Advantages

– Quick way to get information from large number of sources

– Usually easy to quantify

– Relatively low cost

– Generally valid and reliable instruments

– No need for a trained interviewer or observer

Questionnaire Disadvantages

– Incomplete responses (nobody is interviewing or observing actions)

– Responses may be hard to interpret

– Low response rates are possible if there is no supervisory follow-up to get it completed

Interviews

Another available method is the job analysis interview, where questions are asked verbally, usually of the incumbent, and the answers are compiled into a profile of the job. For the interview method, we need a trained interviewer, so that they know how to interpret the answers to their questions and ask follow-up questions if needed. The interviewer asks job-related questions, and the incumbent describes the job based on the questions asked.

Interview Advantages

– The incumbent is most familiar with the job

– Can include qualitative data

– Simple, quick, and more comprehensive than some other forms

– Provides an opportunity to explain the need for the analysis and answer questions

Interview Disadvantages

– Dependent on trained interviewer and well-designed questions

– Workers may exaggerate their job duties

– Time-consuming and may not be cost-efficient

Diaries

We can also have workers maintain a work log, or diary, in which they write down the tasks that they accomplish as they go about their job.[9] This log becomes the document from which we build the description of the job.

Diary Advantages

- Participatory form of analysis

- May collect data as things happen

- The worker knows the job and what is important

- Useful for jobs that are difficult to observe

Diary Disadvantages

- Relies on worker writing all work down

- Worker may rely on memory of things done earlier in the day

- Information distortion

- Data are not in a standard format—makes quantifying difficult

Observation

Finally, we can use observation of the person at work, where an observer shadows the person and logs tasks that are performed over a period of time. If the observer is trained, they will usually identify items that the worker doesn't even think about as they do the tasks, and therefore wouldn't have noted in a log or diary.

Observation Advantages

- Firsthand knowledge

- Allows the analyst to see the work environment, tools and equipment used, interrelationships with other workers, and complexity of the job

- Reduces information distortion common in some other methods

- Relatively simple to use

Observation Disadvantages

- Observer may affect the job incumbent's performance

- Inappropriate for jobs that involve significant mental effort

- May lack validity and reliability

- Time-consuming

- Requires a trained observer

The four methods above are certainly not the only methods of job analysis, and some would say not the best options in a particular situation. There are many other options including work sampling, videotaping of jobs, and others. However, the four types of analysis should show you the basic process of job analysis even if we don't show all possible methods. We also need to be aware that in many cases we may want to use more than one method to analyze a particular job. If one method won't provide a good analysis by itself, then we may use more than one option. However, a caution again is that the more differing methods we use to analyze a single job, the more it costs to do the analysis, so we have to sometimes trade off between

WORK
APPLICATION 4-2

Which of the four job analysis processes would be the most appropriate to use to write the job description and job specifications for a job you hold or held? Explain why, discussing the advantages it has over the over methods.

a better analysis and a less expensive one. The optimal option here would be to do a more thorough analysis, which in turn provides better information on which to make all kinds of decisions about the job such as what kind of employee we would need to look for, what kind of training they need to do the job, and what kind of compensation to offer. But again, sometimes cost to the company matters more than a perfect analysis.

4-1 APPLYING THE CONCEPT

Job Analysis Methods

State which of the following methods would be the most appropriate for the given situation.

a. questionnaire
b. interview

c. diary
d. observation

_____ 1. You have a few hundred employees in a call center taking orders to buy your country greats CD music set sold through TV ads. You have a high turnover rate and would like to improve it.

_____ 2. You have 12 service call employees who repair a variety of major appliances. You would like to have a better idea of what types of appliances they are fixing on the home service calls.

_____ 3. You would like to improve the productivity of your 10 machinists. There is an industrial engineer who is an efficiency expert on your staff.

_____ 4. You have around 100 employees working in Accounts Receivable. They perform data entry to record customer payments of electric bills.

_____ 5. You have seven professionals who conduct complex research to develop new drugs. They mostly work independently and use different methods of developing and testing the various drugs.

Do We Really Have "Jobs" Anymore?

We would be remiss here if we didn't look at a contrasting opinion on job analysis. A number of researchers today are talking about the decline in the value of traditional job analysis, saying that it is static and looks at the past rather than the future.[10] Another argument against job analysis is that stable "jobs" don't exist in today's workplace. Stable jobs are a characteristic of what is often referred to as a *mechanistic* organization, and there are fewer mechanistic organizations today than in the past. The basis of the arguments—that job analysis is static and looks at the job from a historical perspective—is true, but the fact is that job analysis is still valid in many types of jobs for many organizations, such as McDonald's.

As with everything in management, whether job analysis is valuable or not depends on other factors. In general, job analysis is of more value to organizations making a product than those providing a service and those in a more stable unchanging environment. Also, some parts of the firm, such as Production, can be more stable than other parts, such as Research and Development. If jobs in the organization are stable and going to be designed using one of the four basic job design options (we will talk about these shortly), then job analysis is still a valuable part of designing those jobs. If, on the other hand, the organizational structure is going to be highly *organic* in nature, changing rapidly, and there are no well-defined jobs within the structure, then job analysis will be of less value helping us identify the type of person who will need to be hired for a general job category.

Task or Competency Based?

As we go through the process of analyzing jobs, we have to make some other decisions. One decision is whether our job analysis will be task or competency based.[11] What's the difference? In task-based job analysis the job is described as a function of the tasks performed within the job, while in a competency-based job analysis we would look at the capabilities that an individual would need to have in order to be able to succeed in the job. Task-based job analysis tends to be simpler in form and execution, while competency-based job analysis is more complex due to the fact that we have to think about a broader set of skills and abilities as opposed to the ability to do a set task.

So, which is better? Again, it depends on what the organization is doing as its primary function. In more stable, traditional, and bureaucratic organizations, task-based job analysis would usually be the norm. We would use competency-based job analysis in organizations that are less structured and less stable in the work that is accomplished. For example, you would probably choose competency-based job analysis for the jobs in an advertising agency or a research and development laboratory, while manufacturing office furniture would call for more task-based job analysis.

HRM must clearly articulate the job description and job specifications in order to match employees and jobs.

Outcomes: Job Description and Job Specification

So, you now know that job analysis is the process of determining what the position entails and the qualifications needed to staff the position. The primary outcomes that we are looking for in a job analysis are the creation of a *job description* and a *job specification*. As we noted earlier, the job description identifies the tasks and responsibilities of a position. Simply put, it describes the job itself, not the person who will do the job. The person is described in the job specification. The trend today is to describe jobs more broadly in order to design enriched jobs and to allow more flexibility in the work that is assigned. Exhibit 4-2 shows a sample job description.

At www.JobDescription.com, you can create individual, customized job descriptions that meet legal requirements. You work completely online, and it's fast and easy. The job library has more than 3,700 job descriptions that include competencies that you can customize to help define the job. The website also helps you create and place job advertisements on the Web and generate job-specific, behavior-based interview questions; it provides expert advice for each step.[12]

Job specifications, our other job analysis outcome, identify the qualifications needed by the person who is to fill a position. In other words, the job specification tells us *what kind of person* we need in order to successfully do the job. We will use the job specification to go out

| Exhibit 4-2 | Job Description |

DEPARTMENT: Plant Engineering

JOB TITLE: Lead Sheet Metal Specialist

JOB DESCRIPTION:

Responsible for the detailed direction, instruction, and leading of sheet metal department personnel in the construction and repair of a wide variety of sheet metal equipment. Receives verbal or written instructions from foreperson as to sequence and type of jobs or special methods to be used. Allocates work to members of the group. Directs the layout, fabrication, assembly, and removal of sheet metal units according to drawings or sketches and generally accepted trade procedures. Obtains materials or supplies needed for specific jobs according to standard procedures. Trains new employees, as directed, regarding metal-working procedures and safe working practices. Checks all work performed by the group. Usually makes necessary contacts for the group with supervision or engineering personnel. May report irregularities to higher supervision but has no authority to hire, fire, or discipline other employees.

WORK APPLICATION 4-4

Complete a job analysis for a job you hold or held; write a brief job description and job specifications.

and recruit when we have an opening for the job. As discussed throughout this section, job descriptions and job specifications are critical to organizations.

Job Design/Redesign

Tasks to be performed by organizations are grouped by the organization, usually into functional departments, and the tasks are further grouped into jobs for each employee providing structures and processes.[13] **Job design** is *the process of identifying tasks that each employee is responsible for completing as well as how those tasks will be accomplished.* Job design is crucial because it affects job satisfaction and productivity, along with a large number of other functions in HRM.[14]

Job redesign refers to changing the tasks or the way work is performed in an existing job. The nature of work has dramatically changed over the last decade. Many organizations, including GE and Pizza Hut, are asking employees to suggest ways to redesign their work. Job design, which includes redesign, is about working smarter, not harder, to find new ways of doing things that boost productivity.[15]

Organizational Structure and Job Design

SHRM

Guide – D:12
Organizational structure and job design

Recall our discussion of organizational structure in Chapter 2. We said that "the way that we combine the components of organizational structure causes employees within the organization to act in different ways," basically because of the expectations that are created within the structure about how we will be expected to interact with each other. Jobs within the organization have to be designed to fit within the confines of the structure that we have designed.[16]

If we have a more relaxed, flatter structure with lots of autonomy for our workers, we will need to design our jobs to take advantage of that autonomy, or self-direction on the part of our employees. If, on the other hand, we have a rigid bureaucratic organization structure with strong centralized decision making and control (which usually makes it cheaper to run the organization, including Wal-Mart), our jobs have to be designed so that they can be readily controlled by a central authority. So as we design the jobs within the organization we have to keep the structure in mind.

ORGANIZATIONAL STRUCTURE AND JOB DESIGN PREFERENCE

Individuals differ in the type of organizations and job designs in which they prefer to work. To determine your preference, evaluate each of the following 12 statements, using the scale below. Choose a number from 1 to 5 that represents your level of agreement with the statement.

I agree   I disagree

5 _____ 4 _____ 3 _____ 2 _____ 1

_____ 1. I prefer having just one boss telling me what to do, rather than multiple people.

_____ 2. I prefer to just perform my job, rather than being concerned about organizational objectives and being involved in setting them.

_____ 3. I prefer knowing the reporting relationship, knowing who is who's boss, and working through proper channels, rather than just working directly with a variety of people based on the situation.

_____ 4. I prefer having a clear job description so I know just what I need to do at work, rather than the ambiguity of not being sure and doing whatever needs to be done.

_____ 5. I prefer being a specialist doing one job really well, rather than a generalist doing several things not as well.

_____ 6. I prefer doing my own thing that contributes to the organization, rather than coordinating the work I do with that of others in teams.

_____ 7. I prefer slow change, rather than regular fast changes.

_____ 8. I prefer routine at work, rather than being delegated new tasks to perform.

_____ 9. I prefer doing more simple tasks, rather than more complex task that take more time and effort.

_____ 10. I prefer that people get promoted based primarily on seniority, rather than based on performance.

_____ Total

Scoring: To determine your preference, add up the numbers you assigned to the statements (the total will be between 10 and 50) and place it on the continuum below.

        10   15   20   25   30   35   40   50

Organic   Mechanistic

Recall our discussion of mechanistic and organic structures, which you will learn more about throughout this chapter. The higher your score, the more you prefer to work in a more traditional mechanistic stable structure and job design. The lower your score, the more you prefer to work in a more contemporary organic changing structure and job design.

Review your answers knowing that the opening statement applies to mechanistic and the opposite statement (after "rather than") applies to organic organizations' structure and job design. Most firms, and people, prefer organizations somewhere between the two extremes.

Discuss the four major
approaches to job design.

Approaches to Job Design and Redesign

Job design/redesign can follow several different forms, depending on what we are trying to accomplish in the organization. Are we trying to increase motivation levels in our workforce in a customer relations management or direct marketing business? If so, we may choose a specific type of job design that will help motivate the individual worker. Are we trying to simplify the work being done in a manufacturing setting so that the workers are more efficient? If this is the case, we may want to segment the work down into very simple component parts so that the employee can get fast and efficient because they are only being asked to do a few different things. What are our options in how we organization work into jobs? There are four primary approaches to job design: mechanistic, biological, perceptual, and motivations.[17]

1. **Mechanistic job design** *focuses on designing jobs around the concepts of task specialization, skill simplification, and repetition.* In other words, if we are going to design a mechanistic job, we try to make the job simple and repetitive so that the worker can

Organization needs employees with different specializations and skill sets based on the job analysis.

get very good at doing it. This approach is based on the old (early 1900s) concept of *scientific management* by Frederick Taylor. Here we are designing jobs to fit into a mechanistic organizational structure, rather than the opposite end of the continuum, an organic structure. As stated in Self-Assessment 4-1, many firms design jobs that are in between the two extremes of mechanistic and organic. The biggest problem in mechanistic job design is that we might specialize the work to the point that it becomes too repetitive, and as a result it gets very boring. This is not the way to get the best performance from your workforce! An example of mechanistic job design would be a job in a manufacturing plant where the worker attaches the desktop to its base using six fasteners and then goes to the next desk to fasten another identical top to another base.

2. **Biological job design** *focuses on minimizing the physical strain on the worker by structuring the physical work environment around the way the body works.* Here we are trying to make the job easier physically so that the worker can be more efficient and so that it is less likely that they will be injured and have to miss work when they are needed. Again, though, this approach does little to make the worker more motivated or satisfied with their work. An example of biological job design would be if our company installed a conveyor that lifted a vacuum cleaner up to eye level so that a worker could attach wheels to its base, and then the conveyor would drop the vacuum down to about waist level so that another worker could attach the bag to the vacuum. This would allow the workers to do their jobs without physical strain.

3. **Perceptual/motor job design** *focuses on designing jobs that attempt to make sure that we remain within the worker's normal mental capabilities and limitations.* Instead of

trying to minimize the physical strain on the workforce, the goal is to design jobs in a way that ensures they minimize mental strain on a worker. Here again, we may create a job that is not very motivating. (If you want to know why this isn't motivating, look at the two-factor motivation theory by Fredrick Herzberg.) We might use the perceptual/motor approach to break down an Executive Assistant job into Report Writer and Scheduler jobs, because the set of skills needed in these two areas are significantly different.

4. **Motivational job design** *focuses on the job characteristics that affect the psychological meaning and motivational potential, and it views attitudinal variables as the most important outcomes of job design.* The theory is that if the worker is more motivated, they will produce more work. It is in this last approach to job design that we can apply the Job Characteristics Model, which we will discuss next.

The Job Characteristics Model

The **Job Characteristics Model (JCM)**, developed by Richard Hackman and Greg Oldham, *provides a conceptual framework for designing or enriching jobs based on core job characteristics.*[18] The model can be used by individual managers or by members of a team. As Exhibit 4-3 illustrates, users of the JCM focus on core job dimensions, psychological states of employees, and the strength of employees' need for growth. Use of the Job Characteristics Model improves employees' motivation, performance, and job satisfaction and reduces their absenteeism and job turnover. Most of these variables should look familiar to you from Chapter 1, where we discussed the HRM challenges that managers tell us make their jobs more difficult and that they can't *directly* control.[19] Research supports the idea that use of the JCM increases performance by meeting employee needs to grow and develop on the job.[20]

In the model, five core job characteristics can be fine-tuned to improve the outcomes of a job in terms of employees' productivity and their quality of working life:

WORK APPLICATION 4-5

Which of the four approaches to job design/redesign best describes a job you hold or held? Explain how the job incorporates the features of the approach.

LO 4.4

Identify and briefly describe the components of the Job Characteristics Model.

SHRM

Guide – C:1
Job/role design (roles, duties, and responsibilities)

4-2 APPLYING THE CONCEPT

Job Designs

Identify which job design technique is exemplified in each statement.

a. mechanistic
b. organic
c. biological

d. perceptual/motor
e. motivational

_____ 6. This is the 25th tire that I have changed today here at Town Fair Tire.

_____ 7. While loading the trucks at UPS, you have to wear these special belts.

_____ 8. Now that we have grown so much here at Netflix, we are splitting Accounts Receivable and Accounts Payable into two separate departments. So things should be less confusing from now on.

_____ 9. I'd like to change your job so that you can develop new skills, complete entire jobs by yourself so that the job is more meaningful, do the job the way you want to, and know how you are doing here at Titeflex.

_____ 10. Well, Boss, it's 9 o'clock; what are we doing today?

1. *Skill variety* is the number of diverse tasks that make up a job and the number of skills used to perform the job.

2. *Task identity* is the degree to which an employee performs a whole identifiable task. For example, does the employee put together an entire television, or just place the screen in the set?

3. *Task significance* is an employee's perception of the importance of the task to others—the organization, the department, coworkers, and/or customers.

4. *Autonomy* is the degree to which the employee has discretion to make decisions in planning, organizing, and controlling the task performed.

5. *Feedback* is the extent to which employees find out how well they perform their tasks.

Note that if employees are not interested in enriching their jobs, the Job Characteristics Model will fail.

The first three of the core job characteristics lead collectively to the psychological state (in the second column) of "Experienced Meaningfulness of Work." In other words, if we provide the worker with a variety of things to do, so that they need multiple skills in order to accomplish their job; if they can identify what it is that they are accomplishing; and if they think that it is a significant endeavor, they will think that their work has meaning.

The core characteristic of *autonomy,* then, leads to the psychological state of "Experienced Responsibility for Outcomes." If we give a person the ability to make some of their decisions on their own, it is likely that they will feel more responsible for the outcome of those decisions that they make.

Finally, *feedback* leads to the psychological state of "Knowledge of Results." However, it is not the physical knowledge of the result itself that matters. Remember that the second-column characteristics are *psychological states!* So *knowledge of results* is the psychological feeling that we get from knowing the results that create the state of, for lack of a better term, *satisfaction* with the results of our work.

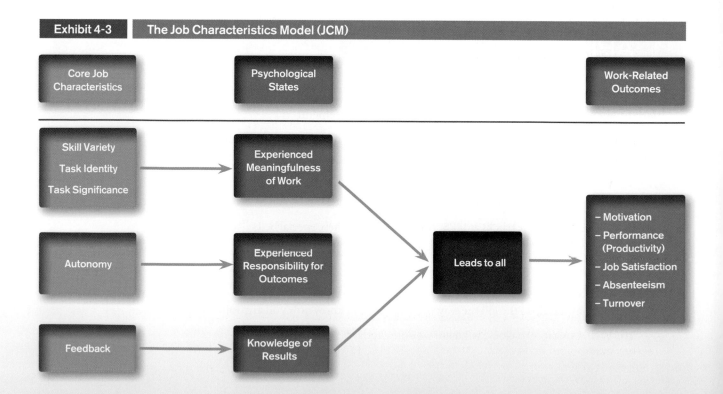

Exhibit 4-3   The Job Characteristics Model (JCM)

| Core Job Characteristics | Psychological States | Work-Related Outcomes |

Skill Variety
Task Identity
Task Significance → Experienced Meaningfulness of Work

Autonomy → Experienced Responsibility for Outcomes

Feedback → Knowledge of Results

Leads to all →

- Motivation
- Performance (Productivity)
- Job Satisfaction
- Absenteeism
- Turnover

All of the psychological states *collectively* lead to all of the outcomes noted on the right side of the diagram. It is an interesting list. If the job is designed correctly, the model says that the worker will quite possibly be more motivated, be more productive, and have higher job satisfaction while also being less likely to be absent or leave the organization.

Designing Motivational Jobs

If we choose to design motivational jobs, we have some tools that are available for our use. A variety of different job tools can be used in different circumstances for this purpose. Our tools include job simplification, job expansion, work teams, flexible work, and, as we discussed, the JCM. Each is discussed next.

LO 4.5

Describe the three major tools for motivational job design.

Job Simplification

The best advice golfer Tiger Woods ever got, and he gives it to you, is to simplify.[21] **Job simplification** is *the process of eliminating or combining tasks and/or changing the work sequence to improve performance.* Job simplification makes jobs more specialized. It is based on the organizing principle of division of labor and Frederick Taylor's scientific management. It's not about hustling to get more done; it's about using our brains.[22] A job is broken down into steps (flowchart), and employees analyze the steps to see if they can:

- *Eliminate.* Does the task, or parts of it, have to be done at all? Is the work actually used?[23] If not, don't waste time doing it.
- *Combine.* Doing similar things together often saves time. Combine similar processes,[24] but don't multitask because it hurts efficiency for complex thinking tasks.[25] Make one trip to the mail room at the end of the day instead of several throughout the day.
- *Change sequence.* Often a change in the order of doing things, or designing new systems, results in a lower total time.[26]

Video Link 4.3

What Motivates People?

Intel managers decided that it was not necessary to fill out a voucher for expenses amounting to less than $100. Thus, fewer vouchers were filled out, saving time and paperwork. GE developed its *WorkOut program* to improve and eliminate work, and Pizza Hut credits increases in store sales to job simplification.

In *some* cases work simplification may be motivational. If an individual is overwhelmed by their job, work simplification allows them to understand the job better, and therefore it becomes more motivational. In other words, we assist them with the task identity factor from the JCM, and potentially the task significance factor as well. In other cases, however, we may make the job less motivational if we simplify the work to the point where the worker becomes bored with their job. We have to strike the right balance.

Job Expansion

Job expansion is *the process of making jobs broader, with less repetition.* Jobs can be expanded through rotation, enlargement, and enrichment. Job expansion allows us to focus on making the work more interesting.[27]

Job Rotation

Job rotation involves performing different jobs in some sequence, each one for a set period of time. For example, employees making cars on a GM assembly line might rotate so that they get to work on different parts of the production process for a set period of time. John might work on the driver's side restraint system for a period of time and

WORK
APPLICATION 4-6

Give one example of how a job you hold or held can be simplified. Explain how the job can eliminate, combine, or change the sequence of tasks.

then move to working on installing the engine and transmission in another rotation. This can assist him even more with the concepts of skill variety, task identity, and task significance. It may also help him with the core characteristic of feedback depending on how we rotate jobs. If John rotates to a job that is affected by his previous work, he will see how his performance in one job affects another—hence he gets feedback on his earlier job performance. Many organizations develop conceptual skills in management trainees by rotating them through various departments. A few of the companies that have used job rotation are Bethlehem Steel, Target, Ford, Motorola, National Steel, and Prudential Insurance.

Related to job rotation is *cross-training*. With cross-training, employees learn to perform different jobs so they can fill in for those who are not on the job. As skills increase, employees become more valuable to the organization.

Job Enlargement

Job enlargement involves adding tasks to broaden variety. For example, rather than rotate jobs, we combined multiple tasks into one job when we made John the driver's side restraint system technician. AT&T, Chrysler, GM, IBM, and Maytag are a few of the companies that have used job enlargement. When we broaden the number of tasks for a worker, we are affecting the core job characteristic of skill variety, and may be helping with task identity and significance. Unfortunately, adding more *similar* tasks to an employee's job is often not a great motivator.

Job Enrichment

Job enrichment is the process of building motivators into the job itself to make it more interesting and challenging, frequently through increasing autonomy. Job enrichment works for jobs of low motivation potential and employees who are ready to be empowered to do meaningful work.[28] A simple way to enrich jobs is for the manager to delegate more authority to employees to make a job satisfying.[29] In this way, the employee becomes more autonomous (another core job characteristic) and can make some decisions that were reserved for management prior to enriching the job. An enriched job may also help the employee with the characteristics of task identity and significance in some cases. Maytag, Monsanto, Motorola, and Travelers Insurance have successfully used job enrichment.

WORK
APPLICATION 4-7

Give one example of how a job you hold or held can be expanded. Explain how the job can use job rotation, enlargement, or enrichment.

Work Teams

The traditional approach to job design has been to focus on individual jobs, but today work teams are the rage[30]—or, to be more accurate, teams are redesigning members' jobs. The purpose of team-based job design is to give the team an entire piece of work. When we provide the team with an entire piece of work, it is a form of job enrichment, and as a result, autonomy, task identity and task significance go up at a substantial rate. Two common types of work teams are integrated teams and self-managed teams.

Integrated Work Teams

Integrated work teams are assigned a number of tasks by a manager, and the team in turn gives specific assignments to members and is responsible for rotating jobs. Students commonly use this approach for group projects. Each member does part of the work, and someone pulls it all together. Unlike with self-managed teams, most members have no input into each other's work.

Self-Managed Work Teams

Self-managed work teams are assigned a goal, and the team plans, organizes, leads, and controls to achieve the goal. Usually, self-managed teams operate without a designated manager; the team is both manager and worker. Teams commonly elect their own members and evaluate each other's performance. W. L. Gore relies on small teams throughout the organization.[31]

WORK APPLICATION 4-8

Give one example of a work team where you work or have worked. Explain why and how it is either an integrated or a self-managed work team.

Applying the Job Characteristics Model

You should realize that job simplification, job expansion, and work teams can all be part of applying the Job Characteristics Model. The JCM helps provide a comprehensive system for designing and redesigning jobs to make them more motivational.[32] Exhibit 4-4 reviews the job design options we have discussed so far as they relate to JCM.

So, let's tie things together by redesigning a job using the JCM and see how we can make it more motivational. John is a worker in an automotive factory. He currently installs the driver's side seat. The job as it currently exists tends to be very boring, so John tends to get distracted. He ends up playing games with his tools and with coworkers, and as a result he may not do this job very well and in fact may waste material and supplies or possibly injure another employee.

We can look at this job and see that John does not have very much skill variety. He probably also doesn't identify very much with the end product—a car—if the only thing he does is install a seat. It is also likely that he doesn't see much significance in his work. He certainly has no autonomy and probably gets very little feedback.

Now let's redesign John's job and make him the "Driver's Side Restraint System Technician." John will now put in the driver's side seat track, the driver's side seat, the seat belt, and the driver's side airbag. What will this do to the five core job characteristics? Certainly John has more skill variety in his new job. It is likely that he'll be able to identify the end product, a car, better than he did before, because he is making a larger part of the overall product. He probably also feels that it's more significant that he do this job well, because he is responsible for the "restraint system" that will determine the safety of the driver. If we allow him to do these jobs in any order he sees fit, then he has greater autonomy. We will also give him feedback concerning how his cars have performed.

4-3 APPLYING THE CONCEPT

Designing Motivational Jobs

Identify which job design technique is exemplified in each statement.

a. job simplification
b. job rotation
c. job enlargement
d. job enrichment
e. work teams

_____ 11. McDonald's stopped requiring customers to sign a credit card slip.

_____ 12. "From now on, you don't have a manager. So share the job together."

_____ 13. "I know you are getting bored, so I'm going to add three new tasks to your job to make it less repetitive."

_____ 14. "I'd like you to learn how to run the cash register so that you can fill in for Juan while he is on vacation."

_____ 15. "I'm delegating a new task to you to make your job more challenging."

| Exhibit 4-4 | Job Design Options, Process, and the JCM |

Option	Process	Core Characteristics Affected (JCM)
Job simplification	Eliminate tasks Combine tasks Change task sequence	Task identity and significance
Job expansion	Rotate jobs Enlarge jobs Enrich jobs	Skill variety, task identity and significance (possibly feedback)
Work teams	Integrated Self-managed	Skill variety, task identity and significance, and feedback

John's supervisor came to him today and told him that one of the cars that he made last week was in an accident. The driver had run into a tree head-on and, as a result of the safety systems in the car, had walked away without serious injuries.

Let's explore John's psychological state. Because of the increased skill variety, task identity, and task significance, John feels that his work has *greater meaning*. He also feels a great sense of *responsibility* for the drivers of the cars that he has manufactured. And by receiving feedback, his *knowledge of the results* of this work shows that his work allowed this driver to survive a bad accident. What kind of outcomes do you think John has gained from this experience? John is almost certain to be more motivated to do his job; he's probably more productive; he is certainly likely to be more satisfied with his work; and he is likely to be absent less, and is not as likely to leave the organization. We have redesigned John's job to make it more motivational. That's the value of the JCM.

We, as managers, have to make decisions over time about what kind of job design process we are going to utilize. It is not always the motivational approach! Sometimes we may need to use the mechanistic job design approach, or the biological approach, or the perceptual/motor approach, or we may be able to use a combination of the above approaches. However, we need to make these decisions during the job design phase so that we understand what end result we are looking for.

Job Design for Flexibility

In addition to the primary tools for designing/redesigning specific jobs, we have another set of tools that can be used in the workplace to improve motivation of entire groups of jobs or maybe even the entire workforce.[33] These tools include flextime, job sharing, telecommuting, and compressed workweeks.[34]

Flextime allows us to provide workers with a flexible set of work hours. We usually create a set of core hours where everyone is at work, and then a set of flex hours where people can be at work or can take that time off. The individual has the opportunity to modify their schedule within the flextime as long as they complete a set number of hours per day/week at work. Flextime has the potential to motivate workers because it allows them much greater autonomy over their schedule.

In *job sharing* we allow two (or more) people to share one whole job, including the workload and any benefits that are associated with that job. Job sharing again allows greater autonomy in the individual's job.

Telecommuting allows workers to work from a location other than the corporate office, usually from home. Telecommuting is another form of autonomy, but we need to make sure that the telecommuter gets good feedback concerning their work, since this is one of the major drawbacks to telecommuting.[35]

Finally, a *compressed workweek* means that we take the normal five-day, 40-hour workweek and compress it down to less than five days. One common example would be a four-day, 10-hour-per-day workweek.

Each of these additional tools allows us to design greater flexibility into our organization in one way or another. As a result, in many cases we can improve both productivity and job satisfaction and in turn lower rates of absenteeism and turnover—a win-win for the organization and the employee within it.

Job Design Is Country Specific

One more thing that we need to make clear in this major section of our text is that job design varies significantly from one country to another as well as from one company to another. While job design in the United States has focused more on designing motivational jobs over the past several years, in many other countries mechanistic job design is still the dominant method. It may come down to the primary types of work being done within different country environments. For instance, if many of the jobs in one country are basic manufacturing or routine service work such as a tech assistance call center, those jobs may be designed in a very mechanistic manner. If, however, jobs in another country tend to be focused more on knowledge creation and innovation, those jobs would almost certainly be designed to be more motivational to that particular workforce.

Alternately, differences may be associated with the cultural differences between countries. For instance, in a collectivist culture, job designs that isolate the individual and their actions (such as mechanistic designs) might not work as well as methods that encourage collaboration (like motivational design).[36] Or it may be for other reasons entirely. Remember, though, that what is motivational as a job design in one country—for example, personal autonomy in the United States—may be absolutely demotivational in another country, such as China or Slovenia (two highly collectivist cultures). Globalization also leads to more competition and the need for using the latest technology, which requires increasing skill requirements and ongoing job redesigning.[37]

HR Forecasting

HR forecasting and labor requirements planning are at the core of our ability to analyze future employment needs for our organizations.[38] Through the process of forecasting future labor requirements we will make determinations, based on both quantitative and qualitative information, of what types of jobs and what number of each type we will need to fill over a particular period of time. If we fail to get it right, we won't get the right people in place at the right time when they are needed and will always be chasing voluntary and involuntary turnover, which causes lower organizational productivity. **HR forecasting** *identifies the estimated supply and demand for the different types of human resources in the organization over some future period, based on analysis of past and present demand.*

Before we get into the forecasting process, we need to understand a couple of terms. You always need to make sure that in any analytical process you use *valid* and *reliable* measures to the best of your ability. If you don't, then your results will always be suspect and will generally be of very little value. So what do these terms mean?

Reliability: Basically, reliability identifies how consistent a particular measure is. In other words, does the measure give a similar result every time it is used, or when it is used by more than one person? If it does, then it is probably reliable. For instance, if I give a

WORK
APPLICATION 4-9

Give one example of how an organization, preferably one you work or have worked for, uses any of the flexible job design tools. State which one is used, explain how it is implemented, and discuss how it affects employee motivation.

SHRM

Guide – K:2
Planning (forecasting requirements and availabilities, gap analysis, action planning, core/flexible workforce)

SHRM

Guide – C:7
HR planning (skill inventories and supply/demand forecasting)

test of comprehension on a set of terms, after teaching those terms in the same manner to several groups of third graders, and the results in each group are similar, then the test is most likely reliable.

Validity: Validity is whether or not we measured what we thought we measured. It seems obvious to us what we are measuring, but we sometimes make mistakes. A good example is measuring job satisfaction. We might give our employees a survey concerning their job satisfaction and get high results. We might not, however, have done the survey anonymously. As a result of the overt nature of the survey, our workers all told us that they were highly satisfied because they might have thought that if we saw that they were disgruntled we would want to fire them. In this case our measure wasn't valid, because we actually measured the level of concern our workers have for the company's honesty and reasons for the survey when we meant to measure their real satisfaction level with their work.

Also, a measure can be reliable but not valid, but it can't be valid if it is not reliable. For example, if I step on my low-quality home scale and weigh 175 pounds, get off and on again several times, and weigh 175 every time, the scale is reliable. However, if I go to a high-quality scale at the doctor's office and weigh 180 repeatedly, my home scale is reliable, but it is not valid. So, remember validity and reliability as you decide on the tools that you are going to use in the forecasting process.

Forecasting Methods

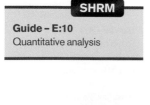

SHRM

Guide – E:13
Forecasting

LO 4.6

Discuss the three most common quantitative HR forecasting methods.

SHRM

Guide – E:10
Quantitative analysis

SHRM

Guide – H:12
Trends and forecasting in HR

SHRM

Guide – E:5
Trend and ratio analysis projections

Forecasting labor requirements is generally completed in two distinct steps. First we complete a quantitative analysis of our workforce using one or more of several methods, and then we adjust the results of the quantitative analysis using qualitative methods. Both of these analyses have value to the organization. The value of quantitative data should be obvious to you by this point in your business education, but qualitative analyses are also important. There is no match for years of expertise when analyzing situations that are unique or different from what has happened in our business environment in the past, and qualitative analysis looks at the differences between the "historical" and the "now." Let's take a little closer look at each type.

Quantitative Forecasting

A **quantitative forecast** utilizes mathematics to forecast future events based on historical data. The three most common quantitative methods for forecasting labor demand are trend analysis, ratio analysis, and regression analysis.[39] Let's take a quick look at each method in Exhibit 4-5, followed by a discussion of each.

Trend analysis is *a process of reviewing historical items such as revenues, and relating those changes to some business factor to form a predictive chart.* For example, we could look at historical revenues and relate those revenue volumes to the number of people in the organization for each year, or, alternatively, we could analyze historical production levels and relate those levels to the number of people used to produce that amount of work. Either of these would give us a historical trend that we could then extend into the future to predict the number of people that would be required for a particular sales or production level.[40] Take a look at the figures in Exhibit 4-5 for an example. **Ratio analysis** is *the process of reviewing historical data and calculating specific proportions between a business factor (such as production) and the number of employees needed.* It generally gives us very similar results to trend analysis, but should be a bit more precise because we are computing an exact value for the ratio. Again, take a look at Exhibit 4-5.

Regression analysis is *a statistical technique that identifies the relationship between a series of variable data points for use in forecasting future variables.* We can use statistical software (most HRISs include this ability) to create the regression diagram. All we would have to do in our example from Exhibit 4-5 is provide the data points for employees and

Exhibit 4-5	Quantitative Forecasting Analysis

Video Link 4.4

Forecasting for New and Vacant Positions

Trend analysis:

Historical data:	2006	2007	2008	2009	2010
Revenues ($MM):	27.84	29.92	25.48	26.3	30.12
Total # of employees:	225	244	215	214	240

We then estimate the number of employees needed based on the historical trend. In this case, how many total employees would you say you would need if we expect 2011 revenues to be $31.8 million? You likely said something around 250 people, because you looked at the historical trend.

Ratio analysis:

Historical data:	2006	2007	2008	2009	2010
Production levels ($MM):	18.62	20.58	17.44	17.23	19.16
Avg. # production workers/yr:	62	71	61	55	61
$ Production/worker (000s)	300	290	286	313	314

The average production per worker for the five years listed would be just under $301,000, so $301,000:worker is our ratio. If we expect production requirements to be $20.2MM in 2011, we could divide $20,200,000 by $301,000, and we would get approximately 67 production workers as an expected complement for 2011. If we had 61 workers at the end of 2010, we would need to recruit six more for 2011.

Regression analysis:

A regression diagram of all of the companies in our industry by year for the past 10 years, plotted for number of employees on the x-axis and revenues on the y-axis, might look like this:

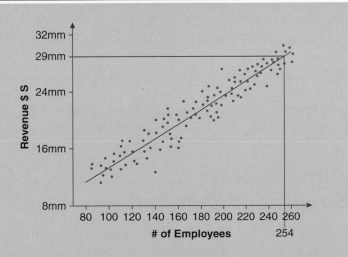

Based on this diagram, if we were expecting to have revenues of $29MM next year, we would need approximately 254 employees.

revenues for each company and each year. The software would calculate and draw the regression line for us. Then it is just a process of looking at the values along the line and applying them to your company's situation in a given year.

Qualitative Forecasting

Qualitative forecasting *uses nonquantitative methods to forecast the future, usually based on the knowledge of a pool of experts in a subject or an industry.* We provide our group of experts with the quantitative predictions that we have created and ask for their assessment of the data, taking into account differences in circumstances within our industry and the general economic climate when comparing the present situation with the historical environment on which the quantitative evaluations are based. The experts will generally come to a consensus about how to adjust the quantitative data for today's environment.

We need to use both quantitative and qualitative analysis to get good forecasts for the future needs of the organization and its human resources.[41] This is because quantitative analysis is based solely on historical data and not on the current business environment, and sometimes situations will occur for which there is no historical precedent—for example, the massive banking and financial services failures of 2008 and 2009. We look at both forecasting methods and identify whether we expect to have a surplus or a shortage of people in the organization over the next few years. More likely we will find that we will have a surplus of some types of people while we have a shortage of others. Regardless of the situation, once we know what to expect we can set up procedures to correct the expected problem.

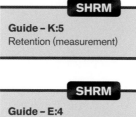

SHRM
Guide – E:12
Analyzing and interpreting metrics

Measuring Absenteeism and Turnover

SHRM
Guide – K:5
Retention (measurement)

SHRM
Guide – E:4
Measuring turnover

SHRM
Guide – E:3
Measuring absenteeism

As we go through the process of forecasting HR needs for the future, we can't lose sight of the fact that we will have some voluntary turnover in addition to any changing personnel needs in the organization. No matter how satisfied our workforce is, we will have some people leave the organization voluntarily—for many different reasons. We will also have some involuntary turnover due to the fact that some people in the organization just can't seem to figure out what is necessary to be successful in their individual jobs, and we have to terminate their employment.

We also have to account for the need for extra employees to cover for hours that are missed within the company due to absenteeism. When individuals miss work, we have to have that job done somehow. We may hire temporary workers, or may redistribute work to other individuals; we may even have an "office pool" of workers available to cover for missing employees, but no matter how we do it we have to cover the hours missed due to absence. As a result of these voluntary absences from work (either permanent or temporary), we have to adjust employment numbers again to get valid and reliable numbers for our future workforce. See Exhibit 4-6 to learn how to calculate absenteeism and turnover.

Reconciling Internal Labor Supply and Demand

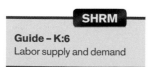

SHRM
Guide – K:6
Labor supply and demand

After completion of the labor requirements planning process, where we create forecasts of our people needs, we end up with either a shortage or a surplus of people in each type of job in the organization. Job supply and demand affect the frequency with which people leave their jobs, and high turnover negatively affects performance.[42] Therefore, balancing our supply and demand for labor affects our firm's productivity.

We have to figure out how to make supply match up with our expected demand. In careers today, we are beginning to experience a major shortage of qualified people able to

Exhibit 4-6	Measuring Absenteeism and Turnover

Absenteeism	
$\dfrac{\text{No. of employees absent}}{\text{Total no. of employees}}$	Percentage or ratio of employees not at work for a specified period of time. Other workers, or temps, often need to do their work.
$\dfrac{10}{100} = 10\%$ or 10:100 ratio	So 1 out of every 10 employees is absent—1:10

Turnover	
$\dfrac{\text{No. of employees leaving}}{\text{Total no. of employees}}$	Percentage or ratio of employees leaving the organization during a specified period of time. They often need to be replaced with new employees.
$\dfrac{14}{100} = 14\%$ or 14:100 ratio	So about 1 out of every 7 (7.14) leaves the company—1:7

4-4 APPLYING THE CONCEPT

Quantitative Methods

Complete each problem below.

_____ 16. Turn to Exhibit 4-5 ("Trend analysis"). Assume that in 2012 you expect revenues to be $35MM. Around how many employees will you need?

a. 210 b. 230 c. 250 d. 270

_____ 17. Turn to Exhibit 4-5 ("Ratio analysis"). Assume that in 2012 you expect the production level to increase to $22MM. Around how many employees will you need, and how many do you need to add to last year's number?

a. 72/5 b. 73/6 c. 74/7 d. 75/9

_____ 18. Turn to Exhibit 4-5 ("Regression analysis"). Assume that in 2012 you expect a recession and revenues to drop to $24MM. Around how many employees will you need?

a. 160 b. 180 c. 210 d. 230

_____ 19. You have 253 employees. Over the past year, there were 26 absences. What is the approximate percentage and ratio of absenteeism?

a. 9.7%, 1:10 b. 10%, 1:10 c. 10%, 1:100 d. 12%, 1:12

_____ 20. You have 1,215 employees. Over the past year, 298 left the firm. What is the approximate percentage and ratio of turnover?

a. 4%, 1:20 b. 40%, 4:10 c. 23%, 23:100 d. 25%, 1:4

fill our jobs. There are many books and articles written on this subject, and they all agree that this shortage of skilled workers will continue to get worse long before it will get better.[43] If all or most of our jobs utilize this type of skilled workforce, we need to understand that it will be increasingly difficult to fill outstanding openings.

However, in other areas, we are experiencing a large surplus of available workers. Most of these jobs tend to require less skill, and many are being replaced by computer-guided equipment or other time-saving and labor-saving tools. If our business works more with less-skilled individuals, we may have a continuing surplus of workers.

Regardless of whether we have a shortage or a surplus of people, we have to make an attempt to get the right numbers of people with the right skill sets into our organization at the right time. What are the options when faced with a shortage of personnel? What options do we have if we have a surplus? What we decide to do will have as much to do with our strategy and our business philosophy and values as it does with the facts of the situation. Some organization will work *very* hard to avoid layoffs of any kind because of their philosophy of caring for their employees. In others, if there is a surplus of people, the first thing they will do is announce and carry out a layoff because it is the most expedient thing to do. What are our options, and how does each of those options affect the company and its workforce? Let's look at this subject next.

Options for a Labor Surplus

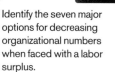

LO 4.7

Identify the seven major options for decreasing organizational numbers when faced with a labor surplus.

If we are in a position where we are predicting a surplus of people going into the future, what can we do about it? We can't usually just hang on to people who aren't needed in the organization. This is too expensive. However, we don't necessarily have to fire a large number of employees either. How we handle the situation will depend on how soon we are able to predict that there will be a surplus, and it will depend on our strategy, values, and philosophy as noted above.

Downsizing and Layoffs

Our first option may be a layoff, especially if we have large numbers of people in surplus. A **layoff** is *a process of terminating a group of employees, usually due to some business downturn or perhaps a technological change, with intent to improve organizational efficiency and effectiveness.* Layoffs go by many names today (downsizing, rightsizing, downscaling, cutback, etc.), but the result is still the same—we are terminating the employment of a reasonably large number of people. Layoffs don't occur person by person! If you are terminating one person, that is typically a disciplinary process, and you should go through the required due process steps to justify that termination. We will discuss how to discipline in Chapter 9. In a layoff, however, we are generally allowed to terminate the employment of a group of individuals with very little advance warning and usually don't have to provide any disciplinary or other justification for why we are doing so. In a few situations we will have to comply with the Worker Adjustment and Retraining Notification (WARN) Act, which we will discuss in some detail in Chapter 10, but other than that we have few documentation needs. We *do* have to document the method by which we determined who should be in the layoff, and would be wise not to be arbitrary in our selection of individuals, but again the requirements are minimal unless there is a union contract that restricts layoffs in some way. We will discuss unions and collective bargaining in Chapter 10.

SHRM

Guide – K:1
Downsizing/rightsizing

What are the business advantages to a layoff? The most satisfying result for management is that the resulting savings are immediately added to the bottom-line corporate performance. In other words, if I lay off people whose salaries total a million dollars, then that million dollars is not spent—it becomes profit or minimized losses, assuming everything else is held constant! This is the reason that companies have tended to overuse layoffs. In some cases, they are trying to dress up the financial statements for investors or the investment community, to make the company look better than it really is. However, investors are starting to catch on to this type of trick, so it isn't working as well as it used to.

Although temporarily improving the financials is probably a shortsighted viewpoint, it is something that the executive frequently thinks about when considering a layoff. Why is the view shortsighted? Because layoffs create all kinds of potential problems for the organization, including lower employee morale and job satisfaction, and a corporate culture of "lying low," or not standing out in any way, so that you don't get caught up in the next downsizing. Alternatively, the remaining employees may have "survivor guilt" where they ask things like "Why Bill? He has a family to feed" and similar questions. So we end up with a lot of stress issues in layoffs that create problems for the organization.

Historically, companies have probably been too fast to use downsizings or layoffs.[44] In the first place, if you are forecasting correctly, you should not have to do layoffs very often. The only reason that you would be in this position is if you hadn't done your job in forecasting the HR needs of the company in the past. In most cases, you should be able to see that you are going to have a surplus in the near future and use some of the other tools that cause less stress and suffering instead. So layoffs are usually performed because HR and the other management in the firm failed to do their jobs. However, recessions can be difficult to forecast, especially how much your sales may drop, and projecting sales is not part of HRM.

An interesting note is in order here, though. There is some pretty good evidence that companies typically do worse financially after a large-scale layoff than they did before. Almost all of the layoff research supports this.[45] One problem is losing good employees not only through the layoff, but good employees may leave when they fear a layoff is coming; the poor workers usually can't get another job anyway, so they stay. It ends up that the layoffs cost more money than they save in many cases. The organization might lay off too many people, or could remove the wrong people and cause greater problems in the organization as a result. So, layoffs are not a cure-all. Sometimes they need to be used, but it will be an unusual case when a layoff is going to be valuable to the organization over the long term.

Pay Reduction, Work Sharing, Natural Attrition, Hiring Freeze, Retraining, and Transfer Options

Another option for mitigating a labor surplus is a *pay reduction* for all or part of the workforce. In many cases, pay reductions may be a valid option for a company. Supply and demand for various types of labor drive the market value of the people who provide that labor. If there is an oversupply of people in a particular field (today, many unskilled and semiskilled positions have oversupplies of people available) or if new technology has made the job less difficult, then those employees may not be worth as much as they were five or 10 years ago. In other cases, economic conditions may demand a cut in organizational expenses, and labor is the biggest organizational expense in many companies. Again, this option can be accomplished fairly quickly, but it certainly is unlikely to improve employee morale or job satisfaction.

A third option for lowering labor costs without terminating employees is some form of *work sharing* arrangement. We may cut the hours available to each worker because fewer jobs are available in the company, but instead of cutting workers we split one job up among more than one worker. This way nobody is laid off, but all of the workers suffer to some extent because of a decrease in income. Some companies would much rather go to a work sharing arrangement than terminate employees because it seems to be fairer to all of their employees, and their corporate philosophy and values may indicate that fairness is a critical concept to them.[46] Everyone in the organization suffers equally as a result of this type of policy. There is certainly still some suffering in the workforce due to a loss in disposable income, but nobody loses their entire paycheck. Plus, when the firm comes out of a recession, it already has the skilled workers to meet the increase in business.

Next, we have the option in some cases to allow *natural attrition* to lower organizational numbers without the need for a layoff of pay reduction. We can just allow positions to stay unfilled as turnover occurs. This option, along with the slightly more stringent option of a *hiring freeze*, causes our number of employees to drop slowly so they can't be used in a situation where speed in reducing expenses is critical, but if we have done our job in the forecasting process, we may have enough time for these options to work for us without massive stress on our workforce.

Retraining and transferring workers from one job to another may be an option in some circumstances. However, this option will only work if we have too many employees in one type of job and too few in another. If there are no positions where we have a shortage, retraining workers will do no good. Here again, the process is a little slow due to the fact that the person has to be retrained in a new field. But if we have a good worker who is willing to try a new job, and a position is available, this can allow us to retain that good employee into the future.

Early Retirement

LO 4.8

Discuss the problems that need to be considered in offering an early retirement program.

The last option that we will discuss here is *early retirement*. Early retirement can be a valuable option in some cases. However, there can be many pitfalls to using early retirement to reduce an organization's workforce. In an early retirement offer, employees are given the choice of leaving the company before they would ordinarily do so (due to reaching the "normal" retirement age of 65, for instance), and in exchange for leaving the employee will receive benefits of some type from the organization.

There are some good reasons to use early retirement as an option to reduce a surplus, but it is a slow method of getting rid of people, and we have to be careful in planning for and offering early retirements. Why do we have to be careful? Problems in early retirement include:

- Too many people may take our early retirement offer. If we make the early retirement offer too good, we may have more people take it than we expected and end up with a shortage of people. Then we will incur additional costs in recruiting and hiring new people because of the newly created shortage.

- Too few may take the offer. What happens if too few people take it? You may have to consider offering a sweetened deal to the rest of the workforce. You really want to avoid this situation. Why? Let's look at an example. Five years ago we offered an early retirement package to our workforce, and the first package wasn't very good, so not too many people took it. So, we decided that we needed to have more people retire. As a result, we offered a better deal, and a second group took that deal, but it was still not enough. Finally, we offered a very good deal, and enough took it that we got the number of retirees that we needed. Now, we come to the present, and we have to reduce the number of people again. What is going to happen when we offer an early retirement deal this time? It's quite possible that nobody is going to take it because they "know" that a better deal is going to come after this one, because that is what happened last time. So if we made multiple offers and sweetened each offer in the past, that is what our employees will expect to happen again.

- The wrong types of people may take the offer. One of the issues with early retirement is that our best people might take the offer and then immediately go to work for a competitor. The best people can usually find work easily. Conversely, the people who are borderline in their capabilities or motivation may be the ones who are afraid that if they take our early retirement offer, they won't be able to find another job. So we may end up losing our good people and keeping our worst performers!

- People may perceive that they are being forced out. We absolutely cannot push people to take an offer of early retirement. Generally, the individuals who would be eligible for early retirement fall within the age group protected by the ADEA (discussed in Chapter 3)—those 40 years of age and older. If there is pressure on these individuals to take the offer, we could be confronted with an EEOC lawsuit for age discrimination.

Generally, if we are going to offer an early retirement option, we have to do some specific things. If we provide an early retirement option, we have to offer it to all people in a particular employee category. For instance, all people in a department that is overloaded, or a division that is overstaffed, or a particular plant within the company would be reasonable options. You can't select individuals who happen to be in a particular category and not offer it to other employees in the same category. If you only offer it to select people, you might create the possibility of legal actions (such as age discrimination complaints if you pick only those older employees). So you need to allow everyone in a category the option for early retirement if you are going to offer it to any. Age *can* be a criterion, but you have to be absolutely sure that you don't push people to accept the offer if you make age a factor.

Another thing that you are required to do is allow people a "reasonable period of time" to accept or not accept the offer. What is a reasonable period of time? Generally, the EEOC and court case history show that if you offer it for about 45–60 days, it is probably a reasonable period of time. If you don't give the employee time to consider their options, it is probably not reasonable. So we have to look at the time frame for acceptance.

LO 4.9

Identify the seven major options for overcoming a labor shortage.

Options for a Labor Shortage

What if our forecasts produce an expected shortage? We need to find some new people. We have some options here too. What we need to look at here is how fast we can solve the problem, but we also want to look at how quickly we can lower our number of employees again if we need to. In other words, how quickly can we reduce numbers in the future if we end up with too many people? The best options here are methods that are really fast in solving the shortage but also can be taken back really quickly if a surplus of employees starts to take form.

In the *surplus* situation discussed in the last section, we want to use the options that we discussed from the bottom up—starting with things like early retirements and attrition, because they are the least disruptive to the workforce and allow us to maintain motivation and job satisfaction levels much better than things like layoffs and pay reductions. Here, though, we want to work from the first options down to the bottom, starting with things like overtime and working down the list as we have to, because again we want the smallest disruption to our workforce.

Overtime

So what is our first option—the quickest and easiest way to fix a personnel shortage? *Overtime*—we can just ask our employees (or force them) to work overtime. Whoa! Can we really force you to work overtime? The answer is yes. No federal law limits the option to require

When there is too much work for the current employees, overtime, temporary, and contract workers can help get the job done.

you to work a "reasonable amount" of overtime if you are an employee of the organization.[47] So, overtime is a very quick method of resolving an employee shortage—we can do it immediately. It's as simple as "We are behind on an order; you need to stay overtime." Tomorrow, when we have finished the order and can go back to a normal schedule, "We are done. Go home at the end of the workday." Overtime is our first and best option until we get to the point where we are starting to stress our people too much because the overtime becomes excessive. When we start to see stress indicators go up, we know that we need to use another method because we know that when stress levels get too high the employee's work will suffer, and we don't want poor work being done. So, if we start to see too much stress, we need to do something else to relieve our personnel shortage, so what other options do we have?

Temporary or Contract Workers

We can frequently use *temporary or contract workers* to overcome a short-term shortage. Since the recession of 2008, many employers are reluctant to hire full-time employees, so many firms are using independent contractors who are not legally employed by the firm. At more than 7% of the workforce, contractors are an important and growing segment of the U.S. population and are increasingly prevalent throughout the developed world.[48]

SHRM

Guide – G:1
Employment relationship
(employees, contractors,
and temporary workers)

Temporary and contract workers are a quick method of overcoming a worker shortage. Well, it's quick if you are hiring someone for general duties. However, if you need someone with a specific high-level skill set, it might take awhile to find a temp worker. For instance, if you need a temporary CEO (yes, they are available!), it might take awhile to find one. There are companies that specialize in providing temporary executive help, including CEOs. But in general this is easy to take back, isn't it? When we no longer need the temporary worker, we just release them back to the temp agency. If we are using contract workers, we allow the contract to lapse in order to release the worker.

However, there are some common problems with temporary and contract workers. First, they have little or no loyalty to you and your organization. And, what are they going to be doing when they are not working for you? They are working for someone else, and that someone else is usually your competition, and the temporary or contract worker who was in your office last week may tell your competitors how you do things, which might help your competitors in some way. So, loyalty to your organization is a problem. What other problems are there?

Temporary and contract workers may not know the job, and they generally don't know the company as well as our permanent workers. They are also frequently not very motivated to work for you because they know that they aren't staying. There can also sometimes be a clash between temp workers and permanent employees. Why? There are a couple of reasons. One is that the permanent workers may think that the temp is trying to take their job. Another is that, if we have had a layoff in the fairly recent past, the permanent worker will resent the temp for taking the job that a friend of the permanent worker used to have.

In addition to the basic problems of loyalty, knowledge of the company and job, and relationships with coworkers, temps can also create legal problems for the organization. If an organization classifies a worker as temporary or contingent and the organization exerts significant control over the actions of that worker, they can be judged guilty of misclassification of the worker as a temporary employee. What does that mean to the employer? It means that the government can penalize them for not withholding employment taxes on the employee. Microsoft had to pay almost $100 million to about 10,000 workers that it had classified as temporary in 2005, and a transportation company was charged $319 million in unpaid employment taxes and penalties in 2007 because it misclassified drivers as contract workers.[49] So, you can see that it can be very expensive to call someone a temporary or contract worker if they are actually working as an employee of the company. These are just a few of the problems with temp workers. However, it is a fast way to overcome a shortage, and it is highly revocable.

Retrain Workers, Outsourcing, or Turnover Reduction

The next options are a bit slower. We can *retrain workers*, but if we retrain people it isn't fast, is it? This option is especially useful if we have a surplus of employees somewhere else. But at least they know the company and they know the work procedures better than someone off the street, so this can be a good option in some cases. It is moderately fast and generally easy to revoke, because the worker is still trained to do their old job.

Outsourcing may be another option. We can outsource a whole function that we currently do in-house to someone outside the organization.[50] For instance, we might outsource all of our computer programming jobs to an outsourcing company that specializes in computer programming. This option is moderately fast, but not extremely fast. Why not? Well, we have to first find a company that can do the job, research the company, negotiate with them, come up with a contract, and then, finally, get them to do the work. It's not going to take forever, but it will probably take a few months. It is also moderately revocable. Why is it only moderately revocable? Because we generally have to create a contract with a specific time period during which we are required to use the services of the outsourcer. Plus, we are now a customer, and we may not get the quick attention that we would from our own in-house operations. The general statement is "Do what you do best, and outsource the rest."

Our next option would be *turnover reduction*. If fewer people voluntarily leave the organization than we had predicted, we can reduce a projected shortage. But, how can we reduce turnover?

There are many ways to reduce turnover. We can increase pay, or do other things that may cause our workforce to become more satisfied. We can shorten work hours (minimally), make benefits packages better, or maybe make their schedule a little better. As discussed, we can use job design flexibility. Any of these things might cause turnover to go down. But this won't happen overnight, because it takes awhile to change people's opinions of the organization. It's going to take awhile to get employee opinion to the point where they aren't willing to leave, so it's a fairly slow method.

We will also probably have trouble if we decide we want to allow turnover to increase again later, perhaps because we are predicting a surplus of workers at that point in time. We can take back some of the above benefits that caused turnover to go down, and over time it will move back up, but we don't want to (in fact, may not be *able* to) take these things back all at once, because we may create some severe problems in motivation and job satisfaction. So this option is very difficult to take back later.

New Hires and Technological Innovation

Our next option is to *hire new employees*. But this option takes awhile, doesn't it? We have to go through a long process of analyzing the job and updating its description, finding out what skills are needed, and then going out and recruiting people. Once we have a pool of recruits, we can select them, train them, and get them up to speed and into the job. We can see that this is a slow method of solving a shortage. It is also not easy to take back. Once we hire new employees and they are beyond their probationary period, it is hard to get rid of them other than for reasons of just cause (we will discuss this concept in Chapter 9). Thus, the trend to using more temporary or contract workers continues.[51]

Finally, we may be able to overcome a shortage of personnel through *technological innovation*. In other words, we may be able to create machinery that can do the job of a human being. But again, this is a slow process. We can't create new equipment and install it and make it operational overnight, can we? If we create a group of robots that are capable

SHRM

Guide – C:8
Work management (work processes and outsourcing)

of assembling our product, we are not going to stop using them and hire a bunch of new assembly workers again, are we? So, it is really not revocable at all once the equipment has been created and installed.

SHRM

Guide – K:7
Succession planning
(workforce planning)

Video Link 4.5

Saving the Day Using
Succession Planning

SHRM

Guide – D:15
Succession planning

Succession Planning

Succession planning is a significant issue in many different situations.[52] Larger organizations need to plan for smooth transitions from one executive and other valuable worker to another in order to minimize disruption in the organization's work. Family businesses are also very concerned with the process of succession, usually from one generation of the family to the next. Even in smaller, nonfamily companies, succession helps the organization survive and succeed over the long term as the owner/founder of the business decides to retire or move on to other businesses. Why are we talking about succession planning at this point? Planning for succession is just another type of forecasting. It is a problem of supply and demand. Do we expect to have a shortage or a surplus of managerial and other valuable candidates over a particular period of time? We know that managers and executives will move through the organization at a certain pace over time, and we have the ability to plan, at least to some extent, for that movement so that we have the people in place to move into the vacated positions as the incumbent manager/executive moves on to other jobs or moves into retirement.

Succession planning is also critical to organizational development over time. As the organization grows and changes, we have to be able to provide the leadership to allow it to succeed. The forecasting process that we use in planning for other human resource needs can also be used to make predictions for leadership requirements over the forecasted time period. Using this forecast information allows us to either prepare new leaders within the company to take on those positions, or alternatively go out and recruit the people that we need in order to ensure smooth transitions in organizational leadership over time.

Trends and Issues in HRM

In this chapter's trends and issues, we will again discuss current questions and problems in organizational HRM. First, how can organizations "think sustainability" in their work flow analysis and job design processes? After that, we will briefly discuss the topic of diversity and job design. Our third and final topic in this chapter will explore the issue of flexibility in job design, especially in high-technology and entrepreneurial organizations.

Work Flows and Job Design for Sustainability

ESR

As in many other areas of business today, we can frequently incorporate sustainability initiatives into our work design processes that will help us to mitigate our effect on our environment as well as saving the organization time and money. How can this happen? First, recall the work flow process. We noted early in this chapter that work flows are designed around the expected end results. Based on the end result, we design the work processes that will be performed and identify the tools, equipment, and human resources that will be used to complete the processes. If we design the work processes with sustainability in mind, we can frequently identify process changes that will lower our impact on critical natural resources. We may be able to use less water in a cooling operation, for instance, by using a more open design that allows for radiational cooling of parts being produced instead of using water to cool those same parts. If we think about sustainability in the work flow analysis and design process, we find many opportunities to lower our effect on the world's resources.

We can also utilize some of our job design options to help with conservation of resources in our organizations. Earlier we discussed options for work including telecommuting, compressed workweeks, and flextime opportunities. Each of these options can lower the need for our workers to commute to and from work.[53] Telecommuting may be able to completely eliminate putting another car on the road at rush hour, but compressed workweeks and flextime can both also lower the number of trips our employees have to make to and from work in a given week/month/year. Each of these options not only minimizes wasted time for the individual; it also lowers the use of fuel for their cars or whatever other conveyances they would use for their commute.

In addition to designing a specific job, we may also be able to lower our effect on the environment by using a fairly recent innovation in the use of office space called "hoteling."[54] Hoteling is *where the organization has less office space than it would in a traditional office arrangement (where everyone has an assigned space) and uses a software program that allows employees to "reserve" office space for particular parts of the workweek when they will need it.* At other times, that same office space will be available to other employees for their use. Hoteling can lower the total amount of office space that we need in an average business, and as a result lower the usage of all of the common services that are needed for that office space such as electricity, heating and air conditioning, water for bathroom facilities, overall energy consumption, and other items. This in turn lowers our effect on the environment.

So if we think about the work flows and processes that have to occur in our organization, we can frequently design changes to those processes that will minimize our use of precious environmental resources. And as a bonus, we can also save money for the organization because we don't use resources that were historically wasted anyway. A win-win situation if there ever was one!

Video Link 4.6
Trends and Issues in HRM

Diversity and Job Design

Throughout the world, there is growing diversity of the labor force.[55] Thus, the next area of discussion for this chapter is the requirement to account for diversity of the workforce in the job design process. More and more, the changing concept of jobs and the requirement for flexibility in the organizational workforce have created challenges to job design. This is on top of the fact that the workforce itself is changing at a rapid rate, creating significant issues in designing jobs that match both the organization's needs and the character and preferred work styles of the workforce.[56]

One recent examination of the job design process looked at whether tasks should be designed to fit preexisting teams, called "design for diversity," or whether teams should be designed based on the requirements of organizational tasks, called "diversity for design."[57] The conclusion, as with most management processes, is "it depends." You have to understand how teams allocate tasks to their membership, how task requirements shape selection of the team's members, and what tenure and continuity characteristics exist in the team. In other words, based on who is selected into the team, who gets what tasks, and how long the team has been together and how it adds and deletes members, the diversity of the team will need to be different. Once you understand these issues, you have at least some of the tools necessary to figure out how diverse to make an organizational team.

The bottom line here is that companies will continue to have to fit people into jobs that have already been designed (with the understanding that the job might need to be modified minimally to account for differences in job incumbent), because organizations are, after all, designed to accomplish certain tasks. If they can't accomplish those tasks, then they will not continue to succeed as viable businesses. Therefore, job design is not going away. It is in fact becoming more critical to "get it right."

High-Velocity and Entrepreneurial Organizations Need Flexibility in Job Design

We noted earlier in the chapter that organic structures need more flexibility with less formal job descriptions focusing on job specification of the types of people we need to hire.

In more mechanistic, stable, traditional, and bureaucratic organizations, task-based job analysis would usually be the norm. We would use competency-based job analysis in organic organizations. So, applying these concepts to entrepreneurial and high-velocity organizations (organic organizations whose company and environment are rapidly and constantly changing), we would conclude that in such organization we have to design flexibility in the business.

Entrepreneurial and high-velocity organizations need such flexibility precisely because of the rapid pace of change that each organization has to participate in if they want to survive and succeed. If we create rigid structures in such businesses, the structure can't allow the employees to adapt to their environment in a timely manner, and if they can't adapt, they can't compete over the long term. A recent researcher noted that employees and entrepreneurs "work hardest, and best, when they perceive what they do as meaningful . . . this often involves providing them with jobs offering high levels of autonomy, task significance, task identity, and other key job characteristics"[58] (you will recall these factors from the Job Characteristics Model earlier in this chapter). So job descriptions and job design will necessarily have to be more fluid and adaptable in these types of organizations.

Wrap-Up

All right! What have you learned in Chapter 4? You have figured out how to analyze work flows and the processes used to create those work flows in the organization. This is important because without understanding processes, we can't figure out the resources, including human resources, that we will need in the organization to get us our desired results. The need for human resources then carried us into a discussion of job analysis and design so that we can make sure that we can do all of the things necessary to accomplish the work flow processes that we identified. We then figured out that there are several different types of job design, depending on what factor or factors we want or need to emphasize within our organizations. Do we want our jobs to be physically more or less demanding? Do we want to make them more motivational or more efficient?

We learned about the Job Characteristics Model to modify jobs to make them more motivational, and some other job tools for increasing worker motivation, such as job simplification, job expansion, telecommuting, and flextime. You have many tools available that can potentially make jobs in your organization more motivating.

Next you learned the process of forecasting future HR requirements for the organization. We discussed what we can do if we foresee a surplus or a shortage of people, and specifically discussed the special issue of succession planning for executive and managerial positions in our companies. Finally, we again closed this chapter out with some interesting issues and trends in HRM for the 21st century. That is definitely enough to absorb for one chapter. Let's close this one and move on to getting the right people into our companies in accordance with our forecasts, after completing the end-of-chapter application and skill development.

Chapter Summary

 Visit www.sagepub.com/lussier for helpful study resources.

4.1 Describe the process of work flow analysis and identify why it is important to HRM.

We start our work flow analysis by determining the end result. Once we identify the result we expect, we can then determine the steps, or activities required in order to create the end result that we've identified. This is basically an analysis of the tasks that are going to have to be performed in order to create the output that we expect. Finally, we can then identify the inputs that are going to be necessary to carry out the steps and perform the same tasks. The inputs are called the 3 Ms. *Material* is any physical resource that we use in production. *Manpower* is the people who are needed in a particular production process. *Money* is the capital that must be spent to perform our processes.

4.2 Identify the four major options available for the job analysis process.

Questionnaires ask questions that help to identify the functions that are a part of a particular job and then, in most cases, assign a point value to that function. In the job analysis interview, questions are asked verbally, usually of the incumbent, and the answers are compiled into a profile of the job. Diaries have the worker maintain a work log, or diary, in which they write down the tasks that they accomplish as they go about their job. This log becomes the document from which we build the description of the job. Finally, we can use observation of the person at work, where an observer shadows the person and logs tasks that are performed over a period of time.

4.3 Discuss the four major approaches to job design.

Mechanistic job design focuses on designing jobs around the concepts of task specialization, skill simplification, and repetition. *Biological job design* focuses on minimizing the physical strain on the worker by structuring the physical work environment around the way the body works. *Perceptual/motor job design* is where, instead of trying to minimize the physical strain on the workforce, we attempt to make sure that we remain within their normal mental capabilities and limitations. *Motivational job design* focuses on the job characteristics that affect the psychological meaning and motivational potential, and it views attitudinal variables as the most important outcomes of job design.

4.4 Identify and briefly describe the components of the Job Characteristics Model.

The five core job characteristics include skill variety, task identity, task significance, autonomy, and feedback. The first three lead

collectively to the psychological state of "Experienced Meaningfulness of Work." In other words, the worker will think that their work has meaning. The fourth core characteristic of autonomy leads to the psychological state of "Experienced Responsibility for Outcomes." If the person is given the ability to make some of their decisions on their own, they will feel more responsible for the outcome of those decisions. Finally, feedback leads to the psychological state of "Knowledge of Results"—the psychological feeling that we get from knowing the results that creates *satisfaction* with the results of our work.

All of the psychological states *collectively* lead to the outcomes: motivation, performance, job satisfaction, absenteeism, and turnover. These can go up or down depending on the design of the job.

4.5 Describe the three major tools for motivational job design.

Job simplification is the process of eliminating or combining tasks and/or changing the work sequence to improve performance. It makes jobs more specialized. Our job is to determine whether or not we can eliminate, combine, or change the sequence of work to improve efficiency. However, we *might* make the job less motivational if we simplify the work to the point where the worker gets bored. *Job expansion,* on the other hand, makes jobs less specialized. Jobs can be expanded through rotation, enlargement, and enrichment. Job rotation involves performing different jobs in some sequence, each one for a set period of time. Job enlargement involves adding tasks to broaden variety. Job enrichment is the process of building motivators into the job itself to make it more interesting and challenging. *Team-based job design* gives the team an entire piece of work. It is a form of job enrichment that can increase autonomy, task identity, and task significance for the worker.

4.6 Discuss the three most common quantitative HR forecasting methods.

Trend analysis allows the company to look at historical trends—for instance, whether employment went up or down in a given year and how number of employees related to revenue or productivity—and make judgments from those trends. *Ratio analysis* calculates specific values by comparing a business factor with the number of employees needed. *Regression analysis* is a statistical technique where we use a regression diagram made from historical data points to predict future needs presented with a y- and x-axis.

4.7   Identify the seven major options for decreasing organizational numbers when faced with a labor surplus.

A *layoff* is the process of terminating a group of employees to improve organizational efficiency and effectiveness. A *pay reduction* lowers the rate of pay for groups of employees within the organization. *Work sharing* is where we cut the hours available to each worker on a per-week or per-month basis, because fewer hours of work are available in the company. The option to allow *natural attrition* may occur. In this case we lower organizational numbers by not refilling jobs when turnover occurs. In a *hiring freeze* we allow natural attrition, but in addition won't create any new jobs, even if they are needed. We stop all hiring—not just rehiring for existing positions. *Retraining and transferring workers* from one job to another may allow us to lower the number of workers in a particular part of our business, but will only work if we have too many employees in one type of job and too few in another. *Early retirement* can be a valuable option in some cases. In an early retirement offer, employees are given the choice of leaving the company before they would normally retire, and in exchange the employee will receive some benefits from the organization.

4.8   Discuss the problems that need to be considered in offering an early retirement program.

Early retirement is a slow method of getting rid of people, and we have to be careful in planning for and offering early retirements.

Problems include the following: Too many people may take our early retirement offer. Too few may take the early retirement offer. Our best people might take the offer and then immediately go to work for a competitor while the people who are borderline or poor performers won't. People may perceive that they are being forced out. There is too great a danger for charges of discrimination.

4.9   Identify the seven major options for overcoming a labor shortage.

The quickest and easiest way to fix a personnel shortage is *overtime*. It is our best option until we get to the point where we are starting to stress our people too much because the overtime becomes excessive. *Temporary workers* are another quick method of overcoming a worker shortage. Remember, though, that temporary workers create some problems for the organization. We may be able to *retrain workers* if we have a surplus of employees in another part of the company. We might be able to utilize *outsourcing* of some of our current in-house functions as another option. We can attempt to *reduce turnover*. If fewer people voluntarily leave the organization than we had predicted, we can reduce a projected shortage. We can *hire new employees*. Finally, *technological innovation* may help alleviate a shortage if we can create machinery that can do the job of a human being.

Key Terms

Biological job design	Job description	Mechanistic job design	Ratio analysis
Hoteling	Job design	Motivational job design	Regression analysis
HR forecasting	Job expansion	Perceptual-motor job design	
Job analysis	Job simplification		Trend analysis
Job Characteristics Model (JCM)	Job specification	Qualitative forecasting	Work flow analysis
	Layoff	Quantitative forecast	

Key Term Review

Complete each of the following statements using one of this chapter's key terms:

_____ is the tool that we use to identify what has to be done within the organization to produce a product or service.

_____ is the process used to identify the work performed and the working conditions for each of the jobs within our organizations.

_____ identifies the major tasks, duties, and responsibilities that are components of a job.

_____ identifies the qualifications of a person who should be capable of doing the job tasks noted in the job description.

_____ is the process of identifying tasks that each employee is responsible for completing as well as how those tasks will be accomplished.

_____ focuses on designing jobs around the concepts of task specialization, skill simplification, and repetition.

_____ focuses on minimizing the physical strain on the worker by structuring the physical work environment around the way the body works.

_____ focuses on designing jobs that attempt to make sure that we remain within the worker's normal mental capabilities and limitations.

_____ focuses on the job characteristics that affect the psychological meaning and motivational potential, and it views attitudinal variables as the most important outcomes of job design.

_____ provides a conceptual framework for designing or enriching jobs based on core job characteristics.

_____ is the process of eliminating or combining tasks and/or changing the work sequence to improve performance.

_____ is the process of making jobs broader, with less repetition.

_____ identifies the estimated supply and demand for the different types of human resources in the organization over some future period, based on analysis of past and present demand.

_____ utilizes mathematics to forecast future events based on historical data.

_____ is a process of reviewing historical items such as revenues, and relating those changes to some business factor to form a predictive chart.

_____ is the process of reviewing historical data and calculating specific proportions between a business factor (such as production) and the number of employees needed.

_____ is a statistical technique that identifies the relationship between a series of variable data points for use in forecasting future variables.

_____ uses nonquantitative methods to forecast the future, usually based on the knowledge of a pool of experts in a subject or an industry.

_____ is a process of terminating a group of employees, usually due to some business downturn or perhaps a technological change, with intent to improve organizational efficiency and effectiveness.

_____ is where the organization has less office space than it would in a traditional office arrangement (where everyone has an assigned space) and uses a software program that allows employees to "reserve" office space for particular parts of the workweek when they will need it.

Quick Check (True-False)

1. Work flow analysis is completed in reverse—the first thing we analyze is the end result of the process. T F

2. The 3 Ms for resources include money, manpower, and manufacturing. T F

3. Job analysis is only important to HR Managers. Line managers don't need to understand it. T F

4. Job analysis methods include diaries, direct observation, and questionnaires. T F

5. The two primary outcomes from job analysis are the job description and job specification. T F

6. Jobs within the organization should be designed to fit within the confines of the organizational structure. T F

7. Perceptual/motor job design attempts to minimize the physical strain on the employee. T F

8. The Job Characteristics Model (JCM) is a mechanistic job design model. T F

9. Feedback (in the JCM) deals with the satisfaction that a worker gets from knowledge of the results of their work. T F

10. In HR forecasting, you should use either quantitative or qualitative methods, not both. T F

11. Three methods of overcoming a predicted shortage of employees are downsizing, early retirements, and pay reductions. T F

Communication Skills

The following critical-thinking questions can be used for class discussion and/or for written assignments to develop communication skills. Be sure to give complete explanations for all answers.

1. Do you agree that "stable jobs don't exist in today's workplace" and as a result we shouldn't worry about job analysis? Why or why not?

2. Looking at the company where you work (use a company that you know well if you are not currently working), does it appear that the organization uses task-based or competency-based job analysis? Why do you think this?

3. Can more than one of the four main approaches to job design be used at the same time to design a job? Can you provide an example of how this could work?

4. Are there any situations in which you might design a job using the JCM and the job would still not be motivational? What circumstances might cause this to happen?

5. Do you think that using flextime, telecommuting, job sharing, or compressed workweeks is really going to motivate employees? Why or why not?

6. Are there situations in which working in teams might be demotivating? How could this occur?

7. Have you seen job simplification, job rotation, or job expansion being used in your workplace (if you aren't currently working, use a workplace that you are familiar with)? Did it work to motivate the employees? Why?

8. Which of the three HR forecasting methods do you think would give you the most accurate forecast? Why did you pick this option?

9. Is a layoff, or downsizing, *ever* the best option to resolve a projected surplus in an organization? Justify your answer.

10. How much overtime is reasonable in a week? How long can the company expect workers to continue to work overtime before they see employee stress levels getting significantly higher than normal?

Video

Please visit the student study site at **www.sagepub.com/lussier** to view the video links in this chapter.

Answers

REVIEW QUESTIONS (TRUE-FALSE) Answers

1. T   2. F   3. F   4. T   5. T   6. T   7. F   8. F   9. T   10. F   11. F

Case

Case 4-1. The Explosion at DHR Construction

A Forced Changing of the Guard

Richard Davis, who handled the corporation's finances at DHR Construction, LLC (the same company discussed in the case in Chapter 2 and again in Chapter 8), had decided some time back that it was time to upgrade from using a part-time bookkeeper to an accountant. A two-year audit conducted by the accountant revealed that about $25,000 of expenses connected to Alan's (their foreman's) corporate credit card account were for non-business items (i.e., Christmas trees), were questionable in multiple cases (i.e., filling up the company truck six times in one day), and, at times, were signed by someone other than Alan (signatures on receipts did not match Alan's signature). After a discussion with their lawyer and Alan, Hodgetts and Davis agreed to let Alan go without pressing criminal charges.

Alan's separation from the business left a wide managerial gap. So who was going to take over as foreman in the short term until they could conduct a thorough search and hire a new one? Davis and Hodgetts agreed that they needed someone immediately (tomorrow) to fill the position so they could focus on conducting their job search. There was only one likely candidate who came to mind, Davis's daughter Delores (nickname RJ).

RJ had the free time, had worked in a very tough and stressful environment (a legal office and a hospital) and excelled, and seemed to have both the interest and the tenacity to try to learn the contracting portion of the business. From Richard Davis's perspective, this would provide RJ an opportunity to determine whether she would want to be the one to eventually take over the family business; she needed to learn the business from the ground up.

Richard Davis then spent a few days at the work site with RJ to introduce her to the numerous subcontractors and to spread the word that RJ was going to take over the job of foreman while the business was searching for an experienced person. Richard also gave RJ a copy of all of the building blueprints, as well as work charts showing which subcontractor had to be working at what time point in each home and what work the subcontractor would perform. RJ was a very quick learner, and after having several question and answer sessions with Davis and Hodgetts, they decided that RJ was ready to go solo on the job site.

The next day RJ was at the construction site checking in with all of the subcontractors to make sure that everyone knew what needed to be done by whom and in what order. RJ came home from the first day of the job exhausted and a bit disgruntled. At the dinner table RJ described how the electrical problems still had not been solved in one home and how the electrician guaranteed that he'd get the job done even if he had to work through the night to do it. Other problems kept creeping up, and RJ had to be "the problem solver." Many of these problems would throw the building schedule off, and RJ had to shuffle the subcontractors between building sites in order to accommodate the numerous mishaps found in each home.

A Failed Inspection and Tempers Flare

After a few days on the job, RJ felt like work was unmanageable. One home in particular was quite problematic since the electrician seemed absolutely baffled as to what the problem was with the wiring in the dining room yet did not inform RJ of this dilemma until the electrical inspector showed up for a scheduled appointment at the work site. Other problems were also evident in other homes, with at least one other home failing a framing inspection. RJ's reaction to all of this was simple. After "playing nice" with the subcontractors who were giving RJ problems, RJ decided to turn hard-hitting and give these subcontractors a tough talking to. Heated words were exchanged, and RJ and the subcontractors angrily parted company.

The Scene Is Set—Action!

That night, after the failed electrical inspection, Hodgetts was invited over to the Davis house for dinner so they could discuss the business and see how RJ's first few days on the job were working out. The dinner conversation started out in its usual jovial manner but eventually moved to a discussion of the progress being made on the construction site.

RJ gave a summary of the past few days, including the failed inspections and the tough time RJ was having managing the contractors. Davis and Hodgetts were absolutely silent

through RJ's description of the situation, and everyone tried to keep their body language as controlled as possible. RJ finally came to an abrupt finish. This left a long pause for everyone else at the dinner table to fill with table talk or comments about the business. Before anyone could ask RJ a question about the building projects, she announced she was quitting the job. "I quit." Those two little words were dropped like an atomic bomb and seemed to burst across the dinner table at the Davis residence. RJ silenced the room, and then she quickly vacated the premises. No one uttered a sound—the devastation was complete and absolute.

Questions

1. Describe RJ's job as foreman in terms of its resource inputs. Which resource was causing her the most difficulties?

2. How would job analysis have helped RJ perform her job as foreman?

3. If Davis and Hodgetts were going to analyze the foreman's job, what method(s) should they employ?

4. If Davis and Hodgetts were going to design (or redesign) the foreman's job, what method(s) should they employ?

5. Describe how the team approach to job design might be helpful to Davis and Hodgetts when considering the foreman's position.

6. How might flexible techniques for job design help the firm better manage the subcontractors?

Case created by Herbert Sherman, PhD, and Mr. Theodore Vallas, Department of Management Sciences, Long Island University School of Business, Brooklyn Campus

SKILL BUILDER 4-1

Job Analysis

Objective

To develop your skill at completing a job analysis; to improve your ability to get ready.

Skills

The primary skills developed through this exercise are:

1. *HR Management skill* – Technical, business, and conceptual and design skills
2. *SHRM 2010 Curriculum Guidebook* – C: Job Analysis/Job Design

Overview

Your output is to arrive at school or work. Your inputs (3 Ms) are each and every task you perform until you arrive at your destination. Through your job analysis flowchart, improve the efficiency of your inputs so you can get more done, in less time, with better results.

Step 1. Make Flowchart

List step-by-step exactly what you do from the time you get up (or start your routine) until the time you start school or work. Get up or start earlier, say 15 minutes, to give yourself time to complete your flowchart without making you late. Be sure to number each step and list each activity separately with its M (don't just say go to the bathroom—list each activity in sequence while in there). For example:

1. Get up at 7:00—manpower
2. Go to bathroom—womanpower
3. Take shower—material
4. Dry hair—material
5. Drive car—material
6. Buy coffee—money
7. Walk in to school at 8:00—manpower

2.   Analyze Flowchart

Later in the day when you have time, do a job simplification analysis of your flowchart of activities to determine if you can:

- Eliminate. Are you doing anything that you don't need to do?
- Combine. Can you multitask any simple tasks, make fewer trips to the bathroom, and so on?
- Change sequence. Will you be more efficient if you rearrange your flowchart of tasks?

3.   Develop New Flowchart

Based on your analysis, make a new flowchart that eliminates, combines, and changes the sequence of tasks you will perform to get ready more efficiently.

4.   Change Routine

Consciously follow the steps of your new flowchart until it becomes your new habit.

Apply It

What did I learn from this experience? How will I use this knowledge in the future?

_____

_____

Your instructor may ask you to do this Skill Builder in class in a group. If so, the instructor will provide you with any necessary information or additional instructions.

SKILL BUILDER 4-2

Job Characteristics Model (JCM)

Objective

To develop your skill at implementing the JCM.

Skills

The primary skills developed through this exercise are:

1. *HR Management skill* – Technical, business, and conceptual and design skills

2. *SHRM 2010 Curriculum Guidebook* – C: Job Analysis/Job Design

Preparation

Select a job you have now or have held in the past. Using the description of the JCM and Exhibit 4-3 and the example of applying the JCM and Exhibit 4-4, apply these concepts to do a job analysis for your job. Be sure to use the exact terms from the text. The two exhibits provide a good summary of the process and terminology.

Apply It

What did I learn from this experience? How will I use this knowledge in the future?

_____

_____

Your instructor may ask you to do this Skill Builder in class in a group. If so, the instructor will provide you with any necessary information or additional instructions.

5

Recruiting Job Candidates

Learning Outcomes

After studying this chapter you should be able to:

5.1 Identify and discuss the primary goal of the recruiting process

5.2 Briefly discuss the main external forces acting on recruiting efforts

5.3 Discuss the major advantages and disadvantages of both internal and external recruiting

5.4 Briefly discuss the major challenges and constraints involved in the recruiting process

5.5 Discuss the value of a Realistic Job Preview

5.6 Discuss the characteristics needed in a capable recruiter

5.7 Discuss the basic methods available for evaluating the recruiting process

5.8 Define the following terms:

Recruiting
Labor market
Internal recruiting
External recruiting

Realistic Job Preview (RJP)
Active listening
Yield ratio

Chapter 5 Outline

E. Outcomes: Metrics and Measurements of HR
    6. Calculating and interpreting yield ratios

G. Staffing: Recruitment and Selection (required)
    2. External influences on staffing (labor markets, unions, economic conditions, technology)
    3. External recruitment (recruiters, open vs. targeted recruitment, recruitment sources, applicant reactions, medium [electronic, advertisement], fraud/misrepresentation)
    4. Internal recruitment (timing, open/closed/targeted recruitment, bona fide seniority systems)
    5. Internal recruitment (promotability ratings, managerial sponsorship, self-/peer assessments, panels/review boards)

Case 5-1. Here a GM, There a GM, Everywhere a GM (or So They Thought)!

SHRM
HR CONTENT

See Appendix A:
SHRM 2010 Curriculum Guidebook for the complete list

Where, Oh Where, Has My Recruit Gone?

Although recruiting is often viewed as an entry-level position, good recruiters are extremely valuable. Some seem to have an innate knack for the job, while others remind me of a former colleague. Jasper was hired to recruit job candidates in a new area for our company expansion. He crafted an elaborate campaign to attract potential candidates using an Internet service. Jasper had experience in white-collar recruiting, and believed what had worked for him in the past should surely transfer successfully to our blue-collar industry. He was ready to commit our company to a contract with an online job posting agency that would absorb the entire recruiting budget. Do you think Jasper's plan was successful? What assumptions was Jasper making about his potential job candidates? Chapter 5 highlights all the factors you need to consider as you endeavor to attract the best qualified candidates for your job search.

The Practitioner's Model for HRM

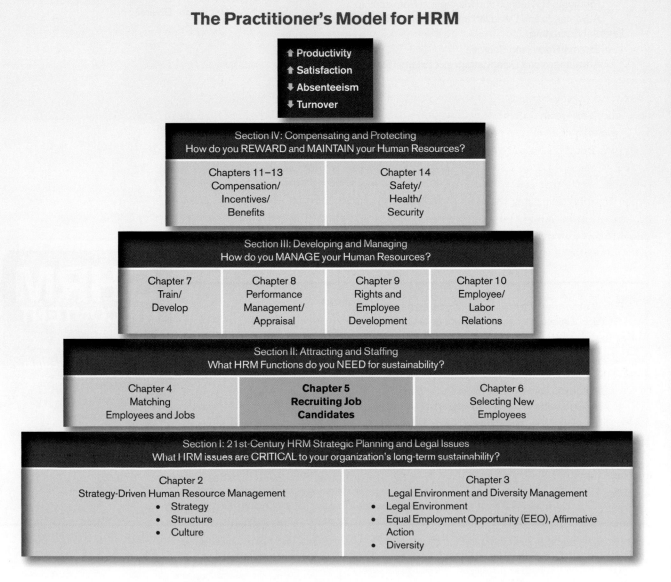

The Recruiting Process

The cost associated with recruiting, selecting, and training new employees is often more than 100% of their annual salary.[1] Recruiting is important for many businesses, but for Groupon it is critical as it went from 37 to 7,100 employees in 21 months.[2] Thus, recruiting is an important HR function.[3]

LO 5.1

Identify and discuss the primary goal of the recruiting process.

After hiring needs have been determined through the forecasting process and after jobs have been analyzed (providing a job description and job specifications), we need to recruit some people to fill our position openings. So the actual first step in matching employees and jobs is recruiting. We can't hire good employees without effectively recruiting them.[4] What are we attempting to do when we begin recruiting? Either we are trying to get people inside the company to apply for different job openings, or we are trying to get outsiders to join the company. In this section, you will learn about the recruiting process. Your college HR staff recruits employees, but who recruits students, and who is the sales team? If you said the admissions counselors are the recruiters and sales team members who get people to apply for admission to your college, you are correct.

So what is the goal in recruiting? Do we want to get a huge pool of people who want to join the organization? Or do we want to find just a couple of skilled people who can do the job—in other words, finely discriminate among reasonably qualified applicants? What is the main goal of the recruiting process? At Groupon, they work to get the best people in the shortest time.[5]

If you think about it for just a minute, you will see that if you find too many applicants it costs the organization too much to go through the selection process, but if you find too few there is no selection process and you don't have the option to find the individual who best fits in the position and the organization. Typically, a good thumb rule might be to find about 15–25 people who want to be a part of the organization *for each opening*. That's just a rule of thumb, but it is probably going to allow a reasonable pool of applicants from whom you can choose an individual who will be a good fit for the job. If you find 15–25 applicants, you can probably cut that to 4 or 5 pretty quickly, and that is a reasonable number of people from which to choose a new member of the organization. You certainly don't want a massive number of recruits because it is too time-consuming and it costs the company too much to cull that number down to a useable pool. However, especially when the unemployment rate is high, you may get more than 100 applications during the recruiting process.

Defining the Process

Recruiting is *the process of creating a reasonable pool of qualified candidates for a job opening.* Notice that the definition identifies the fact that we need *qualified* applicants![6] The process does us no good if the candidates that we attract are not qualified to do the work. One of the most critical things that you have to do very early in the recruiting process is to determine that the individuals who are recruited are qualified. Thus, a good job description is helpful to the company and the people looking for jobs to know if there is a match.

To fill an opening, possible candidates must generally be made aware that the organization is seeking employees. They must then be persuaded to apply for the jobs. We use a series of tools in order to show the candidate why they might want to become a part of the organization. We will discuss these tools as we go through the remainder of this chapter.

External Forces Acting on Recruiting Efforts

LO 5.2

Briefly discuss the main external forces acting on recruiting efforts.

There are a series of external forces that affect our ability to recruit individuals into our organization at a particular point in time.[7] During the 2008–2009 recession, 63% of HR executives said recruiting was cut back, and in 2010 after the recession was over, 30% stated recruiting cutbacks would continue in the future. In 2009, 48% of HR executives had layoffs, but in 2010 only 17% said layoffs will be continued in the future. Also, close to 50% of HR executives said recruiting more temporary and part-time workers will continue in the future.[8]

Think about what is happening around you right now. Is the unemployment rate high, or is it low? Are there government incentives to increase hiring of the unemployed, or is government doing very little to increase employment? Is the available supply of people with advanced skills very large, or are there not enough people with high-level skill sets available to companies? All of these things affect our ability to recruit new workers into our company. Generally, the external forces acting on recruiting fall into two large categories—the available labor market and the social and legal environment. Let's take a quick look at each.

The Labor Market

The availability of talent to fill our needs depends on several items in the labor market.[9] The **labor market** is *the term for the external pool of candidates from which we draw our recruits.*

Supply and demand–unemployment rate. The first item that we have to consider is the *supply and demand* factors in a particular category of jobs. If we are in need of a mechanical engineer, how many mechanical engineers are available in the labor environment? Are there too many for the available number of jobs, or are there more jobs than engineers? If there is a large pool of engineers desiring a job in their field, then our job of recruiting one will be significantly easier than if there are very few available and lots of job openings.

This issue of supply and demand usually ties in directly with the *unemployment rate* in an area. Every business recruits primarily from an identifiable geographic area. Some will recruit locally (perhaps within a metropolitan area or a single city). Others will recruit regionally or nationally for talent that they need. Still others may recruit internationally for people to join the company. We need to identify our recruiting area and then determine what the unemployment rate is in the applicable area. If unemployment is high, the job of recruiting an applicant is generally easier than if unemployment is very low. However, even when the unemployment rate was around 10% and there were thousands of people looking for jobs, there was a shortage of qualified candidates for some highly skilled jobs.

Competitors. We also have to consider our *competitors* and how much they contend with us for the available talent in a particular field. If competition is very strong for available mechanical engineers—if there are a significant number of competitors and each competitor needs a large number of engineers, for instance—then it will be a more difficult recruiting environment. Similarly, if there aren't many competitors who need this particular type of mechanical engineer and are working to attract the applicant to their business, then the recruiting environment will likely be much less difficult. So our environment depends on the labor market.

Social and Legal Environment

The social environment in the country in which we are operating also affects our ability to recruit new people into our organizations.[10] Today people put more weight on "me time" and a higher level of job satisfaction than in past years, and as a result workers look at the social environment in the organization in order to make decisions concerning whether or not to apply for a job within a specific company. In many cases, new employees also expect a high level of benefits and good opportunities for training and development to come with the job in order to consider an organization as a possible employment target. As a result, the social environment drives our ability to recruit our 21st-century workforce.

We also have to take into account the various laws that limit the ways in which we can recruit. First and most obvious, we have to abide by all of the EEO laws that we discussed in Chapter 3 and avoid any issues of discrimination in our recruiting efforts, so this is another area in which we could apply the OUCH test to ensure fairness and equity in our processes. There are also laws in some situations that limit our ability to lure employees away from competitor firms. In other cases, labor agreements may limit our ability to recruit, or the union itself may be able to place limits on our recruiting from outside of the union's ranks. In addition, noncompete agreements might not allow us to recruit certain individuals who are bound by such agreements. State laws might also apply to recruiting in certain industries or in recruiting certain types of employees. The HR Manager must be well versed in the various laws, agreements, and regulations that limit their ability to recruit in any way.

Recruiting Considerations and Sources

Once we become aware of the limitations that are placed on us by the labor market and the legal environment, we can start to consider the internal issues that control our recruiting processes. When should we go through the recruiting process? What alternatives do we have for recruiting (outsourcing, retraining, etc.)? Should we recruit our applicants from internal sources (within the company already) or external sources? We have to set policies on these topics in order to maintain consistency, and we need consistency in order to be fair and equitable and so that we can defend our processes if it becomes necessary. So, what do we have to think about, and in what detail?

What Policies to Set

We have to think about a lot of things as we work to allay a shortage in people within the company. We need to determine how we are going to go through the recruiting process before we start trying to recruit new members into our workforce. Among other things, we have to answer:

- Under what conditions will we recruit new people into the company?
- What alternatives do we have, and when will we use them?
- Should we recruit locally, regionally, nationally, or globally?
- Are we going to recruit from within our own ranks first or go outside the organization?
- What primary recruiting sources will provide us with the best recruits for our company?

and other questions. We have to make these determinations based on our particular company circumstances, taking into account all of the information from our forecasting processes. Let's discuss four of the primary items we will need to think about *before* the recruiting process starts.

When to Recruit

One of the first items that we need to think about is "When do we recruit?" This seems like an obvious question, doesn't it? We recruit when we need someone to fill a job! But it's not that simple. We don't necessarily have to recruit someone when we need a job filled. Remember what we said in Chapter 4. There are all kinds of ways that we can mitigate a shortage in

Video Link 5.1

Overview of Recruiting Process

Recruiting leads to an employment contract, although not all are written and signed.

the organization, and which one we choose depends on a bunch of different factors. Should we recruit or bring in temp workers? Should we add overtime, or outsource some tasks? We need to identify the points at which we would generally go through the process of starting and carrying out a recruitment campaign, because the campaign itself is expensive. We don't want to do it and then figure out that we didn't need to—we would just be wasting money.

Alternatives to Recruitment

Do we have a viable and financially feasible way to solve our shortage other than through recruitment? Is the alternative less expensive or better for our circumstances in some other way? We don't want to recruit new employees into the organization if working a group of people overtime for a week or two, or even a month or two, will solve our problem. We may be prohibited from recruiting because of an attrition policy or a hiring freeze. We might be able to solve our problem with temporary employees instead of new full-time workers.

We have to weigh all of the options available and should generally have a policy that tells us when we would use each option. We need to know what the primary objectives of the organization are so that we can analyze the possibility of outsourcing (we don't want to outsource a critical task). We need to know how much overtime is currently being used—are we working our current employees to the point where their job satisfaction is likely to start going down?

What kind of labor market is our industry in right now? If we are in a market where there are many people out of work, we may be able to get a much better new hire, so it might be best to recruit for new employees. Conversely, if we are in a tight labor market, we might waste a lot of resources trying to recruit new employees and get no good candidates. We are going to analyze each of the options for mitigating a labor shortage other than new hires and create some policy concerning when each of these options is useful in our organization. We have to take all factors that we know into account in making our recruiting decision.

Reach of the Recruiting Effort

Next, we need to identify our effective labor market. Do we plan to recruit only from local sources? Should we consider people all over a particular region (the mid-South or New England)? Do we need to recruit globally or even internationally?[11] The answer, again, is "it depends."

What are the factors that are involved with our decision? The first factor is simple—can we find the right number and types of employees if we recruit locally? If so, then we may be able to work only in our local labor market. If not, we may be forced to recruit from a broader pool of talent. Second, can we get better talent to apply if we recruit regionally, nationally, or globally? Third, do we need this type of talent in order to accomplish our organizational goals (remember that if we are a low-cost producer, we may not want top-notch talent in all areas of our company)? Is the job that we are recruiting for so specialized that we need to recruit from all over the world? Do we want to recruit from locations far away from our organization if we don't have to? Of course not. It is time-consuming and expensive to bring people to the organization from far away. So we only expand our geographic area when we need to. However, remember that multinational corporations tend to hire locally, but many of their total employees are from other countries.

Internal and External Recruiting

What is our policy going to be concerning recruitment from within the current employees in the organization? We can very rarely just say that we will "promote from within" and stick to that policy. So we have to create policies concerning when and how we will recruit

from our current employees and when we will go outside the organization. Why? Probably the biggest reason is so that our employees perceive fairness in our recruiting policies.

If we say we will recruit from within and then we go outside the organization to recruit a new manager, many of our employees will begin to think that we were "just talking" when we said we would promote internally, and they might begin to show less loyalty to the organization because they feel that the organization failed to show them loyalty. However, if our policies say that we will go outside for recruits when it is unlikely that anyone in the organization would have the skill set necessary to do the job identified in our job specification, then we can provide a legitimate answer to someone who would question our recruiting process.

Additionally, we might have a policy that says that when the organization has identified significant resistance to change as an issue in a section of the organization, or when we are instituting new processes, we will bring in new people with new ideas and different skills. We may also identify specific occupations in our organization that will typically be recruited from outside, usually due to a specialized skill set (e.g., nuclear plant operator, corporate attorney, or emergency medical technician). It is unlikely that we would promote from within to these types of positions.

These are just some of the things that we need to consider as we create our recruiting policies. Now, let's take a closer look at internal versus external recruiting efforts. Although we already noted that we need policies concerning these options, we need to look closer at what the advantages and disadvantages are to each.

LO 5.3

Discuss the major advantages and disadvantages of both internal and external recruiting.

Internal Recruiting

Internal recruiting involves *filling job openings with current employees or people they know.* Here we discuss internal recruiting sources, promotability ratings and managerial sponsorship, and the advantages and disadvantages of internal recruiting.

Internal Recruiting Sources

There are two common types of internal recruiting:

- *Promotions from within.* Many organizations post job openings on bulletin boards, in company newsletters, and so on—which can be electronic. Current employees may apply or bid for the open positions. P&G has a promotion-from-within policy that fosters intense competition.[12] Moves today are commonly lateral, rather than an actual promotion. Southwest Airlines has slowed growth and is overstaffed in some areas and is encouraging employees to move about in the company rather than lay them off.[13]
- *Employee referrals.* Employees may be encouraged to refer friends and relatives for positions. About 40% of new hires at Groupon come from employee referrals.[14] Zynga, a social gaming company with 1,500 employees, plans to double that number in a year, and it is focusing on internal recruiting and having employees make the initial recruiting calls.[15] For hard-to-recruit jobs, some firms pay a bonus to employees when their referred applicant is hired.

Open, Targeted, and Closed Recruiting

When it comes to promotion from within as an internal recruiting method, there are several options for the organization. We can use open, targeted, or closed recruiting methods.[16] *Open recruiting* means that we advertise the job openly within the organization and anyone who meets the qualifications can apply for the job opening.

Targeted recruiting is pretty much what it sounds like. We do not openly advertise the position internally. Instead, we ask managers to privately nominate workers who they feel would be able to do the job that needs to be filled. HR will then evaluate the candidates put

SHRM

Guide – G:4
Internal recruitment (timing, open/closed/targeted recruitment, bona fide seniority systems)

WORK
APPLICATION 5-4

Select an organization you work or have worked for and give an example of either an open, a targeted, or a closed recruiting method it uses. List the job(s) it is used to recruit for.

forward by the managers to make sure that they have the required qualifications and then forward the best options to the hiring manager. We have to be more careful with targeted recruiting because it can allow, or appear to allow, bias in the recruiting and selection process.

Finally, *closed recruiting* occurs when hiring managers have a need to fill a position and they communicate that need to HR. HR recruiters will then search the organization's files for people who have the requisite skills and qualifications and send a list of such individuals to the hiring manager. The hiring manager can then select from the applicants identified by the HR Department.

5-1 APPLYING THE CONCEPT

Internal Recruiting

State which of the following recruiting methods was used in each of the given situations.

a. open
b. targeted
c. closed

_____ 1. My manager got promoted, and she recommended me to replace her as the department supervisor.

_____ 2. I'm the Head Teller in a bank. I read the bulletin board, and it described an opening for an Assistant Branch Manager, so I applied for the position.

_____ 3. I went to an interview with the Accounting Department Manager. When I asked him how he got my name for the job, he said the HR Department sent him my name.

_____ 4. I got a job in the Advertising Department because my Sales Manager told the Advertising Manager about me.

_____ 5. At my bank branch, the manager told all us tellers that we could apply to be the new Head Teller. But I don't want the job.

SHRM

Guide – G:5
Internal recruitment (promotability ratings, managerial sponsorship, self-/peer assessments, panels/review boards)

Seniority. One of the difficult issues the organization may run into if they choose an internal recruiting option is the presence of a bona fide seniority system. A bona fide seniority system is simply a system in place within the organization to give preference to individuals with longer tenure in the organization. If we have such a system, we may have to allow people with more seniority to apply for any internal job openings, which would limit our ability to use targeted or closed recruiting.

Promotability Ratings and Managerial Sponsorship

We can do some things within the organization to make the internal recruiting process go a bit smoother in most cases. As part of our annual appraisal process, we can include a "promotability rating" for each member of the organization.[17] This rating evaluates the individual for fitness for higher-level jobs in the organization. If we do it as part of our normal appraisal process, it adds very little to the workload of the managers in the company.

We may use some other tools to assess promotability as well in our efforts to find the best qualified individuals within the organization. We can have each of our employees complete a self-assessment and ask peers to also assess their coworkers for promotability. We can also have people who desire to be considered for promotion put themselves before an organizational review board, which will judge their qualification and readiness for such promotion opportunities. Each of these options strengthens the ability of the organization to get the best possible candidates for internal promotion opportunities.

We can also request "managerial sponsorship" in order for a person to be considered for job opportunities through internal recruiting. In this case, we would ask managers to provide their sponsorship for an individual before they would be considered for a promotion through the internal recruiting process. This sponsorship information would then be used in our internal recruiting efforts. This is a type of mentoring.

Advantages and Disadvantages of Internal Recruiting

Is it generally a good idea to recruit from inside the organization? What are the major advantages and disadvantages to internal recruiting?

Advantages. They include the following:

- The internal recruit may experience possible increases in organizational commitment and job satisfaction based on the opportunity to advance in the organization with commensurate increases in pay.
- The internal recruit will be able to learn more about the "big picture" in the company and become more valuable.
- The individual has shown at least some interest in the organization as well as having knowledge of our operations and processes and feels comfortable continuing employment within the company.
- The company has existing knowledge of the applicant and a record of their previous work.
- The organization can save money by recruiting internally, because of both lower advertisement costs and lower training costs.
- Internal recruiting is usually faster than external.

Disadvantages. What about disadvantages? There are a lot of good things that come from internal recruiting, but there must be some problems or potential problems with the practice, right? Here are some of the disadvantages:

- The pool of applicants is significantly smaller in internal recruiting.
- There is still a job to fill—the employee moved from somewhere else in the organization.
- Success in one job doesn't necessarily mean success in a significantly different job, especially if the prior employee is now a supervisor and knows their subordinates from previous work as a coworker.
- An external candidate may have better qualifications for the job opening.
- Internal employees may feel that they are entitled to the job whether they are capable and qualified or not, especially if we have a strong policy of preferring internal candidates.
- And the biggest threat to the company—we may create or perpetuate a strong resistance to change or stifle creativity and innovation because everyone in the organization, even the "new hires," are part of the old organizational culture.

External Recruiting

Employees changing jobs influence organizational performance, and companies commonly recruit people from other firms to satisfy their HR needs.[18] **External recruiting** *is the process of engaging individuals from the labor market outside the firm to apply for a job.* External recruiting can also be accomplished in either an open or a targeted manner, in much the same way as internal recruiting. If we have an open recruiting effort, we will provide the job information for anyone who wishes to apply. If, however, we are using targeted recruiting (as an example—a headhunter), we would seek out specific individuals with the necessary skills and invite them to apply for the job opening.

SHRM

Guide – G:3
External recruitment
(recruiters, open vs. targeted
recruitment, recruitment
sources, applicant reactions,
medium [electronic,
advertisement], fraud/
misrepresentation)

External Recruiting Sources

When we decide to recruit from external sources, what options do we have? When looking for new employees, where would you recruit? Again, the answer is "it depends." Recall that we are trying to get a good pool of employees. So which option will give you the best pool of applicants for the specific job? We have to look at the type of person that we are trying to find and then go to the source or sources that provide that type of person. Here are our external recruiting options. They are also listed with a summary of strengths in Figure 5.1.

Walk-ins. Without actually being recruited, good candidates may come to an organization "cold" and ask for a job. Those seeking management-level positions generally tend to send a résumé and cover letter asking for an interview. Walk-ins may be a good source of recruits for a couple of reasons. First, they have already selected your organization as an employment target because they took the initiative to come in and ask for a job. Second, this is an inexpensive source for external recruiting. You have no advertising costs, and you don't have to wait for résumés and applications to come in from an external advertisement, so the process can occur much quicker than using other external recruiting methods.

Educational Institutions. Recruiting takes place at high schools, vocational/technical schools, and colleges. Many schools offer career planning and placement services to aid students and potential employers. Educational institutions are good places to recruit people who have no prior experience. We might decide to recruit here for a new external hire if we need somebody with a good basic skill set, and a good degree and education. They will probably have a lot of specialized education in a specific field, which is always good. If you are looking for that type of person, a college/university might be a good place to go. Have you visited your college's Career Services? You don't have to wait for senior year when you are about to graduate to take advantage of what they have to offer.

Employment Agencies. There are three major types of employment agencies:

(1) *Temporary agencies,* like Kelly Services and Accountemps, provide part- or full-time help for limited periods. They are useful for replacing employees who will be out for a short period of time or for supplementing the regular workforce during busy periods. However, today organizations are reluctant to add to their permanent workforces and instead create short- and long-term temporary positions (called permatemps)—almost 3 million each day.[19] Firms are also hiring independent contractors for flexibility and variety.[20]

However, you should be cautioned here concerning the long-term use of temporary workers. There have been a number of lawsuits against employers in the past 10 years dealing with the hiring of "temporary" workers, when in fact these workers were permanent—just without the benefits associated with the company's full-time permanent workforce. Probably the most famous, and one of the most expensive, settlements came in the case of Microsoft using permatemp workers in the 1990s. We briefly noted this case in Chapter 4. A class action lawsuit was filed and was being heard in the U.S. Ninth Circuit Court of Appeals when Microsoft agreed to settle with the permatemp workers for nearly $100 million.[21]

(2) *Public agencies* are state employment services. They generally provide job candidates to employers at no cost or very low cost. One of the best and most often overlooked sources for external recruits, public employment agencies provide potential employees at all levels of the exempt and nonexempt workforce due to the fact that anyone who seeks unemployment assistance must be on the public employment agency roles for possible employment. Too often the public agencies get reputations as havens for the hard-core unemployed—those who do not want to work. However, they can be a strong source for

good quality employees, especially in bad economic conditions where many good workers lose their jobs, and the cost can't be beat.

(3) *Private employment agencies* are privately owned and charge a fee for their services. These agencies generally do a lot of prescreening for the company searching for employees, so they can mitigate some of those screening costs. There are several different types of private employment agencies. These agencies are generally good for recruiting people with prior experience.

- *General employment agencies* operate on a for-profit basis. Some of them charge job seekers for their service, and others charge the employer. These agencies *usually* do not specialize in a particular type of employee, but some may only operate in certain employment categories such as IT or accounting employment.
- *Contingency agencies* offer employees to the employer and are paid when the job candidate is hired by the employer. Contingency agencies frequently work with a more skilled set of clients—those with high-level manufacturing skills or midlevel management skills, for example, would be common candidates for contingency agencies.
- *Retained search firms or executive recruiters* are paid to search for a specific type of recruit for the organization and will be paid regardless of success in their recruiting efforts. Often referred to as *headhunters,* they specialize in recruiting senior managers and/or those with specific high-level technical skills, like engineers and computer experts. They tend to charge the employer a large fee, and will be at least partially paid whether or not there is a successful hire. Usually, the retained search firm will be paid in three installments, with the first installment being nonrefundable. The installments might be split as a percentage—40-30-30—with the first installment due on signing the contract, the second due around 90 days, and the third due on successful completion of the hiring process. "The cost of retaining a search firm can equal about 30 percent of a new hire's signing bonus, moving expenses, and first-year cash salary combined,"[22] so if your organization is looking for a high-level manager at a salary level of about $100,000, it might cost almost that much to find a candidate using a headhunter. Because of their expense, retained search firms won't generally be used for anything but high-level employee searches.

Advertising. It is important to use the appropriate source to reach qualified candidates. A simple help-wanted sign in the window is an advertisement. Newspapers are places to advertise positions, but professional and trade magazines may be more suitable for specific professional recruiting. There are also several online job search websites, such as Monster.com and CareerBuilder.com.

No matter which advertising option we use, however, we have to be aware of the potential for fraud and/or misrepresentation in our advertisement. If we knowingly, or in some cases even unknowingly, provide misleading information, we can cause the organization to have to defend

Advertising is an effective way to recruit job candidates, and more organizations are moving from newspaper to online ads.

a lawsuit over fraud or misrepresentation. This is obviously something that we don't want to have to do, so we need to check our ads for factual errors and exaggeration before we put them out to the public. Once we have checked our ads to ensure accuracy, our options for advertising include the following:

(1) *Local mass media.* Is the *Daily Planet* (thanks, Superman), Channel 5, or the oldies FM radio station a good option for your recruiting dollars? As usual, it depends on what kind of candidate you are looking for. Is mass media a good option if you are looking for a lawyer or a nuclear physicist? Would that be the best place to spend your money? Maybe not. The cost-per-person-reached by this form of advertising is very low, but you might not reach the people you are looking for.

What type of people would you look for through the use of mass media? Semiskilled or skilled line employees might be a good target for this type of advertisement, especially if you need a large number of them for a specific type of job. For example, when Southwest Airlines opened up a call center in Arkansas in the 1990s, they put an ad for customer service representatives in the local newspaper, on the radio, and on television. Southwest wanted to find a large number of people (initially about 400 employees) with a basic skill set—the ability to interact with customers and solve their travel problems. The ads resulted in several thousand people applying for the customer service jobs that Southwest was trying to fill—a good 15-to-1 candidate pool, as we noted earlier.

(2) *Specialized publications.* Publications that target specific groups of people, such as the *Wall Street Journal* and the *Financial Times* or the *APICS* magazine printed by the Association for Operations Management, may be good sources for new recruits. There are many other examples of this type of specialty publication. Almost all of these publications have help-wanted advertisements similar to the local newspaper, but the ads tend to be targeted to a specific group of potential recruits. *APICS* magazine would be a good source if your company was looking for a production or operations manager. The *Wall Street Journal* might be best if you were looking for someone for a senior-level executive position. However, if you are looking for a lower-level employee, these would probably not be the place to go. Ads in such specialty publications are more expensive and have less reach than the local mass media, but they are much more targeted toward the type of recruit that you may be looking for.

(3) *The Internet.* What kind of people would you advertise for using the Internet? Should your company put every job opening up on the Internet? If you do, how many applicants are you going to get for that job opening? In many cases, companies are discovering that they may not want to advertise every job opening on the Internet because of the reach of the World Wide Web.[23] They just don't have the time to wade through thousands of applications for a single opening.

It *seems* that everybody is on the Internet today, but that isn't true, even in the United States. Between 70% and 80% of Americans are on the Internet,[24] but that still leaves one out of every five people that you wouldn't reach via Internet recruitment. And in other countries, the percentage of people without access is significantly higher than in the United States, so international recruiting efforts via the Internet may not give you the results that you desire. The Internet will be a good medium for certain types of jobs, but not for every job.

What kinds of job openings would you want to advertise using the Internet? Jobs requiring computer or other high-level technical skills would probably have good potential for Internet recruitment, because technical people would tend to use the Internet more than people in nontechnical fields. Would you advertise for a five-star chef on the Internet? Unlikely. What about a janitor? Probably not. How is a five-star chef generally going to find a job? Most likely they will find work through the use of recommendations and talking to people that they know in the restaurant business. Word of mouth works well in this type of industry.

For people that you will recruit from the local workforce, and who have general skills (such as construction workers), it is unlikely that you will find them using the Internet. You have to look at what type of recruit you are looking for and ask if the Internet is a logical place to advertise.

You might also want to use the Internet to recruit new employees using professional associations such as SHRM. SHRM puts employment advertisements on its website; go to www.shrm.org and click on SHRM's *HR Jobs* link. So, professional associations give us the ability to reach highly specialized individuals with specific skill sets. See Exhibit 5-1 for a review of the internal and external recruiting sources.

WORK APPLICATION 5-5

Identify the recruiting source and explain how it was used to hire you for your current or a past job.

Exhibit 5-1	Major Recruiting Sources

Internal Sources	Strengths
a. Promotion from within	Provides current employees new job opportunities within the firm
b. Employee referral	Inexpensive recruiting based on employee knowledge of the candidate
External Sources	**Strengths**
c. Walk-ins	Inexpensive and self-selected
d. Educational institutions	Good basic skill sets; typically less expensive than others with more experience
e. Temporary agencies	Prescreened workers; useful in short-term shortage situations
f. Public agencies	At least some prescreening; public employment agencies are very inexpensive
g. Private agencies	Heavy prescreening of recruits, lowering the organization's prescreening costs; typically very well targeted; good for experienced recruits
h. Local mass media	Fairly broad reach if searching for many recruits; cost per person is low; good for semiskilled or skilled line employees
i. Specialized publications	Good targeting to specific types of recruits; fairly good reach; fairly low cost per person
j. Internet	Very broad reach; beginning to be able to target to specific audiences—many professional organizations have sites

5-2   APPLYING THE CONCEPT

Recruiting Sources

Using Exhibit 5-1, select by its letter (a–j) which recruiting source is most appropriate in each of the given situations.

_____ 6. Your Maintenance Department needs a person to perform routine cleaning services.

_____ 7. You need a new secretary.

_____ 8. One of your first-line supervisors is retiring in a month.

_____ 9. Your Sales Manager likes to hire young people without experience in order to train them to sell using a unique approach.

_____ 10. You need an engineer who has very specific qualifications. There are very few people who can do the job.

_____ 11. Jose, Nancy just quit. Do you know anyone who can take her job?

_____ 12. Interest in entrepreneurship is growing, so we need to hire a new professor.

_____ 13. We need another person to keep our computer network running.

_____ 14. One of your workers got hurt on the job and will be out for two weeks.

_____ 15. We need a clerical worker, but we don't have any money for ads.

Advantages and Disadvantages of External Recruiting

What are the advantages and disadvantages of external recruiting?

Advantages. They include the following:

- The first and biggest advantage is the mirror image of the biggest disadvantage in internal recruiting—we *avoid* creating or perpetuating resistance to change, allowing a foothold for innovative new ways of operating.
- We may be able to find individuals with complex skill sets who are not available internally.
- We can lower training costs for skilled positions by hiring in someone with the requisite skills.
- External hires will frequently increase organizational diversity.

Disadvantages. What about disadvantages? There are certainly potential problems in bringing outsiders into the company:

- Disruption of the work team may occur by introducing significantly different ways of operating.
- External recruiting takes much longer, which means it costs more.
- Current employees' motivation and satisfaction might be affected due to the perceived inability to move up in the organization.
- External recruits likely will incur higher orientation and training costs than internal recruits.

- The candidate may look great on paper, but we have no organizational history on them.

Challenges and Constraints in Recruiting

The process of recruiting is expensive and time-consuming. As a result, we want to pay attention to the effectiveness of our recruiting methods. Some methods can give us too many new recruits to review, costing us valuable time and money. Other options will not give us enough of a pool so that we have some flexibility in whom to choose, while still others will cost too much for the results that we get. So the process of recruiting new employees has to be targeted a bit better than what we think it does sometimes.

All management functions are subject to constraints and challenges, and the recruiting function is no different. We have to live within certain rules and policies while still making it possible to bring the right kinds of people in the right numbers into the organization. Let's discuss some of the most significant issues that we face in the recruiting function.

LO 5.4

Briefly discuss the major challenges and constraints involved in the recruiting process.

Budgetary Constraints

Probably the most obvious constraint is money. We have to live within our budgets in all cases, and recruiting is no exception. There are times that we would like to fly half a dozen top-notch recruits in from around the world to interview for a position, but such costs add up very quickly. We would need to look very carefully at whether or not funds were available and whether it was necessary to do this due to the key nature of the job being filled. We might agree to incur the cost if the position being filled was important enough, but would not do so for a less significant job. Our budgets should always be created with the type of job that is being filled in mind.

Organizational Policies and Image

There are many *organizational policies* that can affect our recruiting efforts. We have to be familiar with such policies in detail in order to take them into account as we go through the recruiting process. Below are some of the policies that affect recruiting.

Whether we have a "promote-from-within" policy or not affects how we recruit. Our policies on "temporary-to-permanent" employees would also affect how we recruit in most cases. Do we have policies concerning recruiting and hiring relatives of current employees? If so, this would affect our recruiting efforts. Such a policy might significantly limit our ability to get referrals from current employees. Do we have an Affirmative Action policy in the organization? If so, it will dictate many of our recruiting procedures. We may also have a policy on how and when we communicate with any recruits or job applicants. If so, we need to understand and follow it.

We are also affected in our recruiting efforts by our *organizational image* in the markets from which we source our recruits.[25] You may know of a company in your local community that you would rather not work for because of a bad organizational reputation. Conversely, you might also know of an employer that you would very much like to work for because of a stellar reputation. Organizational image can play a significant part in

WORK
APPLICATION 5-6

Explain how the firm's image played a role in your applying for and accepting a job you have or have held.

determining our ability to source the people we need from the communities around us. A few organizations have lists of the best places to work, including *Fortune*'s "100 Best Companies to Work For"; companies listed include American Express, FedEx, Google, SAS, and Zappos.com.[26] This is just one of many reasons why we want to maintain a strong reputation in the communities that we serve.

<table>
<tr><td>**LO 5.5**</td></tr>
</table>

Discuss the value of a Realistic Job Preview.

Job Characteristics and the Realistic Job Preview

Let's face it. Not every job we need to fill is glamorous. Perhaps you have seen the show *Dirty Jobs* with Mike Rowe. Mike takes on jobs that most of us would not want to do, at least not on a routine basis. Almost all organizations have such jobs, whether it is a facilities job, such as housekeeping, or a nursing aide job where we might be emptying bedpans, or worse. Even though some of our jobs are not glamorous, we still need to find and recruit people to do them. The more difficult, dangerous, or just downright nasty a job is, the more difficult it is to recruit people into it. Still, we have to work to fill these jobs, and there are people out there who are willing to do each of them. We just need to do the work required to find them and get them to apply. As discussed in the last chapter, the key to success is matching the right person to the job.

Speaking of jobs that most of us would not want to do, should we hide the bad side of a job from recruits? This is really not an ethical thing to do and is not a good idea if we are looking at success in filling the job for the long term. Most companies have come to the conclusion that Realistic Job Previews are a necessary part of the recruiting process. A **Realistic Job Preview** (**RJP**) is *a review of all of the tasks and requirements of the job, both good and bad*. A good job analysis (Chapter 4) with a clear job description should provide a good RJP.

Why would we want to tell people the bad parts of the job? Won't that keep them from considering the job if we offer it? We have found that "giving applicants a warts-and-all preview of what a job entails on a day-to-day basis can reduce turnover effectively by making sure the applicant is really a good fit for the job."[27] Keeping information about the job from applicants is unethical and probably not socially responsible, and in most cases, if we don't tell recruits the truth about the job and they agree to work for the organization, they find out the bad parts of the job and feel like they were manipulated into coming to work for the organization. Remember, too, that an individual can sue us in some cases for fraud or misrepresentation if we don't tell them the truth in an advertisement for the job.

Job candidates need a Realistic Job Preview to understand what the job is all about.

What do you think it would do to their job satisfaction, organizational commitment, and productivity levels if we hid the bad part of the job from them? Satisfaction and organizational commitment would almost certainly go down, and this would happen literally right after they took the job. Is this what we want to do in a recruiting situation? How likely is it that this person would quit very early on if they felt like they were lied to in order to get them to accept the job? And if they did quit, we would incur all of our recruiting costs again almost immediately. There is strong research evidence that early turnover in a job is directly related to failure to provide an RJP for that job.[28]

WORK
APPLICATION 5-7

Briefly describe the RJP you received for your present or a past job. How could the RJP be improved?

The Recruiter–Candidate Interaction

LO 5.6

Discuss the characteristics needed in a capable recruiter.

Does the recruiter (or recruiters) affect the job candidate and their willingness to apply for a job in our organization? The obvious answer is yes. The recruiter is, in fact, one of the primary factors responsible for an applicant showing interest in our organization and our jobs.[29] What kind of recruiter do we need in a particular hiring situation? How does the recruiter affect the job seeker, and how can we make sure that the effect is both positive and realistic based on the RJP?

The recruiter is the critical piece in the recruiting process. According to one report, "Recruiters with higher degrees of engagement and job fit dramatically outperform their peers who score lower in those areas. That's measured both in the quality of hires and in productivity."[30] If you think about it, how well do *you* do things if they don't matter to you? So if our recruiters aren't engaged, how can we expect them to perform at a high level for the organization?

In addition to their desire to perform, though, we also have to ensure that our recruiters have certain skill sets. The most important of these skills is probably active listening. **Active listening** is *the intention and ability to listen to others, use the content and context of the communication, and respond appropriately*. What does this mean? It means that recruiters have to want to listen and have developed their active listening skills so that they not only hear the words that someone is saying, but also understand the context of the conversation (what the circumstances are and why the other is communicating this information) so that they can empathize with them and visualize why they are providing this information. If recruiters can do this, they can respond accordingly and, usually, successfully. If not, they will generally not provide the appropriate response to the recruit and as a result may lose a valuable opportunity to bring someone with a strong skill set into the organization. Empathy in this situation (putting yourself in another's position) allows the recruiter to visualize why something is being communicated and is critical if the recruiter is to respond correctly.

Besides active listening skills, recruiters have to have a strong set of communication skills. The recruiter must be able to talk with the recruit "on their level" in order to make them feel comfortable with the process. Recruiters need to learn when to ask probing questions and when to lie back and let the recruit talk. Role-playing training for the recruiter is particularly effective in teaching this skill.

The recruiter's job also includes successfully communicating with the hiring managers in the organization. The same active listening skills that serve them with an applicant can allow them to more clearly define what the hiring manager wants and needs in the new organizational recruit. So we need to create strong training programs in communication with recruiters in the organization.[31]

We also have to train recruiters in the process of the RJP. They need to understand the job in detail so that they can give honest answers and an RJP of the job to the potential candidate. In many cases today, with our complex jobs, we may have a recruiting team with one person on the team having the "technical" knowledge of the job (maybe the supervisor of the job) and the other person having the HR-related knowledge so that we don't inadvertently violate any laws, regulations, or internal policies. This helps us with the RJP because the technical person can explain details that the HR recruiter would generally not know or understand.

So our selection and training of the recruiter is a major factor in our overall recruiting success. We have to find individuals who have the ability to actively listen and empathize with the candidate and then train them in the communication skills that they will need and the roles that they will play with both the hiring manager and the candidate in order for them to be successful.

WORK
APPLICATION 5-8

Briefly describe the interaction you had with the recruiter for your current or a past job. How could the interaction be improved?

5-1 SELF-ASSESSMENT

CAREER DEVELOPMENT

Indicate how accurately each statement describes you by placing a number from 1 to 7 on the line before the statement.

Describes me   Does not describe me

7_____6 _____5_____4_____3_____2_____1

_____ 1. I know my strengths, and I can list several of them.

_____ 2. I can list several skills that I have to offer an employer.

_____ 3. I have career objectives.

_____ 4. I know the type of full-time job that I want next.

_____ 5. I have analyzed help-wanted ads or job descriptions and determined the most important skills I will need to get the type of full-time job I want.

_____ 6. I have, or plan to get, a part-time job, summer job, internship, or full-time job related to my career objectives.

_____ 7. I know the proper terms to use on my résumé to help me get the next job I want.

_____ 8. I understand how my strengths and skills are transferable, or how they can be used on jobs I apply for, and I can give examples on a résumé and in an interview.

_____ 9. I can give examples (on a résumé and in an interview) of suggestions or direct contributions I made that increased performance for my employer.

_____ 10. My résumé focuses on the skills I have developed and on how they relate to the job I am applying for rather than on job titles.

_____ 11. My résumé gives details of how my college education and the skills developed in college relate to the job I am applying for.

_____ 12. I have a résumé that is customized to each part-time job, summer job, or internship I apply for, rather than one generic résumé.

Add up the numbers you assigned to the statements and place the total on the continuum below.

84_____74_____64_____54_____44_____34_____24_____12

Career-ready   In need of career development

Evaluation of Recruiting Programs

LO 5.7

Discuss the basic methods available for evaluating the recruiting process.

We need to measure our recruiting processes the same as we measure every other process in the organization. We need to know how much the process costs, what our results from the process are, and whether or not the results were cost-effective. As we noted above, the recruitment process is expensive, and unless we identify and control these costs, the beneficial results may end up being outweighed by the costs. Remember, recruiting costs for one management position can run as much as 30% of the individual's yearly salary or more (and this doesn't include later costs for things like selection and initial training). So we need to pay attention to cost-benefit results of our recruiting efforts.

See Exhibit 5-2 for an overview of five evaluation methods that we discuss in this section.

Exhibit 5-2	Recruiting Evaluation Methods

Generally, all recruiting evaluation methods are comparisons to historical averages to see whether the organization is improving in its recruiting efforts or is less successful than in the past.

Yield Ratio:
Divide the number of qualified applicants by the number of applicants.

An advertisement yielded 40 applications, and 28 have the basic qualifications. The yield ratio is 28:40 or 70%.

Cost per Hire:
Divide the total cost by the number of applicants hired.

$60,000/10 = $6,000

Time to Hire:
The total time required from a position coming open until a new hire is in place.

A new opening on October 15 was filled on December 5, so our time to hire was 51 days.

New Hire Turnover:
Divide the number of recruits who left within a specified time frame by the number of new hires.

Last year, 84 people were hired, and 13 of those left again within a three-month time frame. Our new hire turnover would be 13/84 or 15.5%.

New Hire Performance:
Divide the difference in performance by new recruits into the average for all employees in the same category to determine percentage above or below average.

The average of all new hire appraisals last year was 3.1 on a 4-point grading scale. The average of all appraisals in the organization last year was 3.2. Therefore, new recruits are 3.3% below average (3.2 − 3.1 = .1 / 3.2 = 3.3%).

Yield Ratio

First, we probably want to look at the *yield ratio*. The recruiting **yield ratio** is *a calculation of how many people make it through the recruiting step to the next step in the hiring process.* For example, we advertise for a job opening and receive 100 résumés and applications. Of these applicants, 50 are judged to have the basic qualifications for the job. As a result, our yield ratio on the advertisement would be 50% (50 of our 100 applicants made it through the first recruiting step). As with all metrics, we then compare to historical data or to other company benchmarks to see how we are doing in the process. If our historic yield ratio for advertisements is 40%, then our ad was much more effective than average.

SHRM

Guide – E:6
Calculating and interpreting yield ratios

Cost per Hire

Another measure that you probably want to use is how much it costs to get each person hired—*cost per hire*. Cost per hire can be calculated based on the formula:[32]

> (Advertising + Agency Fees + Employee Referrals + Travel Cost of Applicants and Staff + Relocation Costs + Recruiter Pay and Benefits = Total Cost)
>
> Total Cost ÷ Number of Hires = Cost per Hire

We needed several new customer service representatives. We were successful in recruiting and hiring 15 fully qualified applicants for the open positions. During the recruiting campaign, the company spent $140,000 on all of the recruiting costs combined. The cost per hire would be $140,000/15 ($9,333.33 per hire).

Time Required to Hire

You also may want to analyze how long it takes to get someone hired. At Groupon with its fast growth, recruiting speed is key to its success.[33] Time required to hire is pretty self-explanatory. How many days/weeks/months did it take to get someone hired into an open position? If our company has a new opening on June 10, and we are able to fill the position on August 28, our time to hire was 79 days (June 30 – 10 = 20 + July 31 + August 28 = 79).

New Hire Turnover

Employee retention remains a critical issue for organizations and HR Managers.[34] You would certainly want to know how often new hires turned over again in a short period of time. In measuring new hire turnover, we need to identify a time frame. We would usually look at turnover within the first three to six months. Any longer than that and it is likely that factors other than the recruiting process were responsible for the turnover. So we identify our time frame and then measure how many new recruits compared to all hires during that period chose to leave the organization.

We had 30 new hires in the past year, and two of them left again within six months of being hired (we are identifying our turnover window as six months). We can calculate the turnover percentage and then compare it to historical averages: 2/30 = 6.7% New Hire Turnover Rate. If our historical new hire turnover is 10%, then we have improved, at least during this annual cycle.

New Hire Performance

You also want to know how well your new recruited employees perform on the new job. We can analyze the performance ratings of new hires versus all employees. Since there are so many ways to evaluate employees, it is a bit difficult to give an example here, but suppose you evaluate employees on an overall 4.0 scale (like college). Further, let's assume the average employee in the organization is judged to be a 3.0 on our 4-point scale. If we review new hires in their first year of service and they fall near the norm (3.0 on a 4-point scale), then our new hires are performing at a rate roughly equal to all employees— probably pretty good results. If, however, our new hires are significantly lower (say, 2.4 on the 4-point scale), we may want to analyze where they are not being successful and provide training opportunities to them and all new hires going forward to increase their chances for long-term success.

To make the measure more objective, we can calculate the percentage above or below average of new recruits to average employees. You divide the difference in performance by new recruits to the average. Let's use the new recruit average of 2.4 compared to the 3.0 average: $3.0 - 2.4 = .6 / 3.0 = .2$ or 20% below average. Don't bother working with negative numbers, you can easily see if the new recruits are above or below average, so just subtract the smaller from the larger number.

WORK
APPLICATION 5-9

Discuss how your present or a past employer evaluates its recruiting programs. If you don't know, contact the HR Department to find out.

5-3   APPLYING THE CONCEPT

Recruiting Evaluation Methods

Do the math.

_____ 16. An advertisement for a job opening receives 62 applications. Of these, 48 have the basic qualifications required for the job. The yield ratio would be _____ .

_____ 17. You hired 7 workers, and it cost you $72,000. The cost per hire is _____.

_____18 . Your company had a new opening on May 5, and you filled the position on June 25. Your time to hire was _____ days.

_____ 19. Your company hired 24 people last year, and 14 of those left again within your three-month time frame. Your new hire turnover would be _____.

_____ 20. The average of all new hire appraisals last year was 4.3 on a 5-point grading scale.

   The average of all appraisals in the organization last year was 4.1. Therefore, new recruits are _____ % above ____ or below ____ average.

Trends and Issues in HRM

In this chapter, the first item that we will discuss is the Internet and its use as a recruiting tool in today's job markets. We also need to consider global recruiting efforts to help us in our continuing search for knowledge workers, and we will finally briefly analyze the process of recruiting for diversity.

Video Link 5.2
Recruiting

Technology–The Internet and Recruiting Efforts

Does the Internet provide us with a valuable tool for recruiting new employees? It seems that this is a silly question. Look at the reach of the Internet; we can find workers in every corner of the country or even all over the world through the use of the Internet. However, does this reach give us better-quality hires and lower costs, or does it in fact increase our overall recruiting costs? The answer, as always, is "it depends." The Internet as a method of simply sourcing recruits has actually started to become a burden, at least in some cases, rather than a boon. When an advertisement goes out on the World Wide Web, we frequently get overwhelmed with online applicants, many of whom have little in common with the job that we are recruiting for. It has become so easy to apply for jobs online that we now have to wade through hundreds or even thousands of applicants for jobs that are posted on the Internet. So, untargeted sourcing of recruits using the Internet is likely on its way out.

What are we doing instead? Organizations are beginning to see that the Internet can and should be used for more than a "shotgun" advertising tool for job vacancies. We are beginning to figure out how to target ads to much narrower groups of applicants through scanning software and other tools that allow us to go out onto the web and find people who match our hiring criteria.

We are also emphasizing the screening and assessment functions using the web. How can we more efficiently screen job candidates? "How can we tell that a candidate has the skills needed before we incur major recruiting expenses? How do we know that a candidate with the right technical skill set is going to be a match for a particular work environment?" What types of online testing can we do to more closely target our recruiting efforts?[35]

Answering the above questions will allow us to continue to gain advantages from the Internet as a recruiting tool without overwhelming our abilities to comb through the applicants that we gain through online advertising. Many companies now use scanning software to prescreen applications and résumés that are completed online, which saves HR specialists time and money. The software is designed to find key words, so if you complete an online application, be sure to read the job description and use the exact key words from it.

Many companies are struggling with how to test applicants without running into questions of impropriety or questions of test validity and reliability. This is another situation in which we can apply the OUCH test to determine, at least on the surface, whether or not a testing practice is acceptable—is it *Objective, Uniformly applied,* and *Consistent in effect* between different protected groups, and does it *Have relatedness to the job?* If the answer to each of these questions is yes, the test is probably a legitimate tool to use in the recruiting process.

Global Recruiting for Knowledge Workers

Technological advancement, globalization, and the increasing shortage of skilled staff and talent workers have made it crucial for companies to implement appropriate recruitment practices to attract the best workers in the global market.[36] In Chapter 1, we noted that there is an expectation of a major shortage of workers with the complex set of required skills to be able to perform in the 21st-century workforce. In a recent study in the United States, HR executives project high worker shortages in many professions in 10 major industries by 2020 and 2030.[37]

As a result, more and more recruiting efforts for knowledge-based jobs are becoming global searches. In fact, it would not be unfair to say that recruiting has become a critical step in a knowledge-based strategy, where global recruiting efforts can yield significant advantages to the successful company.[38] With the shortage of skilled 21st-century workers, the only way to have any real chance of recruiting for open knowledge worker positions is to do so in every corner of the globe.

What factors affect our ability to recruit globally? First, we must understand labor regulations in each market in which we recruit for any positions within our firm. Failing to know and follow country regulations is a quick way to get into legal problems with a country government. Labor regulations also include any immigration laws that must be followed.

Next we need to know how people in a particular country market go about looking for work. The rest of the world does not necessarily follow the U.S. model when it comes to searching for jobs. How does a knowledge worker in China or South Africa look for work? If we are going to find the best talent, we need to know how the worker will search for and find us.

In addition to the issues above, we have to understand the myriad factors that must be dealt with in order to successfully recruit from the global workforce. Some of these factors include a global mind-set for both the organization and the employee; cultural awareness and adaptability; spouse and family challenges; and employee attitudes toward global assignments.[39] So global recruiting is a potential method for overcoming skilled worker shortages, but it is not without its problems and issues that must be overcome. However, more and more, we are going to find that global searches are the only method to find those skilled workers that we need for our 21st-century company.

WORK
APPLICATION 5-10

Discuss how your present or a past employer uses technology in recruiting. If you don't know, contact the HR Department to find out.

Should We Recruit for Diversity?

Should you recruit to increase diversity in your organization? Well, *if* your company already mirrors the communities around you, then you may not need to specifically recruit for diversity. However, in the majority of organizations, this is not the case. Few businesses today actually mirror their outside communities and customer bases. If this is the case, can you afford not to recruit for a more diverse workforce? What are the advantages of greater diversity in your organization?

The first, and arguably largest, advantage would be lower cost of discrimination litigation. If we discriminate over an extended period of time, it is almost guaranteed that someone will file an EEOC complaint against our company. Even if you go all the way and win a suit in court, you still face significant costs associated with defending the company. And if you lose, you face stiff fines, plus the potential for things such as a forced Affirmative Action plan. In addition, once a company is accused of discrimination, it is likely that it will be the target of additional legal actions in subsequent years.

If you are sued for discrimination, it is also likely that your reputation will suffer significantly. Several well-known companies are still haunted by past discrimination lawsuits, such as Abercrombie & Fitch ($47 million),[40] Shoney's ($132.5 million),[41] and Coca-Cola ($192 million).[42] Large settlements to be sure, but can you afford to alienate large numbers of potential customers through such a process, even if the organization wins the lawsuit?

Even if we disregard the issue of potential discrimination, do you serve the company well if you don't evaluate a diverse group of recruits for open positions within the company? If we limit our recruiting to certain groups, we run the risk of not finding the best qualified candidates. By limiting the recruiting pool, we unnecessarily tie our own hands with respect to finding the best talent available, and that is certainly not in the best interest of the organization over the long term.

If we, on the other hand, seek out diverse individuals, we can increase the innovation in the organization as well as increasing the options for solutions to difficult problems, such as how to reach particular customer groups in the most efficient and effective ways. So, looking at the facts, the company that limits its options in the recruiting process also limits its ability to compete with its rivals in an increasingly difficult competitive environment where our people mark the difference between success and failure.

Wrap-Up

What have you learned in this chapter? Based on our job analysis (job description and specifications), the actual first step in matching employees and jobs is recruiting. You know now that recruiting is not searching for anyone who can fill a job. It is about targeting and finding a reasonable pool of talented people who can do a particular job. You learned about some of the many forces acting on the firm's ability to recruit new employees, both inside and outside the organization. You now know that you need to have a thorough understanding of organizational policies in order to know when and how to recruit for a particular job, and you know that we can recruit internally or externally, and that each option has advantages and disadvantages. You also learned which sources are generally preferred in a specific recruiting situation and which options will probably not give you the kind of candidates that you want.

We also discussed the challenges and constraints in the recruiting process, especially the recruiter and the Realistic Job Preview (RJP) and why they are critical in getting the right people to apply to the organization. And lastly, we showed some methods for measuring the success of our recruiting efforts. Again, that's a pretty full chapter, so let's go on now to the selection process, after completing the end-of-chapter application and skill development exercises.

WORK
APPLICATION 5-11

Does your present or a past employer's workforce mirror the communities around you? What effort, if any, is your firm making to increase diversity? If you don't know, contact the HR Department to find out.

Chapter Summary

 Visit www.sagepub.com/lussier for helpful study resources.

5.1 **Identify and discuss the primary goal of the recruiting process.**

Through the recruiting process, we are trying to get people inside the company to apply for different job openings, or we are trying to get outsiders to join the company. The goal is to create a "reasonable pool" of candidates. Typically, a good goal is 15–25 candidates who are qualified and want to work for the organization.

5.2 **Briefly discuss the main external forces acting on recruiting efforts.**

The main external forces are the effective labor market and the social and legal forces that act on us as well as our potential recruits. These forces include *supply and demand* (are there plenty of candidates for the available jobs, or are there more jobs than candidates?); *unemployment rate* (what is the unemployment rate like in an area?); *competitors* (is competition for available workers strong or weak?); *the social environment* (what social factors do recruits emphasize when weighing whether or not to accept employment in a particular company?); and *laws* (what limits are placed on recruiting efforts by laws and regulations?).

5.3 **Discuss the major advantages and disadvantages of both internal and external recruiting.**

The major advantages of internal recruiting include increases in organizational commitment and job satisfaction; ability to learn more about the "big picture" in the company; feeling comfortable working for the company; the company knowing the individual and their work history; lower recruiting costs; and the fact that it is faster than external recruiting. Disadvantages include the fact that the pool of applicants is smaller; there's still another job to fill; success in one job doesn't necessarily mean success in a different job; external candidates may be more qualified; internal candidates may feel that they are entitled to the job whether they are capable and qualified or not; and we may perpetuate resistance to change and stifle innovation and creativity.

Advantages of external recruiting are that we avoid perpetuating resistance to change and encourage innovation and creativity; that we may be able to find individuals with complex skill sets who are not available internally; lower training costs for complex positions; and that we can potentially increase diversity. Disadvantages include potential disruption of the work team; that it takes longer than internal recruiting and costs more; that it may adversely affect current employees' motivation and

satisfaction; higher orientation and training costs; and that the candidate may look great on paper but not perform.

5.4 **Briefly discuss the major challenges and constraints involved in the recruiting process.**

The most obvious constraint is *money*. We have to avoid spending too much for the situation. Additionally, *organizational policies* also affect how we recruit. Our organization's *image* also plays a significant role in our ability to source the people we need from the communities around us. Next is the *type of job*. Not all jobs are clean or fun. Finally, our selection and training of the *recruiter* is a major factor in recruiting success. We have to find the individuals who have the ability to actively listen and empathize with the candidate.

5.5 **Discuss the value of a Realistic Job Preview.**

We have found that the RJP can reduce turnover by making sure the applicant is really a good fit for the job. In most cases if we hide the truth about the job, satisfaction and organizational commitment will almost certainly go down, and it is highly likely that the person will quit. If they do quit, we incur all of our recruiting costs again. There is strong evidence that an early turnover in the job is directly related to failure to provide an RJP for that job. Remember, too, that an individual can sue us in some cases for fraud or misrepresentation if we don't tell them the truth in any advertisement for the job.

5.6 **Discuss the characteristics needed in a capable recruiter.**

Recruiters need a high degree of *engagement and job fit* to be successful. In addition, we also have to ensure that our recruiters have *active listening skills* so that they can empathize with the other person. The recruiter also has to have a strong set of *communication skills* themselves. They need to learn when and how to ask questions and when to lay back and let the recruit talk. Their job also includes successfully *communicating with the hiring managers* in the organization. Finally, we have to *train the recruiter in the RJP* process.

5.7 **Discuss the basic methods available for evaluating the recruiting process.**

The recruiting *yield ratio* calculates how many people make it through the recruiting step to the next step in the hiring process. Another measure is how much it costs to get each person hired— *cost per hire*. You also may want to analyze how long it takes to get someone hired—*time required to hire*. *New hire turnover* is another measure of success. If we have high rates of turnover immediately after recruitment and selection, we probably need to reevaluate our recruiting and selection process. Finally, we can also analyze *new hire performance ratings* and compare them to the organizational norms. If our new hires perform at a significantly lower level than the norm, we may want to analyze where they are not being successful and provide training opportunities to them and all new hires going forward to increase their chances for long-term success.

Key Terms

Active listening

External recruiting

Internal recruiting

Labor market

Realistic Job
Preview (RJP)

Recruiting

Yield ratio

Key Term Review

Complete each of the following statements using one of this chapter's key terms:

_____ is the process of creating a reasonable pool of qualified candidates for a job opening.

_____ is the term for the external pool of candidates from which we draw our recruits.

_____ involves filling job openings with current employees or people they know.

_____ is the process of engaging individuals from the labor market outside the firm to apply for a job.

_____ is a review of all of the tasks and requirements of the job, both good and bad.

_____ is the intention and ability to listen to others, use the content and context of the communication, and respond appropriately.

_____ is a calculation of how many people make it through the recruiting step to the next step in the hiring process.

Quick Check (True-False)

1. The process of recruiting does no good if the candidates that we attract are not qualified to do the work. T F

2. External forces affecting the recruiting effort include the labor market, the legal environment, and the recruiter. T F

3. Unions and labor agreements, where they exist in organizations, don't have much effect on our ability to recruit externally. T F

4. The answer to the question "When should we recruit?" is "When we need someone to fill a job." T F

5. Internal recruiting can occur in one of two primary ways—promotions from within and employee referrals. T F

6. In closed recruiting, HR recruiters actively look for individuals with the correct qualifications for the job opening but don't openly advertise the job opening. T F

7. One of the advantages of external recruiting is that it usually costs less than internal recruiting does. T F

8. No matter which advertising option we use, we have to be aware of the potential for fraud and/or misrepresentation in our advertisement. T F

9. The Internet is probably the best source for any external recruiting effort because of its ability to reach all over the world. T F

10. Organizational image heavily affects our ability to bring in outside recruits. T F

11. A Realistic Job Preview makes it much less likely that a new hire will leave the job in the weeks following their initial hiring. T F

12. The recruiter's job is to get the recruit to join the organization "no matter what else happens."

Communication Skills

The following critical-thinking questions can be used for class discussion and/or for written assignments to develop communication skills. Be sure to give complete explanations for all answers.

1. Should you "shop" for good employees who are out of work in a bad economy and then terminate existing employees who aren't doing their jobs very well after finding a good replacement? What consequences can you see to this course of action?

2. If you were in charge in your company, would you personally rather recruit new employees, or would you rather use some of the other tools for a shortage of employees that were discussed in this and the last chapter? Why?

3. In your personal experience, do you think that internal recruiting really improves organizational morale, job satisfaction, and productivity? Why or why not?

4. Do you think that targeted or closed recruiting leads to the potential for discrimination in recruiting efforts? Why or why not?

5. When would you *definitely* use the Internet as a recruiting tool, and when would you definitely *not* use the Internet to recruit? Why?

6. What could an organization do to improve its image if it has a bad reputation with recruits? Categorize your efforts into immediate items and longer-term items.

7. What would you tell recruiters to do or not do in order to enhance their recruiting efforts if you were in charge of your company? Why?

8. Do you think that you are a good "active listener"? Why or why not, and what could you do to become better?

9. What options do you see as alternatives to recruiting globally for knowledge-based jobs in the coming years?

Video

Please visit the student study site at **www.sagepub.com/lussier** to view the video links in this chapter.

Answers

REVIEW QUESTIONS (TRUE-FALSE) Answers

1. T   2. F   3. F   4. F   5. T   6. T   7. F   8. T   9. F   10. T   11. T   12. F

Case

Case 5-1. Here a GM, There a GM, Everywhere a GM (or So They Thought)!

Hartson Printing Services, Inc.,[1] was a midsized company (revenues of approximately $12 million per year) serving the southern United States. The owners, a husband and wife, had personally managed the company for most of its nearly 25 years in business. However, as the company had grown, it was becoming more and more difficult to personally manage all of the details of daily operations. As a result, Angie and Joe Hartson decided to create and fill a new position as General Manager (GM) of the printing company. The GM would handle all of the day-to-day operations of the facility, leaving the owners free to make more strategic decisions as well as get some needed time off.

Once the decision to recruit a GM had been made, Angie and Joe decided that the best way to find a person for the job was to advertise. They discussed the kind of person that they were interested in hiring in some detail and then sat down and wrote out the following advertisement for the new opening:

Now Hiring: General Manager—Printing Services Industry

Looking for strong leader to aggressively manage and grow a high-quality printing business. Duties include daily management of midsized operations, including projects ranging from personal business cards to small-volume book binding. Candidates must have good leadership, management, and P&L skills and be able to manage in a fast-paced, deadline-driven environment. An Equal Opportunity Employer. Send résumé and cover letter to P.O. Box 66452, Gadsden, AL 35901.

The Hartsons sat back after looking at their work and congratulated themselves on writing their advertisement. They put it in the local newspaper and the *Birmingham News* the next day, and within two weeks had more than 145 responses—many more than they really had anticipated. However, as they started going through all of the responses, they realized that none of the applicants really fit what they needed for their print shop. They had

[1]The name of the printing company and its location have been changed.

received replies from an extremely diverse group of respondents with no real knowledge of an operation of the size of Hartson Printing. The cover letters didn't provide them with any valuable information on the skill sets of the applicants, and the résumés were "all over the map." One of the applicants was currently an Assistant Night Manager at a local fast-food restaurant, but was convinced that she could manage their $12 million print shop. Another was the retired former president of an international multibillion-dollar firm, and neither Angie nor Joe could figure out why he would want such a small-scale job opportunity.

They decided to take some time away from the office to work their way through the other résumés. They scanned through more than 140 of them over the course of two full days and found out that none of the applicants really fit what they needed in a GM. Angie and Joe couldn't figure out what on earth the applicants were thinking! Most had no idea what kind of firm they were applying to, and the few who did didn't fit with the owners' vision of what they would need to be able to do and the background necessary for successfully filling the job. The Hartsons couldn't even find one applicant that they wanted to interview for the job. At this point, Angie suggested and Joe agreed that they might need some professional help, so they called a local consulting firm that had experience in management recruiting.

The next day, Tom, an HR Consultant, came to speak with Angie and Joe. He asked to see the advertisement and the résumés from the respondents. He took one look at the ad and thumbed through some of the résumés, and immediately saw what had happened. He quickly started working with the owners on a new advertisement that ended up looking as follows:

General Manager Wanted—Full P&L Responsibility

Starting salary $60,000+ with opportunity for performance incentives to be determined jointly with company owners.

Hartson Printing Services, a $12 million firm in Gadsden, AL, is seeking an experienced Printing Services Manager who will be responsible for all day-to-day operations for our printing firm. Please review our product and service line at www.hartsonprinting.com for details on the company.

Qualifications will include at least 15 years in printing and/or publishing industries; experience with bid and proposal processes; experience with short run and quick throughput jobs; knowledge of pre-press preparation, pressroom, and binding operations; knowledge of maintenance schedules for common printing equipment used in Hartson's offices; at least 5 years in a management role with responsibility for planning, organizing, and controlling the work of at least 5 employees; knowledge of organizational budgets and experience in a P&L role; 4-year business degree; proven skills in cost containment in a midsized printing firm. Relocation required.

To apply, provide a résumé and cover letter to Hartson Printing Services, 318 Main St., Gadsden, AL 35901. Hartson is proud to be an Equal Opportunity Employer.

The Hartsons reviewed the advertisement, and immediately had some questions for Tom. Once these questions had been answered, the three agreed that they would like to immediately get the ad published in order to get the process of finding a strong GM for the business back on track. The Hartsons were excited about this fresh start and beginning to look forward to the interviewing process (another significant challenge!).

Questions

1. What was wrong with the Hartsons' first recruiting advertisement?

2. What do you think happened to cause the first advertisement to be off target in reaching its intended audience?

3. What problems did this first attempt at advertisement create for the owners?

4. What significant differences do you see between the first ad and the second ad?

5. Would you make any other changes to clarify the job? If so, what changes would you make and why? If not, why not?

6. In what external recruiting sources would you choose to publish the new advertisement? Be specific and provide your reasoning for your choice(s).

Case created by Herbert Sherman, PhD

SKILL BUILDER 5-1

Online Job Search

Objective

To develop your job searching skills and to learn more about job descriptions and specifications.

To get you thinking about your career.

Skills

The primary skills developed through this exercise are:

1. HR *Management skill* – Technical, business, and conceptual and design skills

2. *SHRM 2010 Curriculum Guidebook* – G: Staffing: Recruitment and selection

Preparation

Steps in the Job Search, Which Is Preparation for the Written Assignment

Let's do an exercise related to your professional development. Employers recruit job candidates, so we focus on you.

1. Think about a job or an internship you would like to have. You may also get ideas when you go to a job search website.

2. Go to a job search website of your choice. You may use http://online.wsj.com/public/page/news-career-education-college .html (jobs and tips for new college grads), www.CollegeRecruiter.com (a career test to identify possible jobs; internships and entry-level jobs), www.shrm.org (HR jobs and advice), www.Monster.com (simply a listing of all types of jobs), and www .CareerBuilder.com (jobs and advice). You may want to search using other websites and use more than one job search engine.

If you are interested in working for a specific business or nonprofit organization, you may also visit its website.

3. Read about the job—job descriptions and specifications for the available jobs.

4. Your professor may want copies of the website pages pertaining to your job search.

Written Assignment Instructions

Type the answers to these three questions.

1. What job(s) were you searching for, and which website(s) did you use to search?

2. List three or four things that you learned about job searching.

3. How will you use this information to get a job?

Apply It

What did I learn from this experience? How will I use this knowledge in the future?

_____

_____

Your instructor may ask you to do this Skill Builder in class in a group by sharing your answers to the questions. If so, the instructor will provide you with any necessary information or additional instructions.

SKILL BUILDER 5-2

Résumé

Objective

To develop a résumé you can use for part-time, summer, internship, and full-time employment.

Skills

The primary skills developed through this exercise are:

1. *HR Management skill* – Technical, business, and conceptual and design skills
2. *SHRM 2010 Curriculum Guidebook* – G: Staffing: Recruitment and selection

Preparation

Writing the Résumé

You may go to your college's Career Center and/or visit www.provenresumes.com for help. You should read the tips below before writing your résumé.

Type out your résumé, and keep it to one page, unless you have extensive "relevant" experience. Before finalizing your résumé, improve it by using the résumé assessment below, which may be used to grade your résumé.

Answer these résumé questions (Yes/Somewhat/No):

- Within 10 seconds, can a recruiter understand the job you are applying for and that you have the qualifications (skills/experience and education) to get the position? You should not use the word *I* or *me* on a résumé.

Objective

- Does your résumé have an objective that clearly states the position being applied for (such as Sales Rep)? The job applied for affects all sections of your résumé because your résumé needs to state how you are qualified for the job. If you don't list the job you are applying for on your résumé, it will most likely be tossed out, and you will not get a job with the firm.

Education (describe relevant courses)

- If education is your major qualification for the job, is there detail that states the skills developed and courses taken in school that will qualify you for the position applied for?

- Be sure to state your degree, major and minor, and concentration, if you have them. Don't write bachelor of science or master of business administration; use BS and the name of your degree or MBA. Be sure to list your month and year of graduation.

- Your résumé should do a good job of filling one page. If you don't have extensive experience, list relevant courses that prepared you for the job you are applying for. For relevant courses, don't just include a shopping list. Pick a few "relevant" courses and describe how the course qualifies you for to the job listed in your objective. So if you want to be a Sales Rep, you state that you are a marketing major/concentration and that you have had the sales and selling course. Describe the skills you developed in the sales and other relevant courses.

- Computers. If you list computer courses/skills, be sure to list programs such as Microsoft Word, Excel, Access, PowerPoint (it is one word, not two), Windows, SPSS, HTML, and so on. If used on the job, say so with the program you used.

Experience

- Does your résumé list experience or skills that support that you can do the job stated in your objective?

- Be sure to list names and addresses of employers, with months and years on the job. If you want the company to which you are applying to contact your boss for a reference, list the person's name and telephone number on your résumé.

- Don't just list activities, such as cutting grass. Focus on general skills that can be applied to the job you want. Try to show skills. Did you do any planning, organizing, leading (influencing others, communication skills, motivation), and controlling? Give examples of your skills.

- For the sales job example, if each job doesn't have sales experience, list sales skills developed on the job. List communication skills that you used to successfully interact with customers, stating how you used them, that you enjoy meeting new people, and that you have the ability to easily converse with people you don't know.

Accomplishments (not necessarily a separate section and heading)

- Does your résumé clearly list accomplishments and valuable contributions made during your education and/or experience?

- A high GPA should be listed with education.

- Sports teams. If you are on a college sports team, be sure to list it with any accomplishments (such as Maroon of the Week, Captain, MVP, selection to conference teams). A good place to list sports is under the education section.

- Job. Increased sales by 10% from May to August 2010. Employee of the month. Earned highest tips based on communication skills with customers and superior service.

- Is your résumé neat, attractive, and free of errors? It should have neat columns, so use tables without gridlines. Use high-quality bond paper and ink color for hard copies actually used to get a job.

Apply It

What did I learn from this experience? How will I use this knowledge in the future?

_____

_____

Your instructor may ask you to do this Skill Builder in class in a group by showing others your résumé. If so, the instructor will provide you with any necessary information or additional instructions.

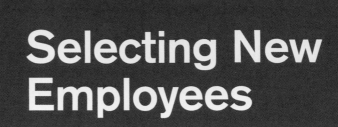

6

Selecting New Employees

Learning Outcomes

After studying this chapter you should be able to:

6.1 Describe why the selection process is so important to the company

6.2 Identify the three main types of "fit" that we look for in the selection process and why they are important

6.3 Discuss the major points in the Uniform Guidelines on Employee Selection Procedures

6.4 Briefly discuss the use of applications and résumés as selection tools

6.5 Briefly discuss the legal considerations in the selection process

6.6 Discuss the major types of written testing available as a selection tool

6.7 Identify the requirements for organizational drug testing programs

6.8 Discuss the value of selection interviews, including the three primary types of interviews

6.9 List and briefly describe the steps taken in conducting interviews

6.10 Identify the common problems that are faced during the selection process

6.11 Define the following terms:

Selection

Negligent hire

Uniform Guidelines on Employee Selection Procedures (UGESP)

Validity

Criterion-related validity

Content validity

Construct validity

Reliability

Skills test

Personality test

Interest test

Cognitive ability test

Physical test

Assessment center

Multiple-hurdle selection model

Compensatory selection model

Chapter 6 Outline

The Selection Process
  The Importance of the Selection Process
  Steps in the Selection Process

Looking for Fit
  Personality-Job Fit
  Ability-Job Fit
  Person-Organization Fit

Uniform Guidelines on Employment
Selection Procedures
  What Qualifies as an Employment Test?
  Valid and Reliable Measures

Applications and Preliminary Screening
  Applications and Résumés
  Preemployment Inquiries

Testing and Legal Issues
  The EEOC and Employment Testing
  Polygraph Testing
  Genetic Testing
  Written Testing
  Physical Testing
  To Test, or Not to Test

Selection Interviews
  Interviewing
  Types of Interviews and Questions
  Preparing for the Interview
  Conducting the Interview

Background Checks
  Credit Checks
  Criminal Background Checks
  Reference Checks
  Web Searches

Selecting the Candidate and Offering the Job
  Problems to Avoid
  Hiring

Trends and Issues in HRM
  Selection With a Global Workforce
  Local Hiring as a Sustainable Business Practice
  HRISs and the Selection Process

B. Employment Law (required)
  32. The Genetic Information Nondiscrimination Act of 2008
  36. The Fair Credit Reporting Act
  39. Negligent hiring

C. Job Analysis/Job Design (required)
  3. Employment practices (recruitment, selection, placement)

D. Organization Development
  14. Social networking

G. Staffing: Recruitment and Selection (required)
  6. Initial assessment methods (résumés, cover letters, application blanks, biographical information, reference/background checks, genetic screening, initial interviews, minimum qualifications)
  7. Discretionary assessment methods
  8. Ability/job knowledge tests, assessment centers
  9. Noncognitive assessments (e.g., personality assessments, integrity tests, situational judgment tests, interest inventories)
  10. Structured interviews
  11. Contingent assessment methods (drug testing, medical exams)
  12. Measurement concepts (predictors/criteria, reliability, validity)
  13. Selection decisions (ranking, grouping/banding, random selection)

L. Workplace Health, Safety, and Security (required–undergraduates only)
  10. Testing for substance abuse

Case 6-1. Who Is Doing the Selling? Gerald Interviews at Washington Home Builders

SHRM HR CONTENT

See Appendix A: *SHRM 2010 Curriculum Guidebook* for the complete list

Eenie, Meenie, Meinie, *You!*

The process of moving a person from job candidate to employee is a matching game for both the candidate and the company. When Kathy, our accounting manager, insisted on conducting her own job interviews, I knew we needed to talk. "I don't want someone hired that I can't get along with," Kathy said. "I need to be the one to decide who we hire." Is Kathy qualified to conduct the interview? What are the pitfalls to avoid and legal restrictions that must be respected? Chapter 6 covers the process that must be followed to properly select employees.

The Practitioner's Model for HRM

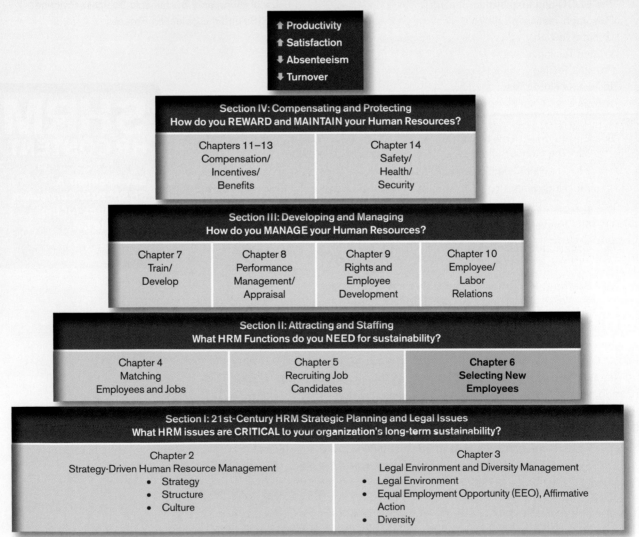

⬆ Productivity
⬆ Satisfaction
⬇ Absenteeism
⬇ Turnover

Section IV: Compensating and Protecting
How do you REWARD and MAINTAIN your Human Resources?

| Chapters 11–13 Compensation/ Incentives/ Benefits | Chapter 14 Safety/ Health/ Security |

Section III: Developing and Managing
How do you MANAGE your Human Resources?

| Chapter 7 Train/ Develop | Chapter 8 Performance Management/ Appraisal | Chapter 9 Rights and Employee Development | Chapter 10 Employee/ Labor Relations |

Section II: Attracting and Staffing
What HRM Functions do you NEED for sustainability?

| Chapter 4 Matching Employees and Jobs | Chapter 5 Recruiting Job Candidates | **Chapter 6 Selecting New Employees** |

Section I: 21st-Century HRM Strategic Planning and Legal Issues
What HRM issues are CRITICAL to your organization's long-term sustainability?

Chapter 2
Strategy-Driven Human Resource Management
- Strategy
- Structure
- Culture

Chapter 3
Legal Environment and Diversity Management
- Legal Environment
- Equal Employment Opportunity (EEO), Affirmative Action
- Diversity

The Selection Process

We learned in Chapter 5 how to go through the recruiting process to get our "reasonable pool" of job candidates. Now we need to select one person from the pool to fill our job opening. Firms always seek to hire the most highly skilled employees to maximize their output,[1] but there is often a mismatch when the job and person don't fit and productivity suffers.[2] Thus, managers' focus on hiring is one of their critical tasks.[3] **Selection** is *the process of choosing the best qualified applicant recruited for a job*. Remember, too, that in most organizations today at least one of their competitive advantages will be their employees, so if we put the wrong people into the wrong jobs, we can have great difficulty in carrying out our strategic plans. So we need to focus on fit.[4]

As with all other decisions that involve people in the organization, we can apply the OUCH test here as a quick test of whether or not we should use a particular tool or measure in the selection process. Is the tool *Objective*—does it use fact and knowledge, or is it based on bias and emotion? If we use a tool or measure, we must be *Uniform in application* of the measure—we need to use it with all of the people in the selection process. Is the tool *Consistent in effect*—does it have an inconsistent effect on one or more protected classes? And finally, the tool or measure must *Have job relatedness*—it must be able to be shown to have a relationship with the primary (essential) factors in the job. The OUCH test will give us an initial analysis of the measure being used, and if it appears that we might not be able to apply the measure so that it meets the OUCH test requirements, we need to do some more investigation before we decide to use it in the selection process.

LO 6.1

Describe why the selection process is so important to the company.

The Importance of the Selection Process

Selection is a critical management task.[5] Here are three reasons why the selection process is so important, and each reason is essentially the result of a mismatch of the job and employee.

Video Link 6.1

Selection Process

Time and money. The first and probably most notable reason is that we want to get the best possible person into the job in every case because of our requirement to improve organizational productivity. It is often important to fill jobs quickly, but hurrying can result in a mismatch; or as the old saying goes, haste makes waste. If we hire someone who is not willing or not able to do the job successfully, we will most likely have to go through the whole process again in a very short time. This obviously costs us more time and money for the new recruiting and selection process, so it is something that we work very hard to avoid.

Lower productivity. Think about your experiences in the past. Have you ever seen (or been a part of) an organization with employees who did the minimum amount of work possible, who didn't ever go out of their way to help customers in any situation, and who didn't cooperate with others in the organization? Do you think that organization started out that way, or did people start out working hard and paying attention? In such an organization, what kind of overall productivity are you going to have? And it is easier than you think to get into this type of situation. Just a few people hired into the company who show this lack of concern for the organization and its customers can be highly contagious. Pretty soon others in the organization decide that "if they are able to do the absolute minimum and still get paid the same amount as me, why should I work so hard?" Once this occurs, morale, job satisfaction, and organizational commitment can drop very quickly. You don't want to put your organization in such a position, so you absolutely must give your full attention to the selection process to make sure you hire only people who fit the jobs.

SHRM

Guide – B:39
Negligent hiring

WORK
APPLICATION 6-1

Select a present or past organization and give an example of how a mismatch of the job and an employee resulted in a negative outcome.

SHRM

Guide – G:7
Discretionary assessment methods

WORK
APPLICATION 6-2

Select a present or past job and list each step in the selection process and state if it was or was not used to hire you.

LO 6.2

Identify the three main types of "fit" that we look for in the selection process and why they are important.

SHRM

Guide – C:3
Employment practices (recruitment, selection, placement)

Negligent hires. Another issue that makes selection critical is the potential for a *negligent hire.* Almost every state in the United States recognizes the concept of *negligent hire*, so HR Managers must understand it as well.[6] A **negligent hire** is *a legal concept that says if the organization selects someone for a job who may pose a danger to coworkers, customers, suppliers, or other third parties and then that person harms someone else in the course of their work for the company, the company can be held liable for the individual's actions.*

For example, if a company hired a salesperson who had a criminal record for assault and who then assaulted a customer, the company could be held liable for the harm done to the customer who was assaulted. Many businesses focus on quick delivery, but when drivers have hurried and been negligent, they have caused accidents involving damage of property and injury to people, resulting in companies being sued for millions. So we have to make every legitimate attempt to find out if someone has the potential to be a danger to others and weed them out during our selection process.

Steps in the Selection Process

The selection process follows a series of steps that are illustrated in Exhibit 6-1. Note that this is a *general guide* that is commonly followed, but there can be exceptions in following the steps in the process. The steps may not be followed sequentially as shown, and some parts may not be included. For example, there may not be any preliminary testing or initial interviewing, and there may not be any drug or physical exam conditions.

There are many tools at our disposal when we are going through the selection process. There are written tests, physical tests, personality tests, honesty tests, drug testing, background checks of various types, and more. Which tools should we use in which circumstances? Almost all of our selection devices are discretionary, or optional. We don't have to do any written or physical ability tests; we don't have to administer any cognitive ability tests; we don't have to provide tests for stamina, honesty, or judgment.

The steps do, however, make logical sense. People apply for jobs, followed by the firm screening the job candidates to narrow down the selection, which can include a test of some type and an initial interview for the top candidates. For lower-level jobs, it is not uncommon for the HR Department to do the screening, conduct any testing and do the background checks, and send the best applicants to the manager the candidate will actually work for. The manager commonly conducts interviews and makes a conditional job offer that may include drug screening and/or a physical exam. The final step ending the process is when the applicant is hired.

In this chapter, we discuss each step in the process. But before we get into the selection steps, let's discuss the importance of selecting the applicant who best matches the job, or what we call looking for fit. Next, we need to understand that the government has Uniform Guidelines on Employment Selection Procedures that affect how we conduct each of the steps in the selection process.

Looking for Fit

Throughout the selection process, we have to keep in mind that we hire for fit.[7] "We hold these truths to be self-evident, that all men are created equal."[8] Is this a true statement? It is what the Declaration of Independence says! However, we all know that people are not equal. We also know that, as managers, if we treat people equally (the same), then we really aren't doing our job. Managers are supposed to get the best productivity out of their workforce, but not everyone can do everything equally well. So we have to treat people differently, but fairly, in order to be successful in our jobs. What do we need to look for in the selection process in order to put "the right person in the right job"? We need to attempt to

| Exhibit 6-1 | Steps in the Selection Process |

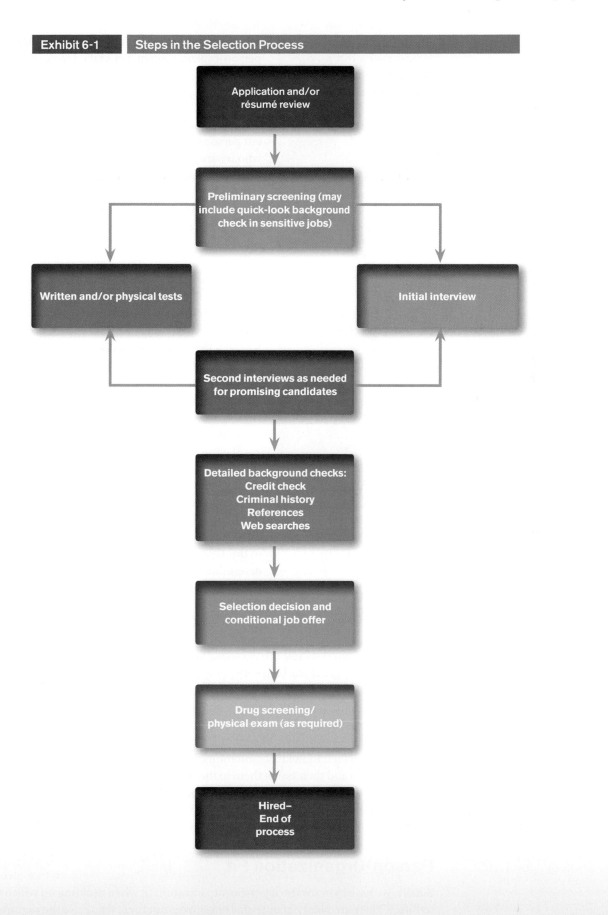

To be successful, the employee must match the job and the organization.

assess three things: personality-job fit; ability-job fit; and person-organization fit. Let's take a look at these items.

Personality-Job Fit

What is personality-job fit? We all have unique and different personalities. Our personality defines to a great extent who we are and how we act and react in certain situations. Some of us are strongly extroverted and enjoy "working the crowd" in a social setting, while others may be fairly introverted and feel extremely uncomfortable in such an environment. Some of us desire to try new things constantly, while others are more comfortable with things that they know well. There are many traits that help define our personalities, but the fact remains that each of us is different. Should you as a manager try to change the basic personality of one of your employees? Of course not! However, does their personality affect the things they enjoy doing and even affect the way that they work? Yes, it does. So you can't change their personality, but it affects how they work, and as a result you have to make an attempt to identify their personality type and then put them in a position that will be enhanced by their particular personality traits. This is called personality-job fit.[9]

If we need to hire an employee who will have to "work the crowd" in, say, a sales job for our company, would we want to hire someone who is very uncomfortable talking with and relating to strangers? If we did hire that person, is it likely that they would succeed or fail in the position? Obviously, it is more likely that such a person would fail in this type of environment. So one of the things we try to determine in the selection process is the personality-job fit.

Ability-Job Fit

In addition to personality-job fit, we want to determine ability-job fit. Every individual has a certain set of physical and intellectual skills, and no two people are exactly alike. Some people are very capable working with computers, while others are more capable in physical work. Still others may be able to successfully perform both physical and computer-based tasks, but have difficulty with analyzing quantitative information. Each of us is more skilled at some things than others.

Managers have to analyze the set of abilities in each of our subordinates or new hires and understand their individual limitations. Using this information, the manager must hire the right person and then assign them to the type of job for which they are best suited. Here again, if we assign the wrong person to a job, we can easily frustrate them and as a result cause motivation and job satisfaction to drop, which in turn will likely cause losses in productivity. So we have to pay attention to ability-job fit.[10]

Person-Organization Fit

Finally, we have to be aware of person-organization fit when deciding on which candidate to hire.[11] There are plenty of potential employees out there who have the required skills to do the jobs that we need them to do, and they may even have the right type of personality to be comfortable in such a job, but they just may not fit well within the organization itself. Person-organization fit deals with the cultural and structural characteristics of the organization and how well the candidate will fit within that structure and culture.[12]

If a candidate works best in a decentralized organization with strong individual reward systems and we are hiring them to work in a tightly controlled and centralized team-based division, it is unlikely that they will be able or willing to conform to the requirements of the company structure and culture. As a result, they will likely be unhappy in this situation and are more likely to leave as soon as they can find another opportunity that more closely matches their desires for a specific type of work environment.

Uniform Guidelines on Employment Selection Procedures

We are now ready to discuss a legal issue that affects each step of the selection process. The **Uniform Guidelines on Employee Selection Procedures (UGESP)** *provide information that can be used to avoid discriminatory hiring practices as well as discrimination in other employment decisions.* Most often called by the term Uniform Guidelines, they were created to guide employers in their efforts to comply with the federal laws concerning all employment decisions, and especially the selection process.[13] Let's discuss some of the most important sections of the UGESP.

What Qualifies as an Employment Test?

The UGESP formalize and standardize the way that the federal government identifies and deals with discriminatory employment practices. They define the concept of "tests for employment" that are used in either the selection process or other employment actions. But, what is a test for employment? It is a pretty broad term. The guidelines define it as applying to "tests and other selection procedures which are used as a basis for any employment decision. Employment decisions include but are not limited to hiring, promotion, demotion, membership (for example, in a labor organization), referral, retention, and licensing and certification . . . training or transfer may also be considered employment decisions if they lead to any of the decisions listed above."[14]

Although the guidelines specifically say that they "apply only to selection procedures which are used as a basis for making employment decisions,"[15] if we look closely at the definition of employment decision above, pretty much any selection procedure that we would use becomes a test for employment, which means that we need to follow the UGESP during every step of the selection process.

Valid and Reliable Measures

The UGESP also discuss the need for any employment test that is used by an employer to be validated and reliable. Let's discuss validity and reliability separately, then put them together. **Validity** is *the extent to which a test measures what it claims to measure.* The UGESP require validity in our selection procedures. They note that "users may rely upon criterion-related validity studies, content validity studies or construct validity studies"[16] in order to validate a particular selection procedure. But what are these validity measures?

Criterion-related validity. **Criterion-related validity** is *an assessment of the ability of a test to measure some other factor related to the test.* Criterion-related validity therefore occurs in selection when we can show a strong relationship between scores on a

WORK APPLICATION 6-3

Select a present or past job and explain in detail how well your personality, ability, and person fit or did not fit the job and organization.

LO 6.3

Discuss the major points in the Uniform Guidelines on Employee Selection Procedures.

Video Link 6.2

Selection Devices

SHRM

Guide – G:12
Measurement concepts (predictors/criteria, reliability, validity)

test prior to being employed in a job and performance on the job once the individual is hired. For example, SAT scores are designed to be one of the predictors of college success. We most often show this through demonstration of a significant statistical relationship between scores on a selection test and job performance of existing workers in that job.[17] One of the issues here is that we need a fairly large number of individuals available included in the analysis in order to get the statistical data necessary to show criterion-related validity.

Content validity. **Content validity** is *an assessment of whether a test measures knowledge or understanding of the items it is supposed to measure.* So, in measuring content validity for selection, we have to show that "the content of a selection procedure is representative of [measures] important aspects of performance on the job."[18] "A selection procedure can be supported by a content validity strategy to the extent that it is a representative sample of the content of the job."[19] So, in other words, if we have good work sample tests or other tests of knowledge, skills, or abilities that are directly applicable to the job, we can probably use content validity to validate our selection procedure.

Construct validity. **Construct validity** *measures a theoretical concept or trait that is not directly observable.* For construct validity to be applicable, we must demonstrate that "(a) a selection procedure measures a construct (something believed to be an underlying human trait or characteristic, such as honesty) and (b) the construct is important for successful job performance."[20] However, the UGESP say that this method of validation is far more difficult to show than the other two options, so it would be best if you can show that a measure has criterion-related or content validity.

You will learn about several different types of tests that must meet criterion-related, content, and/or construct validity in the "Testing and Legal Issues" section. But now let's move on to reliability, because tests also have to be reliable to be legal.

Reliability. **Reliability** *is the consistency of a test measurement.* In addition to validity, for a measure to be useful in any type of testing (including employment testing), it needs to be reliable. On the face of it, what does the word *reliable* mean? It means that the measure is consistent in some way—perhaps consistent when used by two different people (called interrater reliability) or perhaps consistent over time (called test-retest reliability). Let's make it simple. If you go out to your car every day and it starts when you turn the ignition key, it is reliable. If it sometimes starts, but sometimes doesn't, then it isn't reliable. We want our measures when we are working with people to be reliable measures—they are consistent over time and between people.

The relationship between reliability and validity. Let's put validity and reliability together by stating the obvious. If a test is not reliable, it can't be valid. For example, some jobs do include a weight criterion as a job specification. Remember from Chapter 4 that if a job candidate steps on our company scale and weighs 150 pounds, then steps off and on again and weighs 155, then 153, the scale is not reliable. How much does the candidate actually weigh? If our scale is not reliable, then it can't be valid because it doesn't accurately measure what we claim it measures.

Let's make it a bit more complicated by stating that a test can be reliable but not valid, but it can't be valid without being reliable. If a job candidate steps on the company scale and weighs 150 pounds, then steps off, and then weighs 150 pounds three more times, our scale is reliable. However, what if we place the person on a more expensive, better scale and the person weighs 155? Then our scale is reliable, but it is not valid because it doesn't accurately measure a person's weight.

WORK
APPLICATION 6-4

Select a present or past job and explain which one of the three types of validity would be the most relevant for that job.

Now that we have a general overview of the selection process and understand that we need to select for fit and follow the UGESP in every step of the selection process, we are ready to discuss the selection steps illustrated in Exhibit 6-1.

6-1 APPLYING THE CONCEPT

Validity and Reliability

State which of the following validities or reliability is being discussed in each of the given situations.

a. criterion-related validity
b. content validity
c. construct validity
d. reliability

_____ 1. One of your employees wants to get a promotion to another job. You give him a test for the job. He doesn't do well enough to get the job, so he asks to take the test again. The next day he takes the test again, and the score is within a couple of points of the first test. So you don't give him the promotion.

_____ 2. The employee agrees that he didn't pass the test. But now he claims that the test is not a good predictor of the job and that he is confident that he can do the job. What type of evidence do you need to ensure that the test is in fact a good test?

_____ 3. You are running a CPA firm, and you require all your accountants to pass the CPA exam. What does the CPA exam need to do to indicate it is a good test?

_____ 4. You have developed a system for predicting which stocks will go up in value. Your boss wants some proof that it works.

_____ 5. The NFL team makes a recruit take an IQ test. The recruit's IQ is below the acceptable level, so you refuse to hire the player. The player complains, questioning what his IQ score has to do with playing football. What evidence do you need to support not hiring the player?

Applications and Preliminary Screening

LO 6.4

Briefly discuss the use of applications and résumés as selection tools.

The first step in the selection process is to get job applicants to fill out an application or send in their résumé. Then we do preliminary screening that may include a quick background check, testing, and initial interviewing to narrow down the applicants to the best matches, or fit, to the job.

Because these preliminary steps may not be done, or may not be done until later in the selection process, and the process is essentially the same no matter when it is done, we will discuss testing, interviewing, and background checks in three separate sections. Here we will discuss the application and résumé and what you can and can't ask during the preemployment inquiries.

Applications and Résumés

SHRM

Guide – G:6
Initial assessment methods (résumés, cover letters, application blanks, biographical information, reference/background checks, genetic screening, initial interviews, minimum qualifications)

As part of the selection process, the recruited candidates are typically asked to complete an application to provide biographical data.[21] We need data to aid in selecting the best person for the job.[22] Organizations may use different application forms for different jobs. For professional jobs, a résumé may replace the application form. However, even in cases where

Video Link 6.3

Guidelines to Review
Résumés

résumés are appropriate, many companies today will request that the applicant also fill out an application.

Why does the company need candidates to fill out an application if they already have a résumé with the same information? There are a couple of primary reasons. First, the application gives the company information on the applicant that is in a standard form. This makes it easier to quickly scan and evaluate different applicants. Second, applications almost always have some legal language, or "disclosures" that must be agreed to by the applicant. This information will generally include language to inform the applicant of an "employment-at-will" clause; will allow the company to conduct background and reference checks with the applicant's permission; tells the applicant that the company will conduct some mandatory tests prior to final employment (e.g., drug testing); and informs the applicant that any false information provided will be grounds to immediately terminate any relationship between the company and employee. Résumés won't have such language, so the organization will generally require that the application be completed in order to efficiently cover these items.

In reality, we use applications and résumés for much the same reason. We are trying to figure out your basic skill set, background, work history, education, and other basic information. What do we absolutely need to do with applications and résumés? We need to verify them. No one lies on a résumé, right? None of you would ever lie on any applications that you fill out, would you? Well, there is anecdotal evidence from professional recruiters[23] and background screeners[24] that between one third and one half of all applications and résumés have significant fictitious information. And companies have started to check these documents much more thoroughly, because they know that many of their applicants will embellish and outright lie, and the problem has gotten worse over the years.[25]

After several organizations got burned in the last few years—a Notre Dame football coach who got hired and then fired within five days; an MIT dean who claimed a doctorate that she did not have; the former CEO of RadioShack claiming two degrees he hadn't earned; and many others—companies are more concerned about lies on résumés than ever. So, résumés and applications give a good idea of your relevant background for the job, but we always want to check. We want to make sure an applicant did not lie on their application or résumé.[26]

One area that we absolutely want to check is education level, because this is one of the most commonly exaggerated items on a résumé or an application. Does the applicant have a degree, if one is required for the job? How can we check this? If you say you are a graduate and the HR representative calls your university, will the university records office tell them whether or not you are a graduate? The answer is, yes, they will. They can and will tell the recruiter whether or not you graduated and with what degree. They cannot provide your transcript or GPA without your permission, but they can tell the employer whether you graduated or not. And as one politician found out, the college may also state that the applicant was never registered as a student.

Preemployment Inquiries

On a job application or during an interview, no member of an organization can legally ask any questions that can be used to discriminate against the applicant, unless the questions are Bona Fide Occupational Qualifications (see Chapter 3). Exhibit 6-2 lists what can and cannot be asked during the selection process.

It may be hard to memorize the list, but to keep it simple, there are two major rules of thumb to follow: (1) Every question asked should be job related. If the question is not job related, there is a chance that it is discriminatory, so don't ask it. When developing questions, you should have a purpose for using the information. Only ask questions you plan to use in the selection process. (2) Any general question that you ask should be asked of all candidates.

Exhibit 6-2	Preemployment Inquiries

Topic	Can Ask ...	Cannot Ask ...
Name	Current legal name and whether the candidate has ever worked under a different name	Maiden name or whether the person has changed his or her name
Address	Current residence and length of residence there	Whether the candidate owns or rents his or her home, unless one or the other is a Bona Fide Occupational Qualification (BFOQ)
Age	Whether the candidate's age is within a certain range (if required for a particular job; for example, an employee must be 21 to serve alcoholic beverages); if hired, can ask for proof of age	How old are you? What is your date of birth? Can you provide a birth certificate? How much longer do you plan to work before retiring?
Sex	Candidate to indicate sex on an application if sex is a BFOQ	Candidate's sexual preference
Marital and Family Status	Whether candidate can adhere to the work schedule; whether the candidate has any activities, responsibilities, or commitments that may hinder him or her from coming to work	Specific questions about marital status or any question regarding children or other family issues
National Origin, Citizenship, or Race	Whether the candidate is legally eligible to work in the United States, and whether the candidate can provide proof of status if hired	Specific questions about national origin, citizenship, or race
Language	What languages the candidate speaks and/or writes; can ask candidate to identify specific language(s) if these are BFOQs	What language the candidate speaks when not on the job or how the candidate learned the language
Criminal Record	Whether the candidate has been convicted of a felony; if the answer is yes, can ask other information about the conviction if the conviction is job related	Whether the candidate has ever been arrested (an arrest does not prove guilt); for information regarding a conviction that is not job-related
Height and Weight	Whether the candidate meets BFOQ height and/or weight requirements and whether the candidate can provide proof of height and weight if hired	Candidate's height or weight if these are not BFOQs
Religion	If candidate is of a specific religion, if religious preference is a BFOQ	Candidate's religious preference, affiliation, or denomination if not a BFOQ
Credit Rating	For information if a particular credit rating is a BFOQ	Unless a particular credit rating is a BFOQ
Education and Work Experience	For information that is job related	For information that is not job related
References	For names of people willing to provide references or who suggested the candidate apply for the job	For a reference from a religious leader
Military Record	For information about candidate's military service that is job related	Dates and conditions of discharge from the military; draft classification; National Guard or reserve unit of candidate
Organizations	About membership in job-related organizations, such as unions or professional or trade associations	About membership in any non-job-related organization that would indicate candidate's race, religion, or the like
Disabilities	Whether candidate has any disabilities that would prevent him or her from performing the job being applied for	General questions about disabilities

6-2 APPLYING THE CONCEPT

Preemployment Questions

Using Exhibit 6-2, and the general guide not to ask any questions that are not job related unless they are BFOQs, identify whether each question can or cannot be asked on an application form or during a job interview.

a. Legal (can ask)   b. Illegal (cannot ask during preemployment)

_____ 6. Have you ever belonged to a union?

_____ 7. How old are you?

_____ 8. Have you ever been arrested for stealing on the job?

_____ 9. Do you own your own car?

_____ 10. Do you have any form of disability?

_____ 11. Are you a member of the Knights of Columbus?

_____ 12. Can you prove you are legally eligible to work?

_____ 13. What languages do you speak?

_____ 14. Are you married or single?

_____ 15. How many children do you have?

_____ 16. So you want to be a truck driver. Are you a member of the Teamsters union representing truck drivers?

_____ 17. Are you straight or a homosexual?

WORK
APPLICATION 6-5

Have you or anyone you know been asked an illegal question on an application form or during a job interview? What was the question?

LO 6.5

Briefly discuss the legal considerations in the selection process.

Testing and Legal Issues

As shown in Exhibit 6-1, testing can be used during the selection process; however, as discussed, all tests must be valid and reliable. So obviously, the organization must ensure that it follows all applicable federal and state laws concerning employment discrimination. As we noted in Chapter 3, all of the federal EEO laws apply to "any employment action," so clearly they apply in all selection tests. But in addition, managers must know that there are some other significant laws dealing with allowable hiring practices.

In this section, we discuss testing. We begin with a brief overview of the EEOC and testing and then move on to specific testing—polygraph testing, genetic testing, written testing, and physical testing—and end with a discussion of "to test, or not to test."

The EEOC and Employment Testing

The UGESP (covered above) were created to provide a "uniform Federal position in the area of prohibiting discrimination in employment practices on grounds of race, color, religion, sex, or national origin."[27] The guidelines have been formally adopted by the Equal Employment Opportunity Commission, the Department of Labor, the Department of Justice, and the Civil Service Commission. As such, the EEOC will use these guidelines any time they are faced with a discrimination-in-hiring complaint, so every HR Manager needs to be familiar with the UGESP and their requirements. If the EEOC investigates a complaint about employment testing being discriminatory, the company will have to show that the selection procedure that is being used is a valid measure for the job being filled. If the company can't show that the measure is valid, it is likely that the EEOC will consider the test a discriminatory hiring practice.

Polygraph Testing

Can we use a polygraph as a selection test? Yes, but only in a few circumstances. In 1988 the Employee Polygraph Protection Act (EPPA) was passed. The act made it illegal to use a polygraph to test employees' honesty in most circumstances. However, there are two exceptions for corporations and other businesses (there are other exceptions for government and national security). The two exceptions for businesses are[28] (1) the use of polygraph tests on prospective employees by any private employer whose primary business purpose consists of providing armored car personnel; personnel engaged in the design, installation, and maintenance of security alarm systems; or other uniformed or plainclothes security personnel, and (2) the use of a polygraph test by any employer authorized to manufacture, distribute, or dispense a controlled substance listed in Schedule I, II, III, or IV of Section 202 of the Controlled Substances Act (21 U.S.C. 812).

If you own a store and things are being stolen, can you polygraph all of your employees? No—the act says you can't. There *is* one other case, however, where an employer might be allowed to *request* that an employee submit to testing using a polygraph, but the use is severely restricted. This is when:

1. There is an active investigation involving economic loss or injury to the employer's business.

2. The employee had access to the property.

3. The employer has reasonable suspicion that the employee was involved in the incident or activity under investigation.

4. The employer executes and maintains a statement of the facts for a period of three years and provides a copy of the statement to the employee.

However, due to the nature of this exemption for ongoing investigations and the ability of the employee to deny the request, it is probably not generally of significant value to the average employer, and can be the basis for a claim of discrimination. As such, the company would be advised to avoid use of a polygraph in these situations unless there is clear and convincing evidence of the employee's involvement. Exhibit 6-3 provides a summary of exceptions to the EPPA.

> **SHRM**
>
> **Guide – B:32**
> The Genetic Information
> Nondiscrimination
> Act of 2008

Genetic Testing

You should recall our discussion in Chapter 3 about the Genetic Information Nondiscrimination Act (GINA). We noted that a significant number of companies also began to use genetic tests as a result of advances in medicine and genetic testing and analysis. The basis for this testing was an attempt to make sure that a potential employee didn't have the genetic predisposition to certain known illnesses or diseases, which might adversely affect their ability to work. However, many individuals felt that this was a significant invasion of their privacy and as a result shouldn't be allowed to be used by the potential employer. As a result of people's concerns, Congress began looking into the issue of genetic testing, and in 2008 passed GINA.[29] So, GINA protects people from discrimination by health insurers and employers on the basis of their DNA information.

Exhibit 6-3	Exceptions to the EPPA for Polygraph Testing
General Exception	For armored car personnel; personnel engaged in the design, installation, and maintenance of security alarm systems; or other uniformed or plainclothes security personnel
General Exception	Use by any employer authorized to manufacture, distribute, or dispense a controlled substance listed in Schedule I, II, III, or IV of Section 202 of the Controlled Substances Act
Specific Exception—the employer can *request* the employee to submit when:	1. There is an active investigation involving economic loss or injury to the employer's business. 2. The employee had access to the property. 3. The employer has reasonable suspicion that the employee was involved in the incident or activity under investigation. 4. The employer executes and maintains a statement of the facts for a period of three years and provides a copy of the statement to the employee.

Written Testing

LO 6.6

Discuss the major types of written testing available as a selection tool.

Written tests can be used to predict job success, as long as the tests meet EEOC guidelines for validity (people who score high on the test do well on the job, and those who score low do not do well on the job) and reliability (if people take the same test on different days, they will get approximately the same score each time). Illegal tests can result in lawsuits. Some of the major types of written tests include skills tests, personality tests, interest tests, cognitive ability tests (tests of general intelligence or of some type of job-related aptitude), and honesty tests.

Today, written tests are a common part of the selection process.[30] In fact, 80% of mid-size and large companies use personality and ability assessments for entry-level and midlevel management positions to help ensure the right fit between the job candidate and the job.[31]

Skills tests. Skills tests can be either written or done in physical form. For now, let's discuss written skills testing. A **skills test** is simply *an assessment instrument designed to determine if you have the ability to apply a particular knowledge set.* In other words, can you actually *do* something that you have the knowledge to do? How do we create written skills tests, and do they work to show a set of skills? Many of you have gone through a large number of written skills tests as you have progressed through your college courses. Have you ever taken a written test on Microsoft Word or PowerPoint? If so, you have taken a written skills test. Do these tests show us that you have a particular set of skills if you can successfully answer questions concerning those skills? In fact, they do.

When would we use skills tests? We would use them to find out how you would perform a particular job. Can we legitimately use a written skills test? Well, let's see, using the OUCH test. Is a skills test *Objective*? Can we say yes or no as to whether or not you know how to indent and italicize after we give you a test in Microsoft Word, for example? If we can determine this, it would be objective. Is it *Uniform in application*? If we give the same test to everyone in the same situation, it is. Is it *Consistent in effect*? In general, the answer is yes. However, we can certainly design skills tests that are not consistent in effect, whether we do it intentionally or unintentionally, so we have to validate the tests. Does it *Have job relatedness:* a direct relationship to the primary aspects of the job? If the answer is yes, it would be a legitimate test in this case, because it meets the OUCH test. Groupon uses skills testing that's role specific.[32]

Personality and interest tests. Personality tests *measure the psychological traits or characteristics of applicants to determine suitability for performance in a specific type of job.* Myers-Briggs Type Indicator and the Birkman Method are two common personality tests.

Interest tests are similar, but they *measure a person's intellectual curiosity and motivation in a particular field.*

So are we allowed to use personality or interest assessments as selection tools? Is this too personal? Who cares about your personality or personal interests? Can it be legitimate for the employer to care? Yes it can, in some cases. Sometimes we need a certain type of personality for a job. For example, we need to ensure that a flight attendant can be trained not to panic in an emergency situation. We might also need to determine whether someone applying for a job as an outside salesperson is able to operate in unfamiliar environments with customers whom they have never met. An outside salesperson who is an extreme introvert or who has no personal interest in or motivation to sell would not work for the job.

However, if you are hiring an accountant, does having an introverted personality harm their ability to do the job? Not really. If you are a line assembly worker, would it harm your ability to work on the line? It is unlikely. So, in some cases, personality does not matter. Remember, earlier in the chapter, we noted that individual personalities are part of the analysis that we may perform for job fit, but if personality or interests have nothing to do with the job, we probably don't want to do these types of testing.

However, if there is a legitimate reason for a particular type of personality or certain set of interests, we need to be able to support the validity and reliability of the test because if we can't show a relationship between these items and the job, an applicant could potentially take the company to court for discriminatory hiring practices. If the hiring manager is an extrovert, and they use personality testing to find other extroverted people for no reason other than they enjoy being around the same type of person, then they improperly used the test. It would quite likely be illegal to test personality in such a situation. So if we are going to use personality or interest tests, we have to ask if there is a potential association between the test and the job. If there is and it can be shown, then it is probably OK to use it. If not, you shouldn't use it as a selection tool. However, through an interview, you may be able to get a general idea of the applicant's personality and interest without giving a test.

Cognitive ability tests. **Cognitive ability tests** are *assessments of general intelligence or of some type of aptitude for a particular job.* Here again, we need to ensure that the tests that may be used are professionally developed, reliable, and valid indicators of a particular ability or knowledge set, or we should not use them. Can they be used at all? Yes. In fact, there have been a large number of court cases that dealt with the ability to apply cognitive ability testing, even when such testing had a potential disparate impact, as long as the ability being tested was directly related to a *business necessity* and was *job related.*[33]

In fact, the 1964 Civil Rights Act itself provides an exemption to "professionally developed testing" in Section 2000e-2*(h)*: "nor shall it be an unlawful employment practice for an employer to give and to act upon the results of any professionally developed ability test provided that such test, its administration or action upon the results is not designed, intended or used to discriminate because of race, color, religion, sex or national origin."[34] Bill Gates, cofounder of Microsoft, doesn't necessarily give an IQ test, but he developed his business based largely on hiring intelligent people.

Honesty or integrity tests. There are actually two types of honesty tests: pen-and-paper and polygraph, also known as a lie detector test. We discussed the polygraph in the legal section earlier in this chapter, so we won't reiterate that information here.

What about the pen-and-paper honesty or integrity test? How good are these tests? The employee will just tell the employer what they want to hear, right? Is the test valid and reliable? In reality, these tests are better than most people think they are. There is some significant evidence that, at least in personality-based honesty or integrity tests, the applicant has trouble faking answers to the test.[35] The tests ask questions that analyze your philosophy

SHRM

Guide – G:9
Noncognitive assessments (e.g., personality assessments, integrity tests, situational judgment tests, interest inventories)

concerning theft or other forms of dishonesty and what you would do in certain situations. The tests also look for inconsistency in the answers to indicate that an applicant may be trying to give the right answers.

Honesty tests are certainly not infallible and can be faked in some cases, but evidence shows that they have some value in identifying people who may be less honest and allowing the employer to weed some of these individuals out of the selection process. As such, they have value to the business.

Physical Testing

In addition to written testing, we may also want to use some form of physical testing. **Physical tests** are designed to *ensure that applicants are capable of performing on the job in ways defined by the job specification and description.* Physical testing will generally be valuable where there are significant physical skills required in order to perform the job, or where there is a significant safety risk associated with putting an individual into a job if they have physical limitations that are not evident or may be under the influence of substances that could cause their work performance to suffer and create danger for themselves or others. There are many types of physical testing, but we will limit our discussion to some of the most common forms.

Physical skills tests. We reviewed written skills tests earlier and noted that skills tests determine whether or not you have the ability to apply (use) a particular knowledge set. Physical skills tests are designed to establish the same facts. In this case we are trying to determine whether you have the *physical* skills and abilities to apply a particular set of knowledge. Physical skills tests may include tests of strength and/or endurance, tests of dexterity, tests of eye-hand coordination, or tests of other physical abilities. These tests can also be conducted in several different forms, including work sample tests, assessment centers, and using simulations.

Let's take a closer look at some of the common forms of physical testing. *Work sample* tests are basically what they sound like. We provide a sample of the work that the candidate would perform on the job and ask them to perform the tasks under some type of controlled conditions. A simple example of a work sample test might be typing a particular letter, where we judge speed and accuracy of the individual results of the test, or lifting a package of similar size and weight to what would have to be lifted in the actual job for which we are testing.

An assessment center is a more detailed physical testing environment. Internal and external candidates for positions are often tested through assessment centers. **Assessment centers** *are places where job applicants undergo a series of tests, interviews, and simulated experiences to determine their potential for a particular job.* For example, at Great Western Bank, job candidates for a teller job sit before a computer, which asks them to make change, respond to tough customers, and sell products that customers don't ask for. Candidates who perform well are selected for positions. Assessment center tests will be designed to make the candidate use several different groups of skills so that we can evaluate them more thoroughly than we could with a more simple form of testing. Some assessment center tests can go on for more than one day, and in some cases can be as much as several days in length. Longer assessments are more commonly used for higher-level professional and management positions.

We can also use *simulations* for physical testing, especially where there may be a dangerous and emotional component to the function being tested. Simulations are very valuable in cases where a real event could be dangerous or cost a lot of money. They allow us to put the person into a high-pressure situation but still control the environment so that we limit the danger and cost. Simulators and even virtual reality simulators are beginning to be used in many situations such as military training and teaching new doctors how to perform different types of surgery.[36]

For example, commercial airline pilots are required to routinely train in simulators on the type of aircraft that they fly. In this simulator environment we can put the pilot into a situation

WORK
APPLICATION 6-6

Have you or has anyone you know taken a written test when applying for a job or on the job? If so, state the type of test and describe its content.

SHRM

Guide – G:8
Ability/job knowledge tests, assessment centers

where perhaps a control surface of the airplane jams and the pilot has to take certain actions described in the flight manual for that aircraft to control the aircraft and either correct the problem or figure out how to land the aircraft successfully. Neither the Federal Aviation Administration (FAA) nor the airline/employer wants to actually put a pilot in an aircraft that has a major control surface failure! It would be very dangerous and could be expensive if the pilot crashed the aircraft! This is why simulators are so valuable in this type of situation.

Physical exams. Physical examinations may be desired, or in some cases required, with candidates for certain jobs. If the job will heavily stress the individual physically, there may be a legitimate need to have them submit to a physical exam to ensure that they are healthy enough for the stress (think NFL lineman!). In other cases, we may be required by the state or federal government to have individuals who work in specific fields take a physical exam before they are allowed to work in certain jobs such as driving a heavy truck (DOT physical) or flying an aircraft (FAA physical). We may just want to have our candidates take a physical exam before they start work so that we have baseline knowledge of their health at the time of hire. We can then use that baseline later to determine if they were subjected to conditions that harmed them physically.

For instance, if we have a candidate take a physical and the physician finds out that they have significant carpal tunnel problems in their wrists, it makes it harder for them to claim later that the job they are doing for us caused the injury. We have to be very aware of the potential for discrimination based on a disability if we require a physical exam in order to work in our organization, though. If the exam is not directly related to the essential functions of the job, it may not be advisable to require it as part of the selection process, because of the potential to illegally discriminate on the basis of disability.

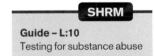

SHRM

Guide – G:11
Contingent assessment methods (drug testing, medical exams)

Drug testing. Most employers have the right to test for a wide variety of substances in the workplace.[37] While drug testing is not required in most cases, employers can put testing programs in place. The primary reasons for drug testing will generally be workplace safety and productivity. Private sector, nonunion companies are generally allowed to require applicants and/or employees to take drug tests in most states. In unionized workforces, however, the implementation of testing programs must be part of contract negotiations. No matter what kind of employer, though, the company needs to follow some guidelines to stay within the law in implementation and maintenance of a drug testing program. What does the company need to do?

In general, testing must be done systematically in one of two forms—either *random* or *universal*. Testing can't be selective using any other form in most states. In other words, we can't decide we want to test "Amy Jones" because we just want to. The selection would have to be random or universal. Testing can be universal in some situations (after a workplace accident or on initial offer of employment, for example) and random in others (quarterly drug testing of a sample of the workforce), but it has to be one or the other, and we have to specify which option we use in each situation.

Most states now require prior authorization for drug testing. In the case of applicants, this authorization is usually part of the job application legal notices that we reviewed earlier in the chapter. For existing employees it will usually be part of the employee handbook.

The organization also must have a drug testing policy. The policy should generally contain the following information:

- Requirement for training and the frequency of training on substance abuse (generally required at least annually, but in some states it is semiannual)
- When individuals will be tested—for example, preemployment; random testing; after any workplace accident; if there is reasonable suspicion
- Substances that will be tested for during any drug tests
- Disciplinary actions that will result from testing positive for a first test, and subsequent tests if applicable

LO 6.7

Identify the requirements for organizational drug testing programs.

SHRM

Guide – L:10
Testing for substance abuse

In many states, the employer is required to "reasonably accommodate" employees who voluntarily submit to an alcohol or drug rehabilitation program. If this is the case, it also needs to be noted in the policy. In most states, the policy is not allowed to exempt managerial employees just because they are at the managerial level.

Remember again, as with all employment tests, we have to identify the relationship of the test to the job that will be, or is being, done—it has to be *job related.* Drug testing almost certainly meets the *Objective, Uniform,* and *Consistent* requirements of the OUCH test, so *Having job relatedness* is the critical concern in this case. In most cases, the relationship is one of concern for safety and productivity in the workplace, but the organization has to make that determination, and if it doesn't look like drug testing will enhance safety in a particular type of job, you may not want to use it as a selection tool.

As related to productivity, over the years research has shown that substance abusers tend to be absent more often, which lowers productivity, as well as having more accidents on the job. Substance abusers are also potentially negligent hires, and they cost employers millions of dollars annually. Therefore, many employers try not to hire candidates who use illegal drugs. On a personal note, if you are using illegal drugs, we suggest you get straight or be sure not to apply to organizations that test for drugs.

WORK
APPLICATION 6-7

Have you or has anyone you know taken a physical test when applying for a job or on the job? If so, state the type of test and describe its content.

6-3   APPLYING **THE CONCEPT**

Type of Test

For each job situation below, identify the type of test that is described.

a. genetic
b. skills
c. personality and interest
d. cognitive ability

e. honesty or integrity—polygraph
f. physical skills
g. physical exam
h. drug

_____ 18. So you want to be a sheet rocker. You will have to take a test to see if you can hang, tape, and paste 10 sheets, while doing a quality job, in three hours.

_____ 19. You will have to take our intelligence test and get at least 100 on it.

_____ 20. To be a firefighter for us, you have to carry this 50-pound bag up this ladder in two minutes or less.

_____ 21. You have to go in the bathroom now and put a sample of your urine in this cup so we can test to see what it contains.

_____ 22. You need to take a test so that we can determine if you might get any known illnesses or diseases.

_____ 23. To get the job, we are going to hook you up to this machine and ask you some questions. You will have to answer the questions to our satisfaction.

_____ 24. You need to take this paper-and-pencil test so that we can determine if you have the right characteristics to succeed on the job.

_____ 25. The last test you will have to pass is an exam by our doctor to determine if you can handle the job.

To Test, or Not to Test

We can choose to have tests or decide not to. A consideration is the test. If you develop your own test, you have to provide support for its reliability and validity, so you have to have experts develop and test the test, which takes time and money. The other option is to use tests that have already been developed and tested for reliability and validity. The problem here is that you usually have to pay a fee for every single test that you give, not to mention the time and effort to give and assess the tests.

So testing can be time-consuming and expensive. Therefore, the testing has to pay for itself through hiring applicants who are in fact a good fit to the job and organization. By developing or spending the money on a good test, you can save time and money by not hiring and losing employees who need to be replaced quickly and often, you can possibly avoid negligent hires, and because the employees fit, productivity should be high, justifying that the investment in the test paid off. Today, tests are common.[38] In fact 80% of midsize and large companies use personality and ability assessments for entry-level and midlevel positions to help ensure the right fit between the job candidate and the job.[39] So testing is a good investment in many companies.

Here again, the OUCH test gives us a quick guide to whether or not a particular test would be appropriate in any given situation. Let's say that we are trying to decide whether or not to use a personality test in a specific hiring situation. Should personality testing be used? Well, if we use a validated test that has proven reliable in assessing basic personality characteristics (*Objective*), give the same test to each applicant (*Uniform in application*), evaluate its effect on the various protected groups that we have to be aware of and find that it is consistent between these groups (*Consistent in effect*), and find, most important, that it is directly applicable to a major function of the job for which we are hiring (*Has job relatedness*), it would be appropriate to use such a test. If this is not the case, then we probably don't want to use a personality test in this case. We can and should go through this thought process in determining the value of each selection tool before we decide to use it in the selection process. Now, let's take a closer look at some of our tests.

Selection Interviews

As stated, during the selection process, some of the steps may be skipped or completed out of sequence. While the initial interview may be skipped, rarely will a candidate get a job without being interviewed by at least one person. In review, the common role of the HR staff specialists for hiring lower-level employees is to conduct screening interviews to pick the top candidates who will continue on in the selection process. This screening step helps save line managers' time when there are large numbers of job applicants. Many organizations today are also using technology to enhance their ability to quickly complete screening interviews. Organizations including Nike and PricewaterhouseCoopers are using computers to conduct screening interviews.

LO 6.8

Discuss the value of selection interviews, including the three primary types of interviews.

Interviewing

The interview is usually the most heavily weighted and generally one of the last steps in the selection process. The interview gives the candidate a chance to learn about the job and organization. The interview also gives a manager a chance to assess things about a candidate that can't be obtained from an application, a test, or references, such as the candidate's ability to communicate and his or her personality, interest, appearance, and motivation. The

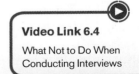

Video Link 6.4

What Not to Do When Conducting Interviews

The job interview is commonly given the most weight in the selection process.

interview is also used to check the accuracy of the application/résumé to make sure the candidates did not embellish or outright lie.[40]

An important focus on the interview is to assess the applicant's personality-job fit, ability- job fit, and person-organization fit. Because job interviewing is so important, you will learn the basics of how to prepare for and conduct a job interview in this subsection. As a manager, you will need to know how to conduct a job interview. You can practice this skill in Skill Builder 6-1.

Types of Interviews and Questions

Exhibit 6-4 shows the types of interviews and questions, which we discuss in this section.

Types of interviews. Three basic types of interviews are based on structure: (1) In a *structured interview*, all candidates are asked the same list of prepared questions. (2) An *unstructured interview* has no preplanned questions or sequence of topics. (3) In a *semistructured interview*, the interviewer has a list of questions but also asks unplanned questions. At Groupon, there are no stock questions; they're trying for a free-flowing conversation.[41]

SHRM

Guide – G:10
Structured interviews

▶ **Video Link 6.5**

Conducting an Interview

The semistructured interview is generally preferred by most interviewers: It helps avoid discrimination (because the interviewer has a list of prepared questions to ask all candidates), but it also allows the interviewer to ask each candidate questions relating to his or her own situation. The interviewer departs from the structure when appropriate. At the same time, using a standard set of questions makes it easier to compare candidates. The amount of structure you should use depends on your experience as an interviewer. The less experience you have, the more structure you need.

Types of questions. The questions you ask give you control over the interview; they allow you to get the information you need to make your decision. As discussed in the pre-employment inquiries sections, all questions should have a purpose and should be job related. You may use four types of questions during an interview: (1) The *closed-ended question* requires a limited response, often a yes or no answer, and is appropriate for dealing with fixed aspects of the job. "Do you have a Class 1 license? Can you produce it if hired?" (2) The *open-ended question* requires a detailed response and is appropriate for determining abilities and motivation. "Why do you want to be a computer programmer for our company?" "What do you see as a major strength you can bring to our company?" (3) The *hypothetical question* requires the candidate to describe what he or she would do and say in a given situation; it is appropriate in assessing capabilities. "What would the problem be if the machine made a ringing sound?" (4) The *probing question* requires a clarification response

WORK
APPLICATION 6-8

Select one of your jobs and identify the type of interview it was. Describe how the interview went in terms of structure.

and is appropriate for improving the interviewer's understanding. The probing question is not planned. It is used to clarify the candidate's response to an open-ended or a hypothetical question. "What do you mean by 'it was tough'?" "What was the dollar increase in sales you achieved?"

Today, HR interviewers prefer behavior-based questions that ask the candidate to describe how they handled specific situations. Here are a few of their favorites: "Tell me about a time you had to work with someone you did not personally like." "Describe your Outlook calendar on a typical day." "How much do you know about our company?" "Tell me about a time when your integrity was challenged; what was the situation, and what did you do?"[42]

WORK
APPLICATION 6-9

Select one of your jobs and identify the type of interview questions you were asked. For each type of question, state some of the questions you were actually asked during the interview.

Exhibit 6-4	Types of Interviews and Questions

Preparing for the Interview

Completing the interview preparation steps shown in Model 6-1 will help you improve your interviewing skills.

Step 1. Review the job description and specifications. You cannot effectively match a candidate to a job if you do not thoroughly understand the job. Read and become familiar with the job description and job specifications. If they are outdated, or do not exist, conduct a job analysis using the guidelines from Chapter 4.

Step 2. Prepare a realistic job preview. Candidates should understand what the job is and what they are expected to do. They should know the good and bad points of the job. Plan how you will present a realistic preview of the job (Chapter 4), based on the job description. It often helps to give candidates a tour of the work area.

Step 3. Plan the type of interview. What level of structure will you use? The interview should take place in a private, quiet place, without interruptions. It may be appropriate to begin the interview in an office and then tour the facilities while asking questions. Decide when the tour will take place and what questions will be asked. Take a list with you if you intend to ask questions during the tour.

Step 4. Develop questions for all candidates. Your questions should be job related, nondiscriminatory, and, in the case of a structured interview, asked of all candidates. Use the job description and specifications to develop questions that relate to each job task and responsibility. Use a mixture of closed-ended, open-ended, and hypothetical questions. Don't be concerned about the order of questions; just write them out at this point.

Step 5. Develop a form. Once you have created a list of questions, determine the sequence. Start with the easy questions. One approach starts with closed-ended questions, moves on to open-ended questions and then to hypothetical questions, and uses probing questions as needed. Another approach structures the interview around the job description and specifications; each responsibility is explained, and then questions relating to each are asked.

Write out the questions in sequence, leaving space for checking off closed-ended responses, for making notes on the responses to open-ended and hypothetical questions, and for follow-up questions. Add information gained from probing questions where appropriate. Make a copy of the form to use with each candidate you will be interviewing and a few extras for future use when filling the same job or for a reference when developing forms for other jobs.

Step 6. Develop questions for each candidate. Review each candidate's application and/or résumé. You will most likely want to add specific questions to a copy of the form to verify or clarify some of the information provided; for example: "I noticed that you did not list any employment during 2009; were you unemployed?" "On the application you stated you had computer training; what computer software were you trained to operate?" Be sure the individual questions are not discriminatory. For example, do not ask only women whether they can lift 50 pounds; ask all candidates, men and women, this question, and plan to have all candidates take this physical test if it hasn't been done before the interview.

Conducting the Interview

Following the steps listed in Model 6-2 will help you do a better job of interviewing candidates.

LO 6.9

List and briefly describe the steps taken in conducting interviews.

Step 1. Open the interview. Develop rapport. Put the candidate at ease by talking about some topic not related to the job. Maintain eye contact in a way that is comfortable for you and the candidate.

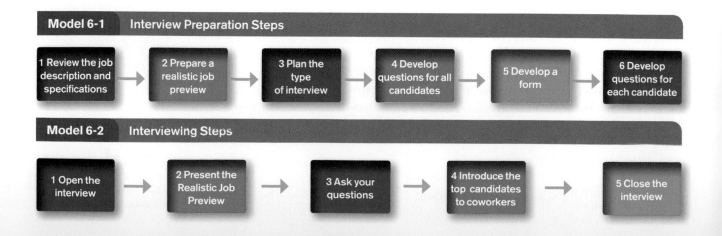

| Model 6-1 | Interview Preparation Steps |

1 Review the job description and specifications → 2 Prepare a realistic job preview → 3 Plan the type of interview → 4 Develop questions for all candidates → 5 Develop a form → 6 Develop questions for each candidate

| Model 6-2 | Interviewing Steps |

1 Open the interview → 2 Present the Realistic Job Preview → 3 Ask your questions → 4 Introduce the top candidates to coworkers → 5 Close the interview

Step 2. Present the Realistic Job Preview. Be sure the candidate understands the job requirements. Answer any questions the candidate has about the job and the organization. If the job is not what the candidate expected, or wants to do, allow the candidate to disqualify him- or herself and close the interview at that point.

Step 3. Ask your questions. Steps 2 and 3 can be combined if you like. To get the most out of a job interview, you must take notes on responses to your questions. Tell the candidate that you have prepared a list of questions you will be asking and that you plan to take notes.

During the interview, the candidate should do most of the talking. Give the candidate a chance to think and respond. If the candidate did not give you all the information you wanted, ask a probing question. However, if it is obvious that the candidate does not want to answer a question, don't force it. Go on to the next question or close the interview. End with a closing question, for example: "I'm finished with my questions. Is there anything else you want to tell me about or ask me?"

Step 4. Introduce top candidates to coworkers. Introduce top candidates to people with whom they will be working to get a sense of the candidates' interpersonal skills and overall attitude. Introductions can also give you a sense of whether the person is a team player. It is also common to have coworkers interview the candidates and give you, the hiring manager, their assessment of the candidates.

Step 5. Close the interview. Do not lead candidates on. Be honest without making a decision during the interview. Thank candidates for their time, and tell them what the next step in the selection process is, if any. Tell candidates when you will contact them. For example, say, "Thank you for coming in for this interview. I will be interviewing over the next two days and will call you with my decision by Friday of this week." After the interview, be sure to jot down general impressions not covered by specific questions.

WORK
APPLICATION 6-10

Select a job, an internship, or an interview that you have had. Describe how each of the five steps of Model 6-2 was conducted and how it could have been improved. If any step was skipped, say so.

Background Checks

Background checks are needed to help prevent unethical negligent hires.[43] During the selection process (Exhibit 6-1), in addition to verification of the information on a candidate's application form and/or résumé that we noted earlier, there are several other types of background checks that may or may not be appropriate in a selection situation. Background checks can become rather expensive depending on which checks we do and how often we have to do them, so they are usually left until we have at least narrowed down the list of candidates to a final few, or in some cases even to the final candidate. It is not unusual for the background check to be a simple pass or fail. We may then offer employment to the candidate conditioned on passing various background checks.

What types of background checks are available, and when should we use them? The types of background checks include credit checks, criminal background checks, reference checks, and web searches. In this section we describe them, and we provide guidelines on when to use them.

LO 6.10

Discuss the use of the various background checks as tests for employment.

Credit Checks

One of the most commonly used background checks is a credit check. Credit checks are subject to the Fair Credit Reporting Act (FCRA). The act requires that employers disclose to

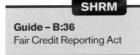

SHRM
Guide – B:36
Fair Credit Reporting Act

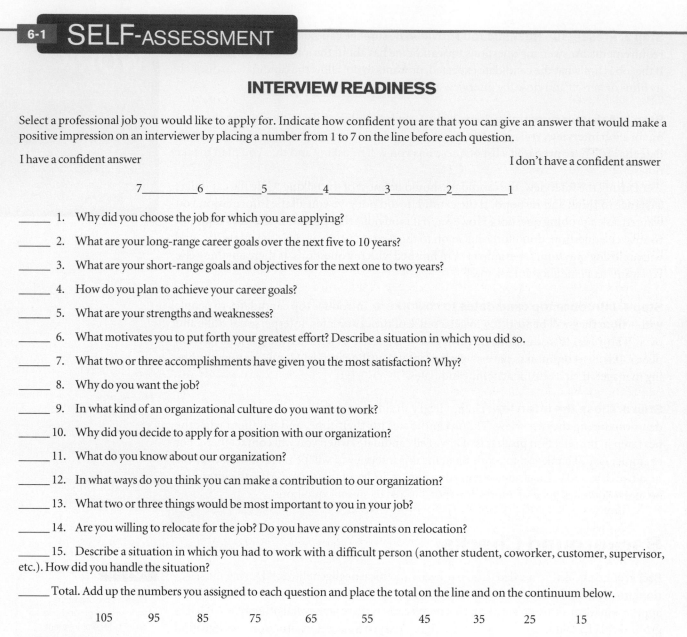

6-1 SELF-ASSESSMENT

INTERVIEW READINESS

Select a professional job you would like to apply for. Indicate how confident you are that you can give an answer that would make a positive impression on an interviewer by placing a number from 1 to 7 on the line before each question.

I have a confident answer   I don't have a confident answer

7_____6_____5_____4_____3_____2_____1

_____ 1. Why did you choose the job for which you are applying?

_____ 2. What are your long-range career goals over the next five to 10 years?

_____ 3. What are your short-range goals and objectives for the next one to two years?

_____ 4. How do you plan to achieve your career goals?

_____ 5. What are your strengths and weaknesses?

_____ 6. What motivates you to put forth your greatest effort? Describe a situation in which you did so.

_____ 7. What two or three accomplishments have given you the most satisfaction? Why?

_____ 8. Why do you want the job?

_____ 9. In what kind of an organizational culture do you want to work?

_____ 10. Why did you decide to apply for a position with our organization?

_____ 11. What do you know about our organization?

_____ 12. In what ways do you think you can make a contribution to our organization?

_____ 13. What two or three things would be most important to you in your job?

_____ 14. Are you willing to relocate for the job? Do you have any constraints on relocation?

_____ 15. Describe a situation in which you had to work with a difficult person (another student, coworker, customer, supervisor, etc.). How did you handle the situation?

_____ Total. Add up the numbers you assigned to each question and place the total on the line and on the continuum below.

    105   95   85   75   65   55   45   35   25   15

Ready for the job interview   Not ready for the job interview

These are common interview questions, so you should be prepared to give a good confident answer. Your Career Services office may offer mock interviews to help you with your interview skills to get the job you are looking for.

the applicant that we will use credit reports for employment decisions, and if the information on the credit report results in an adverse employment action, the employer has to give a copy of the report to the person and tell them of their FCRA rights.

When can employers complete credit checks on applicants, and why would they do so? Credit checks will most likely be done if the applicant will have access to any money or if they will work with the company's financial information. They may also be done with other employees to evaluate their personal responsibility—to see if you have a habit of being dishonest in credit transactions.

If someone has a history of not paying their bills, that gives the organization information that they are likely to be dishonest in other ways as well. Does something like a bankruptcy on your credit report automatically knock you out of contention for a job? No. In fact, by law the company can't refuse to hire you solely because of a bankruptcy.[44] However, again, if the credit report shows a pattern of failure to live up to your credit obligations, the company can and probably will use that information to remove you from the applicant pool, as long as their home state laws allow it.

Credit reports also give the employer other reference information that can be used for background checks. The credit report generally includes historical data on previous addresses, giving the organization information against which they can check your employment history and perform criminal history checks. If you were working at a manufacturing plant in North Carolina, according to your employment history, and you were living in Texas at the time, there is a significant discrepancy. It may show that you are not telling the truth on your employment history. The credit report also provides information on previous employers directly in some cases, although this information may not be complete.

Criminal Background Checks

All states allow criminal background checks in at least some cases. However, the laws vary so significantly that it is difficult to enumerate the circumstances in this text. Most companies today will generally complete a criminal background check when it is allowed, though, due to the issue of negligent hiring that we discussed at the beginning of this chapter. Can, or should, a criminal record keep an individual from being hired? Again, it depends on what type of conviction it was, how long ago it occurred, and what type of job the individual is being considered for by the organization.

We would have a much easier time defending the use of a criminal background check for an individual who would have access to products or funds that are easily stolen than we would in the case of someone with no access to anything of significant value in the company. Similarly, we would be more likely to be able to use a violent criminal history to rule out an applicant if they would have access to children or other innocent persons who could easily be harmed by the employee. As always, we have to look at the entire circumstance and make a decision based on the OUCH test and the defensibility of the selection tool that we are considering.

Reference Checks

Reference checks include not only calls to references that are provided by the applicant, but also reference letters from employers or personal letters of recommendation and possibly cold calls to previous employers. Should the company perform a reference check on applicants? Is it going to be of any value, or are the references that the applicant provides going to say only good things about the applicant?

The basic answer is that the reference letter that is requested by the applicant is almost always going to say good things about them. The applicant will almost never ask anybody to provide a reference unless they know that the reference will be good. Almost! Every once in a while, you will check a reference, and it will not be very good. It is rare, but it does happen, and when it happens, it is usually a good piece of information for the company. The truth is that generally the letters don't give much information, but we want to ask for them anyway. In addition, though, we want to check references that might not have been given to us by the applicant—people such as former employers and coworkers. Does that do any good?

What is a previous employer most likely going to tell you if you call for a reference check? The most common HR answer will be in the form of "Yes, they worked at this company, from [date] to [date] in [job type] job." Why is this a typical response to a reference check with a former employer? It is to protect the company from being sued for providing defamatory information about the former employee; in other words, the company hurt the individual's reputation unfairly. Company lawyers through experience have found that if we provide more information than noted above, we can become the target of lawsuits, so most companies won't provide any more information than they have to. So if you are looking for a true reference, you are better off to bypass the HR Department. Get the title and name of candidates' prior supervisors and try giving them a reference call.[45] Sometimes the supervisor will give you the typical yes and dates of employment, but when the candidate is good the supervisor will often say so; and when they are very vague about their former employee's performance, this may give you the "read between the lines" information that will help in the selection process.

Often, the question comes up concerning whether or not the individual is "eligible for rehire." Think about this question for a moment. As soon as a previous employer says an applicant to your company is *not* eligible for rehire, what do you think? You think that they are probably not a good employee. Another comment that comes up in discussions on employer reference checks is that many states now have laws that allow a previous employer to provide an honest reference with "immunity" from legal action.

Arkansas law, for instance, says that "a current or former employer may disclose the following information about a current or former employee's employment history to a prospective employer of the current or former employee upon receipt of written consent from the current or former employee."[46] However, the law also states that "the immunity conferred by this section shall not apply when an employer or prospective employer discriminates or retaliates against an employee because the employee or the prospective employee has exercised or is believed to have exercised any federal or state statutory right or undertaken any action encouraged by the public policy of this state."[47]

So if the previous employer were to provide an honest reference, assuming immunity under the law, and the former employee claims that the reference was discriminatory or in retaliation for something the employer didn't like, the company can still be sued. This is why most companies still won't provide more than a basic reference on former employees.

On a personal note, if you did an internship or had a job and you know you impressed your boss, ask for a written recommendation. You can provide this letter to prospective employers. Also, for internships and jobs that you list on your résumé, again if you know you will get a good recommendation, be sure to list your supervisor's name and telephone number (a direct-line number if available). Why? Because it is not unusual for a prospective employer to call your prior employer for a reference. So wouldn't you like the caller to speak directly with your boss, rather than the HR Department that will only give the standard answer listed above?

Web Searches

Finally, with the ability to access very large amounts of information via the Internet, more and more companies and other organizations are using the Internet to do research on job candidates. Googling a candidate's name is becoming a standard practice in these organizations.[48] And it is truly amazing what the company finds in many cases.

SHRM

Guide – D:14
Social networking

You may recall that Olympic gold medal swimmer Michael Phelps was seen on YouTube smoking marijuana. Because of the video, Phelps did lose some signed sponsorships, Kellogg's cereal just to list one, and potentially others didn't sign him after the negative publicity. That one video probably cost him more than a million dollars. What do you think a prospective employer will do if they see you online smoking dope, or drunk out of your mind, not to mention vomiting?

Does the organization want to hire an individual if that individual's Facebook page shows pictures of them wearing and drinking from a beer bong hat while they are driving around town? Is there a potential liability to the company if they do hire that person, especially if the individual will be driving a company vehicle? Of course there is.

Many companies are more technologically savvy than many younger applicants believe, and the company will use that tech knowledge to evaluate the candidate. Companies are also seeking to create strong policies on the use of social networking for business purposes, including policies on the use of social networking in recruiting and selection processes. Almost two thirds of businesses worldwide have at least some policy guidance on the use of social media in the workplace.[49] Most legal opinions seem to favor the employer in cases where there might be a question of violation of privacy if the employer is doing a check of social media to avoid negligent hires, but companies need to make sure that they are doing so in an even-handed, equitable manner, or they can be considered liable for invasions of of-duty privacy.[50] So on a personal note, as a potential job applicant, make sure that everything on the web about you is information that

WORK
APPLICATION 6-11

Do an Internet search on yourself. Did you find any material that you or others posted that you would not want a prospective employer to find? Are your e-mail address and telephone message professional?

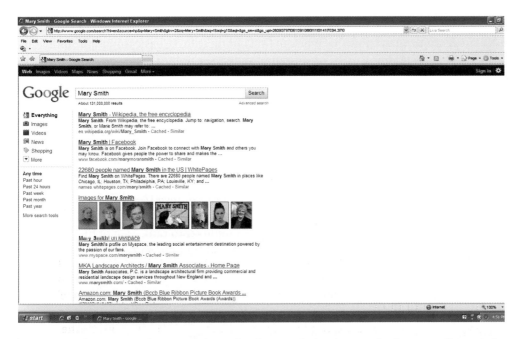

Many organizations today are doing a background check over the Internet. Some job candidates are not offered the job because of content found on the web.

you are comfortable with if the company discovers it in a web search. You may not be putting negative things about you online, but you also need to make sure your friends aren't either. Employers *will* most likely do a web search on you as a candidate in today's 21st-century world. And this goes for part-time jobs, summer jobs, and internships. Also, make sure your e-mail address and telephone message are professional for job searching.

Selecting the Candidate and Offering the Job

We made it to the last step of the selection process. You learned in previous sections that there are different parts available to employers as they go through the selection process. However, even with all of these tools, we can't find out everything about a potential job candidate. People who have been in recruiting and selection for any length of time know this and only try to discover a limited number of answers as they go through the selection process.

HR-savvy people know not to set their sights too high—nobody can find out everything in the selection process. You may want to limit what you want to find out to some basic items that tell whether or not the individual should be hired because they are *really* a good fit. One recruiter may limit his or her searches in the selection process to an attempt to find out three things:

SHRM

Guide – G:13
Selection decisions: ranking, grouping/banding, random selection

1. Does the individual have the basic qualifications for the job—right personality, ability, and person-organization fit?

2. Do they actually *want* to do the job, or do they just want any job? In other words, are they going to be satisfied with the job and stay for some time, will they be productive, and will they be a potential negligent hire?

3. Are they basically honest and telling the truth? If not, they could be a problem employee.

The recruiter may know that if he can find out these three basic things, the individual will be a valuable addition to the organization and can be trained to do any specific job that is necessary.

There are two basic methods that we use to make final selection decisions for the organization. The first type is sometimes called a *multiple-hurdle* selection model, and the second is known as a *compensatory* selection model. The **multiple-hurdle selection model** *requires that each applicant must pass a particular selection test in order to go on to the next test.* If an applicant fails to pass any test in the process, they are immediately removed from the running. The **compensatory selection model** *allows an individual to do poorly on one test but make up for that poor grade by doing exceptionally well on other tests.* Again, each step in the selection process (interviews and background checks) is a test. Using the compensatory model allows the employer to rank each of the candidates based on their overall score from all of the testing. The employer can also group candidates based on this same information.

LO 6.11

Identify the common problems that are faced during the selection process.

Problems to Avoid

Avoid the following problems during the selection process:

- *Rushing.* Try not to be pressured into hiring just any candidate. Find the best fit, or you will have turnover, productivity, and negligent hire problems.

- *Stereotyping.* Don't prejudge or leap to conclusions. Match the candidate to the job based on analysis rather than instinct.
- *"Like me" syndrome.* Don't look for a candidate who is your clone. People who are not like you may do an excellent job. Remember the benefits of diversity.
- *Halo and horn effect.* Do not judge a candidate on the basis of one or two favorable characteristics (the "halo effect") or one or two unfavorable characteristics (the "horn effect"). Make the selection on the basis of the total qualifications of all candidates.
- *Premature selection.* Don't make your selection based only on a candidate's application or résumé or

The final step of the selection process is commonly the job offer.

after interviewing a candidate who impressed you. Do not compare candidates after each interview. The order in which you interview applicants can influence you. Be open-minded during all interviews, and make a choice only after you have finished all interviews. Compare each candidate on each job specification.

Hiring

So after all selection activities are completed, compare each candidate's qualifications to the job specifications, identify whether or not they really want to do the job, and analyze whether or not they have been basically honest during the selection process to determine who would be best fit for the job. Be sure to get coworkers' impressions of each candidate, when appropriate, because they have to work with them and get along (person-organization fit). Diversity should be considered when selecting a candidate.

So to bring the selection process to an end, the best candidate is then contacted and offered the job. If the candidate does not accept the job, or accepts but leaves after a short period of time, the next-best candidate is frequently offered the job.

HRTools offers online help with the selection process. The company's website (www.HRTools.com) can help managers screen applicants and assess their skills, create interview scripts and improve interviewing skills, provide salary information for jobs offered by other organizations, conduct a background check, and make the final selection.[51]

Trends and Issues in HRM

In this chapter's trends and issues in HRM, we're going to take a brief look at the issue of selection with a global workforce, the concept of local hiring as a sustainable business practice, and the use of HRISs in the selection process. Each of these issues has affected the process of selection in a significant way during the past decade, which in turn has caused HR Managers to change the way that they work.

Selection With a Global Workforce

Because we've already reviewed the significant coming shortage of knowledge workers worldwide in earlier chapters, we won't go through that information again here. The shortage certainly affects our ability to select individuals into our workforce. However, we have several other issues of significance when we're dealing with selecting individuals from all over the world into our organizations. The first major issue that HR Managers must deal with is the process of immigration and work visas for the various countries in which the organization operates. Each country has its own requirements for immigration and for foreign workers who want to gain employment in that country. The HR Manager is typically the responsible individual for identifying the requirements and making sure that the individual fulfills them.

The organization, through the HR Department, is also typically responsible for assisting the individual with filling out the forms and in many cases sponsoring the individual's work visa. The most common type of professional work visa in the United States is the H-1B visa for professional employees. Some companies might also use the L-1 for transfer to an affiliate company in the United States. The HR Department also has to maintain records of their employees showing a legal right to work in the United States in accordance with the Immigration Reform and Control Act of 1986. The form required here is the I-9 Employment Eligibility Verification Form. As you can easily see, there is a lot of paperwork involved in moving individuals who are citizens of one country to another country in order to work for your organization—and the above paperwork is just the basics. In some circumstances other forms are required for entry into the United States for the purpose of work.

In addition to the immigration and visa requirements, organizations that hire workers in other countries face issues with the selection process itself. How does HR select somebody who resides in another country? How difficult is it to go through the process of identification of recruits, selection testing, interviewing, and the other pieces of the selection process? In many cases, the HR representative may never even see the individual who's being hired. A large portion of the work of selection will be done virtually, typically using the Internet. This inability to interact directly with the candidate creates an entirely new set of problems for the HR representative. There may also be a language barrier between the candidate and the HR representative, and there are almost certainly cultural differences between the candidate's home country and the organization in the hiring country. Each of these barriers must be overcome, and every company handles these issues a little bit differently. However, the HR Managers must understand and be able to work within the global hiring environment.

Local Hiring as a Sustainable Business Practice

Is local hiring a more sustainable business practice? Many organizations are beginning to consider local hiring as a valuable alternative to searching for workers over great distances. Certainly there are advantages to "hiring local." Both the company and the individual may save time and money because of lower requirements for travel to the organization for purposes of selection testing and interviews. Lessening the requirements for traveling significant distances also lowers the amount of pollution in the environment from either automobile or aircraft used to transport the candidate to the organization. There may also be advantages to the company due to the positive economic impact on the community that surrounds the organization. The organization's reputation as a socially responsible member of the community will almost certainly be enhanced.

The company may also financially gain through the use of sustainable practices such as online recruiting and applications, which lower the amount of paper both used and stored by the organization. Although this may seem trivial, over time the costs associated with this paperwork have a significant effect on the organization and its budgets. The company may also save both the environment and organizational funds through the use of online interviewing. Again, this process lowers the fuel costs associated with the candidate traveling to the organization for the interview.

Of course, not everything that we do to improve environmental sustainability works to the organization's advantage. The practice of hiring local may make it significantly more difficult to find sufficient talent, especially in jobs that have significant skill or knowledge requirements. If the organization is unable to find sufficient talent, they certainly are not getting the best recruits for the open positions. In some cases, this trade-off may be acceptable. However, in other cases (as we noted in earlier chapters), finding the best person for the job may be one of the few ways to create strategic advantage for the organization. If this is the case, the organization may have to consider loosening any rule or policy that designates local hiring as a preferred practice. The bottom line here is that the organization needs to practice sustainable selection whenever possible, but obviously also has to use selection processes as a way to further strategic goals. Here again, the HR Manager has to make decisions about how the HR Department will further the organization's mission and vision.

HRISs and the Selection Process

HRISs continue to become increasingly valuable to the organization in all HRM functions including, of course, the selection process. How do HRISs provide assistance in the selection process? The system allows the organization to automate many of the selection processes such as applications, initial screening, testing, interviewing, and correspondence with the candidate.

Modern HRISs provide organizations with the ability to automate their application process by providing a standard application to candidates by way of the Internet or company intranets. The application can even be varied for different types of jobs within the organization. The applicant identifies which type of job they're interested in, and the system provides them with the online application. Virtually all of the systems are also able to accept résumé files from the applicant that can be stored in the HRIS. This can then allow automated searching of all stored résumés and applications for keywords, which will provide the HR Manager with a first cut of the applicants for a specific job.

Once this first cut is complete, many of the systems can automatically alert each applicant to the need to log in to the company's site for any initial testing that may be required for the position. The system can be set up to score the testing and provide the HR representative with a list of the highest-scoring candidates.

Once all of the automated services are complete, HR representatives can set up and conduct interviews (which can also be graded using the HRIS) and identify any further testing necessary for the applicants. Once finalists are identified for the position, the HR representative identifies those finalists to the HRIS, and the system can create automated letters (e-mails) thanking the applicant for their application but letting them know that they haven't been chosen.

As you can quickly see, the HRIS can save significant amounts of money and time within the HR Department. In addition, the fact that the initial application and testing is done in an automated form allows the organization to limit any human bias that might occur from face-to-face interaction between the HR representative and the candidate. This can act to minimize any potential for discrimination in the selection process, which is obviously something that the HR Department needs to be concerned with.

Wrap-Up

Well, another chapter has come to an end. What have we covered that will be significant to you as you go on in your management career? You now know the steps in the selection process and why it is so important. During the selection process, you understand the need to look for fit, or the applicant has to have personality-job fit, ability-job fit, and person-organization fit. You've probably found out that the selection process in a 21st-century organization is much more complex than you thought it was. You know now that this is another place where you can apply the OUCH test to try to ensure that you are fair and equitable with all applicants, and you know how critical the selection process has become to organizations concerned with the world-class rivals that they must compete against on a daily basis. One of the few places where a modern organization can create a competitive advantage is in the people within the firm. We also have to be concerned with negligent hiring to protect both the organization and its employees and customers.

You learned about the UGESP in this chapter, and what they identify as a test for employment, as well as the criteria necessary to create a valid and reliable test. You also know the many types of tests for fit that we can consider using during the selection process to hire the best match, as well as some guidelines for when and when not to use a test.

Critically important to both the HR staff and line manager job, you have learned what you can and cannot ask during the preemployment inquiry to help avoid legal problems of discrimination. You know the types of interviews and interview questions, and how to prepare for and conduct the job interview. You also learned the different background checks that can be done on applicants, and should now understand the reasons why those checks are typically done prior to selection of an individual into the organization. As usual, that's quite a bit of information for you to digest from one chapter, so let's go ahead and end this one and go to the summary.

Chapter Summary

6.1 Describe why the selection process is so important to the company.

The first reason that selection is important is that we need the best possible person in each job in order to maximize productivity. Unproductive members of the organization can cause lower motivation and job satisfaction in all of a company's employees. Second, organizations have a responsibility to avoid negligent hires—people who may pose a danger to others within the organization or who come into contact with it. The company can incur legal liability if we don't screen potential applicants carefully.

6.2 Identify the three main types of "fit" that we look for in the selection process and why they are important.

The three types of fit are personality-job fit; ability-job fit; and person-job fit. They are important because managers are supposed to get the best productivity out of their workforce, but not everyone can do everything equally well. So managers have to treat people differently, but fairly, in order to put "the right person in the right job." They do this by assessing the three types of fit between the person and the company.

6.3 Discuss the major points in the Uniform Guidelines on Employee Selection Procedures.

The UGESP are guidelines on how to avoid discriminatory hiring practices. They identify what the federal government considers to be an employment test, and how those tests can be used in making employment decisions. The UGESP also identify the acceptable types of validity that can be used to validate employment tests and note that these tests must be reliable.

6.4 Briefly discuss the use of applications and résumés as selection tools.

Applications and résumés are used in a fairly interchangeable manner, except the application gives the company information on the applicant that is in a standard format. This makes it easier to quickly scan and evaluate the different applicants. Applications also typically have some legal language, or "disclosures" that must be agreed to by the applicant. Both documents should be used to review and verify both work experience and education of the applicant. This experience and education should always be verified, though, because evidence shows a high percentage of people exaggerate or lie on applications and résumés.

6.5 Briefly discuss the legal considerations in the selection process.

The biggest legal considerations in the selection process are the measures that are required in order to ensure that we avoid illegal employment discrimination. There are also two laws that deal specifically with the ability to apply certain types of testing to employment candidates—the Employee Polygraph Protection Act of 1988 (EPPA) and the Genetic Information Nondiscrimination Act of 2008 (GINA). The EPPA limits the use of polygraphs in normal businesses to generally two instances: when the employee will be involved in company security operations and when the employee will have access to federally identified controlled substances. GINA protects prospective employees from discrimination by health insurers and employers on the basis of their DNA information.

6.6 Discuss the major types of written testing available as a selection tool.

The major types of written tests are *skills tests*, which evaluate the candidate's ability to apply their knowledge to a specific type of problem; *personality tests*, which evaluate the applicant's personal traits or characteristics so that they can be matched up with an appropriate type of job; *interest tests*, to identify what an applicant is interested in and therefore most likely motivated to learn; *cognitive ability tests*, which are assessments of intelligence or aptitude for a specific type of work; and *honesty or integrity tests*, which evaluate the individual's philosophy concerning theft and other forms of dishonesty.

6.7 Identify the requirements for organizational drug testing programs.

Testing must be done in one of two forms—either *random* or *universal*. Testing can't be done selectively using any other method in most states. Most states also require prior authorization for drug testing, and the organization must have a drug testing policy that is provided to all employees and states the following information: the requirement for training on substance abuse; when individuals will be tested and what substances will be tested for; disciplinary action that could result from a positive test; and the "reasonable accommodations" that the organization will provide to employees who voluntarily submit to a substance abuse rehabilitation program. In unionized workforces, the implementation of drug testing programs *must* be part of contract negotiations.

6.8   Discuss the value of selection interviews, including the three primary types of interviews.

The interview gives the manager a chance to assess the candidate, their ability to communicate, their personality, their appearance, and their motivation face-to-face, and also allows the candidate a chance to learn about the job and the organization. The three primary types of interviews are the unstructured interview, in which the interviewer has no preplanned questions or topics; the semistructured interview, where the interviewer may ask both planned and unplanned questions; and the structured interview, where all candidates are asked the same set of questions. Most interviewers prefer the semistructured interview.

6.9   List and briefly describe the steps taken in conducting interviews.

Step 1: Open the interview—develop rapport and put the candidate at ease. Step 2: Present a Realistic Job Preview—make sure that the candidate understands the job and what will be expected of them if they are selected for the job. Step 3: Ask questions—try to ensure that the candidate does most of the talking; take notes of their answers. Step 4: Introduce top candidates to coworkers—let them talk with people who they will be working with while judging their interpersonal skills and attitude. Step 5: Close the interview—thank the candidate for their time and tell them what the next step in the process will be. Tell them when they will be contacted and, once they leave, make any final notes about the interview.

6.10   Identify the common problems that are faced during the selection process.

Common problems include rushing—caving in to pressure to fill a job; stereotyping—prejudging a candidate based on a perceived group to which they may belong; "like me" syndrome—where the candidate who seems to be like the interviewer is thought to be the best for the job; halo and horn effect—making judgments based on one or two characteristics instead of evaluating the candidate's total qualifications; and premature selection—making a snap decision based on a high-quality résumé or a good interview.

Key Terms

Assessment center	Content validity	Negligent hire	Skills test
Cognitive ability test	Criterion-related validity	Personality test	Uniform Guidelines on
Compensatory selection	Interest test	Physical test	Employee Selection
model	Multiple-hurdle selection	Reliability	Procedures (UGESP)
Construct validity	model	Selection	Validity

Key Term Review

Complete each of the following statements using one of this chapter's key terms:

_____ is the process of choosing the best qualified applicant recruited for a job.

_____ is a legal concept that says if the organization selects someone for a job who may pose a danger to coworkers, customers, suppliers, or other third parties and then that person harms someone else in the course of their work for the company, the company can be held liable for the individual's actions.

_____ provides information that can be used to avoid discriminatory hiring practices as well as discrimination in other employment decisions.

_____ is the extent to which a test measures what it claims to measure.

_____ is an assessment of the ability of a test to measure some other factor related to the test.

_____ is an assessment of whether a test measures knowledge or understanding of the items it is supposed to measure.

_____ measures a theoretical concept or trait that is not directly observable.

_____ is the consistency of a test measurement.

_____ is an assessment instrument designed to determine if you have the ability to apply a particular knowledge set.

_____ measures the psychological traits or characteristics of applicants to determine suitability for performance in a specific type of job.

_____ measures a person's intellectual curiosity and motivation in a particular field.

_____ is an assessment of general intelligence or of some type of aptitude for a particular job.

_____ ensures that applicants are capable of performing on the job in ways defined by the job specification and description.

_____ are places where job applicants undergo a series of tests, interviews, and simulated experiences to determine their potential for a particular job.

_____ requires that each applicant must pass a particular selection test in order to go on to the next test.

_____ allows an individual to do poorly on one test but make up for that poor grade by doing exceptionally well on other tests.

Quick Check (True-False)

1. Failure to select the right person for the job in the selection process leads to higher early turnover (within the first 3–6 months) in the organization. T F

2. The UGESP define a test for employment as only written tests; physical tests are covered by the EEOC. T F

3. A test measure is "reliable" if it tests what it is supposed to test. T F

4. Ability-job fit measures whether a person's personality matches up with the job for which they are being considered. T F

5. Employers can use a polygraph test anytime that they suspect theft in the company. T F

6. The Genetic Information Nondiscrimination Act (GINA) protects people from discrimination by health insurers and employers on the basis of their DNA information. T F

7. Applications and résumés are used for much the same reason—to figure out applicant skill sets, work history, education, and other basic information. T F

8. Skills tests measure whether you can actually do something that you have the knowledge set to do. T F

9. Companies are generally given the ability to test personalities, regardless of the job the applicant may hold. T F

10. There is some evidence that, at least in personality-based honesty or integrity tests, the applicant has trouble faking answers to the test. T F

11. An assessment center is a very quick physical testing method—it usually only takes a few minutes. T F

12. Private sector, nonunion companies are generally allowed to require applicants and/or employees to take drug tests in most states. T F

13. It is legal to ask if a candidate is of a specific religion, as long as religious preference is a BFOQ. T F

14. Credit checks are unfair and should never be used in the selection process. T F

15. Googling a candidate's name is becoming a standard practice in many organizations. T F

Communication Skills

The following critical-thinking questions can be used for class discussion and/or for written assignments to develop communication skills. Be sure to give complete explanations for all answers.

1. Do you agree that selection of a top-quality candidate is a critical process in organizations, or do you think intensive training after the person is selected is more valuable? Explain your answer.

2. Should organizations be held liable by the justice system for negligent hires? Why or why not?

3. In your mind, how critical is the concept of person-organization fit? Why do you think so?

4. Are there cases other than the two instances noted in the chapter when companies should be allowed to use polygraph tests on employees? When and why?

5. Do you feel that it's OK to tell "little white lies" on résumés and applications? Why or why not?

6. Are companies overtesting applicants by using the processes that were discussed in this chapter? Explain your answer.

7. Are background checks including credit checks, criminal history checks, and looking at a candidate's Facebook pages too invasive? Explain your answer.

8. Is the use of an HRIS for narrowing down the list of candidates and sending form letters, including rejection letters, too impersonal? Why or why not?

Answers

REVIEW QUESTIONS (TRUE-FALSE) Answers

1. T   2. F   3. F   4. F   5. F   6. T   7. T   8. T   9. F   10. T   11. F   12. T   13. T   14. F   15. T

Case

Case 6-1. Who Is Doing the Selling? Gerald Interviews at Washington Home Builders

Gerald Mahoney was working in the women's shoe department and doing the best that he could to sell a fairly expensive pair of boots to a young lady who obviously could afford to shop at a much classier store such as Nordstrom or Neiman Marcus. For some unfathomable reason, however, she decided to bestow her good graces on Macy's. After a few minutes of trying on several pairs of boots, Gerald was able to gently persuade Ms. Monahan to buy one of the store's most expensive boots. He rang up the sale and was complimenting himself on his persistence when out of the blue the customer said:

> Why is an obviously highly talented man like you, who has just sold me a pair of shoes I probably don't need or even want, working at a place like Macy's? My name is Ms. Monahan, and I am the Director of Recruiting and Training at Washington Home Builders, and I can tell from the way that you have handled this sale that you would make a superb home salesperson. Here's my card. Why not call me tomorrow morning, and we can arrange a time for you to come in? Our website is also on the card, so feel free to check us out and see our job listings.

Gerald thanked Ms. Monahan for her kind words and told her he certainly would call her in the morning and arrange for an appointment.

Getting the Interview

Gerald called Ms. Monahan the next day as he had promised, and she seemed quite receptive to his call. She asked him to fax over a résumé and said that she would get back to him (or her assistant would), in order to set up an appointment for him to interview with her and some of the key salespeople in the firm. Gerald ended up faxing his résumé three days after he talked with Ms. Monahan. Her office called him back and faxed him a blank job application, which he quickly completed and mailed back. A nerve-racking week went by, and Gerald finally received an appointment for an interview for the following week.

The "Interview Process" at Washington Home Builders

Gerald thought he knew what to expect during an interview since he had been through so many—he was prepared to sell himself to Washington big time. Usually he would meet with a store manager or the head of personnel for about an hour, and they would ask him questions about his previous employment, why he left his last job, and why he wanted to work for their firm. These were routine questions that inevitably led to a discussion of salary (if they thought he was qualified to do the job) and a job offer. Washington's interview process turned out to be far more complex.

It all started at 9 a.m. First, before he met with anyone, Gerald took a battery of exams and filled out a set of questionnaires. The exams included everything from basic math questions (which he hadn't done since his college days, nearly 30 years ago), to what seemed to be an IQ test, to questions about self-image, his honesty, and his preferences about the type of work he liked to do.

Rather than having a long break for lunch, they had a working lunch where HR went through the entire compensation package: a base salary plus commission, medical benefits, and a really good 401(k) plan where the firm contributed 5% of his salary.

His first interview that afternoon seemed to set the tone for the rest of the day. Gerald had a wonderful interview with the Sales Director, Sam Arden, and found Sam's easygoing, laid-back style a refreshing change of pace from the usual salespeople he had dealt with most of his life. Sam, after telling Gerald about the firm and the job, asked Gerald some brief standard questions about his background and sales history and what made Gerald special enough to become a Washington sales associate. Gerald expected these questions and was quite prepared.

The next series of questions, however, were very different from anything Gerald had experienced during an interview, and he found this approach very positive and exciting. Sam would tell him a little story and then ask Gerald what he would do or say if he were the manager or sales associate in the situation. No one had ever asked Gerald's opinion about anything at his prior jobs, and Gerald felt that he had finally found a firm that cared about what he thought and was willing to listen to him. Gerald thought he sailed through these scenarios with flying colors since Sam's tone was always very positive throughout the interview. It was 3 p.m. when Sam finally called an end to the session, and Gerald felt invigorated and ready for more.

Gerald was directed to a small conference room where three people who identified themselves as area managers and one person from HR asked him a series of questions about his selling approach, his work habits, and his ability to work with a sales partner. This session was repeated in another room with another three area managers and another person from personnel. Both of these sessions involved a series of follow-up questions that Gerald was happy to answer. At 5 p.m. the session ended and Sales Director Sam Arden walked in and told Gerald he would contact him in a week to let Gerald know the firm's decision. Gerald thanked Sam for the opportunity to interview for a job with Washington and said he looked forward to hearing from them.

The Letter

A week went by, and Gerald had not heard anything from Washington. Gerald finally called and was told that a letter was in the mail to him and he should await its arrival. Three days later, and with continued impatience at work and at home, Gerald received the destined letter. The first word he read, *congratulations,* sent Gerald into an ecstatic frenzy. He then read further. "Hmmm," mumbled Gerald, "this is not exactly what I was told." Their job offer was commission-based only, and, assuming that medical and dental packages ran about the same cost and that coverage was the same as his current job, Gerald would lose paid vacation time but perhaps gain in terms of contributions to a 401(k) plan. Gerald thought to himself, "Bummer! This is not the same great deal that I was told about during the interview process! Who sold who on the job?"

Questions

1. If Washington Home Builders had Gerald's résumé, why would they need him to complete a blank job application, which requests much of the same information as a résumé?

2. Once they had his job application, why do you think Washington took a week to ask Gerald to come in for an interview?

3. Gerald's morning included taking a series of exams and questionnaires. What was the purpose of the exams/questions, and what legal limitations are there to testing?

4. Analyze Gerald's interviews in light of Model 6-2, "Interviewing Steps." How well did Washington follow those steps?

5. What types of questions did it seem Washington used during the interview process?

6. In reviewing Exhibit 6-1, "Steps in the Selection Process," how successful was Washington in selecting Gerald for the job? Suggestions for improvement?

Case created by Herbert Sherman, PhD, and Mr. Theodore Vallas, Department of Management Sciences, Long Island University School of Business, Brooklyn Campus

SKILL BUILDER 6-1

Questions for a Professor to Teach This Course

Objective

To develop your ability to develop interview questions.

Skills

The primary skills developed through this exercise are:

1. *HR Management skill* – Technical, business, and conceptual and design skills

2. *SHRM 2010 Curriculum Guidebook* – G: Staffing: Recruitment and Selection

Preparation

Assume you are the dean of your college and you need to hire a professor to teach this course next semester. Develop a list of at least 10 questions you would ask the candidates during a job interview for the position.

Apply It

What did I learn from this experience? How will I use this knowledge in the future?

_____

_____

Your instructor may ask you to do this Skill Builder in class in a group by sharing your interview questions. If so, the instructor will provide you with any necessary information or additional instructions.

SKILL BUILDER 6-2

Interviewing

Objective

To develop your ability to develop interview questions.

To develop your ability to interview and to be interviewed.

Skills

The primary skills developed through this exercise are:

1. *HR Management skill* – Technical, human relations, business, and conceptual and design skills

2. *SHRM 2010 Curriculum Guidebook* – G: Staffing: Recruitment and Selection

Preparation

Assume you are the HR Director and you need to hire a new college grad for an entry-level HR position. Because you are not a large company, you have a small staff and the new hire will help out in a wide variety of HR functions. Develop a list of at least 10 questions you would ask the candidates during a job interview for the position.

Apply It

What did I learn from this experience? How will I use this knowledge in the future?

_____

_____

Your instructor may ask you to do this Skill Builder in class by breaking into groups of two to three and actually conducting interviews using your questions. If so, the instructor will provide you with any necessary information or additional instructions.

Developing
and Managing

Part
III

7

Training, Learning, Talent Management, and Development

Learning Outcomes

After studying this chapter you should be able to:

7.1 Discuss the major difference between training and development

7.2 Identify and briefly discuss the common points in the tenure of employees within the organization where training may be needed

7.3 Briefly discuss the steps in the training process and their interrelationship

7.4 Identify the most common challenges to the training and development process

7.5 Identify the three common learning theories, and the type of learning that results from each theory

7.6 Identify and briefly discuss the four methods for shaping behavior

7.7 Identify which training methods are most commonly used with which HRM skill

7.8 Discuss each of the major types of training delivery

7.9 Briefly discuss the Four-Level Evaluation Method for assessing training programs

7.10 Discuss the term *career* and the significance of the definition in the text

7.11 Briefly discuss the three common methods of employee development

7.12 Briefly discuss some of the individual and organizational consequences that can occur as a result of organizational career planning processes

7.13 Define the following terms:

Competency model
Training
Employee development
Orientation
Remediation
Needs assessment
Self-efficacy
Learning

Positive reinforcement
Negative reinforcement
Punishment
Extinction
Career
Career plateau
Emotional intelligence

Chapter 7 Outline

SHRM
HR CONTENT

See Appendix A:
SHRM 2010 Curriculum Guidebook for the complete list

C. **Job Analysis/Job Design (required)**
   5.   Training and development

       Vocational and career counseling
       Needs assessment
       Career pathing

D. **Organization Development (required)**
   2.   Developing human resources

   3.   Emotional intelligence

   4.   Equipping the organization for present and future talent needs

   8.   Measurement systems

  11.   Organizational learning

  13.   Outsourcing employee development

  16.   Training employees to meet current and future job demands

J. **Training and Development (required)**
   1.   Needs assessment

   2.   Competency models

   3.   Learning theories (behaviorism, constructivism, cognitive models, adult learning, knowledge management)

   4.   Training evaluation (Kirkpatrick's model)

   5.   E-learning and use of technology in training

   6.   On-the-Job Training

   7.   Outsourcing (secondary)

   8.   Transfer of training (design issues, facilitating transfer)

   9.   Employee development (formal education, experience, assessment)

  10.   Determining Return on Investment

  11.   The role of training in succession planning

  12.   Human/intellectual capital

Case 7-1. Who Is Managing the Manager?

Is There a Key to Maintaining Employee Loyalty?

The World War II generation expected to start with one company when they entered the workforce and to retire from that same company at the end of their working days. Such expectations are not much in evidence these days as exemplified by Courtney, our newest addition to the HR Department. I overheard her talking to a friend in the lunchroom one day. "I guess I'll hang here for two years or so—get that first job experience, you know. Then I can move up to a better position somewhere else, don't you think?" Her friend replied, "I've heard if you change jobs too frequently you can be branded as a job hopper." "Oh, I'm not worried about that!" exclaimed Courtney. "Nobody stays in the same job anymore for more than a few years." How do HR Departments work to keep someone they consider a valuable employee as a loyal employee who remains with the company? Chapter 7 looks at the ins and outs of managing talent through training and development.

The Practitioner's Model for HRM

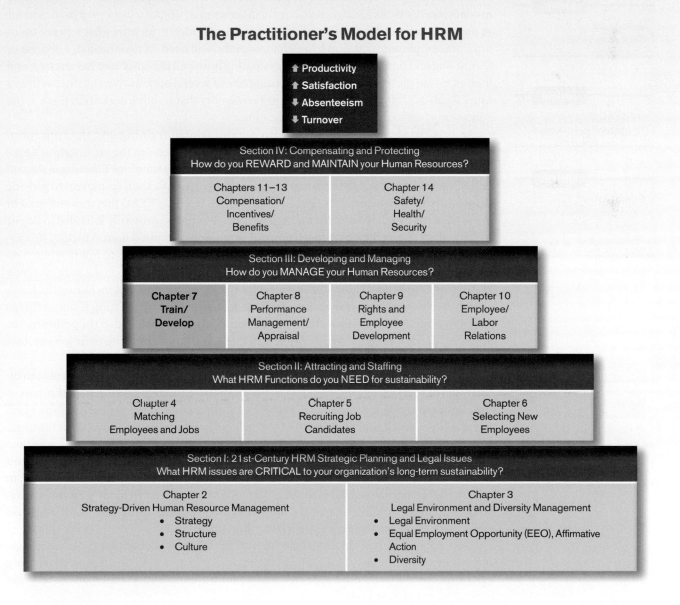

Training and Development and When It Is Needed

LO 7.1

Discuss the major difference between training and development.

Now that we've made it through the process of selecting individuals into the organization, the next thing we need to do is train them to do their new jobs. In all cases, new employees should get at least basic training about the organization and its routine processes as well as the job that they are going to be filling. We can't reasonably expect them to do a job successfully unless they're trained in how to do it, and there is a relationship between training and job satisfaction.[1] Offering training and development generally decreases expensive turnover,[2] and employees are less likely to engage in neglectful behavior.[3] Training is expensive, so it must be done correctly to get the benefits to outweigh the cost.[4] Let's begin by discussing training and development and the difference between them, followed by when training is needed.

Training and Development

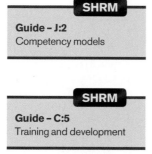

SHRM

Guide – J:2
Competency models

SHRM

Guide – C:5
Training and development

SHRM

Guide – D:16
Training employees to meet current and future job demands

SHRM

Guide – D:2
Developing human resources

Before we get into training and development, we need to understand competency models because training is based on the competencies we want employees to have. **Competency models** *identify the knowledge, skills, and abilities needed in order to perform a particular job in the organization.* We can utilize these competency models to identify what types of training a new employee, or an employee changing jobs, will need. We go through a process of identifying and providing the training, evaluating how well the employee has learned, and then assessing the training process itself using one of several options. We will discuss this in more detail in a little while, but for now just remember that training is a critical piece in the education of each employee in the organization.

In this chapter, we will discuss both organizational training and the concept of employee development. The two are related, but separate pieces of the organization's processes involving the management of its employees. So, what is training? **Training** is *the process of teaching employees the skills necessary to perform a job.* We train employees to provide them with the knowledge, skills, and abilities (known in HR as KSAs) that they will need in order to succeed in their work for the organization. Training is primarily intended to be put to immediate use by the individual being trained. As an example, Amazon focuses on customer service, so it trains its employees by drilling them in what steps to follow when they get everyday questions, as well as fielding more unusual requests. To make sure everyone at Amazon understands how customer service works, each employee, including the CEO, spends two days on the service desk every two years.[5] If the organization is doing things correctly, employee training will also be one of the primary tools used in the performance appraisal of the individual to determine whether or not they are doing their job successfully. We'll discuss employee performance appraisals in the next chapter.

Somewhat in contrast to the training that we do in order for employees to be able to do a new job or to do an existing job better, is the process of employee development. **Employee development** is *ongoing education to improve knowledge and skills for present and future jobs.* So, employee development is designed to teach our workers how to move up in the organization in the future by becoming skilled at those tasks that they will need to know how to do, in order to move into higher-level jobs. Development tends to be less technical, and is aimed at improving human, communication, conceptual, and decision-making skills in managerial and professional employees. To remain competitive in today's dynamic environment, organizations must have employees who maintain up-to-date knowledge and skills, and development plays an important role in this effort.[6]

Both colleges and corporations have been criticized for not doing a good job of developing our business leaders.[7] This is one of the reasons why this book focuses on developing HR skills. Also, GE and others are well known for building leaders based on the fact that their managers are recruited into high-level positions in other companies.[8]

When Is Training Needed?

In order to successfully determine what kind of training needs to be carried out within the organization, HR Managers should begin by completing a needs assessment to determine the training needed. We will discuss needs assessments in the next section. For now, let's review some common points at which we should probably complete a needs assessment and at least consider providing training to our people.

Organizational training and development is a career-long process.

New Employees–Orientation

Orientation is *the process of introducing new employees to the organization and their jobs.* This socialization process is important to both newcomers and organizations as newcomers "learn the ropes" and understand what is expected from them in their work as they assimilate into the organization and attempt to become productive members.[9] Thus, orientation has a long-lasting effect on new employee job attitude and satisfaction, behavior, work mastery, and performance.[10]

Orientation works to acculturate the new employee to the organization and its culture, and to prepare them to do their own job within the organization. It is an introduction of the person to the company. What do we need to think about when we introduce somebody to the company?

We need to think about introducing the new employee to all of the things that exist within the organizational society that they are entering. The process is very similar to someone moving to a different country and having to assimilate into a new culture. What would they need to know in order to be able to go about their daily lives, to do the routine things that they need to do, and to be able to provide for their own personal needs? Orientation should be designed to answer all of the questions necessary to allow the new employee to integrate into the "society" that they are entering.

What things would an individual need to know if they were moving to a new society? Well, one of the first things they would need to know is what the laws, rules, and regulations were in the new society, so we would need to introduce them to the organization's policies and procedures, and its rules and regulations. The second thing that they would probably want to know is how to act and interact with others in the new society. So we would need to introduce them to their job and the ways that they would perform their job within the organization.

We would also want to talk to the individual about the underlying organizational structure and where they would go, and to whom they should talk, in order to get certain things done. To whom should they talk in their department if they have questions about their job or about how things are done within the department? With whom should they speak in other departments if they have questions that can't be answered within their primary work group, and when is it acceptable to go to individuals in other departments?

Next, they would probably want to know how they get the money that they would need in order to survive in society. So we would need to tell them about their pay and benefits, including whom to contact if they have questions. Our person entering this new society would also probably want to know how to stay safe as they go about their business, so we

---

WORK
APPLICATION 7-1

Select a job. Did you receive both training and development or just training? Explain in some detail why it was one or both.

LO 7.2

Identify the common points in the tenure of employees within the organization where training may be needed. Briefly discuss each point.

would need to talk to them about safety in the organization. They would also likely need to fill out paperwork—to get a driver's license, to open a bank account, to identify who they are, or for other purposes. Similarly, there is paperwork that is necessary in order for the organization to function successfully, so in the orientation we would ask the new employee to fill out this paperwork.

As you can see, there are many different things that we need to teach the individual as they are entering our new society, so we can't legitimately perform the orientation process in one day, or a couple of hours. Effective orientation of employees results in lower turnover rates.[11] Orientation to the firm and the new employee's job should be provided over a significant period of time—from approximately one week to as many as two to four weeks, or even more, depending on the complexity of the organization and the jobs. Here are a few examples of world-class companies with long orientation programs: Toyota has a five-week orientation, Honda has a six-week orientation, and Southwest Airlines has a 90-day orientation. However, in most organizations the orientation process is significantly shorter than this, and this is one reason that our 21st-century organizations suffer significant early turnover of new hires.

If our new employee is frustrated because they don't know how to do their job, where their tools are located, whom to go to if they have a problem, or how to fix an issue with their pay, the likelihood of them leaving the organization goes up drastically. Many organizations could significantly reduce their turnover by modestly increasing the orientation period for new hires.

New Job Requirements or Processes

The second common point where training may be necessary occurs when jobs change in some form. Whether our employee is in the same job or they are changing jobs and need to learn new processes, if there is a significant change in any work requirements, we need to train the employee. The change may be based on discovery of new techniques or technologies to perform particular work to make the work more efficient. The organization may have changed its strategic direction, and as a result some or all of the jobs within the organization require new processes or procedures. In any of these cases or any similar situation where the change has significance for that job, we should go through the process of performing a needs assessment. If the result of the needs assessment shows that training is necessary, then an appropriate training program can be designed and implemented.

Remediation

The third common point at which managers need to investigate the requirement for additional training is when there has been some failure of an employee or employees to perform successfully and meet organizational standards. **Remediation** is *the correction of a deficiency or failure in a process or procedure.* In remediation, we work to correct the actions of the individual responsible for the process or procedure so that they can successfully carry out the action in the future. We don't want to make a common mistake, though. Remediation is not about blame for a failure. It is about correcting the actions taken by an employee so that critical organizational activities can be performed successfully. The term comes from the root word *remedy*, which means to cure, fix, or repair a failure or disorder. The emphasis in this case should always be on correcting the actions of the employee to better serve both the employee and the organization's interests. Again, organizational managers act in the same way that a good physician or mechanic would act—they need to diagnose the situation first, and *then* take appropriate corrective action to solve the problem through training.

Employee Development for Advancement

The next point at which we need to evaluate the need for training is in situations where we are working to develop current employee skills and abilities so that they are able to move

---

WORK
APPLICATION 7-2

Briefly describe the orientation you received for a job. How could it be improved?

into higher-level jobs within the organization. Offering development opportunities generally decreases turnover.[12] All organizations have a responsibility to plan for the succession of individuals in management and executive positions, and this planning is usually a function of the HR Department. This is the only way that the organization can be sustainable over long periods of time. In order to successfully carry out a succession process, people at lower levels in the organization must be trained in the knowledge and skills necessary to be able to take on higher-level duties. One area getting more attention today is training and development in ethics and social responsibility, in part because of the litany of ethical failures in the past decade within companies in a variety of industries. While very few organizations will attempt to develop all of the employees within the firm, most organizations go through an informal or a formal process of identifying high-potential individuals for development, and ultimately advancement into managerial and executive slots.

Many 21st-century organizations have rigorous development programs that include job rotation to various departments within the organization, classroom training, On-the-Job Training, assigned mentors, and many other tools, all of which are designed to train the employee and develop their capabilities for future use within the firm. Organizations that neglect succession processes and employee development can find themselves at a competitive disadvantage when senior personnel leave the firm either through retirement or resignation. It is critical that HR lead the process of planning for succession and employee development. Although in this chapter we will focus more on training than development (there are five major sections explaining training, followed by one section on employee development), both are important to the organization.

ESR

SHRM

Guide – J:11
The role of training in succession planning

The Training Process and Needs Assessment

How are we going to go about training our employees? How do we know who needs what training, in what forms, at what point? How do we determine whether or not the employee is ready and willing to participate in the training? Finally, how do we know that the training was effective? In order to answer these questions, we have to plan our training processes very carefully. We need to look at what's currently going on in the organization and how that differs from what needs to happen in the future in order to accomplish our strategic business goals. Once we do this, we can analyze the types of training that will be necessary in order to build new knowledge, skills, and abilities for our workforce.

Steps in the Training Process

This chapter is primarily organized to follow the steps in the training process. Let's take a look at how we go through the training process in Exhibit 7-1, followed by a brief discussion of the steps here, and in more detail throughout the chapter.

Step 1. Assessing Needs. We conduct a needs assessment to determine what training is necessary to improve performance. We will discuss this step in this section.

Step 2. Selecting How to Shape Behavior. We select a method of shaping employee behavior based on learning theories so that we can change employee behavior to improve performance. We will discuss this step in the next major section of this chapter: "Learning and Shaping Behavior."

Step 3. Designing Training. We design the training and development by determining which training methods we will use to shape employee behavior based on the needs assessment. We discuss this step in the fourth major section: "Designing Training Methods." As

LO 7.3

Briefly discuss the steps in the training process and their interrelationship.

we design the training, we must take into account how we will shape behavior and the delivery methods of the training that we will use.

Step 4. Delivering Training. Before we actually conduct the training and development, as part of this step, we must select the delivery method. We will discuss the delivery options in the "Delivering Training" major section.

Step 5. Assessing Training. After the training, our last step is to assess how effective the training was at developing the needed skills by determining our success at shaping behavior. We discuss Step 5 later in this chapter in the "Assessing Training" major section.

Interrelationship of the Training Process Steps. Note in Exhibit 7-1 that Steps 2, 3, 4, and 5 have a double-headed arrow; this is because all the steps are so closely related and based on each other that they are commonly planned together before actually delivering the training. In other words, you are constantly thinking ahead and behind your current step in the training process. If the assessment of the training reveals that the behavior has not been shaped (changed) as needed, we may have to go back to Step 1 and start the training process again.

Needs Assessment

The first major task (Step 1) in the training process, and probably one of the most important, is the *needs assessment*. A **needs assessment** *is the process of analyzing the difference between what is currently occurring within a job or jobs and what is required—either now or in the future—based on the organization's operations and strategic goals.* If a needs assessment is not done correctly, several significant problems can occur. A training course may be poorly designed, or it may cover the wrong information. The wrong employees may be asked to participate in the training, or they may not yet be capable of absorbing the information in the training because of a lack of a knowledge base or skill set. We may end up creating a training program that's unnecessary, or we may fail to determine that an issue is based on poor performance rather than lack of knowledge. These are significant issues that we can avoid if we correctly go through the process of a needs assessment. We absolutely must look at completing a needs assessment and provide training at some particular points in time within the organization.

SHRM

Guide – C:5, J:1
Needs assessment

SHRM

Guide – D:4
Equipping the organization for present and future talent needs

| Exhibit 7-1 | The Training Process |

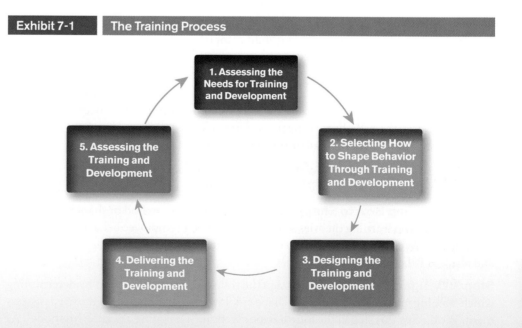

Similar to a good automobile mechanic, organizational managers have to diagnose what may currently be wrong with a process in order to successfully repair and/or tune the process up. If the diagnosis isn't done correctly, again similar to the mechanic working on your car, managers in the organization may create training solutions that don't solve the existing problem. So the manager has to go through a process of identifying where in a current sequence of events things are not working the way they should or determine how they can be done more efficiently. Only by diligently going through the process of looking at that chain of events in the status quo can a manager identify where the process can be changed in order to improve organizational productivity and reach the organization's goals.

Challenges to the Training Process

As part of the needs assessment, let's now discuss some common challenges to the training process that include minimally prepared or unprepared workers, difficulty in identifying the Return on Investment provided from training, employee resistance to change (due at least in part to insecurity on the part of the individual concerning how the change will affect them), matching the training to the strategic goals of the organization, and finally logistics issues—including scheduling and locations available for training courses. Managers have to work through each of these challenges in order for training programs to be successful. Let's do a quick review of each of these factors.

Unprepared workforce. One of the most significant challenges to work process training is the fact that so many of the individuals being hired into the corporate workforce are ill prepared in the educational basics, including reading and math skills. A recent report notes that employers hire substantial numbers of new entrants who are poorly prepared, requiring additional company investment to improve workforce readiness skills.[13] In cases where the employee doesn't have the basic skills necessary to succeed, the organization must train them in those basic skill sets before they can be taught the advanced skills necessary to improve organizational processes.

Return on Investment/cost justification. Businesses today are naturally concerned with the return that they get from any corporate investment. Training is time-consuming and expensive,[14] and training is no different from any other investment. Executives expect, and in fact require, that training provide a positive Return on Investment (ROI). HR Managers have become more familiar with the ROI calculation discussed in Chapter 2, and use it to provide justification for the financial cost of training programs.

Resistance to change and employee insecurity. Since this is not a change management text, suffice it to say that virtually all individuals resist changes to their routine. They resist for a variety of reasons, including insecurity—the insecurity is based on the concern the individual has that they may not be able to successfully adapt to the change in some way. This insecurity, leading to resistance to change, can cause significant difficulty in the training process. Management must overcome the resistance to change exhibited by the workers in order for the training to be successful.

Strategic congruence. Strategic congruence is another challenge to the training process. One of the most critical requirements in corporate training programs is to ensure that the training furthers the strategic goals of the organization. Any training program that does not aim squarely at the strategic goals of the organization is difficult to justify in a corporate environment. As HR Managers, we have to ensure that our training and development programs help to carry out the organization's strategy over the long term.

WORK APPLICATION 7-3

Do a simple needs assessment for a job you have or had. Be sure to state the competency model (knowledge, skills, and abilities) it takes to do the job.

LO 7.4

Identify the most common challenges to the training and development process.

WORK APPLICATION 7-4

Think about the people with whom you have worked. What is your perception of the preparation people have for the workforce?

WORK APPLICATION 7-5

Think about the people with whom you have worked. What is your perception of their resistance to changes in their work routine?

Scheduling. The last of our common challenges, scheduling, involves both the timing and the location of the training. As with most things, there's never an ideal time to schedule a training course, especially if it runs for several days or even weeks. The trainees have to leave their regular jobs undone for the period of the training, and the organization has to be able to operate without those trainees performing their normal tasks. In addition, we may need physical locations for the training that have special equipment or tools and are only available for limited time periods during the year. These logistics issues may seem minimal, but frequently create significant problems for the HR Department in scheduling training courses.

Employee Readiness

Also, as part of our needs assessment, the manager needs to evaluate the employees who would be taking part in the training. The employee may feel insecure about their ability to learn and therefore be unwilling to participate in training for new processes. We must also evaluate whether the employees are physically and mentally ready to go through the training process successfully. In other words, are they *able and willing* to learn? Do they have the skills and competencies necessary to succeed in this training process?

Ability

We have to determine whether or not our employees feel that they are *able* to participate in the training process. Why wouldn't they be able to participate in training? Well, they might feel that they don't have the background training necessary to succeed in training for a more complex process. In other words, they feel that their core set of skills needs to be improved before they can be successful in more intricate training. **Self-efficacy** is *whether a person believes that they have the capability to do something or attain a particular goal.* If the employee's self-efficacy is low, they may not believe that they have the ability to succeed in the training process. Regardless of whether or not it is true, if the employee *believes* they are unable to learn, then it is highly unlikely that they will be successful in any training process because they are unlikely to try.

If the employee feels that they are unable to learn, the job of the manager becomes one of upgrading the employee's abilities if necessary, and then convincing them of their capabilities. In addition, the manager has to analyze the true abilities and limitations of each of the employees who may participate in the training process. Every person has core sets of abilities and limitations. We all have physical abilities and intellectual abilities, but we don't all have the same physical and intellectual abilities. Again, it is management's job to diagnose and determine whether are not an individual has the abilities necessary to succeed in a training process and not put that individual into a scenario where their abilities condemn them to failure.

HR Managers select employees who have the ability and willingness to be trained to succeed on the job.

What happens when people are put into situations where they are certain to fail? What happens to their motivation? What happens to their morale and job satisfaction? What most likely will happen to their productivity? If we as managers put people into this type of situation, we are almost assured of lowering their performance level rather than raising it. This is certainly not the way to get maximum productivity out of your workforce, so we want to avoid putting people in training situations where they are almost certainly going to fail.

Willingness

The second major piece in the employee equation is whether or not they're *willing* to learn what's being taught in a training program. In other words, we have to determine their "motivation to learn." Why would our workers not be motivated to learn? There are several potential reasons. First, the individual may not feel that they need to learn a new process. If they feel that the current process is sufficient and that the new process won't improve their work environment, they may be unwilling to learn.

If they feel that the training process is being done solely for political reasons (many workers think that programs such as diversity training and sexual harassment prevention training are motivated by the perceived need of the organization to be politically correct, even though this is not true, then they may not be interested in the training.

If the individual doesn't feel that the training is related to their job, they may not be motivated to learn. If the employee is concerned that their work will pile up while they're gone, they may not be motivated to train.

If their coworkers or supervisors don't support the fact that the individual will have to be away from the job in order to go through a training course and as a result put pressure on the individual, that person may not be motivated to go through the training. A significant part of willingness to learn is based on the support the individual gets from the people that surround them, including coworkers, supervisors, and even family members.

If one of your employees is going to be away from home for a period of several weeks and their family members are opposed to this extended period of separation, it's extremely unlikely they are going to be willing to participate in the training. So the manager needs to make sure that the employee is willing to go through the training process.

Learning and Shaping Behavior

Step 2 of the training process is to select how to shape or change employee behavior. In order to do so, trainers have to understand how people learn. So in this section we begin by explaining learning. Then we discuss three basic learning theories used to shape employee behavior. Next, we put the theories together in Exhibit 7-2 and discuss how to shape or change employee behavior, and we end with learning styles.

Learning

What is learning? Learning can be many different things, but in a business, we usually need to *know* that our employees have learned something that we are trying to train them to do. How do we know that they have learned a particular thing then? We know because of changes in their behavior at work. So in our case, **learning** is *any relatively permanent change in behavior that occurs as a result of experience or practice.*[15] This is a good definition to use in the organizational learning process due to the fact that it provides us with the visible evidence that an individual has learned something because they *change the way they act* as a result of the learning.

People learn in multiple ways. We learn through trial and error, we learn from the consequences that occur as a result of something we've done, and we learn from the consequences of other people's actions. And what makes this process even more complex is the

LO 7.5

Identify the three common learning theories, and the type of learning that results from each theory.

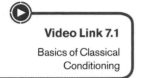

Video Link 7.1

Basics of Classical Conditioning

fact that people prefer to learn differently. We all have preferred learning styles that we use when we have an option to pick one style over another.

Learning Theories

Here we explain the three common learning theories: classical conditioning, operant conditioning, and social learning.

Classical Conditioning

Classical conditioning was made famous by a physiologist named Ivan Pavlov. Probably all of you have heard of Pavlov. He became famous by causing dogs to salivate even when not in the presence of food. Pavlov proved that when dogs were conditioned to associate the ringing of a bell with being fed, they "learned" to salivate when the bell was rung. What does the fact that a dog would salivate on command have to do with human learning? At first glance, it looks a little silly. However, what Pavlov proved was that animals will react *involuntarily* to a stimulus in their environment if they associate that stimulus with something else. OK, but humans are not dogs, are they? Do humans react involuntarily to a stimulus in the environment? Of course they do. Human beings react involuntarily to stimuli the same way all other animals react.

Have you ever walked down a row of restaurants in your hometown and smelled the aroma of fresh food being prepared, and been reminded of a relative's home when they were cooking a favorite dinner of yours? This pleasant memory may change your mood, and in fact may change your behaviors because of the feeling of well-being that's created. Alternately, have you ever heard a sound that caused you to be afraid or to want to run away from it? Why does such a sound cause you to be afraid? If you think for a few seconds, you will probably realize that the sound indicates danger to you, whether you consciously thought about it or not. You've been involuntarily conditioned to the danger associated with the sound. So, Pavlov's *classical conditioning* results in "direct, involuntary, learned behaviors." The behaviors are learned because you have changed the way you act due to some prior experience, and they are *involuntary* because you didn't intentionally learn to act in a particular way in response to the stimulus. Finally, the behaviors are *direct*, because the learning occurs as a result of something happening directly to the individual.

Operant Conditioning and Reinforcement

Video Link 7.2

Positive Reinforcement

The second common learning theory is called *operant conditioning*, which is based on reinforcement. Again, most of us have heard of the individual who made this learning theory famous—B. F. Skinner. Skinner's theory says that behavior is based on the consequences received by behaving in a similar way at an earlier point in time. In other words, if we acted in a certain way previously and received a reward, we will likely repeat that behavior. If, however, we acted in a particular way and received a negative consequence (punishment), then we will probably not repeat the behavior. Skinner tested his theory using his "Skinner Box." He would put animals such as a pigeon or a rat in a box and provide a stimulus such as a light above a lever. If the animal chose the right lever, they were rewarded with food. If the animal chose the incorrect lever, they would receive punishment such as a mild electric shock.

Skinner showed that very quickly the animals would figure out which lever to press in order to receive the reward. So, *operant conditioning* results in "direct, voluntary, learned behaviors." The subject in Skinner's experiments *voluntarily* selected the lever that provided the reward, so they learned to behave in a particular way based on the *direct* consequences of their actions. So Skinner proved that animals will voluntarily act in order to receive a reward and avoid acting in order to avoid receiving punishment.

Social (Vicarious) Learning

Our third type of learning, *social learning,* is similar in form to *operant conditioning.* The difference here is that we are learning not from consequences of our own actions but from consequences of actions of another person. *Social learning* is also called *vicarious learning.* The word *vicarious* means "experienced or realized through imaginative or sympathetic participation in the experience of another."[16] So social or vicarious learning is experienced through watching the actions of another person and witnessing the consequences of their actions. In other words, if a young boy watches his sister receive a cookie as a reward for cleaning her room and he wants a cookie too, he may determine that the best way to get a cookie is to go clean his own room. This would be an example of social learning. Again social learning is based on *voluntary,* learned actions on the part of the individual, but it is based on *indirect* consequences of the actions of another person.

Shaping Behavior

We can use the three types of learning that we have just reviewed, especially Skinner's concept of *operant conditioning,* in order to shape the behaviors of the employees in the organization. In order to shape the behavior of our employees, we will provide reinforcement (rewards, punishment, or as a third alternative neither). Take a look at Exhibit 7-2. It shows four methods of shaping behavior. We can break these methods down into a process of applying a reward, removing a reward, applying punishment, removing punishment, or providing no response to the actions of the individual.

WORK APPLICATION 7-8

Give examples of what you learned in an organization through classical conditioning, operant conditioning, and social learning.

Video Link 7.3

Real Life Experiments

LO 7.6

Identify and briefly discuss the four methods for shaping behavior.

7-1 APPLYING THE CONCEPT

Learning Theories

State which of the following learning theories is illustrated in each of the given situations.

a. classical conditioning
b. operant conditioning
c. social learning

_____ 1. Jamal, I just saw Tom walking around the construction site without his helmet on, and a nail fell and hit him on the head, and now he is bleeding, and they took him to the hospital to get stitches. You better believe that I'm keeping my helmet on from now on when I'm on the job.

_____ 2. Even though the boss didn't ask me to, I stayed late and finished the report she wanted. She gave me a sincere thanks and a $50 gift certificate to Antony's Restaurant. I learned that it is worth putting in extra effort for the boss.

_____ 3. I just landed another good account. The customer commented on my good manners and social skills. Does this have anything to do with my parents continuously telling me how to behave properly as I was growing up?

_____ 4. I was late for work today, and my boss gave me a first warning. The next time I'm late, I will get a second warning, and I will have to pay a $25 fine. So I'm going to get to work 10 minutes early from now on so I don't get another warning.

_____ 5. Karen works harder than anyone and has the highest-level quality and quantity of work in the department. But I've never even seen her get as much as a thank-you for her hard work. So why should I work as hard as she does?

Exhibit 7-2	Shaping Behavior

(A)	**(B)**
Positive Reinforcement Apply a reward	**Punishment** Apply a noxious stimulus— Give bad consequence
(C)	**(D)**
Punishment Remove a reward	**Negative Reinforcement** Avoid or remove or a noxious stimulus

Extinction (E) = The absence of a response, designed to avoid reinforcing negative behaviors Shaping (changing) behavior:

A, D = Increasing target behaviors
B, C, E = Decreasing target behaviors

So, what's the value of understanding Exhibit 7-2 and the four methods of shaping behavior? If we understand each of the four methods, we can use them in order to cause workers to act in ways that are conducive to the improvement and ultimate success of the organization. Let's discuss each part of the exhibit.

Positive reinforcement. If we *apply* a *reward* (the upper left Quadrant A in the exhibit), we're using the concept of positive reinforcement. **Positive reinforcement** is *providing a reward in return for a constructive action on the part of the subject.* For example, if our employee does something that improves the safety of workers in the organization, we may give them a bonus as a reward. This would be positive reinforcement. Applying a reward to a particular behavior is likely to cause the individual to perform that behavior, or similar behaviors, again. So our employee would be likely to provide other suggestions to improve our business operations because of the past reward. We should realize that positive reinforcement is the most commonly used method to shape employee behavior when we train new employees to do their jobs and when existing employees need to learn new job requirements and processes.

Negative reinforcement. Our second option would be to *avoid or remove a noxious stimulus* (the lower right Quadrant D in the exhibit), which is called negative reinforcement. **Negative reinforcement** is *the withdrawal of a harmful thing from the environment in response to a positive action on the part of the subject.* Negative reinforcement is commonly based on rules with punishment for breaking the rules. A rule itself is not a punishment; it is a means of getting people to do or avoid specific behavior, such as coming to work on time. But if the rule is broken, punishment is usually the consequence. An example here would be coming to work on time not because you want to be on time, but because you want to avoid a punishment for being late. It can also be removing an employee from disciplinary probation for tardiness in response to their positive action of showing up for work on time for a period of time after being disciplined. Avoiding or taking away a negative consequence in response to a positive behavior is likely to cause the individual to perform the desired behavior. We should realize that negative reinforcement is commonly used during the new employee orientation to make sure employees know the expected behavior, and the consequences for breaking rules. We certainly don't want to punish an employee for breaking a rule that they didn't know exists.

Punishment. In contrast to reinforcement, we may punish adverse behaviors. **Punishment** is *the application of an adverse consequence or removal of a reward, in order to decrease an unwanted behavior.* One method of punishment would be to *remove a reward* (the lower left Quadrant C in the exhibit) as a result of someone doing something that they shouldn't have done. Think of taking away the car keys for a school-age driver when they do something wrong. Let's say that our organization has a policy of providing free parking for our workers in a crowded downtown area. We might take away the parking privileges of an individual who continually harasses other workers in the parking lot.

Alternately, we can *apply a noxious stimulus* (the upper right Quadrant B in the exhibit), which is also considered to be punishment. An example here would be suspending a worker without pay because of excessive absenteeism. By suspending the worker, we're applying a negative response. The negative response received by the worker is designed to cause the behavior that created such a response to decline. So, in other words, punishment can be the application of something bad (a noxious stimulus), or the removal of something good (a reward).

We should realize that punishment is not a commonly used method when we train employees; rather it is commonly used when employees know how to do the job but just will not meet the job standards and when employees break a rule and get disciplined for doing so. Because we need punishment, not training, in these two situations, and as a manager you will likely have employees in these situations, we will learn how to discipline employees in Chapter 9.

Extinction. We noted earlier in this section that there are four options for shaping behavior. What is the other option? The last option doesn't fit in the diagram itself, because it's the absence of reinforcement or punishment of any kind. **Extinction** is *the lack of response, either positive or negative, in order to avoid reinforcing an undesirable behavior.* It is also called "ignore it and the behavior will stop." How does a lack of response cause behavior to be shaped in a way that we desire?

Problem employee behavior will sometimes be exhibited specifically to cause a reaction from the manager or fellow employees. The employee who exhibits the behavior may delight in causing others concern or consternation. For example, the male employee who continually asks his female manager about organizational sexual harassment policies in front of other workers in order to cause her discomfort as she explains the policy is most likely *intentionally* acting to cause her embarrassment. In such a case, the female manager may be able to ignore the stimulus behavior and provide no reinforcement. If the manager does so for a long enough time, the employee behavior will most likely decline or go away completely, because it is not having the desired negative effect on the manager. We should realize that extinction is also not very commonly used because when we train employees, we don't usually ignore behavior in hopes that it will not be repeated—we correct it.

Shaping (changing) behavior. If you understand these methods of shaping behavior, this becomes a powerful tool in your managerial toolbox for changing behavior to increase performance. These tools allow you to *cause* your employees to act in ways you want them to and to avoid acting in ways that are detrimental to themselves, their division or department, or the organization as a whole. Now let's discuss how to increase and decrease behavior to increase performance.

Increasing targeted behavior. If we want to cause the behavior to increase, we would want to use positive or negative reinforcement (Quadrant A or D in Exhibit 7-2). Reinforcement, whether positive or negative, is designed to cause an increase in the target behavior.

Decreasing targeted behavior. If, on the other hand, we want to cause a particular behavior to decrease, we would use punishment (in either of its forms) or extinction (Quadrant B, C, or E in Exhibit 7-2). Punishment and extinction are designed to cause a target behavior to decrease over time.

WORK
APPLICATION 7-9

Give examples of how an organization uses positive reinforcement, punishment, negative reinforcement, and extinction to shape employee behavior.

Learning Styles

As a last point in our review of the learning process, we need to briefly discuss various learning styles that people prefer to use. There are several common learning style inventories available in psychology literature, and even some questionnaires that track learning style on the Internet. Individual learning styles have to be taken into account when we create training programs so that we ensure the best potential outcomes from the training by utilizing teaching methods that cover each of the major learning styles.

Video Link 7.4

Learning Styles for the Workplace

Fleming learning styles. One of the more common learning style inventories by Neil Fleming provides three primary learner options. These three options are *visual, auditory, and tactile learning*.[17] As you would think, visual learners prefer to have material provided in a visual format such as graphs and charts. Auditory learners, on the other hand, generally prefer to learn information based on hearing that information. Auditory learners tend to perform best in a historical classroom setting where the teacher stands in front of the class and teaches while the students passively listen. Finally, tactile learners prefer to learn by doing. Tactile learners want to physically perform a task in order to learn. Most of us use a mix of all three of the major learning styles. Therefore, in a training situation the trainer should take each of the styles into account when creating the training program. You should realize that we provide multiple tactile learning application and skill building opportunities in this book. Which of the three options do you prefer when learning something?

7-2 APPLYING THE CONCEPT

Shaping Behavior

State which of the following methods is illustrated in each of the given situations.

a. positive reinforcement
b. punishment—give bad consequence

c. punishment—remove reward
d. negative reinforcement
e. extinction

_____ 6. You are breaking the rule of wearing your safety goggles while running the machine. Therefore, I am sending the form to payroll to deduct the $50 fine from your paycheck.

_____ 7. I just overheard you dealing with that angry customer. You got her to calm down and leave the store as a happy customer. This behavior leads to keeping our customers and growing our business. Thanks—keep up the good work.

_____ 8. If you're not more careful and you don't stop burning the steaks, you will have to start paying for them.

_____ 9. I know you like to get out of work for a while and make the coffee run, but because you were late getting back from lunch, Tony will make the coffee run this afternoon.

_____ 10. Jose used to give me that intimidating look when I assigned him a task he didn't like, which made me uncomfortable. So I just ignored it and didn't let him make me feel uncomfortable, and he stopped doing it.

Kolb learning styles. A more complex learning style inventory was developed by David Kolb.[18] To determine your preferred learning style, complete Self-Assessment 7-1.

YOUR LEARNING STYLE

Below are 10 statements. For each statement distribute 5 points between the A and B alternatives. If the A statement is very characteristic of you and the B statement is not, place a 5 on the A line and a 0 on the B line. If the A statement is characteristic of you and the B statement is occasionally or somewhat characteristic of you, place a 4 on the A line and a 1 on the B line. If both statements are characteristic of you, place a 3 on the line that is more characteristic of you and a 2 on the line that is less characteristic of you. Be sure to distribute 5 points between each A and B alternative for each of the 10 statements. When distributing the 5 points, try to recall recent situations on the job or in school.

1. When learning:

_____ A. I watch and listen.   _____ B. I get involved and participate.

2. When learning:

_____ A. I rely on my hunches and feelings.   _____ B. I rely on logical and rational thinking.

3. When making decisions:

_____ A. I take my time.   _____ B. I make them quickly.

4. When making decisions:

_____ A. I rely on my gut feelings about the best alternative course of action.   _____ B. I rely on a logical analysis of the situation.

5. When doing things:

_____ A. I am careful.   _____ B. I am practical.

6. When doing things:

_____ A. I have strong feelings and reactions.   _____ B. I reason things out.

7. I would describe myself in the following way:

_____ A. I am a reflective person.   _____ B. I am an active person.

8. I would describe myself in the following way:

_____ A. I am influenced by my emotions.   _____ B. I am influenced by my thoughts.

9. When interacting in small groups:

_____ A. I listen, watch, and get involved slowly.   _____ B. I am quick to get involved.

10. When interacting in small groups:

_____ A. I express what I am feeling.   _____ B. I say what I am thinking.

Scoring: Place your answer numbers (0–5) on the lines below. Then add the numbers in each column vertically. Each of the four columns should have a total number between 0 and 25. The total of the two A and B columns should equal 25.

1. _____ A. _____ B. (5)   2. _____ A. _____ B. (5)

3. _____ A. _____ B. (5)   4. _____ A. _____ B. (5)

5. _____ A. _____ B. (5)   6. _____ A. _____ B. (5)

7. _____ A. _____ B. (5)   8. _____ A. _____ B. (5)

9. _____ A. _____ B. (5)   10. _____ A. _____ B. (5)

Totals: _____ A. _____ B. (25)   _____ A. _____ B. (25)

Style: Observing Doing   Feeling Thinking

There is no best, or right, learning style; each of the four learning styles has its pros and cons. The more evenly distributed your scores are between the As and Bs, the more flexible you are at changing styles. Understanding your preferred learning style can help you get the most from your learning experiences.

Determining your preferred learning style: The five odd-numbered A statements refer to your self-description as being "observing," and the five odd-numbered B statements refer to your self-description as "doing." The column with the highest number is your preferred style of learning. I described myself as preferring to learn by _____.

The five even-numbered A statements refer to your self-description as being a "feeling" person, and the five even-numbered B statements refer to your self-description as being a "thinking" person. The column with the highest number is your preferred style. I described myself as preferring to learn by _____.

Putting the two preferences together gives you your preferred learning style. Check it off below:

_____ Accommodator (combines doing and feeling).

_____ Diverger (combines observing and feeling).

_____ Converger (combines doing and thinking).

_____ Assimilator (combines observing and thinking)

Designing Training Methods

Once we have completed our needs assessment, and selected how we plan to shape behavior, we are ready to complete Step 3 of the training process—design the training by selecting training methods. So in this section, we will discuss training methods and then identify which types of training are more commonly used with employees and managers.

LO 7.7

Identify which training methods are most commonly used with which HRM skill.

Skills and Training Methods

Recall, back in Chapter 1, we identified four important HRM skills: technical, human relations, conceptual and design (decision making), and business skills. Essentially, all of the training methods are used to develop specific skills that can be classified into one of these four skills categories. So here we present which training methods to use based on which types of skills we are developing. Exhibit 7-3 presents the types of skills, the training methods appropriate for developing each skill, and a description of the training.

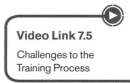

Video Link 7.5

Challenges to the Training Process

Exhibit 7-3	Skills and Training Methods	
Skills Developed	**Methods**	**Description**
Technical skills	a. Written material, lectures, videotapes, question-and-answer sessions, discussions, demonstrations	Questions or problems related to previously presented material are presented to the trainee in a booklet or on a computer screen. The trainee is asked to select a response to each question or problem and is given feedback on the response.
	b. Programmed learning	Depending on the material presented, programmed learning may also develop interpersonal and communication skills.
	c. Job rotation	Employees are trained to perform different jobs. Job rotation also develops trainees' conceptual skills.
	d. Projects	Trainees are given special assignments, such as developing a new product or preparing a report. Certain projects may also develop trainees' interpersonal skills and conceptual skills.
Human relations skills	e. Role-playing	Trainees act out situations that might occur on the job, such as handling a customer complaint, to develop skill at handling such situations on the job.
	f. Behavior modeling	Trainees observe how to perform a task correctly (by watching either a live demonstration or a videotape). Trainees role-play the observed skills and receive feedback on their performance. Trainees develop plans for using the observed skills on the job.
Conceptual and design/ business skills	g. Cases	The trainee is presented with a simulated situation and asked to diagnose and solve the problems involved. The trainee usually must also answer questions about his or her diagnosis and solution.
	h. In-basket exercises	The trainee is given actual or simulated letters, memos, reports, and so forth that would typically come to the person holding the job. The trainee must determine what action each item would require and must assign priorities to the actions.
	i. Management games	Trainees work as part of a team to "manage" a simulated company over a period of several game "quarters" or "years."
	j. Interactive videos	Trainees can view videotapes that present situations requiring conceptual skills or decision making.

7-3 APPLYING THE CONCEPT

Training Methods

For each of the training situations below, identify the most appropriate training method. Use the letters a–j in Exhibit 7-3 as your answers.

_____ 11.   You want to be sure that employees can cover for each other if one or more of them are on break or absent.

_____ 12.   You need to teach employees how to sell products to customers.

_____ 13.   In our strategy course, we are running a company by filling out these forms and getting quarterly results. We are competing with other companies in our industry.

_____ 14.   Your supervisors need to do a better job of handling employee complaints.

_____ 15.   Employees must learn several rules and regulations in order to perform their jobs. You have a large department with a high turnover rate.

_____ 16.   New employees must be trained to handle the typical daily problems they will face on the job.

_____ 17.   You need an employee to prepare a special report.

Employee and Managerial Use of Training Methods

All of the methods listed in Exhibit 7-3 as technical skills are commonly used in training employees to perform their jobs. To develop human relations skills, employees often use role-playing and behavior modeling to develop customer service and sales skills, and managers develop skills in working with employees. Management games and cases are commonly used with managers to develop conceptual and design (decision-making) and business skills to become top-level managers, whereas in-baskets are more commonly used with employees, and interactive videos are used by both. So employees tend to be taught technical skills more than managers, both develop human relations skills, and managers are more commonly taught conceptual and design decision-making and business skills. However, there are always exceptions to these general rules, such as managers being taught the technical business skill of using Excel or other spreadsheets to develop their budgets.

WORK
APPLICATION 7-10

Identify and describe the training method(s) that was used to train and develop you for a job you have or had.

Delivering Training

LO 7.8

Discuss each of the major types of training delivery.

Based on the prior three steps of the training process, before we actually conduct the training, as part of Step 4, the HR Department or other trainers have to select the types of delivery for a training. The choice will depend to some extent on what information is being transferred, as well as the options that are available to the particular organization. We also need to look at the best type of training to use in order to maximize transfer of knowledge while minimizing the cost of the training process. Each of the four training types has advantages and disadvantages that have to be understood in order to assign the correct option to a specific type of training program. In this section, we discuss our four options: on-the-job, classroom, distance, and simulation training.

On-the-Job Training

SHRM

Guide – J:6
On-the-Job Training

On-the-Job Training (OJT) is done at the work site with the resources the employee uses to perform the job. The manager, or an employee selected by the manager, usually conducts the training one-on-one with the trainee. Because of its proven record of success,

Job Instructional Training (JIT), a specific type of On-the-Job Training, is a popular training type used worldwide.

Job Instructional Training

JIT has four steps, presented in Model 7-1 and described here.

Step 1. Preparation of the trainee. Put the trainee at ease as you create interest in the job and encourage questions. Explain the task objectives and quantity and quality requirements, and discuss their importance.

Step 2. Presentation of the task by the trainer. Perform the task yourself slowly, explaining each step several times. Once the trainee seems to have the steps memorized, have him or her explain each step as you perform the task. Prepare a written list of the steps in complex tasks and give a copy to the trainee.

Employees are often given On-the-Job Training, especially in small business.

Step 3. Performance of the task by the trainee. Have the trainee perform the task slowly while explaining each step. Correct any errors and be willing to help the trainee perform any difficult steps. Continue until the employee can perform the task proficiently.

Step 4. Follow-up. Tell the trainee who is available to provide help with any questions or problems. Gradually leave the trainee alone. Begin by checking quality and quantity frequently, and then decrease the amount of checking based on the trainee's skill level. Watch the trainee perform the task and be sure to correct any errors or faulty work procedures before they become habits. Be patient and encouraging.

Model 7-1	Job Instructional Training Steps

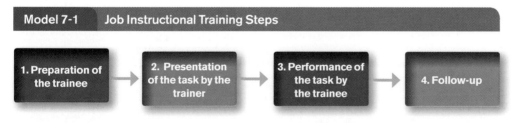

Even though On-the-Job Training is fairly expensive on a per-person basis, many organizations still use it heavily because of the fact that it works very well. What are some of the major advantages and disadvantages of On-the-Job Training? See Exhibit 7-4 to find out.

Classroom Training

Our second training option is classroom training. Classroom training is also a common form of training in organizations. To accomplish classroom training, the organization will create a training course, including content, instruction methods, lesson plans, and instructor materials, and provide all these materials to a qualified instructor who will teach the class.

Classroom training is generally very good for transferring general knowledge or theories about a topic consistently to a large number of people. It is generally not very good for teaching specific hands-on skills because of the passive nature of learning in a classroom. However, it is effective when using the same equipment that is used on the job. For example, many large banks have to train lots of tellers, so they conduct the training in a

Exhibit 7-4	On-the-Job Training Advantages and Disadvantages

Advantages	Disadvantages
• Most people learn best by actually doing a job, in conjunction with how-to explanations.	• The one-to-one aspect of the training means that it is relatively high in cost on a per-person basis.
• The training can be immediately transferred to the job.	• Trainers may not know how to teach, may be unmotivated or unable to transfer their knowledge successfully, or may transfer their own bad habits to the trainee.
• Training occurs person-to-person on the actual job site and includes all of the incidental factors associated with the job.	• The training may be inconsistent unless trainers follow a standardized training plan.
• Training occurs in an interactive environment, with feedback from the trainer.	• If the equipment being used is expensive, it may be dangerous to have the trainee operating and potentially harming it because the trainee is not yet a skilled operator.
• The trainer is typically highly competent in doing the job.	• Training often disrupts the work environment.
• The instructor can customize the training to the trainee's needs.	

classroom setting at headquarters with an expert trainer so that the employee can go to the bank and actually begin work without any training at the branch by people less skilled in training others to use the equipment. Let's do a quick review of some of the advantages and disadvantages of classroom training in Exhibit 7-5.

Distance or E-Learning

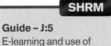

SHRM

Guide – J:5
E-learning and use of technology in training

Our third option is some form of distance learning, also called e-learning—either in a synchronous or in an asynchronous format. *Synchronous distance learning* occurs when all of the trainees sign in to a particular website where their instructor then interacts with the students and teaches the topics for the day. In contrast, *asynchronous distance learning* is a process where the student can sign in to the training site at any point in time and where materials are available for their studies. The instructor may or may not be online at the

Exhibit 7-5	Classroom Training Advantages and Disadvantages

Advantages	Disadvantages
• Classroom training is a good method to provide consistent knowledge or information to a fairly large number of people about a general topic.	• The classroom is often a passive environment, where the learner absorbs the information provided.
• A significant number of students can be trained at the same time.	• The pace of the training may be too fast for some students and too slow for others, causing anxiety or boredom.
• Information provided to the trainees is typically more consistent than OJT.	• It is more difficult to cater to different learning styles in a classroom setting than by using OJT.
• Instructors are usually professional trainers.	
• Classroom training is less expensive than OJT due to the fact that it's one-to-many training.	
• The classroom is a somewhat interactive environment based on question-and-answer sessions.	
• Classroom training does not disrupt the actual work environment.	

same time as the student, but there's no dedicated connection between the two for the purpose of teaching the information.

Distance learning, similar to classroom training, is also valuable for teaching basic concepts and providing general information on the topic. There's typically even less interaction between an instructor and a trainee in this form than in classroom training. Let's analyze some of the advantages and disadvantages of distance learning in Exhibit 7-6.

Self-directed learning is a specific kind of distance learning. In self-directed learning, the individual is going completely at their own pace, and is able to study whatever aspects of the topic they think they need to in order to be successful by leaving other parts of the training uncompleted. Self-directed training tends to have all of the potential advantages and disadvantages of other forms of distance learning. The most significant issue in self-directed learning tends to be the fact that if the individual is not motivated to learn on their own, they will be unsuccessful in the process because nobody else is going to follow their progress and push them to complete the training.

Exhibit 7-6	Distance Training Advantages and Disadvantages
Advantages	**Disadvantages**
• Training may be available 24/7/365. • The students can learn at their own pace. • There's no requirement for a physical classroom space, or necessarily for an instructor to be available at a particular point in time. No time is lost due to commuting. • The option is available to provide multiple media, which can enhance the learning process by matching up with different learning styles. • Distance learning is a reasonably low-cost method to train over time. Once the course is set up, costs to train an additional student are fairly minimal. • It does not disrupt the actual work environment.	• Distance learning requires self-discipline on the part of the trainee. The responsibility for "getting" the information shifts from the instructor to the trainee. • A standardized distance learning course often lacks the ability to respond directly to student needs and questions. • In its basic form, distance learning often lacks immediate feedback to the students on their success or failure. • Distance learning programs tend to have high initial startup costs due to the need to create voluminous online materials. • Student dishonesty is more difficult to identify, and testing usually has to be open book. • The lack of social interaction can inhibit learning in certain fields.

Simulations

A simulation is a training method where we may simulate a real-life situation in order to teach a student what actions to take in the event that they encounter the same or a similar situation in their job. Some common examples of simulations are flight simulators, driving simulators, and firefighting simulations. Simulations would typically be used in situations where actually performing an action or a set of actions could lead to significant financial cost because of lost equipment or could put the trainee in significant danger of injury or death.

In these types of cases, simulations make much more sense than actually performing a particular task. Asking the student to perform in a simulation will also generally cause them to go through the same set of emotions that they would go through in the real-life situation. Training through the use of a simulation allows the student to experience these emotions

WORK
APPLICATION 7-11

Identify and describe the type(s) of training you received for a job you have or had.

Organizations are now offering training and development to employees anytime from anywhere—24/7/365.

SHRM

Guide – D:8
Measurement systems

LO 7.9

Briefly discuss the Four-Level Evaluation Method for assessing training programs.

and learn to control them in order to resolve a complex and dangerous situation. Let's review the advantages and disadvantages of simulations in Exhibit 7-7.

Assessing Training

The fifth and last step of our training process (Exhibit 7-1) is assessment. No matter what the training covers, we always want to evaluate whether or not it achieved the shaped behavior identified through our needs assessment. Training can be designed to cause changes in a variety of employee attitudes and behaviors and as a result can be assessed in a number of different ways, depending on what we were trying to accomplish. A challenge is to develop metrics to assess training.[19] In this section, we present four assessment methods and how to choose an assessment method.

Assessment Methods

One of the most common assessment options, first identified by Donald Kirkpatrick, is called the Four-Level Evaluation Method. The Four-Level Evaluation Method measures *reaction, learning, behaviors,* and *results.*

Reaction evaluations measure how the individual responds to the actual training process. Self-reporting measures are quick and efficient metrics of training.[20] In reaction evaluations, the organization asks the participant how they feel about the training process, including the content provided, the instructors, and the knowledge that they gained by going through the process. They may also be asked about what new skills they have learned during the training process. This is the lowest level of training evaluation, and is frequently discounted due to its subjectivity and because some people overestimate their capabilities.[21] After all, is the trainee

Exhibit 7-7	Simulation Training Advantages and Disadvantages

Advantages	Disadvantages
• Simulation is a low-risk method of training individuals on how to react to a complex situation.	• Simulations can become "a video game" to the student and as a result not be taken seriously.
• Generally a very realistic form of training, simulations can convincingly emulate actual physical situations.	• Simulation systems may be very expensive to create and/or maintain.
• Simulations allow the student to try out experimental solutions to a problem. If the solution fails, the simulation can just be reset.	• Complex computer-based simulations may require a very powerful and expensive processor in order to run the application.
• Results of the student's actions can be analyzed post hoc to determine whether or not different actions may have been more successful.	• Some processes cannot be simulated successfully due to a lack of knowledge of the details of the process.
• Simulation does not disrupt the actual work environment.	

the best person to evaluate the knowledge that's been gained if that knowledge is brand new to them? Certainly reaction evaluations are less rigorous than some other forms, but they still provide the organization with valuable feedback concerning the learner's state of mind at the end of the training process as well as their attitude toward the process at its conclusion. Student course assessments are an example of reaction evaluations.

Learning evaluations are Level 2 measures designed to determine what knowledge was gained by the individual, whether any new skills have been learned because of the training, and whether attitudes toward the person's knowledge or skill set has changed as a result of the training. Learning evaluations are easily done using quizzes, tests, and even topic-based discussions. Learning evaluations help the organization evaluate the skill of the instructor as well as the change in the knowledge set of the trainee. If the instructor is inadequate as a teacher, it should show up in a learning evaluation measurement. We should also be able to see whether or not the individual gained knowledge of the subject because of the training process.

Behavior evaluations are the third level of evaluating training processes. Behavior evaluations are designed to determine whether or not the trainee's on-the-job behaviors changed as a result of the training. Behavior evaluations usually take the form of observation of the individual on the job, after completion of the training process. Did the process of going through the training have a direct effect on the individual's post-training job performance? The behavior evaluation is specifically designed to identify whether or not the individual is able to transfer the knowledge gained into new skills that they then use in their work.

Results evaluation is the fourth and final level. In a results evaluation, we're trying to determine whether or not individual behavioral changes have improved organizational results. In other words, we're looking at the bottom line for the organization to determine whether or not productivity has increased. This is the level at which ROI will be measured and evaluated in order to see whether or not the training has paid off for the company. However, ROI is not the only thing that we will measure at this level. Other results that may be measured include increased quality of work, lower absenteeism and turnover, reductions in rework and scrap, lower on-the-job accident rates, and many others. What we're looking for in a results evaluation is concrete evidence that the training resulted in organizational changes that were valuable in some form.

Choosing Assessment Methods

Why not just evaluate all of our training programs at each of the four levels? The primary reason is that it costs the organization money to go through the evaluation process, so we don't want to evaluate something that isn't necessary. In fact, as we go from Level 1 to Level 4, the cost of evaluating the training process increases. Let's identify when we might use each of the four evaluation levels.

Reaction evaluations, Level 1, help us identify employee attitudes toward the training process. If, in fact, the training process has been designed to change employee *attitudes* such as motivation toward their work or satisfaction with their job, Level 1 evaluation may be critical. The perception of the trainee in this case may be more important in changing their level of motivation and job satisfaction than in any new skills that they actually learned.

Learning evaluations, Level 2, are used if there's a need to evaluate more than employee attitude. Learning evaluations measure new knowledge gained by the employee. We may wish to be certain that the trainee has gained a depth of knowledge of a particular issue to ensure that they are capable of putting their knowledge to use. For instance, to comply with federal harassment statutes, all U.S. businesses need to ensure that their employees are trained on the concept of sexual harassment and how to avoid it. If we want to be certain that our employees know what sexual harassment is, we may choose to do a learning evaluation of that particular training session through giving a test.

SHRM

Guide – J:4
Training evaluation
(Kirkpatrick's model)

SHRM

Guide – J:10
Determining Return
on Investment

WORK
APPLICATION 7-12

Which training assessment methods are used where you work or have worked? Give examples of the training and its assessment method.

SHRM

Guide – J:8
Transfer of training (design issues, facilitating transfer)

Video Link 7.6

Train vs. Development

Behavior evaluation, Level 3, is needed to ensure not only that new knowledge has been gained but also that the individual knows how to apply that knowledge by acting in a certain way. A behavior evaluation is the only way that we can truly measure whether or not the individual has transferred knowledge gained in training into actions that will improve their performance. An example here would be training operators for a nuclear power plant. Determining their attitude toward their work and whether or not they have the innate knowledge necessary to perform the work is insufficient in this case. It would be critical to determine whether or not they could act correctly to maintain and operate the nuclear reactor, so we would observe their actual performance on the job. Can you imagine what might happen if an individual took an incorrect action in response to a failure in some area of a nuclear power plant? You can quickly see here that we need to be absolutely certain that they'll take the correct action—in other words that they will behave in the manner necessary to correct the failure.

Results evaluation, Level 4, is used when measuring reactions, learning, and behavior are not enough. Here we are measuring what happens as a result of the actions of the trainee. Did productivity increase? Did cost go down? Did product quality improve? This is the point at which we measure the return that the organization gets from the training process, usually in dollars and cents. If our trainees learned a new process that should reduce waste and they carried out that process successfully, how much money was saved by the organization? This is the highest of the four levels of evaluation and is certainly the most expensive evaluation form.

Talent Management and Development

Now that you have learned about the five steps of the training process, let's discuss developing employees. We should realize, however, that development programs also follow the same five steps in the training process, as the steps listed in Exhibit 7-1 state both training

7-4 APPLYING THE CONCEPT

Training Assessment Methods

State which of the following assessments are the most appropriate in each of the given situations.

a.   reaction evaluation
b.   learning evaluation

c.   behavior evaluation
d.   results evaluation

_____ 18.   You are the HR Manager and have some new staff members who will be involved in selecting new employees. You want to make sure that they understand what questions they can and can't ask during the selection process to avoid breaking discrimination laws.

_____ 19.   You need to train some employees on how to effectively deal with angry customers at the service desk, primarily for when they return merchandise. You want the employees to remain calm and deal with the customer's emotions to satisfy the customer.

_____ 20.   Diversity is important to your organization, so you develop a training program to help employees better understand each other so they can work well together.

_____ 21.   You are a bank manager, and you want your new tellers to know about the various services you offer to customers and how to provide these services.

_____ 22.   You are a restaurant owner who installed a new food-ordering computer system to speed up the time it takes to serve meals, so you need to train employees or how to use the new system.

and development. Remember from the beginning of the chapter that employee development deals primarily with training workers for *future* jobs, not their current position. In this section, we discuss careers, talk about common methods of development, and present a model of career development consequences.

Careers

We just used the term *career*. What is a career? How do we define this concept in today's organizations? Is a career in the 21st century the same as a career in the 1960s or '70s? Do individuals today go through just one or many careers throughout their work life? Half a century ago, a large number of people would spend their entire work life with one company. How often does that happen today? It obviously does not happen very often in modern organizations. In fact, there's much evidence that says that you will likely have several changes in career throughout your work life.

A Bureau of Labor Statistics survey, which followed individuals born between 1957 and 1964, cited an average of 11 *jobs* per person in this group. The report defined a job as an uninterrupted period of work with a particular employer.[22] So, if we defined a career as we did in the 1960s and said that to have a successful career you had to go to work after graduating from college, stay with that employer for 40 years while moving upward through a progression of jobs from lower levels to higher levels, and then retire with a pension, very few of us today would have a "successful" career. Obviously, then, the concept of career has changed.

So how do we define a job or a career in the 21st-century workforce? Douglas Hall defined *career* as a process where the person, not the organization, is the manager of the process. His definition states, "A **career** is *the individually perceived sequence of attitudes and behaviors associated with work-related experiences and activities over the span of the person's life.*"[23] Whew! Let's break this definition down into its subcomponents.

"Individually perceived." This definition of the term *career* relies heavily on the perception of the individual who is making the judgment concerning success or failure of the career. So, whether or not a career is defined as successful or a failure is determined within the individual's own mind. If you go through four, or five, or 10 different jobs in your lifetime, and if you perceive that as being successful, then you are a success. If you perceive it as a failure, then you have failed.

"Sequence of attitudes and behaviors." A career consists of both attitudes and behaviors, so it is not only *what* you do; it's the way you *feel* about what you do and how well you think you've done over time. What is an attitude? An attitude is simply a positive or negative individual judgment about a particular situation, isn't it? So your career involves not only the things that you do, but also the way you think and how you feel about your progression of jobs over time.

"Associated with work-related experiences and activities over the span of the person's life." The definition of *career* involves not only the direct work that is done, but all work-related experiences and activities. So, even nonwork activities that are work related, such as training off-site, would be included in our definition of *career*. We can even extend this to the way your family and friends interact with you and your job, and say that any interaction of family, friends, and work could help define your career. This is one place where attitudes come into play. Your friends and family know how you feel about your job and how it allows you to interact with others or prevents you from interacting with others in different circumstances. Using this definition of *career* avoids the problem of having to confront the fact that by the 1960s definition most of us would fail to have a *successful* career, and also allows us to take into account the significant factors of perception and attitude.

LO 7.10

Discuss the term *career* and the significance of the definition in the text.

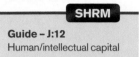

SHRM

Guide – C:5
Training and development
(vocational and career
counseling/career pathing)

SHRM

Guide – J:12
Human/intellectual capital

Video Link 7.7

Training as an Investment

Why Career Development?

Why has career development become such a significant issue to companies, and what problems does career planning need to be designed to solve? Twenty-first-century organizations have a significant need for career planning and development programs. We need to provide our employees with reasonable career paths and career counseling so that they can achieve their personal goals over the course of their career. These services can create significant motivation in our workforce, which, as we noted earlier, can lead to a major improvement in productivity and job satisfaction as well as lower absenteeism and turnover.[24]

The first reason that companies have become more concerned with career development is the nature of jobs in a modern organization. Recall from Chapter 2 that many of our jobs are knowledge management jobs, and the individuals who fill these jobs have to have special skills. Because people with these special skills (human intellectual capital) are in short supply, the organization cannot afford to lose individuals with such abilities. As a result we spend significant amounts of time and money on developing the individuals who have the knowledge sets that we need so that they can progress through the organization and be allowed to do new things, which can help the organization reduce turnover of highly skilled employees.

Another issue is that the national culture of the United States has changed in the past 30–40 years, and the latest generation of workers, called Generation Y or Millennials (many of you), have significantly different expectations of what they are going to be able to do in their careers than did their parents. Millennial workers expect to have significant freedom at work to do what they think they need to do, and make the money that they expect to make. Such high expectations create difficulty for organizations. We have to create policies and procedures that will not harm these individuals' initiative to work, but will also cause them to recognize the realities of the workplace. Through the process of career development, we can show these younger workers how they can progress through the organization, be entrepreneurial, and reach their personal career goals.

The next major reason for career development is because organizations are continuing to get significant pressure from governments to provide career paths for individuals who have historically been disadvantaged. Even though there are many different Equal Employment Opportunity laws on the books, and we have had such laws for over 50 years, there's still a significant disparity between the number of Caucasian male managers and all other groups.[25] Career development programs can create career paths for individuals who are members of these disadvantaged groups and who are qualified to go into management or other professional programs. This not only helps the individual employee, but also assists the organization in its diversity efforts.

Finally, good employee development and career planning programs can help the organization avoid productivity and disciplinary problems associated with employees who are stagnating in a particular job. This may be due to career plateauing. A **career plateau** occurs *when an individual feels unchallenged in their current job and has little or no chance of advancement*. If our employees feel as if their career has stagnated, they are more likely to become disciplinary problems. We may be able to avoid such problems by providing the opportunity for individuals to progress in their career over time. There are many other reasons for career development, but these are some of the most common issues. So, as you can see, there are a number of reasons why career planning has become a really big issue to 21st-century organizations.

LO 7.11

Briefly discuss the three
common methods of
employee development.

Common Methods of Employee Development

OK, so we need to develop our employees. How do we go about doing that? There is a series of common methods that organizations use to develop their employees. The most common forms of employee development include formal education, experience, and assessments. Let's go through a brief description of each of these options for development.

Formal Education

Our first method of employee development, *formal education*, provides employees the opportunity to participate in programs that will improve their general knowledge in areas such as finance, project management, and logistics. These formal education opportunities include such things as degree programs at colleges and universities, short courses of study that are available from many different sources including private training firms and public agencies, and courses in community colleges. Such formal education courses may be held with any of the training and delivery methods discussed earlier.

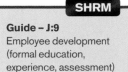

SHRM

Guide – J:9
Employee development (formal education, experience, assessment)

The intent of formal education programs is to provide the student with a specific set of information about a particular topic. Through formal education we can provide programs for every level of individual within the organization, from the executives down to the first line supervisors. At the executive level, we might send a strong midlevel manager from the company to a university executive MBA program. In contrast, at the supervisor level the organization would probably want new first line supervisors to go through courses that teach supervisory skills, leadership, coaching, and basic financial analysis. Many organizations pay part or all of the cost of formal education for their employees.

Experience

Employee development programs that use experience as a method for developing the individual would seek to put the person through a number of different types of job-related experiences over time. Such an experience-based program might include job rotation to provide them with a wide range of experiences within the company. This allows the person to see more of what goes on within the organization, and how each job ties to others.

Experience-based employee development might also include the use of coaches or mentors for the individual. The coach or mentor will work with the person to identify how these different job experiences help them to learn and grow as an individual within the organization. [26]

Putting the individual through different job experiences also allows them to develop new skill sets and new knowledge that will be valuable as they move up in the organization. Development using job experience can successfully be used from the executive level all the way down to the level of work teams within the organization. In fact, there's significant evidence that career experience, team experience, and job-related skills are all related to higher levels of team performance. [27]

In today's flatter organizations, it has become more difficult to climb the old corporate ladder. Plus, younger workers become bored doing the same job. Therefore, giving employees a variety of experiences through lateral jobs that provide new challenges and experience, with pay raises, may help to keep employees satisfied and to stay with the organization.

Employee Assessment

There are a number of different assessment tools that provide individuals with information about how they think, how they interact with others, and how they manage their own actions and emotions. These assessments provide the individual with information that allows them to understand better how they can manage others within the organization. Some of the more common measures include personality tests, emotional intelligence tests, and performance appraisals. Each of these assessments, if properly used, provides the individual with information that can be used to modify the way that they interact with others within the organization. We will review performance appraisals in the next chapter. However, let's take a look at the other two options now.

Psychological assessments. These have gained significant acceptance within the workplace and include tests such as the Myers-Briggs Type Indicator (MBTI), the Birkman Method, and the Benchmarks assessment tool. Each of the psychological assessment tools provides information to the individual and the organization about the person's style of thinking, interacting with others, management, and leadership.

The MBTI is probably the most common personality-type assessment used for employee development, but each of the tests has advantages and disadvantages compared to the other options. However, the validity and reliability of the common forms of psychological assessment have been questioned by various researchers.[28] Even with the weaknesses in validity and reliability, though, several of the personality assessment tools have been in use in businesses for many years and have shown legitimate real-world value in assessing the basic type of personality exhibited by individual employees within the organization.

Emotional intelligence. **Emotional intelligence** is *the way that we identify, understand, and use our own emotions as well as the emotions of others to promote our working relationships.* It is an important part of human relations skills. Emotional intelligence is also referred to as an Emotional Quotient (EQ) making it similar to the Intelligence Quotient (IQ). So testing provides an IQ and an EQ. It is said that to be highly successful a person needs a high IQ, needs a high EQ, and has to have a clue of what to do to succeed.

Emotional intelligence has been described as "Our Most Versatile Tool for Success" in a 2005 SHRM White Paper.[29] The Mayer-Salovey-Caruso Emotional Intelligence Test (MSCEIT) is one of the more common tools used to measure emotional intelligence. The MSCEIT consists of four pieces: perceiving emotion (the ability to identify your own and others' emotions); use of emotion to facilitate thought ("the ability to use emotions to focus attention and to think more rationally, logically, and creatively"); understanding emotion (the ability to analyze and evaluate your own and others' emotions); and managing emotion (the ability to adjust emotions of yourself and others).[30]

Here again, validity and reliability of the test are still in some question. However, as with personality assessments, there's at least some evidence in the business arena that higher levels of emotional intelligence provide employees with a greater chance of success as they move up in the organization.[31]

A Model of Career Development Consequences

Because the organization and the individual have joint responsibility for career planning and development, both will suffer significant consequences if the planning isn't done successfully. Individual employees go through a series of career stages as they progress through their work life. Within each of these stages, the employee has different needs that must be met by the organization in order for the relationship between the two to remain stable and for the worker to continue to be motivated to produce for the organization. Organizations must respond successfully to the individual employee based on the employee's current career stage.

Let's discuss the commonly identified stages of career development first identified by Donald Super and Douglas Hall.[32] You can see them summarized in the first section of Exhibit 7-8.

Exploration. The first career development stage, called the *Exploration* stage, is the period of time during which the individual is identifying their personal needs that will be satisfied by a particular type of work, the types of jobs that interest them, and the skill sets necessary in order to be able to accomplish those types of jobs. This stage is usually identified as being between the ages of 15 and 24.

Establishment. The second stage, called *Establishment*, is the period where the individual has entered into a career and becomes concerned with building their skill set,

SHRM

Guide – D:3
Emotional intelligence

WORK
APPLICATION 7-13

State some of your career goals and the methods you will use to develop yourself to meet these goals.

LO 7.12

Briefly discuss some of the individual and organizational consequences that can occur as a result of organizational career planning processes.

Exhibit 7-8	Career Stages and the Hierarchy of Needs

Exploration	Establishment	Maintenance	Disengagement
Meet personal needs	Career entry	Personal satisfaction	Lower output
Identify interests	Building skills	Continue advancement	Coach/mentor as desired
Evaluate skills	Security/stabilization	Coach/mentor	Balance between work and nonwork
Tentative work choice	Work relationships	Improve policies and procedures	
	Work contributions		
	Advancement		

Maslow's Hierarchy of Needs

Physiological	Safety/Security	Social	Esteem	Self-Actualization
Air, food, water, sleep, etc.	Physical shelter, physical security, financial security, stability, etc.	Friendship, love, relationships, family, belonging to social groups, etc.	Social status, recognition, self-respect, reputation, achievement, etc.	Wisdom and justice—pass knowledge to others because *you* think it is valuable

developing work relationships, advancement, and stabilization within their career. In the Establishment phase, we see the individual begin to make significant personal contributions to their career in the organization and begin to create relationships with coworkers, or alliances, that allow them to become more secure within the organization. This stage is usually identified as covering approximately age 25 to the mid-40s.

Maintenance. This is the third stage of career development. The maintenance stage covers the period from the mid-40s to 60 years old or older. In the maintenance stage, the individual typically continues to advance but begins to seek personal satisfaction in the jobs that they perform for the organization. This is the phase where we see individual employees begin to act as mentors or trainers to their younger coworkers, and to act to improve the organization and its processes and policies because they see a need to do so.

Disengagement. Finally, the fourth stage is identified as the *Disengagement* stage. This stage typically shows lower levels of output and productivity as the individual prepares for life after work. During this stage, because of their desire to balance nonwork with work activities, the individual may begin to choose to work only on efforts that they feel are necessary or worthy of their attention. They may continue to mentor or sponsor other individuals in the organization as those others progress through their own careers. Obviously, this stage goes from the early 60s to whatever point at which the individual finally completely disengages from the organization through retirement.

You may be wondering why these career stages matter. Let's take a look now at the second part of Exhibit 7-8. We have added Abraham Maslow's Hierarchy of Needs below each of the career stages. It's rather surprising how closely Maslow's needs hierarchy matches up with our career stages. We could accomplish a similar matching process with many other motivation theories, but this one serves to illustrate why career stages matter so much to managers in the organization, and especially to HR Management.

What are people most concerned with at the earliest career stage, Exploration? They are typically most concerned with physical and safety issues, right? Are they physically able to get the *basic things* that they need in order to live and work—money for shelter, food to eat, fuel for their car? Are they getting paid enough to *survive and be safe*? Then, as they get into the Establishment and Maintenance stages, they are more concerned with *social*

WORK
APPLICATION 7-14

Identify the level of career development you are on. Using Exhibit 7-8, but in your own words, describe your career stage and the Maslow motivational issues you are dealing with now.

interactions, and then gaining *status and recognition* as organizational leaders. Finally, as they move to the Disengagement stage, they are more concerned with higher-level esteem needs such as *self-respect, achievement* of personal goals, and being able to do the *things that they think are important*. So, we see people go through these different motivational points in their life as they go through their career. It's very interesting that the career stages follow almost exactly with what the motivation theories show us that it does.

Now that we understand a little bit about career stages that individuals go through during their work life and how those stages identify what might motivate workers in a particular stage, let's match those up with organizational HR strategies that are available to reinforce employee behavior. This will give us a general working model of how organizational HR strategies can create either positive or negative consequences for both the individual and the organization, depending on how the HR strategies are applied in a particular situation. Take a look at Exhibit 7-9. We have individual career stages identified on the left inside of the diagram. On the right side are some of the major organizational HR strategies that are available. Depending on how the HR strategies are applied, and based on the individual's career stage and motivating factors, we end up with either positive or negative consequences to both the individual and the organization.

If we apply the correct HR strategy or strategies to an individual employee based on the factors that motivate the employee, we can improve each of the major organizational dependent variables that we identified in Chapter 1—job satisfaction, productivity, absenteeism, and turnover. In addition, there are several other organizational factors that can either improve or decline based on the application (or lack thereof) of the correct HR strategy. These factors include labor costs, organizational safety, employee lawsuits, and organizational reputation, among others.

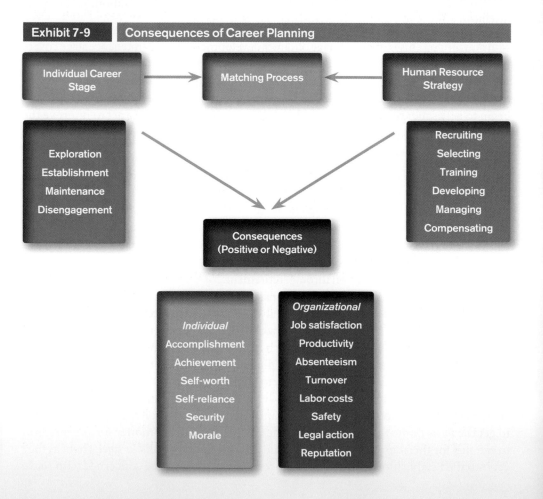

Exhibit 7-9   Consequences of Career Planning

So, as you can see, if the organization fails to apply the correct strategy to motivate the employee (based on the employee's career stages), the consequences can be severe.

On the other side of the diagram, the consequences to the employee are equally significant. If the organization applies the correct types of HR strategies to develop the employee successfully over time, individual feelings of accomplishment and achievement increase, self-worth and self-reliance increase, the employee's sense of security increases, and their morale is likely to increase due to higher individual satisfaction levels. Again, if the strategies applied are unsuccessful, each of these individual consequences can become negative. After looking at the model, it should become obvious that successfully applying HR strategies to individual employees based on their personal motivating factors and career stage is critical to overall organizational success over time.

So, now you know why it's so important to create career paths for our employees within the organization and provide employee development opportunities. If we do these things successfully, we end up with a series of positive consequences for both the organization and the individuals involved. We have better productivity, better job satisfaction and employee engagement, and lower absenteeism and turnover. However, if we fail to do these things successfully, a series of negative consequences can occur that ultimately cost both the organization and the individual time and money. Employee development is a critical piece in the organizational puzzle in order to provide long-term success.

Trends and Issues in HRM

As with each chapter, let's take a look now at some of the trends and issues in training and development. The first issues that we will discuss involve diversity and sustainability training programs. After that, we will identify potential new measures for development success and then evaluate the process of outsourcing training and development.

Does Diversity Training Work?

Competitive organizations always need to work to maximize the talent pool from which they can draw their recruits. If, in fact, the organization arbitrarily limits the number and types of recruits through artificial limits on organizational diversity, it restricts its ability to draw in the best talent available from the at-large workforce. However, most organizations today accept the fact that *unmanaged* diversity can decrease employee commitment and engagement, lower job satisfaction, increase turnover, and increase conflict. Organizations must create a *cultural change* in order for diversity training to be successful. But since cultural change is very difficult, many organizations try to shortcut the process and as a result end up with failed programs.[33]

How can organizations create and deliver a diversity training process that has a chance of being successful? Common diversity initiatives include such things as diversity recruitment, diversity training, and formal mentoring programs. However, plugging these programs into organizational training without providing a process by which they can be integrated into the daily activities of the members of the organization will likely lead to minimal if any success. Let's take a quick look at the history of diversity training and its effectiveness.

Diversity training has been around in some form since the 1960s. In its earlier days, diversity training primarily focused on organizational *compliance* with equal opportunity laws. Later on, diversity training moved through a sequence of options—from attempting to *assimilate* different individuals into an organizational culture, through attempting to make employees sensitive to others and their differences, and more recently to an attempt to create *inclusion* of all individuals, from all backgrounds, into the organization.[34]

In each of the phases of diversity training, there appeared to be significant pushback on the part of one or more groups involved in the training. Whether the pushback was from the White male majority, from feeling that they were being persecuted, or from females or minority individuals, feeling that they had to conform to the organization and its practices, each of the phases had significant hurdles to overcome in order to move the organization forward. Today, organizations are attempting to integrate diversity more directly into the business and its strategies. Companies that lead the diversity initiative are becoming much more involved at all levels of the organization, from the executive suite to the shop floor.

Throughout each phase of its existence, diversity training effectiveness has been questioned by many organizations and researchers. Evidence appears to be growing that diversity training in its present form does add value to the organization, both sociologically and economically.[35, 36] In addition, when diversity training focuses on the *similarities* between individuals rather than their *differences*, trainees appear to become more capable of resolving conflict that may occur as a result of individual diversity.[37] Finally, the bottom line is that most major corporations believe that diversity adds significant value to their organizations, both from the perspective of providing different viewpoints and solutions to problems and from the perspective of providing the organization with a larger talent pool in a period when qualified applicants are becoming less and less available in the at-large workforce.

Sustainability Training Programs

ESR

Look back just a few years and you would probably find that there were very few sustainability training programs in major corporations. Fortunately for all of us, this is no longer the case. While a very small number of organizations have been concerned with social responsibility and sustainability for many years (for example, Ben & Jerry's Homemade Ice Cream, founded in 1978), most larger businesses didn't become concerned with sustainability programs until about the turn of the 21st century. However, the concept of sustainability is increasingly viewed as providing value to "the so-called triple bottom line of economic, social, and environmental performance."[38]

Organizations with sustainability programs tend to gain the trust of their customers and surrounding communities. By doing so, these organizations may gain great competitive advantage over their rivals who are less oriented to the sustainability of the community in the environment. Because a sustainable organization embodies the values of its customers and community, those customers and community members become willing to provide reciprocal concern for the organization. This can create significant loyalty to the organization and its brands.

There is a problem, though. It can be extremely difficult for organizations to embed the concept of social responsibility and sustainability throughout the firm. A sustainability mind-set must be incorporated into the corporate culture, and that can only typically happen from the top of the organization down.[39] So any organizational sustainability training program must begin at the top and change the culture of the executives and managers. Strong organizational cultures that have sustainability as one of their core concepts can begin to create a collective commitment to social responsibility and sustainability within the entire workforce. But, how do corporations disseminate this culture of sustainability down into the employee ranks?

Certainly, training that involves identification of the concept of sustainability and how the organization can affect its environment plays a large part in disseminating this information. In addition, the organization may choose to provide all employees with a code of conduct or code of ethics that identifies sustainability as one of the core principles of the firm.

In conjunction with the training and code of conduct, the organization must measure the impact of their sustainability programs to allow modifications to those programs if necessary. Changes in company policies and procedures, as well as organizational structure,

WORK
APPLICATION 7-15

Select an organization, preferably one you work or have worked for. Describe how it is using training and development to meet the challenges of an increasingly diversified world.

may also assist in improving sustainability within the organization. Again, though, training of employees on the changes in policies, procedures, and structure must occur in order to modify those employees' behaviors.

Several challenges have been identified to teaching employees about sustainability issues.[40] The first challenge concerns organizational resources. All organizations have limited resources, and as a result must make choices concerning which stakeholder issues to address. Overcoming resistance to addressing environmental issues is one of the main challenges in training for sustainability.

Second, raising awareness of sustainability issues may engender optimism concerning the company's ability to "solve the problem." Organizations must ensure in sustainability training that the employees understand that there are limits to what the firm can accomplish on its own.

Third, solutions to some sustainability problems may lie beyond the knowledge and skills of the organization and its members. If the knowledge and skills necessary to solve a problem involve bringing in personnel from outside the firm, the organization may revert to the first challenge above and claim limited resources prevent it from resolving the issue.

The fourth issue concerns employee willingness to learn and commit to change actions to improve organizational sustainability. At this point, the change in culture at the top of the organization can assist in pushing culture change at lower levels. If successful, the culture change that values sustainability will, over time, lower the levels of resistance to change in the employees of the firm.

So, as you can see from these challenges, organizational training must provide both information on the concept of sustainability and the impact of the organization on the sustainability of its environment and training to modify the organizational culture to place greater value on organizational social responsibility and environmental sustainability. If the organization succeeds in these training efforts, corporate sustainability efforts will be likely to significantly improve over time.

Measuring Development Success

As with all things in HRM, we need to measure and evaluate the process of employee development. If the process is not measured, we will not know whether employee development costs outweigh the returns to the organization from such programs. But, how do organizations measure a process that occurs over years, rather than over a few days or weeks?

There are a number of firms that have been successful in creating metrics to do just this. While we certainly can use each of the levels in the Four-Level Evaluation Method that was discussed earlier in the chapter, in evaluating the employee development *process* we should probably focus on the fourth level.

What measures would make sense if we were planning to complete a results evaluation on an employee development program? What organizational returns can be measured and applied to the ROI calculation? All we have to do is focus on Exhibit 7-9 in order to see some of the ROIs and measures that are available. We can begin with measures of productivity, job satisfaction, absenteeism, and turnover, and then move to the other organizational consequences identified in the exhibit.

Each of these organizational consequences can be measured over time, and positive or negative changes to the consequence can provide us with information on the ROI of our employee development programs. If you look, you will notice that most of these organizational consequences will not immediately change because of changes in our employee development process.

So, organizational leadership must understand that the measure of ROI for employee development programs will be delayed, while not being denied. In other words, ROI can be measured, but not immediately. Returns on employee development programs will

WORK
APPLICATION 7-16

Select an organization you work or have worked for. Describe how it is using training and development to meet the challenges of sustainability.

only become evident over time. For instance, employee absenteeism and turnover will not immediately go down as a result of an employee development program. We will have to measure these levels months, and even years, after the onset of the program. Other areas where employee development programs can show change over time include having available successors to fill management positions as they become open; reduction of production errors, accidents or incidents, waste, and damage to equipment; improving customer and community relations; and improvements in quality, among others.

Even though ROI on employee development programs does not occur immediately, organizations need to ensure that they measure the results of these programs. Patient leadership will allow these programs time to show results before the leader becomes inordinately concerned. However, programs that fail to provide positive ROI to the organization over time must either be modified or discontinued.

Outsourcing Employee Training and Development

SHRM

Guide – D:13, J:7
Outsourcing employee
development

As we noted earlier in the book, outsourcing has become the major topic of interest to organizations of all sizes. In fact, based on a recent survey by Hewitt Associates, the outsourcing of one or more major HR functions occurred in more than 90% of respondents to the survey.[41] Outsourcing of the training and development function significantly lags behind other functions in the HR Department, though. In their survey, Hewitt identified only 14% of participants as outsourcing their "learning and development" functions.[42] Even so, modern organizations must evaluate whether or not outsourcing of the training and development functions makes sense. If the company can reduce costs for training and development as well as improving quality of the training function, it may make sense for the organization to consider outsourcing of these functions.

What does the organization need to consider when analyzing whether or not to outsource training and development? We need to consider basically the same things we consider when we outsource any function of the organization. Probably the most significant *strategic* issue in any outsourcing debate is whether or not the organization might lose control of key processes or functions that have historically been performed within the company. If training and development are critical functions within the organization in order to maintain or advance their competitive advantage over rivals, they can ill afford to outsource those functions.

The second likely consideration would be a *financial* analysis concerning expected cost savings from outsourcing training and development. This would depend on how efficient the organization currently is at performing the training and development function. If the organization has a well-developed training department or group and has developed detailed courses concerning the major training and development issues that face the organization, outsourcing companies may not be able to provide much cost savings. If, however, the organization doesn't perform the training function very often or very intensely, outsourcing organizations that specialize in training and development may be able to save significant amounts of money for the firm. Here again, as with so many other HR functions, the organization must evaluate the ROI expected if the process is outsourced and compare that with the internal ROI for the same function.

Finally, the organization will want to evaluate the ability to maintain or improve *service levels* to their employees if outsourcing is utilized. If the organization is unable to provide sufficient training and development programs for their employees through outsourcing, they run significant risks including lower employee morale and job satisfaction, lower productivity over time, and greater absenteeism and turnover within the firm. If, however, the organization can actually increase service levels in training and development through the use of the specialty outsourcing provider, each of the above risks can turn into an advantage for the firm. The organization must carefully evaluate all of the information in an analysis

WORK
APPLICATION 7-17

Select an organization you work or have worked for. What, if any, training and development functions does the organization outsource—including bringing in consults to develop and conduct T&D? If you are not sure, ask the HR Training Specialist.

for potential outsourcing of the training and development function. Without this careful evaluation, significant mistakes can be made, and large amounts of money may be spent without the organization receiving the requisite benefits from the process.

Wrap-Up

So what have you learned in this chapter? Quite a bit, ha! The first things that we discussed were the concepts of training and development, where you learned that training was primarily information to be put to immediate use but development is designed for long-term changes in knowledge, skills, and abilities. We then did a quick review of the four common points when training may be needed, identified the steps in the training process, and quickly reviewed the concept of a needs assessment. We then identified some of the common challenges in the training process, followed by a check of the two factors in employee readiness for training.

As we completed our discussion of the basic training process and needs assessment, we realized that in order to successfully train employees we need to know how they learn. So we defined learning and then reviewed some of the common concepts in learning theory, including classical conditioning, operant conditioning, and social learning. Once we defined these concepts, we showed how they can be used to shape employee behaviors and cause our employees to act in ways that we need them to and avoid acting in ways they can harm the organization. The last thing that we reviewed in that section was the various learning styles that people utilize.

In the next section, we took a brief look at training design and how it relates to the HRM skills that were noted in Chapter 1, and then moved on to review several common training types and identified the advantages and disadvantages of each. Types included OJT, classroom training, distance learning, and simulations, plus we reviewed the value of case studies, behavior modeling, and role-playing. And the last section on training discussed assessment of the process, where we reviewed Kirkpatrick's evaluation method and discussed when to use each level.

As we completed our training discussion, we moved to talent management and development, where we went into more detail about the employee development and career planning processes. We defined the term *career* and identified several reasons why career development has become such a significant issue to 21st-century organizations. We then discussed several common methods of employee development, including formal education, job experience, and employee assessment tools. After this, we identified a model that visually shows the consequences of either good or bad career development processes within the firm.

In the trends and issues for this chapter, we briefly discussed four current issues in the training and development field. The first issue was a question concerning whether or not diversity training works in organizations. Second, we reviewed sustainability programs in organizations, from the perspective of both whether or not sustainability is a valid organizational concern and whether or not the organization can successfully instill a sustainability mind-set in its employees. Our third issue was how to measure development success. In this section we identified several options for measurement of employee development, including ROI measures as well as other measures to analyze safety, waste, damage, customer and community relations, and quality. Finally, we discussed the option of outsourcing employee development and training and came to the conclusion that whether or not outsourcing makes sense must be determined on a company-by-company basis. Once again, we have given you a pretty full plate of information to digest. So, let's go on to our summary of the chapter.

Chapter Summary

 Visit www.sagepub.com/lussier for helpful study resources.

7.1 Discuss the major difference between training and development.

Training is designed to provide employees with the knowledge, skills, and abilities (KSAs) that they need in order to succeed in their work for the organization. Training is primarily intended to be put to *immediate* use by the individual being trained. On the other hand, employee development is designed to teach our workers how to move up in the organization in the *future* by becoming skilled at those tasks that they will need to know how to do in order to perform higher-level jobs.

7.2 Identify and briefly discuss the common points in the tenure of employees within the organization where training may be needed.

The most common points at which managers should consider workforce training include *orientation* to acculturate the new employee to the organization and its culture, and to prepare them to do their own job within the organization; when *processes or procedures have changed*; whenever there has been some *failure to perform* successfully; or for *employee development* opportunities to develop current employee skills and abilities so that they are able to move into higher-level jobs within the organization.

7.3 Briefly discuss the steps in the training process and their interrelationship.

The first step is to conduct a needs assessment to identify the type of training needed. The second step is to select how to shape employee behavior. The third step is to design the training by selecting training methods. The fourth step is to select the delivery method and deliver the training. The last step is to assess the training to determine if employee behavior has changed to improve performance; if not, return to Step 1. The steps are interrelated because these steps are so closely related and based on each other that they are commonly planned together before actually delivering the training.

7.4 Identify the most common challenges to the training and development process.

Common challenges to the training process include unprepared workers, difficulty in identifying the ROI provided from training, employee resistance to changes in processes and procedures, matching the training to the company's strategic goals, and logistics issues, including scheduling and locations available for training courses.

7.5 Identify the three common learning theories, and the type of learning that results from each theory.

The three common learning theories are classical conditioning, operant conditioning, and social learning theory. Classical conditioning results in direct, involuntary, learned behaviors. Operant conditioning results in direct, voluntary, learned behaviors. Social learning is experienced through watching the actions of another person and witnessing the consequences of their actions, so it is *voluntary,* and *learned,* but it is based on *indirect* consequences of the actions of another person.

7.6 Identify and briefly discuss the four methods for shaping behavior.

The four options for shaping behavior include positive reinforcement, negative reinforcement, punishment, and extinction. Positive reinforcement involves the application of a reward in response to a person's behavior in order to increase the chances that that behavior will be repeated. Negative reinforcement involves the withdrawal of a noxious stimulus, or a negative thing, in response to a person's positive behavior in order to increase the chances that the behavior will be repeated. Punishment occurs either when a noxious stimulus is applied or when a reward is taken away in response to a negative behavior. Extinction provides no reinforcement, either positive or negative, to the actions of the subject.

7.7 Identify which training methods are most commonly used with which HRM skill.

Among the most common methods used for *technical skills* training are written material and lectures, programmed learning, projects, job rotation, discussions, and demonstrations. To train individuals in *human relations skills*, some of the most common options are role-playing and behavior modeling. Management games and cases are commonly used to develop *conceptual and design (decision-making) and business skills* for managers, whereas in-baskets are more commonly used with employees, and interactive videos are used by both.

7.8 Discuss each of the major types of training delivery.

On-the-Job Training is done at the work site with the resources the employee uses to perform the job and is conducted one-on-one with the trainee. In *classroom training,* the organization creates a training course, and provides a qualified instructor to teach the class in a single location at a specific time. *Distance learning*, also called e-learning, allows the student to sign in to the training site and provides materials to them for their studies. There's typically less interaction between an instructor and a trainee than in OJT or classroom training. *Simulations* mimic a real-life situation in order to teach a student what actions to take in the event that they encounter the same or a similar situation in their job.

7.9 Briefly discuss the Four-Level Evaluation Method for assessing training programs.

The Four-Level Evaluation Method measures *reaction, learning, behaviors,* and *results*. In *reaction evaluations*, the organization asks the participant how they feel about the training process, including the content provided, the instructor or instructors, and the knowledge that they gained by going through the process. *Learning evaluations* are designed to determine what knowledge was gained by the individual, whether any new skills have been learned, and whether attitudes have changed as a result of the training. *Behavior evaluations* are designed to determine whether or not the trainee's on-the-job behaviors changed as a result of the training. In a *results evaluation*, we try to determine whether or not individual behavioral changes have improved organizational results. This is the level at which ROI will be measured and evaluated.

7.10 Discuss the term *career* and the significance of the definition.

Our definition of *career* is "the individually perceived sequence of attitudes and behaviors associated with work-related experiences and activities over the span of the person's life."

"Individually perceived" means that if you perceive your career as being successful, then you are a success. If you perceive it as a failure, then you have failed. "Sequence of attitudes and behaviors" means that your career involves not only the things that

you do, but also the way you think and how you feel about your progression of jobs over time. "Associated with work-related experiences and activities over the span of the person's life" means that even nonwork activities that are work related would be included in our definition of *career*. Using this definition of *career* avoids the problem of having to confront the fact that by the 1960s definition most of us would fail to have a *successful* career.

7.11 Briefly discuss the three common methods of employee development.

Formal education provides the opportunity to participate in programs that will improve general knowledge in areas such as finance, project management, and logistics. *Experience* as a method for developing the individual seeks to put the person through different types of job-related experiences over time. *Assessment* tools provide employees with information about how they think, how they interact with others, and how they manage their own actions and emotions.

7.12 Briefly discuss some of the individual and organizational consequences that can occur as a result of organizational career planning processes.

Organizational consequences include all of the major organizational dependent variables that we identified in Chapter 1—job satisfaction, productivity, absenteeism, and turnover. In addition, labor costs, organizational safety, employee lawsuits, and organizational reputation can either improve or decline based on the application (or lack thereof) of the correct HR strategy. On the employee side, the consequences are equally significant. If the organization applies the correct HR strategies, individual feelings of accomplishment and achievement increase, self-worth and self-reliance increase, the employee's sense of security increases, and their morale is likely to increase due to higher individual satisfaction levels. If the strategies are unsuccessful, each of these individual consequences can become negative.

Key Terms

Career	Employee development	Negative reinforcement	Remediation
Career plateau	Extinction	Orientation	Self-efficacy
Competency model	Learning	Positive reinforcement	Training
Emotional intelligence	Needs assessment	Punishment	

Key Term Review

Complete each of the following statements using one of this chapter's key terms:

_____ identifies the knowledge, skills, and abilities (KSAs) needed in order to perform a particular job in the organization.

_____ is the process of teaching employees the skills necessary to perform a job.

_____ is ongoing education to improve knowledge and skills for present and future jobs.

_____ is the process of introducing new employees to the organization and their jobs.

_____ is the correction of a deficiency or failure in a process or procedure.

_____ is the process of analyzing the difference between what is currently occurring within a job or jobs and what is required—either now or in the future—based on the organization's operations and strategic goals.

_____ is whether a person believes that they have the capability to do something or attain a particular goal.

_____ is any relatively permanent change in behavior that occurs as a result of experience or practice.

_____ is providing a reward in return for a constructive action on the part of the subject.

_____ is the withdrawal of a harmful thing from the environment in response to a positive action on the part of the subject.

_____ is the application of an adverse consequence or removal of a reward, in order to decrease an unwanted behavior.

_____ is the total lack of response, either positive or negative, in order to avoid reinforcing an undesirable behavior.

_____ is the individually perceived sequence of attitudes and behaviors associated with work-related experiences and activities over the span of the person's life.

_____ is when an individual feels unchallenged in their current job and has little or no chance of advancement.

_____ is the way that we identify, understand, and use our own emotions as well as the emotions of others to promote our working relationships.

Quick Check (True-False)

1. Training and development are basically the same thing. T F

2. A *needs assessment* is designed to identify whether or not there is a need for training in a specific situation. T F

3. ROI calculations can't be done, or even closely approximated, for training programs. T F

4. When looking at employee readiness for training, we have to analyze both *ability* and *willingness* factors. T F

5. We all have physical and intellectual abilities, but we don't all have the same abilities. T F

6. Your family, friends, and coworkers really have no bearing on your willingness to attend training classes for work. T F

7. *Reaction evaluations* measure the instructor's reaction to the student's ability to learn. T F

8. *Behavior evaluation* is the only way that we can truly measure whether or not the individual has transferred knowledge from training into actions that will improve their performance. T F

9. Classical conditioning causes direct, learned voluntary behaviors on the part of the learner. T F

10. The four methods of shaping behavior include positive reinforcement, negative reinforcement, positive punishment, and negative punishment. T F

11. Orientation should be designed to answer all of the questions necessary to allow the new employee to integrate into the "society" that they are entering. T F

12. Very few organizations will attempt to develop all of the employees within the firm, but most go through a process of identifying high-potential individuals for development. T F

13. Advantages of OJT include the fact that it is a very inexpensive training type. T F

14. Distance learning requires significant self-discipline on the part of the student. T F

15. Simulations are a low-risk method of teaching students about complex and dangerous situations. T F

16. Management games and case studies are frequently used to develop decision-making skills. T F

17. Millennial generation workers really don't have very different expectations of what they are going to be able to do in their careers than previous generation workers. T F

18. The motivation evident in the four career stages really matches up very closely with Maslow's Hierarchy of Needs. T F

19. Throughout its existence, diversity training effectiveness has been questioned by many organizations and researchers. T F

20. Sustainability in organizations is increasingly viewed as providing value to the so-called triple bottom line of economic, social, and environmental performance. T F

Communication Skills

The following critical-thinking questions can be used for class discussion and/or for written assignments to develop communication skills. Be sure to give complete explanations for all answers.

1. Is the currently available workforce really not sufficiently trained to participate in knowledge-intensive jobs? Why or why not?

2. Think of and then list all of the items that you think should be included in a new employee orientation. Briefly justify why each item should be included.

3. What learning style is the one that you feel that you use most? Why do you think that you use this style more than the others?

4. Briefly describe a job you have or had. If you were promoted, which training method(s) would you use to train the person to do your current job?

5. Which one of the primary types of training delivery would you use to teach basic accounting to a group of employees? Justify your answer.

6. Have you ever filled out an evaluation form for an employee training class? Which type of evaluation was it? What evidence led you to think it was this type?

7. What management tools or processes would you use in order to evaluate your employees for remediation training?

8. Do you agree with the definition of *career* presented in the text? Why or why not? How would you change it?

9. Which of the reasons for creating career development programs from the text do you feel are most valid, considering the cost of career development programs? Justify your choice.

10. Which method of development, formal education, experience, or assessment do you think is most valuable? Justify your choice.

11. Identify and discuss two or three ways that poor application of HR strategies (Exhibit 7-9) would create negative *employee* consequences.

12. Do you think that diversity training is worth its cost to organizations? Why or why not?

13. If you were the lead trainer for your company, how would you go about trying to create an organization-wide commitment to sustainability? Why?

Video

Please visit the student study site at **www.sagepub.com/lussier** to view the video links in this chapter.

Answers

REVIEW QUESTIONS (TRUE-FALSE) Answers

1. F   2. T   3. F   4. T   5. T   6. F   7. F   8. T   9. F   10. F   11. T   12. T   13. F   14. T   15. T   16. T   17. F   18. T   19. T   20. T

Case

Case 7-1. Who Is Managing the Manager?

Gerald Mahoney, new Sales Manager and sole full-time employee of the Oreck vacuum cleaner store of Red Hook, New York, was relaxing and watching television in the back office. There were no customers in the store at the time, and Gerald was tired of repairing vacuums. There always seemed to be a million machines to repair, and the owner of the store, John

Timmson, was never around to lend a hand. In fact, John would rather be out playing golf or hanging out with his girlfriend than dealing with his business. John never lent a hand with difficult customers, rarely repaired vacuums, and was always "away" when stock came in, and Gerald needed assistance to stack inventory. John refused to complete warranty reports and, most important, never, ever cleaned the store. As Gerald nestled himself into the big comfortable couch in the back office and slowly dozed off, he contemplated his 40-hour, five-day workweek and the unfairness of the situation. His last fading moments of consciousness were focused on the fact that it just didn't seem right that after four months of employment he did all of this work while John was out having a good time.

Those Happy Early Days

"I love my work, and I'm only in my first month here," Mr. Mahoney commented to his friend Stephen Hodgetts. "John is purposely never around, so I can really run the store the way I like it. I can arrange the store in a manner I think is appealing; I can sell the way that I know customers would most like to be sold, not like my old boss Mr. Paulson's hard-nosed methods. I never had a chance to do anything but sell and repair vacuums, and here I run the entire operation from purchasing to return policies. I have never had such responsibility before, but I am learning on the job and enjoying every minute of it. This is like a dream come true. As long as I continue to sell and the store makes money, what can go wrong with this deal?"

The Honeymoon Is Over

A month had passed since Gerald's conversation with Stephen, and Gerald was starting to see what could go wrong. For example, Gerald liked the store to be particularly neat and clean, and it seemed that on Gerald's days off John would let the store become disheveled. He thought, "How can I do my job to the best of my ability if John leaves me all of this extra work? For instance, my rate of completing repairs is way down, creating a backlog because of the extra time I have to spend cleaning the store. Customers are starting to complain, and I don't know what to tell them!"

John Timmson's Fateful Store Visit

It was four months into Gerald's hire, and John had regrets. John had talked with Gerald several times about the condition of the store, and all that Gerald seemed to do was grumble about the lack of support John was giving him. Gerald was sounding more and more like his last girlfriend than a manager, and John was getting fed up with Gerald's "I'm helpless, overworked, and underpaid" routine.

"Unsupportive?" John thought to himself. "As Gerald requested, I reduced his working hours from his old job with Paulson, gave him two days off, and allowed him to run the store the best way he saw fit. I gave him a chance to really be a manager, not the dumb flunky that Paulson regarded him as. And what did I get in return? I get a poorly run store, customer complaints, and reduced profits—so much for me being Mr. Nice Guy."

Gerald had let him down and just had to go, but if John fired Gerald, then John would be stuck in the store seven days a week for a while. But what else could he do? Getting an additional employee to work on weekdays was not cost-effective—the business just did not generate enough income during the week to profitably handle even a second part-time employee's salary for the days that would have to be covered when Gerald was working.

His current part-time employee did not want to work in the store full-time since this employee was semiretired and did not want to commit himself to a full-time job. Subcontracting out the repair work was also not cost-effective since many of the repairs were fairly simple and could be done in 15 minutes by a salesperson during the week, when the store was not busy.

John did not have any good answers to the problem but hoped that just maybe he and Gerald might work out something. Otherwise John's life would be ruined, at least for the next three to four months. John arrived at the store and noticed the untidiness of the store, the poor layout of the displays, and Gerald's slovenly, tired appearance. Repair work from the back office seemed to have invaded the front of the store (meaning there was an ever-growing number of machines to repair) and the tool rack was in total disarray. What a catastrophe! Gerald looked extremely nervous, like a cornered rabbit ready for the hunter to pull the trigger. He must have guessed at what was probably coming and was resigning himself to his fate.

John became furious and highly frustrated with Gerald for not taking better care of the store but decided not to vent his anger. He was the boss, and he was not going to let an employee get his goat, especially an employee who seemed short-lived at best. John also knew he had to do something in order to salvage his business, but what? John gathered himself for what was going to be a difficult discussion but a discussion that nonetheless had to occur.

Questions

1. Gerald Mahoney's attitude and performance dramatically changed after a few months on the job. What type of training should Mahoney have immediately received from John Timmson that might have avoided this?

2. Assuming Timmson keeps Mahoney as the store manager, what should be the first step he institutes in the training process?

3. Assuming that Timmson and Mahoney agree to a training program in order to solve the problem, what are some challenges Timmson might face in conducting this training?

4. According to Exhibit 7-2, there are four methods for increasing and decreasing employee behavior. What are these methods, and which one(s) do you think would work the best for changing some of Mahoney's more problematic behaviors?

5. Look at Exhibit 7-3, "Skills and Training Methods." What are some of the appropriate training techniques that Timmson might use to increase Mahoney's KSAs?

6. Mahoney jumped from being a sales associate under Mr. Paulson to a store manager under Mr. Timmson. How might career planning and development have helped him in making this transition?

Case created by Herbert Sherman, PhD, and Mr. Theodore Vallas, Department of Management Sciences, Long Island University School of Business, Brooklyn Campus

SKILL BUILDER 7-1

The Training Process

Objective

To develop your ability to conduct a needs assessment, to select how to shape employee behavior, to design a training program by selecting training methods, to select a method to deliver training, and to choose an assessment method.

Skills

The primary skills developed through this exercise are:

1.   *HR Management skill* – Conceptual and design skills

2.   *SHRM 2010 Curriculum Guidebook* – J: Training and Development

Assignment

As an individual or a group, select a job and write out your answers. Then follow the steps in the training process below to train a person to do the job.

Step 1. Needs assessment. Conduct a needs assessment for the job by developing a competency model identifying the knowledge, skills, and abilities needed to do the job successfully.

Step 2. Select how you will shape behavior. Be sure to specify if you will use positive reinforcement, punishment, negative reinforcement, or extinction. State the rewards and/or punishment.

Step 3. Design the training. Select and describe in detail the training method(s) you will use to shape the behavior.

Step 4. Deliver the training. Select one of the four methods of delivery that you will use to conduct the actual training and describe how you will deliver the training.

Step 5. Assessment of training. Select one of the four assessment methods and describe in detail how you will determine if the training did in fact shape the behavior.

Apply It

What did I learn from this experience? How will I use this knowledge in the future?

_____

_____

Your instructor may ask you to do this Skill Builder in class by breaking into groups of four to six and doing the preparation. If so, the instructor will provide you with any necessary information or additional instructions.

SKILL BUILDER 7-2

Career Development

Objective

To begin to think about and develop your career plan.

Skills

The primary skills developed through this exercise are:

1. *HR Management skill* – Conceptual and design

2. *SHRM Curricular Guide* – J: Training and Development

Assignment

Write out your answers to the following questions.

1. Do you now, or do you want to, work in HRM? Why? If not, what career do you want to pursue and why?

2. If you want to work in HR, based on your self-assessment back in Chapter 1 or other knowledge, list your highest levels of interest in HR disciplines. If not, what are your highest levels of interests, functions, or disciplines within your chosen career?

3. What methods of employee development (formal education, experience—internships and jobs, and assessment) are you using to prepare for your career?

Apply It

What did I learn from this exercise? How will I use this knowledge in the future?

_____

_____

Your instructor may ask you to do this Skill Builder in class by breaking into groups of two to three and discussing your career plans. If so, the instructor will provide you with any necessary information or additional instructions.

8

Performance Management and Appraisal

Learning Outcomes

After studying this chapter you should be able to:

8.1 Discuss the difference between performance management and performance appraisal

8.2 Identify the necessary characteristics of accurate performance management tools

8.3 List and briefly discuss the purposes for performance appraisals

8.4 Identify and briefly discuss the options for "what" is evaluated in a performance appraisal

8.5 Briefly discuss the commonly used performance measurement methods and forms

8.6 Identify and briefly discuss available options for the rater/evaluator

8.7 Briefly discuss the value and the drawbacks of a 360° evaluation

8.8 Identify some of the common problems with the performance appraisal process

8.9 Identify the major steps we can take to avoid problems with the appraisal process

8.10 Briefly discuss the differences between evaluative performance reviews and developmental performance reviews

8.11 Define the following terms:

Performance management
Performance appraisal
Motivation
Traits
Behaviors
Results
Critical incidents method
Management by Objectives (MBO) method
Narrative method or form

Graphic rating scale form
Behaviorally Anchored Rating Scale (BARS) form
Ranking method
360° evaluation
Bias
Stereotyping
Electronic Performance Monitoring (EPM)

Chapter 8 Outline

SHRM
HR CONTENT

See Appendix A:
SHRM 2010 Curriculum Guidebook for the complete list

Performance Management Miscue

Most managers don't look forward to performance appraisals. As soon as Heather stuck her head in my office and asked me to sit in on her performance appraisal, I knew I had *two* employees who needed some coaching—Heather and her supervisor, Christine. Our company bases many employment decisions on performance appraisals, so the results are important.

When I entered the room, it became apparent that although Heather believed she had been doing a great job, Christine did not agree. Christine recorded Heather's performance as needing improvement overall, but did not offer any reason beyond a vague charge that Heather had a poor attitude and wasn't a team player.

I quickly suggested a small interruption to the meeting, and asked Heather to step out of the room. It soon became clear that the overall problem was Heather's failure to report to work on time. When Heather was late, it impacted her entire work group as the other employees then had to answer Heather's phone calls.

What's going on here? Why don't Heather and Christine agree on Heather's performance? Where did Christine go wrong? How can Christine get Heather to agree with her performance review now? How can this problem be avoided during the next formal performance appraisal session? The answers to these questions are based on having a good performance management system. By reading this chapter, you will learn how you can avoid these problems.

The Practitioner's Model for HRM

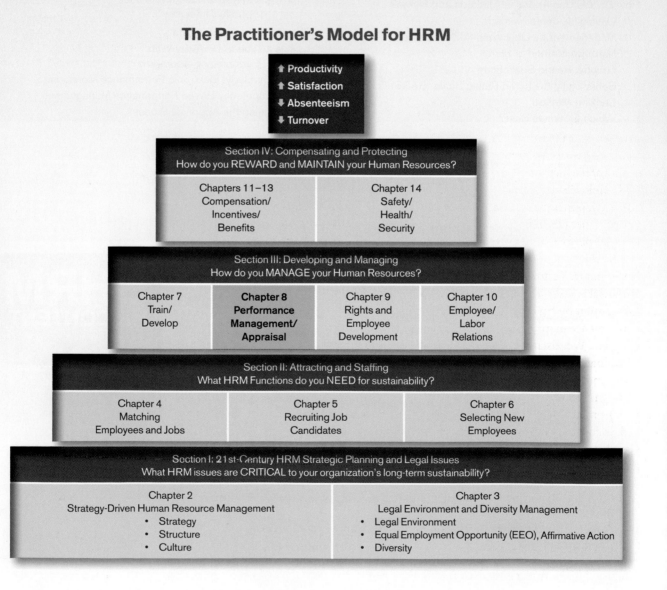

⬆ Productivity
⬆ Satisfaction
⬇ Absenteeism
⬇ Turnover

Section IV: Compensating and Protecting
How do you REWARD and MAINTAIN your Human Resources?

| Chapters 11–13 Compensation/ Incentives/ Benefits | Chapter 14 Safety/ Health/ Security |

Section III: Developing and Managing
How do you MANAGE your Human Resources?

| Chapter 7 Train/ Develop | **Chapter 8 Performance Management/ Appraisal** | Chapter 9 Rights and Employee Development | Chapter 10 Employee/ Labor Relations |

Section II: Attracting and Staffing
What HRM Functions do you NEED for sustainability?

| Chapter 4 Matching Employees and Jobs | Chapter 5 Recruiting Job Candidates | Chapter 6 Selecting New Employees |

Section I: 21st-Century HRM Strategic Planning and Legal Issues
What HRM issues are CRITICAL to your organization's long-term sustainability?

| Chapter 2 Strategy-Driven Human Resource Management • Strategy • Structure • Culture | Chapter 3 Legal Environment and Diversity Management • Legal Environment • Equal Employment Opportunity (EEO), Affirmative Action • Diversity |

Performance Management Systems

LO 8.1

Discuss the difference between performance management and performance appraisal.

At this stage of human resource management (HRM), we now have employees in our organization who can do the work, we've given them at least some initial training, and they are now doing their individual jobs. What's next? The next issue that we need to figure out is how to manage their performance over time to ensure that they remain productive, and hopefully become even more capable, as they progress in their careers. Remember our discussion from Chapter 1 that our human resources are typically one of the few options available to create a sustainable competitive advantage for the firm. So we need to ensure that our human resources perform at the highest possible level. To this end, in this section, we discuss the difference between performance management and performance appraisal, and present the performance appraisal process.

Performance Management Versus Performance Appraisal

SHRM

Guide – C:4
Performance management (performance criteria and appraisal)

"In a knowledge economy, organizations rely heavily on their intangible assets to build value. Consequently, performance management at the individual employee level is essential and the business case for implementing a system to measure and improve employee performance is strong."[1] Management time and effort to increase performance not only meets this goal; it also decreases turnover rates.[2]

How do we manage performance within the organization? The most common part of the process, and the one with which we are most familiar, is the process of the performance appraisal, or evaluation. In this chapter, we will use the phrases *performance evaluation, performance appraisal,* and *appraisal* interchangeably. However, the performance appraisal process is not the only thing that's done in performance management. **Performance management** is *the process of identifying, measuring, managing, and developing the performance of the human resources in an organization.* Basically we are trying to figure out how well employees perform and then to ultimately improve that performance level. When used correctly, performance management is a systematic analysis and measurement of worker performance (*including* communication of that assessment to the individual) that we use to improve performance over time.

Performance appraisal, on the other hand, is *the ongoing process of evaluating employee performance.* Performance appraisals are reviews of employee performance over time[3], so appraisal is just one piece of performance management. Although we will spend most of this chapter discussing performance appraisal, there are several other significant pieces of performance management that we already covered in past chapters and will cover in future chapters. We discussed "strategic planning," which provides inputs into what we want to evaluate in our performance management system, in Chapter 2. We also discussed the major method of identifying performance requirements in a particular job when we went through "job analysis and design" in Chapter 4. In Chapter 7, we discussed "training and development," which obviously play a part in performance management. Additionally, we will discuss motivating employees, employee relations, compensation, and other pieces in Chapters 9–14. Now that we understand the difference between performance management and performance appraisal, let's look at the performance appraisal process.

The Performance Appraisal Process

Exhibit 8-1 illustrates the performance appraisal (PA) process. Note the connection between the organization's mission and objectives and the performance appraisal process. Here we briefly discuss each step of the process.

Video Link 8.1
Performance Appraisal Process

| Exhibit 8-1 | The Performance Appraisal Process |

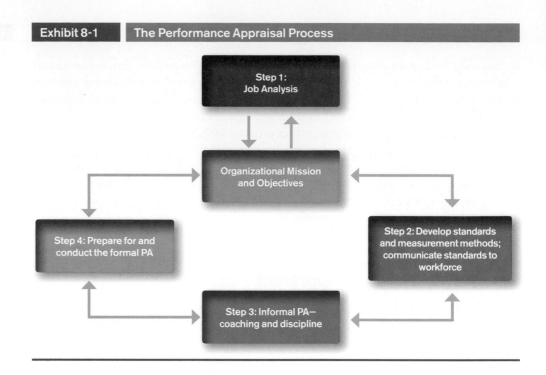

Step 1. Job analysis. This is logically our first step because if we don't know what a job consists of, how can we possibly evaluate an employee's performance? We already learned how to do a job analysis in Chapter 4, but as shown in Exhibit 8-1, we should realize that the job must be based on the organizational mission and objectives, the department, and the job itself.

Step 2. Develop standards and measurement methods. If we don't have standards of acceptable behavior and methods to measure performance, how can we assess performance? We will discuss performance measurement methods in the next part of this section, and in the major section "How Do We Use Appraisal Methods and Forms?" we will discuss these topics in more detail.

Step 3. Informal performance appraisal—coaching and disciplining. Performance appraisal should not be simply a once- or twice-yearly formal interview. As its definition states, performance appraisal is an ongoing process. While a formal evaluation may only take place once or twice a year, people need regular feedback on their performance to know how they are doing.[4] We will briefly discuss coaching in the "Critical Incidents Method" subsection of "How Do We Use Appraisal Methods and Forms?" and in more detail along with teaching how to discipline in the next chapter.

Step 4. Prepare for and conduct the formal performance appraisal. The common practice is to have a formal performance review with the boss once or sometimes twice a year using one or more of the measurement forms we will be learning about. Later in this chapter we will discuss the steps of preparing for and conducting the performance appraisal.

In the major sections to come, we discuss "why" we assess performance, "what" we assess, "how" we assess, and "who" conducts the performance appraisal. Then we discuss performance appraisal problems and how to avoid them, and we end the performance appraisal process with the actual formal review session. But before we leave this section, we need to understand a critically important part of each step in the performance appraisal process—accurate performance measurement.

Accurate Performance Measures

LO 8.2

Performance should be accurately measured so employees will know where they can improve.[5] Knowing where to improve should lead to training employees to develop new skills to improve.[6] To be an accurate measure of performance, our measure must be valid and reliable, acceptable and feasible, specific, and based on the mission and objectives. Let's discuss each here.

Identify the necessary characteristics of accurate performance management tools.

Valid and reliable. As with all areas of our people management process, we must make sure that all of our performance management tools are valid and reliable. Here again, we can pull out and dust off the OUCH test as a quick measure to ensure fairness and equity in the performance management and appraisal process. We remember by now that OUCH stands for *Objective, Uniform in application, Consistent in effect,* and *Has job relatedness,* right? However, we still need to analyze validity and reliability in some detail.

If our method of measurement is not valid and reliable, then it makes no sense to use it. We discussed reliability and validity in Chapter 4. Recall that a valid measure is "true and correct." When a measure has validity, it is a factual measure that measures the process that you wanted to measure. A reliable measure is consistent; it works in generally the same way each time we use it.

Acceptable and feasible. In addition to validity and reliability, we need to look at a couple of other characteristics of our performance measures. We need to analyze acceptability and feasibility. Acceptability means that the use of the measure is satisfactory or appropriate to the people who must use it. However, in performance appraisal, this isn't enough.[7] Acceptability must include whether or not the evaluation tool is feasible. Is it possible to reasonably apply the evaluation tool in a particular case? As an example, if the performance evaluation form is two or three pages long and covers the major aspects of the job that is being evaluated, and both managers and employees believe that the form truly evaluates performance measures that identify success in the job, then they are likely to feel that the tool is acceptable and feasible. If, however, the manager must fill out a 25-page form that has very little to do with the job being evaluated, the manager may not feel that the form is acceptable or feasible, at least partially due to its length, even if the employee does.

Conversely, if managers fill out a two-page evaluation that they feel is a true measure of performance in employees' jobs but the employees feel that the evaluation leaves out large segments of what they do in their work routine, they may not feel that the form is acceptable and feasible. If either management or employees feel that the form is unacceptable, it most likely will not be used correctly. So, we always have to evaluate acceptability and feasibility of a measure.

Specific. Next, we want any evaluation measure to be specific enough to identify what is going well and what is not. The word *specific* means that something is explicitly identified, or defined well

Without accurate measures of performance, the performance appraisal can't be reliable or valid.

WORK
APPLICATION 8-2

Assess the accuracy of the measurements of your performance on your last performance appraisal. Be sure to describe the measures' validity and reliability, their acceptability and feasibility, if they were specific, and if they were based on the organization's mission and objectives.

enough that all involved understand the issue completely. In performance appraisal, *specific* means that the form provides enough information for everyone to understand what level of performance has been achieved by a particular employee within a well-identified job.

Creating specific measures is the only way that we can use a performance appraisal to improve the performance of our employees over time. The employees have to understand what they are doing successfully and what they are not. Many times, evaluation forms may be too general in nature to be of value for modifying employee behaviors because we want the form to serve for a large number of different types of jobs. This can create significant problems in the performance appraisal process.

Based on the mission and objectives. Finally, you want to make sure that your performance management system leads to accomplishment of your organizational mission and objectives. As with everything else we do in HR, we need to ensure that the performance management process guides our employees toward achievement of the company's mission and objectives over time. As managers in the organization, making sure of this connection will allow us to reinforce employee behaviors that aim at achieving organizational goals and to identify for our employees things that they may be doing that actively or unintentionally harm our ability to reach those goals.

Thus, stating specific objectives of exactly what each person in each job should achieve or his or her performance outcomes leads to accurate assessment that can increase performance. For some examples of inaccurate measures of performance, complete Applying the Concept 8-1.

8-1 APPLYING THE CONCEPT

Measurement Accuracy

Which of the following criteria for a measure to be accurate is not met in each of the given situations?

a. valid
b. reliable
c. accepted
d. feasible
e. specific
f. based on the mission and objectives

_____ 1. My boss asked me to fill out a self-evaluation of my performance. But I refused to do it. Evaluation is her job, so let her do it.

_____ 2. My boss told me that I was not doing a very good job of data entry. When I asked him what he meant, he went around in circles and never gave me a good answer.

_____ 3. The boss said I'm not producing as many widgets as I used to. But it's not my fault that the machine jams every now and then and I have to stop working to fix it.

_____ 4. My boss asked to me to evaluate my employees four times a year instead of only once. I told her I don't have the time to do it that many times. It's just not possible to do a good review that often without cutting back other things that are more important.

_____ 5. My boss said I have a bad attitude and gave me a lower overall rating. But I pointed out that I get all my work done well and by the deadline or early, and I questioned what my attitude had to do with my performance.

Why Do We Conduct Performance Appraisals?

LO 8.3

List and briefly discuss the purposes for performance appraisals.

As you can begin to see already, the appraisal process gets extremely complicated very quickly. And remember, anytime a process in an organization is complicated, it costs a lot of money. So why do we even do performance appraisals? What value provided to the organization and to the individual makes the process of evaluating the performance of our workers so critical?

If performance appraisals are done in the correct manner, they can provide us with a series of valuable results. However, done incorrectly, the process of evaluating employee performance can actually lead to lower levels of job satisfaction and productivity. In this section, let's discuss three major reasons why organizations complete performance evaluations—communicating, decision making, and motivating.

Communicating

The first major reason for performance appraisal is to provide an opportunity for formal communication between management and the employees concerning how the organization believes each employee is performing. All of us know intuitively that successful communication requires two-way interaction between people. "Organizations can prevent or remedy the majority of performance problems by ensuring that two-way conversation occurs between the manager and the employee, resulting in a complete understanding of what is required, when it is required and how the employee's contribution measures up."[8]

Communication always requires that employees have the opportunity and ability to provide feedback to their bosses in order to make sure that the communication is understood. So, in performance appraisals the communication process requires that we as managers communicate with the employees to provide them information about how we believe they're doing in their job, but the process also requires that we provide the opportunity for the employees to speak to us concerning factors that inhibit their ability to successfully perform for the organization.

Factors in a job that management may not know about can include many things, including lack of training, poorly maintained equipment, lack of tools necessary to perform, conflict within work groups, and many other things that management may not see on a daily basis. If the communication component of the performance appraisal process does not allow for this two-way communication, managers may not know of the obstacles that the employees have to overcome. The only way that we can resolve problems is to know about them. So, as managers, we need to communicate with our employees to find out when issues within the work environment cause loss of productivity so we can fix them. Thus, two-way communication is a critical component of correcting problems through the performance appraisal process.

Decision Making (Evaluating)

The second major purpose of performance appraisals is to allow management to make decisions about employees within the organization. We need to make decisions based on information, the information we get from our communication. Accurate information is necessary for management decision making and is an absolutely critical component to allow the manager to improve organizational productivity.[9] We use information from annual performance appraisals to make evaluative decisions concerning our workforce including pay raises, promotions, demotions, training and development, and termination. When we have valid and reliable information concerning each individual within our division or department, this gives us the ability to make decisions that can enhance productivity for the firm.

If, for instance, through the process of coaching (the third step of the performance appraisal process) we find that several machine operators are having trouble keeping their equipment in working order, this piece of information would quite likely lead to a *needs assessment* (as discussed in Chapter 7) to determine whether or not maintenance training is necessary for our group of operators. Without our rigorous evaluation process, we might not learn of this common problem as early, and as a result could do some significant damage to very expensive equipment. This and similar types of information frequently come to the forefront as we go through the performance appraisal process. Decision making based on good communication is a very large part of why we take the time to do annual performance appraisals.

SHRM

Guide – F:7
Managing Performance

Motivating (Developing)

The third major purpose for performance appraisal is to provide motivation to our employees to improve the way they work individually for developmental purposes, which in turn will improve organizational productivity overall.[10] What is motivation, and are performance appraisals normally motivational? Well, from a business perspective, **motivation** can be defined as *the willingness to achieve organizational objectives*. We want to create this willingness to achieve the organization's objectives, which in turn will increase organizational productivity.

Our evaluative decisions should lead to development of employees. Returning to the machine operators having trouble keeping their equipment in working order, making the decision to train the employees leads to their development through improving their performance, as well as better utilizing the resources to improve organizational performance.

Evaluating and Motivating (Development)

An effective performance appraisal process has two parts (evaluating and motivating), and it does both parts well. Evaluating is about assessing *past* performance, and motivating is about developing employees to improve their *future* performance. But, are both parts done well? Have you ever been in a position of being evaluated and debriefed as an employee? Was the process motivational? Probably not. Think about the appraisal process and how it was carried out. Here we discuss problems with evaluation and how to overcome them, explain how to motivate, and suggest separating evaluation and motivation.

Problems with evaluation. A common problem in appraisals is overpowering employees during an evaluation debrief with large amounts of negative information that they have not heard during coaching. This tends to cause the employees to "turn off," or stop listening to their managers as they explain what is wrong. Employees will just "raise their shields" to ward off all of the negative information. This is a natural human characteristic. We are naturally suspicious of negative information for a variety of psychological reasons (defense mechanisms), so when employees are presented with a large amount of negative information, they tend to discount or even disbelieve it. They may consider the process unfair or one-sided and not an accurate measure of their performance, and as a result the evaluation may be useless as a motivator.

Avoiding problems with evaluation. To help overcome such problems with evaluation, an effective manager who is a good coach will generally never identify a weakness that the employee has not previously been made aware of during the formal appraisal interview—there are no surprises. The evaluative part of the appraisal should only be a review of what the employee already knows and should be willing to hear. However, avoiding surprises is not enough.[11]

The appraisal debrief must be a well-rounded look at individual employees; it should identify both positive and negative factors in the employees' behaviors and results within their job (and remember that the communication needs to be two-way). As managers, we want to tell employees what they are doing right, but also where they have room for improvement. This more balanced approach to the debriefing process will minimize the potential that the employees will raise those shields and avoid listening.

Motivating development. The important part of development is the need for managers to provide motivational opportunities for employees to improve their performance over time. In other words, we need to tell them how to fix the problem. We need to provide them with tools, training, or other methods that will allow them to improve to the point where their behavior is sufficient, and we then must continually strive to get them to perform at an above-average level and ultimately to be superior through ongoing coaching between formal reviews.

If we provide employees with tools to allow them to improve over time, we're focusing not on the negative past results but on the positive future potential results.[12] If they are given an honest opportunity to fix something that they know is a problem and are given the necessary tools or training, most will take advantage of that opportunity. So performance appraisals *can* be motivational if they are properly used and debriefed.

Separating evaluation and development. To improve both parts of the performance appraisal, we suggest splitting the debriefing into two separate interviews. The first meeting is to evaluate the employees' *past* performance, pointing out strengths and areas for improvement; the employees are asked to think about how they can improve their performance. At the second meeting, manager and employee *jointly* come up with a developmental plan that should lead to increased performance that will result in a higher *future* evaluative rating during the next formal appraisal. We will discuss how to conduct the two separate interviews in the "Debriefing the Appraisal" major section of this chapter.

What Do We Assess?

Now that we know why we conduct performance appraisals, the next step is to figure out what needs to be evaluated. In other words, we have to decide what aspects of the individuals and their performance we're going to measure. The best option for what we evaluate would come from analyzing the essential functions and qualifications required for a particular job—or, in HR terms, our job analysis. We could then use these facts to design an appraisal instrument with measurable and observable factors with which performance can be evaluated.[13] However, we can't evaluate everything that is done over the course of the year. We have to choose what we will focus on because if we can't measure it, we can't manage it, and what gets measured and evaluated gets done.[14] Our three primary options are traits, behaviors, and results.

Trait Appraisals

Traits *identify the physical or psychological characteristics of a person.* We can evaluate the traits of an individual during the performance appraisal process. Can we accurately measure traits that affect job performance, can trait measures pass the OUCH test, are traits commonly used to measure performance, and should we measure traits as part of our performance appraisal process? Here we answer these questions, and we will answer these same questions for our behavior and results options.

Can we accurately measure traits that affect job performance? Certainly, there's *some* evidence that particular types of traits are valuable in jobs that require management and leadership skills. Characteristics such as inquisitiveness, conscientiousness, and general

WORK
APPLICATION 8-3

Assess the effectiveness of an evaluative performance appraisal you had. Did the manager present both positive and negative performance areas? Did you "really" listen? Were there any surprises? Explain any problems and how the evaluation could be improved.

LO 8.4

Identify and briefly discuss the options for "what" is evaluated in a performance appraisal.

cognitive ability have been shown to have a reasonable "link" to job performance.[15] But just how accurate is the link?

Many traits that most of us would be likely to focus on, such as physical attractiveness, height, extroversion, and others, actually have been shown to have very little bearing on job performance. If we're going to use traits in performance evaluation, we must ensure that we focus on traits that have a direct relationship to the essential functions of the job being done, and they have to be accurate measures.

If we decide to use trait-based evaluations, is that a good method for judging work performance? How many of us would want to have judgments made about our work based on our appearance or personality? Would you consider this to be a *valid and reliable* measure of your work performance? In most cases, it's very difficult to show that personal traits are valid and reliable measures of work performance.

Can trait measures pass the OUCH test? Let's take a look at trait-based measurements using the OUCH test. Is a physical characteristic, such as height, or a psychological characteristic, such as attitude, cheerfulness, work ethic, or enthusiasm, an objective measure of an individual's work performance? We would have great difficulty creating a quantifiable and factual link between height or enthusiasm and job performance.

So it's difficult when measuring traits to meet the *objective* requirement of the OUCH test. If we utilized these trait-based measures in all cases in employee evaluations, we would be able to meet the *uniform in application* requirement of the OUCH test. The third test— *consistent in effect*—would likely be extremely difficult to meet due to the fact that different racial, ethnic, social, and gender groups tend to have different physical and psychological characteristics. Remember, reliability is a measure of consistency. Could we meet the *has job relatedness* test? Is a particular trait directly related to the essential functions of the job? In a very few cases this may be true, but in most situations physical and personality characteristics have less to do with success in the job than certain behaviors will. So it's very difficult to meet the *has job relatedness* test.

Finally, we need to ask whether or not different supervisors would evaluate our traits differently, based on their traits. Would their individual biases based on their personalities cause them to evaluate us differently? The answer is, of course, that different people would quite likely evaluate our traits differently.

Are traits commonly used to measure performance? Surprisingly, if you go to the local office supply store and look at standard evaluation forms that are available in pre-printed pads, you will find that they usually contain many traits as part of the evaluation. Why would this be the case? The simple answer is that at least some traits, both physical and psychological, are fairly easy to identify, and we make the *assumption* that they are related to how the individual will perform on the job. Many of us, individually and as managers, value certain things like enthusiasm even if enthusiasm has very little to do with the ability to do a particular job or the actual results of job performance.

Certainly, there are some jobs where enthusiasm is critical. However, in most jobs, being enthusiastic employees may have very little to do with job success. If we evaluated individuals based on the characteristic of enthusiasm, we might make an error in judgment concerning their performance. And if we make errors in analyzing the performance of our employees, the appraisal form becomes much less *acceptable* to both the individual employee and management.

Finally, if our organization happened to be sued by a former employee who claimed that they were fired based on an appraisal process that was unreliable and not valid, it would be very difficult to defend trait-based evaluation forms due to their subjective nature.

Should we measure traits? Author Ken Blanchard says that there are too many evaluation items that can't be objectively measured because they attempt to measure things that no one knows how to accurately measure, such as attitude, initiative, and promotability. An important question is whether both managers and employees will agree that the measured rating is accurate. The bottom-line test (we will call it the Blanchard test) is whether everyone understands why they are assessed at a specific level (evaluation) and what it takes to get a higher rating (development).[16] So we should only assess traits if we meet the bottom-line test of having a direct and obvious objective relationship between the trait and success in the job.

Behavioral Appraisals

Our second option in the assessment process is to evaluate employees based on behaviors. You will recall that **behaviors** are simply *the actions taken by individuals*—the things that they do and say. Behavioral appraisals measure what individuals *do* at work, not their personal characteristics. Is this a good option to use in a performance appraisal process?

Can we accurately measure behaviors that affect job performance? As a general rule, behaviors are a much better option to use in an appraisal than traits. While an individual supervisor or manager may make a mistake in judgment of the traits of an employee, physical actions or behaviors can be directly observed, and as a result they are more likely to be a valid assessment of the individual's performance.

Can behavior measures pass the OUCH test? Let's take a look at a behavioral evaluation using the OUCH test. Would an evaluation based on actions taken by an employee be *objective*? In general, directly observing and evaluating an action is significantly more objective than making an attempt to judge a trait such as effort. If we applied the same evaluation of behaviors to all of the individuals in the same type of job, we would have a reasonable certainty that we were being *uniform in application*. The same thing would be true here in evaluating the concept of *consistent in effect*.

So, we come down to whether or not a behavioral evaluation *has job relatedness*. Would a behavioral evaluation be directly related to the essential functions of a job? It would be if we made sure that we chose behaviors that were necessarily a part of successfully accomplishing a task. For instance, if a person *acted* correctly to fill out a requisition form, putting the proper information in the correct blocks and providing the requisition to the appropriate person who would then order the material, we would be assessing behaviors that are job-related. If, however, we evaluated the action of walking to the lunchroom and back to your workstation, would that be a valid job-related behavior? More than likely it would not. Of course, this is a silly example, but it should help you understand that no matter what we do in the evaluation process, we need to ensure that our actions are job-related.

Would behavioral evaluations be defensible in the situation of our fired employee above? Would it be possible for us to show that our evaluation process was *valid and reliable*? If we choose job-related behaviors, it becomes much easier for the organization to defend the validity and reliability of the appraisal process. Observation of actions that are directly related to a job provides at least some presumption of validity as well as reliability purely because the behaviors are directly job-related. Again, if we chose behaviors that were not able to be directly associated with the job, the validity and reliability would be suspect.

Should we measure behavior? Are behaviors that measure performance more *acceptable* to the individual employee and the managers than personal traits? In fact, evidence shows that most individuals are very comfortable with the evaluation of their performance being based on their behaviors. In general, the most useful and therefore acceptable feedback to employees is considered to be in the form of specific job-related behaviors.[17] As managers, though, we still need to be cognizant of the fact that a behavioral evaluation can be a poor measure of work performance unless the behaviors chosen are directly applicable to being successful in the job. So, like with traits, the Blanchard test is whether everyone understands why they are assessed at a specific level (evaluation) and what it takes to get a higher rating (development).[18]

Results/Outcomes Appraisals

Our final option concerning what we evaluate is the results, or outcomes, of the work process. **Results** are simply *a measure of the goals achieved through a work process.* Using results as an evaluation measure provides management of the organization with an assessment of the goals that were achieved in a particular job over time.

Can we accurately measure results that affect job performance? Is measuring the outcomes of a particular individual's job a valid and reliable measure of that person's performance? Well, certainly results are a concrete measure of what has happened in the organization. However, could results of a job have been skewed based on factors that were outside the control of the individual who is performing that job? The answer is obviously that the results could be affected by many other factors besides the individual. For example, the goals could be set too low and be easy to achieve, or too high and be impossible to achieve.

Even though this is true, the measurement of results is the final organizational measure of success. The results produced through organizational processes provide the company with its return on investment—in this case its investment in the people in the organization. So, organizations really like to measure results.

Can results pass the OUCH test? Let's take a look at the OUCH test concerning results-based evaluations. Is a result achieved in a particular job a concrete, factual measure that can easily be quantified? Obviously, it is a very *objective* measure of what has happened in that particular job. If we apply the same results-based measure to each similar job, then our measure is *uniform in application.* The measure of results would almost certainly be consistent across different groups of employees, so we would meet the *consistency in effect* requirement of the OUCH test. And of course, if we are measuring the results of what happens in a job, we are certainly providing a measure that *has job relatedness.* So, with a quick scan we can see that a results-based performance appraisal meets the requirements of the OUCH test better than either of the other two options.

Should we measure results? Results-based evaluations, like behavior, are also typically very acceptable to both the employee and the manager. Employees readily accept results-based appraisals because they feel that such measures are one of the fairest methods of analyzing their performance. After all, results are the most concrete form of evaluation that can be performed. Either the result was achieved, or it wasn't. We can also defend this type of appraisal much easier than the other two options in court, if necessary. It tends to be very easy for the organization to go into a courtroom and show that an individual's results were absolutely lower than the results achieved by other people in the same or similar jobs, if such an action becomes necessary.

But would a performance evaluation measured on results be valid and reliable? The results-based evaluation would most likely be highly valid and would usually be reliable, assuming that we were able to take into account factors outside of individuals' control that nonetheless affect the performance of their job. So, like with traits and behaviors, the Blanchard test is whether everyone understands why they are assessed at a specific level (evaluation) and what it takes to get a higher rating (development).[19]

Which Option Is Best?

Our three options concerning *what* we evaluate are traits, behaviors, and results. But, which option is best? The answer's not as easy as you might think. Certainly, results-based and behavior-based evaluations are more defensible due to the fact that they are more reliable and valid than trait-based evaluations. But we have to include a large number of factors in order to select which option is best in a particular situation.

8-2 APPLYING THE CONCEPT

Assessment Options

Which of the following assessment options for measuring performance is being described in each of the given situations?

a.   traits
b.   behavior
c.   results

_____ 6. This is the second time you got upset and yelled at customers. This has to stop.

_____ 7. You have produced 15 products again this week. You know the standard is 20, so I'm giving you a formal warning that if you don't get up to standard in two weeks, you will be fired.

_____ 8. When you promote one of the women from waitress to hostess, be sure she is attractive so customers have a good impression of our restaurant and want to come back.

_____ 9. I'm really surprised. Since you started working from home, you have actually increased your data entry numbers by 5 percent.

_____10. On item number 5, willingness to take responsibility, I'm giving you an average rating.

For example, if we need to evaluate employees who work on the assembly line, we may need to evaluate behaviors such as punctuality—do they show up to work on time? If we have employees who, when they are there, produce at 150% of the standard, but only show up two or three days a week, that creates a problem for the whole assembly line. In that case, we may need to evaluate attendance and punctuality (behaviors) because everyone on the assembly line depends on everyone else.

However, if we have individuals who don't do their actual work where managers can measure traits and behaviors—for example, people who work from home (telecommuters) and in independent outside sales positions—we need to rely on results. Other employees are often not affected by the hours that the telecommuters and salespeople work. It will not matter when they are at the office, as long as they get the job done. The firm will be concerned with how much they produced or sold. So circumstances dictate which method we will use; we cannot say one method will always be superior to the other two.

How Do We Use Appraisal Methods and Forms?

SHRM

Guide – F:5
Performance appraisals

The formal performance appraisal usually involves the use of a standard form developed by the HR department to measure employee performance. Again, "If you can't measure it, you can't manage it."[20] But you must be careful how you measure success,[21] as the assessment should be as objective as possible, not subjective.[22] Employees need to know the standards and understand what good performance looks like, and they need to be able to measure their own performance. If you are stuck with a form that has subjective sections, work with your employees to develop clear accurate standards.

LO 8.5

Briefly discuss the commonly used performance measurement methods and forms.

Exhibit 8-2 lists the commonly used performance appraisal measurement methods and forms and displays them on a continuum based on their use in administrative evaluative and developmental decisions. In the following section, we discuss each of them, starting with the developmental methods and working toward the evaluative.

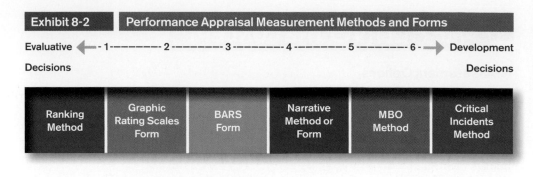

Exhibit 8-2   Performance Appraisal Measurement Methods and Forms

Evaluative ←- 1 ---------- 2 ---------- 3 ---------- 4 ---------- 5 ---------- 6 -→ Development
Decisions   Decisions

| Ranking Method | Graphic Rating Scales Form | BARS Form | Narrative Method or Form | MBO Method | Critical Incidents Method |

Critical Incidents Method

The **critical incidents method** is *a performance appraisal method in which a manager keeps a written record of positive and negative performance of employees throughout the performance period.* There is no standard form used, so it is a method. Here, and for each of the other methods and forms, let's answer two questions: Why and when is it used, and how is it used?

Why and when do we use the critical incidents method? Most formal reviews take place only once or twice a year. Do you want to wait for formal reviews to talk to employees about what they are doing well and when they are not performing up to expectations? Of course you want to let them know how they are doing on an ongoing basis. Also, let's say we are a manager with 12 employees. Can we remember everything each of them did well, and when they messed up, and on what dates, so we can evaluate their total performance for the past 6–12 months? Very few, if any, of us can say yes. However, many managers don't keep a record of critical incidents, which leads to problems of accurate measures during the formal review meeting.

We use critical incidents to do a good assessment of the entire review period, and we coach when needed during the entire review period for developmental decisions. We need to continually conduct informal coaching and disciplining when needed as we make notes of critical incidents to use during the formal review. With clear standards and coaching, you can minimize disagreements over performance during the formal performance appraisal because there are no surprises, because employees know what is coming.[23]

Although critical incidents are commonly used for developmental decisions, they are also used for evaluative decisions. For legal purposes, a list of documented critical incidents is especially important to have leading up the evaluative decision of firing employees. We will discuss discipline and documentation in Chapter 9.

How do we use critical incidents? Managers commonly simply have a file folder for each employee, which can be hard copy or electronic. Critical incidents are important employee actions, not minor ones, which help or hurt performance. Every time employees do something very well, such as beat a tough deadline or save angry customers from terminating their business relationship with the firm, a note goes in the employees' file. Notes also go into the file every time the employees' behavior hurts performance, such as coming to work late or the quality of work not meeting standards.

The note is usually written by the manager and/or is in the form of documentation, such as a warning that is given, performance reports, or a letter from a happy customer thanking the employee for doing a great job. Coaching is part of this ongoing process, and it involves helping employees succeed by monitoring performance through giving feedback to praise progress and to redirect inappropriate behavior as often as needed.[24] One error managers tend to make is to focus on the negative actions of employees. Remember that a good balanced evaluation includes both positive and negative, so look for good performance, not just poor, and praise it when you see it.[25]

Management by Objectives (MBO) Method

The **Management by Objectives (MBO) method** is *a process in which managers and employees jointly set objectives for the employees, periodically evaluate performance, and reward according to the results.* Although it is a three-step process, no standard form is used with MBO, so it is a method. MBO is also referred to as work planning and review, goals management, goals and controls, and management by results.

Why and when do we use the MBO method? The MBO method is one of the best methods of developing employees. Like critical incidents, employees get ongoing feedback on how they are doing, usually at scheduled interval meetings. We can use the MBO method successfully with our employees if we commit to the process and truly involve employees rather than trying to make them believe that our objectives are theirs—accurate measures.

On an organization-wide basis, MBO is not too commonly used as the sole assessment method. It is more commonly used based on the evaluative assessment during the development part of the performance appraisal. One difficult part of MBO is that in many situations, most, if not all, employees will have different goals, making MBO more difficult and time-consuming than using a standard assessment form.

How do we use the MBO method? MBO is a three-step process:

Step 1. *Set individual objectives and plans.* The manager sets objectives jointly with each individual employee.[26] The objectives are the heart of the MBO process and should be accurate measures of performance results. To be accurate, objectives should be SMART.[27] They need to be *Specific, Measurable, Attainable, Relevant,* and *Time-based.* Being specific, measurable, and time-based is fairly easy to determine in a written goal, but being attainable and relevant is more difficult. So we developed a model based on the work of Max E. Douglas with two examples in Model 8-1 that we can use when setting objectives for ourselves or with others.

Step 2. *Give feedback and evaluate performance.* Communication is the key factor in determining MBO's success or failure, and employees should continually critique their own performance.[28] Thus, the manager and employee must communicate often to review progress.[29] The frequency of evaluations depends on the individual and the job performed. However, most managers do not conduct enough review sessions.

Step 3. *Reward according to performance.* Employees' performance should be measured against their objectives. Employees who meet their objectives should be rewarded through recognition, praise, pay raises, promotions, and so on.[30] Employees who do not meet their goals, so long as the reason is not out of their control, usually have rewards withheld and even punishment when necessary.

WORK
APPLICATION 8-5

Select a job you have or had. Did your boss use critical incidents? Assess how well your boss used coaching between formal performance appraisal meetings to review your performance.

Model 8-1	Setting Objectives Model

1. To + 2. Action Verb + 3. Specific and Measureable Result + 4. Target Date

    To + produce + 20 units + per day

    To increase widget productivity 5% by December 31, 2014.

Narrative Method or Form

The **narrative method or form** *requires a manager to write a statement about the employee's performance.* There often is no actual standard form used, but there can be a form, so narrative can be a method or a form.

Why and when do we use the narrative method or form? A narrative gives managers the opportunity to give their evaluative assessment in a written form that can go beyond a simple "check of a box" to describe an assessment item. Managers can also write up a developmental plan of how the employee will improve performance in the future. Narratives can be used alone, but are often combined with another method or form. Although the narrative is ongoing, it is commonly used during the formal review.

How do we use the narrative method or form? The system can vary. Managers may be allowed to write whatever they want (method), or they may be required to answer questions with a written narrative about the employee's performance (form). Let's discuss both here.

The no-form narrative method can be the only assessment method used during the formal review process. But the narrative method, when used alone, is more commonly used with professionals and executives, not operative employees. How we write the formal narrative assessment varies, as writing content and styles are different. A narrative based on critical incidents and MBO results is clearly the best basis for the written assessment.

The narrative is also often used as part of a form. For example, you have most likely seen an assessment form (such as a recommendation) that has a list of items to be checked off. Following the checklist, the form may ask one or more questions requiring a narrative written statement.

Graphic Rating Scale Form

The **graphic rating scale form** *is a performance appraisal checklist on which a manager simply rates performance on a continuum such as* excellent, good, average, fair, *and* poor. The continuum often includes a numerical scale, for example from 1 (*lowest performance level*) to 5 (*highest performance level*). Self-Assessment and Skill Builder 8-1 uses a graphic rating scale form; it is found at the end of this chapter.

Why and when do we use the graphic rating scale form? Graphic rating scales are probably the most commonly used form during the formal performance appraisal (primarily for evaluative decisions), but they should lead to development decisions as well. Why the popularity? Because graphic rating scales can be used for many different types of jobs, they are a kind of "one form fits all" form that requires minimal time, effort, cost, and training. If we walk into an office supply store, we can find pads of them. But on the negative side, graphic rating scales are not very accurate measures of performance because the selection of one rating over another, such as an excellent versus good rating, is very subjective. For example, think about professors and how they measure performance with grades. Some give lots of work and few As, while others give less work and almost all As.

How do we use the graphic rating scale form? It is very simple, and we have most likely all used one. For example, many colleges have student assessments of professors at the end of the course. All we do is check off, or usually fill in a circle for, our rating. One problem is that some of us don't bother to actually read the questions. Based on our biases, some of us just go down the list checking the same rating regardless of actual performance on the item. To be fair, this problem is not common with managers formally evaluating their employees. However, it does tend to occur when customers evaluate products and services, including student assessments of professors.

To overcome this problem, which is unfortunately not commonly done, we can reverse the scale from good to poor on different questions. Why isn't this done all the time? Some HR, or other, managers who make the scales do not know they should do this. Some who do know they should reverse the scales don't because they don't want to end up with overall ratings being pushed to the middle because people don't read the questions.

There shouldn't be any surprises or lack of agreement on performance levels during the formal performance appraisal interview.

Behaviorally Anchored Rating Scale (BARS) Form

The **Behaviorally Anchored Rating Scale (BARS) form** is *a performance appraisal that provides a description of each assessment along a continuum.* Like with rating scales, the continuum often includes a numerical scale from low to high.

Why and when do we use the BARS form? The answer to why and when is the same as for graphic rating scales. So let's focus on the differences between graphic rating scale and BARS forms. BARS forms overcome the problem of subjectivity by providing an actual description of the performance for each rating along the continuum, rather than one simple word (*excellent, good,* etc.) like graphic rating scales. A description of each level of performance makes the assessment a more objective accurate measure. So if BARS forms are more accurate, why aren't they more commonly used than graphic rating scale forms?

It's partly economics and partly expertise. Again, the graphic rating scale can be used for many different jobs, but BARS forms have to be customized to every different type of job. And developing potentially hundreds of different BARS forms takes a lot of time (which costs money) and expertise. Even when a firm has an HR staff, the question becomes whether developing BARS forms is the most effective use of staff members' time. Obviously, it depends on the types of jobs being evaluated and the resources available to complete the evaluation process.

How do we use BARS forms? Like graphic rating scales, we simply select a level of performance along the continuum. College accreditation associations are requiring more measures of student outcomes as assurance of learning, and as part of the process they want more BARS rubrics as evidence. So in college courses, especially for written assignments, professors give out rubrics that describe in some detail the difference between excellent (A), good (B), average (C), poor (D), and not acceptable (F) grades for multiple criteria put together to provide a final grade. Here is a very simple example of making a graphic rating scale item into the more objective BARS form.

Attendance—excellent, good, average, fair, poor
Attendance—number of days missed 1, 2, 3–4, 5, 6 or more

Ranking Method

The **ranking method** is *a performance appraisal method that is used to evaluate employee performance from best to worst.* There often is no actual standard form used, and we don't always have to rank all employees.

Why and when do we use the ranking method? Managers have to make evaluative decisions, such as who is the employee of the month, who gets a raise or promotion, and who gets laid off. So when we have to make evaluative decisions, we generally have to use ranking. However, our ranking can, and when possible should, be based on other methods and forms.

Ranking can also be used for developmental purposes by letting employees know where they stand in comparison to their peers—they can be motivated to improve performance. For example, when one of the authors passes back exams, he places the grade distribution on the board. It does not in any way affect the current grades—but it lets students know where they stand, and he does it to motivate improvement.

How do we use the ranking method? Under the ranking method, the manager compares an employee to other similar employees, rather than to a standard measurement. An offshoot of ranking is the forced distribution method, which is similar to grading on a curve. Predetermined percentages of employees are placed in various performance categories, for example, *excellent,* 5%; *above average,* 15%; *average,* 60%; *below average,* 15%; and *poor,* 5%. The employees ranked in the top group usually get the rewards (raise, bonus, promotion), those not at the top tend to have the reward withheld, and those at the bottom sometimes get punished. In Self-Assessment and Skill Builder 8-1, you are asked to rank the performance of your peers.

Which Option Is Best?

While this section does not contain an exhaustive list, it provides examples of each major method of performance appraisal. Determining the best appraisal method or form to use depends on the objectives of the organization. A combination of the methods and forms is usually superior to any one used by itself. For developmental objectives, the critical incidents, MBO, and narrative methods work well. For administrative decisions, a ranking method based on the evaluative methods and especially graphic rating scale or BARS forms works well.

Remember that the success of the performance appraisal process does not just lie in the formal method or form used once or twice a year. It depends on the manager's human relations skills in ongoing critical incidents coaching, and on effective measures of performance that are accurate so that everyone knows why they are rated at a given level (evaluative), as well as how to improve (develop) for the next assessment.[31]

PerformanceReview.com is a website that has been designed to help managers write complete and effective performance appraisals online. The site offers practical advice to guide managers through the appraisal process.[32]

Who Should Assess Performance?

Now that we've learned the why, what, and how of the performance appraisal process, the next thing we need to discuss is options for the rater, or evaluator. There are a number of different options concerning who should evaluate the individual employee, and the decision needs to be based on a series of factors. Let's take a look at our options for who should evaluate an employee.

WORK
APPLICATION 8-6

Select an organization, preferably one you work or have worked for. Identify and briefly describe the assessment methods and/or forms that are used to assess employee performance.

SHRM

Guide – F:2
Sources of Information (e.g., managers, peers, clients)

8-3 APPLYING THE CONCEPT

Appraisal Methods and Forms

Which of the following assessments is being described in each of the given situations?

a. critical incidents method
b. MBO method
c. narrative method or form

d. BARS form
e. graphic rating scale form
f. ranking method

_____ 11. One of your employees has applied for a better job at another company and asked you for a letter of recommendation.

_____ 12. You are overworked, so you want to develop a performance appraisal form you can use with all 25 of your employees who do a variety of jobs.

_____ 13. You have been promoted from a supervisory position to a middle management position. You have been asked to select your replacement.

_____ 14. One of your employees is not performing up to standard. You decide to talk to her in order to improve her performance.

_____ 15. You want to create a system for developing each of your employees individually.

Supervisor

LO 8.6

Identify and briefly discuss available options for the rater/evaluator.

When we ask who should evaluate employees, the most common response is their immediate supervisor. Why would the supervisor be the best person to evaluate an employee? Well, the supervisor is supposed to know what the employee should be doing, right? Certainly, supervisors are frequently one of the best and most commonly used options to choose as evaluators for the employees under their control. However, this is not always the case due to problems with supervisor performance assessments.

Problems with supervisor evaluations. What if the supervisor doesn't see the employee very frequently? This may not be all that uncommon in a modern organization. Many times today, supervisors may be in a different building or even a different city than the individuals they supervise. Virtual teams, Internet-linked offices, telecommuting, and other factors cause supervisors to not be in constant touch with their employees, unlike the situation 20 or 30 years ago.

There are other problems as well. What if there's a personality conflict? Supervisors are human, just like their employees, and may just not relate well to some of their employees. This may cause a personal bias for, or against, certain employees that may invalidate the appraisal process if it's significant enough.

What if the supervisor doesn't know what employees are supposed to be doing in their jobs? Aren't supervisors always supposed to know every job for which they are responsible? Again, 30 years ago this may have been true. However, in today's work environment, with the amount of information necessary to do the complex tasks that organizations must accomplish in order to compete, nobody can know every job. There's just too much information for any one individual to learn. So jobs have been segmented down into smaller and smaller areas, and the supervisor may not know each of those jobs in great detail. So there are certainly problems that can occur in the case of a supervisor being responsible for a subordinate employee's evaluation process. This being the case, what other options do we have?

Avoiding supervisor review problems. A simple answer to overcome these problems is to have others, in addition to the supervisor, assess performance. Also, multiple measures can make a performance assessment more accurate. For example, using other evaluators can help overcome personal bias and provide information that supervisors don't always know about.

Peers

As discussed, the supervisor is not always knowledgeable enough to make a valid assessment of employee performance. Another possible option is to use coworkers or peers of the individual employee as appraisers. When would it be valuable to use peer evaluations in an organization? If the supervisor is absent or has infrequent contact with the employees, but all employees have multiple coworkers that they interact with on a frequent basis, peer evaluations may be valuable. Peers or coworkers also often know the job of the individual employee better than the supervisor does, and they are more directly affected by the employee's actions, either positive or negative. In addition, peers can evaluate the ability of the individual to interact with others successfully in a group or team setting. This may be very difficult for supervisors to see unless they are intimately involved with the group.

Problems with peer reviews. There are certainly issues that can come up in peer evaluations that can cause the process to become less objective. In fact, research evidence regarding the validity of peer evaluations is really unclear.[33] Personality conflicts and personal biases can affect how individual employees rate their peers. Individuals within a group or team may just have significantly different personality types, and these differences can cause friction within the work group that may spill over when it comes time to evaluate those with whom they are in conflict. Additionally, no matter how much we try and protect against it, personal biases can affect working relationships and may show up in peer evaluations.

Avoiding peer review problems. Because we know that these problems can occur within a peer evaluation, the organization can take the issues into account and adjust rating values as necessary. For example, assume you are the manager of a work group of six people who in your opinion work very well together and provide a quality work product, and you review a set of peer evaluations from the work group. In your review you notice that two of the members of the group gave each other significantly lower-than-average grades—one of the two is a young male, and the other is an older female. However, the other four members of the group gave both of them good marks for their contributions to the group.

This quite likely is a situation where a personality conflict has occurred between the two members, which caused them to lower each other's grades. Knowing that the other four members of the group evaluated these two individuals as valued members of the team, you may want to adjust the individual ratings from the two individuals to more closely match the overall evaluations from the team, noting that it appears that a personality conflict may have lowered their individual grades of each other. Even with the potential for personality conflicts and bias, peer evaluations can give us good insight into the inner workings of a group or team when the supervisor has infrequent contact with the team. In Self-Assessment and Skill Builder 8-1, you will do a performance assessment of your peers.

Subordinates

Our next available option is the subordinates of an individual supervisor in the firm. We would typically only use subordinate evaluators for manager-level employees. However, who within the firm knows, and suffers the consequences of, the actions of supervisors more than the people who work for them? Subordinate evaluations can give us good insight into the managerial practices and potential missteps of people who control other employees in our organization. As a result, subordinate evaluations may give us valuable information that we would be unable to find out using any other means.

Problems with subordinate reviews. Can subordinate evaluations cause a problem within the department or work group? Is the potential for bias, especially from subordinates who have been disciplined by the supervisor, significant in this type of evaluation? Of course there is a potential for bias. Obviously, the subordinates may try to get back at their supervisor for giving them tasks that they did not want to perform, or for disciplining them for failure in their jobs.

There may be a personality conflict, or some subordinates certainly may be biased against their supervisor or manager. So there are certainly negative aspects to subordinate evaluations. On the other end of the scale, the subordinates may inflate the capabilities of the manager, at least partly because of a lack of understanding of all the tasks and duties required of the manager. In fact, in a recent survey, about two thirds of employees rated their managers higher than the managers' self-ratings.[34]

Avoiding subordinate review problems. In all of these problem areas, if we know that there is a potential problem, we can most likely guard against it. In many cases, as we go through a group of subordinate evaluations, we will see one or two outliers providing either very high or very low marks for the supervisor. In such a case we should probably throw those outliers out of the calculation when determining overall marks for the supervisor. It's honestly surprising how often these outliers are extremely easy to spot in a subordinate evaluation process.

Another significant issue in the case of subordinate evaluations is confidentiality. Subordinate evaluations *must* be confidential in nature, or it is unlikely that the subordinates will provide an honest evaluation of their supervisor. Why is this the case? Obviously, if the evaluation is not confidential, the supervisor can and may take retribution on subordinates who provide unflattering evaluations. So, if the evaluation is not anonymous, many of the subordinates will likely inflate the capabilities of the supervisor, which minimizes the value of the evaluation process itself. So, even though subordinate evaluations have the potential for biases and other problems, we can help to overcome these problems, and they can provide us with valuable information about the supervisor's capabilities.

Self

Self-assessment is also an option in the performance appraisal process, or is it? Virtually all employees do a self-assessment whether they are actually formally asked to do so as part of the assessment or not. It is required with MBO. Even when not asked to do a self-assessment, employees will still walk into the review discussion with some informal self-assessment that they compare to the supervisor's rating. But are self-evaluations valuable, or will the employees overestimate their individual capabilities and tell us that they're perfect? (As you know, every chapter of this book has one or more self-assessments, and the one for this chapter is Self-Assessment and Skill Builder 8-1; it is at the end of the chapter. You will assess your performance on a group project. If you want to, you can do the self-assessment now.)

Problems with self-assessments. *Most* of the research evidence shows that self-assessments tend to overestimate the individual's ability to do a job.[35] However, some of the research says that employees either underestimate or accurately estimate their job performance over time. A significant portion of the evidence seems to show that individuals with lower levels of knowledge and skills within their field tend to inflate their self-assessment of their abilities.[36] Conversely, as individuals become more knowledgeable and more skilled, the evidence tends to show that they will either accurately estimate or even underestimate their capabilities in their jobs.[37,38,39]

Avoiding self-assessment problems. Based on the fact that most of the evidence shows that employees overestimate their ability to do their job, is this a valid performance measure? Here again, even though the measure may have validity concerns, if we know that self-evaluations tend to be skewed, we can most likely adjust for this factor. In addition, receiving information from individuals concerning their perception of their skill set is extremely valuable in a number of management processes, including plans for training and development opportunities, providing work assignments, and counseling and disciplinary measures, among others. A big step in overcoming self-assessment problems, as well as other assessment problems, is the Blanchard test—do the employees understand why they are assessed at a specific level (evaluation) and what it takes to get a higher rating (development)?[40]

Customers

We may also want to ask customers to evaluate individuals within the company. We use the word *customers* in a broad sense to include people outside the organization, including customers for our products and services and suppliers to the firm. Customers can also be internal including people in other departments of the firm—for example, the print shop that makes copies for other departments or the mail room that receives and delivers communications and products to the rest of the firm.

When and why would we want to use customers in the evaluation process? We may want to use customers as evaluators when the individual being evaluated has frequent contact with organizational customers, either internal or external to the firm. If employees interact routinely with internal or external customers, we need to know how the customers feel about their interactions with the employees because obviously external customers are the ones who ultimately pay the bills.

It does not matter what else we do successfully if our customers are uncomfortable with their interactions with our employees. If *external* customers are upset about their interactions with our employees, they have the ability to go elsewhere with their business. Even *internal* customers can create significant problems within the firm due to conflict between departments or divisions. So we want to ask customers to evaluate the individuals with whom they come into contact.

Problems with customer assessments. What do you think the major problem is with customer-based evaluations? One problem is that customer assessments commonly use simple rating scales, which we discussed as being very subjective. Also, customers are usually not trained to do an accurate assessment. So bias is a problem. For these and other reasons, the popular opinion is that customer evaluations are almost always skewed to the negative. However, research shows that this is not necessarily the case.[41] In some situations, customer evaluations actually exceed evaluations of the individual that are internal to the firm or department.

Avoiding customer assessment problems. Regardless of whether or not customers will tell us when we're doing an exceptional or acceptable job, customer evaluations provide us with valuable information concerning our employees who have direct customer contact. If this is the case, can we adjust the evaluation process knowing that customer evaluations are frequently skewed either positively or negatively? Obviously, we can. One of the basic methods of adjusting the customer evaluation process is to compare the individuals being evaluated and identify the ratios of negative and positive comments to allow us to identify more successful and less successful employees. Although this is an imperfect measure, it still provides value to the firm in the fact that customers' perception is critical to our relationship with them. So, we need to measure this relationship.

WORK
APPLICATION 8-7

Select your current or a past job. Identify who had input into your performance appraisal.

360° Evaluation

LO 8.7

Briefly discuss the value and the drawbacks of a 360° evaluation.

As a final option, we can do "all of the above." The **360° evaluation**, in effect, *analyzes individuals' performance from all sides—from their supervisor's viewpoint, from their subordinates' viewpoint, from customers' viewpoint (if applicable), from their peers' viewpoint,* *and using their own self-evaluation.* Obviously, the 360° evaluation would give us the most accurate, best possible analysis of individuals and their performance within the company. **DuPont** developed 360° reviews back in 1973, but they are still popular today.[42] With the trend of structuring work in teams, peer evaluations are now being used regularly.[43] Those who fill out the appraisal form usually do so confidentially. The feedback from all these people is used to evaluate and develop the employee.

Problems with 360° evaluations. If they are the best, then why don't we always use 360° evaluations? The simple answer is "time and money." It takes a significant amount of time for a group of individuals to evaluate one person if we use a 360° format. By using up so much organizational time, it obviously also costs us a significant amount of money. If we multiply the numbers based on the time required to evaluate one individual to count everyone in the organization, the costs can quickly become massive.

Avoiding problems with 360° degree evaluations. Unfortunately, there really is no simple way to avoid such problems, besides what is commonly done—not using 360° evaluations. When used, the 360° evaluation format tends to be most valuable if it is used for purposes of individual development, rather than for making administrative evaluative decisions.[44] A good 360° feedback system can provide specific suggestions about how to improve individual competencies.[45] It can also go a long way toward minimizing some of the most common problems with the performance appraisal process, which we will review next.

Who Do We Choose?

Now that we know our options for who should conduct an evaluation of each employee, which option should we use? Again, we need to remember that each of the options costs us money because it takes time for the individual who must perform the appraisal. So, we need to determine which option or options to use. We can use any of these methods combined with any other, all the way up to the point of the 360° evaluation. However, we only want to use a 360° evaluation when it's worth it. If it's not necessary, then it doesn't make a lot of sense due to the cost of this method.

For instance, is there any need to do a 360° evaluation of janitorial or housekeeping staff? Does this make sense? Obviously, in this case we probably don't need to do this type of evaluation. In most cases, with low-level staff members, a supervisor's evaluation is sufficient. We also make this statement because the evaluation is often more than just a supervisor's biased opinion. Even though only the supervisor does the formal assessment, the supervisor often does get informal feedback regarding performance from customers and peers during conversations. Customers will often complain to the supervisor if the service is not satisfactory, and peers will complain about a fellow employee who is not meeting standards for some reason. The supervisor's critical incident file is often written based on information received from peers and customers.

What about the case of an outside salesperson? In this situation, the results tend to speak for themselves. Sales numbers are available to the salesperson and manager. Where the supervisor rarely sees the individual but the customer interacts with our salesperson on a routine basis, we can ask the customer to do an evaluation of the salesperson as well as asking the salesperson for a self-appraisal. With the sales figures, a self-assessment, and customer feedback, we can develop a plan to increase future performance.

Finally, if we are evaluating the marketing manager for the firm, we may want to do a 360° evaluation because this individual would affect all of the groups—subordinates, customers, peers, the organization, and himself or herself. So, we evaluate the specific situation and use the number of methods necessary to get an accurate assessment of the individual.

Once again, we need to do a cost-benefit analysis to determine when the benefits of increasing performance outweigh the cost to give us a return on our investment. In essence, we attempt to maximize performance while minimizing the total cost of the appraisal process.

LO 8.8

Identify some of the common problems with the performance appraisal process.

WORK
APPLICATION 8-8

Select an organization, preferably one you work or have worked for. Identify some of the positions and people who should be evaluated using 360° evaluations. Briefly describe your cost-versus-benefit analysis to justify your selection.

Performance Appraisal Problems to Avoid

During the performance appraisal process, there are common problems that we face. However, knowing these common problems, we can take measures to avoid them. So in this section we discuss the problems first with simple ways to avoid each of them as an individual. Then we discuss what the organization can do to overcome these problems on an organization-wide basis. We can actually overcome multiple problems with the same method. See Exhibit 8-3 for a list of problems and ways to avoid them.

SHRM

Guide – F:3
Rater Errors in Performance
Measurement

Common Problems With the Performance Appraisal Process

Let's briefly discuss each of the common problems during the performance appraisal process listed in Exhibit 8-3 here.

Bias. **Bias** is simply *a personality-based tendency, either toward or against something.* In the case of performance assessment, bias is toward or against an individual employee. All human beings have biases, but supervisors especially cannot afford to allow their biases to enter into their evaluation of subordinates in the firm. This is very easy to say, but very difficult to do. Biases make the evaluation process subjective rather than objective, and certainly provide the opportunity for a lack of consistency in effect on different groups of employees. So to overcome the bias problem, we need to be objective and not let our feelings of liking or disliking the individual influence our assessment.

Stereotyping. **Stereotyping** is *mentally classifying a person into an affinity group, and then identifying the person as having the same assumed characteristics as the group.* Though stereotyping is almost always assumed to be negative, there are many incidents of positive stereotypes. However, regardless of whether the stereotype is positive or negative, making bership in a group, rather than explicitly identifying the characteristics of the individuals, creates the potential for significant error in evaluations. So we can avoid stereotyping by getting to know each employee as an individual and objectively evaluating individual employees based on their actual performance.

Halo error. This error occurs when the evaluator has a *generally* positive or negative (negative halo error is sometimes called "horns error") impression of an individual, and the evaluator then artificially extends that general impression to many individual categories of performance to create an overall evaluation of the individual that is either positive or negative.[46] In other words, if employees are judged by their supervisor to be generally "good" employees, and the supervisor then evaluates each of the areas of their performance as

| Exhibit 8-3 | Performance Appraisal Problems and Avoiding Them |

Common Problems	Avoiding Problems
Bias	Develop Accurate Performance Measures
Stereotyping	Use Multiple Criteria
Halo Error	Minimize the Use of Trait-Based Evaluations
Distributional Errors	Use the OUCH and Blanchard Tests
Similarity Error	Train Your Evaluators
Proximity Error	Use Multiple Raters
Recency Error	
Contrast Error	
Attribution Error	

good, regardless of any behaviors or results to the contrary, the supervisor is guilty of halo error. We can avoid halo error by remembering that employees are often strong in some areas and weaker in others, and we need to objectively evaluate individual employees based on their actual performance for each and every item of assessment.

Distributional errors. These errors occur in three forms: severity or strictness, central tendency, and leniency. They are based on a standard normal distribution, or the bell curve that we are all so familiar with. In *severity or strictness* error, the rater evaluates everyone, or nearly everyone, as below average. *Central tendency* error occurs when raters evaluate everyone under their control as average—nobody is either really good or really bad. Finally, *leniency* error occurs when the rater evaluates all others as above average. Leniency error, therefore, is basically a form of grade inflation. We can avoid distributional errors by giving a range of evaluations. The distribution is often based on the ranking method of evaluation and forced distribution.

Similarity error. This error occurs when raters evaluate subordinates that they consider more similar to themselves as better employees, and subordinates that they consider different from themselves as poorer employees. We all have a tendency to feel more comfortable with people who we feel are more similar to ourselves,[47] and if we are not careful, we can allow this feeling of comfort with similar individuals to be reflected in the performance appraisal process. We can avoid similarity error by embracing diversity and objectively evaluating individual employees based on their actual performance, even if they are different from us and don't do things the same way that we do.

Proximity error. This error states that similar marks may be given to items that are near (proximate to) each other on the performance appraisal form, regardless of differences in performance on those measures. We can avoid proximity error by objectively evaluating employees' actual performance on each and every item on the assessment form.

Recency error. This error occurs when raters use only the last few weeks or month of a rating period as evidence of their ratings of others. For instance, if a warehouse worker has been a strong performer for most of the appraisal period, but right before his annual evaluation he knocks over a stack of high-cost electronic equipment while driving a forklift, he may be rated poorly due to recency error. We can avoid the recency error by evaluating the employee based on the entire assessment period, commonly 6–12 months. Using the critical incidents method really helps our recall and assessment of the entire period more objectively.

Contrast error. In contrast error, the rater compares and contrasts performance between two employees, rather than using absolute measures of performance to measure each employee. For example, the rater may contrast a good performer with an outstanding performer, and as a result of the significant contrast, the good performer may seem to be "below average." This would be a contrast error. We can avoid contrast error by objectively evaluating individual employees based on their actual performance. We must use the ranking method correctly; first we assess each individual based on the items on the assessment form—then we rank the individuals based on their assessments.

Attribution error. In simplified terms, attribution is a process where an individual *assumes* reasons or motivations (such as attitudes, values, or beliefs) for an observed behavior. So, attribution error in performance appraisal might occur when the rater observes an employee action—such as an argumentative answer to a question—and assumes that the individual has a negative attitude toward the job and is a poor performer. This may not be true, and in such a case the rater would be guilty of an attribution error. We need to avoid attribution error because it is based on our subjective conclusion. When in doubt, we shouldn't assume we know why the employee did or didn't do something. We should talk to employees to find out so that we can objectively evaluate employees based on their actual performance.

WORK
APPLICATION 8-9

Identify the major steps we can take to avoid problems with the appraisal process.

8-4 APPLYING THE CONCEPT

Avoiding Appraisal Problems

Which of the following common problems or errors is being described in each of the given situations?

a.   bias
b.   stereotyping
c.   halo error
d.   distributional errors
e.   similarity error

f.   proximity error
g.   recency error
h.   contrast error
i.   attribution error

_____ 16.   My year's performance was not going very well. So I made sure to really push and do a good job for the month of December, and I got a good performance review.

_____ 17.   I did a really good job of coming to all the classes and participating in the discussions, so the professor gave me an A- even though my test-score average was a B+.

_____ 18.   I got an average rating, which is lower than I deserve, because my boss found out I was talking about him behind his back.

_____ 19.   I'm tired of hearing how much Juan is selling and being told I don't measure up.

_____ 20.   My boss gave me a good overall rating instead of an excellent rating. I told her I thought I deserve excellent, but she said everyone gets a good rating and that I'm doing a very good job.

Avoiding Performance Appraisal Process Problems

LO 8.9

Identify the major steps we can take to avoid problems with the appraisal process.

As you can see above, there are a significant number of ways that performance appraisals can fail to provide an accurate assessment of the capabilities and the behaviors of individual employees. Thus far we have only provided simple things we can do to overcome these problems as individuals. How can a firm avoid these problems on an organization-wide basis throughout the performance appraisal process?

Luckily, there are a number of fairly simple steps that we can take within the organization to minimize the negative issues that occur in the performance appraisal process. All we have to do is look at the problems noted, and we can fairly quickly come up with some possible solutions to at least the majority of those problems using the same methods. Let's discuss how the firm can limit the potential for the appraisal process to go astray by developing accurate performance measures, training evaluators, and using multiple raters.

Develop Accurate Performance Measures

As discussed earlier in this chapter, if the performance appraisal methods and forms are not accurate measures, the entire performance appraisal process will have problems. Therefore, the organization should have its own HR specialist or hire consultants to develop the assessment process and measures. Now, let's discuss three things HR specialists commonly do to help ensure accurate measures.

Use multiple criteria. One method of overcoming some of the problems with the appraisal process is to ensure that we use more than one or two criteria to evaluate an individual's performance over time. We should generally have at least one evaluation criterion for each major function within an individual job. As we noted earlier, behaviors and results that occur over the entire course of the evaluation period are typically the best criteria to use in the process of evaluating an individual's performance, but employees behave in many different ways in different circumstances throughout the course of a year, so we shouldn't limit the appraisal process to one or two actions on the part of that individual employee. By evaluating multiple criteria, we have the ability to lower the incidence of halo, recency, contrast, and attribution errors, and may even be able to affect bias and stereotyping, because many criteria, not just one or two, are being analyzed.

Minimize the use of trait-based evaluations. Our next method of overcoming problems within the appraisal process is to minimize the evaluation of individual traits. As we noted in the section on what we have the ability to evaluate, trait-based evaluations tend to be more subjective than behavior- or results-based evaluations and as a result should generally not be used unless there is a specific reason why the particular trait must be exhibited in order to be successful in a job. Only when we have *specific reason* for trait-based evaluations should those traits be measured and evaluated in the appraisal process.

In addition, because of their subjectivity, trait-based evaluations are much more difficult to defend in cases where the organization used the evaluation process for later disciplinary action with an individual employee. By minimizing the evaluation of traits, we lower the incidence of bias, stereotyping, similarity error, and potentially attribution error. So, minimizing trait evaluations lowers the ability of the rater to make some of the most significant mistakes that can occur in the appraisal process.

Give the measures the OUCH and Blanchard tests. Yes. We already stated this with each of the three types of assessment. But these two tests are so important to successful accurate measures that we are repeating them again. With the OUCH test, is the measure objective, uniform in application, and consistent in effect, and does it have job relatedness? With the Blanchard test, does everyone understand why they are assessed at a specific level (evaluation) and what it takes to get a higher rating (development)?[48]

Train Evaluators

Once we have accurate measurement methods and forms, the next thing that we should do to help overcome some of the issues with the appraisal process is to train our evaluators concerning the common errors and problems that occur and how to use the methods and forms.

Train evaluators to overcome the common problems of assessment. Simply through the process of training, many of the common problems are mitigated, if not eliminated. Once evaluators become aware that the common errors occur with some regularity, they almost immediately begin to evaluate such errors and guard against them. Even the bias and stereotyping errors *may* be mitigated through the rater training process. As we've said several times in this book, most of our employees want to do a good job, and once they know that an error is being committed, they will make attempts to correct that error. So, rater training provides them with knowledge of these errors and allows them the opportunity to correct them.

Train evaluators to use the measurement methods and forms. Evaluators should also be trained to use the various performance assessment methods and forms. Because the critical incidents method is not commonly used as a formal assessment method, evaluators should be taught to use it to help overcome recency error. Evaluators need training to effectively use MBO and to write a good narrative. When a rating scale is used, some training should be given to better understand the differences between the word descriptors along the continuum (*excellent, good,* etc.). BARS and ranking forms are fairly straightforward, but when they are used, some training can help overcome problems.

Use Multiple Raters

The next tool to minimize errors in the evaluation process, at least in some cases, is to use multiple raters to evaluate an individual. As we noted earlier, this becomes expensive very quickly, so we must decide whether or not the value inherent in using multiple evaluators

LO 8.10

Briefly discuss the differences between evaluative performance reviews and developmental performance reviews.

WORK
APPLICATION 8-10

Select your current or a past job. Identify and explain how it did or did not use each of the three methods organizations can use to overcome common problems during the performance appraisal process. How could it improve the process?

overcomes the cost of the process. If it does, using multiple evaluators can conquer some significant problems in the appraisal process. What will the process of using multiple evaluators do to improve the appraisal process? Multiple evaluators limit the ability of one individual appraiser to provide a biased opinion concerning an employee's performance, as well as limiting the ability for stereotyping in the appraisal process. In addition, halo, similarity, contrast, and attribution errors become less likely, and distributional errors tend to even out among multiple raters. It is for these reasons that 360° evaluations have gained favor in many organizations over the past 20 years.

Debriefing the Appraisal

The debriefing process is where we communicate the analysis of each individual's performance with that person. Earlier in the chapter, we noted that there are two major reasons for assessing performance: for evaluative decisions and for development. We also suggested breaking the formal performance appraisal debriefing into two separate interviews. In this section, we describe how to conduct both reviews.

The Evaluative Performance Appraisal Interview

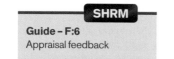

SHRM

Guide – F:6
Appraisal feedback

Planning ahead is critical when it comes to performance appraisal interviews. Therefore, this section is separated into preparing for and conducting the evaluative interview. Because the evaluative interview is the basis for the developmental interview, it should be conducted first.

Preparing for an Evaluative Interview

When preparing for an evaluative interview, follow the steps outlined in Model 8-2. Our evaluation should be fair (ethically and legally not based on any of the problems discussed).[49] If we have had regular coaching conversations with our employees, they know where they stand,[50] and our preparation is mostly done except the form. So our relationship with an employee will directly affect the outcome.[51] Employees should also critique their own performance through a self-assessment using the form.[52]

So Step 1 of Model 8-2 is to simply set up the meeting. Step 2 has employees use the form to conduct a self-assessment of their performance, and in Step 3 we, too, assess employees' performance using the form. In keeping with the balanced evaluation, in Step 4, we identify both strengths and areas for improvement that serve as the basis for the developmental interview. Last, Step 5 is to predict employee reactions to our assessment and plan how to handle them. Using critical incidents will help support our assessment when employees disagree. Don't forget the Blanchard test states that we should be able to explain, and agree on, the employee's level of performance.

▶ Video Link 8.2

Prepare for the Evaluative Interview

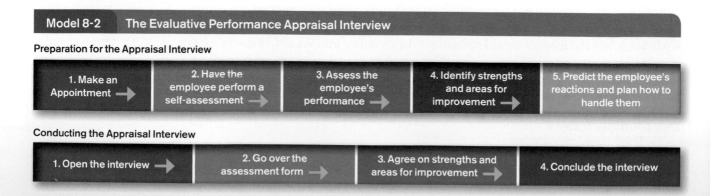

Model 8-2	The Evaluative Performance Appraisal Interview

Preparation for the Appraisal Interview

1. Make an Appointment →	2. Have the employee perform a self-assessment →	3. Assess the employee's performance →	4. Identify strengths and areas for improvement →	5. Predict the employee's reactions and plan how to handle them

Conducting the Appraisal Interview

1. Open the interview →	2. Go over the assessment form →	3. Agree on strengths and areas for improvement →	4. Conclude the interview

Conducting an Evaluative Interview

During the interview, encourage employees to talk and listen to the critique of their performance.[53] Model 8-2 lists the steps for conducting an evaluative performance appraisal interview. We open the meeting with some small talk to put the person at ease in Step 1. Then in Step 2 we go over our evaluation of the items on the assessment form. For Step 3, we identify the employee's strengths and weaknesses, and discuss and agree on them. Our last Step 4 is to conclude the interview, which may be to make the appointment for the developmental interview.

When we are the employee, we should be open to negative feedback, even if we don't agree with it. We shouldn't make excuses or blame others. If we don't agree with the assessment, we should say something like "Thanks for the feedback, but I don't agree with it for the following reasons." Then we should give our objective reasons without being argumentative and disrespectful. We may want to schedule a follow-up meeting to have time to gather facts that support our stance on the assessment.[54]

The Developmental Performance Appraisal Interview

Again, planning ahead is critical when it comes to performance appraisal interviews. Therefore, this section is also separated into preparing for and conducting the interview.

Preparing for a Developmental Interview

After the employee's performance evaluation is completed, we should prepare for the developmental interview based on areas for improvement. Yes—managers are busy, and may question the need for coaching and cost of separate formal developmental interviews, but spending time developing employees leads to increased performance and lower turnover.[55] To do this, follow the steps in Model 8-3, which begins with simply setting up a time to conduct the review. As stated in Step 2, have employees come up with their own objectives and strategies for improvement,[56] and then develop objectives for them (in Step 3).

Conducting a Developmental Interview

The steps to follow when conducting a developmental performance appraisal interview are listed in Model 8-3. Again, we start with small talk to open the interview. In Step 2, it is important to agree on developmental objectives. As part of Step 3, employees need to know exactly what they must do to improve and increase the rating on the next review, and follow-up feedback on progress is essential for changing behavior.[57] So Step 4 is to set up a follow-up meeting to review progress. When conducting Steps 3 and 4, we don't want the employee working on too many things at once, so keep the number of objectives

WORK
APPLICATION 8-11

Assess how well your present or past boss helped develop your knowledge, skills, and competencies through informal coaching and/or the formal performance appraisal interview. Describe how the boss could improve.

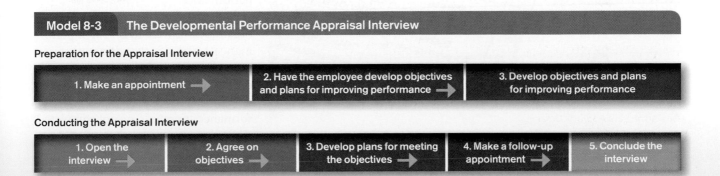

Model 8-3   The Developmental Performance Appraisal Interview

Preparation for the Appraisal Interview

| 1. Make an appointment → | 2. Have the employee develop objectives and plans for improving performance → | 3. Develop objectives and plans for improving performance |

Conducting the Appraisal Interview

| 1. Open the interview → | 2. Agree on objectives → | 3. Develop plans for meeting the objectives → | 4. Make a follow-up appointment → | 5. Conclude the interview |

between 1 and 3. We can always add new objectives later. We end in Step 5 by concluding the interview with some positive encouragement about reaching the objectives.

Trends and Issues in HRM

It's time to take a look at some of the trends and issues in performance appraisal over the past several years. The first item in this chapter's trends and issues is a question: Should we even be using performance appraisals? Second, we will take a look at Electronic Performance Monitoring or EPM—does it improve performance and add value to the organization's performance appraisal process by providing results-based evidence of employee productivity? Our third issue deals with the question of competency-based performance management, rather than the historical task-based evaluation of performance. And finally, we will discuss one method of aligning the organization's performance appraisals so that the variability between managers does not cause one group of employees to suffer relative to another group, due to the fact that the managers don't happen to evaluate consistently.

Is It Time to Do Away With Performance Appraisals?

Samuel Culbert, a clinical psychologist at the University of California at Los Angeles, has written a book called *Get Rid of the Performance Review!*[58] His premise is that performance appraisals are one-sided analyses by the manager of what the subordinate is doing wrong. He notes that if the process can become a two-way communication between the manager and the subordinate, a performance review becomes a "performance preview." The boss and the subordinate "have conversations" that allow the manager to become a coach and tutor for the subordinate.

However, if you take note of the purposes for performance appraisals that we identified early in this chapter, communication is one of the three main aims of the process. As we discussed, we need two-way communication between the supervisor and the subordinate. If it's one-way, the process has very little chance of improving the subordinate's performance over time.

A well-designed form can help managers do a good job during the formal performance appraisal.

In addition, one of our other purposes—motivation—also requires a continuing conversation between the supervisor and the subordinate—coaching. The performance management process does not occur one day a year. If it is going to be successful, it has to occur continuously throughout the year as the supervisor and the subordinate have conversations about ongoing performance.

The most significant problem, if organizations were to get rid of performance reviews, is that these appraisals are used legitimately by organizations in order to make good decisions about their employees and their development. If performance appraisals are not completed, the organization doesn't have valid and reliable information about the human resources in the organization and therefore has no ability to make good decisions about things such as training, promotions, pay raises, and other factors. Going back to the OUCH and Blanchard tests, in *any* personnel action within the organization we need to attempt to be as objective as possible.

An appraisal process that is done correctly (and most aren't) is an absolutely necessary piece if the organization is going to be objective in management of its human resources—one of the most critical pieces of organizational success today. In fact, what Culbert is really saying is if you are not going to do it right with accurate measures and coaching, don't do performance reviews. This is what good managers have been saying for the last 40 years. If we're going to be successful in improving employee performance over time, two-way conversations have to occur that allow employees to identify problems and issues that prevent them from being as successful as possible—coaching. If coaching occurs, individual performance is almost certain to increase, and as a result organizational performance will increase overall over the course of time. We will discuss how to coach in the next chapter.

Technology: Electronic Performance Monitoring

Electronic Performance Monitoring (EPM) is *the process of observing ongoing employee actions using computers or other nonhuman methods.* The number of employees monitored through EPM has increased drastically in the past 20 years. In the early 1990s, about one third of employees were being monitored electronically. By 2001, approximately 78% were monitored electronically,[59] and in 2010 that number more than likely increased even more. The reason for this steep increase is that EPM apparently is an effective means of increasing productivity.[60] EPM allows management to know if employees are actually working or doing personal things during work hours. The biggest upside to EPM seems to be that it provides information for concrete results-based performance evaluations.

Certainly, this is a valuable, outcome. However, some researchers and practitioners argue against EPM because of a number of factors including ethical questions concerning such monitoring, legal concerns over employee privacy, and apparent increases in stress due to constant monitoring of performance. So, the question is whether or not organizations should use EPM systems.

There's no simple answer to such a question. Again, EPM has been shown to increase productivity, and organizations need to maximize employee productivity. However, increases in stress are known to decrease productivity if the stress level becomes too significant. So there's an obvious trade-off between more employee monitoring and controlling stress levels in our workforce. Management must understand this trade-off in order to successfully improve productivity in the organization overall.

In addition, the ethical and legal questions noted in the previous paragraph may be significant enough in some cases to cause individual employees to leave the organization. If these individuals are our more productive workers, and especially if they are knowledge workers, what does the loss of these knowledgeable individuals do to organizational productivity? There doesn't appear to be any current research-based answer to these questions. Therefore, because these questions exist, organizations must be very careful in how they implement EPM processes so that they improve their chances of reaching the stated goal of EPM—improving organizational productivity.

Finally, as these programs are rolled out in the organization, managers must be acutely aware of the potential for increased levels of stress as well as employee feelings concerning invasion of privacy that could lead to decreases in productivity and higher rates of turnover as well.[61] In other words, management must work to overcome the potential problems and costs in order to gain the benefits.

WORK
APPLICATION 8-12

Select an organization you work or have worked for. Does it use formal evaluations? Do you believe the organization should or should not conduct formal evaluations?

SHRM

Guide – F:4
Electronic monitoring

Competency-Based Performance Management

What is competency-based performance management? Historically, the performance appraisal process evaluates specific employee skills and the employee's success in using those skills to produce products or services for the organization. Competency-based performance, on the other hand, evaluates large sets of capabilities and knowledge which, if put to good use, can significantly improve organizational productivity to a much greater extent than just doing a job using an existing skill set. Or, using Chapter 7 terms, development is more effective than simply training.

Because jobs have been changing at a rapid pace over the past 20 years, competency-based performance management is becoming a more useful form for performance appraisal than the historical skill-based, transactional process. How are jobs changing? According to the Society for Human Resource Management (SHRM), the nature of work is changing from single-skilled jobs to multiskilled jobs, from repetitive tasks to problem-solving tasks, from individual work to teamwork, and from functional specialization to collaboration.[62] Taking a look at the ways in which work is changing, we can understand why it may be necessary for the organization to move from skill-based performance appraisal to evaluations based on larger-scale competencies.

Because competencies are becoming so significant in organizations, the performance management systems need to be redesigned so that we evaluate the skills and capabilities that are most important to the business. However, these types of performance management systems can present significant design challenges to the organization. To successfully use competency-based performance management, the organization has to move from an analysis and measurement of the *individual activities* within a process to a more holistic evaluation of the *ability to combine and improve activities* to create the most successful organizational outcomes.

SHRM notes that one of the problems with knowledge workers is that "performance analysts cannot directly observe much of what they do."[63] This being the case, new competency-based evaluation methods that measure the ability to manipulate and manage information and to collaborate across many dimensions must be designed and used.

SHRM explains that because the most common type of historical job (the individual repetitive job) is going away, the organization has an increasing need for competency-based evaluations. They also note that competency-based evaluations are necessary in order to align performance with rewards if the organization is going to use a competency-based pay and incentives program.[64] Competency-based pay programs have been shown to focus individual goals more closely to the organization's overall strategic goals. Because of all these factors, competency-based performance appraisals will likely continue to increase as a percentage of overall performance appraisal processes.

Aligning the Appraisal Process

The last of our trends and issues for Chapter 8 deals with problems that occur because of harder and easier individual evaluators causing the performance appraisal process to be inconsistent. But, what processes can be created in the organization that will minimize this inconsistency? There are two approaches.

One method is to gather all of the raters, within a given division, department, or section of the organization, in one place where they discuss each of the individuals being evaluated. A process called "calibration" provides the organization with a methodology for normalization of grades across raters.[65] Many organizations have done something similar to the process of calibration for years by gathering groups of managers together and, through a series of discussions, coming to an agreement on the rating of each of their employees.

Calibration is done face-to-face with a group of managers who are responsible for one division or department within the organization. However, the end result of the calibration process is not necessarily a ranking of employees. It is designed simply to standardize, or even out, evaluations between multiple managers. There are some issues with this process, though. If one manager is a better communicator or persuader than another, the process can still be inconsistent. Managers who are quiet, and who generally will not speak out in favor of or against something, may be at a disadvantage in these types of meetings. In order for a calibration or ranking meeting to be successful, all of the managers in the room must be given a chance to speak on behalf of their employees.

In fact, a professional facilitator may help to get individual managers the time to speak in support of their employees. There's no perfect method of ensuring that performance appraisals are consistent between different managers in the organization. However, open meetings where managers discuss each of their individual ratings can help to minimize the differences between raters.

On the other side, autocratically dictating a ranking process based on a forced distribution also helps overcome this problem of managers being too hard and easy in their evaluations. But not allowing managers to have input into the method of making raters more consistent in their assessments can lead to other problems within the performance appraisal process. So, two important questions must be considered in deciding on using participation in calibration or dictating a mandatory forced distribution.

First, what are the chances of getting the group of managers to agree on a calibration? If you know you have managers who very firmly disagree on assessment, one being very hard and another being very easy, maybe calibration will not work and could cause problems between managers. Second, dictating a forced distribution is faster and thus costs less. So do the benefits from participation in calibration outweigh the costs of the time and effort to use calibration? In a knowledge-based organization, the answer is often yes, but not always.

Wrap-Up

This chapter has covered the process of managing employee performance. What have we learned that will allow us to become better managers? We discussed the concept of performance management, and noted that it is a continuous process, not a once-a-year evaluation of performance. We then proceeded through a discussion of the steps in the performance appraisal process. We answered the question of why we even do them. Next we looked at what we evaluate—traits, behaviors, and results—and identified and then discussed how the evaluation is typically done using various assessment methods and forms. We then discussed options for who can complete the appraisal, why we would choose one option over others, and when a 360° evaluation is valuable.

After covering the assessment process itself, we then presented some of the common problems that individual evaluators and organizations encounter with the appraisal process and how to minimize or even overcome those problems. Then we discussed the debriefing process, where the manager and the subordinate sit down and discuss the employee's evaluation. Here, we discussed the two types of debriefs—the evaluative and the developmental appraisal interview.

Finally, we examined some of the trends in appraisal of employees in the firm, including whether or not to even complete them, the use of electronic monitoring to evaluate performance, the change in some organizations to a competency-based performance evaluation process, and, finally, how to make the process more consistent across raters. That's another big dose of information, and enough for this chapter, so let's move on to the chapter summary and end-of-chapter material.

WORK
APPLICATION 8-15

For a change, let's use your college professors' grading. Are some professors hard graders (they give few As) and others easy (they give lots of As), or are they all consistent? Assuming there is inconsistency, should the college administration dictate a forced distribution or use calibration?

Video Link 8.3
Performance Evaluation

Chapter Summary

Visit www.sagepub.com/lussier for helpful study resources.

8.1 Discuss the difference between performance management and performance appraisal

Performance management identifies, measures, manages, and develops the performance of people in the organization. It is designed to improve worker performance over time. Performance appraisal is the part of the performance management process that identifies, measures, and evaluates the employee's performance, and then discusses that performance with the employee.

8.2 Identify the necessary characteristics of accurate performance management tools

The performance management tools that we use need to be valid and reliable, acceptable and feasible, and specific. Valid means that it measures the process that we wanted to measure. Reliable means the measure works in a generally consistent way each time we use it. Acceptability and feasibility deal with the measure being a *satisfactory* measure with the people who use it and a *reasonable* measure capable of being successfully applied in a particular situation. Finally, specific means the measure defines the performance well enough that we understand the current level of performance achieved and what, if anything, employees need to do to improve their performance to comply with standards.

8.3 List and briefly discuss the purposes for performance appraisals

Communication is the first purpose. Appraisals need to provide an opportunity for formal two-way communication between management and the employee concerning how the organization feels the employee is performing. The second purpose is "information for evaluative decisions." We need good information on how employees are performing so that we can take fair and equitable actions with our workforce, to improve organizational productivity. Motivation for development is the last major purpose. Used correctly, appraisals can motivate by providing opportunities for employees to improve their performance over time.

8.4 Identify and briefly discuss the options for "what" is evaluated in a performance appraisal

Our three primary options are traits, behaviors, and results. There is *some* evidence that particular types of traits are valuable in jobs that require management and leadership skills, but many traits have been shown to have very little bearing on job performance, making them invalid measures of performance. We can also use behaviors to evaluate our workers. Behaviors are usually a much better appraisal option because physical actions or behaviors can be directly observed and as a result are more likely to be a valid assessment of the individual's performance. Finally, we can evaluate performance based on results. Results are a concrete measure of what has happened in the organization. However, results may be skewed based on factors that are outside the control of the individual who is being evaluated.

8.5 Briefly discuss the commonly used performance measurement methods and forms

The *critical incidents method* utilizes records of major employee actions over the course of the appraisal period in order to complete the employee evaluation. The *MBO method* uses objectives jointly set by the manager and the employee to gauge employee performance during the evaluation period. In the *narrative method*, the manager writes either a structured or an unstructured paragraph about the employee's performance. *Graphic rating scale forms* provide a numerical scale so that the manager can check off where an employee falls on the continuum. *BARS forms* provide a description of the behaviors that make up acceptable performance at each level on the scale. Finally, the *ranking method* creates a hierarchy of employees from best to worst.

8.6 Identify and briefly discuss available options for the rater/evaluator

Supervisors are a logical choice when they have ongoing contact with the subordinate and know the subordinate's job. When the supervisor may not spend lots of time with the individual employee, *peers* may be a better choice as evaluators because they may know the job of the individual employee better than the supervisor does, and are more directly affected by the employee's actions. *Subordinate* evaluations can give us good insight into the managers who control employees in our organization. We may want to use *customers* as evaluators when the individual being evaluated has frequent contact with those customers because we need to know how customers feel about their interactions with our employees. *Self-evaluation* is valuable in a number of management processes, from training and development to counseling and disciplinary measures, among others.

8.7 Briefly discuss the value and the drawbacks of a 360° evaluation

The 360° evaluation gives us the best overall analysis of any employee in the firm, because it looks at the employee's performance in the eyes of all others who are affected by the individual.

The 360° evaluation format is more useful for individual development than it is for administrative purposes. The biggest downside is that the process takes a lot of time, which means that it also costs the company a lot of money.

8.8 Identify some of the common problems with the performance appraisal process

Personal biases and stereotyping are two of the most significant appraisal problems. Other problems include halo error; distributional errors—the grading is either too harsh or too lenient, or everyone is judged to be average; similarity error; proximity error; recency error; contrast error; and attribution error.

8.9 Identify the major steps we can take to avoid problems with the appraisal process

The first step would be to develop *accurate performance measures*. Accurate performance measures use *multiple criteria*, *minimize trait-based evaluations*, and can be analyzed using the OUCH test and the Blanchard test. Next, *train the evaluators*,

because as soon as they know some of the common errors, those errors become less pronounced. *Use multiple raters* to mitigate any potentially biased evaluations and minimize other errors such as similarity, contrast, and attribution errors. Finally, *don't evaluate what you don't know*. Find people in the organization who do know the job and have them evaluate the individual performing that job.

8.10 Briefly discuss the differences between evaluative performance reviews and developmental performance reviews

The evaluative interview is a review of the individual employee's performance over a certain period. The evaluation needs to be fair and equitable, not based on bias. Employees must be given the opportunity to talk as well as listen to the critique of their performance. The developmental interview, on the other hand, will focus on areas for improvement over time. Managers should have employees come up with their own objectives and strategies for improvement, as well as develop their own objectives for employees.

Key Terms

360° evaluation

Behaviorally Anchored Rating Scale (BARS) form

Behaviors

Bias

Critical incidents method

Electronic Performance Monitoring (EPM)

Graphic rating scale form

Management by Objectives (MBO) method

Motivation

Narrative method or form

Performance appraisal

Performance management

Ranking method

Results

Stereotyping

Traits

Key Term Review

Complete each of the following statements using one of this chapter's key terms:

_____ the process of identifying, measuring, managing, and developing the performance of the human resources in an organization

_____ the ongoing process of evaluating employee performance

_____ the willingness to achieve organizational objectives

_____ identify the physical or psychological characteristics of a person

_____ the actions taken by an individual

_____ a measure of the goals achieved through a work process

_____ a performance appraisal method in which a manager keeps a written record of positive and negative performance of employees throughout the performance period

_____ a process in which managers and employees jointly set objectives for the employees, periodically evaluate performance, and reward according to the results

_____ requires a manager to write a statement about the employee's performance

_____ a performance appraisal checklist on which a manager simply rates performance on a continuum such as *excellent, good, average, fair,* and *poor*

_____ a performance appraisal that provides a description of each assessment along a continuum

_____ a performance appraisal method that is used to evaluate employee performance from best to worst

_____ analyzes individuals' performance from all sides—from their supervisor's viewpoint, from their subordinates' viewpoint, from customers' viewpoint (if applicable), from their peers' viewpoint, and using their own self-evaluation

_____ a personality-based tendency, either toward or against something

_____ mentally classifying a person into an affinity group, and then identifying the person as having the same assumed characteristics as the group

_____ the process of observing ongoing employee actions using computers or other nonhuman methods

Quick Check (True-False)

1. The annual performance evaluation process is naturally motivational because the company identifies each employee's weaknesses. T F

2. In performance appraisals, the word *specific* means that the form provides enough information for everyone to understand what level of performance has been achieved by a particular person within a well-identified job. T F

3. As a manager, an important part of your job is to make sure that your employees know exactly what is expected of them—the standards. T F

4. The basic performance appraisal is very simple to carry out. T F

5. To meet the communication purpose of performance appraisals, managers have to allow the employee the opportunity to speak to them concerning factors that inhibit their ability to succeed. T F

6. Without good information on performance of individual workers, managers cannot make reasonable decisions about their workforce. T F

7. Traits that most people would be likely to focus on, such as physical attractiveness, punctuality, and extroversion, have been shown to have very little bearing on job performance. T F

8. Results-based appraisal is the most concrete, or fact-based, form of appraisal. T F

9. The critical incidents and MBO methods tend to be the best appraisal methods for an evaluative interview. T F

10. The immediate supervisor is always the best person to evaluate any employee. T F

11. Personality conflicts and personal biases can affect how individual employees rate their peers. T F

12. Subordinate evaluations *must* be confidential in nature, or it is unlikely that the subordinates will provide an honest evaluation of their supervisor. T F

13. We rarely use 360° evaluations because they are so difficult to coordinate. T F

14. If they are guilty of halo error, evaluators *assume* reasons or motivations (such as attitudes, values, or beliefs) for an observed behavior. T F

15. Using multiple evaluators will limit the ability of one individual appraiser to provide a biased opinion concerning an employee's performance. T F

Communication Skills

The following critical-thinking questions can be used for class discussion and/or for written assignments to develop communication skills. Be sure to give complete explanations for all answers.

1. Other than an annual evaluation, what would you do to "manage" the performance of your employees? Explain why you chose the items that you did.

2. What would you do as the manager in order to make sure that your employees knew the standards that they would be evaluated against? Explain your answer.

3. Do you really think that it is possible for a performance appraisal to be motivational? Why or why not?

4. Can you think of a situation where a trait-based evaluation would be necessary? Explain your answer.

5. You are in charge, and you want to evaluate a group of assembly workers. Who would you choose as the evaluator(s)? What about an evaluation of the director of operation? Explain your answer.

6. How would you minimize the chance that stereotyping could affect the evaluation process in your company?

7. Which of the solutions to performance appraisal problems would you implement first if you were in charge? Second? Why?

8. What would you do to make the performance appraisal debrief more comfortable and less confrontational for your employees? How do you think this would help?

9. Do you agree that performance appraisals should be discontinued in companies? Defend your answer.

10. Is Electronic Performance Monitoring ethical? Would you use it if it was your choice? Why or why not?

Video

Please visit the student study site at **www.sagepub.com/lussier** to view the video links in this chapter.

Answers

REVIEW QUESTIONS (TRUE-FALSE) Answers

1. F   2. T   3. T   4. F   5. T   6. T   7. T   8. T   9. F   10. F   11. T   12. T   13. F   14. F   15. T

Cases

Case 8-1. Beauty and the Beastly Situation at Aerospace Designs' Marketing Department

"Oh no! What now?" said Tom Moore, Director of Human Resources at Aerospace Designs. "Just when I thought this mess was over on how the Marketing Department does performance appraisal, we're smacked with a sexual harassment lawsuit. Well, we've got to do something about this predicament, and fast."

Aerospace Designs Background

Aerospace Designs (AD) was founded in the early 1960s. A privately held company started by two engineers, it was deliberately designed to feed off the blossoming U.S. military budget as the United States fought the Cold War. It became part of the supplier system to the massive Grumman contractor on Long Island, New York, and took on a military-like culture and structure.

Aerospace's Marketing Department

Aerospace Designs was predominantly a population of White males, and the hiring of minorities and women would assist in meeting its government-imposed affirmative action goals. The Marketing Department had never employed women. It was a very flat structure, consisting of three internal salesmen, a sales coordinator on-site, and one road salesman, who all reported directly to Frank Fasting, the Vice President of Sales and Marketing. (See Appendix A for an abbreviated organizational chart of

the Sales and Marketing Department.) Aerospace Designs had hired Frank in hopes that he would be able to bring it out of its recent trend of flat growth. He was expected to grow the existing stable aerospace electronics business, and to firmly establish both a lights product line and a land-based vehicle business for military and commercial operations. The addition of new staff positions to the Marketing Department, of which the Marketing Assistant was one, was designed to help establish a web presence and improve the capabilities for print media and trade show coordination.

Enter Lola

Lola Meyer was above average in height, single, blonde, and 32 years old with lingering aspirations to be a model. Having a four-year degree, and opting out of the education field, she came over to Marketing in an attempt to find a steady job where she might be taken seriously. Although Frank had reservations regarding hiring Lola for the job given her qualifications, Sue Jones, the Human Resources Manager, eventually persuaded him to give Lola a chance. After a few months on the job, Frank approved arrangements for Lola to take courses related to the work that needed to be done, as it became apparent that she lacked some technical marketing skills necessary to be effective in her position.

Lola's Performance Evaluation

The ensuing year went by without fanfare. Lola, Frank, and the rest of the Marketing Department seemed to coexist amicably. Frank proved to be an outgoing, friendly sort, as you might expect of someone who is in Sales. His greatest weakness as a manager seemed to be his lack of administrative follow-through.

Aerospace Designs policies dictated an annual performance evaluation for every employee. This review unfortunately hadn't been done by Frank in a timely manner for Lola. By the time January rolled around, Lola's review was two months late. Frank discussed with Sue that he was not pleased with Lola's performance to date and would indicate such on her review. Sometime in April Frank became ill and needed to take time off to care for his personal health. Lola's review was written by Frank but not formally presented to Lola. Since it was now delayed nearly five months and it was apparent that Frank would be out for several more months, the decision was made to have Mark Gurello (Senior Sales Manager overseeing Marketing in Frank's absence) present Lola with the poor performance evaluation. This took place at the end of April. Lola was rated overall as "less than competent" and was not given a salary increase.

Lola's Reaction

Lola was both shocked and dismayed. In the beginning of May, she met with Sue to discuss her performance review. She handed Sue an 18-page, handwritten rebuttal of her evaluation. Her reply admitted her inability to reach designated goals, but stated that her performance was hindered due to items beyond her control. During this discussion with Sue, Lola alleged that sexual conversations and behavior had occurred in her work environment. Specifically, she cited that Frank had used highly inappropriate language, including nicknames for the President of Aerospace Designs. When she walked in on one of these conversations and was asked to comment, she abruptly left, and immediately filed her rebuttal report with HR.

Sue's Response and Lola's Bombshell

Upon reading about these incidents, Sue conducted a prompt, thorough internal investigation and determined that Lola's performance was marginal and upheld the performance review as written. She also determined that inappropriate conversations had taken place, and Frank received a written reprimand and was required to attend sexual harassment awareness training when he returned to the job. Lola's supervisor was permanently changed to Mark, and her workstation was moved to the other side of the Marketing area, away from Frank's office door. Lola was agreeable to these actions taken by the company. However, three months later Lola filed a sexual harassment lawsuit against the firm, stating that she could not get a fair evaluation given the harassing environment she was working in.

Questions

1. What evidence does this case provide for formulating and implementing a systematic approach to performance appraisal?

2. Do you believe that Lola's performance evaluation was valid and reliable? Do you feel that Frank had a bias or stereotypical mind when filling out the evaluation? Explain your answer.

3. What in the case indicates a problem with this supervisor's evaluation? Please connect examples from this case to what the chapter discusses.

4. How did Lola, her supervisor, and human resources communicate with one another? Do you feel that a performance appraisal interview should have been more formally established and conducted? Why or why not?

5. How can Lola's accusation of sexual harassment affect her personal work performance and her performance evaluation?

Case created by Herbert Sherman, PhD, and Mr. Theodore Vallas, Department of Management Sciences, School of Business Brooklyn Campus, Long Island University

Abbreviated Organizational Chart Sales and Marketing Department, Aerospace Designs, Inc., 2001

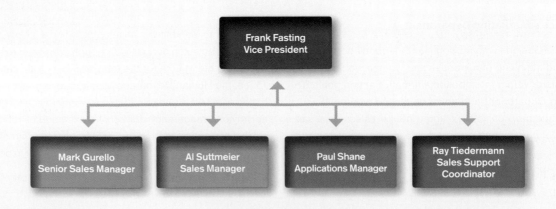

Case 8-2. Performance Evaluation at DHR: Building a Foundation or Crumbling Ruins?

DHR Construction was managed by Richard Davis, operating manager and senior partner. Homes were built on-demand to customer specifications. Richard Davis was in charge of the financial management of the firm including working with suppliers, creditors, and subcontractors (obtaining bids and construction loans). Davis and Richard Hodgetts, the general partner, met on a weekly basis and communicated through phone calls and e-mail. The role of project foreman was delegated to either one of their subcontractors or a hired employee and, in the worst-case scenario, filled by a reluctant Hodgetts (who had a full-time job outside of the business and had minimal free time).

DHR earned a reputation for honesty, promptness in paying bills, and professionalism—rare commodities for a small home builder in the area. However, DHR was also very demanding of suppliers—if you promised a job was going to be completed or supplies were going to be delivered by a certain date and you did not meet the deadline, you were going to hear from the firm. Repeated miscues would result in not being asked to bid on future projects.

Enter James Kennison

James Kennison was a successful corporate executive who was good with his hands; his main hobby and passion was working on his home. His mild-mannered, laid-back approach to life was perfect for the professional environment of his former firm, Micro-Tech, a business that produced specialized electronic parts and gauges. Kennison left the corporate world when he became economically self-sufficient in order to simplify his life, reconnect with nature, and become, as he called it, "self-actualized."

In order to keep busy, Kennison decided that he would put his passion for building to good use and hire himself out as an independent handyman/subcontractor. His aptitude, acumen, and even-tempered style made it very easy for Kennison to fit into any work crew that would hire him. After a few jobs, Kennison decided to work on his own and hired himself out as a finisher on home construction projects. It was in that capacity that Kennison was originally hired by Davis and Hodgetts to work as a subcontractor on the homes in their Mountain Trails project. Kennison's wit, charm, and polished demeanor sat well with Davis and Hodgetts, and he became a fixture at their weekly business meetings.

It was not surprising, then, that Davis and Hodgetts approached Kennison about taking over the position of contractor/foreman when a sudden vacancy occurred. Kennison had a plethora of experience, had a real head for business, and was respected by the other subcontractors as a fellow artisan, one who knew the work and was not afraid to get dirty doing it.

Although Kennison seemed open and honest in his dealings with Davis (with Kennison consistently indicating that all was going well), it didn't take more than a month before Davis realized that all was not going as planned. Davis's Gantt chart indicated that several homes were falling behind schedule with one of the homes failing inspection.

Evaluative Appraisal Interview: Cracks in the Drywall?

Davis and Hodgetts talked about the situation at some length and decided that both of them needed to talk with Kennison at the next dinner meeting and find out exactly what was happening at the job site since Kennison hadn't commented on work delays or problems with the inspectors. At the meeting, Davis reiterated with Kennison what he thought were the job responsibilities, the important tasks to be accomplished, and the need to have open and candid communications between them. Kennison admitted that getting subcontractors to show up as scheduled was starting to become a problem and that he thought that the construction inspections would be quickly dealt with. He apologized for the delays and said that he would keep in better contact with Davis and let him know exactly what was happening, especially if there were any new problems. Davis reminded Kennison that he needed to keep a close watch on the subcontractors since they had a tendency to work for multiple builders simultaneously and therefore would jump from job to job. Kennison assured Davis and Hodgetts that he would manage the situation and that things would improve.

The talk with Kennison seemed to get things back on track. Kennison provided Davis with a list of the subcontractors to invite to their dinner meetings. When the issue was raised with these subcontractors about work scheduling, the subcontractors promised to do the best they could to perform the work as required. The next few days saw a flurry of activity at the work site as the subcontractors, guided by Kennison, tried to catch up with the construction schedule. The next inspection came off without a hitch.

Here's to the New Boss, Same as the Old Boss

After a few days, the subcontractors were back to their old routine of not showing up at the work site when planned. After a few weeks went by, Kennison tried to cover for the work not being done by the subcontractors but to no avail. The situation deteriorated when one of the home purchasers, who visited the work site, reported to Davis that their home was way behind schedule. After a quick talk with Kennison, several of the subcontractors had to be fired by Davis because they continued to not show up when scheduled without notification. Worse, now other subcontractor]s (e.g., painters) were quitting because the homes were not ready to work on.

Questions

1. What appraisal method best describes how Davis and Hodgetts evaluated Kennison's work?

2. Given your answer to Question 1, why do you believe that this method of appraisal did not produce long-lasting results in Kennison's ability to manage the subcontractors?

3. Assume that you are Davis and Hodgetts. What appraisal system would you use for Kennison? Why?

4. Evaluate how well Davis and Hodgetts prepared for and conducted the appraisal interview with Kennison.

5. Discuss "who" evaluated and "who" should be evaluating Kennison's performance. Explain why.

Case created by Herbert Sherman, PhD, and Mr. Theodore Vallas, Department of Management Sciences, School of Business Brooklyn Campus, Long Island University

SKILL BUILDER 8-1

Peer and Self-Assessment

This exercise actually includes the usual self-assessment for each chapter, and an evaluation of peers, plus developing measures of performance.

Objective

To develop your skill at assessing your performance and that of your peers.

To develop your skill at developing measures of performance.

Skills

The primary skills developed through this exercise are:

1. HR *Management skill*—Conceptual and design skills

2. *HRM 2010 Curriculum Guidebook*—F: Performance management

Assignment Part 1–Self-Assessment

During your college courses, you most likely had to do some form of group assignment. Select one group you worked with for this assignment. Based on your performance in your prior group, or it could be for this course, do a self-evaluation using the rating scale form below.

Evaluator (you) _____ (Self-Evaluation)

This exercise can stop with just a self-assessment or continue to also include peer evaluations.

	A A– Always	B+ B B– Usually	C + C C– Frequently	D+ D D– Sometimes	F Rarely
Did a "good" analysis of project					
Developed "good" questions to ask					
Actively participated (truly interested/involved)					
Made "quality" effort and contributions					
Got along well with group members					
Displayed leadership					
List at least 3 of your own measures of performance here					
Class Attendance—number of absences	0–1	2	3	4	5+
Group Meetings Attendance to prepare group project—number of absences	0	1	2	3	4+
Managed the group's time well					

Assignment Part 2–Peer Review

1. Part 2 begins by conducting a peer evaluation using the above form for each of the other members in your group with this heading:

    Group Member _____ (Peer Evaluation)

    Either copy the above form for each group member, do your assessment on any sheet without the form, or your instructor will provide you with a form that includes multiple forms for you to complete for each group member.

2. Below, rank each group member (including yourself) based on his or her performance. The first person listed (number 1) should be the best performer, and the last person listed should be the least effective performer, based on the performance appraisal above. If members are close or equal, you may assign them the same rank number, but you must list the better one first.

3. To the right of each group member (including yourself) place the letter overall grade (A–F) you would assign to this member based on the performance appraisal. You may give more than one member the same grade if he or she deserves the same grade. You may also use plus and minus grades.

Rank   *Name*   *Grade*

_____   _____   _____

_____   _____   _____

_____   _____   _____

_____   _____   _____

_____   _____   _____

SKILL BUILDER 8-2

Debriefing the Appraisal

Note: This exercise is designed for groups that have been working together as part of the course requirements for some time. It is a continuation of Skill Builder 8-1. Based on your peer evaluations, you will conduct performance appraisals for your group members.

Objective

To develop a plan to improve your team performance, and to develop your skills in conducting performance appraisals.

Skills

The primary skills developed through this exercise are:

1. HR *Management skill*—Conceptual and design skills

2. *SHRM 2010 Curriculum Guidebook*—F: Performance management

Assignment

You will be both the evaluator and evaluatee. Get together with group members and beginning with the letter A have each member select a letter. Pair off as follows: A and B, C and D, E and F, etc. If there is an odd number in the group, each member will sit out one round. A, C, and E (etc.) conduct the evaluation interview using the form in Skill Builder 8-1, directly followed by the developmental interview to give suggestions on improve group member's performance for B, D, and F (be sure to follow the evaluative and developmental interview steps in Models 8-1 and 8-2). Be an evaluator and evaluate; do not be peers having a discussion. When you finish, or the instructor tells you the time is up, reverse roles of evaluator and evaluatee—B, D, and F are the evaluators.

When the instructor tells you to, or the time is up, form new groups of two and decide who will be the evaluator first. Continue changing groups of two until every group member has appraised and been appraised by every other group member.

Apply It

What did I learn from this experience? How will I improve my group performance in the course? How will I use this knowledge in the future?

_____

_____

9

Rights and Employee Development

Learning Outcomes

After studying this chapter you should be able to:

9.1 Discuss the difference between a right and a privilege in a work context

9.2 Identify the commonly accepted individual rights in the workplace

9.3 Identify the rights that management has in modern organizations

9.4 Briefly describe the coaching process and how it is used

9.5 Describe the management counseling process and its purpose

9.6 Briefly discuss the purpose of the tests for Just Cause used in disciplinary investigations

9.7 Describe the concept of progressive discipline in the organization, including the stages of progressive discipline

9.8 Discuss the two common situations in which an employee might be immediately discharged from the company

9.9 Identify the factors that positive leadership takes into account in order to be successful

9.10 Briefly discuss the stages of the change process

9.11 Identify the factors that can help overcome resistance to change in organizations

9.12 Define the following terms:

Privileges

Rights

Employment-at-will

Coaching

Management counseling

Employee Assistance
   Program (EAP)

Discipline

Just Cause

Progressive discipline

Gross negligence

Serious misconduct

Leadership

Chapter 9 Outline

Overview

Commonly Accepted Employee Rights
- Rights and Privileges
- Right to Free Consent
- Right to Due Process
- Right to Life and Safety
- Right to Freedom of Conscience (Limited)
- Right to Privacy (Limited)
- Right to Free Speech (Limited)

Management Rights
- Codes of Conduct
- Workplace Monitoring
- Employment-at-Will
- Orientation (Probationary) Periods
- Drug Testing

Developing or Terminating Individual Employees
- Coaching
  - Determining Corrective Coaching Action
  - The Coaching Model
- Counseling
  - Types of Problem Employees
  - Personal Problems and Performance
- Disciplining
  - Just Cause
- Guidelines for Effective Discipline
- Progressive Discipline
- The Discipline Model

Terminating
- Gross Negligence and Serious Misconduct
- Termination of Nonmanagerial Employees
- Managerial or Executive Employees

Employee Coaching, Counseling, and Discipline May Differ Globally

Developing Teams
- Leadership
- Situational Management Model
  - Using the Situational Management Model
  - Applying the Most Appropriate Management Styles
- Building Effective Work Teams
- Managing the Change Process
- Overcoming Resistance to Change

Trends and Issues in HRM
- Positive Leadership and Organizational Discipline
- Facebook, Twitter, and So On @ Work—The Burden of Control
- Does a Commitment to Sustainability Foster Employee Motivation?

A. Employee and Labor Relations (required)
   1. Disciplinary actions (demotion, disciplinary termination)
   7. Managing teams
   22. Investigations
   27. Employee records

B. Employment Law (required)
   20. Employee privacy
   30. Employment-at-will doctrine

D. Organization Development (required)
   1. Coaching
   7. Leadership development

F. Performance Management (required)
   8. Diagnosing problems
   9. Performance improvement programs

G. Staffing: Recruitment and Selection (required)
   14. Job offers (employment-at-will, contracts, authorization to work)

K. Workforce Planning and Talent Management (required)
   3. Retention (involuntary turnover, outplacement counseling, alternative dispute resolution)

L. Workplace Health, Safety, and Security (required—undergraduates only)
   12. Monitoring, surveillance, privacy

Case 9-1. Just One Little Slip

SHRM
HR CONTENT

See Appendix A:
***SHRM 2010 Curriculum Guidebook* for the complete list**

I Can't Take It Anymore!

Not all employees are optimal employees, and sometimes a workplace dynamic needs major adjustment. "I've had it with Jeremy!" Bob, our staffing supervisor, exploded when I returned his phone call one Friday morning. "I've had a lousy day, we're having problems with our end-of-the-month report so it looks as though I will have to stay late today, plus I've got a king-sized headache! If he makes one more mistake, that's it—he's out of here!" Some employees need more supervision than others, and some supervisors do as well. Does Jeremy have certain rights as an employee that might prevent Bob from dismissing him just because Bob is having a "bad day"? Chapter 9 illustrates employee versus management rights and related legal requirements.

The Practitioner's Model for HRM

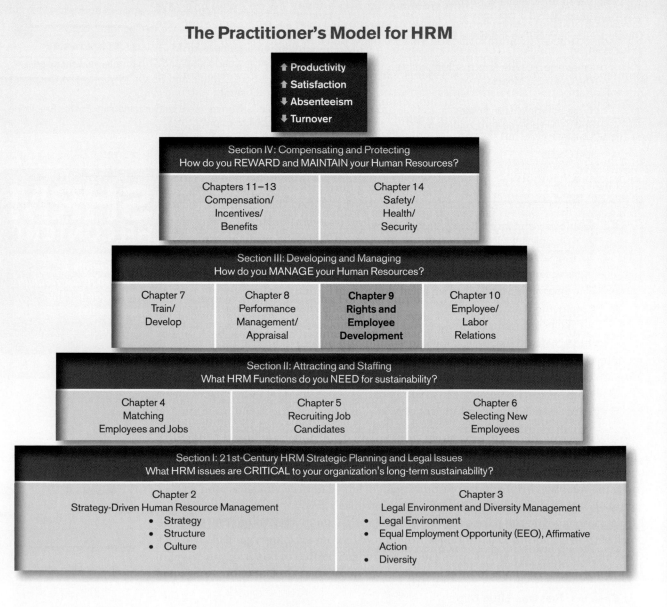

Overview

To remain competitive today, organizations must continually develop their employees' knowledge and skills.[1] Effective employee development leads to committed motivated employees who then increase performance.[2] Now that we understand how to successfully assess our employees' performance from the last chapter, we can use the information to make decisions about our employees' development.

In this chapter we follow up on the developmental interview to continuously improve individual performance through coaching, counseling, and finally disciplining or terminating employees who cannot or will not perform to acceptable standards. In addition to individual development, we also discuss team development through positive leadership, team building, and managing change.

However, before we can develop, discipline, or terminate individual employees and before we can develop high-performance teams, we need to understand employee and management rights to ensure that we don't violate those rights and develop or discipline employees unethically or illegally. So in this chapter we begin by discussing commonly accepted employee rights and management rights. Based on this foundation, we proceed to developing or disciplining individual employees and then to developing teams. As usual, we end with trends and issues in HRM.

Video Link 9.1

Employee Training

Commonly Accepted Employee Rights

In this section, we discuss six employee rights; see Exhibit 9-1 for a list. However, before we discuss employee rights, we need to understand the difference between a right and a privilege; so this is our opening discussion followed by the rights.

Rights and Privileges

Individual rights are the topic of much conversation in our society today. However, how many of us actually know the difference between a right and a privilege? If we listen, we

LO 9.1

Discuss the difference between a right and a privilege in a work context.

Exhibit 9-1	Employee Rights

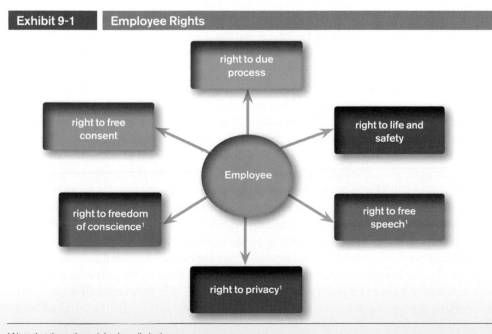

[1] Note that these three rights have limitations.

constantly hear statements such as "I have a right to drive my car the way I want" and "I have a right to go to college." Are such statements correct? In fact, in both of these situations, the actions of the individual would be based on privilege, not rights. What's the difference?

Privileges are *things that individuals are allowed to do based on asking permission from an authority.* In simple terms, a privilege must be earned because the individual does something successfully (like passing a driver's test or getting good grades in high school) while a right is provided to the individual by the society in which they are a member. We don't have a right to drive, especially not any way we want. Driving is a privilege based on the individual showing that they have knowledge of the correct way to drive so that they avoid harm to others.

On the other hand, a right does not require the individual to do anything in order to gain that right *at that time in that society.* **Rights** are *things a person in society is allowed to do without any permission required from an authority.* The right is bestowed upon the individual based on their membership in the society. The simple way to tell the difference between a right and a privilege would be, if the employee has to request permission to do something within the organization, it would be a privilege that they are requesting to exercise; however, they would not need permission to exercise their rights.

What rights do employees have in an organization? In general, employees have several rights; refer back to Exhibit 9-1 for the list. Because these are rights in the sense noted in the above paragraph, the individual employee doesn't have to do anything to gain these rights. Because they're a part of this society (the organization), they gain these rights. Because individual employee rights exist within the organization, the organization has a duty to protect each employee's rights. A duty, or an obligation, is a societal (company) responsibility to protect the individual's (employee) rights. The individual employee *also* has a duty to avoid harming the rights of other employees in the course of exercising their own rights. Rights are always balanced by duties or responsibilities.

So what do these rights allow an individual within the organization to do, and what limitations are there on the three "limited" rights that we noted? Let's break down each of the six rights individually in separate sections.

Right to Free Consent

Individuals in a modern organization have a right to free consent. What does this right provide to the individual? The right to free consent is the right of the individual to know what they're being asked to do for the organization and the consequences of that action to the individual employee or others, either in or outside the organization. People should know what they are being asked to do in their jobs and shouldn't be forced, manipulated, or deceived into working in situations that could cause harm, unless they are aware of the circumstances. The organization's duty would be to ensure that the individual *voluntarily agrees* to do a particular job or task for the organization. The organization would violate the individual's right to free consent if it forced the person to do something against their will or manipulated them in some way to do something that they would not do if they knew all of the circumstances.

A great example of the right to free consent was shown after the Japan earthquake and ensuing tsunami in March 2011. Several nuclear reactors were damaged in northern Japan, and workers were needed to go into areas with significant radiation dangers. The workers would need to be told about the dangers from both radiation and potentially explosive gases that they would encounter by taking on the job of working on the reactors and associated equipment. If the workers had not been told the extent of the danger, the company (Tokyo Electric Power Company) would have violated their rights to free consent. The workers would have to be given enough information so that they could understand the danger that they were placing themselves in, and then freely agree to do the job in order for the right of free consent to be in effect.

WORK
APPLICATION 9-1

Give examples of rights and privileges where you work or have worked.

LO 9.2

Identify the commonly accepted individual rights in the workplace.

Right to Due Process

We have due process so that employees can be treated fairly.[3] People have a right to not be punished arbitrarily. If the organization contemplates a disciplinary action, the employee has a right to know what they are accused of, to know the evidence or proof thereof, and to tell their side of what happened. This is the right to due process. We will review due process and the seven "Tests for Just Cause" a little bit later, but due process is basically the concept of providing fair and reasonable disciplinary actions as consequences of an employee's behavior. So, the organization would have a duty to investigate any disciplinary infractions and explain any disciplinary charges against the individual employee. The employee would have a right to understand the charges against them, the evidence concerning those charges, and the reasons for the conclusions that led to any disciplinary action by the organization.

Right to Life and Safety

Every employee within the organization has a right to be protected from harm to the best of the organization's ability. In 1948 the United Nations declared that every individual has a right to life, liberty, and security of person.[4] Security of person basically means personal safety. This would obviously include individual employees at work in the organization. So the organization would have a general duty to see that every employee would be protected from harm when working within the organization, because the individual has a right to life and safety. We will discuss safety and health in more detail in Chapter 14.

Right to Freedom of Conscience (Limited)

Employees generally should not be asked to do something that violates their personal values and beliefs, *as long as these beliefs generally reflect commonly accepted societal norms.* The person's conscience determines in their mind what is right and wrong. The organization has a general duty to avoid forcing an individual to do something that they consider to be wrong, either morally or ethically, and the individual has a right to avoid doing things within the organization that would violate their personal values and beliefs.

However, this doesn't mean that a person can accept a job in, for example, a medical lab working on cancer cures and then refuse to work with living human cells because of their moral convictions and be free from any threat of termination of their employment. The organization would generally have the right in this case to terminate the worker for noncompliance with legitimate requirements associated with their job, since it would be almost certain that the individual would know of these requirements before accepting the job.

Right to Privacy (Limited)

This right protects people from unreasonable or unwarranted intrusions

Organizations need to make all jobs as safe as possible.

into their personal affairs. This general right to privacy would include the privacy of a personnel file, employee records, or private areas of the person's workplace (such as a personal locker) to an extent. The organization would have a general duty to protect individual employee privacy in most cases. Whether dealing with the employee's private life, personal history, or private areas in the workplace, the organization has an obligation to protect the individual employee's information and privacy.

However, if the employer feels that there might be a hazard to others, a locker or other personal space (e.g., a desk) could be searched. For example, if an employee reports to one of the organization's managers that another employee has a weapon in a personal space (their locker), the organization probably has a right to search the individual's locker.

Another limitation to privacy is in e-mail to and from company addresses. The employer again has a right to review any information in these types of correspondence to protect other employees and the organization. An example of the right to privacy is discussed in our second trend and issue in HRM: "Facebook, Twitter, and So On @ Work."

Right to Free Speech (Limited)

The First Amendment to the Constitution guarantees the right to freedom of speech. What most people don't understand, though, is that the First Amendment only applies to government agencies. In the workplace, individual freedom of speech is limited based on many years of case law. Individuals, whether in an organization or not, generally have the right to freely express themselves in a modern society. Within the organization itself, individuals should be free to express concerns or discontent with organizational policies without fear of harm. Allowing such expression provides the organization an opportunity to see that problems exist, and gives them the opportunity to correct these problems. Employees have legal protection to blow the whistle on an organization that is involved in illegal activities; in other words, employers can't fire or discriminate against an employee for telling others about the organization's illegal activities. We will talk more about whistle-blowers in the next chapter.

However, many types of speech have no protection. If the individual employee exercises their freedom of speech, and in the course of that action harms the organization or other employees, the organization has a right to discipline the employee based on the harm that was done to others. For example, an organization in the private sector can discipline an employee for using demeaning language toward another employee, even though the first employee might assert their right to free speech. This is due to the requirement to maintain good order and discipline in an organization in order for work to be produced.

In another case, a manager might verbally and *publicly* disagree with a corporate policy. They certainly have a right to do so, but the organization would also have a right to discipline or even terminate the manager because of such actions, again based on maintenance of good order and discipline in the organization. Managers, in such a case, are generally held to a higher standard than nonmanagerial employees. So here again, the organization gains a right to limit the rights of the individual employee because of the harm that employee could cause to others in the organization and to the organization itself. Getting back to Facebook, Twitter, and so on, should the organization monitor what employees say about the firm on the web and take disciplinary action when employees hurt the organization?

Management Rights

You notice that, in each of the rights that we identified as limited, we said the organization has a *right* to limit the individual employee's rights in order to protect the firm. Organizations, like individuals, are given rights within the larger society. Organizational rights tend to be provided based on the necessity for the organization to protect itself

9-1 APPLYING THE CONCEPT

Employee Rights

State which of the following rights is being discussed in each of the given situations.

a. free consent
b. due process
c. life and safety
d. freedom of conscience
e. privacy
f. free speech

_____ 1. Wait a minute; you can't dock my pay for coming in late. I'm on salary, and I'm going to the HR Department about this.

_____ 2. I don't want to be transferred to working in the bar. Drinking is against my religion.

_____ 3. Hey boss, what are you doing with your hand in the pocket of my jacket?

_____ 4. My new boss made me sign this form before I could start the job, stating that she told me about the possible side effects from the radiation I'm exposed to by the X-ray machine.

_____ 5. You better take a break from writing those nasty comments online about our company because the boss is getting angrier about it with each posting.

_____ 6. I'm going to teach you how to use the deli slicer. Rule Number 1 is to always make sure this handle is down so you don't cut yourself.

and its employees from persons who might do them harm, whether intentionally or unintentionally.

So, when faced with employee rights to privacy, if the organization had reasonable evidence or proof that an individual had a weapon, or was harassing a coworker, or was providing organizational secrets to a competitor, we would generally have a right to investigate the individual in order to protect the organization and its other employees. Concerning the right of the employee to freedom of speech, the organization has a right to determine whether or not the employee's free speech does harm to the organization or other employees that is greater than the individual's free speech rights. In other words, does the harm to the organization and other employees outweigh the rights of the individual to say what they want?

Managers in the firm have to weigh the individual's rights against the potential harm that could be done to the organization by allowing the individual to express those rights. What other rights do organizations have? In this section we discuss five management rights; see Exhibit 9-2 for a list.

Codes of Conduct

Managers of organizations have a right to create a code of employee conduct. The code of conduct is the organization's mechanism to identify the ethics and values of the firm. The code of conduct serves as a guide to individual action within the firm. It tells the employees what conduct is acceptable within the organization and what is not. Most codes of conduct today also note the consequences that can occur if an employee does not follow the requirements in the code. The code of conduct gives an employee a practical tool that they can use in their daily activities, in order to determine whether or not an action that they are contemplating is within the acceptable boundaries of conduct within their organization.

Virtually all organizations have a code of conduct. Generally, the larger the firm, the more likely the code of conduct will be a written document, or the behaviors will be in

WORK APPLICATION 9-8

How do you feel about employees communicating negative things about the organization to outsiders? Should management monitor employee speech and take action to stop negative speech?

LO 9.3

Identify the rights that management has in modern organizations.

Exhibit 9-2   Management Rights

multiple documents. Most large companies also have a specific section of the code of conduct or separate document known as the code of ethics to spell out what is and is not ethical behavior.

Workplace Monitoring

Managers in the organization have a right to monitor the workplace to ensure that employees are acting both legally and ethically in all of the actions that they take on behalf of the organization. One form of monitoring that we already discussed in earlier chapters is the monitoring of the Internet sites that companies may undertake in an attempt to ensure that employees and others don't defame the organization. Other forms of monitoring may include monitoring and analysis of the use of computers and networks within the firm, video monitoring of work spaces, and recording of phone conversations and e-mails. Workplace monitoring provides the organization with a mechanism to protect itself and its employees from individual actions that might harm them.

Employment-at-Will

Currently, under common law, "employment relationships are presumed to be 'at-will' in all U.S. states except Montana."[5] The concept of **employment-at-will** *allows the company or the worker to break their work relationship at any point in time, with or without any particular reason, as long as in doing so no law is violated.* This is one of management's rights in organizations. In practicality, what this means is that the employer does not have to have *cause* (reasons) to terminate an employment relationship with an individual worker. If an organization states that employment in the firm is "at-will," then it is typically presumed that the worker has no contractual rights to a continuing job with the firm.

However, employment-at-will is in reality a fairly weak law. What has made employment-at-will so weak? Courts in many jurisdictions in the United States have for many years ruled that employment-at-will is limited in when and how we use it. The courts have specifically stated that there are several standard exceptions to employment-at-will. *Public policy exceptions* to employment-at-will would include such things as being terminated for filing a legitimate worker's compensation claim; refusing to lobby for a particular political candidate just because your boss likes them; and refusing to violate a professional code of ethics. In other words, if the organization was violating vital public interests, and the worker refused

ESR

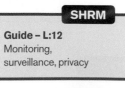

SHRM

Guide – L:12
Monitoring, surveillance, privacy

SHRM

Guide – B:30
Employment-at-will doctrine

SHRM

Guide – G:14
Job offers (employment-at-will, contracts, authorization to work)

to participate, the organization would not have a right to terminate the individual's employment based on employment-at-will.

The courts have also noted that frequently there is at least some evidence of an *implied contract* between the employee and the employer. One of the most common places where we see implications of contract is in the employee manual or handbook. The company must be very careful in the wording that goes into an employee handbook in order to keep from voiding its employment-at-will policies. For instance, if the company were to note in its employee handbook that "our organization values hard work, and many of our employees who perform well have been with us for many years," this *might* be considered an implied contract—in other words, if you work hard, we will continue to employ you.

Keeping the organization's assets and its employees safe takes monitoring.

This implication of a contract could negate the employment-at-will rights of the employer.

A third case in which courts have ruled that there are exceptions to employment-at-will is when employers are suspected of *lack of good faith and fair dealing* in the employment relationship. In other words, if the employer does something that will benefit them significantly but will harm the individual employee, that action would create a lack of good faith and fair dealing. For instance, we might release an older employee shortly before they become eligible for a company-sponsored retirement plan in order to hire a younger (and cheaper) employee in the same position and not have to pay the retirement benefits. This would be lack of good faith and fair dealing, in addition to probably being against age discrimination laws.

Orientation (Probationary) Periods

Organizations have a right to set up an orientation, or introductory, period for new employees. Many of you may be familiar with the older term *probationary period*. This term has fallen out of favor with organizations due to the fact that courts have, in past cases, said that completion of a probationary period may give employees additional rights in the workplace, even if employment in the workplace is ostensibly at-will as noted above. Regardless of what it is called, the orientation or probationary period allows the organization a certain amount of time in which to assess the new employee and their capabilities, before fully integrating the individual into the organization. The orientation period usually runs from 60 to 90 days, but can be much longer in some organizations that provide significant training to new entrants.

Normal activities in the orientation period include job training and socialization into the organization's customs and culture, as discussed in Chapter 7. Usually as an employee nears the end of the orientation period, manager and employee will meet in order to discuss what the new employee has learned and how they feel about their continuing employment in the organization, and determine the individual's performance goals for a preset period of time.

Drug Testing

As we first noted in Chapter 6, "Most employers have the right to test for a wide variety of substances in the workplace."[6] While drug testing is not required in most cases, employers

Video Link 9.2
Management Rights

WORK
APPLICATION 9-10

How long is the typical orientation period where you work or have worked?

WORK
APPLICATION 9-11

How do you feel about companies giving drug tests? Does an organization you work or have worked for give drug tests?

9-2 APPLYING THE CONCEPT

Management Rights

State which of the following rights is being discussed in each of the given situations.

a. code of conduct
b. workplace monitoring
c. employment-at-will

d. orientation period
e. drug testing

_____ 7. I checked your computer, and you have been spending an average of two hours a day on personal things.

_____ 8. I don't like you; you're fired.

_____ 9. In order to get the job, you will have to pass a physical exam that includes a urinalysis.

_____ 10. You are smoking in a restricted area. Come with me to the HR Department for disciplinary action.

_____ 11. You have finished your first six months with us, and you haven't been able to meet the standards of the job, so we are letting you go.

can put testing programs in place. The primary reason for drug testing will generally be workplace safety." So, drug testing is another major employer right. Always remember, though, drug testing needs to be done in either a universal or a random form.

Developing or Terminating Individual Employees

Organizations hire new employees with the hopes that they will become productive workers. Ongoing employee development has three parts: coaching, counseling, and disciplining, but not all three parts are needed in all cases. As discussed in Chapter 8, managers need to continually coach virtually all employees to improve performance. Sometimes employees will have on- or off-the-job problems, and the manager should get them professional counseling through the HR Department. Some employees will break the code of conduct, and the manager will need to take disciplinary action; in some cases, managers will need to terminate these employees. Also, if employees cannot do the job to standards (and during the orientation period performance needs to be monitored very closely), the employee should be terminated. In this section, we discuss employee development through coaching, counseling, disciplining, and if it doesn't work, terminating.

LO 9.4

Briefly describe the coaching process and how it is used.

Coaching

SHRM

Guide – F:9
Performance improvement programs

SHRM

Guide – D:1
Coaching

We know that a great boss can inspire employees to new heights.[7] An important part of coaching is making sure that the employee knows what competencies are most important and to work to continually develop those skills.[8] **Coaching** is *the process of giving motivational feedback to maintain and improve performance.* Coaching focuses on helping employees succeed by monitoring performance through giving feedback to praise progress and to redirect inappropriate behavior with feedback on how to improve.[9] Employees who are given more immediate, frequent, and direct feedback perform at higher levels than those who are not given such feedback.[10] When we coach, we should provide positive feedback that helps the employee improve performance.[11] Some organizations even provide *peer coaching* to help develop employees.[12]

Many people who hear the word *coaching* immediately think of athletes, but coaching is also an important management skill that is used to get the best results from each employee.[13] Training is an important part of coaching, as coaching is about continuously stretching an individual just beyond his or her current abilities.[14] As implied in the definition of coaching, feedback is the central part of coaching, and the feedback should be motivational.[15] In other words, you should give more positive than negative feedback.[16]

Video Link 9.3
What is Coaching?

Determining Corrective Coaching Action

Coaching is needed when performance falls below aspirational levels.[17] When an employee is not performing up to potential, even when acceptable standards are being met, the first step is to determine why, using the performance formula: performance = ability × motivation × resources. When ability is holding back performance, training is needed. A good manager is also a good teacher, so when something isn't done properly, we should teach employees how to do it correctly.[18] Use job instructional training (Chapter 7). When motivation is lacking, motivational techniques, such as coaching, may help.[19] Talk to the employee to try to determine why motivation is lacking, and develop a plan together to improve performance.[20] If motivational coaching does not work, you may have to use discipline,[21] which will be discussed later. Finally, when resources are lacking, work to obtain them.

The Coaching Model

Coaching is a way to provide ongoing feedback to employees about their job performance.[22] However, ask managers what they tend to put off doing, and they'll likely say advising weak employees that they must improve their performance. Many managers are hesitant to confront employees, even to the point of jarred nerves and sleepless nights. Procrastinating managers often hope that the employees will turn around on their own, only to find—often too late—that the situation just continues to get worse. Part of the problem is that managers don't know how to coach or are not good at coaching, so let's take a look at a simple coaching model. Coaching models can improve performance.[23] Model 9-1 presents a four-step coaching model. The four steps in the coaching model are described below.

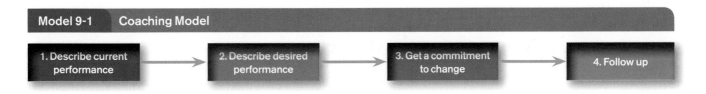

Model 9-1   Coaching Model

1. Describe current performance → 2. Describe desired performance → 3. Get a commitment to change → 4. Follow up

Step 1. Describe current performance. Using specific examples, describe the current behavior that needs to be changed. Tell the employees exactly what they are not doing as well as they can. Notice the positive; don't tell them only what they are doing wrong.

For example, don't say, "You are picking up the box wrong." Say, "Billie, there is a more effective way of picking the box up off the floor than bending at the waist."

Step 2. Describe desired performance. Tell the employees exactly what the desired performance is in detail. Show how they will benefit from following your advice.

If performance is *ability* related, training is needed. Good managers know that training is a large part of their job, and they constantly look at situations as training opportunities.[24] If the employees know the proper way, then the problem is *motivational*, and training is most likely not needed. The manager may just describe the desired performance and ask the employees to state why the performance is important.

For example: Ability—"If you squat down and pick up the box using your legs instead of your back, it is easier, and there is less chance of injuring yourself. Let me demonstrate for you." Motivation—"Why should you squat and use your legs rather than your back to pick up boxes?"

Step 3. Get a commitment to the change. When dealing with an ability issue, it is not necessary to get employees to verbally commit to the change if they seem willing to make it. However, if employees defend their way and you're sure it's not as effective, explain why your proposed way is better. If you cannot get the employees to understand and agree, get a verbal commitment. This step is also important for motivation issues, because if the employees are not willing to commit to the change, they will most likely not make the change.

For example: Ability—the employee will most likely be willing to pick up boxes correctly, so skip this step. Motivation—"Will you squat rather than use your back from now on?"

Step 4. Follow up. Remember that some employees (those with low and moderate capability for self-control) do what managers *inspect* (imposed control), not what they *expect*. You should follow up to ensure that employees are behaving as desired.

When dealing with an *ability* issue, if the person was receptive and you skipped Step 3, say nothing. However, watch to be sure that the activity is done correctly in the future. Coach again, if necessary. For a *motivation* problem, make a statement that you will follow up and that there are possible consequences for repeat performance. You may also want to set up a follow-up meeting to review progress, especially if the behavior is complex.[25]

Counseling

When coaching, you are fine-tuning performance; with counseling and disciplining, you are dealing with an employee who is not performing to standards or is violating the code of conduct. Good organizations realize the need to help employees with problems.[26]

When most people hear the term *counseling*, they think of psychological counseling or psychotherapy. That type of sophisticated help should not be attempted by a noncounseling professional such as a manager. Instead, **management counseling** is *the process of giving employees feedback so they realize that a problem is affecting their job performance and referring employees with problems that cannot be managed within the work structure to the organization's employee assistance program.*

Types of Problem Employees

There are four types of problem employees:

1. Employees who do not have the *ability* to meet the job performance standards. This is an unfortunate situation, but after training reveals that such employees cannot do a good job, they should be dismissed. Many employees are hired on a trial basis; this is the time to say, "Sorry, but you have to go." Keeping an individual who cannot do a particular job harms not only the organization, but also the individual employee. Continued inability to perform will always lead to frustration, and frustration ultimately leads to lower job satisfaction and employee engagement.

2. Employees who do not have the *motivation* to meet job performance standards. These employees often need discipline.

3. Employees who intentionally *violate the rules or the code of conduct.* As a manager, it is your job to enforce the rules through disciplinary action when employees intentionally violate rules, regulations, or procedures.[27]

4. Employees with *problems.* These employees may have the ability to do their job, but they have a problem that affects their job performance. The problem may not be related to the job. It is common for personal problems, such as child care and

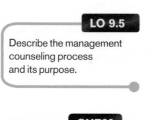

WORK
APPLICATION 9-12

Assess your present or past boss's coaching skills. Did the boss follow the steps in the coaching model?

LO 9.5

Describe the management counseling process and its purpose.

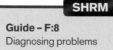

SHRM

Guide – F:8
Diagnosing problems

Video Link 9.4

Counseling

relationship/marital problems, to affect job performance. Employees with problems should be counseled before they are disciplined.

Exhibit 9-3 lists some problem employees you may encounter as a manager. It is not always easy to distinguish between the types of problem employees. Therefore, it is often advisable to start with coaching/counseling and change to discipline if the problem persists.

Personal Problems and Performance

Most managers do not like to hear the details of personal problems, in many cases because they don't know what to do about those problems. Doing so is not a requirement. Instead, the manager's role is to help employees realize that they have problems and that those problems affect their work. The manager's job is getting the employee back on track, back to where they can perform at an acceptable level.

The manager should not give advice on how to solve personal problems such as a relationship difficulty. When professional help is needed, the manager should refer the employee to the Human Resource Department for professional help through the Employee Assistance Program.[28] **Employee Assistance Programs (EAPs)** *provide a staff of people who help employees get professional assistance in solving their problems.* Most large businesses have an EAP to help solve employees' personal problems.

To make the referral, a manager might say something like "Are you aware of our employee assistance program? Would you like me to set up an appointment with Jean in the HR Department to help you get professional assistance?" However, if job performance does not return to standard, discipline is appropriate because it often makes the employee realize the seriousness of his or her problem and the importance of maintaining job performance. Some time off from work, with or without pay, depending on the situation, often helps the employee deal with the problem.

A manager's first obligation is to the organization's performance rather than to individual employees. Not taking action with problem employees because you feel uncomfortable confronting them, because you feel sorry for them, or because you like them does not help you or the employee. Not only do problem employees negatively affect their own productivity; they also cause more work for managers and other employees. Problem employees also lower morale, as others resent them for not pulling their own weight. Thus, it is critical to take quick action with problem employees.

WORK
APPLICATION 9-13

Identify a problem employee you observed on the job. Describe how the person affected the department's performance.

Video Link 9.5

Counseling and Discipline

Exhibit 9-3	Problem Employees

- The late employee
- The absent employee
- The dishonest employee
- The violent or destructive employee
- The alcoholic or drug user
- The nonconformist
- The employee with a family problem
- The insubordinate employee
- The employee who steals
- The sexual or racial harasser
- The safety violator
- The sick employee
- The employee who's often socializing or doing personal work

Disciplining

Coaching, which includes counseling, should generally be the first step in dealing with a problem employee. However, if an employee is unwilling or unable to change or a rule has been broken, discipline is necessary.[29] Managers can't allow employees to engage in counterproductive work behavior,[30] to be uncivil at work,[31] to be revengeful, or to show other deviant behavior.[32] Discipline is also appropriate if an employee is guilty of doing personal things (many employees spend hours per day on the phone and computer for personal reasons) while on company time.[33] Many organizations have also found it necessary to fire employees for inappropriate use of time and resources.[34]

Discipline *is corrective action to get employees to meet standards and the code of conduct.* The major objective of coaching, counseling, and discipline is to change behavior.[35] Secondary objectives may be to (1) let employees know that action will be taken when standing plans or performance requirements are not met and to (2) maintain authority when challenged.

The Human Resource Department handles many of the disciplinary details and provides written disciplinary procedures. These procedures usually outline grounds for specific sanctions and dismissal, based on the violation. Common offenses include theft, sexual or other types of harassment, verbal or substance abuse, and safety violations. However, some union contracts allow employees to delay or block disciplinary action.[36] But, how do we know as managers that we are being fair in applying discipline? Let's take a look at one mechanism for determining whether or not to discipline an errant employee and, if so, what level of discipline is appropriate—Just Cause.

Just Cause

LO 9.6

Briefly discuss the purpose of the tests for Just Cause used in disciplinary investigations.

Just Cause is actually *a set of standard tests for fairness in disciplinary actions that were originally utilized in union grievance arbitrations.* However, many companies other than unionized companies have adopted the tests for Just Cause in their own nonunion disciplinary processes to try to ensure *fairness* and *due process* in applying discipline with their own employees. Basically, Just Cause standards try to ensure that we investigate any disciplinary infraction fully and fairly and provide disciplinary action that matches the level of the offense.

The seven tests for Just Cause are as follows:

1. Did the company give the employee forewarning or foreknowledge of the possible or probable disciplinary consequences of the employee's conduct?

Basically, here we want to know whether or not the employee was given any knowledge beforehand that the action was prohibited. If they were told in some form, such as through the employee handbook or a posting in the workplace, then we meet this first test for Just Cause.

2. Was the company's rule or managerial order reasonably related to (a) the orderly, efficient, and safe operation of the company's business and (b) the performance that the company might properly expect of the employee?

Here we want to find out whether the rule was reasonable. We look at orderly, efficient, and safe operations to see whether the rule or order is reasonable or not. We also look at whether or not the employee should be expected to act in a certain manner in order to follow the rule or order. If the rule was reasonable and the employee should have been expected to act a certain way, we meet the second test.

SHRM

Guide – A:22
Investigations

3. Did the company, before administering discipline to an employee, make an effort to discover whether the employee did in fact violate or disobey a rule or order of management?

Test 3 deals with investigation of the alleged infraction. The supervisor needs to investigate what happened and why it happened. If, upon investigating, the supervisor finds that there is reasonable evidence that the individual did violate the rules, we've met the third test.

4.   Was the company's investigation conducted fairly and objectively?

In Test 4 we're looking for evidence that the investigation was conducted in the same manner as any other investigation into similar circumstances. Are we utilizing facts, figures, and knowledge of the events (OUCH test), or is the supervisor basing their investigation on some emotional reaction to the supposed infraction? If we determine that the investigation was conducted in a reasonably fair and objective manner, we meet Test 4.

5.   At the investigation, was there substantial evidence or proof that the employee was guilty as charged?

Test 5 asks whether or not we have substantial evidence or proof of guilt on the part of the employee. *Substantial evidence* means that we have a large body of circumstantial information showing that the individual probably committed the offense. In a disciplinary action we don't have to meet court standards of proof of guilt. We only have to have a substantial amount of evidence that the infraction was committed. If we have *proof,* then we meet this test, but if we have substantial evidence, we *still* meet the requirements of Test 5.

6.   Has the company applied its rules, orders, and penalties evenhandedly and without discrimination to all employees?

Test 6 tries to identify whether or not the rule is applied in an equitable manner. If the company punishes one person for an infraction by a written reprimand and punishes another person for the same infraction with a disciplinary discharge, then they may not have been evenhanded in their disciplinary action. Does this mean that we have to punish every person the exact same way for the exact same infraction? The answer is no—that is where we get into Test 7.

7.   Was the degree of discipline administered by the company in a particular case reasonably related to (a) the seriousness of the employee's proven offense and (b) the record of the employee's service with the company?

Test 7 is where we are allowed to provide a different punishment to different people based on past history. It says that the discipline has to be related to the seriousness of the offense, but that we also take into account the employee's past record. So if we have two employees who have committed the same infraction and one of the employees has never been in trouble while the other has repeatedly committed the same infraction, we have leeway to provide a different punishment to the two different offenders.

WORK
APPLICATION 9-14

Assess how well your boss and the organization you work or worked for follows the Just Cause standards.

Guidelines for Effective Discipline

Exhibit 9-4 lists eight guidelines for effective discipline.

Exhibit 9-4	Guidelines for Effective Discipline

A.   Clearly communicate the standards and code of conduct to all employees.

B.   Be sure that the punishment fits the crime.

C.   Follow the standing plans yourself.

D.   Take consistent, impartial action when the rules are broken.

E.   Discipline immediately, but stay calm and get all the necessary facts before you discipline.

F.   Discipline in private.

G.   Document discipline.

H.   When the discipline is over, resume normal relations with the employee.

9-3 APPLYING THE CONCEPT

Guidelines for Effective Discipline

Identify which guideline is being followed—or not being followed—in the following statements. Use the guidelines in Exhibit 9-4 as the answers. Place the letter of the guideline (A–H) on the line before its statement.

_____ 12. Come into my office so that we can discuss this matter now.

_____ 13. The boss must have been upset to yell that loudly.

_____ 14. It's not fair. The manager comes back from break late all the time; why can't I?

_____ 15. When I leave the place a mess, the manager reprimands me. When Helen does it, nothing is ever said.

_____ 16. The boss gave me a verbal warning for being late for work and placed a note in my file.

_____ 17. Come on. It's not fair to fire me just for being late for work once.

_____ 18. Give me a break. I didn't know that I'm not supposed to be visiting Facebook while I'm working.

_____ 19. I don't know why, but some days my boss comments about my being late, but other days the boss doesn't say anything about it.

_____ 20. OK, let's get back to the way things were before I had to discipline you.

WORK APPLICATION 9-15

Assess how well your boss and the organization you work or have worked for follow the eight guidelines for effective discipline.

LO 9.7

Describe the concept of progressive discipline in the organization, including the stages of progressive discipline.

Progressive Discipline

If discipline is deemed necessary after going through the Just Cause standards, what type of discipline is warranted? Most organizations today have a series of progressively more severe disciplinary actions that will typically be used for minor disciplinary infractions. **Progressive discipline** is *a process where the employer provides the employee with opportunities to correct poor behavior before the individual is terminated.* Progressive discipline is typically only used in the case of minor behavioral infractions such as arriving late to work or insubordination with a superior. The progressive disciplinary steps are (1) informal coaching talk, (2) oral warning, (3) written warning, (4) suspension, and (5) dismissal. In some *limited* cases we may add a sixth option between suspension and dismissal. We will discuss this option shortly. All five steps are commonly followed for minor violations such as being late for work or excessive absenteeism, but for more important violations, such as stealing, steps may be skipped. At Wal-Mart, any employee with more than three unauthorized absences in six months is disciplined with a warning, and those with seven unauthorized absences are fired.[37] Let's briefly discuss each step in progressive discipline.

Step 1. Informal coaching talk. As we noted, the first option in progressive discipline is an *informal coaching talk.* In an informal talk, we as the supervisor may see an employee coming in late to work and just ask them what is going on and why they were late. Typically the manager won't even write down a recording of this conversation for their own use, although they can do so in the critical incident file (Chapter 8). They're just in an information gathering and recognition mode at this point, and they hope to avoid any further disciplinary problems.

Step 2. Oral warning. In the second option, the supervisor formally tells the employee that their behavior is currently unacceptable and tells them what they need to do to correct the behavior. In this situation, even though the supervisor does not write a report for the individual to sign, they will keep a formal record in their own files of this conversation. The oral warning is the first of our formal methods of disciplining an employee.

Step 3. Written warning. Our third option is a *written warning*. In this situation the supervisor writes on a piece of paper (typically organizations have a standard form for documentation of written warnings) the facts of the situation. They identify the unacceptable behavior for the individual and identify ways to correct the behavior. The supervisor then speaks with the employee using the written document to assist the employee in correcting their actions. Typically here we ask the employee to sign the written warning acknowledging that their actions are under review and not currently acceptable. This paper is then put into the employee's permanent file.

Step 4. Disciplinary suspension. As a fourth stage, we may move on to a *disciplinary suspension* of the employee for a period from one day to typically a maximum of one week. Though most companies use an unpaid suspension, some companies have experimented with a paid day off to allow the employee to think of the suspension not as punishment but as time to figure out whether or not they wish to continue working for the organization. There is *some* evidence that these paid suspensions work although the conclusions are slightly mixed.

Options. Next, we have a couple of limited options we noted at the top of this section—options that would typically not be used but might be valuable in certain cases. We can sometimes *demote* an individual to a lower position in the organization. In some cases this may be valuable because the employee may be overwhelmed at the higher-level position. In general, however, demotion creates even more job dissatisfaction within the individual employee, and we may see their performance deteriorate even further.

We may also choose in some cases to *transfer* an employee from one part of the organization to another. This should typically be used in very limited circumstances. The only time where you should use a transfer as a progressive discipline measure would be where you know that there is a personality conflict between the employee and another employee in the unit or between the employee and their supervisor. Transfers should never be used simply to get rid of a problem employee from your department or division. If this is the reason for the transfer, the manager should not transfer the employee but should correct the problem behavior.

Step 5. Termination. Finally, as a last resort, *discharge* is the final option. If the employee's behavior does not improve over time through verbal and written warnings, suspensions, demotions, or a transfer, we may be forced to let the employee go. However, if we followed the progressive discipline process, we will have sufficient evidence such that the employee will have little opportunity to bring an unlawful termination lawsuit against us.

The Discipline Model

The steps in the following discipline model should be followed each time an employee must be disciplined. The five steps are presented here and summarized in Model 9-2.

Step 1. Refer to past feedback. Begin the interview by refreshing the employee's memory. If the employee has been coached/counseled about the behavior or if he or she has clearly broken a known rule, state that.

> **SHRM**
>
> **Guide – A:1**
> Disciplinary actions (demotion, disciplinary termination)

> **WORK**
> **APPLICATION 1-16**
>
> Describe progressive discipline where you work or have worked.

Model 9-2	The Discipline Model

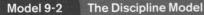

| 1. Refer to past feedback | → | 2. Ask why the undesired behavior was used | → | 3. Give the discipline | → | 4. Get a commitment to change and develop a plan | → | 5. Summarize and state the follow-up |

For example: *Prior coaching*—"Billie, remember my telling you about the proper way to lift boxes with your legs?" *Rule violation*—"Billie, you know the safety rule about lifting boxes with your legs."

Step 2. Ask why the undesired behavior was used. Giving the employee a chance to explain the behavior is part of getting all the necessary facts before you discipline. If you used prior coaching and the employee committed to changing the behavior, ask why the behavior did not change. If the behavior had changed, discipline would not be needed. Again, be sure to describe specific critical incidents to support your contention that behavior has not changed at all or has not changed enough to be at standard.

For example: *Prior coaching*—"Two days ago you told me that you would use your legs, rather than your back, to lift boxes. Why are you still using your back?" *Rule violation*—"Why are you breaking the safety rule and using your back, rather than your legs, to lift the box?"

Step 3. Give the discipline. If there is no good reason for the undesirable behavior, give the discipline. The discipline will vary with the stage in the disciplinary progression.

For example: *Prior coaching*—"Because you have not changed your behavior, I'm giving you an oral warning." *Rule violation*—"Because you have violated a safety rule, I'm giving you an oral warning."

Step 4. Get a commitment to change and develop a plan. Try to get a commitment to change. If the employee will not commit, make note of the fact in the critical incidents file or use the procedures for a written warning. If a plan for change has been developed in the past, try to get the employee to commit to it again. Or develop a new plan, if necessary. A statement such as "Your previous attempt has not worked; there must be a better way" is often helpful. With a personal problem, offer professional help again. Offer recommendations for change and develop a plan to improve.[38]

For example: *Prior coaching or rule violation*—"Will you lift with your legs from now on?" "Is there a way to get you to remember to use your legs instead of your back when you lift?"

Step 5. Summarize and state expected follow-up. Summarize the discipline and state the follow-up disciplinary action to be taken. Part of follow-up is to document the discipline. At all stages, get the employee's signature verifying the disciplinary action taken. If necessary, take the next step in the discipline model: dismissal.

For example: *Prior coaching or rule violation*—"So you agree to use your legs instead of your back when you lift. If I catch you again, you will be given a written warning, which is followed by a suspension and dismissal if necessary."

Terminating

Unfortunately, the coaching, counseling, and disciplining process will not always work to make a problem individual into a productive employee. Because this is the case, HR Managers have to understand the process of termination, which is the final disciplinary step. We do not want to terminate individuals employed by the organization because, as we noted in Chapter 1, turnover is extremely expensive for the organization. However, if an individual cannot be made into a productive member of the workforce, we have no other choice, and there is a benefit to turnover when you replace poor workers with better job matches.[39] First let's take a look at some of the offenses that might be cause for dismissal immediately upon completion of an investigation of the facts, and then we will discuss the dismissal process for nonmanagerial employees, managerial employees, and executives.

WORK
APPLICATION 9-17

Assess how well your present or past boss used the discipline model with employees.

SHRM

Guide – K:3
Retention (involuntary turnover, outplacement counseling, alternative dispute resolution)

LO 9.8

Discuss the two common situations in which an employee might be immediately discharged from the company.

Gross Negligence and Serious Misconduct

Organizations will also set up their own rules listing violations that are grounds for immediate termination, without progressive discipline. For example, many firms list stealing money or other assets from the organization as resulting in immediate dismissal. In one company that promotes open and honest communications, there is a rule that anyone caught lying will be fired.

Two of the more common situations in which we might immediately dismiss employees are in cases of gross negligence or serious misconduct. What constitutes gross negligence or serious misconduct? **Gross negligence** is *a serious failure to exercise care in the work environment*. It is a reckless disregard for circumstances that could cause harm to others; a lack of concern for safety or life. So if someone acted at work, because of their failure to exercise care, in a manner that would be likely to hurt or kill others, then they would be guilty of gross negligence. For example, if we were operating a hospital and an employee who was an electrician left a live, high-voltage electrical line dangling into a hallway, they would be guilty of gross negligence because they could seriously injure or kill someone who happened to come by and contact that live electrical line.

Serious misconduct is a little different from gross negligence. Where negligence is a failure to take care, misconduct is *intentionally* doing something that is likely to harm someone or something else. So, **serious misconduct** would be *intentional behavior by an employee that has potential to cause great harm to another or to the company*. An example of serious misconduct would be bringing a weapon to work. This action has the potential to cause great harm to others. Another example would be a direct assault on another employee by instigating a fight. Each of these could be cause for termination of the individual responsible, of course after an investigation to ensure that they actually did what they are accused of.

Termination of Nonmanagerial Employees

If offenses do not fit into the gross negligence or serious misconduct categories, should we still consider dismissal of an employee? Well, there are certainly times when we have to dismiss employees from the firm, such as when they fail to perform their job satisfactorily even after being thoroughly trained or if they continually disregard rules or policies.

Why do we need to dismiss such employees? Again, it is because these types of behavior can be contagious in the organization, especially in the lower ranks of employees, and we can't afford to have a large number of our employees failing to do their jobs correctly. In some cases, it only takes a few individuals to hurt, or even destroy, job satisfaction and employee engagement throughout the company. As managers in the organization, it is our job to make sure that this doesn't happen, so we sometimes have to go through a termination process.

One of the things that we have to be concerned with is the legal risk to the organization when an employee is terminated. Employment-at-will can mitigate these risks, but it doesn't completely eliminate them. As a result, we would usually want to use Just Cause procedures to analyze the situation and to make a determination concerning whether or not an employee action was sufficiently harmful to the organization to result in termination.

Once the initial determination is made (usually by the individual's immediate supervisor), we would usually want to subject the evidence to a review by another organizational manager. This individual may be the next person up the chain of command from the supervisor, it may be the company's legal counsel, or it may be an HR representative. Regardless of who it is, the second reviewer will make an attempt to ensure that the supervisor's decision was made in an objective fashion (following the OUCH test), and not based on an emotional reaction to the employee or to something they did.

WORK
APPLICATION 9-18

Give examples of reasons why employees can be terminated where you work or have worked.

Video Link 9.6

Steps to Terminate

Losing a job is difficult. But in some cases, people are happy they were terminated because they go on to more satisfying jobs.

Managerial or Executive Employees

What if the individual to be terminated is a manager or an executive for the firm? Do we need to handle this process differently than we would with a lower-level employee? The answer is yes, because management in the organization typically works under different circumstances than do the lower-level employees. The basic process of analyzing the individual's actions using Just Cause procedures should still be followed. However, in many cases managerial employees will be hired through a contractual process. If the manager has a contract with the organization, that contract will typically identify when the individual may be terminated by the firm.

If, however, the individual is not under contract, managerial employees still may need to be dealt with in a slightly different manner than a normal employee. For one thing, managerial employees are usually held to higher standards of behavior by the firm than are lower-level employees. So an action that might not cause a lower-level employee to be terminated could quite possibly create such a situation for a managerial or an executive employee. As would happen in any other case, a judgment concerning the individual's actions will have to be made, and an appropriate level of reaction by the firm will be identified.

There is one more thing that makes managerial terminations different from others. In reality, in most cases when a managerial worker has failed to perform successfully or has committed a disciplinary infraction that would cause termination, they are usually given the option to resign rather than face termination by the organization. Whether this is right or wrong, it is a common practice in most industries. The only time that this would typically not happen is in a case where circumstances are so egregious that the organization is forced to terminate the individual in order to avoid other more serious consequences, such as lawsuits against the organization for the individual's behavior.

Executive termination follows very closely the pattern for managerial actions. In most cases, executives have employment contracts that identify their duties and responsibilities, and also denote circumstances under which they can be terminated by the firm. In public companies, the Board of Directors must agree to dismissal of executives. Another factor that must be considered is the fact that, in many cases, company executives will have a noncompete clause as part of their employment agreement. The reason that this matters is that in some situations if a noncompete case goes to court, the judge will determine whether or not the company is allowing the former executive the opportunity to make a living. If the judge feels that the noncompete clause makes it impossible for the former executive to become gainfully employed, the noncompete clause may be removed from the employment agreement. So we have to be very concerned that we may be creating the ability for a rival firm to compete better against our company because of the knowledge that the executive has about our operations.

One last concern in termination of managerial or executive employees is the fact that these employees typically have access to company files, records, and computers, and may have broad knowledge of the firm's operations. Because of this, there's the potential for managerial or executive employees to be able to harm the organization if they know they're going to be dismissed. So, managerial and executive dismissals must include the concern that company files and records be protected to an extra degree to avoid potential sabotage or misappropriation of information.

Employee Coaching, Counseling, and Discipline May Differ Globally

Do coaching, counseling, and discipline work the same way around the world? Not always. Much of the process of employee development will vary based on country culture, including cultural norms. A recent article notes that "it is clear *cultural competency* will be a prerequisite for managers in the future"[40] in order to become successful coaches, and by extension, counselors and disciplinarians.

There are certainly cultural issues that need to be understood in such coaching and counseling sessions. The coach needs to be "prepared to learn new ways of going about their own learning, so they can readily adapt to new cultures and styles."[41] For instance, in high-power-distance cultures, it may be impossible for the coach to ask a lot of questions of the subject employee about what they might think of a situation. In these societies the manager (coach) is considered to have more and better knowledge of what is necessary in an organizational context than the employee. If the manager then asks the employee what they think should be done, the manager will quite likely lose the respect of the employee.

However, in any coaching or counseling situation, the most important thing in a successful interaction between the coach and the recipient is probably an understanding of the *individual*, not the culture that they come from.[42] This is because no matter what culture a person belongs to, individual personalities may or may not adhere to the cultural norms and values. So we need to look at the individual in order to create a valid and valuable coaching session.

Two of the most significant issues that the coach needs to attempt to determine are therefore the individual's personality type and their motivators.[43] Once we know the individual, we can add in the cultural context that drives, at least in part, the employee's values and norms to understand what is likely to happen based on a specific set of coaching actions. From these pieces of information a good coach can design a program that will improve performance.

Developing Teams

As managers, in addition to developing our individual employees, we also need to develop our employees into effective teams, and this takes leadership and the ability to overcome resistance to change and managing the change process. The three areas of leadership, team building, and change management are critical building blocks for 21st-century organizations.[44] These are the topics of this section.

Leadership

Leadership is *the process of influencing employees to work toward the achievement of organizational objectives.* Here are a few of the thousands of statements being made about leadership. Effective global leaders are a vital asset today.[45] Leaders have a profound impact on organizations' productivity through affecting their employee feelings, thinking, and behaving.[46] The ability to lead is perhaps the most important skill for any manager, but many managers lack leadership skills.[47]

People tend to use the terms *manager* and *leader* interchangeably. However, managers and leaders differ.[48] Leading is one of the major management functions that we originally noted in Chapter 1. Thus, management is broader in scope than leadership. A manager can have this position without being a true leader. There are managers—you may know of some—who are not leaders because they do not have the ability to influence others. There are also good leaders who are not managers. An informal leader, an employee group member, is a case in point. You may have worked in a situation (or been on a sports team) where one of your peers had more influence than the manager.

LO 9.9

Identify the factors that positive leadership takes into account in order to be successful.

SHRM

Guide – D:7
Leadership development

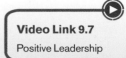

Video Link 9.7
Positive Leadership

So what makes a good, positive leader? There are many leadership theories. However, all of the modern theories of leadership have some commonalities. All modern leadership theories identify the fact that leadership, in its basic form, involves people and goals. A leader has to get individuals and teams in the organization to accomplish organizational goals.[49] This is the basis of leadership, but it isn't enough.[50]

What else do 21st-century leaders have to do? Because of the complexity of modern organizations, leaders have to take into account a variety of *contingency factors*. A contingency factor is a factor that intervenes, or interferes with, the relationship between two variables, in this case the people and the goal. There are many contingency factors in modern organizations. Some of the common contingencies that we deal with in leadership include the leader's personality characteristics and style; follower ability and willingness; complexity of the situation; macro-environmental external factors, such as national economies; and organizational culture and structure, among many others.

Situational Management Model

One model (among many) that takes some of these factors into consideration is the Situational Management Model. But before you learn about the model and how to use it with individuals and teams, complete Self-Assessment 9-1 to determine your preferred management style.

According to contingency theorists, there is no best management style for all situations.[51] Instead, effective managers adapt their styles to individual capabilities or group situations.[52]

Using the Situational Management Model

Now let's learn how to use the Situational Management Model to select the most appropriate management style in a given situation; see Model 9-3.

Employee Capability. There are two distinct aspects of employee capability:

- *Ability.* Do employees have the knowledge, experience, education, skills, and training to do a particular task without direction?
- *Motivation.* Do the employees have the confidence to do the task? Do they want to do the task? Are they committed to performing the task? Will they perform the task without encouragement and support?

Employee capability may be measured on a continuum from *low* to *outstanding*. As a manager, you assess each employee's capability level and motivation on a scale from C1 to C4; see Model 9-3.

Employees tend to start working with low capability, needing close direction. As their ability to do the job increases, managers can begin to be supportive and probably cease close supervision. As a manager, you must gradually develop your employees from low to outstanding levels over time. Most people perform a variety of tasks on the job. It is important to realize that employee capability may vary depending on the specific task. For example, a bank teller may handle routine transactions with great ease but falter when opening new or special accounts.

Manager–Employee Interactions. Managers' interactions with employees can be classified into two distinct categories of behavior:

- *Directive behavior.* The manager focuses on directing and controlling behavior to ensure that tasks get done and closely oversees performance.

9-1 SELF-ASSESSMENT

YOUR PREFERRED MANAGEMENT STYLES

Following are 12 situations. Select the one alternative that most closely describes what you would do in each situation. Don't be concerned with trying to pick the right answer; select the alternative you would really use. Circle a, b, c, or d. (Ignore the C _____ preceding each situation and the S _____ following each answer choice; these will be explained later in Skill Builder 9-3.)

C _____ 1. Your rookie crew seems to be developing well. Their need for direction and close supervision is diminishing. What do you do?

    a. Stop directing and overseeing performance unless there is a problem. S _____

    b. Spend time getting to know them personally, but make sure they maintain performance levels. S _____

    c. Make sure things keep going well; continue to direct and oversee closely. S _____

    d. Begin to discuss new tasks of interest to them. S _____

C _____ 2. You assigned Jill a task, specifying exactly how you wanted it done. Jill deliberately ignored your directions and did it her way. The job will not meet the customer's standards. This is not the first problem you've had with Jill. What do you decide to do?

    a. Listen to Jill's side, but be sure the job gets done right. S _____

    b. Tell Jill to do it again the right way and closely supervise the job. S _____

    c. Tell her the customer will not accept the job and let Jill handle it her way. S _____

    d. Discuss the problem and solutions to it. S _____

C _____ 3. Your employees work well together and are a real team; the department is the top performer in the organization. Because of traffic problems, the president has approved staggered hours for departments. As a result, you can change your department's hours. Several of your workers are in favor of changing. What action do you take?

    a. Allow the group to decide the hours. S _____

    b. Decide on new hours, explain why you chose them, and invite questions. S _____

    c. Conduct a meeting to get the group members' ideas. Select new hours together, with your approval. S _____

    d. Send out a memo stating the hours you want. S _____

C _____ 4. You hired Bill, a new employee. He is not performing at the level expected after a month's training. Bill is trying, but he seems to be a slow learner. What do you decide to do?

    a. Clearly explain what needs to be done and oversee his work. Discuss why the procedures are important; support and encourage him. S _____

    b. Tell Bill that his training is over and it's time to pull his own weight. S _____

    c. Review task procedures and supervise his work closely. S _____

    d. Inform Bill that his training is over and that he should feel free to come to you if he has any problems. S _____

C _____ 5. Helen has had an excellent performance record for the last five years. Recently you have noticed a drop in the quality and quantity of her work. She has a family problem. What do you do?

    a. Tell her to get back on track and closely supervise her. S _____

    b. Discuss the problem with Helen. Help her realize that her personal problem is affecting her work. Discuss ways to improve the situation. Be supportive and encourage her. S _____

    c. Tell Helen you're aware of her productivity slip and that you're sure she'll work it out soon. S _____

    d. Discuss the problem and solution with Helen and supervise her closely. S _____

C ____ 6. Your organization does not allow smoking in certain areas. You just walked by a restricted area and saw Joan smoking. She has been with the organization for 10 years and is a very productive worker. Joan has never been caught smoking before. What action do you take?

   a. Ask her to put the cigarette out; then leave. S ____

   b. Discuss why she is smoking and what she intends to do about it. S ____

   c. Give her a lecture about not smoking and check up on her in the future. S ____

   d. Tell her to put the cigarette out, watch her do it, and tell her you will check on her in the future. S ____

C ____ 7. Your employees usually work well together with little direction. Recently a conflict between Sue and Tom has caused problems. What action do you take?

   a. Call Sue and Tom together and make them realize how this conflict is affecting the department. Discuss how to resolve it and how you will check to make sure the problem is solved. S ____

   b. Let the group resolve the conflict. S ____

   c. Have Sue and Tom sit down and discuss their conflict and how to resolve it. Support their efforts to implement a solution. S ____

   d. Tell Sue and Tom how to resolve their conflict and closely supervise them. S ____

C ____ 8. Jim usually does his share of the work with some encouragement and direction. However, he has migraine headaches occasionally and doesn't pull his weight when this happens. The others resent doing Jim's work. What do you decide to do?

   a. Discuss his problem and help him come up with ideas for maintaining his work; be supportive. S ____

   b. Tell Jim to do his share of the work and closely watch his output. S ____

   c. Inform Jim that he is creating a hardship for the others and should resolve the problem by himself. S ____

   d. Be supportive but set minimum performance levels and ensure compliance. S ____

C ____ 9. Barbara, your most experienced and productive worker, came to you with a detailed idea that could increase your department's productivity at a very low cost. She can do her present job and this new assignment. You think it's an excellent idea. What do you do?

   a. Set some goals together. Encourage and support her efforts. S ____

   b. Set up goals for Barbara. Be sure she agrees with them and sees you as being supportive of her efforts. S ____

   c. Tell Barbara to keep you informed and to come to you if she needs any help. S ____

   d. Have Barbara check in with you frequently so that you can direct and supervise her activities. S ____

C ____ 10. Your boss asked you for a special report. Frank, a very capable worker who usually needs no direction or support, has all the necessary skills to do the job. However, Frank is reluctant because he has never done a report. What do you do?

   a. Tell Frank he has to do it. Give him direction and supervise him closely. S ____

   b. Describe the project to Frank and let him do it his own way. S ____

   c. Describe the benefits to Frank. Get his ideas on how to do it and check his progress. S ____

   d. Discuss possible ways of doing the job. Be supportive; encourage Frank. S ____

C ____ 11. Jean is the top producer in your department. However, her monthly reports are constantly late and contain errors. You are puzzled because she does everything else with no direction or support. What do you decide to do?

   a. Go over past reports, explaining exactly what is expected of her. Schedule a meeting so that you can review the next report with her. S ____

      b. Discuss the problem with Jean and ask her what can be done about it; be supportive. S ____

      c. Explain the importance of the report. Ask her what the problem is. Tell her that you expect the next report to be on time and error-free. S ____

      d. Remind Jean to get the next report in on time without errors. S ____

C ____ 12. Your workers are very effective and like to participate in decision making. A consultant was hired to develop a new method for your department using the latest technology in the field. What do you do?

      a. Explain the consultant's method and let the group decide how to implement it. S ____

      b. Teach the workers the new method and supervise them closely as they use it. S ____

      c. Explain to the workers the new method and the reasons it is important. Teach them the method and make sure the procedure is followed. Answer questions. S ____

      d. Explain the new method and get the group's input on ways to improve and implement it. S ____

To determine your preferred management style, circle the letter you selected for each situation.

	Autocratic	Consultative	Participative	Empowering
1.	c	b	d	a
2.	b	a	d	c
3.	d	b	c	a
4.	c	a	d	b
5.	a	d	b	c
6.	d	c	b	a
7.	d	a	c	b
8.	b	d	a	c
9.	d	b	a	c
10.	a	c	d	b
11.	a	c	b	d
12.	b	c	d	a
Totals	_____	_____	_____	_____

Now add up the number of circled items per column. The column with the most items circled suggests your preferred management style. Is this the style you tend to use most often?

Your management style flexibility is reflected in the distribution of your answers. The more evenly distributed the numbers, the more flexible your style. A total of 1 or 0 for any column may indicate a reluctance to use that style.

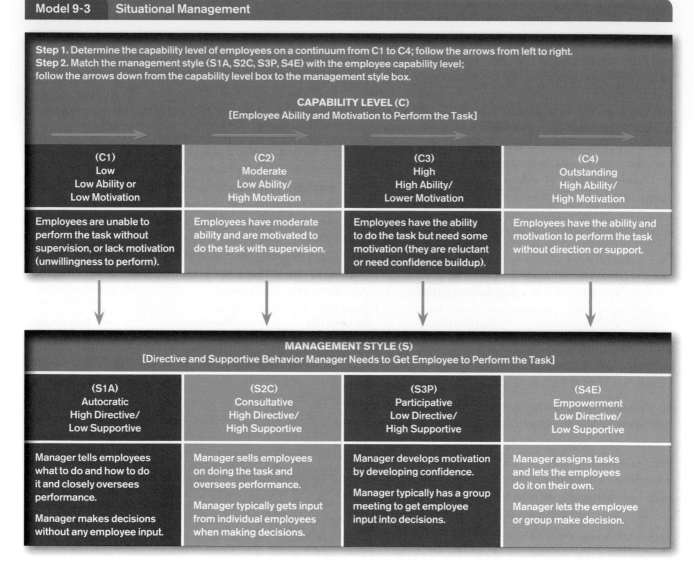

Model 9-3   Situational Management

Step 1. Determine the capability level of employees on a continuum from C1 to C4; follow the arrows from left to right.
Step 2. Match the management style (S1A, S2C, S3P, S4E) with the employee capability level; follow the arrows down from the capability level box to the management style box.

CAPABILITY LEVEL (C)
[Employee Ability and Motivation to Perform the Task]

(C1) Low Low Ability or Low Motivation	(C2) Moderate Low Ability/ High Motivation	(C3) High High Ability/ Lower Motivation	(C4) Outstanding High Ability/ High Motivation
Employees are unable to perform the task without supervision, or lack motivation (unwillingness to perform).	Employees have moderate ability and are motivated to do the task with supervision.	Employees have the ability to do the task but need some motivation (they are reluctant or need confidence buildup).	Employees have the ability and motivation to perform the task without direction or support.

MANAGEMENT STYLE (S)
[Directive and Supportive Behavior Manager Needs to Get Employee to Perform the Task]

(S1A) Autocratic High Directive/ Low Supportive	(S2C) Consultative High Directive/ High Supportive	(S3P) Participative Low Directive/ High Supportive	(S4E) Empowerment Low Directive/ Low Supportive
Manager tells employees what to do and how to do it and closely oversees performance. Manager makes decisions without any employee input.	Manager sells employees on doing the task and oversees performance. Manager typically gets input from individual employees when making decisions.	Manager develops motivation by developing confidence. Manager typically has a group meeting to get employee input into decisions.	Manager assigns tasks and lets the employees do it on their own. Manager lets the employee or group make decision.

- *Supportive behavior.* The manager focuses on encouraging and motivating behavior without telling the employee what to do. The manager explains things and listens to employee views, helping employees make their own decisions by building up confidence and self-esteem.

As a manager you can focus on directing (getting the task done), supporting (developing relationships), or both.

Management Styles. Based on the employee capability level and the type of behavior they need, we select the most appropriate management style for the situation; see Model 9-3, and below for a description of each of the four management styles.

- An *autocratic style* is highly directive and low in supportiveness. The autocratic style is appropriate when interacting with low-capability employees. When interacting with such employees, give very detailed instructions describing exactly what the task is and when, where, and how to perform it. Closely oversee performance and give some support. The majority of time with the employees is spent giving directions and supervising performance. Make decisions without input from the employees.

- A *consultative style* involves highly directive and highly supportive behavior and is appropriate when interacting with moderately capable employees. Give specific instructions and oversee performance at all major stages of a task. At the same time, support the employees by explaining why the task should be performed as requested and answering their questions. Work on relationships as you explain the benefits of completing the task your way. Give fairly equal amounts of time to directing and supporting employees. When making decisions, you may consult employees individually, but retain the final say. Once you make the decision, which can incorporate employees' ideas, direct and oversee employees' performance.

- A *participative style* is characterized by low directive but still high supportive behavior and is appropriate when interacting with employees with high capability. When interacting with such employees, spend a small amount of time giving general directions and a great deal of time giving encouragement. Spend limited time overseeing performance, letting employees do the task their way while focusing on the end result. Support the employees by encouraging them and building up their self-confidence. If a task needs to be done, don't tell them how to do it; ask them how they will accomplish it. Make decisions together or allow employees to make decisions subject to your limitations and approval.

- An *empowering style* requires providing very little direction or support for employees and is appropriate when interacting with outstanding employees. You should let them know what needs to be done and answer their questions, but it is not necessary to oversee their performance. Such employees are highly motivated and need little, if any, support. Allow them to make their own decisions, which can be subject to your approval. Other terms for empowerment are *laissez-faire* and *hands-off*. A manager who uses this style lets employees alone to do their own thing.

Applying the Most Appropriate Management Styles

As part of Skill Builder 9-3, or on your own, return to Self-Assessment 9-1 where you determined your preferred management style. Identify the employee capability level for each of the 12 items; indicate the capability level by placing a number from 1 to 4 on the line marked *C* before each item (1 indicates low capability; 2, moderate capability; 3, high capability; and 4, outstanding capability). Next, indicate the management style represented in each answer choice by placing the letter *A* (Autocratic), *C* (Consultative), *P* (Participative), or *E* (Empowering) on the line marked *S* following each answer choice. Will your preferred management style result in the optimum performance of the task?

Let's see how you did by looking back at the first situation.

C _____ 1. Your rookie crew seems to be developing well. Their need for direction and close supervision is diminishing. What do you do?

    a. Stop directing and overseeing performance unless there is a problem. S _____

    b. Spend time getting to know them personally, but make sure they maintain performance levels. S _____

    c. Make sure things keep going well; continue to direct and oversee closely. S _____

    d. Begin to discuss new tasks of interest to them. S _____

- As a rookie crew, the employees' capability started at a low level, but they have now developed to the moderate level. If you put the number 2 on the *C* line, you were correct.
- Alternative *a* is *E*, the empowering style, involving low direction and support. Alternative *b* is *C*, the consultative style, involving both high

direction and high support. Alternative c is A, the autocratic style, involving high direction but low support. Alternative d is P, the participative style, involving low direction and high support (in discussing employee interests).

- If you selected b as the management style that best matches the situation, you were correct. However, in the business world there is seldom only one way to handle a situation successfully. Therefore, in this exercise, you are given points based on how successful your behavior would be in each situation. In Situation 1, b is the most successful alternative because it involves developing the employees gradually; answer b is worth 3 points. Alternative c is the next-best alternative, followed by d. It is better to keep things the way they are now than to try to rush employee development, which would probably cause problems. So c is a 2-point answer, and d gets 1 point. Alternative a is the least effective because you are going from one extreme of supervision to the other. This is a 0-point answer because the odds are great that this approach will cause problems that will diminish your management success.

The better you match your management style to employees' capabilities, the greater are your chances of being a successful manager.

Building Effective Work Teams

Organizational leaders also have to build strong work teams in 21st-century organizations. Why do we need work teams? Some U.S. workers do not like having to work in teams due to the individualistic nature of American culture. However, today we usually don't have any choice, either as leaders or as followers, in whether or not we work in teams. The major reason is that in most cases, you can't succeed without an effective team effort, and organizations are using teams to create competitive advantage over competitors.[53]

Also, the explosion of available information continues to drive how we operate in business today. This information explosion is caused in large part by technology—computers and their storage and retrieval capabilities. Because of this vast store of information, no one individual can have a broad *and* deep amount of knowledge in any field today, so we put people together in teams so that they can share their expertise with each other.

Team building is probably the most widely used Organizational Development (OD) technique today, and its popularity will continue as more companies use work teams.[54] The effectiveness of each team and how the teams work together directly affect the entire organization.[55] Team building is widely used as a means of helping new or existing groups improve their effectiveness. The goals of team-building programs vary considerably, depending on the group's needs and the change agent's skills.[56] Some typical goals are:

- To clarify the objectives of the team and the responsibilities of each team member
- To identify problems preventing the team from accomplishing its objectives
- To develop team problem-solving, decision-making, objective-setting, and planning skills
- To develop open, honest working relationships based on trust and an understanding of group members

Team-building programs also vary in terms of agenda and length, depending on team needs. Typical programs go through six stages:

1. **Climate building and goals.** The program begins with a change agent trying to develop a climate of trust, support, and openness. The change agent discusses

the program's purpose and goals based on data gathered earlier. Team members learn more about each other and share what they would like to accomplish (goals) through team building.

2. **Evaluation of structure and team dynamics.** The team evaluates its strengths and weaknesses in areas of how the work is done (structure) and how team members work together as they do the work (team dynamics).

3. **Problem identification.** The team identifies its weaknesses or areas where it can improve. Problems may be identified in the change agent's interviews and/or a feedback survey. The team prioritizes the problems based on how solving them will help the team improve performance.

4. **Problem solving.** The team takes the top priority from Stage 3 and develops a solution. It then moves to the other priorities on the list, in order.

5. **Training.** Team building often includes some form of training that addresses the problem(s) facing the group.

6. **Closure.** The program ends with a summary of what has been accomplished. Team members commit to specific improvements in performance. Follow-up responsibility is assigned, and a future meeting is set to evaluate results.

WORK
APPLICATION 9-21

Assess how well your present or past boss developed employees to perform as an effective team.

Managing the Change Process

Managing change has become the ultimate managerial responsibility as firms continuously engage in some form of change.[57] Thus, how firms adopt new practices is a central topic in management.[58] As part of HP's growth strategy to greatly expand technology services, it acquired EDS along with its new technology and people (142,000 workers). With EDS, HP restructured tech services, investing $1 billion in technology to automate their offerings, replacing 34,000 high-cost workers with software that performs certain functions automatically, and cutting its total workforce to 304,000.[59] This restructuring was a massive change to the traditional way in which HP had done business in the past.

People go through four distinct stages when facing change, so we need to manage change through each stage. The four stages of the change process are *denial, resistance, exploration,* and *commitment.* They are presented in Exhibit 9-5 and described using HP as an example below. Notice that the stages in Exhibit 9-5 are in a circular formation because change is an ongoing process, not a linear one. People can regress, as the arrows show.

LO 9.10

Briefly discuss the stages of the change process.

Exhibit 9-5	Stages of the Change Process

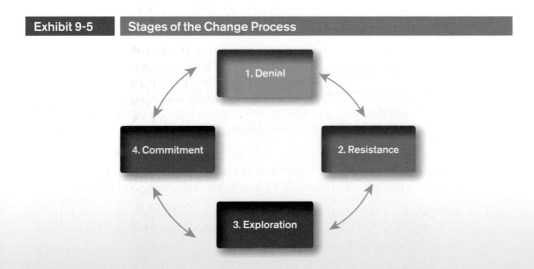

1. **Denial.** When people first hear that change is coming, they may deny that it will affect them. The HP sales force, for example, initially thought that management would focus its change efforts on HP's research and development and engineering departments. When management began changing sales responsibilities and commission structures, many sales representatives were surprised.

2. **Resistance.** Once people get over the initial shock and realize that change is going to be a reality, they often resist the change. When management revealed its plans for restructuring HP, many of the firm's employees expressed doubt that the restructuring was necessary. After management began to implement its plan, employee surveys showed widespread dissatisfaction with and even anger at the changes. This stage is so important that we will present seven ways to help overcome resistance to change in the next subsection.

3. **Exploration.** When the change begins to be implemented, employees explore the change, often through training, and ideally, they begin to better understand how it will affect them. As the restructuring took place, HP employees began to explore the new partnerships developing between engineering and sales and, as a result, began working on new technologies for meeting customer needs. In the first year alone, HP patent applications tripled.

4. **Commitment.** Through exploration, employees determine their level of commitment to making the change a success. The level of commitment can change. After management began restructuring the organization, a fair number of longtime HP employees left the company voluntarily, unwilling to adapt to the changes. Others, however, were excited about the changes.

Overcoming Resistance to Change

Because resistance to change is one of the most difficult factors in successful change management, let's discuss seven things we can do to overcome resistance to changes at work.

1. **Develop a positive trust climate for change.** Develop and maintain good human relations. Make employees realize you have their best interests in mind and develop mutual trust.[60] Constantly look for better ways to do things. Encouraging employees to suggest changes and implementing their ideas are important parts of continuous improvement.

2. **Plan.** Implementing changes successfully requires good planning. You need to identify the possible resistance to change and plan how to overcome it. View change from the employees' position. Set clear objectives so employees know exactly what the change is and how it affects them.[61] The next four steps should be part of your plan.

3. **Clearly state why the change is needed and how it will affect employees.** Communication is the key to change. Employees want and need to know why the change is necessary and how it will affect them, both positively and negatively.[62]

   Be open and honest with employees. Giving employees the facts as far in advance as possible helps them to overcome fear of the unknown. If the grapevine starts to spread incorrect information, correct it as quickly as possible.

4. **Create a win-win situation.** The goal of human relations is to meet employee needs while achieving departmental and organizational objectives. To overcome

resistance to change, be sure to answer the other parties' unasked question, "What's in it for me?" When people can see how they benefit, they are more willing to change.[63] If the organization is going to benefit by the change, so should the employees, so provide incentives for change.[64]

5. **Involve employees.** To create a win-win situation, involve employees. A commitment to change is usually critical to its successful implementation, so make employees part of the process.[65] Employees who participate in developing changes are more committed to them than employees who have changes dictated to them.[66]

6. **Provide support and evaluation.** To overcome resistance to change, employees need to know that managers are there to help them cope with the changes, so relationships matter.[67] Managers need to make the learning process as painless as possible by providing training and other support. To ensure that the change is implemented, and that employees don't regress to old habits, performance appraisals (discussed in the next chapter) need to be tied to successful implementation of the change.[68]

7. **Create urgency.** Many people procrastinate making changes. A feeling of urgency is the primary driver toward taking action. If something is perceived as urgent, it is given a high priority and is often done immediately.[69]

People have different attitudes toward change. Some thrive on it; some are upset by it; many resist it at first but gradually accept it. As a manager of change, you must anticipate whether resistance will be strong, weak, or somewhere in between. Intensity will be lower if you use the seven methods for overcoming resistance to change.

WORK
APPLICATION 9-23

Assess how well your present or past boss overcame resistance to change in each of the seven ways to overcome resistance to change.

Trends and Issues in HRM

In this chapter's trends and issues, we are going to explore issues in motivation and organizational leadership. We will first take a look at positive leadership and how it may minimize the need for disciplinary actions. Next, we'll discuss social media at work, and the burden that such media create for the organization in controlling worker productivity. The final issue in this chapter will deal with organizational commitment to sustainability and the potential that it may help with employee motivation, engagement, and commitment at work.[70]

Positive Leadership and Organizational Discipline

As we noted in this chapter's section on leadership, management and leadership are different. Many managers cannot qualify as true leaders because they do not have the ability to influence others. However, if a manager is a successful leader, can they affect, and potentially lower the need for, disciplinary action in the firm? A significant amount of evidence says that the answer to this question is yes. One study noted that "ethical leaders are 'courageous enough to say "no" to conduct that would be inconsistent with [their] values' . . . conveying information about the importance of standing up for what's right."[71] Research suggests that leaders who possess a variety of positive states (traits, goals, values, and character strengths) are able to positively influence followers' states, behavior, and performance.[72]

We can see from this information that when the leader stands up for the organization's core values and what is right (often called walking the talk), followers see these actions and will frequently act to emulate the leader. The fact is that organizational leaders have

Effective leaders are good teachers who develop employees through using the appropriate management style for each individual.

an outsized effect on organizational culture.[73] This effect on the culture causes a trickle of the leader's values down to the individual employees. Once employees internalize these values, the organizational culture causes them to act in ways that are in concert with the organizational values, which will in turn lower the necessity to discipline organizational members for failing to live up to the standards of their culture. So, by having this strong effect on organizational culture, positive leaders can lower the need for disciplinary action within the firm.

Related to leadership is situational management. Managers who use the appropriate management style for the employee or team capability level do in fact have fewer discipline problems because they provide the appropriate level of directive and supportive behavior to help their employees and teams succeed.[74]

Facebook, Twitter, and So On @ Work—The Burden of Control

Our second issue concerns the use by employees of social media tools at work. As discussed, employees do have a right to privacy, but the right is limited. This chapter's topic deals with developing employees at work, and new social media tools can make this much more difficult than it has historically been. Nearly everyone today carries a cell phone, and most cell phones can link into social media sites including Twitter, Facebook, LinkedIn, Foursquare, and many others.

How does social media create potential problems in the workplace? One of the issues with such social media sites is the fact that they're almost instantaneous in their ability to broadcast information about the company to the outside world. This can cause any number of problems, including the loss of trade secrets, inappropriate or unprofessional posts about the company and its policies, and information inconsistent with the company's public stance. Another issue is the time that can be wasted when employees are participating in social media interactions rather than doing their work. If left unchecked, this can cause a serious loss of productivity within the firm.

So, what can we do about social media at work? According to a recent SHRM article, the organization needs to ensure that it has a strict "lack of privacy policy"[75] to let employees know that they have no expectation of privacy in social media communications in association with their workplace. The same article also identifies the need for a social media policy within the firm that specifically identifies what is classified as a social medium, as well as "the employer's position on the use of social media to discuss the company. Prohibited topics should be specifically identified. Employees should be encouraged not to mix business with personal postings."[76]

ESR

Does a Commitment to Sustainability Foster Employee Motivation?

Can an organization that's committed to a sustainability policy have an effect on employee motivation? A strong sustainability commitment is part of the organization's overall ethical position, so it would make sense that if strong organizational ethics foster employee trust and motivation, then a strong sustainability focus would also create such trust and motivation. But do organizational ethics create motivation in the workforce?

As we noted earlier in the chapter, generally, people who are satisfied with their jobs are more highly motivated.[77] We have recent evidence that shows that there is a strong relationship between organizational ethics and job satisfaction,[78] and we also know that there is a strong relationship between job satisfaction and motivation.[79] As a result, it stands to reason that there is a relationship between ethics (including sustainability) and motivation. Research shows fairly conclusively that ethical leaders enrich the overall work environment, and this enrichment of the work environment translates into extra effort and motivation, and higher levels of job performance.[80]

Wrap-Up

So, what have we covered in this chapter? The chapter's first section discussed worker rights and privileges within the organization, including the right to free consent, the right to due process, the right to life and safety, and limited rights to freedom of conscience, privacy, and free speech. In this section, we identified why three of the individual's rights are limited within the organization based on management's right to protect the organization as well as the other employees of the firm.

Next, we noted that the organization also has a series of rights. These include the right to create and enforce a code of conduct, the right to monitor the workplace, the right to employ workers "at-will," the right to set up orientation periods, and, finally, the right to test for substance abuse in the workplace.

The third major section in this chapter provided a review of developing or terminating individual employees through coaching, counseling, and disciplining or terminating within the firm. We first showed a model for coaching your employees in order to provide them feedback that will allow them to improve their job performance. Next, we discussed the process of counseling workers on poor performance, identified the four common types of problem employees, and showed you some ways to handle these employees. We also covered the process of employee discipline, including the use of the tests for Just Cause and how they are applied. We also identified the potential to use progressive discipline in cases that are not severe, and we noted cases when progressive discipline should probably not be considered. To end this section of the chapter, we discussed the process of termination as a final disciplinary step—one that we do not want to use unless it is necessary. Here we discussed the concepts of gross negligence in serious misconduct and identified what is meant by each of these terms. We then noted the general differences in the process of terminating lower-level employees versus managers or executives of the firm.

The fourth major section of the chapter dealt with leadership, situational management, team building, and change management. Here we discussed the concept of positive leadership and how managers can apply positive leadership within the firm. We explained how to use the Situational Management Model to select the most appropriate management style for the employee or team capability level. We then discussed team building as an organizational development technique and how this technique can improve the effectiveness of the company's work teams. In the last part of this section, we discussed the four stages of managing the change process, as well as methods to overcome resistance to organizational change. That's another big dose of information, and enough for these topics, so let's move on to the chapter summary.

Chapter Summary

 Visit www.sagepub.com/lussier for helpful study resources.

9.1 Discuss the difference between a right and a privilege in a work context.

Rights are things that an individual is allowed to do in a society, or in this case an organization, without asking anyone's permission. On the other hand, the individual is required to get permission from some authority in order to exercise their privileges. So, the easy way to tell the difference would be, if the employee has to request permission to do something within the organization, it is a privilege that they are requesting to exercise. Employees would not need permission to exercise their rights.

9.2 Identify the commonly accepted individual rights in the workplace.

The commonly accepted rights of individuals within the workplace include the *right to free consent*—the right of the individual to know what they are being asked to do and the consequences of their actions; the *right to due process*—a right to not be punished arbitrarily, or without reason (generally we use the seven tests for Just Cause to ensure this right); the *right to life and safety*—everyone in organizations has a right to be protected from harm by the organization while working there; the *right to freedom of conscience*—a right in general to not be forced to violate the individual's personal values and beliefs; the *right to privacy*—a right to protection from unreasonable searches or intrusions into their personal space; and the *right to free speech*—freedom to express their opinions or concerns within the organization without fear of harming their work relationship.

9.3 Identify the rights that management has in modern organizations.

Management first has a right to create and enforce an employee *code of conduct*. Managers also have a right to *monitor the workplace* to protect the organization and its employees. The organization can also identify the relationship with workers as one of *employment-at-will*, which basically allows either party to break the relationship at any time, even without stating a reason. Management also has a right to set up an *orientation period* and require that new employees attend such orientation. Finally, management has a right to *test for drugs* in the workplace. In each case, these rights are offered based on the need for managers to be able to protect the organization and the employees from unnecessary danger or harm.

9.4 Briefly describe the coaching process and how it is used.

Coaching is designed to give employees feedback in order to improve their performance over time. This feedback in general should be designed to improve the employees' motivation to perform for the organization. The coaching process occurs in four basic steps: Step 1—*Describe the current performance*, or what is presently being done by the employee; Step 2—*Describe the desired performance*, or what the manager wants the employee to change about the way they perform; Step 3—*Get a commitment to change*, or ask the employee to verbally commit to make the change the manager has asked for; and Step 4—*Follow up*, to ensure that the employee is behaving in the desired manner.

9.5 Describe the management counseling process and its purpose.

The management counseling process is designed to provide employees with feedback so that they understand that their performance is not currently at an acceptable level, and to provide them with guidance on how to improve their performance over time. The purpose of management counseling is to get the employee back on track with their work so that they can perform at an acceptable, or even exceptional, level.

9.6 Briefly discuss the purpose of the tests for Just Cause used in disciplinary investigations.

Just Cause is a set of standards to test for fairness in an organizational setting in order to ensure that any disciplinary action taken has a reasonable basis. The tests attempt to ensure that the individual knew what the rules were, that they violated or disobeyed those rules based on either reasonable evidence or proof, and if the rules were violated, that the disciplinary action was appropriate and fair.

9.7 Describe the concept of progressive discipline in the organization, including the stages of progressive discipline.

Progressive discipline is usually used for minor disciplinary infractions in the organization. It provides progressively stronger sanctions against an employee who continues to behave in an unacceptable manner in the organization, based on rules or policies. The sequence of progressive discipline is (1) informal talk, (2) oral warning, (3) written warning, (4) suspension, (5) in *some* cases demotion or transfer, and (6) dismissal.

9.8 Discuss the two common situations in which an employee might be immediately discharged from the company.

Probably the two most common situations where an employee might be immediately dismissed from the organization are in cases of gross negligence or serious misconduct. Gross negligence is a major failure to pay attention to the work environment where, as a result of this failure to exercise care, the individual or another employee could likely be hurt or killed. While gross negligence is a failure to pay attention, serious misconduct is an intentional action by an employee that has the potential to seriously hurt or kill another person or cause great harm to the organization. Either of these situations would generally be cause for dismissal from the organization immediately after an investigation showed that the individual did what they were accused of.

9.9 Identify the factors that leadership takes into account in order to be successful.

Modern leadership theories identify the fact that leadership involves people and goals. A leader has to get individuals and teams in the organization to accomplish organizational goals. Because of the complexity of modern organizations, leaders also have to take into account a variety of *contingency factors*. Some of the common contingencies that we deal with in leadership include the leader's personality characteristics and style; follower ability and willingness; complexity of the situation; macro-environmental external factors, such as national economies; and organizational culture and structure.

9.10 Briefly discuss the stages of the change process.

The four stages of the change process include denial, resistance, exploration, and commitment. Denial is frequently the first reaction when people hear the changes are going to be made in the workplace. Employees frequently deny that any change necessary will have any effect on them and their work. Once employees understand that the change will affect their work, resistance to change often occurs. Next, as the change is implemented, employees may begin to explore how the change affects their work and how they can adapt to the necessary changes. Finally, through the exploration stage, the employees determine their level of commitment to the change process. Recall, however, that the change process is ongoing, not linear. Changes continually occur, and organizations are constantly going through new change processes.

9.11 Identify the factors that can help overcome resistance to change in organizations.

There are seven major steps to overcome resistance to change:

1. Develop a positive trust climate for change. 2. Plan the change. 3. Clearly state why the change is needed and how it will affect employees. 4. Create a win-win situation. 5. Involve employees. 6. Provide support and evaluation. 7. Create urgency. As a manager you must anticipate whether resistance will be strong or weak, and should master the seven steps for overcoming resistance to change.

Key Terms

Coaching

Discipline

Employee Assistance Program (EAP)

Employment-at-will

Gross negligence

Just Cause

Leadership

Management counseling

Privileges

Progressive discipline

Rights

Serious misconduct

Key Term Review

Complete each of the following statements using one of this chapter's key terms:

_____ are things that individuals are allowed to do based on asking permission from an authority.

_____ are things a person in society is allowed to do without any permission required from an authority.

_____ allows the company or the worker to break their work relationship at any point in time, with or without any particular reason, as long as in doing so no law is violated.

_____ is the process of giving motivational feedback to maintain and improve performance.

_____ is the process of giving employees feedback so they realize that a problem is affecting their job performance and referring employees with problems that cannot be managed within the work structure to the organization's Employee Assistance Program.

_____ provide a staff of people who help employees get professional assistance in solving their problems.

_____ is corrective action to get employees to meet standards and the code of conduct.

_____ is a set of standard tests for fairness in disciplinary actions that were originally utilized in union grievance arbitrations.

_____ is a process where the employer provides the employee with opportunities to correct poor behavior before the individual is terminated.

_____ is a serious failure to exercise care in the work environment.

_____ is intentional behavior by an employee that has potential to cause great harm to another or to the company.

_____ is the process of influencing employees to work toward the achievement of organizational objectives.

Quick Check (True-False)

1. Exercising individual rights requires permission from an authority while exercising personal privileges requires no permission. T F

2. People in organizations only have a *limited* right to free consent because of organizational rules and policies. T F

3. Organizations, just like societies, have a duty to protect each employee's rights. T F

4. The right to due process attempts to ensure that employees are not punished arbitrarily. T F

5. An employee's right to privacy in the workplace can be overcome by an organization's duty to protect all of its workers. T F

6. Employment-at-will means that the employee can do what they want at work as long as no laws are violated. T F

7. Orientation periods for new employees are illegal in all organizations. T F

8. Coaching, counseling, and discipline are all designed to improve employee performance over time. T F

9. Most managers enjoy providing coaching feedback to weak employees. T F

10. If, after initial training and coaching, new employees do not have the *ability* to do the job, they should be dismissed. T F

11. The tests for Just Cause try to ensure that we investigate any disciplinary infraction fully and fairly, and provide disciplinary action that matches the level of the offense. T F

12. To avoid looking weak, managers should rarely use progressive discipline. Instead, employees who break the rules should generally be dismissed. T F

13. Poor job behaviors can become contagious if allowed to continue, and soon many employees will exhibit the same types of negative work behaviors. T F

14. Once the initial determination to terminate a worker's employment has been made, it should be done with no further review and no delay. T F

15. Managerial or executive employees may have greater ability to harm the organization if their employment is terminated, due to the knowledge that they have of the firm's operations. T F

16. Managers must learn to adapt to the various contingency factors that affect their dealings with their employees in order to become good positive leaders. T F

17. Work teams are generally unnecessary in organizations. They are only created to minimize the manager's workload. T F

18. The four stages of change include denial, evasion, resistance, and commitment. T F

19. Trust is one of the best ways for a manager to overcome resistance to change. T F

Communication Skills

The following critical-thinking questions can be used for class discussion and/or for written assignments to develop communication skills. Be sure to give complete explanations for all answers.

1. Do you think that organizations should provide more rights or fewer rights to employees than those listed in the chapter? If more, what would you add? If fewer, which rights do you think are unimportant?

2. Should companies make a strong attempt to never violate the privacy rights of an employee? Why or why not?

3. Do you think an organization would be more adaptable to changes in its environment if it provides more of a free speech right to all employees? Why or why not?

4. Do you think codes of conduct have any effect on employees' activities? What would make them more or less effective in an organization?

5. Is employment-at-will fair, or should companies have to have a legitimate reason to discharge their employees? Justify your answer.

6. Should coaching, counseling, and discipline processes be utilized by the firm, or should we just terminate the employment of workers who are not doing their job? Explain your answer.

7. Is it really necessary to follow *all* of the Just Cause standards rigorously, or is it a waste of time? Explain your answers.

8. Do you feel that progressive discipline processes actually work to improve employee performance in most cases? Why or why not?

9. In your opinion, should there be any situations in which you might not immediately terminate a worker's employment as a result of gross negligence or serious misconduct? Explain why you feel this way.

10. Do you think leadership can be learned, or is it just a personal characteristic that some people have? Why do you think this way?

11. What would you do as a manager in order to create high-performing work teams in your organization? How would your actions create these high-performance teams?

12. What are some of the methods you have seen managers or others use to overcome resistance to change? Were these methods successful? Why or why not?

Video

Please visit the student study site at **www.sagepub.com/lussier** to view the video links in this chapter.

Answers

REVIEW QUESTIONS (TRUE-FALSE) Answers

1. F   2. F   3. T   4. T   5. T   6. F   7. F   8. T   9. F   10. T   11. T   12. F   13. T   14. F   15. T   16. T   17. F   18. F   19. T

Case

Case 9-1. Just One Little Slip

Charlene Fisher is a market analyst for the Top Cat Apparel Company, a women's boutique clothing store with shops in several southwestern states. She joined the company in early 2007 at the corporate office located in Memphis, Tennessee. Charlene previously lived in Richmond, Virginia, and worked as a market analyst for a major retailer for five years. She was looking for a better job when she found Top Cat's advertisement for a market analyst. After a telephone interview with Alan Jordan, Top Cat's Human Resource Manager, she was invited to interview with Ron McCoy, the Vice President, in Memphis. At the end of the interview, Mr. McCoy offered her the position and said that she would later receive written confirmation of the offer's terms. Within a week, Charlene received a letter of confirmation from Vice President McCoy, detailing the terms of compensation and stating that she would be offered an employment contract from year to year as long as her work performance was satisfactory. She also received a booklet containing the company's benefit plans

as well as a copy of the employee handbook for all new employees. Charlene accepted the offer and moved to Memphis from Richmond, though the moving expenses cost her considerably.

As a market analyst at Top Cat, Charlene's primary function was to anticipate fashion trends and provide the shop managers with purchase recommendations about the type, brand, and quantity of clothing they should have in their store inventories. Her performance was annually rated as being very good during the first three years of her employment with the company, and therefore her contract was extended each year with a salary increase. Charlene recently made a costly forecasting error by recommending the purchase of a large number of coats that didn't sell very well in most stores. Tom Long, her manager, informed Charlene that the top management folks were very unhappy with her decision to recommend the coat purchase, and the company had decided not to renew her contract.

Charlene asked for a meeting with Mr. Long and HR Manager Alan Jordan to appeal the company's decision not to renew her employment contract, which she considered the same as a discharge for poor work performance. She claimed that her job performance should not be based upon one mistake since her performance evaluations had been consistently very good. Charlene felt that since this one error was not a typical example of her work performance throughout her employment with the company, her termination was too severe. She believed that she should have an opportunity to show that she learned from this mistake and that a similar incident would not likely occur again. Charlene pointed out a statement in the company's employee handbook that asserts employees will only be discharged for just or sufficient cause. Charlene felt that some lesser form of discipline should be considered in her case. Mr. Jordan informed her that the decision had already been made by upper management, and they were not willing to reconsider this decision. He explained that Top Cat Apparel Company is an at-will employer, and her employment can be terminated for any reason as long as the decision is not based upon some discriminatory or illegal grounds.

Charlene decided to sue the company for wrongful discharge and breach of contract.

Questions

1. Does Charlene have a good argument that she is a contractual employee and that the company has a relationship with her that is controlled by either express or implied terms? Explain your answer.

2. What reasons would you expect the employer to claim in defense of their action? Thoroughly explain your answer.

3. Charlene expects the company to take a less severe and more gradual course of action. Identify and explain the steps of this process that Charlene hopes the company will follow.

4. What are the factors or questions that should be considered in order to determine if Charlene was afforded due process by the company in their decision to not continue her employment?

5. Explain how the situation may have been different if the company was located in the state of Montana.

Case created by Herbert Sherman, PhD

SKILL BUILDER 9-1

Coaching

Objective

To develop coaching skills using the coaching model.

Skills

The primary skills developed through this exercise are:

1. *HR Management skill* – Conceptual and design

2. *SHRM Curricular Guide* – J: Training and Development

Procedure 1 (2–4 minutes)

Break into groups of three. Make some groups of two, if necessary. Each member selects one of the following three situations in which to be the manager and a different one in which to be the employee. In each situation, the employee knows the standing plans; he or she is not motivated to follow them. You will take turns coaching and being coached.

Three Problem Employee Situations

1. Employee 1 is a clerical worker. The person uses files, as do the other 10 employees in the department. The employees all know that they are supposed to return the files when they are finished so that others can find them when they need them. Employees should have only one file out at a time. The supervisor notices that Employee 1 has five files on the desk, and another employee is looking for one of them.

2. Employee 2 is a server in an ice cream shop. The employee knows that the tables should be cleaned up quickly after customers leave so that new customers do not have to sit at dirty tables. It's a busy night. The supervisor finds dirty dishes on two of this employee's occupied tables. Employee 2 is socializing with some friends at one of the tables.

3. Employee 3 is an auto technician. All employees know that they are supposed to put a paper mat on the floor of each car so that the carpets don't get dirty. When the service supervisor got into a car Employee 3 repaired, the car did not have a mat, and there was grease on the carpet.

Procedure 2 (3–7 minutes)

Prepare for coaching to improve performance. Each group member writes an outline of what he or she will say when coaching Employee 1, 2, or 3, following the steps below:

1. Describe current performance.

2. Describe desired performance. (Don't forget to have the employee state why it is important.)

3. Get a commitment to the change.

4. Follow up.

Round 1 (5–8 minutes)

Role-Playing. The manager of Employee 1, the clerical worker, coaches him or her as planned. (Use the actual name of the group member playing Employee 1.) Talk—do not read your plan. Employee 1, put yourself in the worker's position. Both the manager and the employee will have to ad lib. The person not playing a role is the observer. He or she makes notes as the observer for each step of the coaching model listed above. Try to make positive comments and point out areas for improvement. Give the manager alternative suggestions about what he or she could have said to improve the coaching session. As the supervisor, coach Employee 1.

Feedback. The observer leads a discussion of how well the manager coached the employee. (This should be a discussion, not a lecture.) Focus on what the manager did well and how the manager could improve. The employee should also give feedback on how he or she felt and what might have been more effective in getting him or her to change. Do not go on to the next interview until you are told to do so. If you finish early, wait for the others to finish.

Round 2 (5–8 minutes)

Same as Round 1, but change roles so that Employee 2, the server, is coached. The job is not much fun if you can't talk to your friends. As the supervisor, coach Employee 2. Again, the observer gives feedback after the coaching.

Round 3 (5–8 minutes)

Same as Rounds 1 and 2, but change roles so that Employee 3, the auto technician, is coached. As the supervisor, coach Employee 3. Again, the observer gives feedback after the coaching.

Apply It

What did I learn from this exercise? How will I use this knowledge in the future?

_____

_____

SKILL BUILDER 9-2

Disciplining

Objective

To develop your ability to discipline an employee using the disciplining model.

Skills

The primary skills developed through this exercise are:

1. *HR Management skill* – Conceptual and design

2. *SHRM Curricular Guide* – J: Training and Development

Note that this is a continuation of Skill Builder 9-2. Coaching didn't work, and you have to discipline the employee.

Procedure 1 (2–4 minutes)

Break into groups of three. Make some groups of two, if necessary. Each member selects one of the three situations from Skill Builder 9-2. Decide who will discipline Employee 1, the clerical worker; Employee 2, the ice cream shop server; and Employee 3, the auto technician. Also select a different group member to play the employee being disciplined and the observer.

Procedure 2 (3–7 minutes)

Prepare for the discipline session. Write a basic outline of what you will say to Employee 1, 2, or 3; follow the steps in the discipline model below.

1. Refer to past feedback. (Assume that you have discussed the situation before, using the coaching model.)

2. Ask why the undesired behavior was used. (The employee should make up an excuse for not changing.)

3. Give the discipline. (Assume that an oral warning is appropriate.)

4. Get a commitment to change and develop a plan.

5. Summarize and state the follow-up.

Round 1 (5–8 minutes)

Role-Playing. The manager of Employee 1, the clerical worker, disciplines him or her as planned. (Use the actual name of the group member playing the employee.) Talk—do not read your plan. Both the manager and the employee will need to ad lib. As the supervisor, discipline Employee 1.

   The person not playing a role is the observer. He or she makes notes on the five steps of the discipline model above. For each of the steps, try to make a statement about the positive aspects of the discipline and a statement about how the manager could have improved. Give alternative things the manager could have said to improve the discipline session. Remember, the objective is to change behavior.

Feedback. The observer leads a discussion of how well the manager disciplined the employee. The employee should also give feedback on how he or she felt and what might have been more effective in getting him or her to change. Do not go on to the next interview until you are told to do so. If you finish early, wait until the others finish or the time is up.

Round 2 (5–8 minutes)

Same as Round 1, but change roles so that Employee 2, the ice cream server, is disciplined. Employee 2, put yourself in the worker's position. As the supervisor, discipline Employee 2, and the observer gives feedback.

Round 3 (5–8 minutes)

Same as Rounds 1 and 2, but change roles so that Employee 3, the auto technician, is disciplined. Employee 3, put yourself in the worker's position. As the supervisor, discipline Employee 3, and the observer gives feedback.

Apply It

What did I learn from this exercise? How will I use this knowledge in the future?

_____

_____

SKILL BUILDER 9-3
Situational Management

Objective

To learn how to use the Situational Management Model to develop skill at selecting the most appropriate management style in a given situation.

Skills

The primary skills developed through this exercise are:

1. *HR Management skill* – Conceptual and design

2. *SHRM Curricular Guide* – J: Training and Development

Assignment

As stated back in the chapter section on situational management, select the most appropriate management style for each of the 12 situations in Self-Assessment 9-1 using the Situational Management Model. Be sure to fill in the C _____ (1-2-3-4) and S _____ (1A-2C-3P-4E) lines as instructed in the text.

Apply It

What did I learn from this exercise? How will I use this knowledge in the future?

_____

_____

Your instructor may review the Situational Management Model completing more of the situations in class and/or ask you to do this Skill Builder in class by breaking into groups of two to three and to select or discuss your answers. If so, the instructor will provide you with any necessary information or additional instructions.

10

Employee and Labor Relations

Learning Outcomes

After studying this chapter you should be able to:

10.1 Briefly describe the five steps in the message-sending process

10.2 Briefly describe the three steps in the message-receiving process

10.3 Identify the primary reason why measuring job satisfaction is so difficult, and the best tool for getting employees to tell the truth about their level of satisfaction

10.4 Identify the major labor relations laws in the United States, and the major reasons for each law

10.5 Briefly discuss the difference between wrongful discharge and constructive discharge

10.6 Briefly discuss the NO TIPS rule for labor elections

10.7 What can management do to limit union organizing efforts?

10.8 Identify the five conflict management styles. How is each described in terms of winning and losing?

10.9 Briefly explain the processes of mediation and arbitration and the major difference between the two processes

10.10 Define the following terms:

Trust	Constructive discharge
Communication	Labor relations
Feedback	Collective bargaining
Paraphrasing	Grievance
Active listening	Lockout
Strike	Economic strike
Whistle-blower	Conflict
Express contract	Negotiating
Implied contract	Mediator
Quasi-contract	Arbitrator
Wrongful discharge	Functional conflict

Chapter 10 Outline

A.   Employee and Labor Relations (required)
2.   Alternative dispute resolution
8.   Union membership
9.   Union-related labor laws
10.   Union/management relations
11.   Union decertification and deauthorization
12.   Collective bargaining issues
13.   Collective bargaining process
14.   Negotiation skills
15.   Conflict management
16.   Grievance management
17.   Strikes, boycotts, and work stoppages
18.   Unfair labor practices
19.   Managing union organizing policies and handbooks
21.   Attitude surveys

B.   Employment Law (required)
11.   The Labor Management Reporting and Disclosure Act of 1959
12.   The National Labor Relations Act of 1935
13.   The Labor Management Relations Act of 1947
15.   The Railway Labor Act of 1926
17.   The Worker Adjustment and Retraining Notification Act of 1988
19.   Contractual and tort theories
21.   Employer unfair labor practices
23.   Agency relationships/quasi-contracts
24.   Employment contracts
28.   Whistle-blowing/retaliation

K.   Workforce Planning and Talent Management (required)
4.   Retention (voluntary turnover, job satisfaction, withdrawal, alternatives)

Case 10-1. Decker Deals With the Unions

SHRM
HR CONTENT

See Appendix A:
SHRM 2010 Curriculum Guidebook for the complete list

I Walk the Line

Few issues bring HR professionals out in force to voice their opinion like labor relations. The barriers between management and labor may seem like an impenetrable wall, yet there is a very fine line separating management rights from unacceptable labor practices. My good friend Linda's company was facing a labor organization drive. Her boss's solution was to direct the managers to summon all the employees to a lunch meeting so he could personally impress upon them all the negative things that would befall them and their jobs if they elected union representation. Fortunately, Linda's boss listened to her suggestion that he consult professional legal advice before he reacted to the campaign. Why wasn't such a meeting a great idea? Are there restrictions on the actions a company may take to counter a labor organization campaign? Chapter 10 takes on another critical legal liability portion of HR Management—labor relations.

The Practitioner's Model for HRM

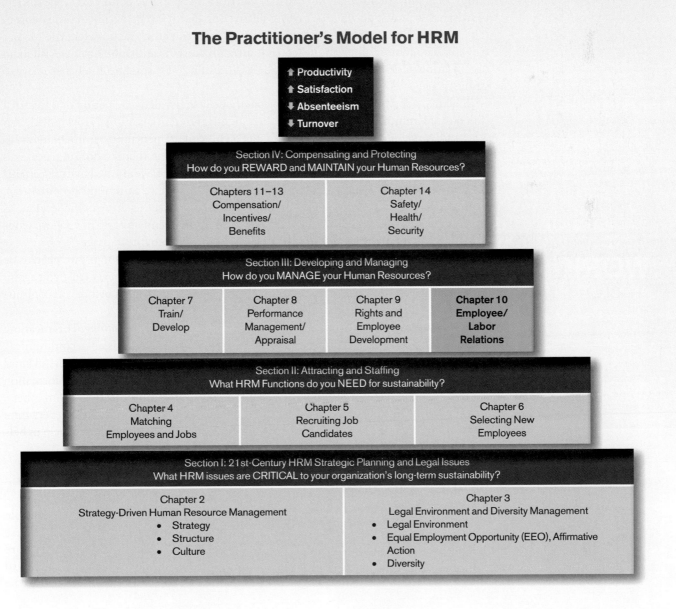

Labor Relations: A Function of Trust and Communication

No matter what else happens in an organization, managers and labor have to work together to accomplish sets of goals. In order for this to happen successfully, people in organizations must be able to communicate with each other. Communication allows us to control the work environment, give and receive important information, express how we feel about a set of circumstances, and motivate ourselves and others. In addition, whenever people have to communicate in order to accomplish a goal, trust must be established between the sender and the receiver, or barriers are created in the communication process. In this section, we begin with an overview of trust and communications and then provide details of sending and receiving messages when communicating.

Trust and Communications

Trust is simply *faith in the character and actions of another*. In other words, it is a belief that another person will do what they say they will do—every time. So, how do we get others to trust us? We must do what we say we will do consistently over a period of time in order to get others to trust our actions—we need to "walk the talk." Jack Welch, the former CEO of GE and now an executive consultant, said trust "is enormously powerful in an organization and people won't do their best without it."[1] Trust is absolutely necessary to strong management-labor relations.

Since a person must consistently do what they say they will over a period of time, trust isn't created immediately. But, ask yourself a slightly different question: "How quickly can we as individuals *lose* trust in another person?" This can happen almost immediately—as soon as the other person fails to do something that we trusted them to do. So, trust takes awhile to create but only takes an instant to lose. As managers, we always have to keep this fact in mind because we need our employees to trust us when we communicate with them. In any communications, receivers take into account the trust they have in the senders, as well as the senders' credibility.[2] When receivers do not trust senders or do not believe senders know what they are talking about, they are reluctant to accept the message.[3]

So the bottom line is, if we want to improve others' level of trust in us, we need to be open and honest with people.[4] If people catch you in a lie, they may never trust you again. To gain and maintain trust and credibility, always get the facts straight before you communicate, and send clear, correct messages.[5]

Communication is *the process of transmitting information and meaning*. This meaning can be transferred verbally, nonverbally, or in writing. Although this is not a communications course, open communications are needed for the organization to be successful,[6] and good managers are good communicators. This involves successfully providing information to others as a sender, as well as being a capable receiver of communications from others. Let's face it—we all like to communicate (we are glued to our cell phones), and every time we communicate we are selling our ideas.[7] Let's take a look at some tips that can help us better communicate as both a sender and a receiver.

Sending Messages

The vast majority of messages you send and receive in the workplace are quite simple and straightforward: "Please copy this document." "I'll call you when I've reviewed these specifications." "I put the report you requested on your desk." Many such messages are transmitted orally and face-to-face or in a brief memo, e-mail, or fax. Such straightforward messages need minimal planning, because they are routine. However, sometimes the

WORK
APPLICATION 10-1

Select a present or past boss and describe how well you trust(ed) him or her. Be sure to give specific examples of things your boss did, or didn't do, that created or destroyed your trust.

message you need to transmit is difficult, unusual, or especially important. For example, you may have the difficult task of communicating to someone that he or she is to be laid off. Or, perhaps you need to communicate to workers at one plant about the changes that will be occurring as a result of closing a second plant and moving its processes to this one—an unusual situation and an important communication.

Before sending a message, we should answer the *what* (set our goal—end result),[8] *who* (which employee/s), *how* (verbal/written), *when* (date and time), and *where* (your place or mine) questions. When planning and sending a message, especially when it's giving advice, as *The One Minute Manager* says, keep it short.[9]

The Message-Sending Process

Oral communication channels (channels where we *speak* to others directly) are richer than other channels, and face-to-face, oral communication is the best channel when the message you must transmit is a difficult or complex one. When sending a face-to-face message, you can follow the steps in Model 10-1, the message-sending process.

LO 10.1

Briefly describe the five steps in the message-sending process.

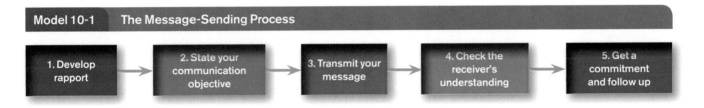

Model 10-1   The Message-Sending Process

1. Develop rapport → 2. State your communication objective → 3. Transmit your message → 4. Check the receiver's understanding → 5. Get a commitment and follow up

Step 1. Develop rapport. Begin by putting the receiver at ease by creating a harmonious relationship. It is usually appropriate to begin communication with an opening conversation related to the message.

Step 2. State your communication objective. It is helpful for the receiver to know the objective (end result) of the communication before you explain the details.

Step 3. Transmit your message. Tell the receiver(s) whatever you want them to know calmly and with respect. It may be helpful to also provide written directives and/or to ask the receiver to take some notes.

Step 4. Check the receiver's understanding. When giving information, ask direct questions and/or paraphrase. Simply asking "Do you have any questions?" does not check understanding. (The next subsection describes how to check understanding.)

Step 5. Get a commitment and follow up. If the message involves assigning a task, make sure that the message recipient can do the task and have it done by a certain time or date. Finally, follow up to ensure that the necessary action has been taken.

Checking Understanding: Feedback

Feedback is *information provided by the receiver that verifies that a message was transmitted successfully.* As you probably already know, when we ask people if they have any questions, they usually don't ask questions for a variety of reasons. So as senders of messages, we need to get feedback from the receiver. Questioning, paraphrasing, awareness of nonverbal communication, and inviting comments and suggestions are all means of obtaining feedback that check understanding. Being asked for their feedback motivates employees to be creative and achieve high levels of performance.[10] The best way to make sure communication has taken place is to get feedback from the receiver of the message through questioning and paraphrasing.

WORK
APPLICATION 10-2

Select a present or past boss and describe how well he or she sent messages. Did he or she essentially follow the steps in the message-sending process?

WORK
APPLICATION 10-3

Select a present or past boss and describe how effective he or she was at getting feedback/paraphrasing. How often did you get the task done right the first time versus having to redo it?

Paraphrasing is *the process of restating a message back to the original sender in the receiver's own words.* Paraphrasing can often avoid the problem of the sender saying "This isn't what I asked for." So taking a minute to get feedback to ensure understanding can help ensure the task gets done right the first time, or save lots of time in not having to do the task again. How we ask for feedback is important because we don't want to make the receiver defensive, so say something like this: "Now tell me what you are going to do so that we will be sure we are in agreement." "Would you tell me what you are going to do so that I can be sure that I explained myself clearly?"

Receiving Messages

We need to be as effective at receiving messages as we are at sending messages. Successfully receiving and interpreting messages is harder than most of us think. Here we discuss listening skills and the message-receiving process so we can round out our communication skills.

Listening Skills

If someone asked us if we are good listeners, most of us would say yes. However, unfortunately, a recent survey found that the number-one thing lacking in new college grads is listening skills.[11] One of the biggest problems in the 21st-century work environment is that constant multitasking is deteriorating our ability to pay attention and listen for very long.[12] Multitasking can cause us to be distracted, whether we realize it or not, and miss the message being communicated. However, there are ways to ensure that you improve your skills in receiving communications. By using the message-receiving process, you can learn to become a better listener. But first, find out how good a listener you are by completing Self-Assessment 10-1.

With mobile technology, employees are constantly connected and communicating 24/7/365.

The Message-Receiving Process

The message-receiving process includes listening in a form that is called *active listening,* analyzing, and then checking understanding. **Active listening** is *the process of paying attention to an entire message, taking into account both the content of the message and the context in which the communication is delivered.* If you apply the following tips, you can improve your listening skills. The message-receiving process is illustrated in Model 10-2.

Step 1. Active Listening

Active listening is all about giving your full (100%) attention to the message sender for the entire time of the message sending. As the speaker sends the message, you should be doing the eight things listed in the first column of Model 10-2. If you find your mind wandering by thinking of other things, and it happens to all of us, bring it back to pay attention. One way to help pay attention is to repeat in your mind what

LISTENING SKILLS

For each statement, select the response that best describes how often you actually behave in the way described. Place the letter *A, U, F, O,* or *S* on the line before each statement.

A = almost always; U = usually; F = frequently; O = occasionally; S = seldom

_____ 1. I like to listen to people talk. I encourage others to talk by showing interest, smiling, nodding, and so forth.

_____ 2. I pay closer attention to people who are more similar to me than to people who are different from me.

_____ 3. I evaluate people's words and nonverbal communication ability as they talk.

_____ 4. I avoid distractions; if it's noisy, I suggest moving to a quiet spot.

_____ 5. When people interrupt me when I'm doing something, I put what I was doing out of my mind and give them my complete attention.

_____ 6. When people are talking, I allow them time to finish. I do not interrupt, anticipate what they are going to say, or jump to conclusions.

_____ 7. I tune people out who do not agree with my views.

_____ 8. While another person is talking or a professor is lecturing, my mind wanders to personal topics.

_____ 9. While another person is talking, I pay close attention to the nonverbal communication so I can fully understand what he or she is trying to communicate.

_____ 10. I tune out and pretend I understand when the topic is difficult for me to understand.

_____ 11. When another person is talking, I think about and prepare what I am going to say in reply.

_____ 12. When I think there is something missing from or contradictory in what someone says, I ask direct questions to get the person to explain the idea more fully.

_____ 13. When I don't understand something, I let the other person know I don't understand.

_____ 14. When listening to other people, I try to put myself in their position and see things from their perspective.

_____ 15. During conversations, I repeat back to the other person what has been said in my own words to be sure I understand what has been said.

If people you talk to regularly answered these questions about you, would they have the same responses that you selected? To find out, have friends fill out the questions using *you* (or your name) rather than *I.* Then compare answers.

To determine your score, give yourself 5 points for each A, 4 for each U, 3 for each F, 2 for each O, and 1 for each S for Statements 1, 4, 5, 6, 9, 12, 13, 14, and 15. For Items 2, 3, 7, 8, 10, and 11 the scores reverse: 5 points for each S, 4 for each O, 3 for each F, 2 for each U, and 1 for each A. Write the number of points on the lines next to the response letters. Now add your total number of points. Your score should be between 15 and 75. Note where your score falls on the continuum below. Generally, the higher your score, the better your listening skills.

Poor listener											Good listener	
15	20	25	30	35	40	45	50	55	60	65	70	75

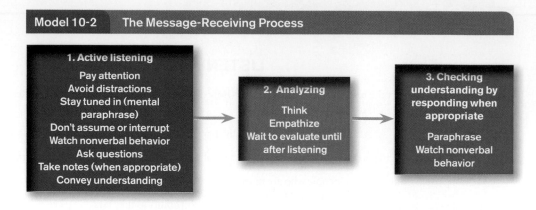

Model 10-2   The Message-Receiving Process

1. Active listening

Pay attention
Avoid distractions
Stay tuned in (mental paraphrase)
Don't assume or interrupt
Watch nonverbal behavior
Ask questions
Take notes (when appropriate)
Convey understanding

2. Analyzing

Think
Empathize
Wait to evaluate until after listening

3. Checking understanding by responding when appropriate

Paraphrase
Watch nonverbal behavior

the sender is saying. Active listening is not easy; most of us have to work hard at it to keep our minds from thinking about other things besides what the actual message is.

Step 2. Analyzing

Analyzing is the process of thinking about, decoding, and evaluating the message. Poor listening is caused in part by the fact that we speak at an average rate of 120 words per minute, but we are capable of listening at a rate of 600 words per minute. The ability to comprehend words more than five times faster than the speaker can talk allows our mind to wander. As the speaker sends the message, we should be doing the three things listed in the second column of Model 10-2. Thinking involves mental paraphrasing, again. Empathy involves putting yourself in the other person's position to understand where they are coming from.

Step 3. Checking Understanding by Responding When Appropriate

Checking understanding is the process of giving feedback to the sender. Although the sender is responsible for conveying the message, it is our job to help them by giving them feedback whether they ask for it or not.

After you have listened to the message (or while listening if it's a long message), check your understanding of the message by paraphrasing. When we can tell the sender their message correctly, we convey that we have listened and understood them. Now we are ready to offer our ideas, advice, solution, decision, or whatever the sender of the message is talking about. As you speak, watch the other person's nonverbal communication. If the person does not seem to understand what you are talking about, clarify the message before finishing the conversation. Roles can continue to change between sending and receiving throughout the conversation.

Improving Listening Skills

Do you talk more than you listen? Ask your boss, coworkers, or friends, who will give you an honest answer. Regardless of how much you listen, if you follow the guidelines discussed in this section, you will become a better listener. Review Items 1, 4, 5, 6, 9, 12, 13, 14, and 15 in Self-Assessment 10-1, which are the statements that describe good listening skills; the other numbered statements are things not to do. Select a couple of your weaker areas (lower numbers), and work to improve them.

Job Satisfaction

Labor relations affect job satisfaction.[13] *Job satisfaction,* as we first noted in Chapter 1, is a feeling of well-being and acceptance of our place in the organization, and it is generally measured along a continuum from satisfied/positive/high to dissatisfied/negative/low.

APPLYING THE CONCEPT

Communications

Identify whether each statement helps or hurts communications.

a. effective   b. ineffective

_____ 1. After giving instructions you should ask the receiver, "Do you have any questions?" to ensure understanding.

_____ 2. When giving instructions, you should tell the receiver your communication objective before giving the details of what is to be done to complete the task.

_____ 3. Multitasking allows us to get more done, so we should multitask while receiving messages.

_____ 4. When you are listening to instructions, if you don't understand something being said, you should not do or say anything until you have received the entire set of instructions.

_____ 5. When you paraphrase, you should repeat back what the other person said word-for-word.

Remember that job satisfaction is important to us because it affects many other factors at work.[14] It can have a direct effect on all of our other dependent variables discussed in Chapter 1—productivity, absenteeism, and turnover—so we need to know in general how satisfied our workforce is at any point in time.

Job Satisfaction/Dissatisfaction and Performance

Job satisfaction is critically important to managers, and especially so to HR Managers, because it will most likely affect worker productivity, absenteeism, and turnover.[15] It is very difficult to have good employee relations when employees don't like their jobs, and job dissatisfaction is a cause of losing good employees and costly turnover.[16] There are many other potential consequences of poor job satisfaction as well, such as lower levels of health and wellness, higher levels of alcohol and other substance abuse, physical or psychological withdrawal on the part of the employee, and high levels of theft and sabotage.[17] Even attempts to unionize a workforce could be the result of collective job dissatisfaction, so managers are wise to pay attention to employee satisfaction levels.

It is known that employees with the personality traits of optimism and positive self-esteem tend to have greater job satisfaction.[18] Although there has long been a debate over the expression that a happy worker is a productive worker, there is support for the idea of a positive relationship between job satisfaction and *citizenship behavior*—employee efforts that go above and beyond the call of duty.[19] However, even though there is no strong evidence for the notion that higher job satisfaction levels lead to higher productivity, there is some support for the assertion that lower levels of job satisfaction (or higher job dissatisfaction levels) can lead to lower productivity,[20] and low job satisfaction is a prominent indicator of the desirability to leave the firm.[21] Also, job satisfaction can affect an individual's satisfaction away from the job, as people tend to take their jobs home with them, which affects their behavior.[22]

Measuring Job Satisfaction

Job satisfaction can be measured through an organizational development survey, but we have to remember that any survey like this is an indirect measurement. Since job

---

SHRM

Guide – K:4
Retention (voluntary turnover, job satisfaction, withdrawal, alternatives)

WORK
APPLICATION 10-6

Select a present or past job. Pick a person who had low job satisfaction and another who had high job satisfaction. How did their level of job satisfaction affect their job performance?

LO 10.3

Identify the primary reason why measuring job satisfaction is so difficult, and the best tool for getting employees to tell the truth about their level of satisfaction.

SHRM

Guide – A:21
Attitude surveys

Video Link 10.1

Measuring Job Satisfaction

satisfaction is an attitude, we can't directly see or measure it. We can only experience *behaviors* directly, not attitudes. With *attitudes*, we have to indirectly evaluate the factor—we have to *ask* about your attitude. This is the primary reason why job satisfaction is so difficult to measure accurately. As a result of the inability to observe job satisfaction, we must rely on the individual to self-report their level of satisfaction. However, this brings up a *big* question: "Will employees tell us whether or not they are satisfied with their job?"

The answer, as with so many management questions, is it depends. If managers and employees trust each other, the employees may tell their managers the truth. However, as noted earlier in the chapter, if there isn't a strong trust between the two, employees may think that if they say they are dissatisfied, their manager will work to get them out of the organization because they are "disgruntled workers."

Because of this question of trust, it's always a good idea to ensure that any job satisfaction surveys that are done within the organization can remain completely *anonymous*. If the surveys are anonymous, and the employees know that is the case, they are much more likely to tell the truth when they take the survey. There are two common types of job satisfaction surveys or questionnaires.

The Faces Scale of Job Satisfaction Measurement

The first and simpler questionnaire is called the *faces scale*.[23] The faces scale is pretty much what it sounds like: a series of pictures of several faces on a sheet of paper, with the face at one end of the scale looking very happy and the face at the other end of the scale looking unhappy or angry. All that the employee is asked to do is circle the face that most closely matches their satisfaction with their job. Exhibit 10–1 shows an example of the faces scale.

The Questionnaire for Job Satisfaction Measurement

The second type of survey or questionnaire—the organizational development survey—is more complex and more comprehensive. An example of this type of survey is the Job Satisfaction Survey (JSS). Take a look at Exhibit 10-2, which shows some of the questions from the JSS.[24] There are many different surveys of this type, but this is one of only a few that have been shown to be valid and reliable when used to measure job satisfaction in a work environment.[25] The JSS includes nine factors: pay, promotion, supervision, benefits, contingent rewards, operating procedures, coworkers, nature of work, and communication.

Which Job Satisfaction Measurement Should We Use?

Since there are two types of measurement options here, which one should we use? The answer, again, is it depends. If we want a quick analysis of the basic level of job satisfaction in our organization, the faces scale has been shown to be quite accurate.[27] However, if we need a more in-depth analysis of job satisfaction, including what aspects of the job our

| Exhibit 10-1 | Female Faces Scale |

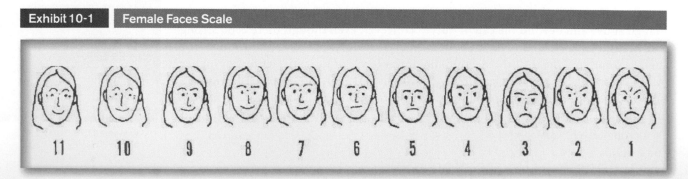

Source: "Development of a female faces scale for measuring job satisfaction" by Randall B. Dunham and Jeanne B. Herman, *Journal of Applied Psychology, 60(5)*, Oct. 1975, 629–631.

Exhibit 10-2	Sample of Job Satisfaction Survey (JSS) Questions[26]					
	Disagree very much	Disagree moderately	Disagree slightly	Agree slightly	Agree moderately	Agree very much
People get ahead as fast here as they do in other places.	1	2	3	4	5	6
My supervisor shows too little interest in the feelings of subordinates.	1	2	3	4	5	6
The benefits package we have is equitable.	1	2	3	4	5	6
There are few rewards for those who work here.	1	2	3	4	5	6
I have too much to do at work.	1	2	3	4	5	6
I enjoy my coworkers.	1	2	3	4	5	6

employees may be dissatisfied with, the more complex and comprehensive JSS (or another longer survey instrument) would be the appropriate choice.

Many organizations will routinely (every few months or every year) ask their employees to take the faces scale survey, and then HR will track the level of *overall* job satisfaction in the workplace. If management sees that job satisfaction is dropping, they may then utilize the JSS or another survey instrument to attempt to determine more exactly *why* the workforce is becoming dissatisfied so that they can take necessary measures to stop any slide in satisfaction. Each tool has its value, and in combination we can keep track of organizational job satisfaction levels over time.

Determinants of Job Satisfaction

Although compensation (pay and benefits) is important for job satisfaction, research does not strongly support that pay is the primary determinant of job satisfaction, or that people in high-paying jobs are more satisfied than employees in low-paying jobs. Money may not necessarily make employees happy.[28] In fact, new college graduates recently ranked other factors as more important in their job selection than compensation.[29] Would you be happy doing a job you don't like (say, washing dishes) for $100,000 a year versus doing a job you really want for, say, $50,000?

Seven major determinants of job satisfaction are presented in Self-Assessment 10-2. Complete it to find out what is important to you and your own level of job satisfaction. You *can* have an overall high level of job satisfaction and still not like some aspects of your job; this is common.

Improving Your Job Satisfaction

Remember that job satisfaction is to a large extent based on personality and perception, so it can be changed. If you work at being more positive by focusing on the good parts of your job and spend less time thinking about problems, and especially complaining to others about your job, you may increase your job satisfaction.[30] Improving your communications and human relationship skills can help you to get along better with coworkers and managers and increase your job satisfaction. It can also increase your chances for growth and your opportunities for advancement and higher compensation.

WORK APPLICATION 10-7

Select a present or past job. Does the organization measure job satisfaction? If yes, state how it is measured and the level of job satisfaction. If not, on a scale of 1 (low satisfaction) to 6 (high satisfaction), what level are employees on?

WORK APPLICATION 10-8

Identify the three most important determinants of your job satisfaction, and explain why they are important to you.

LO 10.4

Identify the major labor relations laws in the United States, and the major reasons for each law.

Legal Issues in Labor Relations

SHRM

Guide – A:9
Union-related labor laws

As with most management processes, there are a number of legal issues that affect labor relations. There are laws that deal with unions and unionization efforts, laws that identify what the organization has to do in the event of a significant layoff in their workforce, and laws that govern collective bargaining between the firm and the employees, plus a series of court decisions and EEOC or other government agency rulings that limit organizational rights in managing the workforce. While each of the labor laws that we will discuss here covers many details, we will only cover the major issues of the laws in this text, and save the details for your employment law class. *Every* manager needs to understand the constraints set up by these labor laws in order to successfully do their job. In this section, we will introduce you to the major labor laws in the United States. See Exhibit 10-3 for a brief overview of the five major labor laws.

10-2 APPLYING THE CONCEPT

Job Satisfaction

Correctly match each statement with its determinant of job satisfaction.

a. personality
b. work itself
c. compensation
d. growth

e. coworkers
f. management
g. communications

_____ 6.   The thing I like best about my job is the great people I work with.

_____ 7.   There is a job opening in the Accounting Department, and I am going to apply for the position.

_____ 8.   I really enjoy selling insurance policies to help protect a family's future.

_____ 9.   Management lied to us about how well the company was doing.

_____ 10. I don't think this is much of a risk; I believe we can achieve this goal.

Exhibit 10-3   Major Labor Laws

The Railway Labor Act of 1926 (RLA)	The act was passed to significantly limit the potential for railroad strikes to affect interstate commerce, and was later expanded to include airlines. In an amendment to the law, the National Mediation Board (NMB) was established to mediate between management and labor so they can come to an agreement.
National Labor Relations Act of 1935 (NLRA, Wagner Act)	The act gave employees the right to unionize without fear of prosecution, as it listed unfair employer practices. The law also established the National Labor Relations Board (NLRB) to enforce the provisions of the act and to conduct elections to determine whether employees will unionize and who will be their representative in collective bargaining.
Labor Management Relations Act of 1947 (LMRA, Taft-Hartley Act)	The act was passed to offset some of the imbalances of power given to labor. It amended the Wagner Act (NLRA) to include a list of unfair practices by unions.
Labor Management Reporting and Disclosure Act of 1959 (LMRD, Landrum-Griffin Act)	The act was passed to protect union members from corrupt or discriminatory union practices.
Worker Adjustment and Retraining Notification Act of 1988 (WARN)	The act was passed to give employees 60 days advanced notice in the case of a plant closing or large-scale layoff.

10-2 SELF-ASSESSMENT

JOB SATISFACTION

Select a present or past job. Identify your level of satisfaction by placing a check at the appropriate position on the continuum for each determinant of job satisfaction.

1. Personality

I have positive self-esteem.   6____ 5____ 4____ 3____ 2____ 1____   I have negative self-esteem.

2. Work itself

I enjoy doing the tasks I perform.   6____ 5____ 4____ 3____ 2____ 1____   I do *not* enjoy doing the tasks I perform.

3. Compensation

I am fairly compensated (pay and benefits). 6____ 5____ 4____ 3____ 2____ 1____   I am *not* fairly compensated (pay and benefits).

4. Growth and upward mobility

I have the opportunity to learn new things and get promoted to better jobs.   6____ 5____ 4____ 3____ 2____ 1____   I have *no* opportunity to learn new things and get promoted to better jobs.

5. Coworkers

I like and enjoy working with my coworkers. 6____ 5____ 4____ 3____ 2____ 1____   I do *not* like and enjoy working with my coworkers.

6. Management

I believe that my boss and managers are doing a good job.   6____ 5____ 4____ 3____ 2____ 1____   I do *not* believe that my boss and managers are doing a good job.

7. Communication

We have open and honest communications.   6____ 5____ 4____ 3____ 2____ 1____   We do *not* have open and honest communications.

Overall Job Satisfaction

When determining your overall job satisfaction, you cannot simply add up a score based on the above seven determinants, because they are most likely of different importance to you. Rank your top three factors below:

1 _____

2. _____

3. _____

Now, think about your job and the above factors, and rate your overall satisfaction with your job.

I am satisfied with my job (high level of job satisfaction).   6____ 5____ 4____ 3____ 2____ 1____   I am dissatisfied with my job (low level of job satisfaction).

The Railway Labor Act of 1926

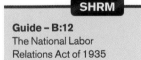

Guide – B:15
The Railway Labor
Act of 1926

The Railway Labor Act of 1926 (RLA) was originally enacted to significantly limit the potential for railroad strikes to affect interstate commerce (in 1926, railroads were the primary means of moving goods from one state to another). It also provides protection for worker rights to join a union.[31] The act requires that in so-called major disputes—disputes involving rates of pay, work rules, or working conditions—management and labor must participate in a fairly long negotiation and mediation process before a labor strike may be called. A **strike** is *a collective work stoppage by members of a union that is intended to put pressure on an employer*. This long process is designed to force the two parties to come to an agreement without resorting to a strike in almost all cases. The obvious reason for this forced negotiation is to limit the ability of a labor action to affect the general public's ability to procure goods and services. Airlines were added to the act in 1936, and are subject to *basically* the same negotiation and mediation processes.[32] Why were airlines added to this law? In the 1930s, much of the U.S. mail was beginning to be delivered with the help of airlines, and an airline disruption would affect the delivery of the mail.

Guide – A:17
Strikes, boycotts, and
work stoppages

In 1934, the National Mediation Board (NMB) was created in an amendment to the RLA. The NMB is an independent executive branch agency made up of three members appointed by the President, and confirmed by the U.S. Senate. Board members "cannot have any interest in an airline or railroad, and not more than two of the board members can be of the same political party."[33] If management and labor fail to negotiate a settlement to their disagreement, the NMB is tasked by the act with mediating the two parties' disagreements. The NMB can, in fact, "keep the two parties in mediation indefinitely, so long as it feels there's a reasonable prospect for settlement."[34]

Even after the NMB determines that there's no reasonable prospect for settlement through mediation, they can push the two parties to submit to an arbitration process. However, both parties must consent to arbitration. Finally, if arbitration is unsuccessful or is rejected, the NMB has the authority to refer the dispute to the President, who can create a Presidential Emergency Board (PEB) as a mechanism to investigate the disagreement.

It should probably be obvious by now that the intent of the act is to draw out the bargaining process between management and labor and push the two sides to resolve a labor disagreement without having to resort to a strike. In fact, in most cases involving *minor* disputes (disputes over items *other than* collective bargaining rights such as pay, work rules, or working conditions), strikes are prohibited under this law, because of the fact that a disruption in railroad or airline traffic could have such a devastating effect on the general public.

The National Labor Relations Act of 1935 (The Wagner Act)

Guide – B:12
The National Labor
Relations Act of 1935

The National Labor Relations Act of 1935 (NLRA), frequently called the Wagner Act, was the first major modern law to deal with the legal issue of unions in the general workforce (workers who were not covered by special laws such as the Railway Labor Act) in the United States. The act states that "employees shall have the right to self-organization, to form, join, or assist labor organizations, to bargain collectively through representatives of their own choosing, and to engage in other concerted activities for the purpose of collective bargaining or other mutual aid or protection, and shall also have the right to refrain from any or all such activities except to the extent that such right may be affected by an agreement requiring membership in a labor organization as a condition of employment."[35] The NLRA was originally considered to be very one-sided by employers, because it identified five "unfair labor practices" (prohibitions) for employers, but it identified no unfair labor practices for employee unions or other labor organizations. The act was later amended to include unfair labor practices by employees and their representatives. We will talk more about unions, other labor organizations, and their processes shortly. The *employer* unfair labor practices identified by the NLRA include (1) to interfere with, restrain, or coerce employees in the exercise of the rights guaranteed in the NLRA; (2) to dominate or interfere with the formation or administration of any labor organization or contribute financial or other support to it; (3) by discrimination in regard to hire or tenure of employment or any term or condition of employment, to encourage or discourage membership in any labor organization (with some specific exceptions); (4) to discharge or otherwise discriminate against an employee because he has filed charges or given testimony under the NLRA; and (5) to refuse to bargain collectively with the representatives of employees.

The NLRA is enforced by the National Labor Relations Board (NLRB). The NLRB was created in its current form by the NLRA in 1935. According to the NLRB website, they have five primary functions: conducting elections, investigating charges, seeking resolution, deciding cases, and enforcing orders.[36] The NLRB has authority over all elections to either certify or decertify unions within a particular employer's workforce. It is also tasked with investigation of any unfair labor practice charges and resolution of those charges. In addition, when complaints of unfair labor practices cannot be settled, the case will typically be heard by an NLRB administrative law judge. The administrative law judge's ruling is subject to review by the NLRB itself. Finally, board decisions may be appealed to a U.S. court of appeals, and ultimately to the U.S. Supreme Court if the parties are still unsatisfied. The last of the NLRB's tasks is enforcing orders. When a U.S. circuit court, an appeals court, or the Supreme Court issue a decision in a labor relations case, the NLRB is the enforcement arm of the U.S. government. Board attorneys act to "secure monetary remedies such as back pay and to obtain protective orders to ensure that assets will not be dissipated in an effort to avoid obligations."[37]

> **SHRM**
> **Guide – A:18, B:21**
> (Employer) unfair
> labor practices

The Labor Management Relations Act of 1947 (The Taft-Hartley Act)

The Labor Management Relations Act of 1947 (LMRA), also called the Taft-Hartley Act, was passed by Congress as an amendment to the 1935 NLRA. Where the NLRA identified a series of employee rights and employer unfair labor practices, the LMRA attempted to rebalance employer and employee rights.

> **SHRM**
> **Guide – B:13**
> The Labor Management
> Relations Act of 1947

The LMRA included a number of new provisions that limited union and labor rights in the United States. It outlawed several types of union actions that had been used since passage of the Wagner Act. These included *jurisdictional strikes*, which were used by union members to push companies to provide them with certain types of jobs; *wildcat strikes*, which are strikes that individual union members participate in that are not authorized by the union; *secondary boycotts*, in which a union participating in a strike against the company would pressure other unions to boycott organizations that did business with that company; and *closed shops*, which provided for "the hiring and employment of union members only."[38] In addition, *union shops*, shops where every employee was required to become a member of the union within a certain time period, were limited by the law. Finally, the LMRA provided that supervisors had no right to be protected if they chose to participate in union activities, so if a supervisor participated in unionizing activities the company was allowed to terminate them.

The LMRA, as noted in the beginning of this section, also created a set of unfair labor practices for unions and labor. The *union/labor* unfair practices include:

- Restraining or coercing (a) employees in the exercise of their rights guaranteed in the NLRA or (b) an employer in the selection of his representatives for negotiations
- Causing or attempting to cause an employer to discriminate against an employee who is not a union member
- Refusal to bargain collectively with an employer, provided the union is the elected representative of its employees

- Engaging in, or encouraging any individual to engage in, a secondary boycott of an employer
- Requiring dues that the NLRB finds excessive or discriminatory
- Causing or attempting to cause an employer to pay for more workers than necessary or for services that are not performed (called *featherbedding*)
- Picketing, or threatening to picket, an employer to force the employer to bargain with a labor organization, unless the labor organization is certified as the employee's representative

In addition to the limitations on unions and labor, the LMRA created mechanisms for decertifying unions through an election process, and it allowed the states to pass something called a "right-to-work law." Right-to-work laws work directly against union shops by declaring that every employee in a company has a "right to work" even if they choose not to join the union representing the shop. If the state passed such a law, union shops could not be set up in that state.

The Labor Management Reporting and Disclosure Act of 1959 (The Landrum-Griffin Act)

SHRM

Guide – B:11
The Labor Management
Reporting and Disclosure
Act of 1959

The Labor Management Reporting and Disclosure Act of 1959 (LMRDA) came about as the result of a congressional investigation in the 1950s that linked organized crime with some national labor unions. The act required a series of disclosures by union officials as well as providing specific rights to union members. The LMRDA is broken down into seven sections, or titles.

Among the important provisions of the law are:[39]

- A statement of worker rights for union members as well as all other workers in organizations whose members are represented by union agreement
- A right of all organization members (not just union members) to receive and evaluate collective bargaining agreements
- Freedom of speech when it comes to union activities
- Requirements for periodic secret ballot elections of union officers
- Requirements for unions to file copies of their constitution and bylaws, as well as annual financial reports with the federal government
- Requirements that any officers of the union who receive loans or other benefits from union funds, or have financial interests in employers whose members the union represents or that deal with the union, must file declaration forms stating such facts
- A prohibition against using union funds to support any specific candidate for union elections
- Declaration that union officers have a duty to manage funds and property of the union solely for the benefit of the members. If union officials fail in this fiduciary duty, they've committed a federal crime, which can be punished with a fine of up to $250,000.

The Worker Adjustment and Retraining Notification Act of 1988

SHRM

Guide – B:17
The Worker Adjustment
and Retraining Notification
Act of 1988

The last of the major federal labor laws that we will discuss here is the Worker Adjustment and Retraining Notification Act of 1988 (WARN). The WARN Act was designed to protect workers in the case of a plant closing or large-scale layoff. The act says that management has to give employees notice of a layoff at least 60 days ahead of time if we are going to lay off more than 50 people and if we employ (full-time) a total of more than 100 people. All workers are entitled to notice under WARN, including hourly and salaried workers, as well as managers.

If we don't give our workers notice of a layoff or plant closing, can we still lay them off? In fact, we can do that by accepting the penalty provision in the law. The penalty provision of the law says that an employer who fails to provide notice "is liable to each aggrieved employee for an amount including back pay and benefits for the period of violation, up to 60 days." What this means is if we lay people off with less than 60 days' notice, we have to pay them as if they were still employed for the 60 days anyway.

So, we can lay them off today, but can't save the money from their salaries and benefits until 60 days later. Why would we consider doing that? Well, some workers might have the ability to sabotage the organization and, as such, we need to get them out of the company before they have a chance to hurt it. If we were to give them 60 days to stay and they have the ability to harm the organization, some of them might take advantage of that time because they feel betrayed by the company. For example, if we were going to lay off a group of computer programmers, should we allow them to have access to the company computer system, knowing that they are going to lose their jobs in 60 days? What could potentially happen in such circumstances? Someone may potentially sabotage the system, because they are mad at the company. So in some cases we will say, "OK, I know that I am going to have to pay you anyway, but I am going to lay you off today even though I am required to give you 60 days' notice." However, if your employees are not likely to do harm to the organization in their last 60 days, you need to give them notice in accordance with the WARN Act, because that is just the right thing, a "fair and reasonable thing to do."

Other Legal Issues in Labor Relations

In addition to the major labor laws, we need to do a quick review of some of the other issues in labor relations. There are several organizational issues that have become items of concern to companies either because of years of common law decisions or because they are associated with other federal laws that limit businesses in their ability to manage their workforce. Some of the more common issues that you might run into in your company include corporate *whistle-blowers, wrongful discharge, constructive discharge,* and *express contracts, implied contracts,* and *quasi-contracts.*

Corporate Whistle-Blowers and the Law

What's a corporate whistleblower? A **whistle-blower** is *someone who tells an authoritative organization outside their own company* (such as a TV station or a government agency) *about actions within the firm that they believe to be illegal.* Among the many laws that deal with protection for whistle-blowers are the Federal False Claims Act and, most recently, the Dodd-Frank Act. In 2010, the U.S. Justice Department collected $3 billion in settlements and judgments from companies that defrauded the federal government. Over $2.3 billion of the $3 billion was recovered with the help of whistle-blowers.[40] This shows the magnitude of the potential loss to organizations from whistle-blowers.

Because there are incentives to whistle-blowing in many federal and state laws, organizations have to devise policies and create cultures that encourage employees to bring complaints of fraud or other illegal activities to the attention of the organization's management. Research shows that about 90% of individuals who ultimately acted as whistle-blowers and reported company wrongdoing outside the firm first reported the illegal actions internally.[41] Companies must also devise training programs to teach management and supervisors how to avoid any perception of retaliation against an organizational whistle-blower.

WORK
APPLICATION 10-9

Select an organization you work or have worked for and explain how the five major labor laws apply to that firm. For each law, what can and can't it do?

SHRM
Guide – B:28
Whistle-blowing/retaliation

10-3 APPLYING THE CONCEPT

Labor Laws

Identify each statement by the law it is discussing.

a. RLA 1926
b. NLRA 1935
c. LMRA 1947

d. LMRDA 1959
e. WARN 1988

_____ 11. The union president knows I am against the collective bargaining contract. He is afraid that I will speak up at the discussion to vote on the contract and influence the members to vote it down. So I think he had a few of his boys warn me that I'd better be quiet or be ready to face severe consequences.

_____ 12. Management is definitely engaging in activities to stop us from creating a union. I think we should call in the National Labor Relations Board to investigate.

_____ 13. This is illegal. They can't tell us today in our paychecks that our branch is being closed and 300 employees are without a job and paychecks anymore.

_____ 14. But we can't go on strike because it is against the law. The National Mediation Board will step in and get involved.

_____ 15. The union can't put in the contract that we have to pay for services that the members don't actually perform. Featherbedding is illegal, and we should call the National Labor Relations Board to investigate.

So, what can the organization do to limit the potential for whistleblowers? Here are six things that can encourage internal reporting and, as a result, limit outside reports of wrongdoing by the firm:[42]

1. Create and maintain a company culture that values reporting of unethical and illegal activities. If the whistle-blower feels that the company listens, they're less likely to take action outside the company.

2. Have a written policy on actions to be taken by the organization when reports of illegal or unethical activities occur. This policy should include information on avoiding adverse employment actions with persons who report such activities. The policy should specifically address retaliation, a direct violation of many of the whistle-blower laws.

3. Routinely train all employees, especially managers and supervisors, on the contents of organizational policies concerning the reporting of illegal and unethical activities.

4. Provide multiple ways to report suspected illegal or unethical activities. As with sexual harassment, in many cases an individual's supervisor may be the person suspected of illegal activity, and as a result should not be the only person designated to take reports of these activities. There needs to be a mechanism to allow the individual to avoid directly confronting the supervisor in such a case. One common way to report suspected wrongdoing is an organizational hotline. Hotlines aren't used very much—in fact evidence says only in about 3% of reporting cases—but they do provide an indirect mechanism to report suspicious activity.

5. Create and follow clear guidelines for investigation of reports and keep the whistle-blower informed of the progress in the investigation. The Just Cause procedures provided in Chapter 9 can be used in this situation to ensure that a fair investigation is conducted.

6. Maintain confidentiality if at all possible during and after the investigation. In some cases, the individual reporting the suspicious activity may have to be identified in order to conduct a thorough investigation or in the case of a criminal complaint, but unless it is absolutely necessary, their identity should be protected.

Express Contracts, Implied Contracts, and Quasi-Contracts

Good labor relations also require an understanding of the concepts of both formal and informal agreements. At this point we need to briefly discuss the concepts of *express contracts, implied contracts,* and *quasi-contracts.* Each of these legal concepts means something slightly different, and all can affect employment contracts. Let's take a quick look at the differences between the terms.

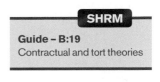

SHRM
Guide – B:19
Contractual and tort theories

An **express contract** is *a transaction in which the agreement between two parties is specifically stated,*[43] whether orally or in writing. Generally, in employment and labor relations, any express contracts should probably be written due to the complex nature of the relationships between individuals. Express contracts are frequently used to delineate terms of employment, labor-management agreements, and the results of other negotiations in labor relations. Express contracts are much easier to implement and follow than implied contracts or quasi-contracts.

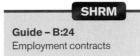

SHRM
Guide – B:24
Employment contracts

Implied contracts, by their nature, are not express contracts. An **implied contract** exists *when "the parties form an agreement from their actions rather than from a specific oral or written agreement."*[44] Every manager needs to understand the concept of an implied contract. Nothing has to be written down; the parties don't have to sign an agreement; all that has to happen is that the two parties act in a way to create an agreement. In many cases, managers and supervisors don't even realize that they have created an implied contract with their employees, but in fact may have done so and as a result may cost the company significant amounts of money.

For instance, if by words and actions a supervisor lets an employee know that if they perform well they will be promoted, the supervisor may have entered into an implied contract that the employee can then require to be enforced, and if not enforced by the supervisor and the organization, the employee may then resort to the courts for enforcement. As managers, we need to be aware of the concept of an implied contract and avoid words or actions that would create such an organizational obligation to our employees.

Finally, a quasi-contract is a contract that doesn't really exist, but a court may create it to avoid an unfair situation. A **quasi-contract** is *a court-ordered implied agreement to prevent one party in an action from benefiting at the expense of another party.* Why would a judge or a court create an implied contract when one doesn't exist? The answer is basically because of a question of fairness for services provided by one party to another. One of the more common examples in HR law of a quasi-contract would be in the case of an agency relationship. Agents are individuals who act on behalf of an organization. We have many agents in companies who act on our behalf, some within the organization and others who are outside of the organization itself.

SHRM
Guide – B:23
Agency relationships/ quasi-contracts

Let's take an example of an agent acting on behalf of the organization where a quasi-contract might be judged to exist. Assume that our organization has a relationship with an employment firm that frequently provides new employees with specific computer talents to our business. Assume further that one of our managers saw the owner of the employment agency at the grocery store two weeks ago on Sunday. During their conversation, our manager mentioned the need for a systems analyst to help with an ongoing project. Due to this conversation, the employment agency owner thought that they were being asked to find a systems analyst, and as a result, following their conversation with our company manager, they started a search. The employment agency spent significant time finding a systems analyst with experience in exactly the type of project that had been described at the grocery store, and presented our manager

WORK
APPLICATION 10-10

Select an organization you work or have worked for and give an example of an express, an implied, and a quasi-contract.

with a candidate's information this morning. Our manager protested that she hadn't asked the employment agency to find this individual, but our manager also had knowledge of the historical informal relationship between the employment agency and our firm, and as a result should have known that such a conversation would result in the employment agency owner beginning a search. In this case, a judge might determine that a quasi-contract existed and cause our company to pay for the search undertaken by the employment agency.

Organizational managers, and certainly HR Managers, must be aware of the concepts of *express contract, implied contract,* and *quasi-contract.* Obviously, managers can obligate the firm to significant expenses by not knowing these terms. We always have to be careful of the way that we phrase communications with others to avoid creating a contractual liability when none is intended.

10-4 APPLYING THE CONCEPT

Labor Contracts

Identify each statement by the type of contract being discussed.

a. express contract
b. implied contract
c. quasi-contract

_____ 16. Sarah, you have been doing a good job. Keep it up, and I will give you the next promotion.

_____ 17. They finalized the deal. The union president and CEO will have an official ceremony and sign the new collective bargaining agreement.

_____ 18. I know I told you we are changing our insurance carrier and that you have our business. But I changed my mind, plus we never signed anything; sorry you did the paperwork for nothing.

_____ 19. If you accept the teaching job, you will not have to join the union, but you must sign the standard one-year contract.

_____ 20. If you push really hard and get the order out today by closing time, I will let you leave an hour early tomorrow.

Wrongful Discharge and Constructive Discharge

LO 10.5

Briefly discuss the difference between wrongful discharge and constructive discharge.

Video Link 10.2

Wrongful Discharge

The last of our legal issues concerns the process of employee termination or discharge. There are two specific issues that we have to be concerned with in order to maintain good labor relations—wrongful discharge and constructive discharge. **Wrongful discharge** is simply *terminating an individual employee for an illegal reason, either due to a violation of a contract or because of violation of a state or federal law.* Even in situations where employment is "at-will," employers can't violate laws or contracts to terminate employees. Many labor contracts have clauses concerning actions that constitute wrongful discharge. Employers must understand the terms of such clauses in order to avoid a contract violation.

Constructive discharge, on the other hand, is not really a direct corporate termination of employment at all. **Constructive discharge** *occurs when an employee is forced to quit their job because of severe and/or pervasive harassment or intolerable working conditions.* In this case, other members of the organization may put significant enough pressure on an individual, or make it so difficult for the individual to continue their normal work activities, that the individual terminates their own employment—they quit. This type of pressure generally occurs in retaliation for some action from the individual that harmed the employees and/or organization.

For instance, if the individual acted as a whistle-blower and reported the company to government authorities, managers or supervisors in the organization might retaliate by making it virtually impossible for the individual to do their assigned work, either by constantly interrupting their work efforts and then reporting poor productivity, or by failing to provide necessary tools and equipment, or by harassing the individual, or by some other means. If the pressure from the other members of the organization is of such duration and/or intensity (severe and pervasive) that the individual can no longer reasonably do their job, constructive discharge has probably occurred. Because such actions frequently occur as a result of retaliation against the individual for some legally protected action, this is a serious offense that company managers need to be aware of. As HR Managers, we cannot afford to allow such actions to be taken against individuals in our organizations. We must guard against constructive discharge.

Video Link 10.3
Constructive Discharge

Unions and Labor Rights

The United States has a fairly strong history of unions and labor rights. Workers in the United States enjoy more freedoms than in many other countries, including the right to form and become members in unions. However, over the past 40 years, union membership has declined.

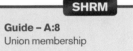

SHRM

Guide – A:8
Union membership

There are certainly both good and bad components to unions and unionization of organizational workforces. On the positive side, unions are tasked with providing their members with jobs in which they are provided fair wages and good benefits, as well as protection from arbitrary disciplinary or other actions by employers. On the negative side, unions frequently drive up employer costs, protect subpar employees, and may disrupt organizational work through strikes and other work stoppages. Let's take a look at unions and their impact on organizations.

People join unions for a variety of reasons including increasing pay and benefits, especially good health care coverage and retirement plans. Unfair management practices that lead to poor labor relations often lead to unionization. A more recent reason for unionizing is job security.

Union Organizing

The most prominent unions are among public sector employees such as teachers and police.[45] Labor union membership in the private sector has decreased dramatically in the past 40 years in the United States to the point where only 7.2% of the U.S. workforce belongs to unions.[46] However, some experts believe that union organizing is currently increasing at a fairly rapid rate. Unions are also targeting industries that they have typically avoided. Most employers work to avoid elections, but when elections are held unions are winning up to 70% percent of the time.[47]

Unions represent their members with management.

If employees decide they want to join a union, what steps do they take? Usually, the employees will go through a union organizing process (Exhibit 10-4). In this process, employees will generally select a union to represent them and then ask for a vote of employees concerning whether or not they desire to be represented by the union. The NLRA (discussed earlier in the chapter) gives employees the right to bargain collectively with their employer, and to choose a union as their representative. It is the primary federal law governing union organizing and elections in private firms. The primary method for union elections is a secret ballot.

An election is authorized if at least 30% of the employees in an appropriate bargaining unit sign "authorization cards" allowing a union to negotiate employment terms and conditions on their behalf. The union then presents these cards to the NLRB, as an election petition. Once this happens, "the NLRB sharply limits what management can say and do. Violating the rules is an unfair labor practice, and the union is likely to complain to the NLRB about any such violations and use them against the employer in the union organizing campaign."[48]

The NO TIPS Rule

What practices are prohibited from the point of providing the authorization cards to the NLRB? A lot of organizations use the acronym NO TIPS to identify what the company and its managers can't do. No Threats; No Interrogations; No Promises; No Spying.[49] An example of each of these factors will help you understand what management can and can't do.

- No Threats—managers in the firm can't threaten employees that the company will shut down a facility that votes for unionization and send the work elsewhere, maybe overseas.
- No Interrogations—the manager is prohibited from calling an individual employee into the manager's office and asking the employee about union organizing activities on the part of others in the workforce.

| Exhibit 10-4 | The Union Organizing Process |

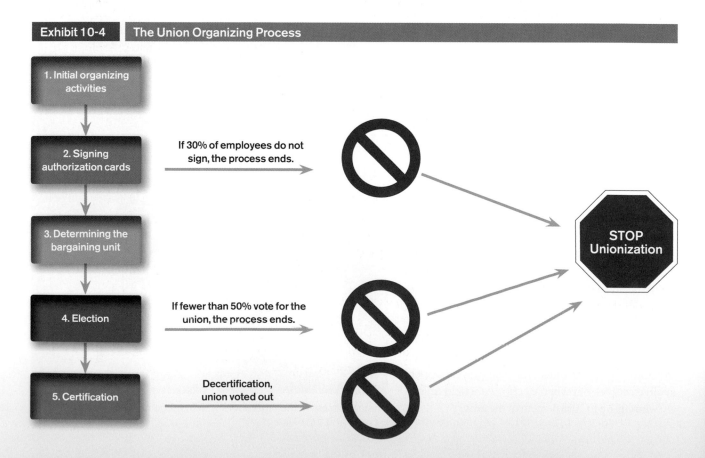

- No Promises—management cannot promise employees that if they vote against union authorization they will receive raises or changes in their benefits package.
- No Spying—management is prohibited from planting individuals in union organizing meetings or other activities so that those individuals can report back to management on what is being discussed or who attends the meetings.

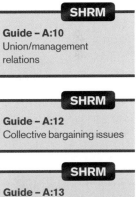

Video Link 10.4

Issues Between Unions and Employers

Remember, however, these are just examples of things that are prohibited by the NLRA.

There is also one final limitation on actions by the organization and its managers in the last 24 hours prior to the union authorization election. Management is prohibited from holding group meetings with employees who will vote on unionization during this 24-hour period.

Once the election is held, a simple majority of those voting determines the success or failure of the campaign. In other words, if only 51 workers in a bargaining unit of 200 vote, and 26 of the voters desire union membership, membership in the union will be authorized. So one tactic that organizations can use in union organizing is to encourage everyone to vote. It is frequently more difficult for the pro-union side to get a majority if everyone votes in an authorization election.

Labor Relations and Collective Bargaining

Labor relations are *the interactions between management and unionized employees.* Labor relations are also called union-management relations and industrial relations. Since there are many more nonunionized than unionized employees, most organizations don't have to deal with labor relations as part of their Human Resource systems.

Collective bargaining is *the negotiation process resulting in a contract between union employees and management that covers employment conditions.* The most common employment conditions covered in contracts are compensation, hours, and working conditions, but a contract can include almost any condition that both sides agree to. Job security continues to be a major bargaining issue for unions.[50]

SHRM

Guide – A:10
Union/management relations

SHRM

Guide – A:12
Collective bargaining issues

SHRM

Guide – A:13
Collective bargaining process

Grievances

As part of a union contract, a **grievance** is a *formal complaint concerning pay, working conditions, or violation of some other factor in a collective bargaining agreement.* In union settings, grievance procedures help protect employees against arbitrary decisions by management regarding discipline, discharge, promotions, or benefits. They also provide labor unions and employers with a formal process for enforcing the provisions of their contracts. Grievance procedures provide a mechanism to allow an individual to bring up a complaint and have the company resolve the complaint in a timely manner.

Providing a grievance mechanism will generally encourage employees to raise concerns about fairness, working conditions, or contract provisions directly with management, which in turn allows managers to resolve such problems quickly and efficiently. The grievance process provides a series of steps that the organization must go through to resolve a problem. Do you remember earlier, in Chapter 9, when we discussed tests for Just Cause? These procedures are used if a grievance involves questions of fairness in disciplinary actions.

As part of a union labor contract, a formal grievance process will usually provide a mechanism to escalate discussion of the issue through successively higher layers of organizational management until the problem is resolved. It begins with an employee making a complaint to their supervisor in accordance with the labor contract provisions. The supervisor has a limited amount of time in which to investigate and respond to the complaint or to send it further up the management chain to his or her manager. If the complaint cannot be resolved quickly to the satisfaction of the employee, a union representative (usually the "shop steward") will become the representative of the employee in further negotiations to resolve the issue. The grievance can continue up the chain until

WORK
APPLICATION 10-11

Describe your experience with a union. If you have no experience, interview someone who has union experience to find out their views of the union (what do they like and dislike?).

SHRM

Guide – A:16
Grievance management

WORK
APPLICATION 10-12

Describe a complaint that you brought to your supervisor and how it was handled. If you never had a complaint, interview someone who has and describe the complaint and how it was handled.

it reaches the head of the firm or the local plant manager. If it still can't be resolved, there is frequently an arbitration clause in the union contract that requires both sides to submit the grievance to an arbitrator—sometimes called an ombud. The arbitrator's decision on the matter is generally final—the parties cannot dispute it legally.

As a manager, when you have an employee come to you with a complaint, you can follow the steps in Model 10-3. Note that in Step 2 you don't have to agree and implement the recommendation, and for Steps 4 and 5, unless the employee is totally wrong in the complaint, you should try to resolve the complaint.

Management Rights and Decertification Elections

Of course, management also has some rights concerning union organizing and labor relations. As in all areas of business, managers have to deal with the protection of the firm and *all* of its stakeholders. What tools do managers have at their disposal to manage their interaction with unions and labor? Let's find out in this section.

Limiting Union Organizing Efforts

LO 10.7

What can management do to limit union organizing efforts?

Management has some rights in limiting union organizing activities in the workplace. What can company managers do to limit union organizing efforts?

No Unionization on Company Time

SHRM

Guide – A:19
Managing union organizing policies and handbooks

The first thing management can do is limit the ability of union organizers to solicit employees during working hours and on company time. The organization is within its rights to prevent solicitation of employees as long as it is consistent with company solicitation policies and the company handbook. In other words, the company cannot limit union organizers' rights to solicit employees, but then later allow a charitable organization to solicit employees for donations. In 1992, a famous case involving Lechmere, Inc., went all the way to the Supreme Court. The court verified the company's right to limit solicitations on company property as long as their policies were consistent with all solicitors.[51] However, the company cannot limit the rights of employees or union organizers to discuss unionization efforts outside of normal work hours, such as during lunch breaks and before or after work.

Management's Position on Unionization

Management can provide the company's position on unionization of the workforce and how it will affect management and labor relationships too. Management of the firm can also identify the costs associated with union membership (such as dues), as well as limits that may be imposed on promotions or compensation increases based on merit if the employees choose to unionize. Management can meet with employees to explain the company's position

Model 10-3	The Employee Complaint Resolution Model

| 1. Listen to the complaint and paraphrase it. | → | 2. Have the complainer recommend a solution. | → | 3. Schedule time to get all the facts and/or make a decision. | → | 4. Develop a plan to resolve the complaint. | → | 5. Implement the plan and follow up. |

on unionizing efforts and tell employees the truth about what might happen to the company and its employees as a result of a successful organizing effort. Remember, though, that the company cannot threaten (No Threats) that the facility will close or that massive layoffs will occur, or make any other threat to try to stop employees from voting for unionization. These types of communications are not protected by the NLRA and LMRA.

Change Agreements and Use of Nonunion Employee Representation

Management also has a right to change working agreements, even during a period when union organizers are soliciting their workforce, in order to show that they are responsive to their employees' needs. This can include something called Nonunion Employee Representation (NER), where management gives employee representatives a voice in such things as working conditions, pay and benefits, job security policies, promotion, and grievance resolution.[52] NER policies can sometimes effectively gut a unionization effort since the areas covered by NER are the most common areas of concern that lead to unionization of the workforce in any organization.

Lockouts and Replacement Workers

Unions have the potential to strike against an employer if collective bargaining efforts have failed, but management also has a right to prevent employees from working in certain cases. Two significant tools in management's arsenal are lockouts and replacement workers.

Employees need to understand the union contract, or NER.

A **lockout** occurs *when management stops work and physically prevents workers from entering the workplace.* Lockouts can put economic pressure on members of the union due to the fact that employees may not be paid during the period of a lockout. If management and union representatives have made a legitimate attempt to come to an agreement on a contract but have reached an impasse in their collective bargaining process, management is allowed to use a lockout. If negotiations have *not* reached a stalemate, the lockout is likely to be illegal.[53] A recent example of a lockout was when the National Football League owners locked out the NFL players in 2011 after negotiations with the players' union failed.[54]

Another tool that management may employ in the case of a strike is the hiring of replacement workers. Is this a legal action on the part of management? In fact, it is. However, whether or not the striking employee has to be offered his or her job back depends on the type of strike action undertaken by the union and its members. An **economic strike** is *a work stoppage over authorized collective bargaining issues such as pay or working conditions.* In the case of an economic strike, "an employer may not discriminate against a striker, but the employer is not obligated to lay off a replacement worker to give a striker his job back."[55] Alternately, a strike may be called because an employer engages in unfair labor practices as defined under the NLRA. In the case of an unfair labor practices strike, the employees are protected from being permanently replaced and must be offered their jobs back when the strike concludes.

WORK
APPLICATION 10-13

Describe any management attempts to stop unionization that you are aware of from any source.

Decertification Elections

Decertification elections can be held to remove a union as the representative of company workers. This cannot happen within a year of a previous attempt at decertification, though, and the company can't bring a decertification petition up on its own. Management cannot even directly encourage this action on the part of the employees, but can provide information to employees regarding decertification processes if requested "as long as the company does so without threatening its employees or promising them benefits."[56]

SHRM

Guide – A:11
Union decertification and deauthorization

Employees or other groups such as another union or labor organization must bring decertification petitions forward; "any impetus for decertification must come from the workers rather than the employer."[57] In general, if there is an existing labor contract in effect and the duration of that contract is three years or less, a petition can't be brought to the NLRB until a window between 60 and 90 days before the end of the contract.[58]

What happens in a decertification process? The first thing that must happen in order for a decertification election to proceed is that 30% of covered employees must sign a petition for decertification of the union. Once this happens, the election process proceeds in pretty much the same way as the process *for* voting for union representation. The petition will be provided to the NLRB, and it will then call an election. If a majority of the employees vote to decertify the union, the union is no longer authorized to bargain collectively for that employee group. In addition, if the election results in a tie, the union will be decertified because it received less than a majority of votes. Remember, though, that the employer cannot directly or indirectly encourage the decertification process. To avoid *any* implications of influence over the process, companies need to require that signatures on the decertification petition must be collected in the same manner as they would require that signatures for a certification petition be collected—on nonwork time and in nonwork areas.

Managing Conflict

No chapter on labor relations would be complete without a discussion of conflict and negotiation. Certainly, conflict between management and labor is not something that is intentionally created, but the chance of conflict occurring is significant when two parties have to work in concert in any circumstance but each party has its own set of opposing goals. As a result of the potential for conflict, we as managers have to understand it and be able to work our way through conflicting goals. Let's discuss conflict and conflict management styles (including negotiation) in this section, and discuss negotiation in more detail in the next section.

Video Link 10.5

Conflict In the Workplace

Conflict

A **conflict** exists whenever people are in disagreement and opposition. So why do we have conflicts, and should they be avoided? Read on to find out.

Why We Have Conflicts

WORK
APPLICATION 10-14

Give an example of when you were in conflict at work. Describe how expectations were not met.

Conflicts are inevitable,[59] and the chance of conflict occurring is significant when two parties have to work together in any circumstance but each party has its own set of goals. Incompatible activities occur,[60] because management wants to keep costs down and employees want to maintain and improve their standard of living. Thus, you need strong conflict resolution skills to be successful in any job.[61]

On a personal level, in any relationship, we have expectations of what we will do and what the other party will do. As long as people meet our expectations, everything is fine. We are in conflict when people don't meet our expectations, and this happens for three major reasons. First, we fail to let others know our own expectations, and we don't ask others' their expectations. Second, we assume that others have the same expectations that we have. Third, sometimes we don't know our expectations until people do things in opposition to us. Thus, it is important to share information and communicate expectations.

Functional Versus Dysfunctional Conflict

People often think of conflict as "fighting" and view it as disruptive. However, conflict can frequently be beneficial, or *functional*, when it helps the organization meet its goals of increasing performance.[62] On the other side, conflict that prevents the achievement of individual and organizational objectives is called *dysfunctional* conflict. Conflict between management and labor often degrades into dysfunctional

Conflict between employees can affect the entire team.

conflict, because of significantly different objectives. This can produce severe negative consequences for individuals and organizations.[63] Employees in conflict can seek revenge and engage in deviant behavior.[64] Conflict within or between groups can also impede group effectiveness.[65] However, conflict management skills can lead to resolving conflicts and maintaining relationships before they become dysfunctional.[66]

Conflict Management Styles

When we are faced with conflict, we have five basic conflict management styles to choose from. The five styles are based on two dimensions of concern: concern for others' needs and concern for our own needs, and being cooperative or not. Various levels of concern and cooperation result in three types of behavior: passive (taking no action or permissively giving in to others), assertive (defending our position while considering others' needs), and *aggressive* (fighting for what we want without others' needs, or taking advantage of them).

SHRM

Guide – A:15
Conflict management

| Exhibit 10-5 | Conflict Management Styles |

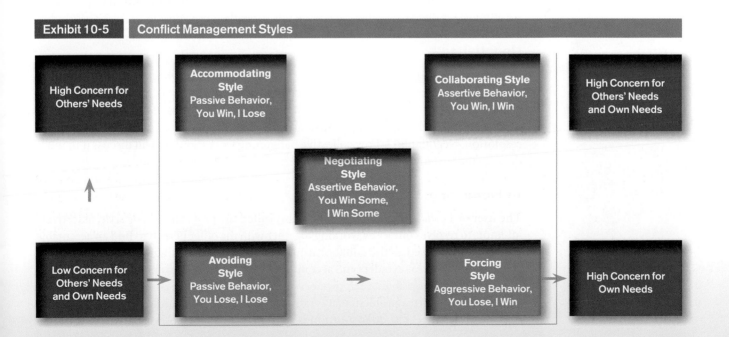

High Concern for Others' Needs

Accommodating Style
Passive Behavior,
You Win, I Lose

Collaborating Style
Assertive Behavior,
You Win, I Win

High Concern for Others' Needs and Own Needs

Negotiating Style
Assertive Behavior,
You Win Some,
I Win Some

Low Concern for Others' Needs and Own Needs

Avoiding Style
Passive Behavior,
You Lose, I Lose

Forcing Style
Aggressive Behavior,
You Lose, I Win

High Concern for Own Needs

LO 10.8

Identify the five conflict management styles. How is each described in terms of winning and losing?

Video Link 10.6

Conflict Resolution

Each conflict management style results in a different win-lose pattern. The five styles are presented in Exhibit 10-5. Note that there is no right or wrong style. Each style has its advantages and disadvantages and is appropriate to use in different situations. However, collaborating is the ideal situation.

Avoiding

The user of an *avoiding conflict style* attempts to passively ignore the conflict rather than resolve it. When we avoid a conflict, we are being passive and generally uncooperative. We avoid conflict when we refuse to take a stance, by mentally withdrawing, or by physically leaving. A lose-lose situation results because the conflict is not resolved.

Accommodating

The user of an *accommodating conflict style* attempts to resolve conflict by passively giving in to the opposing side. When we use the accommodating style, we are being passive but cooperative. We attempt to satisfy the needs of others but neglect our own needs by letting others get their own way. A lose-win situation is created—we lose and allow the other party to win.

Avoid versus accommodate. A difference between the two styles is this. When we avoid, we just don't say or do anything. How many times have you heard someone say something dumb and ignored it, rather than getting in an argument? When we accommodate, we do something we don't really want to do. For example, if you and another person are working on a project together and you go along with that person's way of doing a particular task, even though you disagree with it, you are using the accommodating style.

Forcing

Users of a *forcing conflict style* attempt to resolve conflict by using aggressive behavior to get their own way. When we use the forcing style, we are aggressive and uncooperative; we do whatever it takes to satisfy our own needs at the expense of others. Forcers use authority, threaten, intimidate, and call for majority rule when they know they will win.

Forcers commonly enjoy dealing with avoiders and accommodators. If we try to get others to change without being willing to change ourselves, regardless of the means, then we use the forcing style and create a win-lose situation. Being in a position of authority, some managers tend to use this style frequently to get their way quickly.

Negotiating

The user of the *negotiating conflict style*, also called the *compromising style*, attempts to resolve conflict through assertive give-and-take. When we use the negotiating style, we are moderate in assertiveness and cooperation. A situation in which each side achieves a partial victory is created through compromise, and this is a win some–lose some form of conflict resolution. Negotiation is how collective bargaining works, and we will discuss it in more detail in the next major section.

Collaborating

The user of a *collaborating conflict style*, also called the *problem-solving style*, assertively attempts to resolve conflict by working together with the other person to find an acceptable solution. When we use the collaborating approach, we are being highly assertive and cooperative. Whereas avoiders and accommodators are concerned about others' needs and forcers are concerned about their own needs, the collaborators are concerned about finding the best solution to the problem that is satisfactory to all. Unlike the forcer, the collaborator is willing to change if a better solution is presented. While negotiating is often based on secret information, collaboration is based on open and honest communication. This is the only style that creates a true win-win situation.

Negotiating versus collaborating. A difference between the two options is in the solution each leads to. Again, suppose you and another person are working on a project, and she wants to do a task in a way that you disagree with. With the negotiating style, you might do this task her way and the next task your way; you each win some and lose some. With the collaborating style, you work to develop an approach to the task that you can both agree on. The key to collaboration is agreeing that the solution picked is the best possible one. Thus, a win-win situation is achieved. Unfortunately, we can't always collaborate.

Using the Most Appropriate Styles

Again, there is no one best style for resolving all conflicts. A person's preferred style tends to meet his or her needs. Some people enjoy forcing; others prefer to avoid conflict. Managerial and personal success lies in one's ability to use the appropriate style to meet the situation. For most people, the two most difficult styles to develop are the negotiating and collaborating styles. Thus, these two skills are discussed in more detail next and in the following major section.

Initiating Conflict Resolution

Conflict management skills are important,[67] so managers are often trained to use effective conflict resolution strategies.[68] Conflict resolution models have also been shown to be effective in managing conflict,[69] so when initiating a conflict resolution process, you may want to use the collaborative conflict resolution model. Research suggests that collaborative conflict resolution skills can be developed.[70] The steps are illustrated in Model 10-4.

WORK APPLICATION 10-15

Select a present or past boss and identify which conflict management style the boss uses most often when in conflict with employees. Give a typical example conflict and how the style is used.

WORK APPLICATION 10-16

Which one of the five conflict management styles do you tend to use most often? Should you be using another style more often? Why or why not?

10-5 APPLYING THE CONCEPT

Conflict Management Styles

Identify the most appropriate conflict management style to use in each situation.

a. avoiding style
b. accommodating style
c. forcing style
d. negotiating style
e. collaborating style

_____ 21. You have joined a committee in order to make contacts. You have little interest in what the committee actually does. At a meeting you make a recommendation that is opposed by another member. You realize that you have the better idea, but the other party is using a forcing style.

_____ 22. You are on a task force that has to select a new manufacturing machine. The four alternatives will all do the job, but team members disagree about the brand, price, and service.

_____ 23. You are a Sales Manager. Beth, one of your competent salespeople, is trying to close a big sale. The two of you are discussing the sales call she will make. You disagree on the strategy to use to close the sale.

_____ 24. You're on your way to an important meeting and running late. As you leave your office, at the other end of the work area you see Chris, one of your employees, goofing off instead of working.

_____ 25. You're over budget for labor this month. At the moment, the workload is light, so you ask Kent, a part-time employee, to leave work early. Kent tells you he doesn't want to go because he needs the money.

| Model 10-4 | Initiating Conflict Resolution |

1. State the problem in terms of Behavior, Consequences, and Feelings (BCF statement). → 2. Allow the other person to respond to your BCF statement and acknowledge the problem or conflict. → 3. Ask for and/or present alternative resolutions to the conflict. → 4. Come to an agreement. Determine specific actions to be taken by each person.

Consider an example: Suppose that you don't smoke and are in fact allergic to cigarette smoke. Some of your coworkers do smoke, and although they are allowed to do so in the employees' lounge, most of them avoid smoking when you are in the lounge. One coworker, however, persists in smoking in your presence. This is a problem—you can't always avoid going into the lounge during breaks or lunch. You decide to initiate a collaborative solution to this problem. You begin by asking the smoker to help you solve your problem. This approach reduces defensiveness and establishes an atmosphere that will help maintain a good relationship.

Step 1. The first step in the collaborative conflict resolution model is to express the problem in a BCF statement, that is, a statement that describes a conflict in terms of Behaviors (B), Consequences (C), and Feelings (F) in a way that maintains ownership of the problem.
There are three things you should not do in the BCF statement:

1. Don't make judgments. This can make the person defensive.

2. Don't make threats. This can make the person defensive.

3. Don't give solutions. This is done in Step 3.

Regarding the smoker, you should make statements like "When you smoke around me (B), I have trouble breathing and become nauseous (C), and I feel ill and stressed (F)." You don't want to make statements like "You are inconsiderate of others. You shouldn't smoke. You are going to get cancer. Just quit smoking."

Note that you can vary the sequence if a situation warrants it; for example, "I fear (F) that some viewers will respond negatively to this advertisement (B) and we will lose money by running it (C)."

Now, what exactly does *maintaining ownership of the problem* mean? Think about it: Is it you or the smoker who has the problem? Since the smoker is allowed to smoke in the lounge, the problem is yours. Maintaining ownership of the problem means expressing it without assigning blame or making assumptions about who is right or wrong. Fixing blame only makes people defensive, which is counterproductive in conflict resolution. Your BCF statement should be descriptive, not evaluative, and it should deal with a single issue.

Before confronting the other person, practice your BCF statement. Also, think of some possible solutions you might suggest. But be sure your ideas take into consideration the other person's point of view, not just your own. Remember to practice empathy—try to put yourself in his or her position: If you were the other person, would you like the solutions you have thought of?

Step 2. You cannot resolve a conflict if the other person does not even acknowledge that it exists. After stating the problem, let the other person respond. Your coworker might say, "Oh, I didn't realize you reacted so strongly to cigarette smoke" or "Well, that explains why everybody puts out their cigarettes when you're around." On the other hand, the coworker could say, "What's the big deal? You can just stay away from the lounge if smoke bothers you." If the other person doesn't understand or acknowledge the problem, you'll need to be persistent. Repeat your statement in different terms, if necessary.

Step 3. Once the other person acknowledges the problem, ask him or her how the conflict might be resolved. Perhaps the person will suggest something that you can agree to; if so, you're well on your way to a resolution of the conflict. If not, be prepared with your own suggestions. However, remember that you are collaborating, not simply trying to change the other person. If he or she acknowledges the problem but seems unwilling to resolve it, appeal to common goals. Try to make the other person realize how he or she might also benefit from a solution to this conflict.

Step 4. The final step in the collaborative conflict resolution model is to come to an agreement. Determine what specific actions you will each take to resolve the conflict. Perhaps your coworker will agree not to smoke in your presence, now that he knows how it affects you. Perhaps you'll suggest changing your lunch hour, so you don't run into each other in the lounge. Clearly state whatever actions you each agree to.

Negotiations

In this section, we discuss the negotiation process so you will know how to negotiate effectively in your personal and professional lives.

The Negotiation Process

Negotiating is *a process in which two or more parties in conflict attempt to come to an agreement.* If there is a set "take it or leave it" deal, there is no negotiation, so good managers generally want to try to avoid making such statements.[71] Also, not all negotiations end with an agreement. You have to negotiate in both your personal and your professional life, so it is an important skill.[72] There are times when negotiations are appropriate and maybe even necessary, such as in management-union collective bargaining, when buying and selling goods and services, and when discussing a job compensation offer.

Negotiation is often a *zero-sum game* in which one party's gain is the other party's loss. For example, every dollar less that you pay for a car is your gain and the seller's loss. Ideally, however, negotiation should be viewed by all parties as "I win some, and you win some," rather than a win-lose situation; all parties should believe they got a good deal. If union employees believe that they lost and management won, they may become dissatisfied with their jobs, which could result in lower performance in the long run. You can develop your negotiation skills by implementing the negotiation process as described below.

> **SHRM**
>
> **Guide – A:14**
> Negotiation skills

The Negotiation Process Model

Negotiation is a process.[73] The negotiation process has three and possibly four parts. These steps are summarized in Model 10-5 and discussed throughout this section. We discuss the process in two parts to reflect the planning and actual negotiation in which you may or may not postpone or agree to make a deal. In the course of actual negotiations, you may have to make slight adjustments to the steps in the process.

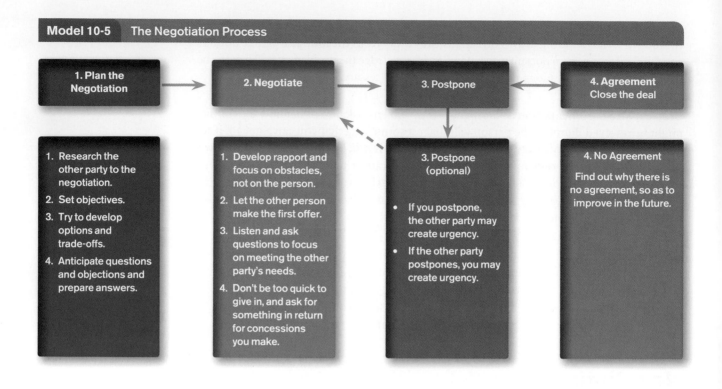

Model 10-5   The Negotiation Process

1. Plan the Negotiation → **2. Negotiate** → **3. Postpone** ↔ **4. Agreement Close the deal**

1. Plan the Negotiation

1. Research the other party to the negotiation.
2. Set objectives.
3. Try to develop options and trade-offs.
4. Anticipate questions and objections and prepare answers.

2. Negotiate

1. Develop rapport and focus on obstacles, not on the person.
2. Let the other person make the first offer.
3. Listen and ask questions to focus on meeting the other party's needs.
4. Don't be too quick to give in, and ask for something in return for concessions you make.

3. Postpone (optional)

- If you postpone, the other party may create urgency.
- If the other party postpones, you may create urgency.

4. No Agreement

Find out why there is no agreement, so as to improve in the future.

Planning the Negotiation

Success or failure in negotiating is usually based on preparation.[74] Planning has four steps:

Step 1. Research the other parties to the negotiation. Do your homework.[75] Know the key power players; make sure you are dealing with the right person.[76] Try to find out what the other parties want and what they will and will not be willing to give up before you negotiate. Find out, through your networking grapevine, their personality traits and negotiation style. You can also Google, Facebook, or otherwise research the person for information.[77] The more you know about those with whom you will be negotiating, the better your chances are of reaching an agreement. If you have worked with some of the people before, think about what worked and did not work in the past. Doing your homework can result in realizing that it's not worth the time and effort negotiating.[78]

Step 2. Set objectives. In some negotiations, your objective will be to change someone's behavior; at other times, you may be negotiating salary or benefits or a better price from a supplier. Know what you want to get out of the deal.[79] Be clear about what it is you are negotiating. Is it price, options, delivery time, sales quantity, or something else entirely? Set limits—what price and other key terms do you need to make a deal?[80] In any case, you want to set three objectives:

- A specific lower limit that you are unwilling to give up (say, a certain behavior on the part of your peer in the department, or a minimum price from your supplier). You must be willing to walk away from negotiations if this lower limit is not agreed to.[81]
- A target objective that represents what you believe is fair.
- An opening objective that is more than you actually expect but that you may achieve.

Remember that the other person or party is probably also setting these kinds of objectives. The key to successful negotiation is for each person or party to achieve something between their minimum objective and their target objective.

Step 3. Try to develop options and trade-offs. In some negotiating situations, you may find that you are in a position of power to achieve your target objective. For example, when negotiating prices with a supplier or applying for jobs, you may be able to quote other prices or salary offers and get the other person to beat them. If you have to give up something or cannot get exactly what you want, be prepared to ask for something in return. When GM, Eastern Airlines, and others were having financial difficulty, the company asked employees to take a pay cut. Rather than simply accept a cut, the employees asked for company stock in a trade-off. Based on your research, you should be able to anticipate the kinds of trade-offs you might expect from the other person.

Step 4. Anticipate questions and objections and prepare answers. Very likely the other party to negotiations wants an answer to the unasked question "What's in it for me?" Focus on how the negotiations will benefit the other person.[82] Speak in terms of *you* and *we* rather than *I*.

There is a good chance that the other person will raise objections. Unfortunately, not everyone will be open about his or her real objections. Thus, you need to listen and ask questions to find out what is preventing an agreement. It will also help to project an attitude of enthusiasm and confidence. If the other person does not trust you, you will not reach an agreement.

Conducting the Negotiation

After you have planned, you are ready to negotiate the deal. Face-to-face negotiations are generally preferred because you can see the other person's nonverbal behavior and better understand objections. However, negotiations by telephone and written negotiations (e-mail) work, too. It will help to keep the following in mind as you negotiate.

Step 1. Develop rapport and focus on obstacles, not on the person. Use the other person's name as you greet him or her. Relationships are always wrapped up in underlying influences.[83] So it is appropriate to open with small talk and develop a relationship.[84] How long you wait before getting down to negotiations will depend on the particular situation and the other person's style.

Never attack the other person's personality or use negative statements such as "You always bad-mouth me to the boss" or "You're being unfair to ask for such a price cut." Statements like these will make the other person defensive, which will make it harder to reach an agreement. During negotiations, people look for four things: inclusion, control, safety, and respect. If people perceive that you are pushing them into something, threatening them, or belittling them, they will not trust you and will be unlikely to come to an agreement with you.

Step 2. Let the other party make the first offer. Of course, the other party may pressure *you* to make the first offer; for example, the person may say, "Give us your best price, and we'll decide whether to take it." If so, you can counter with a question such as "What do you expect to pay?" The reason to let the other party go first is, if you get a better offer than you expected, you can take it and get more than your target. If the offer is lower than your target, you can negotiate to get more.

Step 3. Listen and ask questions to focus on meeting the other party's needs. Create an opportunity for the other person to disclose reservations and objections. Focus on how your deal will benefit the other party.[85] When you ask questions and listen, you gather information that will help you overcome the other party's objections. Determining whether the objection is a "want" criterion or a "must" criterion will help you decide how to proceed.

Step 4. Don't be too quick to give in, and remember to ask for something in return. Those who ask for more often get more. But many people—especially many women—are reluctant to ask for what they deserve.[86] You want to satisfy the other party without giving up too much yourself; remember not to go below your minimum objective, and be prepared to walk away if that minimum can't be met.[87] When you are not getting what you want, having other options can help give you bargaining power.

Though you don't want to be quick to give in, you might want to be the first to make a concession, particularly when you are negotiating complex deals. A concession makes the other party feel obligated, which gives you negotiating power. However, before making a concession, it's essential to know what all of the other party's demands are. And avoid unilateral concessions.

Be reluctant to lower your price.[88] If you have to, ask for something in return, which means giving something and getting something else. For example, if you are offered a job at $30,000 but your target is higher and they will not or cannot come up, ask for more vacation days, more retirement, or more benefits. If you are buying a car, and the sales rep will not come down in price, ask for an extended warranty, new tires, and so on.

Postponing the Negotiation

When there doesn't seem to be any progress, it may be wise to postpone negotiations. A sense of urgency pushes parties to come to an agreement and close the deal.[89]

If the other party is postponing, you can try to create urgency. Suppose the other party says, "I'll get back to you." You may try to create urgency by saying, for example, "This is on sale, and it ends today." However, honesty is the best policy. Or, if you have other options, you can use them to create urgency, such as by saying, "I have another job offer pending. When will you let me know if you want to offer me the job?" Honesty and integrity are the most important assets a negotiator can possess.

If you are unable to create urgency and the other party says, "I'll think about it," say, "That's a good idea." Then at least review the major features the other party liked about your proposed agreement. But the threat of loss is more persuasive than the potential for gain, so tell them what they have to lose.

One thing to remember is that when the other party becomes resistant to making the agreement, a hard sell will not work. Take the pressure off by asking the other person something like "Where do you want to go from here?" or by suggesting "Why don't we think about it and discuss it some more later?"

You also need to learn to read between the lines. Some people will not come right out and tell you that there is no agreement. For example, a Japanese businessperson might say something like "It will be difficult to do business." Americans tend to perceive this to mean that they should keep trying to negotiate, but the Japanese businessperson means stop trying but will not say so directly because doing so is impolite.

If you want to postpone, the other party may try to create urgency. If you feel you cannot agree, tell the other party you want to think about it. You may need to check with your boss, or other people. If the other party is creating urgency, be sure the urgency is real; don't be pressured into agreeing to something you may regret later. If you do want to postpone, give the other party a specific time that you will get back to them.

Agreement or No Agreement

Once you have come to an agreement, stop selling it, and put things in writing, if appropriate. It is common to follow up an agreement with a letter (e-mail) of thanks that restates the agreement. This helps to create an express contract, rather than an implicit one, and provides documentation when a quasi-contract was made.

There will be times when you simply will be unable to come to an agreement. Rejection, refusal, and failure happen to us all; in negotiating conflict, you need to be thick-skinned. The difference between the "also-rans" and the "superstars" lies in how they respond to the failure. Your ability to gain a victory is directly related to your ability to come back from defeat.[90] Successful people keep trying and learn from their mistakes and continue to work hard. If you cannot make a deal, analyze the situation and try to determine where you may have gone wrong so you can improve in the future.

Alternative Dispute Resolution— Mediation and Arbitration

Labor and management are required by law to bargain in good faith, and they need to maintain effective employee relations, but when in conflict we cannot always resolve our dispute alone. In these cases, something called alternative dispute resolution can be used. Alternative dispute resolution includes a series of tools, most commonly either mediation or arbitration, which can be used by parties who are in conflict in order to resolve their disagreements without going through the process of litigation. In some contractual employment agreements, there will actually be a requirement that any disagreement concerning the contract will be subject to arbitration instead of the use of the legal system. The U.S. government's Federal Mediation and Conciliation Service (FMCS) is often used as an alternative dispute resolution resource. For more information about the FMCS, visit its website at http://www.fmcs.gov. At this point, let's take a little more detailed look at both mediation and arbitration.

In many cases in an organization where conflicts occur, a mediator may be used. A **mediator** is *a neutral third party who helps resolve a conflict, but has no authority to impose a solution to the conflict.* As a manager, you may often be called upon to serve as a mediator between two employees. In this case, remember that you should be a mediator, not a judge. Your task is to get the employees to resolve the conflict themselves, if possible. You will need to work diligently to remain impartial, unless one party is violating company policies.

When bringing conflicting employees together, focus on how the conflict is affecting their work. Discuss the issues by addressing specific behavior that bothers the other person, not personalities.[91] If a person says, "We cannot work together because of a personality conflict," ask him or her to identify the specific behavior that is the root of the conflict. The discussion should make the parties aware of their behavior and of how its consequences are causing the conflict. What expectations are not being met?

In the mediation process, the purpose of the mediator is to assist the parties in overcoming barriers to communication as well as other barriers that are keeping the parties from resolving their differences. *Facilitation* is one of the major tools available to the mediator. When a person acts as a facilitator, their primary purpose is to help individuals or groups who are in conflict to overcome hurdles that are keeping the conflict from being resolved.

As in most cases, an example will help you understand how a mediator might act in their role as a facilitator. Let's assume that an individual employee and their supervisor are in conflict over how to resolve a grievance concerning unsafe tools in the workspace. The employee, in fact, filed a grievance based on a concern for their own safety and the safety of others, while the supervisor is under the impression that the employee just wants newer and nicer tools. The employee's grievance was initially denied by the supervisor, and the contract with the labor union allows a mediation process between the direct supervisor and the employee prior to going up the chain of command to higher-level managers.

LO 10.9

Briefly explain the processes of mediation and arbitration and the major difference between the two processes.

SHRM

Guide – A:2
Alternative dispute resolution

Video Link 10.7
Mediation

In this case, the mediator could step in and assist the two parties in communicating their concerns with each other by acting as a facilitator of communication between the two parties. While the employee is concerned with safety, the supervisor was initially concerned with the overall cost of buying new tools or equipment. Part of the supervisor's job is to control costs in their work area, and the tools that would have to be replaced are very expensive. However, the supervisor did not know the details concerning how the existing tools were unsafe, and the employee had not successfully explained the nature of the problem in the initial grievance. The mediator helps each party communicate with the other about their concerns—they help the supervisor relay their concern for cost controls while also providing the employee with assistance in identifying the specific problem with the tools that makes them unsafe. The result might be that both parties successfully communicate their concerns, but the supervisor realizes that the issue of safety is much more significant than the issue of cost, and therefore agrees to buy the new tools that the employee has requested.

If the conflict cannot be resolved by mediation, an arbitrator may be used as a follow-up. An **arbitrator** is *a neutral third party who resolves a conflict by making a binding decision.* Many business contracts require the use of an arbitrator rather than seeking relief by way of the court system. An arbitrator basically acts like a judge in a civil hearing. The arbitrator will hear arguments from both parties in a conflict, may ask questions of each of the parties in order to clarify issues, and then make a decision on which party will "win" the case.

The most significant difference between mediation and arbitration is that the result of an arbitration process is binding on the parties who are in conflict. Mediation, on the other hand, is merely a process to assist the parties in coming to an agreement on their own. The mediator has no authority to impose a solution on the two parties in conflict. Because of this difference, the use of arbitration should be kept to a minimum, because it is not a collaborative process.

Trends and Issues in HRM

It's time to take a look at this chapter's trends and issues. Because the chapter deals with labor relations, we will begin by taking a look at some sample countries around the world and how they handle labor relations. Second, we will review the ethical issue associated with union suppression tactics employed by some companies. The last issue is whether or not Congress should pass a "card check" law.

Variance in Worldwide Labor Relations

In the global village, developing country unionization is just beginning, and it is expanding quickly. For example, in China angry migrant workers have used the Internet. China has 348 million Internet users, which is more than the total population of the United States at around 309 million,[92] and it has 787 million mobile phones to organize. Workers at Honda plants went on strike and won big increases in compensation. Compensation has increased to the point where the United States and other countries, and even Chinese manufacturers, are outsourcing some production to other countries.[93] Let's take a quick look at a few countries around the world and how unions affect work in those countries.

Brazil. As with many South and Central American countries (as well as other countries all over the world), Brazil's labor regulations tend to favor the employee over the employer, and provide strong protection for unions. This is in part a function of the history of the country where privileged employers treated their workers unfairly for many years before a military intervention created the impetus for major changes in the labor laws in the country. In addition

WORK
APPLICATION 10-18

Describe when you were in conflict and could not resolve it and a neutral third party (teacher, coach, boss) got involved to help resolve the conflict. Assess how helpful the mediator or arbitrator was.

to labor laws favoring the employee, Brazil has also seen a significant increase in unionized workers in the past several years. The number of unionized workers stood at 18.35% in 2005, up from 16.73% in 2001.[94] Labor is also guaranteed the right to strike in the constitution, and labor agreements either can be in writing "or may be implied from the relationship between an individual and the company."[95] Labor laws in Brazil also require any disputes between management and workers "to be settled in labor tribunals rather than in the companies involved, so little space is left for direct negotiations between employers and employees."[96]

South Korea. South Korea's basic laws concerning labor relations are similar to those in the United States. The South Korean Trade Union Act allows workers to organize, collectively bargain, and act in concert to achieve labor goals. However, for many years the government had direct control of the major labor union in the country. This is not so any longer, and as a matter of fact, South Korea recently passed legislation that allows multiple unions to represent different workers within the same organization. South Korean employers are concerned that relations with employees will deteriorate due to this multiple-union system.[97] About 10% of South Korea's workforce is currently unionized, but employers are worried that this will increase with the new law on multiple union representation.[98]

Czech Republic. While the numbers of employees who are members of trade unions in the Czech Republic are high compared to most other countries, this number has been steadily declining since the early 1990s. In 1990, more than 80% of workers in the Czech Republic were trade union members. In 2004, the number had decreased to 22%.[99] Part of this decrease is probably due to the continuing transformation of the economy of the Czech Republic from a state-controlled economy (as part of the Soviet bloc) to an open economy vying for its place in world markets. Unions are fighting back, trying to recruit new members from the worker ranks, but have so far had limited success. The country's trade unions are also currently fighting amendments to the labor code, which could weaken the unions' position as negotiators for workers in the country.[100]

France. While in many countries labor unions focus on worker rights and fair pay, French unions have historically played an active part in the political system of the country. Labor unions in France routinely directly advocate for, and support, candidates who are friendly to labor issues. At least partly because of this political activity, unions in France have been able to control the work environment in the areas of pay and benefits as well as work-life balance. Even though only about 5% of French workers are in trade unions, the unions and their supporters have been able to get laws passed at the national level that limit the organization's ability to vary such things as workload, working hours, part-time employment, and compensation.[101] Also, throughout the European Union, labor has won greater benefits, including more paid vacation, than most employees get in the United States.

As we can quickly see from the sample of countries above, union influence affects relationships between labor and management in a significantly different way in different countries. For those working in a business that operates in multiple countries, these differences in labor laws will be significant. You may have to become well informed on the differing laws concerning labor relations and union representation in each of the countries in which your firm works.

Is a Union Suppression Policy Ethical?

Union suppression is using all tactics available in order to avoid unionization of a company's workforce. These tactics can include such things as spreading rumors about potential job losses, hiring consultants who specialize in union avoidance tactics, hiring

ESR

labor lawyers who know the limits to what the company can do to avoid unionization, closing facilities that vote for unionization, bringing in disgruntled current members of the union to talk to your workforce, and many other tactics.

Is this process of union suppression ethical or unethical? Again, the answer has to be it depends. If the organization remains within the law and the NO TIPS guidelines, is management being ethical? Even here you need to look at fair, reasonable, and equitable treatment of employees in the organization and not just at whether or not the company is following the letter of the law.

We have discussed the issue of ethics in several chapters of this text, and noted that just because something is legal it doesn't mean that it is necessarily ethical. Staying within the letter of the law may not provide the company with the kind of workforce it needs in order to compete with other firms in the 21st century. Here again, we return to the question of whether or not actions on the part of management will increase the satisfaction and engagement levels of the employees, or cause it to decrease.

Unions suppression tactics that employ actions such as the Nonunion Employee Representation that we discussed earlier in the chapter can certainly be ethical methods of suppressing unions in some cases. Using these representatives can also increase employee satisfaction and engagement in the organization. So this tactic and other similar tactics would be considered by most to be ethical.

On the flip side, planting rumors concerning the closing of facilities if the workers vote to unionize (whether true or not) would probably be unethical and in some cases could even violate the rule of No Threats in a unionization campaign. Each situation has to be looked at individually, and management needs to make a decision concerning what suppression tactics are ethical and legal, and which tactics might not be.

Should Congress Pass a Card-Check Law?

The last issue we want to take a look at in this chapter is the possibility of a card-check law. The current laws covering union organizing generally require a secret ballot election process that is supervised by the NLRB. Unions and other labor organizations have been pushing for a revision to the law that would allow union representation on completion of a "card check." What this means is that if the union organizers can get more than 50% of the employees to sign cards saying that they want to be represented by the union, there would be no requirement for an election.

The problem that employers have with this process is the issue of peer pressure. If individual employees who want a union could pressure others to sign cards and as a result get signatures from more than 50% of employees, the union would be authorized to represent the workers in the organization. However, there's a significant chance that some of those individuals who signed cards because of peer pressure might vote against the union if a secret ballot election were held. There are even concerns that holdouts within the workforce might be harassed or intimidated by others if they refused to sign an authorization card. Employers that oppose the card-check law feel that the only way to get a fair vote on the question of unionization is by allowing all those involved in the election to vote yes or no in a private setting.

The last version of the legislation that went through Congress would also boost penalties for retaliation against workers who support unions, and it would require binding arbitration within three months if management and the union can't agree on a contract. Businesses are also concerned about the binding arbitration component of the legislation. If the contract agreement is not reached within 90 days of the union being ratified as a representative of the employees, NLRB arbitrators could step in and force a contract on both parties. Business owners have legitimate concerns that the arbitrators will not be well versed in their particular business environment, and as a result the decisions made may be very harmful to the ability of the business to continue operations.

Certainly, both sides in the card-check argument have legitimate concerns. The final question of the argument becomes one of fairness to both the employer and the employees. The current version of the card-check bill may be skewed toward the advantage of the employees and against their employers, while the current law concerning secret ballot elections can be viewed as skewed toward the employer. Hopefully, Congress can find a balance that takes into account the needs of both parties.

The Obama administration is more prounion than business, and the Democratic majority on the NLRB is led by a former lawyer who represented unions. Even without the card-check law getting through Congress, the Obama NLRB has affected and is expected to continue to affect management-labor relations in favor of unions through making new regulations that don't need a law to be passed. For example, it already sided for labor and against business by upholding the rights of unions to set up protest banners outside companies. The board could also rule on cases that would give unions greater access to company property for organizing drives, and it may push for a speedier election after workers petition for a vote, limiting a company's ability to try to prevent unionization.[102]

Wrap-Up

OK, what have we learned in this chapter? This chapter is about relationships between management and the organization's employees. The first thing that we discussed is the need to create trust in order to successfully communicate within and between these two groups. We reviewed the communication process including sending and receiving messages. The next section dealt with the process of analyzing job satisfaction in the workforce. Here, we identified two common methods of measuring job satisfaction and showed when each is appropriate. We also discussed what happens if job satisfaction is too low among the workforce.

The third major section of this chapter dealt with several of the major federal laws that cover labor relations in for-profit businesses. These included the Railway Labor Act, the National Labor Relations Act, the Labor Management Relations Act, the Labor Management Reporting and Disclosure Act, and the Worker Adjustment and Retraining Notification Act. We also covered some of the issues concerning whistle-blowers, and gave you some tools to limit the potential for whistle-blowers in companies that you might work for. In this section, we also discussed express contracts, implied contracts, and quasi-contracts. The last item in the third section discussed two kinds of employee termination—wrongful discharge and constructive discharge—and the legal issues associated with each.

The fourth section provided a little background on unions and labor rights in the United States, and looked at some of the reasons why employees join unions. We also discussed the union organizing process, including the role of the NLRB and prohibitions on employers during the period leading up to a union election. In the last part, we reviewed the process of filing, investigating, and disposing of grievances by members of a unionized workforce.

Our next section reviewed management's rights during the union organizing process, and what management can and can't legally do to limit organizers' efforts within their workforce. We discussed lockouts and replacement workers—in order to deter strike actions on the part of the workforce. Additionally, we discussed the process that workers must go through in order to hold off the certification election to remove union representation from the organization. A reminder here—management cannot initiate this process.

Next we discussed conflict and five conflict management styles we can use when faced with a conflict. You also learned how to initiate a conflict resolution following the steps of a model to get to a win-win solution.

In the next section, we reviewed the processes of planning for and conducting a negotiation, with the steps involved in the process model so that you can improve your negotiation skills. We also discussed the concept of alternative dispute resolution, including two methods—mediation and arbitration. We showed how both mediators and arbitrators facilitate discussions between parties in conflict in order to come to a resolution. We also showed how mediators and arbitrators differ—mediators have no power to enforce a resolution to a conflict, but arbitrators do.

Finally, as with each of our chapters, we took a look at some trends: in this case trends in unionization and labor relations. The first item was a quick trip around the globe to see how unions affect employers and their workforce in different parts of the world. The second trend asked whether or not union suppression efforts on the part of employers are ethical. Lastly, we reviewed some of the recent efforts in Congress to pass a card-check law to simplify the process of unionizing a workforce.

It looks like we have a recurring theme here in providing an awful lot of information in one chapter. That's enough for this chapter, so let's go on to the summary and end-of-chapter material.

Chapter Summary

Visit www.sagepub.com/lussier for helpful study resources.

10.1 Briefly describe the five steps in the message-sending process.

The five steps are (1) Develop rapport—put the receiver at ease; (2) State the communication objective—the end result you want to achieve; (3) Transmit the message—tell the receiver what you want them to know; (4) Check for understanding—ask questions and/or paraphrase; and (5) Get a commitment and follow up—make sure the receiver can do what is required and check to make sure action was taken.

10.2 Briefly describe the four steps in the message-receiving process.

The steps are (1) Active listening—pay attention to the whole message, avoid distractions, take notes if necessary, and convey understanding; (2) Analyzing—think, empathize, and wait to evaluate until after listening is complete; (3) Check understanding—paraphrase back to the sender and watch nonverbal behavior; and (4) (if appropriate) Respond to the sender.

10.3 Identify the primary reason why measuring job satisfaction is so difficult, and the best tool for getting employees to tell the truth about their level of satisfaction.

Job satisfaction is an attitude, not a behavior. We can experience behaviors directly, while attitudes can only be measured indirectly. Because of this we must use some form of survey and ask the employee about their job satisfaction level. When using job satisfaction surveys, we have to ensure that they are anonymous, or employees will most likely not tell the truth about their satisfaction levels.

10.4 Identify the major labor relations laws in the United States, and the major reasons for each law.

1. The Railway Labor Act of 1926 was enacted to force negotiation between labor and management, first in railroads and later in the airlines, to prevent shutdown of these critical services.

2. The National Labor Relations Act of 1935 was the first major law to deal with the rights of labor to form unions in the general workforce and collectively bargain with their employers. It identified unfair labor practices for management in negotiating with labor organizations.

3. The Labor Management Relations Act of 1947 was an amendment to the NLRA that focused on unfair labor practices on the part of unions and other labor organizations, and outlawed or restricted a variety of strikes and boycotts. The LMRA also allowed the states to pass "right-to-work laws."

4. The Labor Management Reporting and Disclosure act of 1959 was passed as a result of congressional investigations linking organized crime with labor unions. The LMRDA required a series of reports from labor unions and created restrictions on their activities.

5. The Worker Adjustment and Retraining Notification Act of 1988 required, based on some qualifying characteristics, that an organization provide 60 days' notice when laying off more than 50 people or closing a plant.

10.5 Briefly discuss the difference between wrongful discharge and constructive discharge.

Wrongful discharge is the process of terminating an individual from employment for an illegal reason. Even when employment is "at-will," employers can't break the law or violate a contract to terminate employees. Constructive discharge is actually not discharge at all. In constructive discharge, an employee quits their job because of severe harassment or "intolerable" working conditions.

10.6 Briefly discuss the NO TIPS rule for labor elections.

The NO TIPS acronym stands for No Threats; No Interrogations; No Promises; and No Spying. This means first that employers cannot threaten employees with a loss of their jobs or the closing of the plant, or in any other manner during the period prior to a labor election. Second, employers cannot question individual employees about union organizing activities on either their part or the part of others within the organization. Third, management cannot promise that if employees vote against unionization, the organization will provide them with benefits because of their votes. Finally, management cannot spy on individual employees taking part in union organizing events, either through planting individuals in such meetings or through electronic or other means.

10.7 What can management do to limit union organizing efforts?

Management can prevent union organizers from soliciting employees on company property during working hours as long as such prohibitions are consistent with the company's general solicitation policies. Management can also identify costs that would be associated with union membership and can provide truthful information concerning how unionization will affect relationships between individual employees and management. These relationships can include things such as performance-based promotions, or merit-based raises or training opportunities.

10.8 **Identify the five conflict management styles. How is each described in terms of winning and losing?**

The first conflict management style is called avoiding. Avoiding is unassertive and uncooperative, leading to a "lose-lose" situation. The second option is accommodating. In accommodation, the individual is unassertive but cooperative, leading to a "lose-win" situation—they lose and the other party wins. The third option is forcing. Forcers are assertive but uncooperative, which creates a "win-lose" situation. Some managers will use this style to get things done quickly because they have a legitimate authority over others. The fourth style is negotiating, which creates a "win some—lose some" situation. Each side gets some of what they want through compromise, but not all that they want. The final

style is collaborating, which creates a true "win-win" situation. Both sides worked together to create a solution that meets all of their needs.

10.9 **Briefly explain the processes of mediation and arbitration and the major difference between the two processes.**

Mediation and arbitration both deal with inserting a third party as an intermediary into a dispute between two other individuals or groups. However, they differ in how much power the third party has. Mediators enter into a conflict to assist the two conflicting parties in coming to a resolution and to act as a facilitator in their negotiations, but the mediator has no authority to force a solution on the opposing parties. In contrast, arbitrators also assist the two parties in attempting to work out a solution to their conflict, but arbitrators have the ability to enforce a decision made by the arbitrator on both of the conflicting parties. This is called a binding decision.

Key Terms

Active listening	Economic strike	Labor relations	Strike
Arbitrator	Express contract	Lockout	Trust
Collective bargaining	Feedback	Mediator	Whistle-blower
Communication	Functional conflict	Negotiating	Wrongful discharge
Conflict	Grievance	Paraphrasing	
Constructive discharge	Implied contract	Quasi-contract	

Key Term Review

Complete each of the following statements using one of this chapter's key terms:

_____ is faith in the character and actions of another.

_____ is the process of transmitting information and meaning.

_____ is information provided by the receiver that verifies that a message was transmitted successfully.

_____ is the process of restating a message back to the original sender in the receiver's own words.

_____ is the process of paying attention to an entire message, taking into account both the content of the message and the context in which the communication is delivered.

_____ is a collective work stoppage by members of a union that is intended to put pressure on an employer.

_____ is someone who tells an authoritative organization outside their own company about actions within the firm that they believe to be illegal.

_____ is a transaction in which the agreement between two parties is specifically stated.

_____ occurs when the parties form an agreement from their actions rather than from a specific oral or written agreement.

_____ is a court-ordered implied agreement to prevent one party in an action from benefiting at the expense of another party.

_____ involves terminating an individual employee for an illegal reason, either due to a violation of a contract or because of violation of a state or federal law.

_____ occurs when an employee is forced to quit their job because of severe and/or pervasive harassment or intolerable working conditions.

_____ are the interactions between management and unionized employees.

_____ is the negotiation process resulting in a contract between union employees and management that covers employment conditions.

_____ is a formal complaint concerning pay, working conditions, or violation of some other factor in a collective bargaining agreement.

_____ occurs when management stops work and physically prevents workers from entering the workplace.

_____ is a work stoppage over authorized collective bargaining issues such as pay or working conditions.

_____ exists whenever people are in disagreement and opposition.

_____ exists where disagreement and opposition support the achievement of organizational and individual objectives.

_____ is a process in which two or more parties in conflict attempt to come to an agreement.

_____ is a neutral third party who helps resolve a conflict, but has no authority to impose a solution to the conflict.

_____ is a neutral third party who resolves a conflict by making a binding decision.

Quick Check (True-False)

1. Trust between two people is created quickly and can be lost just as quickly. T F

2. In communication, planning the message is necessary when the information is difficult, unusual, or especially important. T F

3. Feedback allows you to check whether or not the receiver understood the message. T F

4. Multitasking (working on the computer, watching a video) while listening is easy for workers in their 20s because they have grown up this way. T F

5. Job satisfaction can be measured with organizational development surveys, which are *direct* measures of a person's attitude. T F

6. The faces scale and an organizational development survey are the two primary tools we use to measure job satisfaction. T F

7. Job dissatisfaction leads to many potential negative consequences such as alcohol abuse, lower overall health levels, higher levels of theft, and sabotage. T F

8. The Railway Labor Act also covers airline workers. T F

9. The Taft-Hartley Act (1947) amends the NLRA to include unfair labor practices by labor organizations. T F

10. The WARN Act requires that employers notify their employees in the case of a nuclear accident or incident. T F

11. One action that employers can take to limit whistle-blowers is to have a written policy on what action will be taken on receipt of a report of unethical activity. T F

12. Quasi-contracts become express contracts once both parties realize that they exist. T F

13. If an employee quits due to pervasive harassment or intolerable working conditions, they are guilty of wrongful discharge. T F

14. One of the major reasons that employees vote to join unions is that their friends are doing it. T F

15. NO TIPS means that employers can't Threaten, Interrogate, make Promises to, or Spy on employees during the preelection period for a union vote. T F

16. Grievance procedures call for an individual employee to bring up a complaint and have the company resolve the complaint in a timely manner. T F

17. Management cannot change any working conditions once a petition for a labor election has been filed with the NLRB. T F

18. Replacement workers must be terminated and striking workers reinstated in their original jobs once any type of strike is concluded. T F

19. All conflict should be avoided in order to maintain high employee job satisfaction. T F

20. Avoiding is the best conflict management style for most situations. T F

21. In a successful negotiation, both parties usually get *part* of what they wanted, but don't get all of the concessions that they want from the other party. T F

22. Alternative dispute resolution methods include mediation and arbitration. T F

23. Facilitation is a major tool for mediators and arbitrators. T F

Communication Skills

The following critical-thinking questions can be used for class discussion and/or for written assignments to develop communication skills. Be sure to give complete explanations for all answers.

1. What causes you to trust or distrust someone else? Using this answer, what would you do as a manager to cause your employees to trust you?

2. Good communication skills are critical to a manager. Which do you think is more important: learning to communicate specifically as a sender, or learning to listen well as a receiver? Why?

3. What *specific* things would you think about if you were trying to empathize with an employee telling you about a problem in their work group?

4. What actions would you consider taking, other than increasing pay, if job satisfaction survey data showed that your employees' satisfaction level was dropping significantly?

5. Which side do you think has an easier job when a labor organization is trying to unionize the company's employees—management or the union organizers? Why?

6. Do you think it is ever OK for employees to strike against an employer? If so, in what circumstances? If not, why not?

7. After reviewing both the management and labor "unfair labor practices" noted in the chapter, do you feel that they are fairly well balanced, or do you feel that they are skewed toward either management or labor? Explain your answer.

8. What actions would you take if confronted by a potential whistle-blower employee if they said they had evidence that an executive-level manager in your company was doing something illegal? Explain your answer in some detail.

9. Looking at the concept of constructive discharge, is it ever really possible that an employee could be harassed so severely that they were forced to quit? Can you give an example of the situation that you feel would meet this level of harassment?

10. Assume that you are a fairly high-level manager in your company, and one of your employees comes to you to tell you that other employees are attempting to unionize the company. What would your initial actions be, and why?

11. An employee who works for you confronts you with a formal grievance concerning another employee being promoted over them. What initial actions would you take in order to address this grievance?

12. If you have authority to make decisions for your organization, would you ever use a lockout to prevent workers from entering your business, even after "good faith" bargaining efforts had failed? Why or why not?

13. Can opponents in a conflict ever really come to a collaborative conclusion, or is the best that we can do simply a negotiation where each party wins some of what they wanted and loses other things that they desired? Explain your answer.

14. Would you personally rather have an arbitrator handle a conflict between you and another person, or go to court and have a judge make a decision? Explain your answer.

15. Describe a sample of conflict between people in an organization. How would you as a facilitator assist the people in conflict to resolve their differences?

Video

Please visit the student study site at **www.sagepub.com/lussier** to view the video links in this chapter.

Answers

REVIEW QUESTIONS (TRUE-FALSE) Answers

1. F   2. T   3. T   4. F   5. F   6. T   7. T   8. T   9. T   10. F   11. T   12. F   13. F   14. F   15. T   16. T   17. F   18. F   19. F   20. F   21. T   22. T   23. T

Case

Case 10-1. Decker Deals With the Unions

Tom Decker is Plant Manager of a large fruit and vegetable canning plant owned by a national grocery chain. The plant has 200 full-time production employees staffing three 8-hour shifts. Tom has just recently become aware of an attempt by the United Food and Grocery Workers Union (UFGWU) to organize the production workers in the plant. He is somewhat surprised by the union organizing campaign since he feels that employee relations have always been very good in the plant. Tom believes that employees are somewhat satisfied with the amount of compensation provided, but he thinks that it may be time to consider making some improvements. He intends to meet with management in the corporate office to convince them that improving employee wages and benefits shows that the company will take care of them and that they don't need union representation. Tom plans to hold meetings with small groups of employees in an effort to persuade them that a union is unnecessary and that having a union represent them will not necessarily help them gain better wages or benefits.

Tom asked his shift supervisors to keep their eyes and ears open in order to learn which employees are supportive of the union's organizing attempt. A few days later, the shift supervisors furnished Tom a list of all employees whom they believe have signed union authorization cards. Tom's cousin, who also works in the plant, is attending union organizing meetings and is keeping management informed on the meetings. Lew Spencer, the evening shift supervisor, informed Tom that two employees working on his shift appear to be the plant leaders of a group of union sympathizers because they have been "talking up" the union to all the other employees in the plant. One of the employees, Bill Vance, has only been with the company for two years. A review of his personnel file shows that he has received reprimands for poor attendance and unsatisfactory job performance. The other employee, Jason Higgins, has been with the company for 23 years. A review of his personnel file indicates that he has always performed his job satisfactorily. He has never received

any formal disciplinary action; however, Supervisor Lew Spencer stated that he can be a hothead and occasionally tends to be very vocal and argumentative about any changes in working conditions at the plant. Tom wonders why these two employees have not been fired since they do not appear to be good employees. Corporate management has been considering reducing the workforce through an economic layoff since the plant is currently not operating at full capacity. Tom thinks that this would be an opportunity to get rid of some employees who are union sympathizers including Bill Vance and Jason Higgins.

Questions

1. Why should management personnel be careful regarding comments made to employees during a union organizing campaign? What should managers not say and what could they say to employees during a union organizing attempt?

2. If Tom Decker is correct in his assessment that the production employees are satisfied with their wages and benefits, what other factors may be motivating employees' interest in organizing with the union?

3. Should management take some employment action against any employees during this organizing campaign? Explain your answer.

4. Should management make changes in wages, benefits, and other conditions of employment during a union organizing campaign? Explain your answer.

5. What is meant by the term *exclusive bargaining agent*? What would it take for the UFGWU to become the exclusive bargaining agent if an election is held?

6. What could be a possible outcome concerning the union organizing campaign if the union files an unfair labor practice against the company with the National Labor Relations Board (NLRB)?

Case created by Herbert Sherman, PhD

SKILL BUILDER 10-1

Conflict Resolution

Objective

To develop conflict skills using the initiating conflict resolution model (Model 10-4).

Skills

The primary skills developed through this exercise are:

1.   *HR Management skill* – Human relations

2.   *SHRM Curricular Guide* – A: Employee and Labor Relations

During this exercise, you will be given the opportunity to role-play a conflict you are facing, or have faced, in order to develop your conflict resolution skills. Students and workers have reported that this exercise helped prepare them for successful initiation of conflict resolution with roommates or coworkers. Fill in the following information:

Name the other party/parties (you may use fictitious names):

_____

_____

_____

Describe the conflict situation:

_____

_____

_____

List pertinent information about the other party (i.e., relationship to you, knowledge of the situation, age, and background):

_____

_____

_____

Identify the other party's possible reaction to your confrontation. (How receptive will he or she be to collaborating? What might he or she say or do during the discussion to resist change?)

_____

_____

_____

How will you overcome the resistance to change?

Following the steps in the collaborative conflict resolution model, write out your BCF statement.

_____

_____

_____

Apply It

Your instructor may allow you to role-play the conflict in class, or you may role-play with someone outside of class, or just initiate the conflict resolution in your personal or professional life. If you role-play in class, the instructor will provide directions.

What did I learn from this experience? How will I use this knowledge in the future?

SKILL BUILDER 10-2

Negotiating

Objective

To develop negotiating skills using the negotiation process model (Model 10-5).

Skills

The primary skills developed through this exercise are:

1. *HR Management skill* – Human relations

2. *SHRM Curricular Guide* – A: Employee and Labor Relations

You will role-play being the buyer or seller of a used car.

Procedure 1 (1–2 minutes)

Pair off and sit facing your partner so that you cannot read each other's confidential sheet. Pairs should be as far apart as possible so they cannot overhear other pairs' conversations. If there is an odd number of students in the class, one student will be an observer or work with the instructor. Decide who will be the buyer and who will be the seller of the used car.

Procedure 2 (1–2 minutes)

The instructor will give a confidential sheet to each buyer and seller. (These do not appear in this book.)

Procedure 3 (5–6 minutes)

Buyers and sellers read their confidential sheets and jot down some plans (what your basic approach will be, what you will say) for the negotiation.

Procedure 4 (3–7 minutes)

Negotiate the sale of the car. You do not have to buy or sell the car. After you make the sale or agree not to sell, read your partner's confidential sheet and discuss the experience.

Integration (3–7 minutes)

Planning the Negotiation

Step 1. Research the other party. Did you at least consider the car to be an antique?

Step 2. Set objectives. Did you set a lower limit, target, and opening price?

Step 3. Did you develop options and/or develop trade-offs?

Step 4. Did you anticipate questions and objections and prepare answers?

Negotiating

Step 1. Did you develop rapport and focus on obstacles, not the person?

Step 2. Did you let the other party make the first offer?

Step 3. Did you listen and ask questions to focus on meeting the other party's needs?

Step 4. Were you quick to settle for less than your target price and/or ask for something in return for giving concessions?

Did you postpone? If you did reach a sales agreement, which price did you receive? $_____

Apply It

What did I learn from this experience? How will I use this knowledge in the future?

_____

_____

Compensating and Protecting

11

Compensation Management

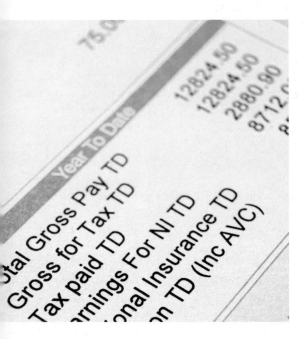

Learning Outcomes

After studying this chapter you should be able to:

11.1 Identify the components of a compensation system

11.2 Briefly describe expectancy theory as it applies to compensation

11.3 Briefly describe equity theory as it applies to compensation

11.4 Identify the seven basic issues that make up the organizational philosophy on compensation

11.5 Discuss the three major provisions of the Fair Labor Standards Act

11.6 Describe the penalties in the FLSA for misclassification of nonexempt employees

11.7 Briefly describe the concept of *comparable worth* and how it compares with *equal pay*

11.8 Identify the three types of job evaluation and discuss whether they are more objective or subjective in form

11.9 Briefly describe the concepts of *job structure* and *pay levels*

11.10 Discuss the concepts of *product market competition* and *labor market competition*

11.11 Briefly describe the concept of a *pay structure*

11.12 Briefly discuss the value of broadbanding to the organization

11.13 Define the following terms:

Compensation	Overtime
Compensation system	Job evaluation
Expectancy theory	Pay structure
Equity theory	Rate range
Wage compression	Delayering
Minimum wage	Broadbanding

Chapter 11 Outline

SHRM
HR CONTENT

See Appendix A:
SHRM 2010 Curriculum Guidebook for the complete list

B. Employment Law (required)
8. The Fair Labor Standards of 1938

C. Job Analysis/Job Design (required)
2. Job evaluation and compensation (grades, pay surveys, and pay setting)
6. Compliance with legal requirements
   Equal pay (skill, effort, responsibility, and working conditions) and comparable worth
   Overtime eligibility (exempt vs. nonexempt work)

E. Outcomes: Metrics and Measurement of HR (required)
11. Benchmarking

G. Staffing: Recruitment and Selection (required)
16. The employment brand (above, at, or below market pay)

I. Total Rewards (required)

A. Compensation
1. Development of a base pay system
2. Developing pay levels
3. Determining pay increases
4. Role of job analysis/job design/job descriptions in determining compensation
6. Compensation of special groups (e.g., executives, outside sales, contingent workers, management)
7. Internal alignment strategies
8. External competitiveness strategies
9. Legal constraints on pay issues
10. Monitoring compensation costs
11. Union role in wage and salary administration
12. Minimum wage/overtime
13. Pay discrimination and dissimilar jobs
14. Prevailing wage
15. Motivation theories (equity, reinforcement, and agency theories)

Case 11-1. Selling the Sales Force on Commission Compensation

It's Not Fair!

Once you have an established pay scale, does it really matter if you worry about compensation levels? Alex stormed into my office and flopped down in the nearest chair. "I hear they hired a new payroll clerk—the same job I've been doing for five years—and this new person is going to be paid more than I make! I've been a loyal employee for years and haven't had a real raise since the downturn in the economy.

This is the thanks I get?" I couldn't fault Alex for his feelings, and I knew it was past time my company examined our compensation guidelines. What do we do when the going market rate for a position outdistances our set pay scale? Chapter 11 answers this question and more as it demonstrates the reasons why compensation management is so vital to attracting and retaining your best employees.

The Practitioner's Model for HRM

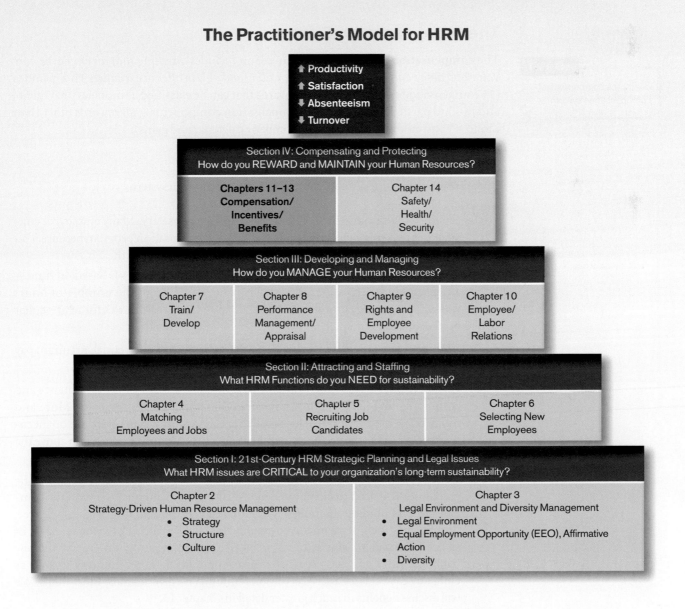

Compensation Management

Compensation costs are frequently 65% to 70% of total production costs in today's firms.[1] **Compensation** is *the total of an employee's pay and benefits.* A business designs and implements a compensation system in order to focus worker attention on the specific efforts the organization considers necessary to achieve its desired goals.[2] However, if rewards are to be useful in stimulating desired behavior, they must also meet the demands of employees whose behavior they're intended to influence.[3] Thus, poor compensation management practices can have negative effects on performance.[4] Why?

Video Link 11.1

Basic Questions
Regarding Compensation

Compensation affects the process of both attracting and retaining employees.[5] Thus, compensation is an important part of HRM.[6] A recent survey revealed that employers may not fully grasp what it takes to retain good workers, as managers consistently rated management climate and supervisor relationships as the top "drivers of retention." However, workers rated pay and benefits as the top drivers to retain them. And only 27% of employees are "very satisfied" with their pay, while just 37% are very satisfied with their benefits.[7] So in order to meet the requirements of the firm, we have to also design the system to meet the various needs of employees.

The Compensation System

LO 11.1

Identify the components of
a compensation system.

The **compensation system** of an organization *includes anything that an employee may value and desire and that the employer is willing and able to offer in exchange.* This includes (1) compensation components—all rewards that can be classified as monetary payments and in-kind payments; and (2) noncompensation components—all rewards other than monetary and in-kind payments (e.g., company cafeterias and gyms).

Types of Compensation

There are four basic kinds of compensation in a compensation system:

1. **Base pay**—typically a flat rate, either hourly wage or salary. Many employees consider this to be the most important part of the compensation program because it's a major decision factor for most employees in deciding to accept the job.

   Wage versus salary. Wages are paid on an hourly basis. *Salary* is based on time—a week, a month, or a year. A salary is paid regardless of the number of hours worked. Wages are common for blue-collar workers and salaries for white-collar professionals and managers.

2. **Wage and salary add-ons**—includes overtime pay, shift differential, premium pay for working weekends and holidays, and other add-ons.

3. **Incentive pays**—also called variable pay. *Incentives* are pay for performance and commonly include piecework in production and commission sales. More and more today, pay for performance is the trend.[8] As more companies develop incentive mechanisms,[9] they give workers more powerful incentives to perform above the standard.[10] We will discuss incentives in much greater detail in Chapter 12.

4. **Benefits**—indirect compensation that provides something of value to the employee. You need to include benefits in your system, because they cost the company a lot of money even though they aren't direct compensation to the employee. Benefits may include payments to employees if they are unable to work because of sickness or accident; payments for medical insurance services; retirement pay contributions; and provision of a wide variety of desired goods and services such as company cars, cafeteria service, tuition reimbursement, and many other items. We will discuss benefits in much greater detail in Chapter 13.

11-1 APPLYING THE CONCEPT

Types of Compensation

Identify each statement by its type of compensation.

a. base pay
b. wage and salary add-ons

c. incentive pay
d. benefits

_____ 1. I like working nights because it pays more.

_____ 2. After I graduate with my BS in accounting, I'd like to work for a firm that will help pay for me to get my Master of Business Administration (MBA) degree.

_____ 3. The company only pays $10 an hour. I need to find a better job.

_____ 4. I like getting paid the same each week. It helps me to budget my expenses.

_____ 5. I'm good at sales, so I like being paid for every sale I make.

Direct versus indirect compensation. The first three compensation components—base pay, any add-ons, and incentive pay—are known as direct compensation. These forms of compensation go directly to the employee as part of their paycheck. Benefits are called indirect compensation. The employee doesn't directly get any funds from a benefits program. Benefits are usually paid for by the company, and the employee never sees these funds.

In for-profit businesses, we want to design the mix of compensation and noncompensation components that provide us with the best productivity return for the money spent. However, in order to do that, we need to understand something about the motivational value of our compensation system. Let's take a look at a few theories that help us understand better how compensation systems can motivate our workers to learn, and act in the way we need them to act.

Motivation and Compensation Planning

When we look at designing our compensation programs, we need to remember that we are trying to motivate the employee to do the things that we need them to do, consistently, over a period of time. Probably the most significant theories that help in compensation planning are *expectancy theory* and *equity theory*, both "process theories" of motivation.[11] However, we also need to look at how our employees learn and carry out their jobs in the organization. To make sense of the implementation of their training we need to remember what we discussed in Chapter 7 about *learning theories*. But let's get started with motivation and how it affects the design of our compensation system.

Expectancy Theory

We said in the introduction to this section that expectancy theory is a *process theory* of motivation. This basically means that we, as human beings, go through a cognitive process to evaluate something and, if we evaluate the process positively, we will likely continue to be

WORK
APPLICATION 11-1

Select a job you have or had. Identify the compensation you received in detail.

Video Link 11.2

Compensation Benefits

SHRM

Guide – I:A15
Motivation theories (equity, reinforcement, agency theories)

LO 11.2

Briefly describe expectancy theory as it applies to compensation.

motivated to do the same thing. Alternately, if we evaluate the process negatively, we will be disinclined to do the same thing in the future. **Expectancy theory** *proposes that employees are motivated when they believe they can accomplish a task and the rewards for doing so are worth the effort.* Expectancy theory is based on Victor Vroom's formula: motivation = expectancy × instrumentality x valence.[12]

For compensation purposes, we have intentionally simplified the theory to show how it affects a person's motivation to perform. *Expectancy* is the person's perception of his or her ability (probability) to accomplish an objective. Generally, the higher one's expectancy, the better the chance for motivation. *Instrumentality* is the perception of the likelihood of a particular level of performance providing the individual with a desired reward. *Valence* refers to the value a person places on the outcome or reward. Not all people value the same reward. Again, generally, the higher the value (importance) of the outcome or reward, the better the chance of motivation. One thing that we need to remember here is that the three components of the theory—valence, instrumentality, and expectancy—are multiplicative. This means that if any one of the three is near zero, the motivating potential is also near zero—*the individual has almost no motivation to perform*!

Salespeople are often given incentive pay to motivate them to sell more.

How does the theory affect compensation of our workforce? The simple way to answer is to show expectancy in action— refer to Exhibit 11-1. An employee will have an *expectation* to put forth some form of *effort* at work. This effort is *expected* to result in some level of *performance*—higher effort should get higher performance levels. The performance level is *expected* to result in some type of desired *reward*, and if it does, the employee *expects* to put out more effort. (Obviously, compensation is at least part of the reward expected by the employee.) The reward must be *significant* to the individual (have valence); if it is, the motivation to put forth effort should continue. As long as the process continues unbroken, the employee will continue to put out effort. In other words, as HR Managers, if we help employees get what they want, they will give us the work we want to help meet the organizational goals.[13]

So the result of expectancy theory is that our employees will either be motivated by their outcomes, including compensation, or be demotivated by them. Knowing how people internally evaluate their outcomes using the cognitive process of expectancy theory helps us when we are structuring the compensation plan.

Motivating employees with expectancy theory. Here are some keys to using expectancy theory successfully:

1. Clearly define objectives and the performance needed to achieve them. In other words, goal setting is part of expectancy theory.

2. Tie performance to rewards. High performance should be rewarded. When one employee works harder to produce more than other employees and is not rewarded, he or she may slow down.

3. Be sure rewards have value to employees. What motivates one employee may not motivate other employees, so managers should get to know employees as individuals.[14]

Exhibit 11-1	Expectancy Theory and Compensation

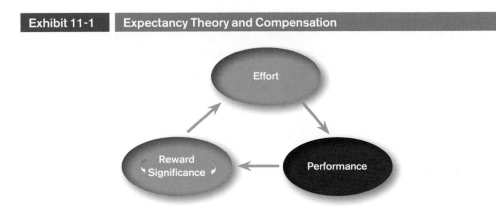

4. Make sure employees believe that management will do what it says it will. For example, employees must believe that management will give them a merit raise if they meet their performance goals. And management must do so to earn employees' trust.

Equity Theory

Equity theory is another real-world concept that affects people in our organizations. People in companies apply equity theory constantly—we all do. Equity theory, particularly the version of J. Stacy Adams, proposes that people are motivated to seek social equity in the rewards they receive (outcomes) for their performance (input).[15] So, **equity theory** *proposes that employees are motivated when the ratio of their perceived outcomes to inputs is at least roughly equal to other referent individuals.*

According to equity theory, people compare their inputs (effort, loyalty, hard work, commitment, skills, ability, experience, seniority, trust, support of colleagues, and so forth) and financial rewards (pay, benefits, perks) and intangible outputs (such as praise, recognition, status, job security, and sense of advancement and achievement) to those of relevant others.[16] A relevant other could be a coworker or a group of employees from the same or different organizations. Notice that the definition says that employees compare their *perceived* (not actual) inputs and outcomes.[17] Equity may actually exist. However, if employees believe that there is inequity, they will change their behavior to create equity. Employees must perceive that they are being treated fairly, relative to others.

Unfortunately, at least in some cases, employees tend to inflate their own efforts or performance when comparing themselves to others.[18] They also tend to overestimate what others earn. Employees may be very satisfied and motivated until they perceive that a relevant other is earning more for the same job or earning the same for doing less work. When employees perceive inequity, they are motivated to reduce it by decreasing input or increasing outcomes. A comparison with relevant others leads to one of three conclusions, which can cause problems.[19] The employee is either underrewarded, overrewarded, or equitably rewarded.

1. ***Underrewarded.*** When employees perceive that they are underrewarded, they may try to reduce the inequity by increasing outcomes (requesting a raise, theft), decreasing inputs (doing less work, being absent, taking long breaks, etc.), rationalizing (finding a logical explanation for inequity), changing others' inputs or outcomes (getting them to do more or receive less), leaving the situation (getting transferred or taking a better job), or changing the object of comparison. There is strong evidence that perceptions of being underrewarded can lead to some very negative consequences for the organization including theft and sabotage, so we have to take perceptions of being underrewarded seriously.[20]

2. *Overrewarded.* Being overrewarded does not disturb most employees. People tend to tolerate overrewarded situations to a much greater extent than underrewarded situations. However, research suggests that if the employee feels *significantly* over-rewarded, they may reduce perceived inequity by increasing input (working harder or longer), decreasing outcomes (taking a pay cut), rationalizing (I'm worth it), or trying to increase others' outcomes.

3. *Equitably rewarded.* When inputs and outcomes are perceived as being equal, the theory says that employees will be motivated to continue to put forth effort for the organization so long as they are content where they perceive these to be in balance.[21]

Motivating employees with equity theory. Using equity theory in practice can be difficult, because you don't know the employees' reference groups and their views of inputs and outcomes. However, the theory does offer some useful general recommendations:

1. Managers should be aware that equity is based on perception, which may not be correct. Possibly, managers can create equity or inequity, so the manager's role is to be the arbiter of equity.[22] If employees believe they are not being treated fairly, there should be procedures to follow to resolve the issue or complaint.[23] A good performance appraisal system (as discussed in Chapter 8) can help.

2. Rewards should actually be equitable. When employees perceive that they are not treated fairly, morale suffers, and performance problems occur. Employees producing at the same level should be given equivalent rewards.

3. High performance should be rewarded, but employees must understand the inputs needed to attain certain outcomes. When using incentive pay, managers should clearly specify the exact requirements to achieve the incentive. As discussed in Chapter 8, a manager should be able to state objectively why one person got a higher merit raise than another.

As HR Managers, we need to understand that people will be demotivated if they feel (perceive) that they are not fairly compensated. As a result, we have to use this information when we begin to structure our compensation plan. We need to "build in" equity, to minimize the problems associated with equity theory.

Learning Theories

We talked about learning at length in Chapter 7, so we want to do just a brief review of those theories here. Remember that learning theories are about how to get people to do the things that we need them to do in the organization. We especially need to remember how *reinforcement* and *social learning* work, because compensation is designed at least partly to reinforce learned behaviors at work.[24]

B. F. Skinner said that if we give an employee something that they want in return for doing what we need them to do, they are more likely to continue to do the same work successfully in the future, because their behavior got *positive reinforcement*. In the same way, if an employee sees another get positive reinforcement for doing something, Skinner says that the person observing this action is more likely to imitate the behavior, because of *social learning*, in order to get a similar reward.

We can also use *negative reinforcement* because, you remember, it also causes a person to repeat a desired action. If employees are less motivated because they have to work too much overtime, we can take the overtime away. Because we take something that the employees don't want away, they are inclined to be more motivated. The whole point of compensation is to motivate employees, so we don't want to demotivate because we are working them too hard.

WORK
APPLICATION 11-3

Give an example of how equity theory has affected your motivation, or that of someone you work with or have worked with. Be sure to specify if you were underrewarded, overrewarded, or equitably rewarded.

WORK
APPLICATION 11-4

Give an example of the types of reinforcement used on a present or past job.

We also set work standards to ensure that employees do a reasonable amount for work for their compensation (avoidance reinforcement). If not, we use punishment, such as pay cuts, demotions, and when necessary firing employees.

Organizational Philosophy

LO 11.4

Identify the seven basic issues that make up the organizational philosophy on compensation.

In addition to understanding our compensation options and how they motivate employees, we need to identify what our compensation philosophy will be. We need to ask ourselves (and get honest answers to) a series of questions concerning the compensation system that we need to design. How much can we afford to pay? What are we willing to pay for? How will we structure our compensation system and why? Will our pay structure be higher or lower than that of our competitors, and why? Let's discuss some of these major organizational issues that we will need to understand and make decisions about before we can set up our system.

Ability to Pay

Probably the first thing we need is an honest assessment of how much we can afford, or are willing to afford, in order to compensate our employees. This of course means we need to complete an assessment of estimated revenues from our business operations, and determine what percentage of revenues can or should realistically go toward compensation costs. There are a number of ways of figuring this out such as building pro forma financial analyses, but it is beyond the scope of this text.

SHRM

Guide – I:A 10
Monitoring compensation costs

In our analysis, we want to calculate the total amount of annual organizational revenue that we expect to be available for all compensation components—wages, incentive payments, and benefits. One of the worst possible situations a company can find itself in is to have promised a particular level of compensation and then not be able to provide what was agreed upon because the funds are not available. This is especially true in the payment of incentives. Incentive promises at the beginning of a year that are then reneged on at the end of the year will almost always cause intense demotivation and potentially high rates of turnover among our workers.[25]

What Types of Compensation?

WORK
APPLICATION 11-5

Assess an organization you work or have worked for in terms of its ability to pay. Explain how you came up with your answer.

Once we identify how much revenue is available for compensation, the next thing we need to do is determine how to break the compensation structure down. We noted earlier in the chapter that we have four basic components to compensation—base pay, wage add-ons, incentives, and benefits. We will need to determine how to divide the funds available between each of the components.

There are some legal requirements for certain benefits such as Social Security (we will discuss these in Chapter 13), so these legal requirements have to be dealt with "off the top"—they have to be subtracted from the available funds. Once we subtract the amount necessary to provide the benefits that are legally required by state and federal requirements, we need to make a determination concerning how much direct compensation will be in the form of a base pay and how much will be incentive pay. We will have to ensure that the direct compensation that we provide will allow us to be competitive in the labor markets from which we must draw our employees. Otherwise we may not be able to get recruits to select jobs with our firm.[26] We'll talk more about how we determine what a competitive amount of compensation will be when we get to pay structures later in this chapter.

The last type of compensation that we will consider is benefits. Here again, we need to analyze competition within the labor market and what benefits each of our close competitors provides. We will most likely have to approximately match the benefits that are provided by our main competitors.[27] In addition, we may determine that other benefits provide us with leverage that allows us to get better employees to commit to work for our firm, and keep the workers who are already part of the organization more satisfied and less likely to quit.[28]

Pay for Performance or Pay for Longevity?

In breaking down base pay versus incentives, we will need to look at whether our organization is going to have a *performance or a longevity philosophy*. What do we mean by performance and longevity? Some companies pay people more for *longevity or seniority*—for attaining years of service to the firm. If we work for this type of organization, we will likely get promotions and raises over time, assuming that we meet minimal organizational standards, regardless of performance, because we have been a "loyal organizational member." Other companies, however, will pay you for *performing*—for completing certain tasks or doing certain things faster or better than average, not for just being there and being loyal to the firm.[29]

Why would anyone pay people just for being in the company for a long time? We may be in an industry where customers have strong relationships with their contact within the firm and they don't feel comfortable when they don't have that contact available anymore. In this case, we might need to reward service because it gives us stability, and our customers rely on this stability. A common example where at least part of direct compensation is based on longevity is in the insurance industry. Customers create a relationship with their insurance agent, sometimes over long periods of time, and may not feel comfortable changing to a new agent every few months. In this type of company, base pay would probably be the largest component of direct compensation. Educators are also commonly paid based on longevity when all teachers get a raise regardless of performance.

Now, there are certainly problems with longevity philosophies. Some of our employees may feel as if "As long as I am here regardless of my performance, I will get more compensation over time." So entitlement-style pay philosophies don't motivate us much. They may cause us to continue to work, but it is unlikely that we will be concerned with performing better over time.

However, if we are in an industry that focuses on performance, where customers want the best possible product or service, then that would probably tell us that we have to lean toward a performance orientation rather than a longevity-based philosophy.[30] What kind of industry might need a strong performance-based pay philosophy? Industries where competition is intense, or where products or services are constantly developing and changing, might need to base at least a significant portion of their pay on performance. An example here might be a company such as Nokia or Sony that is continuously developing new microcircuit-based electronic products. In these firms, speed to market is a critical component of their overall strategy, so major parts of their compensation strategy may be based on worker performance. In companies such as these, incentive pay will likely be a very large component compared to base pay.

One caution here, though. Pay for performance is on the rise, but there is a potential dark side to individual incentives, as linking pay and performance is difficult in many jobs and employees frequently don't think the system is fair.[31] For example, was one of your professors (or physicians) better and another worse than others? Why, and would all the professors and students (or doctors and patients) agree and think it is fair to pay them differently based on performance? Also, many people believe in the egalitarian approach that we are all in this together, we are all equal, it is not fair to treat people differently, and we deserve the same compensation.[32] This is the common mentality of most unions (e.g., teachers' unions that fight merit pay). So the challenging part is to design compensation programs that are perceived as fair to everyone.[33]

WORK
APPLICATION 11-6

Select a job you have or had. Did the firm pay for performance or longevity? Explain in detail.

Skill-Based or Competency-Based Pay?

The next item that we may consider is whether or not we want to utilize *competency-based or skill-based pay*. Competency-based and skill-based pay fall within the incentive component of compensation. While Chapter 12 is the primary chapter covering incentive pay, we need to consider whether or not we're going to use this type of incentive pay before we create the company's pay structure.

If we decide to use skill-based or competency-based pay, we will pay members of the workforce for individual skills or competencies that they bring to work, whether or not those skills are necessary for the individual to do their current job. Competencies involve the individual's knowledge in a particular area while skills involve the ability to apply that knowledge set in that field. Examples of competencies (individual capabilities or knowledge) include such things as an understanding of negotiation and collaboration, an understanding of the basic principles of physics, or problem-solving and decision-making expertise. Examples of skills related to these competencies would include the ability to actually negotiate contract agreements, apply principles of physics to a new equipment design, or make a high-quality decision based on good analysis of a situation.

Should we use competency or skill-based pay? Again, it depends.[34] The biggest thing that we probably need to consider is our generic strategy. As we noted in Chapter 2, if our generic strategy is low in cost, we probably want to hire and train people for specific jobs and will not generally pay them for knowledge and skills outside of that narrow job description. If, however, our strategy says that we're going to act as a differentiator, we may gain significant value from paying individuals extra for bringing skills or competencies to the workplace that can allow them to think, analyze a situation, and come up with good solutions to organizational problems.

We have to think about this, though. We are, in fact, paying our employees for knowledge, skills, and abilities that they may not necessarily ever use in the organization. This obviously drives up our overall costs for compensation. So we have to ask whether it is valuable to have somebody who is well rounded or whether we just need someone who is specifically trained for a job. Thus, skills-based pay is commonly measured based on the number of actual jobs the person can perform. For example, on an assembly line, a person who can only work on one part of the production will be paid less than a person who can work on two or three parts. People who can perform multiple jobs are more valuable because they can help out wherever they are needed at any particular time.

At, Above, or Below the Market?

The next item that must be determined is whether we will pay *above market, at market, or below market.* Are we willing to pay more than necessary to hire individuals? Can we pay less than average and still get people to apply for jobs in our company? What are the advantages and disadvantages of each option?

Why would we want to pay above the market? The simple answer is to attract better workers and enhance our

Organizations commonly pay based on the skills and competencies needed to do the job.

employment brand. We want good employees to have a strong incentive to work for us, and one way to "enhance our employment brand" is to pay above the market rate.[35] We also want better productivity out of our workforce if we are paying more for employees. The philosophy is, when we take good care of our employees (and it is more than just compensation), they will work harder and take good care of our customers, and profits will follow.[36]

Would better workers generally have higher levels of productivity? In fact, there is some evidence that says that this is the case. *Efficiency wage theory* says that if a company pays higher wages, it can generally hire better people who will in turn be more productive.[37] Because of higher-quality employees, we get a productivity increase that more than offsets the higher cost of employment. But, does this theory always work? There's some pretty strong evidence that it does.[38] However, would every company in every industry always want to pay high wages?

Based on efficiency wage theory, would we necessarily get lower productivity from our workforce if we pay below the market? In general, yes, but not always. If our firm is in an industry where unemployment is high and it is easy to find replacement workers, and where most positions require a low-level skill set, we may be able to get away with paying *less* than average. Is this a good or bad idea?

What may happen in our firm if the labor market starts to get tighter—in other words there are fewer unemployed workers with the skills that we require, and it is easier for an employee with such skills to quit one employer and go to work for another—it's quite likely here that we will start to lose at least some of our more skilled employees because of job dissatisfaction and a lack of organizational commitment.[39] If you pay too low and the skill set is in high demand, it will be hard to find people.

So we have to think about our overall pay levels. Are they going to be at the market average, above, or below? However, all competitors can't have higher or lower compensation, or we don't have an average pay. Plus, we can't pay higher than average if we can't afford to do so. HRM professionals consistently conduct research to find out what the average compensation is so they know where they stand, and most of them select the average option.

Wal-Mart, with its Sam's Club subsidiary, is known as a low-paying firm with limited benefits. It has been estimated that it costs $2,500 to recruit and train each of its employees. Costco Wholesale Corporation pays more than Wal-Mart with more generous benefits, but has a lower turnover rate, saving it money. Wal-Mart is clearly a successful company with low pay, but most of the world's most admired companies compensate their employees well and are reluctant to lay them off.[40]

Wage Compression

Wage compression is another concern in setting up a pay structure. **Wage compression** *occurs when new employees require higher starting pay than the historical norm, causing narrowing of the pay gap between experienced and new employees.* It generally occurs over a period of time. We bring workers into the organization in both good economic times and bad. When the economy is doing poorly overall and wages are depressed, people will generally accept jobs within the firm for less than they would if the economy was doing well and they could get higher wages from another employer. Over time their subsequent raises are frequently based on their initial salary or pay rate.

Because we have to pay more to attract new employees when the overall economy is doing well or when their skills are in high demand, we may create a situation where workers with less tenure (less time on the job) might be paid nearly as much or more than employees who have worked for us for many years, but who came into the organization under other circumstances. For example, the supply for accounting professors with PhDs and

SHRM

Guide – G:16
The employment brand (above, at, or below market pay)

WORK
APPLICATION 11-7

Select a job you have or had. Did the firm provide above-average, average, or below-average compensation? Explain how you came up with your answer with comparisons to competitors.

CPAs is far lower than the demand. So at some universities, they hire them without any full-time academic experience and pay them more than some of the tenured full professors in other areas, such as organizational behavior.

This can weaken the desired link between pay and performance, creating significant dissatisfaction on the part of the long-term employees because of the higher or minimal pay differential.[41] Employers are usually unaware that pay compression exists until problems surface. Most companies and organizations don't set out to do this; they just fall into it.[42] If we understand wage compression when creating a pay structure for the organization, we can avoid at least some of the dissatisfaction associated with the pay differentials between short-term and long-term employees.

Pay Secrecy

As managers, we know that based on equity theory, our employees will review both internal and external equity—they will compare themselves to other people both inside the firm and in other companies. Because our employees do this, we too have to pay attention to both types of pay equity. Sometimes we actually do a worse job with internal equity than we do with external equity. We have some knowledge of what a job is worth in other companies or on the open market through the use of pay survey data. However, we can have people working next to each other who have significant differences in salary, possibly because of wage compression or possibly from other factors such as personal productivity. When workers talk to each other and they find out they are getting significantly different pay, they might get upset.

One of the proposed solutions to this is *pay secrecy*. Is it legal to tell employees that they can't discuss their pay with anyone else? Why would we want to force employees to keep quiet about their pay? How do you think employees would generally respond to a pay secrecy clause in their employment contract?

We may want to keep employees from discussing their pay because if we have two people working next to each other, doing the same basic job, and there are big pay differences, there could be a problem. We think we may be able to avoid the problem by not letting them talk about it. But, do we really avoid the problem? Not always. If you're an employee who is required to sign a contract with a pay secrecy clause, what is one of the first things that pop into your head? If we make you sign such a contract, you immediately begin to believe that we must be paying somebody else more than us. So, one of the issues here is that we almost immediately create a motivation and job satisfaction problem because of your perception of inequity (remember, *perception* is the key to equity).[43] We are requiring employees to keep their pay secret and keeping them from seeing what we are paying others.

So there is a perception problem associated with pay secrecy. We may *assume* the job is unfair and biased against us, whether it is the truth or not. Therefore, we may try to balance the equation in a different way. There is also a possible legal problem—potential age, race, or gender discrimination or other issues—right?[44] For example, companies might have pay secrecy rules because they have older employees making less than younger employees. This may actually be because of the wage compression that we discussed in the last section, or it may be because the older worker has fewer current skills than someone who is just out of school. When you get out of college, you should have fairly up-to-date skills. Older employees may not even want to learn those new skill sets. In that kind of situation, the younger person may be worth more to the company, but the older person doesn't feel like it. So there is some potential for discrimination lawsuits.

There are some reasons why companies might want to apply a pay secrecy clause. But, will this really keep everyone from talking about their pay? Of course not—at least some people will talk. So one thing that we create (if we decide to insert a pay secrecy clause into employment contracts) is a whole bunch of rule breakers. This is never a good idea. Well, will it cause people to be more satisfied with their pay, since they don't *know* that anyone

WORK
APPLICATION 11-8

Select a job you have or had. Did people know how much other employees made, or was there pay secrecy?

else is getting paid more than they are? We have already dispelled that assumption, because of perception. All right, won't we have to answer a lot of questions about why someone is getting paid more than someone else in a similar job? Yes, we might, but isn't this something that you should do proactively if you are doing your job and you know that the differential exists because of performance, knowledge, or skills? If we can explain the reason for inequity successfully, we change the equity theory equation. So if we look at all of the evidence, there usually are no defensible reasons for pay secrecy.

Romac Industries, Inc., has an unusual open-book system, whereby all employees can see how much every employee is paid. Romac managers believe everyone finds out how much others make through the grapevine anyway, so they just tell everyone—they address equity head-on. Salary equity is open to public debate at the company. When employees want more pay, their names, pictures, current salaries, and requested increases are given to all employees, who discuss the facts and then vote by secret ballot on what, if any, raise should be given.[45]

Legal and Fairness Issues in Compensation

LO 11.5

Discuss the three major provisions of the Fair Labor Standards Act.

We discussed the Equal Pay Act in Chapter 3, and how it specifically deals with paying women equal to men when all other factors are the same. We have to provide equal pay for equal work unless there is a difference in productivity, seniority, merit, or other factors "other than sex." There are also a number of federal and state laws that directly or indirectly affect pay and compensation systems. Virtually every Equal Employment Opportunity law identifies compensation as one of the employment actions where discrimination is prohibited if it is based on a protected characteristic. See Exhibit 11-2 for a list of some of the major EEO laws and legal concepts that cover compensation.

Fair Labor Standards Act of 1938 (Amended)

SHRM

Guide – B:8
The Fair Labor Standards Act of 1938

Besides the Equal Pay Act and the other EEO laws, there are some specific laws that deal with compensation issues. The grandfather of these laws is the Fair Labor Standards Act (FLSA). We must really understand the FLSA well in order to create a pay system. The law's major provisions cover minimum wage, overtime issues, and child labor rules for most U.S.-based businesses.[46] Let's complete a quick review of the major provisions of the FLSA.

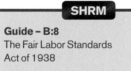

Video Link 11.3

Employers and Labor Standards

Exhibit 11-2	Major EEO Laws and Legal Concepts

Antidiscrimination legislation

1. Equal Pay Act of 1963 (EPA)
2. Title VII of the Civil Rights Act of 1964 (CRA)
3. Age Discrimination in Employment Act of 1967 (ADEA)
4. Vietnam Era Veterans' Readjustment Assistance Act of 1974 (VEVRAA)
5. Americans with Disabilities Act of 1990 (ADA)
6. CRA of 1991
7. Lilly Ledbetter Fair Pay Act of 2009 (LLFPA)

Legal concepts linking employment discrimination and pay discrimination:

1. Disparate impact
2. Disparate treatment
3. Bona Fide Occupational Qualification (BFOQ)

Minimum Wage

The first major provision of the FLSA concerns the federal minimum wage. **Minimum wage** is *the lowest hourly rate of pay generally permissible by federal law.* The current federal minimum wage for most employees in the United States is $7.25 per hour.[47] This is adjusted periodically by Congress, but the FLSA applies the minimum wage provision. It doesn't matter how the employer pays his or her employees; the net value paid per hour can't generally fall below the minimum wage. In other words, we can compensate employees based on a "piece-rate" payment, by commission, or by use of a straight hourly wage, or by any other common form, but the amount has to equal $7.25 per hour or more for the hours worked.[48] Some states have set the minimum wage higher than the federal rate.

Does everyone get paid at least the minimum wage? Not exactly. There are some exemptions to the rules.[49] If someone is *exempt*, by the definitions in the FLSA, they are exempt from the minimum wage requirement, overtime provisions, child labor rules, or possibly all three. People not meeting any of the requirements for an exemption are called *nonexempt* and we have to pay them minimum wage, overtime, and so on.

As an example, a common exemption that most people are aware of is waitresses, waiters, or servers of any kind. The current minimum wage for servers is $2.13 per hour.[50] Why should servers be paid less than $7.25? The obvious answer is that they are usually in a tipped position. Servers would normally expect to get a large portion of their wages by tips. The FLSA says that we can pay servers a minimum of $2.13 per hour as long as their tips make up the difference. If somebody in a restaurant spends 20 hours working in one week and does not make an average of $5.12 an hour in tips, it is illegal to pay them $2.13. Just because there is an exemption, it does not mean that we can pay our servers $2.13 per hour no matter the circumstances. The average tips must make up the difference between the wage paid and the minimum wage.[51] There are also other exemptions for individuals who are live-in child care providers, newspaper carries, seasonal workers, and many others. In fact, there are hundreds of exemptions (see Exhibit 11-3 for examples).

However, there is a set of quick guidelines concerning exempt and nonexempt persons at work. If you make under $23,660, you are pretty much guaranteed to be nonexempt under the current provisions of the FLSA.[52] "Highly compensated employees" paid $100,000 or more (*and* at least $455 per week) are pretty much automatically exempt from the minimum wage and overtime rules if they regularly perform *at least one* of the duties of an exempt executive, administrative, or professional employee identified in the standard tests for exemption.[53] If an individual is paid more than $23,660 but less than $100,000, they usually must meet a set of specific "duties tests" in order to fall within an exemption category (see Exhibit 11-4).

Overtime

Overtime is *a higher-than-minimum, federally mandated wage, required for nonexempt employees if they work more than a certain number of hours in a week.* Overtime is currently set by the FLSA as "time and a half," or 150% of the individual's normal wages. "If somebody is not an exempt employee and works more than 40 hours a week, do we have to pay them overtime?" Yes, in almost all cases we will have to pay them overtime. "What if they work more than eight hours in a day?" No, there is no limit to the number of hours per day for calculation of overtime. With very few exceptions, if a nonexempt employee works more than 40 hours in a week, they are eligible for overtime.

In a few cases the organization may be allowed to average two weeks in order to determine whether an individual is eligible for overtime, but this is an exception, not the rule! Some examples where this may be allowed would be shift work for firefighters, police officers, or medical personnel who may work on 12- or 24-hour shifts, and as a result may work 48 hours one week and 24 the next. In this case, we can calculate their overtime based on a

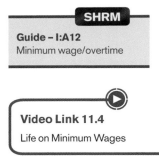

SHRM

Guide – I:A12
Minimum wage/overtime

Video Link 11.4

Life on Minimum Wages

WORK
APPLICATION 11-9

Select a job you have or had. What is the minimum wage in your state? Does the firm pay its lowest-level employees below, at, or above the state minimum wage?

SHRM

Guide – I:A6
Compensation of special groups (e.g., executives, outside sales, contingent workers, management)

WORK
APPLICATION 11-10

Select a job. Give examples of jobs that are exempt and nonexempt. Be sure to state why they are classified as such.

Exhibit 11-3	Common Exemptions

MAJOR CATEGORIES:

Executive
Professional
Administrative
Outside Sales
Computer Employee

SOME OTHER COMMON FLSA EXEMPTIONS:[54]
(MW = minimum wage; OT = overtime; CL = child labor)

- Airline employees: OT
- Babysitters on a casual basis: MW & OT
- Companions for the elderly: MW & OT
- Workers with disabilities: MW
- Domestic employees who live in: OT
- Farmworkers on small farms: MW & OT
- Firefighters working in small (less than 5 firefighters) public fire departments: OT
- Fishing: MW & OT
- House parents in nonprofit educational institutions: OT
- Motion picture theater employees: OT
- Newspaper delivery: MW, OT, & CL
- Newspaper employees of limited circulation newspapers: MW & OT
- Police officers working in small (less than 5 officers) public police departments: OT
- Railroad employees: OT
- Seamen on American vessels: OT
- Seamen on other than American vessels: MW & OT
- Taxicab drivers: OT
- Youth employed as actors or performers: CL
- Youth employed by their parents: CL

SHRM

Guide – C:6
Compliance with legal requirements (overtime eligibility)

WORK
APPLICATION 11-11

Select a job. Who gets paid overtime, why, and how much?

two-week average rather than a one-week average. Remember, though, that these situations are fairly rare and explicitly identified in the FLSA.

What about double time? If an employee works more than 60 hours in a week, do we have to pay them double time? In fact, we don't. The FLSA has no requirement for paying employees double time.[55] Employers are also not required to provide paid holidays or vacation, or extra pay for working on weekends. Many do this, though, because of the issue of job satisfaction and organizational commitment.

Child Labor

The FLSA also has some rules on the use of *child labor*. When can we employ people under 18, and in what jobs? If an individual is 18 or older, we can use them in any normal employment situation. However, we can only employ 16- and 17-year-olds in nonhazardous jobs, although their work hours are unrestricted. Finally, there are significantly different rules for 14- and 15-year-olds.

Minors age 14 and 15 may work outside school hours for no more than "three hours on a school day, 18 hours in a school week, eight hours on a non-school day, and 40 hours in a non-school week."[56] They can't start work before 7 a.m. or work after 7 p.m., except from June 1 through Labor Day, when they can work until 9 p.m. Jobs are limited to retail, food service, and gasoline service establishments specifically listed in the FLSA regulations. Employees 14 and 15 years old may not work overtime. While there are some exceptions

---

11-2 APPLYING **THE CONCEPT**

Employee Exemptions

Identify each job as generally being considered exempt or not from minimum wage or overtime pay.

a.   exempt

b.   nonexempt

_____ 6.   Computer programmer (paid more than $27.63 per hour)

_____ 7.   Hairdresser

_____ 8.   Bank teller

_____ 9.   Auto mechanic

_____ 10.   Fruit picker

_____ 11.   Worker on a foreign-flag cruise ship

_____ 12.   Librarian

_____ 13.   New York taxi driver

_____ 14.   Real estate agent

_____ 15.   Bellhop at a hotle

---

to these rules for businesses such as family businesses or family farms, these are the general guidelines for child labor.

Employee Misclassification Under the FLSA

Misclassification of employees as exempt from minimum wage or overtime is one area where companies can get into serious trouble. In 2008, Department of Labor (DOL) regulators collected $185 million in back wages for more than 228,000 individuals. What is really interesting here is that there were only 23,845 complaints lodged against employers.[57] This means that it cost companies an average of $7,700 per complaint filed. So how did 228,000 people end up getting back wage settlements when fewer than 24,000 complained?

This happened because once a complaint is filed, the Department of Labor Wage and Hour Division (the enforcement arm for wage complaints) will come investigate the situation. If they find evidence of minimum wage or overtime violations with the complainant, they will typically investigate *every employee record* at the company. In the 2008 statistics, this created an almost 10 to 1 ratio of wage settlements to complaints, so we can quickly see how dangerous this is if the company misclassifies even one individual as exempt.

Why does misclassification occur? Obviously, companies want to save money. Many employers think that if you are on salary, they don't have to pay overtime. So they put you on a salary and work you 70 hours per week. Another company might say "all my people are professionals, so they are all exempt," but this is rarely possible in reality if you look at the FLSA rules for exemption. What happens if we exempt someone who is not legitimately in an exempt category? We could end up being investigated by the Wage and Hour Division of the DOL.

What are the penalties for misclassifying employees? If you have inaccurately exempted an employee, what can happen to the organization? The employer can personally be criminally prosecuted and fined up to $10,000 per infraction. That can add up real fast! And, there is no maximum limit to the fines in this law, and most managers don't realize this is the case. A second conviction could result in imprisonment. In addition, employers who willfully or repeatedly violate the exemption rules may be assessed civil penalties of up to $1,100 *per violation*. It's worse for child labor violations. Here the civil penalty can be up to $11,000 per worker *for each violation*. And this can go to as much as $50,000 or even $100,000 if the violation causes the death or serious injury of an employee less than 18 years of age.[58]

WORK
APPLICATION 11-12

Select a job. Does the organization hire child labor? If so, why, and what do they do?

LO 11.6

Describe the penalties in the FLSA for misclassification of nonexempt employees.

Exhibit 11-4	Duties Tests for Employee Exemptions

Executive Exemption

To qualify for the executive employee exemption, *all* of the following tests must be met:

- compensated on a salary or fee basis not less than $455 per week;
- primary duty must be managing the enterprise, or some recognized department or subdivision of the enterprise;
- must regularly direct the work of at least two other full-time employees;
- must have the authority to hire or fire other employees, or their recommendations concerning hiring, firing, advancement, and promotion of others must be given particular weight.

Professional Exemption

To qualify for the professional employee exemption, *all* of the following tests must be met:

- compensated on a salary or fee basis not less than $455 per week;
- primary duty must be the performance of work requiring invention, imagination, originality, or talent in an artistic or other creative field; or
- primary duty must be the performance of work requiring advanced knowledge and exercise of discretion and judgment; and
- the advanced knowledge must be in a field of science or learning; and
- the advanced knowledge must be customarily acquired by a prolonged course of specialized instruction.

Administrative Exemption

To qualify for the administrative employee exemption, all of the following tests must be met:

- compensated on a salary or fee basis not less than $455 per week;
- primary duty must be the performance of office or nonmanual work directly related to the management or general business operations of the employer or the employer's customers;
- primary duty includes the exercise of discretion and independent judgment.

Outside Sales Exemption

To qualify for the outside sales employee exemption, *all* of the following tests must be met:

- primary duty must be making sales, or obtaining orders or contracts for services;
- must be customarily and regularly engaged away from the employer's place of business.

The salary requirements of the regulation do not apply to the outside sales exemption.

Computer Employee Exemption

To qualify for the computer employee exemption, *all* of the following tests must be met:

- compensated either on a salary or fee basis at a rate not less than $455 per week or, if compensated on an hourly basis, at a rate not less than $27.63 an hour;
- employed as a computer systems analyst, computer programmer, software engineer, or other similarly skilled worker in the computer field;
- the employee's primary duty must consist of one of the following:

  1. the application of systems analysis techniques and procedures to determine hardware, software or system functional specifications;
  2. the design, development, documentation, analysis, creation, testing or modification of computer systems or programs;
  3. the design, documentation, testing, creation or modification of machine operating systems;
  4. a combination of the aforementioned duties, the performance of which requires the same level of skills.

The computer employee exemption does not include employees engaged in the manufacture or repair of computer hardware and related equipment.

Source: U.S. Department of Labor.[60]

So what do we need to do as HR Managers? We must try to impress on our company leadership that misclassifying employees as exempt to save a few dollars is not the smart thing to do. Would you rather pay a few extra dollars a week or have a multimillion-dollar liability because of multiple fines?

Finally, states can't allow a lower minimum wage than the federal guidelines of $7.25, but they can require a higher wage. Therefore, we need to remember that many states have a state minimum wage that is higher than the federal minimum wage.[59] About 20 states currently have their own rules that are higher than the federal minimum wage. So we need to make sure that we know our state's laws concerning minimum wage and overtime. Note that it can be complicated for firms with employees in several states, and even more so with international business operations.

Pay Equity and Comparable Worth

One of the more controversial issues in compensation is comparable worth. *Comparable worth* is the principle that when jobs are distinctly different but entail similar levels of ability, responsibility, skills, and working conditions, they are of equal value and should have the same pay scale. Comparable worth legislation has been proposed as a solution to the problem of persistent gender inequity in pay. According to the EEOC, women earn an average of 77 cents for every dollar that men earn.[60] While equal pay for equal work is the law (EPA of 1963), comparable worth is not currently federal law except in some very limited cases.

What is the concept of comparable worth? It is simply *similar pay for similar work*. While this sounds almost like the Equal Pay Act (*equal pay for equal work*), there is a significant difference. The doctrine of comparable worth says that if we can compare your job with that of another person and they are *similar*, we should pay you a similar wage. So this concept is much broader than equal pay. In fact, if comparable worth was a federal law, companies would be required to pay people who are in similar jobs similarly, which leads to a whole bunch of questions: What is similar work? Who determines what work is comparable? How do we take market supply and demand for labor into account? What is comparable pay?

Let's look at an example to see what comparable worth is about. In our firm, we have a female and a male employee—an engineer and a nurse. Both of them are working for our company: Baptist Medical Center. Amanda has a graduate degree in mechanical engineering. She started working at Baptist about five years ago as the head of Heating/Ventilation/Air-Conditioning services. Amanda is paid $85,000 a year. Her primary job is to maintain the HVAC system and reengineer it as necessary when the hospital changes its facilities in any way. Kenny, on the other hand, is a Registered Nurse (RN), and also has a master's degree, in nursing. He has been at Baptist for about five years, too. Kenny's primary job is to work as an RN in one of the intensive care units (ICUs). He is responsible for maintaining the health of the patients in the ICU, and his job frequently involves life and death situations. However, Kenny only gets paid $60,000 a year. He may feel like Amanda's job doesn't involve life and death (although it might in some ways if she did a poor job of engineering something at the hospital and caused an accident) as his job does. How might Kenny feel about the pay differential if he knows about it? He may feel like he is not getting paid enough, right? Kenny is using the equity equation that we talked about earlier in the chapter to determine that he is underpaid, and this is exactly what comparable worth legislation would do. OK, how much *should* Kenny be paid versus Amanda?

There is no simple answer to the question of how much Kenny should be paid, and it would be very difficult to apply comparable worth to determine a dollar value for Kenny's job. Why? It is too hard to classify these jobs and determine what is comparable, because there are too many variables. These jobs are certainly comparable in such things as education (both have graduate degrees), tenure on the job (both about five years), and classification (both are considered professional occupations). But are there other factors? Of course

LO 11.7

Briefly describe the concept of *comparable worth* and how it compares with *equal pay*.

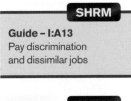

SHRM

Guide – I:A13
Pay discrimination and dissimilar jobs

SHRM

Guide – C:6
Compliance with legal requirements (equal pay and comparable worth)

there are, including thousands of details within each job, *and* the supply and demand for nurses and mechanical engineers.

Who should get paid more if there are too many nurses and not enough engineers? It would be very difficult to deal with the market value factor of a job within a federal law. This is probably the main reason why Congress has not been able to pass a comparable worth law, at least not one that covers most businesses. Almost every year since the mid-1990s, at least some members of Congress have tried to bring up and pass a comparable worth law. The most recent proposed legislation includes the Paycheck Fairness Act and the Fair Pay Act, neither of which has passed in Congress, at least at the point of writing this text.[61] In fact, these attempts have so far been defeated in Congress every time they come up for a vote, mainly because of the issue of market forces and the difficulty of enforcing the laws.

As we noted, though, there are a few exceptions where comparable worth is law. Some states have passed comparable worth legislation within state, county, and city agencies. If individuals are employed by the state or another government agency, they are subject to comparable worth assessment to determine their pay levels. Some states such as Washington and California have also attempted to pass comparable worth laws for businesses, but have not succeeded yet, at least partially because of the market value factor for jobs. Market value simply cannot be estimated completely, so we can't successfully define comparability, yet.

Other Legal Issues

There are a number of other federal laws that place controls on pay and benefits. Recall from Chapter 10 that the National Labor Relations Act allows collective bargaining on the part of workers who join a union. Since the NLRA allows employees to bargain collectively with their employers for wages, benefits, and working conditions, in limited cases the workers can agree to a workweek that is longer than 40 hours. The wages paid must be significantly higher than minimum wage, and other conditions apply, but it is possible for the collective bargaining unit to agree to more than a 40-hour workweek.[62]

Mandatory employee *pension and benefits legislation* also includes the following:

- Social Security
- Worker's compensation
- Unemployment insurance
- FMLA—Family and Medical Leave Act
- PPACA—Patient Protection and Affordable Care Act
- ERISA—Employee Retirement Income Security Act (mandatory for employers who offer pension plans)
- HIPAA—Health Insurance Portability and Accountability Act (mandatory for employers who offer health insurance)

We will discuss each of these laws further in Chapter 13.

Job Evaluation

How much to pay each employee in a company is a difficult decision. An *external approach* is to find out what other organizations pay for the same or similar jobs through available pay surveys, and set pay levels that are comparable. An *internal approach* is to use job evaluation. **Job evaluation** is *the process of determining the worth of each position relative to the other positions within the organization.* Organizations commonly group jobs into pay levels, or grades: The higher the grade of the job, the higher the pay. The external and internal approaches are often used together.

WORK
APPLICATION 11-13

Select a job. Could comparable worth work at your organization? Why or why not?

SHRM

Guide – I:A9
Legal constraints on pay issues

SHRM

Guide – I:A11
Union role in wage and salary administration

LO 11.8

Identify the three types of job evaluation and discuss whether they are more objective or subjective in form.

SHRM

Guide – C:2
Job evaluation and compensation (grades, pay surveys, and pay settings)

How do we accomplish job evaluation? There are several different ways, but the methods usually involve assigning points to activities that occur within a job and totaling the points for the job. Once this is done, we can place the job in a hierarchy and create our pay grades. Let's discuss some of the more popular job evaluation methods.

Job Ranking Method

The easiest and fastest method of job evaluation is the job ranking method. However, it has limited usefulness because it is more subjective than objective in form. Ranking is simply the process of putting jobs in order from lowest to highest or vice versa, in terms of value to the company. We utilize the job descriptions that we discussed in Chapter 4 to identify the factors in each job and then rank those jobs based on content and complexity. We usually do this type of job evaluation without assigning points to different jobs. So we might start at the top of the organization with the CEO as the highest-ranking person and work our way all the way through to the lowest-skilled housekeeping job. But if you look at this method for a second, you will see that somebody has to decide the value of each job, and they do this without any quantitative factors, so it is highly subjective. This means it is difficult to defend if we have to do so.

Point-Factor Method

A second type of job evaluation is the point-factor method. The *Hay Guide* is the most well-known point-factor method, but there are many others.[63] Point-factor methods attempt to be completely objective in form. They break a job down into components, such as a particular skill or ability, and then apply points to each of the factors based on that factor's difficulty. These factors are usually referred to as compensable factors.

Essential functions, defined in the ADA, would certainly be compensable factors to which points would be applied for that job. Many of the factors where we would apply points will be common among a number of different jobs, so once we have identified the number of points the factor is worth, we can then transfer that same value to all other jobs where the factor is present. The value in a point-factor job evaluation method is that we can differentiate jobs based on the difficulty or intensity of a factor, so it becomes easier to determine the total value of the job—in a quantitative form.

Generally, the higher in the organization, the more compensation given.

Factor Comparison Method

The factor-comparison method combines the ranking and point-factor methods to provide a more thorough form of job evaluation.[64] This model is somewhat similar to the point-factor method in that it assigns points to compensable factors. However, the factor comparison method first identifies a group of benchmark jobs—jobs that are identified and evaluated in a large number of organizations and that can generally be found in most pay surveys. Examples of benchmark jobs include Training Specialist I, Accountant II, Lending Officer I, or Hotel Registration Clerk. As you can see, these jobs would be done in many different companies. These benchmark jobs are then analyzed in

11-3 APPLYING THE CONCEPT

Job Evaluation

Identify the job evaluation method for each statement below:

a.   external
b.   job ranking

c.   point factor
d.   factor comparison

_____ 16.   I look at the job and determine the specific skills needed to do the job, and the total point value of the skills is used to set the pay.

_____ 17.   I'm checking the SHRM data to figure out how much to pay the data entry person.

_____ 18.   I just determined what job was worth the most all the way down to the least to determine how much to pay for each position.

_____ 19.   In the fast-food industry, we all pay essentially the same hourly wage.

_____ 20.   I'm an HR professional, so I use two methods together to determine how much to pay each position.

WORK
APPLICATION 11-14

Select an organization. Identify and describe which of the four job evaluation methods are used for determining pay.

SHRM

Guide – I:A1
Development of a base pay system

SHRM

Guide – I:A4
Role of job analysis/job design/job descriptions in determining compensation

---

some detail based on the compensable factors in those jobs. We then rank the benchmark jobs in order, and finally compare all other jobs in the organization to the benchmark jobs in order to determine where each one fits in the rankings. Here again, the primary method of determining the monetary value of the job is through the analysis of the compensable factors. The factor comparison method is more complex and time-consuming than the ranking or point-factor methods, mainly because this model is customized to the individual organization and to the jobs within the organization.[65] Because the factor comparison method uses both point factors and ranking, it has both objective and subjective components to it.

Developing a Pay System

Well, we have finally gotten to the point where we can start to develop our new pay structure. Remember, though, all of the things that we had to review and decide on first. We had to review motivational theories that show us how compensation motivates our workers and why. We also looked at how much revenue we expect to be available for compensation purposes. Then we reviewed each of our *pay policies* to make sure they were fresh in our minds in order to maintain consistency in our compensation system. Remember, we have four main types of compensation—base pay, wage add-ons, incentive pays, and benefits.

We also reviewed each of the major federal laws concerning compensation and equity, and went through the process of ensuring that our job analysis (Chapter 4) files were up to date. This gave us a list of qualifications, skills, and knowledge that allowed us to create job descriptions and specifications, to give us the best possible information on compensable factors. From these, we were able to complete *job evaluations* of each of the jobs in the organization.

In addition, we most likely researched external equity using one or more industry-specific *pay surveys*. There are many different types of pay surveys available to companies. Some surveys are free, such as the Bureau of Labor Statistics National Compensation Survey, and others are sold through companies that specialize in HR and salary research such as Towers Watson, Inc., and the Economic Research Institute. In some cases the free survey information is sufficient, but in many situations a company will need more detail on

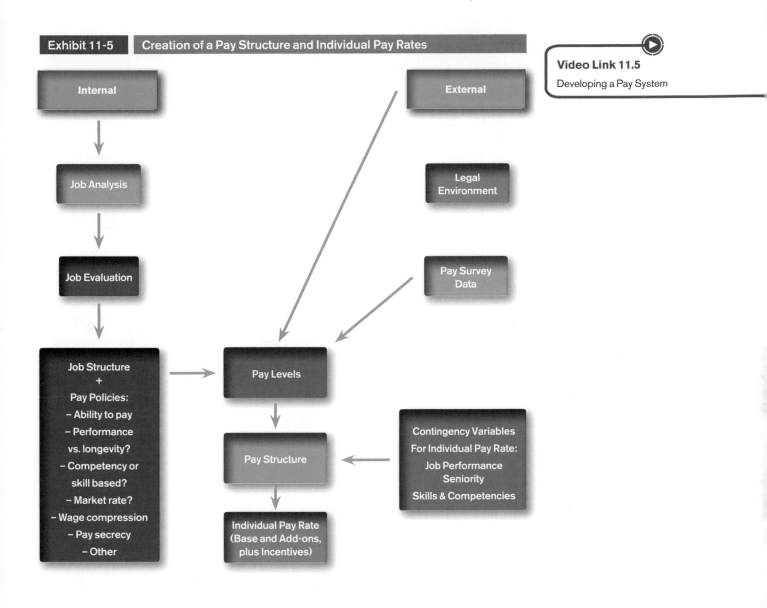

Exhibit 11-5   Creation of a Pay Structure and Individual Pay Rates

Video Link 11.5
Developing a Pay System

jobs that are specific to its organization, and the national data may not be the best information to use in order to get an accurate picture of what pay levels should be within the company. Regardless of the survey mechanism used, the company literally looks for similar jobs from the applicable survey data and brings that information in to help design a pay structure. Take a look at Exhibit 11-5 to see how each of these items comes together to allow us to create a *pay structure*, and finally *individual pay rates* for each job.

Job Structure and Pay Levels

What exactly is a pay structure, though? Basically, **pay structure** is *a hierarchy of jobs and their rates of pay within the organization.*[66] It allows us to identify what the pay range is for each job. Once we have completed the process, we will have the pay range for every job in the hierarchy. From that, managers can determine individual compensation level based on the employee's performance, seniority, skills, and any other significant contingency factors.

So, what is the pay structure composed of? It is made up of both *pay levels* and *job structures.*[67] The job structure is what gives us our job hierarchy. As we noted in the "Job Evaluation" section of this chapter, it is the stacking up of the jobs in the organization from the lowest to the highest levels. Each of the jobs within the job structure will end up at a particular pay level. Let's take a closer look now at what a pay level is and how it is created.

LO 11.9

Briefly describe the concepts of *job structure* and *pay levels*.

Exhibit 11-6	Supply and Demand Curve

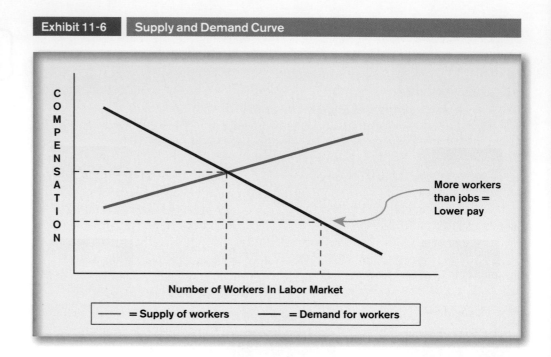

= Supply of workers   = Demand for workers

Creation of Pay Levels

A single pay level (frequently called a pay grade) will be made up of several if not many different jobs. Each pay level has a maximum pay rate and a minimum pay rate. How do we establish these maximum and minimum rates? We have to look at some market factors in order to determine maximum and minimum values for particular jobs. We are looking at external equity again, because if we don't pay attention to external equity we are going to have trouble filling many of our jobs.

Product Market and Labor Market Competition

LO 11.10

Discuss the concepts of *product market competition* and *labor market competition*.

How do we set the minimum value for a particular pay level? We have to look at the applicable *labor market competition*. We need to look at supply versus demand; where they cross is the average pay for a specific type of work. Take a look at Exhibit 11-6, and we can see that when the supply of labor equals the demand for that labor in the workforce, we have equilibrium. The market will pay about what the workers demand to be paid or workers who have the necessary skills won't be willing to fill the job.

What happens when there are more workers available than jobs? The market can get some of them to work for less than the normal rate (where the lines cross) because those workers need to work and earn a living. So the average pay will most likely go down because we have an oversupply situation. Conversely, what if we have more jobs available than we have workers with the requisite skills? In this case, we will usually have to pay more to attract one of the limited number of workers with the skill set that we require. In either case, though, labor market competition will set the minimum pay that a worker will require in order to come to work for us, and recall that we have to pay at least minimum wage to non-exempt employees.

For example, if we need to hire an arc welder for one of our shops and the average pay for a welder is $16 per hour, what will happen if we advertise that we will pay minimum wage ($7.25 per hour)? Will we be able to hire a qualified welder for that wage? It is *really* unlikely, unless there are way too many welders that are out of work. If that were the case, though, we might be able to hire a welder for minimum wage, but we had better understand that as soon as the market for welders recovers, this new employee would likely quit.

What happens if, instead of there being too many welders available, there are too few? If the average pay for a welder is usually $16 per hour and we advertise that we will pay $16 per hour for a welder, are we likely to be able to hire one? We will probably have to raise the minimum amount that we are willing to pay in order to get someone to take the job. If our pay rate is too low in either situation, we will not get anybody. If the market demands $18 an hour and we pay $16, we will probably not get anybody to fill the position. So, we have a base wage—the bottom. We have to compete for people who are willing to do the job. So, *labor market competition sets the minimum amount for any pay level,* but it can be a moving target.

So now, how do we determine the *top* of the pay level? We have to look at something called *product market competition.* This is basically a function of the value of the product or service that you sell to the customer.[68] Again, an example will probably make it clear.

Let's say we manufacture utility trailers (take a look at Exhibit 11-7). The public will pay about $500 for our 5x8-foot utility trailers. To make the problem simple, we will pretend that we only have a couple of components that go into making that trailer: labor (our welder can also assemble other parts of the trailer) and materials (all of the pieces that go into the making of the trailer). Let's assume that all of the materials are going to cost $250 (we might need bolts, axles, angle iron for the basic frame, welding rods, etc.).

What do we have left for labor? Do we have $250? No! We also have some other indirect costs, don't we? And, we would like to make a profit, right? So if we estimate all of our other costs at $50, we now have $200 left. We can pay labor $200 if we only want to break even. However, if we want to make any money, we have to pay less than $200 for labor. Assume again that our welder makes $20 per hour (because they are a good welder and have worked for us for a long time), and it takes them eight hours to build a trailer: $160 for the eight hours of labor costs. So we have a $40 profit left: about 8% profit.

Now, our welder comes to you and says: "Boss, I need more money—I need a raise." What do you just about have to tell them? "We can't pay you more." The trailer can only sell for a certain amount of money. If our trailer is $800 and a competitor's trailer is $500, almost everyone will buy the competitor's trailer. We can't charge much more than the normal rate for a product or service. The labor is only worth so much money, because the sale price of the good or service has to cover the cost of the labor.

Something you always need to keep in mind in HR and as a manager is "How much can you pay for labor?" You need to understand that you can't pay more than the value added to the product or service by the labor. The biggest reason that you need to understand this is so that you can explain it to your employees. The decision on whether or not to pay someone more for a particular job is not a function of liking or disliking the employee; it is a function of only being able to pay a certain amount because of the product's market value. So, *product market competition sets the top of the pay level* for most types of jobs in the company. Other producers will be selling the trailer for about the same amount as we do, and we most likely can't sell our products or services for much more than they can.

SHRM

Guide – I:A2
Developing pay levels

Exhibit 11-7	Product Market Competition Limits

Utility Trailer Manufacturing

$500 - Sale price
−$250 - Material costs
$250 - Remainder

−$50 - Overhead costs
$200 - Remainder

−$160 - Labor (MAXIMUM COST OF LABOR!)
$40 - Before Tax Profit (8%)

So what have we designed here (see Exhibit 11-8)? Now we can see that we have a maximum and a minimum level of pay for a particular class of jobs. So *labor market competition* sets the bottom of the range and *product market competition* identifies the top. Remember that this example was very simplistic—we assumed there were very few other factors.

Exhibit 11-8	Pay Levels

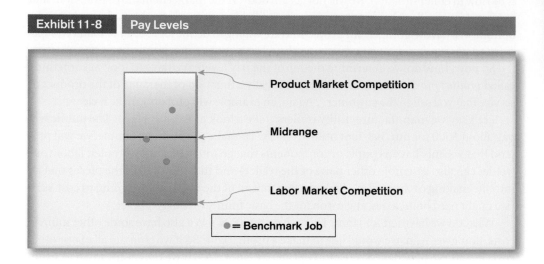

Benchmarking Pay Survey Data

Next, we look at *benchmarks* from the pay survey data that we reviewed earlier and put those benchmark jobs that belong at this level (based on our job evaluations) into the pay level (the blue dots in Exhibit 11-8). Once we place some benchmark jobs in a plot of our pay levels, we can get a *market pay line* (sometimes called a pay curve)—a line that shows the average pay at different levels in a particular industry (see Exhibit 11-9). We use the benchmarks to see whether or not what we are doing is OK. Is the range correct? If yes, we have successfully created a pay level; if not, we have to figure out what is wrong with our range.

We look at all of these things, and at the end, for a particular pay level, we will end up with a rate range. A **rate range** *provides the maximum, minimum, and midpoint of pay for a certain group of jobs.* Once the range is created, we can then go in and add any other jobs that are at approximately the same level based on our earlier job evaluations.

Pay Structure

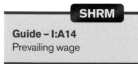

WORK
APPLICATION 11-15

Select an organization. Identify the rate range for a category of jobs.

LO 11.11

Briefly describe the concept of a *pay structure*.

All right! Now we have our first pay level. So what do we do now? We start to lay them out one next to the other. Again, look at Exhibit 11-9. We take our first pay level and put it down: Bottom, Midpoint, Top. The bottom of the range for the first level will probably be near minimum wage in most cases. Then our second tier will start, and the third and the fourth, and so on.

Notice that the ranges overlap each other in Exhibit 11-9. Why do they overlap? What would happen if each pay level started with its minimum pay rate at the maximum rate of the previous level? Would we have any room to pay people differentially in a particular level? Take a look at the market pay line. It would have to go exactly through the corners of each pay level if the levels didn't overlap. That doesn't give us much wiggle room on which to base people's pay rates, does it? So the major reason for the overlap is to give the company some flexibility in each person's pay within a particular pay level.

Once we set up our pay levels, we can actually plot the real pay levels for people in the organization. These are indicated in Exhibit 11-9 as black dots. We identify where people fall within the pay structure, and will sometimes see that we have someone plotted outside our pay level ranges—either high or low. Individuals who fall outside our pay range to the high side are called *red circle rates* (red dots in Exhibit 11-9). If they are lower than the bottom of the

| Exhibit 11-9 | Pay Structure |

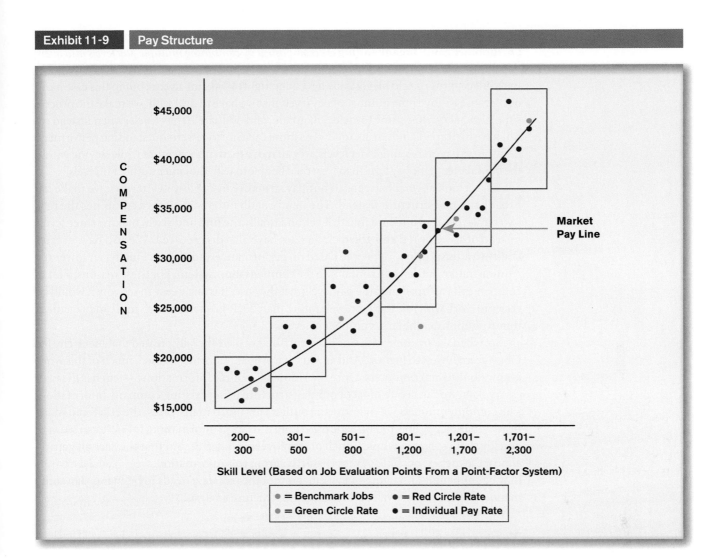

pay range, it is called a *green circle rate* (green dots in Exhibit 11-9). If we find a green circle rate for an individual, the correct thing to do is to raise their pay to at least the minimum for that pay level, because we are not paying them for their skill set.[69]

But, what should we do about a red circle rate? We probably won't cut their pay, but we will not be able to pay them any more unless they move up to a higher skill level, and therefore a higher pay level. For instance, if our welder is making $24 per hour and the maximum for their pay level is $20, but they want a pay raise and haven't had one in several years, we may have to tell them no. However, we can also tell them that if they are willing to become a supervisor for other welders they can get the chance to raise their pay rate, because the skill level for a supervisor is higher than it is for a welder.

Understanding pay levels and our pay structure allows us to provide good answers to our employees about why their pay is at a certain level. If a worker decides to become a supervisor, they are worth more, and we can pay them more. So we are able to tell the employee that "*the job* isn't worth any more than what you are being paid," instead of saying "you are not worth any more than that." It also gives us leverage to get good workers to consider becoming a supervisor or manager. "If you want a pay raise, become a supervisor."

Delayering and Broadbanding

A trend over many years now has been to lower the number of pay levels using one of two options—either delayering or broadbanding. **Delayering** is *the process of changing the*

SHRM

Guide – I:A3
Determining pay increases

LO 11.12

Briefly discuss the value of broadbanding to the organization.

company structure to get rid of some of the vertical hierarchy (reporting levels) in an organization. On the other hand, **broadbanding** *is accomplished by combining multiple pay levels into one.*[70] What is the benefit of combining levels either vertically or horizontally in this way? We can make bigger groups, and bigger is always better, right? Well, not always, but in this case it can be. Because we lower the number of pay levels that we have to deal with, we make the process simpler. It takes a long time to create, maintain, and evaluate 20 pay levels, when instead we can have five broadbands. It also allows us more capacity to reward outstanding performers. Because we have taller and wider levels, we can move them up way more while staying within the boundaries of the pay level than we would be able to with the larger number of levels.

Take a look at what happens to our pay structure in Exhibit 11-10 when we make it a broadband pay structure instead. The new broadband pay structure combines the first two pay levels, the third and fourth level, and finally the fifth and sixth, making three levels instead of six. Our red and green circle rates have also disappeared. We also have greater ability to adjust the pay of people based on performance and ability. Finally, we lower the administrative burden of maintaining the compensation system. For these reasons, a lot of companies have broadened the pay levels that they use. It is fairly easy to see why it would be easier to work with just five pay levels rather than 20. It just takes much more management time to administer the larger number of levels.

So, when we are done with our pay structure, we have literally created that hierarchy for jobs—from lowest to highest. And as you have probably already guessed, much of this work is now done using computers. Once the Human Resource Information System has the necessary data, we can create most of our pay structure using existing company information. The computer models will identify the outliers for us. In many cases, the HRIS can identify the market pay line and provide other compensation information, too. We can see very quickly that we have a whole bunch of employees in Level 3, and that they are all getting almost the highest possible pay for that level. From this information, we can analyze why it may be happening and figure out whether or not the pay scale needs to be changed in some manner. HRISs are very valuable tools for job structure analysis.

Trends and Issues in HRM

All right! It's time for our trends and issues for this chapter. What trends are we seeing in the compensation of our 21st-century workforce? First, we are seeing more discussion over minimum wage versus providing all of our workers with a "living wage." The second significant issue is how to compensate individuals in multinational environments. Third, we will take a look at why there seems to be a strong shift from base pay to variable pay components. Finally, we will briefly discuss some of the things that technology is allowing us to do to keep better track of our compensation programs.

Is Minimum Wage a Sustainable Wage?

In this chapter, we discussed the federal minimum wage, but we all know that it would be very difficult to live for an entire year based on a minimum wage job and only working 40 hours a week. This would only provide a little over $15,000 in a year to the wage earner for food, clothing, housing, and other essential items. However, is the federal minimum wage designed to be a living wage, or is it designed as a minimum amount of compensation that would be fair for performing jobs that require minimal amounts of skill?

Many proponents of living wage legislation argue that a minimum wage that does not allow the individual to survive is unfair and unreasonable to the worker. Some research argues that a living wage is more sustainable for the entire economy than a minimum wage.[71] Other research shows that living wage legislation moderately reduces poverty rates where it has been enacted.[72] However, other evidence suggests that the process of raising

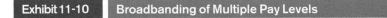

| Exhibit 11-10 | Broadbanding of Multiple Pay Levels |

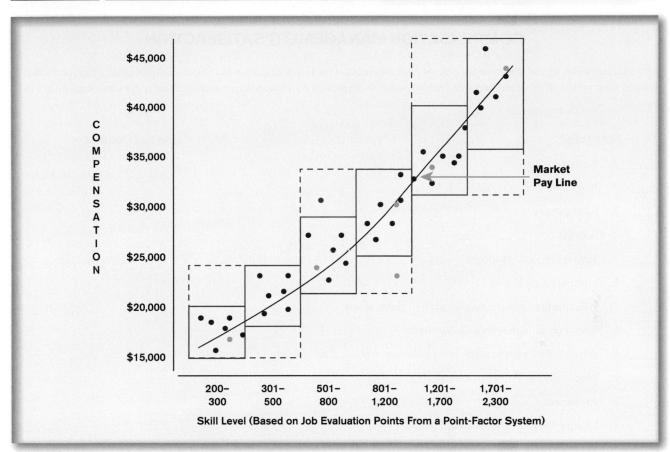

the minimum wage frequently increases unemployment in locations where wages are increased.[73,74] There is probably some room for each of these arguments in the battle over living wages versus the minimum wage.

We have to remember, however, the discussion of *product market competition* in this chapter. Recall that product market competition sets the maximum amount that we can pay for labor if we are planning on selling our goods or services in a competitive market. If we raise prices beyond our competitors in other country markets, we may cause an increase in unemployment over time, which defeats the reason for providing a living wage to employees. While it's beyond the scope of this text to argue for or against a living wage, all companies have to take economic reality into account when pricing the products or services that they sell, and therefore when they set compensation levels.

Many members of Congress say we have to help the poor. So one final question related to this topic is "Does increasing the minimum wage help reduce poverty?" The original minimum wage was 25 cents an hour. Congress has continued to raise the rate up to its current (in 2011) $7.25, and recall that it is higher in many states, but have we come close to eliminating poverty yet? If we pay employees more, and they don't produce any more, what options do we as business managers have in dealing with *product market competition* to maintain our profitability? The common reaction to an increase in the minimum wage is to cut cost, usually labor cost, somehow or to increase prices. When most businesses relying on low-paid workers increase prices, all we get is inflation. So an increase in the minimum wage doesn't tend to increase the standard of living of the poor because it tends to be offset by increased prices or, as stated, fewer workers. Also, employees slightly above the minimum wage want an increase in compensation too.

11-1 SELF-ASSESSMENT

COMPENSATION MANAGEMENT SATISFACTION

This exercise is also a good review of the chapter, as it uses most of the important concepts. Select an organization that you work(ed) for and select your level of satisfaction with each of the following parts of the compensation management system on a scale from 1 to 5.

1	2	3	4	5
Not satisfied				Satisfied

_____ 1. Base pay

_____ 2. Wage and salary add-ons

_____ 3. Incentive pay

_____ 4. Benefits

_____ 5. Meeting expectancy theory

_____ 6. Meeting equity theory

_____ 7. What the firm actually pays based on its ability to pay

_____ 8. Pay for performance versus longevity

_____ 9. What the firm pays based on being below, at, or above market-level pay

_____ 10. Wage compression

_____ 11. Pay secrecy

_____ 12. Meeting the Fair Labor Standards Act

_____ 13. Pay equity and comparable worth

_____ 14. The system used for job evaluation

_____ 15. The job structure

_____ 16. Pay levels

_____ 17. Benchmarking

_____ 18. Pay structure

_____ 19. Pay raises

_____ 20. Benefit increases

_____ Total the points and place the score on the continuum below.

20	30	40	50	60	70	80	90	100
Not satisfied								Satisfied

The higher the score, the greater the level of satisfaction with the compensation management system of the organization. However, to most employees, what really matters most is their answers to questions regarding their own pay and benefits (compensation), and we all are more satisfied when they increase.

Think about the people you worked with as a group. You can select the group's level of satisfaction with each question. Would their answers vary from yours? Would the satisfaction level vary by the level in the organization—executives versus nonmanagers, by departments, or other groupings?

The only way we can increase our standard of living without inflation is to increase our level of productivity. If employees can produce more, we can pay them more without raising our prices and causing inflation to increase. So if we are going to justify asking for a raise, we really need to justify that we are actually contributing more to the business than the cost of our compensation—*product market competition.*

Compensation in the Global Environment

The obvious first question about compensation in a global environment is why compensation in various countries needs to be different. The answer, of course, is that each country has a different standard and cost of living, and if we want to keep high-quality managers and workers in our organization while asking them to work in various countries around the world, we need to compensate them fairly. But, what is fair? Is it fair to take a manager from the high-cost country and send them to a location that has a lower cost of living, and once there lower their pay to match the local norm? If you were the manager, would you accept this?

Conversely, if we bring a manager from a low-cost economy to a higher-cost environment, we probably need to increase their pay to match the country or region in which they work. However, if we return them to their home country or location, should we lower their pay back to the original rate? Another question concerns the currency in which the employee will be paid. Should we pay our employees in their home currency, or should we pay them in the local currency where they are assigned?

As you can see, compensation of a global workforce becomes pretty complex very quickly. One of the common methods to manage expatriate compensation is called *the balance sheet approach.* Using the balance sheet approach, the organization continues to pay the individual at a rate equivalent to their home country salary while providing allowances during an overseas assignment to enable that employee to maintain their normal standard of living. Obviously, this is only necessary when an individual is moving to a higher-cost environment and out of their home country.

A variant on the balance sheet approach is to use *split pay.*[75] In fact, about half the organizations in a recent survey said that they use split pay as part of their compensation strategy.[76] Split pay is a process where the organization pays the individual partly in home country currency and partly in the currency of their work location. This allows the individual to lower currency exchange rate risks in moving money from one location to another, and to pay obligations in both their home location and their work location much easier than if all their pay were in one currency.

Compensation in an environment for workers who are operating all over the world is a very difficult process. However, HR must play a part in the analysis and implementation of a compensation system that will allow the company to attract and retain high-quality managers and employees for their facilities. The only way to do this, based on our discussions of operant conditioning and reinforcement as well as equity and expectancy theories, is to provide reasonable and fair returns to those employees for the job that they do.

A Shift From Base Pay to Variable Pay

As we noted earlier in this chapter, there appears to be a shift away from the majority of an individual's income being in base pay, and toward a larger percentage of that income being provided in variable forms. We also noted, though, that "there is a potential dark side to individual incentives, as linking pay and performance is difficult in many jobs, and employees frequently don't think the system is fair." With this being the case, what reasons do companies have for the shift toward incentive compensation? One of the biggest reasons for the shift to the incentive compensation is to lower the risk to the company when markets fail or economies go into recession. How does incentive compensation do this?

If a large percentage of an employee's pay comes from incentives for performance, when downturns occur the company will not have to pay out as much in overall compensation as is necessary in better economic conditions. An illustration of this fact is the recent recession in the United States (and most of the rest of the world). In a 2010 salary survey it was noted that "spending on variable pay as a percentage of payroll for salaried exempt workers was 11.3 percent, down from a record high of 12.0 percent in 2009. Spending in 2011 is expected to creep upward to 11.8 percent—which would be the second highest increase since Hewitt [a management consulting firm] began tracking the data in 1976."[77]

This provides evidence that when companies were suffering from recession, paid-out incentives dropped, and as the economy recovers, the expectation is that incentives will increase. So, when organizational performance (productivity) is high, the company can afford to pay out more in overall compensation costs (through incentives), and when organizational performance is lower, the company has the ability to cut overall compensation costs if a large percentage of compensation comes from performance incentives. Therefore, the employees, as well as the employers, risk having variable compensation based on changing business conditions.

The Technology of Compensation

Since compensation is typically one of the largest costs in most organizations, management needs to be mindful of what it gets for our money. As labor costs increase and technology costs decrease, replacing people with technology becomes more cost-effective. For a simple example, is it quick and easy to call most large businesses and actually talk to a person?

As related to HRM, like with so many other HR practices, we need to look at things like Return on Investment (ROI) from our compensation programs. New analytical programs, many within our HRIS, allow us to analyze compensation programs in more detail than has historically been possible. These programs and systems can take data from multiple sources including external pay surveys, benchmark jobs, government databases, and company sources, and provide us the ability to measure and monitor organizational costs and benefits.

HRIS analytical programs allow us to measure effectiveness of incentives and compare our compensation information with industry metrics. They also help ensure compliance with various state and federal government regulations on compensation, benefits, medical leave, and labor laws. They can lower administrative costs of managing and maintaining compensation programs and can help create higher organizational productivity too, which can in turn improve employee satisfaction levels, especially when incentive programs are in place to reward productivity increases.

So given all of the capabilities of HRIS programs in compensation management, companies have to look very hard at the costs and benefits of these systems. More and more, it is becoming critical to have these tools available for our use in order to ensure compliance and improve performance.

Wrap-Up

So what have we covered in our first chapter dealing with compensation systems? We began the chapter by defining the concept of compensation and identifying the major components of a compensation system. We then did a quick review of some of the motivation and learning theories that affect the compensation process in companies, including expectancy theory, equity theory, reinforcement theory, and social learning.

The second section of our chapter discussed the main components of organizational philosophy in creating a compensation system. The first component was the ability to pay—we have to understand how much ability we have to pay our employees. The second component discussed the types of compensation—we have to look at what mix of compensation components we will provide to our employees. Third, we discussed pay for performance versus pay for longevity—there are some instances where pay for longevity, or tenure, is necessary. However, in most 21st-century firms it is probably better to pay for performance than longevity. The fourth factor in this section looked at whether or not we might want to provide skill-based or competency-based pay, and we noted that it probably depends on what strategy the company is following whether or not these would be a good idea. We next explored whether to pay at, above, or below the market rate. There is some evidence that paying above market in certain kinds of organizations allows the company to be more productive than competitor firms, but there's also evidence that in some situations companies can get by paying less than market rates, at least in the short term. The sixth topic in this section discussed wage compression and its effect on job satisfaction and organizational commitment when it occurs. Finally, we discussed pay secrecy as a concept, and determined that in most cases the psychological damage done to the employees in the firm outweigh the value of having a pay secrecy clause in employment contracts.

The third major section of the chapter discussed legal and fairness issues in compensation. We started off with a detailed discussion of the Fair Labor Standards Act and its major components—minimum wage, overtime, and child labor. We also defined the concept of an exempt employee and provided information on some of the more common exempt categories. In the last part of the discussion of the FLSA, we noted that misclassification of employees as exempt is a common problem and also discussed the penalties that can be assessed against employers when they misclassify employees as exempt when the employee doesn't really fit in any of the exemption categories.

The second part of this section was a discussion on pay equity and comparable worth. We noted that comparable worth as a concept is much broader than pay equity, and also noted that comparable worth legislation for most businesses has not yet passed in Congress even though comparable worth bills have been brought up virtually every year for nearly 20 years. We also noted that the likely reason for the failure to pass comparable worth legislation is that it is virtually impossible to identify how jobs might be comparable and that it is very difficult to calculate the value of supply and demand for workers in a market economy.

In our fourth major section of the chapter, we discussed the concept of job evaluation and its end result—a hierarchy of organizational jobs. Three major job evaluation methods were discussed, including job ranking, point-factor, and factor comparison methods. We noted that each of these has its own strengths and weaknesses.

In the last major section of this chapter, we finally put all of the previous information together to create a pay system. We discussed the process of creating a pay structure using both external and internal information to price jobs within the firm. We learned how to create individual pay levels and how to identify the maximum pay for each level using product market competition and the minimum pay using labor market competition. We also discussed the value of benchmarking using pay survey data from external sources and how to check the benchmark data against the rate range that we created in each pay level. We then put all of this information together to create a pay structure. Finally, we discussed the concepts of delayering and broadbanding to lower the administrative burden of managing a compensation system.

Lastly, we looked at our trends and issues for this chapter. These included discussions of minimum wage versus a living wage, compensation in different country environments, an apparent shift from base pay to variable pay or incentives, and the value of technology in managing compensation systems. Once again, we've covered a lot of territory for one chapter, so let's get to the chapter summary and some quick check questions.

Chapter Summary

 Visit www.sagepub.com/lussier for helpful study resources.

11.1 Identify the components of a compensation system.

1. Base pay, either an hourly wage or salary. Base pay is frequently a major decision factor for most employees in deciding to accept the job.

2. Wage and salary add-ons include overtime pay, shift differential, premium pay for working weekends and holidays, and other add-ons.

3. Incentive is pay for performance. Incentives give workers strong reasons to perform above the standard.

4. Benefits are indirect compensation that provides something of value to the employee. Benefits cost the company money even though they aren't direct compensation.

11.2 Briefly describe expectancy theory as it applies to compensation.

Employees *expect* to put forth some form of *effort* at work. This effort is *expected* to result in some level of *performance*. The performance level is then *expected* to result in some type of *reward*, and if it does, the employee *expects* to put out more effort. The reward has to be *significant* to the individual, but as long as it is, the employee will continue to put out effort. So employees will either be motivated by their outcomes, including compensation, or be demotivated by them.

11.3 Briefly describe equity theory as it applies to compensation.

According to equity theory, people compare their inputs (the things they *do* in the organization) and outcomes (the things that they *receive* from the organization) to those of relevant others. Employees compare their *perceived* inputs and outcomes to others, though. Whether or not equity actually exists, if employees believe that there is inequity, they will change their work behavior to create equity. Employees must perceive that they are being treated fairly, relative to others. Compensation is obviously a large part of the outcomes that are compared between the employee and relevant others.

11.4 Identify the seven basic issues that make up the organizational philosophy on compensation.

1. Ability to pay—an honest assessment of how much we can afford, or are willing to afford, in order to compensate our employees.

2. Types of compensation—what mix of the four basic components of compensation (base pay, wage add-ons, incentives, and benefits) will we employ? Funds available must be divided among each of the components.

3. Pay for performance or longevity—will we pay people based on organizational loyalty/tenure, or will we pay based on performance in their jobs? There may be reasons for each option.

4. Skill or competency-based pay—will skill- or competency-based pay be used as an employee incentive?

5. At, above, or below the market—what will our general pay structure look like, and why? Efficiency wage theory provides some reason to pay above the market, but sometimes paying below market is also acceptable, at least in the short term.

6. Wage compression—lowers the pay differential between long-term employees and those newly hired. If wage compression occurs, it may weaken the desired link between pay and performance, creating significant dissatisfaction on the part of the long-term employees.

7. Pay secrecy—will we utilize pay secrecy clauses in employment contracts? Pay secrecy may allow us to hide actual wage inequities from employees, but it has the potential to create dissatisfaction and demotivation even if there is not real inequity, because of employee perceptions.

11.5 Discuss the three major provisions of the Fair Labor Standards Act.

1. Minimum wage rates identify the lowest hourly rate of pay generally allowed under the FLSA. There are many exemptions, but if a person is *nonexempt,* minimum wage will apply.

2. Overtime rates are also required for persons who are nonexempt. However, there are different exemptions for overtime than there are for minimum wage, so HR Managers must check the law to make sure who will have to be paid overtime.

3. Child labor requirements within the FLSA identify the jobs and allowable working hours for individuals between 14 and 18 years old. Sixteen- and 17-year-olds can only be employed in nonhazardous jobs, but their work hours are unrestricted. However, 14- and 15-year-olds can only work outside school hours for "three hours on a school day, 18 hours in a school week, eight hours on a non-school day, or 40 hours in a non-school week." In general, they can't start work before 7 a.m. or work after 7 p.m. The jobs that they are allowed to do are limited to retail and other service positions, and they may not work overtime.

11.6 Describe the penalties in the FLSA for misclassification of nonexempt employees.

The employer can personally be criminally prosecuted and fined up to $10,000 per infraction. There is no maximum limit to the allowable fines, so fines in the millions of dollars have been assessed in the past. A second conviction can result in prison. Employers who willfully or repeatedly violate the exemption rules may be assessed civil penalties of up to $1,100 *per violation*. For child labor violations the civil penalty can be up to $11,000 per worker *for each violation* and can go to as much as $50,000 or even $100,000 if the violation causes the serious injury or death of an employee less than 18 years old.

11.7 Briefly describe the concept of *comparable worth* and how it compares with *equal pay*.

Comparable worth is simply *similar pay for similar work*. Although it sounds almost like the Equal Pay Act (equal pay for equal work), there is a significant difference. Comparable worth says that if we can compare your job with that of another person and they are *similar*, we should pay you a similar wage, which makes this concept much broader than equal pay. The biggest problem with comparable worth from a legal standpoint is how to legislate the value of a job while taking supply and demand into account.

11.8 Identify the three types of job evaluation and discuss whether they are more objective or subjective in form.

1. The job ranking method is simply the process of putting jobs in order from lowest to highest or vice versa, in terms of value to the company. However, it has limited usefulness because it is more subjective than objective in form. This means it is difficult to defend if we have to do so.

2. Point-factor methods, on the other hand, attempt to be completely objective in form. They break a job down into component skills or abilities, and then apply points to each of the factors based on that factor's difficulty. The value in a point-factor method is that we can differentiate jobs based on the difficulty or intensity of a factor, so it becomes easier to determine the total value of the job—in a quantitative form.

3. The factor comparison method combines the ranking and point-factor methods to provide a more thorough form of job evaluation. It identifies benchmark jobs that are analyzed and then ranked in order. We then compare all other jobs in the organization to the benchmark jobs to determine where each one fits in the rankings. The factor comparison method is more complex than the ranking or point-factor methods, because it is customized to the individual organization and it has both objective and subjective components.

11.9 Briefly describe the concepts of *job structure* and *pay levels*.

The job structure is what gives us a job hierarchy. The job hierarchy is the stacking of the jobs in the organization from the lowest (simplest) to the highest (most complex) levels. A pay level (frequently called a pay grade) will be made up of several different jobs. Pay levels provide a framework for the minimum and maximum pay for a particular group of jobs in the organization. Pay levels are then laid out one next to another in order to create the entire pay structure for the company.

11.10 Discuss the concepts of *product market competition* and *labor market competition*.

Labor market competition sets the bottom of a pay level. We have to compete with other companies to attract labor, and if we don't pay enough, we will be unable to attract the workers that we need. So we compete in the labor market for available workers. Product market competition sets the top of a pay level. We can only pay someone as much as we can recover from a customer when we sell our goods or services. We can't pay more than the value added to the product or service by the labor. Together, product market and labor market competition identify the maximum and minimum rates of pay for a particular group of jobs in a pay level.

11.11 Briefly describe the concept of a *pay structure*.

A pay structure is created by laying out our pay levels, one next to the other. The entire group of pay levels creates the pay structure. Benchmark jobs can be plotted on the pay structure to get a *market pay line*—a line that shows the average pay at different levels in a particular industry. Once pay levels are set, we can actually plot employee rates of pay on the pay structure to see if any are plotted outside our pay level ranges—either high or low. Individuals who fall outside our pay range to the high side are called *red circle rates,* and those who fall outside low are called a *green circle rate*. Each of these rates out of range should be reviewed and corrected if necessary.

11.12 Briefly discuss the value of broadbanding to the organization.

Broadbanding lowers the number of pay levels that a company administers by combining multiple pay levels into one. Lowering the number of pay levels makes the process simpler. It takes a long time to create, maintain, and evaluate many pay levels, when instead we can have just a few broadbands. Because pay bands are wider and taller, the company also has more flexibility in pay rates for individuals who are overperforming or underperforming, so most red and green circle rates may disappear. Lowering the administrative burden of maintaining the compensation system can significantly lower the man-hours required to manage the compensation system and thus lessen the cost of the system.

Key Terms

Broadbanding	Delayering	Job evaluation	Pay structure
Compensation	Equity theory	Minimum wage	Rate range
Compensation system	Expectancy theory	Overtime	Wage compression

Key Term Review

Complete each of the following statements using one of this chapter's key terms:

_____ is the total of an employee's pay and benefits.

_____ includes anything that an employee may value and desire and that the employer is willing and able to offer in exchange.

_____ proposes that employees are motivated when they believe they can accomplish a task and the rewards for doing so are worth the effort.

_____ proposes that employees are motivated when the ratio of their perceived outcomes to inputs is at least roughly equal to other referent individuals.

_____ occurs when new employees require higher starting pay than the historical norm, causing narrowing of the pay gap between experienced and new employees.

_____ is the lowest hourly rate of pay generally permissible by federal law.

_____ is a higher-than-minimum, federally mandated wage, required for nonexempt employees if they work more than a certain number of hours in a week.

_____ is the process of determining the worth of each position relative to the other positions within the organization.

_____ is a hierarchy of jobs and their rates of pay within the organization.

_____ provides the maximum, minimum, and midpoint of pay for a certain group of jobs.

_____ is the process of changing the company structure to get rid of some of the vertical hierarchy (reporting levels) in an organization.

_____ is accomplished by combining multiple pay levels into one.

Quick Check (True-False)

1. A business designs and implements a compensation system to focus worker attention on the efforts the organization considers necessary to achieve its desired objectives and goals. T F

2. Expectancy theory says that individuals compare their perceived inputs and outcomes to relevant others. T F

3. If employees perceive that they are underrewarded, they may try to reduce the inequity by reducing their outcomes or increasing their inputs. T F

4. HR Managers need to understand that people will be demotivated if they feel that they are not fairly compensated. T F

5. Reinforcement and social learning have no real effect on motivation to perform at work. T F

6. One of the worst possible situations a company can find itself in is to have promised a particular level of compensation and then not be able to provide the amounts agreed upon because the funds are not available. T F

7. Paying employees purely for longevity is never valuable to an organization. T F

8. Efficiency wage theory says that if a company pays lower wages, it can generally save money, and productivity will be about the same as if it pays higher wages. T F

9. It is legal to tell employees that they can't discuss their pay with coworkers. T F

10. The three major components of the FLSA are minimum wage, overtime, and child labor. T F

11. According to the FLSA, nonexempt workers only include those who are not an exception to child labor laws. T F

12. The maximum rate allowable in the FLSA for overtime pay is two times the individual's hourly wage. T F

13. States are allowed to have a minimum wage that differs from the federal minimum wage—either lower or higher—as long as the state legislature votes on it. T F

14. The concept of comparable worth says that companies should "provide similar pay for similar work." T F

15. In the job ranking method of job evaluation, we use quantifiable factors to determine the rank of each job in the organization starting with the lowest-level jobs and working upward. T F

16. Pay surveys are external documents that tell us about pay for comparable job categories in other companies, usually within the same or similar industries. T F

17. Pay structures are composed of two things: job structure and pay levels. T F

18. Labor market competition will help determine the minimum amount that can be paid at a particular pay level and still get people who are willing to do the job. T F

19. A green circle rate is where an individual is being paid less than the minimum for a particular job category and pay level. T F

20. If a company uses broadbands instead of narrower pay levels, this will increase overall costs to administer the compensation system.

Communication Skills

The following critical-thinking questions can be used for class discussion and/or for written assignments to develop communication skills. Be sure to give complete explanations for all answers.

1. Do you believe it is always necessary to provide incentives as part of a pay structure? Why or why not?

2. As the HR Manager, which one would you pay most attention to—expectancy theory or equity theory—in designing your compensation system? Why?

3. If your company had promised an incentive program right before the recession in 2007–2008 and at the end of 2008 could not pay the employees what was promised, how would you explain this to your workforce in order to keep them motivated?

4. Would you rather have higher pay or better benefits? Why?

5. Would you ever consider paying below the market rate for employees if you had control of wages? Why or why not?

6. Do you believe that pay secrecy can ever really work in a business? Why or why not?

7. How would you approach a CEO or company president who insisted on classifying nonexempt workers as exempt? What would you say to get them to stop this practice?

8. Do you think that comparable worth should be made federal law? Why or why not?

9. If you were the lead HR Manager in your company, would you ever consider setting pay levels by just using external pay surveys and no internal analysis? What are the advantages and disadvantages of this?

10. As the head of HR, would you rather change narrow pay levels into broadbands? Can you think of any *disadvantages* to doing so?

Video

Please visit the student study site at **www.sagepub.com/lussier** to view the video links in this chapter.

Answers

REVIEW QUESTIONS (TRUE-FALSE) Answers

1. T 2. F 3. F 4. T 5. F 6. T 7. F 8. F 9. T 10. T 11. F 12. F 13. F 14. T 15. F 16. T 17. T 18. T 19. T 20. F

Case 11-1. Selling the Sales Force on Commission Compensation

Laughter could be heard from the back office as the sales associate and his part-time assistant were jokingly discussing the last sale. "Then the woman said to me, 'Do you absolutely guarantee that your product won't scratch my wood floors and won't mark my kitchen linoleum?' 'Guarantee,' I repeated. 'We not only guarantee that our product won't scuff or muff your wood or vinyl surfaces, but the Oreck vacuum has been scientifically designed with a floating head system that will adjust itself to any surface.' I then demonstrated how the vacuum easily glides from our carpeted portion of the store to the wooden area by the register. I immediately handed her the vacuum and asked her to try it herself. She vacuumed half the store just to test it out.

"She bought the best upright vacuum in the store including extra bags and a room deodorizer. Let's see if you can do any better with your next customer!"

Sales Training

The local Oreck vacuum store was owned by Mr. Paulson who classified himself as a super salesman and took great pains in training his sales force on how to close a deal. The store was always staffed by two employees: one full-timer with one part-timer to cover Paulson's two days off. The training consisted of On-the-Job Training (usually watching Mr. Paulson go through several Oreck vacuum presentations) coupled with take-home material including a sales script and product information. Inventory was computerized, and therefore it was easy for a trainee to check his or her price knowledge using the computer. After several observations of Mr. Paulson's sales techniques, the trainee was then allowed to make a sales presentation on his or her own, with assistance provided by Mr. Paulson as needed. The trainee was then debriefed by Mr. Paulson and asked to make changes in the presentation as needed in order to better close the customer. The full-time employee worked six days, 48 hours per week (including Saturdays and Sundays), with the part-time employee working only on the weekend.

Sales and Service Revenues

There were two distinct revenue streams: sales, which accounted for 90% of the revenues (predominantly of vacuum cleaners), and repair work. In terms of sales, by far the best moving item was the Oreck XL followed by vacuum bags (which were carried for all makes and models) and cleaning accessories. The markup on vacuums and other cleaning equipment was

100% while the markup on cleaning products and ancillary items was 200%. Repair work was priced at 200% over parts costs plus a $29.95 flat labor fee.

Price Flexibility

Unlike most other retail operations, Mr. Paulson allowed his employees some price flexibility on big-ticket items including the Oreck XL. These items did not have prices listed on them, and the sales personnel were instructed not to divulge the price until their sales presentations were completed. Sales personnel were given the option of either dropping the price (e.g., a $499 machine could be lowered to $449) or offering the customer an additional incentive for purchasing the machine (e.g., extra bags, upgrade in the vacuum cleaner). Customers could also receive a trade-in allowance (e.g., $25 for a machine in any condition) at the time of the sale. Mr. Paulson preferred that his sales force drop the price rather than let a customer walk out of the store empty-handed, although he always cautioned his sales force not to drop the price too early in the sale.

Employee Compensation

The average wage earned by employees at the store was considered fairly low for the region. Full-time employees received a straight salary of $500 a week plus benefits (complete medical and dental coverage, two weeks' paid vacation, no sick or personal days, unpaid holidays when available) and earned a commission of 2.5% of gross store sales over $7,000 a week. Part-time employees received $65 a day plus a commission of 2.5% of gross store sales over $1,000 per day they worked, and they received no benefits. Store revenue generally ran about $6,500 for the week with a 20% net profit margin.

Third-party exit interviews with several of the ex-employees indicated that the owner put inordinate pressure on them to sell products and services to the customers. "I felt like I always had to sell the customer something whether they needed it or not. Paulson felt that you could always find a way to overcome customers' objections, even if it meant using pressure sales tactics. I wanted to build up customer loyalty for the store over the long run, but you can't do that by browbeating consumers into sales just to try to make commission. A straight weekly salary would have remedied that problem." Other complaints included tying the commission into total store sales (rather than individual sales), working weekends without a pay differential, working six days a week, and the fact that the commission base was set higher than the store weekly average sales.

The owner indicated that many of the employees who left the job just did not seem to have the selling instinct needed for his sales force, and high turnover was therefore not only expected but desired in order to get the best salespeople. When questioned about the compensation package, Paulson replied, "This scheme is used to motivate my sales force. I want hungry employees who want to sell. If they do a good job in selling, they get rewarded—if they don't sell, they have a base salary to get by on. Many of my employees leave because they cannot sell enough to earn a commission. I know that it's hard to live on $500 a week, but I do not want to have employees who just sit around and collect a paycheck."

Questions

1. What is the compensation package for the full-time sales force at the store? Classify by kind of compensation.

2. Explain Paulson's rationale for the current compensation system using expectancy theory. Why might his ex-employees have disagreed with his rationale?

3. Using equity theory, explain why Paulson's compensation system may be deemed as inequitable by his former employees.

4. Describe Paulson's current compensation philosophy.

5. Do you think this compensation philosophy is an effective one?

6. Construct a new compensation system for Paulson's full-time employees. Make sure to address all four basic kinds of compensation.

Case created by Herbert Sherman, PhD, and Mr. Theodore Vallas, Department of Management Sciences, Long Island University School of Business, Brooklyn Campus

SKILL BUILDER 11-1

Job Evaluation

Objective

To develop a better understanding of the job evaluation process.

Skills

The primary skills developed through this exercise are:

1.   *HR Management skill* – Technical, conceptual and design, and business skills

2.   *SHRM 2010 Curriculum Guidebook* – I: Total Rewards

Assignment

Step 1. You decided to open a restaurant and pub and have five job categories.

- Owner/manager. You are the owner performing all the management functions and also greet and seat people as you oversee all activities.

- Waitstaff. They take food orders and bring food to customers.

- Cook. Prepares the food.

- Helpers. Bus tables, wash dishes, help in food preparation, and bring food to some customers.

- Bartender. Makes the drinks for both the dining and bar areas.

Rank the jobs from 1 to 5, with 5 being the highest-ranking job and 1 the lowest.

Step 2. Using the table below, rank each job for each of the five factors commonly used in job evaluations.

Job	Mental Requirements (education, intelligence, specialized knowledge)	Physical Requirements (effort such as standing, walking, lifting)	Skill Requirements (specific job knowledge/ training to do work)	Responsibilities (for equipment, money, public contact, supervision)	Working Conditions (safety, heat, ventilation, coworkers)
Manager					
Waitstaff					
Cook					
Helper					
Bartender					
Factor Rank (1–5) Weight (100%)					

Step 3. Although we have listed five factors important to jobs, the factors are commonly weighted as some factors are more important than others. (A) Now rank the five factors from 1 to 5 with 5 being the most important and 1 the least important in the above table in the bottom row—Factor Rank.

(B) The five factors can also be weighted as a percentage. For example, based on 100% the highest factor could be 40%, then 30%, followed by 20%, and the other two 5% each. So also include your weights for each factor based on 100% like in the example.

People generally will not agree on all the rankings, and that is a major reason why there is virtually always a committee that conducts job evaluations.

Step 4. Here is the more difficult part that is beyond the scope of this introductory book. So you don't have to do Step 4, but think about it. You would assign pay values to each of the five factors and weight them to determine pay levels for each job.

Apply It

What did I learn from this experience? How will I use this knowledge in the future?

_____

_____

SKILL BUILDER 11-2

Product Market Competition Limits

Objective

To develop a better understanding of product market competition limits.

Skills

The primary skills developed through this exercise are:

1. *HR Management skill* – Technical and business skills

2. *SHRM 2010 Curriculum Guidebook* – I: Total Rewards

Assignment

Complete the math problems below.

_____ 1. Your product sells for $1,000. Materials cost $300, labor $300, and overhead $200. What is the profit in dollars and as a percentage?

_____ 2. Your product sells for $750. Materials cost $250, labor $300, and overhead $150. What is the profit in dollars and as a percentage?

_____ 3. Your product sells for $1,000. Materials cost $300 and overhead $200. What is the maximum amount you can pay labor to make $100 profit with a 10% return?

_____ 4. Your product sells for $750. Materials cost $250 and overhead $150. What is the maximum amount you can pay labor to make a 10% profit return on the sales price?

_____ 5. Your product sells for $800. Materials cost $300 and overhead $200. What is the maximum amount you can pay labor to make a 15% profit return on the sales price?

12

Incentive Pay

Learning Outcomes

After studying this chapter you should be able to:

12.1 Discuss the major reasons why companies use incentive pay

12.2 Identify the advantages and disadvantages of individual incentives

12.3 Identify the advantages and disadvantages of group incentives

12.4 Briefly discuss options for individual incentives

12.5 Briefly discuss options for group-based incentives

12.6 Discuss the major reasons why incentive plans fail

12.7 Discuss the challenges associated with incentive systems

12.8 Identify the guidelines for creating motivational incentive systems

12.9 Discuss the issue of whether or not executive compensation is too high

12.10 Identify the major provisions of the Dodd-Frank Act that affect executive compensation

12.11 Define the following terms:

Variable pay
Individual incentives
Group incentives
Social loafers
Bonus
Commission

Merit pay
Profit sharing programs
Entitlement
Extrinsic rewards
Golden parachutes
Perquisites

Chapter 12 Outline

A. Employee and Labor Relations
24. Promotion
25. Recognition
26. Service awards

I.   Total Rewards

A. Compensation
5.   Pay programs (merit pay, pay for performance, incentives/bonuses, profit sharing, group incentives/gainsharing, balanced scorecard)

B. Employee Benefits
18. Financial benefits (gainsharing, group incentives, team awards, merit pay/bonuses)

Case 12-1. Realtor Reward Plans Gone Haywire

SHRM
HR CONTENT

See Appendix A:
SHRM 2010 Curriculum Guidebook for the complete list

Who Do You Love?

Whether the economy is up or down, the best employees can always find another job. This keeps HR Departments looking for ways to keep their best employees engaged and invested in their positions. One of my colleagues, Terry, is a big advocate of incentive pay. "We have had a good year while many in our industry are struggling," Terry said at one of our strategy meetings. "We need to look at ways to reward our employees now without extending our labor costs into future years." "Well, I've heard lots of complaints against incentive pay," said Arthur, another member of our department. "I'm not sure we want to open our compensation program to those problems." Is incentive pay a good idea? Chapter 12 details the pros and cons plus the methods of implementation for your consideration.

The Practitioner's Model for HRM

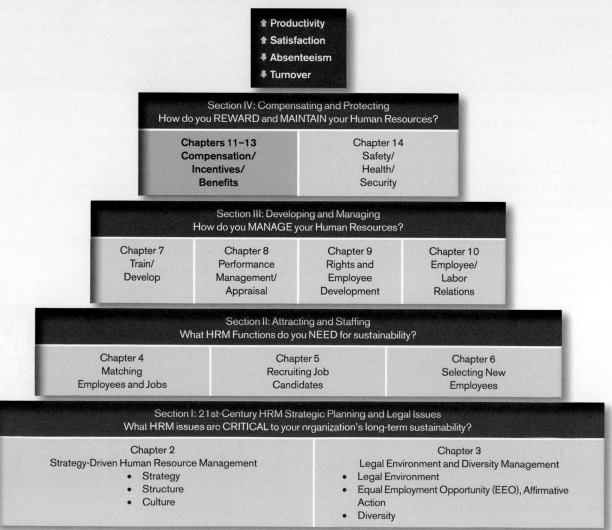

Why Do We Give Incentives?

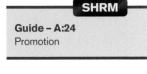

Chapter 11 provided an overview of compensation planning. One component of our compensation system is variable pay, also known as incentives. **Variable pay** is *compensation that depends on some measure of individual performance or results in order to be awarded.* But, why do we need variable pay? Isn't it enough that our employees get a set amount of money each week or month in a paycheck from the organization? While we briefly discussed incentive pay in the last chapter, let's now get into some more detail on why we use incentives, what they are, their advantages and disadvantages, and why they might be successful in motivating our workforce.

In Chapter 11, we identified which employees fit into which pay levels. We noted then, though, that individual effort and performance levels can vary. That is why we have pay ranges in each level. We want to be able to reward our best employees so that they feel that they are being recognized.[1] Recognition is a highly motivational tool.[2] But pay levels only have so much flexibility built into them, so we would sometimes like to have a tool that will allow us to provide greater rewards to the best people in our organization. This is why we create incentives.[3]

What are we attempting to do when we provide employees with incentives? We are rewarding them for their past performance, but we are doing it in the hope that they will want similar rewards in the future and therefore will repeat the desired behaviors.[4] It is simply a reinforcement process like the one we discussed when we covered learning theories in Chapter 7.

There is a second reason why we use variable pay in organizations. Variable pay moves some of the risk associated with having employees (and the associated payroll costs) from the firm to the individual. If the employee has variable pay tied to performance as part of their annual compensation, and the company (and therefore the employee) doesn't do well in that year, the individual loses part of their pay. The company does not have to pay out as much in compensation when the organization's performance in a given year is lower than expected. This effectively moves the risk associated with the incentive payment from the organization to the employee. If all annual compensation was provided in the form of base pay, we would still have to provide it to each employee, no matter how well the company did in a particular year. But, if we have part of the annual compensation budget applied to variable pay, we don't have to pay out as much in lean years.

Our final reason for incentive pay ties into company strategy. We noted in Chapter 2 that "HRM is a critical component of meeting organizational goals, because without the right people with the right types of education and *the right mind-set*, we cannot ever expect to be able to accomplish the objectives that we set for ourselves." However, we can't get the right people to accomplish organizational objectives without providing some incentives to do so.[5] Incentive pay has to aim at the strategic goals of the organization in order to make any sense. Remember that what gets measured gets done, and your people will do what they are rewarded for doing. People will not focus on attaining goals that we don't emphasize as important, and we emphasize what is important by attaching incentives to the achievement of the goal. People respond to incentives and can nearly always be guided toward goals if we find the right incentives.[6] Incentives are so important that they are one of the most written about topics in management.[7]

Individual and Group-Based Incentives

There are two basic choices in incentive pay—individual and group-based incentives. Groups can be small (a work cell of three people who assemble a computer) or large (an entire manufacturing plant or a call center), but all of these divisions are a bit artificial when

LO 12.2

Identify the advantages and disadvantages of individual incentives.

it comes to incentive pay, and, in fact, even the individual and group categories may cross. So in this text we will just divide incentives into individual or group options. You will see as we go through our incentive pay options that a lot of incentives can work in either an individual or a group setting. For example, bonuses have historically been provided as an individual incentive, but they can be, and are being, used as group incentives as well.[8] Let's take a look at the advantages and disadvantages of each and when each option works best.

Individual Incentive Advantages and Disadvantages

Individual incentives *reinforce performance of a single person with a reward that is significant to that person.* What are some of the more common advantages and disadvantages of individual incentive plans to the organization? Let's take a brief look at them (see Exhibit 12-1 for a list).

Exhibit 12-1	Individual Incentive Plan Advantages and Disadvantages

Advantages	Disadvantages
Easy to evaluate individual employees	Many jobs have no direct output
Ability to match rewards to employee desires	May motivate undesirable employee behaviors
Promotes the link between performance and results	Record-keeping burden is high
May motivate less productive employees to work harder	May not fit organizational culture

Advantages of Individual Incentives

Video Link 12.2

Employee Recognition

Easy to evaluate individual employees. Individual incentive programs, if done correctly, make it easier to identify individual efforts. This is because performance goals will be set at the personal level, not the group or organizational level. If goals are reached, it will be due to individual efforts, not those of a larger organizational group.

Ability to match rewards to employee desires. Recall that expectancy theory (Chapter 11) shows the need to reinforce individual performance levels with rewards that are *significant to the individual*. Individualized incentives allow us to do this to a much greater level than group incentives.

Promotes the link between performance and results. Individual incentives provide the direct link between performance levels and the rewards received—pay for performance.[9] A side benefit to this link is that we get equitable (fair) distribution of incentives; higher incentive payments go to those who perform at a higher level.

May motivate less productive employees to work harder. Recall social learning theory: People learn by watching the consequences of others' behavior (Chapter 11). Less productive employees who see others getting valued rewards for performance may be convinced to increase their own performance levels in order to get similar rewards.

Disadvantages of Individual Incentives

Many jobs have no direct output. We don't have any way to directly measure results of some jobs in organizations. We discussed this in Chapter 8 when we discussed results-based performance appraisals. What is a measurable result on which we can base an incentive for most managers? How about equipment maintenance personnel or health care providers? It may be very difficult or even impossible in some jobs to identify individual output on which we can base an incentive.

May motivate undesirable employee behaviors. If rewards are distributed based on personal performance levels, a perception of favoritism may be created. Jealousy can occur because of this perception. Jealousy can then cause other problems, such as dysfunctional conflict or competition, and even sabotage if it is significant enough. Another problem is that even the top performers may focus only on the items that are being measured for incentive payments. So we end up with a situation where only the things that are rewarded get done. Everything else may be allowed to lag.

Record-keeping burden is high. Individual incentive plans require that we keep track of individual efforts. Supervisors must develop and maintain comprehensive records to manage the program. This makes individual incentive programs much more time-intensive than group incentives.

May not fit organizational culture. Individual incentives may not be acceptable in team-oriented organizations or in societies where the culture is highly collectivist. For example, in some Central and South American countries and in many countries in Southeast Asia, the national cultures do not condone the rewarding of individual efforts. In these societies, the team or group is what is valued, and therefore the team or group should be rewarded as a whole. In these situations, individual reward systems go against the norms of the employees and will likely cause significant backlash if implemented.

Criteria for Individual Incentives

Individual incentive plans work best when:[10]

There are distinct, measurable outcomes for individual efforts. If we can isolate individual results, individual incentives can work. If not, they won't be very effective at motivating employees.

Individual jobs require autonomy. In some jobs, autonomy is a necessary condition, because a group effort may just cause confusion or unnecessary conflict. Individual effort is almost always necessary in one-to-one sales situations, for instance. Or think about your professor. Is at least *some* part of teaching an individual effort on the part of the professor?

Group Incentive Advantages and Disadvantages

Individual incentive programs obviously work well in some cases. However, group incentives tend to work better in a number of other situations. CEO Alan Mulally said, "We're aligning compensation with the success of Ford."[11] **Group incentives** *provide reinforcement for actions of more than one individual within the organization.* What are the advantages and disadvantages of group incentive plans? See Exhibit 12-2 for a list.

Advantages of Group Incentives

Better teamwork. Group incentives, to no one's surprise, tend to encourage higher levels of teamwork and group cohesiveness. They can foster loyalty and trust between group members. Rewarding members for successfully working within the group creates an enticement to perform in ways that improve group outcomes, not just individual outcomes.

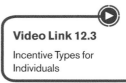

Video Link 12.3

Incentive Types for Individuals

WORK
APPLICATION 12-1

Select a job. Assess the advantages and disadvantages of offering incentives for your job, and whether it meets the criteria for individual incentives to be effective at motivating employees.

LO 12.3

Identify the advantages and disadvantages of group incentives.

12-1 APPLYING THE CONCEPT

Individual Incentives

Identify each statement by its advantage or disadvantage.

Advantages

a. Easy to evaluate individual employees
b. Ability to match rewards to employee desires
c. Promotes the link between performance and results
d. May motivate less productive employees to work harder

Disadvantages

e. Many jobs have no direct output
f. May motivate undesirable employee behaviors
g. Record-keeping burden is high
h. May not fit organizational culture

_____ 1. I've been slacking. If I want more compensation, I will just have to work harder to earn more.

_____ 2. I'm a college professor, and I'm very concerned about how the administration will assess my teaching.

_____ 3. The boss offered me a few different gifts for my good performance, but I took the cash.

_____ 4. Why did they have to go and change this incentive system? Now I'm overworked with having to keep track of everyone's performance.

_____ 5. The new incentive system will be easy for me because all my employees are sales reps and we already keep track of each sale.

Exhibit 12-2	Group Incentive Plan Advantages and Disadvantages

Advantages	Disadvantages
Better teamwork	Social loafing can occur
Broadens individual outlook	Individual output may be discounted
Requires less supervision	Outstanding performers may slacken efforts
Easier to develop than individual incentive programs	Group infighting

Video Link 12.4

Types of Incentives

Broadens individual outlook. Recall the discussion of the Job Characteristics Model in Chapter 4. When we broaden the individual's job by giving them more and different things to do, we can ultimately increase motivation and productivity. By allowing employees to see how their actions affect others, we create positive psychological states that improve performance. Group incentives encourage this type of understanding because the employee has to know what others are doing and how one's individual efforts affect each of the members of the group.

Requires less supervision. Group incentives, at least in some cases, tend to require less supervision. This is due to the tendency for the group to police its own members when they are not performing as well as they can. The "social loafers" in the group will get pressure to improve their efforts from others in the group who are performing up to standards.

Easier to develop than individual incentive programs. If we are developing incentive programs for groups, it is less difficult than creating separate incentives for each individual in the organization. We can cover entire segments of the workforce with one set of incentives in many cases, and may be able to design just a few different incentive program options that will motivate most of our employees.

Disadvantages of Group Incentives

Social loafing can occur. Social loafers (or free riders) may be able to stay hidden within the group while allowing others to do the majority of the group work. **Social loafers** *avoid providing their maximum effort in group settings because it is difficult to pick out individual performance.* This social loafing, if left uncorrected, can cause group morale and ultimately motivation and performance to drop significantly. If you want to learn more about social loafing, look up/Google the Ringelmann effect.

Individual output may be discounted. Individual effort and results may get "lost" in the group. Some individuals may feel as if they are providing most of the group's effort, while others take a "free ride" in the group. Therefore, they may hold back their efforts and commitment,[12] especially when the relationship with other group members is not good.[13]

Outstanding performers may slacken efforts. If the group is highly cohesive and has low performance norms, individual high-level performers may be pressured to lower their output to conform to group norms. Peer pressure can operate on the individual member to force them to stay within the performance boundaries of the rest of the group.

Group infighting. There might be a breakdown of communication and/or cooperation between individuals within the group, and they might begin to compete with each other instead of cooperating. High-performance group members may even sanction or coerce low-performance group members to provide greater efforts.

Criteria for Group Incentives

Group incentive plans work best when:[14]

We need people to cooperate. When a group effort is necessary in order to optimize an outcome or to produce organizational goods or services, group incentives are far more powerful than individual incentives.

Individual contributions are difficult to identify. When an activity requires the work of many individuals, all doing their part of the job, it may be difficult or impossible to identify how important one individual's contribution is compared to others in the group. Think about a team designing software—did the interface engineer do more than the programmer, or vice versa? It may be impossible to tell.

The group members possess either similar or complementary skills. If group members all have similar skill levels (think *comparable worth* from Chapter 11), it may be difficult to determine whose efforts are more significant in creating the desired results. Similarly, if group members complement each other's skill sets, it may be impossible to say that one set of skills was more important than others.

WORK
APPLICATION 12-2

Select a job. Assess the advantages and disadvantages of offering incentives for your work group, and whether it meets the criteria for group incentives to be effective at motivating employees.

12-2 APPLYING THE CONCEPT

Group Incentives

Identify each statement by its group advantage or disadvantage

Advantages

a. Better teamwork
b. Broadens individual outlook
c. Requires less supervision
d. Easier to develop than individual incentive programs

Disadvantages

e. Social loafing can occur
f. Individual output may be discounted
g. Outstanding performers may slacken efforts
h. Group infighting

_____ 6. Listen, Phil, you need to step up your output to keep up with the rest of us. You're not doing your best.

_____ 7. Ever since we've switched to a team-based process, I don't see the boss around very often.

_____ 8. Now that we assemble the product together as a group, we actually make more widgets than when we worked on our own.

_____ 9. Why should I work so hard? Nobody else in the group is busting their tail.

_____ 10. I don't get it. Juan and Carl used to get along so well. Now they are constantly on each other's case about every little thing that goes wrong.

Incentive Options for Individuals

LO 12.4

Briefly discuss options for individual incentives.

SHRM

Guide – I:A5
Pay programs (merit pay, pay for performance, incentives/bonuses, profit sharing, group incentives/gainsharing, balanced scorecard)

There are many different potential incentive programs that can be flexible in their use to meet the award needs of every individual.[15] Remember, each person has to consider the incentive to be significant, or it won't act as a mechanism to motivate that individual to increase their performance. Because of this, sometimes the best thing to do is ask the members of the organization what they want.[16] However, there are some rewards that have become commonplace partially because we as managers believe that they work, at least in some cases. Exhibit 12-3 summarizes some of the more common incentive options. In this section we discuss the individual option, while group incentives are presented in the next section.

Exhibit 12-3	Individual and Group Incentive Options	
Individual	**Group**
Bonus	Profit Sharing
Commissions	Gainsharing
Merit Pay	Employee Stock Ownership Plan (ESOP)
Piecework	Stock Options
Standard Hour	Stock Purchasing
Nonmonetary Awards	
Praise	

We noted earlier that individual incentives work best when we can isolate individual efforts, and when jobs require autonomy. There are six common options for individual incentive programs that are used in a wide variety of companies. Let's take a brief look at each of these six incentives used to reward individual employee performance.

Bonus

A **bonus** is *a lump sum payment, typically given to an individual at the end of a period*.[17] A bonus does not carry over from one time period to the next. Over what type of period do we usually provide bonuses? Generally they will be provided annually. Many companies will call them a Seasonal Bonus or a Holiday or Year-End Bonus or something similar. How would a bonus program have to be designed in order to motivate increased performance? We would need to identify specific and measurable goals that the individual could effect, and a bonus that (assuming we are making this an individual incentive program) would cause the individual to change something that they are doing to perform at a higher level. [18] If they then reached the measurable goal, they would receive the bonus. Bonuses can also be used at the group level, but are generally considered an individual incentive.

Ineffective bonus implementation. Let's look at how motivational the "Year-End Bonus" is *in most companies*—remember that we are talking about things that are supposed to be incentives to perform at a higher level! Three years ago, because the company was doing well, senior management decided to provide a bonus at the end of the year to all employees. Joanna received a $3,000 bonus based on her pay level at the time. Two years ago, she again received $3,000 at the end of the year (because the company was doing well). The same thing happened last year, but then this year she received no bonus. Management explained that the recession had hurt company performance and as a result there would be no bonuses provided at the end of the year, but Joanna had worked hard all year *expecting* to receive her bonus at year end. How do you think Joanna feels? Is she frustrated and demotivated? Wasn't a bonus supposed to do the opposite—make her feel like she wanted to perform better? What happened?

What did the company do wrong? First, they provided the bonus based on a period of time, not based on meeting a performance goal. Reinforcement theory says that variable reinforcement works much better than fixed reinforcement.[19] The end of each year is a fixed reinforcement period. That is one error on the part of the company. What else did they do wrong? What individual goal did they base the bonus on? They based it on individual results, but not on company performance, so the employees most likely did nothing different than they had done in the past. In addition, the individual employees most likely have no idea how to affect the overall performance of the company. Third, because the bonus had been provided on the fixed schedule, as soon as the company provided it to the employees twice, they started to expect it. It became an *entitlement*, or something that they felt the company owed to them because it had been provided in the past. As soon as the bonus became an entitlement (you *owe* me), it ceased to motivate any additional performance on the part of the employees. This is historically how most companies use a bonus payment. And if we use it this way, it just becomes an expected part of your pay.

Effective bonus implementation. However, if we use a bonus as it was originally designed and should be used, what should we do? We create a specific, measurable, and attainable goal that the individual has control over, and communicate that goal to the employee. The goal is continuously measured during the performance period. When the individual meets the goal, the bonus payment is provided—immediately, not at the end of the year.[20] The reward is applied for doing more than was required—it was a bonus! Now, the bonus can act as an incentive to perform. So the biggest problem with a bonus as an incentive is in allowing it to become a time-based entitlement instead of a performance incentive.

In the global competitive environment, many businesses are giving bonuses effectively to keep valuable employees from leaving for other companies. Bonuses are typically paid out over several years based on performance goals. Technology companies are closely looking at their top 10% of performers and asking themselves, are they locked in? What can we do to keep them? Google awarded a $5 million bonus package to a top engineer to keep him from leaving for a job with a startup firm.[21]

Commissions

Commissions are well-known incentive tools for sales professionals. A **commission** is *a payment typically provided to a salesperson for selling an item to a customer* and is usually paid as a percentage of the price of an item that is sold. If you sell a $100 product, and you are on a 10% commission, you would receive $10 for that sale. Salespeople sometimes work on straight commission, where they only get paid when they sell an item, or they can be paid a salary plus commission, where they receive a lower salary and it is supplemented by commissions on sales. Commissions can also be used at the group level in some cases. In general, commissions are good individual incentives to sell.[22]

Selling products over the phone and online is challenging, and it takes the right type of employee to be successful on commission pay.

Ineffective commission implementation. Are commissions sometimes ineffective as individual incentives? If not implemented correctly, they can certainly be unproductive. The salesperson may ignore the customer's needs or desires in order to sell something that makes the salesperson more money. If the salesperson gets the customer to buy something they didn't really want, it may harm the long-term relationship between the company and the customer. The company can also create too much competition within the sales force if the commission structure isn't set up right. We may create dysfunctional conflict between members of the sales force or even provide the opportunity for one salesperson to sabotage another in order to make the sale themselves.[23] However, overall commissions are a strong incentive to perform well in a sales role.

Effective commission implementation. In order for a commission incentive program to work, it must provide a significant return to the salesperson for success in selling to the customer, but it also has to provide a disincentive to harm the customer to make a "quick sale." You may have noticed that more automobile dealerships are now using customer satisfaction surveys after a customer buys a vehicle from the dealer.[24] What they are trying to do is determine whether or not the salesperson may have done anything to damage the long-term relationship between the customer and the company. In some cases, dealers are even making customer complaints part of their commission structure so that if a salesperson gets too many complaints part of their commissions will have to be reimbursed to the dealership.

Merit Pay

The next incentive option is called merit pay. **Merit pay** is *a program to reward top performers with increases in their annual wage that carry over from year to year.* Merit pay is different from most other individual incentives in that if an individual gets merit pay increases consistently over time, their annual pay can be significantly greater than that of others who do not consistently get merit increases.[25]

Merit pay works as follows: The company announces a "merit pool" available for pay increases in a given period, usually annually. The merit raises will be given to the top performers in the company based on performance evaluations. Frequently, individuals who receive either outstanding or excellent marks will get merit increases above the average, while average performers will get a lower raise and those who receive below-average marks will get no raise at all.

Ineffective merit pay implementation. There are some significant potential problems in using merit pay as an incentive. The first issue is that merit pay is typically a very small percentage of the individual's total pay, which makes it very difficult to use it as a motivator to perform. Remember that people need to feel that the reward is "significant" to them in order for it to motivate. In many cases, merit raises may amount to only an extra 1% of pay in any given year. Many employees won't consider this as significant.

Another major issue is inflation of the performance appraisal process. If the company does not set limits to how many employees can be judged as outstanding or excellent, and supervisors know that a pay increase is attached to the individual's performance rating, nearly everyone tends to become outstanding or excellent.[26] While we know this is not true, the supervisor doesn't want to be the person to keep someone in their department from getting a pay raise. Also, when you limit the number of persons that can get a merit raise in any given year, sometimes the manager rotates who will get merit pay, rather than rewarding the best performers, to keep the majority happy.

In order for merit pay to be valuable as an incentive, it must be significant, which means it must be more than 1% of the employee's pay. However, there is another problem here. Remember that merit pay increases the individual's pay from one year to the next and it carries forward, so if merit pay is 5%–10% instead of 1%–2%, we can end up with employees who break right through our maximum wage for a specific pay level very quickly. If we had a pay level (from Chapter 11) that began at $12 per hour and went to $16 and an employee was hired with a base pay of $12, they could "max out," or reach $16 per hour, in only three years on the job if they received a merit raise of 10% each year. So merit pay is difficult to use as an incentive to perform at a higher level.

Effective merit pay implementation. Merit pay is one of the most frequently used individual incentive programs in companies,[27] and it *can* be used in some team-based situations as well. It requires that we pay attention to some details, though. The first and probably most important item that HR needs to develop for a merit pay program is material that communicates the value of merit pay over time. We need to communicate that even what

WORK
APPLICATION 12-4

Select a job. Does the organization offer commissions? If not, how could it offer commissions to be effective at motivating employees? Assess the advantages and disadvantages of offering commissions at your organization. Should it offer commissions?

would normally be considered a small incentive can become a significant boost to an individual's pay when they are judged to have merit over several years. For instance, if we have a merit raise each year of only 2%, because of compounding this becomes an additional *permanent increase* in the pay of an individual employee of nearly 10.5% above cost of living increases if received for five years. Over the employee's entire work life this will make a huge difference in total wages earned. So HR needs to communicate the value of merit pay better than has historically been the case.

Second, we only want to reward true top performers with merit pay. If we do so, this means that those who are rewarded are truly recognized as having exceptional ability, and it also means that limited amounts of merit pay cash can provide a larger merit increase to those who deserve it. Alternately, if we provide all employees with merit raises, the pool of funds must be spread out among everyone, and the small amount of the supposed "merit" increase doesn't amount to much. Let's look at a quick example.

If your company has 1,000 employees and the annual payroll is $60 million, and the leadership decides to provide a 2% merit pool for the coming year, that is almost $1.25 million in available dollars for merit increases. If we spread that money evenly over the entire 1,000 employees, each employee receives about a $100-per-month increase in pay. However, if we truly identify the individuals who are meritorious and limit our payout to the top 30% of the employee group, each individual receives an average merit raise of about $350 per month. Most of us would consider an extra $350 per month to be significant, while $100 is probably not significant to many of us. So if we give "all As" to our employees and say that everyone is meritorious, our actual top performers are demotivated because their efforts aren't being recognized, *and* nobody in the employee group considers the reward to be significant because it is too small to make much difference in their lives.

Piecework Plans

Piecework or piece-rate plans are one of the simplest forms of compensation, and they can act as an incentive to produce at a higher level because the more workers get done, the more they get paid. In a "straight piece-rate" compensation system, the employee gets paid for every "piece" that they complete. If they are faster than the average, they can make more money than other employees.[28] A "differential piece-rate" system (sometimes called a *Taylor plan* after Frederick Taylor of *scientific management* fame) provides the employee with a base wage to complete a certain amount of work, and if they produce more than the standard, a differential wage is paid for the extra pieces produced. In either case, the employee is being paid for increased speed. Take a look at Exhibit 12-4 for an example of a piece-rate system. Piece-rate plans can sometimes be used at the group level, when the group is responsible for completing a "piece" of work.

Ineffective piecework implementation. Are there any problems associated with a piecework incentive program? There is an obvious one—quality.[29] If we pay employees "by the piece," they may make lots of pieces with lots of quality problems because they are trying to work too fast and not paying attention to how well they are doing the work. So quality is an issue in a piece-rate system. There may also be a problem in determining where the standard is going to be set for a differential piece-rate system, and there are other potential problems.

Effective Piecework Implementation. However, in some situations, a piecework plan can be an incentive to produce at a faster rate. The obvious answer to the potential quality

WORK
APPLICATION 12-5

Select a job. Does the organization offer merit pay? If not, how could it offer merit pay to be effective at motivating employees? Assess the advantages and disadvantages of offering merit pay at your organization. Should it offer merit pay?

Exhibit 12-4	Piece-Rate Plans

Straight Piece-Rate

Anji Presser is paid to iron and package new dress shirts in special decorative packaging. She is paid on a basic piece-rate system at $0.65 per shirt ironed and packaged. Anji works 40 hours per week, and the company estimates the value of the job at $13 per hour. Anji's production last week was as follows:

Monday –	182
Tuesday –	165
Wednesday –	188
Thursday –	179
Friday –	163
Total –	877 x $0.65 = $570.05 instead of $13 x 40 = $520.

Anji made an additional $50.05, a 9.6% premium because of being efficient in her job.

Differential Piece-Rate:

Bob Rivette works in a factory assembling folding chairs from parts. He is paid using a differential piece rate. If he assembles 480 chairs or fewer in a day, he is paid $15 per hour (he works eight hours per day). For every additional chair, he is paid an additional $0.25. Last week his statistics were as follows:

Monday –	450 – fewer than 480, so $15 x 8 hours =	$120
Tuesday –	520 – 40 more than production requirement: 40 x $0.25 = $10 + $120 =	$130
Wednesday –	540 – 60 more than production requirement: 60 x $0.25 = $15 + $120 =	$135
Thursday –	532 – 52 more than production requirement: 52 x $0.25 = $13 + $120 =	$133
Friday –	460 – fewer than 480, so $15 x 8 hours =	$120
Total –		$638

Bob made $638 this week instead of $600. This additional $38 is a 6.33% premium in Bob's pay.

problem is to set clear standards that each piece must meet to be accepted and paid for. Thus, if the employees don't do a quality job, they don't get paid. Clear standards tell the employee what they need to do in order to benefit from the piecework pay schedule. If they will not be given credit for items that don't meet quality standards, they need to know this up front. If they will have to rework any items that aren't correct, they need to know this too. They also know that they don't have to "hit a moving target" if the standards are clear from the beginning—that the company isn't going to just lower the amount paid per piece in order to pay the employees what they have always been paid.

The other key to effective piecework plans is feedback. Employees need to know how they are doing as they go through the workweek. In some cases they may see that they are not meeting their own goals of performance and pick up the pace, and in others they may see that their performance is producing a desired result. Many people expect that once the employee reaches a level of production that provides them with an acceptable wage they will slow down, but there is very little evidence that this occurs in more than isolated cases. Feedback gives the employees information about the "significant reward" that they seek, and can motivate continued performance—just as expectancy theory shows.

Standard Hour Plans

Standard hour plans are used quite a bit in some types of service work. In a standard hour plan, each task is assigned a "standard" amount of work time for completion.[30] Generally

WORK
APPLICATION 12-6

Select a job. Does the organization offer piecework? If not, how could it offer piecework to be effective at motivating employees? Assess the advantages and disadvantages of offering piecework at your organization. Should it offer piecework?

this time will be shown in a *standard hour manual*. The individual doing the job will get paid based on the standard time to complete the job, but good workers can frequently complete the work in less than the standard amount of time. If they do, they can get paid for an hour of work while working less than an hour of time. Take a quick look at Exhibit 12-5 for two examples of a standard hour plan. In many cases, good service employees can do better than the standard most of the time, so they get an incentive to work faster.

Exhibit 12-5	Standard Hour Plan

Brant Wrenchright is a master mechanic at the local Honda dealership. He works on a standard hour plan. Brant is paid $32 per standard hour and works 40 hours per week. His last week's work (in standard hours billed) is shown below:

Monday –   8.3
Tuesday –   9.2
Wednesday – 8.1
Thursday –   8.8
Friday –   8.7
Total –   43.1

Even though Brant only worked 40 hours, he completed 43.1 *standard hours* of work. His pay is based on standard hours, so: 43.1 x $32 = $1,379.20. If Brant were paid only for his actual hours, he would have been paid 40 x $32 = $1,280. Brant made an additional $99.20 because of his standard hour completion rates—or a 7.75% premium.

On the other hand, Willy Lugnutty is a young mechanic who is paid $20 per standard hour for his work. He, like Brant, worked 40 hours last week, and his standard hours are shown below:

Monday –   7.3
Tuesday –   8.2
Wednesday – 7.1
Thursday –   7.8
Friday –   6.7
Total –   37.1

Since Willy completed only 37.1 hours of work in a 40-hour week, he is paid $742 (37.1 x $20). If he had been paid on an hourly basis, he would have made $800. So, Willy actually lost $58, or 7.25% of his pay, because of working more slowly than the standard hour plan dictated.

Ineffective and effective standard hour implementation. Like the piecework plan, standard hour incentives can cause quality problems. So most standard hour plans also require that any quality problems require the job to be redone; the worker must do the rework for no additional pay. This is one way to make sure that speed doesn't create poor quality service. Standard hour plans, like most individual incentive programs, can be used for groups if the group is responsible for completion of the work.

Standard hour plans are used heavily in automotive and heavy equipment repair, and in other areas like heating and air-conditioning services. The biggest challenge with standard hour plans is creating the manuals showing the allowable time for a job. We have to have a large baseline measuring the amount of time necessary to perform specific services in order to figure out the average time needed to do a particular job. We can only do this in areas where the same job is done many times in a year. We also need to keep an ongoing record of the actual times to do the jobs so we can adjust the standards accordingly so we don't over- or underpay for each job.

Recognition and Other Nonmonetary Incentives

We also have a nonmonetary option as an individual incentive. Recognition can come in many forms (e.g., service awards), but evidence says that recognition is one of the most

WORK
APPLICATION 12-7

Select a job. Does the organization offer a standard hour plan? If not, how could it offer a standard hour plan to be effective at motivating employees? Assess the advantages and disadvantages of offering a standard hour plan at your organization. Should it offer a standard hour plan?

effective motivational tools that management has at its disposal.[31] Other nonmonetary rewards also increase motivation if the individual considers them to be significant.[32] Some of the more common forms are extra time off, ability to choose tasks or jobs, flexible hours, or extra training in a particular area of interest to the employee. Younger workers especially want more flexible hours and working conditions.[33] Nonmonetary incentives can be, and frequently are, used in group situations.

Ineffective recognition implementation. Wait just a minute! Service awards—things like Employee of the Month—are motivators? How often is an award like Employee of the Month just rotated among the employees? In such a case, is it a motivator, or is it a joke? It is a joke if not used correctly, because everyone knows that there are no criteria that the employee must meet in order to become Employee of the Month. So how do we make an Employee of the Month award a valuable incentive?

Effective recognition implementation. Remember that recognition *is* a powerful incentive, so we need to use it effectively to motivate our employees. In order for this type of recognition to mean something, there has to be a specific set of criteria that must be met in order to receive the recognition. The employee has to *do something extra*, above what others do, in order to be recognized.[34]

How many of you have seen a military awards ceremony where service members receive meritorious awards? Why do military services perform these ceremonies? It takes a lot of time and man-hours to do so. The ceremonies are carried out to recognize special efforts by service members, because in doing so the officers in charge know that other service members will see such ceremonies and (through social learning!) figure that they can perform at a higher level in order to also receive an award.

If service awards have strong requirements for eligibility, they can become a powerful motivational factor in any workforce. So if our company has an Employee of the Month or Year program, it needs specific and measurable criteria, clearly communicated to the workforce, that require performance above the company's standards in order to be eligible for the award. If this is done, these awards can become excellent motivators.

Giving Praise

Another nonmonetary individual incentive that can be very effective is the act of giving praise. Empirical research studies have found that feedback and social reinforcers (praise) may have as strong an impact on performance as pay. Praise actually works by boosting levels of dopamine in the brain, a chemical linked to joy. In the 1940s, a survey revealed that what employees want most from a job is full appreciation for work done. Similar studies have been performed over the years with little change in results. Employees want to know that their organization values their contributions and cares about their well-being.[35] Giving praise creates a win-win situation, and it only takes a minute and doesn't cost anything.[36] It is probably the most powerful, simplest, least costly, and yet most underused motivational incentive there is.

Ken Blanchard and Spencer Johnson popularized giving praise back in the 1980s through their best-selling book, *The One-Minute Manager*. They developed a technique that involves giving one-minute feedback of praise. Blanchard calls it *one-minute praise* because it should not take more than one minute to give the praise. It is not necessary for the employee to say anything. The four steps are described below and illustrated in Model 12-1.

SHRM
Guide – A:25
Recognition

SHRM
Guide – A:26
Service awards

WORK
APPLICATION 12-8

Select a job. Does the organization offer a recognition plan? If not, how could it offer a recognition plan to be effective at motivating employees? Assess the advantages and disadvantages of offering a recognition plan at your organization. Should it offer a recognition plan?

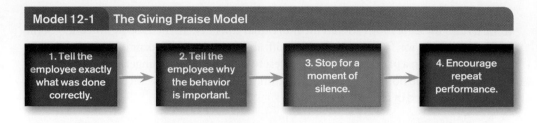

Model 12-1   The Giving Praise Model

1. Tell the employee exactly what was done correctly. → 2. Tell the employee why the behavior is important. → 3. Stop for a moment of silence. → 4. Encourage repeat performance.

Step 1. Tell the employee exactly what was done correctly. When giving praise, look the person in the eye. Eye contact shows sincerity and concern. It is important to be very specific and descriptive. General statements, like "You're a good worker," are not as effective. On the other hand, don't talk for too long, or the praise loses its effectiveness.

Step 2. Tell the employee why the behavior is important. Briefly state how the organization and/or person benefits from the action. It is also helpful to tell the employee how you feel about the behavior. Be specific and descriptive.

Step 3. Stop for a moment of silence. Being silent is tough for many managers. The rationale for the silence is to give the employee the chance to "feel" the impact of the praise. It's like "the pause that refreshes." When you are thirsty and take the first sip or gulp of a refreshing drink, it's not until you stop, and maybe say, "Ah," that you feel your thirst quenched.

Step 4. Encourage repeat performance. This is the reinforcement that motivates the employee to continue the desired behavior. Blanchard recommends touching the employee. Touching has a powerful impact. However, he recommends it only if both parties feel comfortable. Others recommend that you don't touch employees; it could lead to a sexual harassment charge.

WORK
APPLICATION 12-9

Select a job. How often does your boss criticize your work? How often does your boss praise your work? What is the last thing you did that deserved praise? How often do you criticize and praise others at work? Will you give more praise knowing how it affects others?

As you can see, giving praise is easy, and it doesn't cost a penny. Managers trained to give praise say it works wonders. It's a much better motivator than giving a raise or other monetary reward. One supermarket manager stated that an employee was taking his time stacking cans on a display. He gave the employee praise for stacking the cans so straight. The employee was so pleased with the praise that the display went up with about a 100% increase in productivity.

Note that the manager looked for the positive, and used positive reinforcement rather than punishment. The manager could have given a reprimand such as "Quit goofing off and get the display up faster." That statement would not have motivated the employee to increase productivity. All it would have done was hurt human relations, and it could have ended in an argument. The cans were straight. The employee was not praised for the slow work pace. However, if the praise had not worked, the manager should have used another reinforcement method.

In this global environment, it is not always possible to give praise in person, so when you don't see people face-to-face, use written communication, including e-mail, instead. The personal handwritten note is considered to be special.[37] Disney CEO Bob Iger writes personal, handwritten notes on Disney stationery to praise employees, even those he has never met. He says that writing a simple note goes a long way with people.

SHRM

Guide – B:18
Financial benefits (gainsharing, group incentives, team awards, merit pay/bonuses)

Incentive Options for Groups

Individual incentives can work well, but what can we use to motivate higher levels of performance from groups? After all, in most of our 21st-century companies, groups and teams are the norm. Let's take a look at some of the more common group incentive options.

12-3 APPLYING THE CONCEPT

Individual Incentive Options

Identify the individual incentive being discussed below.

a. Bonus
b. Commissions
c. Merit Pay
d. Piecework

e. Standard Hour
f. Nonmonetary Awards
g. Praise

_____ 11. I'm one of only three people in the entire department who will get an extra raise for high performance this year.

_____ 12. They had me go to this dinner and go up in front of everyone to get a plaque for five years of service to the company. The boss listed some of my major accomplishments—it made me kind of proud.

_____ 13. What is going on with the boss? Although I've done it many times, today is the first time in two years the boss thanked me for getting a shipment that was behind schedule out on time.

_____ 14. I complete a job before a stated time so that I can go on to the next job and get paid extra for being faster than the average guy.

_____ 15. I just sold that giant 3D TV set. I can't wait to get my pay this week.

Profit Sharing Plans

LO 12.5

Briefly discuss options for group-based incentives.

Profit sharing programs *provide a portion of company proceeds over a specific period of time* (usually either quarterly or annually) *to the employees of the firm through a bonus payment.* The programs are designed to cause everyone in the company to focus on total organizational profitability.[38] This sounds like a good opportunity for the employee to get a share of the returns that the company receives from their work, right? But, how well does it work? What if the company does not have any profit during a particular period? If this is the case, then there is no profit to be shared.

Ineffective profit sharing implementation. If the company doesn't have any profits, employees may not be motivated to work harder. But, how can a company have no profit? It is actually pretty easy for the company to have no, or a minimal amount of, profit in any given year. The company can, and frequently does, manipulate net profit in many ways in order to pay less in tax on corporate profits at the end of the year, and in some cases to minimize profit sharing.

There are many ways that management can manipulate expenses to minimize profit. Management might put profits back in the company by buying new equipment or other assets. It can decide to pay management an unscheduled bonus, acquire another business, or increase finished goods inventory. However, if the company is manipulating expenses or other cost factors to decrease profit sharing and employees find out, the plan will certainly not be a performance motivator and most likely will cause other problems.

Another issue with profit sharing as a motivator is that it is focused on total organizational profitability. How does the average employee change companywide profitability? If the employee doesn't know what to do in order to increase profits, what will they do differently in their job? The answer is absolutely nothing. Remember that we need to be able to personally affect the desired result in order to be motivated to do anything different. So profit sharing in many cases does not provide the company with the expected boost in productivity.[39]

Effective profit sharing implementation. To motivate employees, we need to be sure that management is not manipulating factors to minimize profits so it doesn't have to pay much in profit sharing. The second thing is to be sure to train all employees on how to increase revenues and decrease cost in their job areas so that they can affect the bottom line and increase their profit share. In addition, a running record of organizational revenues and profitability should be maintained and updated on at least a weekly basis. This record should be posted where everyone can see it and keep track of company performance— some companies post it in the lunch/break room. This allows the employees to see how their efforts are affecting profitability of the firm overall. It can also allow interim payments of incentives, which can assist the company in maintaining high worker efficiency over longer periods of time.

Gainsharing Plans

An alternative to profit sharing is a gainsharing program. Gainsharing is similar to profit sharing because in each case the gain (in either profit or some other factor) is shared with the employees who helped to create the gain. Gainsharing is a bit broader than profit sharing, though. Gainsharing can be accomplished using any organization factor that costs the company money and can be analyzed and modified for performance improvement.[40] Originally, gainsharing usually used corporate revenue, but today many gainsharing options exist. Some of the more common gainsharing options are increased revenues, increased labor productivity or lower labor costs, improved safety (fewer lost-time accidents), return on assets or investment, and increased customer satisfaction.

Ineffective and effective gainsharing implementation. Being somewhat similar to profit sharing, gainsharing has the same potential problems. Here, as with profit sharing, we have to show employees how they can affect the desired outcome in order for them to be motivated to change the way they work.[41] However, different from profit sharing, many of the options for gainsharing are more difficult for management to manipulate, so workers feel that they have more control over their results. It is tougher for management to modify total revenue or days lost to accidents, for instance, than it is to modify net profit. So gainsharing sometimes initiates a stronger reaction and more motivation from the workforce than profit sharing.

How do we incorporate gainsharing effectively in the organization? It's pretty straightforward, but easier said than done. Here is the process. We establish the objective(s), identify the performance measure (usually as a per-unit value), determine how to split the gain between the organization and the employees, and then provide the payout when earned.

Employee Stock Ownership Plans

An Employee Stock Ownership Plan (ESOP) ultimately allows at least part of the stock in the company to be given to the employees over a period of time based on some formula.[42] For example, if you work for the company for a year, you get 10 shares of stock, and for every additional year of employment you receive 10% more than the year before. It is actually a retirement benefits plan because the company puts the tax-deferred stock in a trust for eventual use by employees who retire. But it also has the potential to be an incentive to the company's employees, because they become part-owners of the firm.

Why would the current owners of the firm give away stock in the company? Well, there are a couple of major reasons. Because an ESOP is basically a "qualified" retirement benefits plan, it has some significant tax advantages to both the firm and the employee in most cases.[43] This means that owners can give their employees part of the company and receive a tax break for doing so. A second major reason for giving employees stock in the company is to cause them to act more like owners. It is thought that this will motivate employees to do such things as reduce scrap, increase quality, improve customer service, and pay attention to many other things that cost the company money over the course of a year.

Ineffective and effective ESOP implementation. But does an ESOP always work as intended? Of course not. Because an ESOP is like the other two group incentives, it is subject to the same potential problems and needs the same lack of manipulation and employee training.

Stock does, however, have a unique potential problem. The entire company typically has to improve in order for the value of its stock to increase. But even if the employees are highly motivated and work really hard, the value of the stock can actually go down for many reasons that are outside the control of the individual and groups. For example, stock may not perform well in a bear market, and your company's stock price can go down along with the overall market. A recession may hit, and sales and profits may go down, as may the price of your stock. Competition can take some or all of your business away, like Netflix did to Blockbuster, or the company can go bankrupt like Circuit City did, and you can lose it all.

Stock Options and Stock Purchasing Plans

There are two other common stock plans used by companies as incentives. The first is a stock option plan, and the second is direct stock ownership.

Stock options. Stock options are usually offered to an individual employee to allow them to buy a certain number of shares of stock in the company at a specified point in the future, but at a price that is set when the option is offered. Options can be provided to either executives or to nonexecutive employees.[44] So, we might offer our employees the option to buy stock in the company in a year at today's stock price.

The intent here is to motivate the employees to work to improve the value of the company, so that when the option to buy the stock in a year comes up the price of the stock has increased, giving the employee more value than what they paid for. For example, we may offer our employees the option to buy 100 shares of our stock in one year at today's price of $10. If the company's value increases so that at the end of the year a share of stock is worth $20, the employee can buy $2,000 worth of company stock for $1,000. However, if the value of the stock doesn't go up in a year, the option isn't worth anything.

Stock purchasing. These plans are similar to stock options, but instead of giving you the option to buy stock in the future, they let qualifying employees buy the stock essentially any time, usually at a discount. ESOPs, stock options, and stock purchasing give employees ownership in the company, but the big difference is that with an ESOP the employees are given the stock over time, whereas with stock options or purchases employees have to buy the stock.

Ineffective and effective stock options and purchasing implementation. Like ESOPs, they don't always work as intended for essentially the same reasons. The hope is that if you are an owner you will think more about the long-term value of the company and work to improve its performance. But with stock options, there is a unique potential problem. The employee can simply buy the stock and then quickly sell it for a profit, so that they

WORK
APPLICATION 12-12

Select a for-profit job. Does the organization offer ESOPs? If not, how could it offer an ESOP to be effective at motivating employees? Assess the advantages and disadvantages of offering ESOPs at your company. Should it offer an ESOP?

WORK
APPLICATION 12-13

Select a for-profit job. Does the organization offer stock options and/or stock ownership? If not, how could it offer one or the other to be effective at motivating employees? Assess the advantages and disadvantages of offering stock options and ownership at your company. Should it offer stock options and/or a stock ownership plan?

are no longer owners of the company. The same problem can occur with stock purchases depending on the arrangement; there can be restrictions on the sale of the stock, and if it is part of a qualified retirement plan, there are penalties for selling before retiring.

Evenly Distributed or Fairly Distributed Group Incentives?

The final question concerning group incentives is how to distribute them to the members of the group. There are two schools of thought on this—evenly distribute the reward or "fairly" distribute the reward. If we decide to distribute rewards to employees, we will generally utilize one of these two methods:

1. **Even.** Each member receives the same reward (the same amount of money if our reward is monetary).

2. **Fairly.** Each member receives their *fair share* of the incentive based on their peer evaluations and a formula for their pay level (everyone potentially gets a different reward, based on evaluation of their individual efforts by the other group members).

When to distribute evenly. In many cases, in groups where cohesion may be more important than individual effort, the even distribution of rewards is the method of choice. This avoids singling out individuals where such actions might cause dysfunctional conflict or lack of cooperation within the group.

WORK
APPLICATION 12-14

Select a for-profit job. Does the organization offer an evenly or fairly distributed plan? If not, how could it offer one of the two methods to be effective at motivating employees? Assess the advantages and disadvantages of offering each of the two methods at your company. Should it offer an evenly or fairly distributed plan?

When to distribute fairly. Fairly distributing a reward is much more difficult, but is probably more motivating to our best employees. If we choose to fairly distribute the rewards, we provide a different reward amount to each person based on their contributions to the group. In this case, the highest-level performers in the group get the greatest reward while the slackers (social loafers) get less.

The difficulty here is in determining who did the most work. A common method of fairly distributing rewards to group members is through the use of *peer evaluations*. Each of the coworkers evaluates all other coworkers in the group, and the results of the evaluations are averaged in some form. Rewards are then distributed based on each individual's peer ratings. In cases where individual efforts should be recognized and where group cohesion is not as important as providing returns to the best performers, a fair distribution method rather than an even method would probably work best.

Failure, Challenges, and Guidelines in Creating Incentive Pay Systems

Now that we know a little about the various types of incentives available to the company, let's discuss some of the issues that we will have to deal with in creating an incentive program that works.

Why Do Incentive Pay Systems Fail?

LO 12.6

Discuss the major reasons why incentive plans fail.

Too often incentive systems are poorly designed and badly implemented.[45] If we are not going to carefully manage a system, then we shouldn't even create it. It is worse than no system at all. There are many reasons why incentive plans might fail to motivate the workforce, but let's take a look at some of the more common ones.[46]

12-4 APPLYING THE CONCEPT

Group Incentive Options

Identify the group incentive option being discussed below

a.　Profit Sharing
b.　Gainsharing
c.　ESOP
d.　Stock Options
e.　Stock Purchasing

_____ 16.　My group option plan allows me to buy $100 shares of the company stock for only $25 each next year.

_____ 17.　My group option plan gives me a bonus at the end of the year based on how profitable we were for the year.

_____ 18.　My group option plan allows me to get stock and put it in my retirement account without paying anything for it. Over the years, I have accumulated 1,000 shares of my company's stock.

_____ 19.　My group option plan worked like this. The manager told us that if we could cut cost in our department by 10%, as a group we would get 10% of the savings to the company distributed evenly among the 25 of us.

_____ 20.　My group option allows me to buy company stock for 10% less than the market value.

Poor Management

Even the best incentive plan won't work with bad management.[47] Managers are the core of any incentive program, because they have to keep track of individual and group performance in order to reward those who perform the best. Management also has to monitor the program and adjust things as necessary when the environment or the organizational tasks change.

Complicated Programs

If the employees can't figure out what they need to do in order to receive the incentives, they won't do anything different. Complex programs will almost always lead to failure of an incentive program because the workers don't know how to reach the goals or, in many cases, even what the true goals are.[48] In addition, failure to successfully communicate the plan to employees creates the same problem—the employee won't know how to reach the goals.

The Plan Doesn't Really Increase Rewards, or Provides Insignificant Rewards

If a plan takes away from base pay in order to add incentive pay, the employee isn't gaining anything in reality. The net result is the same, and employees will see right through such a "rewards" program. Even if there is a minimal increase in pay, often employees will figure that the extra effort required is not worth the return—expectancy theory.[49] We have to tailor the incentive program to the things that matter to each specific employee.[50]

Employees Can't Affect the Desired Outcomes

Frequently, we create rewards programs that promise a return to the employee, but we base the promised reward on something the employee can't do anything about. Think about

12-1 SELF-ASSESSMENT

COMPENSATION OPTIONS

Answer each question based on how well it describes you:

1	2	3	4	5

Not like me   Describes me

_____ 1. I enjoy competing and winning.

_____ 2. I usually work faster than others.

_____ 3. I like working alone, versus being part of a group.

_____ 4. I don't need to have approximately the same pay every week; varying income is fine.

_____ 5. I enjoy meeting new people and can strike up a conversation with most people.

_____ 6. I take risks.

_____ 7. I would prefer to get a large sum of money all at once, rather than broken into many payments.

_____ 8. I'm thinking long-term for my retirement.

_____ 9. I like working toward a set of goals and being rewarded for achieving them.

_____ 10. I like knowing that I am one of the best at what I do.

There is no simple sum of this one to add up. Although we would all love to have a high wage or salary with lots of incentive pay on top of it, this is not reality in most jobs today. In general, the higher your number of "Describes me" statements, the more you are open to incentives versus wages and salaries. Below is an explanation of each statement.

For Item 1, if you don't like competing and winning, you may be more comfortable in a job with a wage or salary; you usually have to compete for incentives like merit raises. For Item 2, if you are not faster than others, piecework and standard hour incentives may not be your best option. For Item 3, commissions, piecework, and standard hours are often based on individual performance. For Item 4, wage and salary give you fixed income, whereas incentives provide variance. Item 5 is characteristic of commission salespeople. For Item 6, if you don't like risk, incentives can be risky. For Item 7, getting a large sum at once tends to be a bonus, profit sharing, or gainsharing incentives. For Item 8, ESOPs are retirement plans, and stock purchases can be, too. Item 9 reflects gainsharing and bonuses. Item 10 reflects merit pay and praise.

company profit—what can the housekeeping staff (and many others in the organization) do about company profit? So if the desired outcome is increased profit, the employee doesn't know what to do to affect profitability.

Employees Don't Know How They Are Doing

In order for an incentive plan to motivate, the employee has to know how they are doing compared to the desired outcomes.[51] If you know that you have to reach a certain production goal by the end of next week in order to get a desired reward and you are currently behind schedule, you will likely work harder to reach the goal. However, if you don't know where you stand, you may feel that everything is going well and won't increase your efforts. People have to know how they are doing compared to the program goals.

Challenges to Incentive Pay Systems

There are obviously going to be challenges associated with incentive systems. Employees do respond to incentives, but unfortunately, they don't always respond to incentives in the way we expect them to.[52] Questions covered in this section will discuss four of the major challenges: Do incentives work, do incentives become entitlements, will employees only do what they get paid for, and do extrinsic rewards decrease intrinsic motivation? After we discuss each challenge, we will present guidelines for successful implementation of incentive pay programs to meet these challenges.

Do Incentives Really Work?

The answer here is it depends on who you ask. If you ask the CEO of a company that does incentive planning for other firms, they work great. If you ask some company leaders who have tried them, they don't work at all. For others, they work some of the time, but not always.[53] One of the things that we have found out over the past 20 years or so is that incentives don't work as well as we might have thought they would in at least some cases.[54]

There is some recent evidence that *group incentives* work significantly better than *individual incentives* when people in the organization *have to cooperate* or coordinate with one another in completing a set of tasks.[55] However, there is little clear evidence that supports *companywide* applications of group incentives. One *HR Magazine* article noted that "company incentives do little to drive performance. They're the least effective motivational tool."[56] This is primarily because of the difficulty establishing a link between the individual employee's actions and the success of the firm.

Does this mean companies shouldn't use incentives? No, but managers need to make sure that employees understand the requirements for making the connection between the actions of each employee and the results that are needed. We have to help our people figure out how they can help the group or organization gain. If we can create the connection between how the employee acts and how they gain from it, we can create strong performance incentives. If not, the incentives will not work. We will get into some rules for creating incentives that will motivate later in the chapter.

Incentive to Entitlement—An Easy Step

Remember from our discussion of bonuses that in order for an incentive to continue to motivate, it can't be considered an entitlement. An **entitlement** *is something that the employee feels they have a right to receive from the company.* A common example of an entitlement would be a weekly paycheck. Most employees feel that if they show up to work, the company *owes* them a paycheck. In academia, some students feel they deserve a B for showing up. It doesn't matter whether they *did* anything or not! So we have the same

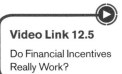

HR needs to create the right incentives to motivate employees to work hard.

challenge with regular pay and incentive compensation. However, an effective incentive makes the employees actually earn the reward based on their performance—it is not automatic like a salary. The current group of younger employees entering the workforce has been called the entitlement generation because of the expectation that they are entitled to certain perquisites just for becoming an employee.[57]

Consultants are seeing that in many cases "what was intended to be 'pay for performance' in many organizations deteriorated into a bland set of rewards based on an entitlement mindset."[58] As soon as this happens, our incentive program ceases to motivate higher levels of performance. Incentive pay of any kind is going to be a significant portion of overall compensation costs in companies where it is used. In fact, it will almost always be at least a few percent of base pay and in many situations can go up to 100% of base pay or even more, so we have to ensure that we get something in return for the cost.

If we take a look at the effectiveness of reinforcement schedules (part of reinforcement theory in Chapter 11), we will note that variable-rate rewards tend to be much better motivators than fixed-rate rewards.[59] So, one of the mechanisms that we can use to avoid creating an entitlement is to avoid basing our reinforcement on a fixed period of time or a fixed number of actions by the employee. We need to base the reward on achieving a particular specific and measurable goal, and provide at least some reinforcement as soon after the goal is achieved as is feasible. Don't wait for the end of the quarter or the end of the year.

Another thing that we can do is to create both short-term and long-term goals. This will both mix up the timing of the rewards provided to the employee, and provide them with incentives to improve company performance over the long term. Finally, avoid linking long-term incentives to only the upper-level employees in the company. Both short- and long-term incentives should be provided at each level in the firm.

"Do Only What Gets Paid For" Syndrome

Another of the challenges associated with incentive programs is the tendency of people to only do what is measured and is paid for. In other words, our people will pay attention to the work that will get them the rewards that they desire. There is a lot of anecdotal evidence that this occurs. However, there is not much empirical evidence that incentive pay fails because of this syndrome. Besides, we have the same challenge with regular compensation. Again, reinforcement theory notes that if we reward an individual for doing something, they are likely to continue to do that thing in the expectation that they will continue to receive a desired reward.

However, assuming that this might be a problem in some cases, one way to combat it is to make the incentive specific, but make overall job performance a part of any variable pay program. The incentive causes the employees to focus on the specific goals that we need accomplished, but the performance component lets everyone know that they still have to do all of the other things that make the organization successful over the long term.

Extrinsic Rewards May Decrease Intrinsic Motivation

Extrinsic rewards are *valued returns* (such as incentive pay for performance) *to the individual in exchange for doing something that the organization desires of the employee.* Intrinsic motivation means that a person does something because they like it, it is interesting and personally satisfying, and they want to do it. More than 100 studies over many years have shown that there is a relationship between the application of extrinsic rewards and a decrease in intrinsic motivation.[60] In other words, when we get an external reward for doing something that we enjoy, the enjoyment level will go down. Some evidence says that this is due to the fact that we may feel like we are being *controlled* externally, and rebel against that control.

However, there is also evidence that in at least some cases we can increase internalization of extrinsic motivators (cause the individual to believe that the rewards are for the "right" things), which lowers the resistance to the external rewards.[61] We always need to be on the lookout for ways to show that the external motivators that we provide are good things both for the employee being rewarded and for others who depend on the actions of the employee being rewarded, to increase this internalization process.

Guidelines for Creating Motivational Incentive Systems

So we now know that we have a number of factors that make incentive programs more or less successful. Anytime we are developing a variable pay plan, we have to consider what we need to do to make it work. What will make the system motivational to the workforce while also improving organizational success overall? Exhibit 12-6 lists some guidelines that researchers have come up with over many years of analyzing incentive programs that can significantly increase the chances for creating a successful program. Let's discuss our guidelines for creation of an effective incentive plan in a little more detail in this section.

Based on Organizational Strategy and Culture

The incentive program must be based on the goals in the strategic plan—the direction of the organization.[62] Think back to when we discussed strategic HR in Chapter 2. We talked about how HR can drive people to do things for the organization that it needs to have done in order to help it reach its goals. If the incentives are not driving our employees to work toward organizational goals, we won't reach those goals. One of the most common problems in incentive systems is in picking an expedient goal that is easy to measure, but doesn't aim at the strategic goals of the company.

We also need to make sure that the program is consistent with the organizational culture.[63] A lot of organizational cultures are egalitarian, where everyone expects that they will be compensated equally with others in similar positions. Many others are collectivist where the group has a strong desire to work together. In an egalitarian culture it will be difficult or impossible to provide different rewards to individuals, even if it is based on performance differences. In collectivist cultures, the group won't accept incentives that focus on the individual. So, culture must be taken into account in designing incentive systems.[64]

WORK APPLICATION 12-18

Select an organization that you know or work for. Do employees only do what they get paid for?

WORK APPLICATION 12-19

Select an organization that you know or work for. Do incentives decrease intrinsic motivation, or would they if the firm offered them?

LO 12.8

Identify the guidelines for creating motivational incentive systems.

Exhibit 12-6	Guidelines for Creating Motivational Incentive Systems

a) Base the system on organizational strategy and culture.
b) Offer incentives for all—managerial and nonmanagerial employees.
c) Make it understandable and clearly communicate the program and expected results.
d) Base the incentive on factors the individual or group can affect.
e) Make sure that you have SMART goals.
f) Clearly separate incentives from base pay.
g) Make the reward a significant piece of overall compensation.
h) Take great care in creating and administering the program.
i) Promptly provide any incentive awards.
j) Don't forget nonmonetary rewards.
k) Don't reward nonperformers.
l) Make the incentive program part of a comprehensive approach to managing.

Incentives for All

Any incentive program needs to provide performance incentives to all individuals involved in the process that is being targeted.[65] We can't just provide incentives to management, because management will attempt to force lower-level employees to perform so that the manager can get rewarded. This is a recipe for frustration and resistance by the line employees. But, what if we only provide incentives for the line workers and not management? Management's job (at least a significant part of it) is to get obstacles out of the way so that line employees can do *their* jobs. If the manager has no incentive to move quickly to get obstacles out of the way, we just end up with frustrated employees who can't meet their incentive goals.

Can the incentive apply differentially? Yes. If one group's job in getting to the goal is more important, then it is OK to give them a differential incentive. However, everyone needs to be rewarded so that they have an incentive to work together.

Understandable and Clearly Communicated

Complexity is a part of many organizational environments in today's businesses. However, our incentive programs have to be set up in such a way that they are able to be understood by every level of employee in the firm. If people can't understand what is expected of them, there is no way that they will reach the goals that we set. In addition, even if the program is understandable, it has to be accurately communicated to everyone in the organization.[66] All of our employees need to know about the program: how to participate, what their goals are, any assistance that is available to help them meet those goals, how their performance ties in with others in the company, and any other pertinent information. Good incentive programs must be clearly and completely communicated to all the personnel affected by the program.[67]

Based on Factors the Target Can Affect

The incentive offered should be based on factors that the individual or group, whichever is the target of the incentive, can affect.[68] If it is an individual incentive, the individual employee should be able to modify their behavior to affect the outcome of the process, and the same for a group of employees. If the individual or group can see no connection between what they do and reaching the goal, they will most likely do nothing different than before the incentive was instituted.

SMART Goals

Remember in Chapter 8 where we talked about goals having to be SMART—Specific, Measurable, Attainable, Relevant, and Time-based? SMART goals provide a clear link

12-5 APPLYING THE CONCEPT

Effective Incentives

Identify each statement by the guideline it is violating using the letters *a–l* as listed in Exhibit 12-6. You should read the explanations of each guideline before completing this application.

_____ 21. Management is really unfair. They get these great bonuses every year, and we do all the work, but they don't give us anything.

_____ 22. What the heck does this mean, "to have the best reputation in the area"?

_____ 23. This system stinks. John didn't meet his work goals, and he gets as much of a bonus as the rest of us get.

_____ 24. We went to the meeting together to find out about the new incentive system, but I haven't got a clue what they were talking about. Do you, Juan?

_____ 25. OK. I understand that if the price of the stock goes up next year, we can buy some stock at today's lower price. What I don't get is how my cleaning the offices can make any difference in the price of the stock.

between performance and payout.[69] Here again, as with any valuable organizational goal, we have to ensure that our incentive program identifies the goals of the plan in SMART fashion. This is the only way that we can then accurately measure and reward our employees for goal attainment. So remember to use our *setting objectives* model—To + action verb + specific and measurable outcome + target date.

Clearly Separate From Base Pay

Base pay is almost always considered an entitlement by the employees in an organization. We utilize base pay to allow our workforce to meet their basic needs (Maslow's physiological, safety, and social needs). This base pay very rarely really causes motivational actions on the part of our employees. Incentives need to be clearly separated from base pay to avoid creating the impression that they too are an entitlement. Employees need to understand that they only receive incentive rewards if they do something extraordinary.

A Significant Piece of Overall Compensation

What is a "significant piece" of compensation? Compensation studies will tell you different things on what is considered to be significant.[70] A good recommendation would be at least 10% of overall pay, and in some cases 20% or more. Why? Let's take a look at an example.

You work for XYZ Co. and are getting paid $40,000 a year. Your manager decides to give you a 2% bonus if you reach your goals this year—$800. You reach your incentive goals at the end of the year, and it is now time to pay you. If we pay you a lump sum at the end of the year, we generally have to take out 25% for federal withholding taxes and may have to take out state tax as well, so your $800 just became $500–$600. At a salary of $40,000 per year, if you are paid twice monthly, you would normally receive about $1,350 or so per paycheck, depending on the state in which you reside. How many of you would work really hard next year if you got a whopping $500, a little more than a third of one month's pay, as a bonus for meeting your goals the year before? To most of us that is an insignificant reward for meeting our goals for an entire year. Remember what we said when discussing merit pay earlier in the chapter—merit pay is typically a very small percentage of the individual's total pay, which makes it very difficult to use it as a motivator to perform.

Alternatively, if we make your base pay $36,000 and provide a 10% incentive for reaching certain goals, you will receive around $2,600 after taxes—a sum that most people making $36,000 per year would consider significant. People need to feel that the reward is "significant" to them in order for it to motivate.

Take Great Care in Administering the Program

Meticulously measure performance using multiple metrics and vigilantly calculate the rewards to be provided to persons who reach their incentive goals.[71] Be careful to do the things that are right, the things that people expect you to do in accordance with your incentive program. If the company owes an individual or a group an incentive award based on reaching their goals, then we must make sure that it is paid. Set attainable standards and then measure them fairly, when and how they are supposed to be measured. Once measured, reward those who attain the goals, as soon as possible. If individuals or groups did not meet their goals, communicate that to them so that they know why they didn't get a reward.

Again, an example helps in understanding what might happen if we fail to be meticulous in our measuring and administration duties. Let's say we have 600 employees in our company and set some ambitious goals at the beginning of the year for the company and for each individual employee. As a company, we met our goals for the year and calculated whether or not each individual employee met their personal goals. But we miscalculated with one person. How fast will the word likely get around the company that we "cheated" that one employee? Via the employee grapevine it will probably be known throughout the company in two days—possibly one. This employee starts telling their friends that "the company cheated me and lied to me." And what will happen as soon as one person starts to complain? As soon as one person makes that claim, others will start to wonder whether or not they were treated fairly—*even though we were correct in calculating their individual payments*! Pretty soon, what was supposed to be a motivational program becomes a massive demotivator due to the fact that people begin to *perceive* that they may not have been treated fairly. We have to be meticulous in our management of any incentive program.

Promptly Apply Any Incentive Award

"Keep the time between the performance and reward as short as possible."[72] If the incentive is based on an annual goal, and we use a calendar year as our organizational fiscal year, our year ends in December, and we should provide any incentive awards on the first payday in January, or even on December 31, if we already have results calculated. If incentives are calculated monthly, pay them at the end of the month. Rewards should be provided as quickly as possible. Why? We provide the reward to reinforce the employee's efforts that led to desired results. If you receive a reward six months after you do something, you don't really see the connection. If you don't see the connection, it does not reinforce your earlier actions.

Don't Forget Nonmonetary Rewards

Remember that not everyone is motivated by cash.[73] There are many other rewards that are available as part of incentive programs. Incentives can include providing a group with the ability to choose between work assignments, providing training and learning opportunities, allowing flexible schedules, providing extra paid time off, personal or group recognition at an awards ceremony, offers to present results to top management, having greater input into future incentive goals, and many others. Anything that employees consider to be significant can become a reward, whether monetary or not. We can use an on-site child care center, or a gym or lounge, as an incentive. If we reach a certain set of organizational goals by the end of the year, we will be able to build the child care center.

To many people in today's workforce, this would be a significant incentive. However, to others, it may not be a reward at all. We have to pay attention to significance.

Nonmonetary rewards often work better than monetary rewards. Having a bit of time off to play with the company's resources, like 3M Company provides, can be a huge incentive. 3M gives 15% of work time to employees to use their resources and labs and to just tinker around and see what they can come up with.[74] Post-It notes were created in just this way in 1974. A 3M employee was tired of bookmarks falling out of his books, so he used an adhesive that had been invented earlier (also in 3M) and applied it to small pieces of paper. The incentive was in being *allowed* to be creative, and avoid being bored. Always think about what your employees consider to be significant. In many cases, it may not be money. And don't forget about giving lots of praise, following the steps of the model, as it doesn't cost anything and only takes a minute of your time.

Don't Reward Nonperformers

When goals are not met, do not apply rewards.[75] It seems silly to have to say this, but in many cases, you will *want* to reward your employees, even when they don't quite meet the goals that were set. Why would this happen? Let's take a look at an example that will explain it.

Andy works for you, and didn't quite meet the goals set for the incentive program at the end of the year. You are a good manager, and you saw Andy consistently come to work and work hard, but he just wasn't able to reach his goal. At the end of the year, you see that he didn't make it, but you know that Andy is a hard worker. So, you sit down and look at everyone in your department, and everyone except Andy met their goals. Then you think about how hard Andy tries and you say, "I know I saw him working all the time. I am just going to give the incentive payment to him anyway because I know that he works hard." How quickly will the word get around about Andy getting the reward even though he didn't meet his goals? Again, the communication grapevine will start working, and within one or two days everyone will know, because Andy is going to tell them.

Well, what will happen next time incentives are being calculated? Next time maybe several workers miss their goals, and they tell you, "Boss, I worked my tail off, but I just couldn't reach my goals. But you gave Andy his incentive last time even though he missed his goal. You can go ahead and give it to me too, right?" You have succeeded in destroying your incentive program because you rewarded a nonperformer. Rewarding nonperformers just cannot be allowed if we want the incentive program to continue to work in the future.

There is, however, a way that we may be able to reward Andy, at least partially, but we have to identify it at the beginning of the program. We can create a series of progressively more difficult goals in our incentive program. This allows us to provide a minimal incentive for meeting goals that are just above a baseline, and provide progressively more significant awards for meeting more difficult goals. This will let us reward Andy for going above the standard, but not quite meeting an aggressive incentive goal. So, progressive or stair-step goals can help us to avoid rewarding people who don't meet the top-level, or most difficult, goals.

Make the Incentive Program Part of a Comprehensive Approach to Managing

Remember that incentives can create a "just do what you get paid for" mentality. So, as we noted earlier in this chapter, we can "make the incentive specific, but make overall job performance a part of any variable pay program." We can't create an incentive for every aspect of every job in most organizations, so we have to continue to evaluate and reward overall performance so that our employees know that they have to do all tasks successfully, even though only some have incentives directly attached to their performance. One easy way to do this is to provide a caveat in the incentive program that receipt of an overall performance appraisal of "Meets Expectations" or higher is required in order to be eligible for incentive rewards.

WORK
APPLICATION 12-20

Select an organization that you know or work for. Which two or three guidelines is your organization strongest and weakest in following to ensure they effectively motivate employees with incentives?

LO 12.9

Discuss the issue of whether or not executive compensation is too high.

Video Link 12.6

Executive Compensation

Executive Compensation

No modern discussion of compensation is complete without at least touching on the topic of executive compensation practices. Executives drive organizational performance more than any other employees. The great debate over how much Chief Executive Officers (CEOs) matter rages on.[76] CEOs, including the late Steve Jobs of Apple, have the power to make or break a company.[77] When Jobs announced his immediate retirement in August 2011, Apple stock lost more than 5% of its market value (about $18 billion!) literally overnight.[78] Research clearly links managerial leadership to positive consequences for both the individual and organizations, including financial performance. Also, substantial evidence demonstrates that sound managerial leadership practice is critical to creating effective organizations.[79] So it just makes sense that executives are well paid for their managerial and decision-making skills. Let's take a brief look at executive compensation today.

Too Much or Just Enough?

There are many cries in the business world today that executives are getting paid too much. In at least some cases, that certainly appears to be true based on the performance of their companies. But are executives generally paid too much, too little, or about right? In order to even attempt to answer such a question we need to look at what executives are paid to do. If we were to ask you if anyone in a company *physically* produces enough products or services to make $1 million or more in any given year, most of you would answer absolutely not. However, executives are not paid to be production employees; they are paid to make decisions for the organization and to guide it toward its goals. In addition, the decisions that executives are paid to make are not easy decisions. It requires a high level of inherent intelligence, knowledge, and skills to analyze the information, and significant experience in making decisions of similar types and consequences.

There is an ongoing debate as to whether or not executives are overpaid.

While many of us think that we could run a billion-dollar company, the reality is that there are very few individuals who have the required skills and abilities to do so. Since labor is always at least partly priced based on supply and demand, and there are very few executives with the high-level skills necessary to run large firms, these individuals are always going to be worth quite a bit of money to the firm. Think of it this way. If you were the owner of a company and had hired somebody to lead the company throughout the year, and at the end of the year this person had made you $1 billion in profit, would you be willing to pay them several million dollars? Most of us would have no problem paying someone this much money if they made us a billion dollars. They deserve a piece of the pie they helped create.[80] However, this is not to say that there have not been some serious excesses in executive pay in the past several years, especially when CEO pay increases while employees are taking pay cuts and getting laid off.[81] The company is not acting ethically or in a socially responsible manner in this situation because they are harming a large number of stakeholders (including employees and shareholders and maybe others) in order to reward a single stakeholder, or a few stakeholders, in the executive suites. Actions such as this are certain to affect the market value of the firm as soon as they become publicly known. The result of some actions of this type is recent federal legislation on executive compensation—the Dodd-Frank Wall Street Reform and Consumer Protection Act.

ESR

The Dodd-Frank Wall Street Reform and Consumer Protection Act of 2010

One of the outcomes of both perceived and actual excesses in executive pay was the Dodd-Frank Wall Street Reform and Consumer Protection Act of 2010. The Dodd-Frank Act placed some significant limits on executive pay in public corporations and also added some new requirements for reporting of both compensation and shareholder involvement with executive compensation.[82]

Shareholder "Say on Pay" and "Golden Parachute" Votes

Among the most significant provisions of the act is that shareholders must be allowed to vote on compensation packages for their executive officers at least once every three years. This provision is called "say on pay." While the vote is nonbinding, it can still serve to put pressure on executives to maintain compensation in line with organizational performance.

Shareholders also have a vote on what's called a "golden parachute" for executives. **Golden parachutes** *provide executives who are dismissed from a merged or acquired firm with typically large lump sum payments on dismissal.* This tool is typically used to discourage a takeover of the firm, because the cost of the takeover becomes much higher due to the high payout to these executives.

Executive Compensation Ratios

Other provisions in Dodd-Frank include a requirement that every public company disclose the total compensation of the CEO and the total median compensation of all employees, and provide a ratio of these two figures.[83] A recent survey on CEO pay found that in the top 10% of all public firms the CEO-to–median employee pay ratio was nearly 200 to 1.[84] It would be very easy to argue that this pay ratio is significantly out of line with performance, even though these firms have revenues well over $1 billion each. However, we should also note that research shows that the *average* CEO pay was only 5.4 times that of the average employee in the United States in 2010.[85]

Another provision of Dodd-Frank is that all public firms will be required to provide information on the relationship between executive compensation and the total shareholder return of the company each year. This will allow shareholders to more easily evaluate the performance of firms in which they hold stock. The act also requires that public companies establish policies to "claw back" incentives in certain cases if the company has to restate financial information that is detrimental to the firm's value. [86] In other words, if the company paid out an executive incentive based on its financial statements and then had to disclose later that those statements were not accurate, the company policy would require that any incentives paid out to the executives be paid back to the company.

Executive pay is obviously not a simple issue. However, there is significant evidence that at least in some industries executive pay has gotten out of line with organizational performance.[87] As a result of this realization, and also new legislation placing limits on organizational compensation for executives, companies have to be more diligent both in creating and in managing their executive compensation packages.

Executive Incentives

As with any other type of incentive, executive incentives are supposed to create a motivation to perform for the organization in certain ways. Executive incentives should be designed to cause the executive receiving them to make decisions that will benefit the organization over both the short and the long term. We need the executive to act as an

WORK
APPLICATION 12-21

Would you say the CEO of an organization you work(ed) for is overpaid, underpaid, or paid fairly for the contribution made to the firm?

LO 12.10

Identify the major provisions of the Dodd-Frank Act that affect executive compensation.

WORK
APPLICATION 12-22

Would you say the Dodd-Frank Act will help, hurt, or have no effect on an organization you work(ed) for?

impartial "agent" for the organization.[88] An agent is someone who acts on the owners' (shareholders') behalf. *Agency theory* says that agents will act in the way that provides the most benefit to them and not the owners, unless we provide the agent with incentives to act in ways that help the owners of the firm. The way to do this is to align the benefits that go to the agent with benefits that accrue to the firm. This is what executive incentives should be designed to do.

What are some of the common incentives that are used to create this alignment? The first and probably most common is the stock incentive.[89] We noted earlier that various types of stock incentives are available as group incentives. These same incentives—primarily stock grants and stock options—are used in executive compensation for basically the same reason. They are supposed to cause the executive to act to increase the value of the company over time, because if this is done, the executive's stock becomes more valuable.

Stock ownership helps to align the executive's goals with the organization's goals. Long-term bonuses attached to company performance goals are another popular incentive for executives.[90] These also help to target the "agent" executive toward goals that will improve the value of the company over several years. In addition to stock awards, executives may be paid retention bonuses for each year they continue in their positions, and are often paid bonuses tied to either short- or long-term company performance.

In addition to incentive packages, executives generally receive compensation in the form of perquisites or "perks." **Perquisites** are *extra financial benefits usually provided to top employees in many businesses.* While perks are not technically incentive pay (they are generally classified as benefits), they do serve to entice top-level executives to consider accepting jobs within an organization in some cases. Common perks include such things as vehicle allowances, memberships in various clubs, the use of company aircraft, tax assistance in various forms, home buying or selling assistance, security systems, and many others.[91] You need to be aware of executive perks and understand that they are a common component of executive compensation systems.

WORK
APPLICATION 12-23

Identify the incentives the CEO of an organization you work(ed) for receives.

Short-Term Versus Long-Term

For many years now, executive incentives have been moving toward more long-term options and fewer short-term payments in order to force the executives to look at the health of the firm over many years.[92] Even though this is the case, there are still many short-term incentives being used by firms.

Most short-term incentives are in the form of bonuses for one or a combination of several company performance measures. These bonuses are designed to focus executive behavior toward managing the performance measure designated in the bonus offering. Examples of short-term bonuses might be providing a 10% bonus of CEO base pay for lowering per-unit labor costs by 7% over one year, or offering a 12% bonus for improving workplace safety (as measured by OSHA reports of lost time accidents) by 3%. These bonuses are designed to focus the CEO's attention on specific problems.

In contrast to short-term incentives, most long-term incentives are made in the form of stock awards or options.[93] Of course there are other long-term incentives such as excess contributions to retirement plans and longevity bonuses mentioned above, but in general, at least for publicly traded companies, long-term incentives tend to be stock based. And there is a relatively new practice with long-term incentives in many companies—the "claw back" provision. The Dodd-Frank Act required this in some cases, but companies are extending the claw back to other instances that are not subject to the law's provisions.

The Goal of Executive Compensation

So what is the goal of executive compensation? Remember that we want to create a system that aligns the behavior of the executive with the interests of the owners of the firm. The best way to do this is to use a combination approach of short- and long-term incentives.

One way companies are making the attempt to better align executive compensation with organizational performance is through the use of performance "scorecards."[94] The use of these performance scorecards came about partly as the result of the 2008–2009 bank crises in the United States. At least part of the crisis was blamed on CEOs who were being rewarded for short-term organizational performance. In a 2010 survey, 68% of the companies who responded had created performance scorecards that measured success of the firm in both financial and nonfinancial terms and rewarded senior executives based on this scorecard.[95] While it is still too early to tell whether this approach will work, it is at least an attempt to put a longer-term focus on executive compensation.

WORK
APPLICATION 12-24

Would you say the CEO of an organization you work(ed) for focuses more on short-term, long-term, or a balance of both types of incentives to run the firm effectively?

Trends and Issues in HRM

In this chapter's trends and issues, we are going to explore recent changes in the mix of base and variable pay, the heavy reliance on incentives to perform in entrepreneurial organizations, and how incentive pay can cause unethical actions, and finally we will take a brief look at how incentives work (or don't work) in various country cultures.

Variable Pay Rising?

As we briefly noted at the beginning of the chapter, variable pay takes some of the risk to the firm away and shifts that risk to the individual. If the employee has variable "pay for performance" as part of their annual compensation plan and the company doesn't do well in that year, the individual loses part of their pay. The company limits its risk by passing on some of the risk of poor corporate performance to the employee.

This is one of the reasons why many companies have increased their variable pay components in recent years. The major recession in most of the world in the 2007–2008 time frame created a very difficult environment for companies all over the globe. Additionally, especially in the financial sector but in other areas as well, companies found that some of their incentive pay was poorly targeted. People were being paid for actions that didn't necessarily help the organization succeed and, in fact, in many instances led to serious internal financial and operational crises. As a result, boards of directors for public companies and the most senior managers in those companies have taken on greater responsibility for decision making on variable pay plans.[96]

Bonuses and other incentive plans are being much more closely managed and are being monitored for their Return on Investment in companies around the world. In addition, boards of directors are spending much more time making sure that incentives are aimed at achievement of the company's strategic goals. In a recent survey, more than 60% of companies said they were changing their variable pay to better align rewards with business strategy.[97] However, we have to be careful to not create a variable pay structure that only rewards short-term financial returns such as Return on Investment. This creates a potential problem of not paying attention to other factors that are necessary to the long-term operation of a business in the 21st century—factors such as brand image, operational excellence, and sustainability. Because incentive pay has the ability to mitigate corporate risk and also allows us to target strategic goals, we are seeing more and more companies creating or modifying their incentive pay programs. It looks like this will be the case for some time to come.

Entrepreneurial Organizations Rely on Incentives to Perform

Why do good, talented individuals choose to work for entrepreneurial organizations instead of established companies? By doing so, the individual increases their personal financial risk but, in turn, expects to have the *opportunity* for greater rewards as a result of their choice. It appears that they make a conscious decision to trade security for a significant potential payoff. Most top performers who leave big companies for new startup tech companies are typically taking a 20% to 40% cut in their base salary in the hope of securing a big payday later, usually through ESOPs and/or stock options.[98]

Entrepreneurial startups have always had fewer slack resources than larger firms. As a result, most entrepreneurial firms tend to have their employees carry out a much broader set of duties within the company, and they need their employees to be talented in multiple areas and driven to perform. In this situation, it makes sense that entrepreneurial firms would need to provide strong incentive pay in order to get strong performance on the part of their employees, and this seems to be the case.

The preferred method of incentive compensation for people who are willing to take a risk with entrepreneurial firms appears to be equity-based incentives in the form of ESOPs or stock options. And entrepreneurs should take note that research shows a relationship between equity incentives and performance of the startup firm.[99] Equity incentives in the form of stock in a new venture have the same advantages that they do in more established firms; plus they have additional value.

Remember that in large businesses, the individual employee may have difficulty figuring out how their work affects the firm overall. But, in new and smaller firms, it is generally easier to see how one person's action can affect the results of the organization. This allows us to provide the desired link between what the individual employee does and the results (and rewards) that they desire. So entrepreneurs need to understand the value of incentive rewards in startup organizations and learn to use them to their advantage.

Incentives to Act Unethically

ESR

How did we get into this mess? What caused the greatest recession of the last 80 years? That is what a lot of people were asking when the financial crisis hit home in the United States in 2008–2009. Well, at least part of it was caused by incentive programs. Recall that any incentive program is designed to cause people to be motivated to act in a certain way because they want a desired reward. So, how did incentive pay contribute to the financial crisis in the first decade of the 21st century?

Mortgage incentives both to individuals looking to buy homes and to banks and other financial firms created a "housing bubble" around 2005–2006. Mortgage brokers encouraged, and in some cases even coached, individuals to apply for loans that were of higher than normal risk because of historically low national interest rates in the United States and because of the fact that they received incentive bonuses for providing the loans.[100] Financial firms have always used large incentive awards to encourage their employees to act in ways that create large commissions and cause higher levels of financial assets to come under their control.

This was the case in many large banks, and as a result they made riskier and riskier loans to individual mortgage applicants. This was assisted by relaxation of documentation requirements at the federal government level, but driven primarily by the bonus payments attached to "writing" the mortgages. Many executives in the large international banks also had their annual incentive bonuses based on assets under their control instead of having their bonus based on long-term increases in the value of the firm. This put further pressure on the employees to write loans that increased the value of the assets under the bank's control.

While this is certainly not the only reason for the financial problems that the majority of the world faced at the end of the first decade of the 21st century, it is without a doubt one of the contributing factors to the meltdown. Bonus payments created a situation where rational individuals acted unethically because of the incentive returns that they received for taking such actions. Incentive payments have the potential to lead to such unethical actions, so we always have to guard against them when we design our incentive programs.

Incentives in Global Firms

Effective global leaders are a vital asset that can offer a competitive advantage within organizations today.[101] CEO Mike Duke of Wal-Mart has stated that his biggest challenge is to continue to develop the leadership talent to grow the company around the world.[102] But do incentive programs work the same worldwide? The answer, briefly, is no, but they are becoming more similar over time. In fact, in some emerging market countries, variable pay is a higher proportion than in most developed markets.[103] However, in other countries, variable pay still has negative connotations, especially as an *individual* incentive. Many country cultures do not mesh well with individual incentive programs, and some do not readily accept even group incentive programs.[104]

One study of two cultures notes that "many multinational companies have 'exported' their human resource practices overseas," but some studies "have revealed that people in different cultures prefer different means of reward distribution." This study analyzed the United States (an individualistic society) compared to Hong Kong (a collectivist culture), and determined that "people in a collective culture more readily relate individual contributions to group performance and they also appreciate linking rewards with group performance."[105] There are many other studies that relate similar information concerning the effectiveness of incentive pay across the globe. The main thing that compensation professionals need to understand is that we cannot provide the same types of incentives to employees regardless of the organizational and country culture and structure. We have to understand the function of "significance" in expectancy theory and always make sure that our system rewards are significant and acceptable to our employees.

Wrap-Up

Another chapter comes to a close. What did we learn about incentives for performance in this chapter? We started off by noting why we use incentive pay. One reason that we need to have incentives is that we want the ability to reward high performers better than average or low performers. Another reason for incentives is to shift some of our payroll risk to the employee when the organization doesn't perform up to expectations. A third reason is to target individual behaviors toward accomplishment of strategic goals.

In our second section, we went through a discussion of both individual and group-based incentives, including advantages and disadvantages of each. We also discussed when each option will tend to work best.

The third and fourth sections took a look at some of the more popular options for both individual and group incentives. Individual options included bonuses, commissions, merit pay, piecework plans, standard hour plans, and nonmonetary rewards, especially recognition and praise. Group incentives included profit sharing, gainsharing, and stock-based incentives of various types, including ESOPs. We also discussed the question of whether to apply group incentives evenly or "fairly," based on individual efforts within the group.

In the fifth section we covered three major related topics: incentive program failure, challenges, and guidelines to overcome them.

1. We started by stating why incentive plans *fail* to motivate performance, with the most obvious issue being bad management of the program. In addition, complex programs, programs that don't really increase the rewards to the employees, inability of the employee to affect the desired outcomes, and a lack of knowledge of how the plan is working are also common items that cause incentive programs to fail.

2. We noted that there are many *challenges* in the creation of successful incentive systems. We noted that, in general, the evidence says that group incentives work better than individual incentives, especially when the group has to cooperate. We also discussed the problem of incentives becoming an expectation, and the fact that once this happens the employee looks upon them as an entitlement—something that the company "owes them." We identified reinforcement schedules as one key to avoiding this problem.

We also took a look at the tendency to do only what is directly rewarded in companies with targeted incentive programs and finally discussed the potential for external rewards, causing us to lose our intrinsic motivation to do things.

3. The last part of this section covered some *guidelines* for creating a motivational incentive pay system. We distilled information from the earlier part of the chapter to provide you with some rules or guidelines for making sure that your company's incentive pay system rewards the right things and aims the incentive program toward the company's strategic goals.

Finally, in our last major section of this chapter, we briefly discussed executive compensation. We identified some of the reasons why executives are highly paid and noted that in many cases that compensation isn't well targeted toward long-term organizational growth and success. We identified some of the more significant factors in a recent federal law (the Dodd-Frank Act) that affect executive pay, and saw that, in fact, the average CEO is paid only 5.4 times the median salary in their company—certainly not an unreasonable premium for the responsibility that they bear.

The second part of the sixth section discussed issues in setting up executive compensation to align the executive's goals with the organizational goals. It also identified some of the more common executive incentives and perquisites. We also took a brief look at both short- and long-term incentives in this section, and noted that one possible way to reach alignment between executive compensation and organizational goals is to use a balanced approach to analyzing executive performance. These balanced scorecards are becoming more popular as tools to measure executive performance against their incentive goals.

In this chapter's trends, we looked at four variable pay issues. The first issue deals with the question of why variable pay is getting so much attention in 21st-century companies and how those companies are using it to their advantage. The second issue is one that entrepreneurs struggle with constantly. Do they provide more compensation to their employees in the form of a paycheck or pay for performance? Evidence shows that incentive pay, and especially equity-based incentives, provide more motivation to employees in entrepreneurial organizations than does base pay. Our third issue explored the problem of incentives creating an impetus for unethical behavior. We used the recent financial meltdown, especially in the housing/mortgage market, to illustrate how this can occur. Our final issue covered incentives in global companies. The bottom line is that we have to take country culture and any other factors that make each country market unique into account when we create our incentive programs.

Chapter Summary

 Visit www.sagepub.com/lussier for helpful study resources.

12.1 Discuss the major reasons why companies use incentive pay.

Incentives are necessary because they give us the opportunity to recognize our best people and provide us with flexibility to provide them with greater rewards than average or low performers. Variable pay systems also shift some of the company risk to the employee when economic downturns affect our businesses. Companies don't have to pay out some incentives if they are tied to organizational performance and the organization underperforms because of problems in the economy. Finally, incentive pay helps us achieve strategic goals, assuming that our incentives are aimed at accomplishing these objectives.

12.2 Identify the advantages and disadvantages of individual incentives.

Individual incentives make it easy to evaluate each individual employee; they provide the ability to choose rewards that match employee desires; they promote a link between performance and results; and they may motivate less productive workers to work harder. Disadvantages include the fact that many jobs have no direct outputs, making it hard to identify individual objectives; we may motivate undesirable behaviors; there is a higher recordkeeping burden than in group incentives; and individual rewards may not fit in the organizational culture.

12.3 Identify the advantages and disadvantages of group incentives.

Group incentives help foster more teamwork; they broaden the individual's outlook by letting them see how they affect others; they require less supervision; and they are easier to develop than individual incentives. Disadvantages include the potential for social loafing; we may discount individual efforts and output; outstanding performers may lessen their efforts; and there may be group infighting.

12.4 Briefly discuss options for individual incentives.

Individual incentives can come in many forms. The first form that we discussed was bonus payments, or lump sum payments for reaching a goal that don't change base pay. Commissions can also be used as incentives for sales. Commissions also only occur based on certain actions on the part of the employee—they don't add to base pay. Merit pay is different. Merit pay is based on past performance (appraisals) and *does* change base pay in future pay periods. However, merit pay is frequently too small

to be considered a significant reward. Piecework and standard hour plans also work as incentives for speed of production. In piecework the employee gets paid for each item produced, and in a standard hour plan they are paid based on a standard time allowed to perform an action. Both may have quality issues if not monitored. Finally, there is recognition and other nonmonetary rewards, which are very powerful incentives if used in the right ways.

12.5 Briefly discuss options for group-based incentives.

Group incentives are mostly based on organizational gains of some kind, or on gaining an ownership stake in the company. First, there is profit sharing, where if the company increases profit over the course of a year, the employees share in that profitability increase. However, in some cases gainsharing may be better, because profit can be easily manipulated. Gainsharing is based on other organizational gains that are more difficult to manipulate such as revenue changes, lost time accidents, or lower per-unit labor costs. If the company gains in these areas, it saves money, and some of the savings is shared with employees. ESOPs are the first stock (ownership) option, where at least part of the company's stock is provided to the employees over time. Other stock incentives are stock ownership awards or stock options, where employees earn stock by meeting goals.

12.6 Discuss the major reasons why incentive plans fail.

Incentive plans usually fail for one or more of five reasons. The first is bad management—managers have to manage the incentive program, and if they fail to do so, employees won't trust the program. Second, programs may be so complex that people can't figure them out, so they don't change their behavior. Third, plans may not really increase the potential rewards available, or the rewards don't appear to the employees to be significant. The fourth problem is that in a lot of cases employees can't affect the desired outcomes by their actions. Finally, in many "reward" programs, employees never know how they are doing, so they don't know whether or not to modify their behavior to change their output.

12.7 Discuss the challenges associated with incentive systems.

There is still some concern that, at least in some cases, incentives don't work. The evidence shows that group incentives do work better than individual incentives when cooperation is required in a work group, but in general it is difficult to tie employee actions to company success. If we fail to do that, incentives will not work. There is also an issue of incentives becoming an expected part of employee compensation—an entitlement. If this occurs, the incentive no longer motivates changed behaviors, which defeats the purpose of the incentive. Third, external incentives to act may lower a person's internal motivation to do something because they "like it." This may mean that we actually lower their performance instead of raising it when we apply incentives. Finally, there is the problem of people only focusing on what they are receiving incentive pay to do. They may neglect the rest of their job.

12.8 Identify the guidelines for creating motivational incentive systems.

1. Base all incentive programs on the company strategy and culture.
2. Make sure that the incentive program has some reward for everyone—nobody should be left out.
3. Make the incentive program easy to understand and clearly communicate it to all involved.
4. Base the incentive on factors that the individual or group can affect.
5. Use SMART goals—Specific, Measurable, Attainable, Relevant, and Time-based.
6. Clearly separate incentives from base pay to avoid the question of entitlement.
7. Make the reward a significant piece of overall compensation.
8. Take great care in program administration and provide rewards in the amount owed, when they are owed.
9. Promptly apply any incentive award—immediate reinforcement works much better than delayed reinforcement.
10. Don't forget to use nonmonetary rewards, too—not everyone is motivated by cash.
11. Don't reward nonperformers, or you risk ruining the incentive system.
12. Make the incentive program part of a comprehensive approach to managing—pay attention to the entire performance of employees, not just specific behaviors tied to incentive payments.

12.9 Discuss the issue of whether or not executive compensation is too high.

There is no doubt that in some cases executive compensation has gotten out of control. There is evidence that at the highest levels it can be more than 200 times the average employee's pay. However, research shows that overall executive pay only runs about 5.4 times the pay of an average employee in most firms, which means that as a general rule executive pay is probably not out of line, considering the pressure on executives to perform at the highest level all the time.

12.10 Identify the major provisions of the Dodd-Frank Act that affect executive compensation.

Dodd-Frank requires that shareholders be allowed a "say on pay" where they vote on executive compensation packages at least once every three years. Shareholders also have a vote on "golden parachute" payments to executives who are forced out of the company because of a merger or an acquisition. In addition, every public company is required to disclose the total compensation of the CEO and provide a ratio of CEO pay to the average pay in the company. Finally, all public companies are required to provide information on executive compensation compared to the company's total shareholder returns every year to allow shareholders to evaluate the performance of companies in which they own stock.

Key Terms

Bonus	Extrinsic rewards	Individual incentives	Profit sharing programs
Commission	Golden parachutes	Merit pay	Social loafers
Entitlement	Group incentives	Perquisites	Variable pay

Key Term Review

Complete each of the following statements using one of this chapter's key terms:

_____ is compensation that depends on some measure of individual performance or results in order to be awarded.

_____ reinforce performance of a single person with a reward that is significant to that person.

_____ provide reinforcement for actions of more than one individual within the organization.

_____ avoid providing their maximum effort in group settings because it is difficult to pick out individual performance.

_____ is a lump sum payment, typically given to an individual at the end of a period.

_____ is a payment typically provided to a salesperson for selling an item to a customer.

_____ is a program to reward top performers with increases in their annual wage that carry over from year to year.

_____ provide a portion of company proceeds over a specific period of time (usually either quarterly or annually) to the employees of the firm through a bonus payment.

_____ is something that the employee feels they have a right to receive from the company.

_____ are valued returns (such as incentive pay for performance) to the individual in exchange for doing something that the organization desires of the employee.

_____ provide executives who are dismissed from a merged or acquired firm with typically large lump sum payments on dismissal.

_____ are extra financial benefits usually provided to top employees in many businesses.

Quick Check (True-False)

1. Incentives are a tool to allow us to provide greater rewards to the best people in our organizations. T F

2. Variable pay shifts some of the compensation-related risk from the individual employee to the company. T F

3. Individual incentives can never be used to reward groups instead. T F

4. Individual incentives may motivate less productive employees to work harder. T F

5. One disadvantage of group incentives is that individual effort may get "lost" within the group. T F

6. Individual incentives work better than group incentives when we need people to cooperate. T F

7. Incentive programs may fail if they are too complex. T F

8. To make a bonus program successful we need to identify specific and measurable goals that the individual could affect. T F

9. Commissions don't really work very well as incentives to sell more products or services. T F

10. When merit pay is used as an incentive, it is typically a large percentage of the individual's total pay. T F

11. Standard hour plans work best in a sales environment. T F

12. Profit sharing plans are great incentives because companies find it difficult to manipulate company profit. T F

13. An ESOP provides a form of stock ownership as an incentive program. T F

14. Distributing group-based incentive awards "fairly" instead of equally is relatively easy to do. T F

15. In many cases what was intended to be pay for performance in an organization has deteriorated into a bland set of rewards based on an entitlement mindset. T F

16. Any incentive program should provide performance incentives to both managerial and nonmanagerial employees. T F

17. We need to provide the incentive reward as quickly as possible after the goal is reached to connect the action with its result. T F

18. All public company chief executives tend to be overpaid. T F

19. The Dodd-Frank Act requires that public companies show the ratio of CEO pay to the pay of an average employee. T F

20. To get company executives to act as impartial agents of the firm, we need to align the benefits that go to the agent with benefits that accrue to the firm. T F

Communication Skills

The following critical-thinking questions can be used for class discussion and/or for written assignments to develop communication skills. Be sure to give complete explanations for all answers.

1. Do you think that incentive programs can really work to align the company's goals with the employees' goals? Why or why not?

2. Would you rather be given the opportunity to receive incentives based on individual performance or group performance? Does it depend on the situation? Why?

3. As a manager, would you rather judge your employees' performance on an individual or a group basis? Why?

4. Have you ever been a "social loafer" in a group? If so, why did you not put out your best effort? What could the group or the company have done to limit your social loafing?

5. Have you ever seen an incentive program that didn't work because management didn't monitor and adjust the program? What could have been done differently?

6. What level of base pay do you think is really necessary in order for people to pay attention to an incentive program—5%, 10%, more than that? Why did you choose your answer?

7. Do you feel that merit pay programs would cause you to work hard, knowing that the average merit award is only between 1% and 2%? If not, how big would they need to be to cause you to pay attention?

8. Would you work on a commission basis if you were in sales, or would you rather have a salary—or a combination of both? Why?

9. How would you monitor quality in a piece-rate program to assemble AM-FM radios from components?

10. Do nonmonetary rewards ever motivate you? Why do you think you answered the way that you did?

11. Would you personally rather participate in a profit sharing plan or a gainsharing plan? Why?

12. Do you think incentive programs in general really work? Why or why not?

13. Which of the 12 guidelines for creating incentive systems is the most important in your mind? Why did you choose this one?

14. If you were a compensation consultant to a company, what would you recommend they do to provide incentives to the CEO and other executives? Why?

15. Is the Dodd-Frank Act a good or bad idea? Why?

Video

Please visit the student study site at **www.sagepub.com/lussier** to view the video links in this chapter.

Answers

REVIEW QUESTIONS (TRUE-FALSE) Answers

1. T   2. F   3. F   4. T   5. T   6. F   7. T   8. T   9. F   10. F   11. F   12. F   13. T   14. F   15. T   16. T   17. T   18. F   19. T   20. T

Case

Case 12-1. Realtor Reward Plans Gone Haywire

Frank is the lead broker at the real estate firm that is located in one large city. The company has a nationally known real estate training program that costs $2,000 to attend. The program motivates real estate agents to sell more, gives tips on how to get leads, and recruits more agents to Frank's brokerage firm.

Each real estate agent in his firm grosses a 3% commission with each transaction involved with buying or selling a house. After the broker's cut, most agents net a commission of 2.1% with each transaction.

Frank's motivation is to build his training program and the size of his brokerage firm by adding real estate agents. To do so, he decided to provide his real estate agents some incentives.

At noon on the first Monday of each month, agents sign up for four hours of floor time for the month via computer. Floor time at the downtown office allows each agent to be the sole person to accept phone calls, answer e-mails, or visit with walk-ins to get possible listings and generate more business. Floor time occurs

from 6 a.m. to 10 p.m. each day. Agents love floor time so much that by noon each Monday sign-up day, all floor times for the month are taken.

There are other ways to get real estate leads such as contacting people who have de-listed their houses or are showing "For Sale by Owner" signs in front of their houses. But floor time in this firm accounts for a third of all leads.

Here is the new incentive policy:

Realtors can receive up to four hours of floor time per month if they have had a transaction in the last three months.

Realtors receive one additional hour of floor time per month for exceeding three transactions in a three-month period. If there are four transactions in a three-month period, Realtors receive one additional hour. If there are five transactions, Realtors receive two additional hours. Six transactions lead to three hours and so on.

Realtors receive one additional hour of floor time per month for referring one person to Frank's training program. They receive two hours for two people, three hours for three people, and so on.

The system worked well for two months after initiation of the program. On the third month, floor time ran out. Agents who had rights to floor time but could not get it were promised extra floor time the next month. The real estate firm added 16 real estate agents (while losing only two) and brought in 18 agents to the training program due to referrals from other agents. The superstar real estate agent Trina was involved with nine real estate transactions during the three-month period.

Frank decided to change the standard one week before Realtors could sign up for the next floor time. Realtors can now receive up to four hours of floor time per month if they have had a transaction in the last two months (effective next sign-up). All other aspects of the incentive program will continue.

Stacey has been a Realtor with Frank's brokerage firm for the last 15 years. She had been on vacation in February and was gone in late March, so she did not get the e-mail on the new incentive policy. She thought she could sign up for floor time because she had a transaction in the last three months. She went on the computer to sign up for floor time as usual on Monday, April 3, at noon. She was locked out. The computer said she had insufficient transactions over the last two months.

Stacey immediately called Frank at 12:05 complaining that she couldn't sign up for floor time. Frank said that she should have been keeping up with all e-mail correspondence from the firm. She said it wouldn't have made a difference. "I went on vacation knowing I was safe for floor time. Now you surprised me. The firm is going to get bigger and bigger, and it is only going to get tougher to get floor time."

She was disgusted by the fact that her friend Trina received 20 hours of floor time in April. The incentive plan was also unfair to newcomers who get no floor time. Stacey said, "Trina is a machine. She has a staff that helps her get sales. She even hired a person to find Realtors to go to your training seminars. How can I compete against Trina who will capture all the floor time in the firm?"

Stacey also wondered about the training seminars. She got into the business of real estate to sell houses, not seminars.

Frank stated that he wants to give the spoils to those in the firm who produce the most. Trina happens to be one of the most productive Realtors in the city and state. Trina also nets 2.5% with each transaction because she passes the magical $3 million threshold each year. Besides, said Frank, floor time is only a small piece of the pie.

Questions

1. What were Frank's strategic purposes for the incentive plan? Did the incentive plan accomplish his purposes? Why or why not?

2. Which incentive option is Frank choosing?

3. Do you think that high-level performers should get the bulk of the rewards in an organization, or should the rewards be meted out in a more egalitarian fashion?

4. Let's say Stacey represents most of the Realtors of the firm. How could Frank have improved the cooperative development of incentives with Stacey prior to incentive initiation?

5. Given Frank's strategic purposes, what alternative incentive plans would be appropriate for this real estate firm? Consider incentive plans mentioned in the chapter.

Case created by Gundars Kaupins, Boise State University

SKILL BUILDER 12-1

Calculating Individual Incentives

Objective

To develop your skill at calculating incentive pay.

Skills

The primary skills developed through this exercise are:

1. *HR Management skill* – Technical and business skills

2. *SHRM 2010 Curriculum Guidebook* – I: Total Rewards

Assignment

Complete the math for the following six incentive programs.

1. **Bonus.** You have a salary of $46,000 per year and you get a 7% bonus at year's end. (1) How much is your bonus, and (2) what is the premium percentage on your annual salary?

2. **Commission.** You are an independent real estate agent in a rural area in the South, and you get a 5% commission on every house you sell. Your monthly expenses are around $10,000. This month you sold two houses: one for $168,000 and the other for $116,000. (1) How much revenue did you earn this month? (2) What was your profit for the month? (3) If this was an average month, what would be your profit for the year?

3. **Merit Pay.** You are the top performer in your department, so you are getting a 2% merit raise over the 2% that everyone else will get. (1) How much is your merit pay if your current salary is $35,000? (2) What is the merit pay premium percentage on your annual salary of $35,000? (3) What will your total pay be for next year? (4) What is the total pay premium percentage for next year?

4. **Straight Piece-Rate.** You make car parts. You get paid $1.10 for every part you make. This week you made 423 parts. (1) What is your pay for the week? (2) The estimated average pay is $450, so how much more or less than average did you make? (3) What is the premium percentage?

5. **Differential Piece-Rate.** You sell cell phones and phone service contracts in a small rural town. You are paid a salary of $7.50 per hour (above minimum wage) for a 40-hour week—$300 weekly or $1,350 for the (180-hour) month. You also get paid $8 for every phone you sell in excess of five for the month. This month you sold 15 phones. (1) What is your total pay for the month? (2) What is your premium if the average pay is $1,400 per month? (3) What is your premium percentage over the average?

6. **Standard Hour.** You rebuild transmissions. The standard rate is six hours each. You are paid $25 per standard hour. During this 40-hour week you rebuilt eight transmissions. (1) What is your pay for the week? (2) What is your premium for the week? (3) What is your premium over the standard as a percentage?

SKILL BUILDER 12-2

Developing a Compensation With Incentives Plan

Objective

To develop a better understanding of creating motivational incentives.

Skills

The primary skills developed through this exercise are:

1. *HR Management skill* – Technical, conceptual and design, and business skills

2. *SHRM 2010 Curriculum Guidebook* – I: Total Rewards

After a few years of selling new cars, you managed to get the funding to start your own small new car dealership as a sole proprietorship. Your starting staff of 10 employees will be as follows:

- You are the Owner-Manager and will oversee everything. You will also be the Sales Manager and do some selling.
- Sales staff. Three sales people reporting directly to you.

- Service and Parts Manager. You will have one person supervise the mechanics and detailer.
- Mechanics. You will need three mechanics to work on the cars.
- Detailer. One person is needed to clean the cars, one to help out the mechanics, and one to work in parts.
- Office staff. Two people must be available to answer phones, greet customers, make up the bills and collect money from sales and service, and do other paperwork including bookkeeping. They will report to you.

Preparing for Skill Builder 12-2–Develop an Incentive System

1. What type of compensation will each classification of employee receive for their work? Will you give them a wage, a salary, or incentive pay (commissions, piecework, or standard hour)?

2. Will you give incentives (recognition and other nonmonetary incentives, merit pay, bonuses, profit sharing, gainsharing, ESOPs, stock options, and/or stock purchase plans)?

3. As the only executive, what will your compensation package include?

SKILL BUILDER 12-3

Giving Praise

Objective

To develop your skills at giving praise.

Skills

The primary skills developed through this exercise are:

1. *HR Management skill* – Human relations skills

2. *SHRM 2010 Curriculum Guidebook* – I: Total Rewards; J: Training and Development

Assignment

Think of a job situation in which you did something well-deserving of praise and recognition. For example, you may have saved the company some money, you may have turned a dissatisfied customer into a happy one, and so forth. If you have never worked or can't think of a situation like this, interview someone who has. Put yourself in a management position and write out the praise you would give to an employee for doing what you did.

1. Briefly describe the situation in writing.

2. Write out the four steps of the *giving praise* model and what you would say to the person for Steps 1, 2, and 4.

In-Class Role-Play

You will give and receive praise.

Procedure *(10–15 minutes)* Break into groups of four to six. One at a time, give the praise you prepared.

1. Explain the situation.

2. Select a group member to receive the praise.

3. Give the praise. (Talk; don't read it off the paper.) Try to select the position you would use if you were actually giving the praise on the job (both standing, both sitting, etc.).

4. Integration. The group gives the praise-giver feedback on how he or she did:

Step 1. Was the praise very specific and descriptive? Did the giver look the employee in the eye?

Step 2. Was the importance of the behavior clearly stated?

Step 3. Did the giver stop for a moment of silence?

Step 4. Did the giver encourage repeat performance? Did the giver of praise touch the receiver (optional)?

Overall. Did the praise take less than one minute? Was the praise sincere?

13

Employee Benefits

Learning Outcomes

After studying this chapter you should be able to:

13.1 Discuss the strategic value of benefits programs

13.2 Identify the major reasons for the growth of benefits as a proportion of overall compensation.

13.3 Briefly discuss the major considerations in providing benefits programs

13.4 Identify and summarize the major statutory benefits required by federal law

13.5 Identify the main statutory requirements that must be followed *if* organizations choose to provide health care or retirement plans for their employees

13.6 Briefly describe the main categories of voluntary benefits available to organizations

13.7 Describe the differences between traditional health care plans, HMOs, PPOs, and HSA/MSA plans

13.8 Discuss the difference between defined benefit and defined contribution retirement plans and the reasons for the shift from defined benefit to defined contribution plans

13.9 Discuss the major retirement plan options

13.10 Discuss organizations' options when providing flexible benefit plans to their employees

13.11 Discuss the need for benefit plans to be communicated to employees

13.12 Define the following terms:

Workers' compensation

Experience rating

Unemployment Insurance (UI)

Serious health condition

Consolidated Omnibus Budget Reconciliation Act (COBRA)

Vesting

Pension Benefit Guaranty Corporation (PBGC)

Traditional health care plans

Health Maintenance Organization (HMO)

Primary Care Physician (PHP)

Preferred Provider Organization (PPO)

Health Spending Account (HSA) or Medical Spending Account (MSA)

High-Deductible Health Plan (HDHP)

Utilization analysis

Defined benefit plan

Defined contribution plan

Domestic partners

Chapter 13 Outline

SHRM
HR CONTENT

See Appendix A:
SHRM 2010 Curriculum Guidebook for the complete list

B. Employment Law (required)
  7. The Employee Retirement Income Security Act of 1974
  9. The Family and Medical Leave Act of 1993
  33. The Consolidated Omnibus Budget Reconciliation Act of 1985
  34. The American Recovery and Reinvestment Act of 2009
  37. The Health Insurance Portability and Accountability Act of 1996

I. Total Rewards (required)

B. Employee Benefits
  1. Statutory versus voluntary benefits
  2. Types of retirement plans (defined benefit, defined contribution, hybrid plans)
  3. Regulation of retirement plans (FLSA, ERISA, Pension Protection Act of 2006)
  4. Types of health care plans (multiple payer/single payer, universal health care systems, HMOs, PPOs, fee-for-service, consumer-directed)
  5. Regulation of health insurance programs (COBRA, HIPAA, HMOs)
  6. Federal insurance programs (OASDI, Medicare)
  7. Disability insurance
  8. Educational benefits
  10. Family-oriented benefits
  11. Global employee benefits
  12. Life insurance
  13. Nonqualified plans for highly paid and executive employees
  15. Time off and other benefits
  16. Unemployment insurance
  19. Managing employee benefits (cost control, monitoring future obligations, action planning, strategic planning)
  20. Domestic partner benefits
  21. Paid leave plans
  22. Workers' compensation

Case 13-1. Defined Benefit Retirement Fades Away

More Value-Added

As a Benefits Administrator for several years, I am a firm believer in educating your employees about their health and welfare benefits. Understanding enables employees to appreciate and to make the best use of their benefits. Tricia popped into my office one morning to quiz me about the finer details of our company health coverage. "During my last new-hire orientation, I had one guy grill me about how our benefits compared to what his last employer offered," Tricia explained. "I was amazed at how passionate everyone else in the session became about what they valued in employee benefits. Some talked about the 401(k) plan, some talked about vacation time, and others just wanted to be sure the medical coverage had low annual deductibles." Why have benefits become so important in total compensation? How do we create benefits packages that provide the greatest value to employees at a price employers can afford? Chapter 13 provides insight into voluntary and involuntary benefits and company benefit plans.

The Practitioner's Model for HRM

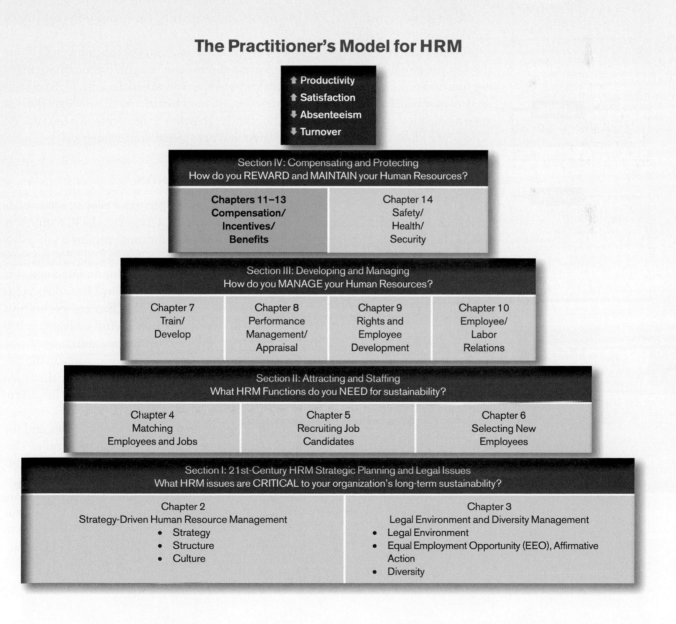

Overview of Benefits Management

SHRM

Guide – I:B1
Statutory versus
voluntary benefits

The last of our chapters on compensation deals with the indirect form—benefits. Benefits, as you remember from Chapter 11, are indirect compensation that provide something of value to the employee. Some benefits are mandatory, due to federal and state statutes, and some are optional, based on the desires of the firm. In addition, we need to understand that if we *choose* to provide some types of benefits to our employees, there are mandatory laws that we have to follow as well. We will get into all of these shortly. First, though, we want to discuss the cost of benefits programs to the company. This should help you to understand why benefits management has become a big issue to organizations in the 21st century and why employment in the benefits function of HRM has grown.

How much would you think that companies spend on benefits packages—5% of direct wages, 10%, more? According to the U.S. Bureau of Labor Statistics (BLS), benefits averaged roughly 30% of total employee compensation cost.[1] Looking at it another way, benefit costs equaled about a 44% premium on top of direct wage costs in March 2011. This means that for every $100 that goes into employee paychecks, another $44 is spent on benefits. So, if you get a full-time job with benefits and your salary is $40,000, you would be getting around $17,600 in benefits, or have a total compensation cost (to the firm) of around $57,600.

LO 13.1

Discuss the strategic value
of benefits programs.

If you became the HR Manager for an organization and you were spending nearly one third of your total compensation dollars on employee benefits, would you want to manage those costs as closely as possible? It makes sense that you would. Luckily, we have *some* control over benefits costs, and as HR Managers we want to make sure that we get the best return possible—in loyalty, job satisfaction, and employee engagement—for our money. So let's take a look at the business of managing employee benefits programs.

The Strategic Value of Benefits Programs

SHRM

Guide – I:B10
Family-oriented benefits

As just noted, the costs of benefits programs are staggering to most people. Many of us have no idea that our firms pay out this much for benefits. Of course, the BLS numbers are just an average cost to companies, but that means that for some employers the costs are even higher than those noted in the previous paragraphs. Because benefits cost our companies so much, we need to plan our benefits programs to add value for our employees and their families as well as provide a strategic advantage to the company.[2] How do benefits programs provide strategic assistance to the firm? As we noted in Chapter 1 of this text, our *human* resources are one of the few potential sources for competitive advantage in a modern, 21st-century organization. What keeps these employees happy and engaged, and willing to create a competitive advantage for our firm? The totality of their compensation—including their benefits packages—is one major factor.[3] While we are all aware that most employees take a job because of the advertised level of pay, many stay with a job because of the benefits package associated with the job.[4]

SHRM

Guide – I:B19
Managing employee
benefits (cost control,
monitoring future
obligations, action planning,
strategic planning)

Today, workers are demanding more benefits, an improved mix of benefits, and the flexibility for benefits to better fit with the lifestyle of the individual and their family.[5] This phenomenon has made it more difficult for the firm to keep track of and control benefits costs. Because people demand more and better benefits to match how they live, companies add new benefits to what they have historically offered. This requires HR to spend more time monitoring the cost as well as the value provided by different types of benefits. But this practice also provides an incentive to our employees to continue working for us due to the fact that they feel as if they are being cared for by the company. We increase job satisfaction and engagement because when employees are taken care of, they work harder and take good care of our customers and the organization.[6]

WORK
APPLICATION 13-1

How important are benefits
to you in selecting and staying
on a job? How do benefits
affect employment where
you work or have worked?

Why Are Benefits Growing as a Portion of Overall Compensation?

Growth in the cost of providing employee benefits has occurred for a number of reasons. Remember that benefit costs average about a 44% premium on employee direct compensation. However, before the 1930s, companies paid virtually no benefits to their employees. Why has the cost of a benefits program grown so much? There are a number of reasons for this growth. Let's take a quick look at some of the biggest reasons for the growth in benefits programs in the United States and worldwide.

Tax advantages. One reason benefits are growing is because of federal and sometimes state tax advantages to companies who provide them. There are federal tax advantages for companies that provide many types of benefits. If the company provides its employees with a benefit, the firm can write off all or part of the cost of providing the benefit. Sometimes the company can get benefits pretax for employees as well. As an example, health insurance premiums are tax deductible for employers and are not taxable as income (pretax) for employees. So providing some benefits can reduce the tax burden on both the company and the individual. Take a look at the table on benefit taxation that is reproduced from IRS Publication 15B in Exhibit 13-1.

Statutory requirements. Federal statutes require companies to provide certain benefits. In 1935, Social Security laws were passed that required companies to provide employees with old-age, survivor, and disability benefits. Over the ensuing years, Congress has added other mandatory benefits such as unemployment, workers' compensation, FMLA leave, and, soon, costs associated with the new health care law—PPACA (we will discuss each of these shortly). Each time Congress requires employers to provide a new benefit, the cost to employers of providing those benefits goes up. So, depending on the company, we could easily add 30%–40% or more to the individual's direct compensation based only on mandatory benefits.

Influence of organized labor. We talked about the National Labor Relations Act in Chapter 9, and noted then that the act allowed employees to "bargain collectively" with their employers. This is another reason that benefit costs have grown for companies over the years. A large part of collective bargaining is usually focused on employee benefits (for a variety of reasons that we don't have time to get into here), and once union members gain such benefits employees in other competing companies use this as leverage to have the same benefits added to their workplace, even if the company is not unionized. Unions also use the tax-favored status of many benefits to make them more palatable to the company during negotiations, and organizations may prefer benefits concessions to wage concessions because of the tax advantages. So unions have also driven up the cost and variety of benefits.

Buying in bulk. Virtually everyone now knows that if you buy things in larger quantities, you get them cheaper (think Sam's Club or Costco). Buying benefits in bulk works the same way. If companies buy benefits in bulk for employees, it is cheaper than if they buy the same benefits individually.

As you can see, there are a variety of reasons why the costs of benefits have grown in the last 80 years. And once a benefit becomes part of the employee's compensation package, it is very hard to delete that benefit in the future. We consider them an *entitlement* (Chapter 12)—the company owes us this benefit.[7] So the cost of providing benefits almost never goes down; it just keeps going up.

LO 13.2

Identify the major reasons for the growth of benefits as a proportion of overall compensation.

Video Link 13.1

Mandatory Benefits

Exhibit 13-1	Special Rules for Various Types of Fringe Benefits

Type of Fringe Benefit	Treatment Under Employment Taxes		
	Income Tax Withholding	Social Security and Medicare	Federal Unemployment (FUTA)
Accident and health benefits	Exempt[1,2], except for long-term care benefits provided through a flexible spending or similar arrangement.	Exempt, except for certain payments to S corporation employees who are 2% shareholders.	Exempt
Achievement awards	Exempt[1] up to $1,600 for qualified plan awards ($400 for nonqualified awards).		
Adoption assistance	Exempt[1,3]	Taxable	Taxable
Athletic facilities	Exempt if substantially all use during the calendar year is by employees, their spouses, and their dependent children and the facility is operated by the employer on premises owned or leased by the employer.		
De minimis (minimal) benefits	Exempt	Exempt	Exempt
Dependent care assistance	Exempt[3] up to certain limits, $5,000 ($2,500 for married employee filing separate return).		
Educational assistance	Exempt up to $5,250 of benefits each year. (See Educational Assistance, later.)		
Employee discounts	Exempt[3] up to certain limits. (See Employee Discounts , later.)		
Employee stock options	See Employee Stock Options , later.		
Group-term life insurance coverage	Exempt	Exempt[1,4] up to cost of $50,000 of coverage. (Special rules apply to former employees.)	Exempt
Health savings accounts (HSAs)	Exempt for qualified individuals up to the HSA contribution limits. (See Health Savings Accounts, later.)		
Lodging on your business premises	Exempt[1] if furnished for your convenience as a condition of employment.		
Meals	Exempt if furnished on your business premises for your convenience.		
	Exempt if *de minimis*.		
Moving expense reimbursements	Exempt[1] if expenses would be deductible if the employee had paid them.		
No-additional-cost services	Exempt[3]	Exempt[3]	Exempt[3]
Retirement planning services	Exempt[5]	Exempt[5]	Exempt[5]
Transportation (commuting) benefits	Exempt[1] up to certain limits if for rides in a commuter highway vehicle and/or transit passes ($120, but see the *Caution* on page 1), qualified parking ($230), or qualified bicycle commuting reimbursement[6] ($20). (See *Transportation*, later.)		
	Exempt if *de minimis*.		
Tuition reduction	Exempt[3] if for undergraduate education (or graduate education if the employee performs teaching or research activities).		
Volunteer firefighter and emergency medical responder benefits	Exempt	Exempt	Exempt
Working condition benefits	Exempt	Exempt	Exempt

[1] Exemption does not apply to S corporation employees who are 2% shareholders.

[2] Exemption does not apply to certain highly compensated employees under a self-insured plan that favors those employees.

[3] Exemption does not apply to certain highly compensated employees under a program that favors those employees.

[4] Exemption does not apply to certain key employees under a plan that favors those employees.

[5] Exemption does not apply to services for tax preparation, accounting, legal, or brokerage services.

[6] If the employee receives a qualified bicycle commuting reimbursement in a qualified bicycle commuting month, the employee cannot receive commuter highway vehicle, transit pass, or qualified parking benefits in that same month.

Source: IRS Publication 15-B, Fully or Partially Tax-Exempt Benefits.

Considerations in Providing Benefits Programs

How do we create and then administer a benefits program in our workforce? There are several things that we need to understand before creating the program so that we create a system that is both valuable to the employees and affordable for the organization. Remember that our goal is to have a program that increases employee motivation and engagement and can help create a competitive advantage.

LO 13.3

Briefly discuss the major considerations in providing benefits programs.

Amounts

The first issue that we need to understand is how much money the company can afford (or is willing to afford) to provide an employee benefits program. How much are we willing to spend on our employees? Many companies will calculate this as a percentage of direct compensation. We may analyze the current situation and come to the conclusion that we are able to provide a 40% premium to direct compensation for the cost of benefits. We have to be very careful in our consideration of the amounts available for employee benefits programs. As with other types of compensation, if we tell our employees that we will provide a benefit that they value and then fail to follow through for any reason, it is just as damaging to motivation and engagement as any other type of management action that breaks the equity theory process discussed in Chapter 11. We need to make absolutely sure that we will have the funds available if we commit to providing the benefit.

Mix

Once we know how much money is available for benefits, we need to decide what types of benefits we will offer. Here again, the number of different types of benefits has exploded over the past 40 years. In the 1960s and 1970s, most companies had limited benefits programs. They might have offered their employees a retirement benefit, health insurance, life and disability insurance, and possibly dental care, but nobody ever thought about providing "doggy day care" or a "nap room" (two modern-day benefits in some companies)! Today, the number and type of benefits available in some company programs are limited only by the imagination of the employees of the firm.

As an example, companies today may provide a transportation subsidy such as a vehicle allowance, a public transportation voucher, free parking near the office, a parking voucher, alternative vehicle allowances (for buying "green" vehicles), allowances for bicycles and places for bike parking, or a van or shuttle service to take employees to work and back home, and this is just benefits associated with transporting the worker to and from work. The company can provide onsite child care, child care vouchers, sick child care, paid child care leave, elder care, and/or pet care. So we can quickly see how large the pool of potential employee benefits can become. We have to decide which of the options is going to provide our workforce with the best benefits package for the money spent.

Flexibility

Finally, we need to consider how much flexibility we are willing to build into our benefits program because flexible options are very important to today's employees. Flexible benefits programs allow employees to pick from a set of benefits in some way. The employee can, at least for a portion of their benefits package, choose one type of benefit over another in flexible benefit plans. In a recent survey, 87% of respondents said that flexibility in the offered benefits package would be extremely or very important in deciding whether to take a new job or not.[8] Why do we need to build flexibility into our benefits programs? Because

Riding a bike to work provides exercise as well as transportation.

the mix of workers is so broad, we need to allow at least some flexibility in our system so that it can be partially tailored to the needs of the worker.

We need to be careful, though. If an unlimited amount of flexibility is allowed in the benefits program, some bad consequences can occur. First, it can cost the company a lot of money to manage. The more choices that we allow and the more we let people mix them to fit their personal needs, the more difficult the paperwork associated with the benefits program becomes. Another major issue in allowing unlimited flexibility is that sometimes our employees don't make the best choices. A young employee may decide that they don't need health care coverage and opt for more vacation time instead. If they then get seriously ill, it can literally bankrupt the employee. Finally, we can lose some of the value in volume buying if we don't have enough employees choose a particular benefit. We will get into the reasons behind these issues later in the chapter. Right now let's get into a review of the mandatory and voluntary benefits available in 21st-century companies.

WORK
APPLICATION 13-2

How important is benefit flexibility to you? How does benefit flexibility affect employment where you work or have worked?

LO 13.4

Identify and summarize the major statutory benefits required by federal law.

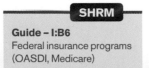

SHRM

Guide – I:B6
Federal insurance programs (OASDI, Medicare)

Statutory Benefits

Statutory benefits are benefits that are required by law. There are a number of benefits that are required by federal laws in the United States and in many other countries. There are also laws that apply if the company chooses certain optional, or nonmandatory, benefits in certain cases. Let's now review the major mandatory benefits that are generally required in U.S. firms.

Social Security and Medicare

By far the largest of the statutory programs, in both size and cost to employers (and employees), are Social Security and Medicare. The combined contributions to the Old-Age, Survivors, and Disability Insurance (OASDI) and Medicare programs were over $860 billion in 2010.[9] To put that in perspective, the total federal revenue collected in 2010 was expected to be about $2.2 trillion.[10] This means that this one group of programs cost almost 40% of all federal revenues in 2010.

Employers and employees are required to provide funds for Social Security benefits. The program was created with the passage of the Social Security Act of 1935. The act created a series of programs for social welfare of the population of the United States, including OASDI, Medicare for the elderly and disabled individuals, and several other lesser-known programs. Since these programs are so complex, and this is an introductory overview of the field of HRM, the best that we can do in this text is to provide some general information on the programs.

How much money does the employee's Social Security benefit cost, and who pays for it? The employer and employee jointly pay into Social Security, through withholdings from the employee's paycheck and a mandatory employer payment. Each of them pays 6.2% of the employee's total pay for a pay period into OASDI and 1.45% of the employee's pay into the Medicare fund. The 6.2% contribution is only withheld up to a maximum salary of $106,800 (in 2010),[11] and then it stops, but the 1.45% tax for Medicare is paid on all income, no matter how large. So the combined amount sent to the federal government is 15.3% of the employee's income, half from the employer and half from the employee.

How does an employee become eligible for OASDI benefits? As a general rule, the individual must receive 40 "credits" in their lifetime in order to become eligible for Social Security *retirement*. They must earn $1,120 in one quarter (in 2010) in order to receive one credit. The amount of earnings required to receive one credit rises each year as average earnings rise. The 40 credits do not have to be in consecutive quarters—the individual does not have to work for 10 years without a break in employment—and more than one credit can be earned in a quarter (if a person made $2,240 in a quarter, they would earn two credits), but a person can only earn four credits per year.[12] However, the 40-credit rule does not necessarily apply to *disability or survivor* benefits. While we would normally need 40 credits in order to be eligible for disability payments, if we were disabled before we could reasonably earn the 40 credits, we might become eligible earlier. For example, if disabled before age 24, you could qualify for disability benefits with as few as six credits in the three years prior to becoming disabled.[13]

Retirement

Once an employee becomes eligible through earning 40 credits and meeting the retirement age requirements, they can receive a monthly check, but is that monthly check supposed to help the employee maintain the lifestyle that they had before retirement? What percentage of preretirement pay was Social Security originally designed to provide upon retirement? It was only designed to pay about 30% of preretirement income. Social Security was never designed to replace 100% of preretirement income. However, many employees plan on it as their only retirement. As HR Managers, part of your job will be to make employees aware that they need to also *save* for retirement. The savings rate in the United States compared to many other developed countries is low. In 1990, the U.S. savings rate was around 7%, but by 2005 had dropped to less than 1.5% and in 2010 had recovered to about 5.8%.[14] This compares with savings rates in excess of 10% in Germany, Switzerland, and Belgium. The common recommendation is to start with your first full-time job by putting 10% of your income into a retirement fund every month, no matter how low or high your income is, and always take advantage of matching benefits from your employer.[15]

The key to having money at retirement is to start saving at a young age to take advantage of compound interest rates of return.

Exhibit 13-2	Full Social Security Retirement Age[16]

Age to Receive Full Social Security Benefits	
Year of Birth	**Full Retirement Age**
1937 or earlier	65 years
1938	65 years and 2 months
1939	65 years and 4 months
1940	65 years and 6 months
1941	65 years and 8 months
1942	65 years and 10 months
1943–1954	66 years
1955	66 years and 2 months
1956	66 years and 4 months
1957	66 years and 6 months
1958	66 years and 8 months
1959	66 years and 10 months
1960 and later	67 years

Source: U.S. Social Security Administration.

WORK
APPLICATION 13-4

Using Exhibit 13-2, at what age can you expect to collect full Social Security?

At what age are we eligible for Social Security retirement? If you were born in 1937 or earlier, you would be eligible for retirement at age 65. If you were born in 1960 or later, your retirement age is 67. For those born between 1937 and 1960, it is based on a sliding scale. Take a look at Exhibit 13-2. If you were born in 1956, you would be eligible for full retirement benefits from Social Security at age 66 years and 4 months.

One of the most interesting things to look at is how many people lived to be age 65 when Social Security was set up. In 1935, approximately 6% of the population was age 65 or older, but in the year 2009 that number was about 12.3%. The Social Security program was designed around a retiree population of 6%, but that has more than doubled. This is one of the issues with the way Social Security is set up today and one of the reasons that the program constantly has to be reevaluated. The changes in life span and changes in income that have occurred over the past 70 years have made the program unsustainable in its current form.

Another major issue in Social Security is the large number of baby boomers who are starting to retire with fewer younger workers paying into the Social Security system. The Social Security Board of Governors has noted that "projected long-run program costs for both Medicare and Social Security are not sustainable under currently scheduled financing, and will require legislative corrections if disruptive consequences for beneficiaries and taxpayers are to be avoided."[17] The Board of Governors estimates that the OASDI component of Social Security will have greater outflows of funds than it takes in beginning in 2023 and will exhaust its funds in 2036 if such legislative corrections are not undertaken.[18]

What about early retirement? Can a person retire earlier than age 65–67? Yes, but their benefits will be *permanently* reduced. For example, if an employee is eligible for retirement at age 65, they can take early retirement and get an 80% benefit at age 62. That 20% reduction is forever, not just until they reach age 65. If an individual is not eligible for full retirement benefits until age 67 (they were born after 1960), the reduction is 30% at age 62—again for the life of the retirement benefit.

Disability and Survivor Benefits

These components are really basically the same benefit. If an employee becomes disabled or dies, and is otherwise eligible, the disability or survivor benefit will apply in most cases. The employee (or their survivors) will get payments each month roughly equal to what the employee would have gotten in retirement based on their historical earnings. If the employee is disabled for at least five months and is expected to be disabled for at least 12 months, Social Security disability will be allowed. The disability must last at least 12 months or be expected to cause the covered person's death.

Survivor benefits can go to a widow/widower over age 60; any child or grandchild who is a dependent of the deceased and is under age 18; or any dependent parent over 62. If an individual has survivors in multiple categories, then the survivor benefit gets split among eligible survivors.

Medicare

Finally, there is the Medicare component. Individuals become eligible for Medicare at the same time as their eligibility for Social Security retirement begins. There are currently four parts to Medicare:

- **Part A** is Hospital Insurance (HI). Hospitalization basically covers the inpatient care of a retiree in a hospital, skilled nursing facility, or hospice.
- **Part B** covers non-hospital-related Medical Services Insurance (MSI).
- **Part C** Medicare recipients can also now choose this option instead of Part A and Part B. Option C combines Part A (HI) and Part B (MSI) coverage in a plan similar to an HMO or a PPO (we will talk about these in detail shortly). Private insurance companies approved by Medicare provide this coverage. Costs may be lower than in the original Medicare Part A and B plans, and the insured may get extra benefits.
- **Part D** is a prescription drug benefit. Parts A and B are basically automatic upon the individual's retirement. The retiree has to elect to participate in Part C and/or Part D.

Medicare is not completely free to the retiree. The covered person has to pay copayments and deductibles of various types, the details of which are beyond the scope of this text. But understand that there are out-of-pocket costs involved with Medicare. There are also limitations on what is covered. So Medicare provides basic medical benefits, but it is not a perfect full-coverage program by any means.

Workers' Compensation

The next statutory benefit is workers' compensation. **Workers' compensation** is *an insurance program designed to provide medical treatment and temporary payments to employees who cannot work because of an employment-related injury or illness.* "Employment-related" means that the illness or injury has to do with the worker's actions for the company, although the injury or illness doesn't have to happen while actually at work. For instance, if an employee is traveling through an airport as part of their job, and picks up their suitcase, injuring their back, this is an "employment-related" injury.

SHRM

Guide – I:B22
Workers' compensation

The workers' compensation program is paid for by employers—employees pay none of the cost of workers' compensation insurance. Workers' compensation payments to sick or injured employees are not permanent in most cases. The program was created to provide workers with *short-term* relief because of work-related injuries or illnesses. Social Security disability, on the other hand, generally provides long-term relief in the form of disability payments. Workers' compensation does, however, pay a survivor benefit in the case of death of the employee.

Workers' compensation is a type of "no-fault" insurance, which means that it doesn't matter which party—the employer or the employee—was at fault. In an accident- or illness-related situation, the insurance will be paid out to the party harmed. Why is no-fault such an issue? The main reason is the problems that would occur if the employee had to sue in court. First, there would almost certainly be animosity between the employer and the employee if the employer were to be sued. It would also take significant time to get the case settled and for the injured party (if the decision went in their favor) to receive compensation. The employer's maximum liability is also limited by workers' compensation. Without it, the employer could potentially be bankrupted by a single employment accident or incident, especially if an employee were killed. In all but situations of gross negligence or intent to harm, neither party can take the other to court over compensation for such an injury or illness because of the no-fault nature of the insurance. So the ability to provide no-fault insurance in this circumstance is valuable to both parties.

Workers' compensation is mandatory in 49 of the 50 United States, and is governed by different laws in each state. It is elective in Texas.[19] In the states where it is mandatory, employers must purchase workers' compensation insurance in order to operate their business. In Texas, companies can choose not to purchase insurance, but in fact many still do. Why would they buy this insurance if it is not mandatory? The simple answer is that it is cheaper than losing a court case concerning an employee injury. Here again, if there isn't an insurance policy in place, the employee can, and likely will, sue the company because they are unable to work. As most of you have seen in the newspaper, these types of court cases may provide very large awards to injured parties. It is likely that workers' compensation insurance is a very low-cost method to insure against a very large potential jury award. Of course, the company can get a blanket liability policy that would cover on-the-job injuries, but it might be much more expensive than workers' compensation insurance, and the company could still be bankrupted by a lawsuit if the liability policy limits were exceeded.

Just how expensive is workers' compensation insurance? It varies, but *as an average* it generally costs between 1.5% and 2% of payroll for most companies.[20] It can go much higher than this, though, in some cases. Rates are primarily determined by three factors:

1. **Occupations.** Within a company, what are the risks of injury associated with each job? Some occupations are much more risky than others. For instance, it costs a lot more to insure firefighters, police officers, and construction workers than it does to cover office workers, sales clerks in a mall, and librarians.

2. **Experience ratings.** An **experience rating** is a measure of *how often claims are made against an insurance policy.* A company's workers' compensation experience rating is basically calculated on the frequency and severity of injuries that occur within that company. There are companies that are in dangerous industries, but they have very few on-the-job injuries because they have very strong safety programs, while other companies in the same industry might have really high injury rates because they don't pay as much attention to safety. Experience ratings can significantly affect a company's workers' compensation costs.

3. **Level of benefits payable.** Injured workers will get compensated based on their particular state's workers' compensation rating manual. This manual provides the required payout rates for various types of injuries. For instance, an amputation of a finger other than the index finger or thumb might provide the employee with a small, one-time payment, but amputation of an arm below the elbow would cost much more. Individual states can set the rates for injuries within the state's boundaries, and these rates affect the cost of workers' compensation insurance.

If you read the previous paragraph closely, you will notice that the company has some control over their workers' compensation rates. The experience rating figures heavily into the company cost of providing this insurance, so if we can lower our experience rating, we can lower our insurance cost as well. And the savings associated with a low experience rating aren't just one-time savings; they continue to lower our costs for as long as we maintain a safer than average work environment (we will discuss safety further in the next chapter). This is an area that HR Managers need to understand so that they can lower company costs for workers' compensation insurance.

Who manages and monitors the workers' compensation programs? State governments have the primary authority for managing their state's program. However, the insurance doesn't come from the state itself. The insurance is almost always provided by a private insurance company that provides workers' compensation insurance in that state. Each state has an insurance commission that authorizes insurance firms to operate in that state, and if insurance companies choose to offer workers' compensation insurance in a particular state, they have to follow that state's guidelines. The company approaches a private insurer for workers' compensation insurance and purchases a policy from whichever state-licensed insurer that they choose.

What if the company has a poor experience rating because of excessive accidents? In such a case, the insurers may choose not to provide insurance to the company because the risk to the insurance firm is too great. In this situation, the company that has been denied insurance can go to the state Workers' Compensation Commission and ask to be covered in the workers' compensation pool. The pool is made up of insurers who provide workers' compensation policies in the state. Each insurer that is licensed to provide such insurance has to be part of the pool. The state commission will then assign the company requesting coverage to one of the insurers, and the insurer will have to write the policy for the company that was previously denied coverage.

The pool assignments are usually based on the percent share of each insurer's policies within the state. For instance, if one insurer writes workers' compensation policies that cover 13% of all employees in the state of Arkansas, they would be asked to cover about 13% of the employees whose companies have to resort to the state pool for coverage. While this is a simplified example, it gives you an idea of how companies can get insured, even if no insurance company is willing to cover the risks associated with an employer with a poor experience rating. Remember, though, that the cost associated with being in the state pool is significantly more in most cases than it is if the company can get insurance coverage without becoming part of the pool.

Because of their industry and their experience rating, there are cases where companies are spending significant amounts of money on workers' compensation. In some cases, as much as 25% of a company's total personnel costs can come from workers' compensation costs if they are in a high-risk business and their experience rating is also high. Obviously, it can be different from company to company. But again, we can actually lower our experience rating by providing safety training as discussed in the next chapter.

WORK
APPLICATION 13-5

How would you rate the risk of occupational injury or illness where you work(ed)? Is it high, moderate, or low? Why?

SHRM

Guide – I:B16
Unemployment Insurance

Unemployment Insurance

The third statutory benefit is Unemployment Insurance. **Unemployment Insurance (UI)** *provides workers who lose their jobs with continuing subsistence payments from their state for a specified period of time.* It is a federally mandated program, but is managed and administered separately by each of the states. UI originated under the Social Security Act of 1935, and is applied as a tax on the *employers*—"Only Alaska, New Jersey, and Pennsylvania levy UI taxes on workers."[21] The basic federal tax rate is set at 6.2% of wages earned (in 2011) for the first $7,000 in individual wages, but this rate can be (and generally is) reduced by up to 5.4% if the employer pays their state unemployment taxes on time and avoids tax delinquencies. A minimum of 5.4% of the first $7,000 paid to each employee goes to the state unemployment fund, and 0.8% goes to the federal government.

In addition to the federal minimum of 6.2%, states can vary the tax rate and effective wage rate within their borders. Here again, as in workers' compensation, the tax rate is also affected by the company's "experience rating." Employers who tend to terminate more employees who are eligible for UI benefits have a higher experience rating and, as a result, a higher UI tax rate.[22] So, within the same state, some employers will pay much more in UI taxes than other employers will.

What is the logic behind UI? It is there to allow people to continue to have at least some purchasing power even when they are unemployed. If UI was not available, when the country experienced a recession, many individuals and families would stop spending, as much as they possibly could. This could cause the recession to deepen even more and make it more difficult for the economy to recover because consumer spending is the largest input into the national economy. If, however, unemployed individuals are provided with some funds, the overall economy is not harmed as much as it would otherwise be. In ordinary times, when unemployment rates are not very high, unemployment payments are capped at 26 weeks per recipient in most states. However, in times of high unemployment this can be (and usually is) extended. In the most recent U.S. recession, some states with very high unemployment rates were allowed to extend unemployment benefits to as long as 99 weeks—nearly two years!

How does an individual become eligible for UI? What has to happen? They have to be terminated from employment, through either downsizing, layoff, or other processes, and in most cases must have worked in four of the last five quarters and meet minimum income guidelines in each of those quarters. What makes them *ineligible*? A series of things can occur that make the individual ineligible:

- They quit voluntarily.

- They fail to look for work.

- They were terminated "for cause" (because they did something wrong).

- They refuse suitable work (work comparable to what they were doing prior to being terminated).

- They, as a member of a union, participated in a strike against the company (in most states).

- They become self-employed.

- They fail to disclose any monies earned in a period of unemployment.

What does the individual receive in the way of UI benefits? Generally the weekly benefit is about 60% of what the person was making when they were employed, but this also varies some by state, and there is a cap on the amount that will be paid out in unemployment benefits. So if the individual was highly paid, in some states they may only receive 25% (or even less) of their prior weekly pay because of the cap.

The Family and Medical Leave Act of 1993

The next mandatory benefit is Family and Medical Leave Act of 1993 leave, more commonly known as FMLA leave. The act requires that the employer provide unpaid leave for an "eligible employee" when faced with any of the following situations:[23]

Leave of 12 workweeks in a 12-month period:

- for the birth of a child and to care for the newborn child within one year of birth;
- for the placement with the employee of a child for adoption or foster care and to care for the newly placed child within one year of placement;
- to care for the employee's spouse, child, or parent who has a serious health condition;
- for a serious health condition that makes the employee unable to perform the essential functions of his or her job; or
- for any qualifying exigency arising out of the fact that the employee's spouse, son, daughter, or parent is a covered military member on "covered active duty."

Leave of 26 workweeks during a single 12-month period to care for a covered service member with a serious injury or illness who is the spouse, son, daughter, parent, or next of kin to the employee (military caregiver leave).

In addition, upon the employee's return from FMLA leave, they must be restored to their original job or one that is equivalent in pay, benefits, and other terms and conditions of employment.

Any private sector employer is covered under the act if they have 50 or more employees who worked at least 20 weeks during the year, working within a 75-mile radius of a central location.

Eligible employees must:

- work for a covered employer;
- have worked for the employer for a total of 12 months (not necessarily consecutive); and
- have worked at least 1,250 hours over the previous 12 months.

The act also exempts some eligible employees. "A salaried eligible employee who is among the highest paid 10 percent of the employees employed by the employer within 75 miles of the facility at which the employee is employed"[24] is exempted from FMLA leave and can be denied restoration of their job if they utilize their "eligible employee" status to take such leave.

Reasons to deny leave include:[25]

- such denial is necessary to prevent substantial and grievous economic injury to the operations of the employer;
- the employer notifies the employee of the intent of the employer to deny restoration on such basis at the time the employer determines that such injury would occur; and
- in any case in which the leave has commenced, the employee elects not to return to employment after receiving such notice.

One of the problems that employers run into with FMLA is the definition of "serious health condition." Under FMLA, a **serious health condition** *means an illness, an injury, an* *impairment, or a physical or mental condition that involves either inpatient care or continuing care for at least three consecutive days*, but there is strong evidence that FMLA leave is heavily abused. In a 2007 survey, SHRM notes that 63% of employers surveyed had reported chronic abuse of intermittent (FMLA) leave by employees.[26] All an employee needs in order to be able to claim FMLA leave is a document from a health care provider that says that they have such a serious health condition. When President Bill Clinton pushed the law through during his first term, the intent of the law was noble. However, the execution left something to be desired for businesses dealing with abuse of this benefit.

Why are there problems with the law? The employer has little leeway when an employee requests FMLA leave and has documentation of a serious health condition. They have to cover the costs of not having the employee at work (and we talked about the costs of absenteeism in Chapter 1). The law also says that we have to give at least 90% (remember, we can exempt the top 10%) of our employees up to 12 weeks of FMLA leave per year and then have to give them their job back, or a comparable job. So if we have 50 employees who work within 75 miles of a central location, we would have to allow up to 45 of those employees to miss up to a quarter of the work year, every year. This puts a huge burden on both HR and operational managers in the firm, and it can easily affect morale of the other employees who have to take up the slack for the employee who is on FMLA leave.

Because of the burden that FMLA can create, employers want to make sure to the best of their ability that employees are not abusing FMLA. One thing that the employer can do to lower abuse is to enforce the requirement that employees give 30 days' advance notice of intent to use FMLA leave if they know that it will be needed. The law also says that if an employee cannot foresee the need 30 days ahead of time, they must provide notice to the company as soon as practicable—usually within one day of learning of the need for FMLA leave, and if the need is emergent (for example, an employee is hurt in a car accident), they must notify the employer as soon as possible. Employers also have the right to require that the reason behind a request for FMLA leave be documented by a health care provider, at the employee's expense. The employer can also require a second or even third opinion on such reasons for FMLA leave (at the *employer's* expense), as well as requiring periodic certification of the continuing need for FMLA leave when the condition lasts for an extended period of time. Employers should typically get a second certification when it is suspected that an employee is abusing FMLA.

Companies can additionally require that employees substitute paid leave and completely use such leave up before taking unpaid FMLA leave as long as that is the employer's normal policy. And they can recover health care premiums that were paid to an employee on FMLA leave if the employee doesn't return to work.

Additional employer requirements include the requirement to post notice of FMLA benefits prominently in the workplace and to also include this notice in either an employee handbook or other written guidance to employees when they are hired. Employers must also maintain health insurance coverage for the employee on FMLA leave if such health benefits are normally provided.

Many employees want to have time to spend with their family.

All in all, even though FMLA requires only *unpaid* leave, the costs to the company are significant. It puts a significant strain on businesses, especially small businesses. The HR Department usually bears a large part of the burden of monitoring and curbing abuses in FMLA leave, and must be aware of the rules and regulations in order to apply the law correctly.

The Patient Protection and Affordable Care Act of 2010

The last mandatory benefit is the Patient Protection and Affordable Care Act of 2010 (PPACA). This act mandates that all employers with more than 50 employees will provide their employees with health care coverage by 2014 or face penalties for failing to do so. While this law is currently being challenged in several different courts for different reasons, for the moment it stands as a statutory benefit that employers have to be aware of and follow. The major provisions of the law are presented in Exhibit 13-3, by the year in which they become effective.

Exhibit 13-3	PPACA

2010

- Children can stay on parents' health care insurance until age 26.
- Insurance companies are banned from rescinding coverage when the covered individual gets sick, and from imposing lifetime caps on benefits.
- Children with preexisting conditions can't be excluded from health care coverage.

2011

- Employers have to disclose the value of employee health insurance on IRS form W-2.
- Flexible Spending Accounts (FSA—we will talk about these later in the chapter) will no longer allow nonprescription medicines to be reimbursed.
- Medicaid will begin providing preventive care services to beneficiaries with no out-of-pocket cost.

2013

- FSA contributions are limited to $2,500 per year.
- High wage earners will have an additional 0.9% Medicare tax on earnings in excess of the current limit. This additional tax starts at $200,000 for individual earnings or $250,000 for joint returns.
- Employers must notify employees of state health insurance exchanges.

2014*

- Employers with more than 50 employees will be required to offer health benefits or face penalties—called "pay or play."
  - Businesses with fewer than 50 Full-Time Equivalents will not be penalized for failing to carry employer health coverage.
  - Businesses with more than 50 Full-Time Equivalents will be fined $2,000 per full-time equivalent minus the first 30 Full-Time Equivalents.
  - Businesses with more than 200 Full-Time Equivalents will be required to offer health insurance.
- State health insurance exchanges must be operational.
- Insurers will be banned from restricting coverage or providing differential premiums based on health of the covered individual.

* Originally, the plan called for employers who offer health insurance to provide vouchers as a choice for health coverage through exchanges if the employer's health plan was between 8% and 9.8% of the individual employee's household income beginning in 2014. This requirement was repealed during a budget compromise in April 2011.

The "pay or play" penalty in Exhibit 13-3 applies to *Full-Time Equivalent (FTE) employees*. Full-Time Equivalents are workers putting in 30 or more hours per week plus the number of part-time hours per month divided by 120. For example, if a company has 42 employees who work 40 or more hours per week, 22 employees who work less than 40 hours per week but more than 30, and 25 employees who work less than 30 hours per week and worked a total of 1,500 hours per month (an average of 68 hours per month, or about 15 hours per week), the calculation of FTEs would be as follows:

42	22 (1,500 / 120)	76.5 (rounded up to 77)
Traditional full-time employees	All employees working more than 30 hours are considered full-time	The number of part-time hours divided by 120

If this company chose not to provide health insurance, they would have to pay a fine of $94,000: 77 FTEs minus 30 FTEs leaves 47; 47 × $2,000 = $94,000.

Another provision of the law is that employees not covered by a health care plan at work will be *required* to go to the state health exchange where they can purchase individual coverage. Individuals who fail to gain coverage will also be fined, although the minimum fine in the first year (2014) is very low ($95 per person), but this amount is indexed based on the individual's earnings, so it can be much higher. In 2015 the minimum individual cost will be $325, and the penalty goes to a minimum of $695 in 2016, and is indexed for inflation after that year. The total amount of the penalty for a family will not exceed $2,250.

Many experts predict that up to one third of businesses may choose to pay the fine rather than provide health insurance, because the fine is less expensive. The average cost for coverage of a full-time worker in 2011 was a little over $4,400,[27] so a $2,000 penalty may be the lesser of two evils for companies that are struggling with profitability.

"Qualified" plans (plans that meet the guidelines of the law) will have to pay at least 60% of allowed charges and meet some minimum benefit standards. The plan must also be "affordable," which means it will not exceed 9.5% of the employee's household income. If an employer offers a plan that is not "qualified and affordable," they will be fined $3,000 annually for each employee who goes to the health care exchange for coverage. So, for an employer with more than 50 employees but fewer than 200, offering *no* plan is cheaper than offering a plan that isn't qualified and affordable—it costs them $2,000 per employee to have no coverage, but $3,000 to have nonqualifying coverage.

Statutory Requirements When Providing Certain Voluntary Benefits

Guide – I:B5
Regulation of health insurance programs (COBRA, HIPAA, HMOs)

Let's take a look now at some legal requirements if we choose to provide certain benefits to our employees. These requirements don't apply unless we make the choice to give our employees health insurance or company-sponsored retirement plans.

The Consolidated Omnibus Budget Reconciliation Act of 1985

SHRM

Guide – B:33
The Consolidated Omnibus Budget Reconciliation Act

If employers choose to provide health insurance, we have to abide by COBRA. The **Consolidated Omnibus Budget Reconciliation Act (COBRA)** is *a law that requires employers to offer to maintain health insurance on individuals who leave their employment (for a period of time)*. The individual former employee has to pay for the insurance, but the employer is required to keep the former employee on their group insurance policy.

Why is this law significant? Primarily because buying an individual health insurance policy is much more expensive than buying insurance for a group of people. According to Smart Money, "Buying individual health insurance isn't as easy as having a clean bill of health and enough cash . . . Should an insurer agree to provide coverage, it will almost certainly be costly and confusing. The average out-of-pocket costs for people insured individually is almost double what people covered by an employer pay."[28] So this option will save people money over buying health insurance on their own. Another reason that it is significant is that in most cases people don't leave one job and start another on the same day, so they will have a gap in their health coverage if they don't utilize COBRA coverage. COBRA allows coverage after termination of employment of at least 18 months and as many as 36 months in some limited cases. This period is usually sufficient to allow an individual to leave one job, gain employment elsewhere, and switch to the new employer's health care plan without losing health coverage for the individual and their family.

COBRA applies to companies with 20 or more Full-Time Equivalent employees. It is required to be offered to both terminated employees and those who voluntarily quit, in most cases. An interesting thing about this law is that it doesn't make failure to comply illegal. It instead denies a tax deduction that employers who provide group health coverage for their employees could otherwise take if they fail to comply with the COBRA regulations and has been amended to charge an excise tax on employers who are not in compliance. So the employer's effective tax rate goes up significantly if they fail to comply with COBRA rules.[29]

There are some other things that you need to understand about COBRA from both an employee and an employer standpoint. The employee, as noted earlier, has to pay the premium for health insurance continuation. The company can also charge the former employee a fee of up to 2% above the premium cost for administration. But even at 102% of the basic premium cost, COBRA coverage is almost always a good deal for the former employee, again because of the power of buying in bulk.

Why don't more former employees choose to continue their insurance under COBRA? In most cases it is because of the cost of paying the premium, especially if they will be out of work for a period of time. We all know that health insurance is becoming more and more expensive, and most individuals can't afford to pay all of the insurance premium if they are out of work. However, as HR Managers, we need to remember that federal law requires that we offer COBRA to individuals who leave our employment. The American Recovery and Reinvestment Act of 2009 (ARRA) also added a new requirement to the COBRA rules that employers need to be aware of—companies will be required to "front" a 65% subsidy of the COBRA cost of health continuation coverage for qualified employees who lost their jobs between September 2008 and December 2009. This means that the employer must pay this cost and then file for a reimbursement of the cost on their quarterly payroll tax deposits. This is significantly different from providing COBRA coverage for individuals who lost their jobs outside of this period.

The Health Insurance Portability and Accountability Act of 1996

The Health Insurance Portability and Accountability Act of 1996 (HIPAA) is another health insurance mandate from the federal government *if* the company provides health insurance to its employees. Only part of the HIPAA law applies directly to all employers. What are the general provisions of HIPAA that all employers need to understand?

First, HIPAA requires that our health insurance be *portable*. This means that if we had group health insurance at our previous employer and if our new employer has health care coverage for their employees, they are required to provide us the opportunity to participate in their health insurance plan. Why wouldn't the new company want us to participate in their plan? Well, if we had a preexisting condition that required a lot of health care expense, the new employer's premiums might go up.

One of the factors that created the impetus for HIPAA was the growing threat of HIV infection and AIDS in the United States in the 1980s and 1990s. If an individual were

LO 13.5

Identify the main statutory requirements that must be followed if organizations choose to provide health care or retirement plans for their employees.

SHRM

Guide – B:34
The American Recovery and Reinvestment Act of 2009

SHRM

Guide – B:37
The Health Insurance Portability and Accountability Act of 1996

infected with HIV, their medical costs and those of their company's group health care plan would go up drastically. If they tried to change jobs, new employers would refuse to cover them on the company's group health plans based on their preexisting condition. This effectively kept the individual employee who was HIV-positive held captive at their current employer, because if they left their health insurance would most likely not be allowed at the new employer. This was considered to be an unfair consequence of being ill, and legislation was created to require businesses and insurance companies to cover new employees who had been covered under their previous employer's plan.

The second issue that is mandatory for all employers under HIPAA is the *privacy* and *security* requirements for medical information on employees. This is the *accountability* part of HIPAA. HIPAA protects "the privacy of individually identifiable health information" from being disclosed to unauthorized individuals.[30] It also provides that employers must take action to ensure the security of personal health information. The *privacy* rule requires that covered firms take "reasonable steps to limit the use or disclosure of, and requests for, protected health information." The *security* rule requires covered firms to have "appropriate administrative, technical, and physical safeguards to protect the privacy of protected health information" for individual employees.[31] So COBRA and HIPAA are mandatory if we as an employer offer health insurance to our employees.

In addition to its effects on COBRA, the ARRA also created new HIPAA privacy and security requirements for companies with group health plans. Most privacy and security rules originally created by HIPAA were limited to the covered entities, including group health benefit plans. The ARRA "has extended HIPAA's privacy and security rules to business associates and other vendors directly, and has enhanced HIPAA's civil and criminal penalties."[32] New "notice requirements" for an inadvertent release of Protected Health Information (PHI) are also included under the ARRA.

The Employee Retirement Income Security Act of 1974

SHRM

Guide – B:7
The Employee Retirement
Income Security Act of 1974

The first two government mandates that we discussed are contingent on company actions in companies that choose to provide *group health insurance* to their employees. However, the last one that we will discuss is contingent on the employer providing a *group retirement plan*. Employee Retirement Income Security Act of 1974 (ERISA) guidance must be followed if the company provides a retirement plan. Let's take a look at the main provisions of ERISA.

SHRM

Guide – I:B3
Regulation of retirement
plans (FLSA, ERISA,
Pension Protection
Act of 2006)

Eligibility. One of the major provisions of ERISA is guidance on retirement (pension) plan eligibility. If the company provides employees with a retirement plan, the guidelines in ERISA say that the plan has to be available to all employees over 21 years of age who have worked in the company for one year. This brings up a common question in such laws. Can the company offer retirement options to employees who are not yet 21 or who haven't worked there for a year? The answer is yes. The company can *relax* the requirements of ERISA, but cannot be more restricting than the law allows. This is the case in many similar laws and federal regulations.

Why was this requirement created? It was done primarily because companies were setting rules for participation in their retirement plans that excluded many of their employees—in fact in some cases only allowing executives and managers to participate, while the work of others subsidized the cost of the plan. This was publicized by various news stories, and ultimately Congress decided to act to make these plans more open and fair to all employees. So, ERISA rules now say that employers who have a pension plan must allow everyone over age 21 who has worked for them for more than one year to participate in the program.

Vesting. A second major provision of ERISA is the vesting rules. **Vesting** *provides for a maximum amount of time beyond which the employee will have unfettered access to their retirement funds, both employee contributions and employer contributions.* Most retirement plans today take in contributions from both the employer and the employee. Of course, the employee's money is available to the employee at pretty much any time. There are rules on how the employee can remove money from a "qualified retirement account" (an account that has federal and sometimes state tax advantages associated with it), including the requirement that they reinvest it into another qualified retirement fund within a certain time period, but the money they contribute can be removed from the account when they leave the employer, or even before as long as they follow some IRS rules. ERISA identifies the maximum amount of time that the company can retain *company* contributions to the employee's retirement account. The rules in ERISA say that the employer must vest the employee in all employer contributions based on one of two options:

- 100% of employer contributions at the end of five years of contributions to the plan; or
- 20% of employer contributions from the end of Year 3 through the end of Year 7.

So if an employer and an employee have been contributing to the employee's retirement fund for five years and the employer has provided $1,000 per year to the account, the employee can take that $5,000 employer contribution out of the retirement fund and move it to any other retirement fund that they choose. Alternately, under the 20%-per-year option, the employee might only be allowed to have access to 20% of $3,000 at the end of Year 3, 40% of $4,000 at the end of Year 4, 60% of $5,000 at the end of Year 5, and so on up until the end of Year 7, when they would have access to all of the employer's contributions to their retirement fund.

Can the company allow the employee to be vested earlier? Of course it can. In some cases companies will immediately vest employees in their own retirement funds as a recruiting incentive. This can be a significant advantage over having to wait five years to have access to employer-provided funds. If we leave the company for a better job after four years and 10 months, we forfeit all of the employer contributions to the fund (in this case about $4,850) if the company doesn't vest us in our retirement fund until five years.

Employers have to be aware that there are a number of factors that may cause retirement plans (as well as other benefits) to be nonqualified. Executive compensation in the form of a deferred contribution to the executive's retirement accounts is one of the most common forms of nonqualified retirement funds. If the benefit doesn't meet the requirements of IRS rules governing qualified retirement plans, the company must treat the contributions to the account as taxable.

> **SHRM**
>
> **Guide – I:B13**
> Nonqualified plans
> for highly paid and
> executive employees

Portability. The third major issue that ERISA addresses is portability of retirement accounts. The portability rule allows us to take our retirement fund and move it from our employer to another qualified fund. The employer cannot require that we keep the funds with them, or under their control. Once the vesting requirements have been met, the employee has the ability to move funds from the employer's control into another qualified retirement account.

Fiduciaries. The next provision of ERISA is the responsibility of individuals acting as fiduciaries for company retirement funds. A fiduciary is a person who has authority over how retirement funds are managed, but also has financial responsibilities associated with that authority. ERISA notes that fiduciaries have the requirement to act under a concept called the *prudent man.* This includes requirements that the fiduciary will act to benefit the fund's participants, will minimize unnecessary expenses to the fund, and will use "care, skill, prudence, and diligence" in managing the funds entrusted to them.

But what is prudence? Is it prudent to put the bulk of retirement investments into dot-com stocks, as many investment managers did prior to the year 2000? What about putting large portions of the fund into financial firm stocks as many did up until 2007–2008? While in hindsight these were probably not good investments, they would have probably passed the *prudent man* standard, so prudence is a pretty minimal standard of diligence for the managers of retirement funds.

PBGC. The last big provision of ERISA is the creation of the Pension Benefit Guaranty Corporation. The **Pension Benefit Guaranty Corporation (PBGC)** is *a governmental corporation established within the Department of Labor whose purpose is to insure retirement funds from failure.* Its main function is to act as an insurer for the benefits promised to employees whose employers go bankrupt or are for other reasons not able to provide the promised retirement benefits to their employees. It covers only "defined benefit" retirement plans (which we will talk about shortly)—plans that have specified benefits that will be paid out to the individual employee on their retirement. The PBGC may not fund 100% of what was promised in the specific retirement plan, but it "guarantees 'basic benefits' earned before the plan's termination date" or the employer's date of bankruptcy.[33] There are also caps on coverage of pensions, which are determined by ERISA.

Who provides funds for the PBGC? In this case, even though the PBGC is a federal government entity, the funds for the program come from employer payments into the program. If an employer chooses to provide "defined benefit" retirement accounts for their employees, they are required to pay into the PBGC. These funds are then used to provide benefits to workers whose employers are unable to pay the promised benefits. So the PBGC acts as a guarantor of these retirement plans.

WORK
APPLICATION 13-6

Which, if any, statutory requirements when providing certain voluntary benefits would be mandatory where you work or have worked?

13-1 APPLYING THE CONCEPT

Statutory Benefit Laws

Identify each statement by its type of statutory benefit law.

a. FMLA
b. PPACA
c. COBRA
d. HIPAA
e. ERISA

_____ 1. I like this law because I can stay on my parents' insurance plan even though I'm out of school and almost 25.

_____ 2. Our company is losing money, so I like this law because it will allow me to move my funds out of my company fund to a new account with the stock broker of my choice.

_____ 3. My father is dying of cancer, so I like this law because it will allow me to take time off from work to take care of him.

_____ 4. I like this law because I am going to quit my job, but I need to continue to have health insurance while I look for a new job.

_____ 5. I like this law because I currently have health insurance and medical problems, but when I change jobs, the new company can't refuse to give me insurance based on my medical problems coming into the firm.

Voluntary Benefits

LO 13.6

Briefly describe the main categories of voluntary benefits available to organizations.

In addition to mandatory benefits, almost all employers provide some group of voluntary benefits to their employees. These can range from a narrow group of commonly provided benefits such as retirement accounts, life insurance, and vacation time, to a very broad group including the company nap rooms to sick-child care services and personal valets. How do companies determine what voluntary benefits they are going to provide? They look at their workforce and the funds available to the company and choose the package that will best allow them to maintain a satisfied and engaged workforce. Let's discuss some of the more common voluntary benefits including Paid Time Off, group health insurance, retirement, and employee insurance.

Paid Time Off

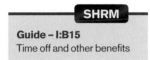

SHRM

Guide – I:B15
Time off and other benefits

Paid Time Off (PTO) benefits include a group of options such as vacation time/annual leave, severance pay, personal time off, sick days, and holidays. Some companies provide an all-encompassing PTO plan that allows the employee to use their Paid Time Off in any way they wish, whether for sick days or vacation, for holidays, or for any other purpose. Others apportion the available days for vacation, sick time, holidays, and others.[34] These benefits contribute approximately 7% of the average employer's total cost of wages and benefits, or 10% of direct wages.[35] Another way to look at this is that the *average cost of paid time off is $1 for every $10 in direct wages*. None of the listed PTO benefits is mandatory in the United States, yet most employers provide at least some holidays off and some vacation and/or sick time. Paid Time Off is commonly viewed as an entitlement (Chapter 12). Let's do a quick review of the most common types of PTO.

Vacation or Annual Leave

SHRM

Guide – I:B21
Paid leave plans

Although federal law does not require any vacation time, the majority of U.S. firms provide paid vacations to their employees, according to the U.S. Bureau of Labor Statistics. In fact, nearly 90% of employers provide vacation time to their full-time workforce.[36] The average vacation time provided was about 15 days in 2007.[37] Why do companies provide this time off? The simple answer is that it refreshes the employee so that they can come back to work and be more productive. There are many studies available that show that when we leave a stressful situation for a period of time, we lower our stress level, which in turn raises our ability to be productive.[38, 39] Good employers know this and, as a result, provide time off to allow their employees to relax.

Sick Leave

The next most popular PTO is sick leave. Approximately three out of four employers in the United States provide sick leave of some type to their employees, whether in an all-encompassing PTO plan or specifically designated as "sick days." Paid sick leave can offer employees relief from loss of income associated with having to miss work due to an illness. However, there is significant evidence that sick leave is abused by employees, especially in the case of a "use it or lose it" sick leave policy. With the entitlement mentality, some employees take every sick day off even though they are not sick. This is one of the reasons why more companies are moving to the total PTO concept instead of designating a specific number of days as sick leave.

Family vacations help employees maintain work and family balance.

Holiday Pay

Nearly all employers provide for at least some paid holidays with their workforce. In 2009, the U.S. government identified 10 federal holidays, and many companies also observe some local, state, and religious holidays as well. Here again, companies can be subject to problems or even charges of discrimination if there is cultural or religious diversity in the firm. Because of these issues, more companies are providing "floating" holidays so that the member can pick which days they will observe as holidays during the work year. About half of companies in the United States currently provide these floating holidays. In addition, about 18% of firms allow employees to swap holidays to observe a holiday of their choice that would normally be unpaid—for instance swapping Christmas day for Yom Kippur.[40]

Paid Personal Leave

Finally, many companies today provide time off for a wide variety of personal needs. Many firms allow employees to use such leave to visit their child at school or accompany them on a field trip. Other options might include funeral leave, family leave that would not be covered under the FMLA, time off on their birthday, and "mental health" days, among others. About two in five organizations provide paid personal leave in addition to vacation and sick leave.[41] Personal leave is an effort on the part of the organization to maintain or improve job satisfaction and organizational commitment on the part of their employees.

Video Link 13.2
Group Health Insurance Benefits

Group Health Insurance

As we have already noted, if a company chooses to provide health care to employees, they have to follow the COBRA and HIPAA rules. Companies also have to look at the rising cost of providing such care. In 1980, health care services accounted for less than 10% of Gross Domestic Product (GDP), in 2000 that figure was 13.8%, and in 2009 (the latest government figures) these services accounted for 17.6% of GDP.[42] It is obvious from these figures that health care expenses are growing at a rapid rate.

A survey by the Bureau of Labor Statistics reported that 71% of private-industry workers receive medical care benefits, and that employers offering health insurance paid an average of 82% of the cost of premiums for single coverage and 70% of the cost for family coverage.[43] Thus, companies that do provide health care have to be concerned with the costs. One of the ways that companies can control costs is to understand what coverage they are buying for what price. Let's look at the major types of group health insurance currently available to companies.

WORK
APPLICATION 13-7

Identify the Paid Time Off benefits offered where you work or have worked.

Traditional Plans (Also Called Fee-for-Service)

Traditional health care plans *typically cover a set percentage of fees for medical services— either for doctors or for in-patient care.* The most common percentage split between the insurance plan and the individual is 80/20. In other words, if the employee has to go to the hospital and is charged $10,000 for services, the insurance would pay $8,000, and the individual would be responsible for the other $2,000. There are, of course, some variations to these plans, but this is basically how they work. One of the issues with traditional fee-for-service plans is that they typically do not cover preventive care, such as an annual physical exam. They do, however, cover most but not all of the costs to treat medical conditions covered by the policy.

One of the biggest advantages of traditional plans is that they allow employees to go to any doctor or provider they want without a referral to see specialists. Also, if the employee has traditional health insurance, they can live anywhere. With some *managed care* health insurance (we will talk about this next), employees are limited to living within a certain range of the network controlled by the insurance company. However, the big problem with such insurance is the high overall cost of medical care today. If a patient went to the hospital for a serious medical problem, such as cancer, it would be very easy to incur bills in excess of $1 million. In such a case, the individual would be responsible for $200,000 of the total charges, unless they had separate gap coverage or other major medical insurance. So traditional plans have somewhat fallen out of favor. Traditional plans do give the employee a lot of choice, but there are some serious issues with potential out-of-pocket costs.

Health Maintenance Organizations

Health Maintenance Organizations are a *managed care* program. A **Health Maintenance Organization (HMO)** is *a health care plan that provides both health maintenance services and medical care as part of the plan.* This is health care that provides the patient with routine preventive care, but in the case of nonpreventive care requires that a review of specific circumstances concerning the individual and their health condition be completed *before* any significant medical testing, medical procedures, or hospital care is approved. Managed care plans generally require that the employee and their family use doctors and facilities that are in the managed care network. In some cases, the managed care plan will allow the insured person to go outside the network, but if this is done the cost of care is usually significantly higher. This allows the managed care company to attempt to ensure that unnecessary tests and procedures are not done, thereby saving both the insured and the insurance company money.

In the HMO form of managed care, the insured person will generally be required to use doctors and facilities in the network. The employee (and their family, if covered) will choose a Primary Care Physician. The **Primary Care Physician (PCP)** will be *the first point of contact for all preventive care and in any routine medical situation, except emergencies.* The PCP will see the patient, and if they feel the need for a specialist to be involved with the case, they will refer the patient to that specialist. The specialists also usually have to be part of the network in order to accept referral patients from the HMO.

In the HMO form of managed care, the patient pays a copayment each time they visit their PCP, and will generally also pay a copayment if they see a specialist after a referral. Once the copayment is paid, all other billable costs for the physician visit will generally be paid by the insurer. In addition, there will almost always be an annual deductible, an

LO 13.7

Describe the differences between traditional health care plans, HMOs, PPOs, and HSA/MSA plans.

SHRM

Guide – I:B4
Types of health care plans

amount that the patient will be required to cover for any care beyond physician office visits (such as an outpatient procedure to have a child's tonsils removed) before the remainder of such costs will be paid by the insurer.

Let's take a look at a common scenario to see what the costs of an HMO would typically be. An employee's child becomes ill and is taken to the family's PCP where the child is diagnosed with tonsillitis. The physician refers the child to an Ear, Nose, and Throat (ENT) specialist who determines that the child's tonsils need to be removed. The child then goes to the local outpatient surgery center for removal of their tonsils. The employee would be responsible for a copayment with their PCP office visit, another copayment for the ENT specialist, and finally an annual deductible for the surgery. The insurance company would pay the remaining cost for both office visits and, assuming the surgery cost more than the employee's deductible, the rest of the outpatient surgery costs.

In an HMO plan, the PCPs are generally paid a flat fee per patient to take care of that patient for the year. This fee is provided to the physician to be the gatekeeper for any other medical services that the employee or their family may need during that year. The PCP will get the same amount of money no matter how many times a patient visits them during the year. Why is this significant? If the physician happens to be selected as the PCP by patients who don't use medical services at the average rate of the overall population, the HMO knows this (because they do a utilization analysis) and will cut payments to the physician the next year because the PCP isn't using up as much of his or her time as the average physician.

The company should always do a similar utilization analysis on its employees. If the HMO can cut payments to the physicians that serve our company, we should share in the cost reduction. If the company fails to complete the utilization analysis itself, the HMO will be happy to keep all of the savings, but if the company is doing a utilization analysis, it can demand some share of the cash saved. This is another place where good HRM can save the company money.

HMOs have some very good characteristics and some bad ones. Preventive care is covered, and there are maximum out-of-pocket costs to the employee in any given year (at least for covered illnesses and injuries). However, the employee may be required to live in certain areas (because of the network of physicians and medical facilities) so that they can be safely covered without having to go long distances in an emergency. There may also be limits to the number and types of procedures that will be covered by the HMO; the employee does not have free choice in doctors, clinics, and hospitals for their care; and there are various copayments and deductibles that are the employee's responsibility before the HMO covers the rest of the costs.

Preferred Provider Organizations

Preferred Provider Organizations (PPOs) are *a kind of hybrid between traditional fee-for-service plans and HMOs.* They have some of the advantages and disadvantages as well as some of the requirements of both. PPOs have networks of physicians and medical facilities, just like HMOs. PPOs act like HMOs in that they *prefer* (but do not require) that you have a PCP within their medical network and that you go to that PCP before going elsewhere for medical care. They also provide preventive care services to their insured members, similar to HMOs, and have similar copayments and annual deductibles.

However, PPOs do not require that you have a referral from the PCP to see a specialist. In this way, they are more similar to a traditional health care plan. They will also allow you to see any provider of care either in or outside the network, although we may be required to pay a larger percentage of the cost of care if we choose to go beyond the network of physicians and facilities.

So if we compare PPOs with HMOs, we see that the advantages of PPOs include the ability to see any physician and use any medical facilities (like a traditional plan), which in turn relieves the individual insured by the PPO of the necessity to live within certain geographical boundaries. The member can live anywhere they want because they can use any medical facilities they choose. In addition, similar to HMOs, PPOs cover preventive care. However, unlike HMOs, the cost of care can be significantly higher if the individual chooses to go outside the preferred providers that are identified as PPO participants. So, PPOs prefer that we use physicians and facilities within their network, but we have a choice to go outside the network and pay at a higher rate if desired.

Health and Medical Savings Accounts

HSAs and MSAs are two very similar savings accounts for health care services. MSAs are medical savings accounts available to self-employed persons and small businesses with fewer than 50 employees. HSAs are available to employees of larger businesses that choose to provide these accounts. A **Health Savings Account (HSA) or Medical Savings Account (MSA)** *allows the employer and employee to fund a medical savings account from which the employee can pay medical expenses each year with pretax dollars.* The money in this account is then used to pay for medical services for the employee (and their family, if desired) over the course of that year. One of the big advantages of HSAs and MSAs is that money remaining in the account at the end of the year can be rolled over to future years without paying a tax penalty as a general rule.[44]

For example, assume that our employer provides an HSA and shares equally in funding our account at the maximum amount allowed for an individual for the year 2013: $3,050. The employer puts in $1,525, and we put in $1,525 (deducted from our pay over the entire year). In February of that year, we go to our physician for our annual physical. The cost of the physical including tests is $465. Our HSA provided us with a debit card for medical expenses at the beginning of the year, so we provide the debit card to our physician, and they bill $465 to our card.

The remaining balance on our card will be $2,585. Our physician reports that it appears that we have a small cancerous growth on our skin that needs to be removed in an outpatient surgery. We go to the outpatient surgery center where they remove the cancer and charge us $1,842, which we pay with our debit card, leaving a balance of $743. The only other medical service that we have that year is a physician's office visit and antibiotics for a sinus infection. We are billed for the full cost of the office visit at $80 and for the full cost of the antibiotics at $34. This would leave a balance of $629 in our HSA. At the end of the year, this $629 will roll over to next year's HSA account and be added to the new contribution of $3,050.

As you can see, in an HSA you pay the full cost of each of the medical services used in a plan year from the HSA account. There are no copayments; there are no deductibles. However, if you don't use the full value of the services, the remaining dollar amounts can be rolled over to future years, so you don't lose that money.

HSAs are also portable, so we can take our HSA balance with us if we change employers. One of the benefits to companies using an HSA or MSA is that it causes the employee to understand the full cost of providing health care for the year. If the full cost of health care is coming out of the employee's pocket through the use of the HSA debit card, it is thought that they might pay more attention to unnecessary medical expenses including such things as going to the doctor's office when they have a cold or if they sprain a finger. The assumption is that if the employees pay more attention to the overall cost of health care, we can lower that cost.

High-Deductible Health Plan (HDHP). One of the problems that we can quickly see with an HSA is that our medical services in a particular year could cost us much more than $3,050, especially if we had to have a surgery. However, federal rules on HSAs and MSAs require that employees who have these accounts also participate in something called a HDHP. A **High-Deductible Health Plan** (**HDHP**) is *basically a "major medical" insurance plan that protects against catastrophic health care costs, and in most cases is paid for by the employer.* A very common HDHP would pay for medical costs in any given year that total more than $10,000. So if an individual exceeded the $3,050 in their HSA, they would be responsible for out-of-pocket costs of a maximum of $6,950, at which time the HDHP would take over and pay the remaining costs of the individual's health care for the year.

At first glance, this looks like a large out-of-pocket expense for the individual employee. However, in other forms of health care, the employee generally has copayments, deductibles, and prescription copayments that come out of their own pocket during the course of the year. Annual deductibles can frequently be as high as $2,000–$4,000; each PCP visit can cost $20–$40; each specialist's office visit costs $40–$50; and prescription copayments typically cost from $25 to $40, or more. So if an individual had large-scale medical costs in any given year, they would most likely have at least as much in out-of-pocket costs as they would under the HSA plan.

One of the big advantages of HSAs and MSAs is that the individual can go to any physician or medical facility. There is no HMO network; there are no preferred providers. If the employee wants to go to the top specialist in their field and is willing to pay the extra cost of the office visit for such a specialist, they have the ability to go. In this way, HSAs and MSAs are much more like traditional fee-for-service plans than HMOs and PPOs. However, they are much more like HMOs and PPOs in the fact that there are maximum out-of-pocket costs per year before the HDHP takes over and pays all other medical expenses.

Because HSAs and MSAs cause the individual employee to see the total cost of their health care, and might cause these employees to use such care at a lower level because it is a direct cost to the employee, many employers have started looking at these accounts in an attempt to control ever-rising health care costs. The HSA can cause people to realize that medical care costs a lot more than their copayments. If the employee only pays $20 to go to the doctor, they will go whenever they feel the slightest problem coming on, but if they have to pay the entire $80 cost of the office visit, they may think much harder before they spend that money to go to the doctor to remove a splinter. Because of the fact that it makes employees aware of the entire cost of health care, it is expected that HSAs and MSAs will continue to become a more significant proportion of the health care plans provided by employers over at least the next several years.

Utilization Analysis

We briefly mentioned utilization analyses earlier. Let's take another look at them now. A **utilization analysis** is *a review of the cost of a program and comparison of program costs with the rate of the program's usage by the members of the company.* In other words, is the company getting a valuable benefit out of the program, or could the same money be spent in a different way to get better returns on money spent?

If, for instance, our average employee is healthier than the national average employee, we might use fewer medical services over time than other companies of similar size in the same industry. But our premiums for health insurance will (at least initially) be based on the "average" employee in our industry. If we investigate and find that our employees do, in fact, use fewer medical services each year than the average, we can ask the insurer to lower our insurance rates to match our utilization rates. Health insurance is one of the easiest things for us to do a utilization analysis on because we are provided information on the

WORK
APPLICATION 13-8

Select a company that offers health insurance and state the type of insurance it offers.

13-2 APPLYING THE CONCEPT

Group Health Insurance

Identify each statement by its type of health insurance option offered.

a. Traditional
b. HMO
c. PPO

d. HSA
e. MSA

_____ 6. I work for a large company, and I like my insurance plan because I am healthy and pay the full cost, but I don't use it all every year, and it has accumulated nicely.

_____ 7. I have the same insurance deal that you have (#6), but my company only has 10 employees.

_____ 8. With my insurance plan, I do have copays and deductibles, but at least I can go to any doctor or hospital I want to at an extra cost.

_____ 9. The thing I don't like about my new insurance plan is that I can only go to doctors and hospitals that are approved by my plan. So I have to stop seeing Dr. Smith after 10 years and start with a new doctor that I'm assigned to.

_____ 10. My insurance plan requires me to pay 20% of my health care cost, and I have medical issues making it very expensive for me.

services that our employees use by the insurance company. If we have a strong case, we need to go to the insurance company and request that they lower our rates to match our utilization of services.

Retirement Benefits

According the Bureau of Labor Statistics, employer-provided retirement plans are available to 74% of all full-time workers and 39% of part-time workers in private industry.[45] They are not mandatory, but if we provide them we have to comply with ERISA. Like with health insurance, companies provide retirement benefits to motivate employees. However, as discussed in Chapter 12, employees may view them as simply an entitlement.[46] Retirement benefits are categorized into two types. Let's discuss both followed by five options for defined contribution plans.

Defined Benefit Versus Defined Contribution Plans

The two options in retirement plans are defined benefit and defined contribution plans.

Defined benefit plan. A **defined benefit plan** *provides the retiree with a specific amount and type of benefits that will be available when the individual retires.* The retiree knows exactly what they are going to receive in benefits when they retire. For instance, a simple defined benefit plan might provide that employees who work in the company for 25 years will get 60% of the average of their two highest years of pay. In addition, they will receive 1% more for every additional year that they work. So if the same employee worked for 35 years, they would receive 70% of the average of their two highest years of pay. If such

LO 13.8

Discuss the difference between defined benefit and defined contribution retirement plans and the reasons for the shift from defined benefit to defined contribution plans.

SHRM

Guide – I:B2
Types of retirement plans (defined benefit, defined contribution, hybrid plans)

an employee made $64,238 in their highest paid year and $63,724 in their second highest paid year, their two highest years' average pay would equal $63,981. If this individual retired with 25 years of service, they would receive $38,388.60 per year in retirement. If they instead retired after 35 years of service, they would receive $44,786.70 per year in retirement. Because it is a defined benefit retirement plan, the employee knows exactly what their retirement will be.

Defined contribution plan. Unlike a defined benefit plan, under a defined contribution plan the employee does not know what their retirement benefit will be. **Defined contribution plans** *identify only the amount of funds that will go into a retirement account, not what the employee will receive upon retirement.* The employee only knows what their contribution into the retirement fund consists of. What will the member who contributes to a defined contribution plan receive upon retirement? The answer to this question will depend on the success of the investment of their retirement funds over the years between the contribution of the funds and the employee's ultimate retirement. If the retirement funds are invested successfully, growing significantly over time, the individual's retirement account will be able to pay much higher benefits than if the funds are not invested successfully and don't grow very much.

Shift from defined benefit to defined contribution plans. Defined benefit plans used to be the most common type of retirement plan, but have been overtaken by defined contribution plans—some would say for legitimate business reasons. For example, Ford got the United Auto Workers (UAW) to move employees from defined benefits to defined contributions, and entry-level wages, making Ford competitive.[47] Providing a defined contribution plan to employees shifts the investment risk from the company to the individual employee. Under a defined benefit plan the employer puts money into retirement accounts and expects that money to grow at a certain rate over time. But if the funds do not grow at the expected rate, the employer is left with a shortage in the retirement accounts and must add money to those accounts in order to be able to pay the promised benefit to retired workers. This happened in the U.S. auto industry as large numbers of retiring employees combined with lower sales and a period of no profits and layoffs, which left fewer employees to cover the cost of those retirees. So the cost of adding funds to the defined benefit plans for their retirees contributed to a cost advantage for foreign automakers, and (when the 2007–2008 recession occurred) to the U.S. government bailout of General Motors and Chrysler.

In the case of a defined contribution plan, the risk of slow growth of the investment shifts to the employee. The company has no obligation to pay a specific amount to the employee so if the fund doesn't grow at the expected rate, the employer is not required to add money to that fund. However, on the downside, the employee may not be able to draw as much in benefits as they had anticipated if the account didn't earn interest or grow at the rate that was expected over time.

There are a number of different defined contribution plans that meet federal and state guidelines for favorable tax treatment, and therefore have added value to both employers and employees. Let's take a look at some of the most common types of defined contribution plans at this point.

LO 13.9

Discuss the major retirement plan options.

401(k) and 403(b) Plans

The most well-known retirement plan in U.S. companies today is the 401(k). These accounts are available to nearly all employees of corporations as well as most self-employed persons. A *401(k) retirement plan* is basically a savings investment account for individual employees of corporations. A *403(b) retirement plan* is a very similar plan to the 401(k) with the exception that it is used for nonprofit entities.

Both the employee and the employer are allowed to contribute funds each year to the employee's 401(k) or 403(b) account, with the *employee* allowed to contribute up to a maximum of $16,500 (for an employee under 50 years of age in 2011). Contributions to these accounts are made on a pretax basis. This means that when funds are put into the account they do not count as taxable income for the individual. Once the individual retires and begins to remove funds from the account, they pay income taxes on the distributions at their current tax rate, which tends to be lower at retirement. The earliest point at which the contributor can withdraw money without incurring a penalty from a 401(k) or 403(b) account is at age 59½.

Matching contributions. Many employers that offer a 401(k) or 403(b) provide a matching contribution up to a set maximum. For example, an employer might allow a 100% match of employee contributions up to a $2,000 maximum. So if the employee put $2,000 of their salary into the retirement account over the course of the year, this plus the employer's matching funds would add $4,000 a year to the individual's retirement account. Because of the tax deferral associated with a 401(k), the individual's taxable income is lowered by the amount of the contribution, so take-home pay is not decreased by the full amount that the employee actually put into their retirement account.

On a personal note, never refuse free money. So when you get a new job with retirement benefits, tell the HR person you want to sign up for the full match. You would be amazed at how many people refuse the retirement match. So taking the full match as early as you can is one of the most important tips in this book. With a $2,000 matching plan, if you start young enough, with good investing, you can retire as a millionaire. Remember the general guide to put 10% of your income every month into your retirement account no matter how low your income is.[48]

IRAs and Roth IRAs

An IRA is an Individual Retirement Account. Under U.S. law, any person who pays taxes can have and contribute to an IRA, and the contributions are tax free (subject to a maximum annual income limit)—they reduce your taxable income by the full amount of the contribution in the year in which they are contributed to the account. Both IRAs and Roth IRAs can supplement the amount that an individual is contributing to a company-sponsored 401(k) account, because we are allowed to contribute to both. An individual can contribute a maximum of 100% of their income up to $5,000 per year (in 2011) into a standard IRA, and can contribute up to $6,000 to a Roth IRA.[49]

The Roth IRA is basically the same type of account as a regular IRA with the exception that the Roth IRA "front-loads," or requires that we pay the taxes immediately for funds put into the retirement account. If we put $6,000 into a Roth IRA in 2011 and were in the 25% federal tax bracket, we would pay $1,500 in tax for 2011, but when we withdrew these funds upon retirement they would be tax free. With the standard IRA, you pay no tax on the funds when you contribute them, but pay taxes at your current tax rate when those funds are withdrawn.

What is the advantage to paying the taxes up front on a Roth IRA? If you expect to be in a much higher tax bracket later in life, it makes sense to pay the taxes at your lower (current) tax rate instead of paying a higher tax rate later. Assume that you are currently in the 15% tax bracket, but your income triples over the next 40 years and you expect that (based on current tax rates) you will be in a 38% tax bracket later. You can pay $750 on your $5,000 Roth IRA contribution today, but might have to pay $1,900 on that same $5,000 contribution (plus any interest earned) when you withdraw it in 40 years. So if you expect your tax bracket to go up over time, a Roth IRA may be advantageous. Also, if we already put in the legal maximum into a tax-deferred retirement account, the Roth IRA is a good alternative for saving more for retirement.

Simplified Employee Pension Plans

The last common retirement plan that we will discuss here is the Simplified Employee Pension (SEP). SEPs are primarily used for self-employed individuals and members of small companies. According to the U.S. Department of Labor, "Under a SEP, an employer contributes directly to traditional individual retirement accounts (SEP-IRAs) for all employees (including the employer). A SEP . . . allows for a contribution of up to 25 percent of each employee's pay" up to a maximum of $49,000 (in 2011) into the person's IRA each year.[50] Because the owner is not an employee with pay, the self-employed person can tax defer a set percentage of the company profits. A SEP can also be used by a person with a job that has retirement benefits and is also self-employed to defer taxes and save more for retirement.

What makes an SEP retirement plan valuable to small business is the lower paperwork burden compared to a 401(k) or 403(b) retirement account. The contributions follow the same basic tax rules as a 401(k): Contributions are not taxed when made, but the individual pays taxes on the money when it is withdrawn during retirement. For self-employed proprietorships without any employees getting SEP retirement benefits, the only records needed are the individual tax return 1040 with a Schedule C for self-employed income showing the SEP deduction from profits going into the SEP, and the SEP account records verifying that the money was actually put into the SEP.

Employee Insurance Coverage

The next major category of voluntary benefits is insurance. There are a number of different types of insurance that are provided as common voluntary benefits to our employees. The largest of these is life insurance, but disability policies (both short- and long-term), supplemental unemployment policies, income continuation (also called supplemental health) policies, travel accident insurance, individual cancer and genetic disease policies, and other insurance options are also available and are part of some companies' voluntary benefit programs. Let's review some of the major employee insurance options.

Life Insurance

In many cases, firms will provide Group Term Life (GTL) insurance policies to provide for survivors of an employee who dies while employed by the company. GTL provides for a survivor payment to occur only if the employee dies during the term that is covered by the insurance policy. It is also a valuable benefit to the employer because it is eligible for an employer tax deduction if it complies with IRS regulations.[51] A fairly standard benefit here would be one to two times the individual's annual compensation. So if an employee dies, on or off the job for most causes of death, the beneficiary would get one to two years' salary. Many companies will allow the employee to add to this coverage at the group rates, which is usually a very good deal for the employee. Generally, once the employee leaves the company, the term insurance policy will be discontinued.

In addition to GTL, employers can provide permanent, or whole life, insurance. Unlike term life policies, this life insurance benefit has no termination or end date. It continues for

---

WORK
APPLICATION 13-9

Select a company that offers retirement benefits and state the type of plan it offers. If it is a defined benefit, describe the plan. If it is a defined contribution, identify the option selected, and if the employer offers any matching contributions, what are they?

SHRM

Guide – I:B12
Life insurance

13-3 APPLYING THE CONCEPT

Retirement Plans

Recommend the appropriate retirement plan based on the person's situation.

a. 401(k)
b. 403(b)
c. IRA
d. Roth IRA
e. SEP

_____ 11. I'm going to work for IBM Corporation. What retirement plan will I get?

_____ 12. I already have a retirement plan at work and put in the maximum tax deferred contribution. So how else can I save for my retirement?

_____ 13. I own my own business with just three employees, and I want to save for retirement. What retirement plan should I use?

_____ 14. I'm going to work for St. John's Church. What retirement plan will I get?

_____ 15. I only work part-time, and the company doesn't offer any retirement benefits. How should I save for retirement?

the life of the individual as long as premiums continue to be paid. Whole life policies can also be used for retirement. However, they are not commonly offered.

Disability Insurance

The other large-scale insurance benefit in many companies is disability insurance. This insurance can be either short- or long-term in nature, and some companies offer both options.

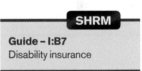

SHRM
Guide – I:B7
Disability insurance

Short-term disability is insurance against being unable to perform the essential functions expected of the employee at work for up to six months due to illness or injury—*not necessarily a work-related illness or injury.* This is valuable because most *long*-term disability policies do not provide replacement income until the employee completes a 180-day "elimination period" (a period during which they are unable to work). Short-term coverage closes this six-month gap. Because 71% of Americans say that it would be difficult to pay their bills if their paycheck were delayed for more than a week, waiting six months would likely create a massive hardship for the disabled worker.[52] Remember, too, that Social Security disability doesn't apply unless the employee is going to be disabled *for at least five months*, so short-term disability can bridge this gap in income.

Long-term disability policies cover employees who are unable to work for more than six months due to illness or injury—again, *not necessarily a work-related illness or injury.* Long-term disability is designed to replace a portion of the disabled employee's income (*typically 50%–60%*) for extended periods of time, or even permanently.[53] This is a supplemental benefit to Social Security disability payments because, remember, Social Security payments are not designed to replace 100% of an employee's preretirement (or predisability) income. Long-term benefits most often begin once the employee has exhausted their short-term disability benefits. Benefits from *group* long-term policies will generally continue until the employee reaches their eligible retirement age under Social Security, or until they are able to return to work.[54]

Other Common Insurance Benefits

In addition to standard life and disability insurance, there are a number of other insurance benefits provided by at least some employers. These can be loosely grouped into two categories: *life and health* and *other* insurance.

Life and health insurance. This category includes insurance policies available for many different issues that may confront the employee and could cause significant consequences to their ability to continue a normal life if a catastrophic situation were to occur (the percentage of firms utilizing coverage is in parentheses). These include the more common vision (53%) and dental (48%) insurance, but also such things as long-term care (51%) for a sick or injured employee or family member; cancer insurance (4%) against the potentially massive costs associated with cancer treatments; critical illness insurance (7%) (much like cancer insurance—other critical illnesses or injuries could wipe out an employee's ability to pay the associated costs); accident insurance (49%), which covers a broad range of accident-related expenses for the insured; and supplemental insurance policies such as AFLAC, which pay for routine expenses (like car payments) not generally covered by health or disability insurance.[55, 56, 57]

Other insurance. Employers provide many types of additional insurance to their members. Some common examples are employer-sponsored automobile (32%) insurance (may be advantageous because of group purchases versus individual auto policies); homeowners' and renters' insurance (29%), again potentially cheaper because of group rates; identity theft insurance (22%), which covers fraudulent use of an employee's personal information, including unauthorized purchases using the employee's personal credit; and pet insurance (19%), which again can be cheaper when purchased in group quantities.[58]

Employee Services

SHRM

Guide – I:B8
Educational benefits

In addition to PTO, insurance, health and retirement benefits, companies provide a wide variety of employee services as benefits for their workforce. *Educational (or tuition) assistance* is one common benefit in this group. In 2008, the last year in which the BLS separately surveyed educational assistance, roughly half of all companies provided some form of educational assistance to their employees. Unfortunately, with the rising cost of benefits and the 2008 recession, this benefit has been cut back at many firms.

Other common employee services include onsite child care or child care vouchers; elder care assistance; company-provided gyms and fitness facilities or vouchers for memberships outside the business; organization-sponsored sports teams; services to mitigate commuting costs including work shuttles, company-provided or -paid parking, "green" vehicle allowances, and public or private transportation vouchers; cafeterias or meal vouchers; plus too many others to name.

Employee services are provided in order to minimize the disruptions to the employee's work life. If the employee isn't worried about their children (because the company has a day care facility on site), they can concentrate on work. If they don't have to deal with figuring out where they can park downtown, they are less stressed when they start their day. If they need 15 minutes' rest, they can take a nap, and if they want to work out to relieve some stress, they can go to the company gym. Companies don't provide these services because they like to throw money away. They provide employee services to lower stress and allow employees to concentrate on the job. Any service that takes the employee away from being able to focus on work is a legitimate target for an employee service benefit, and more and more companies are paying attention to such services.

Before we go on to discuss how to administer and communicate benefits, let's review the list of benefits discussed so far in Exhibit 13-4. Note that there are an unlimited number of voluntary benefits, but only the major ones discussed are listed here.

Exhibit 13-4	Employee Benefits

Statutory Benefits	Voluntary Benefits

• Social Security and Medicare
• Workers' Compensation
• Unemployment Insurance
• Family and Medical Leave (FMLA)
• Patient Protection and Affordable Care (PPACA)
• Statutory Requirements When Providing Certain Voluntary Benefits
   o Consolidated Omnibus Budget Reconciliation (COBRA)
   o Health Insurance Portability and Accountability (HIPAA)
   o Employee Retirement Income Security (ERISA)
	• Paid Time Off
	• Group Health Insurance
	• Retirement Benefits
	• Employee Insurance Coverage
	• Employee Services
	   o Educational (or tuition) assistance
	   o Onsite childcare or child care vouchers
	   o Elder care assistance
	   o Company-provided fitness facilities or vouchers for memberships
	   o Organization-sponsored sports teams
	   o Services to mitigate commuting costs including work shuttles, company-provided or -paid parking, "green" vehicle allowances, and public or private transportation vouchers
	   o Free or low-cost meals

WORK
APPLICATION 13-10

Select a company that offers voluntary benefits. Besides Paid Time Off, retirement, and health and employee insurance, what other benefits does it offer?

Administration and Communication of Benefits

It's time to move on to a discussion of how we manage and administer these benefit programs. Because of their significant cost to the company, HR Managers must pay close attention to the administration of benefit programs in order to get the most return for the money spent. In almost all cases today, benefit programs are not "one size fits all"—they are flexible because that is what employees want.[59] And because they are flexible for the employees, they take more management time. Let's briefly discuss the management of flexible benefits programs now, followed by how to communicate value to employees in this section.

LO 13.10

Discuss organizations' options when providing flexible benefit plans to their employees.

Flexible Benefit (Cafeteria) Plans

What is a flexible benefit plan, commonly known as a *cafeteria* plan? Cafeteria plans are called that because they are similar to a cafeteria restaurant or college dining hall. You get to pick what you want. You may decide that you want more PTO and less insurance, or that you want medical coverage for you and your family, or you may choose to put more money into retirement accounts. Most cafeteria plans fall into one of three categories—each with its own advantages and disadvantages.

Modular Plans

Modular plans are pretty much what they sound like. The employee has several basic modules from which they can choose to provide a set of benefits that match their life and

13-1 SELF-ASSESSMENT

SELECTING EMPLOYEE BENEFITS

Assume you are graduating with your college degree and getting your first or a new full-time job. The organization gives you the list below and asks you to rank order the list of employee benefits from 1 (*the most important to you*) to 11 (*the least important to you*).

_____ Paid Time Off (vacations, sick and personal days, holidays)

_____ Health Insurance (traditional, HMO, PPO, HSA/MSA)

_____ Retirement Benefits (401[k] or 403[b], IRA or Roth IRA, SEP)

_____ Employee Insurance Coverage (life, disability, others)

_____ Educational (or Tuition) Assistance (getting your MBA, another degree, or some type of certification or license like the PHR and SPHR, CPA, FICF)

_____ Child Care (on site or vouchers)

_____ Eldercare (on site or vouchers)

_____ Fitness (organization-provided fitness facilities or vouchers for memberships)

_____ Organization-Sponsored Sports Teams (softball, basketball, bowling, golf, etc.)

_____ Commuting (work shuttles, company-provided or -paid parking, "green" vehicle allowances, public or private transportation vouchers)

_____ Meals (free or low-cost meals on site or meal vouchers)

There is no scoring as this is a personal choice. Think about your selection today. Will your priority ranking change in 5, 10, 15, or 20 years?

family circumstances. Each module has a different mix of insurance, employee services, and retirement options. The employee chooses a module that most closely meets their needs. There may be a module for young single employees that maximizes work flexibility with more time off for personal activities, but has minimal or no benefits in areas such as family health plans, child care, or dental. Another module designed for families with children might have much more emphasis on family health and retirement planning and more life insurance in case the employee were to die and leave the family without income, and still a third module might be designed for workers whose children are grown.

Modular plans are much easier for HR to manage than other types of flexible benefit plans, because there are a limited number of modules to keep track of. Because they are easier to manage, they are cheaper. We also have the advantage of having more people using the same set of benefits, so utilization analyses are a bit easier in this case. However, since there is no flexibility within each module (you get the exact set of benefits specified within the module), the employee may not be able to get the coverage and options that they want or need.

Core Plus Plans

In a *core plus* plan, we have a base set of benefits, called the core, that are provided to everyone, and then they are allowed to choose other options to meet personal needs and desires. The core benefits are there to provide basic protection for all of the company's employees in areas such as health and life insurance, and maybe a minimum amount of retirement funding. The remaining benefits are available for the employee to pick and chose other options that match their personal needs.

If the employee has a family and wants to provide them with coverage, they can choose family health coverage. If they are getting older and didn't save for retirement earlier in their work life, they can provide more funds into their retirement account. The limiting factor is that each employee is provided with a benefits account and once that account is empty they can't pick any additional benefits for their personal plan.

The biggest advantage of *core plus* plans to the employee is, of course, the ability to partially tailor the plan to each person's individual circumstances while providing a minimum level of health and wellness benefits for each employee. The plan is also cheaper than a full choice plan to administer. HRM personnel can still analyze the benefit options and complete utilization analyses on *core plus* plans, but it is more difficult than in modular plans.

Video Link 13.3
Overview of Benefits

Full Choice Plans

The *full choice* plans provide complete flexibility to the organizational member. Each employee can choose exactly the set of benefits that they desire, within specified monetary limitations. If a member chooses to have no health care coverage, they can use the money saved for whatever other available benefit that they want. This is truly a cafeteria plan in that employees can choose any offered benefit they want without a modular or core set of benefits.

Probably the biggest advantage in a *full choice* plan is that it is easy for the employee to understand. However, there are some significant problems with *full choice* plans for both the individual and the organization. One of the problems, "moral hazard," may occur because the employee doesn't fully identify the consequences of their selection. Moral hazard problems can occur when the individual makes bad choices and will be forced to live with those choices in the future. For instance, we may have an employee who decides that they don't need a retirement account because they are going to "work until I die anyway." A few years down the line this same person may be getting tired of working or may even be

Video Link 13.4

Benefits for Domestic Partners

unable to continue to work in the same field because of illness or injuries and want to retire, but may be unable to because of the choices that they made in previous years.

A second disadvantage to *full choice* plans comes from the problem of "adverse selection." For example, most company plans allow changes to the employee's benefits during an open enrollment period at the end of the year. Suppose an employee knows that they have a physical problem that will likely result in the need for surgery in the coming year, and they therefore choose to increase their health care insurance to pay for more of the cost of the upcoming surgery. The next year, with the surgery over and knowing that they have children who are going to need braces, they choose to increase their dental coverage and lower their health care insurance coverage. Through this manipulation of the benefits system, the overall cost of providing these benefits can go up significantly over time. So this problem of adverse selection is an issue of selecting only the benefits that we think will immediately benefit us and then dropping those benefits once we feel that we don't need them. This can cause the utilization rates for the organization to significantly increase over time, which in turn causes an increase in the cost to the organization of providing those benefits.

The third big issue with full choice plans is the cost associated with administration of the plans. It is not too difficult to manage the paperwork of a modular plan—HRM just figures out the number of employees choosing each module and then calculates the total usage for each benefit based on the modules. In *full choice* plans, every employee can change their plan (in its entirety) every year. This is much more difficult to manage, and creates a much larger paperwork burden for HRM.

The bottom line is that flexible plans are really gaining ground because our workforce is much more diverse than it used to be. Benefits need to match the needs of our workers.

WORK
APPLICATION 13-11

Select a company that offers a flexible benefit plan. Identify its type and describe the major benefit options within that category of flexibility.

13-4 APPLYING THE CONCEPT

Flexible Benefit Plans

Identify the type of flexible plan by each person's statement.

a.   modular   c.   full choice
b.   core plus

_____ 16. The thing I like about my benefits package is that I can choose any benefit I want to every year.

_____ 17. My benefit plan is simple. There are five packages, and I get to pick any one of them that I want every year.

_____ 18. I like getting health care and retirement benefits, and in addition selecting a few other benefits with a set dollar value.

_____ 19. The thing I don't like about my benefit plan is that there are so many options to choose from that I have a hard time selecting the ones I may really need.

_____ 20. I'm getting ripped off with our benefit plan because I use my wife's health insurance plan and I just lose the benefit. It subtracts money from what I would have to use on other benefits.

Communicate Value to Employees

In addition to administration of benefit programs, the other major HR activity in benefits management is to communicate the value of such programs to all workers. Many of us may work for a company that provides a summary of benefits and the value of each of them on some routine basis, usually at the end of the year. The basic reason for doing so is that most of us don't understand the true cost and value of the benefits that our organizations provide. And if we don't understand the cost and the return of our benefits programs, we don't perceive the value that we get from having the organization provide us with these benefits.

A recent MetLife study notes that companies have to "reprioritize employee loyalty and satisfaction, or economic recovery may arrive with unanticipated setbacks for retention and productivity."[60] Multiple studies "indicate that employees who are satisfied with their benefits are more satisfied with their jobs."[61] We need to provide employees with knowledge concerning their benefits package, which can then help to engender trust in the organization as well as job satisfaction on the part of those employees.

All we really need in order to communicate the value of benefit programs is a basic, ongoing communication process. We provide information through multiple communication channels and should provide it more often than just once per year during open enrollment. There are a number of methods that have achieved acceptability in HR Departments around the world, and they can reach at least part of our workforce.

We may want to use more than one method because of the multigenerational nature of today's workforce. For older baby boomers standard mailings to the employees' homes may be a good method, but for Generation X and Y employees, searchable knowledge bases and e-mail reminders may work better, while finally with NetGens social media may take the lead. We have to consider the makeup of our workforce and use methods that will be appropriate in reaching each of the groups within it. Finally, if we aren't sure of the best way to communicate with our employees, ask them. On a global basis, the medium of communications may be very different. For example, in underdeveloped countries, most employees will not have a home computer to receive the communications in an e-mail or through a social network. Value communication is one of the most important jobs within HR in the 21st-century workplace. We have to try to help all employees understand their benefits packages, which in turn makes the package more valuable to the individual employee. If they understand the total value of their benefits, we end up with a more loyal and more satisfied workforce. The effort is absolutely worth it.

Trends and Issues in HRM

The first trend that we will discuss is the question of providing benefits for domestic partners who are not spouses of our employees. Second, we will briefly look at some of the differences that we might see in benefits programs in other parts of the world. Third, we want to do a quick review of some of the interesting "sustainability benefits" that are cropping up more and more in business, so let's get going.

Benefits for Domestic Partners

One of the more significant recent issues in benefits management has been the question of providing benefits for domestic partners. Sometimes called significant others, **domestic partners** are *individuals who are not legally married but who are in a one-to-one living arrangement similar to marriage*, whether that arrangement is same-sex or opposite-sex.

LO 13.11

Discuss the need for benefit plans to be communicated to employees.

SHRM

Guide – I:B20
Domestic partner benefits

Should we, or in some cases are we required to, treat such domestic partners the same as spouses for the purpose of providing company benefits?

Our purpose here is not to discuss the validity of domestic partner arrangements and whether or not they are right or wrong. That is up to the organization and the state and country in which they operate. Our analysis has to look at the costs as well as any organizational advantage that might be gained by providing domestic partner coverage. Organizations may choose to provide domestic partner benefits in order to support a more diverse workforce, to recruit the best talent possible, or just to provide equity to all of their employees.

Should we treat domestic partners the same as spouses in determining company benefits? There are several issues that we have to face along with this question. Benefits that are associated with marriage include Social Security survivor benefits, workers' compensation survivor payments, bereavement leave, access to FMLA, and coverage under COBRA and ERISA. Each of these laws has at least some language that provides for benefits only to legal spouses of employees, not to domestic partners. In some cases, federal law would require the employer to tax any benefits to an employee's domestic partner, because the tax code says that to receive favorable tax treatment for benefits, such as an HSA, the coverage has to go to the employee and their immediate family members, not to domestic partners. Employers have to be aware of the language of the laws so that they don't unintentionally violate such laws.

In addition, companies have to be aware that providing domestic partner benefits may cost them significant amounts of money. Allowing domestic partners to be covered under company insurance and other benefit policies will almost always add to the cost of the benefits program. We must weigh the value of the loyalty and satisfaction gained by such actions against the direct monetary cost of this type of coverage. In a 2010 survey, SHRM found that about 37% of organizations provided domestic partner health care coverage, but that about 6% were considering reducing or eliminating such coverage in the coming year.[62] So companies are taking a hard look at the cost of such benefits and in some cases at least deciding that the cost is too high to cover the added value to their employee base.

While we certainly can't resolve this issue here, we need to understand that it is an important question to a number of our employees and therefore must be a question that we ask ourselves when working with our benefit plans. Should we provide these benefits, or is the cost of allowing domestic partner benefits plus the added cost of program administration worth it to the firm? In some cases the answer will be yes, and in others no.

Benefits Programs Around the World

If we just think about it, benefits programs must adapt to the part of the world in which our employees work and live. For one thing, some countries mandate certain benefits that are not required in other countries, and we have no choice but to offer them. In other cases, the living conditions may be such that different benefits packages just make sense. Let's take a look at some samples of differences that we might see in benefits programs in other parts of the world.

One of the most significant factors in international benefits management has been the recent worldwide recession that has put pressure on both governments and companies to reduce their expenses. Because of these cost pressures, governments are looking at reducing the benefits that they provide to workers in their countries, especially in retirement programs and health care expenses. Companies are also feeling the cost crunch around the world, and are looking at ways to cut their expenses while still providing the benefits necessary to attract and retain top-quality employees.

Retirement benefits vary around the world, with some governments providing a strong centralized retirement system (Australia is a good example) while others provide very little in the way of centralized retirement planning and savings. Even in countries where there

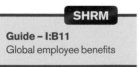

WORK
APPLICATION 13-12

Does any company you know of offer domestic partner benefits? Do you believe these benefits should or should not be offered by a specific organization you work or have worked for? Why or why not?

SHRM

Guide – I:B11
Global employee benefits

is a strong central government plan, though, most employees are concerned that they have not saved enough for retirement. In a survey that included employees in five countries, Australia, Brazil, India, Mexico, and the United Kingdom, in every country "outliving retirement money" was one of the top three worker concerns.[63] One reason for this is that people are living longer today than ever before—all across the globe. Another issue is that in most countries the population is planning on retiring at an earlier age than has historically been the case. In most cases, workers plan to retire in their 60s or earlier.[64] This combination of living longer and retiring earlier is creating the potential for a gap in retirement plan funding. More and more companies are working with employees to narrow this gap through a series of options. Some are providing financial counseling to show workers how much they need to be saving for retirement, and others are providing additional voluntary benefits programs where the employee can fund additional retirement accounts that will help fill the gap in their current retirement plans.

A significant trend is the move by companies toward offering more, and a larger variety of, voluntary benefits that are fully paid by the employee, instead of the employer providing at least part of the money to cover the cost of such benefits. In Brazil, for example, almost a third of female employees expressed interest in accident and pension funds for which they would pay 100% of the cost, and in Mexico 56% of workers said that they would like a wider choice of voluntary benefits and about one fourth said that would pay the *full cost* for life, disability, and health insurance.[65]

Even if there are some significant differences in benefit plans around the world due to differing government policies, the consensus is that a good benefits package is a powerful force in employee satisfaction and retention. Employers worldwide would be well served to start formal communications with their employees to find out what types of benefits will best serve to improve satisfaction and retention in their organizations.

Sustainability-Based Benefits

Another area of current interest is in sustainability-based benefit programs. A number of companies are looking at options for providing benefits to their employees that assist with improving environmental stability and sustainability over the long term. It is not only politically correct; it is an additional way to show the corporation's true concern for the environment as well as their concern for their employees. These programs can range from providing "credits" to employees for riding bicycles or public transportation to work all the way to sharing costs for cars or home appliances that lower energy usage.

ESR

Benefits that will lower the employee's individual "carbon footprint" help the environment and help the employee because such benefits almost always lower the employee's cost of living. An example is a program called HEAL Arkansas. This program was started by the Addison Shoe Factory when they learned that many of their employees spent *up to half of their income* on energy bills.[66] The HEAL program is now offered through the state of Arkansas to selected businesses and provides "facility audits and zero interest retrofit financing of energy efficiency improvements for their facilities."[67] The companies in turn must use part of their energy savings to help employees with home audits and retrofitting of appliances, windows, and other energy-saving items by providing the employees with zero-interest loans for such improvements.

Companies may also provide a variety of other "green" subsidies so that employees can help the environment. These might include assistance to employees in purchasing renewable energy options for their homes, such as solar cells or hybrid, electric, or alternative fuel vehicles. Clif Bar and Company in Berkeley, California, "provides points to employees for selecting alternate modes of transportation to work, such as walking, biking, carpooling, or mass transit."[68] Telecommuting can even be a sustainability benefit because it lowers the number of employees commuting to work. So employers just need to use a bit of imagination and a good search engine to find ways in which they can encourage sustainable practices on the part of their employees as well as practices that they can put into effect within the company.

Wrap-Up

Our final chapter on compensation comes to a close. What have we learned about benefits and their management in organizations? First, we learned that benefits programs have strategic value to the firm by assisting with employee satisfaction and engagement. We also saw that benefits continue to grow as a proportion of overall compensation costs due to a number of factors. We also now know that there are three major considerations when providing benefits—the dollar amounts available, the mix of benefits, and the flexibility of the plans.

The second section of this chapter discussed the statutory requirements for certain benefits. These include Social Security (composed of OASDI and Medicare), workers' compensation, Unemployment Insurance, the Family and Medical Leave Act, and the new Patient Protection and Affordable Care Act. We also took a quick look at some requirements that become mandatory if we offer certain voluntary benefits such as health insurance or retirement programs. These laws include COBRA, which says that we have to offer employees who leave the company continued health insurance coverage for a period of time if they pay the premiums. Another requirement if we provide health coverage is HIPAA, which mandates portability of the individual employee's health insurance, and requires that we maintain privacy and security of personally identifiable health information. In addition, if we offer a retirement plan we have to abide by ERISA, which provides rules on eligibility for such retirement plans, portability of retirement funds, and vesting periods, and requires fiduciaries to act prudently with invested funds.

The third section of Chapter 13 discussed a variety of voluntary benefits, starting with Paid Time Off of various types—vacation, sick leave, holidays, and personal time. This section also reviewed group health insurance options. These options include traditional health care plans, HMOs, PPOs, and HSA/MSA plans. The next part of the section discussed retirement plans. We looked at the difference between defined benefit and defined contribution plans, as well as the major types of plans used in most organizations today. The plan types included 401(k) and 403(b) plans, IRAs, Roth IRAs, and SEP options. We also looked at other voluntary insurance such as life and disability policies, and other, less common, supplemental health insurance options such as dental and vision insurance. The last thing discussed in this section was employee services benefits, of which there are literally too many to count.

Our next section provided a discussion on methods of administering a benefits program and the value in communicating our benefits program to the company's employees. We found that there are three main types of flexible benefit plans—modular, core plus, and full choice plans—and what the advantages and disadvantages of each option are. We also looked at why it is so important to communicate the value of benefits programs to our employees.

Finally, in trends and issues for this chapter, we took a look at three issues in benefits management in the 21st-century world. The first one was the question of whether or not to provide benefits coverage to domestic partners of employees in the same manner as we would for spouses of those employees. The second issue was the question of how benefits programs might differ around the globe and how they are becoming more similar in many ways. The last issue in this section dealt with benefits programs that are aimed at environmental sustainability. And that is another significant amount of information for one book chapter, so now let's move on to the chapter summary.

Chapter Summary

Visit www.sagepub.com/lussier for helpful study resources.

13.1 **Discuss the strategic value of benefits programs.**

Human resources are one of the few potential sources for competitive advantage in a modern, 21st-century organization. The totality of their compensation—including their benefits packages—is one major factor in keeping employees happy and engaged, and willing to create a competitive advantage for our company. Today's workers demand more benefits and a better mix to fit their lifestyles. Because people demand it, companies add new benefits. This allows companies to increase job satisfaction and engagement because when we take care of our employees, they work harder and take good care of our customers and organization, which in turn allows us to create a competitive advantage based on our people.

13.2 **Identify the major reasons for the growth of benefits as a proportion of overall compensation.**

There are four major reasons for benefits growth. First, there are tax advantages to providing employee benefits to both employers and employees. Second, federal laws are requiring companies to provide more benefits than ever before. Third, organized labor has historically bargained for benefits for their workers, and benefits earned in these negotiations carry over to nonunion companies. Finally, buying in bulk can save significant amounts of money, so if companies buy many insurance plans, each plan costs less than if the individual bought the same insurance.

13.3 **Briefly discuss the major considerations in providing benefits programs.**

The three major considerations in providing benefits are amounts, mix, and flexibility. Amount is a function of how much the company is willing to spend on its employees. Many companies will calculate this as a percentage of direct compensation. Mix deals with the types of benefits that will be offered to employees. In many cases today, the number and type of benefits available are limited only by the imagination of the employees of the firm. Finally, we need to consider how much flexibility we are willing to build into our benefits program because flexible options are very important to today's employees. Can different employees choose different benefits from the mix available, or will they all have to get the same benefits?

13.4 **Identify and summarize the major statutory benefits required by federal law.**

The major statutory benefits include the following:

Social Security is composed of Old-Age, Survivors, and Disability Insurance (OASDI) programs and Medicare is the national health care program for the elderly or disabled.

Workers' compensation is a program to provide medical treatment and temporary payments to employees who are injured on the job or become ill because of their job. It is a *no-fault* insurance program that is mandatory in all states except Texas.

Unemployment Insurance is a federal program managed by each state to provide payments for a fixed period of time to workers who lose their jobs.

FMLA leave is leave that must be provided by the employer to eligible employees when they are faced with various medical issues in connection with the employee or their immediate family members. The leave is unpaid, but the employer must maintain health coverage for the employee while they are on leave.

PPACA requires that all employers with more than 50 employees provide health insurance for their employees or face significant penalties levied by the federal government.

13.5 **Identify the main statutory requirements that must be followed if organizations choose to provide health care or retirement plans for their employees.**

The requirements that must be followed if the employer provides health insurance are COBRA—a law that requires employers to offer continuation of health insurance to individuals who leave their employment for up to 18–36 months, if the employee is willing to pay the premium cost of the insurance policy; and HIPAA, which requires that, if the employee had health insurance at their old job and the new company provides health insurance as a benefit, it must be offered to the employee. In other words, the individual's health insurance is "portable." HIPAA also requires that companies take care to protect the health information of employees from unauthorized individuals.

The requirement that must be followed if the employer provides a retirement plan is ERISA. ERISA determines who is eligible to participate in the program and when they are eligible; it provides rules for "vesting" of the employee's retirement funds; it requires portability of those funds; and it requires that the funds are managed "prudently" by the fiduciary that maintains them.

13.6 Briefly describe the main categories of voluntary benefits available to organizations.

Major voluntary benefits include Paid Time Off, group health insurance, retirement plans, other employee insurance coverage, and employee services. Paid Time Off comes in various forms, such as sick leave, vacation time, holidays, and personal days. Group health insurance provides employees with health care coverage, and retirement plans allow them to save for their own retirement, sometimes with some help from the organization. Other employee insurance includes a wider variety of options including group term life insurance, short- and long-term disability policies, dental and vision insurance, group automobile and homeowners' insurance, and many more. Finally, employee services can include a massive range of options from educational assistance to child or adult day care, gyms, cafeterias, transportation and parking assistance, and too many others to list.

13.7 Describe the differences between traditional health care plans, HMOs, PPOs, and HSA/MSA plans.

Traditional health care plans usually cover a percentage of fees (historically 80%) for all medical services. The covered individual can live anywhere and go to any doctor that they choose. Traditional plans do not generally cover preventive care, such as an annual physical exam.

HMOs provide routine preventive care, but in the case of non-preventive care require that a review of specific circumstances concerning the individual and their health condition be completed *before* any significant medical testing, medical procedures, or hospital care is approved. The individual has to go to their PCP first, and if necessary be referred to specialists. There may be limits to where they can live, and there are limits to which doctors and facilities they can use.

PPOs are kind of a hybrid between HMOs and traditional plans. The PPO prefers that you see doctors and use facilities in the network, but you can go outside the network if you are willing to pay a higher percentage of the cost of care. PPOs cover preventive care, like HMOs, but don't limit other choices of the patient as much as do HMO plans.

HSAs/MSAs allow the employer and employee to fund a medical savings account from which the employee can pay medical expenses each year with pretax dollars. The funds can be used for a wide variety of medical expenses, but when the money runs out the individual becomes responsible for all medical costs until they reach a large deductible. Once this deductible is reached, an HDHP plan takes over and pays the remaining costs for the year.

13.8 Discuss the difference between defined benefit and defined contribution retirement plans and the reasons for the shift from defined benefit to defined contribution plans.

Under a defined benefit retirement plan the retiree knows exactly what benefits they will receive when they retire. Defined contribution plans only identify what is going to go into the retirement fund, not what will be received from it upon retirement. If the retirement funds are invested successfully, the individual's retirement account will be able to pay much higher benefits than if the funds are not invested successfully and don't grow very much.

Companies are shifting to defined contribution plans to shift the risk related to the investment of the retirement funds from the company to the individual. Under a defined benefit plan the employer puts money into the employee retirement accounts, but if the funds do not grow at the expected rate, the employer must add money to those accounts to make the promised retirement payments. In a defined contribution plan, the risk of slow growth of the investment shifts to the employee.

13.9 Discuss the major retirement plan options.

In a 401(k) (or 403[b] for nonprofits), the employee and the employer are allowed to contribute funds to the account up to a maximum amount of $16,500 (for an employee under 50 years of age in 2011). Contributions are made on a pretax basis, which means that when funds are put into the account they do not count as taxable income for the individual. Once the individual retires and begins to withdraw their funds, they pay income taxes on the money received.

IRA contributions reduce the employee's taxable income in the year in which they are contributed to the account. When the person withdraws the money in retirement, they pay taxes on it at that time. A Roth IRA works in the opposite way—the employee pays the tax when they contribute the money to the account, but they don't have to pay taxes when the money is withdrawn.

Simplified Employee Pensions are primarily for self-employed persons or owners of small companies. The *employer* contributes directly to traditional individual retirement accounts (SEP-IRAs) for all employees. SEP plans can be used by a person with a job who also has self-employment income to save more for retirement.

13.10 Discuss organizations' options when providing flexible benefit plans to their employees

Companies can choose modular plans, core plus plans, or full choice plans. Modular plans provide several basic modules from which each employee chooses. There is no other option outside one of the modules. Core plus plans provide a base set of benefits to all employees (the core) and then other options that the employee can choose freely from to meet their personal desires and needs. Full choice plans allow the employee the complete freedom to choose, but come with some potential problems such as a "moral hazard" problem, "adverse selection," and high management costs.

13.11 Discuss the need for benefit plans to be communicated to employees.

Most employees don't understand the true cost and value of the benefits that organizations provide and, as a result, don't perceive the value that they get from having the organization provide their benefits. There are many indications that employees who are satisfied with their benefits are more satisfied with their jobs and their companies. Providing employees with knowledge concerning their benefits package will help to create and maintain trust in the organization as well as improving job satisfaction on the part of those employees.

Key Terms

Consolidated Omnibus Budget Reconciliation Act (COBRA)

Defined benefit plans

Defined contribution plan

Domestic partners

Experience rating

Health Maintenance Organization (HMO)

Health Savings Account (HSA) or Medical Savings Account (MSA)

High-Deductible Health Plan (HDHP)

Pension Benefit Guaranty Corporation (PBGC)

Primary Care Physician (PCP)

Preferred Provider Organization (PPO)

Serious health condition

Traditional health care plans

Unemployment Insurance (UI)

Utilization analysis

Vesting

Workers' compensation

Key Term Review

Complete each of the following statements using one of this chapter's key terms:

_____ is an insurance program designed to provide medical treatment and temporary payments to employees who cannot work because of an employment-related injury or illness.

_____ is a measure of how often claims are made against an insurance policy.

_____ provides workers who lose their jobs with continuing subsistence payments from their state for a specified period of time.

_____ is an illness, an injury, an impairment, or a physical or mental condition that involves either inpatient care or continuing care for at least three consecutive days.

_____ is a law that requires employers to offer to maintain health insurance on individuals who leave their employment (for a period of time).

_____ provides for a maximum amount of time beyond which the employee will have unfettered access to their retirement funds, both employee contributions and employer contributions.

_____ is a governmental corporation established within the Department of Labor whose purpose is to insure retirement funds from failure.

_____ typically cover a set percentage of fees for medical services—either for doctors or in-patient care.

_____ is a health care plan that provides both health maintenance services and medical care as part of the plan.

_____ will be the first point of contact for all preventive care and in any routine medical situation, except emergencies.

_____ are a kind of hybrid between traditional fee-for-service plans and HMOs.

_____ allows the employer and employee to fund a medical savings account from which the employee can pay medical expenses each year with pretax dollars.

_____ is a "major medical" insurance plan that protects against catastrophic health care costs, and in most cases is paid for by the employer.

_____ is a review of the cost of a program and comparison of program costs with the rate of the program's usage by the members of the company.

_____ provide the retiree with a specific amount and type of benefits that will be available when the individual retires.

_____ identify only the amount of funds that will go into a retirement account, not what the employee will receive upon retirement.

_____ are individuals who are not legally married but who are in a one-to-one living arrangement similar to marriage.

Quick Check (True-False)

1. Companies can choose whether or not to offer any employee benefits at all. T F

2. Because of benefit costs, HRM needs to plan benefits programs to not only add value for employees, but also to provide strategic advantage to the company. T F

3. The main reason why benefits spending has grown over the past 30 years is that management wants employees to be happy. T F

4. The cost of Social Security and Medicare benefits is currently equal to approximately 40% of all U.S. federal revenues. T F

5. If you claim the correct number of deductions, your monthly Social Security retirement payment should roughly equal your monthly preretirement earnings. T F

6. Every American citizen is eligible to retire with full Social Security benefits at age 65 or earlier. T F

7. Workers' compensation is mandatory in all U.S. states. T F

8. Companies can lower their costs for workers' compensation and unemployment by lowering their "experience rating" in each area. T F

9. In normal economic periods, Unemployment Insurance payments are capped at a maximum of 26 weeks. T F

10. If an individual becomes self-employed, they are still eligible for Unemployment Insurance benefits, but for 13 weeks instead of 26 weeks. T F

11. Companies are required to allow their employees to take up to 12 weeks per year of paid leave under the FMLA. T F

12. The PPACA will require that employers with more than 50 employees "pay or play"—either provide health insurance or pay a fine for failing to provide it. T F

13. Under the PPACA, employees who are not covered by their employers will be required to purchase their own health insurance or face a fine themselves. T F

14. COBRA requires every employer to pay for their former employees to maintain health insurance for a period of 18 months after their employment is terminated if the employee was terminated through no fault of their own. T F

15. One aspect of HIPAA is the employer requirement for protection of individually identifiable health information. T F

16. The vesting requirement in ERISA says that employers must give control over all funds in an individual employee's retirement accounts to the employee after three years. T F

17. Paid Time Off includes the broad categories of vacation, sick days, holidays, and personal time off. T F

18. In 2009, health care services accounted for more than 17% of U.S. GDP. T F

19. Under a PPO plan, employees can see any doctor they choose, but may have to pay more for those physicians outside the preferred network. T F

20. Under HSA/MSA rules, money remaining in the health care account at the end of the year is forfeited back to the federal government. T F

21. Company-sponsored retirement plans are available to virtually all employees in the United States. T F

22. All employers provide at least some matching contribution to 401(k) and 403(b) retirement accounts. T F

23. Educational (tuition) assistance is a commonly known "employee services" benefit. T F

24. Flexible benefit plans are commonly called "cafeteria" plans because the employee gets to pick the benefits that they want, at least to an extent. T F

25. Many studies indicate that employees who are satisfied with their benefits are more satisfied with their jobs. T F

Communication Skills

The following critical-thinking questions can be used for class discussion and/or for written assignments to develop communication skills. Be sure to give complete explanations for all answers.

1. Would you rather have better benefits and a modest salary or a high salary and lower levels of benefits? Why?

2. Based on the high cost of the average benefits package, what would you do if you were the manager in charge of figuring out how to cut benefit costs in your company? Remember that you want to meet the company's strategic goals.

3. How would you "fix" Social Security to allow it to continue as a viable retirement program? Would you raise the retirement age? Would you lower the benefit level? Are there any other options to make the program solvent long-term?

4. Should workers' compensation insurance continue to be no-fault? Why or why not?

5. How would you lower your company's experience rating in the areas of workers' compensation and Unemployment Insurance if you were the HR Manager?

6. What would you do to minimize the abuse of FMLA leave if you became the HR Manager in a company where abuse was rampant? Explain how your answer would help overcome the problem.

7. Based on what is in the chapter, should the PPACA federal health care legislation remain in its current form, or should we rescind the requirement that employers and/or employees have to pay a fine if the employee is not covered by a health care plan? Explain your answer.

8. Is the vesting requirement in ERISA too long, too short, or just about right? Why did you answer the way that you did?

9. Should the United States mandate a certain amount of Paid Time Off per year like many other countries currently do? Why or why not?

10. If you were the head of HR, would you argue for a company-sponsored retirement plan for your employees? What are the pros and cons to such an argument?

11. What employee services can you think of that were not mentioned in the text, but would likely be highly valued by the employees where you work (or have worked)?

12. Do you think that in today's workforce it is becoming necessary to have a "full choice" flexible benefit plan? Why or why not?

Video

Please visit the student study site at **www.sagepub.com/lussier** to view the video links in this chapter.

Answers

REVIEW QUESTIONS (TRUE-FALSE) Answers

1. F   2. T   3. F   4. T   5. F   6. F   7. F   8. T   9. T   10. F   11. F   12. T   13. T   14. F   15. T   16. F   17. T   18. T   19. T   20. F   21. F   22. F   23. T   24. T   25. T

Case

Case 13-1. Defined Benefit Retirement Fades Away

Defined benefit retirement plans appear to be going the way of the dinosaurs. According to the Bureau of Labor Statistics, in 2011 only 20% of all private employees had access to defined benefit retirement plans while 58% had access to defined contribution plans.[1] This shift is also apparent in the amount of money being managed in each type of retirement plan. In 1985, approximately 65% of all retirement savings were held in defined benefit accounts, and only 35% were in defined contribution accounts. In 2005 the percentage had almost reversed to 60% in defined contribution accounts and only 40% in defined benefit plans.[2]

And this phenomenon is not only part of the business land-scape in the United States. Companies around the world continue to shift from defined benefit to defined contribution plans. According to the Canadian Press, the Royal Bank of Canada "is just the latest Canadian company" to end its defined benefit plan for new employees.[3] In the past 10 years, defined benefit plans also fell from about 97% to 60% of all pension funds in Britain, with defined contribution plans taking up the slack.

There appear to be several reasons for this shift. Among them is the fact that defined contribution plans shift the financial risk associated with funding employee retirement from the employer to the employee. The amount paid in retirement is based on the performance of the invested funds over the period of investment instead of being a fixed dollar amount. In addition, moving a defined benefit retirement account from one employer to another is virtually impossible, but defined contribution plans are basically designed for portability.

Companies, of course, are touting the value of defined contribution plans to their employees. They tell employees about defined contribution plans being more portable than defined benefit plans, so for those who will change jobs a number of times in their careers, a defined contribution plan is better. The risk of the employer underfunding the plan also disappears with a defined contribution plan, because the plan is funded directly over time in an account set up for each individual employee. Companies remind employees that defined benefit plans that are underfunded might not be there when the employee actually retires, and the Pension Benefit Guaranty Corporation only guarantees a basic retirement benefit—not 100% of what was promised by the employer. Defined contribution plans also typically have much more flexibility in how the money is invested and managed over the life of the fund, and the individual has direct control over this investment process, unlike defined benefit funds.

On the other hand, many employee associations, unions, and even some academics say that companies have been allowed to pull funding from their defined benefit plans that they knew would eventually be needed to fund employee retirements and that this is the reason that defined benefit plans are having difficulties. Ellen Smith, a *Wall Street Journal* reporter, says that employers have "plundered the nest eggs of American workers" by using their retirement funds as corporate piggy banks.[4] Olivia Mitchell of the Wharton School at the University of Pennsylvania says that companies pulled funds out of their retirement programs in the mid-1980s because of the significant increase in the stock market during that period.[5] When stocks started to take hits to their value several years later, the companies didn't refund their retirement plans, which left them in serious danger of being underfunded when needed.

Opponents to defined contribution plans strongly argue that defined benefit plans are more valuable to the worker because of the guaranteed benefit upon retirement. Since these plans provide a guaranteed income to the worker, it is easier for the employee to plan for their eventual retirement. The employee groups point to the fact that most defined contribution plans have not gained any significant value over the past several years because of the stagnant stock markets worldwide. As a result, employees who put money into such accounts expecting the historical average return on their investment of about 7% have seen virtually no growth in their retirement accounts, and in some case significant declines in the invested monies. Defined contribution accounts may also be subject to inflation risks, which can reduce the actual amounts available in retirement. Finally, many employees choose not to participate in defined contribution plans, and for the ones who do, most are not capable of directly managing their funds with as much success as professional investment managers.

Questions

1. Which side are you on in the debate—should companies be allowed to discontinue existing defined benefit plans or not? Explain your answer.

2. If you were the benefits manager for a large national bank, which defined contribution plan(s) identified in the text would you consider as options for your workforce? Explain your answer.

3. As the benefits manager, what would you need to do to ensure that the retirement plan you chose would have value to both the company and the employees?

SKILL BUILDER 13-1

Developing Flexible Employee Benefit Plans

Objective

To develop your skill at designing flexible benefits.

Skills

The primary skills developed through this exercise are:

1. *HR Management skill* – Technical, conceptual and design, and business skills

2. *SHRM 2010 Curriculum Guidebook* – I: Total Rewards—Employee Benefits

Assignment

1. Using the "Voluntary Benefits" column of Exhibit 13-4, as the HR benefits manager select the benefits to be offered in three different modular plans. Be sure to identify the target group for each of the three modules.

2. Again using Exhibit 13-4, as the HR benefits manager develop a core plus benefit plan.

SKILL BUILDER 13-2

Selecting Flexible Employee Benefit Plans

Objective

To develop your skill at selecting flexible benefits.

Skills

The primary skills developed through this exercise are:

1. *HR Management skill* – Technical, conceptual and design, and business skills

2. *SHRM 2010 Curriculum Guidebook* – I: Total Rewards—Employee Benefits

Assignment

As an employee, rank order the voluntary benefits in Self-Assessment 13-1 from 1 (*most important*) to 9 (*least important*).

14

Workplace Safety, Health, and Security

Learning Outcomes

After studying this chapter you should be able to:

14.1 Identify the responsibilities of both employers and employees under the general duties clause of the OSH Act

14.2 Briefly describe what OSHA does in a work-site inspection

14.3 Discuss employer rights during an OSHA inspection

14.4 Identify the types of violations that OSHA looks for in inspections

14.5 Discuss the primary job of NIOSH as it applies to workplace safety and health

14.6 Briefly discuss EAPs and EWPs and what their value is to companies and employees

14.7 Discuss the concept of ergonomics and identify OSHA's function in ergonomics in the workplace

14.8 Briefly discuss the causes of stress and how it can be managed

14.9 Identify the top concerns for security in the workplace today

14.10 Define the following terms:

Workplace safety	Ergonomics
Material Safety Data Sheet (MSDS)	Stress
	Stressors
Employee health	Burnout
Employee Assistance Program (EAP)	Workplace security
	Cyber security
Employee Wellness Program (EWP)	

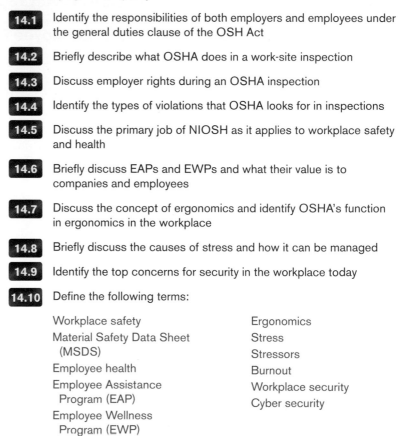

Chapter 14 Outline

SHRM
HR CONTENT

See Appendix A:
*SHRM 2010 Curriculum
Guidebook* for the
complete list

A.   Employee and Labor Relations (required)
   23.   Posting requirements

B.   Employment Law (required)
   14.   The Occupational Safety and Health Act of 1970

C.   Job Analysis/Job Design (required)
   6.   Compliance with legal requirements
      Ergonomics and workplace safety (work hazards and mitigation)

I.   Total Rewards (required)

B.   Employee Benefits
   9.   Employee assistance/wellness programs
   17.   Wellness programs

L.   Workplace Health, Safety, and Security (required–undergraduates only)
   1.   OSHA citations and penalties
   2.   Disaster preparation, continuity and recovery planning
   3.   Employee health
   4.   Inspection
   5.   Protection from retaliation
   6.   Safety management
   7.   Security concerns at work
   8.   Communicable diseases
   9.   Data security
   11.   Ergonomics

Case 14-1. Handling the Unhealthy Employee

Careful, Careful . . . You Can Never Be Too Safe

A safe and healthy workplace is vital for every employee—whether you work in a factory or an office environment. "Did you hear we are finally getting ergonomic keyboards for our computers, and new office chairs too?" Traci asked me excitedly one Monday morning. "We even have a training session scheduled with tips on proper posture and how to prevent fatigue while sitting at the computer.

Should be more fun than the last safety training about lifting boxes properly!" "Well, maybe all training isn't entertaining," I replied with a smile. "But when you lift heavy items at work or at home, I hope you are following the rules!" Why is it an employer's responsibility to provide a safe workplace environment? Chapter 14 explores the issues and ethics behind workplace health, safety, and security.

The Practitioner's Model for HRM

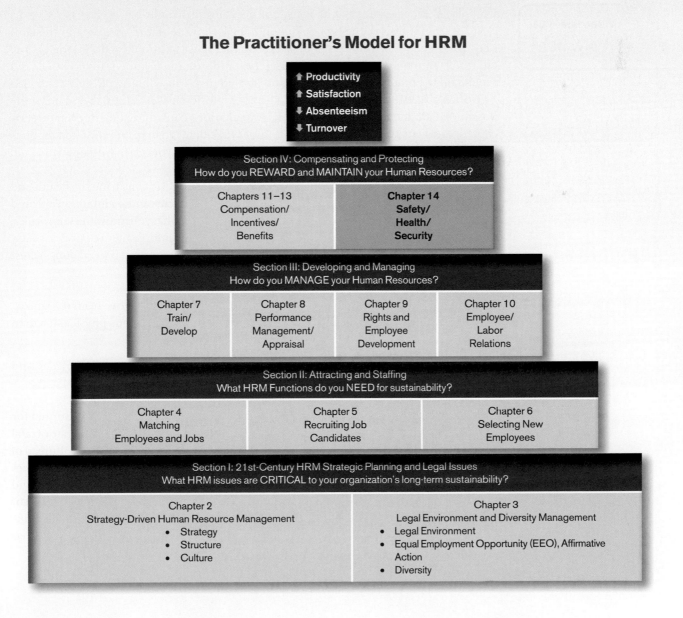

⬆ Productivity
⬆ Satisfaction
⬇ Absenteeism
⬇ Turnover

Section IV: Compensating and Protecting
How do you REWARD and MAINTAIN your Human Resources?

| Chapters 11–13 Compensation/ Incentives/ Benefits | Chapter 14 Safety/ Health/ Security |

Section III: Developing and Managing
How do you MANAGE your Human Resources?

| Chapter 7 Train/ Develop | Chapter 8 Performance Management/ Appraisal | Chapter 9 Rights and Employee Development | Chapter 10 Employee/ Labor Relations |

Section II: Attracting and Staffing
What HRM Functions do you NEED for sustainability?

| Chapter 4 Matching Employees and Jobs | Chapter 5 Recruiting Job Candidates | Chapter 6 Selecting New Employees |

Section I: 21st-Century HRM Strategic Planning and Legal Issues
What HRM issues are CRITICAL to your organization's long-term sustainability?

| Chapter 2 Strategy-Driven Human Resource Management | Chapter 3 Legal Environment and Diversity Management |

Chapter 2
Strategy-Driven Human Resource Management
• Strategy
• Structure
• Culture

Chapter 3
Legal Environment and Diversity Management
• Legal Environment
• Equal Employment Opportunity (EEO), Affirmative Action
• Diversity

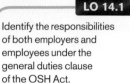

SHRM

Guide – B:14
The Occupational
Safety and Health Act
of 1970 (OSHA)

LO 14.1

Identify the responsibilities
of both employers and
employees under the
general duties clause
of the OSH Act.

Video Link 14.1

Why Was OSHA
Created?

Workplace Safety and OSHA

We now have a workforce that is reasonably compensated, well trained, and productive. The last major management concern is to keep them safe and healthy so that they can continue to perform at high levels. This chapter will first focus on federal workplace safety laws and regulations as well as the governing agencies for industrial safety and health. Later in the chapter, we will also cover employee health issues, including work-life balance for our employees, employee assistance and wellness programs, and stress, and how they affect our employees. Finally we will take a look at the increasingly important topic of workplace security from the organizational perspective, so let's get started.

The Occupational Safety and Health Act of 1970

The Occupational Safety and Health Act (OSH Act) of 1970 requires employers to pursue workplace safety. **Workplace safety** deals with *the physical protection of people from injury or illness while on the job.* Employers must meet all Occupational Safety and Health Administration (OSHA) safety standards, maintain records of injuries and deaths due to workplace accidents, and submit to onsite inspections when notified.

Most of us know of the BP oil spill on their Deepwater Horizon oil rig in the Gulf of Mexico in 2010. A critical safety switch on the rig wasn't functional.[1] BP had many citations from OSHA for violation of safety standards and is known to have deferred repairs on the oil rig that some claim contributed to or caused the explosion that killed 11 workers in 2010; plus BP had a prior deadly explosion in Texas in 2005.[2] So it is quite possible that failure to comply with OSHA regulations contributed to, or even directly caused, the deaths of 11 people. In 2011, under President Obama, OSHA stated that it is taking stronger steps to reduce injuries and illnesses in the workplace with new rules and steeper fines.[3]

Today, the HR Department commonly has responsibility for ensuring the health and safety of employees. HRM works closely with other departments and maintains health and safety records. As HR Managers, it will be absolutely critical that you know the safety rules, that you be sure your employees know them, and that you enforce them to prevent accidents. In addition to many specific requirements in the OSH Act, the *general duties clause* that *covers all employers* states:[4]

1. that each *employer* shall furnish a place of employment that is free from recognized hazards that are causing or are likely to cause death or serious physical harm to employees; and

2. that *employees* have a *duty to comply* with occupational safety standards, rules, and regulations.

In 1970, the year that the OSH Act was passed, job-related accidents accounted for more than 14,000 worker deaths in the United States.[5] The good news is that the rate of fatal work injuries has fallen, but the bad news is that in 2009 (the last year of available Bureau of Labor Statistics information) there were still 4,551 fatalities and nearly 1.25 million injuries or illnesses that required days away from work.[6] This is a rate of almost 12 per thousand full-time workers. Recall from Chapter 1 that absenteeism is one of the major concerns of all managers, and by allowing injuries and occupational illnesses to occur we are contributing to that absenteeism. So, losing this many work days, as well as more than 4,500 lives, has to be a concern for HRM as well as other managers.

The Occupational Safety and Health Administration

OSHA is the division within the Department of Labor that is charged with overseeing the OSH Act. It was created to "ensure safe and healthful working conditions for working men and women by setting and enforcing standards and by providing training, outreach, education and assistance."[7] OSHA has broad authority to investigate complaints and impose citations and penalties on employers who violate the OSH Act.

What Does OSHA Do?

OSHA is responsible for setting federal safety and health standards and promulgating those standards to employers. OSHA is also the responsible agency of the federal government for occupational safety and health inspections. Inspections are made *without any advance notice* to the employer, and are done based on the following issues (in priority order):[8]

- Imminent dangers
- Catastrophes (fatalities or hospitalizations of more than three employees)
- Worker complaints
- Targeted inspections (such as companies with high injury rates)
- Follow-up inspections

Inspectors must identify themselves and tell the employer the reason for the inspection upon arrival at the work site. The employer *can* decide not to allow the inspection without a court order, but this is generally not a very good idea on a number of levels. Besides looking like the company may have something to hide, it wastes time, and the inspector will be less likely to be disposed to assist the employer in immediate correction of discrepancies that might be found during the inspection that *will ultimately occur anyway* after the court order is provided. In general, it makes more sense to allow the inspection to go on, in accordance with OSHA rules.

Employer and Employee Rights and Responsibilities Under OSHA

General rights of employers and employees are shown in Exhibit 14-1. We want to make sure that company management always stays within their rights in interactions with OSHA.

Employer rights. Employer rights during an inspection are a bit more specific. The employer has a right to get the inspector's credentials, including their name and badge number, and to receive information on the reason for the inspection—either the employee complaint or the program inspection information. They also have the right to refuse to allow the inspection without a court order being provided (which we have already said is generally a bad idea).

So assuming that the inspection is allowed, we need to be aware of some things that we have a right to, and should, do during the inspection.

- If the inspection is being conducted due to a worker complaint, we have the right to get a copy of the complaint (without the employee's name), and we want to do so, because we want to know what is being alleged.
- Second, we have a right to have a company representative accompany inspectors as they go through their site visit, and we, as the HR representative, want to accompany them.

There are a few reasons to accompany the inspector. First, we want to understand any violations that the inspector finds and notes because sometimes, no matter how hard a person tries to describe a problem, it will still be unclear unless we see it ourselves. Second,

LO 14.2

Briefly describe what OSHA does in a work-site inspection.

Video Link 14.2
Work Safety and OSHA

WORK
APPLICATION 14-1

Identify any unsafe or unhealthy working conditions that you observed in any organization (business, sports, school, etc.).

LO 14.3

Discuss employer rights during an OSHA inspection.

SHRM

Guide – L:4
Inspection

Exhibit 14-1	Employer and Employee Rights and Responsibilities Under OSHA

Employer Rights	Employee Rights
Know the reason for inspection visits	Working conditions free from unnecessary hazards
Accompany inspectors when on site	Receipt of information and training on workplace hazards
Know the names of employees interviewed in an inspection	File a complaint about hazardous working conditions and request an inspection
Take notes on what is inspected and any discrepancies	Maintain anonymity when filing a complaint
Employer Responsibilities	Use their rights without fear of retaliation or discrimination
General Duty Clause	Object to the time frame for correction of discrepancies
Find and correct safety/health hazards	**Employee Responsibilities**
Inform and train employees about existing hazards in the workplace	Follow employer safety and health rules and keep the workplace free from hazards
Notify OSHA within 8 hours if a fatality occurs or if 3 or more workers are hospitalized	Comply with OSHA standards and regulations
Provide personal protective equipment necessary to do the job at no cost to workers	Report hazardous conditions to their supervisor
Keep accurate records of work-related injuries or illnesses	Report job-related injuries or illnesses to their supervisor
Avoid retaliation against workers who exercise their rights under the OSH Act	Tell the truth if interviewed by an OSHA inspector

Source: OSHA, Department of Labor.

in many cases, we can immediately fix a discrepancy such as loose lines or hoses strung across a workspace. Although the discrepancy will almost surely still be noted, the inspector will see that we are willing to comply with the law and OSHA regulations, quickly and to the best of our ability. This willingness can keep minor infractions from becoming major infractions. Third, we want to make sure that the inspection stays within the scope noted in the complaint or the program inspection guidelines. We don't really want the OSHA representative wandering all over the work site.

An employer representative also has a right to be present when the inspector is interviewing employees (unless the interview is private by request of the employee being interviewed) and the right to stop interviews that are becoming confrontational or disturbing the work environment.

The employer also has a right to inform the employees of their rights during the inspection. The inspector will provide the employer with a list of discrepancies upon completion of their inspection. After an inspection, employers also have a right to contest any citations that they receive through OSHA.

SHRM

Guide – L:5
Protection from retaliation

Employee rights. Employee rights during inspections include the right to refuse to be interviewed, or if they agree to interviews they can request that an employer representative be present *or* that the interview be held in private. The employee also has the right to

14-1 APPLYING THE CONCEPT

Employer Rights and Responsibilities Under OSHA

Identify each statement regarding employer rights and responsibilities.

a. Yes

b. No

_____ 1. Do we have to keep records of work-related injuries or illnesses?

_____ 2. Do I have to accompany the OSHA inspector during the site visit?

_____ 3. Can we require the employees to buy their own safety equipment?

_____ 4. Can I ask the inspector the reason for the inspection?

_____ 5. Now that Tom got us in trouble with OSHA, can we demote him?

_____ 6. Can I write down some notes during the OSHA inspection?

_____ 7. Do we have to inform and train employees about existing hazards in the workplace?

legal representation during the interview if they request it, and they can end the interview at any point in time just by requesting that the interview be discontinued. Finally, employees have a right against retaliation for taking part in an interview with the inspector and telling the truth.

14-2 APPLYING THE CONCEPT

Employee Rights and Responsibilities Under OSHA

Identify each statement regarding employee rights and responsibilities.

a. Yes

b. No

_____ 8. If I see hazardous conditions, do I have to tell my supervisor?

_____ 9. This helmet is heavy and uncomfortable, and I can't see as well with it on. Do I have to wear it?

_____ 10. If I report hazardous conditions to HR, do I have to tell them my name?

_____ 11. If an OSHA inspector interviews me, can I cover up for the company and say we followed OSHA guidelines when we didn't?

_____ 12. I just got hurt, and my supervisor will be mad at me for making him do all the paperwork. Do I have to tell the supervisor about it?

_____ 13. Can I object to the time frame for correction of discrepancies of OSHA standards?

_____ 14. Can I make my employer have working conditions free from "any" hazards?

Hazard Communication Standards

OSHA requires that all employers maintain information at each work site that describes any chemical hazards that may be present on site. Under federal law, "the employer shall maintain in the workplace copies of the required material safety data sheets for each hazardous chemical, and shall ensure that they are readily accessible during each work shift to employees when they are in their work area(s)."[9] **Material Safety Data Sheets** (MSDSs) are *documents that provide information on a hazardous chemical and its characteristics.* The OSHA-recommended MSDS format is provided in Exhibit 14-2. The MSDS provides employees with a quick reference to the hazards of working with chemical compounds. The rule says that electronic versions of MSDSs are acceptable, as long as there are no barriers to immediate access on the work site.

Exhibit 14-2	Material Safety Data Sheet Format

OSHA recommends that MSDSs follow the 16-section format established by the American National Standards Institute (ANSI) for preparation of an MSDS.

Some of the information in this format is not required by the hazard communication standard, but the 16-section MSDS is becoming the internationally accepted standard. The 16 sections are:

- Identification
- Hazard(s) identification
- Composition/information on ingredients
- First-aid measures
- Firefighting measures
- Accidental release measures
- Handling and storage
- Exposure controls/personal protection
- Physical and chemical properties
- Stability and reactivity
- Toxicological information
- Ecological information
- Disposal considerations
- Transport information
- Regulatory information
- Other information

LO 14.4

Identify the types of violations that OSHA looks for in inspections.

SHRM

Guide – L:1
OSHA citations and penalties

Violations, Citations, and Penalties

OSHA violations include the following:[10]

- Willful—a violation in which the employer knew that a hazardous condition existed but made no effort to eliminate the hazard.
- Serious—a violation where the hazard could cause injury or illness that would most likely result in death or significant physical harm.
- Other than serious—a violation where any illness or injury likely to result from the hazard is unlikely to cause death or serious physical harm, but the violation does have a direct impact on employees' safety and health.
- De minimis—violations that have no direct or immediate safety or health danger; this does not result in citations or penalties.

- Failure to abate—violations where the employer has not corrected a previous violation for which a citation was issued and the settlement date has passed.
- Repeated—violations where the employer has been cited for the same type of violation within the previous five years.

Willful and repeated violations can bring the employer up to a $70,000 fine for each violation. *Failure to abate* violations can cost the employer as much as $7,000 per day while the violation continues to exist, and *serious* violations can also cost the employer a $7,000 fine.

The National Institute for Occupational Safety and Health

The National Institute for Occupational Safety and Health (NIOSH) works under the umbrella of the Centers for Disease Control and Prevention (CDC). NIOSH was also created as part of the 1970 OSH Act, and its mission is global in scope. The primary job of NIOSH is "providing research, information, education, and training in the field of occupational safety and health."[11] NIOSH notes three major goals in its strategic plan:

- Conduct research to reduce work-related illnesses and injuries
- Promote safe and healthy workplaces through interventions, recommendations, and capacity building
- Enhance international workplace safety and health through global collaborations

NIOSH routinely works with worldwide government health laboratories and other member nations in the World Health Organization (WHO) to identify workplace issues that can cause illness or injury and to create standards for the WHO member countries. NIOSH also works hand in hand with OSHA to identify workplace illnesses and to track diseases that can be passed from one person to another in the work environment. It also does research on occupational safety and health topics from ergonomics (we will discuss this shortly) to MRSA (methicillin-resistant *Staphylococcus aureus*) infections and workplace violence. NIOSH research frequently provides the data that OSHA uses to create new workplace standards and regulations.

One of the most significant areas of research at NIOSH is communicable disease research. Again, in conjunction with other countries in the WHO, NIOSH has done research on a number of respiratory diseases that can be passed from one person to another, including tuberculosis and various strains of flu virus. NIOSH research attempts to identify methods of transmission and then provide guidelines for minimizing danger of transmission of dangerous diseases that may exist in the workplace. The entire intent of NIOSH research is to make the workplace safer for all employees.

Federal Notice Posting Requirements

There are a number of notices that employers are required to post in a convenient location frequented by employees during normal working hours. The notices or posters contain important information about employee rights and company responsibilities under federal law. OSHA's Job Safety and Health Protection poster is one of these, but there are also other

WORK
APPLICATION 14-2

Identify any organization (business, sports, school, etc.) that has violated, or that was cited and/or penalized for not meeting, OSHA standards. Be sure to provide details of the situation.

LO 14.5

Discuss the primary job of NIOSH as it applies to workplace safety and health.

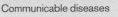

SHRM

Guide – L:8
Communicable diseases

SHRM

Guide – A:23
Posting requirements

Some jobs require safety equipment.

posting requirements. Take a look at the following information for general federally mandated posting requirements.

The Department of Labor provides a number of posting requirements on its website (www.dol.gov), and we have reproduced the major ones in Exhibit 14-3.

Besides the requirements identified by the Department of Labor, SHRM has also identified a series of other required postings, depending on the nature of the employer. We have reproduced part of the SHRM[12] list in Exhibit 14-4 (page 566).

In addition to all of the other requirements, each state has its own posting requirements. Most states have requirements to at least post information on workers' compensation, unemployment insurance, and state minimum wage laws, while many states have a large number of other requirements as well. We need to become aware of and maintain knowledge of our state's requirements. Finally, employers must make certain that they also notify new hires of the above information.

Employee Health

Meeting OSHA requirements is necessary, but there are many other aspects to maintaining good employee health. **Employee health** *is the state of physical and psychological wellness in the workforce.* We have to consider both physical *and* psychological health in order to have a strong workforce. We need to provide our employees with the ability to maintain both. In this section, we are going to complete a quick review of some of the other physical and psychological issues in today's workplace.

Work-Life Balance

With mobile technology, the boundary between work and nonwork hours becomes fuzzy, as employees even check in at work during their vacation and weekends, increasing the likelihood of work-family spillover. Spillover is the effect of work and family on one another that generate similarities between the two domains.[13] Thus, people are seeking work-life balance,[14] and many individuals are even taking classes to learn how to better balance the two.[15] Balance between work and home lives is sought but rarely happens for long because of work-family conflict. This conflict is also linked with some other bad consequences such as stress, absenteeism, burnout, and dissatisfaction with job, family, and life, which can all lead to excessive job turnover and the breakup of families.[16]

To help keep a better work-life balance, the trend is for firms to offer more work-family benefits.[17] For example, employers are offering flexible work schedules, so that employees can start and end work around the times that help them balance work and family, and they also allow their people flexible time off to attend family activities such as parent-teacher meetings and sporting events. Many more firms are offering child care and eldercare on or near their place of work than in the past, and are providing the flexibility for their

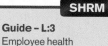

Exhibit 14-3	Department of Labor Posting Requirements for Businesses and Other Employers

POSTER	WHO MUST POST	CITATIONS / PENALTY	OTHER INFORMATION
Job Safety and Health Protection Occupational Safety and Health Administration	Private employers engaged in a business affecting commerce. Does not apply to federal, state, or political subdivisions of states.	Any covered employer failing to post the poster may be subject to citation and penalty.	Employers in states operating OSHA-approved state plans should obtain and post the state's equivalent poster.
Equal Employment Opportunity is the Law Office of Federal Contract Compliance Programs	Entities holding federal contracts or subcontracts or federally assisted construction contracts of $10,000 or more; financial institutions that are issuing and paying agents for U.S. savings bonds and savings notes; depositories of federal funds or entities having government bills of lading.	Appropriate contract sanctions may be imposed for uncorrected violations.	Post copies of the poster in conspicuous places available to employees, applicants for employment, and representatives of labor organizations with which there is a collective bargaining agreement.
Fair Labor Standards Act (FLSA) Minimum wage poster Wage and Hour Division	Every private, federal, state, and local government employer employing any employee subject to the Fair Labor Standards Act.	No citations or penalties for failure to post.	Any employer of employees to whom Sec. 7 of the Fair Labor Standards Act does not apply may alter or modify the poster legibly to show that the overtime provisions do not apply.
Your Rights Under the Family and Medical Leave Act Wage and Hour Division	Public agencies (including state, local, and federal employers), public and private elementary and secondary schools, as well as private sector employers who employ 50 or more employees in 20 or more workweeks per year.	Willful refusal to post may result in a civil money penalty by the Wage and Hour Division not to exceed $100 for each separate offense.	Where an employer's workforce is not proficient in English, the employer must provide the notice in the language the employee speaks. The poster must be posted prominently where it can be readily seen by employees and applicants.
Uniformed Services Employment and Reemployment Rights Act (Notice for Use by All Employers)	The full text of the notice must be provided by each employer to persons entitled to rights and benefits under USERRA.	No citations or penalties for failure to notify. An individual could ask USDOL to investigate and seek compliance, or file a private enforcement action to require the employer to provide the notice to employees.	Employers may provide the notice by posting it where employee notices are customarily placed. However, employers are free to provide the notice in other ways that will minimize costs while ensuring that the full text of the notice is provided.
Notice: Employee Polygraph Protection Act Wage and Hour Division	Any employer engaged in or affecting commerce or in the production of goods for commerce. Does not apply to federal, state, and local governments, or to circumstances covered by the national defense and security exemption.	The Secretary of Labor can bring court actions and assess civil penalties for failing to post.	The act extends to all employees or prospective employees regardless of their citizenship status. Foreign corporations operating in the United States must comply or will result in penalties for failing to post. The poster must be displayed where employees and applicants for employment can readily observe it.
Notification of Employee Rights Under Federal Labor Laws Office of Labor-Management Standards Executive Order 13496	Federal contractors and subcontractors are required to post the prescribed employee notice conspicuously in plants and offices where employees covered by the NLRA perform contract-related activity, including all places where notices to employees are customarily posted both physically and electronically.	The sanctions, penalties, and remedies for noncompliance with the notice requirements include the suspension or cancellation of the contract and the debarring of federal contractors from future federal contracts.	The notice, prescribed in the Department of Labor's regulations, informs employees of federal contractors and subcontractors of their rights under the NLRA to organize and bargain collectively with their employers and to engage in other protected concerted activity. Additionally, the notice provides examples of illegal conduct by employers and unions, and it provides contact information to the National Labor Relations Board (www.nlrb.gov), the agency responsible for enforcing the NLRA.

Source: U.S. Department of Labor.

Exhibit 14-4	Other Required Postings

Federal Posting Requirements

Employers engaged in interstate commerce, state and local governments, federal employees, employment agencies, and labor organizations with 20 or more members:

- Consolidated Omnibus Budget Reconciliation Act (COBRA) Job Loss Poster *(optional but recommended)*

Federal government contractors and subcontractors:

- Rehabilitation Act (private employers with federal contracts or subcontracts of $10,000 or more)
- Executive Order 11246 (federal government contractors, subcontractors and contractors working on federally assisted construction contracts)
- Executive Order 13201—Beck Notice (federal contractors and subcontractors with 15 or more employees)
- McNamara-O'Hara Service Contract Act (private employers with government agency service contracts in excess of $2,500)
- Vietnam Era Veterans' Readjustment Assistance Act (employers with federal contracts of $100,000 or more)
- Davis-Bacon Act (employers working on public construction projects in excess of $2,000)
- Walsh-Healey Act (employers with federal contracts or subcontracts worth $10,000 or more)

Farm labor contractors, agricultural employers, and agricultural associations:

- Migrant and Seasonal Agricultural Worker Protection Act Poster

Source: Society for Human Resource Management (SHRM).

WORK
APPLICATION 14-4

Assess your work- and/ or school-life balance. What percentage of your waking hours are typically devoted to work, school, and personal life? How can you improve the balance?

LO 14.6

Briefly discuss EAPs and EWPs and what their value is to companies and employees.

SHRM

Guide – I:B9
Employee assistance/ wellness programs

employees to select this as a standard benefit. Some organizations are offering courses on how to better balance work and life. Others provide counseling benefits to help improve family life so that it doesn't have a negative impact on work. Such counseling is commonly offered through the HR EAP, our next topic.

Employee Assistance and Wellness Programs

Two significant employee services that can assist with work-life balance and other aspects of employee mental and physical health are Employee Assistance Programs and Employee Wellness Programs, also known as Workplace Wellness Programs (WWPs). These programs continue to grow in popularity in the United States and other countries around the world, most likely because companies are seeing results from the use of such programs.

Employee Assistance Programs

An **Employee Assistance Program (EAP)** is *a set of counseling and other services provided to employees that help them to resolve personal issues that may affect their work.* Almost half of private sector workers have access to an EAP.[18] An EAP is designed to assist employees in confronting and overcoming problems in their personal life such as marital problems or divorce, financial problems, substance addictions, emotional problems, and many other issues. Why do half of all employers pay for these services? The simple answer is that such services can save valuable employees and, as a result, save the company money if they are available to the employee when they are needed.[19,20]

EAPs are confidential services provided to the employee. The employee can contact the company EAP and receive counseling and/or treatment for emotional or other personal issues as necessary. In some cases, EAPs may be regulated by federal laws including meeting the requirements of ERISA and COBRA, so company HR personnel need to be aware of this fact.

Employee Wellness Programs

Employee Wellness Programs (EWPs) are designed to cater to the employee's physical, instead of psychological, welfare through education and training programs. Wellness programs offer health education, training and fitness, weight and lifestyle management, and health risk assessment services to employees. The obvious goal is improving the health of our workforce, but why? EWPs have succeeded in slowing health care cost increases.[21] EWPs can return from $2 to $6 in lower health care and lost productivity costs for every dollar spent.[22] A rate of Return on Investment (ROI) of five is a pretty good investment! Another interesting effect of EWPs appears to be lower turnover—"healthy employees stay with your company . . . organizations with highly effective wellness programs report significantly lower voluntary attrition than do those whose programs have low effectiveness (9% vs. 15%)."[23] So wellness programs provide employers with high ROI and help with productivity, absenteeism, and turnover. No wonder companies continue to institute these programs.

Ergonomics and Musculoskeletal Disorders

According to OSHA, "**Ergonomics** *is the science of fitting workplace conditions and job demands to the capabilities of the working population.*"[24] The CDC identifies the goal of ergonomics as being to "reduce stress and eliminate injuries and disorders associated with the overuse of muscles, bad posture, and repeated tasks."[25] Workplace ergonomics focuses on design of jobs and workspaces to limit the repetitive stresses that employees face in doing their daily work. OSHA provides employers with a set of voluntary guidelines on ergonomics in the workplace. These voluntary guidelines took the place of an earlier set of more rigid rules from OSHA on ergonomics that were rescinded by Congress in 2001.[26]

Several industries, including shipyards, poultry processors, retail stores, and nursing homes, among others, have specific sets of guidelines provided by OSHA. Other industries have the general set of voluntary guidelines published by OSHA.[27] It is wise for the organization to know OSHA's voluntary guidelines for their industry even though the earlier ergonomics rule was rescinded, because the OSHA website notes that "under the OSH Act's General Duty Clause, employers must keep their workplaces free from recognized serious hazards, including ergonomic hazards. This requirement exists whether or not there are voluntary guidelines."[28]

In addition to the potential for enforcement actions on the part of OSHA, it just makes sense to pay attention to ergonomics. Musculoskeletal Disorders (MSDs) "affect the body's muscles, joints, tendons, ligaments and nerves" and can occur in many different work environments. They can take a toll on employee productivity when workers suffer from these issues. MSDs include a commonly known *Repetitive Stress Injury (RSI)* called *carpal tunnel syndrome* where the nerves in the wrist become inflamed and painful, making movement difficult. But there are a large number of other problems that fall under the MSD category including other RSIs like rotator cuff syndrome, tennis elbow, carpet layer's knee, and many others.[29] All of these problems have the potential to cost the organization money in the form of lost productivity as well as the potential for workers' compensation claims. So paying attention to ergonomics at work can both improve productivity and save the company money.

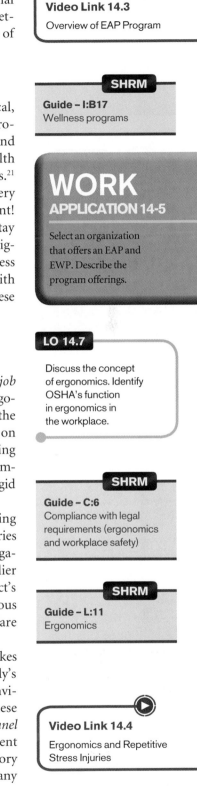

Video Link 14.3
Overview of EAP Program

SHRM
Guide – I:B17
Wellness programs

WORK
APPLICATION 14-5

Select an organization that offers an EAP and EWP. Describe the program offerings.

LO 14.7
Discuss the concept of ergonomics. Identify OSHA's function in ergonomics in the workplace.

SHRM
Guide – C:6
Compliance with legal requirements (ergonomics and workplace safety)

SHRM
Guide – L:11
Ergonomics

Video Link 14.4
Ergonomics and Repetitive Stress Injuries

Identify potential ergonomics and MSDs in an industry that you work or want to work in.

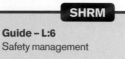

SHRM

Guide – L:6
Safety management

Describe any safety, health, and stress training offered by an organization, preferably one you work(ed) for.

Cornell University has an ergonomics program called CUErgo that has a large number of tools to help design jobs that are less stressful on employees; for a listing, go to its website at http://ergo.human.cornell.edu. It provides information from research by the Cornell Human Factors and Ergonomics Research Group (CHFERG).[30] It also provides information on work environments from hospitals to general workstation design in offices and is a great help in identifying potential ergonomic issues in the workplace.

Safety and Health Management and Training

HR Managers need to understand OSHA rules and standards in order to be able to make the workplace as safe as possible, and offering EAPs and EWPs and stress management training (our next section) is part of safety and health management. In addition, if we understand the OSHA requirements and train our workforce about the rules of safety and health management, we can potentially lower the cost of running the business. Safety and health training is a critical tool used in lowering the rate of injuries and work-related illness, and lowering these factors can significantly improve the bottom line. We discussed training previously, so we will keep this section short; refer back to Chapter 7 for details.

By keeping the number of accidents and incidents low, we lower absenteeism plus increase job satisfaction. Nobody wants to work in an unsafe environment. Because we improve two of our four most important variables at work—absenteeism and job satisfaction—we are almost assured of increasing productivity over time. This is yet another way that HRM can assist in reaching organizational goals while using the least amount of organizational resources possible.

Stress

People often have internal reactions to external environmental stimuli. **Stress** is *the body's reaction to environmental demands.* This reaction can be emotional and/or physical. Americans are putting in some of the longest hours in the global village,[31] and 75% of Americans name work as a stressor.[32] As stated in Chapter 1, absenteeism is costly, and there is a relationship between absenteeism and workplace strain.[33] In this section, we discuss functional and dysfunctional stress, the causes of stress, how to manage it, and the stress tug-of-war.

Functional and Dysfunctional Stress

Video Link 14.5
Workplace Stress

Let's begin by describing the difference between functional and dysfunctional stress, and the consequences of dysfunctional stress.

Functional Stress

Stress is *functional* (also called acute stress) when it helps improve performance by challenging and motivating people to meet objectives. People perform best under some pressure. Stress is an asset that stretches capacity and fuels creativity. When deadlines are approaching, adrenaline flows, and people rise to the occasion. Stress actually provides greater strength and focus than we think we are capable of—so long as we are in control of it.[34]

Dysfunctional Stress

On the other hand, too much stress is dysfunctional because it decreases performance. **Stressors** are *factors that may, if extreme, cause people to feel overwhelmed by anxiety, tension,* *and/or pressure.* Stress that is constant, chronic, and severe can lead to burnout over a period of time. **Burnout** is *a constant lack of interest and motivation to perform one's job.* Burnout results from too much stress. Stress that is severe enough to lead to burnout is dysfunctional stress.

Negative Consequences of Dysfunctional Stress

Some readers may wonder why individual stress is a topic in an HRM text. The fact is that stress has some significant organizational consequences due to its effects on individual employees, so HR Managers need to understand and be able to recognize the symptoms of stress, and especially dysfunctional stress. One major problem with stress is that it is a primary cause of absenteeism.[35] More than 50% of Americans said they were less productive at work because of stress. Stress costs an estimated $300 billion a year in absenteeism, decreased productivity, employee turnover, and medical, legal, and insurance fees.[36] An estimated 85% of lifestyle-related diseases are linked to stress.[37] Stress causes headaches, depression, and illness.[38] Here are some other things dysfunctional stress does to us: It weakens our immune system, it makes us sick more often, it ages us so we look older, it makes us fatter, it decreases our sex drive, it ruins our sleep, and it can even kill us.[39] Stress, like perception, is an individual matter. In the same situation, one person may be very comfortable and stress-free, while another feels stressed to the point of burnout.

Causes of Job Stress

There are five common contributors to job stress: personality type, organizational culture and change, management behavior, type of work, and interpersonal relations.

Personality Type

The *Type A personality* is characterized as fast-moving, hard-driving, time-conscious, competitive, impatient, and preoccupied with work. The *Type B personality* is pretty much the opposite of Type A. In general, people with Type A personalities experience more stress than people with Type B personalities. If you have a Type A personality, you could end up with some of the problems associated with dysfunctional stress. Complete Self-Assessment 14-1 to determine your personality type as it relates to stress.

Organizational Culture and Change

The amount of cooperation and motivation that a person experiences and the level of organizational morale both affect stress levels. The more positive the organizational culture, the less stress there is. Organizations that push employees to high levels of performance but do little to ensure a positive work climate create a stressful situation. A climate with fear of layoffs can also be extremely stressful. Plus, change is stressful to many people, so cultures that continually make major changes can be stressful.[40]

Management Behavior

The better managers are at supervising employees, the less stress there is.[41] Lack of control tends to induce stress. Calm, participative management styles are less stressful. Bad bosses cause employee stress. Workers with bad bosses are more likely to report the stress-related problems that we discussed earlier.

Type of Work

Some types of work are more stressful than others. People who have jobs that they enjoy derive more satisfaction from their work and handle stress better than those who do not. In

WORK
APPLICATION 14-8

Assess your ability to deal with stress. Identify when you tend to get stressed and the negative consequences you experience from dysfunctional stress.

LO 14.8

Briefly discuss the causes of stress and how it can be managed.

14-1 SELF-ASSESSMENT

PERSONALITY TYPE A OR B AND STRESS

Identify how frequently each item applies to you at work or school. Place a number from 1 to 5 on the line before each statement.

| 5 = usually | 4 = often | 3 = occasionally | 2 = seldom | 1 = rarely |

_____ 1. I enjoy competition, and I work/play to win.

_____ 2. I skip meals or eat fast when there is a lot of work to do.

_____ 3. I'm in a hurry.

_____ 4. I do more than one thing at a time.

_____ 5. I'm aggravated and upset.

_____ 6. I get irritated or anxious when I have to wait.

_____ 7. I measure progress in terms of time and performance.

_____ 8. I push myself to work to the point of getting tired.

_____ 9. I work on days off.

_____ 10. I set short deadlines for myself.

_____ 11. I'm not satisfied with my accomplishments for very long.

_____ 12. I try to outperform others.

_____ 13. I get upset when my schedule has to be changed.

_____ 14. I consistently try to get more done in less time.

_____ 15. I take on more work when I already have plenty to do.

_____ 16. I enjoy work/school more than other activities.

_____ 17. I talk and walk fast.

_____ 18. I set high standards for myself and work hard to meet them.

_____ 19. I'm considered a hard worker by others.

_____ 20. I work at a fast pace.

_____ Total. Add up the numbers you assigned to all 20 items. Your score will range from 20 to 100. Indicate where your score falls on the continuum below.

Type A   Type B

100_____90_____80_____70_____60_____50_____40_____30_____20

The higher your score, the more characteristic you are of the Type A personality. The lower your score, the more characteristic you are of the Type B personality.

some cases, changing to a job with more enjoyable work is a wise move that can lower stress levels. This is one major reason that people decide to make career changes.

Interpersonal Relations

Conflicts among people who do not get along can be very stressful. People who don't really like the work they must perform, but who do like the people they work with, can feel less stress and experience higher job satisfaction.

Stress Management

When we continually feel pressured and fear that we will miss deadlines or fail, we are experiencing stress. People watch TV or movies, drink, take drugs, eat, or sleep more than usual to escape stress. But for the most part, these activities don't work in the long run because they are used mostly to escape stress, rather than deal directly with the stress.

We can minimize job stress,[42] so many firms are making wellness a top priority through training employees in stress management.[43] EWPs (mentioned earlier in this chapter) frequently provide stress management programs for employees. Stress management is about taking control of stress and making it functional.[44] We can reduce stress with stress management interventions by better recognizing and managing stress symptoms as they occur.[45] *Stress management* is the process of eliminating or reducing stress and making it functional. Here are *six stress management techniques*. We don't need to use them all because little changes can make big differences, so just implement the techniques that interest you.[46]

Time Management

Generally, people with good time management skills experience less job stress. Vince Lombardi, the famous football coach, said, "Plan your work and work your plan." Remember that procrastinating gives us more time to think about what we have to do and to get stressed before starting. It's a huge relief when we finish the task.[47] If we are perfectionists, we may do a high-quality job, but perfectionism stresses us as we perform the work, so sometimes it's OK to define what is "good enough" and stop there.

How we manage stress affects our job performance and health.

Relaxation

Relaxation is an excellent stress management technique, and we should relax both on and off the job. *Laughter* releases stress-reducing endorphins that lower blood pressure, relax muscles, stimulate our brain, and improve our mood, and also increases our oxygen intake, so laugh it up.[48] In addition, understand that each of us has their own way of relaxing. Some will read a book; others will lie in the sun; still others will play a game. It doesn't matter *how* you relax, as long as you relax in a way that is soothing to you.

Relaxation on the job. Use relaxation on the job, and off, when feeling stress coming on by meditating, deep breathing, and/or muscle relaxation exercises.[49]

- **Meditation.** Keeping mediation simple, when we feel stress, we can close our eyes and think happy thoughts to calm ourselves; for example, we can picture doing something we enjoy, visualize the ocean with waves crashing down, and so on. Meditation works well with deep breathing.
- **Deep breathing.** When feeling stress, simply take five slow deep breaths, preferably through the nose, hold each breath (about 5 seconds), and then let it out slowly (about 7 seconds), preferably through lightly closed lips. To breathe deeply, we must inhale by expanding the stomach, not the chest. Think of the stomach as a balloon; slowly fill and then empty it. We can also breathe deeply while performing relaxation exercises.
- **Muscle relaxation exercises.** When feeling stress, we can also perform relaxation exercises. If we feel tension in one muscle, we may do a specific relaxation exercise. We may relax our entire body going from head to toe, or vice versa. Exhibit 14-5 lists relaxation exercises that we can do almost anywhere.

Relaxation off the job. We need to relax off the job. Try to leave work—don't do any work while away, and don't think about. If you have a Type A personality, slow down and enjoy yourself. Cultivate interests that do not relate to the job.

- **Activities.** Take time for yourself and do things you enjoy to relax and get away from work. What do you enjoy doing?
- **Sleep.** For most people, there is nothing more rejuvenating that a solid seven to eight hours of sleep, and less than six hours makes most people more susceptible to the

Exhibit 14-5	Relaxation Exercises

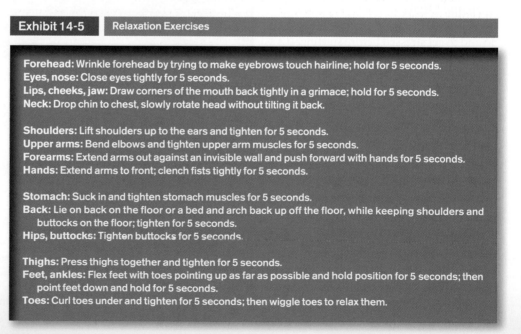

Forehead: Wrinkle forehead by trying to make eyebrows touch hairline; hold for 5 seconds.
Eyes, nose: Close eyes tightly for 5 seconds.
Lips, cheeks, jaw: Draw corners of the mouth back tightly in a grimace; hold for 5 seconds.
Neck: Drop chin to chest, slowly rotate head without tilting it back.

Shoulders: Lift shoulders up to the ears and tighten for 5 seconds.
Upper arms: Bend elbows and tighten upper arm muscles for 5 seconds.
Forearms: Extend arms out against an invisible wall and push forward with hands for 5 seconds.
Hands: Extend arms to front; clench fists tightly for 5 seconds.

Stomach: Suck in and tighten stomach muscles for 5 seconds.
Back: Lie on back on the floor or a bed and arch back up off the floor, while keeping shoulders and buttocks on the floor; tighten for 5 seconds.
Hips, buttocks: Tighten buttocks for 5 seconds.

Thighs: Press thighs together and tighten for 5 seconds.
Feet, ankles: Flex feet with toes pointing up as far as possible and hold position for 5 seconds; then point feet down and hold for 5 seconds.
Toes: Curl toes under and tighten for 5 seconds; then wiggle toes to relax them.

negative effects of stress.[50] But Americans are sleeping less on average today than in the past.[51] If we wake up tired and/or are tired throughout the day, maybe we need more or better sleep. Do you get enough quality deep sleep?

- **Sleeping tips.** Stress can delay sleep or reduce deep sleep. Working, using the Internet, using a cell phone, text messaging, and drinking caffeine close to bedtime can delay sleep and increase alertness. Doing a relaxing activity, like reading, before going to bed helps us sleep. We should shut off the TV, computer, and cell phone because the flickering lights from these devices overstimulate our brain and hurt the quality of our sleep.[52] Alcohol *can* promote sleep initially, but it can contribute to wakefulness later.[53]

Nutrition

Good health is essential to everyone's performance, and nutrition is a major factor in health. Underlying stress can lead to overeating and compulsive dieting, and being over-weight is stressful on the body. Unfortunately, around 34% of Americans are obese, while another 32% are overweight.[54] Men with a waist over 40 inches, and women over 35 inches, are twice as likely to die a premature death.[55] Obesity costs U.S. businesses about $45 billion a year in medical expenses and lost productivity.[56] Are you overweight? Do you need to change your eating habits?

We should watch our intake of junk foods, which contain fat (fried meat and vegetables, including French fries and chips), sugar (pastry, candy, fruit drinks, and soda), caffeine (coffee, tea, soda), and salt. Eat more fruits and vegetables and whole grains, and drink pure juices. Realize that poor nutrition, overeating, and the use of tobacco, alcohol, and drugs to reduce stress often create other stressful problems over a period of time.

When we eat, we should take our time and relax, because rushing is stressful and can cause an upset stomach and weight gain. Also, when people eat more slowly, they tend to eat less. Taking a break generates energy and makes us more productive. So we should avoid eating at our work area.

Breakfast is considered the most important meal of the day for good reason. Getting up and going to work just drinking coffee or soda without eating until lunch is stressful on the body. A good breakfast increases our ability to resist stress.

Exercise

Contrary to the belief of many, proper exercise increases our energy level rather than depleting it. If we are stressed for any reason, the fastest way to tame our anxiety can be physical activity. In fact, exercise is usually more effective than antidepressants in making moderate depression disappear.[57]

Aerobic exercise, in which we increase the heart rate and maintain it for 30 minutes, is generally considered the most beneficial type of exercise for stress reduction. Fast walking or jogging, biking, swimming, and aerobic dance or exercise fall into this category. Playing sports and weight lifting are also beneficial and can be aerobic if we don't take many breaks, and we cross-train by mixing weights with other aerobic exercises.

Before starting an exercise program, check with a doctor to make sure you are able to do so safely. Always remember that the objective is to relax and reduce stress. The "no pain, no gain" mentality applies to competitive athletes, not to stress management.

If we don't enjoy the workout, we most likely will not stick with it anyway, so pick something fun or at least enjoyable, like playing a sport. Having an exercise partner really makes exercise more enjoyable, and it helps motivate us to show up and exercise when we'd rather not. We may also find out that we get in a great workout when we think we were too tired to exercise.

Positive Thinking

People with an optimistic personality and attitude generally have less stress than pessimists because thoughts of gloom and doom (which are often distorted anyway) lead to stress.[58] Once we start having doubts about our ability to do what we have to do, we become stressed. Make statements to yourself in the affirmative, such as "This is easy" and "I will do it." Repeating positive statements while doing deep breathing helps us relax and increase performance.

Support Network

Reaching out to supportive family, friends, and colleagues in our network can help reduce stress.[59] So we can find a confidant at work, and people outside of the workplace, and talk things through.[60] Venting to people that we trust, and their support of our abilities, relieves stress. Being out of work-life balance is stressful, so cultivate a supportive network of family, friends, and colleagues to help maintain that critical work-life balance.[61]

The Stress Tug-of-War

Think of stress as a tug-of-war with you in the center, as illustrated in Exhibit 14-6. On the left are causes of stress trying to pull you toward burnout. On the right are stress management techniques you use to keep you in the center. If the stress becomes too powerful, it will pull us off center to the left, and we may suffer burnout and dysfunctional stress with low performance. If there is no stress, we tend to move to the right and just take it easy and perform at low levels. The stress tug-of-war is an ongoing game. Our main objective is to stay in the center with functional stress, which leads to high levels of performance.

If we try stress management but still experience long-term burnout, we should seriously consider getting out of the situation. Ask yourself two questions: Is my long-term health important? Is this situation worth hurting my health for? If you answer yes and no, respectively, a change of situations may be advisable. Career changes are often made for this reason.

WORK
APPLICATION 14-9

Identify your major causes of stress; then select stress management techniques you will use to help overcome the causes of your stress.

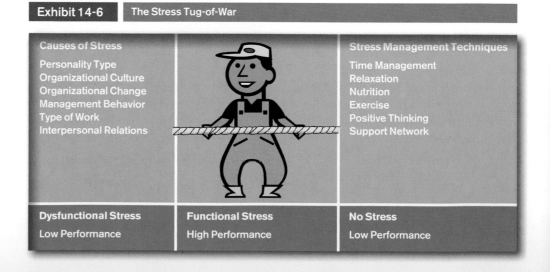

Exhibit 14-6	The Stress Tug-of-War

Causes of Stress		Stress Management Techniques
Personality Type		Time Management
Organizational Culture		Relaxation
Organizational Change		Nutrition
Management Behavior		Exercise
Type of Work		Positive Thinking
Interpersonal Relations		Support Network
Dysfunctional Stress	**Functional Stress**	**No Stress**
Low Performance	High Performance	Low Performance

14-3 APPLYING THE CONCEPT

Stress Management Techniques

Identify each statement by the technique being used.

a. time management
b. relaxation
c. nutrition
d. exercise
e. positive thinking
f. support network

____ 15. I've been getting up earlier and eating breakfast.

____ 16. I've been talking to my colleague Shane about my boss.

____ 17. I've been praying.

____ 18. I've been repeating to myself that "I can meet the deadline."

____ 19. I've started using a to-do list.

____ 20. I've been taking a walk at lunchtime with Karen.

Workplace Security

Workplace security is *the management of personnel, equipment, and facilities in order to maintain their protection.* While workplace safety deals with the issue of minimizing occupational illness and injury, workplace security covers topics such as violence in the workplace, bomb threats, management of natural and man-made disasters, risk to company computer systems and intranets, and many other issues. Workplace security is concerned with mitigating these risks to the organization and its members. Securitas Security Services USA, a large security firm, identified cyber security, workplace violence, business continuity planning, and employee selection and screening as the top security threats to businesses for the year 2010. Prior to 2010, workplace violence was the number-one concern for more than 10 years, but cyber security replaced it as the number-one concern in 2010.[62] Let's take a brief look at some of these major workplace security issues in order of concern.

LO 14.9

Identify the top concerns for security in the workplace today.

SHRM

Guide – L:7
Security concerns at work

Cyber Security

While this is not an information systems text, let's do a quick review of some of the issues companies face today with cyber security. **Cyber security** is *the use of tools and processes to protect organizational computer systems and networks.* This topic has been in the news constantly in the past couple of years, with concerns that amateur and professional hackers, hacktivists, terrorist organizations, and even some governments are working to break into company computer systems for a variety of purposes. Every company has to be concerned with this issue and do what they can to prevent becoming a victim.

HRM is especially concerned with penetrating company computer systems that have sensitive employee information on them, such as information on medical records, payroll and banking data, as well as other personal data. HR Managers must work with company security managers to put up strong roadblocks to outsiders who seek to enter systems with this type of data. While there is no foolproof way to harden company computer systems, we have to do the best that we can to make it as hard as possible for hackers or other unauthorized users to find and exploit employee data. Obviously, the HR Manager won't be the

Video Link 14.6
Workplace Security

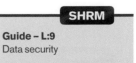

SHRM

Guide – L:9
Data security

Security is of concern to organizations today.

Video Link 14.7

Discussion of
Security Policies

Video Link 14.8

Discussion of
Workplace Violence

person to do the research and implementation on this type of computer security, but we do need to know that it is an issue and that we will work with our company's computer security managers to make it as hard as possible to get access if a person is not an authorized user.

Workplace Violence

Now, let's focus on anger that can lead to violence, and how to prevent it. Human Resource Managers have reported increased violence between employees, stating it can happen anywhere. And don't think that this is just an issue of men harming women. Women commit nearly a quarter of all threats or attacks. There has also been an increase in violence between outsiders and employees, such as customers shooting employees and other customers. One million workers are assaulted each year, and in some years more than 1,000 workers have been killed. The key to preventing workplace violence is to recognize and handle suspicious behavior before it turns violent;[63] that's what this subsection is all about.

Causes of Anger and Violence

Anger can lead to violence. You have most likely heard of road rage. In business we have *desk rage*, which can take the form of yelling, verbal abuse, and physical violence. Frustration, stress, and fear also bring out anger.[64] Unresolved *inter*personal conflicts make people angry.[65] In fact, violence is almost always prompted by unresolved conflict, and the violence is often a form of sabotage on other employees (backstabbing, spreading false rumors) or the organization (damage to property) to get even.[66]

The physical work environment (such as space to work, noise, odors, temperature [hot], ventilation, and color) contributes to making people angry. A bad work environment, called *toxicity*, leads to violence. People also tend to copy, or model, others' behavior. For example, children who have been abused (emotionally and/or physically) are more likely, as parents, to abuse their children. If employees see others being violent, especially managers, and nothing is done about it, they are more apt to also use violent behavior at work. Violence in the community, which also includes family violence, surrounding an organization may be brought into the workplace. Some but not all experts also report that drugs contribute to violence.[67]

Dealing With Anger

Your anger and emotional control. A secondary feeling of anger follows many of our feelings. Your boss may surprise you with extra work, which makes you angry. Disappointment often leads to anger. Your coworkers don't do their share of the work, so you get mad at them. Buddha said, "You will not be punished *for* your anger; you will be punished *by* your anger." Anger can lead to perception problems and poor decisions and hostility, which are stressful and can harm your health.[68]

It is natural to get angry sometimes as we cannot control the feeling of anger, but we can control our behavior, and we can learn to deal with anger in more positive ways to get rid of it. Letting anger build up often leads initially to passively not doing or saying anything, and then later to blowing up at the person. Here are some tips for effectively getting rid of our anger.

- Use objective, rational thinking. For example, when dealing with customers, tell yourself, "Their anger is to be expected. It's part of my job to stay calm."
- Look for positives. In many bad situations, there is some good.
- Look for the humor in the situation to help defuse the anger. Finding appropriate humor can help keep us from moping and getting angry.
- Develop a positive attitude about how to deal with anger. Develop positive affirmations, such as "I stay calm when in traffic" (not "I must stop getting mad in traffic") or "I get along well with Joe" (not "I must stop letting Joe get me angry").
- Use an anger journal. A first step to emotional control of anger is self-awareness. Answer these questions. How often do you get irritated/angry each day? What makes you irritated/angry? How upset do you get? What feelings do you have when you are angry? What behavior (yell, say specific words, pound desk, do and say nothing, accommodate) do you use when you are angry? Are you good at dealing with your irritations/anger? One good way to improve your ability to control your anger is to write the answers to these questions in an anger journal. It is a method of letting out the anger in an effective way. People who use a journal often change their behavior without even trying.

Anger of others and emotional control. Here are some tips from the Crisis Prevention Institute and NIOSH to help us deal with the anger of others through our emotional control to prevent violence. These tips can be very valuable to us as managers.

- Never make any type of putdown statement, as it can make the person angrier. As stated above, you may use appropriate humor to cut the tension, but be careful that it is not viewed as a sarcastic putdown. Such behavior can lead to violence.
- Don't respond to anger and threats with the same behavior. This is the key to success in maintaining your emotional control.
- Don't give orders or ultimatums. This can increase anger and push the person to violence.
- Watch your nonverbal communications to show concern and to avoid appearing aggressive. Use eye contact to show concern, but be aware that staring or glaring can make you appear aggressive. Maintain a calm, soothing tone to defuse anger and frustration. Talking loud and with frustration, anger, or annoyance in your tone of voice will convey aggression. Don't move rapidly, point at the person, get too close (stay 2–5 feet apart), or touch.
- Realize that anger is natural and encourage people to vent in appropriate ways. With the aggressor, the problem is usually to keep the behavior acceptable. With the passive person, you may need to ask probing questions to get them to vent, such as "What is making you angry?" or "What did I do to make you mad?"
- Acknowledge the person's feelings. Using reflective responses by paraphrasing the way the person appears to be feeling shows that we care and helps calm the person so they can get back in control of their emotions.
- Get away from the person if necessary. If possible, call in a third party to deal with the person and leave.

Signs of Potential Violence

Workplace violence is rarely spontaneous; it's more commonly passive-aggressive behavior in rising steps, related to an unresolved conflict. Employees do give warning signs that violence is possible, so it can be prevented if we look for these signs and take action to defuse the anger before it becomes violent.[69]

- Take verbal threats seriously. Most violent people do make a threat of some kind before they act. If we hear a threat, or hear about a threat from someone else, talk to the person who made the threat and try to resolve the issue.
- Watch nonverbal communication. Behavior such as yelling, gestures, or other body language that conveys anger can also indicate a threat of violence. Talk to the person to find out what's going on.
- Watch for stalking and harassment. It usually starts small, but can lead to violence. Put a stop to it.
- Watch for damage to property. If an employee kicks a desk, punches a wall, and so on, talk to the person to get to the reason for the behavior. People who damage property can become violent to coworkers.
- Watch for indications of alcohol and drug use. People can be violent under their influence. Get them out of the workplace and get them professional help from the EAP, if it's a recurring problem.
- Include the isolated employee. It is common for violent people to be employees who don't fit in, especially if they are picked on or harassed by coworkers. Reach out to this employee and help him or her fit in, or get them to a place where they do.
- Look for the presence of weapons or objects that might be used as weapons. You may try talking to the person if you feel safe, but get security involved if you feel the least bit unsafe.

Organizational Prevention of Violence

The number-one preventive method is to train all employees to deal with anger and prevent violence,[70] which is what you are learning now. However, the starting place is with a written policy addressing workplace violence, and a zero-tolerance policy is the best preventive policy. From the HR Manager's perspective, it is very important to take quick disciplinary action against employees who are violent at work. Otherwise, aggression will spread in the organization, and it will be more difficult to stop. Managers especially need to avoid using aggression at work because employees more readily copy managers' behavior than the behavior of other employees.

As discussed in Chapter 10, the organization should have a system for dealing with grievances, and it should also track incidents of violence as part of its policy. Organizations can also screen job applicants for past or potential violence so that they are not hired. They should also develop a good work environment addressing the issues listed above as causes of violence. Demotions, firing, and layoffs should be handled in a humane way following the guidelines to deal with anger, and outplacement services to help employees find new jobs can help cut down on violence.

Individual Prevention of Violence

One thing you should realize is that the police department will not help prevent personal or workplace violence. Police only get involved after violence takes place. We have already given you most of the tips above. But here are a few more tips.[71] Keep in mind that there is always potential violence, and look for escalating frustration and anger to defuse it before it becomes violence. Never be alone with a potentially violent person or stand between the person and the exit. Know when to get away from the person, and utilize the organization's policy of calling in security help if you are concerned. Report any troubling incidents to security staff.

Employee Selection and Screening

We discussed tools concerning employee selection and screening in Chapter 6, but we need to be reminded of some of them again here, because of their importance to company security. The first tool that we want to make sure that we use in employee screening is background checks. Recall that we can be held liable for monetary damages if we are guilty of a "negligent hire." One way to guard against such a hire is through the consistent use of criminal background checks, which specifically look for a history of violent actions or threats of violence on the part of an applicant or employee.

Other background checks can also help with organizational security. Web searches can sometimes turn up negative information on an applicant that may show that they are a potential security risk, even when criminal checks do not. In addition, credit checks might show evidence of a history of unethical behavior that would make it more likely that an applicant might be unscrupulous, and might even intentionally harm other employees if hired. So we do have some tools available in background checks to mitigate the risk of hiring the wrong type of person.

In addition to background checks, substance abuse testing can provide us with a tool to minimize the security dangers in our company. As we noted in Chapter 6, "Most employers have the right to test for a wide variety of substances in the workplace."[72] According to SHRM, "Substance abuse prevention is an essential element of an effective workplace safety and security program. Preventive programs—including drug and alcohol testing—properly implemented, protect the business from liability."[73] The U.S. Department of Justice notes that "the link between drug use and crime has been well-documented in recent years."[74] Screening out substance abusers in the applicant stage can minimize security threats to the organization because there is strong evidence that at least some substance abusers will commit crimes, including violent crimes at work in many cases.

General Security Policies Including Business Continuity and Recovery

Common disasters and emergencies might include such things as fires, floods, earthquakes, severe weather, tsunamis, terrorist attacks, bomb threats, and many others. Some are dependent on the company's geographic location, while others are universal possibilities. One thing is sure, though—disasters and emergencies happen without warning, creating a situation in which the normal organizational services can become overwhelmed or even disappear. During such a crisis, companies require a set of processes that address the needs of emergency response and recovery operations. To address these types of emergencies, the company should establish an emergency response plan, which provides guidelines for immediate actions and operations required to respond to an emergency or disaster.

> **SHRM**
>
> **Guide – L:2**
> Disaster preparation, continuity and recovery planning

The overall *priorities* of any plan in any emergency or disaster should be:

- Protect human life
- Prevent/minimize personal injury
- Preserve physical assets
- Protect the environment
- Restore programs and return operations to normal

The overall *objective* is to respond to the emergency and manage the process of restoring the organization, and its associated programs and services.

But what part does the HRM professional play in this planning process? HRM should be part of the management team that determines the goals of the plan. Once the goals are determined, HR can again help operational management to staff the various key positions in the disaster recovery teams by understanding the types of people that are necessary to do these jobs under crisis circumstances.

Additionally, HR is typically responsible for the training function in the company, and everyone in the organization needs to be trained on the plan and its processes. The training should also become part of the new employee orientation (Chapter 7) so that all personnel are aware of the correct responses to potential emergencies. There are many examples of good emergency response and business recovery plans out there on the Internet for free. All the company needs to do is find a good sample and modify it for their particular circumstances and the likely disasters that would occur based on their geographic locations. A company in Arkansas probably doesn't need a plan for tsunami recovery, while a company on the coast of California is unlikely to need tornado or hurricane sheltering plans.

One final thing that HRM needs to determine is where extra assistance might come from if needed because of a disaster or an emergency. For instance, if severe weather were to kill and injure a number of company employees, grief counseling services might become necessary. Most companies don't routinely have grief counselors on hand, but in this type of case they may need access to such counselors very quickly. HRM can think of likely situations and their aftermaths, and determine where these types of services might be procured if the need presented itself. One potential provider in at least some cases might be the vendor that services the company EAP program. Recall that EAPs are services for the psychological well-being of our employees. Therefore, they may have the needed personnel to handle the psychological aftermath of a disaster.

Trends and Issues in HRM

We come to our last trends and issues segment. What are some of the significant trends and issues in workplace safety and health? First, we will grapple with the issue of smoking and indoor clean air. Our second issue will provide a quick review of good leadership practices and their effect on workplace safety and health. Third, we will take a look at one program that uses the Internet to promote workplace safety—a trend that is occurring with greater frequency in today's 21st-century workplaces, so let's get started.

Smoking and Indoor Clean Air

Video Link 14.9

Benefits of Providing a
Smoke-Free Environment

Many states have passed, and others are continuing to pass, laws concerning the subject of clean air in workspaces, and one of the major issues with indoor clean air is smoking inside buildings. Massive evidence now exists that secondhand smoke is dangerous to all who are exposed to it, and more nonsmokers are becoming vocal about their rights to breathe clean air at work. As a result, even in states where the law allows smoking indoors, many companies are instituting smoking bans at work. In addition, many employers are becoming more concerned with general indoor air quality because modern buildings are built to be almost airtight to improve the efficiency of utilities.

The U.S. Surgeon General's Office completed a study on secondhand smoke in 2006 that noted that secondhand smoke increased heart disease risk by 25%–30% and lung cancer risk by 20%–30% in nonsmokers. It also noted that "current heating, ventilating, and air conditioning systems alone cannot control exposure to secondhand smoke" and "heating, ventilating, and air conditioning systems can distribute secondhand smoke throughout a building."[75] Because of the danger associated with such exposure, many companies have decided on smoking bans anywhere on their premises.

In addition to the research and guidelines on smoking indoors, the WHO has also created sets of guidelines for indoor air quality for some specified pollutants such as benzene, formaldehyde, and carbon monoxide.[76] Also, the U.S. Environmental Protection Agency along with other environmental agencies all over the world have provided more general guidance on indoor air quality improvement.[77] The EPA notes in its publications that "a number of well-identified illnesses, such as Legionnaires' disease, asthma, hypersensitivity pneumonitis, and humidifier fever, have been directly traced to specific building problems."[78]

Because of the gravity of these illnesses, companies have to take indoor air quality seriously. If we see signs that people in our organization are suffering from health problems at a higher than normal rate, we might need to look at the potential that the air quality in the building is compromised. Remember, one of the primary jobs of HR is to maintain worker safety and health. To further identify and possibly remedy the situation, local and state environmental agencies may be able to help analyze the building's air quality, or building management can do their own tests.

Strong Leaders Demand Safe Workplaces

The best leaders almost intuitively know that the success of the organization hinges on all of its people, not just a few at the top. This being the case, all of the people have to be safe in their work environment and have to remain healthy in order to allow the organization to succeed. These leaders understand that a safe and healthy culture doesn't just happen; they have to make it happen. So leaders work to instill a strong safety culture in the company. These leaders commit to putting health and safety in the organizational spotlight and working with their management team to make sure that it stays there.

Leaders such as we just described understand that this is just another aspect of organizational *sustainability*. If our employees are safe and healthy, the organization as a whole is more sustainable. If we allow injuries and occupational illnesses to occur with high frequency, the organization is significantly less sustainable. Employees who are protected from unnecessary hazards will have a higher quality of life, and the organization will enjoy the added benefits of lower workers' compensation rates, lower absenteeism and turnover, and higher levels of employee satisfaction and engagement.

ESR

An additional benefit to strong safety and health cultures is that it is less likely that the organization will be sanctioned by the various government agencies that police workplace safety and health. The direct benefit of a lack of fines, penalties, and other punishments is obvious, but there is another more indirect benefit here as well. Organizations that have strong reputations as good corporate citizens enjoy many benefits with outside stakeholders that poor corporate citizens may not. Cities, counties, and states will frequently work extremely hard to assist good corporate citizens with governmental issues that can hinder productivity. Such programs may include training local citizens to work for the employer if some skill sets are lacking in the local workforce, providing investment funds at a low interest rate so that the employer can expand operations, tax incentives for locating new operations in the local area, and many other types of assistance. It is much more difficult for a "bad corporate citizen" to get these concessions from governments.

eDocAmerica–Health and Wellness Online

One example of new online providers of occupational and employee health-related services is eDocAmerica, found at www.edocamerica.com. eDoc is a health care service provider that "gives individuals and their family members unlimited email access to board certified physicians, psychologists, pharmacists, dentists, dietitians and fitness experts who provide personal answers to all health-related questions."[79] eDoc was started by a physician at the University of Arkansas for Medical Sciences to provide outreach services to employees of client businesses.

The services of eDoc make it much easier as well as significantly quicker for employees of client firms to get answers to most of their routine health questions. This has two major benefits. First, it allows the employee to take more control of their personal and family health, and second, it takes some pressure off of the larger health care system because employees are not running to the doctor's office every time they need a simple question answered.

As a side benefit for the organization, it appears that companies may save money on their group health insurance plans for employees because of the lower utilization rates made possible by the e-mail access to expertise in a quick and easy manner. eDoc has so far been quite successful in creating a more open and accessible health care system with their client company employees. This is just one of the new breed of web-based providers of safety and health services to companies and employees. We will likely continue to see more companies with similar services come online in the near future.

Wrap-Up

Finally! Our *last* chapter comes to a close. Did you learn anything that you didn't already know? We are sure that you did, because *we* did. Let's take a quick look back at this, your last chapter for this book. In our first section we discovered that there is a federal law called the OSH Act that says that employers have a *general duty* to maintain a workplace that is free from unnecessary hazards. We also found that OSHA is responsible for creating safety standards and for enforcing the OSH Act through a process of work-site inspections. We discussed what you want to do as an employer representative if OSHA does come to your workplace, and we talked about both employer and employee rights associated with occupational safety and health.

For the last part of the first section, we told you about NIOSH, which, as part of the CDC, does research on occupational safety and health hazards. We also found out that NIOSH spends a lot of time on communicable disease prevention in workplaces. Next, we went through the major requirements for posting of laws and rules in the workplace.

The second section of this chapter looked at employee health—the state of physical and psychological wellness. We identified work-life balance as a constant challenge here, and discussed how EAPs and EWPs can help employees cope with their jobs as well as their lives outside of work. The second part of this section dealt with ergonomics and some of the problems that repetitive stress can cause at work.

The third section started off with a detailed look at the concept of stress and how it affects our employees. In this section we discussed the main causes of stress at work, what stress does to us, how to manage stress in your life, and the constant stress tug-of-war that we all go through.

In the fourth section, we looked at the issue of workplace security, a concern that has been growing over the past decade for a lot of different reasons. We identified the top security issues that companies are facing today, including cyber security, workplace violence, employee selection and screening, and business continuity in the case of a disaster.

Finally, in our trends and issues for this chapter, we reviewed the issue of indoor clean air and the part smoking plays in this issue, we looked at why strong leaders are so concerned with employee safety and health, and we rounded things up with a look at one new Internet-based vendor providing workplace health services to a broad market of customer companies today. Another full chapter comes to a close, and we hope you enjoyed the ride.

Chapter Summary

Visit www.sagepub.com/lussier for helpful study resources.

14.1 Identify the responsibilities of both employers and employees under the general duties clause of the OSH Act.

Employers have to provide employees with a place of employment free from recognized hazards that are causing or are likely to cause death or serious physical harm and are required to comply with occupational safety and health standards identified in the act.

Employees also have a duty to comply with occupational safety standards, rules, and regulations in all cases while at work.

14.2 Briefly describe what OSHA does in a work-site inspection.

OSHA can inspect a work site without advance notice. The inspector will identify him- or herself and provide the reason for the inspection when they arrive. Once the employer provides access to the work site, the inspector will do an inspection. The inspector has the right to interview employees during the inspection, and may do so unless the interview becomes confrontational or they disrupt the work environment. The inspector will provide the employer with a list of discrepancies upon completion of the inspection.

14.3 Discuss employer rights during an OSHA inspection.

The employer has a right to ask for positive identification from the OSHA inspector, including their badge number. They also have a right to know the reason for the inspection. Employers can refuse to allow the inspector into the work site, unless they have a court order, but this is usually not a very good idea. The employer also has a right to have a representative accompany the inspector while they are on the work site, and has the right to tell employees their rights in the inspection process. The employer can also have a representative in any interviews unless the employee specifically requests that the interview be private, and can stop interviews if they become disruptive. Finally, the employer has the right to contest any citations that they receive.

14.4 Identify the types of violations that OSHA looks for in inspections.

Violations include the following:

Willful—where the employer knew that a hazardous condition existed but made no effort to eliminate the hazard.

Serious—where the hazard could cause injury or illness that would most likely result in death or significant physical harm.

Other than serious—where any illness or injury incurred is unlikely to cause death or serious physical harm, but the violation does have a direct impact on safety and health.

De minimis—violations that have no direct or immediate safety or health danger.

Failure to abate—where the employer has not corrected a previous violation for which a citation was issued and the settlement date has passed.

Repeated—the employer has been cited for the same type of violation within five years.

14.5 Discuss the primary job of NIOSH as it applies to workplace safety and health.

The primary job of NIOSH is providing research, information, education, and training in the field of occupational safety and health. NIOSH notes three major goals in its strategic plan:

- Conduct research to reduce work-related illnesses and injuries
- Promote safe and healthy workplaces through interventions, recommendations, and capacity building
- Enhance international workplace safety and health through global collaborations

14.6 Briefly discuss EAPs and EWPs and what their value is to companies and employees.

EAPs and EWPs both help employees with their work-life balance. EAPs provide confidential counseling and other personal services to employees to help them cope with stress created by personal issues related to either work or home life. EWPs help employees with their physical wellness. They provide programs such as health education, training and fitness programs, and weight management and health risk assessments to employees.

14.7 Discuss the concept of ergonomics and identify OSHA's function in ergonomics in the workplace.

Ergonomics is the science of fitting workplace conditions and job demands to the capabilities of the working population. The goal of ergonomics is to reduce stress and limit injuries due to overuse of muscles, bad posture, and repetitive tasks. OSHA provides guidelines on ergonomics in the workplace that are voluntary, but that can be assessed during an inspection based on the general duties clause of the OSH Act. OSHA also has specific ergonomic guidelines for a number of different industries, so HR representatives should check to make sure that they are following OSHA guidelines based on the industry that they are a part of.

14.8 Briefly discuss the causes of stress and how it can be managed.

The major causes of stress include personality type, organizational culture and change, management behavior, type of work, and interpersonal issues. Type A personalities, weak organizational cultures and rapidly changing organizations, bad management, jobs that employees don't enjoy, and poor interpersonal relations all make stress more prevalent in the workplace. Stress management techniques include good time management skills, the ability to relax once in a while (in whatever form you choose), good nutrition, moderate amounts of exercise, positive thinking skills, and a strong personal support network. All of these tools help us cope with stress successfully.

14.9 Identify the top concerns for security in the workplace today.

The four biggest concerns of employers today are cyber security, workplace violence, business continuity planning, and employee selection and screening. Cyber security deals with the company's computer and network security. Workplace violence is another major issue because of the continuing rise in incidences of violence against employees while on the job. Third, business continuity planning became a much more significant issue to most employers in the past 10 years, partly because of terrorism threats, but also because of a number of large-scale environmental and natural disasters worldwide. Finally, employee selection and screening has become more of an issue because of the problem of negligent hires and the possibility for increased workplace violence if we allow individuals who have a history of violence into our organization.

Key Terms

Burnout

Cyber security

Employee Assistance Program (EAP)

Employee health

Employee Wellness Program (EWP)

Ergonomics

Material Safety Data Sheet (MSDS)

Stress

Stressors

Workplace safety

Workplace security

Key Term Review

Complete each of the following statements using one of this chapter's key terms:

_____ is the physical protection of people from injury or illness while on the job.

_____ are documents that provide information on a hazardous chemical and its characteristics.

_____ is the state of physical and psychological wellness in the workforce.

_____ is a set of counseling and other services provided to employees that help them to resolve personal issues that may affect their work.

_____ is designed to cater to the employee's physical, instead of psychological, welfare through education and training programs.

_____ is the science of fitting workplace conditions and job demands to the capabilities of the working population.

_____ is the body's reaction to environmental demands.

_____ are factors that may, if extreme, cause people to feel overwhelmed by anxiety, tension, and/or pressure.

_____ is a constant lack of interest and motivation to perform one's job.

_____ is the management of personnel, equipment, and facilities in order to maintain their protection.

_____ is the use of tools and processes to protect organizational computer systems and networks.

Quick Check (True-False)

1. OSHA has total authority over employers in all areas of safety and health administration. T F

2. OSHA inspectors must provide a minimum of 24 hours' notice before arriving for an inspection. T F

3. OSHA inspectors can walk on to the work site without identifying who they are and what their purpose is, as long as you know that they are from OSHA. T F

4. OSHA inspections may be initiated because of a worker complaint about unsafe working conditions. T F

5. The employer has a right to know who is interviewed by an OSHA inspector while on a site visit. T F

6. Employees cannot refuse to be interviewed by an OSHA inspector because they have federal authority. T F

7. MSDSs provide documentation of the hazards associated with buildings and equipment. T F

8. "Serious" violations of the OSH Act are hazards likely to cause death or significant physical harm. T F

9. Safety training is a critical tool used in lowering the rate of injuries and work-related illness. T F

10. NIOSH works with OSHA to track diseases that can be passed from one person to another in the work environment. T F

11. Each state has its own workplace posting requirements, with most having at least a requirement to post workers' compensation, unemployment, and state minimum wage information. T F

12. To help keep a better work-life balance, the trend is for firms to offer all employees the same set of benefits. T F

13. EAPs deal with the psychological wellness of employees while EWPs take care of their mental wellness. T F

14. The OSHA guidelines on ergonomics are mandatory only for some specific employers. T F

15. Stress reactions can be either emotional or physical. T F

16. Some of the consequences of dysfunctional stress are a weakened immune system, getting fat, and ruined sleep. T F

17. Workplace security covers everything from bomb threats to violence in the workplace and natural disasters. T F

18. Organizations have gotten very good at cyber security—they are rarely victims of network breaches today. T F

19. A company can almost never be held liable for hiring someone who turns out to have a violent criminal history. T F

20. The first priority in a company's emergency response plan should be to protect human life and minimize personal injury. T F

Communication Skills

The following critical-thinking questions can be used for class discussion and/or for written assignments to develop communication skills. Be sure to give complete explanations for all answers.

1. Are some number of occupational illnesses and injuries an acceptable part of doing business? Why or why not? Explain your answers.

2. Do you foresee a situation in which you would ever refuse to allow an OSHA inspector on your work site? Why or why not?

3. What actions would you take if you were the company representative accompanying an OSHA inspector who found a serious violation in your company? Explain your answer.

4. Is there ever a reason why a company would be charged with a failure to abate a hazard in the workplace? Can you think of any situations that might cause such a charge that would be outside the employer's control?

5. Do you think the OSHA and NIOSH occupational safety and health requirements generally make sense? Why or why not?

6. If you were in charge, would you put an EAP into place at your company? How about an EWP? Why or why not?

7. Can you think of some things that you might be able to institute at work for very little or no cost in order to improve work-life balance for your employees? Be specific in your answers.

8. Have you ever suffered from a Musculoskeletal Disorder injury? Were you able to recover from it? What did you do to help yourself recover or mitigate the problem associated with the MSD injury?

9. Do you think that you suffer from too much stress? Name a few things that you could do to minimize the dysfunctional stress in your life.

10. Go through the process of how you would train your employees on a new business continuity and disaster recovery plan. What do you think the most important part of the training would be? Why?

11. Should smoking be banned in all buildings where smokers and nonsmokers have to work together? Why or why not?

12. What programs would you put into effect as a leader in order to make your employees understand that occupational safety and health are critical to a modern company?

Video

Please visit the student study site at **www.sagepub.com/lussier** to view the video links in this chapter.

Answers

REVIEW QUESTIONS (TRUE-FALSE) Answers

1. F   2. F   3. F   4. T   5. T   6. F   7. F   8. T   9. T   10. T   11. T   12. F   13. F   14. F   15. T   16. T   17. T   18. F   19. F   20. T

Case

Case 14-1. Handling the Unhealthy Employee

Bill is an award-winning newspaper reporter for the city news who can crank out twice as many feature articles as anyone else. To keep relevant in a period of downsizing in the newspaper industry, Bill also maintains the newspaper blog and social network pages. Over time, his work hours grew. He often chain-smoked his way to three hours of sleep or less. He gained weight and started to develop a considerable waist. He always had snacks by his desk because he had little time to go out to a restaurant or make a home-cooked meal.

Bill was known to be irritable and often yelled at his colleagues for not getting information he needed for articles. "Time is important. The second reporter to the story might as well be the last reporter to the story." His colleagues thought he was too pushy and often yelled back at him.

One morning he collapsed at his office desk. He was rushed to the hospital via ambulance. Doctors found that he had a retinal stroke with loss of significant vision in his right eye. Doctors said he would be fine as long as he loses weight and takes better care of himself.

Diane is the owner/manager of the newspaper and is concerned about Bill's condition along with the other overworked reporters and editors who have been survivors of the many downsizings over the years. She has decided to implement several stress and health management policies to help maintain productivity while keeping the employees healthy. In an employee meeting, she mentioned several new initiatives as follows:

First, in the past, smoking has been limited to offices. Now smoking will be banned from the building. If you want to smoke, there will be a designated smoking area in the back of the building.

Second, in the past, vending machines have had junk food. Now the machines have been eliminated. Fresh fruits and vegetables will be provided for free in the cafeteria.

Third, periodically, courses on healthy eating and exercise will be provided by experts. These courses will be regarded as important as mandatory staff meetings. The courses will last for approximately one hour and may involve minor physical activity.

Fourth, health checks by a nearby medical service will be available for free twice a year. This will be totally paid for by our organization.

Finally, if management feels that you are overworked or overstressed, we would like to sit down with you and talk to see what is happening.

Bill was aghast at this new policy. In discussions with a colleague, Bill said the following:

"Diane is trying to impose her will and culture upon me. Smoking relaxes me. I write better when I smoke. Now that there is a no-smoking policy in the office, this is the one thing that would increase my blood pressure through the roof."

"The vending machines were a convenient way to get food. I am a carnivore, and I like my occasional beef jerky. I like my chips. Granola is for the birds."

"The mandatory classes concerning nutrition and exercise are a waste of time for the staff. If there is a great story out there, it is more important to get the story in the middle of the day than waste time on Diane's religion. The newspaper provides significant financial incentives for each feature that is published every week. I write the most features because I am good at it, I write fast, and I need the money. My wife's sick in the hospital, and I've got two teenagers to feed. I might lose my house."

"The 'free' medical service and management visits about health are basically nosy efforts by management to pry into personal business. It is none of management's business to intervene in my personal affairs."

There are several other reporters in the office who feel the same way as Bill and have threatened to resign if Diane's initiatives go through. The reporters offered a very simple alternative of having the newspaper add three days of sick leave benefits per year. They feel that Diane has no right to impose her lifestyle and her culture on them. Diane especially has no right to monitor the lifestyle and personal habits of employees that do not affect work.

Diane counters the group by saying that lifestyle and culture can affect work. "If you are not healthy, in the long term, you will not be productive. I want you around for a long time."

Questions

1. What are the causes of stress in Bill's organization?

2. Has Diane gone too far in imposing a smoking policy, removing junk food from the vending machines, and offering free medical service and management visits?

3. Diane has selected several ways to reduce the stress and improve the health of her employees. What other ways did the chapter mention she could also use to reduce stress and improve employee health?

4. What do you think about the reporters' sick leave proposal?

Case created by Gundars Kaupins, Boise State University

SKILL BUILDER 14-1

Developing a Stress Management Plan

Objective

To develop your skill at managing stress.

Skills

The primary skills developed through this exercise are:

1. *HR Management skill* – Conceptual and design

2. *SHRM 2010 Curriculum Guidebook* – L: Workplace Health

Assignment

Write out the answers to these questions.

1. Identify your major causes of stress.

2. How do you currently manage stress?

3. Select stress management techniques you will use to help overcome the causes of your stress.

SKILL BUILDER 14-2

The Most Important Things I Got From This Course

Objective

To review your course learning, critical-thinking application, and skill development.

Skills

The primary skills developed through this exercise are:

1. *HR Management skill* – Conceptual and design

2. *SHRM 2010 Curriculum Guidebook* – J: Training and Development

Assignment

Think about and write/type the three or four most important things you learned or skills you developed through this course and how they are helping or will help you in your personal and/or professional life.

Appendix A
SHRM 2010 Curriculum Guidebook

Required, Integrated, and Secondary HR Content Areas

(Reordered and numbered for reference)

The Society for Human Resource Management (SHRM), the world's largest Human Resource Management (HRM) association, periodically puts out guidance on college and university curricula for HRM programs (what they think we need to teach you). The latest version of their guidebook is provided below for your information and use. This guidance provides information on what SHRM considers to be critical in the study of HRM. If you choose to pursue HRM as a career choice, this information will help you in the process of certification through the Human Resource Certification Institute (HRCI), SHRM's accreditation arm. Even if you don't decide to pursue HRM as a career, this is the information that will be most pertinent to your success as a manager in any field of business.

It makes sense that an introductory textbook would introduce you to each of the areas that are critical in that field of study. As a result, in this textbook we've chosen to discuss *all* "required content" for undergraduate HR programs from the most recent version (2010) of the curriculum guide. As far as we know, no other introductory HRM textbook does this. This has been done to introduce you to each of the topics that SHRM considers to be critical. We have reordered the information from the SHRM curriculum guide to emphasize the required content first, and then the integrated and secondary content areas, but the content itself is identical to the guidelines from SHRM. If you are already a student member of SHRM, you can call up the guide itself at www .shrm.org/Education/hreducation/Pages/Guidebook.aspx. Unfortunately, you have to be a member to access this content.

This appendix is designed to link back to each of the chapters and identify where each of the required content areas is discussed within the textbook. When you see a box in the chapter titled SHRM Guide, it will have an alphanumeric reference. That alphanumeric reference ties to this appendix by section (*the capital letter*) and subtopic (*the numeral*). For example, if you see this box:

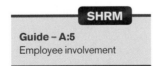

it would lead you to Section A (Employee and Labor Relations), Subtopic 5 (Employee involvement). Next to each of the subtopics is a listing of the page numbers on which the topic is discussed. This should help you if you are looking for information on a particular topic and are having trouble finding it within the chapters.

Note: SHRM's HR curriculum guidelines are revalidated, updated and revised every three years. The next revalidation study is scheduled for quarter 4, 2012 and quarter 1, 2013. The most up-to-date guidelines and appendices showing content outlines appear online at http://www.shrm.org/education/hreducation/pages/guidebook.aspx

Required Content–Undergraduate Curriculum

A. Employee and Labor Relations (required)

1. Disciplinary actions (demotion, disciplinary termination) [Chapter 9, pp. 331–332]
2. Alternative dispute resolution [Chapter 10, pp. 403–404]
3. Managing/creating a positive organizational culture [Chapter 2, p. 57]
4. Employee engagement [Chapter 1, p. 5]
5. Employee involvement [Chapter 1, p. 5]
6. Employee retention [Chapter 1, p. 8]
7. Managing teams [Chapter 9, pp. 354–355]
8. Union membership [Chapter 10, p. 389]
9. Union-related labor laws [Chapter 10, p. 380]
10. Union/management relations [Chapter 10, p. 391]
11. Union decertification and deauthorization [Chapter 10, p. 394]
12. Collective bargaining issues [Chapter 10, p. 391]
13. Collective bargaining process [Chapter 10, p. 391]
14. Negotiation skills [Chapter 10, p. 399]
    Interdependence
    Mutual adjustment
    Cognitive biases
    Communication
    Conflict
    Value claiming
    Value creation
    Distributive bargaining
    Alternative dispute resolution: negotiation, mediation and arbitration
    Contract negotiation
    Framing
    Integrative negotiation
    International negotiation
15. Conflict management [Chapter 10, p. 395]
16. Grievance management [Chapter 10, pp. 391–392]
17. Strikes, boycotts, and work stoppages [Chapter 10, p. 382]
18. Unfair labor practices [Chapter 10, p. 383]
19. Managing union organizing policies and handbooks [Chapter 10, p. 392]
20. Attendance [Chapter 1, p. 9]
21. Attitude surveys [Chapter 10, p. 378]
22. Investigations [Chapter 9, p. 354]
23. Posting requirements [Chapter 14, pp. 563–564]
24. Promotion [Chapter 12, p. 463]
25. Recognition [Chapter 12, p. 475]
26. Service awards [Chapter 12, p. 475]
27. Employee records [Chapter 9, p. 332]

B. Employment Law (required)

1. The Age Discrimination in Employment Act of 1967 [Chapter 3, pp. 85–86]
2. The Americans With Disabilities Act of 1990 and as Amended in 2008 [Chapter 3, pp. 87–88]
3. The Equal Pay Act of 1963 [Chapter 3, p. 82]
4. The Pregnancy Discrimination Act of 1978 [Chapter 3, p. 87]
5. Title VII of the Civil Rights Act of 1964 and 1991 [Chapter 3, pp. 82–83; Chapter 3, pp. 94–95]
6. Executive Order 11246 (1965) [Chapter 3, p. 97]
7. The Employer Retirement Income Security Act of 1974 [Chapter 13, p. 524]
8. The Fair Labor Standards Act of 1938 [Chapter 11, p. 432]
9. The Family and Medical Leave Act of 1993 [Chapter 13, pp. 519–521]
10. The Rehabilitation Act of 1973 [Chapter 3, p. 871]
11. The Labor Management Reporting and Disclosure Act of 1959 [Chapter 10, p. 384]
12. The National Labor Relations Act of 1935 [Chapter 10, p. 382]
13. The Labor Management Relations Act of 1947 [Chapter 10, p. 383]
14. The Occupational Safety and Health Act of 1970 [Chapter 14, p. 558]
15. The Railway Labor Act of 1926 [Chapter 10, p. 382]
16. The Uniformed Services Employment and Reemployment Rights Act of 1994 [Chapter 3, p. 91]
17. The Worker Adjustment and Retraining Notification Act of 1988 [Chapter 10, p. 384]
18. Enforcement agencies (EEOC, OFCCP) [Chapter 3, p. 93; Chapter 3, p. 98]
19. Contractual and tort theories [Chapter 10, p. 387]
20. Employee privacy [Chapter 9, p. 332]
21. Employer unfair labor practices [Chapter 10, p. 383]
22. Professional liability [Chapter 1, p. 24]

23. Agency relationships/quasi-contracts [Chapter 10, p. 387]

24. Employment contracts [Chapter 10, p. 387]

25. Disparate impact [Chapter 3, pp. 83–84]

26. Disparate treatment [Chapter 3, p. 83]

27. Unlawful harassment [Chapter 3, p. 95]

    Sexual

    Religious

    Disability

    Race

    Color

    Nation of origin

28. Whistle-blowing/retaliation [Chapter 3, p. 100; Chapter 10, p. 385]

29. Reasonable accommodation [Chapter 3, p. 93; Chapter 13, pp. 88–89]

    ADA

    Religious

30. Employment-at-will doctrine [Chapter 9, p. 334]

31. The Lilly Ledbetter Fair Pay Act of 2009 [Chapter 3, p. 92]

32. The Genetic Information Nondiscrimination Act of 2008 [Chapter 3, p. 91; Chapter 6, p. 207]

33. The Consolidated Omnibus Budget Reconciliation Act of 1985 [Chapter 13, pp. 522–523]

34. The American Recovery and Reinvestment Act of 2009 [Chapter 13, p. 523]

35. The Immigration Reform and Control Act of 1986 [Chapter 3, p. 92]

36. The Fair Credit Reporting Act [Chapter 6, p. 217]

37. The Health Insurance Portability and Accountability Act of 1996 [Chapter 13, p. 523]

38. The Immigration and Nationality Act of 1952 [Chapter 3, pp. 92–93]

39. Negligent hiring [Chapter 6, p. 198]

C. **Job Analysis/Job Design (required)**

1. Job/role design (roles, duties, and responsibilities) [Chapter 4, pp. 135–136]

2. Job evaluation and compensation (grades, pay surveys, and pay setting) [Chapter 11, pp. 438–439]

3. Employment practices (recruitment, selection, placement) [Chapter 6, p. 198]

4. Performance management (performance criteria and appraisal) [Chapter 8, p. 285]

5. Training and development [Chapter 7, p. 248; Chapter 7, p. 253; Chapter 7, p. 240]

    Vocational and career counseling

    Needs assessment

    Career pathing

6. Compliance with legal requirements [Chapter 3, p. 93; Chapter 11, p. 434; Chapter 11, pp. 437–438; Chapter 14, p. 567]

    Equal employment (job relatedness, Bona Fide Occupational Qualifications, and the reasonable accommodation process)

    Equal pay (skill, effort, responsibility and working conditions) and comparable worth

    Overtime eligibility (exempt vs. nonexempt work)

    Ergonomics and workplace safety (work hazards and mitigation)

7. HR planning (skill inventories and supply/demand forecasting) [Chapter 4, pp. 141–142]

8. Work management (work processes and outsourcing) [Chapter 4, p. 124; Chapter 4, p. 151]

9. Organization design (missions, functions, and other aspects of work units for horizontal and vertical differentiation) [Chapter 2, p. 54]

D. **Organization Development (required)**

1. Coaching [Chapter 9, pp. 336–337]

2. Developing human resources [Chapter 7, p. 240]

3. Emotional intelligence [Chapter 7, p. 266]

4. Equipping the organization for present and future talent needs [Chapter 7, p. 244]

5. Improving organizational effectiveness [Chapter 1, pp. 7–8]

6. Knowledge management [Chapter 1, p. 11]

7. Leadership development [Chapter 9, p. 347]

8. Measurement systems [Chapter 7, p. 260]

9. Ongoing performance and productivity initiatives [Chapter 1, p. 7]

10. Organizational effectiveness [Chapter 1, pp. 7–8]

11. Organizational learning [Chapter 7, p. 247]

12. Organizational structure and job design [Chapter 4, p. 132]

13. Outsourcing employee development [Chapter 7, p. 272]

14. Social networking [Chapter 6, p. 221]

15. Succession planning [Chapter 4, p. 152]

16. Training employees to meet current and future job demands [Chapter 7, p. 240]

E. **Outcomes: Metrics and Measurement of HR (required)**

   1. Economic value added [Chapter 2, pp. 60–61]
   2. Balanced scorecard (HR and organization level) [Chapter 2, p. 61]
   3. Measuring absenteeism [Chapter 4, p. 144]
   4. Measuring turnover [Chapter 4, p. 144]
   5. Trend and ratio analysis projections [Chapter 4, p. 142]
   6. Calculating and interpreting yield ratios [Chapter 5, p. 181]
   7. Return on Investment (ROI) [Chapter 2, p. 61]
   8. HR scorecard [Chapter 2, p. 62]
   9. Organizational scorecard [Chapter 2, p. 61]
   10. Quantitative analysis [Chapter 4, p. 142]
   11. Benchmarking [Chapter 11, p. 444]
   12. Analyzing and interpreting metrics [Chapter 4, p. 144]
   13. Forecasting [Chapter 4, p. 142]

F. **Performance Management (required)**

   1. Identifying and measuring employee performance [Chapter 8, p. 296]
   2. Sources of information (e.g., managers, peers, clients) [Chapter 8, pp. 300–301]
   3. Rater errors in performance measurement [Chapter 8, pp. 306–307]
   4. Electronic monitoring [Chapter 8, p. 313]
   5. Performance appraisals [Chapter 8, p. 295]
   6. Appraisal feedback [Chapter 8, p. 310]
   7. Managing performance [Chapter 8, p. 290]
   8. Diagnosing problems [Chapter 9, p. 338]
   9. Performance improvement programs [Chapter 9, p. 336]

G. **Staffing: Recruitment and Selection (required)**

   1. Employment relationship (employees, contractors, and temporary workers) [Chapter 4, p. 150]
   2. External influences on staffing (labor markets, unions, economic conditions, technology) [Chapter 5, p. 166]
   3. External recruitment (recruiters, open vs. targeted recruitment, recruitment sources, applicant reactions, medium [electronic, advertisement], fraud/ misrepresentation) [Chapter 5, p. 172]
   4. Internal recruitment (timing, open/closed/targeted recruitment, bona fide seniority systems) [Chapter 5, pp. 169–170]

   5. Internal recruitment (promotability ratings, managerial sponsorship, self-/peer assessments, panels/review boards) [Chapter 5, p. 170]
   6. Initial assessment methods (résumés, cover letters, application blanks, biographical information, reference/background checks, genetic screening, initial interviews, minimum qualifications) [Chapter 6, pp. 203–204]
   7. Discretionary assessment methods [Chapter 6, p. 198]
   8. Ability/job knowledge tests, assessment centers [Chapter 6, p. 210]
   9. Noncognitive assessments (e.g., personality assessments, integrity tests, situational judgment tests, interest inventories) [Chapter 6, p. 209]
   10. Structured interviews [Chapter 6, pp. 214–215]
   11. Contingent assessment methods (drug testing, medical exams) [Chapter 6, pp. 211–212]
   12. Measurement concepts (predictors/criteria, reliability, validity) [Chapter 6, pp. 201–202]
   13. Selection decisions (ranking, grouping/banding, random selection) [Chapter 6, p. 222]
   14. Job offers (employment-at-will, contracts, authorization to work) [Chapter 9, p. 334]
   15. Bona Fide Occupational Qualifications (BFOQs) [Chapter 3, pp. 84–85]
   16. The employment brand (above, at, or below market pay) [Chapter 11, p. 430]

H. **Strategic HR (required)**

   1. Strategic management [Chapter 2, p. 46]
   2. Enhancing firm competitiveness [Chapter 2, p. 54]
   3. Strategy formulation [Chapter 2, pp. 52–53]
   4. Strategy implementation [Chapter 2, p. 53]
   5. Sustainability/corporate social responsibility [Chapter 2, pp. 64–65]
   6. Internal consulting (secondary) [Chapter 1, p. 15]
   7. Competitive advantage [Chapter 2, pp. 46–47]
   8. Competitive strategy [Chapter 2, p. 46]
   9. Ethics (integrated) [Chapter 1, p. 21]
   10. Linking HR strategy to organizational strategy [Chapter 2, p. 54]
   11. Organizational effectiveness [Chapter 1, p. 7]
   12. Trends and forecasting in HR [Chapter 4, p. 142]
   13. Mission and vision [Chapter 2, pp. 47–48]
   14. Quality management [Chapter 2, p. 53]

I.   **Total Rewards (required)**

A.   **Compensation**

1.   Development of a base pay system [Chapter 11, p. 440]

2.   Developing pay levels [Chapter 11, pp. 443–444]

3.   Determining pay increases [Chapter 11, p. 445]

4.   Role of job analysis/job design/job descriptions in determining compensation [Chapter 11, p. 440]

5.   Pay programs (merit pay, pay for performance, incentives/bonuses, profit sharing, group incentives/gainsharing, balanced scorecard) [Chapter 12, pp. 468–469]

6.   Compensation of special groups (e.g., executives, outside sales, contingent workers, management) [Chapter 11, p. 433]

7.   Internal alignment strategies [Chapter 11, p. 425]

8.   External competitiveness strategies [Chapter 11, pp. 425–426]

9.   Legal constraints on pay issues [Chapter 11, p. 438]

10. Monitoring compensation costs [Chapter 11, p. 427]

11. Union role in wage and salary administration [Chapter 11, p. 438]

12. Minimum wage/overtime [Chapter 11, p. 433]

13. Pay discrimination and dissimilar jobs [Chapter 11, p. 437]

14. Prevailing wage [Chapter 11, p. 444]

15. Motivation theories (equity, reinforcement, and agency theories) [Chapter 11, pp. 423–424]

B.   **Employee Benefits**

1.   Statutory versus voluntary benefits [Chapter 13, p. 508]

2.   Types of retirement plans (defined benefit, defined contribution, hybrid plans) [Chapter 13, pp. 533–534

3.   Regulation of retirement plans (FLSA, ERISA, Pension Protection Act of 2006) [Chapter 13, pp. 524–525]

4.   Types of health care plans (multiple payer/single payer, universal health care systems, HMOs, PPOs, fee-for-service, consumer-directed) [Chapter 13, p. 529]

5.   Regulation of health insurance programs (COBRA, HIPAA, HMOs) [Chapter 13, p. 522]

6.   Federal insurance programs (OASDI, Medicare) [Chapter 13, p. 512]

7.   Disability insurance [Chapter 13, p. 537]

8.   Educational benefits [Chapter 13, p. 538]

9.   Employee assistance/wellness programs [Chapter 14, pp. 566–567]

10. Family-oriented benefits [Chapter 13, p. 508]

11. Global employee benefits [Chapter 13, pp. 544–545]

12. Life insurance [Chapter 13, pp. 536–537]

13. Nonqualified plans for highly paid and executive employees [Chapter 13, pp. 525–526]

14. Outsourcing (secondary) [Chapter 2, pp. 63–64]

15. Time off and other benefits [Chapter 13, p. 527]

16. Unemployment Insurance [Chapter 13, pp. 518–519]

17. Wellness programs [Chapter 14, p. 566]

18. Financial benefits (gainsharing, group incentives, team awards, merit pay/bonuses) [Chapter 12, p. 476]

19. Managing employee benefits (cost control, monitoring future obligations, action planning, strategic planning) [Chapter 13, p. 508]

20. Domestic partner benefits [Chapter 13, pp. 543–544]

21. Paid leave plans [Chapter 13, p. 527]

22. Workers' compensation [Chapter 13, pp. 515–516]

J.   **Training and Development (required)**

1.   Needs assessment

2.   Competency models [Chapter 7, p. 240]

3.   Learning theories (behaviorism, constructivism, cognitive models, adult learning, knowledge management) [Chapter 7, pp. 247–248]

4.   Training evaluation (Kirkpatrick's model) [Chapter 7, p. 261]

5.   E-learning and use of technology in training [Chapter 7, pp. 258–259]

6.   On-the-Job Training [Chapter 7, pp. 256–257]

7.   Outsourcing (secondary) [Chapter 7, p. 272]

8.   Transfer of training (design issues, facilitating transfer) [Chapter 7, pp. 261–262]

9.   Employee development (formal education, experience, assessment) [Chapter 7, pp. 265–266]

10. Determining Return on Investment [Chapter 7, p. 261]

11. The role of training in succession planning [Chapter 7, p. 243]

12. Human/intellectual capital [Chapter 7, p. 264]

K.   **Workforce Planning and Talent Management (required)**

1.   Downsizing/rightsizing (secondary) [Chapter 4, pp. 146–147]

2. Planning (forecasting requirements and availabilities, gap analysis, action planning, core/flexible workforce) [Chapter 4, p. 141]

3. Retention (involuntary turnover, outplacement counseling, alternative dispute resolution) [Chapter 9, p. 344]

4. Retention (voluntary turnover, job satisfaction, withdrawal, alternatives) [Chapter 10, pp. 377–378]

5. Retention (measurement) [Chapter 4, p. 144]

6. Labor supply and demand [Chapter 4, p. 144]

7. Succession planning [Chapter 4, p. 152]

L. **Workplace Health, Safety, and Security** (required—undergraduates only)

1. OSHA citations and penalties [Chapter 14, pp. 562–563]

2. Disaster preparation, continuity and recovery planning [Chapter 14, pp. 579–580]

3. Employee health [Chapter 14, p. 564]

4. Inspection [Chapter 14, p. 559]

5. Protection from retaliation [Chapter 14, p. 560]

6. Safety management [Chapter 14, p. 568]

7. Security concerns at work [Chapter 14, p. 575]

8. Communicable diseases [Chapter 14, p. 563]

9. Data security [Chapter 14, pp. 575–576]

10. Testing for substance abuse [Chapter 6, pp. 211–212]

11. Ergonomics [Chapter 14, p. 567]

12. Monitoring, surveillance, privacy [Chapter 9, p. 334]

Required Content–Graduate Curriculum

M. **Change Management (required—graduate students only)**

1. Stages of change management
   Indifference
   Rejection
   Doubt
   Neutrality
   Experimentation
   Commitment

2. Dimensions of change
   Culture
   Coaching
   Direction
   Communication
   Accountability
   Resilience
   Skills and knowledge
   Recognition
   Managing projects
   Involvement

3. Communication

4. Building trust

5. Creating a foundation for problem solving

6. Leading change

7. Planning change strategy

8. Implementing change

9. Coping strategies for employees

10. Adjusting to change within the organization

Secondary Content

N. **Career Planning (secondary)**

1. Definition of a career

2. Balancing work and life

3. Career management systems

4. Company policies to accommodate work and nonwork activities

5. Coping with job loss

6. Developing leader skills
   Authentic leadership
   Contingency theory
   Ethical decision making
   Leader-member exchange theory
   Path-goal theory
   Situational approach
   Skills approach
   Style approach
   Team leadership
   Trait approach
   Transformational leadership

7. Plateauing

8. Skills obsolescence

9. Career development

O. **Corporate/Social Responsibility and Sustainability (secondary)**

1. Corporate philanthropy

2. Ethics

3. Diversity
4. Financial transparency
5. Employee relations and employment practices
   Participative decision making
6. Supply chain management
7. Governance
8. Community/employee engagement
9. Green management
10. The business case for CSR
11. Reputation and brand enhancement
12. Accountability and transparency
13. Risk management
14. Linking organizational culture and corporate values

P. Downsizing/Rightsizing (secondary)

1. Employment downsizing
2. Alternatives to employment downsizing
3. Strategies for long-term success
4. Why downsizing happens
5. When downsizing is the answer
6. Effectively managing a downsizing effort
7. Alternatives to downsizing
8. Consequences of employment downsizing
9. Approaches to reducing staff size
10. Identifying and eliminating unnecessary work
11. Prioritizing jobs for combining, streamlining, or eliminating
12. Identifying selection criteria for making downsizing/ rightsizing decisions
13. Importance of focusing on individual jobs versus individual staff members
14. Layoffs
15. Reductions in force

Q. HR Information Systems (secondary)

1. Conducting systems needs assessments
2. Determining system specifications
3. Selecting an HR Information System
4. Using HR data for enterprise management
5. Issues to consider when selecting HRIS software

R. Internal Consulting (secondary)

1. Assess customers' needs
2. Influence cross-departmentally
3. Identify areas for HR intervention and design intervention
4. Advise management and colleagues cross-divisionally
5. Analyze and recommend solutions to business problems

6. Analyze data and prepare reports to inform business decisions
7. Recommend changes for process improvement
8. Conduct periodic audits
9. Lead special and cross-functional project teams

S. Mergers and Acquisitions (secondary)

1. Conducting HR due diligence
2. Integrating HR systems
3. Assimilating work cultures
4. Integrating compensation and benefits structures
5. Merging workplace cultures
6. Integrating performance management systems
7. Cultural compatibility
   Address cultural differences
   Degree of internal integration
   Autonomy
   Adaptability
   Employee trust
   Diversity
8. Integration
   Communication
   Employee anxiety
   Rumors
   Redundancy
   Downsizing
   Morale

T. Outsourcing (secondary)

1. Creating an outsourcing strategy
2. Preparing a Request for Information (RFI) or Request for Proposal (RFP)
3. Identifying third-party providers (contractors)
4. Evaluating proposals from contractors
5. Conducting cost-benefit analyses
6. Negotiating contract terms
7. Retaining management rights
8. Importance of legal review of contracts
9. Managing vendor-staff relationships
10. Managing a vendor's performance under the contract terms
11. Managing communications and deliverables
12. Evaluating effectiveness of outsourcing efforts

Integrated Content

U. Ethics (integrated)

1. Rules of conduct
2. Moral principles

3. Individual versus group behavior
4. Organizational values
5. Guidelines and codes
6. Behavior within ethical boundaries
7. Facing and solving ethical dilemmas
8. Codes of ethics
   General value system
   Ethical principles
   Ethical rules
9. Compliance and laws
10. Confidential and proprietary information
11. Conflicts of interest
12. Use of company assets
13. Acceptance or providing of gifts, gratuities, and entertainment
14. Abusive behavior
    Workplace bullying
15. The Sarbanes-Oxley Act of 2002 (SOX)
    Whistle-blowers
    Fraud
16. The False Claims Act
17. The Foreign Corrupt Practices Act

V. Globalization (integrated)

1. Global business environment
2. Managing expatriates in global markets
3. Cross-border HR Management
4. Repatriating employees post international assignment
5. Global security and terrorism

6. In-shoring
7. Offshoring/outsourcing
8. Global labor markets
9. Cross-cultural effectiveness

W. HR's Role in Organizations (integrated)

1. It is generally expected that faculty will discuss HR's role with regard to each of the individual HR disciplines whenever an individual discipline is taught. This may take the form of describing HR's role in developing human capital, its effect on the organization's success, or the interplay among the various disciplines—meaning how decisions in one HR discipline affect other HR disciplines.

X. Managing a Diverse Workforce (integrated)

1. Equal Opportunity Employment (EEO)
2. Affirmative Action (AA)
3. Aging workforce
4. Individuals with disabilities
5. Language issues
6. Racial/ethnic diversity
7. Religion
8. Reverse discrimination
9. Sex/gender issues
10. Gay, lesbian, bisexual, transgender (GLBT)/ sexual orientation issues
11. The glass ceiling
12. Business case for diversity
13. Cultural competence

Appendix B
Additional Cases

TOYOTA MOTOR COMPANY'S RECALL DEBACLE: DID TOYOTA TAKE A WRONG TURN?

It was a public relations disaster of unimagined proportions for the automotive manufacturing industry icon. On September 29, 2009, Toyota Motor Company (TMC) announced that it would recall 3.8 million vehicles in the United States, due to unintended acceleration. By May 2011, the recall surged to approximately 14 million vehicles.

A media outcry began after an accelerator pedal caught in the floor mat and caused the deaths of a California Highway Patrol officer and three family members in August 2009. Toyota's president of three months, Akio Toyoda, responded to the tragedy by offering a public apology. Both Toyota and the National Highway Traffic Safety Administration (NHTSA) investigated what may have caused the unintended acceleration, and both concluded that a faulty design allowed accelerator pedals to become caught in the floor mat and to stick in the accelerating position. (Toyota also noted, however, that nearly all of the crashes that occurred while the driver was trying to brake resulted from the driver mistakenly pressing the accelerator instead of the brake.) U.S. government regulators fined Toyota nearly $50 million for taking too long to initiate recalls.

On May 23, 2011, a seven-member North American Quality Advisory Panel (NAQAP), created in 2010 by Toyota and headed by former U.S. Secretary of Transportation Rodney E. Slater, released a report that said Toyota had been slow to discover the floor mat and accelerator pedal issues because the company ignored customer and government regulator complaints about sudden acceleration. It also said Toyota had failed to apply its "Toyota Way" manufacturing process principles, which, in part, direct employees to detect and respond to problems quickly, and to encourage timely and effective communications between employees, management, and executives.

The Toyota Way, 2001

In 2001, Toyota executives created corporate principles to encourage the continuous improvement of processes and people through training, teamwork, and management-employee relations, which they dubbed the "Toyota Way." On December 21 of that year, a Toyota press release announced that in January 2002, the company would establish the Toyota Institute, an internal organization for training Toyota Way principles to executives and middle management in Japan's TMC and its overseas affiliates.

The press release stated that these principles considered the effects of globalization and diversity ("people with diverse perceptions") on human resources and "the global Toyota team," and that Toyota conducted a review of its HR training structures to identify best practices for ensuring "a continuous reservoir of personnel with a shared commitment to the Toyota Way." The press release added, "Toyota sees human resource training as one of the most vital issues in today's increasingly challenging age of mega-competition."

The long-term strategic motivation behind the Toyota Way was to identify and develop people who could work "lean" and optimize efficiency, in order to support TMC's aggressive push to become the world's largest automotive manufacturer. TMC executives were well aware that implementing this strategy would require creating a culture in which employees supported the Toyota Way principles worldwide. As Toyota reports on its corporate website (www.toyota-global.com/investors/ir_library/annual_reports/2007/chairman_message.html), its fundamental stance on HR development is "making things is about developing people." The website also states that Toyota's HR development is based on On-the-Job Training in addition to establishing and improving educational systems that focus on sharing and conveying appropriate values in accordance with the Toyota Way.

Putting Principles Into Practice?

The Toyota Way's 14 principles combine a long-term strategic vision with the day-to-day practices that are designed to make the vision a reality. Several principles and their respective practices are especially relevant to Toyota's defective floor mat and accelerator mismanagement. The following summary is a distillation of these principles from Jeffrey Liker's book, *The Toyota Way* (New York: McGraw-Hill, 2004).

Section I: Long-Term Philosophy

Principle 1. Base your management decisions on a long-term philosophy, even at the expense of short-term financial goals.

- Have a philosophical sense of purpose that supersedes any short-term decision making. Work, grow, and align the whole organization toward a common purpose that is bigger than making money.

Principle 5. Build a culture of stopping to fix problems, to get quality right the first time.

- Quality for the customer drives your value proposition.
- Build into your organization support systems to quickly solve problems and put in place countermeasures.
- Build into your culture the philosophy of stopping or slowing down to get quality right the first time to enhance productivity in the long run.

Section III: Add Value to the Organization by Developing Your People

Principle 9. Grow leaders who thoroughly understand the work, live the philosophy, and teach it to others.

- Grow leaders from within, rather than buying them from outside the organization.
- Do not view the leader's job as simply accomplishing tasks and having good people skills. Leaders must be role models of the company's philosophy and way of doing business.
- Good leaders must understand the daily work in great detail so they can be the best teachers of your company's philosophy.

Principle 10. Develop exceptional people and teams who follow your company's philosophy.

- Train exceptional individuals and teams to work within the corporate philosophy to achieve exceptional results. Work very hard to reinforce the culture continually.
- Use cross-functional teams to improve quality and productivity and enhance flow by solving difficult technical problems.
- Make an ongoing effort to teach individuals how to work together as teams toward common goals.

Principle 13. Make decisions slowly by consensus, thoroughly considering all options; implement decisions rapidly (*nemawashi*).

- *Nemawashi* is the process of discussing problems and potential solutions with everyone affected, to collect their ideas and get agreement on how to move forward. This consensus process is time-consuming but broadens the search for solutions, and once a decision is made, implementation can move ahead rapidly.

Toyota's elaboration on the Toyota Way principles on the corporate website describe how these principles support the company's relations with employees.

TMC's Relations With Employees

According to TMC's website (www.toyota-global.com/sustainability/stakeholders/employees/):

- The Toyota Way promotes mutual trust and respect between labor and management, long-term employment stability, and communication.
- The Toyota Institute conducts core training for affiliates worldwide, to teach work methods (problem solving and management expertise), so Toyota personnel around the world can put the shared Toyota Way into practice.

The May 23, 2011, NAQAP report questioned how effectively Toyota followed the Toyota Way principles. The criticisms that are most relevant to HR management reveal flaws in the executive reporting structure, global communications structure, and safety management accountability.

The North American Quality Advisory Panel's Findings

Management and organization analysts generally agree that the oversights that led to Toyota's 2009–2010 recalls stemmed from Toyota setting its own sights, more than 10 years earlier, on becoming the world's largest automaker. Critics propose that the company's focus on global expansion superceded management and employee structures, policies, and processes that the company required in order to keep balanced tabs on the internal and external environments. The NAQAP concurred, adding, "the root causes of Toyota's recent challenges go beyond the issue of growth. They are more complex and more subtle, and in many cases, are not unique to Toyota."

Some of the root causes that the NAQAP cited are rooted in what were possibly misguided or mismanaged HR strategy and management policies.

Executive Reporting and Decision-Making Structures

1. According to the NAQAP, Toyota structured its global operations around functional "silos," each of which reported separately to TMC executives in Japan. Decision-making structures that involved everything from recalls, communications, marketing, and vehicle design and development were centrally managed and tightly controlled by TMC. In North America, instead of having one chief executive in charge of all of its divisions (e.g., sales and marketing, general corporate, engineering, and manufacturing), Toyota placed a separate head in each division, each of whom reported directly to TMC in Japan.

One-Way Communications

2. The NAQAP suggested that Toyota's global "silo" structure contributed to problems with *yokoten*, the part of Toyota's process of continuous improvement that focuses on sharing best practices and transferring knowledge across the organization. For example, Toyota's president, Akio Toyoda, said that the company "failed to connect the dots between problems" with sticking accelerator pedals in Europe and in the United States. A Toyota executive admitted to Congress that "a weakness in our system has been that within this company, we didn't do a very good job of sharing information across the globe. Most of the information was one way. It would flow from the regional markets, like the United States, Canada or Europe back to Japan." A case in point: In 2000 the United Kingdom recalled Lexus IS-200 models due to "a possibility that the driver's side carpet mat may rotate around the central fixing and interfere with the operation of the accelerator pedal." Toyota did not report this recall to North American counterparts. Had North American operations known about the mat and accelerator pedal problem, its specialists could have examined the related safety design issues before they became a widespread problem.

Safety Management Responsibility Oversight

3. The NAQAP suggested that Toyota viewed safety as a subset of quality. As a result, Toyota did not have a senior executive–level position with overall responsibility for safety, and did not appear to have a clear management chain of responsibility for safety issues. Although, from Toyota's perspective, everyone at the company was responsible for safety, the NAQAP suggested that the diffused nature of this responsibility could have thwarted the company's ability to recognize the need to accept responsibility when the public raised safety concerns.

Summary

Critics suggest that TMC's strategy of aggressive growth played a significant factor in how the company mishandled safety concerns raised by U.S. customers who complained that their vehicles' accelerator pedals stuck in an acceleration position. The NAQAP concluded that while they were focusing on global expansion and becoming the world's top automotive manufacturer, TMC executive management (ironically) overlooked the need to redesign the executive reporting and communication structures and to centralize responsibility for safety, and they ignored key principles of the Toyota Way that would have led the company to investigate consumers' and government regulators' complaints sooner.

TMC executives' slow response to customers and regulators who raised vehicle safety concerns (until the media took up the cause) suggests to some critics that Toyota management may have sacrificed Toyota Way principles to try to save money and face.

Questions

1. Based on "the three big strategic questions" of strategic HR (*What is our present situation? Where do we want to go? How do we plan to get there?*), and based on the information provided in this case, how well, in your opinion, did Toyota plan for global expansion back in 2000, in terms of executive reporting structure and corporate communication procedures? Was the structure too centralized and vertical, or not centralized and vertical enough? Should the North American affiliates have had more decision-making autonomy and/or horizontal communication paths? Should there have been more or fewer horizontal communication paths between different divisions and/or countries (e.g., England and the United States)? Explain your position.

2. If you were TMC's HR Director, what design would you choose for an organizational chart that would optimize the flow of communication between the following levels of management at TMC Japan and at plants in the United States and England? Describe how your flow chart works. Your chart should include only the following positions:

   Japan

   Chairman & CEO; President; Vice President; Quality Control Manager; Safety Manager.

   United States

   General Manager; Senior Manager; Section Manager; Production Manager; Plant Manager; Plant Group Leader.

   England

   General Manager; Senior Manager; Section Manager; Production Manager; Plant Manager; Plant Group Leader.

3. What is organizational culture? Was Toyota's response to customer complaints about safety consistent with the organizational culture that TMC executives desired to promote through the Toyota Way principles? Address in your response Principles 1, 5, 9, and 13 as described in this case.

4. Based on what you read in this case regarding executive managers' slow response to consumer complaints about sticking accelerator pedals, how well did managers' training from the Toyota Institute transfer to solving Toyota's real-world safety problem? How might the training they received be improved to better *shape behavior* to achieve Principle 5: "Build a culture of stopping to fix problems . . ."? Consider types of reinforcement, and the challenges of resistance to change and strategic congruence.

5. What challenges might Toyota's *global diversity* create when trying to create and/or change the corporate culture through Toyota Way training programs and reinforcement strategies? Consider how to design training programs that encourage employees from different countries to *conform* to the Toyota Way culture. What role might the need for conformity to the Toyota Way play in recruiting and hiring new Toyota employees?

6. What is your opinion of the Toyota Way principle (#9) of growing (i.e., "developing") leaders from within? How does this principle fit in with the reasoning behind succession planning? If you were Toyota's Director of Human Resources, would you support this practice or recommend recruiting leaders from outside the company, or a combination of both? Explain your reasoning.

7. Some organizational analysts suggest that Toyota managers may have been rewarded for containing costs over ensuring product quality and resolving customer complaints. If you were TMC's HR Director, and you wanted managers to support the Toyota Way principles of promoting safety (product quality) and customer satisfaction over cost containment, would you recommend using a trait appraisal, a behavioral appraisal, and/ or a results/outcome appraisal? Explain why.

8. Based on your response to Question #7, if you were Toyota's Director of Human Resources and money and time were not a concern, would you choose the critical incidents, MBO, narrative, graphic rating scale, or BARS method, or a combination of these methods of performance appraisal, to let managers know how well they are following and promoting the Toyota Way principles? Explain why.

Case study created by Andrea Markowitz

H&H FINANCIAL SERVICES, LLC[1]

H&H Financial was founded in 1997 as a local insurance and investment consulting firm specializing in financial, estate, and retirement planning. The business started as a part-time consulting practice given Mr. Blake's dissatisfaction with his full-time job working for a franchise office affiliated with a large insurance agency. Mr. Blake found that his agency's focus on productivity and numbers precluded his ability to do what he really wanted to do for his clients: provide personalized service that they could trust. He wanted his clients to be faces, not names and numbers. He wanted to offer them the optimal products and services that would best fit their needs, not just the selling needs of a corporation hyping their latest product through their franchises.

Mr. Blake bid his time and learned "the ropes to skip and the ropes to know" about running an agency. He obtained several key financial and insurance licenses and professional certifications (CFP, CFA, CFT, CTEP, etc.) as well as financial product suppliers. When he had developed a sizable private client base, he opened H&H as an independent agency to replace his consulting practice.

The firm started with just Mr. Blake operating out of a cheap storefront, and he was quickly overwhelmed with the paperwork side of the business. Mr. Blake was great at selling and knew the product lines in and out, but he was not an expediter or comfortable with details.

Mr. Blake's solution was to hire a part-time administrative assistant to handle phone calls, deal with foot traffic (what little there was), and do some light computer work. Times were not easy, and Mr. Blake squeaked by on a very limited income.

Early Success Leads to Growth

Mr. Blake's formula for success (personalized service) quickly caught on, and he found that he needed full-time assistance in order to help handle phone calls, process policies, and assist with claims. His office expanded quickly, and he replaced his one part-timer with three full-time employees who buffered him from the mundane paperwork and day-to-day office duties. He remained the sole agent providing sales and expert advice and counseling while the staff provided his clients with all of the support needed (processing bills or claims, answering questions about policies, etc.). His office staff consisted of one office staff person from Mr. Blake's old agency (Ms. Jane Sutton) and Ms. Johnson and Mr. Hayes (two "raw" college graduates: Jen Johnson and Kenneth Hayes). For the most part they all worked independent of Mr. Blake.

Although Mr. Blake never gave any of them titles, job descriptions, or formal authority, it was clear to everyone that Ms. Sutton was the informal leader of the office given her expertise and prior experience in an insurance office. All three employees became flexible generalists, part of a self-managed work team. Work was parceled out through volunteerism and cooperation. Mr. Blake was proud that his team operated so well without his input.

As the business grew, Mr. Blake realized that he would need to bring in new agents (consultants) to help him deal with the increasing flow of customers, and there was just no place to put them in his small back office. Mr. Blake and his team moved into a newly renovated office complex, which had more offices, a main office area that could hold more employees, and a separate waiting area for his clients.

Mr. Blake hired one financial planner and one insurance agent so as to provide more sales and technical expertise to his consulting team. The new associates worked out so well

---

[1] The name of the firm and the case characters have been disguised at the request of the firm's owner.

and his business grew so quickly that within three months, three new staff people (all recent college graduates) had to be hired to help Ms. Sutton, Ms. Johnson, and Mr. Hayes manage the additional workload. Debbie Matthews was one of the three new employees hired.

The Birth of Departments and Continued Growth

The addition of these three new employees altered the structure of the company. As the office manager, Ms. Sutton still managed her two "old rookies" but made each one a supervisor. Jen Johnson became in charge of supplier relations and managed one new employee while Kenneth Hayes ran client relations and managed Ms. Matthews and another new employee (see Figure 1).

Ms. Sutton felt this new structure was highly efficient since it allowed Ms. Johnson and Mr. Hayes the time to develop their own expertise and familiarity with their specific focal group. These new department managers would handle the day-to-day work routine of their own department with their new staff while Ms. Sutton served as coordinator and in-house expert—the answer person. This structure also made the assignment and training of new office personnel much easier since each employee was allocated to one of the two departments where their supervisor would then provide them with basic training within the department.

Mr. Blake was quite happy with Ms. Sutton's work processes and procedures since it allowed him to concentrate on his clients and stay out of the office operations. He could now work with his other specialist consultants to help locate new clients as well as new products and services. This was often voiced by Mr. Blake as a critical operational strategy for continuing to grow the business.

| Figure 1 | Organizational Structure of H&H Financial Services, LLC |

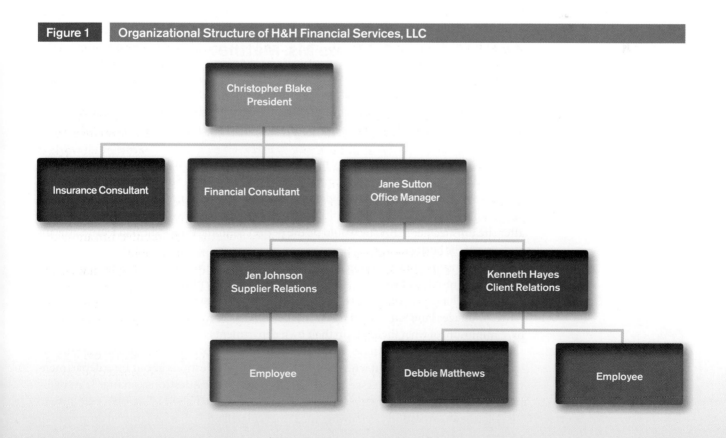

At the department level, Mr. Hayes and Ms. Johnson made the work environment fun, which Ms. Matthews greatly appreciated. Ms. Sutton, however, wanted the office to have a more professional demeanor since she felt that H&H was now an established firm with expert consultants on staff who also seemed to not appreciate the horseplay of the office workers. For Ms. Sutton, maintaining an expert image became everything, and therefore she went to great strides to minimize office antics (like wastebasket basketball) and excessive chatter. Mr. Hayes and Ms. Johnson were not happy with the new rules but went along with them since they spent most of their time in their own work areas and away from the back office where Ms. Sutton stayed and did most of her work. The change in rules did create tension between the newest employees (including Ms. Matthews) and Ms. Sutton. Ms. Matthews quickly learned that she could joke around with Mr. Hayes and Ms. Johnson when Ms. Sutton was out of sight but had to be on her best behavior when Ms. Sutton was around or when they went into the management territory area of the office.

The companywide informal monthly meetings with Mr. Blake, which happened early on in the firm's history, became formal monthly meetings just with Ms. Sutton and all of her subordinates. The monthly meetings consisted of discussions of new products, services, clients, new procedures, and any outstanding problems that either department could not solve alone. These were open meetings, but rarely did anyone but Ms. Matthews raise questions, and these questions were always about work processes and procedures. Everyone else, including the supervisors, only spoke when Ms. Sutton spoke directly to them or asked very general questions about the growth plans of H&H.

With sustained success, the organization continued to grow, adding several more consultants and back office staff while keeping the same basic organizational structure and work flow. Mr. Blake once again needed new office space to contain his firm's growing needs. Mr. Blake announced as part of his growth plan that he was conducting preliminary inquiries as to a possible "number two" who would handle the ever-growing functions of finance, accounting, and Human Resource Management—a job that Ms. Matthews quickly aspired to.

As H&H Grows, So Does Ms. Matthews's Frustration

As a recent college graduate and single mother, Ms. Matthews was excited when she got the job working for H&H Financial as their Assistant Case Manager in the Client Relations Department. In her first month she quickly and eagerly learned all of her required duties and executed them to the best of her ability and therein received more and more demanding work.

In her second month when they moved to a much larger office, Ms. Matthews felt that she had real opportunities for advancement and promotion. She thought, "As the firm grows, so will I." She felt that she had made an excellent choice in a very tough job market. She was aware of Mr. Blake's preliminary search for an Assistant Manager and thought that after she finished her MBA she would be the perfect candidate once she had learned the ins and outs of the business.

Those dreams, however, quickly became a nightmare. Ms. Matthews found that after the first few months of working at H&H Financial, her learning curve came to a complete and sudden halt. Ms. Matthews realized that jobs were very compartmentalized, and the Office Manager Jane Sutton did not want the employees to learn anything more than the bare minimum of what their jobs in their own departments required of them.

Mr. Hayes, her immediate supervisor, was very helpful and supportive about the work in his department, but when Ms. Matthews asked questions about interdepartmental and organizational processes, he deflected most of her questions, saying, "I'm really not sure why we do things this way; check with Ms. Sutton." Ms. Sutton's response to Ms. Matthews's questions was always the same: "I'll tell you what you need to know when you need to know it . . . just do your job, do it well, and you'll get along fine." Ms. Matthews thought that perhaps with a few more months on the job Ms. Sutton would learn to trust her more; but she couldn't have been more wrong.

During her third monthly office meeting, Ms. Matthews became increasingly irate because her questions were still being answered by Ms. Sutton with "You don't need to know that" or "You will never deal with that situation" or, worse, "That's not your concern." Ms. Matthews found that these were the answers to even the simplest of questions dealing with the most essential parts of the business outside of her department. This approach made it difficult for Ms. Matthews to properly do her job because she did not see how her job related to the other jobs in the firm.

Ms. Matthews thought there was a clear lack of communication between the owner, Ms. Sutton, the two supervisors, and the lower-level employees and that this created slow-downs and gaps that bottlenecked the flow of the entire work process of the business. She also noticed that not only was her job compromised by this lack of knowledge, but also, in her opinion, was everybody else's. All of her questions regarding this matter were not only disregarded by Ms. Sutton but discouraged as well. Ms. Matthews thought that for such a small but fast-growing company, the operations would run much smoother if all of the employees were aware and informed about each other's jobs for they were all dependent and interrelated. Overall Ms. Matthews felt that Ms. Sutton was overly controlling and excessively formal.

After several attempts to learn more about her job, Ms. Matthews was starting to lose motivation. She felt like a robot that was programmed to do the same thing day in and day out, and it was starting to affect the quality of her work. She was surprised and disappointed to learn that she no longer cared about her performance, her job, and the firm.

In the meantime, the new large sitting area required the firm to hire a receptionist who then handled walk-ins and who would also orient the new clients to all of the services provided by H&H. The receptionist would also, on occasion, administer customer questionnaires that dealt with customer service satisfaction as well as desired additional services. Ms. Matthews was sorely tempted to take this job because the receptionist reported directly to Mr. Blake; Ms. Sutton would be out of her reporting loop. She quickly let go of the notion, though, since she would be devolving in terms of her career and personal development, not growing.

 This is when she realized, after being with the firm for nearly a year, that by staying at H&H she was starting to compromise her work ethic—her values of always striving to achieve and working to the best of one's ability. Ms. Matthews also found out that she was not the only one feeling less motivated and interested. Both Ms. Johnson and Mr. Hayes confided to her that they felt the same way but never said anything to Ms. Sutton or Mr. Blake.

With all this negativity surrounding her work life, the decision to leave was still a difficult one to make. The company had some great employees in her department that made it fun to come to work every day. Since everybody was about the same age, people got along well. Ms. Matthews also liked the relatively laid-back environment in the department and the flexibility of hours the job offered, especially considering that she was now in graduate school. However, Ms. Matthews was not sure if that was enough; after 11 months of working at H&H she wondered if it was worth it for her to continue working there. On the one hand, Ms. Matthews knew that she had no future at the company. She was pursuing her MBA, and she now knew that that would not make a difference for her future at H&H. Ms. Matthews wondered, "What is the point in spending money and time to get a graduate degree if it is never going to be appreciated or add value to my career at H&H? Should I stay at a place where there was no chance for growth and no value given my curiosity and desire to learn? At the same time, is it a bad decision to try to change jobs right now considering the downturned economic climate, my need for a flexible schedule for graduate school, and my financial responsibilities? Should I stay simply for the money and my flexible schedule?" Ms. Matthews realized that she had an important decision to make, and she had to make it soon before she became completely unmotivated.

Questions

1. Describe H&H Financial's organizational structure. Evaluate the organization's complexity, formalization, and centralization in your answer. How does this structure seem to affect Ms. Matthews's behavior?

2. There are four primary approaches to job design: mechanistic, biological, perceptual, and motivational. How might each approach be employed to better fit Ms. Matthews with her job?

3. Using the Job Characteristics Model, describe the impact Ms. Matthews's job design is having on her work motivation.

4. Suggest how the firm could redesign Ms. Matthews's job so it would increase her work motivation.

5. Ms. Matthews may decide to stay at H&H if a more flexible work environment is created for her. Describe some alternative ways her job could be redesigned for greater flexibility.

6. Describe how formalized training and/or employee development might help Ms. Matthews better fit her job at H&H.

7. How you would you assess Jane Sutton's need for training and development? What training methods you would recommend given her actions in this case?

8. How might career planning help Ms. Matthews decide whether or not to stay at H&H?

9. What would you do if you were Ms. Mathews? Are there options she hasn't considered?

A TEMPORARY SOLUTION AT LOGISTICS[1]

"Steve, Todd, it's Nancy. I'm calling about Annie! I don't think she's going to make it. I don't know how the company could have let this continue and happen," Nancy Ryan cried as she tried to talk to Steve Jones and Todd Wick, managers of the Business Development Group at Logistics. After she hung up, Steve and Todd stared at each other until Todd said, "Steve, what could we have done? What do you think we should do now?"

Background on Logistics

Logistics, a high-tech manufacturer in the Northeast, was a global leader in wireless security and surveillance equipment. Logistics produced wireless audio and video surveillance recording devices. Logistics wireless large-scale products were installed at more than 600,000 customer locations, and its miniaturized ones (more commonly known as "bugs") were installed at more than 10 million locations worldwide. Logistics' global network of business partners provided products and services to both manufacturing- and service-type organizations, including retailers, transportation, banks, health care, and education.

Logistics Inc. was cofounded by Joseph Sergi who was its CEO and President. After obtaining his doctorate in optical physics and with financial support from family and friends, he was able to develop a miniature camera and audio recorder. Soon thereafter the company introduced the LaserTron, a laser security device capable of invisibly detecting intruders. Logistics then launched the LaserBase, which not only identified intruders but also stored the information in a database for future analysis. Logistics then introduced the first commercially available wireless miniature detection devices, making surveillance portability and information storage complete. In recent years, other products emerged to continue Logistics' dominance in the field.

All of Logistics' products required extensive use of highly complex and sophisticated technology supplied from a large pool of vendors. These supply companies were carefully screened for component reliability and quality, adhering to all of Logistics' specifications. Some of these components were microchips, printed circuit boards, lenses, and various microelectronic devices.

The Culture at Logistics: Temporary and Permanent Employees

Temporary employees are everywhere at Logistics. All are hired through temporary employment agencies, which supply people for various positions. Some people are there only for short periods of time (i.e., a week or two) while others may be around for years. It's important to note that it is not uncommon for temporary employees to work at Logistics for at least a year, or longer, before being made the offer of permanent employment. Of course, there are channels that must be adhered to, and procedures that must be followed. In fact, once the paperwork is approved and channeled through the process, an official job description must be compiled and posted onto the bulletin board so that regular Logistics associates have the opportunity to apply for the position as well. What's more, it is not uncommon for temporary workers to put in a year or more on a job, and still not get the position if a more qualified Logistics associate applies for the position instead. This happens because, despite the fact that a temporary worker may build upon an existing position,

---

[1] All events are true. The organization, individuals, and products were changed to provide confidentiality.

or create process flows and a system for a brand-new position, the temporary worker still has to interview with Human Resources and compete for the job once it gets posted. Typically, the temporary worker is not aware of this detail, and it is a well-known norm within the culture of the firm not to associate with temporary workers. This disassociation is not a directive from management; it is simply a norm within the culture.

As a permanent worker at Logistics, it's easy to determine that the corporate culture is cluttered with cliques and peer groups. The corporate culture ostracizes anyone who makes waves, asks for help, or breaks protocol. The longer employees have worked at the company, the better their chances are of being accepted—as long as they follow the rules along the way. Temps and consultants are considered expendable. New employees at Logistics typically feel isolated until they adapt to the unofficial rules of the corporate culture or quit. Accordingly, there is an informal waiting period that all new employees must go through to prove they can adapt to the corporate culture. Acceptance also depends on work ethic and the ability to mind your own business and keep your nose clean. Obviously, the culture is a strong one: Someone is either accepted or not. Ironically, even if an employee makes it through this adjustment period and is accepted, he or she must continue to abide by the rules or risk expulsion from the group. The corporate culture is especially difficult for a new employee or a temporary worker. New employees must navigate the strict corporate culture alone and clumsily find out for themselves about the rules of the game.

The Annie Martin Story

Annie Martin started working at Logistics as a temporary worker in the Business Development Group within the Customer Service Organization. Annie was brought in to work the brand-new position of Database Administrator. On her first day, Annie was introduced by her boss, Steve, to the various associates with whom she would be working. Everyone was informed that Annie would be the Database Administrator. Since the Database Administrator position was never posted on the job opportunities bulletin board, several inquiries were made to Steve about the status of the position. Steve had a uniform response—he simply said that Annie was "just a temp."

After several months, it was easy to assess that Annie was a shy and hardworking individual. Every day she arrived at work early, and stayed late. Although she mostly kept to herself, Annie became friendly with a few of the people at work. Mostly, she got close with Nancy who was Annie's next-door "cube" neighbor. Before long, Annie seemed to be informally accepted into the Business Development (BD) Group of 10 people. She even began attending staff meetings regularly. When the BD Group performed a team-building survey, to develop and help the group work better as a team, Annie was involved. She filled in a survey, and her results were incorporated into the BD Group results just like every other permanent employee in the group. Subsequently, Steve was asked if there were plans to get Annie hired as a permanent worker anytime soon. Steve replied that he was trying to accomplish this feat and get her officially on board as soon as possible. In fact, after about six months on the job, this same question was posed to Steve, by the Director of the BD Group, at one of the staff meetings. With Annie sitting right there in the room, Steve informed the group that he was desperately trying to push through the paperwork, and it was only a matter of time.

Annie continued to develop in the position of Database Administrator, and although people external to the BD Group treated her like an outsider, she was informally accepted into the BD Group. While it became obvious that Steve was having difficulty justifying to Human Resources that the position should be filled permanently by Annie, it became more of a sour topic for the rest of the group.

Over time, Annie started to withdraw once the group seemed to lose interest in the status of her coming on board as a permanent employee. The group hadn't lost interest; it was just that there was absolutely nothing the group could do about the situation. Despite the fact that everyone tried to act as if all was fine and go about business as usual, it was clear something unfair was occurring.

The Incident

After about eight months on the job, Annie was rushed to the hospital. Nancy, Annie's closest friend at Logistics, confided in some of the group that Annie had tried to kill herself. Nancy explained that Annie was in her early 40s, single with no significant other, and extremely lonely. Apparently, Annie was totally alone. Her mother and brother lived in New Jersey, and Annie lived alone in a small apartment on Long Island. Other than being a part of some church group, Annie had no real social connections with anyone. She felt her hopes of becoming a permanent employee at Logistics were dashed. This realization compounded and amplified all the other current difficulties she was facing in life, bringing her problems to a head. Annie felt so hopeless about her life in general that she tried to kill herself.

Nancy was worried when Annie didn't show up for work one day. After trying to call Annie and getting a constant busy signal, Nancy got in her car and drove to Annie's apartment. It was then that she found Annie passed out on the floor as a result of taking a large dose of sleeping pills.

Nancy was visibly upset and, accordingly, needed to talk about the situation and process what had happened. She told a group of people about what Annie had done and how she had found her. Of course, the word spread, and before long, everyone in the department knew that Annie attempted suicide. In a short time, the details were unimportant, and it was just a topic of gossip (e.g., "Did you hear that Annie tried to kill herself because Logistics won't hire her? What a weirdo!").

Steve confided in several of members of the BD Group that he felt somewhat responsible for what Annie had done. In failing to get her hired, he thought he had failed her and it was his fault. Others in the group felt terrible about the whole situation because deep down they felt that they had separated themselves from getting too close to her because of the rules of acceptance.

Return and Recovery

In a few weeks, Steve had Annie return to her position once she had improved, with the promise that he would do everything in his power to get her hired as a permanent employee. The group was sensitive to her return and tried very hard to turn the other cheek to what she had done. Of course, Annie was unaware that everyone knew about her suicide attempt.

Time passed, and subsequently the Business Development Group was restructured. Due to the nature of Steve and Annie's functions within the company, they were placed under a different level of management. Steve helped Annie adjust through the transition by constant reinforcement. Steve watched over her carefully to make sure she was OK. He was worried about her, and he insisted he would help her through until she became permanent.

After a few months, Annie was still a temporary worker. Steve's responsibilities were redesigned, and his new job responsibilities placed him under a new group with new management. Annie's position as Database Administrator and her life situation remained the same. Steve's former responsibilities were removed and given to Todd. Annie started working for Todd who was located in a different part of the building. Subsequently, Annie had to move to a new cube that was closer to Todd, and her old cube, next to Nancy, was reassigned. Steve continued to pushed Todd to get Annie hired. Since Todd was new to the Service Organization, he didn't know Annie's history.

Annie failed to show up to work one day, and Todd didn't receive a phone call. He called her but received no response. He called Steve to see if he had another number, and

Steve told him to contact Nancy, since they were close. Todd called Nancy and explained what had happened. Nancy dropped the phone and ran out of the building. She arrived at Annie's apartment, only to find an ambulance.

Questions

1. Describe the competitive strategy of Logistics and how the HRM function supports this strategy.

2. What are the pros and cons of a temporary workforce? Does this employment status support Logistics' business strategy?

3. Describe the culture of Logistics, specifically its treatment of temporary employees. Does this treatment support their differentiation strategy?

4. Develop some recommendations that would improve Logistics' use of temporary employees and its culture. What changes would need to be made to support the firm's business strategy?

5. Cultural change requires a planned, systemic approach. How does a firm plan for change and overcome resistance to change?

6. What could Annie's boss and coworkers have done to help Annie better cope once she returned to work after her first suicide attempt?

7. How responsible is Logistics for Annie Martin's suicide attempts?

DARIUS D'AMORE'S FRAGRANCES, INC.[1]

"The Position Opening Policy is to first post the job internally, and if no qualified candidate is found, then the open position will be announced to the general public," stated Jeff Juda, Chief Financial Officer of Darius D'Amore, at a Finance Department meeting. "Likewise," he continued, "we fully abide by and support all laws and rules governing employment, especially those from the EEOC."

"What a load of bull!" whispered Rich Rogers to Les Ford. "Juda probably doesn't know what has been going on in his own department!"

"But he will soon," responded Les.

Background

The Darius D'Amore Company was one of the world's leading manufacturers and marketers of quality skin care, makeup, fragrance, and hair care products. Darius and Dante D'Amore founded the company in New York City in 1945. Its products were sold in more than 120 countries and territories under the following brand names: Darius D'Amore, Darius, Dante, Beginnings, Inferno, Heaven, Cleanique, Zodiac, Avalon, *Madeline,* and Seasons. Each division had its own specific and unique image, advertising, and merchandising strategy.

Financial Division Structure

All brands reported their financial information to corporate headquarters in New York City. Some of the corporate executives and departments were located in Huntington, Long Island. The Finance Division reported to the CFO, Jeffery Juda. Each department under Juda was structured slightly differently, but all had a Vice President, a Staff Vice President, an Executive Director(s), directors, managers, supervisors, and the low-level employees.

The Financial Division had a total of 75 employees. The division was broken down into two major departments: Accounts Receivable/Credits/Collections and Accounts Payable/Payroll/Salary/Commissions. Many of the employees were in the same department and position for their entire Darius D'Amore career. (See Exhibit B.)

Human Resource Policy—Posting Open Positions

When a position became available, the policy of Darius D'Amore was to first post the job internally and then, if there was no qualified candidate, to advertise the job to the public. Many low-level positions were filled in this manner. However, when it came to management positions, there were some deviations.

Rich Rogers—No Posting, No Promotion

Rich Rogers, 43, had been with the company as a supervisor in the Corporate Credits and Collections Department for 14 years. Mr. Rogers, a White male, had his bachelor's degree in management and was enrolled in an MBA program at a local university. Rogers was fighting Stage 4 lung cancer, and he made his condition known to the firm because he needed to take a two-month leave to have bilateral lung surgery.

---

[1]The names of the firm and the employees have been changed to protect their anonymity.

Prior to his leave, two people had resigned from the positions of Manager of Credit Returns and Director of Credit Returns. Rogers let Al Savarino (Executive Director for Accounts Receivable/Credits/Collections) know he was interested in both jobs. Both positions were a level up in management and meant more money, responsibility, and status. While on sick leave, Rogers received a call from Mr. Savarino who indicated that the positions had been filled with two people from outside the department. Tony Miceli was the new Director and Tom Mathers was now the Manager of Credit Returns. When Rogers mentioned that he felt he was qualified, at least for the Manager position, Savarino told him that in his estimation he was not qualified and, therefore, Savarino would not post the position internally.

According to Laura Hertz, who works in the Accounts Receivable Department and is a close associate of Rogers, "[Rogers] was devastated because if he was not qualified, why was it his responsibility to train both Miceli and Mathers?" To add fuel to the fire, Hertz had heard that Mathers told Rogers that Rogers did not get the position because Kevin Simmons, Staff Vice President of the Financial Department, said, "He [Rogers] is a dead man and won't return to work."

Kevin Simmons, a White male in his early 50s, had been with the company for eight years. He was esteemed by upper management and his peers because of the dramatic changes he made to improve both the department and the company's profitability. Mary Connors, a Black female who has worked in the Accounts Receivable Department for over 20 years, spoke of how "Kevin came to the department and made many improvements."

Mary Connors revealed that Rogers had taped a conversation with Mathers, who was unaware of the recording. On the tape, Mathers talked about certain employees, including Simmons and some minority employees. Mathers made derogatory comments about Black female employees, implying they were stupid, crazy, inarticulate, and even involved in Voodoo.

Alongside one of his attorneys, Rich Rogers brought the tape to Kevin Simmons. Just a few minutes into the tape, Simmons made him shut it off and asked both of them to leave. Before he left, Simmons asked Rogers how he could continue to work for the company if he was going around taping conversations. Rogers was surprised at the comment and also that Simmons didn't investigate the contents of the tape.

Sometime afterward, Miceli was transferred to the Director of Payroll position. His replacement, Christine Wines, was hired from outside the company without the position being posted internally. Two years later both Wines and Mathers were terminated. As his supervisor, Kevin Simmons, noted, "Mathers was let go because he lacked consideration of others in his interpersonal skills." While Mathers was still the manager, Rogers interviewed a Puerto Rican female for an associate's position. Mathers told Rogers not to hire "the big fat Puerto Rican pig." The female was not hired because Mathers felt "she was unqualified," although Rogers thought differently.

After both Wines and Mathers were terminated, Rogers again let Simmons know he was interested in at least the Manager position (Mathers's job). Simmons did not post the positions internally, and Rogers indicated again he was denied the opportunity to apply. Mary Connors remembered clearly that Rogers was crying when he came out of Simmons's office. While consoling him, Mary reported that Rogers told her that Kevin Simmons said that no matter how hard he worked, he'd never be promoted. "It is probably a good idea if he looked for another job!" Mary was in shock but was even more disturbed by what Rogers said Simmons later told him. With tears coming down his cheeks, Rogers told her, "Simmons has the nerve to tell me that I am using my cancer to cheat the system."

Les Ford's Turndown

Les Ford, a 44-year-old African American employee, worked in the Salary and Commissions Department whose Executive Director was Vic Viola. His Department oversaw the payment of salaries and commissions to the cosmetic personnel. Ford had been with the company for a few years making lateral moves from position to position.

Jasmine Young, a 25-year-old African American female, was hired as a temporary employee to work in the Salary and Commissions Department, with Les Ford.

Les Ford and Jasmine Young worked in a different department than Rich Rogers, and neither of them had cancer. Even though they were from different departments, they were both on the same floor and ultimately reported to the same Staff Vice President, Kevin Simmons.

Linda Evans, a secretary, and Mary Connors both agreed that Les Ford was liked by many of his coworkers. His supervisor, Deborah Jones, left for another position and felt that he was the most qualified for her position. After Ford expressed interest in applying for the promotion, Jones took it upon herself to delegate some of her responsibilities to Ford. After applying for the position he was told by Vic Viola that the position was not going to be filled at the moment, but two new coordinator positions were being created. Ford felt cheated but took one of the positions in order to remain motivated.

One month after Ford began his new position, a White female from the Customer Service Department was named the supervisor. Once again, upper management did not post the position. This was the same position that Ford was told was not being filled. The new hire was Cathy Richards, a White female who had been with the company for more than 24 years. (See Appendix C.) According to Linda Evans and Mary Connors, she was the one who created most of the trouble for minority employees. An unnamed source from the Human Resource Department stated that Cathy was written up on a number of occasions for name-calling, especially to those she supervised. Another minority, Elvin Shane, backed the claim found in the report. He worked in the same department as Ford and Young. Edward indicated that "Cathy, along with other coworkers, would use derogatory racial and sexual slurs. The racial and sexual slurs went on even after people complained to Vic Viola and Kevin Simmons. Mary Connors described an incident where a Black pregnant female employee under Les Ford reported to him that she was tripped and called a derogatory name by Cathy Richards. Ford reported it to the people above him, including Kevin Simmons, but nothing was ever done."

Ford and Young complained to their manager Mike Bonn (Richards's immediate supervisor) and his boss, Director Joe Agnelli, about the verbal and nonverbal abuse by Cathy Richards. Only after numerous complaints did Agnelli decide to bring the issue to John Price, a Human Resource Manager. Ford and Young were stunned when Price told them "to let things slide." Linda Evans remembered a Human Resource secretary, Janice Lawrence, telling Young, "I know that there are people upstairs that do not like certain people, but you just have to ignore it."

Regarding both Rogers and Ford, Mary Connors said, "People in the department started to believe that it was malicious intent by management to keep certain people from moving upward in the company." She continued by saying that it is sad that no one, including herself, took it upon himself or herself to bring the situation to the correct authorities.

Outcomes

Rogers was ultimately fired because of his "refusal to cooperate." Rogers claimed the firing was unjust because he had a great record, and in fact his last bonus was his largest in the 14 years with the company. Young was laid off as a temp. Mary Connors remembered Young telling her she wanted to quit the entire time but she needed the money to support her family. She kept telling herself that her treatment would get better; but it only got worse. Out of frustration, Ford quit after Young's dismissal.

Rich Rogers, Les Ford, and Jasmine Young filed a $70 million lawsuit claiming racial, disability, and gender discrimination.

EXHIBIT A
EXCERPTS FROM CODE OF CONDUCT, DARIUS D'AMORE

Our Workplace

A Safe and Fair Workplace

The continued success of the Company's businesses depends on a safe and equitable workplace in which all employees can perform to the best of their ability.

A. Equal Employment Opportunity

It is the policy and practice of this Company to provide all employees and applicants for employment with equal employment opportunities without regard to race, color, religion, gender, age, national origin, sexual orientation, disability, or veteran status or any other characteristic protected by law. This policy applies to all Company activities, including, but not limited to, recruitment, hiring, compensation, assignment, training, promotion, discipline, and discharge.

The Company will provide reasonable accommodation consistent with the law to otherwise qualified employees and prospective employees with a disability and to employees and prospective employees with needs related to their religious observance or practices. What constitutes a reasonable accommodation depends on the circumstances and thus will be addressed by the Company on a case-by-case basis.

The Senior Vice President, Global Human Resources is the Equal Opportunity Director for the Company and is responsible for implementing this policy. Questions regarding this policy should be directed to that office.

B. Prohibition Against Harassment

The Company endeavors to maintain a working environment in which all employees treat each other with respect. Accordingly, the Company strictly prohibits conduct that constitutes or that could lead or contribute to harassment based on gender (whether or not of a sexual nature), race, color, national origin, religion, age, disability, sexual orientation, or any other characteristics protected by law. Harassment does not require intent to offend. Thus, inappropriate conduct meant as a joke, a prank, or even a compliment can lead or contribute to harassment.

Examples of prohibited conduct are: racial or ethnic slurs; threatening or intimidating acts directed at an individual because of his or her gender or sexual orientation; the posting or distribution of hostile written or graphic materials aimed at a particular sex or religion; the use of computers (including via the Internet) or the e-mail system to view or distribute racially or sexually offensive communications; and the use of an employee's home computer to send racially or sexually offensive communications to another employee at work.

Procedures. If you believe that you have been subjected to prohibited conduct, you are urged and expected to report the relevant facts promptly. You may speak to your supervisor or your supervisor's supervisor (bypassing the chain of command), or, if you feel more comfortable, you may contact your Human Resources Manager, the Senior Vice President, Global Human Resources or the General Counsel. Individuals who have information about inappropriate conduct directed towards others also are expected to report the relevant facts promptly.

Your prompt reporting is very important so that the Company can take action to stop the conduct before it is repeated. All reports will be followed up on promptly, with further investigation conducted where needed to confirm the relevant facts. In conducting its investigations, the Company will strive to keep the identity of individuals making reports as confidential as possible.

Any employee or member of the Board of Directors of the Company found to have violated this policy will be subject to disciplinary action, including termination of employment. Individuals who violate this policy also may be subject to legal and financial liability.

No Retaliation. Threats or acts of retaliation against an individual who in good faith reports inappropriate conduct pursuant to these policies are prohibited. In the event you feel you have been retaliated against for having made such a report, you should report the retaliation as described above.

How to Raise Concerns

Every employee has the responsibility to promptly report any violation or suspected violation of this Code of Conduct, any other Company policy or applicable law or regulation, in order to protect the Company, its stockholders, its employees, and its customers.

If you have information regarding any such violation or suspected violation you should report such information to your supervisor or bring the matter to the attention of:

The General Counsel,

The Senior Vice President, Global Human Resources, or

The Chief Internal Control Officer

You may also call the confidential, toll-free hotline or use the post office box cited below. Callers from outside the United States or Canada must first dial their country's access number. All such submissions will be treated confidentially to the extent possible. To assist and encourage the prompt reporting of suspected violations, we will accept reports made on an anonymous basis.

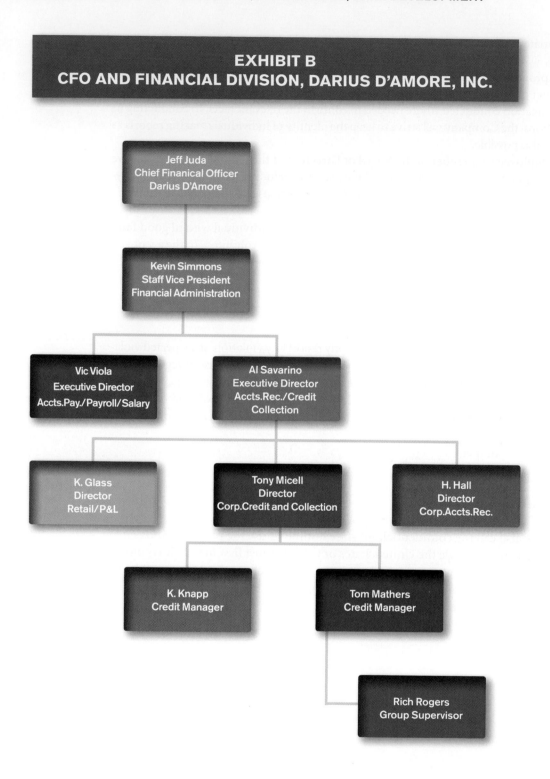

EXHIBIT B
CFO AND FINANCIAL DIVISION, DARIUS D'AMORE, INC.

Jeff Juda
Chief Finanical Officer
Darius D'Amore

Kevin Simmons
Staff Vice President
Financial Administration

Vic Viola
Executive Director
Accts.Pay./Payroll/Salary

Al Savarino
Executive Director
Accts.Rec./Credit
Collection

K. Glass
Director
Retail/P&L

Tony Micell
Director
Corp.Credit and Collection

H. Hall
Director
Corp.Accts.Rec.

K. Knapp
Credit Manager

Tom Mathers
Credit Manager

Rich Rogers
Group Supervisor

EXHIBIT C
ACCOUNTS PAYABLE/PAYROLL/SALARY & COMMISSION DEPARTMENT, DARIUS D'AMORE, INC.

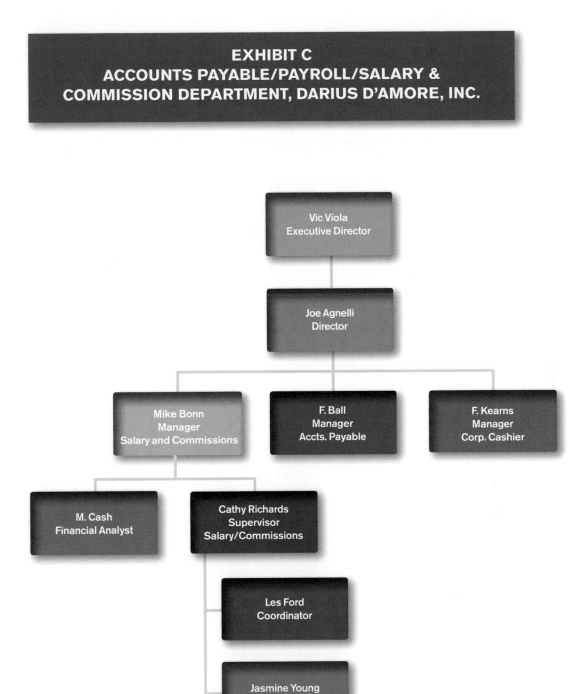

Questions

1. What are the antidiscrimination laws concerning the workplace that apply to this case?

2. In your opinion, do the plaintiffs have a prima facie case for discrimination?

3. If this case were allowed to go forward based upon the prima facie evidence and you were the judge, what would your verdict be, and what would be an acceptable remedy to the complaint?

4. What actions can the firm take in the future to prevent discriminatory actions from occurring again?

5. What actions should Rogers, Young, and Ford have taken in light of the firm's failure to respond to their discrimination complaints?

6. Rather than going to court over their dispute with Darius D'Amore, Rogers, Young, and Ford could have taken an alternative approach: mediation and arbitration. What are these methods of conflict resolution? How might Rogers, Young, and Ford benefit by opting for these methods?

7. Darius D'Amore publicized an internal recruitment and promotion policy. What are the pros and cons of that policy, and how did it partially attribute to the problems in this case?

8. Darius D'Amore's Code of Conduct clearly outlines the firm's policies on Equal Opportunity Employment and Harassment as well as the procedures for how to raise concerns. What is the purpose of a Code of Conduct, and why do you think this code failed to protect Rogers, Young, and Ford?

9. In the case, Rogers was ultimately fired because of his refusal to cooperate while Young was laid off as a temporary employee. Assume that the firm argued in court that under employment-at-will they had the right to fire both workers. Explain their defense and whether you think it is a viable one.

Notes

Chapter 1

1. J. Welch, S. Welch, "How Not to Succeed in Business," *Businessweek* (March 2, 2009), p. 74.

2. A.C. Cosper, "How to Be Great," *Entrepreneur* (March 2010), p. 12.

3. J.C. Santora, "Quality Management and Manufacturing Performance: Does Success Depend on Firm Culture?" *Academy of Management Perspective* (2009), 23(2), pp. 103–105.

4. R. Chia, R. Holt, "The Nature of Knowledge in Business Schools," *Academy of Management Learning & Education* (2008), 7(4), pp. 471–486.

5. K. Pajo, A. Coetzer, N. Guenole, "Formal Development Opportunities and Withdrawal Behavior by Employees in Small and Medium-Sized Enterprises," *Journal of Small Business Management* (2010), 48(3), 281–301.

6. I.R. Gellatly, K.H. Hunter, L.G. Currie, P.G. Irving, "HRM Practices and Organizational Commitment Profiles," *International Journal of Human Resource Management* (April 2009), pp. 869–884.

7. H.L. Sirkin, "New World Disorder," *Time International (Canada Edition)* (October 27, 2008), pp. 41–42.

8. M.J. Brand, E.P.M. Croonen, "Franchised and Small, the Most Beautiful of All: HRM and Performance in Plural Systems," *Journal of Small Business Management* (2010), 48(4), pp. 605–626.

9. R.S. Rubin, E.C. Dierdorff, "On the Road to Abilene: Time to Manage Agreement About MBA Curricular Relevance," *Academy of Management Learning & Education* (2010), 10(1), pp. 148–161.

10. G.P. West, T.W. Noel, "The Impact of Knowledge Resources on New Venture Performance," *Journal of Small Business Management* (2009), 47(1), pp. 1–22.

11. R.E. Ployhart, J.A. Weekley, J. Ramsey, "The Consequences of Human Resource Stocks and Flow: A Longitudinal Examination of Unit Service Orientation and Unit Effectiveness," *Academy of Management Journal* (2009), 52(5), pp. 996–1015.

12. A. Fox, "Raising Engagement," *HR Magazine* (May 2010), p. 36.

13. Ibid.

14. K.W. Mossholder, H.A. Richardson, R.P. Settoon, "Human Resource Systems and Helping in Organizations: A Relational Perspective," *Academy of Management Review* (2011), 36(1), pp. 33–52.

15. K. Blanchard, D. Hutson, E. Wills, *The One Minute Entrepreneur* (New York: Currency, 2008).

16. G.A. Van Kleef, A.C. Homan, B. Beersma, D. Van Knippenberg, F. Damen, "Searing Sentiment or Cold Calculation? The Effects of Leader Emotional Displays on Team Performance Depend on Follower Epistemic Motivation," *Academy of Management Journal* (2009), 52(3), pp. 562–580.

17. J.G. Proudfoot, P.J. Corr, D.E. Guest, G. Dunn, "Cognitive-Behavioural Training to Change Attributional Style Improves Employee Well-Being, Job Satisfaction, Productivity, and Turnover," *Personality and Individual Differences* (January 2009), 46(2), pp. 147–153.

18. P.E. Spector, *Job Satisfaction: Application, Assessment, Causes and Consequences* (London: Blackwell, 1997).

19. M. Riketta, "The Causal Relation Between Job Attitudes and Performance: A Meta-Analysis of Panel Studies," *Journal of Applied Psychology* (March 2008), 93(2), pp. 472–481.

20. R.S. Rubin, E.C. Dierdorff, "On the Road to Abilene: Time to Manage Agreement About MBA Curricular Relevance," *Academy of Management Learning & Education* (2011), 10(1), pp. 148–161.

21. S.S. Culbertson, "Absenteeism: Escaping an Aversive Workplace or Responding to Resulting Illness?" *Academy of Management Perspective* (2009), 23(1), pp. 77–79.

22. Ibid.

23. R.S. Rubin, E.C. Dierdorff, "On the Road to Abilene: Time to Manage Agreement About MBA Curricular Relevance," *Academy of Management Learning & Education* (2011), 10(1), pp. 148–161.

24. "The Talent Hunt: Getting the People You Need, When You Need Them," *Knowledge@Wharton* (University of Pennsylvania, 2008).

25. A. Gupta, J. McDaniel, "Creating Competitive Advantage by Effectively Managing Knowledge: A Framework for Knowledge Management," *Journal of Knowledge Management Practice* (2002), 2, pp. 40–49.

26. M. Porter, N. Siggelkow, "Contextuality Within Activity Systems and Sustainability of Competitive Advantage," *Academy of Management Perspectives* (2008), 22(2), pp. 34–56.

27. E.E. Gordon, *The 2010 Meltdown: Solving the Impending Jobs Crisis* (Westport, CT: Praeger, 2005).

28. G.W. Loveman, J.J. Gabarro, "The Managerial Implications of Changing Work Force Demographics: A Scoping Study," *Human Resource Management* (2006), pp. 7–29.

29. Pew Research Center, *Recession Turns a Graying Office Grayer* (Washington, DC: Author, 2009).

30. M. Toossi, "A Century of Change: The U.S. Labor Force, 1950–2050," *Monthly Labor Review* (2002), pp. 15–28.

31. R.S. Rubin, E.C. Dierdorff, "On the Road to Abilene: Time to Manage Agreement About MBA Curricular Relevance," *Academy of Management Learning & Education* (2011), 10(1), pp. 148–161.

32. R.B. Kaiser, R.B. Kaplan, "The Deeper Work of Executive Development: Outgrowing Sensitivities," *Academy of Management Learning & Education* (2006), 5(4), pp. 463–483.

33. A.C. Cosper, "How to Be Great," *Entrepreneur* (March 2010), p. 12.

34. M. Hilton, "Skills for Work in the 21st Century: What Does the Research Tell Us?" *Academy of Management Perspective* (2008), 22(4), pp. 63–78.

35. L. Dragoni, P.E. Tesluk, J.E.A. Russell, I. Oh, "Understanding Managerial Development: Integrating Developmental Assignments, Learning Orientation, and Access to Developmental Opportunities in Predicting Managerial Competencies," *Academy of Management Journal* (2009), 52(4), pp. 731–742.

36. G.A. Van Kleef, A.C. Homan, B. Beersma, D. Van Knippenberg, F. Damen, "Searing Sentiment or Cold Calculation? The Effects of Leader Emotional Displays on Team Performance Depend on Follower Epistemic Motivation," *Academy of Management Journal* (2009), 2(3), pp. 562–580.

37. R.S. Rubin, E.C. Dierdorff, "How Relevant Is the MBA? Assessing the Alignment of Required Curricula and Required Managerial Competencies," *Academy of Management Learning & Education* (2009), 8(5), pp. 208–224.

38. R.B. Kaiser, R.B. Kaplan, "The Deeper Work of Executive Development: Outgrowing Sensitivities," *Academy of Management Learning & Education* (2006), 5(4), pp. 463–483.

39. K. Pajo, A. Coetzer, N. Guenole, "Formal Development Opportunities and Withdrawal Behavior by Employees in Small and Medium-Sized Enterprises," *Journal of Small Business Management* (2010), 48(3), pp. 281–301.

40. P. Berrone, L.R.G. Mejia, "Environmental Performance and Executive Compensation: An Integrated Agency-Institutional Perspective," *Academy of Management Journal* (2009), 52(1), pp. 103–126.

41. S. Ambec, P. Lanoie, "Does It Pay to Be Green? A Systematic Overview," *Academy of Management Perspectives* (2008), 22(4), pp. 45–62.

42. Definition developed by the Brundtland Commission. Cited from Colvin Interview of Linda Fisher, *Fortune* (November 23, 2009), pp. 45–50.

43. A.A. Marcus, A.R. Fremeth, "Green Management Matters Regardless," *Academy of Management Perspectives* (2009), 23(3), pp. 17–26.

44. www.shrm.org (retrieved June 4, 2010).

45. http://www.shrm.org/about/pressroom/PressReleases/Pages/AssuranceofLearningAssessment.aspx (retrieved August 15, 2011).

46. www.astd.org (retrieved May 28, 2010).

47. www.worldatwork.org (retrieved May 28, 2010).

48. www.shrm.org/TemplatesTools/Toolkits/Pages/AvoidingIndividualLiability.aspx (retrieved August 14, 2011).

49. "New Models of High-Performance Work Systems: The Business Case for Strategic HRM, Partnership and Diversity

and Equality Systems," *National Centre for Partnership and Performance (NCPP) Equality Authority* (Ireland, 2008).

50. J. Tomer, "Understanding High-Performance Work Systems: The Joint Contribution of Economics and Human Resource Management," *Journal of Socio-Economics* (2001), 30 (1), pp. 63–73.

51. www.supremecourt.gov/opinions/08pdf/07-1428.pdf (*retrieved June 18, 2010*).

52. www.careerbuilder.com/share/aboutus/pressreleases detail.aspx?id=pr519&sd=8/19/2009&ed=12/31/2009&sit eid=cbpr&sc_cmp1=cb_pr519_&cbRecursionCnt=1&cbs

id=8412d5b32ef54ce6854a035cf3a59d12-303995843-x3-6 (retrieved July 16, 2010).

53. www.careerbuilder.com/Article/CB-916-Getting-Ahead-Will-Your-Social-Networking-Profile-Get-You-Hired-or-Fired/?ArticleID=916&cbRecursionCnt=1&cbsid=0fa 19ddd2a354b07ae679ad83583f35a-332624691-x7-6&ns_ siteid=ns_us_g_fired_or_not_hired_be_ (retrieved July 16, 2010).

54. http://bits.blogs.nytimes.com/2009/08/20/more-employers-use-social-networks-to-check-out-applicants/ (retrieved July 16, 2010).

Chapter 2

1. K. Blanchard, D. Hutson, E. Wills, *The One Minute Entrepreneur* (New York: Currency, 2008).

2. J.C. Santora, "Quality Management and Manufacturing Performance: Does Success Depend on Firm Culture?" *Academy of Management Perspective* (2009), 23(2), pp. 103–105.

3. S. Latham, "Contrasting Strategic Response to Economic Recession in Start-Up Versus Established Software Firms," *Journal of Small Business Management* (2009), 47(2), pp. 180–201.

4. D. Sirmon, M.A. Hitt, R.D. Ireland, "Managing Firm Resources in Dynamic Environments to Create Value: Looking Inside the Black Box," *Academy of Management Review* (2007), 32(1), pp. 273–292.

5. J. Skinner, "A View From the Top," *Fortune* (March 16, 2009), p. 110.

6. G.T. Payne, K.H. Kennedy, J.L. Davis, "Competitive Dynamics Among Service SMEs," *Journal of Small Business Management* (2009), 47(4), pp. 421–442.

7. M. Bustillo, T.W. Martin, "Wal-Mart Bets on Reduction in Prices," *Wall Street Journal* (April 9, 2010), p. B1.

8. T. Yu, M. Subramaniam, A.A. Cannella, "Rivalry Deterrence in International Markets: Contingencies Governing the Mutual Forbearance Hypothesis," *Academy of Management Journal* (2009), 52(1), pp. 127–147.

9. H.L. Smith, R. Discenza, K.G. Baker, "Building Sustainable Success in Art Galleries: An Exploratory Study of Adaptive Strategies," *Journal of Small Business Strategy* (2005/2006), 16(2), pp. 29–41.

10. K.D. Dea Roglio, G. Light, "Executive MBA Programs: The Development of the Reflective Executive," *Academy of Management Learning & Education* (2009), 8(2), pp. 156–173.

11. "Dell Plans," *The Wall Street Journal* (August 15, 2006), p. A1; "Toshiba and Fujitsu," *The Wall Street Journal* (September 30, 2006), p. A1.

12. www.google.com (accessed July 14, 2010).

13. M.J. Canyan, "Executive Compensation and Incentives," *Academy of Management Perspectives* (2006), 20(1), pp. 25–44.

14. J.W. Webb, L. Tihanyi, R.D. Ireland, D.G. Sirmon, "You Say Illegal, I Say Legitimate: Entrepreneurship in the Informal Economy," *Academy of Management Review* (2009), 34(3), pp. 492–510.

15. Margin Note, *Entrepreneur* (November 2006), p. 105.

16. A. McWilliams, D. Siegel, "Corporate Social Responsibility: A Theory of the Firm Perspective," *Academy of Management Review* (2001), 26(1), pp. 117–127.

17. P.M. Vaaler, "How Do MNCs Vote in Developing Country Elections?" *Academy of Management Journal* (2008), 51(1), pp. 21–43.

18. G.F. Keller, "The Influence of Military Strategies on Business Planning," *International Journal of Business and Management* (May 2008), p. 129.

19. D.F. Kuratko, D.B. Audretsch, "Strategic Entrepreneurship: Exploring Different Perspectives of an Emerging Concept," *Entrepreneurship Theory and Practice* (2009), 33(1), pp. 1–17.

20. M.J. Brand, E.P.M. Croonen, "Franchised and Small, the Most Beautiful of All: HRM and Performance in Plural Systems," *Journal of Small Business Management* (2010), 48(4), pp. 605–626.

21. M Kornberger, S. Clegg, "Strategy as Performative Practice," *Strategic Organization* (May 2011), 9(2) pp. 143.

22. J. Welch, S. Welch, "Inventing the Future Now," *Business Week* (May 11, 2009), p. 76.

23. W. Bennis, "Acting the Part of a Leader," *Business Week* (September 14, 2009), p. 80.

24. University of Arkansas at Little Rock website (http://ualr .edu/cob/index.php/home/about-us/vision/), retrieved July 10, 2010.

25. *The American Heritage College Dictionary* (New York: Houghton Mifflin, 1993).

26. University of Arkansas at Little Rock website (http://ualr .edu/cob/index.php/home/about-us/mission/), retrieved July 10, 2010.

27. M. Porter, *Competitive Strategy: Techniques for Analyzing Industries and Competitors* (New York: The Free Press, 1980), p. 15.

28. M. Bustillo, T.W. Martin, "Wal-Mart Bets on Reduction in Prices," *Wall Street Journal* (April 9, 2010), p. B1.

29. L. Liu, "Europe's New McCafe Culture," *Businessweek* (October 5, 2009), p. 70.

30. H.L. Smith, R. Discenza, K.G. Baker, "Building Sustainable Success in Art Galleries: An Exploratory Study of Adaptive Strategies," *Journal of Small Business Strategy* (2005/2006), 16(2), pp. 29–41.

31. J. Cazier, B. Shao, R. St. Louis, "E-Business Differentiation Through Value-Based Trust," *Information and Management* (September 2006), 43(6), pp. 718–727.

32. E.K. Clemons, P.F. Nunes, M. Reilly, "Six Strategies for Successful Niche Marketing," *Wall Street Journal* (May 24, 2010), p. R6.

33. N. Byrnes, "Why Dr. Pepper Is in the Pink of Health," *Businessweek* (October 26, 2009), p. 59.

34. M. Porter, "How Competitive Forces Shape Strategy," *Harvard Business Review* (1979), 57(2), pp. 137–145.

35. G. Hirst, D. Van Knippenberg, J. Zhou, "A Cross-Level Perspective on Employee Creativity: Goal Orientation, Team Learning Behavior, and Individual Creativity," *Academy of Management Journal* (2009), 52(2), pp. 280–293.

36. L. Dragoni, P.E. Tesluk, J.E.A. Russell, I. Oh, "Understanding Managerial Development: Integrating Developmental Assignments, Learning Orientation, and Access to Developmental Opportunities in Predicting Managerial Competencies," *Academy of Management Journal* (2009), 52(4), pp. 731–742.

37. S. Covy, "Time Management," *Fortune* (September 19, 2009), pp. 28–29.

38. K. Kelly, M. Marr, "Marvel Defection Deals Blow to Shares," *Wall Street Journal* (June 12, 2006), p. C1.

39. "Nike," *Businessweek* (May 10–16, 2010), p. 25.

40. "Dell," *Wall Street Journal* (February 27, 2009), p. A1.

41. N. Byrnes, "Why Dr. Pepper Is in the Pink of Health," *Businessweek* (October 26, 2009), p. 59.

42. M. Pirtea, C. Nicolescu, C. Botoc, "The Role of Strategic Planning in Modern Organizations," *Annales Universitatis Apulensis Series Oeconomica* (2009), 11(2), pp. 953–957.

43. P. Jarzabkowski, "Shaping Strategy as a Structuration Process," *Academy of Management Journal* (2008), 51(4), pp. 621–650.

44. S. Postrel, "Multitasking Teams With Variable Complementarily: Challenges for Capability Management," *Academy of Management Review* (2009), Vol. 34(2), pp. 273–296.

45. M.S. Wood, "Does One Size Fit All? The Multiple Organizational Forms Leading to Successful Academic Entrepreneurship," *Entrepreneurship Theory and Practice* (2009), 33(4), pp. 929–947.

46. P. Fiss, E. Zajac, "The Symbolic Management of Strategic Change: Sensegiving Via Framing and Decoupling," *Academy of Management Journal* (2006), 49(6), pp. 1173–1193.

47. M. Rhee, "An Educated Work Force," *Wall Street Journal* (January 23, 2009), p. R3.

48. K. Swisher, "A Question of Management," *Wall Street Journal* (June 2, 2009), p. R4.

49. www.americanexpress.com (accessed July 12, 2010).

50. C. Chen, J. Huaung, "How Organizational Climate and Structure Affect Knowledge Management—The Social Interaction Perspective," *International Journal of Information Management* (2007), 27(2), pp. 104–118.

51. "Deep Trouble," *Wall Street Journal* (May 28, 2010), pp. A1, A6.

52. Ibid.

53. Bill Gates, "The Best Advise I Ever Got," *Fortune* (July 6, 2009), p. 43.

54. P. Drucker, *Management: Tasks, Responsibilities, Practices* (Oxford, UK: Butterworth-Heinemann, 1999), p. 546.

55. M. McDermott, "Listening With a Purpose," *Chief Executive* (U.S.) (February 2001), p. 35.

56. C. Hymowitz, "Executives Who Build Truth-Telling Cultures Learn Fast What Works," *The Wall Street Journal* (June 12, 2006), p. B1.

57. D. West, Retired Executive of Toyota, Lecture at Springfield College (November 23, 2009).

58. R.M. Kanter, "Values Investing," *Wall Street Journal* (January 25, 2010), p. R2.

59. G. Colvin, "How to Build Great Leaders," *Fortune* (December 7, 2009), pp. 70–72.

60. D. Ravasi, M. Schultz, "Responding to Organizational Identity Threats: Exploring the Role of Organizational Culture," *Academy of Management Journal* (2006), Vol. 49(3), pp. 433–458.

61. R.M. Kanter, "Values Investing," *Wall Street Journal* (January 25, 2010), p. R2.

62. www.shrm.org/Publications/hrmagazine/EditorialContent/Pages/0808hrsolutions.aspx (accessed July 7, 2010).

63. A. Gumbus, R.N. Lussier, "Entrepreneurs Use a Balanced Scorecard to Translate Strategy Into Performance Measures," *Journal of Small Business Management* (2006), 44(3), pp. 407–425.

64. A. Gumbus, R.N. Lussier, "Developing and Using a Balanced Scorecard," *Clinical Leadership & Management Review* (2003), 17(2), pp. 69–74.

65. R. Kaplan, D. Norton, *Alignment* (Boston: Harvard Business School, 2006).

66. www.shrm.org/TemplatesTools/hrqa/Pages/WhatisaBalancedScorecard.aspx (accessed July 7, 2010).

67. Ibid.

68. "New Models of High-Performance Work Systems: The Business Case for Strategic HRM, Partnership and Diversity and Equality Systems," *National Centre for Partnership and Performance (NCPP); Equality Authority* (Ireland, 2008), p. 46.

69. K.W. Mossholder, H.A. Richardson, R.P. Settoon, "Human Resource Systems and Helping in Organizations: A Relational Perspective," *Academy of Management Review* (2011), 36(1), pp. 33–52.

70. D. Mueller, S. Strohmeier, C. Gasper, "HRIS Design Characteristics: Towards a General Research Framework," *Third European Academic Workshop on Electronic Human Resource Management* (May 2010).

71. W. Felps, T.R. Mitchell, D.R. Hekman, T.W. Lee, B.C. Holtom, W.S. Harman, "Turnover Contagion: How Coworkers' Job Embeddedness and Job Search Behaviors Influence Quitting," *Academy of Management Journal* (2009), 52(3), pp. 545–561.

72. B. Lombardi, Y. Ono, "Professional Employer Organizations: What Are They, Who Uses Them, and Why Should We Care?" *Economic Perspectives* (4th Quarter, 2008), 32(4), pp. 2–14.

73. B. Leonard, "IRS Plans to Examine Employee Leasing" *HR Magazine* (April 2004), 49(4), retrieved from SHRM website www.shrm.org/Publications/hrmagazine/EditorialContent/Pages/0404hrnews.aspx, July 10, 2010.

74. R.N. Lussier, C.E. Halabi, "A Three-Country Comparison of the Business Success Versus Failure Prediction Model," *Journal of Small Business Management* (2010), 48(3), pp. 360–377.

75. P. Berrone, L.R.G. Mejia, "Environmental Performance and Executive Compensation: An Integrated Agency-Institutional Perspective," *Academy of Management Journal* (2009), 52(1), pp. 103–126.

76. S. Ambec, P. Lanoie, "Does It Pay to Be Green? A Systematic Overview," *Academy of Management Perspectives* (2008), 22(4), pp. 45–62.

77. A.A. Marcus, A.R. Fremeth, "Green Management Matters Regardless," *Academy of Management Perspectives* (2009), 23(3), pp. 17–26.

78. Definition developed by the Brundtland Commission. Cited from Colvin Interview of Linda Fisher, *Fortune* (November 23, 2009), pp. 45–50.

79. A.A. Marcus, A.R. Fremeth, "Green Management Matters Regardless," *Academy of Management Perspectives* (2009), 23(3), pp. 17–26.

80. D. Esty, A. Winston, *Green to Gold: How Smart Companies Use Environmental Strategy to Innovate, Create Value and Build Competitive Advantage* (New York: Wiley and Sons, 2006).

81. J. Bennett, "Are We Headed Toward a Green Bubble?" *Entrepreneur* (April 2010), pp. 51–54.

82. R. Plant, "How Green Should My Tech Be? It Depends on the Tech," *Wall Street Journal* (January 25, 2010), p. R6.

Chapter 3

1. J. Hendon, "Hiring and the OUCH Test," *Arkansas Business* (May 3, 2010). p. 7

2. www.dol.gov/dol/allcfr/title_41/Part_60-3/41CFR60-3.4.htm (retrieved July 20, 2010).

3. www.eeoc.gov/laws/statutes/epa.cfm (retrieved July 20, 2010).

4. Ibid.

5. archive.eeoc.gov/policy/vii.html (retrieved July 20, 2010).

6. www.dol.gov/dol/allcfr/title_41/part_60-3/41CFR60-3.11.htm (retrieved July 20, 2010).

7. www.dol.gov/ofccp/regs/compliance/fccm/ofcpch7.htm#7E (retrieved July 20, 2010).

8. www.dol.gov/dol/allcfr/title_41/Part_60-3/toc.htm (retrieved July 20, 2010).

9. www.eeoc.gov/laws/statutes/titlevii.cfm (retrieved July 21, 2010).

10. 442 F2d 385 *Diaz v. Pan American World Airways* Inc.

11. www.eeoc.gov/laws/statutes/titlevii.cfm (retrieved July 21, 2010).

12. Ibid.

13. www.dol.gov/dol/allcfr/title_41/Part_60-3/toc.htm (retrieved July 20, 2010).

14. United States Code, 29 U.S.C. § 621 through 29.

15. www.eeoc.gov/eeoc/statistics/enforcement/charges.cfm (retrieved July 21, 2010).

16. www.hr.com (retrieved July 20, 2010).

17. www.dol.gov/compliance/laws/comp-vevraa.htm (retrieved July 20, 2010).

18. www.eeoc.gov/facts/fs-preg.html (retrieved July 21, 2010).

19. www.answers.com/topic/pregnancy-discrimination-act (retrieved July 21, 2010).

20. "All Things Being Equal . . . *General Electric Co. v. Gilbert*: An Analysis," *Journal of Law and Education* (January 1978), 7(1), pp. 21–30.

21. www.dol.gov/compliance/laws/comp-rehab.htm (retrieved July 21, 2010).

22. www.ada.gov/pubs/adastatute08.htm (retrieved July 20, 2010).

23. Ibid.

24. www.ada.gov/employmt.htm (retrieved July 21, 2010).

25. www.ada.gov/pubs/adastatute08.htm (retrieved July 21, 2010).

26. www.dol.gov/odep/pubs/fact/diverse.htm (retrieved July 20, 2010).

27. www.eeoc.gov/eeoc/statistics/enforcement/charges.cfm (retrieved July 21, 2010).

28. Civil Rights Act of 1991 (Public Law 102-166).

29. www.eeoc.gov/employers/remedies.cfm (retrieved July 21, 2010).

30. www.eeoc.gov/eeoc/history/35th/thelaw/cra_1991.html (retrieved July 21, 2010).

31. www.dol.gov/elaws/vets/userra/userra.asp (retrieved July 20, 2010).

32. www.dol.gov/vets/regs/fedreg/final/2005023960.htm#regs (retrieved July 20, 2010).

33. www.eeoc.gov/laws/statutes/gina.cfm (retrieved July 22, 2010).

34. Ibid.

35. http://thomas.loc.gov/home/gpoxmlc111/s181_enr.xml (retrieved July 20, 2010).

36. www.dol.gov/compliance/guide/h1b.htm (retrieved July 20, 2010).

37. Ibid.

38. www.eeoc.gov/eeoc/history/35th/thelaw/irca.html (retrieved July 21, 2010).

39. http://eeoc.gov/eeoc/ (retrieved July 20, 2010).

40. Ibid.

41. www.eeoc.gov/laws/statutes/titlevii.cfm (retrieved July 21, 2010).

42. www.eeoc.gov/laws/types/retaliation.cfm (retrieved July 20, 2010).

43. www.eeoc.gov/laws/practices/index.cfm (retrieved July 21, 2010).

44. Pennsylvania State Police v. Suders (03-95) 542 U.S. 129 (2004) 325 F.3d 432.

45. Ibid.

46. http://ecfr.gpoaccess.gov/cgi/t/text/text-idx?c=ecfr&tpl=/ecfrbrowse/Title29/29cfr1608_main_02.tpl (retrieved July 21, 2010).

47. 41 CFR Part 60-1.

48. Ibid.

49. www.dol.gov/ofccp/aboutof.html (retrieved July 20, 2010).

50. C.L. Holladay, M.A. Quinones, "The Influence of Training Focus and Trainer Characteristics on Diversity Training Effectiveness," *Academy of Management Learning & Education* (2008), 7(3), pp. 343–354.

51. A. Joshi, H. Roh, "The Role of Context in Work Team Diversity Research: A Meta-Analytic Review," *Academy of Management Journal* (2009), 52(3), pp. 599–627.

52. "The World Population," *Wall Street Journal* (June 20, 2008), p. A1.

53. B. Caplan, "The Breeders' Cup," *Wall Street Journal* (June 19–20, 2010), pp. W1–W2.

54. C. Dougherty, "U.S. Nears Racial Milestone," *Wall Street Journal* (June 11, 2010), p. A3.

55. "What the Next Census Will Tell Marketers," *Businessweek* (November 9, 2009), p. 8.

56. C. Dougherty, "U.S. Nears Racial Milestone," *Wall Street Journal* (June 11, 2010), p. A3.

57. "Whites Will Constitute," *Wall Street Journal* (August 14, 2008), p. A1.

58. C. Dougherty, "The End of White Flight," *Wall Street Journal* (June 11, 2010), p. A3.

59. E. Kearney, D. Gebert, S.C. Voelpel, "When and How Diversity Benefits Teams: The Importance of Team Members' Need for Cognition," *Academy of Management Journal* (2009), 52(3), pp. 581–598.

60. C.L. Holladay, M.A. Quinones, "The Influence of Training Focus and Trainer Characteristics on Diversity Training Effectiveness," *Academy of Management Learning & Education* (2008), 7(3), pp. 343–354.

61. C.T. Kulik, L. Roberson, "Common Goals and Golden Opportunities: Evaluation of Diversity Education in Academic and Organizational Settings," *Academy of Management Learning & Education* (2008), 7(3), pp. 309–331.

62. S.D. Sidle, "Building a Committed Global Workforce: Does What Employees Want Depend on Culture?" *Academy of Management Perspectives* (2009), 23(1), pp. 79–80.

63. S. Horwitz, I. Horwitz, "The Effects of Team Diversity on Team Outcomes: A Meta-Analytic Review of Team Demography," *Journal of Management* (December 2007), 33(6), pp. 987–1015.

64. M. Mayfield, J. Mayfield, "Developing a Scale to Measure the Creative Environment Perceptions: A Questionnaire for Investigating Garden Variety Creativity," *Creativity Research Journal* (April 2010), 22(2), pp. 162–169.

65. J. Guilford, *The Nature of Human Intelligence* (New York: McGraw-Hill, 1967).

66. F. Stevens, V. Plaut, J. Sanchez-Burks, "Unlocking the Benefits of Diversity," *Journal of Applied Behavioral Science* (March 2008), 44(1), pp. 116–133.

67. A.A. Cannella, J.H. Park, H.U. Lee, "Top Management Team Functional Background Diversity and Firm Performance: Examining the Roles of Team Members Collocation and Environmental Uncertainty," *Academy of Management Journal* (2008), 51(4), pp. 768–784.

68. S.D. Sidle, "Building a Committed Global Workforce: Does What Employees Want Depend on Culture?" *Academy of Management Perspectives* (2009), 23(1), pp. 79–80.

69. A.A. Cannella, J.H. Park, H.U. Lee, "Top Management Team Functional Background Diversity and Firm Performance: Examining the Roles of Team Members Collocation and Environmental Uncertainty," *Academy of Management Journal* (2008), 51(4), pp. 768–784.

70. K.Y. Ng, L. Van Dyne, and S. Ang, "From Experience to Experiential Learning: Cultural Intelligence as a Learning Capability for Global Leader Development," *Academy of Management Learning & Education* (2009), 8(4), pp. 511–526.

71. L.A. Nardo, K.A. Morris, S.A. Goodwin, "The Confronting Prejudiced Responses (CPR) Model: Applying CPR in Organizations," *Academy of Management Learning & Education* (2008), 7(3), pp. 332–342.

72. L.A. Nardo, K.A. Morris, S.A. Goodwin, "The Confronting Prejudiced Responses (CPR) Model: Applying CPR in Organizations," *Academy of Management Learning & Education* (2008), 7(3), pp. 332–342.

73. C.T. Kulik, L. Roberson, "Common Goals and Golden Opportunities: Evaluation of Diversity Education in Academic and Organizational Settings," *Academy of Management Learning & Education* (2008), 7(3), pp. 309–331.

74. L.A. Nardo, K.A. Morris, S.A. Goodwin, "The Confronting Prejudiced Responses (CPR) Model: Applying CPR in Organizations," *Academy of Management Learning & Education* (2008), 7(3), pp. 332–342.

75. www.eeoc.gov/facts/fs-sex.html (retrieved July 20, 2010).

76. www.law.cornell.edu/supct/html/historics/USSC_CR_0477_0057_ZS.html (retrieved July 20, 2010).

77. E.L. Perry, C.T. Kulik, A.C. Bourhis, "The Reasonable Woman Standard: Effects on Sexual Harassment Court Decisions," *Law and Human Behavior* (February 2004), 28(1), pp. 9–27.

78. www.law.cornell.edu/supct/html/96-568.ZO.html (retrieved July 20, 2010).

79. www.eeoc.gov/policy/docs/currentissues.html (retrieved July 21, 2010).

80. Ibid.

81. http://archive.eeoc.gov/types/sexual_harassment.html (retrieved July 21, 2010).

82. www.shrm.org/TemplatesTools/Samples/PowerPoints/Documents/2008 Religion in the Workplace.ppt (retrieved July 13, 2010).

83. www.nytimes.com/2009/09/01/world/europe/01france.html (retrieved July 22, 2010).

84. www.eeoc.gov/laws/statutes/titlevii.cfm (retrieved July 22, 2010).

85. www.eeoc.gov/policy/docs/religion.html (retrieved July 22, 2010).

86. D. Nguyen, S. Slater, "Hitting the Sustainability Sweet Spot: Having It All," *Journal of Business Strategy* (2010), 31(3), pp. 5–11.

87. www.eeoc.gov/facts/multi-employees.html (retrieved July 22, 2010).

88. Ibid.

89. www.sba.gov/aboutsba/sbaprograms/sbdc/index.html (retrieved July 22, 2010).

Chapter 4

1. A.L. Kallenbert, "The Mismatched Worker: When People Don't Fit Their Jobs," *Academy of Management Perspectives* (2008), 22(1), pp. 24–40.

2. J. Eder, E. Panagos, M. Rabinovich, "Time Constraints in Workflow Systems," *Lecture Notes in Computer Science* (2010), 1626, pp. 286–300.

3. H.C.W. Lau, G.T.S. Ho, K.F. Chu, William Ho, C.K.M. Lee, "Development of an Intelligent Quality Management System Using Fuzzy Association Rules," *Expert Systems With Applications* (March 2009), 36(2), pp. 1801–1815.

4. O. Henry, "Organisational Conflict and Its Effects on Organisational Performance," *Research Journal of Business Management* (2009), 2(1), pp. 16–24.

5. P. Singh, "Job Analysis for a Changing Workplace," *Human Resource Management Review* (2008), 18(2), pp. 87–89.

6. www.onetcenter.org/overview.html (retrieved August 22, 2010).

7. M. Robinson, "Work Sampling: Methodological Advances and New Applications," *Human Factors and Ergonomics in Manufacturing & Service Industries* (2010), 20(1), pp. 42–60.

8. J. Kilgour, "Job Evaluation Revisited: The Point Factor Method: The Point Factor Method of Job Evaluation Consists of a Large Number of Discretionary Decisions That Result in Something That Appears to Be Entirely Objective and, Even, Scientific," *Compensation & Benefits Review* (July/August 2008), 40, pp. 37–46.

9. M. Robinson, "Work Sampling: Methodological Advances and New Applications," *Human Factors and Ergonomics in Manufacturing & Service Industries* (2010), 20(1), pp. 42–60.

10. P. Singh, "Job Analysis for a Changing Workplace," *Human Resource Management Review* (2008), 18(2), pp. 87–89.

11. K. Soderquist, A. Papalexandris, G. Ioannou, G. Prastacos, "From Task-Based to Competency-Based: A Typology and Process Supporting a Critical HRM Transition," *Personnel Review* (2010), 39(3), pp. 325–346.

12. www.jobdescription.com (retrieved June 29, 2010).

13. R.M.J. Wells, "The Product Innovation Process: Are Managing Information Flows and Cross-functional Collaboration Key?" *Academy of Management Perspectives* (2008), 22(1), pp. 58–60.

14. M. Jokisaari, J.E. Nurmi, "Change in Newcomers' Supervisor Support and Socialization Outcomes After Organizational Entry," *Academy of Management Journal* (2009), 52(3), pp. 527–544.

15. J. Lahart, "Moment of Truth for Productivity Boom," *Wall Street Journal* (May 6, 2010), pp. A1 and A16.

16. F.P. Morgeson, E.C. Dierdorff, J.L. Hmurovic, "Work Design In Situ: Understanding the Role of Occupational and Organizational Context," *Journal of Organizational Behavior* (2010), 31(2–3), pp. 351–360.

17. P. Carayon, "The Balance Theory and the Work System Model . . . Twenty Years Later," *International Journal of Human-Computer Interaction* (2009), 25(5), pp. 313–327.

18. R. Hackman, G. Oldham, *Work Redesign* (Reading, MA: Addison-Wesley, 1980).

19. J.G. Proudfoot, P.J. Corr, D.E. Guest, G. Dunn, "Cognitive-Behavioural Training to Change Attributional Style Improves Employee Well-Being, Job Satisfaction, Productivity, and Turnover," *Personality and Individual Differences* (January 2009), 46(2), pp. 147–153.

20. C.E. Shalley, L.L. Gilson, T.C. Blum, "Interactive Effects of Growth Need Strength, Work Context, and Job Complexity on Self-Reported Creative Performance," *Academy of Management Journal* (2009), 52(3), pp. 489–505.

21. T. Woods, "The Best Advice I Ever Got," *Fortune* (July 6, 2009), p. 43.

22. J. Lahart, "Moment of Truth for Productivity Boom," *Wall Street Journal* (May 6, 2010), pp. A1 and A16.

23. S. Postrel, "Multitasking Teams With Variable Complementarity: Challenges for Capability Management," *Academy of Management Review* (2009), 34(2), pp. 273–296.

24. Ibid.

25. C. Penttila, "Best Practices—Rush Hour," *Entrepreneur* (August 2008), p. 74.

26. Ibid.

27. K. Swisher, "A Question of Management," *Wall Street Journal* (June 2, 2009), p. R4.

28. E. Gibson, "The Stop-Managing Guide to Management," *Businessweek* (June 15, 2009), p. 73.

29. C. Tuna, "Micromanagers Miss Bull's-Eye," *Wall Street Journal* (November 3, 2008), p. B4.

30. J.S. Santora, W.J. Seaton, "The Weakest Link: Can Inferior Members Raise the Bar in Work Groups?" *Academy of Management Perspectives* (2008), 22(2), pp. 104–106.

31. G.T. Lumpkin, C.C. Cogliser, D.R. Schneider, "Understanding and Measuring Autonomy: An Entrepreneurial Orientation Perspective," *Entrepreneurship Theory and Practice* (2009), 33(1), pp. 47–69.

32. C.E. Shalley, L.L. Gilson, T.C. Blum, "Interactive Effects of Growth Need Strength, Work Context, and Job Complexity on Self-Reported Creative Performance," *Academy of Management Journal* (2009), 52(3), pp. 489–505.

33. L. McNall, A. Masuda, J. Nicklin, "Flexible Work Arrangements, Job Satisfaction, and Turnover Intentions: The Mediating Role of Work-to-Family Enrichment," *The Journal of Psychology: Interdisciplinary and Applied Issue* (January–February 2010), 144(1), pp. 61–81.

34. L. Thompson, K. Aspinwall, "The Recruitment Value of Work/Life Benefits," *Personnel Review* (2009), 38(2), pp. 195–210.

35. www.opm.gov/perform/articles/2001/win01-1.asp (retrieved August 21, 2010).

36. T. Ng, K. Sorensen, F.H.K. Yim, "Does the Job Satisfaction—Job Performance Relationship Vary Across Cultures?" *Journal of Cross-Cultural Psychology* (2009), 40(5), pp. 761–796.

37. A.L. Kallenbert, "The Mismatched Worker: When People Don't Fit Their Jobs," *Academy of Management Perspectives* (2008), 22(1), pp. 24–40.

38. S. Mayer, "Strategic Human Resource Management Practices of High Performance Organizations," *Newsletter* (2008), pp. 1-4. Available from www.innovativehumandynamics.com.

39. www.referenceforbusiness.com/management/Gr-Int/Human-Resource-Information-Systems.html (retrieved August 22, 2010).

40. J. Ranjan, D. Goyal, S. Ahson, "Data Mining Techniques for Better Decisions in Human Resource Management Systems," *International Journal of Business Information Systems* (2008), 3(5), pp. 464–481.

41. Ibid.

42. W. Felps, T.R. Mitchell, D.R. Hekman, T.W. Lee, B.C. Holtom, W.S. Harman, "Turnover Contagion: How Coworkers' Job Embeddedness and Job Search Behaviors Influence Quitting," *Academy of Management Journal* (2009), 52(3), pp. 545–561.

43. E.E. Gordon, *The 2010 Meltdown: Solving the Impending Jobs Crisis* (Westport, CT: Praeger, 2005).

44. J. Pfeffer, "Layoff the Layoffs," *Newsweek* (February 15, 2010), pp. 34–37.

45. K. Mellahi, A. Wilkinson, "Slash and Burn or Nip and Tuck? Downsizing, Innovation and Human Resources," *International Journal of Human Resource Management* (2010), 21(13), pp. 2291–2305.

46. R. Zeidner, "Cutting Hours Without Increasing Risk," *HR Magazine* (April, 2009), pp. 44–48.

47. www.dol.gov/whd/overtime_pay.htm (retrieved August 22, 2010).

48. M.J. Bidwell, F. Briscoe, "Who Contracts? Determinants of the Decision to Work as an Independent Contractor Among Information Technology Workers," *Academy of Management Journal* (2009), 52(6), pp. 1148–1166.

49. M. Greco Danaher, "Temps, in Name Alone: Just Because You Call Them Temps Doesn't Mean Courts Will," *HR Magazine* (November 2008), pp. 117–120.

50. M.J. Bidwell, F. Briscoe, "Who Contracts? Determinants of the Decision to Work as an Independent Contractor Among Information Technology Workers," *Academy of Management Journal* (2009), 52(6), pp. 1148–1166.

51. Ibid.

52. N. Davis, "Succession Planning Not Limited to the C-Suite," *HR Magazine* (April 2008), pp. 69–70.

53. N. Landrum, S. Edwards, *Sustainable Business, An Executive's Primer* (New York: Business Expert Press, 2009).

54. Ibid.

55. A.L. Kallenbert, "The Mismatched Worker: When People Don't Fit Their Jobs," *Academy of Management Perspectives* (2008), 22(1), pp. 24–40.

56. A. Grant et al., "Putting Job Design in Context: Introduction to the Special Issue," *Journal of Organizational Behavior* (2010), 31, pp. 145–157.

57. D. Harrison, S. Humphrey, "Designing for Diversity or Diversity for Design? Tasks, Interdependence, and Within-Unit Differences at Work," *Journal of Organizational Behavior* (2010), 31, pp. 328–337.

58. R. Baron, "Job Design and Entrepreneurship: Why Closer Connections = Mutual Gain," *Journal of Organizational Behavior* (2010), 31, pp. 370–378.

Chapter 5

1. D.G. Allen, P.C. Bryant, J.M. Vardaman, "Retaining Talent: Replacing Misconceptions With Evidence-Based Strategies," *Academy of Management Perspectives* (2010), 24(2), pp. 48–64.

2. V. Elmer, "Hiring Without a Net: Groupon's Recruiter Speaks," *Fortune* (July 25, 2011), p. 34.

3. D.G. Allen, P.C. Bryant, J.M. Vardaman, "Retaining Talent: Replacing Misconceptions With Evidence-Based Strategies," *Academy of Management Perspectives* (2010), 24(2), pp. 48–64.

4. R.E. Ployhart, J.A. Weekley, J. Ramsey, "The Consequences of Human Resource Stocks and Flow: A Longitudinal Examination of Unit Service Orientation and Unit Effectiveness," *Academy of Management Journal* (2009), 52(5), pp. 996–1015.

5. V. Elmer, "Hiring Without a Net: Groupon's Recruiter Speaks," *Fortune* (July 25, 2011), p. 34.

6. S. D. Maurer, D. P. Cook, "Using Company Web Sites to E-recruit Qualified Applicants: A Job Marketing Based Review of Theory-Based Research," *Computers in Human Behavior* (forthcoming).

7. M. Guthridge, A. Komm, E. Lawson, "Making Talent a Strategic Priority," *The McKinsey Quarterly* (January 2008), www.dnlglobal.com/includes/repository/newsitem/TheMcKinseyQuarterly01_08.pdf (retrieved September 20, 2010).

8. S. Woolley, "New Priorities for Employers," *Buessinessweek* (September 13–19, 2010), p. 54.

9. D. Autor, L. Katz, M. Kearney, "Trends in U.S. Wage Inequality: Revising the Revisionists," *The Review of Economics and Statistics* (May 2008), 90(2), pp. 300–323.

10. S. Sorenson, J. Mattingly, F. Lee, "Decoding the Signal Effects of Job Candidate Attraction to Corporate Social Practices," *Business and Society Review* (Summer 2010), 115(2), pp. 173–204.

11. K. Lundby (Ed.), *Going Global: Practical Applications and Recommendation for HR and OD Professionals in the Global Workplace* (San Francisco: Jossey-Bass, 2010), pp. 114–115.

12. E. Byron, J.S. Lublin, "Appointment of New P&G Chief Sends Ripples Through Ranks," *Wall Street Journal* (June 11, 2009), p. B3.

13. G. Kelly, "A View From the Top," *Fortune* (March 16, 2009), p. 107.

14. V. Elmer, "Hiring Without a Net: Groupon's Recruiter Speaks," *Fortune* (July 25, 2011), p. 34.

15. J. Helyar, D. MacMillan, "In Tech, Poaching Is the Sincerest Form of Flattery," *Businessweek* (March 7–13, 2011), pp. 17–18.

16. www.shrm.org/Research/Articles/Articles/Pages/RecruitingInternallyandExternally.aspx (retrieved September 20, 2010).

17. I. De Pater, A.E.M. Van Vianen, M. Bechtoldt, U. Klehe, "Employees' Challenging Job Experiences and Supervisors' Evaluations of Promotability," *Personnel Psychology* (Summer 2009) 62(2), pp. 297–325.

18. D. Somaya, I.O. Williamson, N. Lorinkova, "Gone but Not Lost: The Different Performance Impacts of Employee Mobility Between Cooperators Versus Competitors," *Academy of Management Journal* (2008), 51(5), pp. 936–953.

19. V. Smith, E.B. Neuwirth, "Temporary Help Agencies and the Making of a New Employment Practice," *Academy of Management Perspectives* (2009), 23(1), pp. 56–72.

20. M. Hendircks, "Work Force Hired Help," *Entrepreneur* (October 2008), p. 89.

21. M. Greco Danaher, "Temps, in Name Alone: Just Because You Call Them Temps Doesn't Mean Courts Will," *HR Magazine* (November 2008) pp. 117–120.

22. www.cfo.com/article.cfm/4288677 (retrieved September 6, 2010).

23. E. Parry, S. Tyson, "An Analysis of the Use and Success of Online Recruitment Methods in the UK," *Human Resource Management Journal* (2008), 18(3), pp. 257–274.

24. www.internetworldstats.com/top20.htm (retrieved September 6, 2010).

25. W.-C. Tsai, I.W.-F. Yang, "Does Image Matter to Different Job Applicants? The Influences of Corporate Image and Applicant Individual Differences on Organizational Attractiveness," *International Journal of Selection and Assessment* (2010), 18(1), pp. 48–63.

26. "100 Best Companies to Work For," *Fortune* (May 3, 2010).

27. S. Overman, "Hiring Candidates Who Will Stay," *Staffing Management Magazine* (2010), 6(3), pp. 14–17.

28. J. Kammeyer-Mueller, C. Wanberg, T. Glomb, D. Ahlburg, "Turnover Processes in a Temporal Context: It's About Time," *Journal of Applied Psychology* (2005), *90*, pp. 644–658.

29. J. Breaugh, "Employee Recruitment: Current Knowledge and Important Areas for Future Research," *Human Resource Management Review* (2008), 18(3), pp. 103–118.

30. S. Overman, "Help Recruiters Vault Ahead," *Staffing Management Magazine* (2006), 2(2), pp. 32–35.

31. J. Breaugh, "Employee Recruitment: Current Knowledge and Important Areas for Future Research," *Human Resource Management Review* (2008), 18(3), pp. 103–118.

32. www.shrm.org/hrdisciplines/Pages/CMS_005910 .aspx (retrieved September 11, 2010).

33. V. Elmer, "Hiring Without a Net: Groupon's Recruiter Speaks," *Fortune* (July 25, 2011), p. 34.

34. D.G. Allen, P.C. Bryant, J.M. Vardaman, "Retaining Talent: Replacing Misconceptions With Evidence-Based Strategies," *Academy of Management Perspectives* (2010), 24(2), pp. 48–64.

35. www.shrm.org/hrdisciplines/technology/Articles/Pages/ CMS_006511.aspx (retrieved September 11, 2010).

36. L. Hooi, "Integrating Global Recruitment Trends: The Effect on Employee Satisfaction," *International Journal of Knowledge, Culture and Change Management* (2008), 8(4), pp. 151–164.

37. S. Woolley, "New Priorities for Employers," *Buessinessweek* (September 13–19, 2010), p. 54.

38. Global Talent for Competitive Advantage, *SHRM Research Quarterly* (3rd Quarter 2010), p. 1

39. Ibid.

40. www.eeoc.gov/eeoc/newsroom/release/11-18-04 .cfm (retrieved September 14, 2010).

41. R. Austin, "'Bad for Business': Contextual Analysis, Race Discrimination, and Fast Food," *John Marshall Law Review* (Fall 2000), pp. 207–244.

42. http://money.cnn.com/2000/11/16/companies/coke/ (retrieved September 14, 2010).

Chapter 6

1. C.B. Cadsby, F. Song, F. Tapon, "Sorting and Incentive Effects of Pay for Performance: An Experimental Investigation," *Academy of Management Journal* (2007), 50(2), pp. 387–405.

2. A. Kallenberg, "The Mismatched Worker: When People Don't Fit Their Jobs," *Academy of Management Perspectives* (2008), 22(1), pp. 24–40.

3. C. Tuna, "Micromanagers Miss Bull's-Eye," *Wall Street Journal* (November 3, 2008), p. B4.

4. V. Elmer, "Hiring Without a Net: Groupon's Recruiter Speaks," *Fortune* (July 25, 2011), p. 34.

5. D.G. Allen, P.C. Bryant, J.M. Vardaman, "Retaining Talent: Replacing Misconceptions With Evidence-Based

Strategies," *Academy of Management Perspectives* (2010), 24(2), pp. 48–64.

6. P. Babcock, "Spotting Lies," *HR Magazine* (October 2003), 48(10), pp. 46–52.

7. D.G. Allen, P.C. Bryant, J.M. Vardaman, "Retaining Talent: Replacing Misconceptions With Evidence-Based Strategies," *Academy of Management Perspectives* (2010), 24(2), pp. 48–64.

8. www.archives.gov/exhibits/charters/declaration_transcript.html (retrieved October 10, 2010).

9. C. O'Reilly III, "Personality-Job Fit: Implications for Individual Attitudes and Performance," *Organizational Behavior and Human Performance* (1977), 18(1), pp. 36–46.

10. N. Van Yperen, M. Hagedoorn, "Do High Job Demands Increase Intrinsic Motivation or Fatigue or Both? The Role of Job Control and Job Social Support," *The Academy of Management Journal* (2003), 46(3), pp. 339–348.

11. D.G. Allen, P.C. Bryant, J.M. Vardaman, "Retaining Talent: Replacing Misconceptions With Evidence-Based Strategies," *Academy of Management Perspectives* (2010), 24(2), pp. 48–64.

12. M. Morley, "Person-Organization Fit," *Journal of Managerial Psychology* (2007), 22(2), pp. 109–117.

13. www.eeoc.gov/policy/docs/factemployment_procedures.html (retrieved October 10, 2010).

14. www.justice.gov/crt/emp/uniformguidelines.php (retrieved September 29, 2010).

15. Ibid.

16. Ibid.

17. www.justice.gov/crt/emp/uniformguidelines.php (retrieved September 29, 2010).

18. www.uniformguidelines.com/questionandanswers.html#3 (retrieved September 29, 2010).

19. www.justice.gov/crt/emp/uniformguidelines.php (retrieved September 29, 2010).

20. www.uniformguidelines.com/questionandanswers.html#3 (retrieved September 29, 2010).

21. D.G. Allen, P.C. Bryant, J.M. Vardaman, "Retaining Talent: Replacing Misconceptions With Evidence-Based Strategies," *Academy of Management Perspectives* (2010), 24(2), pp. 48–64.

22. V. Elmer, "Hiring Without a Net: Groupon's Recruiter Speaks," *Fortune* (July 25, 2011), p. 34.

23. www.inc.com/news/articles/2008/08/résumés.html (retrieved October 10, 2010).

24. www.accuscreen.com/résumé-falsifications.html (retrieved October 10, 2010).

25. M. Henricks, "Interview for Integrity," *Entrepreneur* (April 2009), p. 22.

26. Ibid.

27. www.uniformguidelines.com/questionandanswers.html#5 (retrieved September 29, 2010).

28. www.dol.gov/whd/regs/statutes/poly01.pdf (retrieved October 10, 2010).

29. www.genome.gov/10002328 (retrieved October 10, 2010).

30. D. Potosky, "A Conceptual Framework for the Role of the Administration Medium in the Personnel Assessment Process," *Academy of Management Review* (2008), 33(3), pp. 629–648.

31. T. Gutner, "Applicants' Personalities Put to the Test," *Wall Street Journal* (August 26, 2008), p. D4.

32. V. Elmer, "Hiring Without a Net: Groupon's Recruiter Speaks," *Fortune* (July 25, 2011), p. 34.

33. supreme.justia.com/us/487/977/case.html (retrieved October 10, 2010).

34. www.eeoc.gov/laws/statutes/titlevii.cfm (retrieved October 10, 2010).

35. C. Berry, P. Sackett, S. Wiemann, "A Review of Recent Developments in Integrity Test Research," *Personnel Psychology* (Summer 2007), 60(2), pp. 271–201.

36. www.scienceclarified.com/scitech/Virtual-Reality/The-Virtual-Classroom-Virtual-Reality-in-Training-and-Education.html (retrieved October 10, 2010).

37. www.dol.gov/elaws/asp/drugfree/drugs/screen92.asp (retrieved October 23, 2011).

38. D. Potosky, "A Conceptual Framework for the Role of the Administration Medium in the Personnel Assessment Process," *Academy of Management Review* (2008), 33(3), pp. 629–648.

39. T. Gutner, "Applicants' Personalities Put to the Test," *Wall Street Journal* (August 26, 2008), p. D4.

40. M. Henricks, "Interview for Integrity," *Entrepreneur* (April 2009), p. 22.

41. V. Elmer, "Hiring Without a Net: Groupon's Recruiter Speaks," *Fortune* (July 25, 2011), p. 34.

42. M. Crouch, "Their Favorite Interview Questions," *Readers Digest* (April 2011), p. 135.

43. M. Henricks, "Interview for Integrity," *Entrepreneur* (April 2009), p. 22.

44. www.law.cornell.edu/uscode/11/usc_sec_11_00000525----000-.html (retrieved October 15, 2010).

45. M. Henricks, "Interview for Integrity," *Entrepreneur* (April 2009), p. 22.

46. www.ramsaylaw.com/research/Spencer%20Robinson/11-3-204.htm (retrieved October 15, 2010).

47. Ibid.

48. www.forbes.com/2010/02/23/job-search-trends-personal-finance-resume.html (retrieved October 15, 2010).

49. www.cio.com.au/article/352087/workplace_social_networking_rises_despite_lack_guidelines/ (retrieved August 16, 2011).

50. K. Schoening, K. Kleisinger, "Off-Duty Privace: How Far Can Employers Go?," *Northern Kentucky Law Review* (2010), 37, p. 287 .

51. www.HRTools.com (retrieved June 30, 2010).

Chapter 7

1. K. Pajo, A. Coetzer, N. Guenole, "Formal Development Opportunities and Withdrawal Behavior by Employees in Small and Medium-Sized Enterprises," *Journal of Small Business Management* (2010), 48(3), pp. 281–301.

2. D.G. Allen, P.C. Bryant, J.M. Vardaman, "Retaining Talent: Replacing Misconceptions With Evidence-Based Strategies," *Academy of Management Perspectives* (2010), 24(2), pp. 48–64.

3. K. Pajo, A. Coetzer, N. Guenole, "Formal Development Opportunities and Withdrawal Behavior by Employees in Small and Medium-Sized Enterprises," *Journal of Small Business Management* (2010), 48(3), pp. 281–301.

4. D.G. Allen, P.C. Bryant, J.M. Vardaman, "Retaining Talent: Replacing Misconceptions With Evidence-Based Strategies," *Academy of Management Perspectives* (2010), 24(2), pp. 48–64.

5. H. Green, "How Amazon Aims to Keep You Clicking," *Businessweek* (March 2, 2009), pp. 34–40.

6. T. Sitzmann, K. Ely, K.G. Brown, K.N. Bauer, "Self-Assessment of Knowledge: A Cognitive Learning or Affective Measure?" *Academy of Management Learning & Education* (2010), 9(2), pp. 169–191.

7. J. Podolny, "Ten New Gurus You Should Know," *Fortune* (November 24, 2008), p. 155.

8. "GE Response," *Fortune* (March 21, 2011), p. 17.

9. D.G. Allen, P.C. Bryant, J.M. Vardaman, "Retaining Talent: Replacing Misconceptions With Evidence-Based Strategies," *Academy of Management Perspectives* (2010), 24(2), pp. 48–64.

10. M. Jokisaari, J.E. Nurmi, "Change in Newcomers' Supervisor Support and Socialization Outcomes After Organizational Entry," *Academy of Management Journal* (2009), 52(3), pp. 527–544.

11. D.G. Allen, P.C. Bryant, J.M. Vardaman, "Retaining Talent: Replacing Misconceptions With Evidence-Based Strategies," *Academy of Management Perspectives* (2010), 24(2), pp. 48–64.

12. Ibid.

13. J. Casner-Lotto, E. Rosenblum, M. Wright, "The Ill-Prepared U.S. Workforce," *The Conference Board* (2009), p. 4.

14. T. Sitzmann, K. Ely, K.G. Brown, K.N. Bauer, "Self-Assessment of Knowledge: A Cognitive Learning or Affective Measure?" *Academy of Management Learning & Education* (2010), 9(2), pp. 169–191.

15. www.edpsycinteractive.org/topics/behsys/behsys.html (retrieved December 18, 2010).

16. http://mw1.meriam-webster.com/dictionary/vicarious (retrieved December 19, 2010).

17. W. Leite, M. Svinicki, Y. Shi, *Attempted Validation of the Scores of the VARK: Learning Styles Inventory With Multitrait–Multimethod Confirmatory Factor Analysis Models* (Thousand Oaks, CA: Sage, 2009), p. 2.

18. The material in this section is adapted from David Kolb Learning Style Inventory, which is sold through the Hay Group. For more information visit www.haygroup.com.

19. T. Sitzmann, K. Ely, K.G. Brown, K.N. Bauer, "Self-Assessment of Knowledge: A Cognitive Learning or Affective Measure?" *Academy of Management Learning & Education* (2010), 9(2), pp. 169–191.

20. Ibid.

21. Ibid.

22. www.bls.gov/news.release/pdf/nlsoy.pdf (retrieved December 26, 2010).

23. D.T. Hall, *Careers in and Out of Organizations* (Thousand Oaks, CA: Sage, 2002).

24. D.G. Allen, P.C. Bryant, J.M. Vardaman, "Retaining Talent: Replacing Misconceptions With Evidence-Based Strategies," *Academy of Management Perspectives* (2010), 24(2), pp. 48–64.

25. http://www1.eeoc.gov/eeoc/statistics/employment/jobpat-eeo1/2009/index.cfm#select_label (retrieved December 24, 2010).

26. S. Teicher, "To Make Your Career Soar, Get a Mentor; Eager to Retain *Employees*, US Firms Are Matching Senior Workers With Newer Hires," *The Christian Science Monitor* (September 27, 2004), p. 13.

27. S. Humphrey, F. Morgeson, M. Mannor, "Developing a Theory of the Strategic Core of Teams: A Role Composition Model of Team Performance," *Journal of Applied Psychology* (2009), 94(1), pp. 48–61.

28. J. Connolly, E. Kavanagh, C. Viswesvaran, "The Convergent Validity Between Self and Observer Ratings of Personality: A Meta-analytic Review," *International Journal of Selection and Assessment* (March 2007), 15(1), pp. 110–117.

29. E. Guss, "Emotional Intelligence: Our Most Versatile Tool for Success," *SHRM White Paper*, www.shrm.org/Research/Articles/Articles/Pages/CMS_014158.aspx (retrieved December 27, 2010).

30. M. Brackett, P. Salovey, "Measuring Emotional Intelligence With the Mayer–Salovey–Caruso Emotional Intelligence Test (MSCEIT)," *Psicothema* (2004), 18(Suppl.), pp. 34–41.

31. L. Summerfeldt, P. Kloosterman, M. Antony, D. Parker, "Social Anxiety, Emotional Intelligence, and Interpersonal Adjustment," *Journal of Psychopathology and Behavioral Assessment* (March 2006), 28(1), pp. 57–68.

32. D. Super, D. Hall, "Career Development: Exploration and Planning," *Annual Review of Psychology* (1978), 29, pp. 333–372.

33. A. Brief (Ed.), *Diversity at Work* (Cambridge, UK: Cambridge University Press, 2008), pp. 265–267.

34. R. Anand, M. Winters, "A Retrospective View of Corporate Diversity Training From 1964 to the Present," *Academy of Management Learning & Education* (2008), 7(3), pp. 356–372.

35. Ibid.

36. C. Holladay, M. Quinones, "The Influence of Training Focus and Trainer Characteristics on Diversity Training Effectiveness," *Academy of Management Learning & Education* (2008), 7(3), pp. 343–354.

37. Ibid.

38. M. Porter, M. Kramer, "Strategy & Society: The Link Between Competitive Advantage and Corporate Social Responsibility," *Harvard Business Review* (December 2006), 84(12), pp. 78–92.

39. O. Branzei, A. Nadkarni, "The Tata Way: Evolving and Executing Sustainable Business Strategies," *Ivey Business Journal* (March/April 2008), 72(2), pp. 1–8.

40. H. Haugh, A. Talwar, "How Do Corporations Embed Sustainability Across the Organization?", *Academy of Management Learning & Education* (2010), 9(3), pp. 384–396.

41. Jon Hay (Ed.), "HR Outsourcing Trends and Insights 2009," *Hewitt Associates* (2009), p. 8.

42. Jon Hay (Ed.), "HR Outsourcing Trends and Insights 2009," *Hewitt Associates* (2009), p. 10.

Chapter 8

1. T. Daniel, "Managing Employee Performance," Society for Human Resource Management (June 15, 2009), www.shrm.org/Research/Articles/Articles/Pages/ManagingEmployeePerformance.aspx (retrieved January 3, 2011).

2. D.G. Allen, P.C. Bryant, J.M. Vardaman, "Retaining Talent: Replacing Misconceptions With Evidence-Based Strategies," *Academy of Management Perspectives* 24(2), 2010, pp. 48–64.

3. M. Gusdorf, "Performance Management and Appraisal," Society for Human Resource Management (2009), www.shrm.org/Education/hreducation/Documents/ Performance_Management_PPT_SL_Edit_BS.ppt (retrieved January 2, 2011).

4. L. Schjoedt, "Entrepreneurial Job Characteristics: An Examination of Their Effect on Entrepreneurial Satisfaction," *Entrepreneurship Theory and Practice* 33(3), 2009, pp. 619–644.

5. S.A. Culbert, "Get Rid of the Performance Review," *Wall Street Journal* (October 20, 2008), p. R4.

6. D.G. Allen, P.C. Bryant, J.M. Vardaman, "Retaining Talent: Replacing Misconceptions With Evidence-Based Strategies," *Academy of Management Perspectives* 24(2), 2010, pp. 48–64.

7. D. Murphy, D. Bruce, S. Mercer, K. Eva, "The Reliability of Workplace-Based Assessment in Postgraduate Medical Education and Training: A National Evaluation in General Practice in the United Kingdom," *Advancements in Health Science Education* 14, 2009, pp. 219–232.

8. T. Daniel, "Managing Employee Performance," Society for Human Resource Management (June 15, 2009), www.shrm.org/Research/Articles/Articles/Pages/ManagingEmployeePerformance.aspx (retrieved January 3, 2011).

9. Society for Human Resource Management/Personnel Decisions International, "2000 Performance Management Survey," *SHRM Research* (2000), p. 7, www.shrm.org/Research/SurveyFindings/Documents/Performance%20Management%20Survey.pdf (retrieved January 3, 2011).

10. R. Hastings, "Performance Appraisals Used to Motivate, Weed Out," *Society for Human Resource Management* (July 20, 2009), www.shrm.org/hrdisciplines/employeerelations/articles/Pages/UsedtoMotivateWeedOut.aspx (retrieved January 3, 2011).

11. A. DeNisi, R. Pritchard, "Performance Appraisal, Performance Management and Improving Individual Performance: A Motivational Framework," *Management and Organization Review* 2(2), July 2006, pp. 253–277.

12. Ibid.

13. D. Sharinger, "Performance Appraisal: An Overview," SHRM White Paper (November 1, 1996), www.shrm.org/Research/Articles/Articles/Pages/CMS_000105.aspx (retrieved January 3, 2011).

14. K. Blanchard, D. Hutson, E. Wills, *The One Minute Entrepreneur* (New York: Currency, 2008).

15. C. Viswesvaran, D. Ones, "Perspectives on Models of Job Performance," *International Journal of Selection and Assessment* 8(4), 2000, pp. 216–226.

16. K. Blanchard, D. Hutson, E. Wills, *The One Minute Entrepreneur* (New York: Currency, 2008).

17. J. Goodale, "Behaviorally-Based Rating Scales: Toward an Integrated Approach to Performance Appraisal," *Contemporary Problems in Personnel* (Chicago: St. Clair Press, 1977), p. 247.

18. K. Blanchard, D. Hutson, E. Wills, *The One Minute Entrepreneur* (New York: Currency, 2008).

19. Ibid.

20. Ibid.

21. R. Youngjohns, "How Can I Keep My Sales Team Productive in a Recession?" *Fortune* (March 2, 2009), p. 22.

22. S.A. Culbert, "Get Rid of the Performance Review," *Wall Street Journal* (October 20, 2008), p. R4.

23. K. Blanchard, D. Hutson, E. Wills, *The One Minute Entrepreneur* (New York: Currency, 2008).

24. Ibid.

25. D.G. Allen, P.C. Bryant, J.M. Vardaman, "Retaining Talent: Replacing Misconceptions With Evidence-Based Strategies," *Academy of Management Perspectives* 24(2), 2010, pp. 48–64.

26. S. Shellenbarger, "Does Avoiding a 9-to-5 Grind Make You a Target for Layoffs?" *Wall Street Journal* (April 22, 2009), p. D1.

27. Wikipedia.com (information retrieved January 17, 2011). The first known uses of the term *SMART goals* occur in the November 1981 issue of *Management Review* by George T. Doran.

28. E. Gibson, "The Stop-Managing Guide to Management," *Business Week* (June 15, 2009), p. 73.

29. S. Shellenbarger, "Does Avoiding a 9-to-5 Grind Make You a Target for Layoffs?" *Wall Street Journal* (April 22, 2009), p. D1.

30. S. McCartney, "How US Airways Vaulted to First Place," *Wall Street Journal* (July 22, 2009), p. D3.

31. K. Blanchard, D. Hutson, E. Wills, *The One Minute Entrepreneur* (New York: Currency, 2008).

32. PerformanceReview.com, https://www.performancereview.com/pfasp/main.asp (retrieved January 27, 2011).

33. A. Sudarsan, "Concurrent Validity of Peer Appraisal of Group Work for Administrative Purposes," *The IUP Journal of Organizational Behavior* IX(1 & 2), 2010, pp. 73–86.

34. R. Hastings, "Manager, Employee Perceptions of Performance Differ," Society for Human Resource Management (April 20, 2009), www.shrm.org/hrdisciplines/employeerelations/articles/Pages/ManagerEmployeePerceptions.aspx (retrieved January 4, 2011).

35. J. Breidert, J. Fite, "Self Assessment: Review and Implications for Training," U.S. Army Research Institute for the Behavioral and Social Sciences (June 2009), Research Report 1900.

36. N. Castle, H. Garton, G. Kenward, "Confidence vs. Competence: Basic Life Support Skills of Health Professionals," *British Journal of Nursing* 16, 2007, pp. 664–666.

37. M. Matthews, S. Beal, "Assessing Situation Awareness in Field Training Exercises," U.S. Army Research Institute for the Behavioral and Social Sciences (2002), Research Report 1795.

38. K. Sullivan, C. Hall, "Introducing Students to Self-Assessment," *Assessment & Evaluation in Higher Education* 22, 1997, pp. 289–305.

39. B. McKinstry, H. Peacock, D. Blaney, "Can Trainers Accurately Assess Their Training Skills Using a Detailed Checklist? A questionnaire-based comparison of trainer self-assessment and registrar assessment of trainers' learning needs," *Education for Primary Care* 14, 2003, pp. 426–430.

40. K. Blanchard, D. Hutson, E. Wills, *The One Minute Entrepreneur* (New York: Currency, 2008).

41. G. Macintosh, "Customer Orientation, Relationship Quality, and Relational Benefits to the Firm," *Journal of Services Marketing* 21(3), 2007, pp. 150–159.

42. J. McGregor, "There Is No More Normal," *Businessweek* (March 23 & 30, 2009), pp. 30–34.

43. M. Gordon, C. Musso, E. Rebentisch, N. Gupta, "The Path to Developing Successful New Products," *Wall Street Journal* (November 30, 2009), p. R5.

44. G. Toegel, J. Conger, "360-Degree Assessment: Time for Reinvention," *Academy of Management Learning and Education* 2(3), 2003, pp. 297–311.

45. H. Aguinas, *Performance Management* (Upper Saddle River, NJ: Pearson Education Inc., 2007), p. 184.

46. A. Thomas, J. Palmer, J. Feldman, "Examination and Measurement of Halo Via Curvilinear Regression: A New Approach to Halo," *Journal of Applied Social Psychology* (February 2009) 39(2), p. 350–358.

47. J. Becton, H. Feild, W. Giles, A. Jones-Farmer, "Racial Differences in Promotion Candidate Performance and Reactions to Selection Procedures: A Field Study in a Diverse Top-Management Context," *Journal of Organizational Behavior* 29(3), 2008, pp. 265–285.

48. K. Blanchard, D. Hutson, E. Wills, *The One Minute Entrepreneur* (New York: Currency, 2008).

49. E.C. Hollensbe, S. Khazanchi, S.S. Masterson, "How Do I Assess If My Supervisor and Organization Are Fair? Identifying the Rules Underlying Entity-Based Justice Perceptions," *Academy of Management Journal* 51(6), 2008, pp. 1099–1116.

50. J. McGregor, "Job Review in 140 Keystrokes," *Businessweek* (March 23 & 30, 2009), p. 58.

51. D.G. Allen, P.C. Bryant, J.M. Vardaman, "Retaining Talent: Replacing Misconceptions With Evidence-Based Strategies," *Academy of Management Perspectives* 24(2), 2010, pp. 48–64.

52. E. Gibson, "The Stop-Managing Guide to Management," *Businessweek* (June 15, 2009), p. 73.

53. Ibid.

54. T. Gutner, "Ways to Make the Most of a Negative Job Review," *Wall Street Journal* (January 13, 2009), p. D4.

55. D.G. Allen, P.C. Bryant, J.M. Vardaman, "Retaining Talent: Replacing Misconceptions With Evidence-Based Strategies," *Academy of Management Perspectives* 24(2), 2010, pp. 48–64.

56. E. Gibson, "The Stop-Managing Guide to Management," *Businessweek* (June 15, 2009), p. 73.

57. T. Gutner, "Ways to Make the Most of a Negative Job Review," *Wall Street Journal* (January 13, 2009), p. D4.

58. S.A. Culbert, *Get Rid of the Performance Review!* (New York: Business Plus, 2010).

59. W. Carroll, "The Effects of Electronic Performance Monitoring on Performance Outcomes: A Review and Meta-analysis," *Employment Rights & Employment Policy Journal* 29, 2008, pp. 29–47.

60. Ibid.

61. D.G. Allen, P.C. Bryant, J.M. Vardaman, "Retaining Talent: Replacing Misconceptions With Evidence-Based Strategies," *Academy of Management Perspectives* 24(2), 2010, pp. 48–64.

62. L. Weatherly, "Competency Models Series Part III: Competency-Based Performance Management," www.shrm.org/Research/Articles/Articles/Pages/Competency_20Models_20Series_20Part_20III__20Competency-Based_20Performance_20Management.aspx (retrieved January 8, 2011).

63. Ibid.

64. Ibid.

65. J. Sammer, "Calibrating Consistency: Sessions Ensure That One Manager's 'competent' rating isn't another manager's 'superior,'" *HR Magazine* (January 21, 2011), http://find-articles.com/p/articles/mi_m3495/is_1_53/ai_n24267399/ (retrieved January 29, 2011).

Chapter 9

1. T. Sitzmann, K. Ely, K.G. Brown, K.N. Bauer, "Self-Assessment of Knowledge: A Cognitive Learning or Affective Measure?" *Academy of Management Learning & Education* (2010), 9(2), pp. 169–191.

2. R.E. Johnson, C.D. Chang, L.O. Yang, "Commitment and Motivation at Work: The Relevance of Employee Identity and Regulatory Focus," *Academy of Management Review* (2010), 35(2), pp. 226–245.

3. J. Hughes, C. Babcock, F. Bass, "You're Fired, Now Get Back to Work," *Businessweek* (August 1–7, 2011), pp. 31–32.

4. Universal Declaration of Human Rights, adopted by the General Assembly on 10 Dec. 1948, UN Doc. GA/RES/217 A (III).

5. www.ncsl.org/?tabid=13344 (retrieved January 22, 2011).

6. www.dol.gov/elaws/asp/drugfree/drugs/screen92 .asp (retrieved October 28, 2011).

7. J. Welch, S. Welch, "An Employee Bill of Rights," *Businessweek* (March 16, 2009), p. 72.

8. A.R. Connell, "Eye of the Beholder: Does What Is Important About a Job Depend on Who Is Asking?" *Academy of Management Perspective* (2010), 24(2), pp. 83–85.

9. K. Blanchard, D. Hutson, E. Wills, *The One Minute Entrepreneur* (New York: Currency, 2008).

10. G. Colvin, "Why Talent Is Over Rated," *Fortune* (October 27, 2008), pp. 138–147.

11. D.G. Allen, P.C. Bryant, J.M. Vardaman, "Retaining Talent: Replacing Misconceptions With Evidence-Based Strategies," *Academy of Management Perspectives* (2010), 24(2), pp. 48–64.

12. P. Parker, D.T. Hall, K.E. Kram, "Peer Coaching: A Relational Process for Accelerating Career Learning," *Academy of Management Education & Learning* (2008), 7(4), pp. 487–503.

13. R. Hooijbert, N. Lane, "Using Multisource Feedback Coaching Effectively in Executive Education," *Academy of Management Learning & Education* (2009), 8(4), pp. 483–493.

14. G. Colvin, "Why Talent Is Over Rated," *Fortune* (October 27, 2008), pp. 138–147.

15. T. Gutner, "Ways to Make the Most of a Negative Job Review," *Wall Street Journal* (January 13, 2009), p. D4.

16. K. Blanchard, D. Hutson, E. Wills, *The One Minute Entrepreneur* (New York: Currency, 2008).

17. D.W. Lehman, R. Ramanujam, "Selectivity in Organizational Rule Violations," *Academy of Management Review* (2009), 34(4), pp. 643–657.

18. J. Sinegal, "Show Don't Tell," *Fortune* (July 6, 2009), p. 44.

19. K.W. Mossholder, H.A. Richardson, R.P. Settoon, "Human Resource Systems and Helping in Organizations: A Relational Perspective," *Academy of Management Review* (2011), 36(1), pp. 33–52.

20. R. Hooijbert, N. Lane, "Using Multisource Feedback Coaching Effectively in Executive Education," *Academy of Management Learning & Education* (2009), 8(4), pp. 483–493.

21. S.D. Sidle, "Personality Disorders and Dysfunctional Employee Behavior: How Can Managers Cope?" *Academy of Management Perspective* (2009), 25(2), pp. 76–77.

22. G. Colvin, "Why Talent Is Over Rated," *Fortune* (October 27, 2008), pp. 138–147.

23. E. De Haan, C. Bertie, A. Day, C. Sills, "Clients' Critical Moments of Coaching: Toward a 'Client Model' of Executive Coaching," *Academy of Management Learning & Education* (2010), 9(4), pp. 607–621.

24. J. Sinegal, "Show Don't Tell," *Fortune* (July 6, 2009), p. 44.

25. T. Gutner, "Ways to Make the Most of a Negative Job Review," *Wall Street Journal* (January 13, 2009), p. D4.

26. N. Tocher, M.W. Rutherford, "Perceived Acute Human Resource Management Problems in Small and Medium Firms: An Empirical Examination," *Entrepreneurship Theory and Practice* (2009) 33(2), pp. 455–479.

27. D.W. Lehman, R. Ramanujam, "Selectivity in Organizational Rule Violations," *Academy of Management Review* (2009), 34(4), pp. 643–657.

28. S.D. Sidle, "Personality Disorders and Dysfunctional Employee Behavior: How Can Managers Cope?" *Academy of Management Perspective* (2009), 25(2), pp. 76–77.

29. D.W. Lehman, R. Ramanujam, "Selectivity in Organizational Rule Violations," *Academy of Management Review* (2009), 34(4), pp. 643–657.

30. R.S. Dalal, H. Lam, H.M. Weiss, E.R. Welch, C.L. Hulin, "A Within-Person Approach to Work Behavior and Performance: Concurrent and Lagged Citizenship-Counter Productivity Associations and Dynamic Relationships With Affect and Overall Job Performance," *Academy of Management Journal* (2009), 52(5), pp. 1051–1066.

31. S.D. Sidle, "Workplace Incivility: How Should Employees and Managers Respond?" *Academy of Management Perspective* (2009), 23(4), pp. 88–89.

32. P.H. Kim, K. Dirks, C.D. Cooper, "The Repair of Trust: A Dynamic Bilateral Perspective and Multilevel Conceptualization," *Academy of Management Review* (2009), 34(3), pp. 401–422.

33. C. Matsuda, "Hello? You've Got a Job to Do," *Entrepreneur* (March 2010), p. 73.

34. W.P. Smith, F. Tabak, "Monitoring Employee E-mail: Is There Any Room for Privacy?" *Academy of Management Perspectives* (2009), 23(4), pp. 33–48.

35. M. Goldsmith, "What Got You Here Won't Get You There: How Successful People Became Even More Successful," *Academy of Management Perspective* (2009), 23(3), pp. 103–105.

36. J. Hughes, C. Babcock, F. Bass, "You're Fired, Now Get Back to Work," *Businessweek* (August 1–7, 2011), pp. 31–32.

37. K. Hudson, K. Maher, "Wal-Mart Adjusts Attendance Policy," *The Wall Street Journal* (October 14, 2006), p. A3.

38. T. Gutner, "Ways to Make the Most of a Negative Job Review," *Wall Street Journal* (January 13, 2009), p. D4.

39. W.S. Siebert, N. Zubanov, "Searching for the Optimal Level of Employee Turnover: A Study of a Large U.K. Retail Organization," *Academy of Management Journal* (2009), 52(2), pp. 292–313.

40. M. Moral, P. Warnock, "Coaching and Culture: Toward the Global Coach," in M. Goldsmith & L. Lyons (Eds.), *Coaching for Leadership: The Practice of Leadership Coaching From the World's Greatest Coaches* (2nd ed.,, San Diego, CA: Pfeiffer & Company), pp. 126–135.

41. Ibid.

42. D. Peterson, "Executive Coaching in a Cross-Cultural Context," *Consulting Psychology Journal: Practice and Research* (2007) 59(4), pp. 261–272.

43. S.D. Sidle, "Personality Disorders and Dysfunctional Employee Behavior: How Can Managers Cope?" *Academy of Management Perspective* (2009), 25(2), pp. 76–77.

44. D.S. DeRue, S.B. Sitkin, J.M. Podolny, "Call for Papers—Teaching Leadership," *Academy of Management Journal* (2010), 33(4), pp. 922–923.

45. K.Y. Ng, L. Van Dyne, S. Ang, "From Experience to Experiential Learning: Cultural Intelligence as a Learning Capability for Global Leader Development," *Academy of Management Learning & Education* (2009), 8(4), pp. 511–526.

46. G.A. Van Kleef, A.C. Homan, B. Beersma, D. Van Knippenberg, F. Damen, "Searing Sentiment or Cold Calculation? The Effects of Leader Emotional Displays on Team Performance Depend on Follower Epistemic Motivation," *Academy of Management Journal* (2009), 52(3), pp. 562–580.

47. Staff, "Leaders of Tomorrow," *Fortune* (November 24, 2008), p. 27.

48. S. McVanel, "Review Subject: How to Grow Leaders: The Seven Key Principles of Effective Leadership Development," *Leadership & Organization Development Journal*, 31(1), pp. 98–99.

49. E.A. Locke, G.P. Latham, "Has Goal Setting Gone Wild, or Have Its Attackers Abandoned Good Scholarship?" *Academy of Management Perspective* (2009), 23(1), pp. 17–23.

50. L.D. Ordonez, M.E. Schweitzer, M.H. Bazerman, "Goals Gone Wild: The Systematic Side Effects of Overprescribing Goal Setting," *Academy of Management Perspective* (2009), 23(1), pp. 6–16.

51. M. Farjoun, "Beyond Dualism: Stability and Change as a Duality," *Academy of Management Review* (2010), 35(2), pp. 202–225.

52. R. Greenwood, D. Miller, "Tackling Design Anew: Getting Back to the Heart of Organizational Theory," *Academy of Management Perspectives* (2010), 24(4), pp. 78–84.

53. Ibid.

54. P. Navarro, "The MBA Core Curricular of Top-Ranked U.S. Business Schools: A Study of Failure?" *Academy of Management Learning & Education* (2008), 7(1), pp. 108–123.

55. E. Kearney, D. Gebert, S.C. Voelpel, "When and How Diversity Benefits Teams: The Importance of Team Members' Need for Cognition," *Academy of Management Journal* (2009), 52(3), pp. 581–598.

56. J.D. Ford, L.W. Ford, A. D'Amelio, "Resistance to Change: The Rest of the Story," *Academy of Management Review* (2008), 33(2), pp. 362–377.

57. L.S. Luscher, M.W. Lewis, "Organizational Change and Managerial Sensemaking: Working Through Paradox," *Academy of Management Journal* (2008), 51(2), pp. 221–240.

58. M.T. Kennedy, P.C. Fiss, "Institutionalization, Framing, and Diffusion: The Logic of TQM Adoption and Implementation Decisions Among U.S. Hospitals," *Academy of Management Journal* (2009), 52(5), pp. 897–918.

59. J. Scheck, "HP Revamps Service Unit," *Wall Street Journal* (June 2, 2010), pp. B1 and B6.

60. M. Goldsmith, "What Got You Here Won't Get You There: How Successful People Became Even More Successful," *Academy of Management Perspective* (2009), 23(3), pp. 103–105.

61. J. Welch, S. Welch, "How Not to Succeed in Business," *Businessweek* (March 2, 2009), p. 74.

62. J. Welch, S. Welch, "Transforming the Family Business," *Businessweek* (May 25, 2009), p. 72.

63. J. Welch, S. Welch, "How Not to Succeed in Business," *Businessweek* (March 2, 2009), p. 74.

64. S.S. Chakravorty, "Where Process-Improvements Projects Go Wrong," *Wall Street Journal* (January 25, 2010), p. R6.

65. M. Splinter, "The Buck Stops Here," *Fortune* (September 28, 2010), p. 58.

66. L.S. Luscher, M.W. Lewis, "Organizational Change and Managerial Sensemaking: Working Through

Paradox," *Academy of Management Journal* (2008), 51(2), pp. 221–240.

67. J.D. Ford, L.W. Ford, A. D'Amelio, "Resistance to Change: The Rest of the Story," *Academy of Management Review* (2008), 33(2), pp. 362–377.

68. S.S. Chakravorty, "Where Process-Improvements Projects Go Wrong," *Wall Street Journal* (January 25, 2010), p. R6.

69. B. Farber, "Close the Deal With Urgency," *Entrepreneur* (May 2009), p. 60.

70. R.E. Johnson, C.D. Chang, L.O. Yang, "Commitment and Motivation at Work: The Relevance of Employee Identity and Regulatory Focus," *Academy of Management Review* (2010), 35(2), pp. 226–245.

71. L. Treviño, M. Brown, L. Pincus Hartman, "A Qualitative Investigation of Perceived Executive Ethical Leadership: Perceptions From Inside and Outside the Executive Suite," *Human Relations* (2003), 56(5), pp. 5–37.

72. F. Walumbwa, S. Peterson, B. Avolio, C. Hartnell, "An Investigation of the Relationships Among Leader and Follower Psychological Capital, Service Climate, and Job Performance," *Personnel Psychology* (2010), 63, pp. 937–963.

73. G. Yukl, "How Leaders Influence Organizational Effectiveness," *The Leadership Quarterly Yearly Review of Leadership* (December 2008), 19(6), pp. 708–722.

74. R.N. Lussier, *Management Fundamentals: Concepts, Applications, Skill Development* (5th ed., Cengage/Irwin, 2011).

75. J. Deschenaux, "Employee Use of Social Media: Laws Fail to Keep Pace With Technology," www.shrm.org/LegalIssues/FederalResources/Pages/EmployeeUseofSocialMedia.aspx (retrieved March 20, 2011).

76. Ibid.

77. C. Zatzick, R. Iverson, "High-Involvement Management and Workforce Reduction: Competitive Advantage or Disadvantage," *Academy of Management Journal* (2006), 49(5), pp. 999–1015.

78. S. Valentine, G. Fleischman, "Ethics Programs, Perceived Corporate Social Responsibility and Job Satisfaction," *Journal of Business Ethics* (2008), 77(2), pp. 159–172.

79. R. Piccolo, R. Greenbaum, D. Hartog, R. Folger, "The Relationship Between Ethical Leadership and Core Job Characteristics," *Journal of Organizational Behavior* (2010), 31, pp. 259–278.

80. Ibid.

Chapter 10

1. "Jack Welch's Lessons for Success," *Fortune* (1993), 127(2), pp. 86–93.

2. M.E. Graebner, "Caveat Venditor: Trust Asymmetries in Acquisitions of Entrepreneurial Firms," *Academy of Management Journal* (2009), 52(3), pp. 435–472.

3. E.C. Tomlinson, R.C. Mayer, "The Role of Causal Attribution Dimensions in Trust Repair," *Academy of Management Review* (2009), 34(1), pp. 85–104.

4. N. Gillespie, G. Dietz, "Trust Repair After an Organization-Level Failure," *Academy of Management Review* (2009), 34(1), pp. 127–145.

5. P.H. Kim, K. Dirks, C.D. Cooper, "The Repair of Trust: A Dynamic Bilateral Perspective and Multilevel Conceptualization," *Academy of Management Review* (2009), 34(3), pp. 401–422.

6. www.dreamworksstudios.com (retrieved May 16, 2011).

7. Blanchard, D. Hutson, E. Wills, *The One Minute Entrepreneur* (New York: Currency, 2008).

8. R. Hooijbert, N. Lane, "Using Multisource Feedback Coaching Effectively in Executive Education," *Academy of Management Learning & Education* (2009), 8(4), pp. 483–493.

9. K. Blanchard, D. Hutson, E. Wills, *The One Minute Entrepreneur* (New York: Currency, 2008).

10. J. Ewing, "Nokia: Bring on the Employee Rants," *Businessweek* (June 22, 2009), p. 50.

11. Public Radio, News Broadcast, WFCR 88.5 (aired May 28, 2010).

12. J. Robinson, "E-mail Is Making You Stupid?" *Entrepreneur* (March 2010), pp. 61–63.

13. D.B. Montgomery, C.A. Ramus, "Calibrating MBA Job Preferences for the 21st Century," *Academy of Learning & Education* (2011), 10(1), pp. 9–26.

14. G. Chen, R.E. Ployhart, H.C. Thomas, N. Anderson, P.D. Blasé, "The Power of Momentum: A New Model of Dynamic Relationships Between Job Satisfaction Change

and Turnover Intentions," *Academy of Management Journal* (2011), 54(1), pp. 159–181.

15. R. Ivies, K.S. Wilson, D.T. Wagner, "The Spillover of Daily Job Satisfaction Onto Employees' Family Lives: The Facilitating Role of Work-Family Integration," *Academy of Management Journal* (2009), 52(1), pp. 87–102.

16. G. Chen, R.E. Ployhart, H.C. Thomas, N. Anderson, P.D. Blasé, "The Power of Momentum: A New Model of Dynamic Relationships Between Job Satisfaction Change and Turnover Intentions," *Academy of Management Journal* (2011), 54(1), pp. 159–181.

17. M. Mount, R. Ilies, E. Johnson, "Relationship of Personality Traits and Counterproductive Work Behaviors: The Mediating Effects of Job Satisfaction," *Personnel Psychology* (2006), 59, pp. 591–622.

18. A. Makikangas, U. Kinnunen, "Psychosocial Work Stressors and Well-Being: Self-Esteem and Optimism as Moderators in a One-Year Longitudinal Sample," *Personality and Individual Differences* (August 2003), 35(3), pp. 537–557.

19. D.R. Soriano, "Can Goal Setting and Performance Feedback Enhance Organizational Citizenship Behavior?" *Academy of Management Perspective* (2008), 22(1), pp. 65–66.

20. J. Buitendach, S. Rothmann, "The Validation of the Minnesota Job Satisfaction Questionnaire in Selected Organizations in South Africa," *SA Journal of Human Resource Management* (2009), 7(1), Art. #183.

21. M.S. Direnzo, J.H. Greenhaus, "Job Search and Voluntary Turnover in a Boundaryless World: A Control Theory Perspective," *Academy of Management Review* (2011), 36(3), pp. 567–589.

22. C.H. Chang, C.C. Rosen, P.E. Levy, "The Relationship Between Perceptions of Organizational Politics and Employee Attitudes, Strain and Behavior: A Meta-Analytic Examination," *Academy of Management Journal* (2009), 52(4), pp. 779–801.

23. R. Dunham, J. Herman, "Development of a Female Faces Scale for Measuring Job Satisfaction," *Journal of Applied Psychology* (1975), 60(5), pp. 629–631.

24. P. Spector, "Measurement of Human Service Staff Satisfaction: Development of the Job Satisfaction Survey," *American Journal of Community Psychology* (1985), 13(6), pp. 693–713.

25. N. van Saane, J. Sluiter, J. Verbeek, M. Frings-Dresen, "Reliability and Validity of Instruments Measuring Job Satisfaction—a Systematic Review," *Occupational Medicine* (2003), 53(3), pp. 191–200.

26. P. Spector, "Measurement of Human Service Staff Satisfaction: Development of the Job Satisfaction Survey," *American Journal of Community Psychology* (1985), 13(6), pp. 693–713.

27. C. Fisher, "Mood and Emotions While Working: Missing Pieces of Job Satisfaction," *Journal of Organizational Behavior* (2000), 21(2), pp. 185–202.

28. D.C. Wyld, "Does More Money Buy More Happiness on the Job?" *Academy of Management Perspective* (2011), 25(1), pp. 101–102.

29. D.B. Montgomery, C.A. Ramus, "Calibrating MBA Job Preferences for the 21st Century," *Academy of Learning & Education* (2011), 10(1), pp. 9–26.

30. C.H. Chang, C.C. Rosen, P.E. Levy, "The Relationship Between Perceptions of Organizational Politics and Employee Attitudes, Strain and Behavior: A Meta-Analytic Examination," *Academy of Management Journal* (2009), 52(4), pp. 779–801.

31. www.nmb.gov/documents/rla.html (retrieved April 9, 2011).

32. Ibid.

33. www.fra.dot.gov/pages/955.shtml (retrieved March 25, 2011).

34. Ibid.

35. www.nlrb.gov/national-labor-relations-act (retrieved March 27, 2011).

36. www.nlrb.gov/what-we-do (retrieved March 27, 2011).

37. Ibid.

38. www.dol.gov/oasam/programs/history/glossary.htm (retrieved April 9, 2011).

39. www.shrm.org/LegalIssues/FederalResources/FederalStatutesRegulationsandGuidanc/Pages/Labor-ManagementReportingandDisclosureAct%28LMRDA%29.aspx (retrieved April 16, 2011).

40. D. Meinert, "Whistle-Blowers: Threat or Asset?" *HR Magazine* (April 2011), 56(4), pp. 27–32.

41. www.whistleblowers.org/storage/whistleblowers/documents/DoddFrank/nwcreporttosecfinal.pdf (retrieved April 16, 2011).

42. D. Meinert, "Whistle-Blowers: Threat or Asset?" *HR Magazine* (April 2011), 56(4), pp. 27–32.

43. A. Goldman, W. Sigismond), *Business Law: Principles and Practices* (Mason, OH: Cengage Learning, 2011), p. 124.

44. Ibid.

45. www.wikipedia.com (retrieved May 17, 2011).

46. H. Rosenkrantz, "What Andy Stern Leaves Behind," *Businessweek* (April 25, 2010), p. 23.

47. www.shrm.org/LegalIssues/FederalResources/Pages/ UnionOrganizingActivity.aspx (retrieved April 29, 2011).

48. www.google.com/url?sa=t&source=web&cd=8&sqi =2&ved=0CE8QFjAH&url=http%3A%2F%2Fwww .velaw.com%2FuploadedFiles%2FVEsite%2FReso urces%2FUnionOrganizationProcess(5-501-0280) .pdf&rct=j&q=unionization%20process%20 TIPS&ei=ms29TZPnPMHytge_uoXCBQ&usg=AFQjCNFX nYfHA5szJc2NOV3JU_LpZ_pjFA&sig2=ZMZpkSQa0feL1Z JnyXcUNw&cad=rja (retrieved April 29, 2011).

49. Ibid.

50. M. Bartiromo, "Union Leader Andy Stern on the Future of Big Labor," *Businessweek* (September 28, 2009), pp. 11–13.

51. caselaw.lp.findlaw.com/scripts/getcase.pl?court=us& vol=502&invol=527 (retrieved May 9, 2011).

52. P. Butler, "Non-union Employee Representation: Exploring the Riddle of Managerial Strategy," *Industrial Relations Journal* (2009), 40(3), pp. 198–214.

53. J. Beatty, S. Samuelson, *Introduction to Business Law,* 3rd ed. (Mason, OH: Cengage Learning, 2009), p. 320.

54. J. Battista, "Judge Returns Players and N.F.L. to Mediation," *New York Times* (April 12, 2011), p. B11.

55. J. Beatty, S. Samuelson, *Introduction to Business Law,* 3rd ed. (Mason, OH: Cengage Learning, 2009), p. 319.

56. www.shrm.org/TemplatesTools/hrqa/Pages/decertify-aunion.aspx (retrieved May 10, 2011).

57. Ibid.

58. Ibid.

59. E. Gibson, "The Stop-Managing Guide to Management," *Businessweek* (June 15, 2009), p. 73.

60. H. Ren, B. Gray, "Repairing Relationship Conflict: How Violation Types and Culture Influence the Effectiveness of Restoration Rituals," *Academy of Management Review* (2009), 34(1), pp. 105–126.

61. H.G. Barkema, M. Schijven, "Toward Unlocking the Full Potential of Acquisitions: The Role of Organizational Restructuring," *Academy of Management Journal* (2008), 51(4), pp. 696–722.

62. K.A. Eddleston, R.F. Otondo, F.W. Kellermanns, "Conflict, Participative Decision-Making, and Generational Ownership Dispersion: A Multilevel Analysis," *Journal of Small Business Management* (2008), pp. 456–464.

63. H. Ren, B. Gray, "Repairing Relationship Conflict: How Violation Types and Culture Influence the Effectiveness of Restoration Rituals," *Academy of Management Review* (2009), 34(1), pp. 105–126.

64. P.H. Kim, K. Dirks, C.D. Cooper, "The Repair of Trust: A Dynamic Bilateral Perspective and Multilevel Conceptualization," *Academy of Management Review* (2009), 34(3), pp. 401–422.

65. E.G. Foldy, P. Rivard, T.R. Buckley, "Power, Safety, and Learning in Racially Diverse Groups," *Academy of Management Learning & Education* (2009), 8(1), pp. 25–41.

66. R.S. Rubin, E.C. Dierdorff, "How Relevant Is the MBA? Assessing the Alignment of Required Curricula and Required Managerial Competencies," *Academy of Management Learning & Education* (2009), 8(5), pp. 208–224.

67. R.S. Rubin, E.C. Dierdorff, "How Relevant Is the MBA? Assessing the Alignment of Required Curricula and Required Managerial Competencies," *Academy of Management Learning & Education* (2009), 8(5), pp. 208–224.

68. C.L. Holladay, M.A. Quinones, "The Influence of Training Focus and Trainer Characteristics on Diversity Training Effectiveness," *Academy of Management Learning & Education* (2008), 7(3), pp. 343–354.

69. C.M. Fiol, M.G. Pratt, E.J. O'Connor, "Managing Intractable Identity Conflicts," *Academy of Management Review* (2009), 34(1), pp. 32–55.

70. C.L. Holladay, M.A. Quinones, "The Influence of Training Focus and Trainer Characteristics on Diversity Training Effectiveness," *Academy of Management Learning & Education* (2008), 7(3), pp. 343–354.

71. S. Wilson, "Think Like a Negotiator," *Entrepreneur* (May 2009), p. 28.

72. P. Navarro, "The MBA Core Curricular of Top-Ranked U.S. Business Schools: A Study of Failure?" *Academy of Management Learning & Education* (2008), 7(1), pp. 108–123.

73. M. Cording, P. Christmann, D.R. King, "Reducing Causal Ambiguity in Acquisition Integration: Intermediate Goals as Mediators of Integration Decisions and Acquisition Performance," *Academy of Management Journal* (2008), 51(4), pp. 744–767.

74. S. Boras, "Be Effective, Not Popular," *Fortune* (July 6, 2009), p. 46.

75. M. Port, "Know Who You Want to Know," *Entrepreneur* (April 2010), p. 48.

76. S. Waterhous, "How Can I Keep My Sales Team Productive in a Recession?" *Fortune* (March 2, 2009), p. 22.

77. M. Port, "Know Who You Want to Know," *Entrepreneur* (April 2010), p. 48.

78. B. Farber, "It's Always Your Lucky Day," *Entrepreneur* (July 2008), p. 71.

79. S. Wilson, "Think Like a Negotiator," *Entrepreneur* (May 2009), p. 28.

80. W. Ross, "Good Execution Beats a Bad Idea," *Fortune* (November 23, 2009), p. 42.

81. B. Farber, "It's Always Your Lucky Day," *Entrepreneur* (July 2008), p. 71.

82. M. Port, "Know Who You Want to Know," *Entrepreneur* (April 2010), p. 48.

83. M. Port, "Know Who You Want to Know," *Entrepreneur* (April 2010), p. 48.

84 B. Farber, "Be All You Can Be," *Entrepreneur* (August 2008), p. 69.

85. S. Wilson, "Think Like a Negotiator," *Entrepreneur* (May 2009), p. 28.

86. M. Buckingham, "How Women Handle Success," *Businessweek* (November 2, 2009), pp. 70–71.

87. B. Farber, "Constructive Criticism," *Entrepreneur* (November 2008), p. 73.

88. S. Waterhous, "How Can I Keep My Sales Team Productive in a Recession?" *Fortune* (March 2, 2009), p. 22.

89. B. Farber, "Close the Deal With Urgency," *Entrepreneur* (May 2009), p. 60.

90. B. Farber, "Constructive Criticism," *Entrepreneur* (November 2008), p. 73.

91. E. Berstein, "Honey, Do You Have to . . ." *Wall Street Journal* (April 20, 2010), p. D1.

92. www.wikipedia.com (retrieved May 19, 2011).

93. D. Roberts, "A New Labor Movement is Born in China," *Businessweek* (June 14–20, 2010), pp. 7–8.

94. www.wharton.universia.net/index.cfm?fa=viewArticle&id =1349&language=english (retrieved May 11, 2011).

95. "Brazil: Labor Relations," *TozziniFriere Advogados* (2007), p. 1.

96. J. Almeida, *Brazil in Focus* (New York: Nova Science Publishers, 2008), pp. 124–125

97. "75% of Employers Expect Worse Labor Relations in 2011," Korea Times (December 19, 2010), www.koreatimes .co.kr/www/news/nation/nation_view.asp?newsIdx=78249 &categoryCode=113 (retrieved May 11, 2011).

98. "Outlook for Industrial Relations After Allowing of Union Pluralism," *Labor in Focus* (February 7, 2011), Vol. 1.

99. www.eurofound.europa.eu/eiro/studies/tn0901028S/ cz0901029q.htm (retrieved May 12, 2011).

100. Ibid.

101. A. Gregory, S. Milner, "Trade Unions and Work-Life Balance: Changing Times in France and the UK?" *British Journal of Industrial Relations* (March 2009), 47(1), pp. 122–146.

102. S. Armour, "Beyond the Reach of Republicans?" *Newsweek* (Winter 2011), pp. 57–58.

Chapter 11

1. C.B. Cadsby, F. Song, F. Tapon, "Sorting and Incentive Effects of Pay for Performance: An Experimental Investigation," *Academy of Management Journal* (2007), 50(2), pp. 387–405.

2. J. DeVaro, "A Theoretical Analysis of Relational Job Design and Compensation," *Journal of Organizational Behavior* (2010), 31(2–3), pp. 279–301.

3. R. E. Johnson, C.D. Chang, L.O. Yang, "Commitment and Motivation at Work: The Relevance of Employee Identity and Regulatory Focus," *Academy of Management Review* (2010), 35(2), pp. 226–245.

4. R.S. Rubin, E.C. Dierdorff, "On the Road to Abilene: Time to Manage Agreement About MBA Curricular Relevance," *Academy of Management Learning & Education* (2011), 10(1), pp. 148–161.

5. J. Helyar, D. MacMillan, "In Tech, Poaching Is the Sincerest Form of Flattery," *Businessweek* (March 7–13, 2011), pp. 17–18.

6. A.M. Grant, J.E. Dutton, B.D. Rosso, "Giving Commitment: Employee Support Programs and the Prosocial Sensemaking Process," *Academy of Management Journal* (2008), 51(5), pp. 898–918.

7. P. Coy, "Are Your Employees Just Biding Their Time?" *Businessweek* (November 16, 2009), p. 27.

8. D. Foust, "The Business Week," *Businessweek* (April 6, 2009), pp. 40–63.

9. J. He, H.C. Wang, "Innovation Knowledge Assets and Economic Performance: The Asymmetric Roles of Incentives and Monitoring," *Academy of Management Journal* (2009), 52(5), pp. 919–938.

10. R. Markadok, R. Coff, "Both Market and Hierarchy: An Incentive-System Theory of Hybrid Governance Forms," *Academy of Management Review* (2009), 34(2), pp. 297–319.

11. J. DeVaro, "A Theoretical Analysis of Relational Job Design and Compensation," *Journal of Organizational Behavior* (2010), 31(No. 2–3), pp. 279–301.

12. V. Vroom, *Work and Motivation* (New York: John Wiley & Sons, 1964).

13. K. Blanchard, D. Hutson, E. Wills, *The One Minute Entrepreneur* (New York: Currency, 2008).

14. G.A. Van Kleef, A.C. Homan, B. Beersma, D. Van Knippenberg, F. Damen, "Searing Sentiment or Cold Calculation? The Effects of Leader Emotional Displays on Team Performance Depend on Follower Epistemic Motivation," *Academy of Management Journal* (2009), 52(3), pp. 562–580.

15. J.S. Adams, "Toward an Understanding of Inequity," *Journal of Abnormal and Social Psychology* (1963), 67, pp. 422–436.

16. "How to Apply Adam's Equity Theory," www.mindtools.com (retrieved June 6, 2011).

17. E.C. Hollensbe, S. Khazanchi, S.S. Masterson, "How Do I Assess If My Supervisor and Organization Are Fair? Identifying the Rules Underlying Entity-Based Justice Perceptions," *Academy of Management Journal* (2008), 51(6), pp. 1099–1116.

18. M. Crouch, "Get Hired, Not Fired," *Reader's Digest* (April 2011), pp. 130–139.

19. S. Anand, P.R. Vidyarthi, R.C. Linden, D.M. Rousseau, "Good Citizens in Poor-Quality Relationships: Idiosyncratic Deals as a Substitute for Relationship Quality," *Academy of Management Journal* (2010), 53(5), pp. 970–988.

20. J. Greenberg, "Employee Theft as a Reaction to Underpayment of Inequity: The Hidden Cost of Pay Cuts," *Journal of Applied Psychology* (1990), 75, pp. 561–568.

21. "How to Apply Adam's Equity Theory," www.mindtools.com (retrieved June 6, 2011).

22. J. Welch, S. Welch, "Layoffs: HR's Moment of Truth," *Businessweek* (March 23 and 30, 2009), p. 104.

23. C.O. Trevor, A.J. Nyberg, "Keeping Your Headcount When All About You Are Losing Theirs: Downsizing, Voluntary Turnover Rates, and the Moderating Role of HR Practices," *Academy of Management Journal* (2008), 51(2), pp. 259–276.

24. S.Y. Moon, S.I. Na, "Psychological and Organizational Variables Associated With Workplace Learning in Small and Medium Manufacturing Businesses in Korea," *Asia Pacific Education Review* (2009), 10(3), pp. 327–336.

25. H. Yang, "Efficiency Wages and Subjective Performance Pay," *Economic Inquiry* (2008), 46(2), pp. 179–196.

26. http://handle.dtic.mil/100.2/ADA499480 (retrieved May 19, 2011).

27. T. Davis, G. Gabris, "Strategic Compensation: Utilizing Efficiency Wages in the Public Sector to Achieve Desirable Organizational Outcomes," *Review of Public Personnel Administration* (December 2008), 28(4), pp. 327–348.

28. S. Anand, P.R. Vidyarthi, R.C. Linden, D.M. Rousseau, "Good Citizens in Poor-Quality Relationships: Idiosyncratic Deals as a Substitute for Relationship Quality," *Academy of Management Journal* (2010), 53(5), pp. 970–988.

29. P.M. Madhani, "Rebalancing Fixed and Variable Pay in a Sales Organization: A Business Cycle Perspective," *Compensation Benefits Review* (2010), 42(3), pp. 179–189.

30. M. Diaz-Fernandez, A. Lopez-Cabrales, R. Valle-Cabrera, "What Companies Pay For: The Strategic Role of Employee Competencies," *European Journal of International Management* (2009), 3(4), pp. 439–456.

31. S.A. Culbert, "Get Rid of the Performance Review," *Wall Street Journal* (October 20, 2008), p. R4.

32. M. Conlin, "The Case for Unequal Perks," *Businessweek* (March 23 and 30, 2009), pp. 54–55.

33. C.B. Cadsby, F. Song, F. Tapon, "Sorting and Incentive Effects of Pay for Performance: An Experimental Investigation," *Academy of Management Journal* (2007), 50(2), pp. 387–405.

34. Y.-C. Wei, T.-S. Han, I.-C. Hsu, "High-Performance HR Practices and OCB: A Cross-Level Investigation of a Causal Path," *The International Journal of Human Resource Management* (2010), 21(10), pp. 1631–1648.

35. J. Helyar, D. MacMillan, "In Tech, Poaching Is the Sincerest Form of Flattery," *Businessweek* (March 7–13, 2011), pp. 17–18.

36. K. Blanchard, D. Hutson, E. Wills, *The One Minute Entrepreneur* (New York: Currency, 2008).

37. E. Krassoi Peach, T. Stanley, "Efficiency Wages, Productivity and Simultaneity: A Meta-Regression Analysis," *Journal of Labor Research* (2009), 30, pp. 262–268.

38. T. Davis, G. Gabris, "Strategic Compensation: Utilizing Efficiency Wages in the Public Sector to Achieve Desirable Organizational Outcomes," *Review of Public Personnel Administration* (December 2008), 28(4), pp. 327–348.

39. K. Evans, "A Nation of Quitters? Could Be a Good Sign," *Wall Street Journal* (February 8, 2011), p. C1.

40. G. Colvin, "How Are Most Admired Companies Different? They Invest in People and Keep Them Employed—Even in a Downturn," *Fortune* (March 22, 2010), p. 82.

41. J. Nickerson, T. Zenger, "Envy, Comparison Costs, and the Economic Theory of the Firm," *Strategic Management Journal* (2008), 29(13), pp. 1429–1449.

42. S. Ladika, "Decompressing Pay," *HR Magazine* (December 2005), 50(12), pp. 79–82.

43. S. Fischer, E. Steiger, "Exploring the Effects of Unequal and Secretive Pay," *Jena Economic Research Papers* (2009), 107, p. 25.

44. M. Wesson et al., "Exposing Pay Secrecy," *Academy of Management Review* (2007), 32(1), pp. 55–71.

45. R. Daft, D. Marcic, *Understanding Management*, 5th ed. (Mason, OH: South-Western, 2007).

46. www.dol.gov/whd/regs/statutes/0002.fair.pdf (retrieved May 21, 2011).

47. www.dol.gov/compliance/guide/minwage.htm (retrieved May 21, 2011).

48. www.dol.gov/whd/regs/compliance/whdfs23.pdf (retrieved May 21, 2011).

49. www.dol.gov/compliance/guide/minwage.htm (retrieved May 21, 2011).

50. Ibid.

51. www.dol.gov/whd/regs/compliance/whdfs15.pdf (retrieved May 21, 2011).

52. www.dol.gov/elaws/esa/flsa/screen75.asp (retrieved May 21, 2011).

53. www.dol.gov/whd/regs/compliance/fairpay/fs17g_salary.htm (retrieved May 21, 2011).

54. www.dol.gov/whd/regs/compliance/fairpay/fs17h_highly_comp.pdf (retrieved May 21, 2011).

55. www.dol.gov/elaws/esa/flsa/screen75.asp (retrieved May 22, 2011).

56. www.dol.gov/elaws/faq/esa/flsa/016.htm (retrieved May 22, 2011).

57. www.dol.gov/compliance/guide/childlbr.htm (retrieved May 22, 2011).

58. www.dol.gov/whd/statistics/2008FiscalYear.htm (retrieved May 22, 2011).

59. www.dol.gov/compliance/guide/minwage.htm#Penalites (retrieved May 22, 2011).

60. www.dol.gov/whd/minwage/america.htm (retrieved May 22, 2011).

61. www.eeoc.gov/eeoc/newsroom/equalpayday2011.cfm (retrieved May 20, 2011).

62. http://law.jrank.org/pages/5478/Comparable-Worth.html (retrieved May 24, 2011).

63. www.dol.gov/oasam/programs/history/flsa1938.htm (retrieved May 24, 2011).

64. www.haygroup.com/ww/services/index.aspx?id=1529 (retrieved May 24, 2011).

65. www.shrm.org/Research/Articles/Articles/Pages/Compensation_20Series_20Part_20II__20Job_20Evaluation.aspx (retrieved May 24, 2011).

66. Ibid.

67. www.shrm.org/Education/hreducation/Pages/DesigningaPayStructureACaseStudyandIntegratedExercises.aspx (retrieved May 24, 2011).

68. Ibid.

69. M. Guadalupe, J. Wulf, "The Flattening Firm and Product Market Competition: The Effect of Trade Liberalization on Corporate Hierarchies," *American Economic Journal: Applied Economics* (2010), 2(4), pp. 105–127.

70. www.shrm.org/TemplatesTools/HowtoGuides/Pages/HowtoEstablishSalaryRanges.aspx (retrieved May 26, 2011).

71. www.shrm.org/hrdisciplines/compensation/Articles/Pages/CMS_000067.aspx (retrieved May 26, 2011).

72. N. Landrum, S. Edwards, *Sustainable Business, An Executive's Primer* (New York: Business Expert Press, 2009).

73. S.H. Clain, "How Living Wage Legislation Affects U.S. Poverty Rates," *Journal of Labor Research* (2008), 29, pp. 205–218.

74. http://ezinearticles.com/?Economics-101—Minimum-Wage-and-Living-Wage&id=4571254 (retrieved October 29, 2011).

75. http://articles.moneycentral.msn.com/CollegeAndFamily/LoveAndMoney/LivingWageHowAbout9AnHour.aspx?page=1 (retrieved May 30, 2011).

76. T. Shelton, "Global Compensation Strategies: Managing and Administering Split Pay for an Expatriate Workforce," *Compensation and Benefits Review* (January/February 2008), 40, pp. 56–60.

77. ORC Worldwide, *2006 Worldwide Survey of International Assignment Policies and Practices* (New York, 2007).

78. www2.hewittassociates.com/Intl/NA/en-US/AboutHewitt/Newsroom/PressReleaseDetail.aspx?cid=9000 (retrieved May 30, 2011).

Chapter 12

1. R.E. Johnson, C.D. Chang, L.O. Yang, "Commitment and Motivation at Work: The Relevance of Employee Identity and Regulatory Focus," *Academy of Management Review* (2010), 35(2), pp. 226–245.

2. D. Hantula, "What Performance Management Needs Is a Good Theory: A Behavioral Perspective," *Industrial & Organizational Psychology* (2011), 4(2), pp. 194–197.

3. www.sibson.com/publications/surveysandstudies/P4P.pdf (retrieved June 1, 2011).

4. R. Gray, "The Return on Incentives," *Human Resources* (October 2010), pp. 49–50, 52.

5. Hay Group, *The Changing Face of Reward* (2010), www.haygroup.com/downloads/ww/misc/cfr_global_report.pdf (retrieved October 31, 2011).

6. R. Pinheiro, "SuperFreakonomics: Global Cooling, Patriotic Prostitutes, and Why Suicide Bombers Should Buy Life Insurance," *Academy of Management Perspectives* (2011), 25(25), pp. 86–87.

7. E. Morrison, "From the Editors," *Academy of Management Journal* (2010), 53(5), pp. 932–936.

8. J. Kragl, "Group vs. Individual Performance Pay in Relational Employment Contracts When Workers Are Envious," *European Business School Research Paper No. 09-09* (January 13, 2010).

9. R. Karlgaard, "Scary Smart," *Forbes* (October 25, 2010), p. 26.

10. J.J. Martocchio, *Strategic Compensation* (Upper Saddle River, NJ: Prentice Hall, 2011), pp. 84–85.

11. C. Rose, "Charlie Rose Talks to Alan Mulally," *Businessweek* (August 1–7, 2011), p. 27.

12. R.E. Johnson, C.D. Chang, L.O. Yang, "Commitment and Motivation at Work: The Relevance of Employee Identity and Regulatory Focus," *Academy of Management Review* (2010), 35(2), pp. 226–245.

13. S. Anand, P.R. Vidyarthi, R.C. Linden, D.M. Rousseau, "Good Citizens in Poor-Quality Relationships: Idiosyncratic Deals as a Substitute for Relationship Quality," *Academy of Management Journal* (2010), 53(5), pp. 970–988.

14. J.J. Martocchio, *Strategic Compensation* (Upper Saddle River, NJ: Prentice Hall, 2011), p. 89.

15. S. Anand, P.R. Vidyarthi, R.C. Linden, D.M. Rousseau, "Good Citizens in Poor-Quality Relationships: Idiosyncratic Deals as a Substitute for Relationship Quality," *Academy of Management Journal* (2010), 53(5), pp. 970–988.

16. C. Chynoweth, "How to Provide Incentives for Your Staff," *The Times* (London, July 8, 2009), p. 49.

17. J.J. Martocchio, *Strategic Compensation* (Upper Saddle River, NJ: Prentice Hall), p. 293.

18. C. Heinrich, "False or Fitting Recognition? The Use of High Performance Bonuses in Motivating Organizational Achievements," *Journal of Policy Analysis and Management* (2007), 26(2), pp. 281–304.

19. R. Hogarth, M. Villeval, " Intermittent Reinforcement and the Persistence of Behavior: Experimental Evidence," *Groupe d'Analyse et de Théorie Économique Working Paper No. 1018* (July 1, 2010).

20. Ibid.

21. J. Helyar, D. MacMillan, "In Tech, Poaching Is the Sincerest Form of Flattery," *Businessweek* (March 7–13, 2011), pp. 17–18.

22. M. Mallin, E. Bolman Pullins, "The Moderating Effect of Control Systems on the Relationship Between Commission and Salesperson Intrinsic Motivation in a Customer Oriented Environment," *Industrial Marketing Management* (October 2009), 38(7), pp. 769–777.

23. www.allbusiness.com/sales/360273-1.html (retrieved June 1, 2011).

24. http://edweb.sdsu.edu/people/ARossett/pie/Interventions/od_1.htm (retrieved June 1, 2011).

25. S. Park, M. Sturman, "The Relative Effects of Merit Pay, Bonuses, and Long-Term Incentives on Future Job Performance," *Cornell University Compensation Research Initiative, Paper 7* (January 1, 2009).

26. F. Christensen, J. Manley, L. Laurence, "The Allocation of Merit Pay in Academia," *Economics Bulletin* (2011), 31(2), pp. 1548–1562.

27. K. Scott, J. Shaw, M. Duffy, "Merit Pay Raises and Organization-Based Self-Esteem," *Journal of Organizational Behavior* (2008), 29(7), pp. 967–980.

28. W. Neilson, J. Stowe, "Piece-Rate Contracts for Other-Regarding Workers," *Economic Inquiry* (2010), 48(3), pp. 575–586.

29. K. Pokorny, "Pay—but Do Not Pay Too Much: An Experimental Study on the Impact of Incentives," *Journal of Economic Behavior & Organization* (2008), 66(2), pp. 251–264.

30. R. Heneman, *Strategic Reward Management: Design, Implementation, and Evaluation* (Information Age Publishing, 2002), p. 85.

31. J. Paterson, "Breeding Loyalty," *Employee Benefits* (February 2011), pp. 27–28.

32. C. Chynoweth, "How to Provide Incentives for Your Staff," *The Times* (London, July 8, 2009), p. 49.

33. S. Anand, P.R. Vidyarthi, R.C. Linden, D.M. Rousseau, "Good Citizens in Poor-Quality Relationships: Idiosyncratic Deals as a Substitute for Relationship Quality," *Academy of Management Journal* (2010), 53(5), pp. 970–988.

34. R.E. Johnson, C.D. Chang, L.O. Yang, "Commitment and Motivation at Work: The Relevance of Employee Identity and Regulatory Focus," *Academy of Management Review* (2010), 35(2), pp. 226–245.

35. D.R. Hekman, G.A. Bigley, H.K. Steensma, J.F. Hereford, "Combined Effects of Organizational and Professional Identification on the Reciprocity Dynamic for Professional Employees," *Academy of Management Journal* (2009), 52(3), pp. 506–526.

36. "Using the Maslow Hierarchy of Needs Theory," www .mindtools.com (retrieved June 7, 2011).

37. K.H. Queen, "Carrot or Stick?" *Costco Connection* (December 2010), pp. 19–20.

38. A. Bayo-Moriones, M. Larraza-Kintana, "Profit-Sharing Plans and Affective Commitment: Does the Context Matter?" *Human Resource Management* (2009), 48, pp. 207–226.

39. Ibid.

40. Alexander C. Gardner, "Goal Setting and Gainsharing: The Evidence on Effectiveness," *Compensation & Benefits Review* (2011), 20(10), pp. 1–9.

41. Ibid.

42. S. Freeman, "Effects of ESOP Adoption and Employee Ownership: Thirty Years of Research and Experience," *University of Pennsylvania Organizational Dynamics Working Papers #07-01* (January 2007).

43. www.nceo.org/main/article.php/id/30/ (retrieved June 3, 2011).

44. Y. Hochberg, L. Lindsey, "Incentives, Targeting, and Firm Performance: An Analysis of Non-executive Stock Options," *The Review of Financial Studies* (2010), 23(11), pp. 4148–4186.

45. C. Chynoweth, "How to Provide Incentives for Your Staff," *The Times* (London, July 8, 2009), p. 49.

46. J. Sammer, "Weighing Pay Incentives," *HR Magazine* (June 2007), 52(6), pp. 64–68.

47. T. Daniel, G. Metcalf, "Fundamentals of Employee Recognition," *SHRM White Paper* (May 1, 2005).

48. J. Sammer, "Weighing Pay Incentives," *HR Magazine* (June 2007), 52(6), pp. 64–68.

49. Ibid.

50. J. Paterson, "Breeding Loyalty," *Employee Benefits* (February 2011), pp. 27–28.

51. J. Moniz, "The Basics for Building and Maintaining Incentive Plans at Smaller Firms," *Compensation Benefits Review* (July/August 2010) ,42(4), pp. 256–264.

52. R. Pinheiro, "SuperFreakonomics: Global Cooling, Patriotic Prostitutes, and Why Suicide Bombers Should Buy Life Insurance," *Academy of Management Perspectives* (2011), 25(25), pp. 86–87.

53. M. Kroumova, M. Lazarova, "Broad-Based Incentive Plans, HR Practices and Company Performance," *Human Resource Management Journal* (2009), 19(4), pp. 355–374.

54. www.shrm.org/hrdisciplines/compensation/Articles/Pages/ EntitlementPay.aspx (retrieved June 4, 2011).

55. T. Libby, L. Thorne, "The Influence of Incentive Structure on Group Performance in Assembly Lines and Teams," *Behavioral Research in Accounting* (2009), 21(2), pp. 57–72.

56. D. Cardrain, "Put Success in Sight," *HR Magazine* (May 2003), 48(5), p. 84.

57. J. Halpern, "The New Me Generation," *The Boston Globe* (September 30, 2007).

58. www.shrm.org/hrdisciplines/compensation/Articles/Pages/ EntitlementPay.aspx (retrieved June 4, 2011).

59. R. Hogarth, M. Villeval, "Intermittent Reinforcement and the Persistence of Behavior: Experimental Evidence," *Groupe d'Analyse et de Théorie Économique, Working Paper No. 1018* (July 1, 2010).

60. E. Deci, R. Ryan, "Facilitating Optimal Motivation and Psychological Well-Being Across Life's Domains," *Canadian Psychology/Psychologie Canadienne* (February 2008), 49(1), pp. 14–23.

61. Ibid.

62. Hay Group, *The Changing Face of Reward* (2010), www .haygroup.com/downloads/ww/misc/cfr_global_report. pdf (retrieved October 31, 2011).

63. www.sibson.com/publications/surveysandstudies/P4P.pdf (retrieved June 1, 2011).

64. J. Sammer, "Weighing Pay Incentives," *HR Magazine* (June 2007), 52(6), pp. 64–68.

65. A. Thompson, Jr., A. Strickland, III, J. Gamble, *Crafting and Executing Strategy*, 17th ed. (New York: McGraw-Hill Irwin, New York, 2010), p. 379.

66. J. Sammer, "Weighing Pay Incentives," *HR Magazine* (June 2007), 52(6), pp. 64–68.

67. www.sibson.com/publications/surveysandstudies/P4P.pdf (retrieved June 1, 2011).

68. M. Rosenthal, R. Adams Dudley, "Pay for Performance: Will the Latest Payment Trend Improve Care?" *Journal of the American Medical Association* (2007), 297(7), pp. 740–744.

69. J. Sammer, "Weighing Pay Incentives," *HR Magazine* (June 2007), 52(6), pp. 64–68.

70. Ibid.

71. www.sibson.com/publications/surveysandstudies/P4P.pdf (retrieved June 1, 2011).

72. A. Thompson, Jr., A. Strickland, III, J. Gamble, *Crafting and Executing Strategy*, 17th ed. (New York: McGraw-Hill Irwin, p. 379.

73. www.shrm.org/hrdisciplines/compensation/Articles/Pages/PinkMoney.aspx (retrieved June 3, 2011).

74. www.fastcodesign.com/1663137/3ms-key-to-innovation-give-everyone-the-day-off (retrieved June 3, 2011).

75. A. Thompson, Jr., A. Strickland, III, J. Gamble, *Crafting and Executing Strategy*, 17th ed. (New York: McGraw-Hill Irwin, 2010), p. 379.

76. The Atlantic, "The CEO Conundrum," *Businessweek* (June 15, 2009), p. 12.

77. Ibid.

78. www.washingtonpost.com/business/steve-jobs-resigns-as-apple-ceo-tim-cook-named-successor/2011/08/25/gIQA-zLCsgJ_story.html (retrieved August 27, 2011).

79. R.S. Rubin, E.C. Dierdorff, "On the Road to Abilene: Time to Manage Agreement About MBA Curricular Relevance," *Academy of Management Learning & Education* (2011), 10(1), pp. 148–161.

80. M. J. Canyan, "Executive Compensation and Incentives," *Academy of Management Perspectives* (2006), 20(1), pp. 25–44.

81. M. Krantz, B. Hansen, "CEO Pay Soars While Worker's Pay Stalls," *USA Today* (April 1, 2011), pp. B1–B2.

82. Executive Compensation Group Advisory, *Vedder Price P.C.* (July 2010).

83. www.shrm.org/hrdisciplines/compensation/Articles/Pages/PayRatios.aspx (retrieved June 4, 2011).

84. Ibid.

85. www.ft.com/intl/cms/s/0/304564c4-531d-11e0-86e6-00144feab49a.html#axzz1PB0uFmWB (retrieved June 6, 2011).

86. Executive Compensation Group Advisory, *Vedder Price P.C.* (July 2010).

87. www.businesswire.com/news/home/20110203006706/en/Companies-Set-Failing-Grades-Pay-Performance-Test (retrieved June 6, 2011).

88. M. Friedman, "The Social Responsibility of Business Is to Increase Profits," *Corporate Ethics and Corporate Governance* (2007), Part IV, pp. 173–178.

89. www.shrm.org/hrdisciplines/compensation/Articles/Pages/CMS_014050.aspx (retrieved June 4, 2011).

90. Ibid.

91. www.salary.com/advice/layouthtmls/advl_display_nocat_Ser300_Par454.html (retrieved June 6, 2011).

92. www.shrm.org/hrdisciplines/compensation/Articles/Pages/PerformTies.aspx (retrieved June 4, 2011).

93. Ibid.

94. www.shrm.org/hrdisciplines/compensation/Articles/Pages/FinancialFirms.aspx (retrieved June 4, 2011).

95. Ibid.

96. Hay Group, *Work on Your Winning Strategy* (2010), www.haygroup.com/downloads/ww/misc/variable_pay_report.pdf (retrieved October 31, 2011).

97. Ibid.

98. J. Helyar, D. MacMillan, "In Tech, Poaching Is the Sincerest Form of Flattery," *Businessweek* (March 7–13, 2011), pp. 17–18.

99. J. Arbaugh, L. Cox, S.M. Camp, "Employee Equity, Incentive Compensation, and Growth in Entrepreneurial Firms," *New England Journal of Entrepreneurship* (2004), 7(1), pp. 15–25.

100. http://graphics8.nytimes.com/packages/pdf/business/20110428-docs/allstate.pdf (retrieved June 11, 2011).

101. K.Y. Ng, L.V. Dyne, S. Ang, "From Experience to Experiential Learning: Cultural Intelligence as a Learning Capability for Global Leader Development," *Academy of Management Learning & Education* (2009), 8(1), pp. 511–526.

102. C. Rose, "Charlie Rose Talks to Mike Duke," *Businessweek* (December 2–6, 2010), p. 30.

103. Hay Group, Work on Your Winning Strategy, (2010), www.haygroup.com/downloads/ww/misc/variable_pay_report.pdf (retrieved October 31, 2011).

104. M. Segalla, D. Rouzies, M. Besson, B. Weitz, "A Cross-National Investigation of Incentive Sales Compensation," *International Journal of Research in Marketing* (2006), 23(4), pp. 419–433.

105. S. Fong, M. Shaffer, "The Dimensionality and Determinants of Pay Satisfaction: A Cross-Cultural Investigation of a Group Incentive Plan," *International Journal of Human Resource Management* (2003), 14(4), pp. 559–580.

Chapter 13

1. www.bls.gov/news.release/ecec.nr0.htm (retrieved June 29, 2011).

2. D.B. Montgomery, C.A. Ramus, "Calibrating MBA Job Preferences for the 21st Century," *Academy of Management Learning & Education* (2011), 10(1), pp. 9–26.

3. G. Moran, "The Business of Better Benefits," *Entrepreneur* (May 2011), pp. 81–82.

4. J.C. Santora, "The Psychology of Defined-Benefits Pensions: When Do They Affect Employee Behavior?" *Academy of Management Perspectives* (2010), 24(2), pp. 85–86.

5. G. Moran, "The Business of Better Benefits," *Entrepreneur* (May 2011), pp. 81–82.

6. K. Blanchard, D. Hutson, E. Wills, *The One Minute Entrepreneur* (New York: Currency, 2008).

7. J.C. Santora, "The Psychology of Defined-Benefits Pensions: When Do They Affect Employee Behavior?" *Academy of Management Perspectives* (2010) 24(2), pp. 85–86.

8. G. Moran, "The Business of Better Benefits," *Entrepreneur* (May 2011), pp. 81–82.

9. www.ssa.gov/OACT/STATS/table3c3.html (retrieved June 29, 2011).

10. www.cbo.gov/ftpdocs/108xx/doc10871/Chapter4.shtml (retrieved June 29, 2011).

11. www.ssa.gov/oact/cola/cbb.html (retrieved June 30, 2011).

12. http://ssa-custhelp.ssa.gov/app/answers/detail/a_id/356/kw/eligibility (retrieved June 30, 2011).

13. www.socialsecurity.gov/dibplan/dqualify3.htm (retrieved June 30, 2011).

14. http://stats.oecd.org/Index.aspx?QueryId=29820 (retrieved June 30, 2011).

15. K. Blanchard, D. Hutson, E. Wills, *The One Minute Entrepreneur* (New York: Currency, 2008).

16. www.socialsecurity.gov/pubs/retirechart.htm (retrieved June 30, 2011).

17. www.socialsecurity.gov/oact/trsum/index.html (retrieved June 30, 2011).

18. Ibid.

19. National Academy of Social Insurance, *Workers' Compensation: Benefits, Coverage, and Costs, 2008* (Washington DC: Author, September 2010), p. 8.

20. National Academy of Social Insurance, *Workers' Compensation: Benefits, Coverage, and Costs, 2008* (Washington DC: Author, September 2010), p. 5.

21. http://workforcesecurity.doleta.gov/unemploy/pdf/uilawcompar/2010/financing.pdf (retrieved October 31, 2011).

22. Ibid.

23. www.dol.gov/whd/fmla/index.htm (retrieved July 2, 2011).

24. www.law.cornell.edu/uscode/29/usc_sec_29_00002614----000-.html (retrieved August 31, 2011).

25. http://finduslaw.com/family_and_medical_leave_act_fmla_29_us_code_chapter_28 (retrieved July 2, 2011).

26. www.shrm.org/Research/SurveyFindings/Documents/FMLA%20And%20Its%20Impact%20On%20Organizations%20Survey%20Report.pdf (retrieved July 2, 2011).

27. www.bls.gov/news.release/ecec.nr0.htm (retrieved July 2, 2011).

28. www.smartmoney.com/plan/insurance/10-things-your-health-insurance-company-wont-say-1299280540906/ (retrieved October 31, 2011).

29. www.law.cornell.edu/uscode/html/uscode29/usc_sup_01_29_10_18_20_I_30_B_40_6.html (retrieved July 5, 2011).

30. www.hhs.gov/ocr/privacy/ (retrieved July 5, 2011).

31. www.hhs.gov/ocr/privacy/hipaa/understanding/coveredentities/index.html (retrieved July 5, 2011).

32. www.shrm.org/LegalIssues/FederalResources/Pages/BenefitPlanChanges.aspx (retrieved October 31, 2011).

33. www.pbgc.gov/wr/benefits/guaranteed-benefits.html (retrieved July 5, 2011).

34. Society for Human Resource Management, *Examining Paid Leave in the Workplace,* Survey Report (October 2008).

35. www.bls.gov/news.release/ecec.t01.htm (retrieved July 5, 2011).

36. Society for Human Resource Management, *Examining Paid Leave in the Workplace,* Survey Report (October 2008).

37. http://money.cnn.com/2007/06/12/pf/vacation_days_worldwide/ (retrieved July 5, 2011).

38. E. DiNovella, "Off on Vacation," *Progressive* (July 2009), 73(7), pp. 24–26.

39. D. Etzion, "Annual Vacation: Duration of Relief From Job Stressors and Burnout," *Anxiety, Stress & Coping* (June 2003), 16(2), p. 213.

40. Society for Human Resource Management, "Examining Paid Leave in the Workplace," Survey Report (October 2008).

41. www.bls.gov/news.release/pdf/ebs2.pdf (retrieved July 5, 2011).

42. www.cms.gov/NationalHealthExpendData/downloads/tables.pdf (retrieved July 8, 2011).

43. Bureau of Labor Statistics, reported in G. Moran, "The Business of Better Benefits," *Entrepreneur* (May 2011), p. 82.

44. www.irs.gov/pub/irs-pdf/p969.pdf (retrieved August 31, 2011).

45. Bureau of Labor Statistics, reported in G. Moran, "The Business of Better Benefits," *Entrepreneur* (May 2011), p. 82.

46. C. Santora, "The Psychology of Defined-Benefits Pensions: When Do They Affect Employee Behavior," *Academy of Management Perspectives* (2010), 24(2), pp. 85–86.

47. C. Rose, "Charlie Rose Talks to Alan Mulally," *Businessweek* (August 1–7, 2011), p. 27.

48. Blanchard, D. Hutson, E. Wills, *The One Minute Entrepreneur* (New York: Currency, 2008).

49. www.irs.gov/retirement/article/0,,id=202510,00.html (retrieved July 8, 2011).

50. www.dol.gov/ebsa/publications/sepplans.html (retrieved July 8, 2011).

51. "Group-Term Life Insurance: How to Keep These Benefits Plans in Compliance," *Payroll Practitioner's Monthly* (May 2007)5, pp. 1, 4–9.

52. N. Griswold, "The Death of Worksite Voluntary Benefits," *Employee Benefit Advisor* (February 2011), 9(2), pp. 26–28.

53. http://pueblo.gsa.gov/cic_text/employ/lt-disability/insurance.htm (retrieved July 8, 2011).

54. Ibid.

55. B. Shutan, "In View of Voluntary Value," *Employee Benefit Advisor* (December 2009), 7(12), pp. 26–29.

56. www.metlife.com/about/press-room/us-press-releases/2010/index.html?SCOPE=Metlife&MSHiC=65001&L=10&W=cancer%20insurance%20&Pre=%3CFONT%20STYLE%3D%22background%3A%23ffff00%22%3E&Post=%3C/FONT%3E&compID=24584 (retrieved July 11, 2011).

57. N. Griswold, "The Death of Worksite Voluntary Benefits," *Employee Benefit Advisor* (February 2011), 9(2), pp. 26–28.

58. B. Shutan, "In View of Voluntary Value," *Employee Benefit Advisor* (December 2009), 7(12), pp. 26–29

59. G. Moran, "The Business of Better Benefits," *Entrepreneur* (May 2011), pp. 81–82.

60. Metropolitan Life Insurance Company, *9th Annual Study of Employee Benefits Trends* (2011) p. 3.

61. E. Halkos, "The Importance of Benefits Communication—A Key Differentiator," *Voluntary Benefits Magazine* (June 1, 2011), www.voluntarybenefitsmagazine.com/article-detail.php?issue=issue-24&article=the-importance-of-benefits (retrieved July 12, 2011).

62. www.shrm.org/Research/SurveyFindings/Articles/Documents/10-0280%20Employee%20Benefits%20Survey%20Report-FNL.pdf (retrieved July 12, 2011).

63. www.metlife.com/assets/institutional/services/insights-and-tools/ebts/intl-ebts/intl-ebts.pdf (retrieved July 12, 2011).

64. Ibid.

65. Ibid.

66. N. Landrum, S. Edwards, "Sustainable Business: An Executive's Primer," *Business Expert Press* (New York, 2009), p. 32.

67. http://arkansasenergy.org/industry/incentives-and-programs/home-energy-assistance-loan-%28heal%29-program.aspx (retrieved July 28, 2011).

68. N. Landrum, S. Edwards, "Sustainable Business: An Executive's Primer," *Business Expert Press* (New York, 2009), p. 32.

Chapter 14

1. "A Critical Safety," *Wall Street Journal* (July 23, 2010), pp. A1, A4.

2. G. Chazan, F. Casselman, B. Casselman, "Safety and Cost Drives Clashed as CEO Hayward Remade BP," *Wall Street Journal* (June 30, 2010), pp. A1, A18.

3. S. Armour, "Labor, Beyond the Reach of the Republicans?" *Businessweek* (Winter 2011), pp. 57–58.

4. www.osha.gov/pls/oshaweb/owadisp.show_document?p_id=2743&p_table=OSHACT (retrieved July 20, 2011).

5. www.osha.gov/doc/outreachtraining/htmlfiles/introsha
    .html (retrieved July 20, 2011).

6. www.bls.gov/news.release/archives/osh2_11092010
    .pdf (retrieved July 20, 2011).

7. www.osha.gov/about.html (retrieved July 20, 2011).

8. www.osha.gov/Publications/3439at-a-glance.pdf (retrieved
    July 20, 2011).

9. www.osha.gov/pls/oshaweb/owadisp.show
    _document?p_table=STANDARDS&p_id=10099#
    1910.1200%28g%29 (retrieved July 22, 2011).

10. www.osha.gov/Publications/osha3000.pdf (retrieved July
    22, 2011).

11. http://cdc.gov/niosh/about.html (retrieved July 22, 2011).

12. www.shrm.org/LegalIssues/StateandLocal
    Resources/StateandLocalStatutesandRegulations/
    Documents/stateposting.pdf (retrieved July 22, 2011).

13. R. Ilies, K.S. Wilson, D.T. Wagner, "The Spillover of
    Daily Job Satisfaction Onto Employees' Family Lives: The
    Facilitating Role of Work-Family Integration," *Academy of
    Management Journal* (2009), 52(1), pp. 87–102.

14. S. Covy, "Time Management," *Fortune* (September 19,
    2009), pp. 28–29.

15. M. Conlin, "Work-Life Balance," *Businessweek* (December 7,
    2009), p. 57.

16. G.E. Kreiner, E. Hollensbe, M.L. Sheep, "Balance Borders
    and Bridges: Negotiating the Work-Home Interface Via
    Boundary Work Tactics," *Academy of Management Journal*
    (2009), 52(4), pp. 704–730.

17. A.M. Grant, J.E. Dutton, B.D. Rosso, "Giving
    Commitment: Employee Support Programs and the
    Prosocial Sensemaking Process," *Academy of Management
    Journal* (2008), 51(5), pp. 898–918.

18. www.bls.gov/opub/cwc/cm20110519ar01p1.htm
    (retrieved July 25, 2011).

19. G. Hargrave et al., "EAP Treatment Impact on Presenteeism
    and Absenteeism: Implications for Return on Investment,"
    Journal of Workplace Behavioral Health (2008), 23(3),
    pp. 283–293.

20. "EAP Effectiveness and ROI," *EASNA Research Notes*
    (October 2009), 1(3).

21. G. Moran, "The Business of Better Benefits," *Entrepreneur*
    (May 2011), pp. 81–82.

22. L. Berry, A. Mirabito, W. Baun, "What's the Hard Return
    on Employee Wellness Programs?" *Harvard Business
    Review* (2010), 88(12), pp. 104–112.

23. Ibid.

24. www.osha.gov/SLTC/ergonomics/ (retrieved July 29,
    2011).

25. www.cdc.gov/workplacehealthpromotion/assessment/poten
    tial_data/injuries.html (retrieved July 29, 2011).

26. www.osha.gov/ergonomics/FAQs-external.html (retrieved
    July 29, 2011).

27. www.osha.gov/SLTC/ergonomics/guidelines.html
    (retrieved July 29, 2011).

28. www.osha.gov/SLTC/ergonomics/faqs.html (retrieved July
    29, 2011).

29. http://ehs.okstate.edu/kopykit/Office%20Ergonomics1
    .PDF (retrieved July 29, 2011).

30. http://ergo.human.cornell.edu/ (retrieved August 1, 2011).

31. C.M. Barnes, J.R. Hollenbeck, "Sleep Deprivation and
    Decision-Making Teams: Burning the Midnight Oil or
    Playing With Fire?" *Academy of Management Review*
    (2009), 34(1), pp. 56–66.

32. K.E. Spaeder, "Time to De-Stress," *Entrepreneur* (October
    2008), p. 24.

33. S.S. Culbertson, "Absenteeism: Escaping an Aversive
    Workplace or Responding to Resulting Illness?" *Academy of
    Management Perspective* (2009), 23(1), pp. 77–79.

34. L. Holloway, "Stress Case," *Entrepreneur* (August 2008),
    p. 35.

35. S.S. Culbertson, "Absenteeism: Escaping an Aversive
    Workplace or Responding to Resulting Illness?" *Academy of
    Management Perspectives* (2009), 23(1), pp. 77–79.

36. K.E. Spaeder, "Time to De-Stress," *Entrepreneur* (October
    2008), p. 24.

37. L. Holloway, "Stress Case," *Entrepreneur* (August 2008),
    p. 35.

38. S.S. Culbertson, "Absenteeism: Escaping an Aversive
    Workplace or Responding to Resulting Illness?" *Academy of
    Management Perspective* (2009), 23(1), pp. 77–79.

39. Staff, "Preserve Your Health Like Your Wealth," *Wall Street
    Journal* (April 15, 2009), pp. D5–D6.

40. L.S. Luscher, M.W. Lewis, "Organizational Change
    and Managerial Sensemaking: Working Through
    Paradox," *Academy of Management Journal* (2008), 51(2),
    pp. 221–240.

41. M. Jokisaari, J.E. Nurmi, "Change in Newcomers' Supervisor
    Support and Socialization Outcomes After Organizational
    Entry," *Academy of Management Journal* (2009), 52(3),
    pp. 527–544.

42. E. Monsen, R.W. Boss, "The Impact of Strategic
    Entrepreneurship Inside the Organization: Examining Job

Stress and Employee Retention," *Entrepreneurship Theory and Practice* (2009), 33(1), pp. 71–104.

43. K.E. Spaeder, "Time to De-Stress," *Entrepreneur* (October 2008), p. 24.

44. L. Holloway, "Stress Case," *Entrepreneur* (August 2008), p. 35.

45. S.D. Sidle, "Workplace Stress Management Interventions: What Works Best?" *Academy of Management Perspective* (2008), 22(3), pp. 111–112.

46. Staff, "Preserve Your Health Like Your Wealth," *Wall Street Journal* (April 15, 2009), pp. D5–D6.

47. Ibid.

48. Ibid.

49. S.D. Sidle, "Workplace Stress Management Interventions: What Works Best?" *Academy of Management Perspective* (2008), 22(3), pp. 111–112.

50. Staff, "Preserve Your Health Like Your Wealth," *Wall Street Journal* (April 15, 2009), pp. D5–D6.

51. C.M Barnes, J.R. Hollenbeck, "Sleep Deprivation and Decision-Making Teams: Burning the Midnight Oil or Playing With Fire?" *Academy of Management Review* (2009), 34(1), pp. 56–66.

52. Staff, "Preserve Your Health Like Your Wealth," *Wall Street Journal* (April 15, 2009), pp. D5–D6.

53. Staff, "When Sleep Leaves You Tired," *Wall Street Journal* (June 9, 2009), p. D5.

54. Staff, "Over 34% of Americans," *Wall Street Journal* (January 10–11, 2009), p. A1.

55. R. Tomsho, "Bulging Waist Carries Risk," *Wall Street Journal* (November 13, 2008), p. D4.

56. C. Arnst, "Taxing the Rich—Food, That Is," *Businessweek* (February 23, 2009), p. 62.

57. Staff, "Preserve Your Health Like Your Wealth," *Wall Street Journal* (April 15, 2009), pp. D5–D6.

58. S.D. Sidle, "Workplace Stress Management Interventions: What Works Best?" *Academy of Management Perspective* (2008), 22(3), pp. 111–112.

59. J. Welch, S. Welch, "Finding Your Inner Courage," *Businessweek* (February 23, 2009), p. 84.

60. Staff, "Preserve Your Health Like Your Wealth," *Wall Street Journal* (April 15, 2009), pp. D5–D6.

61. S. Covy, "Time Management," *Fortune* (September 19, 2009), pp. 28–29.

62. *Top Security Threats and Management Issues Facing Corporate America: Survey of Fortune 1000 Companies* (Securitas Security Services USA, 2010), pp. 6–7

63. R. Lussier, "Dealing With Anger and Preventing Workplace Violence," *Clinical Leadership & Management Review* (2004), 18(2), pp. 117–119.

64. R. Lussier, "Maintaining Civility in the Laboratory," *Clinical Leadership & Management Review* (2005), 19(62), pp. E4–7.

65. D. Geddes, R.R. Callister, "Crossing the Lines: A Dual Threshold Model of Anger in Organizations," *Academy of Management Review* (2007), 32(3), pp. 721–746.

66. R. Lussier, "Dealing With Anger and Preventing Workplace Violence," *Clinical Leadership & Management Review* (2004), 18(2), pp. 117–119.

67. R. Lussier, "Maintaining Civility in the Laboratory," *Clinical Leadership & Management Review* (2005), 19(62), pp. E4–7.

68. "How to Manage Anger," *TopHealth* (May 2007), p. 2.

69. R. Lussier, "Dealing With Anger and Preventing Workplace Violence," *Clinical Leadership & Management Review* (2004), 18(2), pp. 117–119.

70. Ibid.

71. Ibid.

72. www.dol.gov/elaws/asp/drugfree/drugs/screen92.asp (retrieved October 31, 2011).

73. www.shrm.org/hrdisciplines/safetysecurity/Pages/SafetyIntro.aspx (retrieved August 4, 2011).

74. www.ojp.usdoj.gov/programs/substance.htm (retrieved August 4, 2011).

75. www.surgeongeneral.gov/library/secondhandsmoke/report/chapter1.pdf (retrieved August 4, 2011).

76. www.euro.who.int/__data/assets/pdf_file/0009/128169/e94535.pdf (retrieved August 4, 2011).

77. www.epa.gov/iaq/ia-intro.html (retrieved August 4, 2011).

78. www.epa.gov/iaq/pubs/insidestory.html (retrieved August 4, 2011).

79. www.edocamerica.com/about/ (retrieved August 5, 2011).

Photo Credits

Index

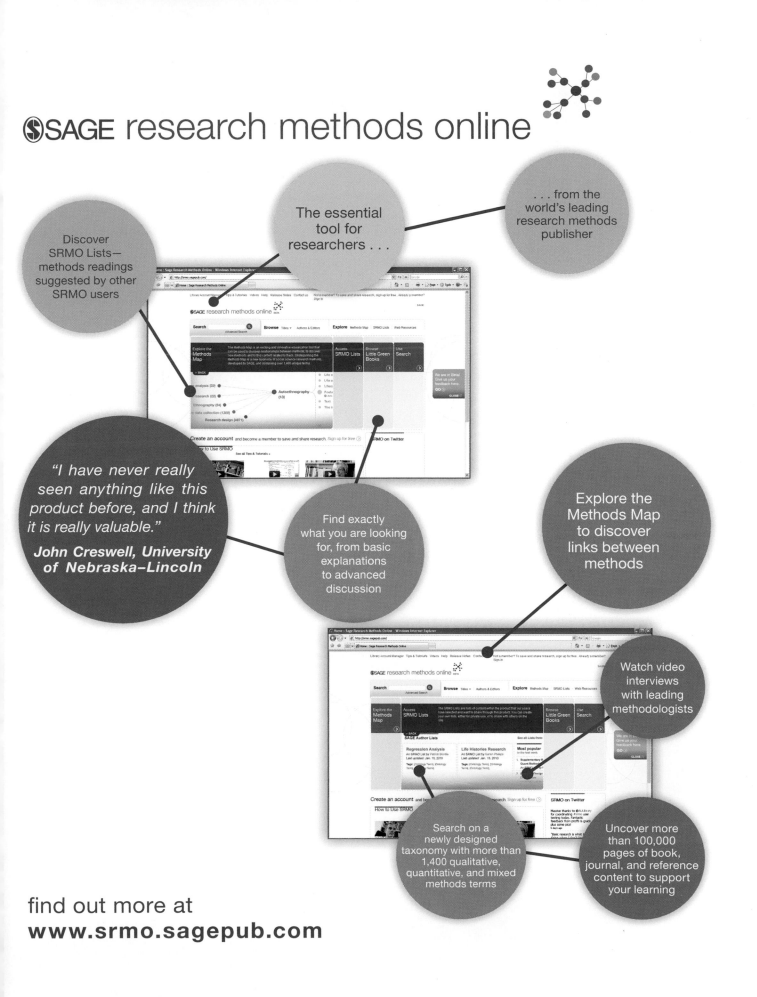

SAGE research methods online

The essential tool for researchers . . .

. . . from the world's leading research methods publisher

Discover SRMO Lists—methods readings suggested by other SRMO users

"I have never really seen anything like this product before, and I think it is really valuable."

John Creswell, University of Nebraska–Lincoln

Find exactly what you are looking for, from basic explanations to advanced discussion

Explore the Methods Map to discover links between methods

Watch video interviews with leading methodologists

Search on a newly designed taxonomy with more than 1,400 qualitative, quantitative, and mixed methods terms

Uncover more than 100,000 pages of book, journal, and reference content to support your learning

find out more at
www.srmo.sagepub.com